MCGRAW-HILL

ONLINE RESOUR

IMPORTANT:

HERE IS YOUR REGISTRATION CODE TO ACCESS YOUR PREMIUM McGRAW-HILL ONLINE RESOURCES.

For key premium online resources you need THIS CODE to gain access. Once the code is entered, you will be able to use the Web resources for the length of your course.

If your course is using **WebCT** or **Blackboard**, you'll be able to use this code to access the McGraw-Hill content within your instructor's online course.

Access is provided if you have purchased a new book. If the registration code is missing from this book, the registration screen on our Website, and within your WebCT or Blackboard course, will tell you how to obtain your new code.

38QU-7CES-9V3S-7077-SNNT

Registering for McGraw-Hill Online Resources

To gain access to your McGraw-Hill web resources simply follow the steps below:

1. USE YOUR WEB BROWSER TO GO TO: **www.mhhe.com/rourke10**
2. CLICK ON **FIRST TIME USER**.
3. ENTER THE REGISTRATION CODE* PRINTED ON THE TEAR-OFF BOOKMARK ON THE RIGHT.
4. AFTER YOU HAVE ENTERED YOUR REGISTRATION CODE, CLICK **REGISTER**.
5. FOLLOW THE INSTRUCTIONS TO SET-UP YOUR PERSONAL UserID AND PASSWORD.
6. WRITE YOUR UserID AND PASSWORD DOWN FOR FUTURE REFERENCE. KEEP IT IN A SAFE PLACE.

TO GAIN ACCESS to the McGraw-Hill content in your instructor's **WebCT** or **Blackboard** course simply log in to the course with the UserID and Password provided by your instructor. Enter the registration code exactly as it appears in the box to the right when prompted by the system. You will only need to use the code the first time you click on McGraw-Hill content.

Thank you, and welcome to your McGraw-Hill online resources!

Higher Education

Mc Graw Hill

* YOUR REGISTRATION CODE CAN BE USED ONLY ONCE TO ESTABLISH ACCESS. IT IS NOT TRANSFERABLE.

0-07-297264-5 T/A ROURKE: INTERNATIONAL POLITICS ON THE WORLD STAGE, 10E

THIRTY YEARS' WAR (1618–1648)

- **1555** — Treaty of Augsburg
- **1588** — Spanish Armada defeated
- **1618** — Tokugawa Era of premodern Japan begins
- **1625** — Grotius publishes first book on international law
- **1648** — Treaty of Westphalia; Manchu dynasty founded in China
- **1651** — Hobbes publishes *Leviathan*
- **1661** — Louis XIV begins to govern
- **1750** — Industrial Revolution under way
- **1762** — Rousseau's *Social Contract*
- **1776** — American Revolution; Popular nationalism begins/divine right challenged
- **1789** — French Revolution
- **1800** — World population 1 billion
- **1804** — Napoleon emperor
- **1815** — Napoleon defeated
- **1824** — Most of Latin America independent; Shaka establishes modern Zulu nation in southern Africa
- **1842** — Great Britain acquires Hong Kong; Era of modern European imperialism in Africa and Asia begins
- **1848** — Marx's *Communist Manifesto*

BIPOLAR ERA (1947–1969)

U.S.–USSR Peaceful Coexistence (1954–1958)

- **1947** — India and Pakistan independent; Cold war; Containment
- **1948** — Israel independent
- **1949** — NATO established; Chinese Communists take power
- **1953** — Stalin dies
- **1954** — Vietnam independent and divided
- **1957** — Ghana independent; Beginning of African independence
- **1958** — European Common Market formed
- **1960** — World population 3 billion
- **1962** — Cuban missile crisis
- **1964** — U.S. enters war in Vietnam
- **1969** — First man on the Moon

BIPOLAR SYSTEM DECLINES (1972–1989)

- **1972** — SALT I; Nixon visits China
- **1974** — World population 4 billion
- **1975** — U.S. out of Vietnam; South Vietnam falls to North; First personal minicomputer (Altier 8800) advertised
- **1976** — Mao dies; Chinese reforms begin
- **1979** — Soviets invade Afghanistan
- **1981** — Reagan in power
- **1985** — Gorbachev in power; Soviet reforms begin
- **1987** — World population 5 billion
- **1989** — Berlin Wall opened; Tiananmen Square massacre

BIPOLAR ERA ENDS (1989–1991)

- **1990** — Germany reunites
- **1991** — War in Persian Gulf; Soviet Union collapses

For all my friends through nine editions at
Dushkin Publishing Group in Guilford, Connecticut

John T. Rourke, Ph.D., is a professor in the Department of Political Science at The University of Connecticut. He is a coauthor with Mark A. Boyer of *International Politics on the World Stage, Brief,* Fifth Edition (McGraw-Hill, 2003); the author of *Presidential Wars and American Democracy: Rally 'Round the Chief* (Paragon House, 1993); a coauthor of *Direct Democracy and International Politics: Deciding International Issues Through Referendums* (Lynne Rienner, 1992); the editor of *Taking Sides: Clashing Views on Controversial Issues in American Foreign Policy,* Second Edition (McGraw-Hill/Dushkin, 2002) and *Taking Sides: Clashing Views on Controversial Issues in World Politics,* Eleventh Edition (McGraw-Hill/Dushkin, 2003), the author of *Making Foreign Policy: United States, Soviet Union, China* (Brooks/Cole, 1990), *Congress and the Presidency in U.S. Foreign Policymaking* (Westview, 1985), and numerous articles and papers. He enjoys teaching introductory classes. His regard for students has molded his approach to writing—he conveys scholarship in a language and within a frame of reference that undergraduates can appreciate. Rourke believes, as the theme of this book reflects, that politics affects us all and we can affect politics. Rourke practices what he propounds; he is involved in the university's internship program, advises one of its political clubs, has served as a staff member of Connecticut's legislature, and has been involved in political campaigns on the local, state, and national levels.

International Politics on the World Stage

TENTH EDITION

John T. Rourke

University of Connecticut

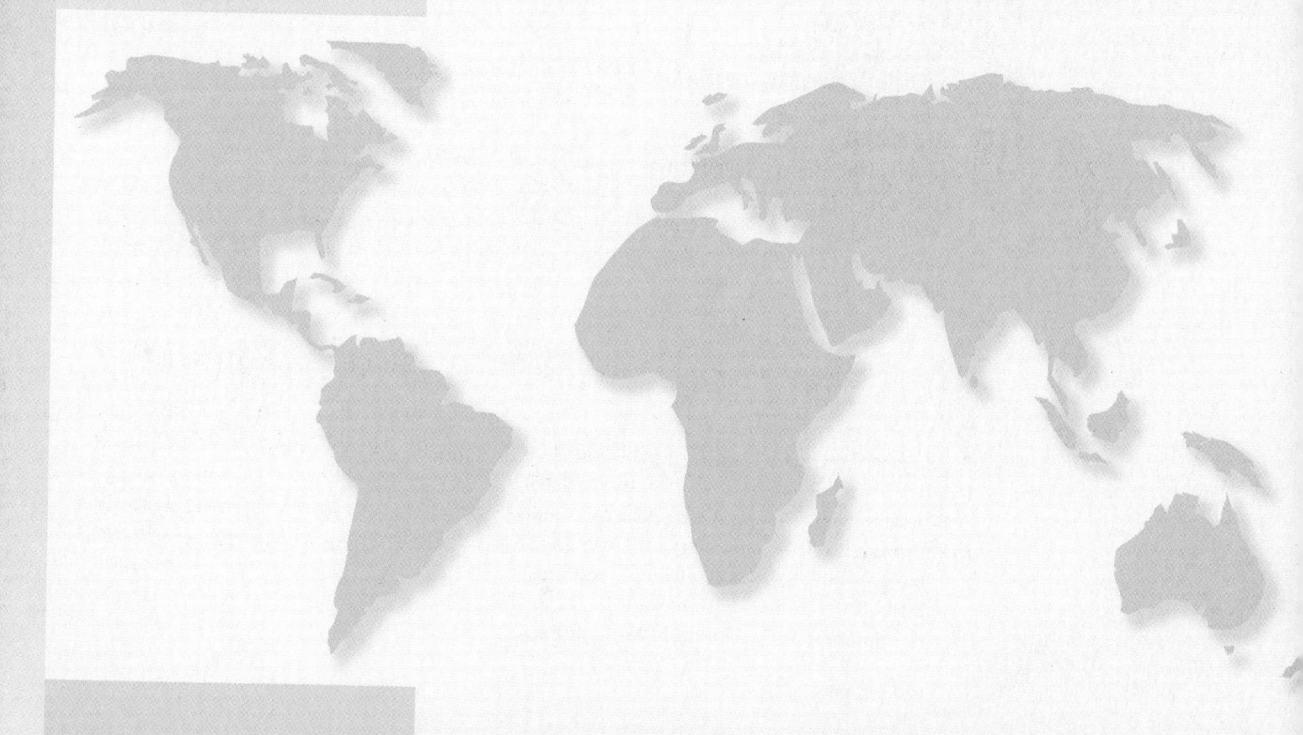

Boston Burr Ridge, IL Dubuque, IA Madison, WI New York San Francisco St. Louis
Bangkok Bogotá Caracas Kuala Lumpur Lisbon London Madrid Mexico City
Milan Montreal New Delhi Santiago Seoul Singapore Sydney Taipei Toronto

The McGraw·Hill Companies

International Politics on the World Stage, Tenth Edition

Published by McGraw-Hill, an imprint of The McGraw-Hill Companies, Inc., 1221 Avenue of the Americas, New York, NY 10020.

1 2 3 4 5 6 7 8 9 0 VNH / VNH 0 9 8 7 6 5 4

ISBN 0-07-289036-3

Editor-in-chief: *Emily Barrosse*
Publisher: *Lyn Uhl*
Senior sponsoring editor: *Monica Eckman*
Senior developmental editor: *Jim Strandberg*
Freelance developmental editor: *Ava Suntoke*
Developmental editor, supplements: *Angela Kao*
Marketing manager: *Katherine Bates*
Permissions coordinator: *Marty Granahan*
Media producer: *Sean Crowley*
Production editor: *Brett Coker*
Production supervisor: *Tandra Jorgensen*
Design manager and cover designer: *Preston Thomas*
Interior designer: *Glenda King*
Art editor: *Emma Ghiselli*
Freelance photo researcher: *Pam Carley*
Cover illustration: © *Digital Vision*
Compositor: *Thompson Type*
Typeface: *10/12 Bembo*
Paper: *45# Publishers Matte*
Printer and binder: *Von Hoffmann Press*

The credit section for this book appears on page C-1 and is considered an extension of the copyright page.

Library of Congress Cataloging-in-Publication Data
Rourke, John T., 1945–
International politics on the world stage / John T. Rourke.—10th ed.
p. cm.
Includes bibliographical references and index.
ISBN 0-07-289036-3 (softcover)
1. International relations. 2. World politics—1989- I. Title.

JZ1305.R68 2004
327—dc21

2003063530

www.mhhe.com

Preface

This Edition: Changes and Organization

Taking the view that our lives are inescapably affected by world politics, *International Politics on the World Stage,* Tenth Edition, stresses the impact that world events and global interdependence have on your students' lives. In addition to highlighting this interconnection, the text points out how the events of current history relate to the theories of international politics that have been formulated by political scientists.

Each time I revise this text I think to myself, "The world will settle down and the next edition will be easier." Wrong! This edition proved to be a major challenge and effort. You will see that there is a continued emphasis on being current in order to engage the students without being journalistic. The American-British invasion of Iraq and the postwar struggle to establish a democratic, unified country, the looming threat of terrorism, the arrival of SARS and other diseases in the United States and elsewhere from Asia, the formation of the International Criminal Court, disclosures about the corrupt trafficking of nuclear weapons information and technology from North Korea and China through Pakistan to Libya and elsewhere, and other recent events are all extensively detailed. It is also important to be as current as possible with the massive amount of changing data on economic performance and capacity, weapons levels and transfers, and other statistical aspects of world politics. I have used original sources for my data when possible so that students will have the most recent information available.

The organization of the text flows from this conception of the world as a primitive, but developing, political system. Therefore, the chapters not only analyze world division and conflict but also focus on cooperation both as a goal and in practice. Indeed, the organizational scheme reflects this text's view that the world is at a juncture echoing Robert Frost's poem, "Two Roads Diverged in a Wood." One road is the traditional way of sovereign states pursuing their self-interests in an often inequitable and conflict-filled world. The alternative, less-traveled-by path is the way of cooperation in a system in which states are less sovereign and international organizations play a wider and more authoritative role.

The introduction to the text discusses the importance of world politics and the methods, theories, and purposes of political science (chapter 1), the evolution of and current instability in the world political system (chapter 2), and the three levels of analysis that need to be studied simultaneously—the system, state, and individual levels (chapter 3). Instructors who have used this text before will undoubtedly notice that what had been three chapters on levels of analysis in previous editions has been consolidated here into one chapter. The change came about as a result of outside reviews of the text that McGraw-Hill and I sought. Most of the comments were gratifying and confirmed the strengths that this book has had since the first edition was published in 1986. But a number of reviewers commented that the book was a bit long and had more chapters (18) than the usual academic semester had weeks (14 to 16). As far as where to tighten up, the consensus was that a chapter each on system-level analysis, state-level analysis, and individual-level analysis provided greater depth than needed for a one-semester introductory course. I was not sure I agreed, and so I sent e-mail inquiries to a dozen or so instructors who were using the text at other colleges and universities. I asked them whether they favored keeping the three chapters as is or consolidating them. To my surprise, frankly, their overwhelming response was the same as that of the first set of reviewers. So, bowing to the greater wisdom, I consolidated the three chapters.

From this point, the remaining organization of the book has remained as it has been for the last few editions. Beginning with chapter 4, the two roads theme organizes the remaining chapters of this edition, with usually alternating discussions of national conflict and international cooperation in successive chapters. In this way, equal attention can be given to the two roads without losing sight of the fact that they lead in divergent directions.

Chapters 4 and 5 deal with two divergent political orientations. The traditional orientation is nationalism (chapter 4); the alternative orientation comprises transnational ideas, identifications, and processes (chapter 5). Alternative ways of organizing the world politically are the subject of the next two chapters, with chapter 6 focusing on the traditional political unit, the state, and chapter 7 taking up international organizations, with particular emphases on the European Union and the United Nations.

Then chapters 8 and 9 explore divergent approaches to the conduct of world politics. Chapter 8 covers the traditional approach, national diplomacy; chapter 9 examines the alternative road of international law and morality. This pair of chapters is followed by another pair that introduce two approaches to physical security in the world political system: national security (chapter 10) and international security and other alternative approaches (chapter 11).

The text then turns to international political economy. The commentary begins with an overview of global economic conditions and trends (chapter 12), then turns to a chapter on traditional national economic competition (chapter 13) and contrasts that with the alternative of international economic cooperation (chapter 14). The final two chapters look into current conditions and ways to preserve and enhance human rights and dignity (chapter 15) and the environment (chapter 16).

I have made substantial changes in this edition so that it reflects more accurately the changing nature of world politics. The more I study the subject, the more I am impressed with the idea that the world is a primitive political society. As such, it is a political system that is marked by little organization, frequent violence, and a limited sense of global responsibility. It is a world of conflict. But there is also a world of cooperation, a countertheme, based on a still-limited desire among states and their people to work together globally as they begin to realize that their fates are inextricably entwined with one another and with the political, economic, social, and environmental future of our planet.

Writing Style and General Approach

The single greatest factor that prompted me over two decades ago to begin to write my own introductory text was the desire to use one that, in today's jargon, was "user friendly." Over the years, I have tried to accomplish that in a number of ways. One is to make my theoretical points in a straightforward, "plain language" way, and then to illustrate them with an interesting and usually current example. Being up-to-date is a major goal of this book. Sometimes, heeding the advice of Mary Poppins that "a spoonful of sugar makes the medicine go down," I even take time to include a joke or tell a "story" (such as the box in chapter 7 "When Is a Banana a Banana?") that make a point in a light way. This is meant to show the student readers that international relations can be fascinating, even fun. A third thing that makes this book user friendly for students is the "road signs" to provide reference points and guidance during the journey through the text and semester. These road signs include an outline (a map, so to speak) to begin each chapter, lots of headings; an array of boldface glossary words, and judicious use of italicized phrases to highlight concepts and points. I am pleased to report that the feedback from instructors and from the occasional student who writes or e-mails me is that most students are delighted with the book's accessibility and readability.

Data and Graphics

This text presents students with an extensive array of tables, figures, photographs, maps, and other graphics to emphasize, expand, and give visual life to ideas. Each photograph is picked personally by me, and I have designed almost all the figures and tables, often making my own calculations to create them from the data. Another part of my approach is to present a significant amount of data to students so that they can see for themselves what the statistics indicate rather than accept my interpretations or those of any other scholar.

Research, Citations, Bibliography, and Suggested Readings

One of the aims of this text is to bring together a representative sampling of the latest research in international relations. Scholarly articles, so often ignored in survey texts, are particularly emphasized. This research is documented by extensive references using the "in-text" style and by a significant reference list/bibliography. In addition to recognizing my intellectual debt to a host of scholars, the references and bibliography also serve as a reading list for students, as explained to them in the "To the Student" section following this preface. As such, references are often meant to serve as suggestions for further reading and do not necessarily mean that the cited author(s) propounded what is being said at the point of reference. Using this approach instead of the end-of-chapter placement gives inquisitive students immediate thoughts for additional reading.

For those instructors whose organization differs from mine, I have taken care to provide a detailed table of contents and index in order to facilitate the integration of this text with your syllabus. You will find, for example, that:

Economics is discussed, among other places, in chapters 1 (how it affects students), 2 (globalization), 12 (general global conditions), 13 (national economic competition), 14 (international economic cooperation), and 16 (sustainable development).

Terrorism is addressed in chapters 1, 5, 9, and 10.

Moral and humanitarian issues are taken up extensively in chapters 9 and 15 and also form an important part of the discussions of national interest, coercion, and economic challenges in, respectively, chapters 4, 10, 13, and 14.

Supplements

Several supplements are available to assist both instructors and students in the use of this text. For instructors, the Instructor's Manual to accompany *International Politics on the World Stage* contains chapter outlines and objectives, sample lectures, discussion questions, and analytical exercises. The Test Bank that accompanies the book provides approximately 1,400 multiple-choice and essay questions organized by chapter and degree of difficulty. The Instructor's Manual and Test Bank are both available on the Instructor's Resource CD-ROM along with a computerized version of the Test Bank and a PowerPoint Slide presentation that includes figures and tables from the book. To get a copy of the Instructor's Resource CD-ROM, contact your local McGraw-Hill representative or McGraw-Hill Customer Service (1-800-338-3987) for details concerning availability.

Online Learning Center

Students and instructors will find additional resources at *www.mhhe.com/rourke10.* For students, the site offers free access to current course-specific articles by leading authorities in the field, daily news feeds from a variety of media outlets including *The New York Times,* interactive exercises, research links, chapter quizzes, and interactive exercises to enhance the classroom and learning experience of students. The password-protected instructor's edition of the site also contains the Instructor's Manual and PowerPoint slides available for easy download. Contact your local McGraw-Hill representative or McGraw-Hill Customer Service (1-800-338-3987) for a username and password.

To the Student

The world, familiar to us and unknown.
—William Shakespeare, *Henry V*

The world is changing at breathtaking speed! That reality is one of the most important things for you to understand about international politics. Yet I have found that most undergraduate students, having been born into this era of warp-speed change, consider it normal. It is not. Recorded history dates back over 30 centuries. A great deal of what we will discuss in this text has happened in the last century, even within your lifetime. But truly understanding this rate of change—maybe *feeling* the rate of change is a better way to put it—is hard without perspective.

As a way of trying to convey the dramatic pace of change, I will introduce you to Charlotte Benkner, of North Lima, Ohio. At 115 years old, she is the world's oldest living person whose birth can be documented. Among other things, Ms. Benkner gives us a sense of how quickly the world is changing. Benjamin Harrison was the U.S. president when she was born on November 16, 1889. There was an emperor in China and an Ottoman Empire ruled by a sultan. Russia's czar, Germany's kaiser, and Austria-Hungary's emperor ruled much of Central Europe, and Queen Victoria reigned over the British Empire. Most of Africa and Asia were still colonies of European powers. There were less than 1.5 billion people in the world; only birds (and insects and bats) could use wings to fly, and the world's most ferocious weapons were the Gatling gun and the long-range artillery piece.

The communist revolution in Russia occurred when she was 28; the Soviet Union disappeared when she was 102. For me, communism and the cold war were the totality of my historical experience; for Ms. Benkner they were mere interludes. For many who read this book they are not even memories, only matter learned about in history books.

If you think about events, trends, and technology in this way—in terms of what one person has seen and experienced—you can begin to grasp how fast they are moving. When Ms. Benkner was born people were basically earthbound. She was 14 when the first airplane flew, 53 when the first jet plane took off, 72 when Soviet cosmonaut Yuri Gagarin became the first human in space, and 81 when Neil Armstrong stepped onto the Moon's surface. There are many other things to consider. Ms. Benkner is more than twice as old as atomic weapons; the world's population has quadrupled during her life; she is older than three-quarters of the countries that exist today. Radios, televisions, computers, and some of the other technological innovations that affect us so profoundly now did not exist when Ms. Benkner was born.

One of the strong themes in this book is the challenges that face the world and the alternative approaches to addressing those challenges. Use Ms. Benkner to help you think about these issues. If, for example, it took all of human history—tens of thousands of years—to reach a world population of less than 1.5 billion in 1880, and if, during her life, we have added another 4.5 billion people, then how much time do we have to get the world population under control? If you live as long as Ms. Benkner (and you might, given modern medical technology), then what will the world population be when you are 115 years old?

In this sense of contemplating the future by pondering the past, thinking about Ms. Benkner is really more about tomorrow than about yesterday or even today. When I talk about her, my thoughts are on our 21st century more than on her 19th and 20th centuries.

Using This Text

The text that follows is my attempt to introduce you to the complex and compelling study of international politics. Prefaces are often given scant attention, but they can be a valuable learning tool for you. They let you in on the author's conceptions, the mental pictures behind a text. What is the author's approach? What are the author's orientations and biases? Does the text have one or more basic themes? How is the text organized? In this preface I have addressed these issues. I hope you'll read it.

In writing this text I have tried to use straightforward prose and have assumed that students who take this course know little about international politics. To help you further, I have included an outline at the beginning of each chapter. Before you read the chapter, pay attention to its outline. It is axiomatic that if you know where you are going, you will find it a lot easier to get there! Additionally, I have written a numbered summary at the end of each chapter to help you quickly review the scope of the chapter. This, of course, is no substitute for carefully studying the chapter.

There are many figures, tables, maps, and photographs in this book. Pay close attention to them. You will find that they graphically represent many of the ideas presented in the text and will help you understand them. But if you really want to know all about something, you will have to read a lot more than just this book and to involve yourself in more than just the course for which it has been assigned. To make it easier for you to do this, I have chosen an "in-text" reference system that gives you citations as you read. Thus (Croucher, 2003:6) refers to page 6 of the book or article written by (in this case, Professor Sheila) Croucher in 2003, which is listed alphabetically in the references and bibliography at the end of the book.

I have also noted studies that helped me think about and organize various topics and those that might be informative to you. I encourage you to utilize the references and bibliography to advance your knowledge beyond the boundaries of this text. You will find a list of the abbreviations that I have used throughout the book on page A-1. Explanations for terms set in **boldface** will be found in the glossary at the end of the text.

Some note should be made of this book's title, *International Politics on the World Stage*, and the Shakespearean quotations that begin each chapter and are used from time to time to highlight a point. The idea behind this motif is to convey some of the sweep and complexity of the world drama. No one who has ever read William Shakespeare can dismiss his masterpieces as easily understood or inconsequential. The events on the world stage are similar—complex, full of drama, sometimes hopeful, often tragic, and always riveting. But you, the reader, would be mistaken to assume that the play analogy means that, as a member of the audience, you can be content to sit back and watch the plot unfold. Quite the contrary—part of what makes the world drama so compelling is that the audience is seated onstage and is part of, as well as witness to, the action that is unfolding. And that is one reason why I have also quoted more recent world players. Shakespeare's plays are of the past; the world drama is ongoing. Furthermore, as in an improvisational play, you in the audience can become involved, and, given the consequences of a potentially tragic rather than a happy ending, you ought to become involved. If there is anything that this text proposes, it is that each of us is intimately affected by international politics and that we all have a responsibility and an ability to become shapers of the script. As we shall see, our play has alternative scripts, and what the next scene brings depends in part on us. There is wisdom, then, in Shakespeare's advice in *All's Well That Ends Well* that "Our remedies oft in ourselves do lie."

I am sincerely interested in getting feedback from the faculty members and students who use this text. My pretensions to perfection have long since been dashed, and your recommendations for additions, deletions, and changes in future editions will be appreciated and seriously considered. People do write me, and I write or call them back! You are encouraged to join this correspondence by writing to me at the Department of Political Science U1024, University of Connecticut, Storrs, CT 06269-1024 or sending me an e-mail at John.Rourke@uconn.edu. This book, just like the world, can be made better, but its improvement depends heavily on whether or not you are concerned enough to think and act.

John T. Rourke

Acknowledgments

It is a difficult task to keep this acknowledgment of those who have contributed to the text down to a reasonable length. There are many who have played an important part, and my debt to each of them is great. I have tried to make adjustments wherever possible. Some contributors have pointed out specific concerns about matters of fact or interpretation, and a number of corrections were made. On a larger scale, this edition's organizational changes; its greater coverage of constructivism, postmodernism, and other critical approaches; and several other shifts in coverage are responses in part to suggestions. Adding to the long list of those who have reviewed earlier editions and made this text better, I would like to thank the following for contributions to this edition:

Karen R. Adams
Louisiana State University

Desmond Arias
John Jay College of Criminal Justice, City University of New York

Dlynn Armstrong-Williams
North Georgia College and State University

Charles T. Barber
University of Southern Indiana

Lowell Barrington
Marquette University

Amanda Bigelow
Illinois Valley Community College

Daniel Breen
Framingham State College

E. Donald Briggs
University of Windsor

Mary Jane Burns
Idaho State University

Richard Byrne
Kirkwood Community College

Sophie M. Clavier
San Francisco State University

John A. C. Conybeare
University of Iowa

Katy Crossley-Frolick
DePaul University

Elizabeth Crump Hanson
University of Connecticut

A. Claire Cutler
University of Victoria

Robert Denemark
University of Delaware

Roxanne Lynn Doty
Arizona State University

Dennis S. Driggers
California State University, Fresno

Douglas Durasoff
Seattle Pacific University

David A. Frolick
North Central College

Clifford Griffin
North Carolina State University

Gregory Hall
St. Mary's College of Maryland

Clinton Hewan
Northern Kentucky University

George Kent
University of Hawaii

Kent Kille
The College of Wooster

Jeffrey P. Krans
Keuka College

Timothy C. Lim
California State University, Los Angeles

Paul McCartney
Rutgers University

Rajan Menon
Lehigh University

D. Allen Meyer
Mesa Community College

John Queen
Glendale Community College

G. Hossein Razi
University of Houston

Karl Schonberg
St. Lawrence University

Wayne A. Selcher
Elizabethtown College

Rosemary Shinko
University of Connecticut, Stamford

Stacy VanDeveer
University of New Hampshire

Kimberly Weir
Northern Kentucky University

I also owe a debt to each author listed in the bibliography of this and the previous editions. The work that these scholars have done on specific subjects forms the intellectual building blocks that are a significant part of the final structure of this, or any, worthwhile introductory textbook. This text is also evolutionary, and I want to continue to express my appreciation to all those who read and commented on the previous editions. Additionally, I also want to thank the colleagues who have taken the time at International Studies Association meetings or other conferences to give me the benefit of their views. I have even, on occasion, taken off my name tag and helped the staff at the publisher's booth at professional meetings. The comments I have received in this anonymity have been sometimes encouraging, sometimes humbling, but always helpful.

Best of all, I have received many good suggestions from students. My own students have had to both read the text and listen to me, and their often obviously candid comments have helped the generations of students who will follow. My favorite was a sophomore who did not do well on his first exam and came to my office to lay blame at the door of the blankety-blank textbook. As we talked, he made some interesting, if pointed observations. It was also clear that he had not connected the author's name on the front of the book with his professor. Boy, was he surprised when it finally dawned on him that he was grumping about the book to its author!

I owe special thanks to Jason Rich of the University of Connecticut, who is responsible for revising the Instructor's Manual and Test Bank to accompany *International Politics on the World Stage.* Jason shouldered the task of preparing, revising, and updating this instructor's tool for the tenth edition with the utmost care and good nature. Another exciting feature of this text is the supplementary material and exercises that can be found on the Online Learning Center. For this I thank Natalie Florea of the University of Connecticut for her meticulous updates and polish. Thanks are also due to Alice and Will Thiede of Carto-Graphics in Eau Claire, Wisconsin, for their standard of excellence in producing the maps in the book.

Then there is the staff of McGraw-Hill. They have encouraged me and supported me. Having shifted from the Dushkin division of McGraw-Hill to the main higher education division, this is the first edition I have done with McGraw-Hill's political science editor, Monica Eckman, and with developmental editor Jim Strandberg. More familiar is my general editor, Ava Suntoke. She has gently and expertly guided me through several editions, and I am continually delighted with her unusual combination of substantive expertise and editing expertise. Sheryl Rose, copyeditor, with her amazing eye for technical detail and substantive consistency, added to the process of ensuring accuracy. I also want to thank Brett Coker and the rest of the McGraw-Hill production staff and Thompson Type for their diligence and for not threatening my life through innumerable changes.

One of the things I like best about this edition is "its look." Pamela Carley has assembled photographs and editorial cartoons that bring powerful visual life to the concepts

I express in words. Glenda King was the interior designer for the tenth edition. Preston Thomas designed its striking cover. Thompson Type performed the difficult but crucial task of layout, arranging text and illustrations; Charles Vitelli drew the original cartoons in this book. He took my raw mental images and turned them into wonderful representations of the issues being discussed in the text. In the same area, Emma Ghiselli and Rennie Evans did an extraordinary job with the exacting art of creating the text's many figures and maps. I owe a great debt to those who have created such a visually attractive, educationally effective package for my words.

To all of you:

I can no other answer make but thanks, thanks, and ever thanks.

—William Shakespeare, *Twelfth Night*

Visit the Online Learning Center with PowerWeb at

http://www.mhhe.com/rourke10/

Contents in Brief

Preface v
To the Student ix
Acknowledgments xii

PART I Approaches to World Politics

CHAPTER 1 Thinking and Caring about World Politics 1
CHAPTER 2 The Evolution of World Politics 27
CHAPTER 3 Levels of Analysis 57

PART II Two Roads: Divergent Political Orientations

CHAPTER 4 Nationalism: The Traditional Orientation 97
CHAPTER 5 Globalization and Transnationalism: The Alternative Orientation 126

PART III Two Roads: Divergent Organizational Structures

CHAPTER 6 National States: The Traditional Structure 163
CHAPTER 7 International Organization: An Alternative Structure 190

PART IV Two Roads: Divergent Approaches to Conduct

CHAPTER 8 National Power and Diplomacy: The Traditional Approach 227
CHAPTER 9 International Law and Morality: An Alternative Approach 265

PART V Pursuing Peace

CHAPTER 10 National Security: The Traditional Road 297
CHAPTER 11 International Security: The Alternative Road 338

PART VI Pursuing Prosperity

CHAPTER 12 The International Economy: A Global Road Map 373
CHAPTER 13 National Economic Competition: The Traditional Road 404
CHAPTER 14 International Economic Cooperation: The Alternative Road 441

PART VII Pursuing Preservation

CHAPTER 15 Preserving and Enhancing Human Rights and Dignity 476
CHAPTER 16 Preserving and Enhancing the Global Commons 510

An Epilogue to the Text/A Prologue to the Future 551
Explanatory Notes N-1
Endnotes E-1
Glossary G-1
Abbreviations A-1
References R-1
Index I-1
Credits C-1

Contents

Preface v
To the Student ix
Acknowledgments xii

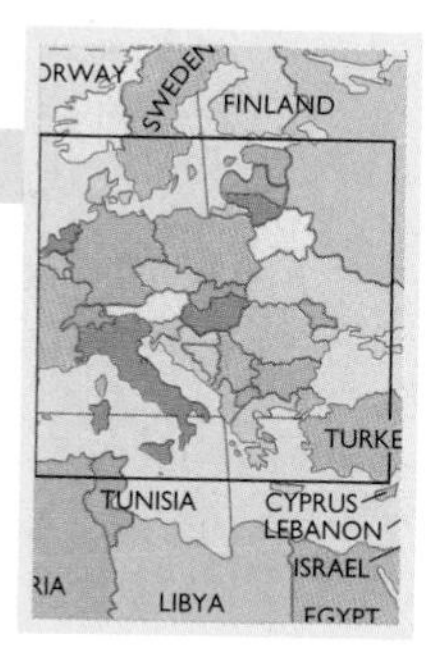

MAPS

1. Dependence on Trade 5
2. World Countries 34
3. The Colonization and Decolonization of Africa: 1878, 1914, 2004 37
4. Global Distribution of Minority Groups 106
5. Kurdistan 109
6. 500 Years of Russian Expansion 118
7. Countries with a Majority Muslim Population 154
8. The Gender Gap: Inequalities in Education and Employment 158
9. Sovereign States: Duration of Independence 164
10. Political Systems 173
11. The Membership and Organizational Structure of the European Union 201
12. The International Court of Justice (ICJ) 275
13. International Conflicts in the Post–World War II World 310
14. The Spread of Nuclear Weapons 349
15. Current UN Peacekeeping Missions 363
16. Per Capita Gross National Product 380
17. Exports of Primary Products 429
18. Regional Trade Organizations 465
19. The Index of Human Development 500
20. World Ecological Regions 514
21. Population Growth Rate 523
22. Per Capita Water Availability 533

PART I Approaches to World Politics

CHAPTER 1 Thinking and Caring about World Politics 1

The Importance of Studying World Politics 3
World Politics and Your Finances 5
World Politics and Your Living Space 8
World Politics and Your Life 10
Can We Make a Difference? 12

The World Tomorrow: Two Roads Diverge 15
Realism and Liberalism: Some Travel Notes on Two Roads 16
The Nature of Politics: Realism and Liberalism 16

The Roles of Power and Principles: Realism and Liberalism 19
Prospects for Competition and Cooperation: Realism and Liberalism 21
Assessing Reality: Realism and Liberalism 23

How to Study World Politics 23
Political Scientists and World Politics 23

Chapter Summary 25

Key Terms 26

CHAPTER 2 The Evolution of World Politics 27

The Evolving World System: Early Development 28
Ancient Greece and Rome 28
After the Fall of Rome in A.D. 476 to 1700 29
The 18th and 19th Centuries 32

The Evolving World System: The 20th Century 36
The Eclipse of the Multipolar System 38
The Cold War and the Bipolar System 39

The 21st Century: The Genesis of a New System 42
The Structure of Power in the 21st Century 42
Security in the 21st Century 47
Global Economics in the 21st Century 48
Quality of Life in the 21st Century 50

Chapter Summary 54

Key Terms 56

CHAPTER 3 Levels of Analysis 57

System-Level Analysis 58
Structural Characteristics 59
Power Relationships in the International System 63
Economic Patterns in the Political System 67
Norms of Behavior in the International System 68

State-Level Analysis 70
Making Foreign Policy: Type of Government, Situation, and Policy 70
Making Foreign Policy: Political Culture 72
Foreign Policy–Making Actors 73

Individual-Level Analysis 81
Humans as a Species 81
Organizational Behavior 86
Leaders and Their Individual Traits 87

Chapter Summary 94

Key Terms 96

PART II Two Roads: Divergent Political Orientations

CHAPTER 4 Nationalism: The Traditional Orientation 97

Understanding Nations, Nationalism, and Nation-States 99
Nations, Nationalism, and Nation-States Defined 99
The Rise and Ascendancy of Nationalism 102

Nationalism in Practice: Issues and Evaluation 105
Nation-States: More Myth than Reality 105

Nationalism: Builder and Destroyer 112
Self-Determination as a Goal 117

Nationalism and the Future 121
The Recent Past and Present of Nationalism 121
The Future of Nationalism 122

Chapter Summary 124

Key Terms 125

CHAPTER 5 Globalization and Transnationalism: The Alternative Orientation 126

Globalization 127
Globalization of Communications and Transportation 128
Economic Globalization 131
Cultural Globalization 131

Transnationalism 137
Early Transnationalism 138
Contemporary Transnational Thought 139

Transnationalism in Action 144
Transnational Organizations 145
Regional Transnationalism 147
Cultural Transnationalism 148
Transnational Religion 150
Islam and the World 151
Transnational Movements 157

Transnationalism Tomorrow 161

Chapter Summary 161

Key Terms 162

PART III Two Roads: Divergent Organizational Structures

CHAPTER 6 National States: The Traditional Structure 163

The Nature and Purpose of the State 165
The State Defined 165
Purposes of the State 170

The State as the Core Political Organization 172
Theories of Governance 172
Democracy and World Politics 176
National and Other Interests 181

States and the Future 184
The State: The Indictment 184
The State: The Defense 187
The State: The Verdict 188

Chapter Summary 188

Key Terms 189

CHAPTER 7 International Organization: An Alternative Structure 190

The Evolution and Roles of International Organization 191
The Origins of IGOs 191
The Growth of IGOs 193
Roles That IGOs Play 195

Regional IGOs: Focus on the European Union 200
The Origins and Evolution of the European Union 200
The Government of the European Union 202
The Future of the EU 204

Global IGOs: Focus on the United Nations 208
IGO Organization and Related Issues 208
IGO Leadership, Administration, and Finance 213
IGO Activities 217
Evaluating IGOs and Their Future 223

Chapter Summary 225

Key Terms 226

PART IV Two Roads: Divergent Approaches to Conduct

CHAPTER 8 National Power and Diplomacy: The Traditional Approach 227

National Power: The Foundation of National Diplomacy 229
The Nature of Power 229

The Elements of Power 234
The National Core 234
The National Infrastructure 239

The Nature of Diplomacy 241
The Functions of Diplomacy 241
The Diplomatic Setting 245

The Evolution of Diplomacy 248
Early Diplomacy 248
Modern Diplomacy 249

The Conduct of Diplomacy 255
Diplomacy as a Communications Process 255
The Rules of Effective Diplomacy 256
Options for Conducting Diplomacy 257

Chapter Summary 263

Key Terms 264

CHAPTER 9 International Law and Morality: An Alternative Approach 265

Fundamentals of International Law and Morality 266
The Primitive Nature of International Law 266
The Growth of International Law 267
The Practice of International Law 267
The Fundamentals of International Morality 268

The International Legal System 269
The Philosophical Roots of Law 269
How International Law Is Made 270
Adherence to the Law 272
Adjudication of the Law 273

Applying International Law and Morality 277
Law and Justice in a Multicultural World 277
Applying International Law and Morality to States 280

Applying International Law and Morality to Individuals *288*
The Prudent Application of Law and Morality *292*
The Future of International Law and Morality 295
Chapter Summary 295
Key Terms 296

PART V Pursuing Peace

CHAPTER 10 National Security: The Traditional Road 297

War and World Politics 298
War: The Human Record *298*
The Causes of War: Three Levels of Analysis *299*
National Military Power 302
Levels of Spending *302*
Weaponry: Quantity versus Quality *303*
Military Morale and Leadership *303*
Military and Political Reputation *304*
Military Power: The Dangers of Overemphasis *305*
Force as a Political Instrument 306
Levels of Violence: From Intimidation to Attack *307*
The Effectiveness of Force *307*
The Changing Nature of War *309*
Classifying Warfare *312*
Unconventional Warfare 313
Arms Transfers *313*
Special Operations *316*
Terrorism *317*
Conventional Warfare 325
Goals and Conduct *326*
Avoiding Unchecked Escalation *327*
Warfare with Weapons of Mass Destruction 328
Biological Weapons *328*
Chemical Weapons *329*
The Potential for Nuclear War *329*
Nuclear Weapons, Deterrence, and Strategy *331*
Chapter Summary 336
Key Terms 337

CHAPTER 11 International Security: The Alternative Road 338

Thinking about Security 339
A Tale of Insecurity *339*
Seeking Security: Approaches and Standards of Evaluation *340*
Limited Self-Defense through Arms Control 343
Methods of Achieving Arms Control *343*
The History of Arms Control *345*
The Barriers to Arms Control *356*
International Security Forces 360
International Security Forces: Theory and Practice *360*
International Security and the Future *366*

Abolition of War 369
Complete Disarmament 369
Pacifism 369
Chapter Summary 371
Key Terms 372

PART VI Pursuing Prosperity

CHAPTER 12 The International Economy: A Global Road Map 373
Theories of International Political Economy 374
Economic Nationalism 374
Economic Internationalism 376
Economic Structuralism 377
Two Economic Worlds: North and South 379
Two Economic Worlds: Analyzing the Data 379
Two Economic Worlds: Human Conditions 381
The Growth and Extent of International Political Economy 383
Trade 383
International Investment 387
Monetary Relations 388
Globalization and Interdependence: Debating the Future 391
Chapter Summary 402
Key Terms 403

CHAPTER 13 National Economic Competition: The Traditional Road 404
National Economic Power: Assets and Utilization 405
National Economic Power 405
Methods of Manipulating Economic Interchange 409
Applying Economic Power 413
The North and International Political Economy 416
The National Economies of the North 417
National Economic Issues and Policies of the North 418
The South and International Political Economy 422
Development in the South: Status 422
Development in the South: Capital Needs 425
Development in the South: LDC Perspectives and Policies 431
The Future of National Economic Policy 438
Chapter Summary 439
Key Terms 440

CHAPTER 14 International Economic Cooperation: The Alternative Road 441
Global Economic Cooperation: Background 442
The Origins of Economic Cooperation 442
Global Economic Cooperation: EDC Prosperity 443
Global Economic Cooperation: LDC Development 444
Global Economic Cooperation: The Institutions 449
The United Nations and Economic Cooperation 449
Trade Cooperation: The GATT and the WTO 451

Monetary Cooperation: The IMF 456
Development Cooperation: The World Bank Group 462
Regional Economic Cooperation 464
Europe 466
The Western Hemisphere 467
Asia, the Pacific, and Elsewhere 471
The Future of Regionalism 472
Chapter Summary 474
Key Terms 475

PART VII Pursuing Preservation

CHAPTER 15 Preserving and Enhancing Human Rights and Dignity 476
The Nature of Human Rights 478
Negative Human Rights: Freedom from Abuses 481
Abuse of Individual Rights 481
Abuse of Group Rights 482
The International Response to Individual and Group Human Rights Issues 491
Positive Human Rights 498
Food 499
Health 503
Education 505
Chapter Summary 509
Key Terms 509

CHAPTER 16 Preserving and Enhancing the Global Commons 510
Toward Sustainable Development 511
The Ecological State of the World 511
Sustainable Development 513
Sustainable Development: Population and Resources 521
Population Issues and Cooperation 521
Resource Issues and Cooperation 527
Resource Conservation: The Global Response 534
Sustainable Development: The Environment 537
Environmental Issues 537
Environmental Protection: The International Response 546
Chapter Summary 549
Key Terms 549

An Epilogue to the Text/A Prologue to the Future 551
Explanatory Notes N-1
Endnotes E-1
Glossary G-1
Abbreviations A-1
References R-1
Index I-1
Credits C-1

CHAPTER

1

Thinking and Caring about World Politics

THE IMPORTANCE OF STUDYING WORLD POLITICS

World Politics and Your Finances

World Politics and Your Living Space

World Politics and Your Life

Can We Make a Difference?

THE WORLD TOMORROW: TWO ROADS DIVERGE

Realism and Liberalism: Some Travel Notes on Two Roads

The Nature of Politics: Realism and Liberalism

The Roles of Power and Principles: Realism and Liberalism

Prospects for Competition and Cooperation: Realism and Liberalism

Assessing Reality: Realism and Liberalism

HOW TO STUDY WORLD POLITICS

Political Scientists and World Politics

CHAPTER SUMMARY

KEY TERMS

An honest tale speeds best being plainly told.

—William Shakespeare, *Richard III*

Be not too tame neither, but let your own discretion be your tutor: suit the action to the word, the word to the action.

—William Shakespeare, *Hamlet*

We will have to repent in this generation not merely for the vitriolic words and actions of the bad people, but for the appalling silence of the good people.

—Martin Luther King Jr., "Letter from Birmingham City Jail"

We are entering a new millennium, a new world, a global economy. [The world] is shrinking all the time.

—Secretary of State Colin Powell, Senate confirmation hearings, 2001

CHAPTER OBJECTIVES

After completing this chapter, you should be able to:

- Analyze the interconnection of all the actors in the international system and the effects that events taking place in one country have on other countries.
- Describe some of the effects of world politics on individuals.
- Describe how the world is interconnected economically.
- Analyze how world politics affects the way countries distribute their economic resources.
- Explain how global problems and challenges, such as population increases, pollution, and resource depletion, affect individuals and their living space.
- Discuss the role of political cooperation as a response to environmental degradation.
- Show how individuals can make a difference in world politics.
- Summarize realist beliefs and assess their impact on the world political system.
- List the tenets and goals of idealism as a present and future force in world politics.
- Identify the analytical orientations of political scientists.
- Identify the goals and research methods of political scientists.
- Describe the three levels of analysis used in the study of world politics.

"All the world's a stage, and all the men and women merely players," William Shakespeare (1564–1616) wrote in *As You Like It*. The Bard of Avon was a wise political commentator as well as a literary giant. Shakespeare's lines are used here to help convey the drama of world politics. The characters on today's world stage and those of Shakespeare's time and imagination are different, of course. Meet the new ensemble in the Global Actors box "Meet the Cast," below. Beyond this change in cast, though, there are remarkable parallels between international relations and the master's plays. Both are cosmic and complex, with many new twists and turns in the plot, as captured by In the Spotlight boxes in this text. The characters are sometimes heroic, sometimes petty, even evil. The action is always dramatic and often tragic. As the audience was drawn into the action at the Globe, the London theater where Shakespeare staged his works, the global theater of international politics also draws us in. Indeed, we are seated on the stage, no matter how remote the action may seem or how much we may want to ignore it. Thus, the progress of the play, whether it continues its long run or closes early, is something we will all enjoy or endure.

Another quotation from Shakespeare—this time from *Macbeth*—is also worth pondering. Macbeth despairs that life "struts and frets his hour upon the stage" in a tale "full of sound and fury." Again the playwright hits the mark! The global drama has a cast of national actors (countries) that are often at odds with one another. It is true that many

GLOBAL ACTORS

Meet the Cast

Unlike those in a play, most of the actors in the world drama are not people. We will meet these global actors regularly. Just as you get a playbill that lists the cast when you enter the theater, we will briefly introduce the cast you will meet in the following pages.

States (countries) are undoubtedly the starring actors. There are nearly 200 of them, and just like some theatrical stars, states can be self-absorbed and jealously guard their claim to fame, which for states is their independence (sovereignty). It is this sovereign status that separates states from the other actors. Of course, sovereignty also means that there is no director who can bring order to the interaction among the stars, which often leaves the actors in conflict with one another. Also, while all the states are legally equal, the reality is that some are bigger stars than others. The United States would certainly head the "A list" of top stars, with China, Japan, and a few other countries also major players. Andorra, Mauritius, Vanuatu, and many other countries, despite their equal billing in the UN General Assembly and elsewhere, are usually consigned to bit parts.

Joining the states onstage is a host of international organizations. Perhaps the most prominent of these are the 300 or so international governmental organizations (IGO) whose membership is made up of states. Some are global (the United Nations); others are regional (the European Union). Even more numerous are the transnational organizations. One type, nongovernmental organizations (NGOs), has individuals as members. These NGOs range in character from the laudable (Human Rights Watch) to the villainous (al-Qaeda). They also range from the ancient (the Roman Catholic Church) to the nearly new (Families of Victims of Involuntary Disappearance—FIND). Multinational corporations (MNCs) are another type of transnational actor. The annual earnings of some of these companies rival many midsize states' GDPs and dwarf most of the smaller ones. In a largely unregulated drama where money is an important source of power, MNCs can be important cast members.

Finally, as in all dramas, people are sometimes actors. Usually the roles they play are as decision makers, protesters, voters, or other forms of political participants in a state or international organization. Sometimes, however, the part an individual plays transcends or predates those institutional boundaries. Later in the book you will meet Jody Williams, a native of Putney, Vermont, who decided that land mines are evil. She joined with others who felt the same, established an IGO to campaign against land mines, was responsible for an international treaty to ban them, and won the 1997 Nobel Peace Prize for her efforts. For a political actor, it is like getting a Tony, Emmy, and Oscar all rolled into one.

That's our cast. Now let's bring up the curtain.

examples of cooperation and humanity can be found. But they are also full of ambition, self-serving righteousness, and greed, and it is a rare day when some of the countries are not in open conflict. And even when they are not threatening one another, they are forever calculating what is good for themselves and taking action based on their national interests.

The Importance of Studying World Politics

The last line from Macbeth's soliloquy is where this text and Shakespeare part company. The Bard pessimistically pronounces the action of life as "signifying nothing." That thought has a certain fatalistic appeal. "What the hell," we can say, "why bother with a complicated subject about faraway places that have little to do with me?"

If Americans did not know it already, they learned on September 11, 2001, that world politics can dramatically impact them. That morning between 8:45 A.M. and 10:00 A.M. four commercial airliners that had been turned into terrorist weapons shattered Americans' sense of security. Two planes demolished the twin towers of the World Trade Center in Manhattan; another plummeted into the Pentagon just outside Washington, D.C.; the fourth crashed into a field near Pittsburgh despite the heroic efforts of the passengers to retake control of the aircraft. Aboard the airliners, 33 crew members, 214 innocent passengers, and 19 terrorists died. More than 3,000 others on the ground perished, many before the horrified, almost disbelieving eyes of Americans who had turned on their televisions as news of the attacks spread. When they had awakened that morning, most Americans had never heard of Osama bin Laden or al-Qaeda; by noon those names were seared in the American psyche.

What is important here is to see that we are all on the world stage where the ebb and flow of the action affects us all every day in large and small ways. It is hard to find a proverbial silver lining in the 9/11 tragedy. If there is one, though, it is the possibility that columnist Robert Samuelson was correct when he wrote that there had been an "end of illusion," and that "what was destroyed was not just the World Trade Center and part of the Pentagon but also Americans' . . . dreamlike . . . feeling [of being] insulated from the rest of the world."[1]

The 9/11 attack, the U.S.-led retaliation against Afghanistan, and the invasion of Iraq 18 months later all worked to focus Americans' interest on foreign affairs. History casts doubt, however, on whether Samuelson was right that in the long run Americans will sustain their interest in the world around them. Studies before 9/11 found that only about 20% of Americans followed foreign news and that most Americans knew little about global politics or world geography.[2] Even after 9/11, knowledge seems woefully limited. One October 2002 study tested 18–24-year-olds in nine countries with 56 questions about world geography and 8 questions about world affairs. As Figure 1.1 details, the study found that the percentage of correct responses by Americans was next to last. On the geography questions, 62% of the Americans got more than half wrong. Unbelievably, only 13% of American young adults could point to Iraq on a blank world map, even though war was brewing with that country. On a multiple-choice question about the size of the U.S. population, not only did a scant 25% of Americans select the correct answer, but their score was lower than that of the respondents in any of the other eight countries.[3]

Is this widespread lack of information about or interest in world events justifiable? The answer is no! This text does not often try to tell you what to think or do. But one message is stressed: The world drama is important and deserves our careful attention.

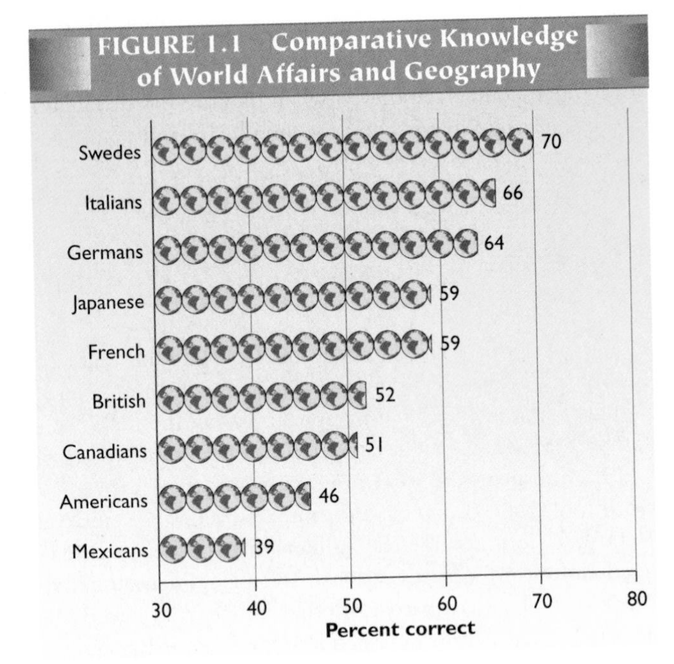

How much people know about the world around them varies from country to country. This figure shows the average percentage of correct answers given by people aged 18 to 24 in nine countries about world geography and affairs. Note that Americans finished next to last, only somewhat ahead of Mexicans, who live in a poor country in which only about half of all youths finish high school (compared to 90% in the United States).

Note: The data are based on the average of the scores on two questionnaires: one with 10 questions on world affairs and another with 56 questions on geography. On the world affairs questionnaire, two questions (one on the world's largest religion, the other on the euro) were factored out by the author for methodological reasons.

Data source: National Geographic—Roper 2002 Global Geographic Literacy Survey, November 2002, available on the Web at http://www.nationalgeographic.com/geosurvey/. Calculations by author.

Did You Know That:

With an average turnout of just 35% during five presidential elections between 1980 and 2000, Americans aged 18 to 24 had the lowest voting turnout of any age group. A young adult is about half as likely to vote as an adult aged 45 to 64. This gap affects whose voices are heard by politicians.

We are more than mere observers. We are all on the stage along with everybody else, and, whether we like it or not, we are all caught up in the flow of global events.

This does not mean that you are stuck with the world as it exists or as it is evolving. The Irish literary lion, Oscar Wilde (1854–1900), once observed wryly, "The world is a stage, but the play is badly cast." If you agree, do not stand idly by. You can play an active part; you can make a difference! The script is not set. It is an improvisational play with lots of room for ad-libbing and even for changing the story line. To help you think about whether you agree with Wilde, you will find a number of boxes in this text that follow the theme, You Be the Playwright, and ask you to think about how the script should be written.

It is also important to realize that we do not have to accept playing the role of a walk-on with no lines. We can speak up if we wish and join the action if we try, a reality captured in the Play a Part boxes. Capturing center stage is difficult, and even the great have not held it for long. But we can all play a part. The important message of this text is that your efforts to become knowledgeable about the world and to try to shape its course to your liking are worthwhile because international politics does matter. It plays

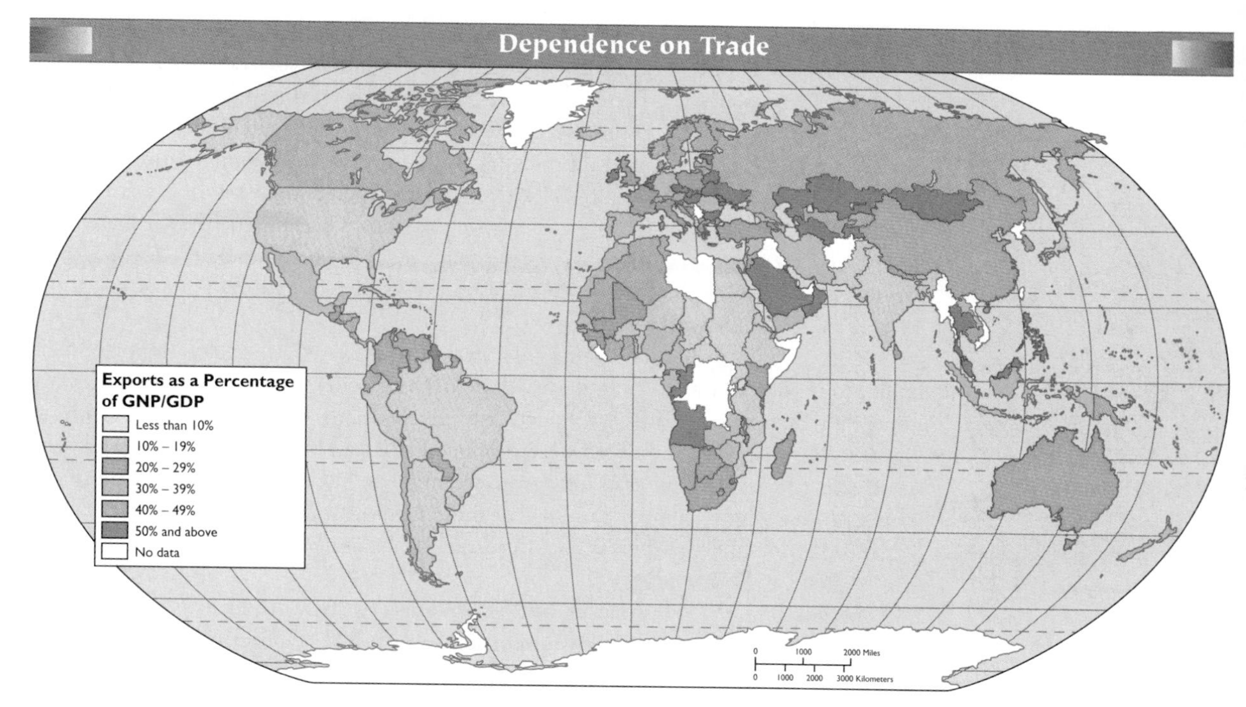

All countries, even the most economically powerful ones, are becoming increasingly dependent on trade for their economic health. Whether you are American or Zimbabwean, there is a good chance that your job, the price you pay for the goods you buy, and other factors in your economic well-being are dependent on global trade.

an important role in your life, and you should be concerned. To understand that further, let us turn to a number of ways, some dramatic, some mundane, in which international politics affects your economic well-being, your living space, and your very life.

World Politics and Your Finances

World politics affects each of our personal economic conditions in many ways. The human toll of the attacks of September 11, 2001, on those who died, their families, and their friends was, of course, the most devastating impact. But the economic impact was also staggering. Just in the first four months, the 9/11 attacks cost the United States at least $81 billion in destroyed property, lost business earnings, lost wages, increased security expenditures, and other ways.

More routinely, the impact of international economics on individuals continues to expand as world industrial and financial structures become increasingly intertwined. Indeed, as we shall see, the ties between national and international affairs are so close that many social scientists now use the term **intermestic** to symbolize the merger of *inter*national and do*mestic* concerns. To illustrate the increasingly ubiquitous connections between your own personal financial condition and world politics, we will briefly explore how international trade, the flow of international capital, and defense spending affect your finances.

International Trade and Your Finances

The global flow of goods (tangible items) and services (intangible items such as revenues from tourism, insurance, and banking) is important to your financial circumstances. One example is U.S. dependence on foreign sources for vital resources. That reality was brought sharply into focus as crude oil prices rose more than 300%, from $12 a barrel in January 2002 to over $36 a barrel in March 2004, driving up the prices of gasoline, heating oil, and other petroleum products to record highs in the United States. Thus, every time you pumped gas, you paid more thanks to the realities of the international system.

Trade also wins and loses jobs. There is a steadily increasing likelihood that international trade and your job are related. Exports create jobs. The United States is the world's largest exporter, providing other countries with $972 billion worth of U.S. goods and services in 2002. Creating these exports employed some 16 million Americans, about 13% of the total U.S. workforce.

While exports create jobs, other jobs are lost to imports. Americans imported $1.4 trillion in goods and services in 2002. Many of the clothes, toys, electronics, and other items they bought were once produced extensively in the United States by American workers. Now most of these items are produced overseas by workers whose wages are substantially lower. Jobs are also lost to service imports. For example, software programmers in India, who earn less than 25% of their American counterparts, provide about $60 billion annually in services to Microsoft, IBM, and other software giants in the United States and elsewhere.

Did You Know That:

Tourist spending is a service export. During 2002, some 45 million foreign visitors created jobs for Americans by spending more than $91 billion in the United States.

Lost jobs are a serious matter, but before you cry "Buy American!" and demand barriers to limit foreign goods, it is important to realize that inexpensive foreign products improve your standard of living. For example, the United States annually imports more than $73 billion worth of clothes and footwear. What Americans pay for shirts, sneakers, and other things they wear would be much higher if they were all made by American workers earning American wages.

The Flow of International Capital and Your Finances

The global flow of international finance affects you in more ways than you probably imagine. These are covered in detail in chapter 12, but to begin to see the impact we can look at two examples.

International Investment Capital

Each year, individuals and companies invest many billions of dollars abroad in business and real estate. For Americans, one thing this means is that many familiar U.S. companies have foreign owners. For example, the British firm Pearson P.L.C. owns Addison Wesley, Longman, Prentice Hall, and other American publishers that produce many of the textbooks American college students read. Check the texts you have purchased this semester. It would not be surprising to find one or more of these imprints among them. Such investment from overseas arguably creates a degree of foreign control over the U.S. economy and how Americans live, but foreign capital also provides jobs and other benefits. This is true, for example, for American workers who make Nissan automobiles in Tennessee, Hondas in Ohio, Toyotas in Kentucky, and Mitsubishis in Illinois.

International Financial Markets

Yet another of the multitudinous connections between your pocketbook and the global economy stems from the huge sums that are invested across national borders in stocks and in private and government bonds each year. One way that affects Americans relates to the U.S. government estimates that the national debt will increase by $2.3 trillion between **fiscal year (FY)** 2002 and FY2009 due to annual federal budget deficits. In 2002, foreign investors owned 32% of the $3.5 trillion U.S. debt, and Americans need them to buy at least as high a percentage of the new bonds that the federal government will sell to finance its soaring debt. If foreigners do not invest in U.S. bonds, then the law of supply and demand will drive up the interest rates on those bonds. Since they compete for dollars, rising U.S. bond rates will drive up other interest rates, meaning that Americans will pay more each month on new mortgages, car loan payments, college tuition loans, and other forms of borrowing.

Defense Spending and Your Finances

The budget of your national government and the taxes to fund it are yet another way that world politics affects you economically. At the very least, you pay taxes to support your country's involvement in world affairs. In FY2002 the U.S. government spent $2 trillion (that's right, trillion, not billion). Spending on general foreign affairs (such as foreign aid) was minor, accounting for only about 1% of the budget. Defense spending was considerably more important. It amounted to $349 billion, approximately 17% of the U.S. budget. This equals about $1,200 per American for national defense.

As more of a country's wealth is devoted to military spending, less is available for private use and for domestic government spending. Table 1.1 compares several countries by a number of defense spending criteria. As you can see, some countries devote huge sums to defense; others spend little. Countries also vary widely in their defense expenditures compared to such measures as their **gross domestic product (GDP)**: the value of all goods and services produced within a country).

One way to think about defense spending and how it relates to you is to compare it with federal spending on higher education. With about 5% of the world's population, the United States accounts for more than a third of the world's military spending. Even after the 9/11 attacks, some

Did You Know That:

Even limited military operations are very costly. Recent U.S. interventions and their costs are:

Grenada	1983	$76 million
Panama	1989	$164 million
Persian Gulf	1990–1991	$61 billion
Somalia	1992–1994	$675 million*
Haiti	1994–1995	$427 million
Bosnia	1996	$1.3 billion*
Kosovo	1999–2000	$5.2 billion*
Afghanistan	2001–2003	$10 billion*
Iraq	2003–2004	$85 billion*

*first year of multiyear operation

TABLE 1.1 National Military Expenditures

Country	Total (US$ Billions)*	As Percentage of Budget	As Percentage of GDP	Per Capita (US$)
Canada	7.8	4.8	1.1	245
China	55.0	+25.0	4.2	43
India	12.1	15.5	2.5	12
Israel	9.0	21.2	8.8	1,493
Japan	40.8	5.7	1.0	322
Kenya	0.2	6.2	1.8	6
Mexico	4.0	2.9	1.0	39
Russia	56.8	+50.0	5.1	380
Sweden	4.4	4.0	2.1	449
United States	348.6	17.4	3.6	1,200

*Defense spending figures for most countries tend to be less reliable than most other data. The data for China and Russia are especially controversial. The + sign before the percentage of budget for China and Russia denotes that with both expenditures and overall budget uncertain, the percentages are at least that high.

Data sources: CIA (2002), *World Almanac* (2003).

The range of government spending on defense as an overall amount, as a percentage of a country's budget or of its gross national product, and as a per capita expenditure varies widely. Whatever the exact figures, defense spending affects your economic conditions in a number of areas, such as jobs, taxes, and budget choices.

people question the need to spend more than $300 billion a year with no hostile, extraordinarily powerful country facing the United States. Yet the government has now built 21 B-2 bombers at a cost of over $2.1 billion each, and has begun to develop the next generation of fighter aircraft, which may eventually cost $1 trillion to deploy.

Although there is no one-to-one relationship between reduced defense spending and increased higher education spending, it is worth thinking about what would be possible if some defense spending were reallocated to higher education. In 2001 about 15 million students were enrolled in U.S. colleges. The annual cost of room, board, and tuition at the average four-year private college was $27,711; at the average public college it was $9,326. If the Pentagon deleted just one B-2 bomber from its budget (a savings of $2.1 billion), that money would be enough to give an all-expenses-paid scholarship at the average private college to 75,782 students or at the average state university to 225,177 students.

Yet the reallocation of defense spending that might bring economic relief to some people would harm the economic circumstances of other people. Many industries and their workers and families depend heavily on defense spending, which declined in the United States from about 6.2% of the GDP in 1985 to 3.6% in 2002. This cost many jobs. In the late 1980s some 8 million people were employed in military uniform, as civilian employees of the Department of Defense, or as defense industry workers. Now the combined uniformed and civilian U.S. workforce stands at 5.2 million wage earners, a decline of 35%. The economic impact of jobs gained or lost creates strong pressure from individuals, communities, and businesses for the government to maintain defense spending. To a degree, as former Assistant Secretary of Defense Lawrence J. Korb commented, "Both the administration and Congress . . . view defense as a federal jobs program."[4]

World Politics and Your Living Space

International politics can affect far more than your pocketbook. It can determine the quality of the air you breathe, the water you drink, and many other aspects of the globe you inhabit.

The growth of the world's population and its pressure on resources threaten to change the quality of life as we know it. It took 100,000 years of human existence for the world population to reach 6 billion, a dubious mark that the UN calculates occurred on October 12, 1999. What is worrisome, as Figure 1.2 depicts, is that each additional billion people have been added in shorter and shorter periods of time. The growth rate has declined a bit, so that it could be as late as 2015 before the world population reaches 7 billion. Still, this represents a tidal wave of new humans. In 2002, for example, the world added over 133 million people, more than the population of Africa's most populous country, Nigeria (129 million).

Among other concerns, Earth's expanding population presents serious environmental dangers. Burning oil and other fossil fuels to warm, transport, and otherwise provide for this mass of people annually creates more than 6 billion tons of carbon dioxide and other gas emissions. These, most scientists believe, are causing global warming. The decade of the 1990s was the warmest in recorded history, with 1998 the warmest year since records were first kept in 1856. The new century has not brought relief. With the first four years almost as warm as 1998, the decade is on track to exceed the record set by the 1990s.

Warmer temperatures may be welcome to some, but the overall ramifications are worrisome. Among other things, many scientists claim that global warming is melting the polar ice caps, thereby raising sea levels and threatening to flood coastal areas of the world. Some Pacific island countries could even disappear under the rising seas. Scientists

FIGURE 1.2 Number of Years to Add Each Billion People

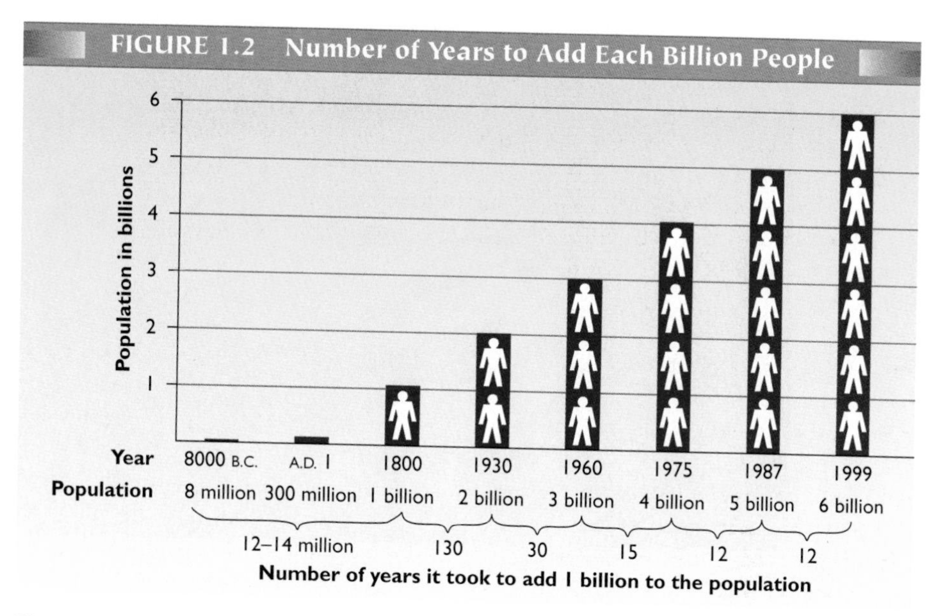

The world population is growing at an alarming rate. In October 1999 it passed the 6 billion mark and is expanding at a rate of about 210,728 people a day, 8,764 an hour, 146 a minute, 2.4 a second. You can go to a world population clock at http://metalab.unc.edu/lunarbin/worldpop and enter the day you were born to see how much the world population has grown in the intervening years.

Data sources: U.S. Census Bureau at http://www.census.gov/ipc/www.worldhis.html; United Nations Population Fund (2003).

project that global warming will also increase the frequency and intensity of torrential rainfall, hurricanes, and other forms of violent weather. The *World Disasters Report, 2002* issued by the International Red Cross/Red Crescent found that globally, "Weather-related disasters have been the most pervasive in the past ten years." The report went on to focus particular concern on the fact that "the number of people in the Oceania [South Pacific] region affected by weather-related disasters has soared by 65 times over the past 30 years. Cyclones, droughts and floods threaten to make life unviable on many islands long before rising seas swallow them up."[5]

An important factor in the weather changes that many people are having to endure are the El Niño/La Niña (unusual warming/cooling) conditions that have been occurring with increasing frequency and intensity in the equatorial Pacific Ocean. Among other impacts in the last decade, scientists say, these conditions caused the torrential rains and horrendous flooding in Central and South America in 1999, which cost billions of dollars in damage and killed thousands, followed in 2001 by a prolonged drought in Central America that caused further economic ruin by severely damaging the region's crops. These El Niño/La Niña conditions also affect areas beyond the Pacific Rim. On the U.S. east coast, for example, years in which El Niño predominates can be drought prone, but they have fewer, milder hurricanes. La Niña can bring flooding and is likely to foster more frequent and violent hurricanes.

There are numerous other proven or suspected deleterious environmental trends that are also despoiling our living space. The United Nations Environment Programme (UNEP) reports that in addition to the perils already mentioned, erosion destroys 25 billion tons of topsoil each year, 900 million urban dwellers breathe dangerous levels of sulfur dioxide, and more than half the world's population could be facing critical water shortages by

Many scientists believe that global warming caused by the discharge of carbon dioxide and other greenhouse gases is increasing the frequency and intensity of storms, droughts, and other undesirable weather patterns. Storms, such as Hurricane Isidore being traced here in 2002 at the U.S. National Hurricane Center in Miami, Florida, pose a serious threat to the lives and property of people in many parts of the world.

midcentury. "Our world is characterized by . . . the accelerating loss of the environmental capital that underpins life on Earth," warns UNEP Executive Director Klaus Toepfer.[6]

Certainly, world politics has not caused most environmental problems. However, we are unlikely to be able to stem, much less reverse, the degradation of the biosphere without global cooperation. As Toepfer put it, "We suffer from problems of planetary dimensions. They require global responses." These are being initiated, but only slowly and somewhat uncertainly, as detailed in chapter 16.

World Politics and Your Life

Not only our lives are affected by world politics, so too in some cases is whether we live at all. Disease control and political violence are just two events that intertwine your very life with world politics.

Disease Control

Politics may not directly cause diseases, but we are increasingly in need of global responses to counter health threats that ignore national borders. One example relates to the environment. Chlorofluorocarbons (CFCs) and other chemicals we have spewed into the air have significantly depleted the Earth's ozone layer, which helps shield us from the Sun's deadly ultraviolet rays. Because higher exposure to ultraviolet rays increases the risk of developing melanoma, the deadliest form of skin cancer, the rate of new melanoma cases has skyrocketed. For Americans, this means that more than 54,000 of them will be diagnosed with melanoma each year, and almost 8,000 will die of the disease. Certainly there are things that you can do, like wearing sunscreen, to reduce the chances of becoming a skin cancer victim. But achieving that goal can also be greatly helped by international agreements, such as the UN-sponsored Montreal Protocol (1987) to phase out the use of CFCs and other ozone-attacking chemicals that were once used in such common items as air conditioners and deodorant sprays.

We also increasingly rely on global cooperation to prevent the spread of infectious diseases. Such diseases have always been international travelers. Italian sailors carried bubonic plague (the Black Death) to Europe in 1347 after contracting it during a voyage to the Black Sea region from people who, in turn, had been infected through their

Diseases have always been international travelers, but the vast number of people traveling today and the speed with which they do so is making disease prevention, containment, and cure a global concern. Severe acute respiratory syndrome (SARS) may have originated in China in 2003, but it soon became an international problem, as represented by this photograph of an official from the U.S. Centers for Disease Control and Prevention speaking at a SARS conference in Hong Kong.

trade contacts with people in China. During the next three years, the Black Death killed between a third and one-half of the people in Europe.

Diseases still travel today, but they do so in part by high-speed airliners rather than by sedate sailing ships. The Black Death took years to spread; severe acute respiratory syndrome (SARS) spread around the world in weeks during 2003. According to a top epidemiologist, the new number of infectious diseases and their ability to spread rapidly has made the "period from the 1970s without precedent in the history of the annals of medicine."[7] Of course each country took steps to contain SARS and treat its victims, but it fell to the World Health Organization (WHO) to coordinate the global effort.

Political Violence

War, terrorism, and other forms of political violence are in many ways more threatening today than ever before (Horne, 2002). Until the 20th century, the vast majority of war deaths were soldiers. Civilian casualties began to rise drastically as noncombatants increasingly became a target of military operations. Nearly as many civilians as soldiers were killed during World War II. Now more civilians than soldiers are killed. According to the UN, civilians accounted for more than 85% of everyone killed during wars in the 1980s and 1990s. Most tragically, these casualties included 2 million children, who died from wounds and other war-related causes. In a nuclear war, military casualties would be a mere footnote to the overall death toll. And terrorists almost exclusively target civilians.

The attacks of September 11, 2001, also brought into sharp focus the reality that violent international attacks are not confined to those launched by countries using their military forces. Americans found that they were vulnerable to terrorism anywhere and at any moment in their daily lives. It must also be said that this unsettling reality has long been felt more acutely in other parts of the world that have been subjected to more frequent acts of international terrorism (Heymann, 2002).

War is a special concern for college-age adults because they are of prime military age. An examination of the ages of U.S. Marines killed during the Vietnam War shows that of those who died, 84% were aged 18 to 22. Some soldiers killed in war are volunteers, but not all are. Many countries have a draft to staff their military services. The United States abandoned the draft in the early 1970s, but draft registration is still required of all military-age males.

It is also the case that military combat is a matter that increasingly affects women directly as well as men. In the United States and elsewhere, the types of combat units in which women are allowed to serve are expanding. As a result, many more women may fight and die in future wars. For example, American women now serve as combat pilots and as officers on warships. Moreover, public attitudes are moving slowly toward accepting the idea of women in units that are even more dangerous. A recent poll of Americans found that 52% were willing to see women serve in ground forces such as the infantry. When asked if women should be subject to the draft, 46% of Americans said yes, 50% said no, and 4% were undecided.[8]

Even if they are not allowed into ground combat units, women are serving in military roles that bring more of them ever closer to the fighting. Thousands of women took part in the war against Iraq in 2003. The story of three of those women and some issues to ponder are in the You Be the Playwright box "Women Warriors."

More than anything, the lesson that you should draw here is that world politics plays a role in your everyday life and sometimes can also have a dramatic, very individual impact on you. We are all involved economically and environmentally. Furthermore, world politics can threaten our very lives. Wars will continue to be fought. Young men—and increasingly young women—will be called upon to fight them. Some will die. In the worst possible circumstance, nuclear war, it will not matter whether you are in the military or not. Furthermore, terrorism is no longer a remote event for Americans, as those unfortunate souls in the twin towers found out as they stared in stunned horror at an airliner hurtling toward them.

Can We Make a Difference?

The next logical question is, "Can I make a difference?" Yes, you can! It is true that we cannot all be president or secretary of state, but we can take action and we can make our views known.

Direct action is one way to influence global relations. This happens more frequently than you might think (Sharp, 2001). Among the activists, students have often been important agents of political change. The sum of millions of individual student actions—ranging from burning draft cards, to massive demonstrations in front of the White House, to protesting and even dying on U.S. campuses—helped end American involvement in Vietnam. College students were also often at the forefront of both the protests against and the rallies for the U.S.-led war with Iraq in 2003, as related in the Play a Part box "For and Against the War in Iraq." In this case, those who demonstrated against the war were not successful, but the more important point is that they and those who rallied in support of action against Iraq did more than sit passively in the political audience.

Consumer boycotts and other forms of pressure can also be effective. Individuals have made a difference by refusing to eat tuna fish that does not bear the "dolphin safe" label. More recently, students on U.S. college campuses have participated in protests and brought consumer pressure to bear on clothing and footwear companies that sell products manufactured in so-called sweatshops in Asia and elsewhere. These factories pay little, require long hours, and have poor safety records. Adding to the pressure, colleges began to follow the lead of their students. The University of Notre Dame, for one, banned the manufacture of its licensed products in 13 countries that have unfair labor standards. As a result of such efforts, Nike and other companies have joined the Fair Labor Association (FLA), a coalition organization of human rights groups, manufacturers,

Did You Know That:

You can find out if your school is a member of the Fair Labor Association by going to the FLA Web site at http://www.fairlabor.org/.

YOU BE THE PLAYWRIGHT

Women Warriors

Throughout history, most of the women killed, wounded, or otherwise traumatized in war have been civilians who met their fate when it came to them. In what is a growing trend, the cruelties of combat befell Shoshana Johnson, Jessica Lynch, and Lori Piestewa when they went to war.

These three women were all enlisted members of the U.S. Army's 507th Maintenance Company when it deployed in February 2003 from Fort Bliss, Texas, to Kuwait. In many ways, they represented a model of American diversity. Lynch, age 19 and of Irish heritage, grew up in Palestine, West Virginia. Johnson, a 30-year-old African American and the mother of a 2-year-old daughter, was raised in El Paso, Texas, and followed the footsteps of her father, a retired veteran, into the Army. Piestewa, who was serving her country as her father had in Vietnam and her grandfather had in World War II, was 23, a Hopi from Tuba City, Arizona, and the mother of a son (age 4) and a daughter (age 3).

On March 23, soon after the war began, the three women were part of a convoy providing support for the U.S.-British offensive. Iraqi forces attacked the U.S. unit near Nasiriyah, Iraq, and more than a dozen American soldiers, including all three women, were killed, wounded, and/or captured. Most tragically, Lori Piestewa died in combat. Lynch suffered multiple injuries (a head wound, a spinal injury, and fractures to her right arm, both legs, and her right foot and ankle), was captured, and was later rescued by U.S. commandos. Johnson was also captured and paraded by her captors before television cameras in violation of the Geneva convention. She remained a prisoner of war until freed by U.S. troops near the end of the war.

The saga of Johnson, Lynch, and Piestewa highlights the reality that the chances of women being killed, captured, or wounded as combatants have grown as the United States and many other countries increasingly gender-integrate their armed forces. Some applaud this change. Others want to take it even further by abolishing the rules in the U.S. and most other armed forces that bar women from infantry, artillery, and armored units. Still others find women in combat abhorrent and would eliminate the possibility.

Ask yourself how you feel about women warriors. One option is to maintain current policy, with women serving in most military positions, but not with the most perilous ground units. A second possibility is to eliminate all barriers to women in the military by opening all positions to them. Your third choice is to remove women from all military jobs that might take them near the front lines. If you were the playwright, how would the next act unfold?

World politics can affect your life if you join or are drafted into the military. This is increasingly true for women as well as men. On March 23, 2003, Pfc. Lori Piestewa of Arizona was killed in action near Nasiriyah, Iraq, and two other women in her unit, Pfc. Jessica Lynch of West Virginia and Pfc. Shoshana Johnson of Texas, were captured and injured in the firefight. In this photo, Johnson, who had been shot in both ankles, is being escorted by U.S. Marines to an evacuation airplane soon after she and six other American prisoners of war were freed when U.S. forces captured Samarra, 75 miles north of Baghdad, where they had been held for three weeks.

and 175 universities and colleges, who work together to help protect the rights of factory workers worldwide.

Voting for candidates is another way to affect policy. Leaders do not always follow campaign promises, but who gets elected usually does influence policy. At this writing, it is clear that the 2004 U.S. presidential election between George Bush and John Kerry, the presumptive Democratic nominee, will be waged in part over their differences on

PLAY A PART

For and Against the War in Iraq

Abbie Hoffman, a prominent protester against the U.S. intervention in Vietnam (1964–1975) and founder of the Youth International Party ("Yippies"), had it right when he told his followers, "Democracy is not something you believe in or a place to hang your hat, but it's something you do. You participate. If you stop doing it, democracy crumbles."[1]

Faced in 2003 with the prospect of a different war, the college students in the two accompanying pictures and the many others like them across the United States and indeed around the world, who demonstrated for and against the U.S.-led invasion of Iraq, were laudably following Hoffman's maxim that democracy is something you do. The students and others who waved signs, debated one another, and took other actions were an important part of the national dialogue about the war.

In the end, war came. By the day before it began, 70% of Americans had come to support action, 27% were opposed, and 3% unsure.[2] It is important to understand, though, that the decision to go to war and even the support of a majority of Americans for war did not mean that those who rallied in favor of it had "won" and those who protested against the war had "lost" and wasted their time. Antiwar protesters did not ultimately prevail, but their influence was evident in the Bush administration's domestic campaign to build public opinion support among Americans. There is also evidence that activism, as Hoffman advocated, has an impact beyond the immediate issue. For example, one study of 37 democracies during the period 1919–1992 found that the higher a country's level of citizen political activity, the less likely it was to initiate international disputes.[3] Most importantly, those who demonstrated their opposition to the war, as well as those who rallied to support it, strengthened democracy. As U.S. Senator J. William Fulbright, another opponent of the Vietnam War, put it, "In a democracy, dissent is an act of faith [that the democracy works]. . . . To criticize one's country is to do it a service and pay it a compliment."[4]

You can make a difference in world politics, and you should try. This does not mean your view will always prevail. As these photographs of University of Minnesota students show, some opposed the war in Iraq and some supported it. That the war occurred did not mean that the opponents wasted their time. Instead, they improved democracy, which rests on a politically active citizenry.

such foreign policy issues as the U.S. attack on Iraq and post-war policy, the value of free trade to the U.S. economy, the wisdom of unilateralism versus multilateralism, and the Bush Doctrine of preemptive action. U.S. foreign policy during 2005–2009 will be different under a Kerry than a Bush administration.

Direct voting on international questions is also possible in some countries (Setala, 1999; Rourke, Hiskes, & Zirakzadeh, 1992). During 2003, citizens in Hungary, Lithuania, Malta, and Slovenia decided directly what their country's foreign policy should be when a majority of voters in each consented to their country's membership in the European Union (EU). The year before, the people of Gibraltar opted to remain a British dependency, the Swiss voted by referendum to join the United Nations, and Irish voters agreed to ratify the Treaty of Nice, which changes the fundamental rules governing the EU. The ability of citizens to make direct decisions about foreign policy is still not common, but it is becoming more so, and there is strong support in the United States, the countries of Europe, and other democracies for greater use of referendums and other such **direct democracy** techniques (Dalton, Burklin, & Drummond, 2001; Qvortrup, 2002).

The point is that you count— by voting, protesting, joining issue-oriented groups, donating money to causes you support, or even by having your thoughts recorded in a political poll. Few individual actions are dramatic, and by themselves few significantly change world politics, but the sum of many smaller actions can and does make a difference. Do not consider politics a spectator sport. It is more important than that. Treat politics as a participant—even a contact—sport.

The World Tomorrow: Two Roads Diverge

The imperative to be active is particularly important as the world begins a new millennium. Many observers believe that we have arrived at a crucial junction in the paths by which we organize and conduct our global politics. Contemplation of that junction brings to mind Robert Frost's famous poem, "The Road Not Taken" (1916). Frost concluded his poem with this thought:

> I shall be telling this with a sigh
> Somewhere ages and ages hence:
> Two roads diverged in a wood, and I—
> I took the one less traveled by,
> And that has made all the difference.

Like the works of Shakespeare, Frost's lines have implications that challenge the reader's intellect. We can build on Frost's imagery of two roads—one the traditional, "more traveled" road, the other an alternative, "less traveled" road—to discuss two possible paths for the future. The traditional road is a continuation of the political path that the world has mostly followed for at least five centuries. This route has been characterized by self-interested states using their power to struggle against one another in a largely anarchistic international system.

The alternative road entails significant changes that will take the world in a new direction. Those who favor the less traveled path argue that states should abandon their pursuit of short-term self-interest and take a more cooperative, globalist approach. Advocates of this direction contend that one reason to follow it is that the advent of nuclear weapons, the deterioration of the global environment, and other looming problems could spark an epic disaster unless the world changes the way it governs itself.

Some of those who advocate the alternative road believe that it entails a decline in the central role states play in the international system (Sørenson, 2001). By the same token, these analysts also see a rise of global institutions (such as the UN) and regional organizations (such as the EU) as authoritative actors capable of constraining individual countries. At its extreme, this process could lead to regional governments or even to a global government, as discussed in chapter 7. Such ideas are not new, but they represent the road less traveled by in world politics.

Frost leaves his reader with the thought that choosing the less familiar road "made all the difference." We do not know whether Frost was content with his choice or regretted it. He wisely left that to the reader's imagination and judgment. Similarly, a major challenge that this text presents to you is deciding which road you think the world should travel by.

Realism and Liberalism: Some Travel Notes on Two Roads

To help you begin to make your choice, the following section describes and contrasts the two paths and discusses those who advocate each direction (Jackson & Sørenson, 2003). Those who believe that the world is and/or should continue on the traditional road are often associated with a theory called realism (associated terms: realpolitik, balance of power, nationalism, conservative, and state-centric). Those who believe that the world is beginning to chart a new course are frequently identified with another theory, liberalism (associated terms: liberal institutionalism, globalism, idealist, cosmopolitan, and internationalist). You will also find the prefix "neo" attached to some of these words (as in neorealism or neoliberalism) to designate recent variations on the classic concepts (Mansbach, 1996).

The world is at one of those rare junctions in the course of global affairs when it has the opportunity to make basic decisions about its future. Liberals and realists suggest very different paths to that future. Which one do you favor?

Some comments on the terms are appropriate. First, do not be fooled by the connotations of realism and liberalism. One school of theorists labeled their position "realism" and the sobriquet stuck, but they do not necessarily see things as they "really" are. It would also be an error to equate the use of "liberal" here with its application to domestic politics. There are some parallels, but there are also differences. It is best, perhaps, to think of realists as "pessimists." Conversely, "optimists" is probably a more descriptive label for liberals. The point is not to prejudge books by covers or theories by labels.

Second, the effort to group theories together is merely a helpful vehicle to introduce them to beginning students of international relations. Table 1.2 summarizes the main points of realism, liberalism, and their two "neo" offshoots. Still, putting theories into neat categories partly obscures their range and subtleties. As one study noted, "If you put four IR theorists in a room you will easily get ten different ways of organizing theory, and there will also be disagreement about which theories are relevant in the first place" (Jackson & Sørenson, 2002:34). Thus, if you delve into theory you will find many nuances in the writings of the leading realist and liberal scholars as they try to describe how the world works politically. You will also discover that there are a number of related approaches, such as international political economy (IPE), feminism, postmodernism, and constructivism, which vary from general realism and liberalism in part because they have different assumptions about what is important and, therefore, stress different things. Each of these approaches is taken up in detail later in the text. IPE scholars focus on wealth as the key unit of analysis and have their own range of theories, which are found in chapter 12. The other three approaches challenge the traditional ways we perceive ourselves, our relations to others, and the supposed realities of world around us. All are examined in chapter 5.

The Nature of Politics: Realism and Liberalism

The disagreement between realists and liberals about the nature of politics is perhaps the most fundamental division in all of political discourse. The two schools of thought disagree over the very nature of *Homo politicus* (political humankind).

Realism and the Nature of Politics

At root, **realists** are pessimistic and liberals are optimistic about human nature (Beitz, 1999; Osiander, 1998; Rose, 1998; Schmidt, 1998). Realists believe that political struggle

TABLE 1.2 Comparing Theories of International Relations

Theory	Realism/Neorealism	Liberalism/ Neoliberalism
View of human nature	Largely pessimistic: Humans aggressive and self-serving; skeptical about possibilities of change.	Largely optimistic: Humans want to cooperate and can learn to do so.
Main cause of conflict	Aggressive human nature, failure of great powers to use power wisely and manage system. Neo-realists focus on unequal state power in anarchical system. Attempts to increase power and counterattempts to restrain power lead to war.	National greed and insecurity prevent positive human instincts from prevailing. Neoliberals emphasize the impact of anarchy, few restraints on power, and few conflict resolution methods.
Role of conflict in international relations	Central and inevitable, at least in the long run.	Central, but does not have to be. Can be decreased by building cooperative relationships.
Analytical focus	States, their leaders, and the ability to make wise policy in dangerous world. Neorealists emphasize the structure of the statecentric system, especially its distribution of power.	Norms (such as justice, freedom, self-determination, democracy) and international organizations (IOs). Over the long term, these more cooperative norms and IOs will help move past systemic anarchy.
Role of state in system	States are core, and their leaders work to promote national self-interest.	States still central but cooperate through IOs to create better system. State role will diminish over time as norms and IOs become more central.
Role of international organizations	May pose danger through illusion of cooperation. Can be tools of the state to pursue national interest.	Promote norms, provide vehicle for states to learn cooperation, provide protection and help for small states. Facilitate cooperation and promote global governance.
Policy prescriptions	Pursue pragmatic self-interest; preserve or expand power; do not squander power on marginal interests or moral/ideological crusades.	Create norms of justice and peace; promote democracy; promote and strengthen IOs.
Key concepts	Power, struggle, self-help, self-interest, systemic anarchy, balance of power.	Peace, justice, democracy, self-determination, global/regional organization and processes, norms, global governance.
Role of morality	State and individual morality different. Highest morality of state is to safety and welfare of its citizens.	State and individual morality the same. Important standard of conduct.
How to achieve interests of people	Promote the power of own state. Only the state can achieve "positive" results for individuals.	Create norms, IOs and processes to regulate behavior, provide justice, and improve social and economic conditions for all.

The author gratefully acknowledges the important contribution of Mark Boyer at the University of Connecticut to this table.

among humans is probably inevitable because people have an inherent dark side (Spegele, 1996). Many realists would trace their intellectual heritage to such political philosophers as Thomas Hobbes (1588–1679), who believed that humans possess an inherent urge to dominate, an *animus dominandi*. In his book *Leviathan* (1651), Hobbes argued that "if any two men desire the same thing, which nevertheless they cannot both enjoy, they become enemies and . . . endeavor to destroy or subdue one another." Taking the same point of view, one leading realist scholar, Hans Morgenthau, wrote that an "ubiquity of evil in human actions" inevitably turns "churches into political organizations . . . revolutions into dictatorships . . . and love of country into imperialism" (Zakaria, 1993:22).

A relatively recent variation on realism is the neorealist (or structural realist) school of thought (James, 2002; Schweller & Priess, 1997). **Neorealists** focus on the anarchic nature of a world system based on competition among sovereign states; classic realists stress human nature as the factor that shapes world politics. As one neorealist puts it, the international system based on sovereign actors (states), which answer to no higher authority, is "anarchic, with no overarching authority providing security and order." The result of such a self-help system is that "each state must rely on its own resources to survive and flourish." But because "there is no authoritative, impartial method of settling these disputes—i.e. no world government—states are their own judges, juries, and hangmen, and often resort to force to achieve their security interests" (Zakaria, 1993:22) What unites both realists and neorealists is that they doubt whether there is any escape from conflict. Classical realists believe human nature is immutable, and neorealists are skeptical about the ability of interdependence or international organizations to promote cooperation (Cox, 1997). In the words of one scholar, "Even in a world that is clearly becoming more interconnected, the game *is* domestic politics for national policymakers" who continue to make policy based on national interests. As for the impact of interdependence and the role of international organizations, the scholar contends that, "Far from transposing the practice of autonomy and unilateral policymaking, cooperation in interdependent conditions can serve merely as an avenue for policymakers to continue business as usual." In the end, she concludes, "Anarchy trumps us in every social act" (Sterling-Folker, 2002).

Liberalism and the Nature of Politics

Liberals reject the notion that all or most humans are inherently political predators. Instead, liberals believe that humans and their countries are capable of achieving more cooperative, less conflictive relations, either through current government structures or through new models of governance. In this sense, many liberals trace their intellectual lineage to political philosophers such as Jean-Jacques Rousseau (1712–1778). He argued in *The Social Contract* (1762) that humans had joined together in civil societies because they "reached the point at which the obstacles [to bettering their existence were] greater than the resources at the disposal of each individual." Having come to that point, Rousseau reasoned, people realized that their "primitive condition can then subsist no longer; and the human race would perish unless it changed its manner of existence." Like Rousseau, contemporary liberals not only believe that people long ago joined together in civil societies to better their existence; they are confident that now and in the future people can join together to build a cooperative and peaceful global society.

There is also a neoliberal school of thought. **Neoliberals**, like neorealists, ascribe world conflict largely to the competition among sovereign states in an anarchical world system (Jervis, 1999; Legro & Moravcsik, 1999). Like all liberals, neoliberals believe that humans can cooperate in order to achieve mutual benefits. Because neoliberals think that the anarchic system hinders cooperation, they further believe that the best way to achieve cooperation is to build effective international organizations. This prescription is why neoliberals are often also called "liberal institutionalists." Typically, two theorists of this school contend that "when states can jointly benefit from cooperation . . . we expect governments to attempt to construct" international organizations to facilitate cooperation. The two scholars go on to argue that, in turn, international organizations add to the growth of cooperation by providing various benefits to member-states that "facilitate the operation of reciprocity" (Keohane & Martin, 1995:42). In sum, realists view the world as a dangerous political jungle filled with untamable predators. Liberals agree that the jungle exists, but they believe that its denizens can learn to live in peace, especially if a way is found to construct a good zoo that will serve to forestall their less civilized tendencies (Jackson & Sørenson, 2002).

The Roles of Power and Principles: Realism and Liberalism

Realists and liberals also disagree in how they describe the roles of power and principles as standards of international conduct (Goldsmith & Krasner, 2003). The two schools are even more at odds over the role that these standards should play. Realists could be styled the "might makes right" school of thought. Liberals would contend that "right makes right."

Realism: An Emphasis on Power

Realists contend that struggles between states to secure their frequently conflicting national interests are the main action on the world stage. This is hardly a new thought (Boesche, 2002). Over 2,000 years ago, Kautilya, minister to the first Maurya emperor of India, wrote, "The possession of power in a greater degree makes a king superior to another; in a lesser degree, inferior; and in an equal degree, equal. Hence a king shall always endeavor to augment his own power."

Given the realists' view of politics as a struggle for power, they maintain that countries should and usually do base their foreign policy on the existence of what realists see as a Darwinian, country-eat-country world in which power is the key to the national survival of the fittest. In the words of one scholar, "In an environment as dangerous as anarchy," those who ignore realist principles will "ultimately not survive" (Sterling-Folker, 1997:18). From this point of view, realists define national interest mainly in terms of whatever enhances or preserves a state's security, its influence, and its military and economic power. For realists, then, might makes right—or at least it makes success.

Where realist theoreticians depart from one another somewhat is on the question of how the dictates of power are applied to policy. Classic realists see them translated through the decisions of national leaders. As such, these realists do not believe that countries necessarily follow the dictates of power. Instead they believe that decision makers can and do err by allowing morality, ideology, or anything else other than power realities to govern foreign policy. Morgenthau, for instance, was critical of Woodrow Wilson's liberal tendencies, as found in his "Fourteen Points" and elsewhere, discussed on page 20. By contrast, neorealists pay little attention to the internal policy making in countries. This is because neorealists believe that countries are "rational actors" and therefore will react similarly and predictably to power realities in a given situation no matter who is in office. Because neorealists see states reacting predictably to power, these theorists are interested in ascertaining rules about how states will react in a given set of circumstances. Examples of how these rules work can be found in the discussion of the international system in chapter 3.

With respect to justice and morality, Morgenthau reasoned that it is unconscionable for a state to follow policy based on such principles. He argued that "while the individual has a moral right to sacrifice himself" in defense of an abstract principle, "the state has no right to let its moral disapprobation . . . get in the way of successful political action, itself inspired by the moral principle of national survival" (Morgenthau, 1986:38). This does not mean that realists are amoral (Murray, 1996). Some argue that the highest moral duty of the state is to do good for its citizens. More moderately, other realists argue that surviving and prospering in a dangerous world requires that morality be weighed prudently against national interest. One scholar has summed up this realist rule of action with the maxim, "Do 'good' if the price is low" (Gray, 1994:8).

Liberalism: An Emphasis on Principles

Liberals do not believe that acquiring, preserving, and applying power must be or even always is the essence of international relations. Instead, liberals argue, foreign policy should be and sometimes is formulated according to cooperative and ethical standards.

IN THE SPOTLIGHT

Woodrow Wilson's Liberalism

Liberalism is not just an academic theory. It has sometimes been advocated by such global leaders as U.S. President Woodrow Wilson (1913–1921). His liberalism was perhaps clearest when he addressed Congress on January 8, 1918, to explain his vision of the peace that should follow World War I (1914–1918).

The following paragraphs are excerpts from Wilson's "Fourteen Points" speech. Note that several of the 14 points related specifically to the fate of the warring powers and not directly to Wilson's liberal vision. The remaining seven, noted below, do, however, speak to Wilson's condemnation of the traditional path of power politics and to his advocacy of an alternative, less-traveled road. Also ponder the president's view in the last paragraph that the conflict in Europe was "the culminating and final war for human liberty." We know now that it was not. The question is whether liberals are naïve (as realists would contend) or whether (as liberals would reply) conflict continues because the realist leaders of most countries have not had the foresight to follow Wilson's clarion call. In Wilson's words:

> What we demand in this war . . . is that the world be made fit and safe to live in; and particularly that it be made safe for every peace-loving nation . . . [to] be assured of justice and fair dealing by the other peoples of the world as against force and selfish aggression. All the peoples of the world are in effect partners in this interest, and for our own part we see very clearly that unless justice be done to others it will not be done to us. The program of the world's peace, therefore, is our program; and that program, the only possible program, as we see it, is this [paraphrased]:
>
> - No secret negotiations or treaties
> - Freedom of the seas
> - Eliminate economic barriers among countries
> - Significantly reduce national armaments
> - Eliminate colonialism
> - Allow national groups to govern themselves
> - Establish a world body to ensure security
>
> For such arrangements and covenants we are willing to fight . . . but only because we . . . desire a just and stable peace such as can be secured only by removing the chief provocations to war, which this program does remove. . . .
>
> An evident principle runs through the whole program I have outlined. It is the principle of justice to all peoples and nationalities, and their right to live on equal terms of liberty and safety with one another, whether they be strong or weak.
>
> Unless this principle be made its foundation no part of the structure of international justice can stand. The people of the United States could act upon no other principle; and to the vindication of this principle they are ready to devote their lives, their honor, and everything they possess. The moral climax of this the culminating and final war for human liberty has come, and they are ready to put their own strength, their own highest purpose, their own integrity and devotion to the test.

President Woodrow Wilson was a classic liberal president, as evident in the In the Spotlight box "Woodrow Wilson's Liberalism."

More recently, President Bill Clinton also regularly espoused a liberal philosophy. For example, he asked Americans to support sending U.S. troops to Bosnia because "it is the right thing to do," as he called up images of "skeletal prisoners caged behind barbed-wire fences, women and girls raped as a tool of war, [and] defenseless men and boys shot down in mass graves." "We cannot save all these people," Clinton declared, "but we can save many of them. . . , [so] we must do what we can."[9]

The views of Clinton and other liberals do not mean that they are out of touch with reality. When, for example, Clinton sought the presidency in 1992, he assailed President George H. W. Bush for his realpolitik approach to relations with China and other autocracies. Clinton castigated Bush, charging that he had consistently "sided with the status quo instead of democratic change, with familiar tyrants rather than those who would overthrow them." Clinton promised that he would "assert a new [more liberal] vision for our role in the world."[10] As president, though, Clinton learned that his power to change China's behavior was limited and that he could not afford to overly antagonize another major power. As a result, he tempered his liberalism, and, as he admitted near the end of his first term, "it would be fair to say that my policies with regard to

China have been somewhat different from what I talked about in the [1992 presidential] campaign."[11]

Liberals also dismiss the realists' warning that pursuing ethical policy often works against the national interest. The wisest course, liberals contend, is for Americans and others to redefine their interests to take into account the inextricable ties between the future of their country and the global pattern of human development. If, as is true, every country's national interest is peace and prosperity for its people, then, liberals argue, the best way for any country to achieve that is to cooperate so that all countries can reach that goal.

Prospects for Competition and Cooperation: Realism and Liberalism

The previous two sections have examined how realists and liberals describe the nature of politics and their respective views on the roles of power and principles. This section addresses the even more important question of whether countries should follow the dictates of realism or strive to establish a new world order based on greater international cooperation.

Realism and the Competitive Future

There are many implications to the realist view that the drive for power and resulting conflict are at the heart of politics and that there is "little hope for progress in international relations" (Brooks, 1997:473). Based on this view, realists advocate a relatively pragmatic, realpolitik approach to world politics. One principle of realpolitik is to secure your own country's interests first and worry about the welfare of other countries second, if at all, on the assumption that other countries will not help you unless it is in their own interest. This makes realists wary of what they see as the self-sacrificing policies advocated by liberals. Such policies are not just foolish but dangerous, according to Morgenthau (1986:38), because countries that shun realpolitik will "fall victim to the power of others."

A second tenet of realpolitik holds that countries should practice balance-of-power politics, which is explained further in chapter 3. This standard counsels diplomats to strive to achieve an equilibrium of power in the world in order to prevent any other country or coalition of countries from dominating the system. This can be done through a variety of methods, including building up your own strength, allying yourself with others, or dividing your opponents.

A third realist policy prescription is that the best way to maintain the peace is to be powerful: "Peace through strength," as President Ronald Reagan was fond of saying. President George W. Bush is very much of that school."We will build our defenses beyond challenge, lest weakness invite challenge," was the way he put it during his January 20, 2001, inaugural address. Thus, realists believe that it is necessary for a country to be armed because the world is dangerous. Liberals would reply that the world is dangerous because so many countries are so heavily armed.

It is important to say that this does not cast realists as warmongers. Instead, a fourth realist tenet is that you should neither waste power on peripheral goals nor pursue goals that you do not have the power to achieve. This frequently makes realists reluctant warriors. It is worth noting, for instance, that Morgenthau was an early critic of U.S. involvement in the war in Vietnam as a waste of resources in a tangential area. More recently, two leading realist scholars opposed the invasion of Iraq in 2003 on the grounds that Saddam Hussein had been successfully contained and that ousting him would require an unsupportable expenditure of U.S. power (Mearsheimer & Walt, 2003). In sum,

It would be a mistake to think that realists are militarists or that President George W. Bush fits easily into the realist model. Many realists opposed the war against Iraq in 2003 as an unwise expenditure of U.S. power and worried that Bush's policy was being driven by ideological neoconservatives (neocons) trying to impose the "American way" on other societies.

they wrote, "Saddam Hussein needs to remain in his box—but we don't need a war to keep him there."[12] Prudence, then, is a watchword for realists.

Liberalism and the Cooperative Future

Liberals believe that humanity can and must successfully seek a new system of world order. They have never been comfortable with a world system based on sovereignty, but they now argue that it is imperative to find new organizational paths to cooperation. Liberals are convinced that the spread of nuclear weapons, the increase in economic interdependence among countries, the decline of world resources, the daunting gap between rich and poor, and the mounting damage to our ecosphere mean that humans must learn to cooperate more fully because they are in grave danger of suffering a catastrophe of unparalleled proportions.

Liberals are divided, however, in terms of how far cooperation can and should go. Classic liberals believe that just as humans learned to form cooperative societies without giving up their individuality, so too can states learn to cooperate without surrendering their independence. These liberals believe that the growth of international economic interdependence and the spread of global culture will create a much greater spirit of cooperation among the world countries.

Neoliberals are more dubious about a world in which countries retain full sovereignty. These analysts believe that countries will have to surrender some of their sovereignty to international organizations in order to promote greater cooperation and, if necessary, to enforce good behavior. "The fundamental right of existence," Pope John Paul II told the UN General Assembly, "does not necessarily call for sovereignty as a state." Instead, the pontiff said, "there can be historical circumstances in which aggregations different from single state sovereignty can . . . prove advisable."[13]

As for the future, liberals are encouraged by some recent trends. One of these is the growth of interdependence. Liberals also support their case by pointing to the willingness of countries to surrender some of their sovereignty to improve themselves. The EU, for instance, now exercises considerable economic and even political authority over its member-countries, and it has even established a convention to draft an EU constitution. Member-countries were not forced into the EU; they joined it freely. This and other indications that sovereignty is weakening will be discussed at length later in the text. Liberals are also buoyed by the spread of democracy and interdependence. They believe that both tend to lessen the chances of conflict among states, and research that shows there is substantial validity to this notion (Kinsella & Russett, 2002).

Liberals also condemn the practice of realpolitik. They charge that power politics leads to an unending cycle of conflict and misery in which safety is temporary at best. They look at the last century with its more than 111 million deaths during two world wars and innumerable other conflicts and deride realists for suggesting that humanity should continue to rely on a self-help system that has failed to provide safety so often and so cataclysmically. Liberals further assert that the pursuit of power in the nuclear age may one day lead to ultimate destruction.

This does not mean that liberals are unwilling to use military force, economic sanctions, and other forms of coercion. They are not so naive as to think that the potential for conflict can be eliminated, at least in the foreseeable future. Therefore most liberals are willing to use coercion when necessary to halt aggression or to end oppression. The use of coercion to restore right is especially acceptable to liberals if it is accomplished through cooperative efforts such as UN peacekeeping forces or sanctions.

Assessing Reality: Realism and Liberalism

Before we leave our discussion of realism and liberalism, it is worth pausing to ask which theory better explains how the world has operated and how it operates now. On balance, it is safe to say that throughout history competition, not cooperation, has dominated international relations. Not being at war is not necessarily the same as being at peace in a cooperative way, and suspicion, tension, and rivalry, rather than cooperation, have been the most common traits of what we euphemistically call international peace. Thus, realpolitik is still usually the order of the day, especially where important national interests are involved. Most political leaders tend toward realism in their policies, and even those who lean toward liberalism often take the realpolitik road (Elman, 1996).

Does this mean that liberalism is a sterile theory confined largely to the halls of academia and the utopian dreams of those without power? It does not. While realpolitik self-interest has been the dominant impulse of countries, it is also true that countries can be cooperative and even altruistic at times. Moreover, it may well be that the liberal approach is gaining ground as states recognize that competition and conflict are increasingly dangerous and destructive and that peaceful cooperation is in everyone's self-interest. It would be naive to argue that the world is anywhere near the point of concluding that self-interest and global interests are usually synonymous. But it is not fatuous to say that an increasing number of people have decided that working toward the long-term goal of a safe and prosperous world is preferable to seeking short-term national advantage. Thus, while the question "what is" should engage our attention, the far more important questions are "what should be" and "what will be." What should be is for you to decide after reading this book and consulting other sources of information. What will be is for all of us to see and experience.

How to Study World Politics

"Well, OK," you may say, "international politics is important and it affects me. And, yes, there are important choices to make. So I'll agree that I should know more about it and get active in the world drama. But where do I start?"

The first thing you should do, if you have not already, is to read the preface. This will tell you how I have structured this text and will help you understand what follows. The next chapter will give you more help in establishing a base for understanding world politics by laying out a brief history of the world system and its current trends.

Political Scientists and World Politics

Before getting to the chapter on global history and trends, it is important that you understand something about what political scientists are attempting to do and how they go about doing it. This knowledge will help you understand the efforts and goals of the many studies that are cited in this text and others that you may read. Evaluating the research of scholars may also help you conduct your own studies of international relations or any other subject.

Why Political Scientists Study World Politics

There is a long history of international relations as an intellectual focus, and concepts such as anarchy and sovereignty were at its core long before realism, liberalism, and other schools of thought were articulated and labeled. Like all political scientists, scholars study world politics in order to formulate theories—generalizations—about politics. The goal is to identify patterns that occur over time or that occur in many places at the same time. There are many ways to do this, but whatever the approach, theory is at the heart of political science (Hermann, 1998; Lepgold, 1998). It is theory that allows us to think systematically. Fitting events into theory and using theory to explain and perhaps predict events is what separates political science from current events.

Within this emphasis on theory, international relations scholars have three subsidiary goals: description, prediction, and prescription. *Description* is the oldest and most fundamental of these goals. This task sounds a whole lot easier than it is. Events are complex and information is often difficult to obtain. Political scientists also have to strive for objectivity and not, for example, let their cultural or national biases color how they evaluate their own or other countries (Oren, 2003; Chan, Mandaville, & Bleiker, 2001). Moreover, when a political scientist studies a single event (a case study) or, better yet, a series of events across time or over space, the object is not to just describe the event(s). Instead, the goal is to relate them to a pattern of other events. One illustrative area of political science research has been to try to prove or disprove the hypothesis that "democracies do not fight each other" (Hensel, Goertz, & Diehl, 2000; Wear, 1998; Gartzke, 1998). By studying history, many political scientists have concluded that, indeed, democracies tend not to go to war with one another. This research is discussed fully in chapter 6.

Political scientists sometimes practice world politics as well as study it. Before heading to Washington in 2001 to become the president's national security adviser, Condoleezza Rice was provost at Stanford University, where she also taught political science. She holds a PhD in political science from the University of Denver.

Prediction is even more difficult than description because of the complexity of human nature. Nevertheless, political scientists can use careful research as a basis for "analytical forecasting," or making "a reasoned argument for what they expect to happen" (George, 1994:172). If, for instance, we believe the descriptive studies concluding that democracies are peaceful toward one another, then it is possible to predict that a democratic Russia will be less likely to be antagonistic toward the United States and other democracies than was the nondemocratic Soviet Union.

Prescription is a third goal. Some political scientists go beyond their objective studies, come to normative (what is right or wrong) conclusions, and prescribe policy (Kelman, 2000). Those who believe that democracies have not been (description) and will not be (prediction) aggressive toward one another may advocate (prescription) policies that promote the adoption or preservation of democracy. Such advocates might, for example, urge extending massive economic aid to Russia in order to avoid the economic turmoil that is so often associated with a slide toward authoritarian government. Some political scientists take their prescriptions a step farther by entering directly into the policy-making realm. Among them is Condoleezza Rice, who left her position as a professor of political science at Stanford University to become the national security adviser to President George W. Bush. In the preceding administration, President Bill Clinton, Vice President Al Gore, and Secretary of State Madeleine Albright all had one or more degrees in political science. Other political scientists try to influence policy indirectly through such methods as serving in so-called think tanks dedicated to policy advocacy, writing op-ed pieces in newspapers, and testifying before legislatures.

How Political Scientists Conduct Research

The most fundamental thing that political scientists need to gather is evidence. They do so by three basic research methodologies: logic, traditional observation, and quantitative analysis. All research should apply logic, but valuable contributions can be made by relatively pure logical analysis (Bueno de Mesquita & Morrow, 1999). Aristotle and the other great political philosophers who are mentioned in this book relied primarily on logical analysis to support their political observations. This technique is still important. Some of the best work on nuclear deterrence has been done by analysts who employ deductive logic (from the general to the specific) to suggest how nuclear deterrence works.

A second methodology, traditional observation, uses a variety of techniques to study political phenomena and draws on a wide range of disciplines such as anthropology, economics, history, and sociology (Mandaville, 2002). One method is historical analysis, using sources such as archives, interviews, and participant observation. Traditional observation is an old and still valuable methodology. There are many modern studies of why wars occur, but we can all still learn much by reading *The Peloponnesian War,* written by the Greek historian Thucydides in about 410 B.C. Realists, for instance, are persuaded by his analysis that a struggle for power caused the Peloponnesian War (intermittently between 431 and 404 B.C.) between Athens and Sparta. "What made war inevitable," Thucydides wrote, "was the growth of Athenian power and the fear which this caused in Sparta." What this historian did is called a case study, and many modern studies use this method to look at one or more events or other political phenomena in order to add to what we can say about international relations theory.

Quantitative analysis is a third methodology. Political scientists who use this method are interested in measurable phenomena and use mathematical techniques. The studies on war and democracy cited in chapter 6 are able to use quantitative methods because countries and wars are relatively measurable.

It would be nice, at least from the author's perspective, if all the students who read this book got so fired up about the captivating drama of world politics that they went on to become political scientists. What is important and possible, however, is that you become an informed observer of world politics, think carefully about it, and take an active role in shaping your world. Just watching it unfold as a passive member of the audience is riveting, but it is even better to get up, go onstage, and play a part.

Chapter Summary

The Importance of Studying World Politics

1. This book's primary message is captured by Shakespeare's line, "All the world's a stage, and all the men and women merely players." This means that we are all part of the world drama and are affected by it. It also means that we should try to play a role in determining the course of the dramatic events that affect our lives.
2. Economics is one way that we are all affected. The word *intermestic* has been coined to symbolize the merging of *inter*national and do*mestic* concerns, especially in the area of economics. Countries and their citizens have become increasingly interdependent.
3. Economically, trade both creates and causes the loss of jobs. International investment practices may affect your standard of living in such diverse ways as determining

how much college tuition is, what your income is, what interest rate you pay for auto loans and mortgages, and how much you can look forward to in retirement. The global economy also supplies vital resources, such as oil. Exchange rates between different currencies affect the prices we pay for imported goods, the general rate of inflation, and our country's international trade balance.

4. Our country's role in the world also affects decisions about the allocation of budget funds. Some countries spend a great deal on military functions. Other countries spend relatively little on the military and devote almost all of their budget resources to domestic spending.
5. World politics also plays an important role in determining the condition of your living space. Politics, for the most part, has not created environmental degradation, but political cooperation almost certainly will be needed to halt and reverse the despoiling of the biosphere.
6. Your life may also be affected by world politics. You may be called on to serve in the military. Whether or not you are in the military, war can cost you your life.
7. There are many things any one of us can do, individually or in cooperation with others, to play a part in shaping the future of our world. Think, vote, protest, support, write letters, join organizations, make speeches, run for office—do something!
8. There are demands for and predictions of a new world order. The future path of the world can be thought about as analogous to Robert Frost's poem about two roads diverging in a wood. The poet wrote that the path he chose made all the difference. So too will the road that the world chooses make all the difference. Therefore it is important to think about the direction in which you want the world to go.

The World Tomorrow: Two Roads Diverge

9. One road is the traditionalist approach, which focuses on the continuing sovereign role of the state as the primary actor in the international system. The traditionalist approach is associated with many terms; "realism" is perhaps the best known. Realism focuses on the self-interested promotion of the state and nation. Realists believe that power politics is the driving force behind international relations. Therefore, realists believe that both safety and wisdom lie in promoting the national interest through the preservation and, if necessary, the application of the state's power.
10. The second, alternative road is advocated by those who stress the need for significant change, including both a restructuring of power within states and international cooperation and global interests. One term associated with this approach is "liberalism." Liberals believe that realpolitik is dangerous and outmoded. They believe that idealpolitik should be given greater emphasis and that everyone's "real" interest lies in a more orderly, more humane, more egalitarian world.
11. Political scientists have numerous orientations, including realist and liberal (and their variations neorealist and neoliberal), discussed in this chapter.

How to Study World Politics

12. Political scientists study international relations to describe and predict political phenomena and to prescribe courses of action. Scholars use a variety of methodologies, including logic, traditional observation, and quantitative techniques, to analyze phenomena and test hypotheses. Scholars also have several orientations, which include focusing on power, human social relations, and economics.

For a chapter quiz, interactive activities, web links, PowerWeb articles, and much more, visit **www.mhhe.com/rourke10/** and go to chapter 1. Or, while accessing the site, click on Course-Wide Content and view recent international relations articles in the *New York Times.*

Key Terms

direct democracy
fiscal year (FY)
gross domestic product
intermestic
liberals
neoliberals
neorealists
realists

CHAPTER

2

The Evolution of World Politics

THE EVOLVING WORLD SYSTEM: EARLY DEVELOPMENT

Ancient Greece and Rome

After the Fall of Rome, A.D. 476 to 1700

The 18th and 19th Centuries

THE EVOLVING WORLD SYSTEM: THE 20TH CENTURY

The Eclipse of the Multipolar System

The Cold War and the Bipolar System

THE 21ST CENTURY: THE GENESIS OF A NEW SYSTEM

The Structure of Power in the 21st Century

Security in the 21st Century

Global Economics in the 21st Century

Quality of Life in the 21st Century

CHAPTER SUMMARY

KEY TERMS

I am amazed, methinks, and lose my way
Among the thorns and dangers of the world.

—William Shakespeare, *King John*

Whereof what's past is prologue, what to come,
In yours and my discharge.

—William Shakespeare, *The Tempest*

To believe that what has not occurred in history will not occur at all is to argue disbelief in the dignity of man.

—Mohandas K. (Mahatma) Gandhi

We have need of history in its entirety, not to fall back into it, but to see if we can escape from it.

—José Ortega y Gasset, *The Revolt of the Masses*

CHAPTER OBJECTIVES

After completing this chapter, you should be able to:

- Recognize major trends in the evolving world system from the birth of states to the present.
- Describe the origin of the current world system and the importance of the Treaty of Westphalia (1648).
- Identify the changes that occurred during the 18th and 19th centuries and that continue to have an important impact on the international system.
- Discuss the pace of world political evolution at the beginning of the 20th century and describe the weakening of the multipolar system.
- Discuss the transition from a bipolar system to the most likely form of a modified multipolar system.
- Analyze the potential shift in the international system away from a strictly Western orientation.
- Identify both international and domestic challenges to the authority of the state.
- Discuss the implications of following either the traditional national security or alternative international security approach in the quest for peace.
- Identify the implications of economic interdependence and the counterpressures to pursue more traditional national economic policies.
- Discuss the implications of the growing economic disparity between the North and South.
- Analyze the future of human rights and environmental issues in the face of national resistance to international solutions.

This chapter has two purposes. The first is to establish a historical foundation on which to build our analysis of international relations. To this end the following pages give a brief historical narrative that emphasizes the themes and events you will encounter repeatedly in this book.

The second goal of this chapter is to sketch the evolution of the current, rapidly evolving world political system. The concept of an **international system** represents the notion that (1) the world is more than just the sum of its parts, such as countries, (2) that world politics is more than just the sum of the individual interactions among those parts, and (3) that there are general patterns of interactions among the system's actors. These patterns and their causes are explored in chapter 3.

Be patient as you read this chapter. You will find that it often introduces a topic briefly and then hurries on to another point. "Wait a minute," you may think, "slow down and explain this better." Hang in there! Other chapters fill in the details.

The Evolving World System: Early Development

There have been numerous global and regional international systems, with some scholars dating them back to the southern Mesopotamian region of Babylon (in what is now Iraq) some 7,500 years ago (Cioffi-Revilla, 2000). Modern politics is vastly different than it was, but that change has, for the most part, evolved slowly.

Ancient Greece and Rome

We can begin tracking the international system with a brief exploration of the era that included the Greek city-states (about 700 B.C. to 300 B.C.) and the rise of Rome in about 500 B.C. to its fall in A.D. 453. It was during this period that four of today's important political characteristics were first seen. Each of them subsequently almost disappeared, only to flourish more than a thousand years in the future.

Territorial State: Before the city-states, political organization was based on a ruler (and the dominions of that individual) or on a cultural group, such as a tribe. Each controlled territory, but the political connection was to the ruler or group, not the territory, which was often in flux. Certainly, the people themselves had no sense of "owning" (as opposed to controlling) the territory. With the rise of the Greek city-states, territory as such defined a political entity, its people felt some permanent ownership of the land, and that connection became part of their political identity. As a result, the concept of citizenship first developed. After 450 B.C. Athenian citizens included only those born of two citizens or approved through what may have been the world's first naturalization process. Athenians, then, were not those living in Athens, only those legally accorded citizenship (membership) in the territorially defined unit.

Sovereignty: Artistotle (384–322 B.C.), in his epic work, *Politics,* advanced the idea that supreme authority can rest with law (a system of government), not just rulers or religion. In line with this notion, each city-state *(polis)* considered itself to have **sovereignty** under its own law. This meant that it recognized no legitimate higher authority, either secular or religious.

Nationalism: As one history puts it, each city-state "generated intense loyalty from its citizens" who regarded the polis "as a state of mind," as well as the place they lived (Sherman & Salisbury, 2004:56). Indeed the strength of the connection between people and polis gave Aristotle license to comment, "Man is an animal of the polis." This state of mind was a precursor of nationalism, today's most important sense of political identity and one that interconnects people, government, and territory.

Democracy: Also for the first time in history, the people, not a ruler or a religion, became the source of political authority. As two historians note, the Athenians and others "did not think of themselves as subjects of a king. . . . Instead they were 'citizens' who were actively responsible for guiding their polis" (Sherman & Salisbury, 2004:56). This idea of citizen participation reached its fullest extent in Athens, where the first known democracy existed for approximately 150 years beginning in the mid-fifth century B.C.

Just about the time Athens was at its zenith, Rome was beginning to grow far to the west. Like Athens, it was a city-state that expanded into an empire, and then itself was eventually invaded and conquered. Also like the Athenians, the Romans had a democracy until it was throttled by military dictatorship. It would be incorrect to try to closely correlate the Greek and Roman political systems with modern ones. For example, Athenian democracy was limited to the small percentage of people in the city who were male citizens, while women, slaves, and foreigners were excluded from participation. Still, the outlines of things to come can be traced to the founding of these two political innovations some 2,700 years ago.

After the Fall of Rome, A.D. 476 to 1700

After more than five centuries as the hub of the known Western world, Rome fell in 476. The remaining vestiges of democracy, nationalism, and the other traits that had not already been extinguished by Roman tyranny and empire were swept away as Rome crumbled and collapsed. These ideas did not die, however, they merely lay moribund for a millennium awaiting the right historical circumstances to reemerge. During this extended period called the Middle Ages (to about 1500), political power in the West was wielded at two levels of authority—one universal, the other local.

Universal Authority in the Middle Ages

Governance during the Middle Ages rested in part on overarching authority that controlled territory and people but was defined by neither. There were both religious and secular aspects to this universalistic authority.

Religious Authority The Roman Catholic Church was one source of universalistic authority. Christianity as interpreted by the Catholic Church and its pope served as the integrating force in several ways. The Church provided a common language among intellectuals by keeping Latin alive. Christian doctrine underlay the developing concepts of rights, justice, and other political norms. Even kings were theoretically (and often substantially) subordinate to the pope. For example, it was Pope Leo III who crowned Charlemagne "Emperor of the Romans" in 800. Charlemagne was Germanic, not Roman, and his empire did not long survive him, but the idea of a new Christian-Roman universal state was established. This notion was furthered in 936 when Otto I was crowned head of what became known as the **Holy Roman Empire**.

Secular Authority As the Middle Ages proceeded, the overarching authority of the Catholic Church came to be supplemented and, in some cases, supplanted by great multiethnic empires. The Austro-Hungarian, British, Chinese, Dutch, French, German, Ottoman, Russian, Spanish, and other empires controlled people in their immediate areas and in distant lands. Most of the people within these empires were not culturally related to the emperors, and ruling classes did not feel a strong political identification with or an emotional attachment to the commoners. Many of these empires lasted into the

20th century, but they and the degree of macrolevel integration they provided were all eventually swept away by the rising tide of nationalism.

Local Authority in the Middle Ages

The local, microlevel of authority was called the **feudal system**. It was organized around principalities, dukedoms, baronies, and other such fiefdoms that were smaller than the states that would one day evolve. Nobles ruled these fiefdoms, exercising near complete sovereignty over them. In theory, these nobles were vassals of a king or an emperor, but in fact they were usually autonomous and sometimes even more powerful than the monarch they supposedly served.

It is important to understand that the concepts of territory and political authority during the medieval period were much different from what they are now. As one scholar explains, fiefdoms and other political units "were nonterritorial, and sovereignty was, at best, disputed" (Spruyt, 1994:35). Certainly monarchs and nobles controlled specific pieces of territory, but in theory they did not exercise sovereignty over them. Instead, kings granted land to lords, and God and God's Church gave license to the monarch to rule. Although these theories were often not true in practice, political authority was based on a hierarchy of relationships that determined both status and land. Thus the very nature of the feudal system, in which vassals were theoretically subservient to kings and kings were theoretically subservient to emperors and popes, meant that sovereignty did not exist legally and often did not exist in fact.

By the 13th century the fabric of universalism and feudalism had begun to fray. During the next few centuries, according to one scholar, "the international system went through a dramatic transformation in which the crosscutting jurisdictions of feudal lords, emperors, kings, and popes started to give way to territorially defined authorities" (Spruyt, 1994:1). The existing nonterritorially defined, hierarchical system was replaced by a system based on territorially defined states whose sovereignty made them equals legally.

The Decline of the Feudal System

The forces of change in the Middle Ages that eroded the feudal system were many. Of these, two factors stand out—military technology and economic expansion.

Military Technology Advances in military capabilities, especially the introduction of gunpowder, diminished the ability of the relatively small feudal manors to provide security. The first mention of guns in Europe is contained in a manuscript written in Florence in 1327. Thereafter, an armored knight, the epitome of the feudal warrior elite, could be shot off his horse by a commoner armed with a primitive firearm; and the castle, the centerpiece of feudal defense, could be demolished easily by cannons. These and other factors meant that static defenses of small territories needed to be replaced by a defense based on the ability to maneuver, which could be provided only by a territorially larger unit, the state.

Economic Expansion The growth of Europe's economy also undermined the feudal system and promoted the state system. *Improved trade* was one factor. The consolidation of the huge Mongol Empire in much of Asia and the Middle East in the late 13th century created the stability that trade needs to flourish. Expanded trade with Asia led Europeans to build larger ships, which, in turn, created even greater possibilities for trade. The journeys of Marco Polo to China and other lands far from his native Venice between 1271 and 1295 were an early manifestation of this new commercial activity. Soon thereafter, the Europeans' search for better trade routes led, among other things, to the journey of Christopher Columbus to the Caribbean in 1492.

The beginning of *mass production* was a second factor driving economic expansion. Individual craftsmen began to give way to primitive factories. Full-scale industrialization did not take place for several hundred more years, but the early stages of this new mode of production were in place by the 1200s.

The growth of trade and manufacturing had important political consequences. First, it created a wealthy and powerful commercial class, the burghers, who increasingly dominated the expanding urban centers of trade and manufacturing. Second, the burghers became dissatisfied with the prevailing political system because to prosper they needed broad access to both raw materials and markets. This access was hampered by the impediments to commerce inherent in the maze of feudal entities. Third, the desire to create larger political units to facilitate their commercial ventures made the burghers natural allies with kings, who were constantly striving to increase their control over their often-fractious feudal lords. The burghers and the kings each had something the other needed. The kings could legitimize the destruction of fiefdoms; the burghers had the money the kings needed to finance the men and arms to overcome the nobles. The resulting alliance helped to create the modern state.

In sum, changes in military technology rendered the feudal manor obsolete as a defensive unit, and changes in manufacturing and commerce rendered the feudal manor obsolete as an economic unit. Larger political units were needed to provide protection and to operate efficiently.

States became the dominant form of political organization for several pragmatic reasons. One of these was that the advent of military uses of gunpowder in territorially larger states came to be more defensible than feudal realms and their castles.

The Decline of Universalistic Authority

At the same time that the micropolitical feudal system was decaying, the macropolitical claims of universalistic authority by the pope and the Holy Roman Emperor were also increasingly challenged. In part, political-religious authority began to wane as the authority of kings grew at the expense of their nobles. As kings became more powerful, they were emboldened to reject the real, or even titular, political authority of the pope.

The decline of papal authority and the increase in royal power were reinforced by a period of cultural and intellectual rebirth and reform called the **Renaissance** (about 1350–1650). Many of the concepts that emerged, including scientific inquiry and personal freedom, tended to undermine the authority of the Church.

One significant outcome was the **Protestant Reformation**. Influenced in part by Renaissance thinking, Martin Luther rejected the Catholic Church as the necessary intermediary between people and God. In 1517 Luther protested Catholic doctrine and proclaimed his belief that anyone could have an individual relationship with God. Within a few decades, nearly a quarter of the people of Western Europe became Protestants.

The first great secular break with the Catholic Church occurred in England, where King Henry VIII (r. 1509–1547) rejected papal authority and established the Anglican Church. The Reformation also touched off political-religious struggles elsewhere in Europe. The ostensible issue was religious freedom, but there were also important political causes and consequences. When the century-long struggle between the imperial and Catholic Holy Roman Empire and the nationalist and Protestant ethnic groups ended with the **Treaty of Westphalia** (1648), centralized political power in Europe was over. The Holy Roman Empire had splintered into two rival Catholic monarchies (Austria and Spain); a number of Protestant entities (such as Holland and many German states) gained independence or autonomy; and other countries, such as Catholic France and Protestant England, were more secure in their independence. Therefore, many scholars regard 1648 as marking the births of the modern national state and of the world political system based on sovereign states as the primary political actors (Philpott, 1999).

The Victory of the Sovereign State

The breakdown of the feudal-universalistic system of governance did not, however, lead immediately to the uncontested role of the **state** as the dominant political actor. Instead, the people of the Middle Ages experimented with several types of political organizations to see how well they would meet the security and economic needs of the time.

The Early State and Its Competitors The revival of city-states, such as Venice, was one alternative scheme of political organization. Another was the formation of loosely confederated city-leagues based on common economic interests. The most famous of these mercantile alliances, the Hanseatic League, was founded in 1358 to protect commerce against piracy. It eventually included 70 northern European cities stretching from Bruges (in modern Belgium) to Novograd (in modern Russia) and became a major economic force.

What is important is that states, not city-states or city-leagues, became the successor of the feudal-universalistic system of political organization. The Hanseatic League ended in 1667. The fortunes of Venice and other city-states ebbed more slowly, but they eventually faded also. The failure of these experiments and the survival of the state occurred for identifiable, pragmatic reasons. Reviewing the complex factors behind this victory of the state is beyond our telling here, but the essential point, as one scholar puts it, is that in time "sovereign states displaced city-leagues and city-states . . . because their institutional logic gave them an advantage in mobilizing their societies' resources"(Spruyt, 1994:185). States were best equipped to conduct commerce, provide defense, and meet other needs.

Consequences of the Victory of the State The triumph of the state as the dominant mode of governance had profound consequences for the international system (Opello & Rosow, 1999). Of these, two are key for our story here.

Most obviously, states became the primary actors in the post-Westphalia international system. They continue in that starring role today. Therefore, much of the action on the world stage is about states and groups of states interacting with one another.

More subtly, the fact that states recognize no higher authority necessarily means that the international system has no central authority to maintain order and dispense justice. Therefore, international relations occur within an **anarchical political system**. This does not mean that the international system is a scene of unchecked chaos. To the contrary, the system operates with a great deal of regularity. It exists, however, mostly because countries find it in their interests to act according to expectations. When a state decides that it is in its interests to break the largely informal rules of the system, as Iraq did in 1990 when it invaded Kuwait, there is little to stop it except countervailing power.

The 18th and 19th Centuries

The emergence of the sovereign state as the primary actor was just the beginning of the evolution of the modern international system. In the aftermath of the Peace of Westphalia, national states continued to gather strength as monarchs such as Louis XIV of France (r. 1643–1715), Frederick II of Prussia (r. 1740–1786), and Peter the Great of Russia (r. 1682–1725) consolidated their core domains and even expanded them into empires. If anything, the pace of change began to quicken in the 18th and 19th centuries. Three themes stand out: the advent of popular sovereignty, the Westernization of the international system, and the zenith of the multipolar system.

Popular Sovereignty

At the beginning of the 18th century, most kings claimed to rule their realms by "divine right." Emblematic of that view, France's Louis XIV could proclaim, "*L'état, c'est moi*" (I am the state). Perhaps it was so then, but in 1793 another French king, Louis XVI, lost his head over this presumption, and the people claimed the state for themselves under the doctrine of **popular sovereignty**.

The reassertion of the concept of popular sovereignty, which seemingly had vanished with the demise of Athenian democracy and the Roman republic, marked a major change in the notion of who owned the state and how it should be governed. Until this time, the prevailing principle of governance held that kings ruled by divine right over both territory and people, who were subjects, not citizens. Given that the political unit was the monarch's, not the people's, the people had little emotional attachment to it (Guibernau, 1996). The American (1776) and French (1789) revolutions challenged this philosophy. *Democracies* were established on the principle that sovereign political power rests with the people, not the monarch. The notion of popular sovereignty also changed and expanded the concept of *nationalism* to include mass identification with and participation in the affairs of the state. If the people owned the state, then they had both a greater emotional attachment to it and a greater responsibility to support it. One symbol of this change was that Napoleonic France (1799–1815) was the first country to have a true patriotic draft that raised an army of a million strong.

From its beginnings in America and, particularly, in France, democratic nationalism spread throughout Europe and steadily undermined monarchical government and its concept of divine right. The collapse of the dynasties in China, Germany, Austria-Hungary, Russia, the Ottoman Empire, and elsewhere early in the 20th century marked the real end of strong monarchical government. The multiethnic and in some cases colonial empires held by several of these monarchies also disintegrated. The British, French, and other remaining colonial empires fell apart in the mid-20th century, and the last great multiethnic empire imploded in 1991 when the Soviet Union fragmented into 15 independent countries.

These fighter aircraft over the Arc de Triomphe in Paris are trailing blue, white, and red smoke to represent the colors of the French flag during the annual celebration of Bastille Day, the anniversary of the fall of the Bastille prison on July 14, 1789, and the beginning of the French Revolution. That uprising was a key event in the growth of popular sovereignty, the idea that political authority ultimately rests with the people, not with the monarch.

Westernization of the International System

The domination and shaping of the international system by the **West** was a second important characteristic of the 18th and 19th centuries. Somewhat earlier, the growth of European power had enabled Great Britain, France, and other European countries to thrust outward and take control of North and South America and some other regions. The Arab, Aztec, Chinese, Incan, Mogul (Indian), Persian, and other non-European empires or dynasties began to decline and fall. The process accelerated in the 19th century, and Europeans came to dominate the globe and to see themselves "as forming an exclusive club enjoying rights superior to those of other political communities" (Bull & Watson, 1982:425).

One reason for the **westernization of the international system** was the scientific and technological advances that sprang from the Renaissance in Europe. This

World Countries

The international system includes many types of actors. Of these, states (or countries) are the most important. National boundaries are the most important source of political division in the world, and for most people nationalism is the strongest source of political identification.

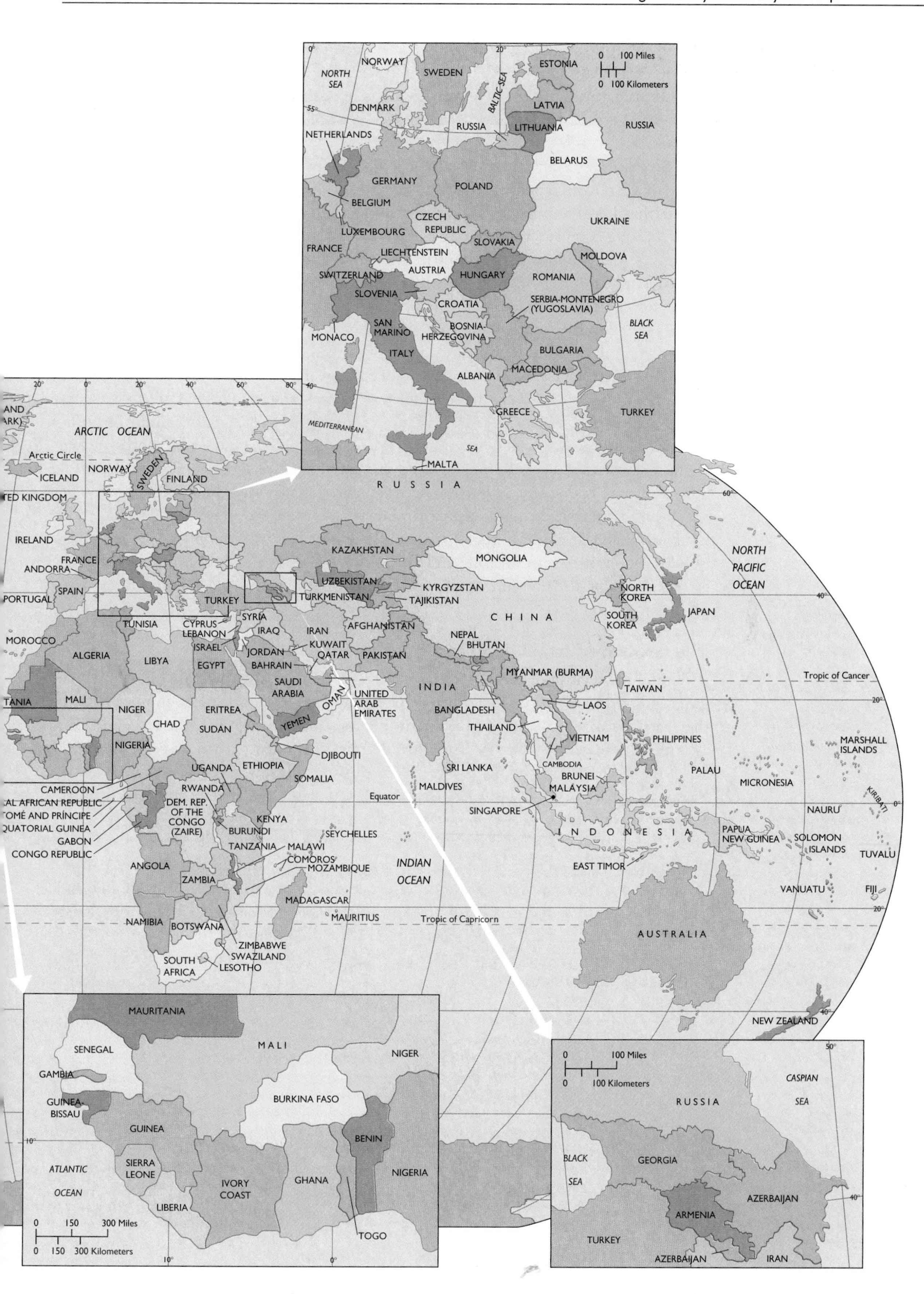
NORTH SEA
NORWAY
SWEDEN
BALTIC SEA
ESTONIA
LATVIA
LITHUANIA
RUSSIA
DENMARK
NETHERLANDS
BELARUS
GERMANY
POLAND
BELGIUM
CZECH REPUBLIC
LUXEMBOURG
UKRAINE
SLOVAKIA
FRANCE
LIECHTENSTEIN
MOLDOVA
AUSTRIA
SWITZERLAND
HUNGARY
ROMANIA
SLOVENIA
CROATIA
SERBIA-MONTENEGRO (YUGOSLAVIA)
SAN MARINO
BOSNIA-HERZEGOVINA
BLACK SEA
MONACO
ITALY
BULGARIA
MACEDONIA
ALBANIA
GREECE
TURKEY
MEDITERRANEAN SEA
MALTA
0 100 Miles
0 100 Kilometers
ARCTIC OCEAN
Arctic Circle
ICELAND
NORWAY
SWEDEN
FINLAND
RUSSIA
IRELAND
FRANCE
ANDORRA
SPAIN
PORTUGAL
KAZAKHSTAN
MONGOLIA
UZBEKISTAN
KYRGYZSTAN
TURKMENISTAN
TAJIKISTAN
NORTH KOREA
SOUTH KOREA
JAPAN
NORTH PACIFIC OCEAN
CHINA
TUNISIA
CYPRUS
LEBANON
SYRIA
IRAQ
IRAN
AFGHANISTAN
MOROCCO
ISRAEL
JORDAN
KUWAIT
NEPAL
BHUTAN
ALGERIA
LIBYA
EGYPT
BAHRAIN
QATAR
PAKISTAN
SAUDI ARABIA
UNITED ARAB EMIRATES
OMAN
YEMEN
INDIA
MYANMAR (BURMA)
TAIWAN
Tropic of Cancer
MALI
NIGER
CHAD
ERITREA
SUDAN
BANGLADESH
LAOS
THAILAND
VIETNAM
PHILIPPINES
MARSHALL ISLANDS
NIGERIA
DJIBOUTI
ETHIOPIA
UGANDA
SOMALIA
SRI LANKA
CAMBODIA
BRUNEI
MALAYSIA
PALAU
MICRONESIA
CAMEROON
RWANDA
MALDIVES
Equator
SINGAPORE
KIRIBATI
NAURU
DEM. REP. OF THE CONGO (ZAIRE)
KENYA
BURUNDI
SEYCHELLES
INDONESIA
PAPUA NEW GUINEA
SOLOMON ISLANDS
TUVALU
GABON
CONGO REPUBLIC
TANZANIA
MALAWI
COMOROS
MOZAMBIQUE
INDIAN OCEAN
EAST TIMOR
ANGOLA
ZAMBIA
VANUATU
FIJI
MADAGASCAR
MAURITIUS
Tropic of Capricorn
NAMIBIA
BOTSWANA
ZIMBABWE
SWAZILAND
AUSTRALIA
SOUTH AFRICA
LESOTHO
NEW ZEALAND
MAURITANIA
SENEGAL
MALI
NIGER
GAMBIA
BURKINA FASO
GUINEA-BISSAU
GUINEA
BENIN
SIERRA LEONE
ATLANTIC OCEAN
NIGERIA
IVORY COAST
GHANA
LIBERIA
TOGO
0 150 300 Miles
0 150 300 Kilometers
0 100 Miles
0 100 Kilometers
CASPIAN SEA
RUSSIA
BLACK SEA
GEORGIA
AZERBAIJAN
ARMENIA
TURKEY
AZERBAIJAN
IRAN

sparked the **industrial revolution**, which began in the mid-1700s in Great Britain. Thereafter industrialization rapidly spread during the 1800s, but it was not global in its reach. Instead, it was mostly a Western phenomenon, and in the few non-Western countries, such as Japan, where it did occur, industrialization came later and usually much less completely.

Industrialization and associated advances in weaponry and other technology had a profound impact on world politics. The European powers gained strength compared with non-industrialized Asia and Africa. Industrialization also promoted colonialism, because the manufacturing countries needed to expanded resources and markets to fuel and fund their economies. Many industrialized countries also coveted colonies as a matter of prestige. The result was an era of Euro-American **imperialism** that subjected many people to colonial domination. The fate of Africa is graphically displayed in the map on page 37. Many Asian cultures were similarly subjected to **Eurowhite** domination. China, it should be noted, was never technically colonized, but after the 1840s it was divided into spheres of influence among the Western powers. Only Japan and Siam (now Thailand) remained truly sovereign.

Americans soon joined in the scramble for colonial possessions. The United States acquired such Pacific territories as Hawaii and Samoa in the 1890s. Victory in the Spanish-American War (1898) added Guam, Puerto Rico, and the Philippines. Additionally, during the next several decades, U.S. domination over many of the Caribbean and Central American countries became so strong that their true independence was compromised.

Even though these colonial empires were, for the most part, not long-lived, they still had a major and deleterious impact that continues to affect world politics. The imperialist subjugation of Asians, Africans, and others by Europeans and Americans set the stage for what became the division of the world into two spheres—one wealthy, one poor—that continue to exist.

The Growth of the Multipolar System

A third characteristic of the 1700s and 1800s was that the **multipolar system**, which governed political relations among the globally dominant major European powers from the Treaty of Westphalia in 1648 through the mid-20th century, reached its zenith. For example, in the century between the final defeat of Napoleon (1815) and the outbreak of World War I (1914), the major powers, or **power poles**, were Great Britain, France, Prussia/Germany, Austria-Hungary, Russia, and to a lesser extent Italy and the Ottoman Empire/Turkey.

The multipolar system was characterized by shifting alliances designed to preserve the **balance of power** by preventing any single power or combination of powers from dominating Europe and, by extension, the world. Prime Minister Winston Churchill once clearly enunciated balance-of-power politics as a governing principle of British foreign policy when he explained that "for four hundred years the foreign policy of England has been to oppose the strongest, most aggressive, most dominating power on the Continent" (Walt, 1996:109).

The Evolving World System: The 20th Century

The 20th century was a time of momentous and rapid global change (Chan & Weiner, 1998). The *rapid pace of change* that continues today is an important theme to keep in mind. When the 20th century began monarchs ruled most countries; there were no

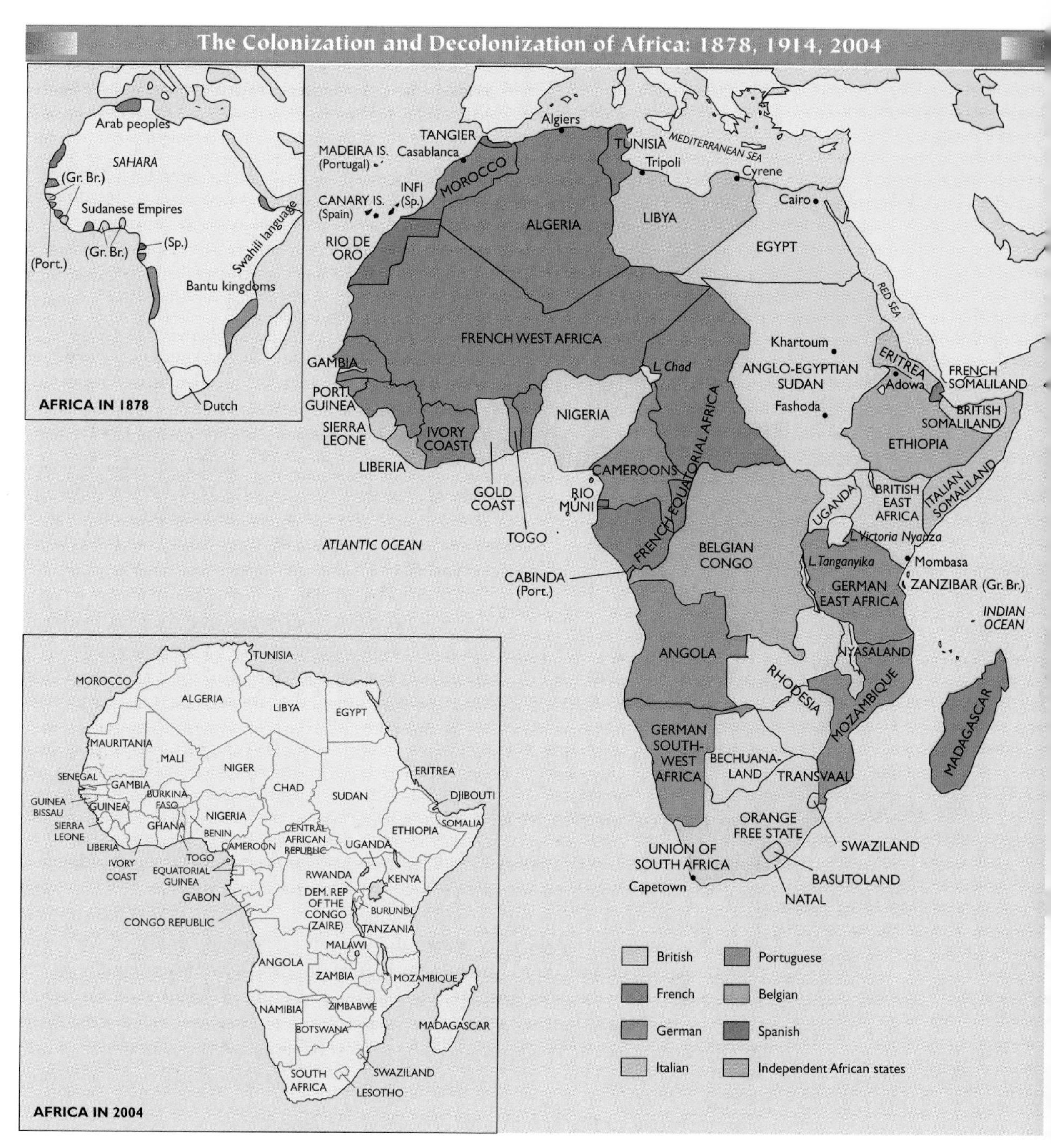

The industrialization of the West was one factor that caused the colonization of Asia and Africa in the late 1800s and early 1900s. This map and its insets show that Africa was largely controlled by its indigenous peoples in 1878 (inset) but had by 1914 (larger map) become almost totally subjugated and divided into colonies by the European powers. Then, after World War II, the momentum shifted. Independence movements led to decolonization. Now there are no colonies left in Africa. Thus the West's domination of the world has weakened.

Source: Perry Marvin, Myra Chase, James R. Jacob, Margaret C. Jacob, and Theodore H. Von Laue. *Western Civilization: Ideas, Politics and Society*, Fourth Edition. Copyright 1992 by Houghton Mifflin Company. Adapted with permission.

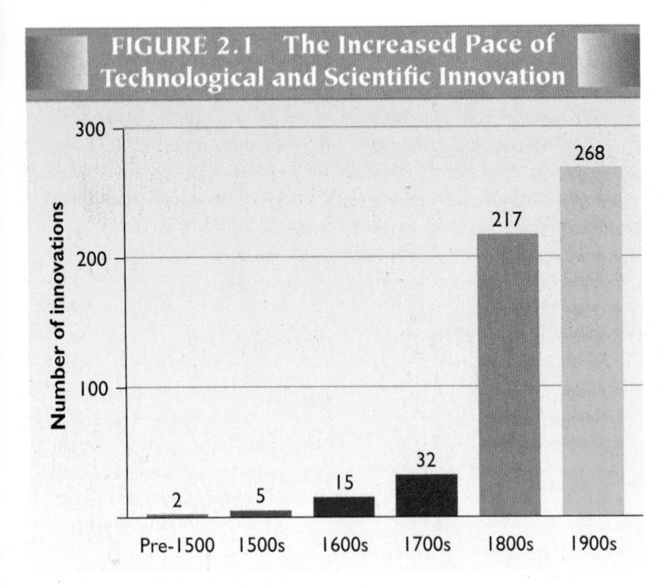

The escalating pace of technological and scientific change has had a major impact on human beings in general and on world politics in particular. This figure depicts important innovations whose dates of discovery or invention are known. As you can see, only about 10% of these occurred before 1800. Another 40% occurred in the 1800s, and about 50% during the 1900s.

Data source: World Almanac (2003).

important global organizations; and there were about 1.5 billion people in the world. By the time the century ended, elected officials governed most countries; the UN and other international organizations were prominent; and the world population had quadrupled to 6 billion people. All this happened in just one century, a time period that represents only about 3% of the approximately 3,500 years of recorded human history.

Many of these and other such changes are at least partly the result of what seems to be an ever-increasing pace of technological and scientific innovation, as evident in Figure 2.1. The 20th century saw the creation of television, computers, the Internet, nuclear energy, air and space travel, missiles, effective birth control, antibiotics, and a host of other innovations that benefit or bedevil us. Technology is both creating and solving problems. Advances in modern medicine, for one, mean that many more babies survive and people live much longer, but those changes have also contributed to the explosive population growth of the last century or so. New technologies have also been a key component in the expansion of the world economy by dramatically improving our ability to extract raw materials, turn them into products, and transport them. Here again, some changes have been positive, others not. Material possessions are available that a person living a century ago could not have imagined. But economic expansion has also brought pollution, deforestation, depletion of the ozone layer, and other ills.

Did You Know That:

The world is changing at an amazing pace. The world's oldest person is Charlotte Benkner, of North Lima, Ohio. Benjamin Harrison was the U.S. president when she was born Nov. 16, 1889. She was 14 years old when Orville and Wilbur Wright first flew and 77 when Neil Armstrong stepped on the Moon. Ms. Benker is older than 75% of the world's countries.

The Eclipse of the Multipolar System

The pace of world political evolution began to speed up even more by the beginning of the 1900s. Democracy was rapidly eroding the legitimacy of monarchs. In 1900 there were still czars and kaisers; they would be gone in less than two decades. **Nationalism** increasingly undermined the foundations of multiethnic empires. World War I was a pivotal point. Two empires, the Austro-Hungarian and Ottoman, were among the losers. From their rubble, countries such as Czechoslovakia, Poland, and Yugoslavia (re)emerged. Other countries like Jordan, Lebanon, Syria, and Palestine/Israel came under the mandate (oversight) of the League of Nations and finally became independent after World War II.

The Collapse of Europe as a Global Power Center

The end of the balance of power that had governed European relations during the 1800s was marked by the tragedies of two world wars. The reasons for the end of the multipolar system are complex and subject to dispute. What is important, however, is that the European-based multipolar system lost its ability to maintain a balance of power as the major powers coalesced into two rigid, nearly bipolar alliances that soon engaged in a death struggle. In World War I (1914–1918) the Central Powers included Germany, Austria-Hungary, and Turkey. The Allied Powers consisted of France, Russia, Great Britain, and Italy. After its defeat in the war, Germany was at first treated severely, but the multipolar system soon led to a **realpolitik** attempt to reestablish balance by allowing

Germany to rebuild its strength in the 1930s. That suited the British, who worried that France might once again dominate Europe and threaten them as it had under Napoleon. The seizure of power in Russia by Lenin's Bolsheviks in 1918 also prompted London and Paris to tolerate German revitalization. The French were especially alarmed by the specter of Communist ideology combined with Russian military might and saw a rearmed Germany as a bulwark against the "Red menace." For the British and French, these balance-of-power maneuvers constituted a near-fatal mistake.

The grotesqueness of World War I was another reason why Great Britain and France did not seriously try to restrain resurgent Germany. The two victors had each lost almost an entire generation of young men. When Adolf Hitler came to power (1933) and rearmed his country, Great Britain and France vacillated timorously. The **Munich Conference** (1938) became synonymous with this lack of will. In that conference, Great Britain and France gave way to Hitler's demands for the annexation of part of Czechoslovakia based on the false hope of British Prime Minister Neville Chamberlain and other leaders that an **appeasement policy** toward Germany would satisfy it and maintain the peace.

The overthrow of the czarist government in Russia in March 1917 was applauded widely in the West. But when the Bolsheviks, as the early communists were called, came to power in November of that year, the specter of communism alarmed many Europeans and Americans. This early cartoon (1920) depicts the frightening image of Soviet communism common in the West at the time.

The Rise of Non-European Powers

While all this was occurring in Europe, the rest of the world community expanded and changed during the first 40 years of the 20th century. Some states gained independence; other existing states, especially Japan and the United States, gradually began to play a more significant role and to undercut European domination of the international system. China began the century saddled with a decaying imperial government and foreign domination, but it overthrew its emperor in 1911 and started a long struggle to rid itself of foreign domination and to reestablish its role as a major power. Also during the first four decades of the century, the League of Nations was established, and many non-European countries became active in world diplomacy through membership in the League. Although international relations still focused on Europe during the early decades of the 1900s, a shift was under way. The voices of Africa, Asia, and Latin America began to be heard, and two non-European powers, the United States and Japan, readied themselves to take center stage.

The Cold War and the Bipolar System

World War II was a tragedy of unequaled proportions. It also marked major changes in the nature and operation of the world political system. On the political front, a series of shifts in the system occurred in the decades after 1945 that involved the actors and, indeed, the polar structure of the system itself. World War II finally destroyed the European-based multipolar structure. It was replaced by a **bipolar system** dominated by the Soviet Union and the United States. To those who experienced its anguished intensity, the hostility between the two superpowers seemed to augur an unending future of bipolar confrontation and peril. As is often true, the view that the present will also be the future proved shortsighted. The bipolar era was brief. Significant cracks in the structure were evident by the 1960s; by 1992 it was history.

The Rise and Decline of the Bipolar System

World War II devastated most of the existing major actors. In their place, the United States emerged as a military and economic **superpower** and the leader of one power pole. The Soviet Union, though incredibly damaged, emerged as the superpower leader of the other pole. The USSR never matched the United States economically, but the Soviets possessed a huge conventional armed force, a seemingly threatening ideology, and, by 1949, atomic weapons. The uneasy alliance that had existed between the United States and the Soviet Union during World War II, followed by suspicious maneuvering during the first few years after the war, was replaced by overt hostility. Indeed, the rivalry that divided much of the world into two antagonistic spheres was so bitter that it became known as the **cold war**, a conflict with the hatred but not the military clashes of a "hot war."

The exact causes of the confrontation termed the cold war are complex and controversial. It is safe to say, however, that varying economic and political interests and the power vacuum created by the collapse of the old balance-of-power structure created a bipolar system in which a great deal of world politics was centered on the confrontation between the two superpowers.

The American reaction to the perceived world Soviet/communist threat was the **containment doctrine**. This principle transformed U.S. foreign policy from a prewar norm of isolationism to postwar globalism, a policy of opposing the Soviet Union (and later Communist China) diplomatically and militarily around the world. The United States sponsored a number of regional alliances, most notably the **North Atlantic Treaty Organization** (**NATO**, established in 1949). The Soviets responded in 1955 with the Warsaw Treaty Organization (or Warsaw Pact). Both sides also vied for power in the developing countries (known as the **Third World**), and both Soviet and American arms and money flowed to various governments and rebel groups in the ongoing communist-anticommunist contest.

Despite intense rivalry marked by mutual fear and hatred, the reality that both superpowers possessed nuclear weapons usually led them to avoid direct confrontations. Of the few that did occur, the scariest was the Cuban missile crisis of 1962. The Soviets had begun building nuclear missile sites in Cuba, and President John F. Kennedy risked nuclear war to force them out.

The containment doctrine also led to the U.S. involvement in Vietnam. Vietnamese forces led by nationalist/communist Ho Chi Minh defeated France's colonial army in 1954 and achieved independence. But the country was divided between Ho's forces in the north and a nondemocratic, pro-Western government in the south. The struggle for a unified Vietnam soon resumed, and the United States intervened militarily in 1964. The war quickly became a domestic trauma for Americans as casualties mounted on both sides. Perhaps the most poignant symbol of opposition to the war was the death in May 1970 of four students at Kent State University during clashes between antiwar demonstrators and the Ohio National Guard. War-weariness finally led to a complete U.S. disengagement. Within a short time Ho's forces triumphed and Vietnam was unified in 1975.

Vietnam caused a number of important changes in American attitudes. One was increased resistance to the cold war urge to fight communism everywhere. Second, Americans saw more clearly that the bipolar system was crumbling, especially as relations between the Soviet Union and China deteriorated.

Beginning approximately with the administrations of Soviet leader Leonid I. Brezhnev (1964–1982) and American President Richard M. Nixon (1969–1974), U.S.-Soviet relations began to improve, albeit fitfully. Nixon accurately assessed the changing balance of power, especially the rise of China, and he moved to improve relations through a policy of **détente** with Moscow and Beijing. They came to similar realpolitik conclusions about the changing power configuration of the international system and sought improved relations with Washington.

The end of the bipolar system and the accompanying demise of communism in the Soviet Union and Eastern Europe is symbolized here by the flag of the fallen superpower hanging nearly forgotten in a window whose architecture, like the Soviet Union, is of a bygone era.

The End of the Bipolar System

During the 1970s and early 1980s, relations between Moscow and Washington continued to warm, fitfully at first, then more rapidly. Mikhail S. Gorbachev became the Soviet leader in 1985 and instituted a range of reforms designed to ease the Soviet Union's oppressive political system and to restructure its cumbersome bureaucratic and economic systems. While Gorbachev's goals were limited, he opened a Pandora's box for the communist Soviet Union and unleashed forces that were beyond his control.

Gorbachev also sought better relations with the West in an effort to reduce the military's burdensome share of the USSR's economy, to receive more favorable trade terms, and to accrue other economic benefits. Among other things, Gorbachev announced that the USSR was willing to let Eastern Europeans follow their own domestic policies. They responded by moving quickly to escape Moscow's orbit. This was symbolized most dramatically in East Germany, where the communist government fell apart rapidly. East Germany dissolved itself in October 1990, and its territory was absorbed by West Germany into a newly reunified Germany. Other communist governments in the region also fell, and the Warsaw Pact dissolved in early 1991.

It was hard to believe then, but the Soviet Union was next. It soon collapsed, as its constituent republics declared their independence. On December 25, 1991, Gorbachev resigned as president of a country that no longer existed. That evening, the red hammer-and-sickle Soviet flag was lowered for the last time from the Kremlin's spires and replaced by the red, white, and blue Russian flag. Few novelists could have created a story of such sweep and drama. The Soviet Union was no more.

The 21st Century: The Genesis of a New System

"What is past is prologue," Shakespeare comments in *The Tempest*. That is as true for the real world of today and tomorrow as it was for the Bard's literary world of yesterday. One hopes that no future historian will write a history of the 21st century under the title *The Tempest*. Titles such as *As You Like It* or *All's Well That Ends Well* are more appealing possibilities for histories yet to be.

Whatever the future will bring, we are in a position similar to that of Banquo in *Macbeth*. He sought to know the future, and we can sympathize with him when he pleads with the three witches to "look into the seeds of time, / And say which grain will grow and which will not." Unfortunately for Banquo, the witches gave him a veiled prophecy he neither understood nor was able to escape. We are luckier, though. As Shakespeare tells us in *Julius Caesar*, "It is not in the stars to hold our destiny but in ourselves."

The sections that follow are meant to help you determine your script for the destiny of the coming decades by examining the factors and trends that will benefit or beset the world during your lifetime and into the future. To facilitate the discussion, these topics are divided into four areas: political structure, security, international economics, and quality of life.

The Structure of Power in the 21st Century

There are a number of important changes occurring in the shape of the international system. A new polar structure is emerging, the Western orientation of the system is weakening, and the authority of the state is being challenged from without and from within.

The Polar Structure

Clearly the bipolar system is gone. What is not certain is how to characterize the current, still evolving system. Although not all scholars would agree, the view here is that what exists in the first decade of the 21st century is best described as a limited unipolar system that is struggling to become a multipolar system.

A Unipolar Moment Just before the Soviet Union's final collapse, analyst Charles Krauthammer (1991:23) wrote an article entitled "The Unipolar Moment." In it he argued that the widespread assumption that "the old bipolar world would beget a multipolar world with power dispersed" among several countries was wrong. "The immediate post–Cold War world is not multipolar," he observed. "It is unipolar. The center of world power is the unchallenged superpower, the United States."

Many other analysts scoffed at Krauthammer's view and some still do, but he had a point. Since then, U.S. global economic dominance has grown further, especially as Japan and Europe have struggled. Militarily, U.S. arms with some allied support twice defeated Iraq (1991, 2003) and overwhelmed Yugoslavia (1999) in wars that were wildly one-sided, mostly because of the vast and growing lead of U.S. military technology.

Others concur with Krauthammer's view that a unipolar system exists. For one, scholar Joseph Nye (2002:545) has written of the United States that "not since Rome has one nation loomed so large above the others." Nye observes that the U.S. status as the **hegemonic power** is not just based on military dominance. Instead, he quotes the observation of France's foreign minister that "U.S. supremacy today extends to the economy, currency, military areas, lifestyle, language, and the products of mass culture that inundate the world, forming thought and fascinating even the enemies of the United States."[1]

The dominance, and some would say hubris, of U.S. power in what many analysts think is a unipolar world is captured in this April 2003 photograph of a U.S. Marine covering the face of the fallen Iraqi leader, Saddam Hussein, with an American flag in Baghdad just after U.S. forces captured the city.

The Multipolar Urge In his famous poem, "Mending Wall," Robert Frost wrote about the seemingly inexorable forces of nature that repeatedly topple stone walls. Wisely he observed:

> Something there is that doesn't love a wall,
> That wants it down.

Similarly, there is something in the balance-of-power nature of the international system that does not like unipolarity. U.S. dominance rankles many countries, whether they were allies, enemies, or neutrals in the cold war era (Malone & Khong, 2003). As evidence, consider the following three statements, all made within three days in mid-2003. In Moscow, Russia's President Vladimir Putin, with China's President Hu Jintao at his side, told reporters that the two leaders believed that "the world order can and should be multipolar."[2] The following day, some 2,700 miles to the southeast in New Delhi, Prime Minister Shri Atal Behari Vajpayee of India commented that his discussions with visiting German Chancellor Gerhard Schröeder made it clear that "our two countries . . . share a vision of a cooperative multipolar world order."[3] And two days after that, over 4,000 miles to the northwest in France, President Jacques Chirac assured the press, "I have no doubt whatsoever that the multipolar vision of the world that I have defended for some time is certainly supported by a large majority of countries throughout the world."[4]

These expressions of support for a multipolar world by the leaders of China, France, Germany, India, and Russia do not mean that the leaders are anti-American, merely anti-unipolarity. The reason is that a world in which there is one dominant power, the United States in this case, is an international system in which all other countries are at least partly subordinate. We will see in chapter 3 that unipolarity arguably has some benefits, but it is a difficult state of affairs for any sovereign country (other than the hegemon, of course) to accept.

Limited Unipolarity There is no precise line where unipolarity begins and ends, which is one reason why not all agree that the world is unipolar now. Perhaps it is more accurate to depict the current state of affairs as a **limited unipolar system**, which means

FIGURE 2.2 American Opinion on the U.S. Global Role

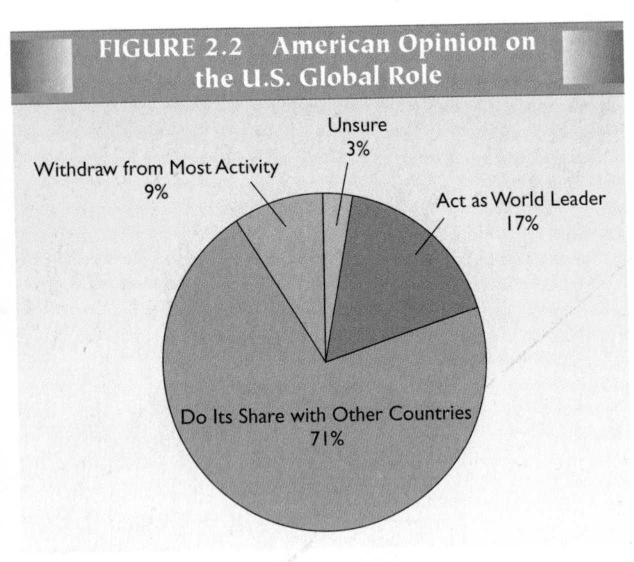

Americans typically say they favor an active U.S. role in world affairs, but only a small minority want their country to play the preeminent role of a unipolar power.

Note: The question was: "Which statement comes closest to your position? As the sole remaining superpower, the U.S. should continue to be the preeminent world leader in solving international problems, the U.S. should do its share in efforts to solve international problems together with other countries, or the U.S. should withdraw from most efforts to solve international problems."

Data source: Harris Poll, 2002, found in *Public Perspective*, March/April, 2003, p. 21.

that one power center dominates, but the extent of that control is restrained (Huntington, 1999). In the current international system, there are many restraints on U.S. power. The most important of these result from the extensive degree to which the United States, like all countries, is intertwined with and reliant on other countries. For example, the U.S. war on terrorism will make little progress unless other countries cooperate in identifying and arresting terrorists within their borders and dismantling the financial networks on which terrorists often rely. Similarly, the U.S. economy may be the world's most powerful, but it depends heavily on favorable trade relationships with other countries for its prosperity. A third example, involves the frequent U.S. need for diplomatic support. The simmering crisis with North Korea is likely to be resolved much more easily if the region's countries, especially China, cooperate with Washington in persuading Pyongyang to desist from building nuclear weapons. The point is that because the United States frequently benefits from the cooperation of others, it can only go so far in riding roughshod over their preferences on a range of issues. Currently, there are probably not too many issues on which a determined Washington cannot get its way, but there is a price to pay for unbridled unilateralism (Patrick & Forman, 2002).

The extent of U.S. unipolar power is also limited by Americans themselves (Sobel, 2001). If you ask them whether they think their country should take an active part in world affairs, about two-thirds will usually respond "yes."[5] If, however, you ask Americans whether they favor a dominant U.S. role, which is what a unipolar power must play if it wishes to retain its status, then you find a much more cautious approach, as depicted in Figure 2.2. Thus, the unipolar role of the United States is limited by what the public will tolerate, and presidents risk a politically dangerous backlash if they follow a policy that Americans feel overly involves their country.

Future Polarity Predicting the future configuration of world power is difficult beyond Krauthammer's safe-bet prediction that, "No doubt, multipolarity will come in time. . . . [when] there will be great powers coequal with the United States" (Krauthammer, 1991:23). Certainly, as the statements by Chirac and others demonstrate, a great deal of the diplomatic strategy of many second-tier powers (such as France, Russia, China) centers on hastening the arrival of that multipolar time (Kapstein & Mastanduno, 1999). For example, many observers expressed the not unreasonable suspicion that the German and French opposition in 2003 to war with Iraq, which prevented the United States from getting UN Security Council support of the invasion, was based in part on a desire to assert their own authority in the system.

Particularly if overly aggressive and unilateral U.S. policy alarms the next tier of powers and drives them into alliance with one another and opposition to the United States, or if the United States is a reluctant hegemon, then a multipolar system could quickly reemerge (Ikenberry, 2002, 2001; Bender, 2003). Some scholars believe that such a system will be statecentric and look and function much like the *traditional multipolar system* that existed in the 19th century (Mearsheimer, 2001). Yet other scholars believe that the system is evolving toward becoming a *modified multipolar system*. They think that it will not look or operate like a traditional multipolar system because states and alliances are now being joined as important actors by regional and global international organizations, such as the European Union (EU) and the United Nations (UN). Analysts believe that these new types of major actors will change the dynamics of the international system in ways that are discussed in chapters 3 and 7.

The international system has become less Westernized in the last several decades. More and more African, Asian, and other countries have gained independence and strength, and they and their leaders have taken on increasingly important roles on the world stage. This shift is represented by this photo taken in 2003 during a meeting of world leaders on economic affairs. U.S. President George Bush and British Prime Minister Tony Blair lead Western powers, but they have been joined on the world stage by Nigerian President Olusegun Obasanjo, Egyptian President Hosni Mubarak, Brazilian President Luiz Inácio Lula da Silva, and Japanese Prime Minister Junichiro Koizumi.

The Weakening Western Orientation of the International System

Another dynamic of the early 21st century is that the dominant Western orientation of the international system continues to weaken as a result of the expansion of the number and power of non-Western states. The colonial empires established by the imperial Western powers collapsed after World War II, and in the ensuing years over 100 new countries have gained independence. The vast majority of these new countries are located in Africa, Asia, and other non-Western regions. A few, especially China, have achieved enough power to command center stage. Even the smaller non-Western countries have gained a stronger voice through their membership in international organizations. For example, non-Western countries now command a majority in the UN General Assembly, and in the Security Council the U.S. attempt in 2003 to gain support for war with Iraq failed because Washington was unable to persuade such Council members as Angola, Mexico, and Pakistan to support the U.S. position.

While the non-Western countries have many differences, they share several commonalities. Most struggle economically, are ethnically/racially not Eurowhite, and share a history of being colonies of or being dominated by Eurowhites. Furthermore, the value systems of many of these countries differ from Western values, which form the basis of current international law, concepts of human rights, and other standards in the international system.

It should not be surprising, then, that many of these new or newly empowered countries support changes in the international system. The result of all this is that the perspectives and demands of these countries are considerably changing the focus and tone of world political and economic debate.

Challenges to the Authority of the State

Along with the changing polar configuration and the rise of non-Western states, the 21st century system is also being affected by the fact that states' starring role in the world drama has become somewhat less secure. This idea is captured by Benjamin Barber (1996) in a book, *Jihad vs. McWorld: How Globalism and Tribalism Are Reshaping the World.* He contends that the authority of states is being eroded by antithetical forces, some of which are splintering states into fragments (jihad, tribalism) and others of which are merging states into an integrated world (McWorld, globalism). As Barber (p. 4) puts it, if the first set of forces prevail, there is a "grim prospect of a retribalization of large swaths of humankind by war and bloodshed: a threatened balkanization of nation-states in which culture is pitted against culture, people against people, tribe against tribe, a Jihad in the name of a hundred narrowly conceived [identifications and loyalties]." The other trend, if it triumphs, melds "nations into one homogeneous global theme park, one McWorld tied together by communications, information, entertainment, and commerce." For now, Barber believes, "Caught between Babel and Disneyland, the planet is falling precipitously apart and coming reluctantly together at the very same moment." If he is correct, it is worth noting that just as the pre-Westphalian system collapsed under the forces of disintegration and integration, so the current system is being challenged by a reverse process of disintegration of the state into smaller units, and integration of states into more regional or universalistic wholes.

The Forces of McWorld Many analysts believe that the political, economic, and social pressures that constitute the forces of **McWorld** are breaking down the importance and authority of states and moving the world toward a much higher degree of political, economic, and social integration.

Political integration, for example, is evident in the increasing number and importance of international organizations such as the World Trade Organization (WTO). When there are trade disputes, countries are no longer free to impose unilateral decisions. Instead, they are under heavy pressure to submit disputes to the WTO and to abide by its decisions.

Economic interdependence, the intertwining of national economies in the global economy, means that countries are increasingly less self-sufficient. This loss of economic control diminishes the general authority of a state. There is a lively debate over what this means for the future of states (Hout, 1997; Strange, 1997; Hirst & Thompson, 1996). But some scholars believe that, as one puts it, "globalization will markedly constrain the autonomy and effectiveness of states and, at a minimum, raise serious questions about the meaning of internal and external sovereignty" (Korbin, 1996:26).

Social integration is also well under way, in the view of many scholars. They believe that the world is being integrated—even homogenized—by rapid travel and communication and by the increased interchange of goods and services. People of different countries buy and sell each other's products at an ever-increasing rate; Cable News Network (CNN) is watched worldwide; the World Wide Web provides almost instant global access to a wealth of information; e-mail has revolutionized communications; English is becoming something of a lingua franca. At a less august level, it is possible to travel around the world dining only on Big Macs, fries, and shakes at the more than 30,000 McDonald's outlets in 118 countries that serve fast food to about 17 billion customers each year. Thus, despite some worrisome culinary trends, there are indications that the world's people are moving toward living in a more culturally homogenized global village. This outward trend works to weaken inward-looking nationalism, the primary basis of identification with and loyalty to one's country.

Did You Know That:

Television is promoting transnational culture and a common global frame of reference. CNN, for example, is now available in virtually every country through some 400 million television sets that are watched, at least occasionally, by more than 1 billion people.

The Forces of Tribalism States are also being tested by and are sometimes collapsing because of a number of pressures, including erosive ethnic rivalries. Barber's main title refers to this as *jihad* (an Arabic word that means struggling to spread or defend the faith), but because of the particular connotation of jihad, this text will use his other term, **tribalism**, to refer to the process of disintegration.

The important point is that whatever one calls the process, the world has recently seen an upsurge of states splintering and collapsing under the pressure of secessionist forces. This is easily evident in events since 1990. Most momentously, the Soviet Union dissolved into 15 independent countries in 1991, and some of them are ethnically unstable. The Chechen people, for instance, seek to carve an independent Chechnya out of Russia. Similarly, Yugoslavia broke apart, and one of its new republics, Bosnia, itself collapsed in ethnic warfare. In 1998 an already diminished Yugoslavia further convulsed when ethnic Albanians, who are a majority in Kosovo Province, rose up and achieved autonomy. Then in 2003, what was left of Yugoslavia further fragmented into a confederation named Serbia and Montenegro after its two dominant **ethnonational groups**. Elsewhere, Somalia in the early 1990s fell into chaos among warring clans and remains a shell; what was Czechoslovakia is now two countries; the people of East Timor declared their independence from Indonesia; Afghanistan is suffering grievously from the incessant power struggle among its dozen or more ethnonational groups; the Hutu massacre in 1994 of hundreds of thousands of Tutsis exposed the myth of a single Rwandan people; and the role of the Kurds in defeating Iraq in 2003 heightened that group's desire to unite their people in Iraq, Turkey, Iran, and elsewhere into an independent Kurdistan. The list could go on, but that is not necessary to stress the point that in all these places and elsewhere, states were in trouble.

Security in the 21st Century

Military security in today's world is provided primarily by individual countries. Each state is responsible for its own protection and tries to maintain a military capability to defend its national interests. Other countries normally come to the aid of a country that has been attacked only if they find it in their national interest to do so. Kuwait provides a good example. The United States came to Kuwait's aid in 1991 mostly because of oil. If Kuwait produced tropical fruit, it is unlikely that a half-million U.S. troops would have rushed to defend the world's banana supply from Iraqi aggression.

Whatever the advantages of national security based on self-reliance may be, there are also disadvantages. *Cost* is one. Even with the cold war over, world military expenditures between 1992 and 2002 amounted to about $10 trillion, about one-third of which was U.S. spending. *Uncertain effectiveness* is the second drawback to the traditional way of providing security. Critics of the traditional approach think that "national security" is an oxymoron, given the fact that over 111 million people were killed in wars during the 20th century alone. This staggering total is almost 6 times more people than were killed in the 19th century and 16 times the number of people slain during the 18th century. Thus, even taking population growth into account, war is consuming a greater percentage of human lives each successive century. Most ominously, the advent of nuclear weapons has raised the curtain on the possibility that the next major war could be humankind's final performance. Moreover, the possibility of such an apocalyptic scene being played out has been increased by the proliferation of **weapons of mass destruction (WMDs)** in the form of biological, chemical, and nuclear weapons, and by the spread of the missile technology to rapidly deliver these WMDs over long distances (Brown, 2003).

> ***Did You Know That:***
> World military expenditure in 2001 amounted to $839 billion. That was only slightly less than the combined gross national product produced by the 2.1 billion people who live in the world's two poorest regions, sub-Saharan Africa ($311 billion) and South Asia ($618 billion).

The limited ability of national forces alone to provide security was also highlighted by the terrorist attacks of September 11, 2001, on the World Trade Center and the Pentagon. The devastation raised global awareness of what has been termed **asymmetrical warfare**. As one analyst explained, "Pentagon and military intellectuals have long talked about . . . the notion of 'asymmetrical warfare'—using unconventional tactics in combat rather than using forces of comparable size and employing similar tactics in battle. Terrorism takes the concept of asymmetrical warfare to another level by not even engaging military forces in battle."[6] And if terrorists with conventional explosives and even airliners transformed into missiles were not scary enough, there is increasing concern about the possibility of terrorists acquiring WMDs.

The increased ability of terrorists to operate globally and to inflict massive damage has created new security challenges for states. This image of a Massachusetts state trooper stationed with an automatic weapon in Boston's Logan Airport, from which the planes that dove into the World Trade Center towers took off, is part of the U.S. effort to guard against terrorism. Some question, however, whether states can adequately meet the security threats posed by terrorists and weapons of mass destruction.

In the face of these realities, the world is beginning to work toward new ways of providing security, which chapter 11 details. *Arms control* is one trend. The high cost of conventional war and the probable cataclysmic result of a war using WMDs have forced the political system toward trying to avert Armageddon. During the last decade alone, new or revised treaties have been concluded to deal with strategic nuclear weapons, chemical weapons, land mines, nuclear weapons proliferation, and several other weapons issues.

International security forces are another relatively new thrust in the quest for security. UN peacekeeping forces provide the most prominent example of this alternative approach to security. Prior to 1948 there had never been a peacekeeping force fielded by an international organization. In 2003 there were 15 under way, with over 37,000 military and police personnel from 89 countries deployed. Using such forces is in its infancy, but they may eventually offer an alternative to nationally based security. There are even calls for a permanent UN army that would be available for immediate use by the UN.

The Bush administration came to office in 2001 with a skeptical view of international security cooperation, and that attitude was enhanced in 2003 when the Security Council refused to support the American and British resolution authorizing immediate force against Iraq. At least part of the inability of Washington to win support for action against Iraq was the disagreement of many countries and even many Americans with the idea of preemptive war contained in the **Bush Doctrine** and discussed in the You Be the Playwright box "The Bush Doctrine."

Global Economics in the 21st Century

The years since World War II have included a number of trends in international economics that will continue to affect the international system as this century evolves. Economic interdependence and economic disparity between the wealthy countries and the relatively poor ones are two matters of particular note.

Economic Interdependence

One important economic change in the international system that has gained momentum since World War II is the growth of **economic interdependence**. The trade in goods and services during 2001 exceeded $7.6 trillion; Americans alone own more than $6.9 trillion in assets (companies, property, stock, bonds) located in other countries, and foreigners own more than $9.2 trillion in U.S. assets; the flow of currencies among countries now exceeds $1.5 trillion every day. The impact of this increasingly free flow of trade, investment capital, and currencies across national borders is that countries have become so mutually dependent on one another for their prosperity that it is arguably misleading to talk of national economies in a singular sense.

To deal with this interdependence, the world during the last half-century has created and strengthened a host of global and regional economic organizations. The three most important global economic organizations are the World Bank, the International Monetary Fund (IMF), and the World Trade Organization (WTO). And among the numerous regional economic organizations are the Association of Southeast Asian Nations (ASEAN), the European Union (EU), and the Southern Common Market (Mercosur) in South America.

YOU BE THE PLAYWRIGHT

The Bush Doctrine

One of the challenges of the 21st century for Americans is how to use U.S. power. President Bush thinks he has the right script, and in 2002 he outlined it in a document entitled, "The National Security Strategy of the United States of America."[1] In what soon was dubbed the Bush Doctrine, the president trumpeted the U.S. "position of unparalleled military strength and great economic and political influence," and he pledged to use U.S. power to "defend the peace by fighting terrorists and tyrants." Moreover, he proposed using preemptive force to do so. "Given the goals of rogue states and terrorists, the United States can no longer solely rely on a reactive posture," Bush argued. Instead, he proclaimed, "To forestall or prevent hostile acts by our adversaries, the United States will, if necessary, act preemptively."

The Bush Doctrine set off an immediate national debate, with criticism coming from realists and liberals alike. From the realist perspective, one critic wrote, "Although the word 'empire' is not used, the Bush administration's ambitious new [doctrine] seems to embrace the notion of neoimperialism" (Eland, 2002:1). The realist critic saw two particular dangers. First, "The strategy of empire is likely to overstretch and bleed America's economy . . . and hasten the decline of the United States as a superpower." Second, "The strategy could also . . . alarm other nations and . . . create incentives for [them] to acquire weapons of mass destruction as an insurance policy against American military might."

From the liberal perspective, another analyst wrote that using preemptive "force against implacable evil may be emotionally satisfying, but it is hardly the basis for responsible policy." "If coercive pre-emption is to be done at all," the liberal critic contended, "it must be done by the international community as a whole for common benefit, not by the United States alone for its own exclusive purposes" (Steinbruner, 2003).

Yet other analysts were full of praise. "The Bush administration's doctrine—imperial or not—is a positive response to the likely proliferation of wildcat violence in a context of state disintegration and dangerously unpredictable states (such as North Korea and Iraq) . . . [with] insidious weapons," one supporter wrote."If the Bush administration's policy is one of identifying, intimidating, and possibly eliminating wildcat violence with global reach and horrendous consequences," he continued, "then I favor it—even if that effort includes new imperial notions of extraterritoriality and spheres of influence" (Jowitt, 2003).

The U.S.-led invasion of Iraq was clearly the first application of the Bush Doctrine. With one member of the so-called axis of evil defeated, there are those who would apply the doctrine to the other members, Iran and North Korea. Beyond those countries . . . well, that is taking the script too far into the future without giving you a chance to be the playwright. How should the drama move forward? Should the Bush Doctrine govern U.S. action on the world stage or is a rewrite needed?

Before leaving our discussion of economic interdependence, it should be noted that the road to integration is not smooth nor is its future certain. There are numerous difficulties. Trade and monetary tensions exist among countries. Many people oppose surrendering any of their country's sovereignty to the UN, the WTO, or any other international organization. Other people worry that free trade has allowed multinational corporations to escape effective regulation to the detriment of workers' rights, product safety, and the environment (Cutler, Haufler, & Porter, 1999). As one analyst puts it, the move to create an unfettered global economy "pulls capital into corners of the globe where there is less regulation, which in turn makes it harder for advanced nations to police their capital markets and social standards" (Kuttner, 1998:6). Indeed, these and other worries have sparked a growing opposition to further interdependence and occasionally violent protests against it. There are, in short, significant choices to be made in how to order financial relations among countries.

Economic Disparity between North and South

There is a wide disparity in economic circumstance between the relatively affluent life of a small percentage of the world population who live in a few countries and the majority of humanity who live in most countries. The terms North and South are used to designate the two economic spheres that divide the world. The **North** symbolizes the wealthy and industrialized **economically developed countries (EDCs)**, which lie mainly in the Northern Hemisphere. By contrast, the **South** represents the **less developed countries (LDCs)**, the majority of which are near or in the Southern Hemisphere.

This categorization does not mean that the world can be divided precisely between countries that are wealthy and those that are poor. Instead their economic circumstances range from general opulence (the United States) to unbelievable poverty (Bangladesh). There are a few countries, such as Portugal, grouped with the North that are far from rich. And there are some countries of the South, such as Singapore, that have achieved substantial industrialization and whose standards of living have risen rapidly. These countries are called **newly industrializing countries (NICs)**. Moreover, there are some wealthy people in LDCs and numerous poor people in EDCs.

Nevertheless, such details cannot disguise the fact that there is a vast economic gap between North and South. In 2001, the per capita **gross national product (GNP)** of the North was $26,510, which is 23 times as much as the per capita wealth of the South, $1,160. This immense gulf in wealth has devastating consequences for the LDCs. Their children, for instance, suffer an unconscionable mortality rate that is almost 12 times greater than the infant mortality rate in the North. As Figure 2.3 shows, the people in countries of the North and those in the South live in virtually different worlds. The North is predominantly a place of reasonable economic security, literacy, and adequate health care. By contrast, the lives of the people of the South are often marked by poverty, illiteracy, rampant disease, and early death.

One ramification of the weakening Western orientation of the international system discussed earlier is that this economic inequity is causing increased tension between the North and South. The LDCs are no longer willing to accept a world system in which wealth is so unevenly distributed.

Many people in the South blame much of their poverty on past colonialist suppression and on what they believe to be continuing efforts by the EDCs to dominate the LDCs by keeping them economically and politically weak. While such feelings do not justify terrorism, it is important to understand that the widespread grinding poverty among the LDCs is one of the factors that led to the rage behind the September 11, 2001, attacks on the United States. President Bush later indirectly acknowledged that by pledging to take such actions as doubling the size of the Peace Corps so that it could "join a new effort to encourage development and education and opportunity in the Islamic world," with the goal of "eliminating threats and containing resentment" in order to "seek a just and peaceful world beyond the war on terror."[7]

The point, whether or not you believe that the EDCs oppress the LDCs, is that choices must be made. One option for the wealthy countries is to ignore the vast difference in economic circumstances between themselves and the LDCs. The other option is to do more, much more, to help. Both options carry substantial costs.

Quality of Life in the 21st Century

The last few decades have spawned several changes involving the quality of human life that will continue to affect world politics in the new century and the choices we must face. Preserving human rights and the environment are two matters of particular note.

Human Rights

It borders on tautology to observe that violations of human rights have existed as far back into history as we can see. What is different is that the world is beginning to take notice of human rights violations across borders and is beginning to react negatively to them.

International tribunals are trying individuals accused of war crimes and crimes against humanity in Sierra Leone, Rwanda, and the Balkans. Importantly, the reach of the law is extending to the highest levels. The former president of Yugoslavia, Slobodan

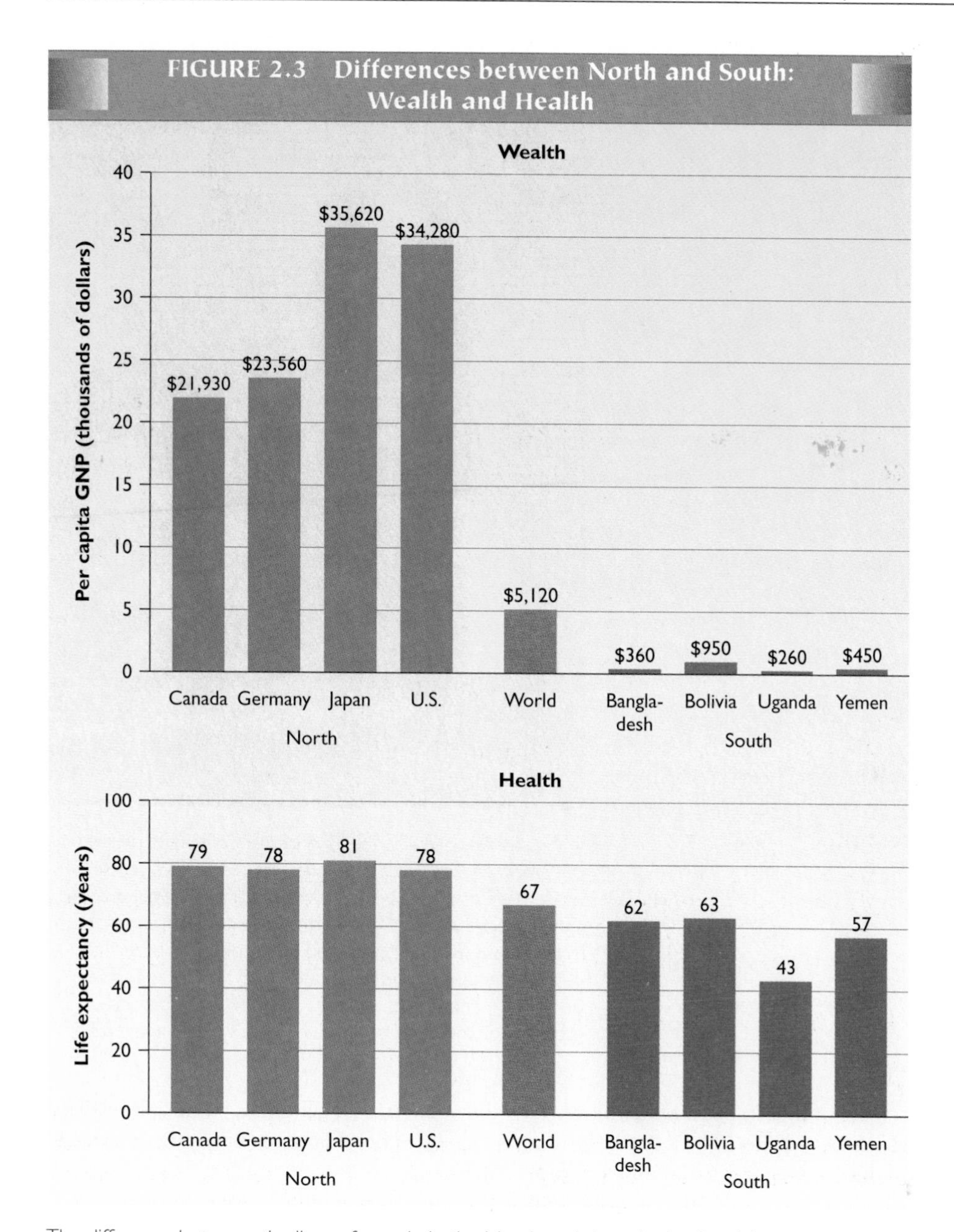

The difference between the lives of people in the North and those in the South is measured by per capita GNP wealth and life expectancy. By these, and many other standards, the people of the South are severely disadvantaged compared to those who live in the North.

Data source: World Bank (2003).

Milosevic, is on trial for war crimes in the Balkans, and President Charles Taylor of Liberia has been indicted for contributing to war crimes in Sierra Leone. Such prosecutions may become even more common when the newly created and permanent International Criminal Court (ICC) completes its organizational process and begins to operate in The Hague, the Netherlands, in 2004.

In numerous other areas the demand for the protection of human rights is louder and stronger. The rights of women are just one of the subjects that have recently become a focus of international concern and action, and women have become increasingly active in

In the past few decades, the advancement of human rights and of democracy have become more prominent issues on the world stage than ever before. As one indication of this change, the Nobel Peace Prize committee gave its 2003 award to Iranian lawyer and activist Shirin Ebadi, pictured here. The committee's announcement cited Ebadi for "her efforts for democracy and human rights . . . [which have] focused especially on the struggle for the rights of women and children."

defense of their rights around the world. Women are "no longer guests on this planet. This planet belongs to us, too. A revolution has begun," is how Tanzanian diplomat Gertrude Mongella has put it with considerable accuracy.[8]

As with many of the other issues that challenge us, it would be naive to pretend that the end of human rights abuses is imminent or that progress has not been excruciatingly slow. Yet it would also be wrong not to recognize that there is movement. Leaders at least discuss human rights concerns; that was virtually unheard of not many years ago. Sometimes, if still not usually, countries take action based on another country's human rights record. Human rights conferences are no longer unnoticed, peripheral affairs. A significant number of human rights treaties have been signed by a majority of the world's countries. In sum, what was once mostly the domain of do-gooders has increasingly become the province of presidents and prime ministers.

The Environment

The mounting degradation of the biosphere has its origins in the rapidly expanding world population and the industrial revolution and, therefore, like the abuse of human rights, is not new to the world stage. Also like human rights, what has changed is the

How can countries develop without harming the environment? This conundrum of sustainable development, especially for economically less developed countries, is depicted in this photograph of Brazilians burning the rain forest in the Amazon River Basin in 2003 to convert it into farmland. The poor farmers need the land to earn their meager living, and Brazil needs the food to feed its expanding population. Yet the massive destruction of the world's forests adds to global warming and other environmental problems that affect everyone.

attention that is now being paid to the subject and the international efforts to protect the environment that have begun.

The greatest challenge is to achieve **sustainable development**, that is, to (a) continue to develop economically while (b) simultaneously protecting the environment. In a further parallel with human rights, progress on the environment has been slow, but it is being made. Among other advances, the subject has shifted from the political periphery to presidential palaces. Leaders have come to realize that their national interests are endangered by environmental degradation, as well as by military and economic threats. This understanding was evident in a White House national security report that portrayed the ability of environmental problems to "compromise our national security," and warned, "We face potentially . . . devastating threats if we fail to avert irreparable damage to regional ecosystems and the global environment. Other environmental issues, such as competition over scarce fresh water resources, are a potential threat to stability in several regions."[9]

The need to balance economic development and environmental protection is recognized by almost everyone, yet achieving sustainable development will not be easy. Among other challenges, the LDCs need extensive assistance to develop in an environmentally responsible way. UN officials have placed that cost as high as $125 billion a

FIGURE 2.4 CO_2 Emissions and the Conundrum of Sustainable Development

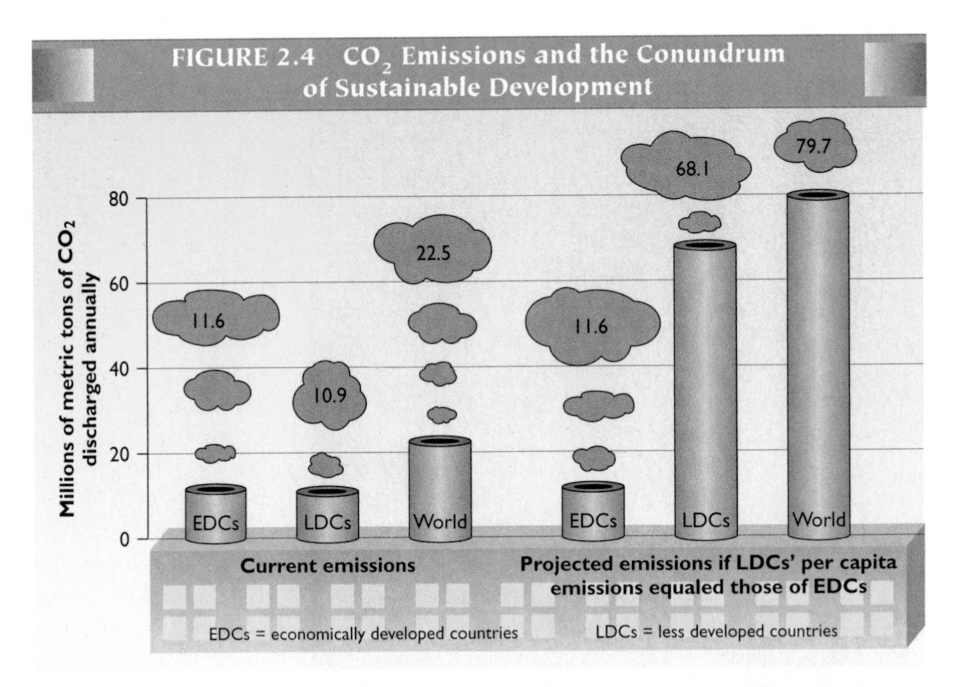

The 16% of the world's population who live in EDCs currently produce 52% of the carbon dioxide (CO_2) emissions. If the LDCs were to reach the same level of economic development as the EDCs, the emissions of the LDCs would increase 625%, and total world emissions would grow 354%, thereby hyperaccelerating global warming. The conundrum of sustainable development is to help the LDCs develop economically in an environmentally acceptable way.

Data source: World Bank (2003).

year, and many observers believe that the North should bear a great deal of the cost for three reasons. One is that the North is much wealthier than the South. The second reason is that over the last 250 years, the industrialized North has emitted a substantial majority of most pollutants, despite having less than one-fifth of the world population. "You can't have an environmentally healthy planet in a world that is socially unjust," Brazil's president noted.[10]

Third, even if you do not agree with the social justice view, it is arguable that the North should assist the South out of sheer self-interest. To better understand the North's stake in LDC development and its impact on the environment, consider Figure 2.4. On the left you can see that with about 84% of the world population, the LDCs still emit less than half as much carbon dioxide (CO_2) as the EDCs. On the right you can see that if the LDCs produced on a per capita basis the same amount of CO_2 as the EDCs, then the annual discharges of the LDCs would soar from an already too high 22.5 billion tons to an astronomical 79.7 billion tons.

Chapter Summary

The Evolving World System: Early Development

1. This chapter has two primary goals. One is to establish a reference framework from which the historical examples used in this book can be understood in context. The second goal is to sketch the evolution of the current world political system.
2. The genesis of the modern world system can be traced to the classical civilizations of ancient Greece

and Rome. Four important political concepts—the territorial state, sovereignty, nationalism, and democracy—have evolved from these ancient states.

3. Following the fall of the Roman Empire, governance during the Middle Ages until 1500 rested in a universalistic authority on the one hand, and a local, microlevel authority on the other.
4. The current world system began to develop in about the 15th century, when modern states started to form due to a process marked by both integration and disintegration of earlier political authority. The Treaty of Westphalia (1648), more than any other event, demarcated the change between the old and the new systems. With the sovereign state at its center, the newly evolving system is anarchical.
5. Several changes occurred during the 1700s and 1800s that had an important impact on the international system. The emergence of the concept of popular sovereignty involved a shift in the idea of who legitimately controls the state. The divine right of kings gave way to the notion that political power does, or ought to, come from the people. During these two centuries, the system also became Westernized and the multipolar configuration reached its apogee.

The Evolving World System: The 20th Century

6. The 20th century witnessed the most rapid evolution of the system. The multipolar system tottered, then fell. The bipolar system declined as other countries and transnational actors became more important, as the expense of continuing confrontation strained American and Soviet budget resources, and as the relative power of the two superpowers declined. The bipolar system ended in 1991 when the Soviet Union collapsed.
7. During the 20th century, nationalism also undermined the foundations of multiethnic empires. European contiguous empires, such as the Austro-Hungarian Empire, disintegrated. The colonial empires dominated by Great Britain, France, and other Eurowhite countries also dissolved.

The 21st Century: The Genesis of a New System

8. There are numerous new trends, uncertainties, and choices to make as we enter the 21st century. One significant question is what will follow the bipolar system. For now a limited unipolar system exists, with the United States as the dominant power, but numerous forces are working to undermine U.S. power and move the system toward a more multipolar configuration. That could be a classic state-centric system or a modified multipolar system, in which global and regional international organizations, as well as states, play key roles.
9. Another shift in the international system is its weakening Western orientation. The number and strength of non-Western countries have grown substantially, and the strength of these states will almost certainly continue to grow in this century. These countries often have values that differ from those of the Western countries.
10. Challenges to the authority of the state represent a third shift in the international system, which has strong implications for the 21st century. There are both disintegrative internal challenges to the state and integrative external challenges.
11. The pursuit of peace is also at something of a crossroads. The destructiveness of modern weaponry has made the quest for peace even more imperative. There are two overriding issues. One is how to respond to the challenge that asymmetrical warfare presents to traditional national defense strategies. The second is whether to seek overall security through the traditional approach of self-reliance or to place greater emphasis on international peacekeeping, arms control, and other alternative international security approaches.
12. The international economy is also changing in ways that have important implications for the 21st century. Economic interdependence has progressed rapidly. The transnational flow of trade, investment capital, and currencies has economically entwined all countries. There are, however, counterpressures, and countries have important choices to make in the near future. One is whether to continue down the newer path to economic integration or to halt that process and follow more traditional national economic policies. If the decision is to continue toward greater economic integration, then a second choice is how to regulate the global economy to deal with the legitimate concerns of those who are suspicious of or even outright opposed to greater globalization.
13. The effort to resolve the wide, and in many ways growing, gulf between the economic circumstances of the countries of the economically developed North and the less economically developed South is also a mounting issue in the new century.
14. A final set of issues that must be addressed in the new century involves the quality of life: human rights and the environment. Both issues have become the subject of much greater international awareness, action, progress, and interaction. Yet ending the abuses of human rights and protecting the environment are still distant goals.

For a chapter quiz, interactive activities, web links, PowerWeb articles, and much more, visit **www.mhhe.com/rourke10/** and go to chapter 2. Or, while accessing the site, click on Course-Wide Content and view recent international relations articles in the *New York Times.*

Key Terms

anarchical political system
appeasement policy
asymmetrical warfare
balance of power
bipolar system
Bush Doctrine
cold war
containment doctrine
détente
economically developed countries (EDCs)
economic interdependence
ethnonational groups
Eurowhite
feudal system
gross national product (GNP)
hegemonic power
Holy Roman Empire
imperialism
industrial revolution
international system
less developed countries (LDCs)
limited unipolar system
McWorld
multipolar system
Munich Conference
nationalism
newly industrializing countries (NICs)
North
North Atlantic Treaty Organization (NATO)
popular sovereignty
power poles
Protestant Reformation
realpolitik
Renaissance
South
sovereignty
state
superpower
sustainable development
Third World
Treaty of Westphalia
Tribalism
weapons of mass destruction (WMDs)
West
westernization of the international system

CHAPTER 3

Levels of Analysis

SYSTEM-LEVEL ANALYSIS
- Structural Characteristics
- Power Relationships in the International System
- Economic Patterns in the Political System
- Norms of Behavior in the International System

STATE-LEVEL ANALYSIS
- Making Foreign Policy: Type of Government, Situation, and Policy
- Making Foreign Policy: Political Culture
- Foreign Policy–Making Actors

INDIVIDUAL-LEVEL ANALYSIS
- Humans as a Species
- Organizational Behavior
- Leaders and Their Individual Traits

CHAPTER SUMMARY

KEY TERMS

Search, seek, find out; I'll warrant we'll unkennel the fox.

—William Shakespeare, *The Merry Wives of Windsor*

Dazzle mine eyes, or do I see three suns?

—William Shakespeare, *King Henry VI, Part 3*

The beginning of knowledge is the discovery of something we do not understand.

—Frank Herbert, *God Emperor on Dune,* 1981

One may say the eternal mystery of the world is its comprehensibility.

—Albert Einstein, "Physics and Reality," 1936

CHAPTER OBJECTIVES

After completing this chapter, you should be able to:

- Describe the structural characteristics of the international system and list the types and characteristics of the actors.
- Analyze the power relationships and discuss characteristics and effects of balance of power in the four systems.
- Define economic patterns in the political system.
- Outline the norms of behavior in the international system.
- Discuss the major emphases of state-level analysis.
- Analyze the foreign policy process based on the type of government, situation, and policy.
- Discuss the importance of political culture to foreign policy.
- List the foreign policy–making actors and evaluate the role and influence of subnational actors.
- Define individual-level analysis in world politics.
- Examine how fundamental human characteristics influence policy.
- Show how organizational behavior, including role playing and group decision making, can influence policy decisions.
- Analyze the idiosyncratic or personal characteristics of leaders that influence their decision making and policy outcomes.

For more than 50 years, the "whodunit" board game Clue has challenged players to figure out who murdered poor Mr. Boddy in his nine-room mansion. This chapter is a bit like Clue. What we want to know is who or what is responsible for what occurs in international relations. As in Clue, we gather evidence and try to understand why an event or events occurred. In a murder mystery, "why" involves motives. In our exploration here, "causal factors" are what we seek to identify. If, for example, the United States and Iraq go to war, as they did in 1991 and again in 2003, our task is to explain why.

There are, of course, differences between the game and world politics. Clue revolves around a murder. Fortunately our tale does not, although violence and death are sometimes part of the drama. Another difference between our endeavor here and Clue is that the game presents nine rooms to explore for clues; this chapter presents three **levels of analysis** to examine: (1) the nature of the world (system-level analysis), (2) how countries make foreign policy (state-level analysis), and (3) people as individuals or as a species (individual-level analysis). Just as you may find clues to solve Mr. Boddy's murder in any of his mansion's rooms, so too are you apt to find clues in one, two, or even all three levels of analysis to explain an event.

System-Level Analysis

System-level analysis involves looking for clues in the biggest of the three areas: the international system. This concept encapsulates the global actors and the social-economic-political setting in which they interact. As such, system-level analysts adopt an essentially "top-down" approach to studying world politics by examining the social-economic-political-geographic characteristics of the system and how they influence the actions of countries and other actors (Moore & Lanoue, 2003). Systems analysts believe that each system's specific characteristics cause its actors to behave in somewhat predictable ways.

Because the concept of a system is abstract, it may help to bring the focus down to a personal level. Each of us is an actor in one or more local systems. Moreover, we behave in reasonably predictable ways because of the system in which we are operating. For example, you have free will, the mental ability to make choices. One way you could exercise that free will on a hot, humid day is by deciding to keep cool by coming to class naked. Neither you nor any of your classmates is likely to do that, however. Why? There are two reasons. Social values (**norms**) are one. Society dictates that people almost always wear clothes in public places, and you would be stared at and probably embarrassed if you were naked. So in the morning you decide what to wear, not whether to wear clothes. The second reason everyone gets dressed before coming to class is the power of the authority structure in which you live; your local system of authority (college, city, state, country) has rules against public nudity and the power to enforce them. Thus even if you were personally disposed to come to class *au naturel,* you almost certainly would be deterred. And if you were not, the police would come and cart you away. So even though you have the ability to decide whether to attend class clothed or not, the system in which you live makes your choice predictable. Therefore you would study the local system to explain why everyone is wearing clothes and even dresses pretty much alike (anyone wearing a tuxedo or ball gown in class today?).

In many ways, the international system influences the behavior of countries and other actors just like your local system helps determine your behavior. Countries, like you, have free will. In 1991 and again in 2003, the United States could have chosen to remain at peace instead of going to war with Iraq. It did not, though, and a system-level analyst would argue that the U.S. decisions to go to war were reasonably predictable, given the realities of the international system. That system, like your local milieu and every other system, can be analyzed according to four factors: structural characteristics, power relationships, economic realities, and norms.

Structural Characteristics

Whether it is the international system or your college international relations class, all systems have identifiable structural characteristics. These include the organization of authority, the actors, and the scope and level of interaction among the actors.

The Organization of Authority

The structure of authority for making and enforcing rules, for allocating assets, and for conducting other authoritative tasks in a system can range from hierarchical (vertical) to anarchical (horizontal). Most systems, like your class and your country, tend toward the hierarchical end of the spectrum. They have a **vertical authority structure** in which subordinate units are substantially regulated by higher levels of authority. Other systems are situated toward the **horizontal authority structure** end of the continuum. There are few, if any, higher authorities in such systems, and power is fragmented. The international system is a mostly horizontal authority structure. It is based on the sovereignty of states. *Sovereignty* means that countries are not legally answerable to any higher authority for their international or domestic conduct (Jackson, 1999). As such, the international system is a **state-centric system** that is largely anarchic; it has no overarching authority to make rules, settle disputes, and provide protection.

To see how horizontal and vertical structures operate differently, ask yourself why all countries are armed and why few, if any, students bring guns to class. One reason is that states in the international system (unlike students in your college) depend on themselves for protection. If a state is threatened, there is no international 911 to call for help. Given this anarchical self-help system, it is predictable that states will be armed.

While the authority structure in the international system remains decidedly horizontal, change is under way. Many analysts believe that sovereignty is declining and that even the most powerful states are subject to an increasing number of authoritative rules made by international organizations and by international law. In 2003, for example, the World Trade Organization (WTO) ruled in favor of a U.S. charge that Canada was violating trade rules by subsidizing its dairy industry, thereby allowing Canadian exports to undercut U.S. producers. But in another case that year, the United States lost when the WTO found the European Union (EU) justified in its complaint that "emergency" U.S. tariffs placed on steel imports were a violation of world trade rules. Countries still resist and often even reject IGO governance, but that does not negate the slowly growing authority of IGOs in the international system.

The Actors

All systems have actors. You, other students, faculty, student organizations, and various administrative units are among the actors in your college system. At the international system level, we can divide the actors into three general categories: states, intergovernmental actors, and transnational actors.

States as Actors **States** (countries) are the principal actors on the world stage. This has been the case for about five centuries, and they continue to dominate the action and to act with independence in a largely anarchical, horizontally structured international system. Yet despite the pivotal role of sovereign states, they are not the only system-level actors. Moreover, there are significant centralizing forces that are slowly transforming the system into a somewhat more vertical authority structure.

TABLE 3.1 Select Intergovernmental Organizations

anization	Mission	Members	Headquarters	Chief Officer
o League	Political, cultural, and economic cooperation	22	Egypt	Egyptian
ociation of Southeast Asian Nations	Economic and other forms of cooperation	10	Indonesia	Singaporean
opean Union	Multipurpose	15	Belgium	Italian
rnational Atomic Energy Agency	Peaceful use of nuclear energy	134	Austria	Egyptian
rnational Cocoa Organization	Cocoa production and trade	42	Great Britain	Dutch
rnational Criminal Police Organization	Investigation of global crime	181	France	American
rnational Monetary Fund	Currency cooperation and stability	184	United States	German
rnational Whaling Commission	Regulation of whaling	51	Great Britain	Danish
rth Atlantic Treaty Organization	Military security	19	Belgium	Dutch
ice International des Epizooties	Animal health	164	France	French
ganization of Petroleum Exporting Countries	Oil production and prices	11	Austria	Venezuelan
ted Nations	Multipurpose	191	United States	Ghanaian
rld Bank	Economic development	184	United States	American
rld Trade Organization	Free economic interchange	146	Switzerland	Thai

There are nearly 300 intergovernmental organizations (IGOs) and they perform a wide variety of functions. Some sense of the range of IGO activities and their global, regional, or specialized membership basis can be gained from this selection. As you can see, membership ranges from near universal to only a few countries, and the functions of IGOs range from the UN's broad range of missions to the single purpose of the International Cocoa Organization.

The United Nations is an important example of the many international organizations that have come on the world scene since 1945. Their roles, importance, and authority in the international system have increased greatly.

Intergovernmental Organizations as Actors A second group of system-level actors is made up of an array of **intergovernmental organizations (IGOs)**. These are international organizations, such as the WTO, whose membership consists of countries. During the past century, IGOs have increasingly come to share the stage with states (Tarrow, 2001). One indication is the steep rise in the number of IGOs. In 1900 there were 30. Now there are nearly 300 IGOs. Not only are IGOs more numerous, they are also playing a larger role in the system, as the U.S. cases before the WTO indicate. Yet another indication of the growing importance of IGOs is their range of activities, as evident in Table 3.1.

Transnational Organizations as Actors Nongovernmental organizations, multinational corporations, and terrorist groups make up a third category of actors in the international system, **transnational actors**. Like IGOs, these organizations operate internationally, but unlike IGOs their membership is private.

Nongovernmental organizations (NGOs) are increasing in their number, range of activity, and importance. In 1900 there were 69 NGOs. Now there are more than 2000 with UN consultative status and many thousands of others. Each of these represents an organized effort by private citizens and voluntary groups conducted across national boundaries to influence one or another aspect of international relations. The diversity of these activities is evident in NGOs with such names as Greenpeace, the International Alliance of Women,

PLAY A PART

Join an NGO

Are you happy with the way that everything, absolutely everything, is going in the world? If you are not, then do something about it!

Each of us has an opportunity to play a part in world affairs by joining one of the multitude of nongovernmental organizations (NGOs). There is almost certainly one and probably several of these voluntary groups that address any transnational issue that you are interested in from almost any policy perspective that you have.

A great way to find a group to your liking is to check the UN site that lists the more than 2,000 NGOs that have consultative status with the UN. The Web address is http://www.un.org/partners/civil_society/ngo/ngoindex.htm.

When you get to the page, you will see a grid that looks very much like the one below that lists 48 interest areas. Each of these and other reference points on the page will lead you to a site that has, in most cases, three columns. The left column lists subtopics, the middle column directs you to "UN Focal Points," and the right column, labeled "Links to Civil Society," will connect you to NGOs active in your area of interest. As a backup, a URL that leads to an alphabetical listing of all NGOs that have consultative status with the UN Economic and Social Council (ECOSOC) is http://www.un.org/esa/coordination/ngo/pdf/INF_List.pdf.

Global Issues—UN System Partnership

Africa	Development Cooperation	Food	Labor	Statistics
Ageing	Disabilities, Persons with	Governance	Law of the Sea and Antarctica	Sustainable Development
Agriculture	Disarmament	Health	Least Developed Countries	Terrorism
AIDS	Drug Control and Crime Prevention	Human Rights	Millennium Assembly	Trade and Development
Atomic Energy	Education	Human Settlements	Question of Palestine	Volunteerism
Children	Elections	Humanitarian Affairs	Peace and Security	Water
Climate Change	Energy	Indigenous People	Population	Women
Culture	Environment	Information Communications Technology	Refugees	Youth
Decolonization	Family	Intellectual Property	Social Development	
Demining	Financing, International	International Law	Outer Space	

the Muslim World League, Socialist International, the International Miners Organization, and the International Union of Students. Most importantly, the influence of these transnational actors on both national governments and on international diplomacy is growing as their numbers increase and as technological advances allow them to operate more effectively across political boundaries. As one analyst has put it, the NGO "role in global negotiations and global governance has been emerging stealthily and slowly over the last quarter century" (Phan, 1996:2). These NGOs are also providing increased opportunities for individuals to become involved in global affairs, as the Play a Part box "Join an NGO" details.

Multinational corporations (MNCs, or **transnational corporations, TNCs**) with production facilities, sales outlets, and other operations in more than one country are a second important type of transnational actor. MNCs have long existed, but their number and size has grown rapidly in the last half century because of the vast expansion of international trade, investment, and other financial interactions. In an international system where money is a source of power, these economic giants exercise considerable influence over the course of events. Some idea of the economic power of the MNCs can be gained from comparing their gross corporate product (GCP: total revenue) to the **gross national product (GNP**: a measure of all goods and services produced by a country's citizens and businesses) of various countries. As you can see in Figure 3.1, some MNCs are economically larger than many countries.

Terrorist groups are a third type of transnational actor with which we must deal. These organizations bring together private individuals who attack civilians and use other methods to inflict physical and psychological pain in an attempt to make it seem better to give in to the terrorists' specific demands or adhere to their political agenda than to risk further suffering. Terrorism is not new, but a number of changes in the international system have made it easier for such groups to operate. Increasingly, terrorist groups are able to travel, move funds, and communicate globally with ease. Even more alarmingly, terrorists are increasingly able to inflict massive damage. The advent of jet airliners and the crowding together of people into skyscrapers were necessary precursors to the 9/11 attack on the World Trade Center. Making matters worse is the possibility of terrorists using biological, chemical, nuclear, or radiological (spreading radioactive material) weapons. According to the International Atomic Energy Agency, there are 130 terrorist organizations with the potential to mount an attack using such weapons. These organizations include 55 ethnic groups, 50 religious groups, 20 left-wing groups, and five right-wing groups.[1]

Did You Know That:

The term *al-Qaeda* (or *al-Qa'ida*) is Arabic for "the base."

Scope, Level, and Intensity of Interactions

A third structural characteristic of any political system is the scope (range), frequency, and intensity (level) of interactions among the actors. In your class, for example, the scope of interactions between you and both your professor and most of your classmates (1) is probably limited to what happens in the course; (2) is not very intense; and (3) is confined to two or three hours of class time each week over a single semester.

At the international system level, the scope, frequency, and level of interaction among the actors is not only often much higher than in your class but has grown extensively during the last half century. Economic interdependence provides the most obvious example. Countries trade more products more often than they did not long ago, and each of them, even the powerful United States, is heavily dependent on others as sources of products that it needs and as markets for products that it sells. Without foreign oil, to pick one obvious illustration, U.S. transportation and industry would literally come to a halt. Without extensive exports, the U.S. economy would stagger because exported goods and services account for about 15% of the U.S. GNP.

Data about expanding trade does not, however, fully capture the degree to which the widening scope and intensifying level of global financial interaction are increasing transnational contacts at every level. For individuals, modern telecommunications and travel have made once relatively rare personal international interactions commonplace. For example, between 1990 and 2000 the number of foreign visitors to the United States jumped 29% from 39.4 million to 50.9 million. During the same period, the number of Americans traveling overseas increased 35% from 44.6 million to 60.2 million. Trillions of phone calls, letters, and e-mail messages add to the globalization of human interactions.

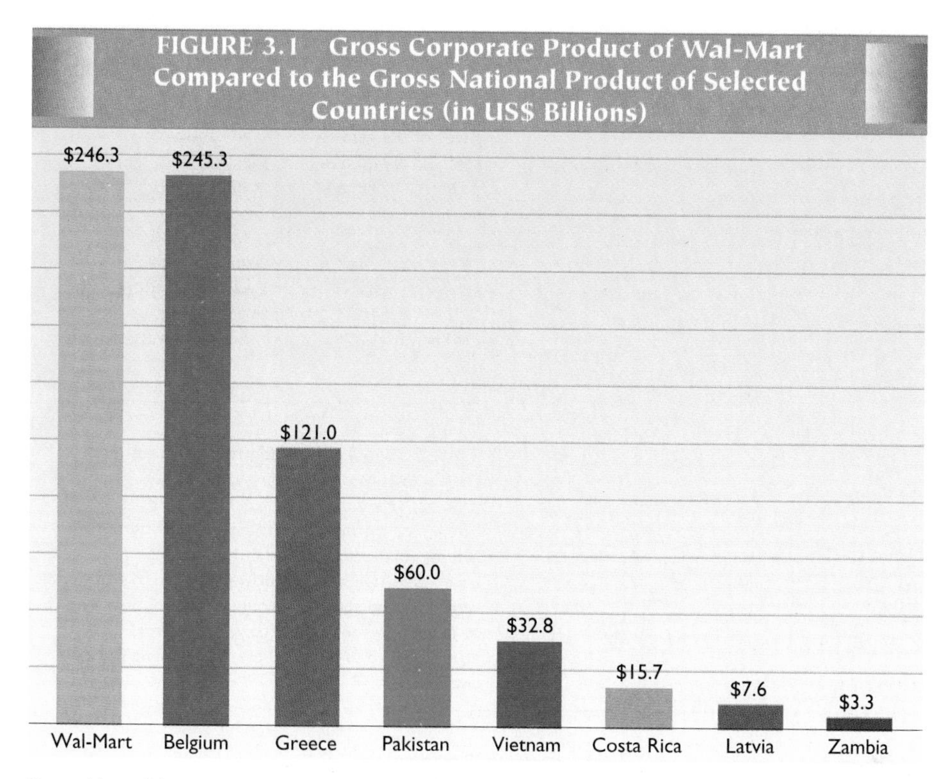

Some idea of the enormous economic power of multinational corporations can be gained by comparing their gross corporate product (revenues) with the gross national products of countries. With revenues of $246.3 billion in 2002 from operations in 10 countries, Wal-Mart is the world's largest MNC. As this figure shows, its GCP is about equal to the GNP of Belgium and much larger than GNPs of many other countries. At the furthest extreme, Wal-Mart's GCP dwarfs the $43 million GNP of São Tomé and Principe, the world's smallest national economy, by an astronomical ratio of 5,728:1.

Data sources: World Bank, 2003; *Forbes*, July 21, 2003.

Power Relationships in the International System

It is very probable that the distribution of power in your class is narrow. There is apt to be one major power, the professor, who decides on the class work, schedules exams, controls the discussion, and issues rewards or sanctions (grades). Sometimes students grumble about one or another aspect of a class, and they might even be right. But the power disparity between students and their professor makes open defiance exceptionally rare. Similarly, the conduct of the international system is heavily influenced by power relationships.

Number of System Poles

Historically, international systems have been defined in part by how many powerful actors each has. Such an actor, called a **power pole**, can be (1) a single country or empire, (2) an alliance, or could be (3) a global IGO, such as the UN, or (4) a regional IGO, such as the EU. We will concentrate on global polar relations, but regions sometimes have more localized polar structures (Zhang & Montaperto, 1999).

One reason that the number of power poles makes a difference is that it is possible, according to some scholars, to identify patterns or rules of the game for unipolar, bipolar, tripolar, and multipolar systems. Figure 3.2 displays four types of system structures

FIGURE 3.2 Models and Rules of the Game of Various International System Structures

Unipolar System

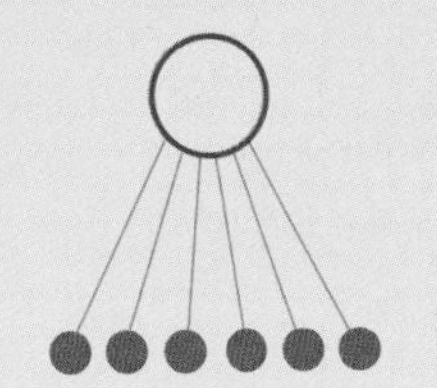

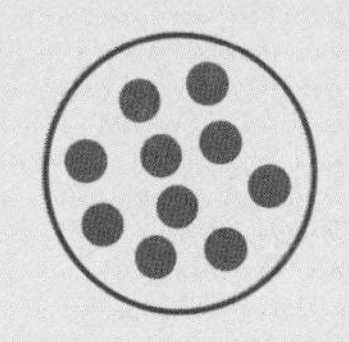

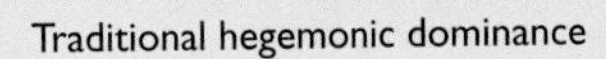

World federal system

One pole
Rules of the game are: (1) The central power establishes and enforces rules and dominates military and economic instruments. (2) The central power settles disputes between subordinate units. (3) The central power resists attempts by subordinate units to achieve independence or greater autonomy and may gradually attempt to lessen or eliminate the autonomy of subordinate units.

Bipolar System

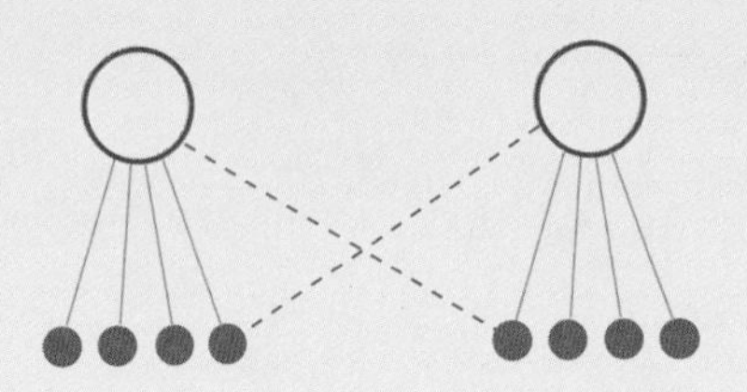

Two poles
Acute hostility between the two poles is the central feature of a bipolar system. Thus primary rules are: (1) Try to eliminate the other bloc by undermining it if possible and by fighting it if necessary and if the risks are acceptable. (2) Increase power relative to the other bloc by such techniques as attempting to bring new members into your bloc and by attempting to prevent others from joining the rival bloc.

Tripolar System

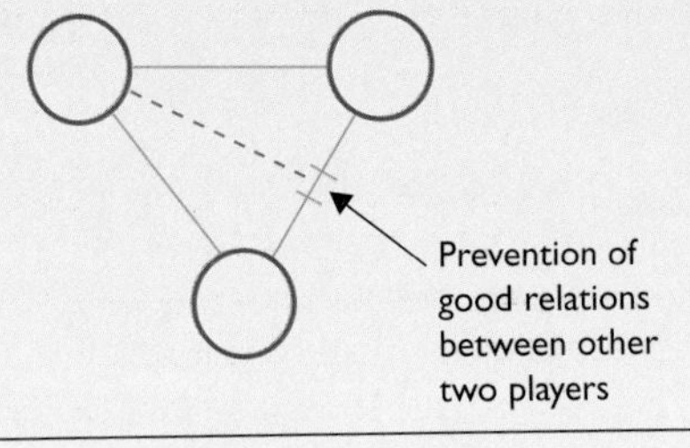

Three poles
The rules of play in a triangular relationship are: (1) Optimally, try to have good relations with both other players or, minimally, try to avoid having hostile relations with both other players. (2) Try to prevent close cooperation between the other two players.

Multipolar System

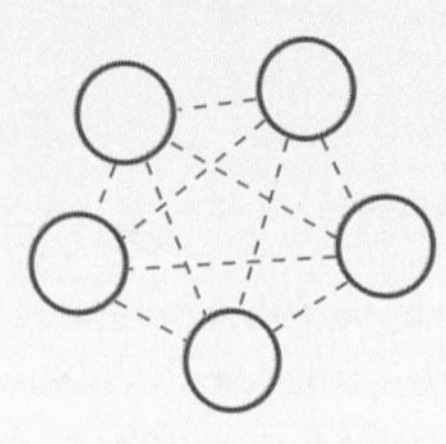

Four or more poles
Rules of the game are: (1) Oppose any actor or alliance that threatens to become hegemonic. This is also the central principle of balance-of-power politics. (2) Optimally increase power and minimally preserve your power. Do so by negotiating if possible, by fighting if necessary. (3) Even if fighting, do not destabilize the system by destroying another major actor.

● Small power
-------- Short-term or potential link
○ Large power
——— Dominant and lasting link

The relationships that exist among the actors in a particular type of international system structure vary because of the number of powerful actors, the relative power of each, and the permitted interactions within the system. This figure displays potential international system structures and the basic rules that govern relationships within each system. After looking at these models, which one, if any, do you think best describes the contemporary international system?

and ways in which the patterns of interaction differ across them. Bear in mind that these rules indicate what actors are apt to try to do. The rules are neither ironclad nor do actors always succeed in implementing them.

As a sample of how these rules work, note that in a **unipolar system**, which exists in many ways today with the United States as the single pole, the **hegemonic power** tries to maintain control, while lesser powers try to escape dominance. Arguably, that explains why the United States seeks to preserve, even expand NATO, which it dominates, and why many Europeans favor transforming the existing 60,000-soldier Eurocorps (with troops from Belgium, France, Germany, Luxembourg, and Spain) into a de facto EU army to rival or even to replace NATO. As former British Prime Minister Margaret Thatcher put it, "The real drive towards a separate European defense" is based on the unstated goal of "creating a single European superstate to rival America on the world stage."[2]

A **bipolar system**, the rules tell us, tends to be marked by intense hostility between the two competing poles. That was true in the ancient world, when the two superpowers of their time, Rome and Carthage (in modern Tunisia), fought the bitter, 118-year-long Punic Wars. "Carthage must be destroyed," Cato the Elder thundered in the Roman Senate in 150 B.C., and that literally came to pass. When Carthage finally fell four years later, according to one historian, "Romans stormed the town and the army went from house to house slaughtering the inhabitants. . . . Carthaginians who weren't killed were sold into slavery. The harbor and the city were demolished, and all the surrounding countryside was sown with salt in order to render it uninhabitable."[3] Some 21 centuries later in another bipolar system, the same visceral hatred and fear were evident in the United States and the USSR, which, atomic scientist J. Robert Oppenheimer wrote, were like "two scorpions in a bottle, each capable of killing the other" (Jones, 1988:523).

A second possible impact of the number of poles is the propensity of a system for instability and war. There is a lively academic debate about whether the number of poles in a system has an impact on the likelihood of war. For example, one scholar believes that "a unipolar system will be peaceful" (Wohlforth, 1999:23). Not all political scientists agree with that, but if unipolarity does make for a stable system, then a continued hegemonic role by the United States could usher in a period of relatively little major conflict (Owen, 2001).

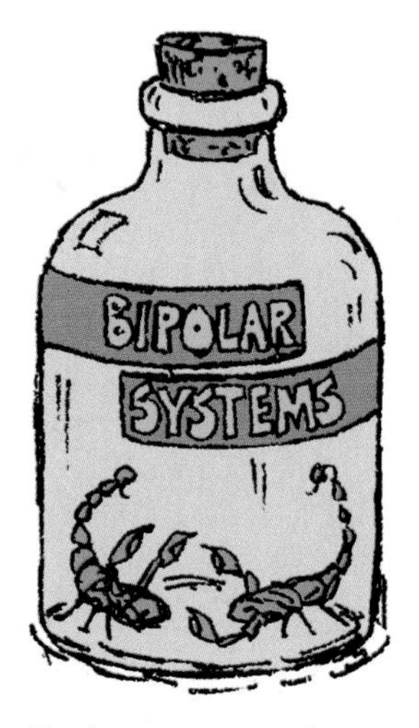

Bipolar systems are often characterized by intense conflict between the two major powers, which has been equated to the death struggle of two scorpions trapped together in a bottle.

Concentration of Power

George Orwell wrote in *Animal Farm:* "All animals are equal, but some animals are more equal than others." Much the same can often be said about power poles, and many scholars believe that system stability varies in part according to the degree to which there is relative power equality or power inequality between poles (Heo, Christensen, & Karaman, 2003; Schweller, 1998). Unfortunately, there is no consensus about which patterns are more or less stable. Some scholars argue that war is more likely when antagonistic poles have relative power equality, creating "a situation in which [every power] can perceive the potential for successful use of force" (Geller, 1993:173). Taking the opposite view, other scholars contend that conflict is more likely between countries of relative power inequality because the more dominant power will confront the weaker power, which, because of emotion and pride, may choose to fight rather than submit (Lemke & Reed, 2001). Such an explanation could explain why the United States was willing to confront Iraq in 1991 and 2003 and why the Iraqi leadership chose war despite the objective odds against them. Still other scholars conclude that conflict is least likely when power is equal or very unequal and most likely when there are moderate power differences between antagonists (Powell, 1996). Less dramatic differences may lead countries either to miscalculate their power relative to that of their opponent or to gamble.

Power Changes and Their Causes

What is more certain than the impact of one or another power configuration on system stability is the fact that the power equation is always in flux. No pole, no matter how powerful, has maintained its status permanently. They eventually decline and sometimes even vanish, as did the USSR. Other countries rise from humble beginnings to the rank of major power, as has the United States. Still others, like China today, may reemerge from a period of eclipse and strive to recapture their lost status (Tammen et al., 2002).

Cycle theories also provide some insight into how power changes in the international system. Some scholars believe that power cycles occur over a period of a few decades, or even as much as a century (Colaresi, 2001). The cycles are demarcated by great-power or "systemic" wars, such as the two world wars, that reflect strains or power shifts within the system and act as political earthquakes, altering the system by destroying the major power status of declining powers and elevating rising powers to pole status. Then the process of power decay and formation begins anew. Another study uses the idea of "chaos theory" to argue that while there is an evolution of power in the system, "this evolution is chaotic [in that] the patterns of global power are not strict chronological cycles, but variable patterns influenced by . . . small random . . . effects" that can change the timing and impact of the cycle (Richards, 1993:71).

Several factors account for the rise or fall of a country's power. One involves the *sources of power*. When a country develops nuclear weapons capability, for instance, its relative power increases. From this perspective, the potential proliferation of biological, chemical, nuclear, and radiological weapons of mass destruction (WMDs) from a relative handful of countries to a wide array of them threatens not only to unleash horrific new levels of death and destruction but also to upset the balance of power. This possible shift is arguably part of what made Iraq's alleged WMD program so alarming to President Bush as leader of the world's dominant power. Whether or not Iraq had WMDs was not the point. The point was that the Bush administration thought Iraq did and was intent on getting more; the administration was willing to accept the lack of conclusive evidence that the Iraqis did not have WMDs as proof that they did.

Conditions within major actors also affect their power. The Soviet Union collapsed in part because it no longer commanded the loyalty of most of its citizens. Most Americans are patriotic, but the country cannot remain a superpower if its people are unwilling to bear the cost of being a leader in the international system. That does not mean the United States should lead, only that it cannot remain dominant if it acts, as one scholar puts it, like a "reluctant sheriff" (Haass, 1997).

Balance-of-power politics is a third cause of change in the system. Countries form alliances and take other actions to avoid being dominated. For example, given U.S. dominance in the system today, it is likely that second-rank powers will try to enhance their status by cooperating in ways that will restrain U.S. power. As noted, this reaction may help explain why France, Germany, Russia, and China were all opposed to U.S. action against Iraq in 2003. Certainly those countries objected to the war as such, but it was also a chance to resist the lead of the hegemonic power. In this context, it was not surprising that several European countries met soon after the Iraq war to discuss how to increase their military cooperation. "In order to have a balance, we have to have a strong Europe, as well as a strong U.S.," is how French President Jacques Chirac explained the conference.[4] Moreover, surveys indicate that Europeans agree with him, as evident in Figure 3.3. None of this means that Europe will be antagonistic toward the United States, only that Washington needs to exercise power carefully to avoid driving its former allies together with its former enemies in an anti-hegemony, not an anti-American, alliance (Carter, 2003; Owen, 2001).

The Impact of Power Changes

Changes in power affect the system in many ways. A *new polar configuration*, with its resulting change in the operation of the system, is the most obvious alteration. Before the early 1990s, the U.S. ability to operate with relative impunity in the Middle East did not exist because of the second superpower, the USSR, and its potential for intervening on behalf of Iraq or some other thorn in the U.S. side. By 1991, although the Soviet Union still existed, it was so weakened that it could not oppose U.S. action, and soon thereafter the USSR collapsed altogether. By 2003, there was no power that could deter U.S. intervention in Iraq.

System instability is a second impact of power changes. "Great powers are like divas. They enter and exit the stage with great tumult," one analyst observes (Zakaria, 1996:37). What this means, and what many studies have concluded, is that the world is most prone to violence during times of system transitions. The rules are uncertain during these times. A declining power may turn to aggression to try to maintain its status. Similarly, a rising power may become more assertive to improve its status. Times of change may also lead to mistakes about the rules of the system. Arguably, Iraq's defiance of the United States was in part a miscalculation of the realities of the new, unipolar system dominated by American power and the willingness of the hegemon to act without UN authorization.

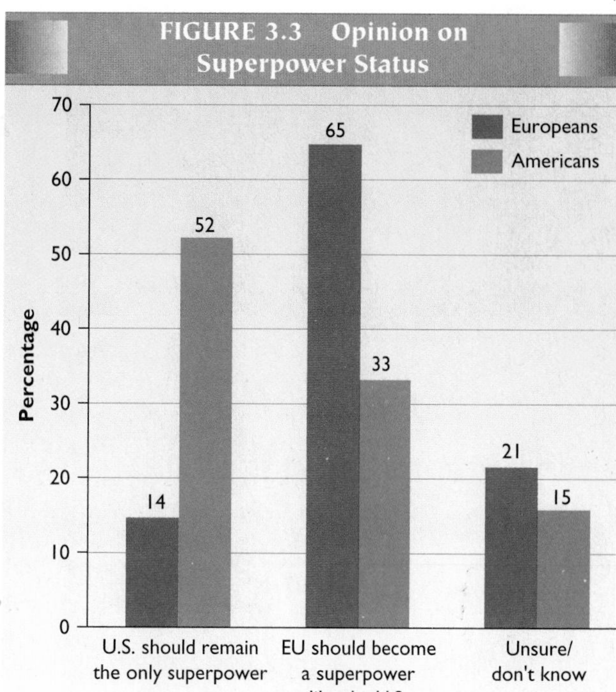

"Uneasy lies the head that wears a crown," Shakespeare tells us in *Henry I, Part II*. This advice may be appropriate for the United States, which, at least for now, is the world's dominant country. Dominance by one means being dominated for others, however, and as this figure shows, Europeans are much less likely than Americans to approve of the current balance of power (or lack thereof) in the international system.

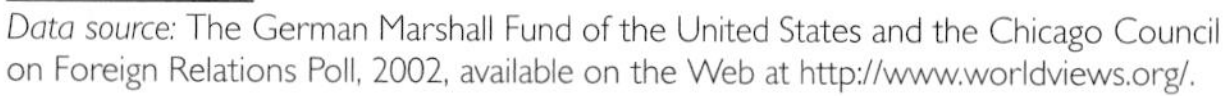

Data source: The German Marshall Fund of the United States and the Chicago Council on Foreign Relations Poll, 2002, available on the Web at http://www.worldviews.org/.

Rules changes can also occur from power shifts. For example, the advent of nuclear weapons may also have shifted the rules of the game for bipolar and perhaps all systems. In contrast to earlier bipolar systems, which were marked by warfare between the two "superpowers" and the eventual defeat of one by the other, the cold war bipolar system did not result in a military death struggle. Why? The answer may be that the devastation that each superpower could wreak on the other changed the rule and kept the two powers from attacking each other because mutual annihilation was predictable.

Economic Patterns in the Political System

Here is a prediction: After graduation or graduate school, you will get a job and spend a significant part of the rest of your life working instead of pursuing whatever leisure activities you enjoy the most. How can such a prediction be made about someone the author has never met? Easy! The economic realities of your local system require money to get many of the things you want, and most of us need a job to get money. Similarly, the international system has economic facts of life that help shape behavior.

Economic interdependence is one pattern that scholars agree influences states' behavior (Gartzke, Li, & Boehmer, 2001; Mansfield & Pollins, 2001). For example, many studies conclude that increasing economic interdependence promotes peace as countries

The pattern of vital natural resources—where they are produced and where they are consumed—influences the operation of the international system. Although the Bush administration denied it, some Americans, including the New York University student pictured here, and many people in other countries believed that the desire to dominate the Iraqi oil fields was at least one motivation behind the U.S.-led attack on Iraq in 2003.

become more familiar with one another and need each other for their mutual prosperity (Schneider, Barbieri, & Gleditsch, 2003).

Natural resource production and consumption patterns also influence the operation of the system. A system-level analyst would say that the U.S. military reaction to Iraq's attack on Kuwait in 1990 and its threat to the rest of the oil-rich Persian Gulf region was virtually foreordained by the importance of petroleum to the prosperity of the United States and its economic partners. As U.S. Secretary of State James A. Baker III explained to reporters, "The economic lifeline of the industrial world runs from the Gulf, and we cannot permit a dictator . . . to sit astride that economic lifeline."[5]

By contrast, U.S. officials repeatedly denied that petroleum was connected to the war in 2003. Secretary of Defense Donald Rumsfeld, for one, asserted that the U.S. campaign against Iraq "has . . . literally nothing to do with oil."[6] Nevertheless, numerous analysts believe that it was an underlying factor. Some contend that Washington sought to ensure continued supplies at a stable price by adding control of Iraq to its already strong influence over Saudi Arabia, Kuwait, Qatar, and other oil-rich states in the region. The administration "believes you have to control resources in order to have access to them," argues Chas Freeman, a former U.S. ambassador to Saudi Arabia.[7] Other analysts believe that the motive behind U.S. policy was a power play. As one scholar put it, "Controlling Iraq is about oil as power, rather than oil as fuel. Control over the Persian Gulf translates into control over Europe, Japan, and China. It's having our hand on the spigot."[8]

There has also been speculation that the opposition of France, Russia, and some other countries to the U.S.-led invasion and their support for easing sanctions on Iraqi oil exports were in part oil related. The contention is that these countries were concerned with the contracts their oil companies had with Iraq to develop its oil production once sanctions were lifted, and they feared that those agreements would be abrogated and given to U.S. firms in the wake of a U.S. occupation of the country. As one U.S. oil expert put it before the war, "Most of these governments . . . have [a financial] interest in the current Iraqi government surviving. It's not trivial. . . . Once it's developed, the oil will be 2.5 million barrels [worth about $70 million] per day."[9]

Uneven distribution of wealth is a third economic pattern that has consequences for the international system. States, which are the main actors in the system, are divided into relative haves and have-nots. At the most general level, this economic division pits the less developed countries (LDCs) of the South and their demands for equity against the economically developed countries (EDCs) of the North. More specifically, as we shall see, there is a connection between the poor economic conditions in LDCs and such problems as political instability, population growth, and environmental degradation that often spill over to affect people in the North, as well as those in the South.

Did You Know That:

Iraq contains 11% of the world's petroleum.

Norms of Behavior in the International System

Just as we concluded that norms (widely accepted standards of behavior) help make it predictable that students will come to class (a) dressed and (b) dressed similarly, so too do norms play a part in determining actions within the international system. In a world in

The United States could have used weapons of mass destruction to quickly kill everyone in Iraq. But the norms of the international system, including criticism of the U.S.-led aerial assault used exclusively to pound Yugoslavia into submission in 1999, helped persuade the Bush administration to quickly send ground forces into Iraq. This occurred even though doing so was more expensive and resulted in more U.S. casualties, including the wounded American soldier pictured here being evacuated to a hospital after a battle near Nasiriya, Iraq, in March 2003.

which absolutely horrendous things sometimes happen, it is hard for some to accept that norms exist, but they do. Certainly it would be far too strong to say there is anything near a universally accepted standard of behavior, but it is the case that values are a more important part of international conduct and are becoming more globally uniform.

For example, one hypothetical option that President George Bush had in 2003 was "nuking" Iraq's main cities and military sites and killing most Iraqis. It surely would have ended the regime of Saddam Hussein, it would have been quick, and it would have cost fewer American lives and dollars than the conventional attack. Yet the president chose to send American troops to Iraq at great expense and at great risk, especially given the perceived threat of a chemical or biological attack on the oncoming U.S. forces. Why?

Norms were one reason that Bush predictably did not choose the nuclear course. The global population would have been horrified, and it is probable that Americans themselves would have risen up and removed Bush from office. Indeed, the norm against using nuclear weapons, especially against a non-nuclear power, is so strong that only massive Iraqi use of chemical or biological weapons might have prompted such a response.

Moreover, even within the parameters of a conventional invasion, it is noteworthy that U.S. and U.K. military forces generally conducted operations in a way to keep civilian casualties much lower than they might otherwise have been. That reflected the growing norms in the world, including those of Americans, 75% of whom, according to one poll, believed there should be a "very high" or "high" priority on minimizing civilian casualties.[10]

It is easy in a long section, such as this one on system-level analysis, to lose track of its main message. So before moving on to state-level analysis, it is worth recapping our focus: Looking for clues (causal factors, independent variables) that will help us explain and evaluate what has happened and is happening in the world. With enough understanding of these causal factors, it is sometimes even possible to make reasonable predictions about what is likely to happen in a given set of circumstances.

As we have seen, system-level analysis offers many insights into the question, Why? Just like individuals, states have free will. But what individuals and states are likely to do is constrained by the social-economic-political systems in which they operate. Understanding those systems helps explain what individuals and states have done and, to a degree, what they may do. Certainly, it remains hard to predict the behavior of either individual or international actors. One reason is that our analytical abilities have only advanced so far. Social science is still a relatively new endeavor. The second reason is that actors sometimes do the unexpected for inexplicable reasons. For countries, it is a phenomenon that one scholar labeled "crazy states" (Dror, 1971). Still the action is not random, and, as the old saying goes, exceptions do not disprove the rule.

State-Level Analysis

To pick up our analogy between levels of analysis and the game Clue, you would not want to search for clues only in the deceased Mr. Boddy's study during the game. So too you should not limit yourself to system-level analysis in your effort to understand international relations. In fact, many scholars believe that you would be well advised to explore for clues at the level of the state because, as one study puts it, "much of what goes on in world politics revolves around interactions between governments" (Hermann & Hagan, 1998:133). Therefore, we should also conduct **state-level analysis**, which emphasizes the characteristics of states, what states do, and how they make foreign policy choices. Most state-level analysts acknowledge the existence of pressures from the system, but they argue that the proper focus for scholars is to examine how states decide to react (Bueno de Mesquita, 2002). What is important from this perspective, then, is the **foreign policy process**: the influences and activities within a country that cause its government to decide to adopt one or another foreign policy (Chittick & Pingel, 2002).

Making Foreign Policy: Type of Government, Situation, and Policy

Those who study how foreign policy is made over time in one country or comparatively in several countries soon realize there is no such thing as a single foreign policy process. Instead, how policy is made varies considerably.

Type of Government and the Foreign Policy Process

One variable that affects the foreign policy process is where a country is on a scale that has **authoritarian governments** on one end and **democratic governments** on the other. The more authoritarian a government is, the more likely it is that foreign policy will be centered in a narrow segment of the government, even in the hands of the president or whatever the leader is called. It is important to realize, though, that no government is absolutely under the thumb of any individual. States are too big and too complex for that to happen, and thus secondary leaders (such as foreign ministers), bureaucrats, interest groups, and other domestic elements play a role in even very authoritarian political systems.

At the other end of the scale, foreign policy making in democracies is much more open with inputs from legislators, the media, public opinion, and opposition parties, as well as those foreign policy–making actors that influence even authoritarian government policy. President Bill Clinton wanted the United States to adhere to the Comprehensive Test Ban Treaty, for example, but the Senate disagreed and in 1999 refused to ratify it. Yet even in the most democratic state, foreign policy tends to be dominated by the country's top leadership.

FIGURE 3.4 Public Opinion and the Rally Effect

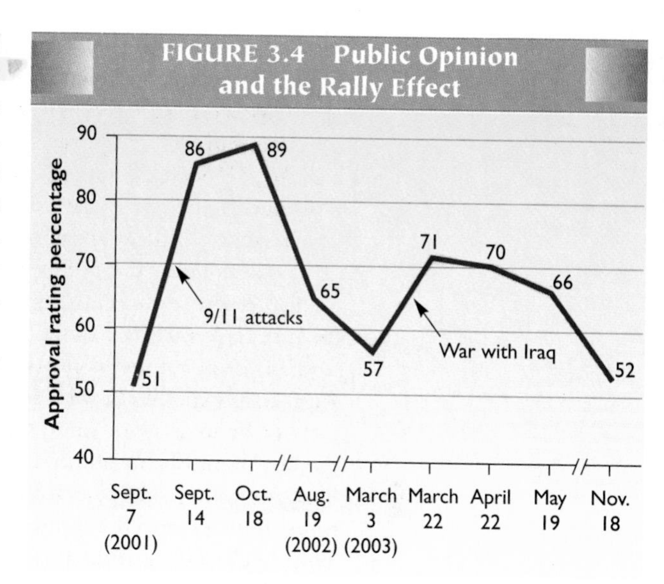

The public tends to rally behind the leader during times of crisis. Public approval of President Bush's performance in office skyrocketed 34 points after the 9/11 attacks and rose 14 points after the onset of war with Iraq on March 19, 2003. As you can see, support tends to drop off markedly after the crisis subsides.

Note: The poll date reflects the first day the poll was being taken. All polls took two or three days to complete.

Data source: CNN/USA Today/Gallup Polls found on the Web site of PollingReport.com at http://www.pollingreport.com/BushJob.htm.

Type of Situation and the Foreign Policy Process

The policy-making process is not even consistent within a country, whatever its form of government (Amadife, 1999; Astorino-Courtois, 1998). Situation is one variable that causes variations in the process. For example, there are important differences in how policy is made during crisis situations compared to noncrisis situations. A **crisis situation** is a circumstance in which decision makers are (1) surprised by an event, (2) feel threatened (especially militarily), and (3) believe that they have only a short time to react (Brecher & Wilkenfeld, 1997). The more intense each of the three factors is, the more acute the sense of crisis.

During a crisis, policy making is likely to be dominated by the political leader and a small group of advisers. By contrast, noncrisis situations will often involve a much broader array of domestic actors trying to shape policy toward their liking. One reason this occurs involves the **rally effect**, whereby the public and other domestic political actors are prone to support the leader during time of crisis. This was evident at the time of the 9/11 attack on the United States and again when it began its war against Iraq on March 23, 2003. As Figure 3.4 shows, Americans' support of President Bush increased in both cases (Hetherington & Nelson, 2003). There was no significant dissent from the actions the president took after 9/11. And although U.S. action against Iraq engendered substantial domestic opposition, it declined markedly once the fighting began. A similar pattern was evident in Great Britain, the only major U.S. ally. There support for the way Prime Minister Tony Blair was handling the crisis with Iraq rose from 48% before fighting began to 63% after hostilities commenced.[11]

Type of Policy and the Foreign Policy Process

How foreign policy is decided also varies according to the nature of the **issue area** involved. Issues that have little immediate or obvious impact on Americans can be termed pure foreign policy. Such issues are usually made by a narrow range of decision makers in the executive branch with little or no domestic opposition or even notice. For instance, President Clinton agreed in 1997 to add three new countries (the Czech Republic, Hungary, and Poland) as members of NATO, and President Bush consented to having yet another seven new members (Bulgaria, Romania, Estonia, Latvia, Lithuania, Slovakia, and Slovenia) join in 2004. Even though these treaty revisions substantially added to U.S. defense commitments, they were nearly invisible within the United States. Polls during the first expansion indicated that 71% of Americans had heard "not very much" or "nothing at all" about the change.[12] And the issue seemed so acceptable in 2003 that pollsters did not even bother to ask the public what it thought. Neither did the expansions arouse much interest in the Senate. After perfunctory debates, it ratified the first expansion by a vote of 80–19 and the second expansion unanimously.

By contrast, foreign policy that has an immediate and obvious domestic impact on Americans is called **intermestic policy**. This type of policy is apt to foster substantial activity by legislators, interest groups, and other foreign policy–making actors and thereby diminish the ability of the executive leaders to fashion policy to their liking. Foreign trade is a classic example of an intermestic issue because it affects both international relations and the domestic economy in terms of jobs, prices, and other factors. Therefore trade legislation is often subject to great controversy in Washington, D.C. and across the country. For example, in 1974 Congress gave up its authority to modify trade agreements when it granted U.S. presidents "fast-track" authority to negotiate such agreements subject only to a "take it or leave it" congressional vote. Then in 1994, amid growing objections from labor unions, environmental groups, human rights groups, and others opposed to various aspects of U.S. trade policy, Congress refused to renew the president's fast-track authority. For the next eight years, Presidents Clinton and Bush fought to have it restored. Bush, with his party in control of both houses of Congress, was finally able to do so in 2002, but only after a concerted effort that included personally going to Capitol Hill to lobby legislators and to offer inducements to gain support. Even this was barely enough, with the final vote in the House of Representatives a razor-thin 215 to 212.

Making Foreign Policy: Political Culture

Each country's foreign policy tends to reflect its **political culture**, that is, a society's widely held, traditional values and its fundamental practices that are slow to change (Paquette, 2003; Jung, 2002). Leaders tend to formulate policies that are compatible with their society's political culture because the leaders share many or all of those values. Also, even if they do not share a particular value, leaders want to avoid the backlash that adopting policies counter to the political culture might cause. To analyze any country's political culture, you would look into such things as how a people feel about themselves and their country, how they view others, what role they think their country should play in the world, and what they see as moral behavior.

One aspect of political culture that affects China's foreign policy is Sinocentrism, the tendency of the Chinese to see themselves and their country as the center of the political and cultural world. This self-image is represented by these Chinese characters. They are Zhong Guó, the Chinese name for their country, which translates as middle (Zhong, on the left) place (Guó, on the right).

How Americans and Chinese feel about themselves and about projecting their values to others provide examples. Both Americans and Chinese are persuaded that their own cultures are superior. In Americans, this is called *American exceptionalism,* an attitude that, for instance, led 81% of Americans in a recent poll to say that the spread of their values would have a positive effect on other parts of the world.[13] A similar sense of superiority among the Chinese is called *Sinocentrism.* This tendency of the Chinese to see themselves as the political and cultural center of the world is expressed, among other ways, in their word for their country: "Zhong Guó" means "middle place" and symbolizes the Chinese image of themselves.

Where American and Chinese differ based on their respective political cultures is in their beliefs about trying to impose it on others. Americans are sometimes described as having a *missionary impulse*, that is, possessing a zeal to reshape the world in the American image. For example, it is this aspect of American political culture that has led the United States to try not only to defeat hostile regimes in Afghanistan, Iraq, and elsewhere, but additionally, to replace them with democratic governments. There is also evidence that the United States makes other decisions, such as foreign aid allocations, based in part on how closely countries adhere to American conceptions of human rights (Apodaca & Stohl, 1999).

Chinese attitudes about projecting values are very different. Despite China's immense pride in its culture, there is no history of trying to impose it on others, even when China dominated much of the world that it knew. The orientation is based in part on Confucianism's tenet of leading by example rather than by forceful conversion. It also has to do with the Sinocentric attitude that the "barbarians" are not well suited to aspire to the heights of Chinese culture and are best left to themselves as much as possible. Among other current ramifications, this *nonmissionary attitude* makes it very hard for the Chinese to understand why Americans and some others try to insist that China adopt what it sees as foreign values and standards of behavior on human rights and other issues. Instead of taking these pressures at face value, the Chinese see them as interference or, worse, as part of a campaign to subvert them.

Foreign Policy–Making Actors

"Washington is like a Roman arena [in which] gladiators do battle," Secretary of State Henry Kissinger (1982:421) wrote in his memoirs. As his analogy implies, foreign policy making is not a calm, cerebral process. Instead it is a clash of ideas and a test of political power and skills to determine which of many policy proposals will prevail. The combatants of which Kissinger wrote are the **foreign policy–making actors**, including political executives, bureaucracies, legislatures, political opponents, interest groups, and the people.

Heads of Government and Other Political Executives

President Harry S. Truman once remarked that in the realm of foreign and defense policy, he had policy-making authority that would make "Caesar, Genghis Khan or Napoleon bite his nails with envy" (Rossiter, 1960:9). That was an overstatement, but it does highlight the fact that the most important of actors in virtually every country's foreign policy process is its **head of government** (most commonly titled president, prime minister, or premier) and his or her supporting cast of other **political executives** (officials whose tenure is variable and dependent on the political contest for power in their country).

Whatever their specific titles, heads of government have important **formal powers** granted by statutory law or the constitution. Most chief executives, for example, are designated as the commander in chief of their country's armed forces. This gives them important and often unilateral authority to use the military. President Bush received supporting resolutions from Congress for military action against Afghanistan in 2001 and Iraq in 2003, but he claimed the right to act with or without support, "pursuant to my constitutional authority to conduct U.S. foreign relations as commander in chief and chief executive."[14] In fact, Bush had built up momentum toward war with Iraq long before he went to Congress, as explained in the In the Spotlight box "The Decision for War."

Political executives also frequently possess important **informal powers**. Their prestige as national leader is often immense, and skillful leaders can use that status to win political support for their policies. This is especially true in world affairs and doubly so

IN THE SPOTLIGHT

The Decision for War

In the months before war broke out with Iraq in 2003, President George Bush sought and obtained support for military action from Congress and from a majority of the American public. He also went to great, if mostly unsuccessful, lengths to rally international support for toppling the government of Saddam Hussein if it did not reveal the location of its alleged weapons of mass destruction and halt other alleged objectionable policies. Arguably, however, the decision for war was a foregone conclusion.

When he assumed office, Bush appointed to high positions a number of "neocons" (neoconservatives). This group already believed that Saddam Hussein's regime should be toppled.[1] Their view had been clearly articulated in 1998 by a public letter to President Bill Clinton. They argued, "Removing Saddam Hussein and his regime from power. . . needs to become the aim of American foreign policy."[2] The letter was written under the auspices of a policy-advocacy organization (a "think tank") called the Project for the New American Century (PNAC), whose Web site expresses its view that "American leadership is good both for America and for the world" and that "such leadership requires military strength, diplomatic energy and commitment to moral principle." Among the PNAC associates who signed the letter (and their soon-to-be titles under Bush) were Secretary of Defense Donald Rumsfeld, Deputy Secretary of Defense Paul Wolfowitz, Chairman of the Defense Policy Board Richard Perle, Deputy Secretary of State Richard Armitage, under secretaries of state John Bolton and Paula Dobriansky, National Security Council staff member Elliott Abrams, and Assistant Secretary of Defense Peter W. Rodman. Not a signatory of the letter but almost certainly supporting it was PNAC founding member, Vice President Dick Cheney.

We cannot be certain of what might have ensued had the 9/11 attacks not occurred, but the terrorist attacks gave momentum to this group. Their pressure on the president to remove Saddam Hussein was so intense that Secretary of State Colin Powell reportedly once returned from a meeting with them, rolled his eyes, and complained, "Jeez, what a fixation about Iraq."[3] In April 2002, still almost a year before the war, Bush revealingly told a British reporter, "I made up my mind that Saddam needs to go."[4] Intense military planning for a campaign against Iraq also began at this time, and by late spring 2002 the eventual commander of military operations, General Tommy Franks, was meeting every few weeks with the president to brief him on the progress of the war plan.

One interpretation is that the neocons in the administration found a president ready to be persuaded. In particular, the neocon view that there is a moral superiority in the American system may have appealed to the deeply religious president. "I do believe certain people have grown theological about this," one administration official worried about the intense focus on Iraq. "It's almost a religion that it will be the end of our society if we don't take action now." Others argue that Bush was swept toward war by his phalanx of advisers. "The issue got away from the president," a senior official commented to a reporter. "He [Bush] wasn't controlling the tone or the direction" and was influenced by people who "painted him into a corner" by encouraging ever more confrontational rhetoric that, eventually, the president could not have backed away from without a huge loss of credibility "even if he had developed second thoughts."[5]

Whichever version is correct, little but an Iraqi capitulation could have prevented war. The president gave the final order to begin military operations at about 6:30 P.M. on March 19, 2003, but the real decision for war had been made long before that.

in crises where a president is the chief "we" in dealings with "them." Chief executives understand this advantage and use it. "The way to do that," former U.S. secretary of state Dean Acheson once admitted, "is to say politics stops at the seaboard—and anyone who denies that postulate is a son-of-a-bitch or a crook and not a true patriot. Now, if the people will swallow that, then you're off to the races" (Rourke, 1983:81).

Fortunately, people do not always swallow that, and in democracies at least, chief executives do not exercise unlimited foreign policy power. Indeed, the spread of democracy and the increasingly intermestic nature of policy in an interdependent world mean that political leaders must often engage in a **two-level game** in which "each national leader plays both the international and domestic games simultaneously" (Trumbore, 1998:546). The strategy of a two-level game is based on the reality that to be successful, diplomats have to negotiate at the international level with representatives of other countries and at the domestic level with legislators, bureaucrats, interest groups, and the public in the diplomat's own country. The object is to produce a "win-win" agreement that satisfies both the international counterparts and the powerful domestic actors so that both are willing to support the accord. Reflecting this reality, one former U.S. official has recalled that "during my tenure as Special Trade Representative, I spent as much time negotiating with domestic constituents (both industry and labor) and members of the U.S. Congress as I did negotiating with our foreign trading partners" (Lindsay, 1994:292).

Bureaucracies

Every state, whatever its strength or type of government, is heavily influenced by its **bureaucracy**. The dividing line between decision makers and bureaucrats is often hazy, but we can say that bureaucrats are career governmental personnel, as distinguished from those who are political appointees or elected officials.

Although political leaders legally command the bureaucracy, they find it difficult to control the vast understructures of their governments. President Vladimir Putin of Russia and President George W. Bush candidly conceded that gap between legal and real authority during a joint press conference. The two presidents were optimistically expounding on a new spirit of U.S.-Russian cooperation when a reporter asked them if they could "say with certainty that your teams will act in the same spirit?" Amid knowing laughter, Bush replied, "It's a very good question you ask, because sometimes the intended [policy] doesn't necessarily get translated throughout the levels of government [because of] bureaucratic intransigence." President Putin agreed. "Of course, there is always a bureaucratic threat," he conceded.[15]

Bureaucrats sometimes do not agree with their country's foreign policy. Instead they may favor another policy option based on their general sense of their unit's mission. How any given policy will affect the organization is also an important factor in creating bureaucratic perspective. Often what a given bureaucracy will or will not favor makes intuitive sense. The military of any country will almost certainly oppose arms reductions or defense spending cuts because such policies reduce its resources and influence. But the stereotypical view of the military as always gung ho for war is not accurate (Gelpi & Feaver, 2002). Whether the area was Kosovo, Bosnia, Haiti, or elsewhere, the U.S. military has often been a reluctant warrior within the council of government, especially regarding the use of ground forces. A common view, expressed by then chairman of the Joint Chiefs of Staff, General Colin Powell, is that "politicians start wars. Soldiers fight and die in them."[16]

Filtering information is one way that bureaucracies influence policy. Decision makers depend on staff for information, and what they are told depends on what subordinates choose, consciously or not, to pass on. The importance of the information flow was illustrated in the months after the U.S. war with Iraq by the uproar over President Bush's assertion in his 2003 State of the Union message that Iraq "recently sought significant quantities of uranium from Africa." As it turns out, the statement was based on shaky British sources with which the CIA did not agree. Yet it wound up in the president's speech when his speechwriters used information from an intelligence report that cited the British report but buried the CIA's objections in a footnote. Why that happened is not yet clear, but it is known that the dubious assertion went unchallenged by the staff member in the National Security Council (NSC) who reviewed the speech and who also was known to strongly favor action against Iraq. This occurred even though the staff member had had an earlier telephone conversation with the director of the CIA, who said that the agency doubted that Iraq had sought uranium from Africa. The NSC official, Stephen J. Hadley, later conceded, "I should have recalled . . . that there was controversy associated with the uranium issue," but many observers doubted that it was a mere oversight.[17]

This image symbolizes the importance of the bureaucracy in the flow of information to policy makers. Massive amounts of information are often available, and what the bureaucracy decides to "capture" as important and pass on to leaders helps determine what the final policy decision will be.

Recommendations are another source of bureaucratic influence on foreign policy. Bureaucracies are the source of considerable expertise, which they use to push the agency's preferred position. One scholar, after analyzing bureaucratic recommendations in several countries, concluded that leaders often faced an "option funnel." This means that advisers narrow the range of options available to leaders by presenting to them only those options that the adviser's bureaucratic organization favors. This recommendation strategy, the analyst continued, "often decided what national leaders would do even before they considered a situation" (Legro, 1996:133).

Implementation is another powerful bureaucratic tool. There are a variety of ways that bureaucrats can influence policy by the way they carry it out (McKeown, 2001). As the investigations into the 9/11 attacks have proceeded, it has become clear that the terrorists were able to carry them off, with the resulting seismic impacts on U.S. foreign policy, in part because of various flaws in the implementation of U.S. antiterrorist policy. Evidence shows that various government agencies often failed to share information or otherwise cooperate, that they discounted the terrorist threat, and that they did not pursue information that pointed to an impending attack. For example, according to a congressional report, an FBI agent warned in July 2001 that "an inordinate number of individuals of investigative interest" were taking flight training. Yet, the report noted, this alert "generated little or no interest" among FBI officials and was not passed on to the CIA or other relevant agencies. The following month the CIA's Counter-Terrorism Center followed with a report admitting that "for every [al-Qaeda operative] that we stop, an estimated 50 . . . slip through . . . undetected. . . . It is clear that [al-Qaeda] is building up a worldwide infrastructure which will allow [it] to launch multiple and simultaneous attacks with little or no warning." The agency also predicted, "The attack will be spectacular and designed to inflict mass casualties against U.S. facilities or interests."[18] These and numerous other signals went unheeded, however, leading the congressional committee to conclude that because government agencies "failed to capitalize" on available information, they had "missed opportunities to disrupt the September 11 plot and . . . to generate a heightened state of alert and thus harden the homeland against attack."[19]

Legislatures

In all countries, the foreign policy role of legislatures is less than that of executive-branch decision makers and bureaucrats. This does not mean that all legislatures are powerless (Scott & Carter, 2002; Leogrande, 2002). They are not, but their exact influence varies greatly among countries. Legislatures in nondemocratic systems generally rubber-stamp the decisions of the political leadership. China's National People's Congress, for example, does not play a significant role in foreign policy making.

Legislatures play a larger foreign policy role in democratic countries, but even in these states legislative authority is constrained by many factors. One of these is that chief executives usually have *extensive legal powers* in the realm of foreign policy. American presidents, for instance, are empowered by the U.S. Constitution to negotiate treaties, to extend diplomatic recognition to other countries, to appoint diplomatic and military personnel, to use U.S. forces as commander in chief, and to take numerous other actions with few or no checks by Congress or the courts. *Tradition* is a second factor that works to the advantage of chief executives in foreign policy making. The leadership has historically run foreign policy in virtually all countries, especially in time of war or other crises.

Third is the *belief that a unified national voice is important to a successful foreign policy*. This is particularly true during a crisis, when Congress, just like the public, tends to rally behind the president (Baker & O'Neal, 2001). This emotional response helped win support for a congressional resolution in late 2001 giving the president almost unchecked authority to use military forces against terrorism by votes of 98 to 0 in the Senate and 420 to 1 in the House of Representatives. Just 13 months later, by votes of 77–23 in the Senate and 296–133 in the House, Congress authorized military action against Iraq. Surely, many members agreed with the war, but at least some voted "aye" despite their misgivings because they agreed, as Senate Democratic leader Tom Daschle explained, commenting on his vote, that "it is important for America to speak with one voice."[20]

Did You Know That:

The only U.S. legislator to vote against the U.S. declarations of war in both World War I and World War II was Jeannette Rankin (R-MT), the first woman elected to Congress.

Fourth, *legislators tend to focus on domestic policy* because, accurately or not, most voters perceive it to be more important than foreign policy and make voting decisions based on this sense of priority. For this reason, legislators are apt to try to influence intermestic policy issues, such as trade, and are apt to be much less concerned with pure foreign policy issues, such as the membership of the NATO alliance.

Nato?

By this logic, though, legislative activity is especially likely and important when a high-profile issue captures public attention and public opinion opposes the president's policy. Even more commonly, intermestic issues that directly affect constituents and interest groups spark legislative activity (Marshall & Prins, 2002). As one member of the U.S. Congress put it, "Increasingly all foreign policy issues are becoming domestic issues. As a reflection of the public input, Congress is demanding to play a greater role."[21]

Political Opposition

In every political system, those who are in power face rivals who would replace them, either to change policy or to gain power. In democratic systems, this opposition is legitimate and is organized into political parties. Rival politicians may also exist in the leader's own party. Opposition is less overt and/or less peaceful in nondemocratic systems, but it exists nonetheless and in many varied forms. One distinction divides opposition between those who merely want to change policy and those who want to gain control of the government. A second division is between those who are located inside and outside of the government.

Interest Groups

Interest groups are private associations of people who have similar policy views and who pressure the government to adopt those views as policy. Traditionally, interest groups were generally considered to be less active and influential on foreign policy than on domestic policy issues. The increasingly intermestic nature of policy is changing that, and interest groups are becoming a more important part of the foreign policy–making process. We can see this by looking at several types of interest groups.

Cultural groups are one type. Many countries have ethnic, racial, religious, or other cultural groups that have emotional or political ties to another country. For instance, as a country made up mostly of immigrants, the United States is populated by many who maintain a level of identification with their African, Cuban, Irish, Mexican, Polish, and other heritages and who are active on behalf of policies that favor their ancestral homes (Saideman, 2001; de la Garza & Pinchon, 2000; Henry, 2000).

There is a rapidly growing American Muslim community that is becoming increasingly active on behalf of its co-religionists, just as the Jewish-American community often supports Israel. Indeed, many estimates place the number of American Muslims as approaching the 6 million Jewish Americans, although these figures are imprecise because U.S. law prohibits the Census Bureau from asking mandatory questions on religious affiliation. The political activity of Muslim Americans is represented by this photograph of a woman in Los Angeles trying to rally support behind the Palestinian cause.

Economic groups are another prominent form of interest activity. As international trade increases, both sales overseas and competition from other countries are vital matters to many companies, their workers, and the communities in which they live (Chrystal, 1998). They lobby their governments for favorable legislation and for support of their interests in other countries. President George W. Bush advocates free trade, but that did not prevent him in 2002 from increasing tariff barriers on imported steel. Republican control of Congress hinged in part on several electoral races in Pennsylvania, Ohio, and elsewhere in districts with steel companies and unions pressing for protection from what they argued was unfair competition.

Issue-oriented groups make up another category of interest group. Groups of this type are not based on any narrow socioeconomic category such as ethnicity or economics. Instead they draw their membership from people who have a common policy goal. The concerns of issue-oriented groups run the gamut from the very general to the specific and from liberal to conservative. Just one of the multitude of groups, the neoconservative Project for the New American Century, is discussed in the box "The Decision for War" on page 74.

Transnational interest groups also deserve mention. Increasing interdependence and modern communications give interest groups the need and ability to lobby across borders. For example, lobbyists representing virtually every country in the world and even their subdivisions operate in the United States and are on the list compiled under the U.S. Foreign Agents Registration Act. During the first six months of 2002, a selection of countries (and the amounts they spent lobbying the U.S. government) were: Colombia ($153,000), Israel ($266,000), Latvia ($251,000), Mexico ($226,000), Pakistan ($300,000), Sri Lanka ($58,000), and Ukraine ($130,000). There are also NGOs of like-minded individuals from many countries who pool their resources to press their own and other governments to adopt policies desired by the group. MNCs and trade groups also conduct extensive lobbying efforts in countries where they have interests.

The People

Like legislatures, the public plays a highly variable role in foreign policy. Public opinion is a marginal factor in authoritarian governments. In democracies, the role of the people is more complex (Everts & Isernia, 2001). On occasion, public opinion plays a key role. The United States got out of Vietnam in the 1970s in significant part because of the determined opposition of many Americans to continued involvement in that war. Yet even in democracies, the public usually plays only a limited role in determining foreign policy (Powlick & Katz, 1998).

Public Interest in Foreign Policy One reason for the public's limited role is that few citizens ordinarily pay much attention to international issues. Instead, whatever political interest they do have tends to focus on domestic issues. During the 2000 U.S. presidential election, for instance, one poll asked Americans how important each of four domestic issues (education, health care, Social Security and Medicare, and the economy and jobs) and one foreign issue (America's role overseas) would be in their deciding whom to support for president. More than 75% of the respondents said that each of the four domestic issues would be very important; only 43% said that the U.S. global role would be very important.[22]

This is not to say that all of the public pays little heed to foreign policy all of the time. First, there is a segment of the public, the "attentive public," that regularly pays attention to world events. Second, crisis issues, such as the war with Iraq, and intermestic issues, such as trade, are apt to draw significantly greater public attention. Third, studies show that although the public is not versed in the details of policies, its basic instincts are neither disconnected from events nor unstable (Isernia, Juhasz, & Rattinger, 2002).

Channels of Public Opinion Influence on Foreign Policy There are a few countries, as discussed in chapter 1, in which the public occasionally gets to decide a foreign policy issue directly through a national referendum (Dalton, Burklin, & Drummond, 2001). However, all democracies are basically republican forms of government in which policies and laws are made by elected officials and their appointees. Therefore, it is more common for public opinion to have an indirect democratic influence on policy through voting for officials and through the sensitivity of those officials to public attitudes.

Even if they cannot usually decide policy directly, voters do sometimes have a choice of candidates for national leadership positions who have different foreign policy goals and priorities (Fordham, 2002). The change of Spain's prime ministers from conservative José Maria Aznar to liberal José Luis Rodríguez-Zapatero in 2004 distinctly changed that country's policy toward keeping its troops in Iraq.

Additionally, research shows that both elected and appointed officials are concerned with public opinion and that it constrains what they do (Reiter & Tillman, 2002). One reason is that most decision makers in a democracy believe that public opinion is a legitimate factor that should be considered when determining which policy is to be adopted. Second, leaders also believe that policy is more apt to be successful if it is backed by public opinion. Third, decision makers are wary of public retribution in the next election if they ignore majority opinion. "I knew full well that if we could rally the American people behind a long and difficult chore, that our job would be easier," President Bush commented about ordering military action against Afghanistan in 2001. "I am a product of the Vietnam era," the president explained. "I remember presidents trying to wage wars that were very unpopular, and the nation split."[23]

Bush also followed this philosophy in the movement to war with Iraq. As the box "The Decision for War" indicates, there was strong momentum within the Bush administration to go to war over a year before action commenced in March 2003. One important obstacle, though, was U.S. public opinion. Most polls found that a majority of Americans wanted Saddam Hussein removed, and they tentatively supported military action. But the surveys also showed that Americans wanted the president to present a stronger case for action, to give UN inspectors more opportunities, and to try to build an international coalition to participate in the invasion. These "conditions" for public support were important factors that explain the efforts of the Bush administration to meet the public's demands during the latter part of 2002 and early 2003.

Dimensions of Foreign Policy Opinion Most polls only report overall public opinion on a topic, but it is important to realize that opinion is not split evenly across all segments of the public. There is, for example, a **leader-citizen opinion gap** in the United States and other countries, whereby the opinions of those who are the leaders of government, business, the media, and other areas often vary from the opinions of the general

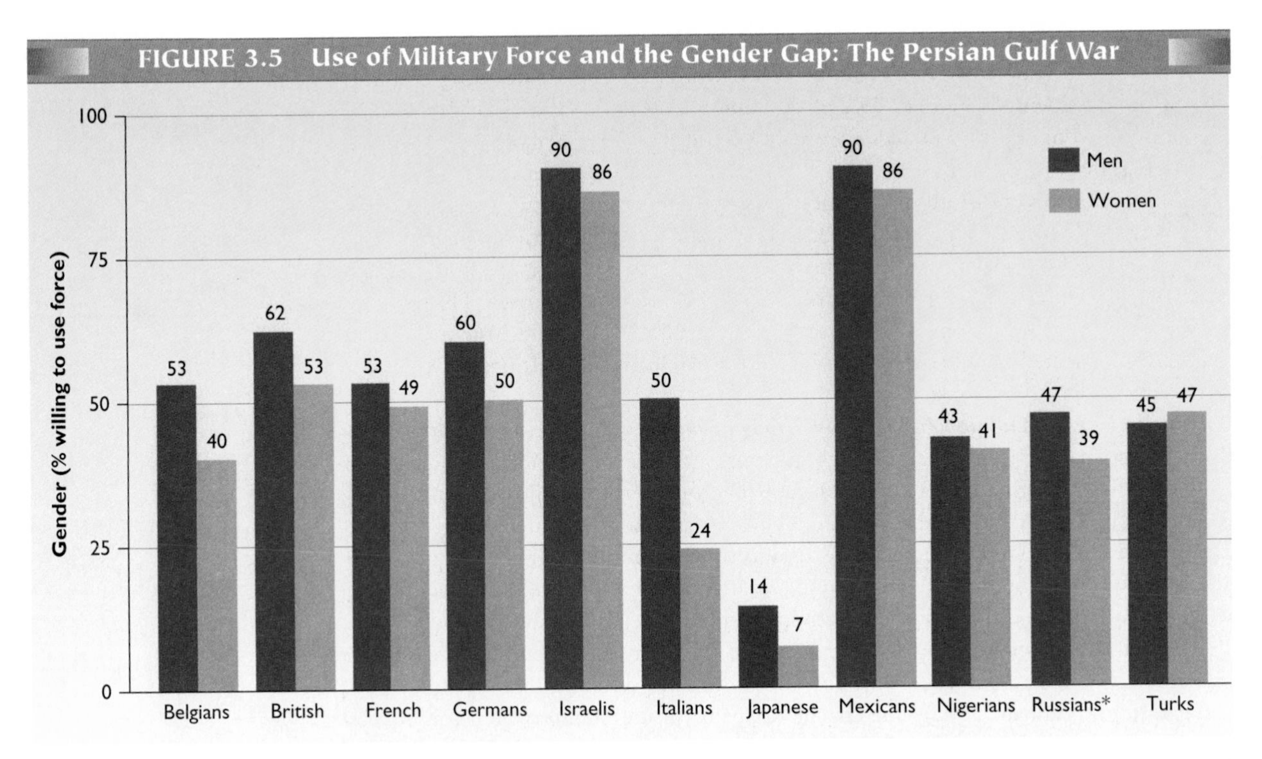

Take note of several things in this figure. One is the gender opinion gap. The men in all but one of the countries, Turkey, were more likely to favor war than were the women. Second, notice the variations between countries. Women, on average, cannot be described as anitwar, nor can men be characterized as pro-war because both men and women in some countries favored war and opposed it in others. Americans were not included in this poll, but the gap existed for them also. One representative poll taken in January 1991 just before the U.S. counteroffensive began found 62% of men in favor of military action, compared with only 41% of women.

Note: The question was: Should UN soldiers fight if the [economic] embargo [on Iraq] fails?

*The Soviet Union still existed, but the survey was taken in Moscow. Respondents were almost certainly Russians.

Data source: Wilcox, Hewitt, & Allsop (1996).

public. According to one survey taken in 2002, most Americans, for instance, would rate improving the global environment a high priority goal; most leaders would not. A majority of citizens also would decrease the legal immigration rate; place protecting Americans' jobs from imports as a top foreign policy goal; see AIDS as a critical threat; would use U.S. troops against foreign drug lords; consider strengthening the UN a high priority; and would de-emphasize foreign aid. Most leaders took the opposite view.[24]

Another of the many dimensions of foreign policy opinion is the **gender opinion gap**. This is most obvious on questions of war. In the United States, for example, polls going back as far as World War II have consistently found that women are less ready than men to resort to war or to continue war. Just before the Persian Gulf War in 1991, for example, 62% of American men compared to 41% of American women favored military action. This gender opinion gap also existed internationally, as evident in Figure 3.5, which shows gender opinion differences in 11 countries. The same pattern occurred in 2003. A poll taken just before the war with Iraq began found two-thirds of American men compared to half of American women supporting military action.[25] This gender gap was also found internationally; for example, men in Australia, Canada, Great Britain, and Italy all were more favorable toward war by 10% to 15% than their female counterparts.

Individual-Level Analysis

Humans as a species and as individuals are the focus as we search for clues in the last area of our mini-whodunit exploration into causality in world politics. **Individual-level analysis** begins with the view that at the root it is people who make policy. Therefore, individual-level analysts argue, understanding the human **decision-making process**, how people (as a species, in groups, and idiosyncratically) make decisions, will lead to understanding how international politics works.

Humans as a Species

The central question is this: How do fundamental human characteristics influence policy? To answer that, a first step is to understand that humans seldom if ever make a purely rational decision. For example, think about how you decided which college to attend. Surely you did not just flip a coin. But neither did you make a fully rational decision by considering all colleges worldwide and analyzing each according to cost, location, social atmosphere, class size, faculty qualifications, living arrangements, program requirements, postgraduate placement record, and other core considerations. Nor is it likely that you consulted a wide range of experts. And almost certainly your choice was influenced by a range of "irrational" emotions, such as how far away from home the school was and how that interacted with your desire to be near, or perhaps far away from, your family, friends, or romantic partner. To make things a bit less rational, you probably had to make a decision without knowing some key factors of your college experience, such as who your dorm roommate would be.

It may be comforting to imagine that foreign policy decision making is fully rational, but the truth is that in many ways it does not differ greatly from your process in deciding which college to attend and many of the other important choices you make in life. They, like foreign policy decisions, are influenced by cognitive, emotional, psychological, and sometimes even biological factors, as well as by rational calculations.

Cognitive Factors

What you did in choosing your college and what national leaders do when deciding foreign policy is to engage in **cognitive decision making**. This means making decisions within the constraints of "bounded rationality." *External boundaries*, such as missing, erroneous, or unknowable information, are one limitation on rationality. To cite just one example, President Bush and Prime Minister Blair had to decide whether to invade Iraq in March 2003 without knowing whether Saddam Hussein would respond with chemical or biological attacks on U.S. and British forces. *Internal boundaries* on rationality are established by the limits that all humans have on the physical stamina and intellectual capacity to study exceptionally complex issues. Whatever the "realities" were during the crisis leading up to the war with Iraq in 2003, the universe of information available was far more than President Bush, Prime Minister Blair, President Saddam Hussein, any other leader, or any human for that matter, could absorb.

Needless to say, none of us likes to think that we are not fully rational, so we are apt to adopt one of a range of mental strategies for coping with our cognitive limits. As illustrations, three such strategies are seeking cognitive consistency, wishful thinking, and using heuristic devices.

Seeking Cognitive Consistency Decision makers tend to seek cognitive consistency by discounting ideas and information that contradict their existing views. The controversy about the snarl of information and misinformation about Iraq's abilities and intentions

Saddam Hussein came to believe that he had been victorious in the Persian Gulf War of 1991 because he had survived in power. The comments from captured senior Iraqi officials indicate that such wishful thinking may have been part of his calculations during the crisis prior to the U.S.-led invasion in March 2003. As this photograph taken three weeks later in Baghdad of a damaged mosaic portrait of the Iraqi president indicates, wishful thinking may influence policy decisions, but it does not influence policy outcomes.

will continue for years, but it is informative to ask why top decision makers in London and Washington were willing to accept British intelligence that Baghdad was attempting to buy uranium from Africa and to ignore the substantial doubts expressed by the CIA. One reason is that the British finding "fit" with the existing negative images of Saddam Hussein and his intentions, whereas believing information that there was no nuclear program would have created uncomfortable cognitive inconsistency.

Wishful Thinking To justify in their minds decisions that they have made or wish to make, humans often tell themselves that their choice will succeed. Given the overwhelming forces he faced, it is hard to understand why Saddam Hussein chose to fight rather than go safely into exile. The answer, according to the reported commentary of some of his bodyguards who were captured after the war, is that the Iraqi president believed that he would win. After all, his regime had survived the Persian Gulf War in 1991, and, as he told CBS anchor Dan Rather in a February 2003 interview, standing up to the United States and surviving the confrontation was a victory. Saddam Hussein's wishful thinking may have been that, once again, he would dodge the bullet and remain in power.

Using Heuristic Devices As a third strategy to deal with cognitive limits, humans utilize **heuristic devices**, which are mental shortcuts that allow us to skip long and detailed gathering and analysis of information and come to decisions quickly. *Stereotypes* are one type of heuristic device. During the tense months after the September 11 terrorist attacks, a few American policy makers fell into the trap of stereotyping Muslims as terrorists based on their religion. For instance, Attorney General John Ashcroft told a columnist, "Islam is a religion in which God requires you to send your son to die for him. Christianity is a faith in which God sends His son to die for you."[26] Ashcroft's office later complained that his remark was misconstrued but did not deny that he had made it.

Analogies are another heuristic shortcut (Breuning, 2003). We make comparisons between new situations or people and situations or people that we have earlier experienced or otherwise have learned about. One such mental connection that frequently figures in policy debates is the **Munich analogy**. This refers to the decision of France and Great Britain to appease Nazi Germany in 1938 when it threatened Czechoslovakia. For many later decision makers, the subsequent traumatic events of World War II in which the United States and its allies fought the three Axis powers (Germany, Italy, and Japan) "taught" that compromise with dictators would only encourage them. The supposed lesson of Munich was clearly in the mind of President George H. W. Bush in 1990 when, after Iraq invaded Kuwait, he told Americans, "As was the case in the 1930s, we see in Saddam Hussein an aggressive dictator threatening his neighbors. Half a century ago the world had a chance to stop a ruthless aggressor and missed it. I pledge to you: We will not make that mistake again" (Rourke, 1993:30). His son, George W., also viewed Iraq partly through the perspective of the Munich analogy, as was evident in his 2002 State of the Union message when he charged that three countries (in this case Iraq, Iran, and North Korea) "constitute an axis of evil." Other administration figures were even more explicit. Secretary of Defense Rumsfeld, in an effort to justify action against Iraq despite the lack of definitive evidence of Iraqi WMDs, urged listeners to "Think of the prelude to World War II . . . [and] all the countries that said, 'well, we don't have enough evidence.'" After all, Rumsfeld admonished, "*Mein Kampf* had been written. . . . [in which] Hitler . . . indicated what he intended to do. [Still, the British, French, and others thought,] 'Maybe he won't attack us.' . . . Well, there were millions of people dead because of the miscalculations."[27]

Emotional Factors

As much as it might be comforting to imagine decision makers as coolly rational, the reality is that they are subject to the same array of emotions as everyone else. Sometimes, for instance, presidents simply get angry. During the crisis after Iran seized the U.S. embassy and American hostages in 1979–1980, President Jimmy Carter was outraged when Iranian students studying at American colleges picketed the White House. Carter fumed about "those bastards . . . in front of the White House. If I wasn't president," Carter growled to an aide, "I would go out on the streets myself and take a swing at any demonstrator I could get my hands on" (Vandenbroucke, 1991:364). Carter could not go out on Pennsylvania Avenue and beat up protesters, but his anger and desperation to do something arguably led to his ill-advised and ill-fated attempt to rescue the hostages.

Understandably, President Bush was also angry on the day of the 9/11 terrorist attacks. "We're going to find out who did this," he told Vice President Cheney, "and we're going to kick their asses."[28] At other times leaders become overwhelmed with human emotion and cry, and more than once during the 9/11 crisis President Bush did that, too.

Psychological Factors

Humankind has a number of common psychological traits that also help explain why feelings and decisions are usually less than fully rational. One such approach is **frustration-aggression theory**, which argues that individuals and even societies that are frustrated sometimes become aggressive.

"Why do they hate us?" President Bush rhetorically asked Congress soon after the 9/11 attacks.[29] "They hate our freedoms," was the answer the president supplied to his own question. Perhaps, but one American analyst puts the source of rage in a very different light. Instead of a hatred for freedom, he suggests that "the disproportionate feelings of grievance directed at America have to be placed in the overall context of the sense of humiliation, decline, and despair that sweeps the Arab world."[30] Polls confirm the analyst's view of widespread negativity among Muslims toward the United States. One Gallup Poll conducted in nine Muslim countries in January 2002 revealed that 53% of the respondents had an unfavorable opinion of the United States, compared to only 22% with a favorable view, and the rest were undecided. In the view of Frank Newport, editor-in-chief at Gallup, the poll results indicate that most Muslims view the United States as "ruthless, aggressive, conceited, arrogant, easily provoked, [and biased against Muslims]." In sum, Newport concluded, "The people of Islamic countries have significant grievance with the West and the United States in particular."[31]

To understand the sense of frustration among Muslims, especially Arabs, it is not necessary to agree with the frustrations many Muslims feel because of the lack of a Palestinian homeland, the lack of development that characterizes most of the Muslim countries, or the sense of being dominated and sometimes subjugated by the Christian-led West. Nor, it must be said, does that frustration justify the aggression that has arguably resulted. Nevertheless, if the old maxim that an "ounce of prevention is worth a pound of cure" has any worth, then an efficacious way of reducing the chances of future terrorism may well be to address the root causes and not simply build defenses.

The banner carried by this group of Pakistanis in Islamabad on September 15, 2001, urges Americans to think about why they are hated by some people. That question, "Why do they hate us?" was also asked rhetorically by President Bush during a speech to the nation after the 9/11 attacks. Bush said it was because the United States represents freedom. Many observers have suggested that there are other reasons. What is important is to understand the views of others, even if they hate you.

Biological Factors

Although they are highly controversial, various biological theories provide yet another way to explain why human decisions fall short of being fully rational. One of the most important issues in human behavior is the degree to which human actions are based on animal instinct and other innate emotional and physical drives or based on socialization and intellect. With specific regard to politics, **biopolitics** examines the relationship between the physical nature and political behavior of humans. Biopolitics can be illustrated by examining two approaches: ethology and gender.

Ethology The comparison of animal and human behavior is called **ethology**. Konrad Lorenz (*On Aggression,* 1969), Desmond Morris (*The Naked Ape*, 1967), Robert Ardrey (*The Territorial Imperative*, 1961), and some other ethologists argue that like animals, humans behave in a way that is based partly on innate characteristics. Ardrey (pp. 12–14), for example, has written that "territoriality—the drive to gain, maintain, and defend the exclusive right to a piece of property—is an animal instinct" and that "if man is a part of the natural world, then he possesses as do all other species a genetic . . . territorial drive as one ancient animal foundation for that human conduct known as war."

It is clear that territorial disputes between neighboring countries are a common cause of war. As one study puts it, "empirical analyses consistently show that territorial issues . . . are more likely to escalate to war than would be expected by chance"(Vasquez & Henehan, 2001:123). To an outsider, some of these territorial clashes may seem rational, but others defy rational explanation. One inexplicable war was the 1998–2000 conflict between two desperately poor countries, Ethiopia and Eritrea, over tiny bits of territory along their border. The land was described in one press report as "a dusty terrain of termite mounds, goatherds, and bushes just tall enough for a camel to graze upon comfortably."[32] It was, said one observer, "like two bald men fighting over a comb."[33] Even the leaders of the two countries could not explain why war was waged. "It's very difficult to easily find an answer," Eritrea's president, Isaias Afwerki, admitted. "I was surprised, shocked, and puzzled," added a perplexed Meles Zenawi, the prime minister of Ethiopia.[34]

Whether it is because of nature or socialization, gender makes a difference in political attitudes. For example, with few exceptions, polls taken during recent crises have found women in many countries more averse on average to war than the men in their country. Depicting this gender gap is the woman pictured here protesting in Bloomington, Indiana, against the impending war with Iraq in 2003.

Gender A second biopolitical factor that interests many analysts is the possibility that some differences in political behavior are related to gender. An adviser to President Lyndon Johnson has recalled that once when reporters asked him why the United States was waging war in Vietnam, the president "unzipped his fly, drew out his substantial organ, and declared, 'That is why.' "[35] Such earthy explanations by male leaders are far from rare in private, and they lead some scholars to wonder whether they represent a gender-based approach to politics or are merely gauche.

Political scientists are just beginning to examine whether gender makes a difference in political attitudes and actions. One such inquiry is the extent of the aforementioned gender opinion gap on issues related to war. A more general question is whether any gender differences that do exist are inherent (biological, genetic) or the product of differences in male and female socialization. The ultimate question is whether an equal representation (or perhaps dominance) of women in foreign and defense policy making would make an appreciable difference in global affairs. Many scholars answer yes and say that the change would be for the good. Francis Fukuyama (1998:33), for one, contends that political violence is a product, in part, of male-dominated politics because, "statistically speaking it is primarily men who enjoy the experience of aggression and the camaraderie it brings and who revel in the reutilization of war." This view leads Fukuyama to speculate that a world dominated by women "would be less prone to conflict and more conciliatory and cooperative than the one we inhabit now." Supporting this view, one recent study found that women tend to adopt more collaborative approaches to negotiation and conflict resolution, while men pursue more conflictual ones (Florea et al., 2003). Other studies, however, have found more mixed results about the potential impact of women decision makers and contend that a future world dominated by women "would not be as rosy as Fukuyama suggests" (Caprioli, 2000:271; Caprioli & Boyer, 2001; Ehrenreich & Pollitt, 1999).

What do you think? Would the U.S. invasion of Iraq have occurred if Laura Bush, not her husband, George W., had been president of the United States; if the long-time head of Iraq had been Sajida Khairallah Telfah, not her husband, Saddam Hussein; and if most of the other top diplomatic and national security posts in the United States and Iraq had been held by women, not men?

Organizational Behavior

A second approach to individual-level analysis examines how people act in organizations. Two concepts, role behavior and group decision-making behavior, illustrate this approach.

Role Behavior

We all play a variety of **roles** based on our attitudes about the positions we have and the behaviors we adopt in them. For example, how you act when you are in class, on the job, or in a family situation varies depending in part on your role—on whether you are a professor or a student, a manager or a worker, a parent or a child.

Presidents and other policy makers also play roles. The script for a role is derived from a combination of *self-expectations* (how we expect ourselves to act) and *external expectations* (how others expect us to behave). For leaders, these latter expectations are transmitted by cues from advisers, critics, and public opinion. One common role expectation is that leaders be decisive. A leader who approaches a problem by saying, "I don't know what to do" or "We can't do anything" will be accused of weakness.

Whatever President Bush's thoughts about his own safety may have been on the morning of September 11, 2001, his sense of his role as president soon prevailed. He was in Florida when the attacks occurred, but his security detail quickly hurried him aboard Air Force One to fly to a more secure location, first at one, then another Air Force base. Soon, however, Bush was irritably telling his chief of staff, "I want to go back [to Washington] ASAP." The senior Secret Service agent objected that the situation was "too unsteady still," but the president insisted, and was back in the White House by 7:00 P.M., less than 11 hours after the terror attacks began. Ninety minutes later, he was addressing the nation from the Oval Office. Among other things, Bush felt it was his job to reassure the public by being visible at his post in the White House. "One of the things I wanted to do was to calm nerves," he later said. "I felt like I had a job as the commander in chief" to show the country "that I was safe . . . not me, George W., but me the president."[36]

Did You Know That:

During the 2000 presidential campaign, George W. Bush said his favorite book was *The Raven*, a 1929 biography of Sam Houston (1793–1863), who had a drinking problem until age 40, when he moved to Texas and became a heroic military leader and president of the Republic of Texas.

Probably it was a wise decision by Bush to override the concerns of the Secret Service in this instance. It is also the case that Bush felt that his role as president required him to take quick action after the terrorist attacks. Most Americans agreed with his response. But there are also times when the role creates pressure to take action even when it might be better to wait or not to act at all. Reflecting on this, former secretary of state Dean Rusk (1990:137) recalled, "We tended then—and now—to exaggerate the necessity to take action. Given time, many problems work themselves out or disappear."

Group Decision-Making Behavior

People behave differently in organizations than they would act if they were alone (Hagen, 2001; Hermann, 2001). There are complex and extensive theories about decision making in a group setting. One of the most important of these is the tendency toward **groupthink**, a concept that denotes pressure within decision-making groups to achieve consensus even if there is none (Schafer & Crichlow, 2002).

Causes of Groupthink *Avoiding psychological isolation* is one cause of groupthink. Most of us are not comfortable with being the "odd person out" and are apt to suppress our views if they strongly diverge from the views of a group. An instinct for *bureaucratic* *survival* is the second cause of groupthink. Especially if a leader has a well-known and firmly held policy preference, individuals and even agencies are wary of telling their boss what he or she does not want to hear. They fear that doing so may cause them to fall out of favor and suffer negative outcomes, such as budget cuts for agencies or being fired for individuals. In some cases, not giving a leader unpleasant advice may even involve physical survival. Interviews with a number of senior Iraqi military officers after the war in 2003 indicate that one reason that Saddam Hussein miscalculated his chances of success was that his generals misled him about their ability to repel U.S. and British forces. The officers have said they knew they could not withstand the allied onslaught, but they were afraid that they might be executed by Saddam Hussein if they told him the truth.

Although there is no indication anyone in Washington would have been shot for telling the president what he did not want to hear, there are indications of groupthink. For example, the phenomenon offers an explanation of how the dubious assertion that Iraq had tried to purchase uranium in Africa wound up in President Bush's 2003 State of the Union address. There was little doubt among mid-level staff members in the White House and the various national security agencies that top administration officials favored taking action against Iraq. As early as August 2002, White House Chief of Staff Andrew H. Card, Jr. formed the White House Iraq Group (WHIG). According to Card, the taskforce's purpose "from a marketing point of view" was to "introduce [a] new product" (the campaign to justify action against Iraq) to the American people and the world. In this atmosphere of finding reasons for action, rather than finding if there was a reason to act, speechwriters downplayed or ignored doubts about Iraqi threats and highlighted worrisome indications.[37] There is yet no evidence that top officials told the analysts and speechwriters what to emphasize and what to discount. That was unnecessary. Groupthink arguably ensured that the "facts" fit the predispositions of the leadership, and it is very possible that the president, just like most other Americans, believed the facts that were in the speech written for him.

Effects of Groupthink One impact of groupthink is that it *limits policy choices*. Anthony Lake, who served as national security adviser to President Clinton, recognized that "there is a danger that when people work well together" and are of the same mind, it can lead to "groupthink . . . [with] not enough options reaching the president."[38] There is no evidence that anyone was able or willing to recommend to President Bush that he give UN arms inspectors more time or that he do nothing immediately in the face of doubts about the existence and extent of Iraq's WMD program. As one adviser has commented about the flow of information in the Bush White House, "The president finds out what he wants to know, but he does not necessarily find out what he might need to know."[39]

Choosing the least objectionable policy, rather than the optimal one, is another common result of groupthink's drive for consensus. During the Cuban missile crisis, President Kennedy and his advisers did not decide to blockade Cuba because they thought it was the best thing to do. In fact, few of the decision makers really liked the idea of a blockade. Instead, it was a compromise between those who wanted to use military force to destroy the missiles and those who preferred to use diplomacy to persuade Moscow to withdraw the missiles.

Poor decisions are frequently a third impact of groupthink. This characteristic is evident in Figure 3.6 on page 88. Thus developing strategies to avoid such decision-making pathologies should improve the quality of the output.

Leaders and Their Individual Traits

A third approach to individual-level analysis focuses on humans as individuals and how each leader's personal (idiosyncratic) characteristics help shape his or her decisions and,

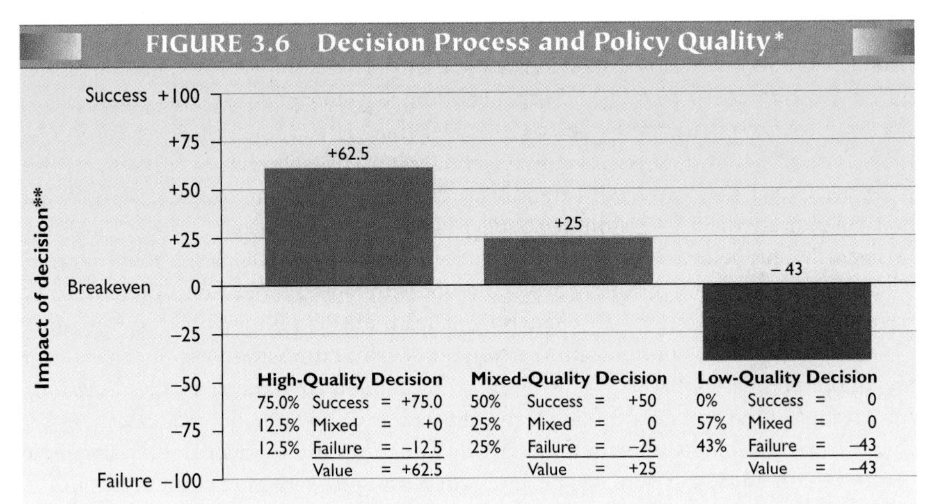

FIGURE 3.6 Decision Process and Policy Quality*

* **Quality:** The quality of the decisions (based on the number of symptoms of groupthink) were high (0–1 symptoms), medium (2 or 3 symptoms) and low (4 or more symptoms).

** **Outcome:** The outcome of policy (based on later evaluations by a balanced team of experts assigning +1 for a success, 0 for a mixed outcome, and –1 for a failure).

Decisions characterized by a lack of groupthink tend to result in better policy than decisions with medium or high instances of groupthink. The research represented in this figure examined the decision making of various policies for evidence of groupthink and then asked experts to evaluate the success or failure of the resulting policy. As this figure indicates, decisions with little or no evidence of groupthink worked well in the estimate of 75% of the experts, with another 12.5% each adjudging the policy a mixed outcome or a failure. By contrast, decisions with significant examples of groupthink were evaluated to be a failure by 43% of the experts, to have only mixed results by the other 57%, with none of the analysts seeing the policy as a success.

Data sources: Herek, Janis & Huth (1987:217). Also see Purkitt (1990) and Welch (1989).

therefore, events (Renshon & Larson, 2002; Hermann et al., 2001). As one study puts it, "The goals, abilities, and foibles of individuals are crucial to the intentions, capabilities, and strategies of a state. Indeed individuals not only affect the actions of their own states but also shape the reactions of other nations, which must respond to the aspirations, abilities, and aggressiveness of foreign leaders" (Byman & Pollack, 2001:111). In its simplest form, **idiosyncratic analysis** includes examining biographies and memoirs as political histories. More recently, analysts have written sophisticated "psychobiographies" that explore the motivations of decision makers. Scholars are also using increasingly sophisticated methodologies such as content analysis, which involves analyzing the content of decision makers' statements and writings to understand the basic ways they view the world.

Whatever the specific methodology of such studies, the fundamental question each asks is how the personal traits of a leader affected decisions. The list of possible factors is long, but the thrust of idiosyncratic analysis can be illustrated by considering five: personality, physical and mental health, ego and ambition, political history and personal experiences, and perceptions.

Personality

When studying personality types and their impact on policy, scholars examine a leader's basic orientations toward self and toward others, behavioral patterns, and attitudes about such politically relevant concepts as authority. There are numerous categorization schemes. The most well known places political personality along an active-passive scale and a positive-negative scale (Barber, 1985). Active leaders are policy innovators; passive leaders are reactors. Positive personalities have egos strong enough to enjoy (or at least accept) the contentious political environment; negative personalities are apt to feel burdened, even abused, by political criticism. Many scholars favor active-positive presidents, but all four types have drawbacks. Activists, for example, may feel compelled to try to solve every problem even though not doing something might be preferable. That was arguably true for President Clinton, who admitted to being "almost compulsively overactive" (Renshon, 1995:59). As for President George W. Bush, one early assessment is that he is an active-positive personality who "loves his job and is very energetic and focused" (DiIulio, 2003:3).

Whatever the best combination may be, there is wide agreement that the worst is active-negative. The more active a leader, the more criticism he or she encounters. Positive personalities take such criticism in stride, but negative personalities are prone to assuming that opponents are enemies. This causes negative personalities to withdraw into an inner circle of subordinates who are supportive and who give an unreal, groupthink view of events and domestic and international opinion. Adolf Hitler and Josef Stalin and, to a lesser degree, Lyndon Johnson and Richard Nixon were all active-negative personalities who showed symptoms of delusion, struck out at their enemies, and generally developed bunker mentalities.

Physical and Mental Health

A leader's physical and mental health can be important factors in decision making. Many analysts believe, for example, that Woodrow Wilson was afflicted by severe cerebral arteriosclerosis late in his presidency. This condition (whose traits include intransigence, memory loss, and other emotional and cognitive impairments) may have contributed to the president's uncompromising behavior and his inability to persuade the Senate to ratify the Treaty of Versailles. At the end of the next world war, according to historian Robert Farrell's *The Dying President* (1998), Franklin Delano Roosevelt was so ill from hypertension that he was "in no condition to govern the republic." Some analysts believe that Roosevelt's weakness left him unable to resist Stalin's demands for Soviet domination of Eastern Europe when the two, along with British Prime Minister Winston Churchill, met at Yalta in February 1945, just two months before Roosevelt died from a massive stroke.

Occasionally leaders also suffer from psychological problems. Initial Soviet defenses against the attack by Germany in 1941 were hampered by what appears to many analysts to have been a nervous breakdown by Stalin. His nemesis, Adolf Hitler, was also arguably unbalanced as a result of ailments that may have included advanced syphilis and by such medically prescribed drugs as barbiturates, cardiac stimulants, opiates, steroids, methamphetamine, and cocaine (Hayden, 2003). According to one analysis, "The precise effects of this pharmaceutical cocktail on Hitler's mental state [are] difficult to gauge. Suffice it to say, in the jargon of the street, Hitler was simultaneously taking coke and speed."[40] The drug combinations Hitler used offer one explanation for the bizarre manic-depressive cycle of his decision making late in the war. Alcohol abuse can also lead to problems. For example, there are persistent stories that President Richard Nixon, whom Secretary of State Henry Kissinger once called "my drunken friend," alarmed advisers with his drinking and was once incapacitated during an international crisis with the Soviet Union (Schulzinger, 1989:178). And it is well established that Russia's President Boris Yeltsin regularly drank to wild excess.

Ego and Ambition

The egos and personal ambitions of political leaders can also influence policy. Ego, especially the male variety, sometimes works to make leaders want to appear tough. This trait may well have figured in the onset of the Persian Gulf War. There is something telling in the fact that former president Saddam Hussein's original name was Hussein al-Takrit, but he dropped al-Takrit and added Saddam, an Arabic word that means "one who confronts." The ego of the first President Bush also may have influenced policy. He came to office in 1989 with a reputation for being wishy-washy, and *Newsweek* even ran a picture of him with a banner, "The Wimp Factor," on its cover. Arguably an ego-wounded Bush responded by being too tough. He soon invaded Panama, and the following year in the Persian Gulf crisis his fierce determination not to negotiate with Iraq left it little choice but to fight or capitulate. Certainly, it would be outrageous to claim that Bush decided on war only to assuage his ego. But it would be naïve to ignore the possible role of this factor. In fact, after defeating Panama and Iraq, the president displayed a prickly pride when he told reporters, "You're talking to the wimp . . . to the guy that had a cover of a national magazine . . . put that label on me. And now some that saw that we can react when the going gets tough maybe have withdrawn that allegation."[41]

Personal Experiences

Decision makers are also affected by their personal experiences. One might think that General Colin Powell would have been an advocate of using military force in crises he had to face as chairman of the Joint Chiefs of Staff under presidents George H. W. Bush and Bill Clinton, and as secretary of state under President George W. Bush. The reality is that he has proven to be a very reluctant warrior.

Powell was one of the generation of junior officers who served in Vietnam and who were frustrated, even traumatized, by their sense of political restraints denying them the chance to achieve victory, by seeing their men die in an ultimately futile war, and by the opprobrium heaped on the military by many critics of the war. Arguably as a result, Powell has been consistently wary of committing U.S. troops to action, was the last major foreign policy/national security figure in the Bush administration to strongly support the war with Iraq in 2003, and has been quoted as being uncomfortable with President Bush's "Texas, Alamo macho."[42] As Powell himself has said about the impact of Vietnam on the officers who served there, "Does it affect our thinking? Sure, it was the most definitive military event in our lives and in our career. . . . What those of us in the military are trying to do is . . . to make sure that our political leaders understand the consequences of going to war and how to go to war well and do it well."[43]

It is also worth speculating how much the personal experiences of President Bush influenced his determination in 2003 to drive Saddam Hussein from power. It is clear that Bush is very close to his family (Greenstein, 2003; Helco, 2003). That connection, in the view of some, made him especially sensitive to the criticism of his father for not toppling the Iraqi dictator in 1991, and may have created in the younger Bush an urge to complete the business of his father (Wead, 2003).[44] Moreover, it is widely believed that Saddam Hussein tried to have the first President Bush assassinated when he visited Kuwait in 1993. Nine years later, his son told a gathering, "There's no doubt [that Saddam Hussein] can't stand us. After all, this is the guy that tried to kill my dad at one time." White House officials quickly issued assurances that the president did not mean "to personalize" his campaign to depose the Iraqi dictator, but it is hard to totally discount the antipathy of a devoted son toward a man who "tried to kill my dad."[45]

Perceptions

Decision makers' images of reality constitute a fifth idiosyncratic element that influences their approach to foreign policy. These images are called **perceptions**, which, in sum, create a decision maker's worldview. One scholar who served briefly on the staff of President George W. Bush has written, "By the time I left the White House . . . I was con-

As evident in this picture, President George W. Bush and his father, former president George H. W. Bush, have a close relationship. Some analysts wonder if the allegation that Saddam Hussein tried to have the senior Bush assassinated in 1993 might have played what role in his son's determination to drive the Iraqi dictator from power in 2003.

vinced . . . [that] the sitting president's 'world view'—'his primary, politically relevant beliefs, particularly his conceptions of social causality, human nature, and the central moral conflicts of the time'—probably explain as much or more about . . . foreign policy than any other single variable" (DiIulio, 2003:3).

Perceptions have a multitude of sources. Many, such as belief systems and historical analogies, are related to the cognitive limits discussed earlier in this chapter or to the idiosyncratic characteristics of decision makers that we have been analyzing in this section. The information that decision makers receive from their bureaucracies or elsewhere, also discussed in this chapter, is another important source of perceptions. Whatever their source, perceptions have a number of characteristics and impacts that are important to world politics.

Characteristics of Perceptions Numerous common perceptual characteristics influence the policy making of individuals and even the policy preferences of whole nations. To demonstrate this, we can take a look at four common characteristics of perceptions.

We often assume that others see the world the same way that we do. Many Americans could not understand why other countries did not see Saddam Hussein as a threat in the way that the Bush administration and a majority of Americans did. Any future crisis with Iran and North Korea, the other two members of the axis of evil, could find the same perceptual gap. A survey in 2003 found that 71% of Americans considered Iran a

Perceptions play a major role in decision making. One common characteristic of perceptions is that we tend to assume that others see our good intentions and are not afraid of us. When President George W. Bush labeled Iran, Iraq, and North Korea as the axis of evil, many people feared that the rhetoric presaged a U.S. attack. When President Bush traveled to South Korea in 2002, he met protesters, including these Roman Catholic nuns in Seoul, displaying a sign that indicates their perceptions of the president and his views.

threat to regional stability and 77% saw North Korea in the same way. By contrast, in the other 20 countries surveyed, only 40% believed Iran to be a force for instability and just 47% perceived North Korea in that light.[46]

We tend to see the behavior of others as more planned and coordinated than our own. Former secretary of state Henry Kissinger (1979:1202) has described the United States and Soviet Union during the cold war as behaving like "two heavily armed blind men feeling their way around a room, each believing himself in mortal peril from the other whom he assumes to have perfect vision." Each, according to Kissinger, "tends to ascribe to the other side a consistency, foresight, and coherence that its own experience belies. Of course, over time even two armed blind men in a room can do enormous damage to each other, not to speak of the room."

We find it hard to understand why others dislike, mistrust, and fear us. President George W. Bush captured this overly positive sense of oneself when at a press conference he asked a rhetorical question, "How do I respond when I see that in some Islamic countries there is vitriolic hatred for America?" In response to his own question, the president pronounced himself "amazed that there's such misunderstanding of what our country is about that people would hate us. I am—like most Americans, I just can't believe it because I know how good we are."[47] Others are less sure of Americans' innate goodness. One recent survey found that 60% or more of poll respondents in countries as diverse as Indonesia, Nigeria, Turkey, and Russia thought that the United States posed a military threat to them.[48]

FIGURE 3.7 Mirror Images: Americans, French, and Germans

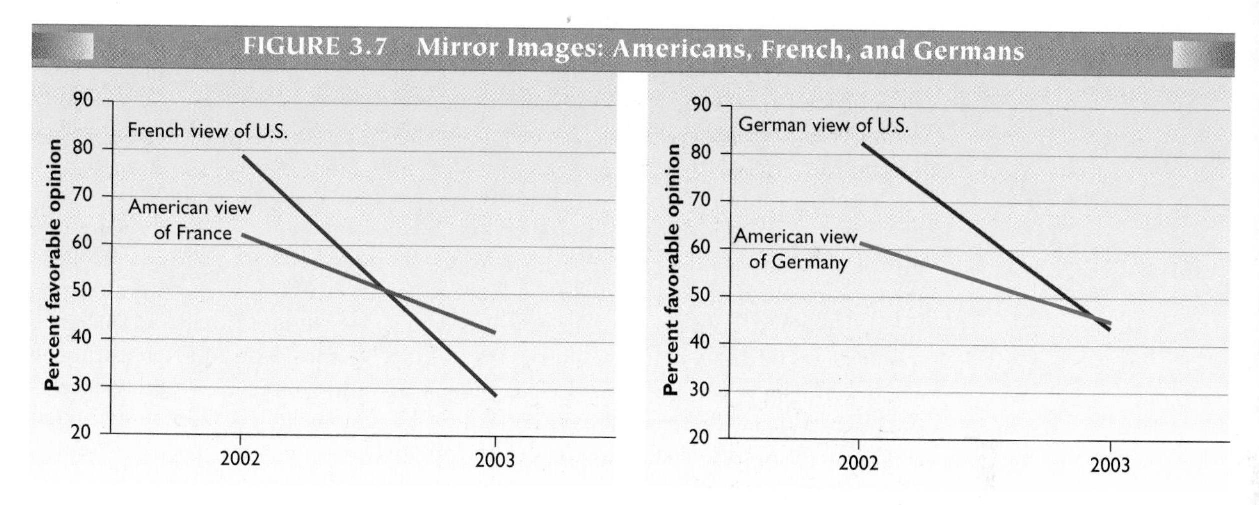

Countries and even leaders often have a mirror image of one another. Disagreements over policy toward Iraq led to a reciprocal decline in postive trans-Atlantic feeligs between Americans, on the one hand, and French and Germans on the other.

Data source: Pew Research Center, "Views of a Changing World 2003: War with Iraq Further Divides Global Publics," June 3, 2003, on the Web at http://people-press.org/reports/display.php3?ReportID=185.

We and others tend to have similar images of one another. Between countries and even between leaders, it is common to find a **mirror-image perception** in which each side perceives the other in roughly similar terms, as shown in Figure 3.7. A poll in late 2002 found that 60% of Americans responded yes to the question, "Do you think the Muslim world considers itself at war with the United States?" Only 33% said no, with 7% unsure.[49] A few months later, a poll in seven overwhelmingly Muslim countries found a remarkably similar mirror image. An average of 61% of the respondents said they felt threatened by U.S. military power, only 36% did not feel threatened, and 3% were unsure. A majority was worried in six of the seven countries (including Kuwait), with only Moroccans (46% worried) feeling relatively safe.[50]

Perceptions and Policy Perceptions translate into policy because they form an **operational reality**. Policy makers tend to act or operate based on perceptions, whether they are accurate or not. For example, the operational reality of perceptions among most ranking officials in the Bush administration that Iraq had WMD capabilities and intended to develop them more fully was a key factor in the U.S.-led intervention. Whether those perceptions were accurate or not is an important question in its own right. But as far as the causes of the war itself are concerned, the operational reality (whatever the objective reality may have been) was determined by the belief of President Bush, Prime Minister Blair, and others that Saddam Hussein did have such weapons and that they presented a long-term threat.

There is a related perceptual phenomenon called an **operational code**. This idea describes how any given leader's worldview and "philosophical propensities for diagnosing" how world politics operates influence the "leader's . . . propensities for choosing" rewards, threats, force, and other methods of diplomacy as the best way to be successful (Walker, Schafer, & Young, 1998:176). To some degree, for example, a leader's operational code reflects whether that leader leans toward the liberal or the realist end of the spectrum, as discussed in chapter 1.

President Bill Clinton's worldview saw the United States as operating in a complex, technology-driven, interconnected world, in which conflict was more likely to result from countries' internal conditions (such as poverty, civil strife, and autocracy) than from traditional power rivalries between states. Among other things, this led Clinton to favor a multilateral approach to diplomacy, to often view the motives and actions of other countries in nuanced shades of gray, and to delve deeply into the intricacies of policy (Harnisch, 2001; Jewett & Turetzky, 1998).

George W. Bush's operational code is very different. Whereas Clinton took a cerebral approach to policy, Bush has described himself as more a "gut" player than an intellectual (Daalder & Lindsay, 2003:7). Perhaps stemming from his profound religious convictions, Bush, more than Clinton, is apt to see the world in right-versus-wrong terms.[51] For him, not only were the terrorists who launched the 9/11 attacks analogous to the fascists of the 1930s, but countries suspected of abetting terrorism were part of an axis of evil. This belief also disposes Bush to see the world as a more inescapably dangerous place than did Clinton. It also makes Bush much more willing to follow a unilateralist path in pursuit of what he believes to be right, whereas the less doctrinaire Clinton was more open to multilateral diplomacy. In this sense Bush is something of a classic realist. Yet there is also a liberal element in his strong sense of what he sees as the goodness of America and its mission to make the world into a better place by promoting democracy, free enterprise, and generally what he might term the "American way" (Rhodes, 2003). This urge is very much part of the Bush doctrine, and it also played a role in his decision to invade Iraq to begin a process of democratization in the Middle East, as well as oust Saddam Hussein. As one analyst has written, "it is impossible to understand Bush's presidential character without fully appreciating his profoundly small 'd' democratic beliefs" (DiIulio, 2003:3).

Finally, analysts have noted that Bush draws a strong sense of duty to lead and sacrifice from the history of the Bush family's public service dating back several generations. For the president this sense of personal leadership translates into feeling responsible to use his position as the leader of what he sees as a great and good country to reshape the world. As one scholar has noted, for Bush, "With 9/11, the long-hidden mission, the purpose for everything that had gone before [in becoming president], seemed to snap into place. In the political ethos of the Bush family, the charge to keep was to behave with responsibility. The terrorist attack filled in the blank space as to what responsibility required in the new post–Cold War era. . . . The Bush Doctrine . . . was born" (Helco, 2003:20).

Chapter Summary

System-Level Analysis

1. It is important to explore each level of analysis (system, state, and individual) for clues about causality in world politics.
2. System-level analysis is an approach to the study of world politics that argues that countries are often compelled to take certain courses of action by the realities of the world in which they exist.
3. Many factors determine the nature of any given system. Systemic factors include its structural characteristics, power relationships, economic patterns, and norms of behavior.
4. One structural characteristic is how authority is organized. The international system is horizontal, based on state sovereignty, and therefore it is anarchical. There are, however, relatively new centralizing forces that are changing the system toward a more vertical structure.
5. Another structural characteristic of a system is its actors. Currently, sovereign states are the dominant actors, but intergovernmental actors and transnational actors are becoming more numerous and important.
6. A third structural characteristic is a system's frequency, scope, and level of interaction. The current system is becoming increasingly interdependent, with a rising

number of interactions across an expanding range of issues. Economic interdependence is especially significant.

7. When analyzing power relationships, an important factor is the number of poles in a system. Bipolar systems, for instance, may operate differently and be more or less stable than multipolar systems.
8. The pattern of concentration of power is another system characteristic. Whether poles are relatively equal or unequal in power, the shifts in relative strength influence behavior in the system.
9. Power changes in the system when there are shifts in the sources of power or when conditions within major actors affect their tangible or intangible power assets.
10. A system's economic patterns, such as the distribution of natural resources, also affect its operation.
11. Norms are the values that help determine patterns of behavior and create some degree of predictability in the system. The norms of the system are changing. Many newer countries, for instance, are challenging some of the current norms of the system, most of which are rooted in Western culture.
12. It is clear that there are significant changes occurring in all the determining elements (structural characteristics, power relationships, economic patterns, and norms of behavior) of the international system. The current system most closely resembles a limited unipolar system dominated by the United States. What is not clear is exactly what the new system will look like in the future.

State-Level Analysis

13. State-level analysis assumes that since states are the most important international actors, world politics can be best understood by focusing on how states decide foreign policy.
14. Foreign policy is not formulated by a single decision-making process. Instead, the exact nature of that process changes according to a number of variables, including the type of political system, the type of situation, the type of issue, and the internal factors involved.
15. States are complex organizations, and their internal, or domestic, dynamics influence their international actions.
16. One set of internal factors centers on political culture, which is the fundamental, long-held beliefs of a nation.
17. Another set of internal factors centers on the policy-making impact of various foreign policy–making actors. These include political leaders, bureaucratic organizations, legislatures, political parties and opposition, interest groups, and the public. Each of these influences foreign policy, but their influence varies according to the type of government, the situation, and the policy at issue. Overall, political leaders and bureaucratic organizations are consistently (although not always) the strongest foreign policy–making actors.

Individual-Level Analysis

18. Individual-level analysis studies international politics by examining the role of humans as actors on the world stage.
19. Individual-level analysis can be approached from three different perspectives. One is to examine fundamental human nature. The second is to study how people act in organizations. The third is to examine the motivations and actions of specific persons.
20. The human nature approach examines basic human characteristics, including the cognitive, psychological, emotional, and biological factors that influence decision making.
21. The organizational-behavior approach studies role (how people act in their professional position) and group decision-making behavior, such as groupthink.
22. The idiosyncratic-behavior approach explores the factors that determine the perceptions, decisions, and actions of specific leaders. A leader's personality, physical and mental health, ego and ambitions, understanding of history, personal experiences, and perceptions are all factors.
23. Perceptions are also important to understanding how leaders react to the world. These spring from such sources as a group's or an individual's belief system, an individual's values, and the information available to the individual.
24. The application of perceptions to policy can be explained by exploring operational reality and operational codes.

For a chapter quiz, interactive activities, web links, PowerWeb articles, and much more, visit **www.mhhe.com/rourke10/** and go to chapter 3. Or, while accessing the site, click on Course-Wide Content and view recent international relations articles in the *New York Times.*

Key Terms

authoritarian governments
biopolitics
bipolar system
bureaucracy
cognitive decision making
crisis situation
decision-making process
democratic governments
ethology
foreign policy–making actors
foreign policy process
formal powers
frustration-aggression theory
gender opinion gap
gross national product (GNP)
groupthink
head of government
hegemonic power
heuristic devices
horizontal authority structure
idiosyncratic analysis
individual-level analysis
informal powers
interest groups
intergovernmental organizations (IGOs)
intermestic policy
issue area
leader-citizen opinion gap
levels of analysis
mirror-image perceptions
multinational corporations
Munich analogy
nongovernmental organizations (NGOs)
norms
operational code
operational reality
perceptions
political culture
political executives
power pole
pure foreign policy
rally effect
roles
state-centric system
state-level analysis
states
system-level analysis
terrorist groups
transnational actors
transnational corporations (TNCs)
two-level game
unipolar system
vertical authority structure
weapons of mass destruction (WMDs)

CHAPTER 4

Nationalism: The Traditional Orientation

UNDERSTANDING NATIONS, NATIONALISM, AND NATION-STATES

Nations, Nationalism, and Nation-States Defined

The Rise and Ascendancy of Nationalism

NATIONALISM IN PRACTICE: ISSUES AND EVALUATION

Nation-States: More Myth than Reality

Nationalism: Builder and Destroyer

Self-Determination as a Goal

NATIONALISM AND THE FUTURE

The Recent Past and Present of Nationalism

The Future of Nationalism

CHAPTER SUMMARY

KEY TERMS

I do love
My country's good with a respect more tender,
More holy and profound, than mine own life.

—William Shakespeare, *Coriolanus*

If he govern the country, you are bound to him indeed; but how honourable he is in that, I know not.

—William Shakespeare, *Pericles, Prince of Tyre*

Our country! In her intercourse with foreign nations may she always be in the right; but our country, right or wrong.

—Stephen Decatur, 1816

You're not supposed to be so blind with patriotism that you can't face reality. Wrong is wrong, no matter who does it or who says it.

—Malcolm X, *Malcolm X Speaks,* 1965

CHAPTER OBJECTIVES

After completing this chapter, you should be able to:

- Define nationalism.
- Identify the elements that make up a state.
- Describe how a nation differs from a state.
- Identify and explain the ideal concept of nation-state and its relationship to nationalism.
- Explain nationalism as the product of historical development.
- Identify the ideal and actual relationships between nation and state.
- Define multistate nationalities and explain when they occur.
- Discuss why nationalism is said to be both a cohesive and a divisive force.
- List and discuss positive and negative aspects of nationalism.
- Discuss the origins of microstates and the problems that their existence presents to the statecentric system.
- Explain the place of nationalism and the nation-state in today's world where transnational and other structures and identifications are also increasing in scope and intensity.
- Identify arguments predicting the end of nationalism and the demise of the territorial state, and note post–World War II trends that have contradicted these predictions.

Aliens fascinate us. Not the aliens that immigration officials worry about, but the ones that come from other planets. Whether it is movies such as the *Men in Black* films, television such as the *Stargate* series, sci-fi novels, or comics, our entertainment media are filled with "others." These aliens can do more than amuse or scare us; they can teach us something. For instance, take E.T., the extraterrestrial being. Now, there was one strange-looking character. He—she?—had a squat body, no legs to speak of, a large shriveled head, saucer eyes, and a telescopic neck. And the color! Yes, E.T. was definitely weird. Not only that; there was presumably a whole planet full of E.T.s—all looking alike, waddling along, with their necks going up and down.

Or did they all look alike? They might have to us, but probably not to one another. Perhaps on their planet there were different countries, ethnic groups, and races of E.T.s. Maybe they had different-length necks, were varied shades of greenish-brown, and squeaked and hummed with different tonal qualities. It could even be that darker-green E.T.s with longer necks from the country of Urghor felt superior to lighter-green, short-necked E.T.s from faraway and little-known Sytica across the red Barovian Sea. If E.T. were a Sytican, would the Urghorans have responded to the plaintive call, "E.T. phone home"?

We can also wonder whether E.T. could tell Earthlings apart. Was he aware that some of his human protectors were boys and some were girls and that a cross section of racial and ethnic Americans chased him with equal-opportunity abandon? Maybe we all

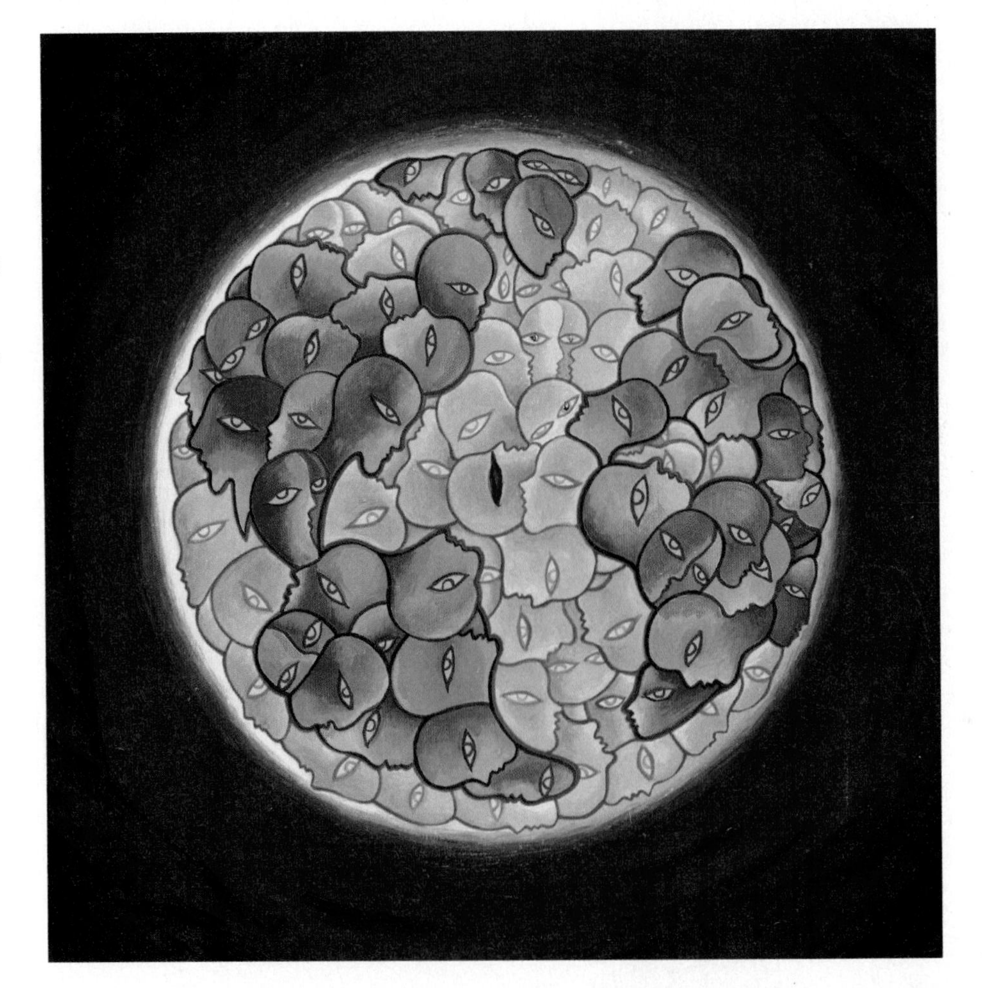

Nationalism tends to make us view people from other cultures and countries as different from ourselves. One has to wonder, though, whether a being from another world, such as E.T., would see people from different regions of the world as dramatically different or would see them, like the representation in this picture, as having some slight differences but, in essence, being very much alike.

looked pretty much the same to E.T. If he had been on a biological specimen-gathering expedition and had collected a Canadian, a Nigerian, and a Laotian, he might have thrown two of the three away as duplicates.

The point of this whimsy is to get us thinking about our world, how we group ourselves, and how we distinguish our group from others. This sense of how you are connected politically to others is called **political identity**. What we humans mostly do is to ignore our many and manifest similarities and perceptually divide ourselves into Chinese, Irish, Poles, and a host of other national "we-groups."

Understanding Nations, Nationalism, and Nation-States

Political division is a key characteristic of traditional global politics, and this chapter is about an important source of that division, **nationalism**. It is the sense of political self that makes people feel patriotic about their country. Certainly, most people have more than one political identity. For example, President Lyndon B. Johnson once said, "I am an American, a Texan, and a Democrat—in that order." Like Johnson, we emotionally rank our identities, and also like LBJ, most of us put our country first. Thus you probably see yourself first and foremost politically as a citizen of the United States or some other country. You might even be willing to fight and die for your country. Would you do the same for your hometown? Or Earth?

Nationalism is the world's "most powerful political idea" (Taras & Ganguly, 1998:xi). It is the primary political identity of most people. As such, nationalism has helped configure world politics for several centuries and will continue to play a crucial role in shaping people's minds and global affairs in the foreseeable future. Despite its strength, however, nationalism today is not as dominant a political orientation as it once was. As we shall see, some even doubt whether it will or should continue and predict or advocate various transnational alternative orientations. Think about this debate. At the end of the chapter you will find a You Be the Playwright box, "*J'Accuse!* Nationalism on Trial." Be ready to prosecute or defend nationalism and ultimately to judge it.

This juxtaposition of the traditional nationalist orientation and the alternative transnational orientation represents one of this book's main themes: that the world is at or is approaching a critical juncture where two roads diverge in the political wood. The two paths to the political future—traditional and alternative—are mapped out briefly in chapter 1.

Nations, Nationalism, and Nation-States Defined

The political segmentation of the world rests in great part on three concepts: nation, nation-state, and nationalism (Mortimer & Fine, 1999). Understanding both the theory and reality of what they are and how they relate to one another is central to our analysis of international politics.

Nations

A **nation** is a people who (a) share demographic and cultural similarities, (b) possess a feeling of community (mutually identify as a group distinct from other groups), and (c) want to control themselves politically. As such, a nation is intangible; it exists because its members think it does. A state (country) is a tangible institution, but a nation, as a French scholar put it, is "a soul, a spiritual quality" (Renan, 1995:7). Americans, for one, are a nation; the institutional vehicle of their self-governance is their state, the United States.

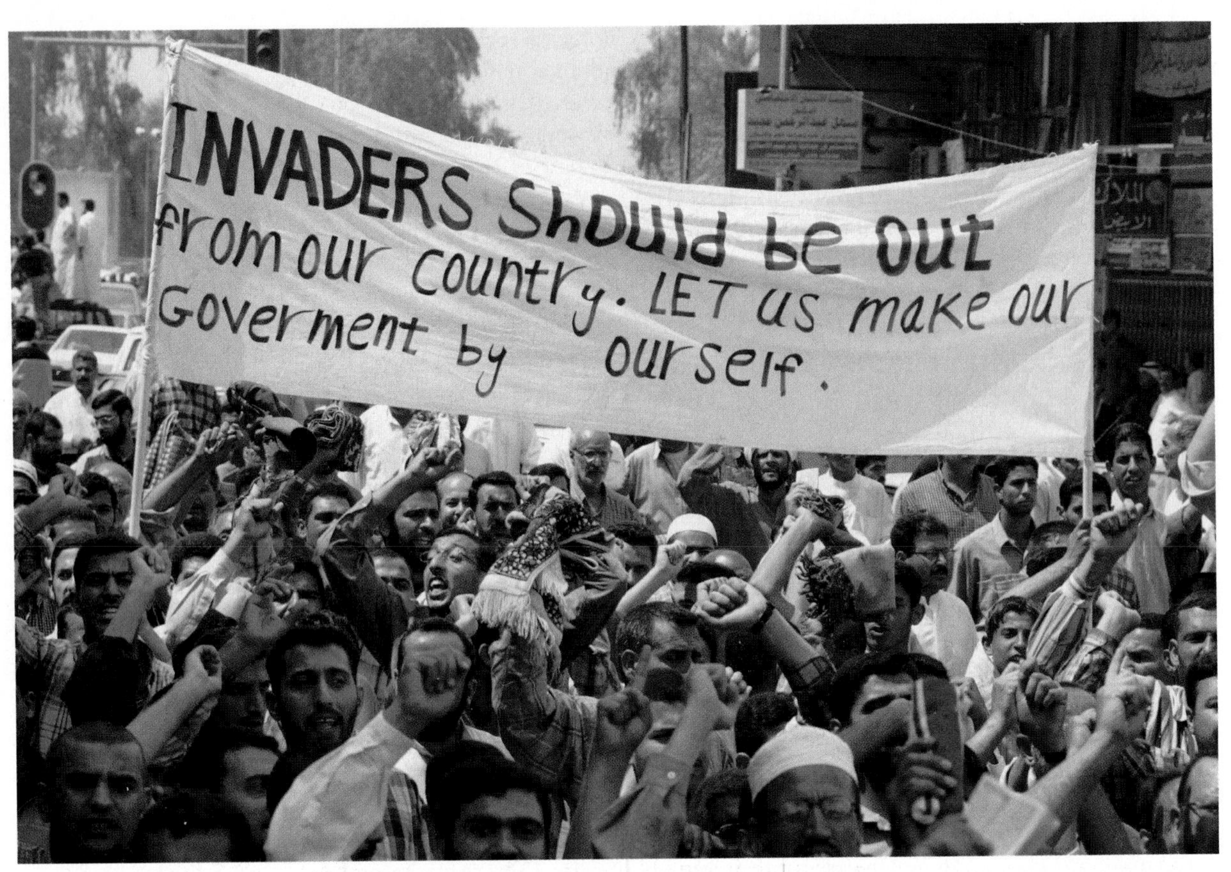

Undergoing common experiences and having a common opponent are among the building blocks of nationalism. In these ways, the war against and occupation of Iraq in 2003 may have strengthened Iraqi nationalism. The United States and Great Britain soon discovered that as much as many Iraqis detested Saddam Hussein, they also chafed at being invaded and occupied by outside, Christian-heritage powers. This feeling led, at its mildest, to demonstrations such as the one depicted here in Baghdad, and, at its worst, helped precipitate the deadly post-war attacks on foreign military and civilian personnel.

Demographic and Cultural Similarities The similarities that a people share are one element that helps make them a nation. These similarities may be demographic characteristics (such as language, race, and religion), or they may be a common culture or shared historical experiences. It could be said that the American nation is the outcome of Valley Forge, Martin Luther King, the interstate highway system, McDonald's, MTV, the Super Bowl, Jennifer Lopez, the 9/11 terrorist attacks, and a host of other people, events, and processes that make up the American experience.

Feeling of Community A second thing that helps define a nation is its feeling of community. Perception is the key here. For all the objective similarities a group might have, it is not a nation unless it subjectively feels like one. Those within a group must perceive that they share similarities and are bound together by them. Thus a nation is an "imagined political community," according to one scholar. As he explains, "It is *imagined* because the members of even the smallest nation will never know most of their fellow-members, meet them, or even hear of them, yet in the minds of each lives the image of their communion" (Anderson, 1991:5).

The central role of perceptions in defining a nation leads, perhaps inevitably, to a "we-group" defining itself not only by the similarities of those in the nation but also in terms of how those in the nation differ from others, the "they-groups." The group members' sense of feeling akin to one another and their sense of feeling different from others are highly subjective.

Desire to Be Politically Separate The third element that defines a nation is its desire to be politically separate. What distinguishes a nation from an ethnic group is that a nation, unlike an ethnic group, desires to be self-governing or at least autonomous. In the United States there are many groups, such as Italian Americans, who share a common culture and have a sense of identification. They are not nations, however, because they are not separatists. In nationally divided states (like Cyprus, with its majority Greek and minority Turkish communities), the minority nationalities refuse to concede the legitimacy of their being governed by the majority nationality.

It should be noted that the line between ethnic groups and nations is not always clear. In many countries there are ethnic groups that either teeter on the edge of having true nationalist (separatist) sentiments or that have some members who are nationalists and others who are not (Conversi, 2002). Canada is one such country where the line between ethnic group and nation is uncertain. There is an ongoing dissatisfaction among many French Canadians in the province of Quebec about their status in the Canadian state. Some Québécois favor separation; others do not. Once the prevailing opinion of the ethnic group perceives the group to be distinct politically as well as culturally, then it becomes an **ethnonational group**.

A key characteristic that separates nations from ethnic groups is that nations have the desire to be separate and to govern themselves. In the former Yugoslavia, it would have been hard for the average outsider to distinguish among Serbs, Bosnian Muslims, Croats, and other national groups; but they could, and each nation desired to be separate.

Nationalism

The second aspect of the traditional political orientation is nationalism, which is the separatist political impulse of a nation. It is hard to overstate the importance of nationalism to the structure and conduct of world politics (Beiner, 1999). Nationalism is an **ideology**, a complex of related ideas that establish values about what is good and bad, directs adherents on how to act (patriotism), link together those who adhere to the ideology, and distinguish them from those who do not. Specifically, nationalism connects individuals, their sense of community, and their political identity in contradistinction to other nations. The links are forged when individuals (1) "become sentimentally attached to the homeland," (2) "gain a sense of identity and self-esteem through their national identification," and (3) are "motivated to help their country" (Druckman, 1994:44). As such, nationalism is an ideology that holds that the nation should be the primary political identity of individuals. Furthermore, nationalist ideology maintains that the paramount political loyalty of individuals should be patriotically extended to the nation-state, the political vehicle of the nation's self-governance.

Nation-States

A third element of our traditional way of defining and organizing ourselves politically is the **nation-state**. This combines the idea of a nation with that of a state. A state, about which much more will be said in chapter 6, is a country, a sovereign (independent) political organization with certain characteristics, such as territory, a population, and a government. Canada and China, for example, are states.

Ideally, a nation-state represents the joining of a nation and state. In this arrangement, virtually all of a nation is united within its own state, and the people of that state overwhelmingly identify with the nation. Thus the ideal nation-state is one in which one nation and one state are within the same boundaries. This connection between nation and state engenders powerful emotions called patriotism, the extension of identification with the nation to loyalty to the state.

The Rise and Ascendancy of Nationalism

Nationalism is such a pervasive mindset in the world today that it is difficult to believe that it has not always existed. But it has not. Indeed, most scholars contend that nationalism is a relatively modern phenomenon. Certainly, as one scholar notes, "there have always . . . been distinctive cultures." It is also the case that in some very old societies the "upper classes have had some sense of shared ethnic solidarity." What is modern, the scholar continues, is the "nationalist idea," the belief that people who share a culture should "be ruled only by someone co-cultural with themselves" (Hall, 1995:10).

This reality that nationalism is not a timeless phenomenon is important because if something has not always been, it does not necessarily always have to be. As we shall see later in the chapter, nationalism has its pluses and minuses, and numerous observers believe that it is an outmoded, even dangerous, orientation that should be abandoned. Understanding that nationalism is not an absolute also leads to a discussion of how it has evolved over time.

Early Nationalism

It is impossible to establish precisely when nationalism began to evolve, but in the West the fall of Rome set the stage. Under Rome something of common culture, language (Latin), and law prevailed, at least among the elite in the various parts of the empire. After Rome's collapse the common cultural and political ties deteriorated. Some sense of universality (such as keeping Latin alive) survived in the Roman Catholic Church. There were also various attempts to reestablish a Western empire. For example, the king of the Franks, Charlemagne (742–814), gained control over most of western and central Europe and in 800 was proclaimed by Pope Leo III to be *Imperatori Augustus,* a symbolic title reminiscent of the Roman emperors. This led to the concept of the Holy Roman Empire (HRE), which lasted in theory until 1806. Yet despite its pretentious title, the HRE never wielded the power of Rome and sometimes had little power at all.

As a result, the universality that had existed under Rome, and which the Church and the HRE tried to maintain, fragmented into different cultures. The use of Latin, a language spoken by all elites across Europe, declined, and the local languages that supplanted Latin divided the elites. This was but the first step in a process that eventually created a sense of divergent national identities among the upper classes. By dividing Western Christendom, the Protestant Reformation beginning in 1517 further fragmented European culture.

The growth of nationalism became gradually intertwined with the development of states and with their synthesis, the nation-state. The history of states is reviewed in chapter 6, but we can say here that some of the earliest evidence of broad-based nationalism occurred in England at the time of King Henry VIII (1491–1547). His break with the centralizing authority of the Roman Catholic Church and his establishment of a national Anglican Church headed by the king were pivotal events. The conversion of

English commoners to Anglicanism helped spread nationalism to the masses, as did the nationalist sentiments in popular literature. In an age when most people could not read, plays were an important vehicle of culture, and one scholar has characterized the works of William Shakespeare (1564–1616) as "propagandist plays about English history" (Hobsbawm, 1990:75). "This blessed plot, this earth, this realm, this England," Shakespeare has his *King Richard II* exult. In another play, *Henry VI,* Shakespeare notes the end of the authority of the pope in Rome over the king in London by having Queen Margaret proclaim, "God and King Henry govern England." This sounds commonplace today, but omitting mention of the authority of the papacy was radical stuff 450 years ago.

Ascendant Modern Nationalism

The evolution of nationalism took an important turn in the 1700s and began to change into its modern form, which is based on the close association of the people and the state. Until that time, the link between the states and their inhabitants was very different from what it is today. Most people were not emotionally connected to the state in which they lived. People were subjects who were ruled by a monarch anointed by God to govern (the divine right theory). This changed when, under the doctrine of **popular sovereignty**, people became citizens who had a stake in and were even owners (no matter how tangentially) of the state. Moreover, rulers governed by the consent of the people, at least in theory if often not in fact.

Popular sovereignty had been evolving slowly in Switzerland, England, and a few other places. But it accelerated when the American and French revolutions dramatically shifted the basis of theoretical political authority in states away from the divine right of kings and toward the idea, as the American Declaration of Independence proclaimed, that governments derive their "just powers from the consent of the governed." While the impact of the American Revolution took time to spread from the isolated United States, the French Revolution's doctrine of "liberty, equality, fraternity" was more immediate. The pens of such French philosophers as Rousseau, Voltaire, and Montesquieu spread the idea of popular sovereignty far beyond France's borders. Soon France's powerful legions added the sword to the tools that spread the philosophy of the national state throughout Europe.

From these beginnings, the idea of popular sovereignty and the belief in the right to national self-determination began to spread around the globe. Within 200 years of the American and French Revolutions, absolute monarchism, which had persisted as a common mode of governance from time immemorial, had virtually disappeared. The sense of public ownership of the state and even the transnational ties among the elites waned. It was still possible in 1714 for Great Britain, when the royal house of Stuart died out, to import a German nobleman, the Elector (ruler) of Hanover, to become King George I. Such a transplanted monarch or president would be virtually unthinkable today.

Did You Know That:

National flags are relatively modern inventions that replaced flags of royal dynasties. The French tricolor, for example, dates only to 1794, when it replaced the white flag with the gold fleur-de-lis of the royal house of Bourbon.

Spreading nationalism also dramatically changed the political map. Consolidation occurred in some cases where nations overspread many political units. The formation of Germany and Italy in the 1860s and 1870s serve as examples. In other cases, national states were established on the ashes of empire. The Spanish empire fell apart in the 1800s, and the Austro-Hungarian and Ottoman empires collapsed after World War I. By the mid-twentieth century, nearly all of Europe and the Western Hemisphere had been divided into nation-states, and the colonies of Africa and Asia were beginning to demand independence. The doomed British and French empires soon vanished also. Finally, the last of the huge multiethnic empires, Russia/the Soviet Union, collapsed in 1991, with 15 nation-states emerging. Nationalism reigned virtually supreme around the world.

These developments were widely welcomed. An image of "populist-romantic nationalism" appealed to liberals on two grounds (Gellner, 1995:6). First, the idea of a nation contains an implied equality for all members. Liberal philosophers such as Thomas Paine in *The Rights of Man* (1791) depicted the nation and democracy as inherently linked in the popularly governed nation-state. Liberals also welcomed nationalism as a destroyer of empires. Among other important expressions of this view is Article 55 of the United Nations Charter, which states that "the principle of . . . self-determination of peoples" is one of the "conditions of stability and well-being which are necessary for peaceful and friendly relations among nations."

Patterns of Nation-State Formation

As the discussion of the rise and ascendancy of nationalism suggests, the pattern of nations, nationalism, and nation-states coming together varies. Sometimes nations and nationalism precede states; sometimes states precede nations and nationalism; and at other times nations and nationalism evolve along with states. The various patterns have been characterized as unification nationalism, state-building nationalism, and irredentist nationalism.

Nation and Nationalism Precede Nation-States When a strong sense of cultural and political identity exists among a people, the formation of the nation often precedes that of the state. In Europe, nations generally came together first and only later coalesced into states. One scholar has called this pattern "unification nationalism" (Hechter, 2000:15).

As noted, for example, Germans existed as a cultural people long before they came together as Germany in the 1860s and 1870s. Similarly, the Italian peninsula had not been united since the fall of the Roman Empire until *risorgimento,* the resurgent sense of Italian cultural unity, led to the political movement that unified most of the peninsula in a new country, Italy, in 1861. Similarly, on the other side of the world in Japan, an upsurge of nationalism set off the chain of events that ended the Tokugawa Shogunate (1603–1867), the political division of the Japanese islands among the *daimyo* (feudal nobles), and restored real power to the figurehead emperor.

Nation-States Precede Nations and Nationalism Elsewhere and in other circumstances, the formation of the state has sometimes come first. In such cases, a critical task of the state is to promote internal loyalty and to create a process whereby its diverse citizens gradually acquire their nationalism through common historical experiences and the regular social/economic/political interactions and cooperation that occur among people living within the same state. This effort has been termed "state-building nationalism" (Hechter, 2000:15).

This form of **state building** has several problems. One is that rulers sometimes try to build support and foster nationalism by whipping up hatred of minority groups (Marx, 2003). Second, even when state building is benign, it is very difficult. For example, many states in Africa are the result of boundaries that were drawn earlier by colonial powers and that took in people of different tribal and ethnic backgrounds. These former colonial states often do not contain a single, cohesive nation, and the diverse cultural groups find little to bind them to one another once independence has been achieved. Rwanda and Burundi are neighboring states in which Hutu and Tutsi people were thrown together by colonial boundaries that, with independence, became national boundaries, as depicted in the map of Africa on page 37. The difficulty is that the primary political identifications of these people have not become Rwandan or Burundian. They have remained Hutu or Tutsi, and that has led to repeated, sometimes horrific, violence.

Nations, Nationalism, and Nation-States Evolve Together Frequently nation-building and state-building are not locked in a strict sequential interaction, when one fully precedes the other. Sometimes they evolve together. This approximates what occurred in the United States, where the idea of being American and the unity of the state began in the 1700s and grew, despite a civil war, immigration inflows, racial and ethnic diversity, and other potentially divisive factors. Still, as late as 1861, the limits of nationalism could be seen when Colonel Robert E. Lee declined President Abraham Lincoln's offer of the command of the United States Army and accepted command of the militia of his seceding home state, Virginia.

The point is that American nationalism was not an instant phenomenon in 1776. As has happened elsewhere, living within a state over time allowed a demographically diverse people to come together as a nation through a process of *e pluribus unum* (out of many, one), as the U.S. motto says.

Nationalism in Practice: Issues and Evaluation

The idea of a community of people coming together as a political nation to establish their own nation-state in order to govern themselves is an attractive one that brings to mind the nun Isabella in Shakespeare's *Measure for Measure,* exclaiming warmly, "The image of it gives me content already; and I trust it will grow to a most prosperous perfection." Alas, nationalism has not grown to prosperous perfection. Surely, it has brought benefits, as we shall discuss. But the reality of nationalism is far from the ideal, and there are even aspects of it that would make Isabella shudder. As it turns out, nation-states are more myth than reality, nationalism has a troubled face as well as a beneficent one, and the idea of self-determination (each nation governing itself) may not always be a sound goal.

Nation-States: More Myth than Reality

Like many, perhaps most ideological images, the ideal nation-state is more myth than reality. The reason is that the territorial boundaries of nations and states often do not coincide (MacIver, 1999). In fact, most states are not ethnically unified, and many nations exist in more than one state. This lack of "fit" between nations and states is a significant source of international (and domestic) tension and conflict. There are five basic patterns: (1) The first is the ideal model of one nation, one state; the other four are lack-of-fit patterns including (2) one state, multiple nations; (3) one nation, multiple states; (4) one nation, no state; and (5) multiple nations, multiple states.

One State, One Nation

The ideal nation–state is a rarity. Indeed, only about 10% of all countries are both nationally unified (have a population that is 90% or more of one nation) and also have 90% of that nation living within its borders. The United States comes fairly close to the ideal. More than 99% of all Americans live in the United States, and there are no large ethnonational groups seeking independence or autonomy. There is some such sentiment among Native Americans (including Aleuts, American Indians, Inuits, and Native Hawaiians and other Pacific Islanders), but combined they make up only a bit more than 1% of the population. Indeed, polls show that the vast majority of U.S. residents, citizens and noncitizens alike, express considerable attachment to the United States. This was evident in a U.S. poll conducted in 2003 in which 98% of the respondents said they were "proud . . . to be an American."[1]

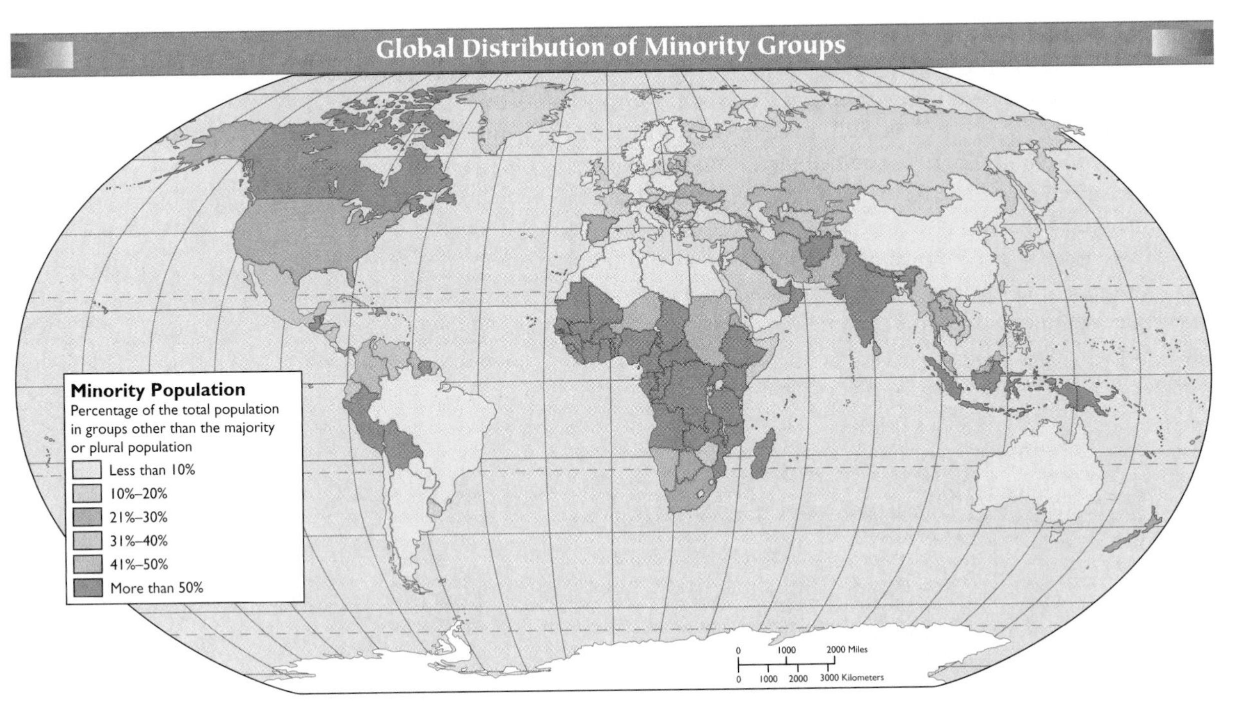

The presence of minority ethnic, national, or racial groups within a country's population can add a vibrant and dynamic mix to the whole. Plural societies with a high degree of cultural and ethnic diversity should, according to some social theorists, be among the world's healthiest. Unfortunately, the reality of the situation is quite different from theory or expectation. The presence of significant minority populations played an important role in the disintegration of the Soviet Union; the continuing existence of minority populations within the new states formed from former Soviet republics threatens the viability and stability of those young political units. In Africa, national boundaries were drawn by colonial powers without regard for the geographical distribution of ethnic groups, and the continuing tribal conflicts that have resulted hamper both economic and political development. Even in the most highly developed regions of the world, the presence of minority ethnic populations poses significant problems: witness the separatist movement in Canada, driven by the desire of some French-Canadians to be independent of the English majority, and the continuing ethnic conflict between Flemish-speaking and Walloon-speaking Belgians. This map, by arraying states on a scale of homogeneity to heterogeneity, indicates areas of existing and potential social and political strife.

One State, Multiple Nations

The number of **multinational states**, those in which more than one nation lies within a state, far exceeds that of nationally unified states. In fact, 30% have no national majority. The map above showing the degree of demographic unity of each country, indicates racial and ethnic, as well as national, diversity. Most of these minority groups do not have separatist tendencies, but many do or could acquire them.

Canada is one of the many countries where national divisions exist. About one-fourth of Canada's 32 million people are ethnically French (French Canadians) who identify French as their "mother tongue" and first language (Francophones). The majority of this group resides in the province of Quebec, a political subdivision rather like (but politically more autonomous than) an American state. Quebec is very French; of the province's 7.2 million people, more than 80% are culturally French.

Many French Canadians have felt that their distinctive culture has been eroded in predominantly English-culture Canada. There has also been a feeling of economic and other forms of discrimination. The resulting nationalist sentiment spawned the separatist *Parti Québécois* and led to a series of efforts in the 1980s and 1990s to obtain autonomy, even independence, for the province. The most recent of these was a referendum on separation held in 1995. The voters in Quebec rejected independence, but did so by only a razor-thin majority, with 50.6% voting *non* to sovereignty and 49.4% voting *oui*.

Since then, nationalist feelings have continued in Quebec, but they have eased because of reforms that have improved economic and cultural conditions for the Francophones (Seymour, 2000). A poll conducted in 2001 that presented Québécois with the same question that was on the 1995 referendum and asked them how they would vote found that support had dropped to 42%.[2]

Canada has avoided bloodshed over its national division, but many other multinational states have not been as fortunate. Some have suffered extraordinary violence. Rwanda, for one, is divided between two ethnonational groups, the minority (but politically dominant) Tutsi tribe and the majority Hutu tribe. In 1994 this split led to an intense orgy of killing when some 800,000 Tutsis and their sympathizers were slaughtered over about 100 days and well over 1 million Tutsis and moderate Hutus fled for their lives to neighboring countries. The horrific massacre was given voice by Prime Minister Agathe Uwilingiyamana: "There is shooting. People are being terrorized. People are inside their homes lying on the floor. We are suffering," she said in a broadcast from the capital, Kigali, appealing for help.[3] Those were her last public words; soon after, she was dragged from her refuge in a UN compound and gunned down by Hutu militia.

One Nation, Multiple States

Another departure from the nation-state ideal occurs when nations overlap the borders of two or more states. When a **multistate nation** exists, nationalist sentiments create strong pressures to join the politically separate nation within one state. This often creates conflict because the process of uniting a divided nation threatens the territorial integrity of one or more of the involved states. Even if a nation-state is not (yet) seeking to incorporate all the members of the nation, surrounding states with minority segments of that nationality may react with worried hostility.

One multistate nation pattern occurs when *one nation dominates two or more states.* The cold war created a number of such instances, including North and South Vietnam, North and South Korea, East and West Germany, and the two Yemens. The Irish in Ireland and Northern Ireland provide another possible example of a multistate nation, although the Scottish heritage of many of the Protestants in the North makes the existence of a single Irish nationality controversial. In any case, a single nation that dominates two states has an urge to unite the states and, thus, itself. Today only Korea (and arguably Ireland) remain as examples of such a division. But there is often conflict over union, a tension that led to fighting between the two halves of the nation in four of the examples (Vietnam, Korea, Ireland, and Yemen).

Another multistate nation pattern is where a *nation is a majority in one state and a minority in one or more other states.* The 5.7 million Albanians provide a good example of this type of multistate nation. Only 3.6 million of them live in Albania, where they are the overwhelming majority of the population. Another 1.6 million Albanians live in and make up 90% of the population in Kosovo, a province of Serbia and Montenegro (the newly renamed remnant of the former Yugoslavia). A third concentration of about 500,000 Albanians live in Macedonia, making up almost a quarter of that country's inhabitants. The Albanians' lack of fit in the states of Serbia and Montenegro and Macedonia has caused serious instability. Fighting broke out in 1997 when Albanian Kosovars asserted their autonomy from the central government in Belgrade. The brutal campaign waged by Serbian-led forces eventually sparked a U.S.-led NATO air war against Serbia and Montenegro in 1999 and the insertion of a NATO security force, Kosovo Force (KFOR), into the province, where it remains.

There has also been unrest in neighboring Macedonia to the south, where the country's Albanian minority has clashed bloodily with the Macedonian-dominated government. "We must also fight for our freedom in Macedonia, just as Albanians are fighting for their freedom in Kosovo," proclaimed one ethnic Albanian in Macedonia.[4] Calm was restored in 2001 by another international peacekeeping force (run first by NATO, then beginning in March 2003 by the European Union), but it is not certain that peace in either Kosovo or Macedonia would survive the withdrawal of the external security forces.

To complicate matters in the region further, the Macedonians are also a multistate nation. The Macedonians in Yugoslavia declared their independence in 1991. However, about 1 million Macedonians, or 40% of that nation, live across the border to the south, in northern Greece. This leaves the Greeks understandably wary about the possibility that independent Macedonia might have designs on the Macedonians in Greece. In such situations where a nation is a majority in one state and a minority in one or more other states, "irredentist nationalism" is common (Hechter, 2000:16). **Irredentism,** the drive to bring outlying members of the nation and their territory into the main nation-state, is a term based on the Italian word *irredenta* (unclaimed).

One Nation, No State

Yet another pattern where the state and nation are incongruent is called a **stateless nation**. This occurs when a national group is a minority in one or more states, does not have a nation-state of its own, and wants one (Hossay, 2002). This drive has been termed "peripheral nationalism" (Hechter, 2000:16). Two such stateless nations that have been much in the news in recent years are the Kurds and the Palestinians.

The possibility of peace in the Middle East rests on the knife-edge of Israeli-Palestinian relations. During the past few decades there have been interludes of hope; at other times the conflict between the two nations has seemed as intractable as the angry confrontation seen here between a Palestinian policeman and an Israeli soldier in the West Bank city of Hebron.

The In the Spotlight box, "The Elusive Quest for Kurdistan," on the next page details the first of these two stateless nations. As for the Palestinians, their story centers on the fact that they and another nation, the Jewish people, have long existed in the same area. The Jewish nation through its state, Israel, now controls most of that territory; the Palestinians mean to get enough of it back to create their own state. The ancient dispute dates back many millennia to Abraham and his two sons: Isaac, who founded the Jewish nation, and Ishmael, the symbolic father of all Arabs. The historical ebb and flow in the region of Jews and Palestinians is cloudy and far too complex to unravel here, but we can pick up the story in 1920 when Palestine was governed by Great Britain. At that time, Palestinian Arabs were about 90% of the population.

In Europe, however, Zionism gathered strength in the 19th century. **Zionism** is the nationalist, not strictly religious, belief that Jews are a nation that should have an independent homeland (Shlaim, 1999). This belief and an upsurge of virulent anti-Semitism in Nazi Germany and elsewhere in Europe caused increasing Jewish emigration to Palestine, swelling the Jewish population there from 56,000 in 1920 to 650,000 by 1948 (along with about 1 million Arabs). In rapid succession, fighting for control erupted, the British withdrew, and Arab leaders rejected a UN plan to partition Palestine into a Jewish state and an Arab state. Israel won the ensuing war in 1948 and acquired some of the areas designated for the Arab state. About 500,000 Palestinians fled to refugee camps in Egyptian-controlled Gaza and elsewhere; another 400,000 came under the control of

IN THE SPOTLIGHT

The Elusive Quest for Kurdistan

The Kurds are an ancient non-Arab people of the Mesopotamian region, who are mostly Sunni Muslims. The most famous of all Kurds was Saladin, the great defender of Islam who captured Jerusalem from the Christians (1187) and then defended it successfully against England's King Richard I (the Lion-Heart) and the other invading Christians during the Third Crusade (1189–1192).

Estimates of the Kurdish population range between 14 million and 28 million. As the accompanying map shows, the Kurds are now spread among several states and have no country of their own. About half of them are in Turkey; Iran and Iraq each have another 20 to 25%; and smaller numbers reside in Armenia, Azerbaijan, and Syria.

Sporadic and continuing attempts to establish an independent Kurdistan have caused conflicts with the countries in which the Kurds live. These disputes sometimes also have involved outside countries. The United States and other countries protected the Kurds in the UN-designated Kurdish Security Zone in northern Iraq from attack by Saddam Hussein's regime in Baghdad. This arrangement lasted from soon after the Persian Gulf War in 1991 to the fall of Saddam Hussein in 2003.

During the war with Iraq in 2003, Kurdish forces fought against the Iraqi army, thereby strengthening the autonomy they have enjoyed in the northern part of the country since 1991. What remains to be seen, and what worries Turkey and other neighbors of Iraq with Kurdish populations, is whether the Kurds in Iraq will be content to remain part of a reformed Iraq, or whether the autonomous region will serve as a base to militate for an independent Kurdistan that includes all or most of the Kurds in other countries and the territories where they live.

For a number of political reasons, the major Kurdish groups maintain a studied ambiguity about whether to seek a fully independent Kurdistan. Doing so overtly would almost certainly spark a military response from the countries in which the Kurds reside. This would be particularly likely for Turkey, whose troops have fought in recent years with Kurdish guerrillas. Indeed, during the early the days of the U.S.-led war with Iraq in 2003, Turkey threatened to intervene in northern Iraq to prevent the establishment of the nucleus of an independent Kurdistan after the fall of Saddam Hussein's regime.

The United States forestalled that potential crisis with Turkey, its NATO ally, by assuring Ankara that, as Secretary of State Colin Powell said after meeting with Turkish foreign minister Abdullah Gul, "We do not see any armed groups controlling territories, areas or resources in northern Iraq, and any moving in. The United States military will make sure that's the case." Later in a news conference in Pakistan, Powell went on to stress, "We have made it clear to all the various parties who have an interest . . . [including] Kurdish leaders . . . that [we are] committed to the territorial integrity of Iraq."[1] That may have been the politically prudent thing to do, but it also denied the Kurds the U.S. blessing to "assume among the powers of the earth, the separate and equal station to which the laws of nature and of nature's God entitle them," as the Americans put it in their own Declaration of Independence in 1776.

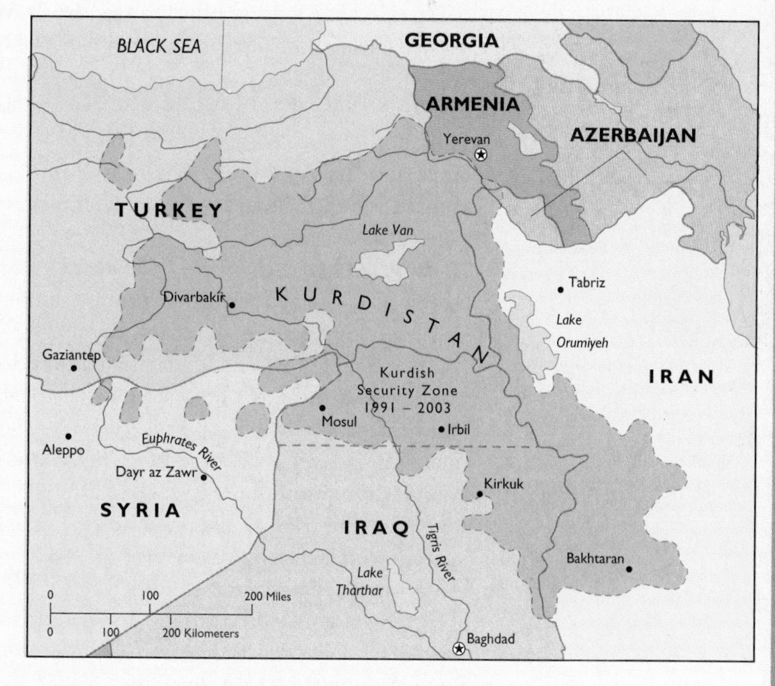

Jordan in an area called the West Bank (of the Jordan River), and 150,000 remained in the new state of Israel.

Since then, Israel has fought and won three more wars with its Arab neighbors. In the 1967 war Israel captured considerable territory, including Gaza from Egypt and the West Bank (including East Jerusalem) from Jordan. Both these areas had major Palestinian

Did You Know That:

A poll found that 16% of Israelis and 22% of Palestinians answered yes to the question, "Have you had a member of your immediate family killed in the fighting?"

populations. Victory, however, did not bring Israel peace or security. The key reason is the unresolved fate of the West Bank, which is central to Palestinians' quest for an independent homeland.

The struggle between Israelis and Palestinians for land, security, even survival has created an explosive situation that has defied resolution for over half a century. Surely, there have been times of progress. Most significantly, a majority of Israelis now grudgingly accept the idea that the Palestinians should have their own state. And most Palestinians, with equal reluctance, now concede the permanent existence of Israel and that a Palestinian state will be largely confined to the West Bank. However, each time of hope has been followed by renewed violence.

Such was the pattern in 2004 at this writing. Ghastly terrorism in Israel, often carried out by suicide bombers, and Israeli reprisals in the West Bank and Gaza finally brought yet another U.S. attempt to mediate a peace. The Bush administration's "road map" to peace once again occasioned an upwelling of hope. "Maybe history is such that now we can achieve it," President Bush told reporters.[5] The path proved largely irrelevant, though, because progress soon lost its way when Hamas and other extremist Arab groups launched new terrorist attacks inside Israel, and Israeli forces reacted with renewed deadly strikes in the West Bank that killed suspected terrorists including Hamas leader Sheikh Ahmad Yassin and many Palestinian bystanders alike. Within months the U.S. road map was in tatters and the latest quest for peace was at yet another dead end.

What the future will hold cannot be foretold. The strife in the region from Gaza to the West Bank is part of the ancient as well as current history of the Middle East. It reverberates globally in the hatred directed against the United States and other supporters of Israel, which, among other things, drives Muslim terrorists. Thus the ongoing agony of the Israelis and Palestinians is a global problem, not just a regional one.

Multiple Nations, Multiple States

Still another lack-of-fit pattern emerges when one examines the global demographic and political map closely. The most common configuration of nations and states is a complex one in which several states and several nations overlap.

Afghanistan and Neighboring Countries Afghanistan, the countries around it, and their ethnonational groups provide a prime example of the volatile mix created by overlapping borders among nations and states. Certainly Afghanistan exists as a legal state. Yet it would also be accurate to term Afghanistan a **failed state**, a country so fragmented that it cannot be said to exist as a unified political or national entity. Some scholars believe that the word "Afghan," which dates back over 1,000 years, is derived from an ancient Turkic word meaning "between." This sense of being a juncture helps to explain the ethnonational complexity within the country and the links that many of its groups have to nearby nations and countries. While there have been brief periods of some unity in the face of invaders or under strong rulers, the sense of being an Afghan has been much less central to the political identification of most people in the country than their ethnic identification.

Afghanistan's ethnic groups (and their percentage of the population) include the Pashtuns (38%) Tajiks (25%), Hazaras (19%), and Uzbeks (6%), with smaller groups making up the remaining 12%. Even this diverse recounting projects more ethnic internal unity than really exists. For example, the Pashtuns are divided into some 60 clans or tribes, each of which has a traditional territory and many of which have a history of armed conflict.

Extending the focus outward to include the neighboring countries makes the ethnonational tangle even more complex. To begin, there are 10 million Pashtuns in Afghanistan and another 18 million in neighboring, Punjabi-dominated Pakistan. Together this stateless Pashtun nation has some aspirations to found its own state, Pashtunistan. Further to the north are the Tajiks, the Uzbeks, and a small number of Turkmen, who are linked respectively to their ethnic brethren in the neighboring countries of Tajikistan, Uzbekistan, and Turkmenistan. Then there are the Hazaras, who claim descent from Genghis Khan and the Mongols and harbor some dreams about an independent Hazarajat. These groups speak some 31 different languages and dialects. Pashto is the language of the Pashtuns. Tajiks, Hazaras, and some others groups speak variations of Dari, which is akin to Farsi, the language of Iran. The Uzbeks and Turkmen speak different, but related, Turkic dialects.

One ramification of this is that the United States has found that it was far easier to take over the country in 2001 and oust the Taliban regime than to create a viable, united Afghani state. The central problem, as one expert put it, is that, "You don't have a functioning state [in Afghanistan]. There is no sense of nationhood. . . . Blood [kinship] is much more important."[6]

Russia and Neighboring Countries Czarist Russia and its successor state, the Soviet Union, were a multiethnic empire that dissolved in 1991 into Russia and 14 other former Soviet republics (FSRs). This left a hodgepodge of nations and states that frequently resembles a *matryoshka,* the classic nested Russian folk art doll in which each doll has a smaller one inside. For example, in addition to living in their own nation-state, Russians make up 10% or more of the populations of seven other FSRs (Belarus, Estonia, Kazakhstan, Kyrgyzstan, Latvia, Moldova, and Ukraine).

Russia itself is predominantly Russian, but it has some difficult ethnonational problems. The status of the Chechens is the most serious of these. The approximately 1 million Chechens are a largely Islamic people living in the northern Caucasus region just west of the Caspian Sea. Chechnya (or the Chechen Republic) encompasses about 6,000 square miles (a bit larger than Connecticut). Imperial Russia began a campaign in 1783 that eventually conquered the territory, but the Chechens' ongoing resistance was so strong that one Russian military governor warned there would be "no peace as long as a single Chechen remains alive."[7]

During World War II, Moscow deported the entire Chechen population to Siberia in the east because Soviet dictator Josef Stalin suspected the Chechens might assist the invading Germans in return for independence. More than one-third of all Chechens died during their time in Siberia, but they remained defiant. The Chechens were allowed to return to their native land in the mid-1950s but remained restive. Once the USSR dissolved, their quest for self-rule redoubled. Amid ferocious fighting that has cost between 60,000 to 100,000 lives, they achieved a level of autonomy in 1996, then lost it in early 2000 when Russian arms again overran them. The struggle continues, however, with sporadic, often brutal fighting in Chechnya and occasional Chechen terrorist attacks in Russia. One of these in late 2002 cost the lives of over 100 Russians when Chechens took over a theater during a performance and Russian forces launched an ill-fated rescue mission. In February 2004 another attack killed 39 Russians and injured more than 130 others when a bomb exploded on a Moscow subway train. For now, Russia maintains a tenuous hold on Chechnya, but current Russians leaders, like czars and commissars before them, are finding it daunting to subdue a people whose national anthem asserts in part:

> Never will we appear submissive before anyone,
> Death or Freedom—we can choose only one way. . . .
> We were born at night, when the she-wolf whelped.
> God, Nation, and the Native land.

Many of the other FSRs also have complicated ethnonational compositions. As noted above, Uzbeks and Tajiks not only live in Uzbekistan and Tajikistan respectively,

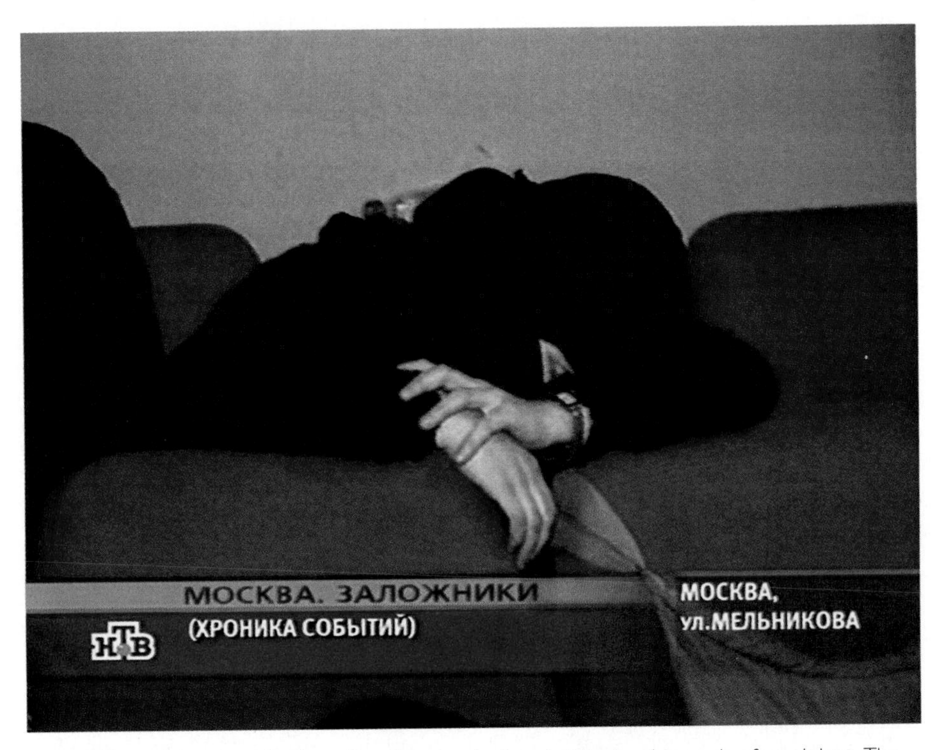

Nationalism encourages rejection of outside domination, but that resistance is often violent. The image here, taken from Russian television in October 2002, depicts this duality. The individual is not sleeping; she is dead. She and other Chechens seized a theater and its patrons in Moscow and demanded an end to Russian control of their homeland, Chechnya. Russian Spetsnaz troops used an immobilizing gas to retake the theater after a three-day siege. While 650 hostages survived, 116 others died from inhaling the gas. Fifty hostage-takers, including 18 women who said their husbands had been killed in Chechnya by Russian forces, also died. They were either killed battling the oncoming security forces or were rendered unconscious by the gas and shot where they lay.

they also live in Afghanistan. To complicate matters more, numerous Tajiks live in Uzbekistan, and many Uzbeks live in Tajikistan. To cite just one more example, the Moldovan ethnic majority in Moldova is ethnically akin to the Romanians. Therefore, there is some urge for closer association with neighboring Romania. Not everyone in Moldova feels that way, however. The ethnic Russians and Ukrainians (14% each of the population) dominate western Moldova and have formed a breakaway area styled the Transdniester Republic with the support of the Russian army. But this region itself contains 40% Moldovans, who would have irrendentist ties to greater Moldova or, perhaps, a greater Romania that had incorporated Moldova.

Nationalism: Builder and Destroyer

During an address to the UN General Assembly, Pope John Paul II spoke of two nationalisms. One was "an unhealthy form of nationalism which teaches contempt for other nations or cultures . . . [and] seeks to advance the well-being of one's own nation at the expense of others." The other nationalism involved "proper love of one's country . . . [and] the respect which is due to every [other] culture and every nation."[8] What the pope could see is that nationalism, like the Roman god Janus, has two faces. Nationalism has been a positive force, but it has also brought despair and destruction to the world.

The Beneficent Face of Nationalism

Most scholars agree that in its philosophical and historical genesis, nationalism was a positive force. It continues to have a number of possible beneficial effects.

Nationalism promotes democracy. Popular sovereignty, the idea that the state is the property of its citizens, is a key element of modern nationalism. If the state is the agent of the people, then the people should decide what policies the state should pursue. This is democracy, and in the words of one scholar, "Nationalism is the major form in which democratic consciousness expresses itself in the modern world" (O'Leary, 1997:222). In short, nationalism promotes the idea that political power legitimately resides with the people and that governors exercise that power only as the agents of the people. The democratic nationalism that helped spur the American Revolution has spread globally, especially since World War II, increasing the proportion of the world's countries that are fully democratic from 28% in 1950 to 46% in 2003.

Nationalism discourages imperialism. During the past 100 years alone, nationalism has played a key role in the demise of the contiguous Austro-Hungarian, Ottoman, and Russian empires and of all or most of the colonial empires controlled by Belgium, France, Great Britain, Italy, the Netherlands, Portugal, and the United States. More recently, nationalism was the driving force behind the birth of the newest state, East Timor.

East Timor was one of the last remnants of the more than 450-year-old Portuguese empire when its people declared their independence in 1975. That independence was stillborn, however, when the Indonesian military annexed it in a bloody takeover that cost some 60,000 East Timorese lives. For the East Timorese, Indonesian overlords were no more acceptable than European colonial masters, and their campaign for self-determination continued. This drive and considerable international pressure finally persuaded Indonesia to allow a referendum on independence in 1998, which resulted in a 79% vote in favor of independence. In response, an army of thugs armed by Indonesia's military went on a rampage, killing thousands and destroying vast amounts of property. The devastation was finally stopped when Australia and then the United Nations intervened militarily. The UN created a transitional administration for East Timor, then turned the government over to a fully independent East Timor on May 20, 2002.

Nationalism has also strengthened the resolve of countries and their nation(s) to resist foreign domination. Less than a century ago, the establishment of a colonial government controlled by the victorious power might have followed a conflict such as the Iraq war of 2003. There were some charges that the United States might try to set up a puppet regime in Baghdad, but there was never any question that power soon would have to be turned over to Iraqis. Global norms would have reacted too strongly against a colonial takeover. Moreover, even if that had been the U.S. intention, it soon became clear that Iraqis, whatever their ethnic and religious internal divisions, were opposed to control of their country by any outside power.

Nationalism allows for economic development. Many scholars see nationalism as both a facilitator and a product of modernization. Nationalism created larger political units in which commerce could expand. The prohibition of interstate tariffs and the control of interstate commerce by the national government in the 1787 American Constitution are examples of that development. With the advent of industrialization and urbanization, the local loyalties of the masses waned and were replaced by a loyalty to the national state.

Subordinate nations have usually been shortchanged economically. This has been true in colonial empires, like those once controlled by the British and French. It has also been the case in theoretically integrated multiethnic empires, such as the Soviet Union, where the six predominantly Muslim FSRs (Azerbaijan, Kazakhstan, Kyrgyzstan, Tajikistan, Turkmenistan, and Uzbekistan) were neglected under Russian/Soviet control and still have an average per capita gross domestic product (GDP) that is only about 37% of

Russia's and an infant mortality rate that is 62% higher than that of Russia. It is certain that these new countries face years of economic hardship, but, from their perspective, at least their efforts will be devoted to their own betterment.

Nationalism allows diversity and experimentation. It has been argued that regional or world political organization might lead to an amalgamation of cultures or, worse, the suppression of the cultural uniqueness of the weak by the strong. By contrast, diversity of culture and government promotes experimentation. Democracy, for instance, was an experiment in America in 1776 that might not have occurred in a one-world system dominated by monarchs. Diversity also allows different cultures to maintain their own values. Political culture varies, for example, along a continuum on which the good of the individual is at one end and the good of the society is at the other end. No society is at either extreme of the continuum. Americans are among those who tend toward the individualism end and its belief that the rights of the individual are more important than the welfare of the society. By contrast, the Chinese provide an example of people who tend more toward the communitarian end of the continuum and hold that the rights of the individual must be balanced against those of the society and sometimes even be subordinated to the common good.

The Troubled Face of Nationalism

For all its contributions, nationalism also has a dark side. "Militant nationalism is on the rise," President Clinton cautioned not long ago, "transforming the healthy pride of nations, tribes, religious, and ethnic groups into cancerous prejudice, eating away at states and leaving their people addicted to the political painkillers of violence and demagoguery."[9] Clinton's warning was based on fact. The number of ongoing ethnonational conflicts over self-determination rose steadily from four in 1956 to 41 in 1990. Since then, the number declined steadily to 22 in 2002. It is possible that ethnonational conflict has peaked and will continue to decline, but it is too early to tell whether the drop since 1990 is an anomaly or a positive sign (Fearon & Laitin, 2003). Unfortunately, whatever the number of conflicts, the intensity and magnitude of ethnonational conflicts remain high, as evident in Figure 4.1 (Marshall & Gurr, 2003). Moreover, these internal conflicts can become internationalized given the evidence that "states suffering from ethnic rebellions are more likely to use force and to use force first when involved in international disputes than states without similar insurgency problems" (Trumbore, 2003:183).

Although it has a number of aspects, the troubling face of nationalism begins with how nations relate to one another. By definition, nationalism is feeling a kinship with the other "like" people who make up the nation. Differentiating ourselves from others is not intrinsically bad, but it is only a small step from the salutary effects of positively valuing our we-group to the negative effects of devaluing they-groups. Four aspects of negative nationalism are lack of concern for others, exceptionalism and xenophobia, internal oppression, and external aggression.

Lack of Concern for Others The mildest, albeit still troubling, trait of negative nationalism is a lack of identification with others. Because we identify with our we-group, we tend to consider the they-group as apart from us. As a result, our sense of responsibility—even of human caring—for the "theys" is more limited than for our we-group. People in most countries accept significant responsibility to assist the least fortunate citizens of their national we-group through national social welfare budgets. The key is that we not only want to help others in our we-group, but that we feel we have a duty to do so.

Internationally, most of us feel much less responsible. Horrendous conditions and events can occur in other countries that evoke little notice relative to the outraged reaction that would be forthcoming if they happened in our own country. In sub-Saharan

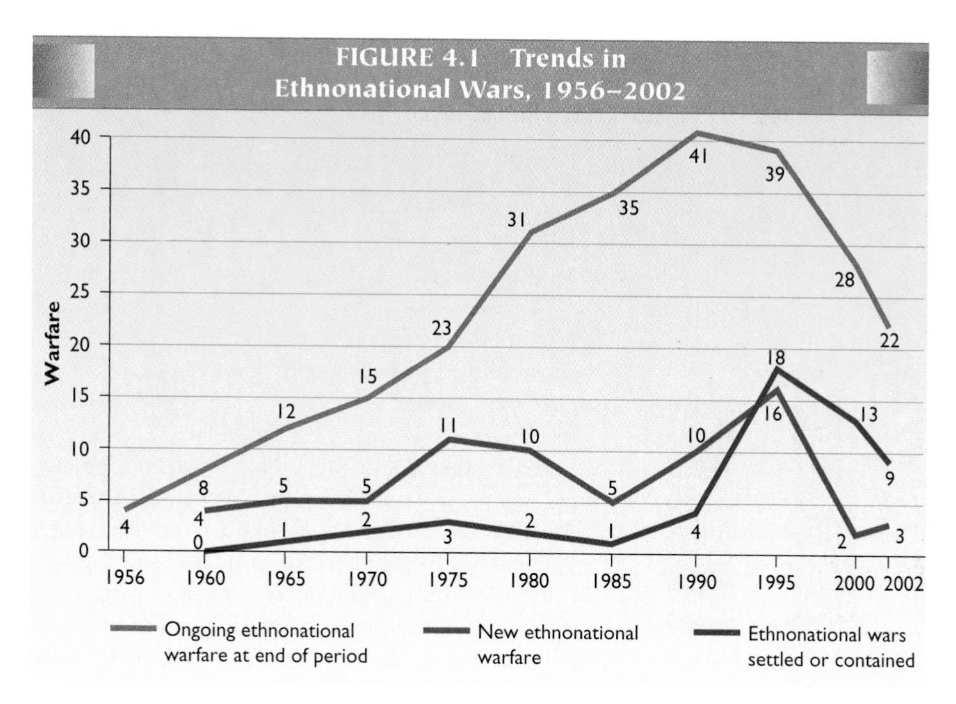

FIGURE 4.1 Trends in Ethnonational Wars, 1956–2002

The number of ethnopolitical conflicts within countries rose steadily from the 1950s to 1990, and these conflicts were much more common than wars between countries. Then the number began to decline in the 1990s. Notice that the number of new wars reached a five-year high of 16 in 1991–1995, but 18 existing conflicts were settled or won during the period, slightly reducing the number of continuing wars at the end of the period. With only five new conflicts in the 1996–2000 and 2001–2002 periods, and with 22 wars concluded, the number of conflicts at the end of 2002 was the lowest in more than three decades. Whether this trend represents a short-term anomaly or a new period of much reduced domestic conflict remains to be seen.

Note: New wars are those beginning since the end of the previous earlier date. Completed wars are those settled or won since the previous earlier date.

Data source: Marshall and Gurr (2003).

Africa, for example, the prevalence of HIV/AIDS is 371 times higher than in the United States. Only 41% of that region's people live to age 55, compared to 80% of Americans. And the chances of an infant in sub-Saharan Africa perishing before his or her first birthday are 15 times greater than the risk to American babies. The grim data could continue, but that is not necessary.

The U.S. response to this ongoing human tragedy is largely limited to sending about $1 billion in economic aid to the region. That comes to about $1.48 per person in sub-Saharan Africa or about $3.51 per American. Is this enough? Some 60% of Americans polled in 2002 thought their country was spending too much on foreign aid. Only 9% thought it too little.[10] In part, that is because, on average, Americans think that 31% of the federal budget goes to foreign aid.[11] The actual percentage is about 1% for all foreign aid, with about six-tenths of 1% for economic assistance. Ironically, the average respondent thought foreign aid should be cut to 19% of the federal budget, which would actually be a monumental increase. None of this is meant to paint Americans as particularly mean spirited. They are not. It is simply that they, like people in other countries, have a sense of responsibility for citizens of their own country, but not toward those of other countries. Therefore, most people contend, government aid should go primarily toward addressing needs "at home" rather than abroad.

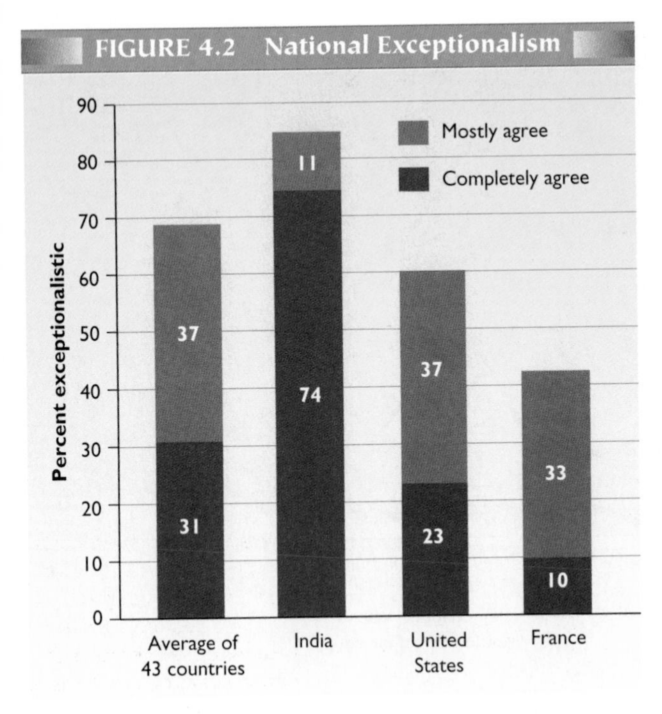

Exceptionalism, feeling that your culture is superior to others, is one negative aspect of nationalism. One recent survey of 43 countries found that 68% of people "completely agree" or "mostly agree" that "our people are not perfect, but our culture is superior to others." This included majorities in all but four countries (Angola, France, Germany, and Great Britain). The people of India were the most exceptionalistic. Especially note the astounding 74% of Indians who completely agreed. The French were the least exceptionalistic, with Americans expressing that view a bit less than average.

Data source: Pew Research Center (2003).

Exceptionalism and Xenophobia If the positive emotion of valuing one's nation is one face of nationalism, its other side involves feeling superior to or even fearing and hating others. **Exceptionalism** is the belief by some that their nation is better than others. A global survey taken in 43 countries found that a majority of people in 39 of them "completely" or "mostly" agreed with the statement, "Our people are not perfect, but our culture is superior to others." On average, 68% of people felt this way. Indians were the most exceptionalistic, and, defying a common stereotype, the French were least exceptionalistic. The view of people in these two countries and others is shown in Figure 4.2.

Fortunately less frequent, but an even more negative way some people relate to they-groups is **xenophobia,** the suspicion, dislike, or fear of other nationalities. Negative nationalism also often spawns feelings of national superiority and superpatriotism, and these lead to internal oppression and external aggression (Kateb, 2000). It is this reality that moved Voltaire to lament in 1764 that "it is sad that being a good patriot often means being the enemy of the rest of mankind."[12]

Feelings of hatred between groups are especially apt to be intense if there is a history of conflict or oppression. Past injuries inflicted "by another ethnic group [are] remembered mythically as though the past were the present," according to one scholar.[13] Understanding the depths that xenophobia can reach helps explain much of what has happened in the Balkans since the early 1990s. For Serbs, this heroic lore centers on the battle of Kosovo in 1389, in which the Ottoman Turks defeated Serbia's Prince Lazar, thus beginning five centuries of Muslim domination. The battle, according to one commentary, is "venerated among the Serbs in the same way Texans remember the Alamo." Adds Serb historian Dejan Medakovic, "Our morals, ethics, mythology were created at that moment, when we were overrun by the Turks. The Kosovo cycle, the Kosovo myth is something that has permeated the Serbian people."[14] The festering mythic wound of 1389 for the predominately Christian Orthodox Serbs spilled its poison through so-called ethnic cleansing attacks by Serbs on Bosnian Muslims in the early 1990s, then on Kosovar Muslims later in the decade.

Oppression and Aggression If negative nationalism were confined to feelings, it might not be so worrisome. But a sense of superiority or unreasoned fear or loathing often leads to domestic oppression and external aggression.

Internal oppression is common. Indeed, it is rare to find a multinational country in which the dominant ethnonational group does not have political, economic, and social advantages over the other group or groups. Perhaps inevitably, this inequality of circumstance causes the disadvantaged groups to become restive. This often leads to conflict because the complaints of the oppressed are not easily resolved. The reason, as UN

Secretary-General Kofi Annan has pointed out, is that the minority group's social and economic inequality "tends to be reflected in unequal access to political power that too often forecloses paths to peaceful change."[15]

Domestic nationalist intolerance can also lead to conflict when, as one scholar notes, it becomes "a scavenger [that] feeds upon the preexisting sense of nationhood" and seeks "to destroy heterogeneity" by trying to suppress the culture of minority groups, or by driving them out of the country (Keane, 1994:175). This aptly characterizes the Serbs' ethnic cleansing frenzy in Bosnia and Kosovo and also the genocidal attacks on the Tutsis by the Hutus in Rwanda.

The earlier, multinational state of Yugoslavia, since renamed Serbia and Montenegro, collapsed because it did not command the internal loyalty of most of its people. Instead, Yugoslavia atomized amid deadly conflict into the states and restive provinces shown here.

At its farthest extreme, nationalism engenders the sense of superiority and hatred of the kind that festered in Nazi Germany. The Germans thought that their "Aryan nation" was at the top of a ladder that descended to the Slavic peoples at the bottom, who were considered marginal humans, to be kept as virtual and expendable slaves in segregated and degrading conditions. Jews and Gypsies were "nonpeople" and "racial vermin" to be exterminated, along with the insane and homosexuals. "The highest purpose of a *folkish* state," Hitler preached in *Mein Kampf,* is "preservation of those original racial elements which bestow culture and create the beauty of a higher humanity. We, as Aryans, can conceive of the state only as a living organism of [German] nationality."

External aggression can also be the product of negative nationalism. Exceptionalism, for example, can lead to the belief that it is acceptable to conquer "lesser" nations or, indeed, even to the notion that they will be improved by being subjugated and having their cultures replaced by that of the conqueror.

Underneath its ideological trappings, the Soviet Union was a classic multiethnic empire built on territories seized by centuries of czarist Russian expansion and furthered by Soviet arms. From its beginning 500 years ago as the 15,000-square-mile Duchy of Moscovy (half the size of Maine), Russia, and then the USSR, ultimately grew to be the world's largest country. This expansion is shown in the map on page 118.

Many of those territories have been lost, but there are strong suspicions that a rejuvenated Russia will try to reclaim them. Such concerns have been heightened by a number of actions or statements, including the 1996 passage by Russia's parliament, the Duma, of a resolution expressing the view that the dissolution of the Soviet Union had been illegal and, by inference, that all the now-independent FSRs should once again come under Moscow's control.

Russia's current weakened position means that it is not in a position even to consider trying to reassert the earlier domination of its neighbors that existed during the days of czars and communist cadres. Indeed, old-fashioned imperialism may have become too costly economically and diplomatically to pursue in the future. Yet there is gnawing concern that the German theoretician Karl Marx was prescient when he warned long ago that "the policy of Russia is changeless. Its methods, its tactics, its maneuvers may change, but the polar star of its policy—world domination—is a fixed star."[16]

Self-Determination as a Goal

Along with the fact the ideal nation-state is more myth than reality and that nationalism has a troubled as well as beneficent face, a third issue related to nationalism is the wisdom of self-determination as a goal (Danspeckgruber, 2002). **Self-determination** is the idea that every nation should be able to govern itself as it chooses. If being a proud member

Nationalism has positive and negative effects, and both are illustrated in the history of Russia. Among the negative effects, nationalism often prompts expansionism. The Grand Duchy of Moscovy was about half the size of Maine when it was founded in about 1480. It expanded under Russian czars and then Soviet commissars to become what was the world's largest country.

of a nation is good for you, and if the nationalistic urge of your people to govern itself in its own nation-state is laudable, then should not that privilege—or perhaps right—be extended to everyone?

Positive Aspects of Self-Determination

Many observers have argued that self-determination is a lofty goal that should be supported. For one, American philosopher William James (1842–1910) judged "the attempt of a people long enslaved to attain the possession of itself, to organize its laws and government, to be free to follow its internal destinies, according to its own ideals" to be "the sacredest thing in this great human world."[17] Similarly, President Woodrow Wilson told Congress in 1918 that "self-determinism is not a mere phrase. It is an imperative principle of action."[18] Moreover, the origins of many of the nation-states that exist are rooted in the demand for self-determination of their nation. For example, the Declaration of Independence asserts in its first sentence the determination of Americans to "assume among the powers of the earth, the separate and equal station to which the laws of nature and of nature's God entitle them."

Certainly, there are numerous good reasons to support self-determination. In addition to the benefits of nationalism noted earlier, self-determination ends many of the abuses that stem from ethnic oppression. If all ethnic groups were allowed to peacefully found their own sovereign units or join those of their ethnic brethren, then the tragedies of Bosnia, Chechnya, East Timor, Kosovo, Rwanda, and many other strife-torn peoples and countries would not have occurred.

Concerns about Self-Determination

The ideal of self-determination becomes more problematic when its application is examined in detail. Although it is impossible to determine exactly where the ultimate limits of national identification are, there are thousands of ethnic groups worldwide (Levinson, 1998). Each has the potential to develop a national consciousness and to seek independence or autonomy. Before dismissing such an idea as absurd, recall that political scientists widely recognize the existence of Barber's (1996) tribalism tendency: the urge to break away from current political arrangements and, often, to form into smaller units. To do so involves several potential problems.

Untangling Groups Untangling groups is one challenge presented by self-determination. Various nations are intermingled in many places. Bosnia is such a place; Bosnian Muslims, Croats, and Serbs often lived in the same cities, on the same streets, in the same apartment buildings. How does one disentangle these groups and assign them territory when each wants to declare its independence or to join with its ethnic kin in an existing country?

A second problem that the principle of self-determination raises is the prospect of dissolving existing states, ranging from Canada (Quebec), through Great Britain (Scotland and Wales), to Spain (Basque region and Catalonia). Americans also need to ponder this problem. They have long advocated the theory of a right of self-determination. One has to wonder, however, how Wilson would have applied this principle to national minorities in the United States. Should, for example, the principle of self-determination mean that Americans should support those native Hawaiians who claim correctly that they were subjugated by Americans a century ago and who want to reestablish an independent Hawaii?

In other places, creating ethnically homogeneous states would have multiple complexities. To create nation-states out of the various ethnonational groups in Afghanistan would require disentangling many places where the groups overlap. It would also include some groups joining neighboring countries such as Tajikistan and Uzbekistan. But then what would happen to the Tajiks who live in Uzbekistan and the Uzbeks who live in Tajikistan? And in the case of the Pashtuns, a Pashtunistan would have to be created by pieces taken out of Pakistan and Iran, as well as Afghanistan.

Did You Know That:

There is an active native Hawaiian independence movement. When a referendum was held in 1996 among native Hawaiians about their preferences for the future, 73% voted for independence. More information is available at http://www.hawaii-nation.org/.

Microstates A third problem of self-determination relates to the rapidly growing number of independent countries, many of which have a marginal ability to survive on their own. Is it wise to allow the formation of **microstates**, countries with tiny populations, territories, and/or economies? Such countries have long existed, with Andorra, Monaco, and San Marino serving as examples. But in recent years, as colonialism has become discredited, many more of these microstates have become established.

Many microstates lack the economic or political ability to stand as truly sovereign states. One set of measures can be seen in Table 4.1's comparison of a tiny Western Pacific island country, the smallest U.S. state, and the one-hundredth most populous U.S. city.

It is important to realize that Kiribati is not an isolated example. There are 40 microstates, countries with populations of less than 1 million. These microstates comprise about 20% of all the world's countries. In fact, as Figure 4.3 depicts, their combined population equals only that of Ecuador, itself a small country; it is smaller than the number of people living in Mexico City, the world's most populous city, and it is a mere 38% of California's population.

The perplexity about microstates is: Can we simultaneously support the theory of self-determination and worry about the political liability that microstates cause? This

TABLE 4.1 Characteristics of a Microstate, a U.S. State, and a U.S. City

	Kiribati	Rhode Island	Irving
Population	96,335	1,058,920	191,615
Territory (sq. mi.)	226	1,545	67
Per capita wealth*	830	29,984	35,216

*Per capita GDP for Kiribati; per capita personal income for Rhode Island and Irving, Texas.
Data source: World Almanac (2003); World Bank (2003).

Some analysts worry about instability associated with the limited ability of microstates to sustain themselves economically or to defend themselves. The sovereign state of Kiribati is smaller in most ways than the geographically smallest U.S. state, Rhode Island, and Irving, Texas, the U.S. city with only the one-hundredth largest population.

quandary is exacerbated by the fact that larger predatory powers, not the microstates, are the real source of danger. In a perfect world, the military strength of a state would not matter and its economic strength would be of less concern. But the world is not perfect. Therefore it is reasonable to evaluate microstates within the reality of the international system that exists. Most microstates have scant ability to defend themselves against internal or external attack. The world's newest country, East Timor, needed outside military help to achieve independence from Indonesia, and if that country sought to reassert control, the 228 million Indonesians would quickly vanquish the 753,000 East Timorese unless they once again received external military assistance.

Many microstates also lack a sustainable economic base. "Impoverished" is the best word to describe East Timor. Its annual per capita GDP is about $520, one of the lowest in the world. Its only significant export is coffee. One bright spot is that Australia has agreed to begin paying East Timor $180 million in annual oil and gas royalties once energy begins to flow from undersea drilling in the so-called Timor Gap between the two countries. Even those revenues, however, would only increase the per capita income to $759. This profound poverty has serious consequences for East Timor's citizens. Life expectancy is only 55 years. Over 12% of East Timorese children die before they reach their fifth birthday. There are only about 30 physicians and another 400 or so health professionals in the country. The question then is: Objectively, is the global community better off with yet another microstate?

This question is not abstract. Existing countries face important choices when deciding whether to recognize new countries. Among other things, as new countries come into existence, the global community, through its commitments to the United Nations and to the integrity of the international system, acquires some obligation to assist them in the face of external aggression. Similarly, new and impoverished states add

FIGURE 4.3 The Combined Populations of 40 Microstates Compared to California, Mexico City, and Ecuador

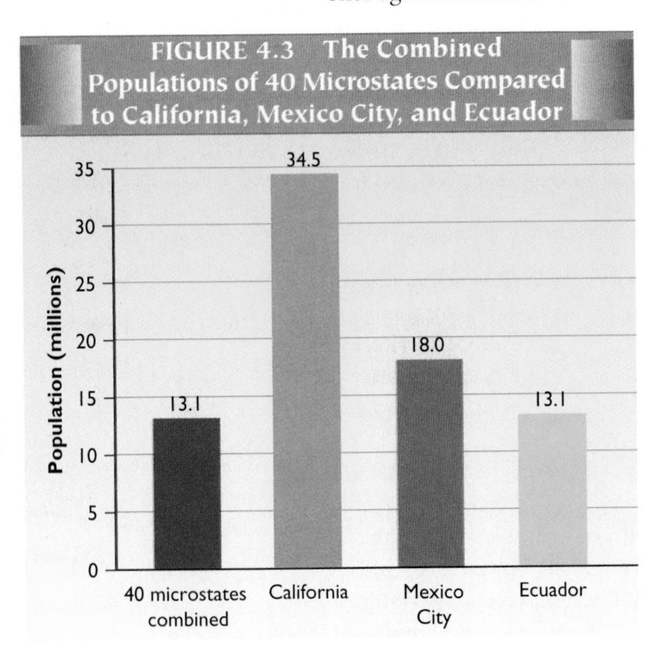

The combined population of the world's 40 countries with populations less than 1 million is equal to the population of Ecuador, smaller than that of Mexico City (the world's most populous city), and 38% that of California.

Data sources: World Almanac, 2003; World Bank (2003); author's calculations.

pressure on already inadequate international economic assistance through donor countries and international organizations. Furthermore, recognizing secessionist movements as new states arguably encourages yet more ethnonational groups to seek independence.

Given that there is a large array of ethnonational groups with aspirations that arguably are just as legitimate as were American goals in 1776, the issue is whether to support them at all, or if not, which ones and why? Some commentators advocate broad support of self-determination, which one analyst calls "the most powerful idea in the contemporary world" (Lind, 1994:88). Others reply that "self-determination movements . . . have largely exhausted their legitimacy. . . . It is time to withdraw moral approval from most of the movements and see them for what they mainly are—destructive" (Etzioni, 1993:21; Dahbour, 2003). Between these two ends of the spectrum of opinion, many seek a set of standards by which to judge whether or not a claim to the right of secession is legitimate. One such standard is whether a minority people is being discriminated against by a majority population (Hannum, 1999). Perhaps it would be wiser for the international community to guarantee human and political rights for minority cultural groups than to support self-determination to the point of *reductio ad absurdum*. Whatever the standard, though, it is certain that applying the principle of self-determination is difficult in a complex world (Ramet, 2000; Talbott, 2000).

Self-determination, the idea that every nation should be free to govern itself, is a noble thought. In practice, though, it can lead to difficulties, including the creation of microstates that have little ability to defend or support themselves. The newest country, East Timor, was born on May 20, 2002, but the joy that the East Timorese felt was soon overtaken by the country's crushing problems. With an annual per capita gross domestic product of just $520, many East Timorese are as poor as this mother and child shown here in the country's capital, Dili.

Nationalism and the Future

People have almost certainly always identified with one or another group, be it based on family, extended clan, religion, or some other basis. However, nationalism, the particular form of political identification that welds a mutually identifying people, their territory, and self-governance is much more recent. Some scholars find traces of nationalism extending back to ancient times, but there is little disagreement that nationalism has only been an important political idea for the past 400 to 500 years and that it did not reach its current ascendancy as a source of primary political identification until the 19th and 20th centuries.

What of the future, though? Since nationalism has not always been, it is not immutable. It could weaken or even disappear as our dominant sense of political identification. In addition to exploring this possibility, we should ask ourselves how we would evaluate the persistence or demise of nationalism. Would that be positive or negative?

The Recent Past and Present of Nationalism

Nationalism and our attitudes about it have continued to evolve over the last half-century or so. Attitudes toward it have weakened in some circles, and there are those who both predict and advocate its diminution or extinction as the primary focus of

Some analysts predicted after World War II that nationalism was dying. The obituary notice proved premature, and nationalism continues to determine most people's political identification. Now, however, there are signs that nationalism and the related concept of sovereignty are weakening.

political identification. Yet in many ways nationalism continues to thrive and dominate our political consciousness.

The Predicted Demise of Nationalism

World War II marked a sharp change in liberal philosophy about nationalism. Many observers blamed fascism and other forms of virulently aggressive nationalism for the horrors of the war and argued that the second global war in 30 years demonstrated that the state system based on national antagonism was not only outdated but dangerous. The advent of weapons of mass destruction seemed to add urgency to the case. As one scholar put it, "the nation and the nation-state are anachronisms in the atomic age."[19] Serving as a counterpoint, the newly established (1945) United Nations symbolized the desire to progress from conflictive nationalism toward cooperative globalism.

The thrust of this thinking led numerous scholars to predict the imminent demise of the national state or, at least, its gradual withering away. As it turned out, such retirement announcements and obituaries proved reminiscent of the day in 1897 when an astonished Mark Twain read in the paper that he had died. Reasonably sure that he was still alive, Twain hastened to assure the world: "The reports of my death are greatly exaggerated." Similarly, after reviewing the predictions of nationalism's impending extinction, one scholar notes that "this infuriatingly persistent anomaly . . . refused to go away" (Wiebe, 2001:2). Instead, nationalism gained strength as a world force.

Persistent Nationalism

The continued strength of nationalism is summarized in Figure 4.4, which shows that between 1940 and 2003 the number of states increased 278%. For most of this time, the primary force behind the surge of nationalism was the anti-imperialist independence movements in Africa, Asia, and elsewhere. More recently, nationalism has reasserted itself in Europe. Germany reemerged when West Germany and East Germany reunited. More commonly, existing states disintegrated. Yugoslavia dissolved into five countries and Czechoslovakia became two states. Soon another state became 15 countries when the last great multiethnic empire, the vast realm of Russia, then the USSR, sank under its own ponderous weight like a woolly mammoth in the La Brea tar pits. Except for East Timor, Eritrea, Namibia, and Palau, all of the states that have achieved independence since 1989 are in Eastern Europe or are FSRs. There are also nationalist stirrings—in some cases demands—among the Scots, Irish, and Welsh in Great Britain; the Basques and Catalans in Spain; and among other ethnonational groups elsewhere in Europe.

The Future of Nationalism

It may seem contradictory, but the continuing strength of nationalism does not necessarily mean that those who earlier predicted its demise were wrong. Perhaps they were only premature. That possibility is raised by numerous signs that nationalism is waning and that states are weakening. Therefore, a critical question is whether nationalism will significantly weaken or even die out.

The answer is unclear. The existence of divergent identities based on language and other cultural differences extends as far back into time as we can see. From a biblical perspective, there may have been a single people at the time of Adam and Eve and their immediate descendants. But later in the first book of the Bible, God divides them after they attempt to build the Tower of Babel up to the heavens. To defeat that pretentious plan, God creates different languages to complicate communication. "Behold," God

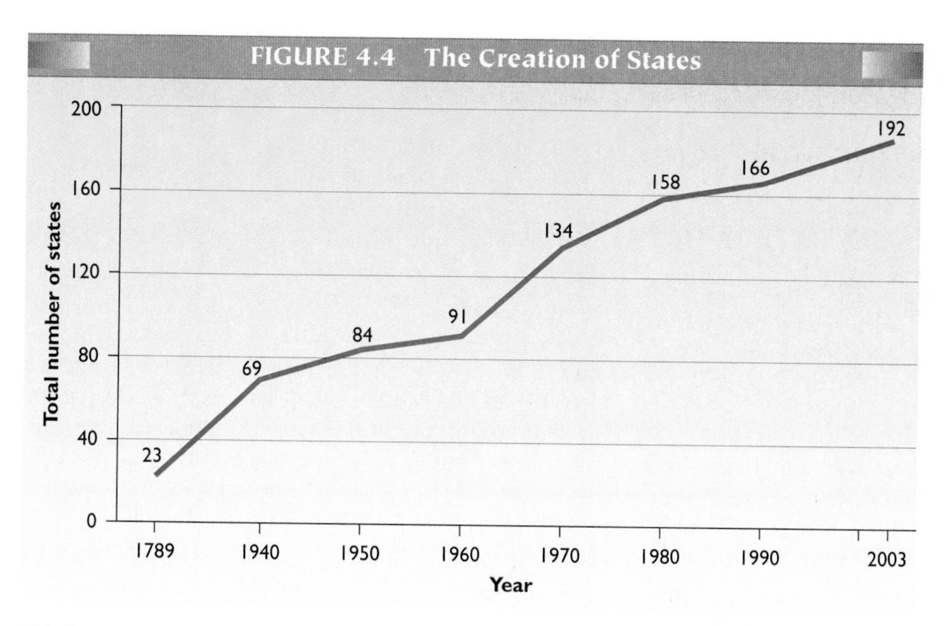

This figure portrays the rapid growth in the number of countries in the international system. From the beginning of the sovereign states about 500 years ago, it took until 1940 for 69 states to evolve. In the intervening 60 years, that number has nearly tripled.

commands, "the people is one, and they have all one language. . . . [L]et us go down, and there confound their language, that they may not understand one another's speech" (Genesis 11:6–7).

Whether this tale is taken literally or symbolically, the point is that diverse cultural identities are ancient and, some analysts would say, important, perhaps inherent, human traits, stemming from the urge to have the psychological security of belonging to a we-group. One scholar contends, for example, that being a member of a nation both "enables an individual to find a place . . . in the world [in] which he or she lives" and also to find "redemption from personal oblivion" through a sense of being part of "an uninterrupted chain of being" (Tamir, 1995:432). Yet it must also be said that group identification and nationalism are not synonymous. The sense of sovereignty attached to cultural identification is relatively modern. "Nationalism and nations have not been permanent features of human history," as one scholar puts it (O'Leary, 1997:221). Therefore, nationalism, having not always existed, will not necessarily always be the world's principal form of political orientation.

Did You Know That:

There are 6,809 languages spoken in the world. That is a decline of 306 since 1600, with another 7% currently in danger of extinction.

What does the future hold? Some scholars believe that nationalism will continue to flourish as the main source of political identification. "Given that globalization has done little to diminish the nation's political [and] ideological . . . appeal—and in many cases has invigorated it," one scholar writes, "we are stuck with the nation—politically, academically, practically, and theoretically" (Croucher, 2003:21). Other scholars expect nationalism to eventually cease to be an important political phenomenon. The most common view among political scientists is a middle position that holds that nationalism will persist for the foreseeable future as a key sense of the political identification of most people but that it will not enjoy the unrivaled center stage presence it has had for several hundred years (Ishiyama & Breuning, 1998).

Also unclear is what would follow if state-centric nationalism were to die out. Some scholars believe that it will be replaced by culture, religion, or some other demographic characteristic as the primary sense of political self. Yet another group of scholars argues

YOU BE THE PLAYWRIGHT

J'Accuse! Nationalism on Trial

"*J'Accuse!*" (I accuse) Émile Zola entitled an open letter written to the president of France and published in 1898 in the newspaper *L'Aurore*. In his letter, Zola charged that the French military had conspired to falsely convict Captain Alfred Dreyfus of treason and to send him to life imprisonment on Devil's Island.

Like Dreyfus, nationalism has been condemned by many as a danger, while others reject the charges as baseless, even subversive. The criticisms of nationalism enumerated in this chapter—that it is a divisive, destructive, and anachronistic concept—are only representative of the scorn heaped on it by some. "Nationalism appeals to our tribal instincts, to passion and to prejudice," one scholar has written. According to another, nationalism has a "built-in capacity for descent into dementia."[1] And Albert Einstein wrote, "Nationalism is an infantile disease. It is the measles of mankind."[2]

The chapter has also presented the positive aspects of nationalism as our primary political identity. Giuseppe Mazzini, one of the founders of modern Italy, argued, "Without country you have neither name, token, voice, nor rights, nor admission as brothers into the fellowship of the peoples." The American patriot Nathan Hale faced the gallows regretting only "that I have but one life to give for my country." In a more contemporary light, analyst Michael Lind has written that in a time of transnational terrorism, predatory multinational corporations, and other aspects of globalism, "old-fashioned nationalism is looking better and better."[3]

How do you think the ongoing script in the drama of global politics should read? Would you write nationalism out of the script as a tired character that only detracts from the play? Or are the critics of nationalism as wrong as the French military was about Captain Dreyfus? He was freed from Devil's Island and eventually exonerated. Now nationalism is in the dock. How say you: *innocent ou coupable* (innocent or guilty)?

that a sense of global nationalism could emerge based on the similarities among all humans and their common experiences, needs, and goals. One such scholar envisages "a nation coextensive with humanity" that would then come together in a "United States of the World" (Greenfeld, 1992:7).

What can we conclude from this scholarly disagreement? Will nationalism persist "until the last syllable of recorded time," to borrow words from Shakespeare's *Macbeth*? The answer is that the script for tomorrow's drama on the world stage is still being written by the world's political playwrights. If we think the world drama important, each of us should lend a hand to establish the plot, cast the actors, and write the dialogue. Join in as urged by the You Be the Playwright box "*J'Accuse!* Nationalism on Trial."

Chapter Summary

Understanding Nations, Nationalism, and Nation-States

1. Nationalism is one of the most important factors in international politics. It defines where we put our primary political loyalty, and that is in the nation-state. Today the world is divided and defined by nationalism and nation-states.
2. Nations, nation-states, and nationalism are all key concepts that must be carefully defined and clearly differentiated and understood.
3. The political focus on nationalism has evolved and become ascendant over the last five centuries.

Nationalism in Practice: Issues and Evaluation

4. There are differences between the theory of nationalism and its application. These must be considered to evaluate nationalism objectively.
5. One issue is that the ideal nation-state is more myth than reality. In practice the boundaries of nations and the borders of states are seldom congruent.

6. Another issue is negative aspects, as well as positive aspects of nationalism.
7. The problems associated with nationalism also raise issues about self-determination and the question of whether this liberal ideal is always wise in the real world.

Nationalism and the Future

8. After World War II, some predicted an end to nationalism, but they were wrong. Today nationalism is stronger, and the independence of Afro-Asian countries, the former Soviet republics, and other states has made it even more inclusive.
9. In a world of transnational global forces and problems, many condemn nationalism as outmoded and perilous. Some even predict its decline and demise. Such predictions are, however, highly speculative, and nationalism will remain a key element and a powerful force in the foreseeable future.

For a chapter quiz, interactive activities, web links, PowerWeb articles, and much more, visit **www.mhhe.com/rourke10/** and go to chapter 4. Or, while accessing the site, click on Course-Wide Content and view recent international relations articles in the *New York Times.*

Key Terms

ethnonational group
exceptionalism
failed state
ideology
irredentism
microstates
multinational states
multistate nation
nation
nationalism
nation-state
political identity
popular sovereignty
self-determination
state building
stateless nation
xenophobia
Zionism

CHAPTER

5

Globalization and Transnationalism: The Alternative Orientation

GLOBALIZATION
Globalization of Communications and Transportation
Economic Globalization
Cultural Globalization
TRANSNATIONALISM
Early Transnationalism
Contemporary Transnational Thought
TRANSNATIONALISM IN ACTION
Transnational Organizations
Regional Transnationalism
Cultural Transnationalism
Transnational Religion
Islam and the World
Transnational Movements
TRANSNATIONALISM TOMORROW
CHAPTER SUMMARY
KEY TERMS

A speedier course than lingering languishment
Must we pursue, and I have found the path.
—William Shakespeare, *Titus Andronicus*

Not all those that wander are lost.
—J. R. R. Tolkien, *The Fellowship of the Ring*

An invasion of armies can be resisted, but not an idea whose time has come.
—Victor Hugo, *Histoire d'un Crime,* 1852

CHAPTER OBJECTIVES

After completing this chapter, you should be able to:

- Define the concepts of globalization and transnationalism.
- Identify the various aspects of globalization and indicate how they relate to transnationalism.
- Analyze the changes in transportation, communications, international economic exchange, and cultural amalgamation, which have promoted globalization.
- Explain the evolution of transnational thought and the current theories related to transnationalism, including postmodernism, constructivism, and feminism.
- Comment knowledgeably on the growth, activity, and transnational impact of nongovernmental organizations.
- Indicate the progress of regional transnationalism in Europe.
- Examine the cohesive and divisive effects of transnational culture.
- Discuss the transnational elements of religion.
- Examine both the positive and negative roles of religion in world politics.
- Analyze, as a case study, the role of Islam in world politics.
- Discuss transnational movements.
- Outline the philosophy of the transnational women's movement.
- Identify transnational activity of the women's movement and trace its progress.

In an attempt to appeal to a new generation of car buyers and boost sagging sales a few years ago, General Motors ran an ad campaign with the slogan, "This is not your father's Oldsmobile." Something like that might be said about global realities because, for good or ill, what exists today is definitely not your father's world. To the contrary, according to one study, we are in a period of "sweeping and revolutionary changes" (Klare & Chandrani, 1998:vii).

This chapter is about the changes that the international system and its actors are undergoing, and how these new realities represent an alternative to the inward focus of nationalism, as discussed in chapter 4. These changes are increasingly taking human interaction and political identification beyond traditional national boundaries and creating myriad regional and global links. To simplify a very complex phenomenon, it is possible to divide what is occurring into two related trends: globalization and transnationalism.

Globalization is a multifaceted concept that represents the increasing integration of economics, communications, and culture across national boundaries. It is in large part the product of technological changes that have rapidly expanded the speed with which merchandise, money, people, information, and ideas all move over long distances. Certainly international trade and investment is not new, nor are travel, the exchange of knowledge and ideas, and the spread of culture across national borders. What is different, though, is the speed at which globalization is now proceeding. As discussed in chapter 2 (see Figure 2.1), about half of history's significant technological advances have occurred since 1900, and another 40% happened in the century before that. Be it the Internet, jet travel, or some other advance, a great deal of this technological innovation is moving the world away from the national orientation that has dominated for several centuries and toward a growing global connectedness.

Transnationalism both preceded and has been spurred by globalization. The two terms are closely linked, but while globalization is a process and a state of affairs, transnationalism is attitudinal and includes a range of political identities and interactions that connect humans *across nations and national boundaries.* Transnationalism is, therefore, substantially counternationalist. To a significant degree, it undermines nationalism (and its tangible manifestation, the national state) by promoting cross-national political activity and even political loyalties.

As we shall see presently, transnationalism, like globalization, is ancient. But also like globalization, the rapid growth of transnationalism is a very modern phenomenon that arguably is combining with globalization to transform global politics. In fact, some scholars believe that the antithesis of transnationalism, nationalism, could share the fate of Oldsmobiles. The carmaker's ad campaign was a monumental flop, and after 107 years of production, the last Oldsmobile rolled off an assembly line during the 2004 production year. Some believe that the drawbacks of nationalism discussed in chapter 4 make it as vulnerable to decline and perhaps even extinction as the Oldsmobile.

Globalization

Ready or not, globalization has arrived! The morning activities of your author include beginning to revise the chapter you are now reading and working on lecture notes for an afternoon introduction to international relations class. Globalization permeates these activities. The computer keyboard I am working on was made in Thailand, the mouse came from China, the monitor was produced in South Korea, and the CD I use to back up my files was manufactured in Taiwan. Both my phone and desk calculator are from Malaysia. The work I have done this morning has led me to connect with Internet sites of more than a half-dozen countries, and the top Web news story on my Web browser is about a speech President George W. Bush will make to the United Nations General Assembly today, trying to get more of its 191 member-countries to assist in the stabilization of postwar Iraq (a process costing me and other Americans billions of dollars each month). The Internet also tells me that the stock market (and thus the value of my retirement account) is down today, in part because of investor worries about the burgeoning U.S. trade deficit and the sagging value of the U.S. dollar against the euro, the yen, and other major currencies. Getting back to my immediate activities, this book will be produced in the United States, but there is a good chance the paper started as a tree in Canada, and my editor is originally from India. The shirt I am wearing is from Mauritius, my shoes are of Mexican origin, and my sweater began its existence in Ireland. My class this afternoon has students from a variety of countries beyond the United States, and my graduate assistant is Israeli.

If you think about it, globalization is probably entwined with your daily economic, communications, and cultural existence as much as it is with mine. We all live in an increasingly interconnected and, in many ways, ever more amalgamated world.

Globalization of Communications and Transportation

Globalization could not exist to the extensive degree it does without the technological ability to transport our products and ourselves rapidly and in large numbers across great distances. Similarly, globalization is dependent on the technology that permits us to transmit images, data, the written word, and sound easily and rapidly on a global basis.

Global Transportation

Modern transportation carries people and their products across national borders in volume and at a speed that would have been incomprehensible not very long ago. Ocean-going transport provides a good example. The most famous merchant vessel of the mid-1800s was the *Flying Cloud* (1851–1874), a 229-foot-long sailing ship. Now the oceans are being plied by such modern megaships as the tanker *Jahre Viking,* which at almost one-third of a mile long is so large that crew members often use bicycles on board to travel from one point to another. The immense ship can carry 564,763 tons of cargo, more than could have been carried by 900 *Flying Clouds.* Yet the *Jahre Viking* is but one of the vast world merchant fleet of almost 28,000 freighters and tankers with a total capacity to carry, at any one moment, over 733 million tons of goods. These behemoths not only can carry more cargo, but also they have expanded trade by reducing seagoing transportation costs, and thus the price of the goods they carry, from an average of $95 per ton in 1900 to $29 per ton in 1990.

Advances in transportation have been important in moving people as well as goods. When the first English settlers traveled from the British Isles to what would be Jamestown, Virginia, in 1607, the only way to make the trip was by ship, and their three tiny ships took four-and-one-half months to carry 101 settlers to their destination. Now, air transportation has reduced the time to cross the Atlantic from months to hours. As late as 1895, Lord Kelvin, president of the Royal Society, Great Britain's leading scientific advisory organization, dismissed as "impossible" the idea of "heavier-than-air flying machines."[1] Just eight years later, in 1903, Orville and Wilbur Wright proved Lord Kelvin wrong. Now the largest airliners, such as the Boeing 747-400, can carry over 500 passengers between New York and Europe in as little as seven hours.

These advances have made international travel almost routine, with hundreds of millions of travelers flying between countries each year. For example, about 25 million Americans traveled beyond North America in 2000, and about 26 million non–North

To understand the speed of technological change, think about what has occurred during the life of Charlotte Benkner of North Lima, Ohio, who was born in 1889. Flight eluded humans until she was 14 and the Wright brothers first flew in the biplane at the bottom of the poster. She was 38 when Charles A. Lindbergh made the first trans-Atlantic flight in the *Spirit of St. Louis* (second from the bottom), and she was 80 when astronauts first journeyed to the moon in the space capsule at the top. Amazing change in one lifetime!

Americans came to the United States. If travel to and from Mexico and Canada is added to these numbers, they increased to over 58 million Americans traveling out of their country and more than 48 million foreign visitors coming to the United States.

Global Communications

It is almost impossible to overstate the impact that modern communications have had on international relations (Tehranian, 1999; Vlahos, 1998). In only a century and a half, communications have made spectacular advances, beginning with the telegraph, followed by photography, radio, the ability to film events, telephones, photocopying, television, satellite communications, faxes, and now computer-based Internet contacts and information through e-mail and the World Wide Web.

The Growth of Communications Capabilities The flow of these communications is too massive to calculate precisely, but if the growth of international telephone calls are any indication, we are increasingly able to "reach out and touch someone" internationally, as the AT&T advertising slogan went. In 1993 about 1.9 billion phone calls were made from the United States to another country. That number had grown 274% to over 5.2 billion calls by 1999.

Did You Know That:

In 1900 it cost $74.89 a minute to call London from New York City. The charge was $1.32 in 1990. Now it is about 8 cents per minute.

The technological revolution in communications has also meant that more and more people around the globe are getting their news from the same sources. The most obvious example is CNN, which now reaches virtually every country in the world and broadcasts in nine languages. And while CNN carries something of an American perspective to the rest of the world, non-U.S. news networks are bringing foreign news perspectives to Americans. Al-Jazeera, which translates as "The (Arabian) Peninsula," is

Modern technology has made transnational communications an important factor in global politics. Among the news media, CNN broadcasts globally in several languages, and other news networks are extending their reach. Representing this change, this photograph shows U.S. National Security Adviser Condoleezza Rice being interviewed on Al-Jazeera, the Qatar-based Arab-language network, which also has an English-language Web site.

based in Qatar and began operations in 1996 as the first Arabic language television news network. Since then it has become well known around the world for its broadcasts of, among other things, video and audio tapes of Osama bin Laden and Saddam Hussein after those two figures were driven into hiding by U.S. forces in 2001 and 2003, respectively. The news agency has also added Internet news sites in both Arabic and English, and it claims to have more than 160 million visits a year to these sites by Internet users and to be "amongst the 50 most visited sites worldwide."

Not only are almost instantaneous news and information available over the Internet, but the number of people using the Internet is growing exponentially. As recently as 1990 there were only 2.7 million Internet users. By 2001 there were 530.2 million. Furthermore, today's Internet users are not only able to access the Web, they can communicate on it to one another via e-mail and create Web sites for themselves or their groups to share information and to promote their causes globally.

The Impact of Globalized Communications The communications revolution that has occurred in recent decades and the continuing spread of global access to information and interactive communications are of immense importance. China's Communist Party leader, Chairman Mao Zedong (1893–1976), once disingenuously encouraged intellectual inquiry and political debate by quoting a classical Chinese poem, "Let one hundred flowers bloom and one hundred schools of thought contend." Free inquiry and debate did not bloom in China in 1957 after Mao's speech, but the Internet has provided fertile ground nearly everywhere for the growth of extraordinarily diverse information, opinion, and interactive exchanges on virtually every subject.

One impact has been to facilitate the formation and growth of a multitude of transnational groups espousing causes of nearly every imaginable type. These groups, discussed in more detail later in this chapter, are flourishing and having an important impact on policy at the international level through the UN and other international organizations and on the national level through the pressure brought on governments by the groups' national chapters.

Another impact of the communications revolution is that it enables people to seek alternative information and opinions from what is normally available to them. Arabs in the Middle East can gain different views of the policy issues related to Iraq, Israel, the Palestinians, and other subjects by, for example, watching CNN or accessing its Web site. Similarly, Americans can get a reasonably firsthand view of the very different Arab perspective on these issues by accessing the Al-Jazeera site.

Yet a further effect of global communications is that they undermine authoritarian governments. As such, the rapid mass communications that are taken for granted in the industrialized democracies are still greeted with suspicion by authoritarian governments. In China, Internet users must register with the police, and fines or imprisonment await those who air dissent. Chinese authorities are also distributing required software that will block access to more than a half million international Web sites and will also track each site any user attempts to access. In the end, though, Beijing's efforts to control the Internet are probably doomed to failure. Whereas only one crimson political flower used to bloom in China, many more are now beginning to sprout.

In a process that has been labeled "democratic internationalism," transnational communications have provided citizens from different countries with the ability to interact, exchange views, organize political activity, and undertake political action (Gilbert, 1999). There are now so many examples that are facilitated through modern communications, especially the Internet, that it is tempting to say that almost any cause you might think of has a transnational network. To get some sense of this, try going to a Web search engine such as Google and keyboard in "Students for a Free Tibet," "Students United for a Responsible Global Environment," "Students for Peace," "United Students Against Sweatshops," or virtually any other political cause, and you will find college student groups organizing themselves and communicating across the world on behalf of their beliefs.

Transnational communications have enabled people from around the world to exchange information and views, organize political activity, and undertake political action. One transnational cause is the campaign against sweatshops, which employ low-wage workers in harsh conditions to make expensive products for consumers in wealthy countries. This photograph shows members of United Students Against Sweatshops unfurling a banner in front of a Nike store in a New York City mall, accusing the company of using sweatshop labor.

Economic Globalization

Economic interchange across borders is bringing the world together in many ways. The intensifying reality of economic interchange and interdependence is detailed in chapters 1, 2, and 12 and, thus, need not be reiterated beyond two basic points. First, the international economy affects each of us through our jobs, what we pay for the goods and services we consume, and many other economic aspects of our lives. Second, as economically intertwined as we are today, it is likely that the connections will grow even more complex and comprehensive. As just one indication, the degree to which we are absorbing one another's products and capital investments is evident in Figure 5.1, which shows that the increased amount of wealth both the world and the United States produce each year is related to trade and foreign investments.

What is important to see here is that economic interchange has a transnational impact that extends beyond dollars and cents. Many analysts believe that economic interchange is bringing people together transnationally through familiarity with one another and one another's products. Some of these contacts are interpersonal; more have to do with the role of international economics in narrowing cultural differences and creating a sense of identification with trading partners. About half of Japan's annual foreign trade is with the Western industrialized countries. The impact of this trade flow is evident in Japan's sense of affinity with others. One study found that when Japanese people were asked whether they more closely associated with Asian or Western countries, 54% of those willing to make a choice replied "Western countries." When asked why they identified with Western countries, 89% said it was because of "economic interaction" (Namkung, 1998:46).

Cultural Globalization

To an important degree, the early development of diverse languages, practices, and the other aspects of the world's diverse cultures was a product of the isolation of groups of people from one another. It is not surprising then that a degree of cultural amalgamation has occurred as transportation and communication have improved, thereby bringing

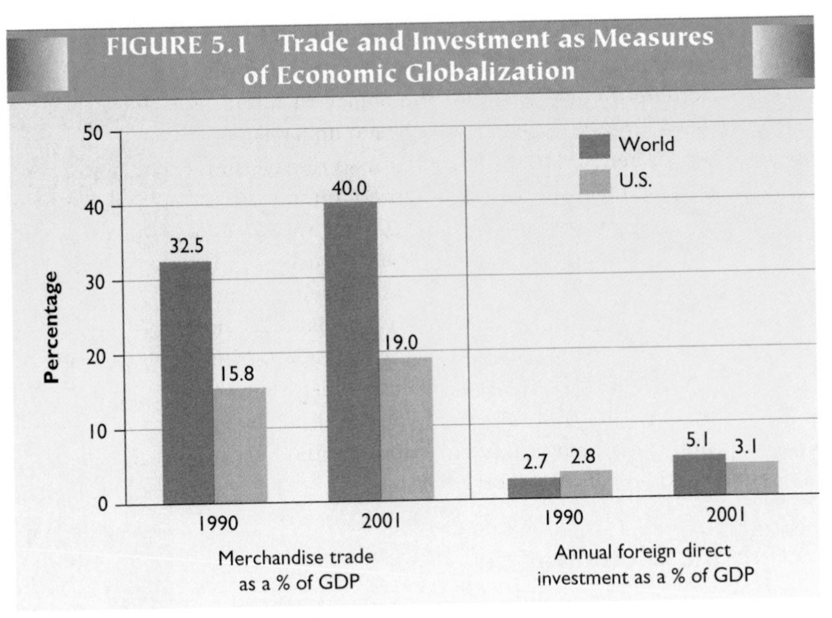

Economic globalization is characterized by the increasing economic interdependence of countries. Global merchandise (goods) trade increased between 1990 and 2001 to 40% of the world's collective economic production (gross domestic product, GDP). Even for the United States, the world's largest and perhaps most insular major economy, exports and imports are an increasing part of overall economic activity. Much the same can be said about investments. Note that for the world, the flow of direct investment (ownership of companies and real property) in and out of countries nearly doubled as a percentage of GDP during the period.

Data source: World Bank (2003).

people of various societies into ever more frequent contact. While it is far too early to speak of a world uniculture, global cultural differences have decreased substantially during the last half-century. It is also the case, though, that the drift toward cultural homogenization—McWorld in Barber's (1996) term—is meeting substantial resistance.

Discussions of the evolution of an amalgamated global culture inevitably include a great deal about fast food, basketball, rock music, e-mail, and other such aspects of pop culture. It would be an error to suppose that such examples trivialize the subject. Instead, a long line of political theory argues that the world will come together through myriad microinteractions rather than through such macroforces of political integration as the United Nations. This school of thought believes that a political community is a furtherance of **civil society**, which one scholar defined as those "areas of social life—the domestic world, the economic sphere, cultural activities and political interaction—which are organized by private or voluntary arrangements between individuals and groups outside the direct control of the state" (Held, 1987:281). From this perspective, it is arguable that a global civil society could emerge through a process of intercultural familiarization and amalgamation based on various private and voluntary interactions across national boundaries. If this occurs, then regional and even global schemes of governance could conceivably supplement or supplant the territorial state. This evolution is akin to the sequence discussed in chapter 4, whereby an ethnic group forms, becomes a nation as it acquires a desire to govern itself, and eventually carves out its own state. Scholars who examine this bottom-up process of integration on a regional or global level look for evidence in such factors as the flow of communications and commerce between countries and the spread across borders of what people wear, eat, and do for recreation.

The Spread of Common Culture

There is significant evidence of cultural amalgamation in the world. The leaders of China once wore "Mao suits"; now they wear Western-style business suits. When dressing informally, people in Shanghai, Lagos, and Mexico City are more apt to wear jeans, T-shirts, and sneakers than their country's traditional dress. Young people everywhere listen to the same music, with "Crazy in Love" by Beyoncé and Jay-Z on the top ten charts in Brazil, Sweden, Taiwan, and many other countries in addition to the United States in 2003. And whatever it means to our gastronomic future, Big Macs, fries, and milk shakes are consumed around the world.

Before looking further at the evidence of cultural amalgamation, one caution is in order. You will see that a great deal of what is becoming world culture is Western, especially American, in its origins. That does not imply that Western culture is superior; its impact is a function of the economic and political strength of Western Europe and the United States. Nor does the preponderance of Western culture in the integration process mean that the flow is one way. American culture, for example, is influenced by many "foreign imports," ranging from fajitas, through soccer, to acupuncture.

Language One of the most important aspects of converging culture is English, which is becoming the common language of business, diplomacy, communications, and even culture. President Hamid Karzai of Afghanistan and many other national leaders can converse in English. Indeed, a number of them, including Jacques Chirac of France, learned or improved their English while enrolled at U.S. universities. A bit more slowly, English is spreading among common citizens. This is evident in differences among various age groups. Among Europeans, for instance, 89% of all school children now have English instruction, and 67% of those between 15 and 24 speak at least some English compared to only 18% of Europeans over age 55 who can do so.

Modern communications are one driving force in the spread of English. There are certainly sites on the World Wide Web in many languages, but most of the software, the search engines, and information in the vast majority of Web sites are all in English. One estimate is that 90% of all Internet information and traffic is in English. As the Web master at one site in Russia comments, "It is far easier for a Russian . . . to download the works of Dostoyevsky translated in English to read than it is for him to get [it] in his own language."

Business is also a significant factor in the global growth of English. The United States is the world's largest exporter and importer of goods and services, and it is far more common for foreign businesspeople to learn the language of Americans than it is for Americans to learn other languages. A report issued by the Japanese government declared that "achieving world-class excellence demands that all Japanese acquire a working knowledge of English."[2]

English will probably continue to expand its use throughout the world. A recent survey of people in 42 countries around the world found that 85% of them "completely" or "mostly" agreed with the statement, "Children need to learn English to succeed in the world today." Moreover, as Figure 5.2 demonstrates, an overwhelming majority of people in every region of the world held that view.[3]

Consumer Products The interchange of popular consumer goods is another major factor in narrowing cultural gaps. American movies are popular throughout much of the world. Hollywood is pervasive, earning 50% of its revenue abroad—a 20% jump in 20 years. American movies dominate many foreign markets, earning 50% of all film revenues in Japan, 70% in Europe, and 83% in Latin America. By contrast, foreign films account for just 3% of the U.S. market. It is not surprising then that at one point in 2003, some countries (and their most popular movies) for the week were: Argentina (*Finding*

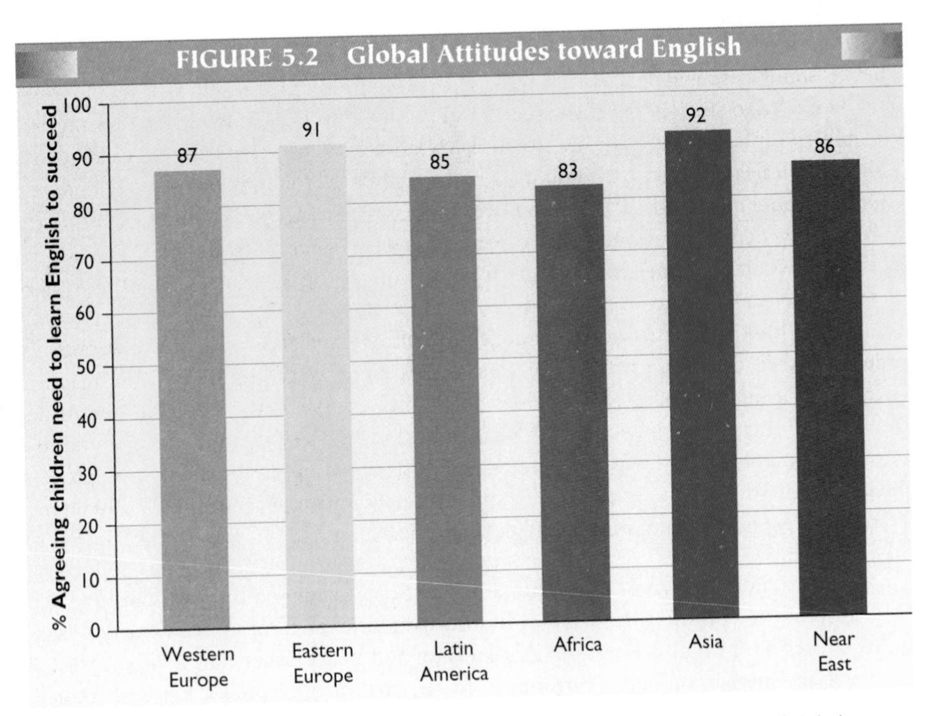

The growth of English as the language of business, the Internet, and other aspects of global communications are likely to spur the continued increase in the number of English speakers because strong majorities of people worldwide believe that it is important for their children to learn English in order to succeed in the modern world.

Note: The Near East is broader than the Middle East and stretches from Egypt to Pakistan.

Data source: Pew Research Center (2003).

Nemo), France (*Bruce Almighty*), Japan (*Terminator 3*), Russia (*Lara Croft: Tomb Raider*), South Africa (*Bad Boys II*), and Turkey (*The Matrix Reloaded*). Joining the tidal wave of visual common culture, American television programming is also increasingly omnipresent. For example, 62% of all television programs in Latin America originate in the United States.

Older American movies are available, among other places, through the more than 2,600 Blockbuster Video stores in 27 countries outside the United States. And if non-Americans want to look authentic at an American movie, they can get a pair of jeans or Dockers distributed through Levi Strauss's sales outlets in more than 100 countries, which account for about half the company's annual sales. China provides just one example of the degree to which diverse cultures have succumbed to many things American, as the In the Spotlight box "And Never the Twain Shall Meet: Until Now" relates.

To reemphasize the main point, there is a distinct and important intermingling and amalgamation of cultures under way. For good or ill, Western, particularly American, culture is at the forefront of this trend. The observation of the director-general of UNESCO, that "America's main role in the new world order is not as a military superpower, but as a multicultural superpower," is probably an overstatement, but it captures some of what is occurring (Iyer, 1996:263). What is most important is not the specific source of common culture. Rather, it is the important potential consequences of cultural amalgamation. As noted, some analysts welcome it as a positive force that will bring people and, eventually, political units together. Others see transnational culture as a danger to desirable diversity.

IN THE SPOTLIGHT

And Never the Twain Shall Meet: Until Now

"Oh, East is East, and West is West, and never the twain shall meet." Perhaps these words seemed true when Rudyard Kipling penned them in "The Ballad of East and West" (1889), but they hardly apply anymore.

As in many countries, Western pop culture has made significant inroads in China. Children there successfully pester their parents to buy them Mi Loushu (Mickey Mouse) comic books, and in January 2003 ground was broken for a $2.9 billion Hong Kong Disneyland that will begin operations in 2006. Kentucky Fried Chicken has also won many converts and now has over 900 outlets in more than 150 cities. McDonald's, with 566 outlets in about 75 cities, is the second largest fast-food company in China (Watson, 2000). A Big Mac in China in 2003 cost $1.26, a significant amount in a country where the average urban worker makes about $850 a year and the average rural worker only a third of that. Still, fast food is popular. "It's a bit expensive to eat here," one diner commented about McDonald's, "but I guess for a high-fashion restaurant like this, the prices are O.K."[1] After fortifying themselves with a *jishi hanbao* (cheeseburger), Chinese can rock and roll *(gun shi)* at a Hard Rock Cafe in Beijing or Shanghai. Finally, exhausted revelers might choose to get some rest at one of the scores of hotels in China operated by Hilton, Holiday Inn, Sheraton, and other Western chains. While at the hotel relaxing, patrons can turn on the television and watch CNN in English or change channels to watch MTV-China or catch a National Basketball Association (NBA) game. Finding one will be easy, because state television regularly broadcasts NBA games.

American YMCA missionaries brought basketball to China in the late 1890s, soon after the game was invented in the United States, which arguably makes China the second-oldest basketball playing country. Chinese fans are considered near fanatics. They shout *pee-ow liang!* (pretty) for 3-point jump shots, but their favorite is the awesome *kou qui* (slam dunk). Until recently, the now retired Michael "Air" Jordan was the favorite NBA player in China, and one observer cited a survey showing that Jordan was more popular among Chinese than Chairman Mao Zedong.[2]

Now, 7'5" Yao Ming is China's round-ball idol. Ming plays for the NBA's Houston Rockets and was the starting center for the Western Conference in the league's 2004 All-Star game. He is also a member of China's national team. If he is joined on it by China's two other NBA players, Wang Zhi-zhi (7'1") of the Los Angeles Clippers and Mengke Bateer (6'11") of the Toronto Raptors, in an anticipated front line that has already been dubbed the "Great Wall of China," their team could overcome the favored Americans and win an Olympic gold medal during the games in Athens in 2004 or when the team will be the home favorite at the 2008 Olympics in Beijing. Basketball may have begun in Springfield, Massachusetts, but American dominance of the sport will be threatened from now on whenever East meets West on the hardwood floor.

Sports are one of the many aspects of culture that are bridging the gap between East and West. The Chinese are huge basketball fans, and some Chinese players are now in the National Basketball Association. Baseball is also becoming popular in China, and Chinese players may someday join the Japanese and South Korean players already in Major League Baseball. Although it is out of the reach of most Chinese, golf has also captured their interest. Tiger Woods (seen here consulting on a shot with a five-year-old girl, who was serving as his honorary caddy during an exhibition in China) is a particular favorite in China, perhaps because of his Asian heritage through his mother, who was born in Thailand.

Global Reactions to Cultural Homogenization

What are the reactions around the world to the spread of English, the expansion of Western fast-food chains, and other aspects of cultural amalgamation? The answer is mixed, perhaps even contradictory.

If you ask people, as one survey did in over 40 countries, about the influx into their country of one of the strongest agents of cultural homogenization, entertainment media (foreign movies, television, and music), reactions are quite positive. Overall, 75% of respondents said such cultural imports are good, 21% thought they are bad, and 4% were unsure. This support of cultural homogenization appears a bit less enthusiastic when those saying "very good" (30%) and only "somewhat good" (45%) are distinguished. Also important is the fact that reactions do not differ dramatically among the world's regions. Americans and Canadians are the most likely (82%) to perceive cultural imports positively, but as Figure 5.3 shows, all the other regions but one have positive reactions above 70%. People are less happy about the spread of fast-food chains. But even on this aspect of cultural amalgamation, a plurality of people (40%) saw it as good, 30% viewed it as negative, 20% thought it made no difference, and 10% were unsure.

People globally also recognize that cultural imports and other aspects of cultural amalgamation are eroding their traditional way of life. Worldwide, 75% feel that way, and as also shown in Figure 5.3, strong majorities in every region have that view. This seems to create a sense of loss, though, which causes people to favor protecting their traditional way of life against foreign influence (which contradictorily includes the movies, television, and music that they find good). This contradictory reaction is additionally detailed in Figure 5.3.

The ambivalent feelings evident in Figure 5.3 have set the stage for strong reactions against cultural amalgamation. In what seems to be a norm of politics, it is those who dislike something who are the most vocal. The strength of the opposition to outside cultural influences also stems from the generation gap, with older people usually more averse to cultural imports than younger people. In the West African country of Senegal, for example, 76% of young adults (age 18 to 29) favor cultural imports; only 47% of adults aged 50 and over support that view. Since it is usually older adults who occupy leadership positions in government, organized religion, and other societal structures, it is their views, rather than those of younger adults, that are most likely to influence policy.

France provides a good example of both the ambivalence about and resistance to cultural amalgamation. Among the French, 91% favor popular entertainment imports, but 55% think that foreign fast food has made life worse. This mixed reaction is evident in French attitudes toward cultural exclusion. A small majority (53%) think their way of life should be protected against foreign influences, with 46% disagreeing, and 1% uncertain.

Nevertheless, France has often been a hotbed of resistance to cultural amalgamation. For example, the French newspaper *Le Figaro* has called fast food gastronomic "new terrorism" and charged that the United States "doesn't just intend to stuff our heads with its diplomatic obsessions. It also means to cram our bellies in its own way."[4] The French also worry that their language is under siege. For one, President Jacques Chirac has warned that a "major risk for humanity" is posed by the "linguistic uniformity and thus cultural uniformity" that may result from the spread of English.[5]

French traditionalists have fought back (Carruthers, 1998; Grantham, 1998). France has amended its constitution to declare, "The language of the republic is French," and has passed several laws requiring that only French be used in teaching, business, and government. It is probably a losing battle. In everyday speech, the French are more apt to say *le e-mail* or *le laptop* than *un message electronique* or *un ordinateur portative*. Moreover, 32% of them already speak English, and it is spreading quickly, with 90% of the French agreeing that learning English will enhance their childrens' chances of success. Then, to make matters worse for language purity, the European Union ruled in 2002 that France could not

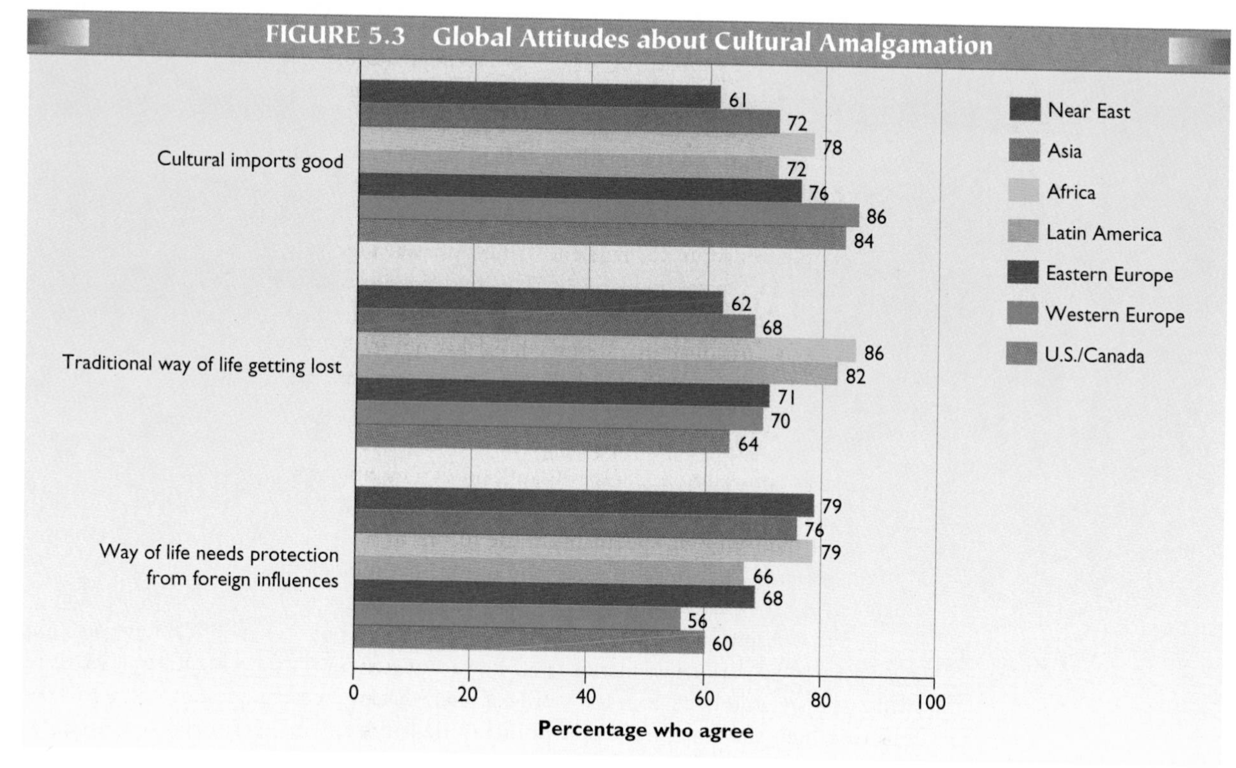

FIGURE 5.3 Global Attitudes about Cultural Amalgamation

People have a degree of ambivalence about cultural amalgamation. As the top series of bars shows, most people around the world like cultural imports, such as foreign movies, television programming, and music. Yet the middle group of bars indicates that most people believe their traditional way of life is getting lost, and it is likely that they would recognize that the cultural imports they favor are playing a role in that deterioration. Therefore, as evident in the bottom group of bars, a strong majority of people in every region wants to protect their way of life from foreign influences. The reactions are reminiscent of the old saw about wanting to have your cake and eat it too.

Note: The Near East is broader than the Middle East and stretches from Egypt to Pakistan.

Data source: Pew Research Center (2003).

require labels of imported food products to be exclusively in French. Now, to the horror of some, French shoppers can buy chicken wings, not *ailes de poulet,* at the supermarket.

Transnationalism

Transnationalism springs from two sources. Globalization is one. Economic interdependence, mass communications, rapid travel, and other modern factors are fostering transnationalism by intertwining the lives of people around the world. As the world becomes evermore interconnected, people interact more often transnationally, become more interdependent on one another, and become cognizant of the extent to which their future is intertwined with global forces. As an extension of these connections, a growing number of people have begun to reconsider their sense of who they are politically.

Human thought is the second source of transnationalism. The philosopher René Descartes argued in *Discourse on Method* (1637) that intellect is the essence of being human. "I think, therefore I am," he wrote. People can think abstractly. This allows them to imagine—to see themselves beyond what they have experienced and to define how they wish to be connected to people, ideas, and institutions. Transnationalism, indeed any political sense, is based on this abstract self-awareness.

While globalization is something that is happening and that exists, transnationalism is a more political term that relates to how people identify, interact, and organize themselves politically. However far globalization may proceed, its political impact will be limited if people continue to have the same political identities, to interact, and to see themselves as they have traditionally. This traditional way, at least for the last five centuries or so, has been to most often identify primarily with your nation and state in a relationship called nationalism. As one scholar has put it, this traditional approach assumes "that where you are [geographically] tells us something about who (politically) you are" (Mandaville, 2000:1).

As an alternative to nationalism, transnationalism may focus on ideologies (such as communism), on religion (such as Islam), on demographic characteristics (such as ethnicity or gender), on region (such as the European Union), or on virtually any another concept or trait. We will speculate on the future of transnationalism at the end of the chapter, but it is important to say at the outset that most people will not abandon nationalism in the foreseeable future. But it is also important to see that things are changing, and that at least some people are shifting some or all of their political identification away from their nationalist identity and toward one or more other identities. There are many scholars who believe, in the words of one, "that we need to question today the extent to which the imagination of political identity remains territorialized—that is, whether political identity remains the exclusive reserve of a single territorial referent" and to explore "the ways in which international socio-political life manages increasingly to escape the constraints of the territorial nation-state" (Mandaville, 2000:10).

Early Transnationalism

Although the process of globalization has spurred transnationalism, it is not new. Instead, what may seem to be a very modern idea has ancient origins.

The Origins of Transnational Thought

Transnational thought in Western culture can be traced to Stoicism, a philosophy that flourished in ancient Greece and Rome from 300 B.C. to A.D. 200. The Stoics saw themselves as part of humanity, not as members of one or another smaller political community. As such, Stoics were cosmopolitan, a word derived from combining the Greek words *cosmos* (world) and *polis* (city). One of those who had a sense of being a global citizen was the Roman emperor Marcus Aurelius, who wrote in *Meditations,* "my . . . country, so far as I am [the emperor], is Rome, but so far as I am a man, it is the world."

Other ancient, non-Western great philosophical traditions contain teachings that are similar to the cosmopolitan thrust of Stoicism. Philosophies such as Confucianism and religions such as Buddhism and Hinduism all contain transnational elements. For example, Siddhartha Gautama (ca. 563–483 B.C.), who became known as the Buddha, urged that we adopt a universal perspective. "Whatsoever, after due examination and analysis, you find to be conducive to the good, the benefit, the welfare of all beings," he taught, "that doctrine believe and cling to, and take it as your guide."

Later Transnational Thought

Although Stoicism declined, the idea of transcending local political structure and power remained alive over the centuries. "We have it in our power to begin the world over again," the revolutionary Thomas Paine proclaimed in *Common Sense* (1776). Americans remember Paine as a patriot, but that is an ill-fitting description. Instead, he was committed to a philosophy, not to any country. Paine described himself as a "citizen of the world" and was dubious about countries because they "limited citizenship to the soil, like vegetation." It is true that Paine's writing helped galvanize Americans during their struggle for independence, but he wrote in *The Rights of Man* (1779) that he would have played "the same part in any other country [if] the same circumstances [had] arisen."[6] Putting this view into practice, he also supported the French Revolution, which he saw as continuing the work of its American counterpart and leading a "march on the horizon of the world" that "neither the Rhine, the [English] Channel, or the ocean . . . can arrest" (Fitzsimons, 1995:579). That transnational march, Paine predicted, would lead to free trade and to establishing an international congress to resolve differences among states. Thus today's globalization would have neither surprised nor dismayed Paine.

During the same era, the philosopher Immanuel Kant took the idea of international cooperation for peace even further. Kant wrote in *Idea for a Universal History from a Cosmopolitan Point of View* (1784) that countries should abandon their "lawless state of savagery and enter a federation of people in which every state could expect to derive its security and rights . . . from a united power and the law-governed decisions of a united will."

The thinking of nineteenth-century German communist philosophers such as Friedrich Engels and Karl Marx also contained a strong element of transnational thought. They believed that all human divisions were based on economic class and that the state was a tool of the wealthy bourgeoisie to oppress the proletariat. Therefore, *The Communist Manifesto* (1848) explained, "Workingmen have no country." Moreover, Engels predicted that "as soon as class rule . . . [is] removed, nothing more remains to be repressed, and a special repressive force, a state, is no longer necessary" and, being "superfluous," would "die out of itself."

Contemporary Transnational Thought

After existing on the periphery of political thought during the halcyon days of nationalism, transnational thought came increasingly to the fore in the 20th century. To a degree this perspective is covered in the extensive discussion of liberalism in chapter 1. As noted there, liberals contend that a transition from a conflictive, state-centric system to a cooperative, interdependent system is both under way and desirable.

Realism and liberalism are not the only theoretical approaches to international relations, and in recent decades several other ways of thinking about world politics have gained standing among scholars. Three of especial note are postmodernism, constructivism, and feminism. Analysts who take one or another of these approaches view realism and liberalism as paths that merely perpetuate the current international system and offer nothing, as one analyst put it, "to assure a day of peace for international relations" (Der Derian, 1988:191). To create change, the critics of realism and liberalism want to reinvigorate the role of individuals in politics. From this point of view, international organizations and states limit the possibilities for individual political involvement. All three critical approaches advocate changing the way we speak, the way we think, and the way we organize our society and our institutions.

Each of the three alternative approaches begins from the perspective that the only truths are those which we create. There is no objective political reality waiting to be discovered. Instead, we have created all political attitudes and structures. Those who follow any of these approaches would agree with Albert Einstein's observation, "Reality is merely an illusion, albeit a very persistent one." Since each of the three approaches portrays people as the creators of everything that is political, each also believes that we can change what we have constructed. Thus each approach encourages us not to accept what seem to be immutable truths. Rather they want us to "re-imagine" our reality and thereby recreate it. Among other things, these alternative approaches challenge us to examine and perhaps redefine our **political identity**, the connection(s) we perceive between ourselves as individuals and various political structures (such as states) and groups (ranging from nations to gender). A brief synopsis of the core concepts of the three theories is in Table 5.1.

Postmodernism

At its core, **postmodernism** contends that reality is created by the ways that we think and by our discourse (writing, talking) about our world. Postmodernists believe that we have become trapped by stale ways of conceiving how we organize and conduct ourselves. In other words, according to one scholar, "postmodernism seeks to understand how . . . the way we think about the world and our place in it, impose[s] limits on us, and how we might be able to resist and eventually transgress those limits."

Postmodernists seek to deconstruct the discourse of world politics. For example, when we speak of "national interest," the meaning that most people give to that concept is nationally selfish in terms of gaining, increasing, and keeping wealth, military might, and status. Postmodernists reject such a meaning because, they contend, there is no such thing as an objective national interest. If that is true, we can change what it is by conceiving of national interest differently. Although he certainly did not mean to, Shakespeare inserted a very postmodern view in *Hamlet* when the Prince of Denmark mused, "there is nothing either good or bad, but thinking makes it so." For example, postmodernists reject the validity of the "we" and "they" discourse in international politics that distinguishes between ethnonational groups. They would also dispute the conception of progress that seeks to impose notions of scientific/technological modernity on people of traditional cultures.

Postmodernists even doubt the reality of the "metanarratives" (overarching stories) of history. The standard portrayal is of the rise and fall of powerful states based on the power struggles among them. Is that real? Perhaps the real story, as Marx and Engels suggested, has been the struggle of the propertied classes to amass more wealth and to oppress the proletariat. Or maybe politics has been driven, as some feminist postmodernists suggest, by creating structures (such as states and organized religion) that have allowed men to oppress women in the supposed interest of protecting them. Because you have not heard such alternative stories, your instinct may be to dismiss them as nonsense. But do not be so sure of what is fairy tale and what is documentary.

One of the numerous contributions that postmodernists make is providing an alternative way to think about how to achieve peace. In the words of one scholar, "postmodernism seeks to reveal the presumption of violence that underlies the founding of all governments. . . . It is force that holds the state together." Therefore, to achieve peace, this scholar argues, we must examine the relationship of violence to our current political structure and "encourage individuals to actively engage in politics" in order to change the discourse (Shinko, 2004).

If even some of the postmodernism argument is true, then it is important for transnationalism because it seeks to examine the ways we organize ourselves politically. Postmodernists believe that organizing ourselves politically around a geographically defined country is only an image in our mind reinforced by the way that we discuss politics. Postmodernists want to change political discourse so that political identity could also include, for instance, being a human, a North American, a woman, or a human, as well as being American, Mexican, or some other national identity.

TABLE 5.1 Contemporary Transnational Theories

Theory/Issue	Constructivism	Postmodernism	Feminism
View of the individual	Identities and interests of agents (individuals and organizations, including states) emerge out of their interactions.	Identities are uncertain, open, and unsettled. Meanings are multiple and fluid. There is no universal, abstract standard of truth.	Sex and gender are distinct. Gender is a socially created set of practices, attitudes, and ideas about biology (sex).
View of international politics	Agents create international structures (rules and images), which reciprocally impact the agents' actions. Thus agents and structures are co-constituted through reciprocal interaction.	Politics is agonistic (an ongoing struggle) process, a "will to power." Knowledge practices (our understanding of the world) determine identities and power relationships.	Unequal gender relations profoundly impact the actions of states and the lives of individual women and men who live within those states.
Area of focus	The way in which agents and structures reciprocally interact.	Deconstructing the concept of sovereignty. Reinvigorating individual political practices.	Gendered social relations and how these unequal power relations adversely affect the economic, social, and political security of women, children, and men.
View of the state	The state is a social construction. A state's identity and interests emerge out of their interactions.	States are neither necessary nor inevitable. States have established themselves as the privileged center of meaning and control in order to discipline politics.	The interests and identity of states reflect patriarchal power structures.
Key concepts	Agent, structures, co-constitution, intersubjective meanings (shared images)	Agonistic politics, power/knowledge, resistance and/or transgression of (going beyond) limits	Gender, security, patriarchy
View of change	Agents created the structures, therefore agents can change them by changing the rules and/or their practices.	The key political activity is to resist and transgress state-imposed limits on our ways of thinking, being, and acting.	Change is contingent upon mitigating the gender biases and the gendered nature of the state.
Summary	Constructivism attempts to redescribe international politics as a social process.	Postmodernism is a radically critical approach to the practice of international politics.	Feminism focuses on socially defined relations in order to transform how we conceptualize gender and international politics.

Compiled and created by Rosemary E. Shinko of the University of Connecticut, Stamford Campus, to whom the author also owes a debt for her contribution to the sections on constructivism, postmodernism, and feminism.

Constructivism

Another group of scholars position themselves between liberalism and postmodernism and are known as constructivists (Jacobensen, 2003; Zehfuss, 2002). **Constructivism** focuses on explaining the dynamic in international relations between "agents" (individuals and other actors) and "structure" (treaties, laws, international organizations, and other aspects of the international system). These scholars explore the dynamic and reciprocal process whereby agents participate in the creation of the various international structures and, in turn, are affected by those structures.

Constructivism shares with postmodernism the view that realities are socially constructed to a substantial degree. However, constructivists also accept the reality of such tangible parts of the international system as states and are even willing to concede certain existing elements of the system, such as its lack of central authority. For constructivists, the key is the ways in which we communicate (speak and write) and think about the world. They believe that language calls things into existence. For them, choosing one label over another (foreigner, fellow human), then attaching certain values to that label (foreign = different, not my responsibility; fellow human = similar, my responsibility) is profoundly important politically because we act on the basis of what things mean to us (Tsygankov, 2003). Constructivists believe that we should reject traditional meanings because they have led to division and conflict. As one put it, "A path cannot be called a path without the people who walk it" (Simon, 1998:158). For example, constructivists do not believe that the anarchical condition of the international system forces states to take certain actions (like being armed). Instead, constructivists think that how we conceive of the lack of central authority is what determines interactions. In the words of one leading constructivist, "Anarchy is what states make of it" (Wendt, 1992:335). From this point of view, conflict is not the result of structural power politics. Rather it stems from the discordant worldviews and the inability of people to communicate in ways that will allow them to construct a mutually beneficial vision and create the structure to accomplish that vision. From this perspective, according to another constructivist analyst, "Constructivism is about human consciousness and its role in international life . . . [and] rests on . . . the capacity and will of people to take a deliberate attitude towards the world and to lend it significance [by acting according to that attitude]" (Ruggie, 1998:855).

The good news is that if values and perceptions change, then so too can relations, structural realities, and other aspects of the international system. Political identification can be among these changes. How people define themselves and the values they place on that identification in relationship to others can, according to constructivists, reshape the structures by which people organize themselves and the interactions among those structures.

Whereas postmodernism is more of a methodological critique than a research agenda, advocates of constructivism pursue research, particularly at the state and individual levels of analysis, into the use of language and symbols, communications flows, and other factors that create the mindsets from which individuals and communities construct their social realities.

Feminism

Yet another alternative to realism and liberalism is provided by feminist theory. It is a diverse theory containing elements of liberal, postmodernist, and constructivist thought. To bridge these, we will adopt the strategy of one feminist author and use the term **feminism** "in its original meaning: the theory of, and the struggle for, equality for women" (Fraser, 1999:855). From this perspective, it is possible to highlight a number of common points in feminist thought about world politics. First, feminism argues that women have been left out of the process and even the conceptualization of world politics. Feminist scholars maintain that the definition of what is relevant to the study of international relations, as presented in textbooks and most other scholarship written by men, is a product of the male point of view and ignores or underrepresents the role of women, their concerns, and their perspectives. The problem, advocates of women's equality say, is that the scholarly definition of international relations has "excluded from that conception, quite comprehensively . . . the [lives] of most women," who "experience societies and their interactions differently" than do men (Grant & Newland, 1991:1). In this sense, many feminist scholars would agree with the postmodernists that mainline scholarship has presented a metanarrative of world politics that is not real and instead reflects just one set of perceptions (male, in this case). The overarching story from a feminist perspective would be very different.

One of the goals that most feminist scholars and activists share is improving the human rights of women. The discrimination that women face is evident in this photograph of an Afghan woman, Zarghona, and her seven-month-old son, Balal, looking out of their cell window in Kabul in early 2003. Zarghona's first husband abused her and then left her penniless. When she married another man without being divorced, she was imprisoned.

Concepts such as peace and security are prime examples of how, according to feminists, men and women perceive issues differently. One feminist scholar suggests that "from the masculine perspective, peace for the most part has meant the absence of war" (Reardon, 1990:137). She terms this "negative peace." By contrast, Reardon (138) continues, women think more in terms of "positive peace," which includes "conditions of social justice, economic equity and ecological balance." Women, more than men, are apt to see international security as wider than just a military concept, as also including security from sexism, poverty, domestic violence, and other factors that assail women (Razavi, 1999). Women favor this more inclusive view of security because, according to another study, "the need for human security through development is critical to women whose lives often epitomize the insecurity and disparities that plague the world order" (Bunch & Carillo, 1998:230).

This inclusive view of violence is supported by women's experiences. "The most painful devaluation of women," according to one UN report, "is the physical and psychological violence that stalks them from cradle to grave" (UNDP, 1995:7). Fewer women than men may die or be wounded as soldiers, but women are at least as likely to be casualties in military and terrorist attacks on economic and population centers. Many other women die from the starvation and disease that frequently accompany war, and yet others fall victim to sometimes widespread sexual abuse that occurs in some wars. During the early 1990s, the campaign against the Bosnians by the Serbs included an officially orchestrated campaign of sexual attack on many thousands of women and girls as young as 13 in an effort to terrorize the Bosnians. Yet another sign of violence against women is the fact that about 80% of the world's refugees are women and their children. Statistics also show that annually "an estimated 1 million children, mostly girls in Asia, are forced into prostitution. And an estimated 100 million girls suffer genital mutilation" (UNDP, 1995:44). Globally, the national incidence of women who have been the victim of abuse by an intimate partner averages 25% and ranges up to 58%.

Feminism is related to political identity in two ways (Croucher, 2003). One is to create womanhood as a focus of women's sense of who they are politically. This does not mean that women are apt to try to forge an independent feminist state somewhere in the world, but it does mean that women may view their country and its policies through a heightened feminist consciousness. Second, the political identity of some women is influenced by their suspicion that states and other political structures are designed to maintain male dominance. This view, one feminist scholar writes, "strips the [state's] security core naked so that we can see its masculine-serving guises" (Sylvester, 1994:823).

Reacting to Transnational Thought

Virtually everyone who reads this book will have been inculcated with nationalism from a very early age and will also tend to believe that the metanarrative (the portrayal of political history and reality) presented to them in school and elsewhere represents a reasonably true image of events. This background makes for great skepticism toward transnational thought. Indeed, different—perhaps seemingly radical—ideas have often alarmed those who travel the traditional path. For example, many Americans who in the 1770s welcomed Thomas Paine's revolutionary fervor later criticized him. Former president John Adams wrote in 1807 that he doubted that "any man in the world has had more influence on its inhabitants or affairs for the last thirty years than Tom Paine." That worried Adams, who condemned Paine's efforts to revolutionize the world as being "a career of mischief" conducted by "a mongrel between pig and puppy, begotten by a wild boar and a bitch wolf" (Fitzsimons, 1995:581).

Despite the fulminations of Adams and other traditionalists about the alternative path propounded by the Stoics, Immanuel Kant, Paine, and others, the ideal of transnationalism has persisted. Think about the critical approaches with an open mind; they just may offer a better path for the future and give us deeper insights into our past and present. While pondering, it would be appropriate to remember a bit of wisdom from Albert Einstein: "We can't solve problems by using the same kind of thinking we used when we created them."

Transnationalism in Action

Although nationalism still dominates how we identify and organize ourselves politically, transnationalism is making inroads. We will explore these advances by first surveying transnational organizations, then turning our attention to regional transnationalism, cultural transnationalism, religious transnationalism, and transnational movements.

One point the discussion of these various aspects of transnationalism will make is its potential to significantly restructure the international system and its conduct. Some aspects of transnationalism tend to undermine nationalism and, by extension, the state. One example is the degree to which citizens of the European Union identify as Europeans, instead of simply as French, German, or some other nationality. In other cases, transnational identification and organization focuses on changing attitudes and policies around the world related to a specific area of concern. This will be illustrated by examining the global women's movement.

Our discussion of transnationalism in action will also indicate that it is neither an inherent force for peace nor for discord. There are some elements of transnationalism that involve greater global interdependence and harmony. This impact of transnationalism is very much in accord with the vision of the liberal school of political thought discussed in chapter 1 and, in most cases, with postmodernism and the other alternative theories discussed earlier in this chapter.

Unfortunately, there is another, less welcome road down which transnationalism may take us. This involves an antithetical, negative image of transnational culture, one that envisions a world divided and in conflict along cultural lines. Those who see transnationalism in this light tend to be realists, many of whom would strengthen the national state as a bulwark against the dangers of hostile transnational alignments.

Transnational Organizations

Ideas only become powerful when those who hold them begin to take action. This is what has increasingly taken place. There is good evidence of this change in the phenomenal growth in the number and activities of transnational organizations called **nongovernmental organizations (NGOs)**. These are organizations that operate across national boundaries and whose membership is composed of individuals, and who do not answer to any government.

The Growth of NGOs

In 1900, there were 69 NGOs. Now the Union of International Associations lists more than 47,000 NGOs. Of these, 2,143 hold consultative status with the United Nations, up from 928 such groups in 1992 and 222 such groups in 1952. The diversity of interests represented by these groups touches on human rights, the environment, and virtually every other public concern. One way to grasp this breadth is by reviewing the list of UN-accredited NGOs on the Web site of the Conference of Non-Governmental Organizations at http://www.ngocongo.org/.

The growth in the number of NGOs and the range of their interests and activities reflect globalization in several ways. First, there is a growing awareness that many issues are in part or wholly transnational, rather than just national. For instance, the discharge of gases in one country that attack the Earth's vital ozone layer increases the rate of skin cancer globally, not just in the country that emitted the gases. Similarly, many women believe that the status of women in any one country is linked to the treatment of women everywhere. For example, they see domestic violence as a global, not just a national, problem. Second, NGOs have flourished because advances in transportation and communication have made transnational contacts easy, rapid, and inexpensive. Third, the growth of NGOs reflects disenchantment with existing political organizations based in or dominated by states in an age of globalization."Stifled by the unwillingness of nations and international organizations to share decision making, and frustrated by the failure of political institutions to bring about reform," one study explains, "political activists began to form their own cross-border coalitions in the 1970s and 1980s" (Lopez, Smith, & Pagnucco, 1995:36).

The Activities of NGOs

There is little doubt that NGOs are having a mounting impact on policy making at the national and international levels. In essence, NGOs are organized interest groups that operate singly or in combination with one another to promote their causes. In the realm of environmental politics, for example, there are such groups as Friends of the Earth International, headquartered in the Netherlands. It coordinates a transnational effort to protect the environment and also serves as a link among Friends of the Earth member groups in 67 countries and 20 affiliated groups, such as Amigos de Terra in Brazil. Similarly,

Greenpeace International, which is also located in the Netherlands, has regional and national offices in 41 countries. Just like more conventional interest groups, NGOs try to promote their goals by such techniques as attempting to raise public awareness and support for their causes and by providing information and argumentation to policy makers in national governments and intergovernmental organizations (IGOs, international organizations in which the members are states).

At least one measure of the increased activity of NGOs and their presence in the international policy-making process is their participation in major multinational conferences convened by the United Nations and other NGOs to address global problems. Since the early 1990s, all such conferences have two parts. One is the official conference that includes delegates from governments. The second is the parallel NGO conference. The first major conference to follow this pattern, the UN Conference on Environment and Development (UNCED) held in Rio de Janeiro in 1992, brought not only governments together in Brazil, but also approximately 15,000 delegates representing 1,100 NGOs. Three years later, the NGO conference that paralleled the fourth UN World Conference on Women (WCW) in Beijing attracted about 30,000 delegates from 2,000 NGOs. More recently, the 2002 World Conference on Sustainable Development in Johannesburg, South Africa, also included an NGO conference that drew some 41,000 delegates from more than 6,600 NGOs.

Thousands of transnational nongovernmental organizations (NGOs) are active in the world, trying to change it. The Friends of the Earth is one such NGO. Its activities have included helping poor South Africans create the statues seen here and some 6,000 similar ones arrayed near the World Summit on Sustainable Development in Johannesburg, South Africa, in 2002. The statues served as a silent protest against what the group believes is the betrayal of all people by governments and business that do not protect the environment.

These conferences are both the result of the work done by NGOs and a vehicle that promotes their role by enhancing their visibility and by serving as a place where they can create **transnational advocacy networks** (**TANs**) groups of NGOs and IGOs that share an interest in a specific aspect of global society. For example, the Partnership for Principle 10 (PP10) is a TAN that includes government agencies (from Africa, Europe, and Latin America), transnational groups (such as Corporación Participa in Chile), and IGOs (such as the UN and World Bank). The TAN is dedicated to accelerating implementation of Principle 10 of the Rio Declaration (1992). That clause expressed the view of the 178 countries attending the conference: "Environmental issues are best handled with participation of all concerned citizens" and everyone "shall have appropriate access to information concerning the environment that is held by public authorities."

The Impact of NGOs

It is hard to measure the impact of NGOs or any other single factor on policy making, but there is evidence that NGOs are gaining recognition as legitimate actors and are playing an increased role in the policy process. One measure is funding. The amount of private and government aid flowing through NGOs to economically less developed countries (LDCs) increased from $1 billion in 1970 to more than $7 billion in 2001. As part of this increase, the U.S. Agency for International Development increased its funding of the "civil society" (NGO) sector from $56 million in 1991 to $230 million in 1999.

NGOs have also helped move some of their causes to the center of the political stage. Fifty years ago, the environment received little political attention. Now it is an important issue that generates world conferences (such as those in Rio in 1992 and Johannesburg in 2002), it is a frequent topic of conversation among heads of government, and it is the subject of numerous international agreements. For example, one indication of the implementation of the Rio Declaration's Principle 10 is the Aarhus Convention, named after the city in Denmark where it was signed in 1998. The convention, which so far has been ratified by 26 European countries, pledges its adherents to grant access to environmental information to citizens of any of the adhering states and to promote public participation in making environmental laws and regulations.

Transnational NGOs and their national chapters also individually and collectively bring pressure on governments. In the United States, for example, the League of Conservation Voters lobbies legislators and agency officials and takes such public relations steps as maintaining a "scorecard" that rates the voting record of members of Congress on the environment. It should also be noted that some forms of NGO activity can be destructive and, therefore, illegitimate in the view of most. For example, al-Qaeda and many other terrorist groups are transnational organizations.

Did You Know That:

A 2002 survey taken in 43 countries around the world found that 74% of all respondents said NGOs were a good influence in their country. Only 13% said they were a bad influence, and another 13% were unsure.

Regional Transnationalism

Chapter 7 on international organizations examines the European Union (EU) as an example of a regional organization. The EU has evolved since its genesis soon after World War II to the point now where there is advanced economic integration. Although at a slower rate, political integration has also proceeded. The EU has its own diplomatic representation in the United States and elsewhere, citizens in all EU member-countries can travel on EU passports if they wish, and EU citizens living in other countries can vote in local elections and even hold some political offices in an EU country in which they reside. Being an EU "citizen" has meaning.

When Europeans are asked about their political identification, their replies indicate continuing strong attachments to their country and a much lower sense of primary identification to the European Union. Forty percent define themselves only as citizens of their country, and another 44% define themselves as citizens of their country first and Europeans second. Eight percent feel more European than national, and 4% perceive themselves as exclusively European (with 3% unsure).

There are two ways to interpret this data. One is that the transnational sense of being European first or exclusively is swamped by the traditional nationalist sense. The other way is that one out of every eight people in the EU has transferred his or her traditional national identification to a primary or exclusive sense of being European. This can be interpreted as a notable shift, given that such loyalties change slowly and given that the movement to integrate the EU politically (as compared to economically) has only been underway for about two decades. It is also notable that 60% of EU citizens have some sense of political identification with it, even if it is secondary.[7]

Some other indications that political identification may increase include a higher percentage of people (18%) with a primary or exclusive European identity in the six countries that in 1958 founded what became the EU than in the newer member-countries, and a stronger European identification (15%) among younger Europeans (age 15 to 24), with support dropping off with age to only 8% among Europeans aged 55 or more. Also, almost two-thirds of all EU citizens support drawing up an EU constitution, a move that the most ardent supporters of political integration see as an important step toward creating a united Europe.

Although still a small minority, many Europeans identify politically with the European Union. It is possible that this sense of political identity will increase as children who do not remember pre-EU times grow up. This boy in Budapest is holding an EU flag on the day in 2003 when the Hungarian people voted in a referendum to approve their country's membership in the EU. When in the late 2020s the boy is his father's age, he may consider himself a European first and a Hungarian second.

There is no other area of the globe with a regional organization that even approaches the economic, much less the political integration of the EU. Thus, to date any sense of regional political identity is almost exclusively confined to Europe. But in the 1950s, Europe's Common Market was just beginning, and it was limited to trade, much as several regional organizations such as the North American Free Trade Agreement (NAFTA, which links Canada, Mexico, and the United States) are today. What has evolved in Europe could occur elsewhere.

Cultural Transnationalism

The familiarity among different cultures that globalization is bringing to people and even the blending of those cultures holds the prospect, according to many analysts, of reducing conflict in the world. There is considerable scholarship in a range of disciplines that demonstrates that greater intercultural familiarity reduces stereotyping, suspicion, fear, and other divisive factors that promote domestic and international conflict. Advocates of cultural amalgamation may concede that it will lead to the "yawn of McWorld," but at least it will be a more peaceful existence.

There is, however, a less sanguine view of the course that cultural transnationalism will take. The best-known proponent of this view is Samuel P. Huntington's (1996, 1993) image of a coming "**clash of civilizations**." Huntington's (1993:22) thesis is that "the fundamental source of conflict" in the future will "be cultural" and that "the battle lines of the future" will pit "different civilizations" against one another. He projects (25) that world politics will be driven by the "interactions among seven or eight major civilizations," including "Western, Confucian, Japanese, Islamic, Hindu, Slavic-Orthodox, Latin American, and possibly African."

Like many analysts, Huntington (26) believes that nationalism will "weaken . . . as a source of identity" and that new cultural identifications will emerge "to fill this gap" and to group countries into cultural blocs. His prediction for such alignments is dark. "Over the centuries," according to Huntington (25–27), "differences among civilizations have generated the most prolonged and the most violent conflicts," because "cultural characteristics and differences are less mutable and hence less easily compromised and resolved than political and economic ones." What should we make of this image of a future world torn asunder by the clash of civilizations?

Some unsettling signs suggest that Huntington's theory is not totally unthinkable. One example is the current conflicts that arguably could be characterized as clashes between Huntington's "Western" and "Islamic" cultures. Whatever the perspective may be from the United States or other Western, largely Christian-heritage countries, there is considerable suspicion among Muslims that there is a concerted campaign under way to undermine their religion and its cultural traits. As is discussed later in the chapter, there is a history of conflict between Christendom and Islam that goes back more than a millennium, and to some Muslims current policy by the U.S.-led West is an extension of that conflict. Muslims making that case might point, among other things, to their perceptions of the following U.S. and/or European policies:

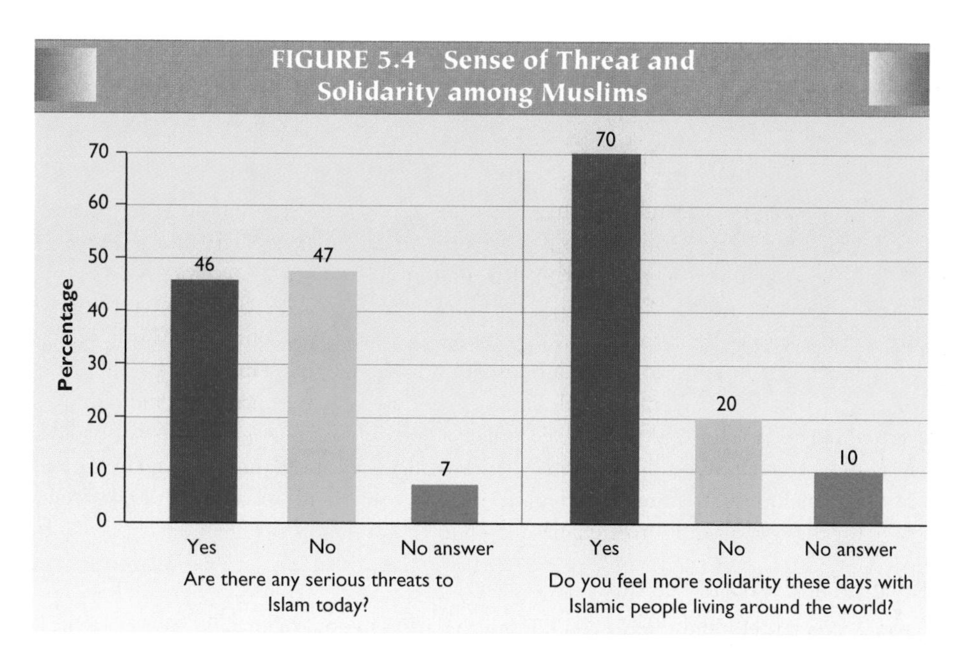

Whatever the cause, about half of all Muslims believe that their religion is under attack. This sense of threat is especially high in the Middle East, where 78% perceived serious threats. Perhaps as part of a defensive reaction, 70% of Muslims indicated that they are currently feeling greater solidarity with other Muslims around the world.

Note: The survey was conducted in 2002 among Muslims in Jordan, Lebanon, Pakistan, Turkey, Uzbekistan, Bangladesh, Indonesia, Ghana, Ivory Coast, Mali, Nigeria, Senegal, Tanzania, and Uganda.

Data source: The Pew Research Center for People and the Press, "Views of a Changing World" (June 2003).

- Inaction (1992–1995) while Christian Serbs slaughtered Bosnian Muslims
- Exclusion of Muslim Turkey from the mostly Christian EU
- Opposition to Iraq or Iran getting nuclear weapons while ignoring Israeli nuclear weapons
- Two invasions of Iraq and one of Afghanistan
- Sanctions on Iraq after 1991 that lasted longer than those on Germany after 1945
- Lack of sanctions on largely Christian Russia for its often brutal campaign against the Muslim Chechens
- Support of Israel

It is important to note that the view of such actions as anti-Islam or, at least, reflecting cultural insensitivity is not confined to Muslims. Just before his death, Richard Nixon wrote, "It is an awkward but unavoidable truth that had the [mostly Muslim] citizens of Sarajevo [the capital of Bosnia] been predominantly Christian or Jewish, the civilized world would not have permitted [the atrocities that occurred]."[8]

Whether such charges are true or not, it is important to see that they are perceived to be true by many Muslims. A survey taken in 2002 of Muslims in 14 countries in Africa, Asia, and the Middle East found that nearly half felt their religion to be in danger. This perception has arguably fostered the greater sense of solidarity that a strong majority of Muslims also expressed in the survey.[9] These findings are detailed in Figure 5.4.

Whether such evidence presages a future that fits with Huntington's prediction is speculative. Some analysts disagree with Huntington. Others argue that racism, ethnic and religious intolerance, and other forms of culturalism have persisted throughout human history and, thus, do not augur increased cultural clashes. Yet other analysts believe that the forces bringing the world together will overcome those that are driving it apart.

Transnational Religion

Most of the world's great religions have a strong transnational element. It is particularly apt to exist when a religion, which is a basis of spiritual identity, becomes a source of political identity among its members. When religion and political identities become intertwined, members of a religion may take a number of political actions. One is to try to conform the laws of their country to their religious values. A second is to provide political support for the causes of co-religionists in other countries. This sense of support is why, for example, Jews from around the world are likely to support Israel and Muslims everywhere are apt to support the Palestinians. Religion also helps explain why Osama bin Laden, a Saudi, was able to recruit Muslims from Egypt, Pakistan, Chechnya, and elsewhere, including the United States and Europe, to the ranks of al-Qaeda and to find a base for the organization in Afghanistan.

Religion and World Politics

"You're constantly blindsided if you consider religion neutral or outside world politics," cautions international relations scholar the Reverend J. Bryan Hehir of Harvard. It is "better to understand the place that religion holds in the wider international framework," he advises.[10]

Religion plays many roles in world politics. Often, it is a force for peace, justice, and humanitarian concern. It is also true, though, that religion has been and continues to be a factor in many bloody wars, conflicts, and other forms of political violence. For example, religion is an element of the conflict between mostly Jewish Israelis and the mostly Muslim Arabs. Religion is also part of what divides Pakistan and India and has led to what some people believe is the world's most dangerous situation, as the In the Spotlight box "India, Pakistan, Religion, and the Bomb" relates.

Religion also causes or exacerbates conflict within countries. What was Yugoslavia disintegrated partly along religious lines into Catholic Croats, Muslim Bosnians, and Eastern Orthodox Serbs. More recently, religion plays a role in the cultural divide between Serbs and Muslim Albanians in Yugoslavia's Kosovo Province and between Macedonians and Muslim Albanians in Macedonia. Yet another example is the long struggle between the Roman Catholics and Protestants of Northern Ireland that killed over 3,000 people between 1969 and the establishment in 1998 of a still tenuous peace.

Organized religion also plays a range of positive roles as a transnational actor, projecting its values through a range of intergovernmental organizations (IGOs). Among Christians, the World Evangelical Alliance, founded in 1846, is an early example of a Protestant NGO. Even older, the Roman Catholic Church is by far the largest and most influential religion-based NGO. The Vatican itself is a state, and the pope is a secular as well as a spiritual leader. The political influence of Roman Catholicism, however, extends far beyond the Vatican. Under John Paul II, the Church has been active on a variety of fronts. Early in the pope's reign, this included attempts to weaken communist governments in Poland and other countries in Eastern Europe with a Roman Catholic heritage. More recently, the Church has played a role in preventing the inclusion of language supporting abortion and other practices it opposes in the programs supported by various UN conferences on women. Additionally, John Paul II has made over 100 apostolic visits to countries outside the Vatican, and he has been active on such issues as seeking an end to economic sanctions against countries, claiming that such sanctions are injurious to civilians, pressing for nuclear arms restraint, and calling on the world's wealthy countries to do more to aid the developing countries.

The Strength of Religious Fundamentalism

One aspect of religion that appears to have gained strength in many areas of the world is **fundamentalism** (religious traditionalism). As used here, a fundamentalist is someone who holds conservative religious values and wishes to incorporate those values into national law. There is also a transnational element to some fundamentalists, whose primary political identity is their religion, not their nation-state or some other focal point. This perspective promotes political cooperation among co-religionists across borders; it may also mean driving out people of another or no faith or suppressing their freedoms within borders.

There is considerable debate over whether the rise of fundamentalism is a series of isolated events or related to a larger global trend. Taking the latter view are scholars who believe that at least part of the increase in the political stridency of religion is based on a resistance to the cultural amalgamation that fundamentalist traditionalists believe is undermining the values on which their religion is based. This sense of siege increases people's awareness of their religious identity and their solidarity with their co-religionists across national borders.

As part of this process, political conservatism, religious fundamentalism, and avid nationalism often become intertwined. Its presence in India is discussed in the box "India, Pakistan, Religion, and the Bomb" and Islamic fundamentalism is detailed later in this chapter. Religious traditionalism also influences Israel's politics through the role played by orthodox Jewish groups. With respect to international affairs, Israel's religious right tends to favor a hard-line stance with the Palestinians, no compromise on the status of Jerusalem, and the continuation of Jewish settlements in Gaza and the West Bank. Indeed, this political faction claims that the West Bank and the Golan Heights are part of the ancient land given in perpetuity to the Jewish nation by God. Whether the policy ramifications are domestic or international, "the issue," according to a Hebrew University scholar, "is whether Israel will shape a way of life according to Western, democratic concepts, or one infected by Middle Eastern fundamentalism and theocratic impulse." Others dismiss such concerns. "We're not going to make a second Iran in the Middle East," a rabbi who also heads a religion-oriented political party assures listeners.[11]

While a number of the world's major religions illustrate the intersection of religion and global politics, more can be gained from a closer examination of one religion. To that end, let us turn our attention to Islam because of its growing sociopolitical impact and because its history and tenets are too often unknown or misrepresented in the Western world.

Islam and the World

Islam is a monotheistic religion founded by Muhammad (ca. 570–632). The word *Islam* means "submission" to God (Allah), and *Muslim* means "one who submits." Muslims believe that Muhammad was a prophet who received Allah's teachings in a vision. These divine instructions constitute the Koran (or Qur'an), meaning "recitation."

It is the political application of Islam by Muslims that interests us here. A traditional Islamic concept is the *ummah,* the idea of a Muslim community that is unified spiritually, culturally, and politically. Muhammad was the first leader of the ummah. Muslims distinguish between Muslim-held lands, *dar al-Islam* (the domain of Islam), and non-Muslim lands, *dar al-harb* (the domain of unbelief). One tenet of Islam is the *jihad,* "struggle"

IN THE SPOTLIGHT

India, Pakistan, Religion, and the Bomb

Relations between India and Pakistan are a volatile mix of religion and nationalism that has led to three wars and numerous other military clashes for nearly 60 years. The two countries and the rest of the subcontinent (Bangladesh, Nepal, and Sri Lanka) were part of British India until 1947. Independence was accompanied by partition, the creation of two states, Hindu India and Muslim Pakistan, which unleashed horrific religious conflict and left hundreds of thousands of people dead. Many Muslims living in Hindu areas fled to the two halves of Pakistan: West Pakistan (current Pakistan) and East Pakistan (now Bangladesh), while Hindus in Muslim areas sought safety in India.

War immediately broke out between India and Pakistan over Kashmir, a large area along the northern part of the two countries' 1,800-mile border. Kashmir's ruler was Hindu and opted to join India; most Kashmiris were Muslim and

Religion, the intractable dispute over Kashmir, and other divides keep India and Pakistan in a state of near perpetual confrontation interrupted occasionally by fighting. These Pakistani and Indian border guards, with headgear arrays reminiscent of the plumage displayed by avian combatants, symbolize what may be the world's most dangerous border because of the nuclear weapons each side possesses.

carried on in the name of Allah by *mujahedin*. It is important to stress that jihad does not necessarily mean armed struggle. It can also mean peacefully spreading Islam or defending the faith. This reality has too often been lost in false stereotypes of Islam as intrinsically violent. Certainly, there are militant Muslims. But virtually every religion is afflicted by fanatics who distort its meaning and commit unimaginable atrocities in its name.

The political ramifications of Islam are important because there are over 1 billion Muslims spread widely over the world, as demonstrated by the map on page 154 of countries in which Muslims are more than half of the population. They are a majority among the Arabs of the Middle East and also in non-Arab countries in Africa, Southwest Asia, and South Asia. Additionally, there are other countries, such as Nigeria and the Philippines, in which Muslims constitute an important political force. Indeed, only about one of every four Muslims is an Arab, and the world's most populous Muslim country is Indonesia, with 235 million people.

The Political Heritage of Muslims

The attitudes of Muslims toward the non-Muslim world are shaped by three historical elements. A *triumphant beginning* is the first element. During Islam's early period, it experienced rapid religious and political expansion by peaceful conversion and violent wished to be part of Pakistan. The war continued for two years, with India retaining most of the territory. A second Indo-Pakistani war occurred along the northern frontier in 1965, and a third war erupted in 1971 when India helped the Muslim Bengalis of East Pakistan, who had revolted against Pakistan's Punjabi-dominated government in Islamabad, gain independence. Full-scale war has not occurred since then, but there is no peace. Instead there have been periodic clashes and continual tension, especially over Kashmir.

More recently, increased religious fundamentalism in both India and Pakistan also escalated the danger. The change in Pakistan is part of the increase in religious traditionalism throughout the Muslim world as discussed elsewhere in this chapter. India has also seen a rise of nationalist religious traditionalism, politically represented by the Bharatiya Janata Party (BJP), which came to power in 1998. It was founded in 1980 as a Hindu nationalist party. Many members wish to create *Hindutva*, a theocratic Hindu India, or even *Akband Bharat* (Old India), a mythical concept of a unified Indian subcontinent under Hindu Indian leadership (Bouton, 1998). According to one BJP leader, "Muslims are converted Hindus, but they have forgotten their Hinduness. So we will awake them to their Hinduness."[1] Prime Minister Atal Behari Vajpayee is a moderate by BJP standards, but even he has warned that "appeasement" of Muslims and other minorities in India would "injure the Hindu psyche."[2] This attitude has increased tension between Hindus and India's sizeable (14%) Muslim population and led to repeated sectarian violence that could spread to war with Pakistan.

Escalating the danger even further, nuclear war became a horrendous possibility when India and Pakistan both tested nuclear weapons in 1998. "I cannot believe that we are about to start the 21st century by having the Indian subcontinent repeat the worst mistakes of the 20th century," a distressed President Clinton said.[3] Both countries have also developed the missile capacity to rain their weapons down on each other's cities with virtually no warning, thereby creating a hair-trigger level of anxiety during times of crisis. One of these times occurred in 1999 when the two countries' armed forces fought a heavy engagement in the Kashmir region for 11 weeks. Then in 2002 the two countries again approached the abyss after terrorists bombed India's national parliament building. "The chance of war between these two nuclear-armed states is higher than at any point since 1971," a worried CIA Director George Tenet told a congressional committee at the time. The greatest danger, Tenet continued, is that "a conventional war once begun, could escalate to a nuclear confrontation."[4] Fortunately, a strong diplomatic push by the United States and other countries persuaded both sides to exercise constraint. Nothing was settled, though, and it is probably just a matter of time before the world once again watches anxiously as the mix of India, Pakistan, religion, and the bomb edges the region toward a potential catastrophe.

conquest. At their farthest, the boundaries of Muslim domination encompassed the Middle East, North Africa, southwestern Asia to the Ganges River, Spain, and central Europe to just south of Vienna.

Conflict with Christian powers, especially those of Europe, is a second element of Muslim political heritage. Eight crusades were launched by Europe's Catholic kings against Muslims between 1195 and 1270, and other lesser expeditions lasted into the 1400s. Muslims also clashed for hundreds of years with Christianity's Orthodox emperors of Byzantium and later with the Orthodox czars of Russia.

The domination of Muslims by others is the third key historical element of Muslims' political heritage. After about the year 1500, Muslim secular strength declined, and by the late 1800s a variety of European powers had come to dominate many Muslim areas. The last vestige of Muslim power was eclipsed when the Ottoman Empire collapsed after World War I, and the British and the French became the colonial overlords of the Middle East. As a result, most Muslim countries, whatever their location, share an experience of recent colonial domination by mostly European, Christian-heritage powers.

During the last half century, direct political domination ended with the collapse of colonialism. New countries came into being; others moved from autonomy to full independence. Yet there is a strong sense among many Muslims that Western dominance, led

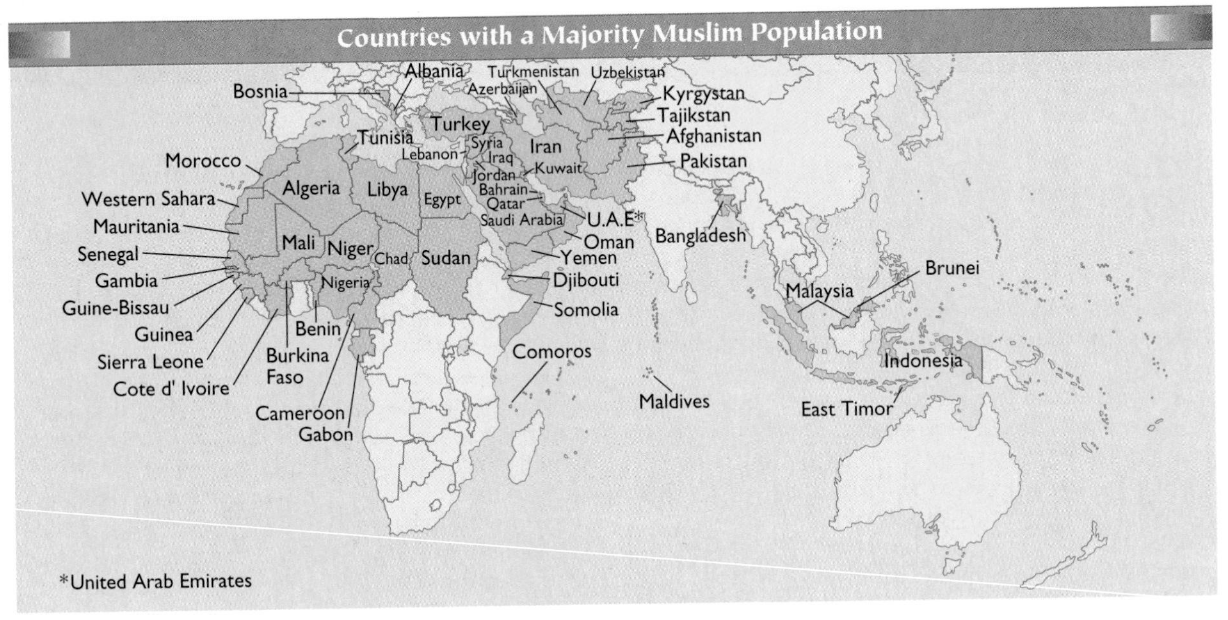

This map of the countries in which Muslims constitute a majority of the population illustrates that Islam is not confined to the Arab states in the Middle East. In fact, most Muslims are not Arabs. The largest predominantly Muslim state is Indonesia, where 87% of the country's 235 million people are Muslims. The people of Pakistan and Iran, the second and third most populous predominantly Muslim countries, are also not Arabs.

by the United States, has continued through alleged neocolonialist practices such as protecting authoritarian pro-Western regimes in Saudi Arabia and Kuwait and using military force to smite Muslim countries that defy U.S. demands to support its interests. For example, a 2002 poll in Turkey asking about the possible U.S. use of force to remove Saddam Hussein from power found that a majority (53%) believed that it was a part of the "U.S.'s war against Muslim countries that it sees as unfriendly." Only 34% thought Washington's policy had to do with a desire for stability in the Middle East, and 13% were unsure or refused to answer.[12]

Islam and Nationalism

There are elements of contemporary Islam that support unification by creating a true ummah. After centuries of outside domination, the people in the region that stretches from Gabon to Indonesia have begun to reclaim their heritage in what might be called a "Muslim pride" movement. This includes Islamic solidarity efforts, which have ranged from coordination in protecting Islamic holy places, through support of the Palestine Liberation Organization, to support of Pakistan's possession of nuclear weapons. Among Arab Muslims, the common tie of Islam has helped promote Pan-Arab sentiment. This Pan-Arab feeling has led to the establishment of some regional cooperation (the Arab League, for example) and even attempts to merge countries.

Nevertheless, it is very unlikely that Muslims will reestablish the ummah in the foreseeable future. Nationalism is one factor that will prevent this. Many Muslim countries have sharp differences and vie with one another for regional influence. Iraq and Iran, for example, fought an eight-year-long war in the 1980s that claimed about 1 million lives. Further solidifying nationalism, there are major ethnic differences within Islam.

Culturally, Indonesians are no more like Syrians than are Canadians. Even neighboring Muslim countries can be quite diverse. Iranians, for example, are ethnic Persians who speak Farsi; Iraqis are ethnic Arabs who speak Arabic. Furthermore, there is a strong sense of patriotic pride in many Muslim countries. This nationalism is particularly strong when faced by an outside influence, as the United States found out in postwar Iraq. Whatever their views of the departed Saddam Hussein, a substantial percentage of Iraqis chafed at the idea of an extended American presence in their country.

Islam and the Non-Islamic World

The political history of Muslims influences their current attitudes toward *dar al-harb,* the domain of unbelief, in several ways. One is the frequent evidence of anti-Western feeling. In the eyes of many Muslims, as noted, the United States is the most recent dominant Euro-Christian heritage power. Americans have therefore inherited Muslim resentment based on what one Arab leader describes as "Western behavior over centuries that has been unfair to Muslims."[13] Muslims also see the struggle with Israel and what they perceive as U.S. bias toward Israel as part of a long, ongoing history of attempted Western domination of their region. "There is a deep feeling that when it comes to the Arabs, it's always very harsh treatment, and when it comes to the Israelis, it's easy," notes an Egyptian analyst.[14]

The degree to which these feelings are held widely among Muslims was confirmed by a 2002 poll of nine Muslim countries. Of the Muslims surveyed, 53% had an unfavorable opinion of the United States; only 22% expressed a positive opinion. Just 12% of Muslims thought the West respects Islamic values. As for the question of Israel and the Palestinians, as few as 1% of Muslims in some countries (Kuwait and Morocco) and at most 12% of Muslims in any country (Indonesia) felt that the United States was dealing fairly with the Palestinians.[15] It is hard for most outsiders to understand how powerfully this issue affects Arab views of the United States. Some insight can be gained, however, from a recent poll conducted by the respected Arab American pollster James Zogby in eight Middle Eastern countries. Among its findings was that most Arabs placed the fate of the Palestinians high up on the list of issues of personal importance to them. This result led Zogby to conclude that the Palestinian question "is not a foreign policy issue [for Arabs]. It defines almost existentially their sense of who they are."[16]

Before leaving this topic of perceptions, it is worth noting that Americans held a negative mirror image of Muslims. Only 24% of the Americans polled in early 2002 held a favorable opinion of Muslim countries, while 41% expressed an unfavorable view. The poll also confirmed that most Americans have little respect for Muslim culture, with about two-thirds of Americans saying Muslim countries would be better off if they adopted U.S. and Western values.[17]

Islamic Sectarianism

Religion is not always a source of Islamic unity. Instead, religious conflict has been sparked by sectarian splits within Islam. The most important of these separates the majority Sunnis and the minority Shiites (Fuller & Francke, 2000). The issues between the two sects involve doctrinal matters beyond our scope of inquiry. What is important here is that the sometimes quiescent Sunni-Shiite rivalry was reignited in 1979 when the Ayatollah Ruhollah Khomeini led fundamentalist Shiites to power in Iran. One result was Iran's war with Iraq (1980–1988). There were territorial and other nationalistic causes behind the war, but Khomeini's determination to overthrow the Sunni-dominated regime of Saddam Hussein was also a cause of the war and of the more than 2 million casualties that occurred.

Whatever Americans may believe or intend, the protest here in Pakistan in March 2003 represents the belief of many Muslims that the recent attacks on Muslim Afghanistan and Iraq, the threats against Muslim Syria and Iran, and other U.S. actions are evidence that Islam is once again being threatened by a crusade led by the dominant, European-heritage, largely Christian power.

The death of Khomeini in 1989 eased, but did not end, Sunni-Shiite strife. Among other places, Muslim sectarianism has spelled continuing tragedy for Afghanistan. For example, there have been frequent charges that Iran is supporting the Shiite Hazara ethnonational group's resistance to the control of the Sunni-dominated central government in Kabul. Even more recently, events in Iraq show the interrelationship of sectarian and national forces. The downfall of Saddam Hussein, a Sunni, raised worries that Iran might try to gain influence in Iraq through the country's Shiite majority. Yet the possibility of that happening is severely constrained by the fact that Iraqis are Arab, Iranians are Persians, and historically the two groups have often clashed.

Islamic Traditionalism and Secularism

A second point of division within Islam separates Muslim traditionalists and secularists. Traditionalist (fundamentalist) Muslims want to preserve or, in some cases, resurrect their cultural traditions. Many of these, such as banning alcohol and having women cover their faces in public, have been weakened under the influence of Western culture. Fundamentalists also want to establish legal systems based on the *shari'ah* (the law of the Koran) rather than on Western legal precepts. The traditionalists also look forward to the reestablishment of the ummah. "The notion that a majority should rule and the notion of the political party are all Western notions," explains one ranking Muslim theologian. What "Islam calls for," he continues, is "obedience to the ruler, the unification of the nation, and advice by religious scholars."[18]

Secularists, by comparison, believe that within Islam there can be many Muslim states and that religious and secular law should be kept separate. A top Arab jurist argues, for example, that "politicized Islamic groups proclaim Islam to be a nation when in fact Islam is a religion."[19] Whatever may be theologically correct, the fact is that since the early 1990s traditionalist Muslim movements have gained strength in Algeria, Iran, Turkey, and several other Muslim countries.

What the average Muslim thinks is unclear, with variations in poll questions bringing very different results. For example, a recent poll that asked Muslims in 14 countries,

"How much of a role do you think Islam should play in the political life of your country?" revealed that 57% (including a majority in 13 of the countries) replied a "large" role. Only 35% said a "small" role, and 8% declined to answer. Yet the same poll found that an average of 71% of the respondents in seven overwhelmingly Muslim countries agreed with the statement, "Religion is a matter of personal faith and should be kept separate from government policy."[20]

What does all this mean about the possible existence of a "green peril," a term that relates to the traditional association of the color green with Muslims? The first answer is that it is equally wrong to ignore the role of religion in politics and to make dire and misleading predictions based on the false assumption of pan-Muslim solidarity. For example, it is probable that much of the strong sense of Muslim solidarity that exists is a defensive reaction prompted by the perception of many Muslims that their religion is being threatened. People who feel threatened by a common enemy often unite in opposition to that antagonist. In particular, there are numerous indications that the issue of the Palestinians and the U.S. support of Israel is a key element in the opinion of Muslims, especially Arabs, toward the United States. Given that, a peaceful solution that addresses the needs and rights of both Jews and Arabs in the region will benefit not only those two groups, but the United States and the rest of the world as well. Perhaps the best lesson to draw is that religion is a significant factor in international relations. Like any set of coherent ideas, religion helps define who is on which side and thus often plays a powerful role in shaping the perceptions of political leaders and the actions of the countries they command.

Transnational Movements

A wide range of transnational movements focus on one or another general aspect of the human condition. Many of these can even claim a role in people's political identity, but they are not inherently linked to the redrawing of territorial political boundaries around the movement's supporters in the same way as regional and some other forms of transnationalism are. Some of these movements focus on specific issues, such as the transnational environmental movement. Others are organized around demographic groups, such as women. The women's movement provides an excellent case study of the organization and operation of transnational movements.

Women in the World

It strains the obvious to point out that women globally have been and remain second-class citizens economically, politically, and socially. Historical data is scant, but current statistics show that no country has achieved socioeconomic or political gender equality. There are relative differences between countries, with the gap between men and women generally greater in less developed countries (LDCs) than in economically developed countries (EDCs). Still, the country-to-country differences are not all explained by economics. Socioeconomic gender differences are represented in the map on page 158.

We will say much more about the status of women in chapter 15's section on human rights, but for now consider the following barrage of facts: Women constitute 70% of the world's poor and 64% of the world's illiterate adults. They occupy only about 1 in 7 of the world's managerial and administrative jobs and constitute less than 40% of the world's professional and technical workers. Worldwide, women are much less likely to have access to paid employment, and the average women who does have a job earns only about half of what the average man does. As noted earlier, women are much more likely than men to be refugees, the victims of domestic violence, and the targets of

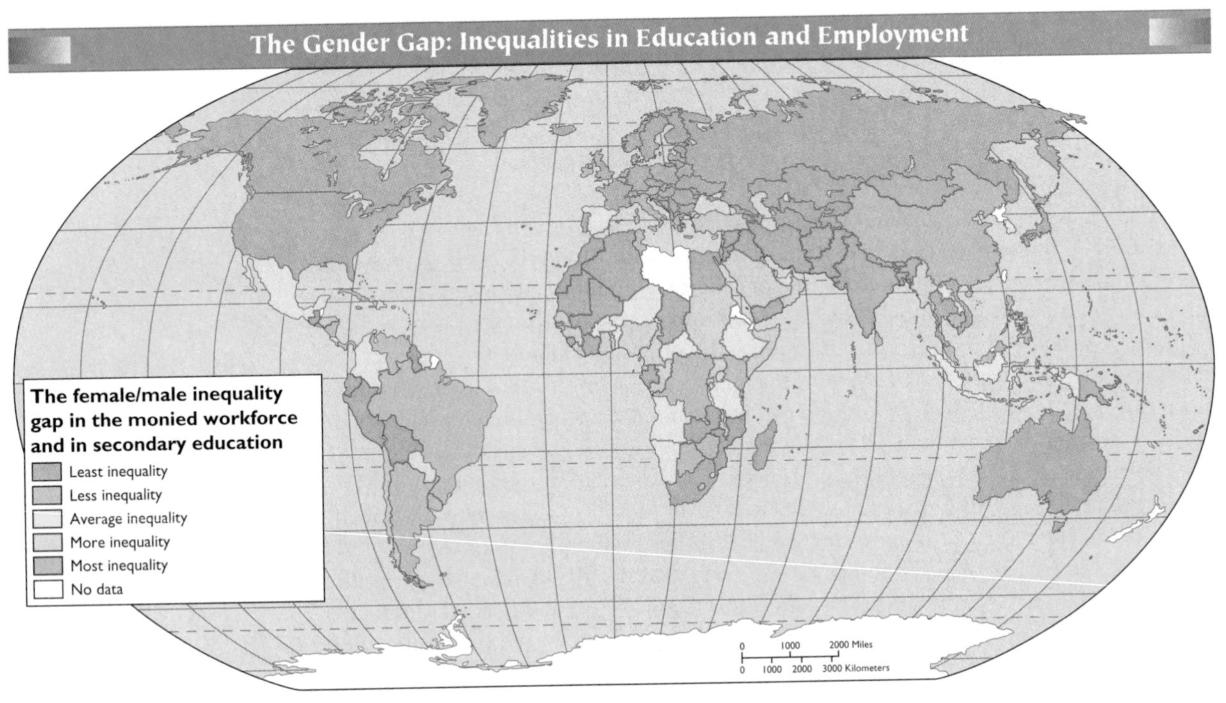

The day may come when one end of a scale of male/female equality is labeled "equal." That time has not arrived yet. This map classifies countries on a scale of relative inequality, ranging from least inequality to most inequality. All societies are held back by legally or socially restricting the educational and work opportunities of females, who make up half the population. While every country does this, the less developed countries, those that need "people power" the most, tend to be the most restrictive and to waste more of the talents of their women.

organized sexual assault during conflicts. A recent survey of 35 cities globally found that 2.2% of the women reported having been the victim of a sexual assault (UNDP, 2003). With such crimes often going unreported, the real percentage is almost surely substantially higher.

Such economic, social, and political deprivations of women are not new. What has changed is women's ability to see their common status in global terms through transnational communication and transportation. What is also new is the focused determination of women and the men who support the cause of gender equality to work together through transnational NGOs to address these issues. As one UNDP report (1995:1) points out, "Moving toward gender equality is not a technocratic goal—it is a political process." The global women's movement is the driving force in this political process.

Goals of the Transnational Women's Movement

Transformation is a term that captures the goals of the transnational women's movement. Chapter 6 takes up the role of women as national leaders, but we can say here that only about 1 in 20 countries is led by a woman, only about 1 in 10 national cabinet ministers is a woman, and only about 1 in 7 national legislators is a woman.

International organizations are no less gender skewed. No woman has ever headed the UN, the International Monetary Fund (IMF), the World Trade Organization (WTO), or the World Bank; and women occupy only about 15% of the senior management positions in the leading IGOs. Like male political leaders, some females have been successful in office; others have not. Yet, as the longtime (1980–1996) president of Iceland, Vigdis Finnbogadottir, has remarked, the stereotype remains that "women are not competitive enough or women do not understand economics." "If you do something wrong," she warned other women at a conference, "you will be attacked with the strongest weapon—mockery."[21]

Advocates of women's political activism see their goal as more than simply a drive for power. For them, increased power for women is also a way to change policy based on their view that, overall, women have different values than men on a variety of issues. While history demonstrates that women leaders can and have used military force, it is also the case, as discussed in chapter 3, that women have been generally less inclined to advocate force than men have been. There are also other differences. A recent poll found, for instance, that American women consistently place more emphasis than do men on international social and economic programs. One illustrative question asked men and women to prioritize whether countries should get U.S. foreign aid based on whether the recipient was important to U.S. security, was important as a U.S. trading partner, or was poor.[22] The rankings (and percentages of those expressing a preference) were:

Men	*Women*
1. Security (39%)	1. Poverty (37%)
2. Trade (35%)	2. Security (36%)
3. Poverty (26%)	3. Trade (27%)

The transnational women's movement additionally addresses the normative issue of how to improve the lot of women—and everyone else—in the international system. As such, the concern extends beyond sexism's deleterious effect on women to include the impact of discrimination on the entire society. Feminists point out correctly that keeping women illiterate retards the entire economic and social development of a society. It is not a coincidence, for example, that the percentage of women in the paid workforce is lowest in those countries where the gap between male and female literacy is the highest. Educating these illiterate women would increase the number of ways that they could contribute to their countries' economic and social growth. Beyond this, there is a correlation between the educational level of women and their percentage of the wage-earning workforce, on the one hand, and restrained population growth, on the other. In other words, one good path to population control is creating a society of fully educated men and women who are employed equally in wage-earning occupations.

Programs and Organization of the Transnational Women's Movement

Women have been and are politically active in a large number of organizations that focus all or in part on women's issues. These organizations and their members interact transnationally at many levels ranging from the Internet through global conferences. For instance, women can now find out more about their common concerns through such sites as that of the UN's WomenWatch at http://www.un.org/ womenwatch/. Collectively, women are now frequently gathering in such global forums as the UN Conference on Population and Development (UNCPD), held in Cairo in 1994, the 1995 **World Conference on Women (WCW)** in Beijing, and the **Beijing + 5 Conference** that convened in New York City in 2000. Beyond the substantive proceedings of such conferences, they facilitate transnational contacts among women. Parma Khastgir, a Supreme Court justice in India and a delegate to the 1995 WCW, stressed this contribution, noting that "what appealed to me most [about the WCW] was that people

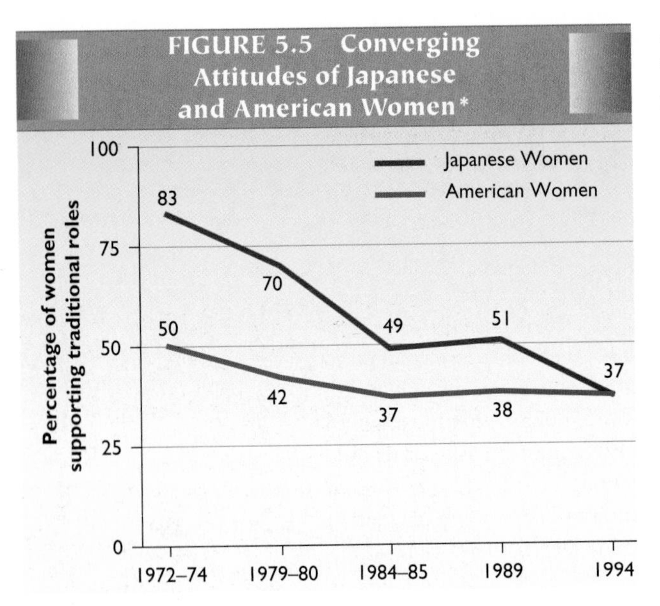

Transnational communications help create similar values across national boundaries. Changes in attitudes about the roles played by women began earlier in the United States, Canada, and Europe than elsewhere. Feminist attitudes have, however, spread globally even to very traditional societies, such as Japan's, as this figure shows.

*This figure incorporates data from surveys that asked similar, but not always the same, questions about accepting or rejecting traditional roles for women and men. Questions were not always asked in the same year in both countries.
Data source: Ladd and Bowman (1996).

overcame their ethnic barriers and were able to discuss universal problems. They showed solidarity."[23] Even more importantly, women draw on their contacts and experiences through NGOs to promote and influence national and international policy (Jutta, 2003).

It is difficult to measure the precise impact that transnational communications among women is having through individual interactions, world and regional conferences, and the mass media (Shaheed, 1999). There is evidence, however, that cultural differences among women relating to their roles are narrowing (Inglehart & Norris, 2003). Figure 5.5 shows, for example, that the views of Japanese women, who had been very traditional compared to American women, came to parallel the attitudes of American women.

Advances of Women in Politics

Another standard by which to judge the impact of the transnational feminist movement is the advancement of women in politics. "Never before have so many women held so much power," writes one scholar. "The growing participation and representation of women in politics is one of the most remarkable developments of the late 20th century" (Jaquette, 1997:23).

Both these statements are certainly factual, but it is also the case that progress is slow, and that women remain a political minority part of both national and international governance. The changes within national governments, which are detailed in chapter 6, parallel the uphill climb of women to political power in international organizations (Meyer & Prügel, 1999). The UN Charter pledges equal opportunity for men and women. The reality a half century after the charter was adopted is that women hold only 36% of the professional staff positions and only 15% of all top UN administrative posts. Just 10% of the ambassadors to the UN are women. "We are a collection of all the world's chauvinisms," one UN staff member has commented bluntly.[24] Still, progress is being made. The secretary-general has appointed a number of women to high UN posts. Most notably, Kofi Annan in 1998 named Canadian diplomat Louise Fréchette as deputy secretary-general, the UN's second highest post. She and six other women make up 23% of the 30 administrators who are members of the UN's Senior Management Group chaired by the secretary-general. Thus, things are changing, although 23% of the senior managers is not half. Former UN executive Nafis Sadik has recalled that in the 1970s, when she first came to work at the UN, "Western men saw me as an Asian woman; very decorative, but I couldn't possibly have any ideas."[25] When she retired in 2000 after 13 years as head of UNFPA, no one any longer saw Executive Director Sadik as an adornment.

The accomplishments of these women have been, of course, personal. Many of the other advances of women have been made through national efforts. It is also the case, however, that the progress of women almost everywhere has been facilitated by and, in turn, has contributed to the transnational feminist movement. Women have begun to think of themselves politically not as only American, or Canadian, or Zimbabwean women, but as women with a transnational identity and ties. This is both transforming national politics and weakening the hold of nationalism.

Transnationalism Tomorrow

It is impossible to predict how far transnationalism will progress. It is not inconceivable that a century from now humans will share a common culture and perhaps even a common government. That is, however, far from certain. There are those who doubt that the trend of today toward transculturalism will continue into the future. Some analysts believe, for example, that English will cease to be the common language of the Internet as more and more non-English-speaking people gain access. "Be careful of turning astute observations about the current state of the Web into implications for the future," one observer cautions wisely.[26]

E Pluribus Unum?

Moreover, nationalism is proving to be a very resilient barrier to globalization and to transnational movements. For example, it is true to some degree that a transnational identity has evolved among Europeans in connection with the EU. Yet those with that new political identity remain a small minority that is dwarfed by the percentage of people living in the EU countries who retain their traditional loyalty to the nation-state.

Thus we can say that the world is changing and even that it has been changing during recent decades at a rapid pace relative to the normal rate of change throughout history. If anyone had 50 or 60 years ago predicted that globalization and transnationalism would progress as far as they have by the middle of the first decade of the 21st century, critics would have called that person hopelessly befuddled. So what has occurred is remarkable. That does not mean, however, that the transnational trend will continue.

Chapter Summary

Globalization

1. The development of transnationalism springs from two sources: human thought and global interaction. Transnationalism includes a range of loyalties, activities, and other phenomena that connect humans across nations and national boundaries. This chapter explores the bases and evidence of how globalization has furthered transnationalism in the world.
2. The world has become much more interdependent and interconnected through transportation and communications globalization, economic globalization, and cultural globalization. This globalization has spurred transnationalism.

Transnationalism

3. The lineage of transnational thought extends in Western culture back to the Stoics of ancient Greece and Rome and to Buddhism in Eastern culture. Transnational thought is evident today in many aspects of postmodernism, constructivism, and feminism.

Transnationalism in Action

4. Evidence of the advance of transnationalism is provided by the rapid growth, in number and range of activities, of transnational nongovernmental organizations.
5. Regional transnationalism, so far evident only in Europe, could lead to the growth of political identification with regions, rather than nation-states.
6. Many observers believe that cultural transnationalism will lead to greater harmony in the world. There are other analysts, however, who think that we are not moving toward a common culture but, instead, toward a future in which people will identify with and politically organize themselves around one or another of several antagonistic cultures or so-called civilizations.

7. Most religions have a strong transnational element. Some religions assert universalistic claims; other religions create an urge to unite all the members of that religion across countries.
8. Religion has played many roles in world politics, both positive and negative. The current rise in religious fundamentalism in many areas of the world is worrisome.
9. To understand the role of religion in world politics, a case study of Islam discusses the global impact of a transnational religion.
10. An important modern trend in international relations is the growth of transnational movements and organizations that are concerned with global issues. This includes the transnational women's movement and its associated organizations.
11. Although women's attitudes and emphases may vary, the transnational women's movement shares a similar philosophy and goals. These center on the idea that women around the world should cooperate to promote gender equality and to transform the way we think about and conduct politics at every level, including the international level.
12. Feminists, both women and the men who support gender equity, are pursuing numerous projects and making progress. The fourth World Conference on Women and its follow-up Beijing +5 Conference are examples of activity in this area.

Transnationalism Tomorrow

13. For all the transnational change that has taken place, there is resistance to it. Nationalism remains a powerful, resilient force, and it still dominates people's political identification.

For a chapter quiz, interactive activities, web links, PowerWeb articles, and much more, visit **www.mhhe.com/rourke10/** and go to chapter 5. Or, while accessing the site, click on Course-Wide Content and view recent international relations articles in the *New York Times.*

Key Terms

Beijing + 5 Conference
civil society
clash of civilizations
constructivism
feminism
fundamentalism
globalization
nongovernmental organizations (NGOs)
political identity
postmodernism
transnational advocacy networks
transnationalism
World Conference on Women (WCW)

CHAPTER

6

National States: The Traditional Structure

THE NATURE AND PURPOSE OF THE STATE

The State Defined

Purposes of the State

THE STATE AS THE CORE POLITICAL ORGANIZATION

Theories of Governance

Democracy and World Politics

National and Other Interests

STATES AND THE FUTURE

The State: The Indictment

The State: The Defense

The State: The Verdict

CHAPTER SUMMARY

KEY TERMS

For the whole state, I would put mine armour on,
Which I can scarcely bear.

—William Shakespeare, *Coriolanus*

Something is rotten in the state of Denmark.

—William Shakespeare, *Hamlet*

Who saves his country, saves himself, saves all things, and all things saved do bless him! Who lets his country die, lets all things die, dies himself ignobly, and all things dying curse him!

—Senator Benjamin H. Hill Jr., 1893

Man exists for his own sake and not to add a laborer to the state.

—Ralph Waldo Emerson, *Journals,* 1839

CHAPTER OBJECTIVES

After completing this chapter, you should be able to:

- Define states as political organizations.
- Explain various theories of governance.
- Analyze forms of authoritarian governance.
- Analyze standards of democracy.
- Discuss the importance of balancing individualism and communitarianism in democracies.
- Examine the drive to institute democracy globally and the related implications for global and national security.
- Outline the democratic peace thesis.
- List various types of interests in determining international activity.
- Discuss the future of states as principal actors in the world system.

How to organize global governance is the subject of this and the next chapter. Each examines one of the two divergent roads that we can take toward politically organizing the world stage. This chapter focuses on the traditional path that we have been following for several centuries. Organizationally, it features the state (nation state, national state) as the core political actor. It is to one of these states that children in many American schools daily "pledge allegiance," and it is to nearly 200 other states that other people in this politically fragmented world direct their patriotic feelings. The role of the state is so important that you will find commentary on its history and operation in other parts of this book. For example, the origins and evolution of the state are detailed in chapter 2, and state-level analysis in chapter 3 explores how countries make foreign policy. In this chapter we will add to that analysis by looking at the operation of the state as the most important political actor in the international system.

For all the importance of states, it is essential to understand that they have not always existed. Humans have organized themselves in cities, leagues, empires, and other political structures at various times in history. States, as evident in chapter 2, are actually relatively recent organizational innovations. Moreover, as evident in the map below, most current states are less than 200 years old. The importance of these facts—that the state as a form of governance has a beginning and that most states are relatively young—underscores the implication that the state as the core of political organization may not be permanent.

If not the state, then what? To answer this question, chapter 7 takes up the United Nations, the European Union, and other international governmental organizations, which are the most likely alternatives in the globalized world of today and in what will almost certainly be the even more interconnected world of tomorrow.

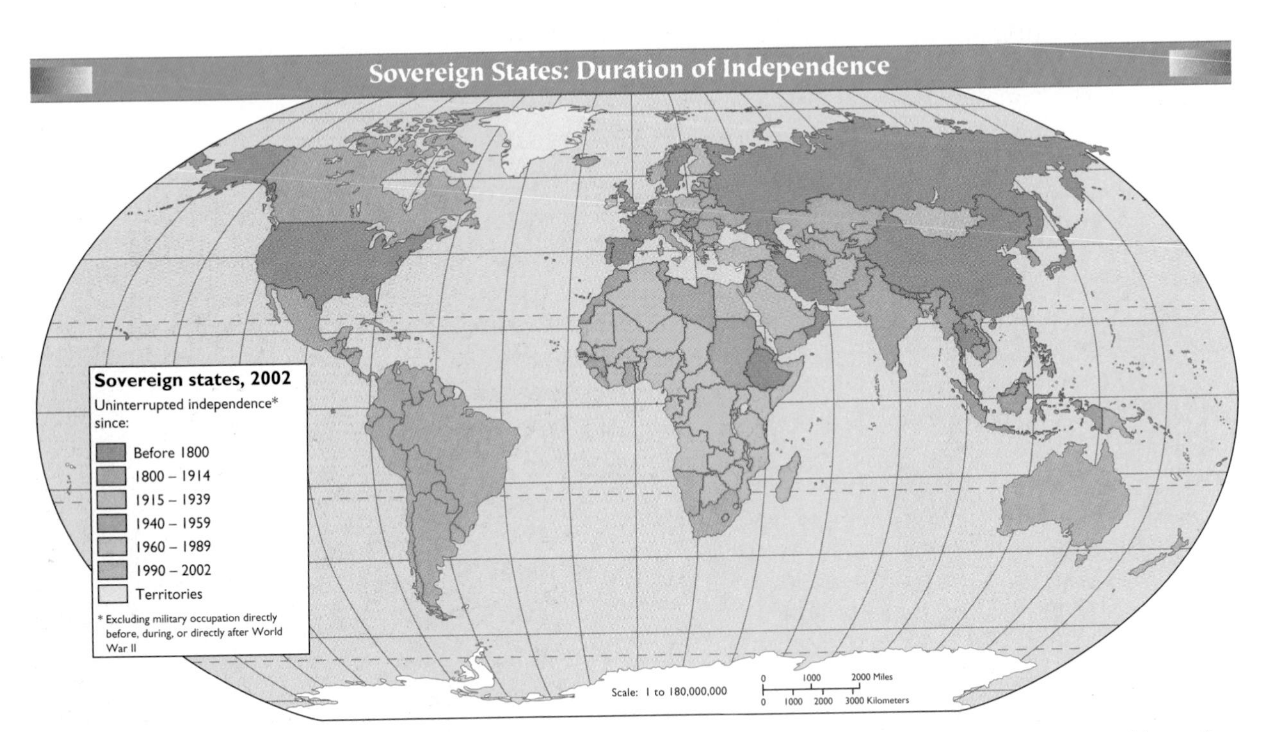

This map gives you an opportunity to see the geographic dimensions of the recent rapid growth in the number of countries. Notice that Asia and Africa have seen the most change. Most of the countries that now exist on those continents were colonies of a European country in 1940.

The Nature and Purpose of the State

In considering states, it is important to understand how their existence as sovereign actors affects world politics and also their political future. Discussing these matters, however, requires that we first establish a foundation of knowledge about states and their purpose.

The State Defined

States are territorially defined political units that exercise ultimate internal authority and that recognize no legitimate external authority over themselves. States are also the most important units in defining the political identity of most people. When an Olympian steps atop the ceremonial stands to receive his or her gold medal, the flag of the victor's country is raised and its national anthem is played. States are also the most powerful of all political actors. Some huge companies approach or even exceed the wealth of some poorer countries, but no individual, company, group, or international organization approaches the coercive power wielded by most states. Whether large or small, rich or poor, populous or not, states share all or most of six characteristics: sovereignty, territory, population, diplomatic recognition, internal organization, and domestic support.

Sovereignty

The most important political characteristic of a state is **sovereignty**. This term means that the sovereign actor (the state) does not recognize as legitimate any higher authority. Sovereignty also includes the idea of legal equality among states. As discussed in chapter 2, sovereign states developed late in the Middle Ages (ca. 500–1350) from a consolidation and simultaneous expansion of political power. First, the rulers of Europe expanded their political authority by breaking away from the secular domination of the Holy Roman Empire and the theological authority of the pope. Second, the kings also consolidated political power by subjugating feudal estates and other competing local political organizations within their realms. The resulting states exercised supreme authority over their territory and citizens; they owed neither allegiance nor obedience to any higher authority.

It is important to note that sovereignty, a legal and theoretical term, differs from independence, a political and applied term (James, 1999). Independence means freedom from outside control, and in an ideal, law-abiding world, sovereignty and independence would be synonymous. In the real world, however, where power is important, independence is not absolute. Sometimes a small country is so dominated by a powerful neighbor that its independence is dubious at best. Especially in terms of their foreign and defense policies, legally sovereign countries such as Bhutan (dominated by India), the Marshall Islands (dominated by the United States), and Monaco (dominated by France) can be described as having only circumscribed independence (Clapham, 1999).

For several centuries the state has been and remains the primary actor on the world stage.

While independence has always been relative, the weakening of the doctrine of state sovereignty is more of a recent phenomenon. It is one of the most important changes under way in the international system. The world community is beginning to reject sovereignty as a defense of a government's mistreatment of its citizens. During the early 1990s, global condemnation coupled with economic and other forms of sanctions forced the Eurowhite-dominated government of South Africa to end the apartheid system of oppression of its non-European-heritage citizens, especially its blacks. The UN also rejected the sovereignty defense when in 1994 it condemned the military overthrow of Haiti's elected president and authorized UN members "to form a multinational force . . . [and] to use all necessary means" to topple the military junta. Soon thereafter, a U.S.-led force sent the generals packing into exile. The international community in the late 1990s demanded that the Yugoslav government cease its brutal attacks on rebellious Albanians in Kosovo, even though that province is clearly part of Yugoslavia. When diplomacy and sanctions failed, NATO warplanes went into action. The Serbs were driven from Kosovo, and the province was occupied by KFOR, the multinational Kosovo Force. Even more recently, the UN authorized the use of international force to topple the government of Afghanistan if it did not comply with demands that it surrender accused al-Qaeda terrorists. When that did not happen, the UN supported the military overthrow of that regime.

A related and dramatic demonstration of the diminution of sovereignty is the trial of Slobodan Milosevic, the former president (1989–2000) of Yugoslavia (officially renamed Serbia and Montenegro in February 2003), on war crimes charges. The action marks the first time in history that an elected president has had to answer in an international court for actions taken while in office. The 29-count indictment against Milosevic includes genocide, murder, torture, and other crimes against humanity and violations of the Geneva Conventions (1949) and characterizes him as having "participated in a joint criminal enterprise" that led to the death and inhumane treatment of tens of thousands of people in Bosnia, Croatia, and Kosovo during the 1990s. It is said that the wheels of justice grind slowly, and in April 2004 with the trial of Milosevic in its twenty-sixth month, that seems particularly true in his case. Still, if convicted, as he almost certainly will be, by the International War Crimes Tribunal for the Balkans located in The Hague, the Netherlands, Milosevic could be sentenced to life in prison.

Expressing a widespread view, one human rights advocate hailed the prosecution of Milosevic as evidence that "even the highest government officials are vulnerable to international prosecution for the most heinous human rights crimes. . . . It will begin to force would-be tyrants to think twice before replicating Milosevic's atrocities."[1] Other observers worried, however, that whatever crimes Milosevic allegedly has committed, putting him on trial before a UN-sponsored tribunal and similar actions have, as one U.S. senator put it, "turned the principle of national sovereignty on its head."[2] Taking a similar view, a member of the U.S. House of Representatives asserted that "the prosecution of Milosevic, a democratically elected . . . leader of a sovereign country . . . threatens U.S. sovereignty." The representative went on to explain, "We cannot have it both ways. We cannot expect to use [war crimes tribunals] when it pleases us and oppose [them] where the rules would apply to our own acts of aggression."[3]

What should we make of these restraints on internal sovereignty in South Africa, Haiti, Yugoslavia, and Afghanistan? It would be naive to imagine they mean that in the foreseeable future the world community will regularly ignore sovereignty to take a stand against racism or authoritarianism whenever and wherever they occur. It would be equally wrong, however, not to recognize that the actions against racial oppression, military coups, ethnic cleansing, and neofascism were important steps away from the doctrine of unlimited state sovereignty.

Sovereignty also implies legal *equality* among states. That theory is applied in the UN General Assembly and many other international assemblies, where each member-state has one vote. Are all states really equal, though? Compare San Marino and China (Table 6.1). San Marino lies entirely within Italy and is the world's oldest republic, dating back to the fourth century A.D. After years of self-imposed nonparticipation, the San

TABLE 6.1 San Marino and China: Sovereign Equals

	San Marino	China	Ratio
Territory (sq. mi.)	24	3,705,400	1:154,392
Population	27,730	1,292,068,842	1:46,595
Gross domestic product	$860,000,000	$1,131,200,000,000	1:1,315
Military personnel	0	2,310,000	1:∞
Vote in the UN General Assembly	1	1	1:1

The legal concept of sovereign equality is very different from more tangible measures of equality, as is evident in this comparison of two countries: San Marino and China.

Note: Data for China includes now-incorporated Hong Kong. San Marino has a police force with an annual budget of about $37 million. ∞ = infinity

Data sources: World Bank (2003); CIA (2003).

Marinese decided to seek membership in the UN. "The fact of sitting around the table with the most important states in the world is a reaffirmation of sovereignty," explained the country's foreign minister.[4] The General Assembly seated San Marino in 1992 as a sovereign equal. Nevertheless, it is obvious that whatever sovereignty may mean legally, in many ways the two countries are not equal.

Territory

A second characteristic of a state is territory. It would seem obvious that a state must have physical boundaries, and most states do. On closer examination, though, the question of territory becomes more complex. There are numerous international disputes over borders; territorial boundaries can expand, contract, or shift dramatically; and it is even possible to have a state without territory. Many states recognize what they call Palestine as sovereign, yet the Palestinians are scattered across other countries such as Jordan. An accord that the Israelis and Palestinians signed in 1994 gave the Palestinians a measure of autonomy in Gaza (a region between Israel and Egypt) and in parts of the West Bank, and these areas have been expanded through subsequent negotiations. However, the spiral downward in Israeli-Palestinian relations in 2002 and 2003 brought numerous Israeli military operations within the Palestinian areas. Indeed, at times the Israeli army had the headquarters of Palestinian leader Yasser Arafat under siege. In sum, depending on one's viewpoint, the Palestinians have some territory, no territory, or have been expelled from the territory now occupied by Israel. It is also possible to maintain, as the United States and most other countries currently do, that the Palestinians still have no state of their own.

Did You Know That:

Other than the United States, countries have a two-letter national "domain" designation of their cyberspace territory. Evolving statehood for Palestine has prompted the private Internet Corporation for Assigned Names and Numbers to grant the domain designation ".ps" to the Palestinian National Authority (PNA), whose URL is now http://www.pna.gov.ps/.

Population

People are an obvious requirement for any state. The populations of states range from the 911 inhabitants of the Holy See (popularly referred to as the Vatican) to China's approximately 1.3 billion people, but all states count this characteristic as a minimum requirement.

What is becoming less clear in the shifting loyalties of the evolving international system is exactly where the population of a country begins and ends. Citizenship has become a bit more fluid than it was not long ago. For example, a citizen of one European Union (EU) country who resides in another EU country can now vote in local elections and even hold local office in the country in which he or she resides. Similarly, recent changes in the laws of Mexico allow Mexicans who have emigrated to the United States and become citizens to retain their Mexican citizenship, vote in that country's presidential election, and even have their children who are born in the United States claim dual citizenship.

Diplomatic Recognition

A classic rhetorical question is, If a tree fell in the forest and no one heard it, did it make a sound? The same question governs the issue of statehood and recognition by others. If a political entity declares its independence and no other country grants it diplomatic recognition, is it really a state? The answer seems to be no.

How many countries must grant recognition before statehood is achieved is a more difficult question. When Israel declared its independence in 1948, the United States and the Soviet Union quickly recognized the country. Its Arab neighbors did not extend recognition and instead attacked what they considered to be the Zionist invaders. Was Israel a state at that point? It certainly seems so, because which countries, as well as how many of them, extend recognition is important.

Yet a lack of recognition, even by a majority of other countries, does not necessarily mean a state does not exist. Diplomatic recognition by most countries of the communist government of Mao Zedong in China came slowly after it took power in 1949. U.S. recognition was withheld until 1979. Did that mean that the rechristened People's Republic of China did not exist for a time? Clearly the answer is no because, as one scholar comments, "power capabilities are equally or more important than outside recognition" in establishing the existence of a state (Thompson, 1995:220).

The issue of recognition remains a matter of serious international concern. Taiwan is for all practical purposes an independent country, with more than two dozen countries recognizing it as such. Yet Taiwan itself does not claim independence from China, and thus is a *de facto* (in fact) but not *de jure* (in law) state. Tibet provides another example in the region of what might be called a state-in-waiting, as the Play a Part box "The Future of Tibet" explains.

Another contemporary issue involves the Palestinians. Many states recognize a Palestinian state and did so even before the Palestinians acquired any autonomous territory in Gaza and the West Bank beginning in the mid-1990s. Currently, according to the Palestine National Authority (PNA), almost 100 countries (including China and India) recognize an "independent State of Palestine," some 79 (including the United States) accept Palestinian passports, and 22 countries maintain representative missions in Gaza or the West Bank. Moreover, the United Nations Security Council passed a resolution in 2002 calling for a separate Palestinian state. Somewhat less definitively, President George W. Bush has also declared his support under the right conditions for a Palestinian state, although one "whose borders and certain aspects of its sovereignty will be provisional until resolved as part of a final settlement in the Middle East."[5] Yet since the PNA has not declared an independent Palestine, it would be hard to construe these diplomatic ties as recognizing Palestinian sovereign statehood. When the final step toward independence comes, as seems increasingly likely to occur, the degree to which countries recognize that independence and establish full diplomatic relations will have important legal and political ramifications for the nascent state of Palestine.

Certainly, the standard of diplomatic recognition remains hazy. Nevertheless, it is an important factor in the international system for several reasons. One is related to psychological status. History has many examples of new countries and governments, even those with revolutionary ideology, that have assiduously sought outside recognition and, to a degree, moderated their policies in order to get it. Second, external recognition has important practical advantages. Generally, states are the only entities that can legally sell

PLAY A PART

The Future of Tibet

China claims Tibet is a province. Most Tibetans and many others maintain that their homeland is an occupied state. If you agree, you can join celebrities such as Richard Gere and many other less well-known people who support Tibet's self-rule. Tibet is almost twice the size of Texas and sits 15,000 feet high in the Himalayas. There are about 2.5 million Tibetans in their homeland, and nearly as many in adjacent areas in China and northern India. The spiritual leader of Tibetan Buddhism and the former secular leader of Tibet is the fourteenth Dalai Lama, who was born Lhamo Dhondrub and enthroned in 1940 when he was just five years old.

Tibet was independent from the 800s to the 1300s. It then came under Mongol rule for over 300 years, but exercised considerable autonomy under its theocratic leader, who in 1577 was designated as the Dalai Lama (lama of all within the seas) by the Mongols. That autonomy ended when the Chinese emperor launched an invasion and in 1751 established his suzerainty over Tibet. A new era of independence began in 1911, after imperial China collapsed, and lasted until 1950, when Chinese forces again seized control. At first, the Dalai Lama remained in Tibet and exercised some authority. Then in 1959 the Tibetans revolted against China. They were crushed, and the Dalai Lama and his supporters fled south to India.

No country recognizes Tibet, but the Dalai Lama continues to try to build support while emphasizing, "I am not seeking independence, I am seeking genuine autonomy." That message does not assuage China. It characterizes him as "a political exile engaged in separatist activities," and warned after he conferred in May 2001 with President George W. Bush that the meeting constituted "rude interference" in China's internal affairs.[1] For his part, President Bush has been cautious, declaring his "strong support for the Dalai Lama's tireless efforts to initiate a dialogue with the Chinese government," expressing his "hope that the Chinese government would respond favorably," and praising "the Dalai Lama's commitment to nonviolence."[2] In the parlance of diplomacy, this means that Washington is not willing to upset relations with Beijing by pressing it too hard on the status of Tibet.

While near-term Tibetan autonomy seems unlikely, politics is often a place of sudden, unexpected changes. So if you want to take the question, What is a state? from the realm of political theory to political action, and you support the Tibetan cause, get involved. There are numerous groups, many on college campuses, that would welcome your support. A starting place is to visit the Web site of the Tibet government in exile at http://www.tibet.com/, where the "How you can help Tibet" hyperlink offers suggestions. Among other sites worth checking out are those of Students for a Free Tibet (http://www.studentsforafreetibet.org/), and the International Campaign for Tibet (http://www.savetibet.org/). Just two of the many examples of campus-based organizations are the University of Washington chapter of Students for a Free Tibet (http://students.washington.edu/tibet/) and the University of Georgia chapter (http://www.uga.edu/sft/).

Numerous groups and individuals support Tibetan independence from China. The protesters here are the members of the dramatic company at London's Globe Theater, where William Shakespeare staged his plays. The actors hope that they can one day emulate the character Cinna in Julius Caesar *and exclaim, "Liberty! Freedom! Tyranny is dead! / Run hence, proclaim, cry it about the streets."*

For China's perspective on the status of Tibet, visit the Web sites of the China Internet Information Center at http://www.tibet-china.org/indexE.html and the China Tibet Information Center at http://www.tibetinfor.com.cn/english/.

government bonds and buy heavy weapons from another state. Israel's chances of survival in 1948 were enhanced when recognition allowed the Israelis to raise money and purchase armaments in Europe, the United States, and elsewhere. Also, it would be difficult for any aspirant to statehood to survive for long without recognition. Economic problems resulting from the inability to establish trade relations are just one example of the difficulties that would arise. The case of Taiwan shows that survival while in diplomatic limbo is not impossible, but it is such an oddity that it does not disprove the general rule.

Internal Organization

States must normally have some level of political and economic structure. Most states have a government, but statehood continues during periods of severe turmoil, even anarchy. Afghanistan, Liberia, Sierra Leone, Somalia, and some other existing states dissolved into chaos during the last decade or so, and none of them can be said to have reestablished a stable government that can exercise real authority over most of the country. Yet none of these "failed states" has ceased to exist legally. Each, for instance, continued to sit as a sovereign equal, with an equal vote, in the UN General Assembly. In the case of Afghanistan, the United Nations never recognized the de facto control of most of the country between 1995 and 2001 by the Taliban government. Instead, the UN continued to seat a representative of what had become the rebel Northern Alliance until the establishment of a tenuous new government under President Hamid Karzai in mid-2002.

An associated issue arises when what once was, and what still claims to be, the government of a generally recognized or formerly recognized state exists outside the territory that the exiled government claims as its own. There is a long history of recognizing governments-in-exile. The most common instances have occurred when a sitting government is forced by invaders to flee. A current and controversial example of what claims to be a government-in-exile involves Tibet, as explained in the earlier box, "The Future of Tibet."

Domestic Support

The final characteristic of a state is domestic support. At its most active, this implies that a state's population is loyal to it and grants it the authority to make rules and to govern (legitimacy). At its most passive, the population grudgingly accepts the authority of the government. For all the coercive power that a state usually possesses, it is difficult for any state to survive without at least the passive acquiescence of its people. The dissolution of Czechoslovakia, the Soviet Union, and Yugoslavia are illustrations of multinational states collapsing in the face of the separatist impulses of disaffected nationalities. One of the challenges facing the U.S. effort to stabilize postwar Iraq is whether it will be possible to create sufficient domestic support for any government among the badly divided Shiites, Sunnis, and Kurds, all of whom, in turn, have their own internal divisions.

As is evident from the foregoing discussion of the characteristics of a state, what is or is not a state is not an absolute. Because a state's existence is more a political than a legal matter, there is a significant gray area. No country truly imagines that the Palestinians control a sovereign state, yet many countries recognize it as such for political reasons. By the same political token, Taiwan is a functioning state, but China's power keeps it in a legal limbo. And no matter what the Tibetans and their Dalai Lama say and no matter what anyone's sympathies may be, Tibet is not and has never been recognized as a sovereign state by any government. Then there are the failed states that remain legal sovereign entities by default because there is nothing else that can be easily done with them.

Purposes of the State

Have you ever stopped to think about why we humans organize ourselves into political units with governments? After all, governments are expensive and they are perpetually telling us what we must and must not do. Yet, despite these arguable drawbacks, humans have subjected themselves to one or another governing authority as far back in history as we can see.

Although political philosophers have disagreed over why humans create societies and establish governments, *individual betterment* is a common theme among them (Baradat, 2003). For example, this theme is evident in the writing of such classical theorists as Thomas Hobbes (1588–1679) and John Locke (1632–1704), both of whom are also discussed in chapter 1. Each contended that people had once lived as individuals or in family groups in a **state of nature**. Communities of unrelated individuals did not exist, and people possessed individual sovereignty, that is, they did not grant authority (legitimate power) to anyone or anything (a government) beyond their families to regulate their behavior. They also argued that people eventually found this highly decentralized existence unsatisfactory. Therefore, the theory continues, it was the desire to improve their lives that prompted individuals and families to join together in societies, to surrender much of their sovereignty, and to create governments to conduct the society's affairs. All this was based on an implicit understanding called a **social contract** that specified the purposes of governments and the limitations on them.

Hobbes and Locke disagreed about what was so unsatisfactory that it persuaded people to abandon the state of nature and merge into societies. Hobbes argued that the problem was that life without government was so dangerous that constant fear led people to create strong governments to provide protection. From a very different perspective, Locke contended that people left the state of nature and joined in societies because they came to realize that they could improve their lives more easily through cooperation than by individual, but isolated, effort.

Such notions did not go unnoticed, and the ideas of Hobbes and Locke are clearly evident, for example, in the fundamental documents of the American Revolution and the new United States. The idea in the Declaration of Independence that people had a right to "life, liberty, and the pursuit of happiness," and "that to secure these rights, governments are instituted among men," is drawn closely from Locke. And the preamble to the U.S. Constitution combines Hobbes's emphasis on protection and Locke's focus on individual advancement in its words that the purpose of the new government is to "insure domestic tranquility, provide for the common defense, [and] promote the general welfare."

The significant point about Hobbes and Locke is that they agreed that political units and their governments were not just givens. Instead, they saw them as instruments created for a utilitarian purpose and believed that these organizations were legitimate and should survive only as long as they fulfilled the purposes for which they had been established in the first place and did not overstep the limits placed on them by the social contract. This approach is called the **instrumental theory of government**. The idea, as President Woodrow Wilson put it, is that "government should not be made an end in itself; it is a means only—a means to be freely adapted to advance the best interest of the social organism. The state exists for the sake of society, not society for the sake of the state."

A final point in this discussion of the purpose of government is to address the question, What does this have to do with world politics? The answer is that having some sense of what states and their governments are meant to do is a necessary step to evaluating how well they are operating. For example, we address the topic of national interest later in this chapter, and since national refers to the interests of the nation, not the state, you will be asked to think about whether the interests of the nation and those of the state are always synonymous.

At the end, this chapter also takes up the question of the future of the state, an issue that is present throughout the text's analysis of the traditional versus alternative paths to the future. You will see that there are analysts who do not believe that the state can fulfill the purposes for which it was created and that new forms of political organization will and/or should supplement or replace states as the basic unit of governance. These analysts would argue (and Hobbes and Locke would agree) with the contention in the Declaration of Independence: "That whenever any form of government becomes destructive [or incapable] of these ends, it is the right of the people to alter or to abolish it, and to institute a new government, laying its foundations on such principles and organizing its powers in such form, as to them shall seem mostly likely to effect their safety and happiness."

The State as the Core Political Organization

Having explored the nature and purpose of states, our next task is to look at the state as our primary political organization. Chapter 3 points out that the anarchical nature of the international system stems from the fact that the sovereign state is the key actor in the system. The chapter then looks inside the state to illuminate the foreign policy–making process. What we can add here is an examination of differing theories of governance and of national and other interests.

Theories of Governance

It is possible to divide theories of governance into two broad categories. One includes types of **authoritarian government**, which allow little or no participation in decision making by individuals and groups outside the upper reaches of the government. The second category includes **democratic government**, which allows much broader and more meaningful participation. As with many things we discuss, the line between authoritarian and democratic is not precise. Instead, using broad and meaningful participation as the standard, there is a scale that runs from one-person rule to full, direct democracy (or even, according to some, to anarchism). The map on p. 173 provides one way to order types of government, with the countries in shades of green being generally democratic and the countries in other colors being generally authoritarian.

Authoritarian Theories

The world has witnessed the coming, dominance, and passing of a number of nondemocratic political theories about how societies should be organized and governed. These can be grouped under general authoritarian theory and a number of more specialized theories. One thing to notice about them with regard to the purpose of the state is that they all (except communism in theory, although not in practice) work to control the people to benefit the state and its government, rather than work to control the state and its government to benefit the people, as is the case in democratic forms of government. Still, it is also the case that democracy has not always appealed to all political theorists. Before turning to the authoritarian theories, it should be noted that many garden-variety dictatorships are based on an urge to power by an individual or a group and not on any overarching theory of how societies are best governed.

General Authoritarian Theory Political theorists who have favored one or another form of authoritarian rule share a skeptical view of the intellectual or moral ability of the general public to govern itself. They believe, therefore, that people and their political structures (such as states) are best governed either by dictators or other forms of one-person rule or by oligarchies, which means rule by the few. Oligarchies can include hereditary aristocracies, plutocracies (rule by the wealthy class), or one-party rule (such as the Communist Party), among other schemes.

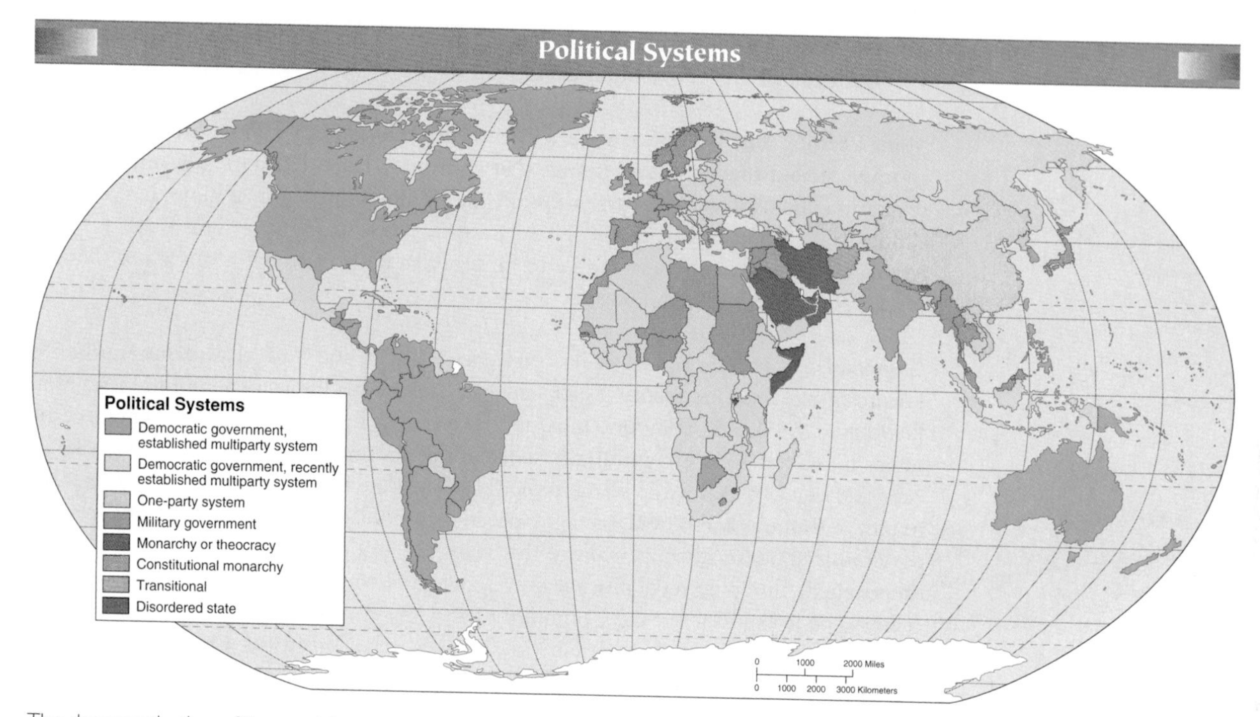

The democratization of the world's countries, which began symbolically with the American (1776) and French (1789) revolutions, progressed slowly for 150 years, then accelerated after World War II. Now, as this map indicates, the majority of countries are full-fledged or quasi-democracies.

Source: From John Allen and Elizabeth Leppman, *Student Atlas of World Politics,* 6th Edition, Dushkin/McGraw-Hill, p. 24. Reprinted with permission from Dushkin/McGraw-Hill.

Authoritarianism dates back to the beginning of political theory. The Greek philosopher Plato (ca. 428 B.C.–347 B.C.), in his famous work *The Republic,* dismissed democracy as "full of . . . disorder and dispensing a sort of quality of equals and unequals alike." He contended that the common citizenry trying to direct the state would be analogous to sailors on a ship "quarrelling over the control of the helm; each thinks he ought to be steering the vessel, though he has never learned navigation . . . ; what is more, they assert that navigation is a thing that cannot be taught at all, and are ready to tear in pieces anyone who says it can." Plato's conclusion was that ships needed strong captains and crews that took orders and that "all those who need to be governed should seek out the man who can govern them."

In more contemporary times, Juan Donoso Cortés, a Spanish legislator and political theoretician, outlined authoritarian theory in his "Speech on Dictatorship" (1849) to Spain's parliament. According to one study, he "viewed human beings as essentially and naturally depraved and irrational." Therefore, he believed that the order and, indeed, the survival of civilization depend on "the will of those who rule to demand and impose obedience . . . as well as upon the willingness of subjects to obey and believe their rulers."[6]

Theocracy The practice of theocratic rule by spiritual leaders is ancient. Now, however, it has virtually disappeared, and the Holy See (the Vatican) is the world's only pure **theocracy**. There are, however, some elements of theocracy left in the popular, if not the legal, status of Japan's emperor, Thailand's king, and (most strongly) Tibet's exiled Dalai Lama. Iran's government also contains an element of theocracy, as did the Taliban government of Afghanistan before it was toppled in 2001. Furthermore, the increased strength of religious fundamentalism in many places means that it is not unthinkable that a rejuvenation of theocracy might occur.

Monarchism The system of governance through hereditary rulers, **monarchism**, is another ancient theory of governance that continues. It has faded greatly, however, and strong monarchism, which rests on the theory of the divine right of kings, has declined almost to the point of extinction. There are only a few strong monarchs (such as Saudi Arabia's king) scattered among a larger number of constitutional monarchies that severely restrict the monarch's power.

Communism In the original works of Friedrich Engels and Karl Marx, **communism** is essentially an economic theory. As applied, however, by Vladimir Lenin and Josef Stalin in the USSR, by Mao Zedong in China, and by other Communist leaders elsewhere, communism also falls squarely within the spectrum of authoritarian governance. Even Marx expected that a "dictatorship of the proletariat" over the bourgeoisie would follow communist revolutions and prevail during a transitional socialist period between capitalism and communism. Lenin institutionalized this view. He argued that "without revolutionary theory there can be no revolutionary movement," and, therefore, it was necessary for leadership to be in the hands of the Communist Party (Gaus, 2000:225). Stalin further concentrated political authority in his person and in a small group of associates. Even the Communist Party lost its control, and, another study explains, "After 1930, not a single protest was raised; not a single dissenting voice or vote expressed" any difference with what Stalin decided (Macridis & Hulliung, 1996:117). Indeed the encompassing social, economic, and political control that Stalin claimed was termed "totalitarian." In sum, whether authority focused on the individual leader or a bit more broadly on the party, and whatever communist theory propounded, "inequality of authority remained a defining feature of these societies" (Gaus, 2000:256). In practice, communism peaked in the later part of the twentieth century when communist governments controlled the Soviet Union, China, the countries of Eastern Europe, and other countries whose combined populations equaled about 30% of the world population. Since then it has been swept aside in most countries, remaining the government system only in China, Cuba, North Korea, and Vietnam. Nevertheless, Communist parties remain active in many countries.

Fascism Another authoritarian political philosophy that in some of its manifestations embraces totalitarianism is **fascism**. The term is often used loosely to describe almost anyone far to the right. That approach is wrong, for the term should be used with some precision. Modern fascism can be traced to Italy and the ideas of Benito Mussolini and to a variant, National Socialism and Adolf Hitler and his Nazi followers in Germany. Its basic tenets include (1) rejecting rationality and relying on emotion to govern; (2) believing (especially for Nazis) in the superiority of some groups and the inferiority of others; (3) subjugating countries of "inferior" people; (4) rejecting individual rights in favor of a "corporatist" view that people are "workers" in the state; (5) demanding that economic activity support the corporatist state; (6) viewing the state as a living thing (the organic state theory); (7) believing that the individual's highest expression is in the people (*volk* in German); and (8) believing that the highest expression of the *volk* (and, by extension, the individual) is in the leader (*führer* in German, *duce* in Italian), who rules as a totalitarian dictator.

This approach, which we will generically call fascism, spread beyond Italy and Germany to include such other countries as Spain under Francisco Franco (1939–1975) and Argentina under Juan Perón (1946–1955). What makes fascism of contemporary interest is that it is again astir in a variety of countries. The term *fascist* is so tainted by

Did You Know That:

Some Italian neofascists believe that J.R.R. Tolkien's work promotes fascist values. The right-wing National Alliance (NA) has run so-called Hobbit camps for youngsters and acclaimed the 2002 opening of the movie *The Lord of the Rings*. "There is a deep significance to this movie as a parable about the battle between community and individuality," explained one NA leader.[1]

history that few admit to being fascist. That does not, however, diminish the worry, expressed by an official of the UN Commission on Human Rights, that "neo-fascism and neo-Nazism are gaining ground in many countries—especially in Europe."[7]

There are many recent areas of concern in Europe, but just three—Austria, France, and Italy—will suffice to make the point. In Austria, the Freedom Party led by Jörg Haider won 27% of the vote in the 1999 parliamentary elections in a campaign based in part on virulent anti-immigrant rhetoric. Freedom Party posters warned against *überfremdung,* a term coined in Nazi Germany, which translates as "foreign infiltration." Haider's party suffered an electoral reversal in the 2002 elections when it received only 10% of the vote, but he remains the governor of one of Austria's provinces, and the Freedom Party continues as a member of the coalition on which the government rests.

Neofascism also exists in France, where in 2002 Jean-Marie Le Pen, head of the ultra right-wing National Front Party, finished second in the first round of presidential voting. Le Pen advocates xenophobic, anti-immigrant policies and has dismissed the extermination of 6 million Jews and others in the Holocaust as a mere "detail of history."[8] Although Le Pen received only 17% of the vote in a 16-candidate field, his second-place finish behind President Chirac (who received 20% of the vote) stunned France and, indeed, much of the rest of the world. Chirac easily beat Le Pen in the second round of voting, but Le Pen's strong showing was indicative of strong rightist sentiment in France.

The threat of fascism remains in Europe and elsewhere. Right-wing leader Jean-Marie Le Pen finished second in France's presidential election in 2002. The view held of Le Pen by a majority of the French is captured here. Note the young woman with a swastika painted on her hand in front of a poster of Le Pen and the warning "threatened democracy." She was among the 10,000 students who demonstrated against Le Pen in Strasbourg, eastern France.

Numerous observers worry that Italy is also flirting with the fascism that gripped it before and during World War II. The government of Prime Minister Silvio Berlusconi includes numerous members of such neofascist parties as the Italian Social Movement (MSI) and the National Alliance (NA). Among other things, and in words that Benito Mussolini would have approved, Berlusconi has urged Europeans to "be confident of the superiority of our civilization," and he has expressed the conviction that "the West will continue to conquer peoples, like it conquered communism."[9] Berlusconi has even given the fascist dictator Mussolini a favorable review, commenting in 2003, "Mussolini never killed anyone. Mussolini sent people on holiday in internal exile."[10]

Thus, in the first years of the 21st century, it is possible to give only a mixed report on the prospects for the end of authoritarian government. Generally democracy has progressed in recent decades, and, despite a few relapses, authoritarianism has been held in check. Yet retrograde political philosophies are far from extinct. As one analysis notes gloomily, "ideologies often go through a process of ebb and flow. Right-wing extremism and authoritarianism have deep roots" (Macridis & Hulliung, 1996:183). Democracy has become more prevalent, but it is also far from triumphant.

Democratic Theory

The existence of democratic government (which is derived from the Greek word *demos,* meaning "the citizenry") dates from the ancient Greek city-states circa 500 B.C. For

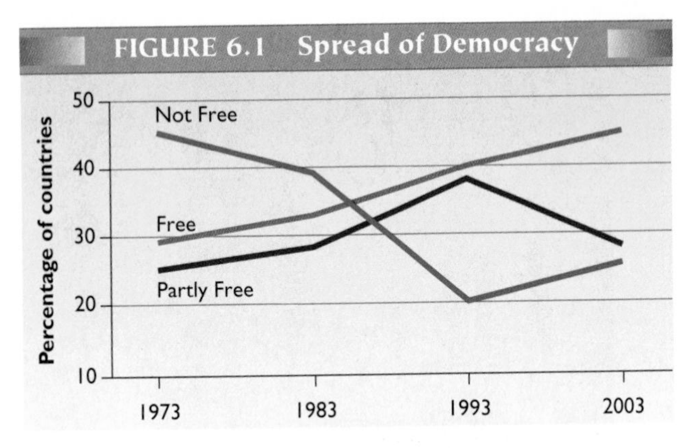

The spread of democracy worldwide is evident in the upward trend from 29% of all countries being free, as Freedom House terms it, in 1973 to 46% being free in 2003. Meanwhile the percentage of countries not free in 2003 was about half of what it was 30 years earlier.

Data source: http://www.freedomhouse.org/.

more than 2,000 years, however, democracy existed only sporadically and usually in isolated locations. The gradual rise of English democracy, then the American and French revolutions in the late 18th century, marked the change of democracy from a mere curiosity to an important national and transnational political idea. Still, the spread of democracy continued slowly. Then, during the late 1980s and early 1990s, dictatorship fell on hard times, and many observers tentatively heralded the coming of a democratic age. This view was captured by Francis Fukuyama's essay "The End of History?" (1989:3). In it he suggests that we may have come to "the end of mankind's ideological evolution and the universalization of Western liberal democracy as the final form of government." Some scholars agree that we are in sight of universal democracy (Diamond, 2003). Others are less optimistic about democracy's strength or the future spread of democracy (Inglehart, 2003).

Whoever is correct in the long run, data show that for now the spread of democracy has not stalled. One periodic study has found that both the number and percentage of democratic countries increased between 1973 and 2003. At the same time, the percentage of authoritarian countries declined, with most of those that changed transitioning to the mixed category, and some in the mixed category becoming fully democratic. These shifts are evident in Figure 6.1.

Democracy and World Politics

How states are governed has a number of ramifications for world politics. To explore that, we will examine democracy. Even if you do not agree with Fukuyama's thesis about Western-style democracy representing the end of political history's evolution, there can be little doubt that democracy has spread substantially in recent decades and is now the dominant form of governance. The issue here is whether this change is good, bad, or irrelevant with regard to world politics.

When President Woodrow Wilson asked on April 2, 1917, for a declaration of war against Germany, he told Congress that America should fight because, among other reasons, "The world must be made safe for democracy." Clarion calls to defend and expand the number of democratic countries continue. Yet, without denying the benefits of democracy, several issues exist with regard to the efforts to export it. Three such difficulties relate to the standards of democracy, the possibility of democracy, and the impact of democracy on domestic security.

Standards of Democracy

One difficulty with promoting democracy is that it is not always clear what is democratic and what is not. We can see that by investigating a number of standards. Be aware that each represents a scale, rather than an either-or categorization.

Individualism-Communitarianism Which is more important: individual rights or society's welfare? Americans, Canadians, Western Europeans, and some others tend to emphasize **individualism.** This is the belief that the rights and liberties of the individual are paramount. By contrast, **communitarianism** contends that the welfare of the collective (the community, the society) must be valued over any individual's benefit. Leaders of economically disadvantaged countries often argue that their struggle to feed, clothe, and otherwise attend to the needs of their people does not allow the "luxury" of Western-style democracy, with its incessant political bickering and its attention to the individual. As chapter 9 on international law and morality discusses, the different perspectives of human rights are sometimes the cause of considerable debate among countries.

Process-Outcome A second scale to measure democracy ranges from an emphasis on process to a focus on outcome. **Procedural democracy** stresses process. If citizens have free speech, periodically get to choose among competing candidates, and follow other such procedures, then by this standard there is democracy. Using procedure to evaluate the extent of democracy is particularly evident in Western concepts, but many other cultures in the world stress **substantive democracy**. They see democracy as a substantive product associated with equality.

Critics of procedural democracy contend that a country has failed democratically if, despite meeting procedural requisites, it produces a perpetual socioeconomic underclass (such as exists in the United States) based on race, ethnicity, gender, or some other factor. Such a system, they contend, although going through the motions of democracy, in the end denies the most important element of democracy: the substantive human right to equality. Critics further argue that any system with such vastly different economic circumstances is inherently undemocratic because the theory of government "of the people, by the people, and for the people" is undercut by the ability of wealthy individuals, groups, and corporations to spend large sums to hire professional lobbyists, to wage public relations campaigns, to donate money to electoral campaigns, to pay attorneys to sue opponents in court, and otherwise to use economic muscle unavailable to most citizens. This, the critics say, makes the contest unfair and undemocratic, no matter what the theory may be.

Exclusiveness-Inclusiveness In an ideal democracy, each person who wished to participate would have an equal opportunity to do so and an equal chance of rising to a position of influence. Such opportunities would exist in fact, not just in theory. No country has ever achieved this ideal. Instead they range along a scale. On one end, meaningful participation is very limited; at the other end such participation is broadly distributed, with such factors as race, ethnicity, and gender irrelevant to democratic processes and outcomes.

Gender provides a good and important focus for looking at this standard. By this criterion, most countries are still far toward the exclusiveness end of the scale. Historically, women won the right to vote in national elections a little more than a century ago. In 1893 New Zealand was the first country to recognize the right of women to vote. Other countries followed suit slowly. Switzerland in 1971 was the last economically developed country to allow female suffrage. Now, almost all countries do, although there are still some exceptions, such as Saudi Arabia.

Voting was a significant political step for women, but access to political office has come more slowly. Australia in 1902 became the first country to constitutionally assure women the right to stand for election, and the world's first elected female national legislators took their seats in Finland's parliament in 1907. The first woman other than a monarch to become a head of state was President of the Presidium Yanjamaa Nemendeyen Sbaataryn of Mongolia in 1953, and the first woman prime minister, Sirimavo Ratwatte Dias Bandaranaike of Ceylon (now Sri Lanka), did not take office until 1960. From these beginnings, the ranks of female political leaders have grown, although slowly (Reynolds, 1999). As former Norwegian prime minister Gro Harlem Brundtland commented dryly, "I was the first woman in 1,000 years [to head Norway's government]. Things are evolving gradually."[11]

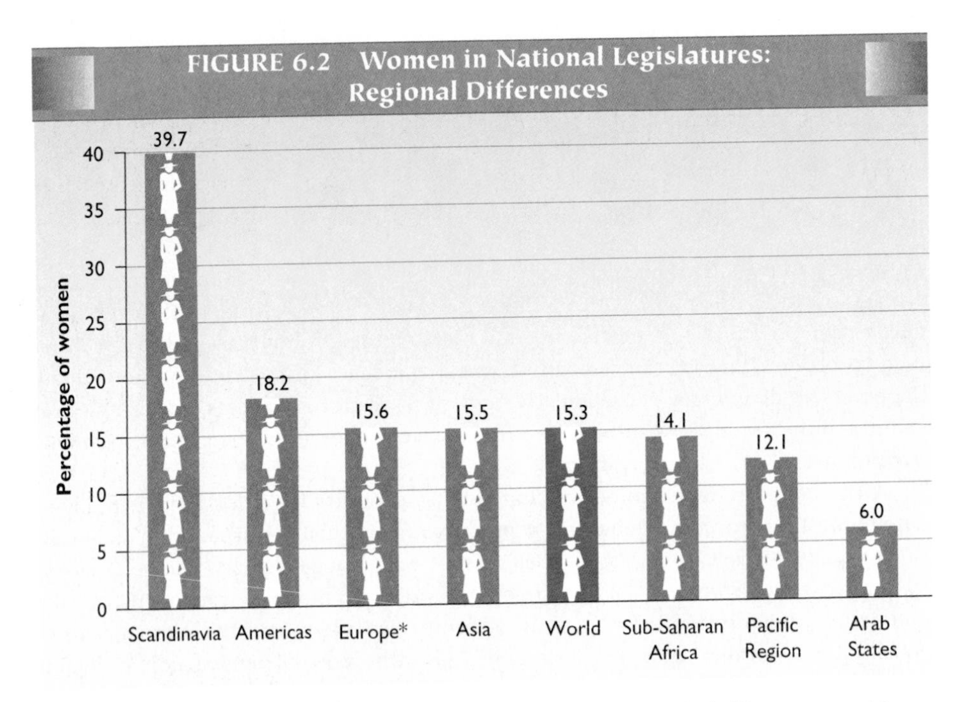

By one measure, women have made significant strides toward being included in government by increasing their global share of national legislative seats from 3% in 1955 to 15.3% in 2003. But there is still a long way, 34.7%, to go to reach equality. This goal is clearly nearer in some regions than in others.

*Excluding Scandinavia

Data source: Interparliamentary Union at http://www.ipu.org/.

In late 2003, only 10 women were serving as the presidents or prime ministers of their countries. In other leadership positions, only about 8% of all cabinet ministers are women, and they make up a scant 15% of the members of the world's national legislatures and 9% of the world's judiciary. Moreover, these overall figures do not reveal that women have an even smaller political presence in some regions, as Figure 6.2 indicates.

What the gradual rise in the number of women in positions of political leadership, assuming it continues, will mean for the course of international politics is an important question. The propensity for conflict provides an interesting example. Certainly, there have been women leaders who have shown themselves to be determined defenders of their country when they need to be. The derogatory whisper campaign that women make weak leaders has been repeatedly disproved by the records of female leaders such as Prime Minister (1966–1977, 1980–1984) Indira Gandhi of India, Prime Minister (1969–1974) Golda Meir of Israel, and Prime Minister (1979–1990) Margaret Thatcher of Great Britain, each of whom led her country to victory in war. Similarly, women who have served among the ranks of such key international relations officials as foreign minister and defense minister have also proven their mettle when necessary. The first woman to serve as U.S. secretary of state, Madeleine Albright, was at times so enthusiastic about using military force that the more cautious chairman of the Joint Chiefs of Staff, Colin Powell, has remembered thinking he "would have an aneurysm."[12] Still, for all these examples of toughness, it is also the case, as chapter 3 notes, that statistics show women in different countries and during different crises have been on average less bellicose than are the men of their country. Given this, some analysts believe that increased female participation through a more inclusive democratic model could reduce global conflict.

Promoting Global Democracy

Yet another connection between democracy and world politics is the effort to promote democracy globally. This presents a number of issues. One is whether democracy is always possible, at least in the short term. In most of the West, where democracy has existed the longest and seems the most stable, it evolved slowly and often fitfully. More recently, other parts of the world have experienced increased degrees of democratization, but the likelihood that any single country will adopt democratic values and practices is at least partly linked with internal factors, such as attitudes about democracy and a country's educational and economic level.

Among the women who head their country is President Chandrika Kumaratunga of Sri Lanka. She has been in office since 1994 and has proven herself a determined leader during the long civil war with the Tamil insurgents in the northern part of the country. Kumaratunga made world headlines in November 2003 when she suspended parliament, which is headed by Prime Minister Ranil Wickremesinghe (seen here just behind her), because she felt he was not being tough enough in his negotiations with the rebels.

Democracy and Economic Development It is clear that there is a strong relationship between democracy and economic development. This is evident in Figure 6.3, which shows that democratic countries have a much higher per capita gross domestic product than do mixed democratic/authoritarian countries and authoritarian countries. As for economic and education levels, it may be that attempting to promote full-fledged democracy in countries with poor economic and educational conditions is tantamount to trying to impose an alien political system on a socioeconomic system that is not ready for it. Doing so may even prove counterproductive. As one analyst has put it, "The democracy we are encouraging in many poor parts of the world is an integral part of a transformation toward new forms of authoritarianism" (Kaplan, 1999:178). Or, in another scholar's succinct phraseology, "Democracy can be bad for you" (Hobsbawm, 2001:25).

Other scholars take exception to this view and argue that democracy enhances development. The recipient of the 1998 Nobel Prize in economics, for one, contends that democracy promotes economic growth by pressing leaders to invest their countries' capital in education, consumer production, and other areas that will build economic strength and stimulate production instead of in military spending and other less productive economic paths (Sen, 1999).

Attitudes about Democracy It would be a mistake to assume that everyone, everywhere is yearning to be free. But nearly everyone, everywhere wants to be able to criticize the government. A survey taken in 2002 of people in 36 countries found that over 75% of the respondents in 35 of the countries said that it was important to be able to do so, and even Jordan (53%) eked out a slim majority for that view.[13] Yet when another survey asked people in 77 countries their opinion about "having a strong leader who does not have to bother with parliament and elections," a majority of respondents in 21% of the countries approved of the idea, as did between a third and half the people in another 21% of the countries (Inglehart, 2003). A third question in yet another survey tested priorities by asking people what they would prefer if they had to choose between democracy and a strong economy. People in 14 countries chose a strong economy, again with that choice within a few percentage points of democracy in several other countries.[14] Such responses lead one scholar to conclude that while "today almost everyone gives lip service to democracy . . . when one probes deeper, one finds disturbing evidence that mass support is not as nearly solid [as one would hope]" (Inglehart, 2003:52).

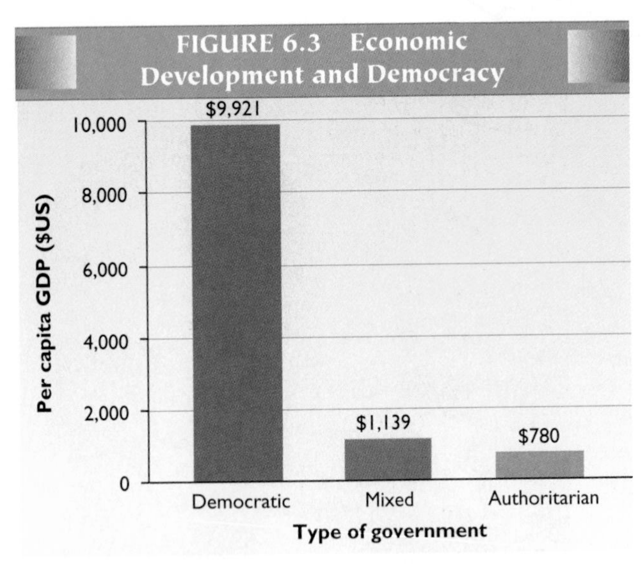

Economic development and democracy are closely related, as this figure demonstrates. Almost all states that are even moderately prosperous are democratic, and with the exception of a few oil-producing countries, almost all autocracies are very poor. Scholars do not agree on whether prosperity helps build democracy, democracy helps promote prosperity, or the two build upon each other.

Data source: http://www.freedomhouse.org/.

Another error would be to assume that the United States or any other country can successfully export its model of democracy to all other countries. In the first place, priorities differ. The standards of Americans, the British, and others tend to favor individualism and procedural democracy. Others disagree. For example, consider American and French responses to a survey in 2002 that asked if it was better for government to interfere in society as little as possible in order to let people pursue their goals or better for the government to take an active role in society to guarantee that nobody was in need. A majority (58%) of Americans chose the limited government option, compared to just 34% wanting an activist government and 8% unsure. Taking a very different view, 62% of the French chose an activist government, just 36% favored limited government, and 2% were uncertain. Yet another survey found that globally more people than not disliked "American ideas about democracy." Taken in 16 countries in 2003, the survey almost surely reflected a degree of anger at the United States over the war with Iraq, but it did reveal 50% of all respondents not liking American-style democracy, compared to 41% liking it and 9% uncertain.[15]

Democracy and Security

In addition to some of the issues raised above about the possibility and wisdom of promoting democracy, that effort also has important implications for domestic and international security.

Democracy and Domestic Security Some observers also contend that the move from authoritarian to democratic government can produce very negative domestic side effects because domestic conflict can spill over into the international sphere. It is possible to argue, for example, that the turmoil that engulfed what was once Yugoslavia was a result of the end of the authoritarian control of the communist government. Once that control was relaxed, the multiple ethnonational rivalries that had been dormant soon erupted into bloody conflict. Similar patterns can be seen in several African countries, in the former Soviet Union, and elsewhere in cases where independence or the coming of democracy has unleashed bloody ethnic clashes.

To this contention, supporters of global democratization respond that any bloodshed that it brings pales when compared to the brutality inflicted by authoritarian regimes. One study of "democide," the killing of unarmed residents by governments, demonstrates that the degree to which a government is totalitarian "largely accounts for the magnitude and intensity of genocide and mass murder" committed by that government. Therefore, the study reasons, "the best assurances against democide are democratic openness, political competition, leaders responsible to their people and limited government. In other words, power kills, and absolute power kills absolutely" (Rummel, 1995:25).

Democracy and International Security One issue regarding democracy and international security centers on the long-standing debate over whether one form or another of government is more successful in foreign affairs, especially war. The noted French observer Alexis de Tocqueville argued in *Democracy in America* (1835) that "it is most especially in the conduct of foreign relations that democratic governments appear to me to be decidedly inferior to governments carried on upon different principles." The drawbacks, Tocqueville wrote, are that democracies tend "to obey the impulse of passion rather than the suggestions of prudence" and also that "a democratic people is less capable of sustained effort than another."

Recent scholarship disputes this view. One study found that democracies have won about 75% of the wars they have fought since 1815 and concluded, "It appears that democratic nations not only might enjoy the good life of peace, prosperity, and freedom; they can also defend themselves against outside threats from tyrants and despots" (Reiter & Stam, 2002:2).

An even more compelling connection between democracy and world politics relates to **democratic peace theory**. This argument of German philosopher Immanuel Kant in *Perpetual Peace* (1795) holds that the spread of democracy to all countries would eliminate war. Kant reasoned that a democratic peace would occur because "if the consent of the citizens is required in order to decide that war should be declared . . . , nothing is more natural than that they would be very cautious in commencing such a poor game, decreeing for themselves all the calamities of war."

Modern scholarship tends to confirm Kant's theory. Using empirical methods, contemporary studies have established, as one scholar puts it, that "democracies are unlikely to engage in any kind of militarized disputes with each other or to let any such disputes escalate into war. They rarely even skirmish" (Russett, 2000:232; Oneal & Russett, 1999; Schultz, 1999). This view is accepted by many scholars "as 'the closest thing to an empirical law' in world politics" that exists (Henderson, 1999:482).

Several caveats about democratic peace theory should be noted. First, democracies do go to war, although only with autocracies. The easy example is the United States, which is both a leading democracy and the country that has most often been at war since 1945. Second, not all scholars agree with democratic peace theory (Caprioli, 1998). For example, some analysts are skeptical that the absence of war between democracies is anything more than a historical anomaly that may not persist in the future (Henderson, 2002; Gartzke, 1998). Future history may prove democratic peace theory wrong. For now, though, there is broad, albeit not complete, agreement among scholars that democracies have more peaceful relations with each other than do democracies with authoritarian states or authoritarian states with one another. From this perspective, even if a world in which all countries were democratic did not produce perpetual peace, as Kant thought it would, it might produce preponderant peace and, thus, should be promoted (Huntley, 1998).

National and Other Interests

Whatever the system of governance of any state, a key factor that governs its affairs and interactions on the global stage are its interests. The concept of national interest is used almost universally to argue for or against any given policy. Most political leaders and citizens still argue that it is paramount. Indeed, it is hard to imagine a national leader announcing that he or she had taken an important action that was counter to the national interest but in the world's interest. Even if such an aberration occurred, it is improbable that the leader would remain in office much longer.

National Interest as a Standard of Conduct

The use of national interest as a cornerstone of foreign policy is a key element of the road more traveled in world politics. Realists contend that it is a wise basis for foreign policy. Henry Kissinger (1994:37), for one, regrets what he sees as the current U.S. "distrust of America's power, a preference for multilateral solutions and a reluctance to think in terms of national interest. All these impulses," Kissinger believes, "inhibit a realistic response to a world of multiple power centers and diverse conflicts."[16]

Realpolitik nationalists further contend that we live in a Darwinian political world, where people who do not promote their own interests will fall prey to those who do. Nationalists further worry about alternative schemes of global governance. One such critic of globalism notes that in intellectual circles "anyone who is skeptical about international commitments today is apt to be dismissed as an isolationist crank." Nevertheless, he continues, globalization should be approached with great caution because "it holds out the prospect of an even more chaotic set of authorities, presiding over an even more chaotic world, at a greater remove from the issues that concern us here in the United States" (Rabkin, 1994:41, 47).

Other analysts reject the use of national interest as a guide for foreign policy. Their objections are:

There is no such thing as an objective national interest. Critics say that what is in the national interest is totally subjective and "approximates idiosyncrasy" (Kimura & Welch, 1998). Analysts can accurately point out that national interest has been used to describe every sort of good and evil. As used by decision makers, it is a projection of the perceptions of a particular regime or even a single political leader in a given international or domestic environment. For example, President George W. Bush and the neoconservatives in his administration (see the "Decision for War" box in chapter 3) have a pronounced unilateralist approach to foreign policy. A majority of the American public disagrees, according to one survey, which found that only 31% of respondents said that the United States should "act alone" in an international crisis if it did not have the support of its allies. A majority (61%) said the United States "should not act alone," and 8% were uncertain. The president is also on record as favoring the use of U.S. forces to protect Taiwan from China and South Korea from North Korea, a position favored by only 35% and 39% respectively of the American public.[17]

Using national interest as a basis of policy incorrectly assumes that there is a common interest. The contention here is that every society is a collection of diverse subgroups, each of which has its own set of interests based on its political identity (Chafetz, Spirtas, & Frankel, 1999). Furthermore, the concept of national interest inherently includes the assumption that if a collective interest can be determined, then that interest supersedes the interests of subgroups and individuals. Writing from the feminist perspective, for example, one scholar has noted that "the presumption of a similarity of interests between the sexes is an assumption" that cannot be taken for granted because "a growing body of scholarly work argues that . . . the political attitudes of men and women differ significantly" (Brandes, 1994:21).

National interest is inherently selfish and inevitably leads to conflict and inequity. The logic is simple. If you and I both pursue our national interests and those objectives are incompatible, then one likely possibility is that we will clash. Another possibility is that the interest of whichever of us is the more powerful will prevail. That is, power, not justice, will win. Certainly, we might negotiate and compromise, as countries often do. But in an anarchical international system that emphasizes self-interest and self-help, the chances of a peaceful and equitable resolution are less than in a hierarchical domestic system that restrains the contending actors and offers institutions (such as courts) that can decide disputes if negotiation fails.

The way that national interest is applied frequently involves double standards. This criticism of the idea of national interest charges that countries often take actions that they would find objectionable if applied to themselves. As noted, President George W. Bush follows a fairly unilateralist U.S. policy. Yet he has bridled when other countries have insisted on their own unilateral interpretations of policy and have refused to support Washington on such issues as the invasion of Iraq. When France and Germany led the effort to block the UN Security Council from authorizing an invasion, U.S. Secretary of Defense Donald Rumsfeld undiplomatically referred in public to the two countries as "problems" and representing "old Europe." That sparked a counterbarrage from the offended French and Germans, including the view of French Minister of Defense Michèle Alliot-Marie, "We are no longer in prehistoric times when whoever had the biggest club would try to knock the other guy out so he could steal his mammoth skin."[18]

National interest is often shortsighted. This line of reason argues, for example, that because economically developed countries (EDCs) are mostly concerned with their immediate, domestic needs, they give precious little of their wealth to less developed countries (LDCs) in the form of foreign aid. This is shortsighted, some analysts contend, because in the long run the EDCs will become even more prosperous if the LDCs also become wealthy and can buy more goods and services from the EDCs. Furthermore, the argument goes, helping the LDCs now may avoid furthering the seething instability and violence born of poverty.

Alternatives to National Interest

Global interest as a standard of conduct is one alternative to national interest. Proponents of this standard contend that the world would be better served if people defined themselves politically as citizens of the world along with, or perhaps in place of, their sense of national political identification. One such advocate writes, "The apparent vast disjunction between what humankind must do to survive on the planet in a reasonably decent condition . . . and the way world society has typically worked throughout history . . . points to the need . . . for substantial evolution of world society in the direction of world community" (Brown, 1992:167).

Those who advocate a more global sense of our interests do not reject national interest as such. Instead, they say that national interest is usually defined in a counterproductive, shortsighted way, as noted above. In the long run, globalists argue, a more enlightened view of interests sees that a state will be more secure and more prosperous if it helps other states also achieve peace and prosperity. This is the line of reasoning taken by those who contend that if the economically developed countries (EDCs) do more now to help less wealthy countries develop economically, the EDCs will win in the long run through many benefits, such as better trade markets and less political instability and violence. That is essentially the point that Han Seung-soo, president of the UN General Assembly, made to world leaders who had gathered in Monterrey, Mexico, in 2002 to discuss world economic and political development. Especially "in the wake of September 11," the South Korean diplomat told the conference, it is imperative to recognize "that development, peace, and security are inseparable," because the poorest countries are "the breeding ground for violence and despair."[19]

Individual interests are another alternative to national interest. Virtually all individuals are rightly concerned with their own welfare. To consider your own interests could be construed as the ultimate narrow-mindedness, but it also may be liberating. It may be that your interests, even your political identification, may shift from issue to issue.

It is appropriate to ask, then, whether your individual interests, your nation's interests, your country's interests, and your world's interests are the same, mutually exclusive, or a mixed bag of congruencies and divergences. Only you, of course, can determine where your interests lie.

Some analysts argue that state-centric interpretations of national interest inherently generate conflicts among countries and that, in the long run, the optimal national interest of every country is the same: a peaceful and prosperous world.

States and the Future

Sovereign, territorially defined states have not always existed, as we have noted. Therefore, they will not necessarily persist in the future. The questions are, Will they? Should they? The future of the state is one of the most hotly debated topics among scholars of international relations. As one such analyst explains, "Central to [our] future is the uncertain degree to which the sovereign state can adapt its behavior and role to a series of deterritorializing forces associated with markets, transnational social forces, cyberspace, demographic and environmental pressures, and urbanism" (Falk, 1999:35). As you ponder your verdict about states, recall the discussion above about the purpose of government and apply your own conclusions about what governments should do to your evaluation of the success or failure of the state as the continued central model of governance.

The State: The Indictment

In rough division, there are two main lines of reasoning by those scholars who foresee or advocate the decline, perhaps the demise, of states as principal actors on the world stage. One contention is that states are obsolete; a second argument is that states are destructive (Lugo, 1996).

States Are Obsolete

The argument that states are obsolete begins with the premise that they were created in the middle of the last millennium as utilitarian political organizations to meet security, economic, and other specific needs and to replace the feudal and other forms of political organization that no longer worked effectively. "The nation-state is a rough and ready mechanism for furnishing a set of real services," one scholar writes. The problem, he continues, is that "the relation between what a state is supposed to do and what it actually does is increasingly slack" (Dunn, 1995:9). An interesting line of reasoning suggests that states are too large to do the small things people want and need and too little to do the big things (Cusimano, 1998). Whatever the immediate cause, the view of many scholars, as one puts it, is that "the separate nation-states have become ever more impotent in dealing on their own . . . with material and political realities that are increasingly threatening the safety and well-being of their citizens" (Brown, 1998:3).

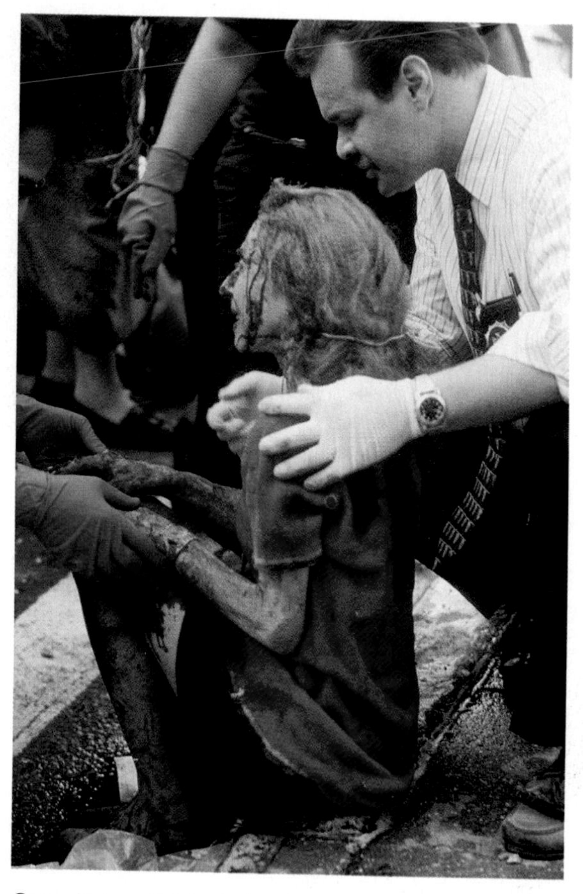

One criticism of states is that they cannot provide adequate security against many threats, especially weapons of mass destruction and terrorism. This woman is one of the victims of the al-Qaeda suicide attack on the World Trade Center towers on September 11, 2001. U.S. security has improved since then, but Americans are still vulnerable to attack, as are people everywhere.

Providing physical safety is one key role of the state. Yet the ability of states to protect their citizens is limited at best (Betts, 1998). If we date the sovereign-state system to its symbolic beginning in 1648 with the Treaty of Westphalia, it is possible to argue that the ability of states to protect their people is horrendous and getting worse. Since the mid-1600s, there have been almost 600 wars that have killed over 140 million people. Moreover, the victim totals have risen rapidly through the centuries as humankind "improved" its killing capabilities. Indeed, 75% of all the people killed in wars during the last 500 years died in the 20th century. Therefore, the question is: In an era of nuclear, chemical, and biological weapons of mass destruction, against which there is little or no defense, does the state protect people or simply define them as targets for other states in an anarchical international system?

Providing economic prosperity is a second key role of the state. The same genre of questions applies to the economic functions of a state. The tidal wave of trade and capital that moves across national borders means that states are increasingly less able to provide for the prosperity of their residents. For example, jobs are won or lost depending on a variety of factors, such as where transnational corporations decide to set up manufacturing, choices over which national governments have little or no control.

Providing for the general welfare is a third key role of the state. Health is one such concern, and states as independent entities are finding themselves increasingly unable to contain the spread of disease in an era when people and products that may carry the threat of disease with them move quickly and in massive numbers around the globe.

AIDS has become the greatest transnational health disaster since the bubonic plague epidemic, commonly called the Black Death, spread throughout Europe. Beginning in 1347 and over the next several years, the plague killed 25 million people, about one-third of Europe's population. AIDS, thought to have its origins in Africa, threatens people everywhere. According to *AIDS Epidemic Update, December 2003,* a report issued jointly by the UN and the World Health Organization, more than 60 million people have been infected by the HIV virus and nearly one-third of those have died of AIDS-related diseases since the epidemic began. The morbid statistics are getting worse. In 2003, 40 million people were HIV positive, about 5 million new cases were reported that year, and 3 million people died. Such statistics not only pose a moral challenge to those countries that can help, they also pose a national security threat. This has been

The ability of diseases to spread rapidly across the globe raises questions about the adequacy of states acting alone to protect the health of their citizens. One new health threat to Americans in recent years is West Nile virus, a disease that is spread when infected birds are bitten by mosquitoes that then carry the disease to humans. In the United States during 2003, there were 9,858 reported cases of the virus in 45 states. This picture shows Mary Tilger of Colorado selling T-shirts to benefit the Make-a-Wish Foundation. The 32-year-old mother was stricken with West Nile virus, leaving her incapacitated for three weeks. She was luckier than the 262 Americans who died of the disease that year.

widely recognized, as in a U.S. Central Intelligence Agency report, "The Global Infectious Disease Threat and Its Implications for the United States." It concluded, "New and reemerging infectious diseases will pose a rising global health threat and will complicate U.S. and global security over the next 20 years" because, "These diseases will endanger U.S. citizens at home and abroad, threaten U.S. armed forces deployed overseas, and exacerbate social and political instability in key countries and regions in which the United States has significant interests."[20]

Whether it is AIDS, West Nile virus, SARS, or another microbial enemy, the reality, according to a U.S. physician, is that "today, in 30 hours, you can literally travel to the other side of the world. And likewise, while you are there, you can pick up a germ or a micro-organism that may not exist on this side of the globe and within 30 hours you can have that back in the United States."[21] National borders provide increasingly scant protection against these globally transportable diseases, which, if they are to be contained, must be attacked through an international effort.

Did You Know That:

That disease respects no borders has long been a problem, as reflected in the children's rhyme that dates back to the 14th century:

Ring-around the rosy
Pocket full of posies
Ashes, ashes!
We all fall down!

It refers to the Black Death plague (1347–1350), which spread from Asia to Europe. "Ring-around the rosy" refers to a circlet of Roman Catholic rosary beads used during prayers for God's deliverance from the plague. Europeans often had a "pocket full of posies," hoping the flowers' perfume would mask the stench of the rotting bodies. "Ashes, ashes" relates to burning the corpses of plague victims. As for "We all fall down," the unspoken final word is "dead."

States Are Destructive

The essence of the sovereign state is to pursue its interests. Those interests clash. There is little in the system other than power to determine which states' interests will prevail. That was amply demonstrated in the events that led up to the U.S./U.K. invasion of Iraq in 2003. Therefore, the argument continues, states too often use economic coercion or military force to settle disputes. Critics of the state system contend that whatever the wins and losses for states, the most likely losers are average citizens, who bear the brunt of war and economic sanctions to a far greater degree than do leaders.

To make matters worse, states are often perpetrators of violence on those they are supposed to protect (Burgess, 1998). "Political regimes—

governments—have probably murdered nearly 170 million of their own citizens and foreigners in this century—about four times the number killed in all international and domestic wars and revolutions," one scholar charges (Rummel, 1995:3).

The State: The Defense

While those who predict or advocate the diminishment or demise of the state as a primary political organization are able to make a strong argument, it is hardly an open-and-shut case leading to a verdict against the state (Paul, Ikenberry, & Hall, 2004).

First, as we noted in chapter 4, nationalism has proven resilient, and its political vehicle, the state, still has many resources at its disposal. This leads some analysts to doubt the substantial weakening, much less the disappearance, of states as sovereign actors. As two such scholars write, "Reports of its demise notwithstanding, sovereignty appears to us to be prospering, not declining. . . . It still serves as an indispensable component of international politics" (Fowler & Bunck, 1995:163). Another scholar observes that while borders are becoming less and less meaningful as barriers to economic interchange, the flow of information, and some other transnational functions, "states are responding to globalization by attempting to restore meaning to national borders, not as barriers to entry, but as boundaries demarcating distinct political communities" (Goff, 2000:533).

Second, states may be able to adjust to the new realities by learning to cooperate and live in peace with other countries. Analysts who hold this view point to the increasing creation of and membership in numerous IGOs, like the WTO, as evidence that states are willing to give up some of their sovereignty in return for the benefits provided by free trade and other transnational interactions.

Third, states are arguably being strengthened as increasingly complex domestic and international systems create new demands for services. From this perspective, globalization and the strength of states "may be mutually reinforcing rather than antagonistic" (Weiss, 1998:204). "Empirical evidence demonstrates that the roles of the state are changing rather than diminishing," according to two scholars. "The state remains crucially involved in a wide range of problems," they continue, and "in each of these areas, specific initiatives may make state policies more efficient . . . as the roles of the nation-state continue to evolve" (Turner & Corbacho, 2000:118–119).

Fourth, sovereignty has always been a relative, not an absolute, principle and a dynamic, rather than static, concept (Sorensen, 1999). States and their leaders have long violated the principle when it suited their interests in what one scholar terms "organized hypocrisy" (Krasner, 1999). This leads some analysts to conclude that states will survive by adapting the parameters of sovereignty to international norms.

Fifth, it is possible to defend sovereign states as better than the other forms of political organization. States do provide some level of defense, and some states have been relatively effective at shielding their citizens from the ravages of war. Sometimes that is a matter of power, as is true for the United States. But in other cases, it is related to geography, diplomatic skill, or a simple resolution not to take sides under almost any circumstances. Sweden and Switzerland, for example, managed to avoid becoming involved in any war, including either world war, during the 20th century.

Sixth, it is yet to be proven that international governmental organizations (IGOs) provide an effective alternative to the state. Peacekeeping by the United Nations and other IGOs has had successes, but also notable failures. The WTO and other economic IGOs are under attack for benefiting rich countries, corporations, and individuals at the expense of less developed countries, small businesses, and workers. It may well be, as we will discuss in the next chapter, that IGOs can prove to be more effective and just instruments of governance as they evolve. That remains an open question, though.

The State: The Verdict

For now, the jury is still out on whether states will and should continue to dominate the political system and be the principal focus of political identity. States continue to exercise great political strength and most of them retain the loyalty of most of their citizens. Yet it is also true that the state exists in a rapidly changing political environment that is creating great pressures, whether they are those of Barber's (1995) tribalism or McWorld. Opinion surveys in the European Union, for instance, show that when people are asked if their primary political identity rests with their region (within their country), their country, or the EU a majority (61%) still chooses their country. But 16% identify first with the EU, and 22% define themselves politically in terms of their region.[22]

Such data and the other changes that are occurring cast doubt on whether the state will survive based on its record or on residual loyalties. As one scholar notes, "history sides with no one. . . . [The] lesson to be drawn [from the rise and evolution of states] is that all institutions are susceptible to challenges." Therefore, the sustainability of states depends in substantial part on whether they provide "efficient responses to such challenges" (Spruyt, 1994:185).

Where does this leave the future of sovereign states in the early 21st century? The answer that most political scientists would probably give is, "Although the system of sovereign states is likely to continue [in the foreseeable future] as the dominant structure in world politics, the content of world politics is changing" (Keohane & Nye, 1999:118). Those changes are well captured in the view of one scholar:

> A new epoch is evolving. It is an epoch of multiple contradictions: . . . States are changing, but they are not disappearing. State sovereignty has eroded, but it is still vigorously asserted. Governments are weaker, but they can still throw their weight around. . . . Borders still keep out intruders, but they are also more porous. Landscapes are giving way to ethnoscapes, mediascapes, ideoscapes, technoscapes, and financescapes, but territoriality is still a central preoccupation for many people (Rosenau, 1998:18).

Chapter Summary

The Nature and Purpose of the State

1. States are the most important political actors. States as political organizations have these defining characteristics: sovereignty, territory, population, diplomatic recognition, internal organization, and domestic support.
2. There are various theories about why humans formed themselves into political units with governments. These theories give insight into what the purpose of these units is and, therefore, what people should expect from them.

The State as the Core Political Organization

3. Monarchism, theocracy, communism applied politically, and fascism are four forms of authoritarian governance. The percentage of countries ruled by authoritarian regimes has declined, but dictatorial governments are still common.
4. Democracy is a complex concept. Different sets of standards serve as a basis to determine the degree to which a political system is democratic.
5. There are disputes over when it is possible or advisable to press all countries to quickly adopt democratic forms of government.
6. There are a number of connections between democracy and domestic and international security.
7. The most important of these links, democratic peace theory, argues that democracies are unlikely to enter into conflict with one another. The reasons why democracies do not fight one another remain disputed among scholars, with explanations given from institutional, normative, and interest perspectives.
8. There are many types of interests—national, state, governmental, global, and individual—and it is important to distinguish among them. National interest has been and is the traditional approach to determining

international activity, but some people contend that national interest is synonymous with destructive self-promotion and should be diminished or even abandoned.

States and the Future

9. The future of the state is a hotly debated topic among scholars of international relations.
10. Some analysts predict the demise of states as principal actors, claiming that states are obsolete and destructive.
11. Other analysts of nationalism contend that the state is durable and has many resources at its disposal. These analysts doubt that the states will weaken substantially or disappear as sovereign actors.
12. One key question that will help determine the fate of states is whether they can cooperate to address global problems, such as environmental degradation.
13. A second key question that will help determine the fate of states is whether they can remain at peace in an era of nuclear arms and other weapons of mass destruction.

For a chapter quiz, interactive activities, web links, PowerWeb articles, and much more, visit **www.mhhe.com/rourke10/** and go to chapter 6. Or, while accessing the site, click on Course-Wide Content and view recent international relations articles in the *New York Times.*

Key Terms

authoritarian government
authoritarianism
communism
communitarianism
democratic government
democratic peace theory
fascism
individualism
instrumental theory of government
monarchism
procedural democracy
social contract
sovereignty
state of nature
states
substantive democracy
theocracy

CHAPTER 7

International Organization: An Alternative Structure

THE EVOLUTION AND ROLES OF INTERNATIONAL ORGANIZATION

The Origins of IGOs

The Growth of IGOs

Roles That IGOs Play

REGIONAL IGOS: FOCUS ON THE EUROPEAN UNION

The Origins and Evolution of the European Union

The Government of the European Union

The Future of the EU

GLOBAL IGOS: FOCUS ON THE UNITED NATIONS

IGO Organization and Related Issues

IGO Leadership, Administration, and Finance

IGO Activities

Evaluating IGOs and Their Future

CHAPTER SUMMARY

KEY TERMS

Friendly counsel cuts off many foes.

—William Shakespeare, *Henry VI, Part 1*

[The United Nations is] group therapy for the world.

—Antonio Montiero, Portuguese ambassador to the UN

No nation needs to face or fight alone the threats which this organization was established to diffuse.

—UN Secretary-General Kofi Annan

CHAPTER OBJECTIVES

After completing this chapter, you should be able to:

- Discuss the nature and development of international organization as an alternative form of organizing and conducting international relations.
- Identify the roots of international organization as a primarily modern phenomenon.
- Trace the growth of intergovernmental organizations and nongovernmental organizations during the 20th century.
- Summarize the traditional goals and activities of international organizations.
- Examine and discuss the current and expanding roles of IGOs.
- Discuss the concept of world and regional government.
- Explain the prospect of effective supranational organizations for international governance, referring to the evolution of the European Union.
- Describe IGO structure by evaluating the experience of the United Nations.
- Identify the promotion of international peace and security as the primary IGO activity, as exemplified by the United Nations.
- Outline major social, economic, environmental, and other roles of intergovernmental organizations.
- Speculate regarding the shape of international organization in the future.

Although the state is and has been the primary actor in the international system, it is not the only option for governance. **International organization (IO)** is one alternative to what some analysts are convinced is the outmoded and even destructive traditional approach of basing global relations on self-interested states operating in an anarchical international system. These critics believe that international organizations can and should increasingly regulate the behavior of states in order to better address world problems. From this perspective, there is wise counsel given by Shakespeare in *Henry VI, Part III*: "Now join your hands, and with your hands your hearts." Such advice may be right. It is just possible that ongoing organizations will serve as prototypes or building blocks for a future, higher form of political loyalty and activity.

The Evolution and Roles of International Organization

Because this chapter addresses governance, it will concentrate on international **intergovernmental organizations (IGOs)**. The membership of this type of IO consists of national governments. As such, IGOs are distinct from the transnational (or international) nongovernmental organizations (NGOs), whose members consist of private individuals or groups and which function more like interest groups than governing bodies, and which are discussed in chapter 6.

There are various ways to classify the growing number of these organizations. Table 7.1 on page 192 presents one categorization. It includes the two IGOs that are highlighted in this chapter's exploration of the current roles of IGOs and their future potential. One, the European Union, is a regional organization. The other, the United Nations, is a global organization.

The Origins of IGOs

IGOs are primarily a modern phenomenon. Nearly all of them were created in the last 50 years or so. Yet the origins of IGOs extend far back in history to three main sources.

Community of Humankind

IGOs are rooted in part in a universalistic concept of humankind dating back perhaps to 300 B.C. and the Stoics, as discussed in chapter 5 (Pagden, 1998). As early as 478 B.C., the Greek city-states established the Delian League to create a unified response to the threat from Persia. Although mostly an alliance, it had two IGO characteristics. First, it was permanent and supposed to last until "ingots of iron, thrown into the sea, rose again." Second, the League had an assembly of representatives appointed by the city-states to decide policy. Although Athens dominated, the assembly was a precursor of such current structures as the UN General Assembly.

Such ideas began to resurface in the late Middle Ages. For example, a French official, Pierre Dubois, proposed in *The Recovery of the Holy Land* (1306) that disputes among Christian kingdoms be arbitrated by an international council. In Dubois's words, "If it seems fitting to establish a league of universal peace" and there is "a unanimous decision by the council," then all should "solemnly swear to uphold with all their power this league of peace and its penalties, and in every possible way see that it is observed."

In modern times, the first example of an IGO based on keeping peace was the **Hague system**, named for the 1899 and 1907 peace conferences held at that city in the Netherlands (Best, 1999). The 1907 conference was more comprehensive, with

TABLE 7.1 Types and Examples of IGOs

	Purpose	
Geography	General	Specialized
Global	United Nations	World Trade Organization
Regional	European Union	Arab Monetary Fund

International intergovernmental organizations (IGOs) can be classified according to whether they are general purpose, dealing with many issues, or specialized, dealing with a specific concern. Another way of dividing IGOs is into global and regional organizations.

44 European, North American, and Latin American states participating. Organizationally, it included a rudimentary general assembly and a judicial system. The conferences also adopted a series of standards to limit the conduct of war.

The next step on the path was the creation of the **League of Nations** after World War I. The League had a more developed organizational structure than that of the Hague system. It was intended mainly as a peacekeeping organization, although it did have some elements aimed at social and economic cooperation. Unfortunately, the League could not survive the turbulent post–World War I era that included the Great Depression and the rise of militant fascism. After only two decades of frustrated existence, the League died in the rubble of World War II.

The collapse of the League did not, however, persuade people to abandon the idea behind it. Instead, at war's end more than 50 countries joined together to try again and established the **United Nations (UN)**. Like the League, the UN was founded mainly to maintain peace. Nevertheless, it has increasingly become involved in a broad range of issues that encompasses almost all the world's concerns. In addition, the UN and its predecessor, the League of Nations, represent the coming together of all the root systems of international organizations. They are more properly seen as the emergent saplings of extensive cooperation and integration.

Big-Power Peacekeeping

IGOs also evolved from the idea that powerful countries have a special responsibility to cooperate and preserve peace. Hugo Grotius, the "father of international law," suggested as early as 1625 in his classic *On the Law of War and Peace* that the major Christian powers cooperate to mediate or arbitrate the disputes of others or even, if required, to compel warring parties to accept an equitable peace.

This idea first took on substance with the Concert of Europe, an informal coalition of the major European powers, and the following balance-of-(big)-power diplomacy managed generally to keep the peace for the century between the fall of Napoleon in 1815 and the outbreak of World War I in 1914. The philosophy of big-power responsibility (and authority) carried over to the Council of the League of Nations. It had authority (Covenant Article 4) to deal "with any matter within the sphere of activity of the League or affecting the peace of the world." Significantly, five of the nine seats on the council were permanently assigned to the principal victors of World War I. The council was thus a continuation of the Concert of Europe concept.

When the United Nations succeeded the League of Nations, the special status and responsibilities of the big powers in the League were transferred to the UN Security Council (UNSC). Like the Council in the League, the UNSC is the main peacekeeping organ and includes permanent membership for five major powers (China, France, Great

Britain, Russia, and the United States), an arrangement that is a conceptual descendant of the Concert of Europe.

Pragmatic Cooperation

Sheer necessity has also driven the evolution of IGOs. An increasingly complex and intertwined world created the need for specialized agencies to deal with specific economic and social problems. The six-member Central Commission for the Navigation of the Rhine, established in 1815, is the oldest surviving IGO, and the International Telegraphic (now Telecommunications) Union (1865) is the oldest surviving IGO with global membership. As detailed below, the growth of specialized IGOs has been phenomenal. This aspect of international activity is also reflected in the UN through the 22 specialized agencies (such as the World Health Organization) associated with it.

Intergovernmental organizations (IGOs) play a wide range of needed roles around the world. Demonstrating just one of these, health care, is this United Nations Children's Fund (UNICEF) worker, who is giving succor to a Rwandan child stricken with cholera.

The Growth of IGOs

The 20th century saw rapid growth in the number of all types of IGOs. Just in terms of sheer quantity, the number of well-established IGOs increased sevenfold from 37 in 1909 to 251 in 2000, according to the Union of International Associations. Indeed, about one-third of all major IGOs are younger than the average American, whose age in 2002 was 36.

Even more important than the quantitative growth of IGOs is the expanding roles that they play. More and more common governmental functions are being dealt with by IGOs. Indeed, there are now few if any major political issues that are not addressed at the international level by one or more IGOs. In some cases, existing IGOs take up new roles. Just as the U.S. government and other national governments have assumed new areas of responsibility over the years as problems have arisen, so too has the United Nations moved to create units to deal with terrorism, biological warfare, environmental degradation, and a range of issues that were not part of the UN's realm when it was founded.

At other times, new areas of global concern are dealt with by creating new IGOs. For example, the development of satellites and the ability to communicate through them and the need to coordinate this capability led to the establishment of the International Mobile Satellite Organization (IMMARSAT) in 1979.

Theories of IGO Growth

A first step in analyzing the growth in the number of IGOs and the expansion of their roles is to look at two ideas about how IGOs develop. These two schools of thought are functionalism and neofunctionalism.

Functionalism The term **functionalism** represents the idea that the way to global cooperation is through a "bottom-up," evolutionary approach that begins with limited, pragmatic cooperation on narrow, nonpolitical issues. One such issue was how to deliver the mail internationally. To solve that problem, countries cooperated to found the Universal Postal Union in 1874. Each such instance of cooperation serves as a building block to achieve broader cooperation on more and more politically sensitive issues. Plato's description of "necessity" as "the mother of invention" in *The Republic* (ca. 380 B.C.) might well serve as a motto for modern functionalists.

Functionalists support their view about how global cooperation is being achieved by pointing to hundreds, even thousands of IGOs, multilateral treaties, NGOs, and other vehicles that have been pragmatically put in place to deal with specific international concerns. Functionalists further hold that by cooperating in specific, usually nonpolitical areas, countries and people can learn to trust one another. This, in turn, will lead to ever broader and ever higher levels of cooperation on the path to comprehensive cooperation or even global government.

Neofunctionalism The "top-down" approach to solving world problems is often called **neofunctionalism**. Its advocates are skeptical about the functionalist belief that nonpolitical cooperation can, by itself, lead eventually to full political cooperation and to the elimination of international conflict and self-interested state action. Neofunctionalists also worry that the functionalists' evolutionary approach will not move quickly enough to head off many of the world's looming problems. Therefore, neofunctionalists argue for immediately establishing IGOs and giving them independence and adequate resources so that they can address political issues with an eye to fostering even greater cooperation.

Reasons for Growth

The 20th century's rapid growth of international organizations, both in number and in scope of activity, is the result of both functionalist and neofunctionalist forces. Those forces were summarized by two scholars who examined why states act through international organizations (IOs). Their conclusion was that "by taking advantage . . . of IOs, states are able to achieve goals that they cannot accomplish [alone]" (Abbot & Snidal, 1998:29). In other words, the growth of international organizations has occurred because countries have found that they need them and that they work. We can note six specific causes for this expansion.

Increased international contact is one cause. The revolutions in communications and transportation technologies have brought the states of the world into much closer contact. These interchanges need organizational structures in order to become routine and regulated. The International Telegraphic Union, founded over a century ago, has been joined in more modern times by the IMMARSAT and many others.

Increased global interdependence, particularly in the economic sphere, is a second factor that has fostered a variety of IGOs designed to deal with this phenomenon. The International Monetary Fund (IMF) and the World Bank are just two examples. Regional trade and monetary organizations, cartels, and, to a degree, multinational corporations are other examples.

The expansion of transnational problems that affect many states and require solutions that are beyond the resources of any single state is a third cause of the growth of international organizations. One such issue (and its associated IGO) is nuclear proliferation (International Atomic Energy Agency).

The failure of the current state-centered system to provide security is a fourth incentive for the expansion of IGOs. The agony of two world wars, for instance, convinced many that peace is not safe in the hands of nation-states. The United Nations is the latest attempt to organize for the preservation of peace. The continuing problems in health, food, human rights, and other areas have also spurred the organization of IGOs.

The efforts of small states to gain strength through joint action is a fifth factor. The concentration of military and economic power in a handful of countries has led less powerful actors to join coalitions in an attempt to influence events. Vulnerability has thus motivated countries to come together in such organizations as the 113-member Nonaligned

Rapidly expanding interdependence has spurred the functionalist growth of IGOs, which have been created to deal with global issues that require international cooperation and organization.

Movement (NAM) and the Group of 77 (G-77), now a 135-member organization of less developed countries (LDCs) interested in promoting economic cooperation and development. Currently, the emphasis of the G-77 is to use what it describes as its "joint negotiating capacity" to represent the needs of the LDCs in the globalization process. The G-77's strategy, according to the declaration of its 2003 ministerial meeting, is the "strengthening of multilateralism and emphasiz[ing] the need to work towards a key and decisive role of the United Nations in international economic policy-making and global and economic development issues."[1]

The successes of international organizations is a sixth reason for their expansion. People and countries have learned that they can sometimes work together internationally, and this has created even more IGOs and NGOs to help address an ever greater range of transnational issues.

Roles That IGOs Play

Given the expanding number and importance of international organizations, we should ask ourselves what it is that we want IGOs to do (Muldoon, 2003; Diehl, 2001). So far, IGOs have mostly played limited, traditional roles. There are, however, a range of more far-reaching activities that some people believe IGOs should take up. It is possible to arrange these roles along a scale that measures how close each is to the traditional road or to the alternative road of international politics. Starting at the traditional end of the scale and moving toward the alternative end, the four roles are: interactive arena, creator and center of cooperation, independent international actor, and supranational organization.

Interactive Arena

The most common function of IGOs is to provide an interactive arena in which member-states pursue their individual national interests. This approach is rarely stated openly, but it is obvious in the struggles within the UN and other IGOs, where countries and blocs

Among other roles, IGOs serve as an interactive arena in which countries maneuver for diplomatic position. The intensity of this interaction during the efforts of the United States to persuade the UN Security Council to back a war with Iraq is captured in this assertive image of U.S. Secretary of State Colin Powell as he speaks to reporters outside the Security Council Chamber in March 2003.

of countries wage political struggles with a vengeance (Foot, MacFarlane, & Mastanudo, 2003). For example, research on the UN General Assembly during the 1990s indicated that its principal dimension of conflict is between the dominant West, led by the United States, and a "counterhegemonic" bloc of countries (Voeten, 2000:185).

Many observers also believe that the maneuvering in the UN Security Council in 2003 over the war with Iraq and its postwar rebuilding demonstrates that the counterhegemonic effort now includes a number of countries—particularly France—that are part of the West. As war hung in the balance in early 2003, France and Russia (both of which have a veto) along with Germany were at the forefront of resisting the U.S. efforts to win UN support for military action against Iraq. Certainly, these countries opposed an attack for substantive reasons, but there was also a palpable sense that they did not want to be seen as U.S. pawns and therefore used the crisis to demonstrate their diplomatic independence and to isolate the United States. "It's better to have only a few friends than to have a lot of sycophants," French President Jacques Chirac commented at the time. "France considers itself one of the friends of the Americans," he continued, "not necessarily one of its sycophants. And when we have something to say, we say it."[2] Putting the issue in perspective, a Russian analyst noted, "Russia has clearly made its choice, and it will stand with the Franco-German [position on Iraq in opposition to the United States]. We do not want to see the United Nations downgraded or the advent of a world order based on U.S. hegemony."[3] In a similar way, the U.S. effort to get UN support for policing and economically rebuilding Iraq while maintaining U.S. control of the process met with staunch resistance in the Security Council. As France's deputy UN ambassador explained, "Sharing the burden and the responsibilities in a world of equal and sovereign nations means also sharing information and authority."[4]

The use of IGOs to gain national advantage is somewhat contradictory to the purpose of these supposedly cooperative organizations, and it has disadvantages. One negative factor is that it sometimes transforms IGOs into another scene of struggle rather than utilizing them as forums to enhance cooperation. Furthermore, countries are apt to reduce or withdraw their support from an international organization that does not serve their narrow national interests.

The use of IGOs as an interactive arena does, however, also have advantages. One is based on the theory that international integration can advance even when IGOs are the arena for self-interested national interaction. The reasoning is that even when realpolitik is the starting point, the process that occurs in an IGO fosters the habit of cooperation and compromise.

A second advantage is that it is sometimes politically easier to take an action if an IGO has authorized it. For example, there was considerable consensus behind military action against Iraq in 1991 (unlike what occurred in 2003), and taking action under UN auspices made it easier for Muslim countries and some others to participate in an invasion conducted primarily by Christian-heritage powers (the United States, Great Britain, and France). Third, debate and diplomatic maneuvering may even provide a forum for diplomatic struggle. This role of providing an alternative to the battlefield may promote the resolution of disputes without violence. As Winston Churchill put it once, "To jaw-jaw is better than to war-war."[5]

Center of Cooperation

A second role that IGOs perform is to promote and facilitate cooperation among states and other international actors. Secretary-General Kofi Annan has observed correctly that the UN's "member-states face a wide range of new and unprecedented threats and challenges. Many of them transcend borders. They are beyond the power of any single nation to address on its own."[6] Therefore, countries have found it increasingly necessary to cooperate to address physical security, the environment, the economy, and a range of other concerns. The Council of the Baltic Sea States, the International Civil Aviation Organization, and a host of other IGOs were all established to address specific needs and, through their operations, to promote further cooperation.

Regime Theory What sometimes occurs is that narrow cooperation expands into more complex forms of interdependence. International regimes are one such development. A regime is not a single organization. Instead, **regime** is a collective noun that designates a complex of norms, rules, processes, and organizations that, in sum, have evolved to help to govern the behavior of states and other international actors in an area of international concern, such as the use and protection of international bodies of water (Heasley, 2003). Some regimes may encompass cooperative relations within a region. Other regimes are global, and we will use one of these, the regime for oceans and seas, as an example.

The Regime for Oceans and Seas The regime that is currently evolving to govern the uses of the world's oceans and other bodies of international water is represented in Figure 7.1. Note the regime's complex array of organizations, rules, and norms that promote international cooperation in a broad area of maritime regulation. Navigation, pollution, seabed mining, and fisheries are all areas of expanded international discussion, rule-making, and cooperation. The UN Convention on the Law of the Sea (1994) proclaims that the oceans and seabed are a "common heritage of mankind," to be shared according to "a just and equitable economic order." To that end, the treaty contains provisions for increased international regulation of mining and other uses of the oceans' floors. It established (as of 1994) the International Seabed Authority, headquartered in Jamaica, to supervise the procedures and rules of the treaty.

In addition to the Convention on the Law of the Sea, the regime of the oceans and seas extends to include many other organizations and rules. The International Maritime Organization has helped create safeguards against oil spills in the seas, which declined over 80% annually between the early 1970s and the late 1990s. The International Whaling Commission, the Convention on the Preservation and Protection of Fur Seals, and other efforts have begun the process of protecting marine life and conserving resources. The Montreal Guidelines on Land-Based Pollution suggest ways to prevent fertilizer and other land-based pollutants from running off into rivers and bays and then into the oceans. Countries have expanded their conservation zones to regulate fishing. The South Pacific Forum has limited the use of drift nets that indiscriminately catch and kill marine life. NGOs such as Greenpeace have pressed to protect the world seas. Dolphins are killed less frequently because many consumers only buy cans of tuna that display the "dolphin safe" logo. It is not necessary to extend this list of multilateral law-making treaties, IGOs, NGOs, national efforts, and other programs that regulate the use of the seas to make the point that in combination they are part of an expanding network that constitutes a developing regime of the oceans and seas.

FIGURE 7.1 Regimes for Oceans and Seas

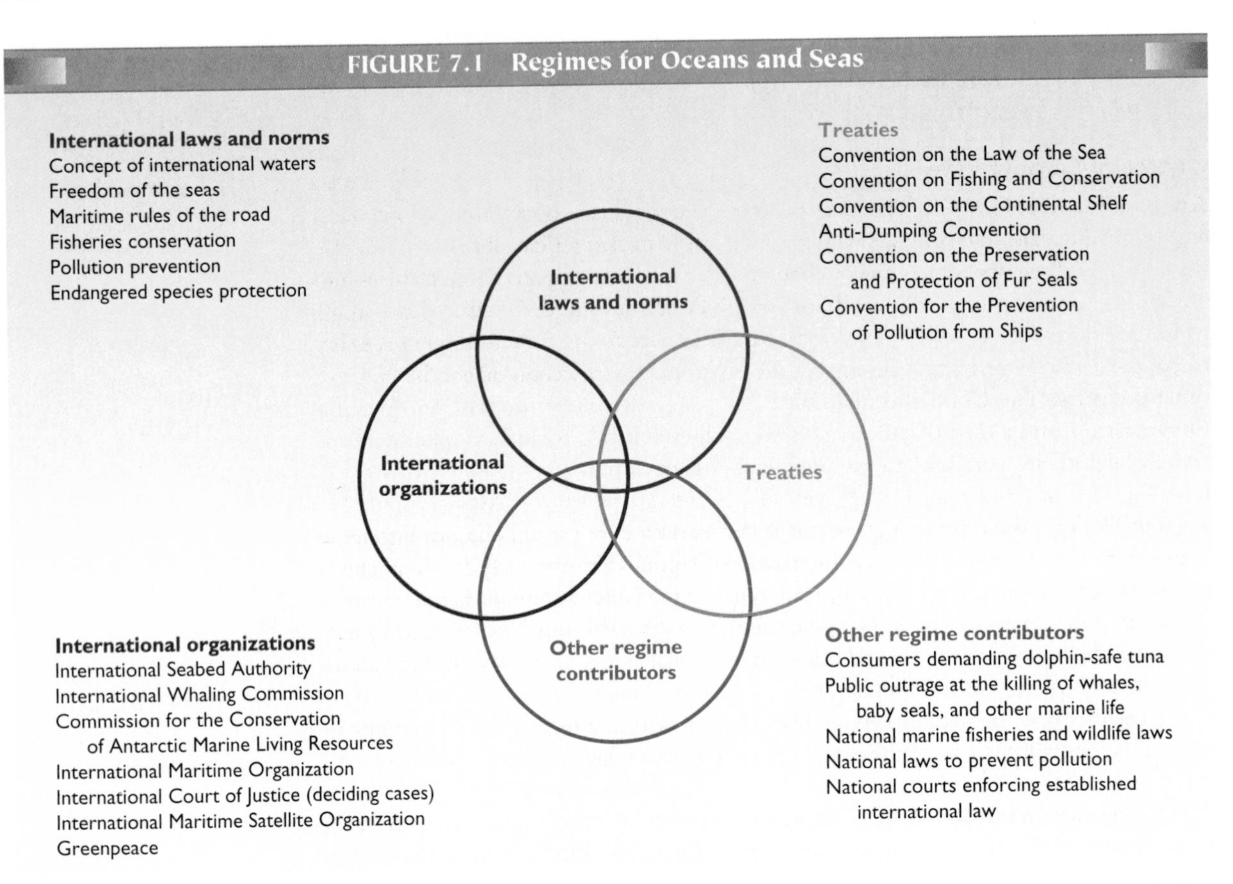

The concept of an international regime represents the nexus of a range of rules, actors, and other contributors that regulate a particular area of concern. This figure shows some of the elements of the expanding regime for oceans and seas.

Note: Entries are only a sample of all possibilities.

Independent International Actor

The third of the existing and possible IGO roles is that of an independent international actor. This role is located toward the alternative end of the traditional-alternative scale of IGO activities. Technically, what any IGO does is controlled by the wishes and votes of its members. In reality, many IGOs develop strong, relatively permanent administrative staffs. These individuals often identify with the organization and try to increase its authority and role. Global expectations—such as "the UN should do something"—add to the sense that an IGO may be a force unto itself. Soon, to use an old phrase, the whole (of the IGO) becomes more than the sum of its (member-country) parts. Sometimes this independence is controversial, as we shall see in the discussions of the EU and UN that follow. In other cases, a degree of organizational independence is intended and established in the charters of various IGOs, such as the International Court of Justice (ICJ).

Supranational Organization

There are many people who believe that the world is moving and should continue to move toward a more established form of international government. As one scholar notes, "The very complexity of the current international scene makes a fair and effective system of world governance more necessary than ever" (Hoffmann, 2003:27). This model envisions a fourth role for IGOs, that of a **supranational organization**, one that has legal authority over its members. Such supranational government could be regional or global in scope.

Specialized Supranational Governance In theory some IGOs already possess a degree of supranationalism in specialized areas, even if that supranationalism is extremely limited. While few states concede any significant part of their sovereignty to any IGO, there are some signs that this is giving way to limited acceptance of international authority in a realm one scholar calls "everyday global governance" (Slaughter, 2003:83). For example, countries now regularly give way when the World Trade Organization (WTO) rules that one of their laws or policies contravene the WTO's underlying treaty (the General Agreement on Tariffs and Trade, GATT).

Regional Government The idea of **regional government** meets some of the objections to global government. Regions would still have to bring heterogeneous peoples together and overcome nationalism, but the regional diversity is less severe than is global heterogeneity. Moreover, regional governments would allow for greater cultural diversity and political experimentation than would a global government. Some proponents of regional governments also suggest that they might serve as a stepping-stone toward world government. The EU is an example.

World Government The most far-reaching alternative to the current state-based international system is the possibility of a **world government** that governs a global political system. The arguments for such a global government begin with the criticism of the current state-based system detailed in chapter 6 and then projects international governance as a more likely path to a positive future. As the World Federalist Association puts it on its Web site, "We believe that a world federation should be given adequate powers to abolish war by keeping disputes between nations from erupting into war, to put an end to crimes against humanity, and to deal with those other urgent global problems that clearly are not manageable by nations acting separately in an ungoverned world."[7]

There is also strong opposition to the one-world idea. First, critics argue that there are practical barriers to world government. Their assumption is that nationalism has too strong a hold and that neither political leaders nor masses would be willing to surrender independence to a universal body (Taylor, 1999). Are we ready to "pledge allegiance to the United States of the World"? Second, critics of the world government movement pose political objections. They worry about the concentration of power that would be necessary to enforce international law and to address the world's monumental economic and social problems. A third doubt is whether any such government, even given unprecedented power, could succeed in solving world problems any better than states can. Fourth, some skeptics further argue that centralization would inevitably diminish desirable cultural diversity and political experimentation in the world. A fifth criticism of the world government movement is that it diverts attention from more reasonable avenues of international cooperation, such as the United Nations and other existing IGOs.

Gradually through history our primary political loyalty has shifted from smaller units such as tribes and villages to larger units, especially countries. Some people believe that this trend should continue and that a world government should be established. The image of children starting out their day by saying "I pledge allegiance to the flag of the United States of the World" may seem strange, but a global government may evolve.

Structuring a World or Regional Government Global government might take one of three forms based on the degree of power sharing between the central government and the subunits. *Centralized government* is one structure. In such a system, countries would be nonsovereign subunits that serve only administrative purposes. *Federal government* would be a less dramatic alternative. A federal government is one in which the central authority and the member units share power. Models of federalism include the relations between the United States and its 50 states and between Canada and its 10 provinces. *Confederal government* is the least centralized of the three arrangements. In a confederal government, members are highly interdependent and join together in a weak directorate organization while retaining all or most of their sovereign authority. The European Union provides a current example of what is, or at least approaches, a **confederation**.

Regional IGOs: Focus on the European Union

The growth of regional IGOs has been striking (Mansfield & Milner, 1999). Prior to World War II there were no prominent regional IGOs. Now there are many. Most of these are relatively specialized, with regional economic IGOs, such as the Arab Cooperation Council, the most numerous. Other regional IGOs are general purpose and deal with a range of issues. These include, for example, the African Union (AU, formerly the Organization of African Unity, OAU) and the Organization of American States (OAS).

Another noteworthy development regarding regional IGOs is that some of them are transitioning from specialized to general-purpose organizations. The Association of Southeast Asian Nations (ASEAN) was founded in 1967 to promote regional economic cooperation. More recently, though, ASEAN has begun to take on a greater political tinge, and, in particular, may serve as a political and defensive counterweight to China in the region (Ahmad & Ghoshal, 1999). A more obvious change in role is evident for the Economic Community of West African States (ECOWAS). It was created in 1975 to facilitate economic interchange, but it has since established a parliament and a human rights court. Also, beginning in the 1990s ECOWAS took on regional security responsibilities through interventions in civil wars raging in the Ivory Coast, Liberia, and Sierra Leone.

Beyond any of these examples of regional IGOs, the best example of what is possible is the regionalism in Europe. There, the European Union, with its 25 member-countries, has moved toward full economic integration. It has also traveled in the direction of considerable political cooperation (McCormick, 1999).

The Origins and Evolution of the European Union

The **European Union (EU)** has evolved through several stages and names. "What's in a name?" you might ask, echoing Shakespeare's heroine in *Romeo and Juliet*. As she discovered, the names Capulet and Montague proved important. So too, the name changes leading up to the current EU are important in the tale they tell.

Economic Integration

The EU's genesis began in 1952 when Belgium, France, (West) Germany, Italy, Luxembourg, and the Netherlands created a common market for coal, iron, and steel products, called the European Coal and Steel Community (ECSC). Its success prompted the six countries to agree to the Treaties of Rome (1958), which established the **European Economic Community (EEC)** to facilitate trade in many additional areas and the European Atomic Energy Community (EURATOM) to coordinate matters in that realm.

FIGURE 7.2 Membership and Organizational Structure of the European Union

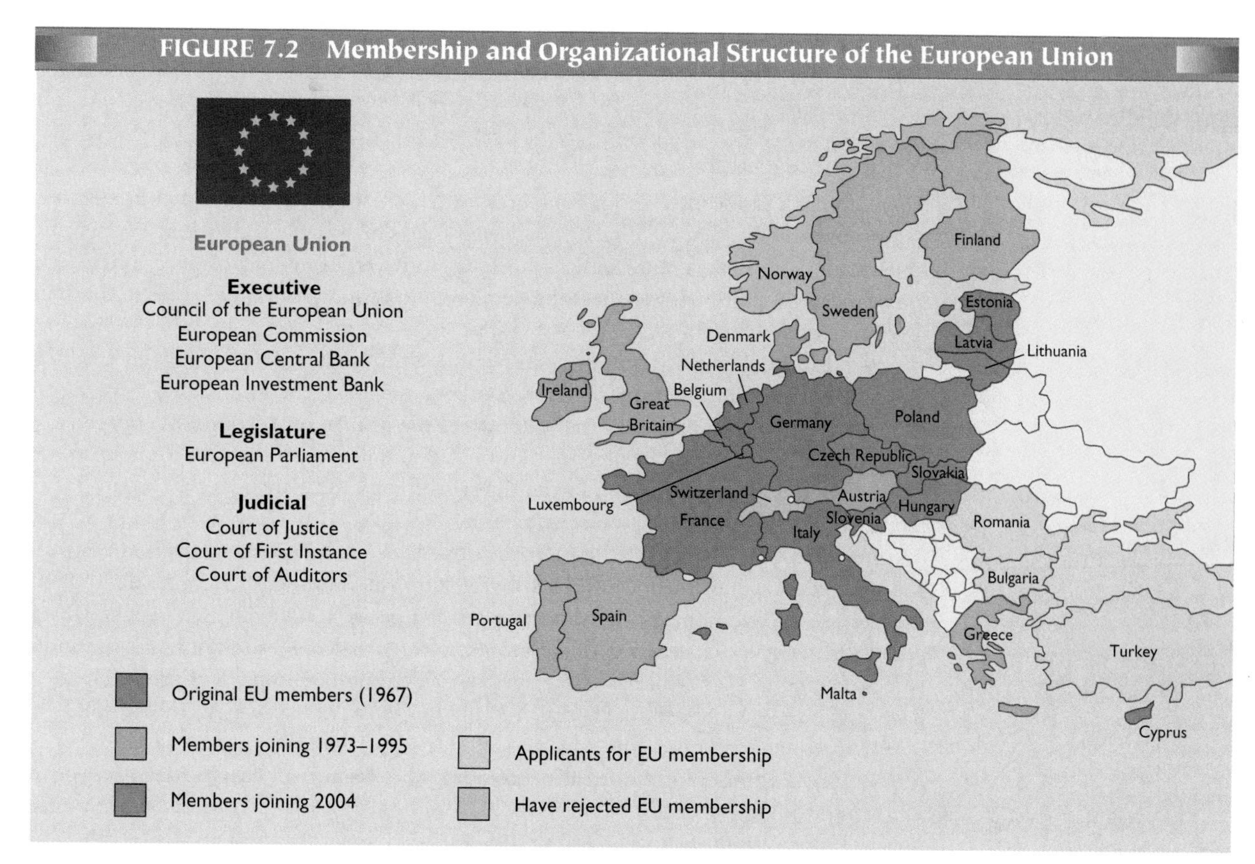

The world's most integrated regional organization is the European Union. It has expanded from the six original countries that established the European Economic Community in 1958 to 25 countries today. The EU's focus is primarily economic, but it has become increasingly integrated on matters of the environment, human rights, and other policy areas.

Even more economic success led the six countries to found an overarching organization, the **European Communities (EC)**, in 1967. Each of the three preexisting organizations became subordinate parts of the EC. Success also brought additional members, as detailed in Figure 7.2, bringing the total to 25 with the addition of 10 new members in 2004. Three more countries have applied for EU membership, and the eventual, if not quite stated, goal of the EU is to encompass all the region's countries. Jacques Santer, president of the European Commission (1995–1999), insisted that no country that met the EU economic and political standards should be kept out. "There will be no such things as 'in countries' and 'out countries'; rather there will be 'ins' and 'pre-ins'," he said.[8]

For about 30 years, the integrative process in Europe focused on economics. Members of the EC grew ever more interdependent as economic barriers were eliminated. In 1968 the members of the EC abolished the last tariffs on manufactured goods among themselves and established a common EC external tariff. The EC also began to bargain as a whole with other countries in trade negotiations. On another economic front, members agreed in 1970 to fund the EC with a virtually independent revenue source by giving it a share of each country's value-added tax (VAT, similar to a sales tax) and all customs duties collected on imports from non-EC countries.

Did You Know That:

The European Union's equivalent of a national anthem is the European Anthem. Its music is the prelude to "Ode to Joy," the fourth movement of Ludwig van Beethoven's Ninth Symphony (1823), but the anthem has no words in recognition of the EU's linguistic diversity. Beethoven's music was inspired by Friedrich von Schiller's poem, "Ode to Joy" (1785), which celebrated the future time when despite "All that custom has divided, / All men become brothers." You can hear the anthem at: http://europa.eu.int/abc/symbols/anthem/index_en.htm.

The last major step in the pre-EU evolution toward economic integration was the Single European Act (SEA) of 1987, which committed the EC to becoming a fully integrated economic unit.

Political Integration

There comes a point in economic integration when taking steps toward political integration becomes necessary. This occurs because it is impossible to reach full economic integration among sovereign states whose domestic and foreign political policies are sometimes in conflict. Moreover, as the people unite economically, it is easier to think of becoming one politically.

The EC reached this point in its integrative evolution, and to address the need for greater political coordination, the EC members agreed to the far-reaching Treaty on European Union (effective 1993), also known as the **Maastricht Treaty**. It changed the name of the EC to the EU, reflecting not only the important provisions to increase the EU's economic integration even further but also the political changes that began under the treaty. The concept of European citizenship was expanded. Citizens of EU countries can now travel on either an EU or a national passport, and citizens of any EU country can vote in local and European Parliament elections in another EU country in which they live. In addition, the EU acts increasingly as a political unit. The Maastricht Treaty called for the eventual creation of a common foreign and defense policy and common policy relating to such issues as crime, terrorism, and immigration. Gradually, such ideas have begun to become reality. The EU and the United States exchange ambassadors.

Since the adoption of the Maastricht Treaty, EU integration and expansion has moved forward through other treaties including the **Treaty of Amsterdam** (effective 1999) and the Treaty of Nice (effective 2003). The Amsterdam treaty creates stronger political integration of the EU and strengthens the powers of the president of the EU Commission and the European Parliament (EP). The Treaty of Nice anticipated the further expansion of the EU's membership by detailing political arrangements—such as the distribution of seats or votes in the EP, the Commission, and the Council of Ministers—that would occur as new member-countries join the EU.

The Government of the European Union

The EU's organizational structure is complex, but a brief look at it is important to illustrate the extent to which a regional government has been created (Hix, 1999; Peterson & Bomberg, 1999). As with all governments, the structure and the authority of the various EU units play an important part in determining how policy is made and which policies are adopted (Meunier, 2000). Figure 7.2 gives a brief overview of this structure. The EU's government can be divided for analysis into the political leadership, the bureaucracy, the legislature, and the judiciary.

Political Leadership

Political decision making occurs within the **Council of the European Union**, usually called the Council of Ministers. The Council meets twice a year as a gathering of the prime ministers and other heads of government and decides on the most important policy directions for the EU. The Council meets more often with lesser ministers (such as agriculture or finance ministers) in attendance to supplement the prime ministerial meetings. Most sessions are held in Brussels, Belgium, which is the principal site of the EU administrative element. Decisions are made by a weighted-vote plan (termed "qualified majority voting"). Under this plan, there are 345 votes, with four countries (France, Germany, Great Britain, and Italy) each having 29 votes, and the other 21 members having a number of votes ranging from 27 (Spain and Poland) to 3 (Malta). Voting procedures are complex, but in some cases unanimity is required. In other cases, passage of a measure requires both 245 votes and that these votes represent at least 62% of the EU's population.

Bureaucracy

The EU's bureaucracy is organized under the **European Commission**. With 25 members (as of 2005), the Commission administers,policy adopted by the Council. Individual commissioners are selected from the member-states on the basis of one each. The commissioners are not, however, supposed to represent the viewpoint of their country. They serve five-year terms and act as a cabinet for the EU, with each commissioner overseeing an area of administrative activity. One of the commissioners is selected by the Council of the European Union to be **president of the Commission**. This official serves as the EU's administrative head and is the overall director of the EU bureaucracy headquartered in Brussels.

The post of president of the Commission has evolved into one of the most significant in the EU. A great deal of that evolution can also be attributed to Jacques Delors, a French national who served as president from 1985 through 1994 and who became known as "Mr. Europe" because of his strong advocacy of European integration. Delors and his staff created a core structure, informally referred to as "Eurocracy," which has a European point of view, rather than a national orientation.

Delors's aggressive stance dismayed some countries, and when he stepped down the British and some others pressed for the election of a president who would be more restrained. This led the Council of Europe to choose Luxembourg's prime minister, Jacques Santer, who took a lower profile than did Delors. Santer's successor, Romano Prodi of Italy (to 2004), followed suit. Nevertheless, the size and power of the EU bureaucracy mean that anyone serving as its president will be a person of significant influence.

Yet another indication of the importance of the commission, as well as the political integration of Europe, is the emergence of an ever larger, more active, and more powerful EU infrastructure. The EU's administrative staff has almost quintupled since 1970 to about 29,000 today. The number of EU regulations, decisions, and directives from one or the other EU body has risen from an annual 345 in 1970 to over 600. The EU's 2003 budget was about $100 billion, raised primarily from payments by member governments (37%), tariff revenues (15%), and the VAT (33%).

Legislature

The **European Parliament (EP)** serves as the EU's legislative branch and meets in Strasbourg, France. It has 732 members, apportioned among the EU's 25 countries on a modified population basis, who are elected to five-year terms. The most populous country (Germany) has 99 seats; the least populous country (Malta) has 5 seats. Unlike most international congresses, such as the UN General Assembly, the EP's members are elected by voters in their respective countries (Scully & Farrell, 2003). Furthermore, instead of organizing themselves within the EP by country, the representatives have tended to group themselves by political persuasion. The 1999 elections, for example, resulted in the moderately conservative coalition, called the European People's Party (EPP), winning 36% of the seats and the moderately liberal coalition, the Socialist Party of Europe (SPE), winning 28% of the seats. It was the first time in the EU's history that the EPP had gained more seats than the SPE. The remaining seats were scattered among seven identifiable groupings of legislators and a few dozen unaffiliated members.

The EP has had mostly advisory authority, but it is struggling to carve out a more authoritative role. That goal was advanced under the Treaty of Amsterdam, which extends the EP's "co-decision" authority with the Council of the European Union to a greater number of matters. The EP can also veto some regulations issued by the commission and it confirms the president of the Commission. A key power, albeit one that is

One indication that the European Parliament is slowly gaining authority within the European Union is the upsurge of people pressing the EP to favor their causes. The area around the EP is now the scene of many demonstrations, including this one in which farmers brought their cattle to the EP building (in the background) to emphasize their demand that the EU do more to protect agriculture.

so far little used, is the EP's ability to accept or reject the EU budget proposed by the commission (Maurer, 2003).

Judiciary

The **Court of Justice** is the main element of the judicial branch of the EU (Alter, 1998; Garrett, Kelemen, & Schulz, 1998; Mattli & Slaughter, 1998). The 15-member court hears cases brought by member-states or other EU institutions and sometimes acts as a court of appeals for decisions of lower EU courts. The combined treaties of the EU are often considered its collective "constitution," and there is a move, discussed later, to consolidate and expand the treaties' various provisions in a single EU constitution. Like the EU's other institutions, the courts have gained authority over time. In one illustrative case, the Court of Justice ruled that certain VAT exemptions in Great Britain violated EU treaties and would have to be eliminated. The ruling prompted some members of the British Parliament to grumble that it was the first time since Charles I's reign (1625–1649) that the House of Commons had been compelled to raise taxes. Another bit of evidence of the mounting influence of the court is that its workload became so heavy that the EU created a new, lower court, the Court of First Instance, which hears cases related to the EU brought by corporations and individuals.

The Future of the EU

The next phase in the movement toward an even more politically integrated EU began when the Convention on the Future of Europe convened in Brussels, Belgium, in 2002.

Chaired by former French president Valery Giscard d'Estaing, the "constitutional convention" was charged with drafting an EU constitution. In mid-2003, the convention presented its draft document to the EU member-countries. Whether the constitution will be adopted and, if so, in what form and, indeed, the general future of the EU rests on a number of factors (Calleo, 2003; Gabel, 1998).

The Specifics of the EU Constitution

Not unexpectedly, the draft constitution, which is trying to increase political integration at the expense of national sovereignty, is controversial, and there are important differences among the leaders of the EU's member-countries on its provisions. The 1,037-page document includes provisions to increase the authority of the European Parliament, to further reduce the need for unanimity in the Council of the European Union, to create a foreign ministry for the EU, and to establish a European public prosecutor to deal with transnational crime. At least immediately, the most controversial point was the qualified voting scheme for the Council of the European Union. The document retained it, but reduced the supermajorities needed to take action. Some smaller countries favor even greater reductions than the draft constitution anticipates, while some larger countries were unwilling to give up any of their current voting power. Spain was particularly adamant about maintaining its advantage, with Prime Minister José Maria Aznar telling reporters, "There is no consensus on this issue [of reducing the supermajority]. We are going to maintain this position."[9]

Some who favor moving quickly toward a truly federal European Union were disappointed, but convention chairman Giscard d'Estaing was probably accurate in this observation, "Our proposal goes, I think, as far as is possible in the political, social and cultural climate of Europe today."[10] As for a name, the convention suggested one of four: the European Community, the European Union, United Europe, or the United States of Europe. According to one British diplomat, the recent strain in U.S.-European relations means that the final choice being the United States of Europe "has not a cat in hell's chance of success."[11]

A 2003 poll by the Eurobarometer, which tracks opinion in Europe, indicates that support or opposition to a European constitution remains unsettled. More than two-thirds of the public supported the concept of a constitution, but when asked about the work of the Convention on the Future of Europe, only 30% of the EU public expressed support, while 20% opposed it. Most importantly, 50% had yet to form an opinion.

General Public Support for EU Integration

Beyond the public's uncertain or undecided reaction to the draft constitution, its more general attitude toward integration is another factor that will determine the EU's future. The Eurobarometer finds somewhat mixed signals about how Europeans feel about the EU. For example, popular support for their country's membership in the EU can be viewed in two ways. From one perspective, only about half of Europeans voice support. But only 29% voice opposition, with others uncertain.

Economic Well-Being One matter that influences how Europeans feel about EU integration is on their perceptions of its impact on their prosperity. During the 1980s, the average annual growth of the EU's GDP was 2.2% and on average 55% of poll respondents said that their country benefited from EU membership. More recently, with the EU's average annual GDP growth at 1.7%, the public perception that that their country benefits from EU membership has dropped by about 5%.

While the potential for the European economy is immense, there are numerous possible obstacles to overcome. One is economic disparity. The original six members

The attitudes of many Europeans toward the European Union is influenced by how prosperous the EU economy is at any given time. Representing that connection, this labor union demonstration near the EU's administrative headquarters in Brussels, Belgium, notes the coming of the EU currency, the euro, but asks, "And what about employment?"

were relatively close in their economic circumstances. The addition of new countries has changed that and will continue to do so. As it stands, the average annual per capita GDPs of EU countries ranges from Luxembourg's $39,840 to Latvia's $3,230.

Just as expanding EU membership has potential pluses and minuses, so does the implementation of the euro as the official currency and the abolishment of the German mark, French franc, Italian lira, and the other national currencies of the EU members (McKay, 1999). A common currency is necessary to achieve full economic integration and to move further toward political integration. Still, the introduction of the euro has created major issues as the EU struggles to resolve longstanding national differences over fiscal policy. Three of the older 15 EU countries (Denmark, Great Britain, and Sweden) are not in the "euro zone," that is, they have not substituted the euro for their national currencies. This resistance was underlined in 2003 when 56% of Sweden's voters rejected adoption of the euro. The 10 newest members will decide on the euro issue in time as their economies integrate with the EU.

Satisfaction with EU Institutions The degree to which the EU's rule-making and administrative institutions function effectively also influences general attitudes about EU integration. Some European voters oppose expansion of EU functions because of their sense that so-called Eurotaxes are too high and that the EU bureaucracy, the "Eurocracy," is too powerful, unresponsive, and even corrupt. Some of the tales of Eurocratic excess that circulate are related in the In the Spotlight box "When Is a Banana a Banana?"

In 2003, according to the Eurobarometer, 44% of respondents indicated confidence in the EU's institutions, while 38% expressed a lack of confidence, and 18% were unsure. This is hardly a ringing vote of confidence in the EU, but it was better than the level of confidence Europeans had in their national government's institutions (37% confident, 53% not confident, 10% unsure).

IN THE SPOTLIGHT

When Is a Banana a Banana?

Many people consider Europe the epicurean center of the world, and the EU's "food fights" bear out the intensity of that continent's focus on gastronomical policy.

During one discussion in the Council of Ministers in 2002 over a proposal to locate the new EU food safety agency in Finland, Italy's Prime Minister Silvio Berlusconi argued that it should be put in Parma, Italy, on the grounds that "Parma is synonymous with good cuisine. The Finns don't even know what proscuitto is." Premier Guy Verhofstaadt of Belgium pointed out reasonably that "the gastronomic attraction is no argument for the location of an EU agency," but Berlusconi was unpersuaded. "My final word is no," he proclaimed, and the conferees put off the decision until after lunch.[1]

This focus on food by the leaders also appeals to what critics condemn as the regulatory gluttony of the EU's bureaucrats, an expansive appetite for power that has become part of the political lore of Europe. First there was the time when Danes were offended to the core and left red-cheeked with anger when the pride and joy of their apple crop, the Queen Bridgette, was declared too small to move in trade among EU members. Intense negotiations re-polished Danish-EU relations. This was followed by the EU's banana contretemps. The details are slippery, but it all stemmed from a bunch of regulations promulgated by the EU bureaucracy that, among other things, specified that imported bananas had to be at least 5.5 inches long and 1.1 inches wide, and could not be abnormally bent. "Brussels bureaucrats proved yesterday what a barmy bunch they are—by outlawing curved bananas," protested the British newspaper, the *Sun*. An EU spokesperson replied that while, indeed, bananas of an abnormal shape could not be imported, that "in no sense" meant that EU regulation banned "curved bananas because a curve is a normal shape for a banana."[2] Soon this too was straightened out—the regulation, that is, not the bananas.

The reputation of the Eurocracy was further darkened by the chocolate imbroglio. Having decided that bananas could indeed be bent, EU policy makers turned to the sticky issue of what constitutes chocolate. The battle line was drawn between those EU countries that require chocolate to consist entirely of cocoa butter and the other EU members that allow up to 5% vegetable oil in chocolate. Representing the purists, the head of the Belgian chocolate company, Godiva, proclaimed that only "100% chocolate should be called . . . chocolate." Answering back for the nondoctrinaire chocolatiers, a representative of Great Britain's largest chocolate maker, Cadbury, urged, "Let's celebrate Europe's regional diversity and recognize that there are different ways of making chocolate." The purists won the first round when the European Parliament voted in favor of their position. But the war was not over, for the Council of the European Union had to make the final gooey decision. "Whatever we do will be attacked from one side or the other," an EU spokesperson has complained. Compromise was the sweet solution. A ruling declared that chocolate with vegetable oil could be shipped throughout the EU. Moreover it could be labeled chocolate, but only in the nonpurist countries. In the purist countries, it would have to be labeled "family milk chocolate." Not that it has anything to do with families or milk. Ah well, as Forrest Gump mused, "Life is like a box of chocolates."

Political Identity How Europeans identify politically is a fourth factor that will affect EU integration (Zielonka, 1998). It will be necessary for Europeans to shift their political loyalties away from their national states and toward the EU for integration to proceed much further. As discussed in chapter 5, the political identity of only about one in eight people in the EU focuses exclusively or primarily on the EU, but six out of ten EU citizens have at least some sense of political identification with it, even if it is secondary.

Nationalism-rooted resistance is especially evident in the newer EU members, but it is an important emotion in even the original six EU members. "Our nations are the source of our identities and of our roots," President Chirac of France recently proclaimed. "The diversity of our political traditions, cultures and languages is one of the strengths of the union. In the future, our nations will stay the first reference point for our people."[12]

Perceptions of Germany Although it is not often spoken of officially, wariness of Germany is yet another factor that impinges on attitudes toward EU integration. Germany has the most people and the largest economy of all the EU countries, and that fact coupled with Germany's past leave some Europeans worried that integration could mean

German domination. That was evident when the German foreign minister, Joschka Fischer, expressed his support for "nothing less than a European Parliament and a European government which really do exercise legislative and executive power within [a] . . . federation."[13] Reaction was swift and sharp. "There is a tendency in Germany to imagine a federal structure for Europe which fits in with its own model," warned France's Minister of the Interior Jean-Pierre Chevènement. "Deep down, [Germany] is still dreaming of the Holy Roman Empire. It hasn't cured itself of its past derailment into Nazism."[14] Fischer later protested he had spoken as an individual, not as German foreign minister, and Chevènement apologized for his undiplomatic reference to Germany's Nazi past. Still, the incident reflected a concern that is not far below the surface in Europe.

Overall, the evolution of the EU has been one of the remarkable events of the past half century (Gilbert, 2003). It does not take much imagination to foresee a day when the once-antagonistic states of Europe are forged into a United States of Europe. That is just one possibility, however. What is certain is that the progress of the EU toward further economic and political integration, whether or not it leads to true federation, will be difficult.

Global IGOs: Focus on the United Nations

The growing level and importance of IGO activity and organization at the regional level is paralleled by IGOs at the global level. Of these, the United Nations is by far the best known and most influential (Ryan, 2000). Therefore, we will focus in this section on the UN, both as a generalized study of the operation of IGOs and as a specific study of the most prominent member of their ranks.

IGO Organization and Related Issues

Constitutions, rules of procedure, finance, organization charts, and other administrative details are often crucial in determining political outcomes. It is, for example, impossible to understand how the UN works without knowing that five of its members possess a veto in the Security Council and the other 186 do not. An outline of the UN's structure is depicted in Figure 7.3.

Structure is also important because to be successful, an organization's structure must reflect realities and goals and have the flexibility to change if it becomes outmoded. "Clearly we cannot meet the challenges of the new millennium with an instrument designed for the very different circumstances of the middle of the 20th century," the UN's secretary-general, Kofi Annan, points out.[15] To examine the structure and rules of IGOs, we will take up matters of general membership, the structure of representative bodies, voting formulas, the authority of executive leadership, and the bureaucracy. Then we will turn to the matter of IGO finance.

Membership Issues

Theoretically, membership in most IGOs is open to any state that is both within the geographic and functional scope of that organization and also subscribes to its principles and practices. In reality, politics is sometimes an additional standard. Today the UN has nearly universal membership, as Figure 7.4 on page 210 shows, but that was not always the case.

Standards for admitting new members is one point of occasional controversy. One instance occurred in 1998 when the General Assembly gave the Palestinians added legitimacy by voting overwhelmingly to give them what amounts to an informal associate

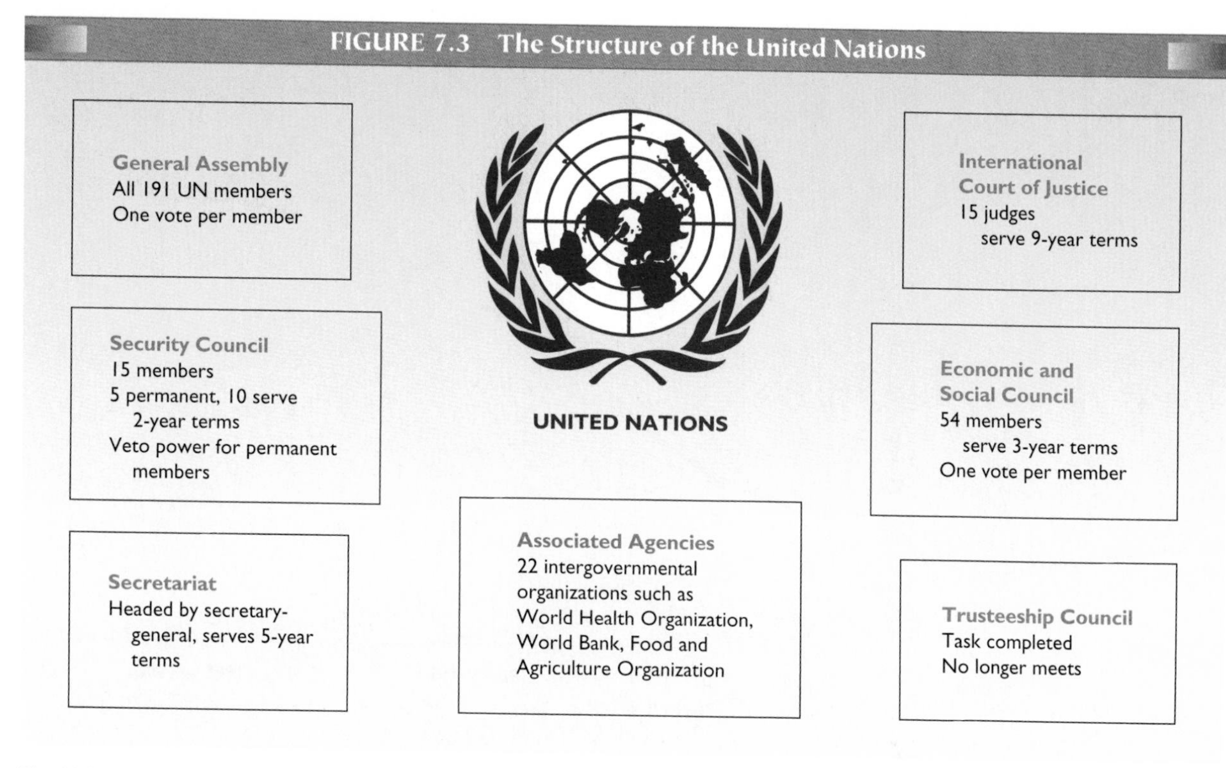

The United Nations is a complex organization. It has six major organs and 22 associated agencies.

membership. The Palestinians cannot vote, but they can take part in debates in the UN and perform other functions undertaken by states.

Successor state status can also sometimes be a political issue. With little fanfare, the UN agreed to recognize Russia as the successor state to the Soviet Union. This meant, among other things, that Russia inherited the USSR's permanent seat and veto on the Security Council. Taking the opposite approach, the UN in 1992 refused to recognize the Serbian-dominated government in Belgrade as the successor to Yugoslavia once that country broke apart. Instead, the General Assembly required Yugoslavia to (re)apply for admission. Once dictator Slobodan Milosevic was toppled, Yugoslavia (since renamed Serbia and Montenegro) did reapply, and it was (re)admitted in 2000.

Withdrawal, suspension, or expulsion is another membership issue. Nationalist China (Taiwan) was, in effect, ejected from the UN when the "China seat" was transferred to the mainland. In a move close to expulsion, the General Assembly refused between 1974 and 1991 to accept the credentials of South Africa's delegate because that country's apartheid policies violated the UN Charter. The refusal to recognize Yugoslavia in 1992 as a successor state was, in effect, an expulsion of that country based on its bloody repression of Bosnians, Croats, and others.

Basis of Representation Issues

There are important issues that relate to the structure of representative bodies of IGOs. Most have a **plenary representative body** that includes all members. The theoretical basis for plenary bodies is the mutual responsibility of all members for the organization and its policies. The **UN General Assembly (UNGA)** is the UN's plenary organ, but in other IGOs it may be termed a council, a conference, a commission, or even a parliament.

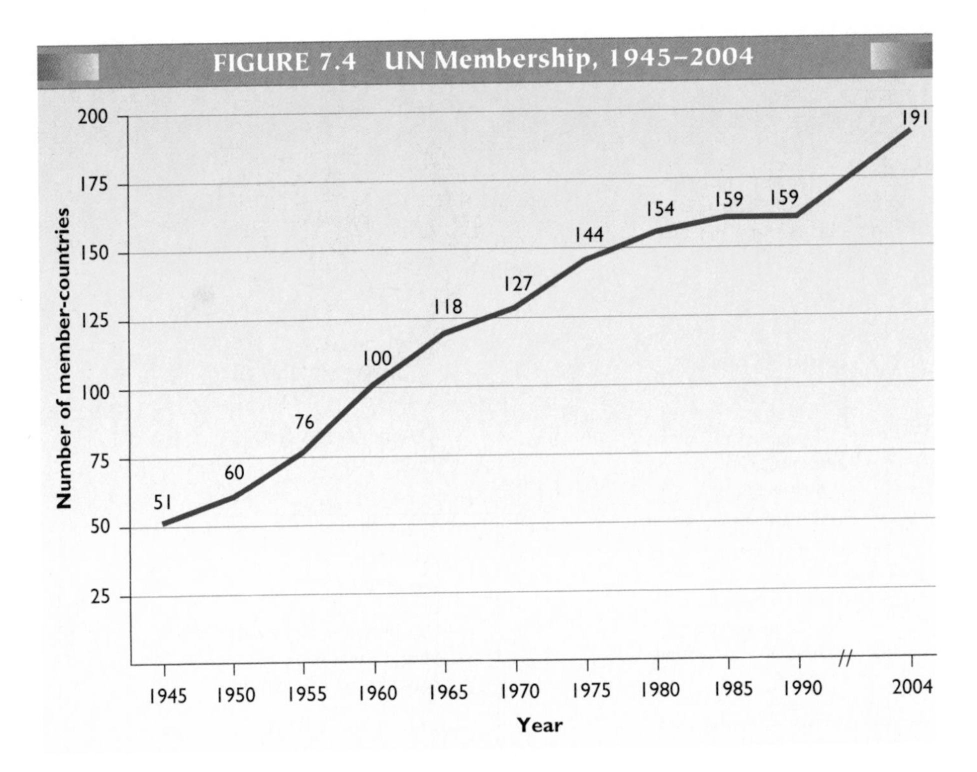

Membership in the United Nations has risen rapidly. The 375% growth in UN membership is an indication of the increased number of states in existence and also of the UN's nearly universal membership.

Data source: UN Web site at http://www.un.org/overview/growth.htm.

These plenary bodies normally have the authority to involve themselves in virtually all aspects of their organizations. Thus, in theory, they are the most powerful elements of their organizations. In practice, however, the plenary organization may be secondary to the administrative structure or some other part of the organization.

A second type of representative body is a **limited membership council**. It is based on the theory that some members have a greater concern or capacity in a particular area. For example, the **UN Security Council (UNSC)** has 15 members. Ten are chosen by the UNGA for limited terms, but five are permanent members. These five (China, France, Russia, the United Kingdom, and the United States) were the leading victorious powers at the end of World War II and were thought to have a special peacekeeping role to play. They have served continuously since 1945 as permanent members on the Security Council; more than half of the other 186 members have never served on the council.

The special status enjoyed by the five permanent members of the UNSC is a simmering issue in the UN. Some charge that it is an *inaccurate reflection of power realities.* As the German mission to the UN puts it, "The Security Council as it stands does not reflect today's world which has changed dramatically since 1945."[16] Given current realities, Germany, India, Japan, and some other powerful countries have begun to press for permanent seats for themselves.

Geographic and demographic imbalance is another issue. Geographically, Europe and North America have four of five permanent seats, and those four permanent members are also countries of predominantly Eurowhite and Christian heritage. Many countries in Africa and elsewhere agree with the view expressed by the president of Zambia that the council "can no longer be maintained like the sanctuary of the Holy of Holies with only the original members acting as high priests, deciding on issues for the rest of the world who cannot be admitted."[17]

What some critics charge is an *inequitable veto* is a third issue. Speaking in the General Assembly, a Venezuelan diplomat described the veto as "an anti-democratic practice . . . not in accordance with the principle of the sovereign equality of states."[18]

Whatever may be just, however, change will be hard to achieve. One difficulty is that any Charter revision must be recommended by a two-thirds vote of the UNSC (in which each of the five permanent members has a veto), adopted by a two-thirds vote of the UNGA, and ratified by two-thirds of the members according to their respective constitutional processes. The permanent UNSC members are opposed to surrendering their special status. It will also be difficult to arrive at a new formula that satisfies the sensitivities of other countries and regions. For example, the thought of India having a permanent seat alarms Pakistan, whose UN representative has characterized those seeking permanent status as motivated by "an undisguised grab for power and privilege."[19] Therefore, the prospects for reform remain dim. Speaking in late 2003, Secretary-General Kofi Annan noted that many of the "structures of the United Nations reflect an earlier age," that "this is most clearly the case in the Security Council," and that there is "widespread agreement that the council should be enlarged." Yet he had to concede, "There is no consensus on the details."[20]

Voting Issues

One of the difficult issues that any international organization faces is its formula for allocating votes (Bohman, 1999). Three major alternatives as they exist today are majority voting, weighted voting, and unanimity voting. The implications of various voting formulas are evident in Figure 7.5 on page 212.

Majority voting is the most common formula used in IGOs. This system has two main components: (1) each member casts one equal vote, and (2) the issue is carried by either a simple majority (50% plus one vote) or, in some cases, a supermajority (commonly two-thirds). The theory of majoritarianism springs from the concept of sovereign equality and the democratic notion that the will of the majority should prevail. The UNGA and most other UN bodies operate on this principle.

The problem with the idea of equality among states is that it does not reflect some standards of reality. Should Costa Rica, with no army, cast an equal vote with the powerful United States? Should San Marino, with a population of thousands, cast the same vote as China, with its more than 1 billion people? It might be noted, for example, that in the UNGA, some 127 states, whose combined populations are less than 15% of the world's population, account for two-thirds of membership and, thus, the available votes. By contrast, the 10 countries with populations over 100 million (Bangladesh, Brazil, China, India, Indonesia, Japan, Nigeria, Pakistan, Russia, and the United States), which combined have 60% of the world's population, have just 5% of the available votes in the General Assembly.

Weighted voting, or a system that allocates unequal voting power on the basis of a formula, is a second voting scheme. Two possible criteria are population and wealth. As noted earlier, the European Parliament provides an example of an international representative body based in part on population. A number of international monetary organizations base voting on financial contributions. Voting in the World Bank and the International Monetary Fund is based on member contributions. The United States alone commands about 17% of the votes in the IMF, and it and France, Germany, Great Britain, and Japan together can cast almost 40% of the votes in that IGO, yet combined have only 10% of the world population. By contrast, China and India, which combined

FIGURE 7.5 Equal, Population-Based, and Wealth-Based Voting Formulas

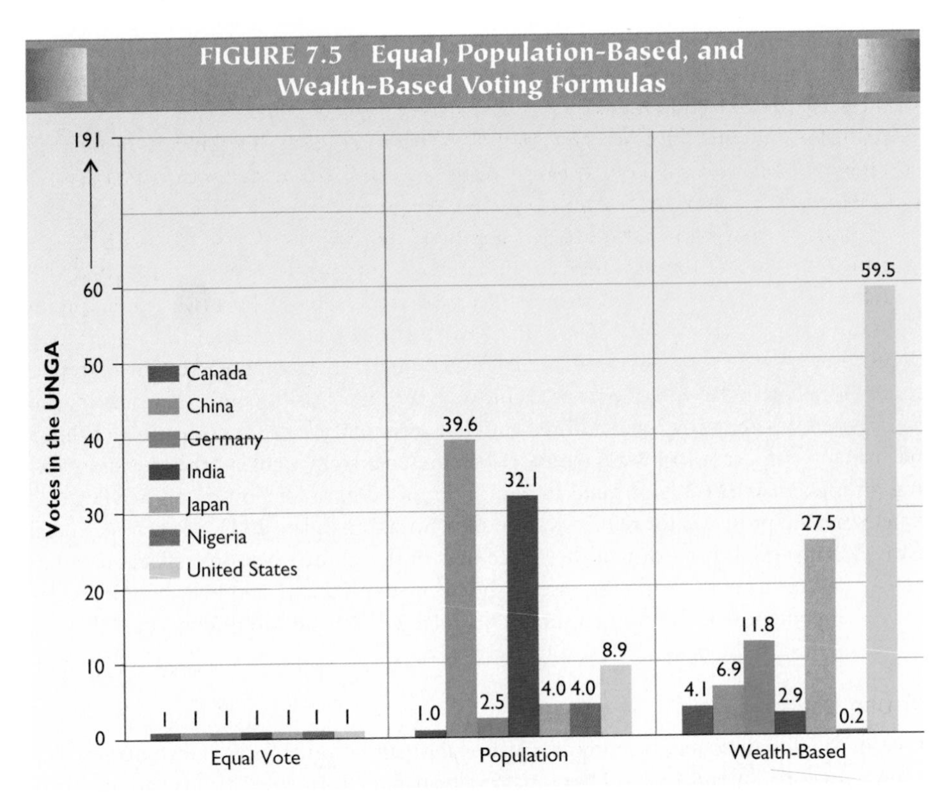

To see the impact of various voting formulas, imagine that the current 191 votes in the UNGA were allocated on the basis of equality, population, and wealth. Voting power would vary widely. Compare the United States and China, for example. Both, of course, would have the same vote in a one-country, one-vote system. In a population system, China would have far more votes than the United States. The reverse would be true in a wealth-based voting scheme, in which the United States would have almost nine times as many votes as China. Are any of these formulas fair? What would be a fair formula?

Data sources: World Bank (2003) and author's calculations.

have 38% of the world's population, together have 4.9% of the IMF votes. This "wealth-weighted" voting is especially offensive to LDCs, which contend that it perpetuates the system of imperial domination by the industrialized countries.

Unanimity voting constitutes a third scheme. This system requires the assent by all, although sometimes abstaining from a vote does not block agreement. The Organization for Economic Cooperation and Development (OECD) and some other IGOs operate on that principle. Unanimity preserves the concept of sovereignty but can easily lead to stalemate.

The voting formula in the UNSC by which any of the five permanent members (the P5) can **veto** proposals while the other 10 members cannot is an unusual variation on the unanimity scheme (O'Neill, 1997). Vetoes were cast frequently during the cold war, but have been infrequent since 1990. Nevertheless, the power remains important. First, a veto is still sometimes cast. In September 2003, a resolution calling on Israel not to expel Palestinian Yasser Arafat from the West Bank received 11 votes, with three countries abstaining. The United States was the lone no vote, but that was sufficient to defeat the resolution. Second, the threat of a veto can sometimes forestall action. For example, the United States and Great Britain wanted to secure Security Council authorization to take military action against Iraq in 2003. But they did not try to push a resolution through the Security Council when it became clear that even if majority support could be gathered (which was doubtful), France and Russia would exercise their veto power.

Many Americans were angry to find that the U.S. effort to gain UN support for action against Iraq faced a veto in the Security Council, but as Figure 7.6 shows, the United States has itself often exercised its own veto. As is evident, the USSR cast many more vetoes than the other four permanent members of the Security Council during the early years of the cold war. Since 1980, however, the veto has become a particular tool of the United States, with votes against resolutions condemning Israel being the most frequent use of the U.S. power.

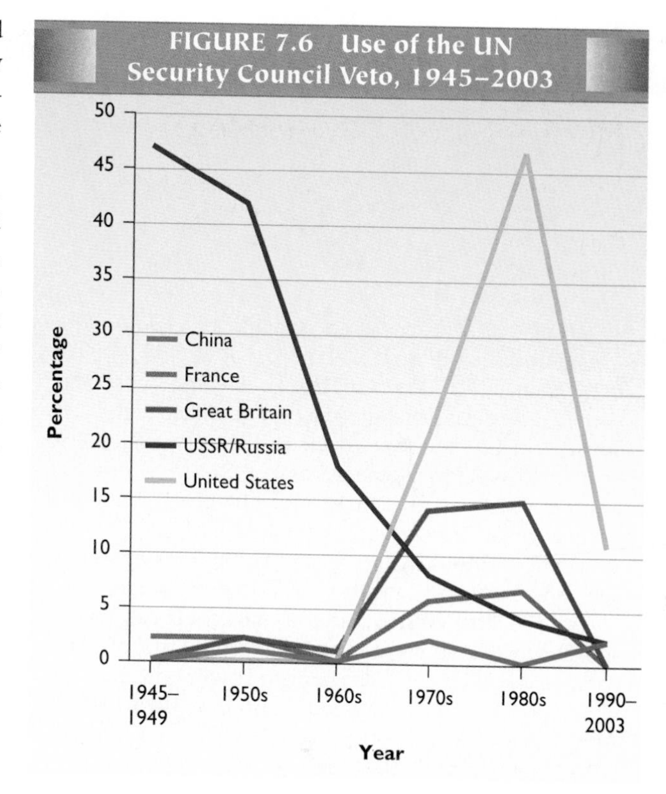

The use of the veto in the UN Security Council has changed over the years. In the first two decades of the cold war, Russia cast the vast majority of vetoes, and it accounts for 48% of the 254 vetoes in UN history through 2003. In more recent years, it has been the United States that has cast the preponderant number of vetoes.

Note: China was represented by the Taipei government until 1971 and by the Beijing government since then. Russia assumed the seat of the USSR in 1992. Many of the votes on which a veto was cast had more than one permanent member casting a no (veto) vote, leaving 215 measures vetoed and 256 veto votes cast.

Data sources: Global Policy Forum at http://www.globalpolicy.org/security/membship/veto/vetosubj.htm and calculations by author.

IGO Leadership, Administration, and Finance

It is difficult for any organization to function without a single administrative leader, and virtually all IGOs have a chief executive officer (CEO). The UN's administrative structure is called the **Secretariat**, and the secretary-general is the CEO. In this section we will take up the selection and role of the UN secretary-general and other CEOs of IGOs. Then, in the next section, we will address the bureaucratic understructure of IGO secretariats (Barnett & Finnemore, 1999).

The Selection of IGO Leaders

The UN secretary-general is nominated by the UNSC, then elected by the General Assembly for a five-year term. This simple fact does not, however, adequately emphasize the political considerations that govern the appointment of administrators. One sign of the importance of IGOs is that who will head them has often been, and seems increasingly to be, the subject of intense struggle among member-countries. This is taken up in the Global Actors box "Much Ado about Something" on page 214.

The Role of IGO Leaders

An issue that swirls around IGO executives is their proper role. The role orientations of the UN secretary-general and other IGO leaders can range between activism and restraint (Kille & Scully, 2003). For the most part, the documents that established IGOs anticipated a restrained role. In the UN Charter, for example, the Secretariat is the last major organ discussed. That placement indicates the limited, largely administrative role that the document's drafters intended for the secretary-general.

Former UN Secretaries-General Whatever was intended, the first two secretaries-general, Trygve Lie of Norway (1946–1953) and Dag Hammarskjöld of Sweden (1953–1961), were activists who steadily expanded the role of their office. Hammarskjöld argued that he had a "responsibility" to act to uphold the peace "irrespective of the views

GLOBAL ACTORS

Much Ado about Something

The argument that IGOs are marginal to world politics is belied by the frequent conflict over who will head them. Clearly, there must be much ado about something. There are several reasons that battle lines have sometimes been drawn over the appointment or reappointment of the UN secretary-general or the head of some other IGO.

The selection of Boutros Boutros-Ghali (1992–1996) began with African discontent that no one from that continent had yet been secretary-general. The United States and some other countries were dubious about the political orientation of a secretary-general from sub-Saharan Africa, but also did not want to alienate Africa by being "the 900-pound gorilla," in the words of one U.S. official.[1] In this atmosphere, Boutros-Ghali, an Egyptian and the only non-sub-Saharan African candidate, was an ideal compromise. He was the most Westernized of all the African candidates, spoke several languages, and had been a professor of international law in Egypt and a Fulbright scholar at Columbia University. Any possible alarm that Boutros-Ghali was an Arab was eased by the fact that he is a Coptic Christian, not a Muslim, and his wife, Leah, is Jewish.

Boutros-Ghali proved to be an assertive, sometimes acerbic secretary-general who often rankled some members, especially the United States. Washington was particularly piqued by his criticism of the Eurowhite-dominated Security Council for what he saw as a racially tinged tendency to pay more attention to some matters (such as the Balkans crisis in Europe) than others (such as the crises in Somalia and Rwanda in Africa). Whatever the validity of such charges, the result was that the United States tacitly vetoed a second term for Boutros-Ghali.

Since Boutros-Ghali had been appointed to remedy the fact that there had been no previous secretary-general from Africa, and since most recent secretaries-general have served two terms, the African countries felt that it was still their "turn." Washington did not want to offend Africa, but also worried about the political views of potential African candidates. After extensive maneuvering, the final choice for the seventh secretary-general was Kofi Annan, a career UN diplomat from Ghana. He had a reputation as a capable and moderate diplomat and administrator, and his personal history (a B.A. degree in economics from Macalaster College in St. Paul, Minnesota, an M.A. in management from MIT) helped assuage Washington's concern that a secretary-general from black Africa might prove too radical. Annan is married to Nane Lagergren, a Swedish lawyer, who is a niece of Raoul Wallenberg, the heroic Swedish diplomat noted for trying to save Jewish lives during World War II.

The often sharp political contests that are waged when picking UN secretaries-general underlines the importance of that office. This standard can also be applied to the heads of other IGOs. For example, there have been spirited contests each time there has been a leadership change at the World Trade Organization. During the most recent round in 1999, the struggle featured a determined effort by the LDCs to break the EDCs' monopoly on the top jobs in the leading financial IGOs. The result was a compromise: an EDC national, Mike Moore of New Zealand, was selected with the understanding that in 2002 he would step down in favor of Thailand's Supachi Panitchpakdi, who would serve until 2005.

There have been similar contests over who would become president of the Commission of the European Union, the World Bank, the International Monetary Fund, and other IGOs in recent years, but recounting these dramas is not necessary to make the basic point that the jostling among the major powers to appoint one of their own or someone of their liking to the top jobs indicates how important these IGOs are. All that sound and fury must signify something.

and wishes of the various member governments" (Archer, 1983:148). Hammarskjöld's approach was epitomized during the civil war that followed the independence of the Belgian Congo in 1960. The secretary-general aggressively used UN military forces to try to restore peace. It is somehow sadly fitting that he died in the area when his plane crashed after reportedly being shot down by one of the warring factions.

The Soviets were so upset at the activist and what they saw as a pro-Western stance of Hammarskjöld that they pressed for successors with more restrained conceptions of the role of secretary-general. Over time, however, secretaries-general have once again tended toward activism. The sixth secretary-general, Egypt's Boutros Boutros-Ghali (1992–1996), believed that "if one word above all is to characterize the role of the secretary-general, it is independence. The holder of this office must never be seen as acting out of fear or in an attempt to curry favor with one state or groups of states."[21] Just as Hammarskjöld's activism had led him into disfavor, so to did Boutros-Ghali's views. As a result, Boutros-Ghali was forced from office after one term, as related in the box "Much Ado about Something."

The Current UN Secretary-General In the aftermath of the ouster of Boutros-Ghali, the Security Council nominated and the General Assembly elected Kofi Annan of Ghana as the UN's seventh secretary-general. Annan is the first secretary-general to have spent almost his entire career as a UN diplomat rather than as a diplomat for his country. He joined UN service at age 24 and served in a variety of positions, including undersecretary-general for peacekeeping. Also, as you will see in the box "Much Ado about Something," Annan was chosen because of Washington's view that he would be a cautious bureaucrat, and this coupled with his quiet demeanor led many observers to speculate that he would not act independently.

Those predictions were inaccurate. Since taking office in 1997, Annan has demonstrated a willingness to exercise leadership and even to differ with the United States. He has done so more diplomatically, however, than the sometimes sharp-tongued Boutros-Ghali. This has earned Annan generally smooth relations with Washington and other major capitals, and he was easily reappointed for a second term beginning in 2002. Adding to his accolades at this time, Annan was awarded the Nobel Peace Prize for 2001 in recognition of his work toward making "a better organized and more peaceful world."

Although Annan is quite soft-spoken, he has proved to be a capable and, at times, tough diplomat and administrator who strongly supports the idea that the UN and its secretary-general should act with independence when necessary. During a commencement speech at the Massachusetts Institute of Technology (MIT), Annan told graduates that his years at MIT had given him "not only the analytical tools but also the intellectual confidence . . . to be comfortable in seeking the help of colleagues, but not fearing, in the end, to do things my way."[22]

This independence was clearly in play during 2003 when Annan repeatedly took on his organization's most powerful member, the United States, over its policy toward Iraq. Before the attack in March, he rejected the U.S. stance that it had the legal authority to act, instead arguing, "If the U.S. and others were to go outside the [Security] Council and take military action, it would not be in conformity with the Charter."[23] Afterwards, speaking to the General Assembly about the preemptive action aspects of the Bush Doctrine, the secretary-general criticized "this logic" as representing "a fundamental challenge to the principles on which, however imperfectly, world peace and stability have rested for the last 58 years," and worrying aloud that if other countries also assumed the right to take preemptive action, "it could set precedents that resulted in a proliferation of the unilateral and lawless use of force, with or without credible justification."[24]

When the U.S. effort in postwar Iraq ran into trouble, and Washington tried to involve the UN while still maintaining tight American control, Annan also opposed that effort

Since coming to office in 1997, Secretary-General Kofi Annan of Ghana has shown himself to be a skilled and assertive leader. The UN secretary-general and the heads of many other international organizations are more than mere administrators; many are important diplomatic figures in their own right.

as "obviously . . . not going in the direction I had recommended."[25] That made it all the more difficult for the United States to win the support it needed in the Security Council. Although the secretary-general has no vote, it is also the case that many countries agree with the comment of Mexico's UN ambassador, Adolfo Aguilar Zinser, "We always look for the guidance of the secretary-general and this is no exception."[26]

Annan has gained such stature in his years as secretary-general that reaction from the Bush administration to his position on Iraq was muted, but the White House was doubtlessly fuming. Such tensions, which also exist over the role of top officials in other IGOs, are in substantial part a struggle between the traditional approach versus the alternative approach to world politics. Traditionally, national states have sought to control IGOs and their leaders. As IGOs and their leaders have grown stronger, however, they have more often struck out independently down the alternative path. As Secretary-General Annan has commented, he and his predecessors have all carried out their traditional duties as chief administrative officer, but they have also assumed another, alternative role: "an instrument of the larger interest, beyond national rivalries and regional concerns."[27] Presidents and prime ministers are finding, comments one U.S. diplomat, that "you can't put the secretary-general back in the closet when it's inconvenient."[28]

Bureaucracy

The secretary-general appoints the other principal officials of the Secretariat, but he must be sensitive to the desires of the dominant powers in making these appointments and also must pay attention to the geographic and, increasingly, to the gender composition of the Secretariat staff. Controversies have occasionally arisen over these distributions, but in recent years the focus of criticism has been the size and efficiency of the staffs of the UN headquarters in New York and its regional offices (Geneva, Nairobi, and Vienna). In this way, the UN is like many other IGOs and, indeed, national governments, with allegedly bloated, inefficient, and unresponsive bureaucracies that have made them a lightning rod for discontent with government.

Certainly, as with almost any bureaucracy, it is possible to find horror stories about the size and activities of IGO staffs. But the charges that the UN and its associated agencies are a bureaucratic swamp need to be put in perspective. For instance, the UN Secretariat has trimmed its staff over 25%, from 12,000 in 1985 to 8,700 currently. Some perspective on such data can also be gained by comparing the UN bureaucracy to local governments and to companies. The city of New Orleans (pop. 485,000), for instance, employs more people (10,100) than does the UN (pop. 6,100,000,000). Even if one were to count all 64,700 employees of the UN and its 22 affiliated agencies (like the World Health Organization), they would only be roughly equal in number to the municipal employees of Baltimore and San Francisco combined, and just slightly more than the combined workers at Disney World and Disneyland. Indeed, McDonald's has more than five times as many employees devoted to serving the world hamburgers, french fries, and shakes as the UN has people devoted to serving the world's needs for peace, health, dignity, and prosperity.

Finance

All IGOs face the problem of obtaining sufficient funds to conduct their operations. National governments must also address this issue, but they have the power to impose and legally collect taxes. By contrast, IGOs have very little authority to compel member-countries to support them.

The United Nations is beset by severe and controversial financial problems. There are several elements to the extended UN budget. The first is the *core budget* for headquarters operations and the regular programs of the major UN organs. Second, there is the *peacekeeping budget* to meet the expenses of operations being conducted by the Security Council. These two budgets were, respectively, $1.6 billion and $2.6 billion in fiscal year 2003 (FY2003) (July 1, 2002–June 30, 2003). The third budget element is called the *voluntary contributions budget,* which funds a number of UN agencies such as the United Nations Children's Fund (UNICEF) and the United Nations Environment Programme (UNEP). The combined FY2003 expenditures of these agencies are about $1.8 billion.

The UN depends almost entirely on the assessment it levies on member-countries to pay its core and peacekeeping budgets. This assessment is fixed by the UNGA based on a complicated formula that reflects the ability to pay. According to the UN Charter, which is a valid treaty binding on all signatories, members are required to meet these assessments and may have their voting privilege in the General Assembly suspended if they are seriously in arrears. Nine countries each have assessments of 2% or more of the budget. They and their percentages of the core budget assessment are: the United States (22.0%), Japan (19.5%), Germany (9.8%), France (6.5%), Great Britain (5.6%), Italy (5.1%), Canada (2.6%), Spain (2.5%), and Brazil (2.4%). Another nine countries pay between 1 and 2%. At the other end of the financial scale, about 70% of the UN's members are assessed below .01%, including about 20% paying the minimum assessment of 0.001%. The "target" voluntary budget payments are the same as the core budget. Because of their special responsibility (and their special privilege, the veto), permanent UNSC members pay a somewhat higher assessment for peacekeeping, with the U.S. share at 25%.

The assessment scheme is criticized by some on the grounds that while the 18 countries with assessments of 1% or higher collectively paid 90% of the UN budget in FY2003, they cast just 9% of the votes in the UNGA. One result of the gap between contributions and voting power has been disenchantment with the organization by a number of large-contributor countries who sometimes find themselves in the minority on votes in the UNGA.

Such numbers are something of a fiction, however, because some countries do not pay their assessment. Member-states were in arrears on the core and peacekeeping budgets by $2.3 billion at the beginning of FY2004. As a result, the UN's financial situation constantly teeters on the edge of crisis at the very time it is being asked to do more and more to provide protection and help meet other humanitarian and social needs. "It is," said a frustrated Boutros-Ghali just before he stepped down, "as though the town fire department were being dispatched to put out fires raging in several places at once while a collection was being taken to raise money for the fire-fighting equipment."[29] The analogy between the UN's budget and fire fighting is hardly hyperbole. During FY2003, for example, the UN's peacekeeping budget is only about half the public safety (police and fire departments) budget of New York City.

Just as it determines many things in this world, U.S. policy toward the UN's budget is a key to its financial stability. Some Americans think that their country overpays; others see the United States as a penurious piker. The You Be the Playwright box "Santa Claus or Scrooge? The United States and the UN Budget" on page 218 asks you to sort out this controversy and decide whether Washington should be lauded or lambasted.

IGO Activities

The most important aspects of any international organization are what it does, how well this corresponds to the functions we wish it to perform, and how well it is performing its roles. The following pages will begin to explore these aspects by examining the scope of IGO activity, with an emphasis on the UN. Much of this discussion will only begin to touch on these activities, which receive more attention in other chapters.

YOU BE THE PLAYWRIGHT

Santa Claus or Scrooge? The United States and the UN Budget

From one perspective, Americans may feel like Santa Claus for their support of the United Nations. After all, with just 5% of the world's population, and just 0.5% of the votes in the UN General Assembly, the United States' assessment is 22% of the UN's core budget and 25% of its peacekeeping budget. For FY2003 that came to about $352 million for the core budget and about $658 million for the peacekeeping budget, for a total of approximately $1 billion.

The billion dollars sounds a bit less extravagant from other perspectives. One is that the total assessment comes to only about $35.59 per American. This is about 25% less than the average American spent in 2002 buying indoor plants. In another context, the $1 billion UN assessment is a microscopic 0.04% (1/2,500th) of the FY2003 federal budget of $2.128 trillion. Focusing on security, the U.S. defense budget of $368 billion for FY2003 would fund that fiscal year's UN peacekeeping budget for 559 years.

Ratcheting down the image of Santa Claus even more, and perhaps even casting Americans as Scrooge, is the fact that the United States is also the UN's biggest debtor. At the end of FY2003, the United States owed $1.1 billion to the UN, accounting for 47% of all UN arrearages. This debt persists even after the United States in 2002 pressured the UN into reducing the U.S. assessments from 25% to 22% for the core budget and from 30% to 25% for the peacekeeping budget. The persistent U.S. failure to meet its obligation has drawn frequent criticism, even from Washington's allies. In a line that British diplomats must have been waiting for over 200 years to deliver, the British foreign secretary said that for Americans to continue to vote in the UN without paying their assessment was tantamount to "representation without taxation."[1]

Most Americans think that their government should pay its debt. One poll that asked them whether they favored or opposed the United States paying off its UN debt found 58% in favor, 32% opposed, and 10% unsure.[2] This willingness to pay held good in spite of the possibility of UN and U.S. policy being at odds. A survey just before the war with Iraq asked people if the United States should stop paying its dues if the UN did not enforce its resolutions on Iraq. Only 37% of Americans favored stopping payments, while 53% wanted to continue them, and 10% were unsure.[3] As for the annual payments, a 2003 survey found that 11% of Americans wanted to increase UN funding, 50% wanted to keep it the same, 37% wanted to decrease it, and 2% were uncertain.[4]

Now it's your turn. How would you rewrite the script for the U.S. approach to the UN budget? Would you quickly pay off the U.S. debt or ignore it? How about the level of funding—Should Santa Claus give less? Should Scrooge give more? Or is the current UN assessment about right?

Activities Promoting Peace and Security

The opening words of the UN Charter dedicate the organization to saving "succeeding generations from the scourge of war, which . . . has brought untold sorrow to mankind." The UN attempts to fulfill this goal by creating norms against violence, by providing debate as an alternative to fighting, by intervening diplomatically to avert the outbreak of warfare or to help restore peace once violence occurs, by instituting diplomatic and economic sanctions, by dispatching UN military forces to repel aggression or to act as a buffer between warring countries, and by promoting arms control and disarmament.

Creating Norms against Violence One way that the United Nations helps promote international peace and security is by creating norms (beliefs about what is proper) against aggression and other forms of violence. To accomplish this, the UN works in such areas as promoting nuclear nonproliferation through the International Atomic Energy Agency, limiting chemical and biological weapons, and fostering rules for the restrained conduct of war when it occurs.

Countries that sign the charter pledge to accept the principle "that armed force shall not be used, save in the common interest" and further agree to "refrain in their international relations from the threat or the use of force except in self-defense." Reaffirming the charter's ideas, the UN (and other IGOs) have condemned Iraq's invasion of Kuwait in 1990, Serbian aggression against its neighbors, and other such actions. These denunciations and the slowly developing norm against aggression have not halted violence, but they have created an increasing onus on countries that strike the first blow. When, for example, the United States acted unilaterally in 1989 to depose the regime of Panama's strongman General Manuel Noriega, the UN and the OAS condemned Washington's action. Five years later, when the United States toppled the regime in Haiti, Washington took care to win UN support for its action.

Whatever the niceties of various legal arguments, when the United States and Great Britain invaded Iraq in 2003 they violated the general intent of the UN Charter to refrain from taking unilateral action except when under attack or in some other extreme situation. Violating a norm does not disprove its existence, however. Indeed, the efforts of U.S. and British diplomats to get a supportive UN resolution underlined the existence of the norm. Moreover, the angry reaction in many parts of the globe to the Anglo-American preemptive action and the postwar difficulties that the two occupying powers have experienced may, in the long run, actually serve to reinforce the norm. One lesson of the experience is that UN involvement in the postwar stabilization of Iraq, which the U.S. administration and 68% of the American public wanted, was much more difficult to obtain given the earlier U.S. disdain for the Security Council. Having not been in on the takeoff, the UN was wisely wary of taking responsibility for the crash landing.

Providing a Debate Alternative A second peace-enhancing role for the United Nations and some other IGOs is serving as a passive forum in which members publicly air their points of view and privately negotiate their differences. The UN thus acts like a safety valve, or perhaps a sound stage where the world drama can be played out without the dire consequences that could occur if another "shooting locale" were chosen. This grand-debate approach to peace involves denouncing your opponents, defending your actions, trying to influence world opinion, and winning symbolic victories. The British ambassador to the UN has characterized it as "a great clearinghouse for foreign policy," a place where "We talk to people . . . whom we don't talk to elsewhere because we have fraught relations with them."[30]

Diplomatic Intervention International organizations also regularly play a direct role in assisting and encouraging countries to settle their disputes peacefully. Ideally this occurs before hostilities, but it can take place even after fighting has started. The United Nations and other IGOs perform the following functions: (1) *Inquiry*: Fact-finding by neutral investigators; (2) *Good Offices*: Encouraging parties to negotiate; acting as a neutral setting for negotiations; (3) *Mediation*: Making suggestions about possible solutions; acting as an intermediary between two parties; (4) *Arbitration*: Using a special panel to find a solution that all parties agree in advance to accept; and (5) *Adjudication*: Submitting disputes to an international court such as the ICJ. These activities do not often capture the headlines, but they are a vital part of maintaining or restoring the peace.

Sanctions The increased interdependence of the world has heightened the impact of diplomatic and economic sanctions. In recent years, these have been applied by the UN, the OAS, and other IGOs against such countries as Haiti, Iraq, Libya, South Africa, and Yugoslavia. As we will see in chapter 13, sanctions are controversial and often do not work. But there have been successes. For example, in 2003 the sanctions that had been in place against Libya for 15 years finally persuaded it to pay $2.7 billion in reparations to the families of the 280 people killed when a bomb planted by Libyan agents destroyed Pan Am Flight 103 over Lockerbie, Scotland, in 1988. The wheels of justice sometimes grind slowly, but grind they did.

Peacekeeping The United Nations additionally has a limited ability to intervene militarily in a dispute. Other IGOs, such as the OAS, have also occasionally undertaken collective

The UN and other IGOs are playing an increasing role in providing security. Wearing the familiar blue helmet or hat, as prominent in the foreground, UN peacekeepers have served on every populated continent except Australia since their first deployment in 1948 to the Middle East. Since then, 130 countries have contributed military and police personnel to UN peacekeeping missions. In one of the most recent new missions, peacekeepers from the predominantly Muslim countries of Mali, Nigeria, Gambia, and Bangladesh pray together in this 2003 picture at a makeshift mosque in Liberia. The troops were part of the UN force trying to bring an end to Liberia's long and brutal civil war.

military action. In the UN, this process is often called peacekeeping. It is normally conducted under the auspices of the UNSC, although the UNGA has sometimes authorized action.

Peacekeeping as a form of international security is extensively covered in chapter 11, but a few preliminary facts are appropriate here. Through early 2004, the United Nations had mounted 56 peacekeeping operations that had utilized military and police personnel from 130 countries. These operations ranged from very lightly armed observer missions, through police forces, to full-fledged military forces. Never before have international forces been so active as they are now. The number of UN peacekeeping operations has risen markedly in the post–cold war era, as shown in Figure 7.7. As of March 2004, there were 13 UN peacekeeping forces of varying sizes in the field at locations throughout the world. These forces totaled about 49,000 troops and police from 94 countries.

United Nations peacekeeping seldom involves a stern international enforcer smiting aggressors with powerful blows. Few countries are willing to give any IGO that much power and independence. Rather, UN peacekeeping is usually a "coming between," a positioning of a neutral force that creates space and is intended to help defuse an explosive situation. This in no way lessens the valuable role that the UN has played. It has, for example, been a positive force in helping East Timor first escape the violence inflicted on it when it was seeking independence from Indonesia and then helping the East Timorese transition during the period between the final withdrawal of Indonesia's troops to the date of the country's independence in May 2002. Fortunately, UN peacekeeping forces have suffered relatively few casualties, but almost 1,900 have died in world service. For these sacrifices and contributions to world order, the UN peacekeeping forces were awarded the 1988 Nobel Peace Prize.

Arms Control and Disarmament Promoting arms control and disarmament is another international security function of IGOs. The International Atomic Energy Agency, an affiliate of the UN, helps promote and monitor the nonproliferation of nuclear weapons. The UN also sponsors numerous conferences on weapons and conflict and has also played an important role in the genesis of the Chemical Weapons Convention and other arms control agreements.

Social, Economic, Environmental, and Other Activities

In addition to maintaining and restoring the peace, IGOs engage in a wide variety of other activities. During its early years, the UN's emphasis was on security. This concern has not abated, but it has been joined by social, economic, environmental, and other nonmilitary security concerns. This shift has been a result of the ebb and eventual end of the cold war, the growing number of LDCs since the 1960s, realization that the environment is in danger, and changing global values that have brought an increased focus on human and political rights. "Peacekeeping operations claim the headlines," Secretary-

FIGURE 7.7 The Growth of UN Peacekeeping Operations

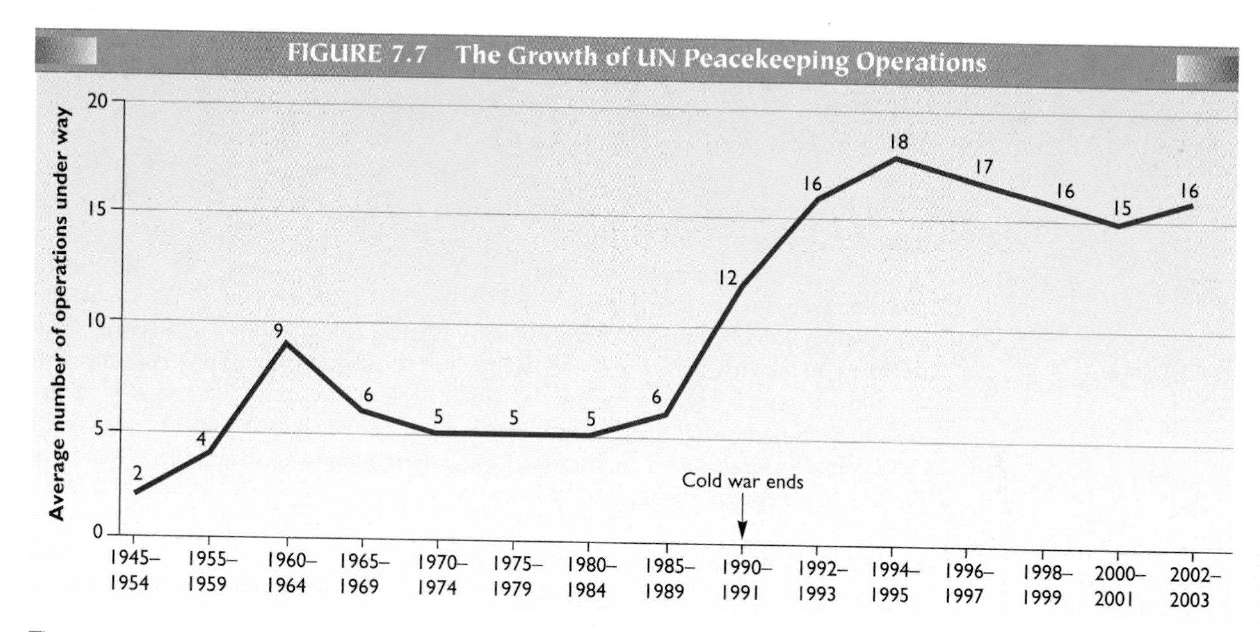

The end of the cold war and its standoff between the United States and the Soviet Union in the Security Council has allowed the UN to mount a significantly increased number of peacekeeping operations since the early 1990s.

Note: 13 missions were underway in early 2004. Number for each two years is the most missions during that period.

Data source: UN, Department of Peacekeeping Web site, http://www.un.org/depts./dpko/.

General Annan has observed astutely, "but by far the lion's share of our budget and personnel are devoted to the lower-profile work of . . . helping countries to create jobs and raise standards of living; delivering relief aid to victims of famine, war, and natural disasters; protecting refugees; promoting literacy; and fighting disease. To most people around the world, this is the face of the United Nations."[31] This effort has recently included the UN's sponsorship of a conference of aid donors to coordinate assistance to rebuild Afghanistan; coordination of the delivery of humanitarian relief to its people; and the repatriation of hundreds of thousands of Afghanis who had fled the country into Pakistan and other neighboring countries.

It would be impossible to list here, much less fully describe, the broad range of endeavors in which the UN and other IGOs are involved. Suffice it to say that they cover most of the issues that humans address at all levels of government. Many of these activities will be highlighted in subsequent chapters, so this discussion is limited to a few of the programs and successes of the UN and other IGOs.

> **Did You Know That:**
> The UN, other IGOs, and foreign aid donors annually give about $12 per human to spend on economic and social development. The world defense ministries have about $131 per human for military expenditures.

IGOs and Economic Development The United Nations Development Programme (UNDP), the World Bank, and a significant number of other global and regional IGOs work to improve the economic well-being of those who are deprived because of their location in an LDC, their gender, or some other cause. The UNDP alone supports more than 5,000 projects globally with a budget of $1.3 billion. The UN Development Fund for Women (UNIFEM) focuses on improving the lives of women in LDCs.

IGOs and Human Rights Beginning with the Universal Declaration of Human Rights in 1948, the UN has actively promoted dozens of agreements on political, civil, economic, social, and cultural rights. The UN Commission on Human Rights has used its power of investigation and its ability to issue reports to expose abuses of human rights and to create pressure on the abusers through a process that one scholar has termed the "mobilization of shame" (Weisband, 2000). Currently, for example, the UN is at the heart of the global effort to free the estimated 250 million children who are forced to work instead of being sent to school, to end the sexual predation of children that is big business in some parts of the world, and to eliminate other abuses that debase the meaning of childhood.

IGOs and the Environment Beginning with the UN Conference on Environment and Development (dubbed the Earth Summit) in 1992, the UN has sponsored several global meetings on the environment. These have resulted in the initiation of programs that will slow down, stop, or begin to reverse the degradation of the environment. IGOs are increasingly also requiring that environmental impact statements accompany requests for economic development aid and in some cases are refusing to finance projects that have unacceptable negative impacts on the biosphere.

IGOs and International Law and Norms An important and increasing role of the UN and other IGOs is defining and expanding international law and international norms of cooperation. International courts associated with IGOs help establish legal precedent. Also, the signatories to the UN Charter and other IGO constitutions incur obligations to obey the principles of these documents. International organizations additionally sponsor multinational treaties, which may establish the assumption of law. Over 300 such treaties have been negotiated through the UN's auspices. As one scholar sees the norm-building function of IGOs, "The procedures and rules of international institutions create information structures. They determine what principles are acceptable as a basis for reducing conflicts and whether governmental actions are legitimate or illegitimate. Consequently, they help shape actors' expectations" (Keohane, 1998:91).

IGOs and the Quality of Human Existence More than 30 million refugees from war, famine, and other dangers have been fed, given shelter, and otherwise assisted through the UN High Commissioner for Refugees. A wide variety of IGOs also devote their energies to such concerns as health, nutrition, and literacy. For example, UNICEF, WHO, and other agencies have undertaken a $150 million program to develop a multi-immunization vaccine. This vaccine program is designed to double the estimated 2 million children who now annually survive because of such international medical assistance. The Food and Agriculture Organization (FAO) has launched a program to identify, preserve, and strengthen through new genetic techniques those domestic animals that might prove especially beneficial to LDCs. Western breeds of pigs, for example, usually produce only about 10 piglets per litter; the Taihu pig of China manages 15 to 20. The FAO hopes to use the latter and other appropriate animals to increase protein availability in the LDCs.

IGOs and Independence Yet another role of IGOs has been to encourage national self-determination. The UN Trusteeship Council once monitored numerous colonial dependencies, but the wave of independence in recent decades steadily lessened its number of charges. Then, in October 1994, the United States and Palau notified the council that, as Kuniwo Nakamura, Palau's president, put it, "We have made our own decision that we are ready to embark on the journey of independence with confidence."[32] Inasmuch as Palau was the last trust territory, the announcement meant that the Trusteeship Council's mission was fulfilled and, while it continues to exist technically, it no longer meets.

Trying to improve the quality of life for refugees is one of the many worthwhile roles of the UN. The Office of the United Nations High Commissioner for Refugees is at the forefront of that effort. In 2003, the UNHCR was assisting nearly 20 million people, such as this Afghani family arriving at a UNHCR refugee camp in Pakistan.

Evaluating IGOs and Their Future

The United Nations has existed for more than fifty years. Most other IGOs are even younger. Have they succeeded? The answer depends on your standard of evaluation.

Ultimate goals are one standard. Article 1 of the UN Charter sets out lofty goals such as maintaining peace and security and solving economic, social, cultural, and humanitarian problems. Clearly, the world is still beset by violent conflicts and by ongoing economic and social misery. Thus, from the perspective of meeting ultimate goals, it is easy to be skeptical about what the UN and other IGOs have accomplished.

One has to ask, however, whether the meeting of ultimate goals is a reasonable standard. There is, according to one diplomat, a sense that "failure was built into [the UN] by an extraordinary orgy of exaggerated expectations."[33]

Progress is a second standard by which to evaluate the UN and other IGOs. Is the world better off for their presence? That is the standard Kofi Annan appeals for when he implores, "Judge us rightly . . . by the relief and refuge that we provide to the poor, to the hungry, the sick and threatened: the peoples of the world whom the United Nations exists to serve."[34] Between its 40th and 50th anniversaries, the United Nations surpassed all previous marks in terms of numbers of simultaneous peacekeeping missions, peacekeeping troops deployed, and other international security efforts. During the 1990s alone, the UN also sponsored 12 conferences on a range of global concerns. This activity has continued apace, with conferences on racism (Durban, 2001), aging (Madrid, 2002), sustainable development (Johannesburg, 2002), financing for development (Monterrey, 2002), and the information society (Geneva, 2003) among those held in the first three years of the new century. These meetings have all focused attention on global problems and have made some contribution to advancing our knowledge and to enhancing our

FIGURE 7.8 Public Evaluation of the UN in 43 Countries

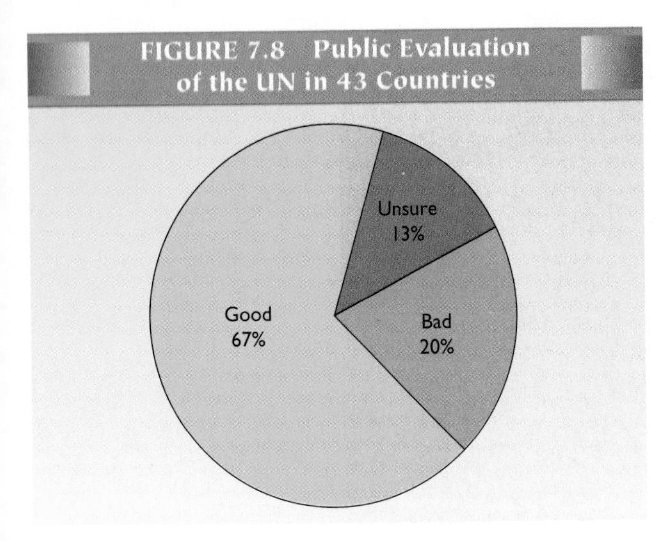

The United Nations enjoys strong popularity around the world. When asked about the impact of the UN on their country, an average of 67% of the people in 43 countries characterized it as good. Kenyans were the most positive, with 93% saying good. There were only two countries (Argentina and Jordan) in which more people said bad than good. As for Americans, 72% responded good, 19% replied bad, and 9% were unsure.

Note: The question was, "Is the influence of the United Nations very good, somewhat good, somewhat bad, or very bad in your country?"

Data source: The Pew Research Center for People and the Press, "Views of a Changing World" (June 2003).

attempts to deal seriously with a wide range of economic, social, and environmental global challenges. Moreover, the people of the world tend to recognize these contributions, as Figure 7.8 shows. Thus, by the standard of progress, the UN and other IGOs have made a contribution.

What is possible is a third standard by which to evaluate the UN and other IGOs. Insofar as the UN does not meet our expectations, we need to ask whether it is a flaw of the organization or the product of the unwillingness of member-states to live up to the standards that countries accept when they ratify the charter. When the Security Council would not authorize action against Iraq, there were angry charges that the UN was not living up to its obligation to make Baghdad surrender its weapons of mass destruction (WMDs) and that it was weak and irrelevant. Raising the specter of the UN's defunct predecessor, President Bush told an audience, "We'll see whether or not the United Nations will be [like] the League of Nations when it comes to dealing with [Saddam Hussein] who for 11 years has thumbed his nose at resolution after resolution [to end Iraq's WMD program]."[35] Such derision is heard less frequently as the months after the war have dragged on with no evidence that there was a WMD program to be discovered. Thus the question must be asked whether the crisis and war showed the UN to be impotent or prudent. At a less dramatic level, simply paying their assessments regularly and on time is another thing more countries could do. The UN will also work better if countries try to make it effective. It is a truism, as Kofi Annan put it, that there is a "troubling asymmetry between what the member-states want of the [UN] and what they actually allow it to be."[36]

Whether alternatives exist is a fourth standard by which to evaluate the UN and other IGOs. One must ask, If not the UN and other international organizations, then what? Can the warring, uncaring world continue unchanged in the face of nuclear weapons, persistent poverty, an exploding population, periodic mass starvation, continued widespread human rights violations, resource depletion, and environmental degradation? Somehow the world has survived these plagues, but one of the realities that this book hopes to make clear is that we are hurtling toward our destiny at an ever-increasing, now exponential speed. In a rapidly changing system, doing things the old way may be inadequate and may even take us down a road that, although familiar, will lead the world to cataclysm. At the very least, as Secretary of State Madeleine Albright noted, "The United Nations gives the good guys—the peacemakers, the freedom fighters, the people who believe in human rights, those committed to human development—an organized vehicle for achieving gains."[37] This returns us to the question, If not the UN, then what? There may be considerable truth in the view of the British ambassador to the UN that "it's the UN, with all its warts, or it's the law of the jungle."[38] It is through this jungle that the road more familiar has passed, and following it into the future may bring what Shakespeare was perhaps imagining when he wrote in *Hamlet* of a tale that would "harrow up thy soul, [and] freeze thy young blood."

To repeat an important point, the UN and other IGOs are, in the end, only what we make them. They do possess some independence, but it is limited. Mostly their successes and failures reflect the willingness or disinclination of member-countries to cooperate and use them to further joint efforts. Kofi Annan urged support of the UN by quoting what Winston Churchill said to Franklin Roosevelt in 1941: "Give us the tools and we will do the job."[39] In the same vein, Dag Hammarskjöld aptly predicted, "Everything will be all right—you know when? When people, just people, stop thinking of the United Nations as a weird Picasso abstraction and see it as a drawing they made themselves."[40]

Whether or not that occurs is uncertain. What is clear is that critics of IGOs are too often narrowly negative. They disparage the organizations without noting their contributions or suggesting improvements. IGOs hold one hope for the future, and those who would denigrate them should make other, positive suggestions rather than implicitly advocating a maintenance of the status quo. There is a last bit of Shakespeare's wisdom, found in *Julius Caesar,* that is worth pondering. The playwright counsels us:

> There is a tide in the affairs of men
> Which, taken at the flood, leads on to fortune;
> Omitted, all the voyage of their life
> Is bound in shallows and in miseries.

Chapter Summary

The Evolution and Roles of International Organization

1. One sign of the changing international system is the rapid rise over the last century in the number of intergovernmental organizations (IGOs). There are many classifications of international organizations, including global, regional, and specialized IGOs.
2. Current international organization is the product of three lines of development: the idea that humans should live in peace and mutual support, the idea that the big powers have a special responsibility for maintaining order, and the growth of specialized international organizations to deal with narrow nonpolitical issues.
3. The rapid growth of all types of international organizations stems from increased international contact among states and people, increased economic interdependence, the growing importance of transnational issues and political movements, the inadequacy of the state-centered system for dealing with world problems, small states attempting to gain strength by joining together, and successful IGOs providing role models for new organizations.
4. There are significant differences among views on the best role for international organizations. Four existing and possible roles of IGOs are: providing an interactive arena, acting as a center for cooperation among states, evolving into an independent national actor, and becoming a supranational organization.
5. Some observers argue that international organizations are best suited to promoting cooperation among states rather than trying to replace the state-centered system. Still others contend that international organizations should concentrate on performing limited functional activities with the hope of building a habit of cooperation and trust that can later be built upon. Finally, many view international organizations as vehicles that should be manipulated to gain national political goals. The UN serves as an example of how current IGOs are organized and operate.
6. Some observers favor moving toward a system of supranational organization, in which some form of world government, or perhaps regional governments, would replace or substantially modify the present state-centered system.

Regional IGOs: Focus on the European Union

7. The EU provides an example of the development, structure, and roles of a regional IGO. The EU has evolved considerably along the path of economic integration. The movement toward political integration is

more recent and is proving more difficult than economic integration.

Global IGOs: Focus on the United Nations

8. The United Nations provides an example of the development, structure, and roles of a global IGO.
9. There are several important issues related to the structure of international organizations. One group of questions relates to membership and criteria for membership.
10. Voting schemes to be used in such bodies are another important issue. Current international organizations use a variety of voting schemes that include majority voting, weighted voting, and unanimity voting.
11. Another group of questions concerns the administration of international organizations, including the role of the political leaders and the size and efficiency of IGO bureaucracies. The source of IGO revenue and the size of IGO budgets are a related concern.
12. There are also a number of significant issues that relate to the general role of international organizations. Peacekeeping is one important role. Others include creating norms against violence, providing a debate alternative, intervening diplomatically, imposing sanctions, and promoting arms control and disarmament.
13. Other roles for the UN and other international organizations include promoting international law, promoting arms control, bettering the human condition, promoting self-government, and furthering international cooperation.
14. However one defines the best purpose of international organization, it is important to be careful of standards of evaluation. The most fruitful standard is judging an organization by what is possible, rather than setting inevitably frustrating ideal goals.

For a chapter quiz, interactive activities, web links, PowerWeb articles, and much more, visit **www.mhhe.com/rourke10/** and go to chapter 7. Or, while accessing the site, click on Course-Wide Content and view recent international relations articles in the *New York Times.*

Key Terms

confederation
Council of the European Union
Court of Justice
European Commission
European Communities (EC)
European Economic Community (EEC)
European Parliament (EP)
European Union (EU)
functionalism
Hague system
intergovernmental organizations (IGOs)
international organization (IO)
League of Nations
limited membership council
Maastricht Treaty
majority voting
neofunctionalism
plenary representative body
president of the Commission
regime
regional government
Secretariat
supranational organization
Treaty of Amsterdam
UN General Assembly (UNGA)
UN Security Council (UNSC)
unanimity voting
United Nations (UN)
veto
weighted voting
world government

CHAPTER

8

National Power and Diplomacy: The Traditional Approach

NATIONAL POWER: THE FOUNDATION OF NATIONAL DIPLOMACY
- The Nature of Power

THE ELEMENTS OF POWER
- The National Core
- The National Infrastructure

THE NATURE OF DIPLOMACY
- The Functions of Diplomacy
- The Diplomatic Setting

THE EVOLUTION OF DIPLOMACY
- Early Diplomacy
- Modern Diplomacy

THE CONDUCT OF DIPLOMACY
- Diplomacy as a Communications Process
- The Rules of Effective Diplomacy
- Options for Conducting Diplomacy

CHAPTER SUMMARY

KEY TERMS

Then, everything includes itself in power,
Power into will, will into appetite.

—William Shakespeare, *Troilus and Cressida*

Bid me discourse, I will enchant thine ear.

—William Shakespeare, *Venus and Adonis*

We thought, because we had power, we had wisdom.

—Stephen Vincent Benét, *Litany for Dictatorships,* 1935

All politicians make their decisions on the basis of national or political interest and explain them in terms of altruism.

—Former Israeli diplomat Abba Eban, 1996

CHAPTER OBJECTIVES

After completing this chapter, you should be able to:

- Characterize diplomacy as an activity conducted by a state to further its interests.
- Discuss power as the foundation of diplomacy.
- Analyze the characteristics of power.
- List the major elements of a country's power.
- Explain the functions of diplomacy.
- Describe the various settings of diplomacy.
- Summarize the evolution of diplomacy from ancient Greece to 19th-century Europe.
- Describe and characterize diplomatic practice in the modern era.
- Explain the increase in high-level, leader-to-leader diplomacy.
- Analyze the growing importance of public diplomacy in world politics.
- Discuss the art of diplomacy and the importance of choosing among various options in its practice.
- Identify the various rules of diplomacy as well as diplomatic alternatives.

"Once upon a time," began a fable told by the great British diplomat and prime minister Winston Churchill, "all the animals in the zoo decided that they would disarm." To accomplish that laudable goal, the animals convened a diplomatic conference, where, Churchill's tale went:

> The Rhinoceros said when he opened the proceeding that the use of teeth was barbarous and horrible and ought to be strictly prohibited by general consent. Horns, which were mainly defensive weapons, would, of course, have to be allowed. The Buffalo, the Stag, the Porcupine, and even the little Hedgehog all said they would vote with the Rhino, but the Lion and the Tiger took a different view. They defended teeth and even claws, which they described as honourable weapons of immemorial antiquity. The Panther, the Leopard, the Puma, and the whole tribe of small cats all supported the Lion and the Tiger. Then the Bear spoke. He proposed that both teeth and horns should be banned and never used again for fighting by animals. It would be quite enough if animals were allowed to give each other a good hug when they quarreled. No one could object to that. It was so fraternal, and that would be a great step toward peace. However, all the other animals were very offended by the Bear, and the Turkey fell into a perfect panic. The discussion got so hot and angry, and all those animals began thinking so much about horns and teeth and hugging when they argued about the peaceful intentions that had brought them together, that they began to look at one another in a very nasty way. Luckily the keepers were able to calm them down and persuade them to go back quietly to their cages, and they began to feel quite friendly with one another again.[1]

Sir Winston's allegory is instructive, as well as colorfully entertaining. It touches on many aspects of diplomacy discussed in this chapter. *Power* is the first thing we will explore. It remains an essential element of diplomacy in a system based on self-interested sovereignty. In our world, like the zoo, the actors that possess the power to give rewards or inflict punishment are able to influence other actors. Power has many forms. Physical strength is one, and the rhino and the lion were both powerful in this way. Skill is another aspect of power. The turkey had little tangible strength, but perhaps it possessed guile and other intangible diplomatic skills to persuade the other animals to adopt its views. Economic power is also important in diplomacy. The zookeepers controlled the food supply and may have used food as a positive incentive (more food) or negative sanction (less or no food) to persuade the animals to return to their cages.

The general nature of diplomacy is a second topic. It naturally follows our exploration of the power foundations of diplomacy. This topic involves the overall system, the setting in which modern diplomacy occurs. The zoo was the system in which the animals negotiated. Like the current international system, the zoo system was based on self-interest, with each group of animals selecting goals that were advantageous to itself, giving little thought to how they affected others. The zoo system also apparently allowed some potential for fighting and thus based success in part on the Darwinian law of the jungle. Yet the animals were also partly constrained by the zookeepers with, perhaps, some protection afforded by cages.

Modern diplomacy is the third major topic in this chapter, and we will look at how it has evolved and at some of its characteristics. Multilateral diplomacy, for example, has become a much more prominent part of diplomacy than it once was. In Churchill's story, the animals conducted multisided negotiations instead of bilateral diplomacy between, say, just the rhino and the tiger. Those two animals might have made a bilateral agreement that both horns and fangs were acceptable; once hedgehogs, turkeys, and others became involved, the diplomatic dynamic changed greatly. In such a circumstance, diplomatic coalition building is one aspect of gathering support. It may well have been that, before the conference, the rhino had met with the buffalo, stag, porcupine, and hedgehog to convince them that they should support the rhino's position that horns were defensive weapons, while teeth and claws were offensive weapons.

Options in the conduct of diplomacy make up the fourth and final part of this chapter. Direct negotiation is one method, and the animals were engaged in that. Signaling is another method. This occurred when the animals "began to look at each other in a very nasty way." Public diplomacy to win the support of public opinion is yet another diplomatic method, and it is possible to see in Churchill's story how a clever diplomatic proposal can create an advantage. One can imagine the bear's proposal emblazoned in the *Zoo News* headline the next day: "Bear Proposes Eliminating All Weapons. Suggests Hugging as Alternative to Fighting." World opinion might have rallied to the bear; this would have put pressure on the other negotiators to accede to a seemingly benign proposal to usher in a new world order based on peace, love, and hugging.

Before proceeding, we should take a moment to put this chapter in context. It is the first of two chapters that look at the traditional and the alternative bases for establishing what policies will prevail in the world. In the traditional approach countries practice national diplomacy by applying power in the pursuit of their self-interest. This approach does not mean that might makes right, but it surely means that might usually makes success. The alternative approach, discussed in chapter 9, is to apply the standards of international law and justice to the conduct of international relations so that right, rather than who is mightiest, will more often determine who prevails.

National Power: The Foundation of National Diplomacy

"Until human nature changes, power and force will remain at the heart of international relations," a top U.S. foreign policy adviser has commented.[2] Not everyone would agree with such a gloomy realpolitik assessment, but it underlines the crucial role that power plays in diplomacy. When the goals and interests of states conflict, states often struggle to determine who will prevail. The resolution rests frequently on who has the most power. The confrontation between Iraq and the United States that had simmered and often seethed during most of the 1990s and into the new century finally led to a U.S. ultimatum. "Saddam Hussein and his sons must leave Iraq within 48 hours. Their refusal to do so will result in military conflict, commenced at a time of our choosing," President George W. Bush declared on March 17, 2003. The following day, the Iraqi government retorted, "Iraq doesn't choose its path through foreigners and doesn't choose its leaders by decree from Washington."[3] Soon thereafter U.S. bombs and cruise missiles rained down on Iraq.

The Nature of Power

Social scientists struggle to define and measure power and to describe exactly how it works. Harvard University dean and former top U.S. Defense Department official Joseph Nye (2000:55) writes that power "is like the weather. Everyone talks about it, but few understand it." Alluding to an even greater mystery, Nye confides that power is "like love . . . easier to experience than to define or measure." He also warns that if we always try to intimidate others, "we may be as mistaken about our power as was the fox who thought he was hurting Brer Rabbit when he threw him into the briar patch." Weather, love, briar patches? Yes, power is perplexing! If its intricacies can throw a Harvard dean and assistant

The ability of a country to get its way rests in part on its power. In the end, the United States prevailed in its diplomatic confrontation and war with Iraq in 2002–2003 because of the massive U.S. advantage in weaponry, which included B-2 stealth bombers. The one seen here is dropping a B61-11 "bunker buster" bomb. This type of munition was used to begin the war with Iraq, when it was dropped on the underground bunker headquarters in Baghdad where U.S. intelligence sources believed Saddam Hussein was staying.

secretary of defense into such a morass of mixed metaphors and similes, then how can we understand power? The first step is to define the way this text uses the word.

Power as an Asset

Power can be understood to equal national capabilities. Power is a political resource, which encompasses the sum of the various attributes of a state that enable it to achieve its goals even when they clash with the goals of other international actors. Power is multifaceted. It includes tangible elements, such as numbers of weapons; it also includes intangible elements, such as public morale.

One way to comprehend power is to think about *power as money,* as a sort of political currency. Equating power and money is helpful because both are assets that can be used to acquire things. Money buys things; power causes things to happen. Like money, power is sometimes used in a charitable way. But also like money, power is more often used for self-interest. It is also true that acquiring money and power both often require sacrifices. Furthermore, those who use their financial or power assets imprudently may lose more than they gain. As with any analogy, however, you should be wary of overusing the comparison. There are differences between money and power. One is that political power is less liquid than money; it is harder to convert into things that you want. A second difference is that power, unlike money, has no standard measurement that allows all parties to agree on the amount involved.

As with money, one of the confusions about power is whether it is an asset (an end, goal) that you try to acquire and maintain or a tool (a means, instrument) that you use. It is both. Countries seek both to acquire power and to use it in international politics.

Although this chapter concentrates on power as an asset, it is important to realize that countries sometimes treat power as a goal.

One important issue about any asset is, How much is enough? If you think about money as a physical object, it is pretty useless. It is inedible, you cannot build anything useful out of money, and it will not even burn very well if you need to keep warm. Yet some people are obsessed with having money for its own sake. For them, acquiring money is an end in itself. Literature is full of such stories, ranging from Molière's *The Miser* to Dickens's classic *A Christmas Carol* and its tragic tale of Ebenezer Scrooge. The misers give up love, friendships, and other pleasures to get and keep money only to discover, in the end, that their money becomes a burden. Similarly, some people believe that countries can become fixated on acquiring power, especially military power, beyond what is prudently needed to meet possible exigencies. This, critics say, is unwise because power is expensive, it creates a temptation to use it, and it spawns insecurity in others.

Measuring Power

At a general level, it is possible to measure or at least estimate power. There can be no doubt, for example, that China is more powerful than Mongolia. Beyond such broad judgments, however, scholars and policy makers have not been successful at anything approaching precise measurements of power. One problem is creating a formula that allocates realistic relative weights to military might, economic capacity, leadership capability, and other factors in the power equation. This was well illustrated by a study that reviewed four attempts by various scholars to devise formulas to measure national power (Taber, 1989). There were numerous disagreements based on the imprecise ability to measure power. Two studies rated the Soviet Union the most powerful. One each rated the United States and China most powerful. One ranked China only seventh. Brazil ranked number three in one study, and India ranked number four in another study; yet two studies did not place either country in the top ten. The list need not go on to make the point that different formulas for measuring power yielded very different results.

A second problem with measuring power precisely is a result of the fact that many aspects of power are difficult to quantify. Gathering data on some aspects of power (such as number of weapons, GDP, or population) is easy. Quantifying other aspects of power, such as leadership, borders on the impossible.

Does this mean that we should abandon trying to estimate national power? No, it does not. To repeat a point, there are clearly differences in national power. Ignoring them would be foolish, but it would also be a mistake to ignore the complexity and fluidity of power and to underestimate or overestimate the power of others based on one or more simple calculations.

Characteristics of Power

Power is not a simple and stable phenomenon. Indeed, it is very much a political chameleon, constantly changing even while it remains the same. The last part of this section explores the impact of the various characteristics of power.

Power Is Dynamic Even simple measurements show that power is constantly in flux. Economies prosper or lag, arms are modernized or become outmoded, resources are discovered or are depleted, and populations rally behind or lose faith in their governments. The USSR was a superpower; it collapsed. Its successor state, Russia, is far from commanding superpower status.

Adding to the dynamism of power, some scholars believe that its very nature is changing. They contend that military and other assets that contribute to **coercive power** (also called "hard power," the ability to make another country do or not do something) are declining in importance as military force and economic sanctions become more costly and less effective. Simultaneously, according to this view, **persuasive power** (also called "soft power," assets such as moral authority or technological excellence that enhance a country's image of leadership) is increasing in importance (Nye, 2000; Hall, 1999).

Some scholars even believe that war has become so destructive that it is a fading phenomenon, especially among economically developed countries (EDCs). As evidence they point to the fact that interstate wars have become less frequent and have not involved major military powers on opposite sides. Perhaps coercive diplomacy will someday become a relic of humankind's barbaric past, but that day, if it comes at all, is probably far in the future for two reasons. First, as one study notes, the incidence of violence during the 1990s was so high and so often sparked outside intervention that conflict was a "growth industry" (Bloomfield & Moulton, 1997:34). Second, there are still times when force or the threat of force is needed to resolve an international crisis. Even UN Secretary-General Kofi Annan has conceded, "You can do a lot with diplomacy, but of course you can do a lot more with diplomacy backed up by firmness and force."[4]

Did You Know That:

Frederic the Great, the king of Prussia (1712–1786), once commented, "Diplomacy without arms is like music without instruments."

Power Is Both Objective and Subjective We have seen on several occasions that international politics is influenced both by what is true and by what others perceive to be true. **Objective power** consists of assets that you objectively possess and that you have both the capacity and the will to use. As such, it is a major factor in determining whose interests prevail, as Iraq found out in 2003 in its war with the U.S.-led coalition forces.

Subjective power is also important. It is common to hear politicians argue that their country cannot back down in a crisis or get out of an ill-conceived military action because the country's reputation will be damaged. Research shows that concern to be overdrawn (Mercer, 1996). Still, a country's power is to a degree based on others' perceptions of its current or potential power or its reputation for being willing (or not willing) to use the power it has. Sometimes the perception that a country is not currently powerful can tempt another country. When asked for his evaluation of the U.S. military in 1917, a German admiral replied, "Zero, zero, zero." Based on this perception of U.S. power, Germany resumed submarine warfare against U.S. merchant shipping, a move that soon led to war with the United States.

Power Is Relative Power does not exist in a vacuum. Since power is about the ability to persuade or make another actor do or not do something, calculating power is of limited use except to measure it against the power of the other side. When assessing capabilities, then, **relative power**, or the comparative power of national actors, must be considered. We cannot, for example, say that China is powerful unless we specify in comparison to whom. Whatever Beijing's power resources may be, China's relative power compared to another major power, such as Japan, is less than is China's relative power compared to a smaller neighbor, such as Vietnam.

A related issue is whether power is a **zero-sum game**. If a gain in power of one actor inevitably means a loss of power for other actors, the game is zero-sum. If an actor can gain power without the power of other actors being diminished, then the game is non-zero-sum. Realists tend to see power as zero-sum; idealists usually portray it as non-zero-sum. Without delving too far into this controversy, we can say that the relative nature of power implies that sometimes, especially between antagonists, power approaches zero-sum. When China's Asian rival India tested nuclear weapons in 1998, it decreased China's relative power compared to India and arguably reduced China's influence in the countries to its southwest. Yet India's advance in power was non-zero-sum relative to another of its regional rivals, Pakistan, because that country tested its own nuclear

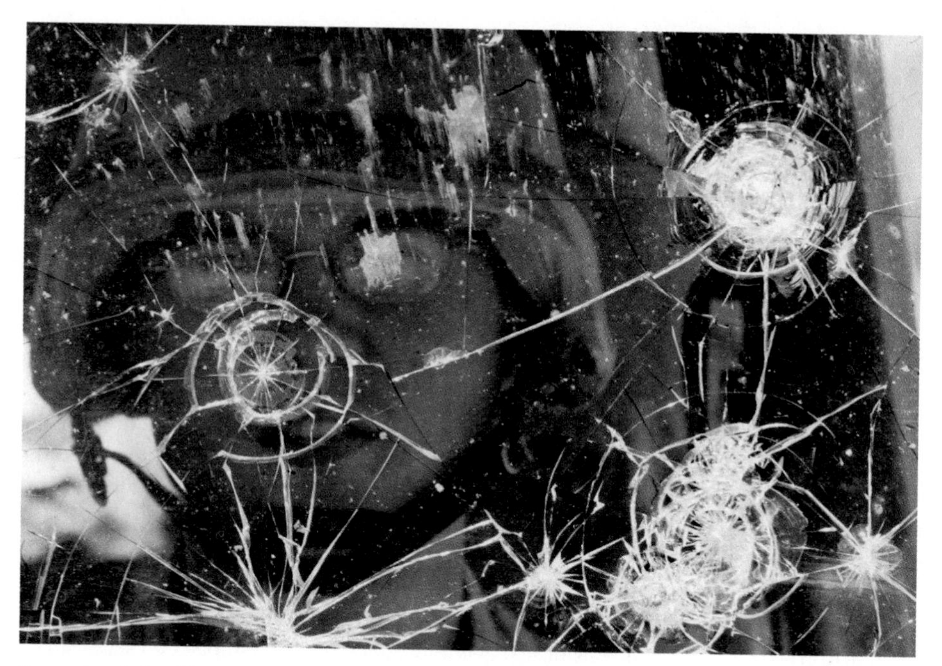

Power is relative. The value of B-2 bombers, Abrams tanks, and other powerful U.S. weapons systems was much less relevant to the postwar clashes with insurgent Iraqis than to the initial clash with Iraq's armed forces. After the war was over and President Bush had declared victory, many American soldiers found themselves attacked by forces using guerrilla tactics. A member of the U.S. 4th Infantry Division, pictured here looking through the shattered window of his Humvee after it was damaged in such an attack near Tikrit in September 2003, was one of the lucky ones. He survived unhurt.

weapons almost simultaneously with India. When the nuclear dust settled, India and Pakistan were in the same relative power position vis-à-vis one another as they had been before the blasts.

Power Is Situational A country's power varies according to the situation, or context, in which it is being applied. A country's **situational power** is often less than the total inventory of its capabilities. Military power provides a good example. During the last weeks of March and first weeks of April 2003, American and British forces faced those of Iraq in a classic conventional war situation. In that context, the conflict was one-sided with the U.S./U.K. forces quickly destroying and dispersing those of Iraq. During the postwar period, the conflict situation changed when forces opposed to the U.S./U.K. presence in the country began to use guerrilla warfare and terrorist tactics. By late 2003, more U.S. soldiers had died in the "postwar" period than during the war, and U.S. policy was in considerable disarray even though the American forces in Iraq were virtually the same ones that had so easily toppled the regime of Saddam Hussein only a few months earlier. The difference was that in the very different situation after "victory," a great deal of the U.S. high-tech weapons inventory, its heavy armored vehicles, and its air power were of no use in countering the resistance tactics in Iraq.

Power Is Multidimensional Power is multifaceted. Therefore, to analyze power well it is important to consider *all* the dimensions of power *and* to place them in their proper relative and situational contexts. Only then can we begin to answer the question of who is powerful and who is not. To help with that process, the next step is to identify the various determinants of national power.

The Elements of Power

There are many ways to categorize the multitudinous elements of power. One common way that we have mentioned is to distinguish between objective (easily measurable, tangible) elements of power and subjective (hard-to-measure, intangible) facets of power. Another approach is to group both the tangible and the intangible power assets into various functional categories. Two such categories, the national core and the national infrastructure, are central to the power of all countries because they serve as a foundation for the more utilitarian categories of national power, specifically military power and economic power. In the following sections, we will analyze these two central categories of national power; military and economic power will be discussed in chapters 10 and 13, respectively.

The National Core

The national state forms the basis of this element of power. The essence of a state can be roughly divided into three elements: national geography, people, and government.

National Geography

Shakespeare's King Henry VI proclaimed:

> Let us be backed with God and with the seas
> Which He hath given for fence impregnable, . . .
> In them and in ourselves our safety lies.

It is not clear what, if anything, God has done for England over the centuries, but King Henry's soliloquy reminds us that the English Channel has helped save England from European conquest for nine centuries. The country's most important physical characteristic is being separated from the continent by a narrow expanse of water. Without it the British might have been conquered by Napoleon in the early 1800s or by Hitler's army in 1940. Geographic factors include location, topography, size, and climate.

The *location* of a country, particularly in relation to other countries, is significant. The Chinese army's significance as a power factor is different for the country's relations with the United States and with Russia. The huge Chinese army can do little to threaten the United States, far across the Pacific Ocean. By contrast, Russia and China share a border, and Chinese soldiers could march into Siberia. Location can be an advantage or a disadvantage. Spain was able to avoid involvement in either world war partly because of its relative isolation from the rest of Europe. Poland, sandwiched between Germany and Russia, and Korea, stuck between China and Japan, each has a distinctly unfortunate location. The Israelis would almost certainly be better off if their promised land were somewhere—almost anywhere—else. And the Kuwaitis probably would not mind moving either, provided they could take their oil fields with them.

A country's *topography*—its mountains, rivers, and plains—is also important. The Alps form a barrier that has helped protect Switzerland from its larger European neighbors and spared the Swiss the ravages of both world wars. The rugged mountains of Afghanistan bedeviled British and Soviet invaders in the past, and since 2001 they have frequently frustrated the efforts of U.S. and other coalition troops to corner and capture or kill remnants of the al-Qaeda and Taliban forces. Topography can also work against a country. For example, the southern and eastern two-thirds of Iraq is a broad plain that provided a relatively easy invasion avenue for the mechanized U.S. and British forces in 2003. The Tigris and Euphrates river systems and the associated swampy areas provided some topographical defenses, but too few to make a difference.

A country's *size* is important. Bigger is often better. The immense expanse of Russia, for example, has repeatedly saved it from conquest. Although sometimes overwhelmed at first, the Russian armies have been able to retreat into the interior and buy time in exchange for geography while regrouping. By contrast, Israel's small size gives it no room to retreat.

A country's *climate* can also play a power role (Eichengreen, 1998). The tropical climate of Vietnam, with its heavy monsoon rains and its dense vegetation, made it difficult for the Americans to use effectively much of the superior weaponry they possessed. At the other extreme, the bone-chilling Russian winter has allied itself with Russia's geographic size to form a formidable defensive barrier. Many of Napoleon's soldiers literally froze to death during the French army's retreat from Moscow, and 131 years later Germany's army, the Wehrmacht, was decimated by cold and ice during the sieges of Leningrad and Stalingrad. In fact the Russian winter has proved so formidable that Czar Nicholas I commented, "Russia has two generals we can trust, General January and General February."

People

A second element of the national core is a country's human characteristics. Tangible demographic subcategories include number of people, age distribution, and such quantitative factors as health and education. There are also intangible population factors such as morale.

Population As is true for geographic size, the size of a country's population can be a positive or a negative factor. Because a large population supplies military personnel and industrial workers, sheer numbers of people are a positive power factor. It is unlikely, for instance, that Tonga (pop. 108,000) will ever achieve great-power status. A large population may be disadvantageous, however, if it is not in balance with resources. India, with 1 billion people, has the world's second-largest population, yet because of the country's poverty ($460 per capita GNP), it must spend much of its energy and resources merely feeding its people.

Age Distribution It is an advantage for a country to have a large percentage of its population in the productive years (15–64 by international reporting standards). Some countries with booming populations have a heavy percentage of children who must be supported. In other countries with limited life expectancy, many people die before they complete their productive years. Finally, some countries are "aging," with a geriatric population segment that consumes more resources than it produces.

Worldwide, 30% of the Earth's population in 2001 was less than 15 years old; 7% was 65 or over; 63% was in the working-age years (15–64). Figure 8.1 shows the age distributions of several countries, which you should compare. The figure also shows the dependency ratio of young and old people combined compared to the working-age population. Many analysts would contend that South Korea is relatively advantaged by its large working-age population, while Uganda, with numerous children, and Italy, with a high percentage of senior citizens, are relatively disadvantaged.

Countries like Italy that have such low birthrates that they are in a zero or even a negative population growth pattern are also disadvantaged in that they may experience economic difficulty because of future labor shortages. A growing geriatric population

FIGURE 8.1 Age Distribution and Dependency Ratios

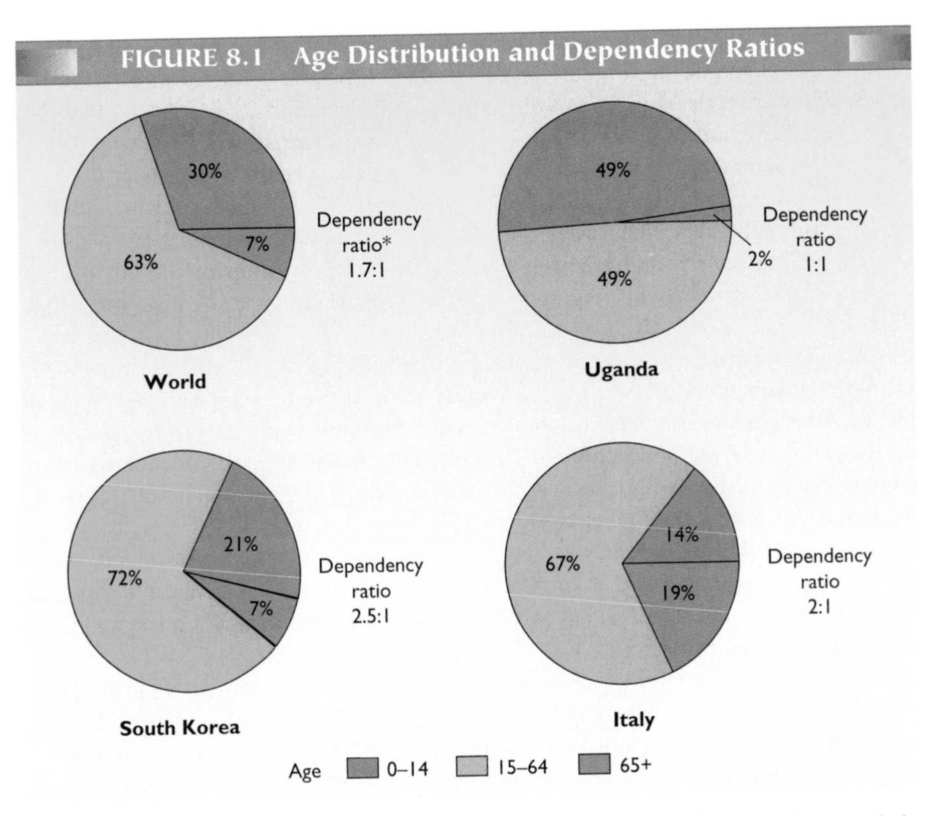

Most economically less developed countries (LDCs), like Uganda, are disadvantaged because their population has a high percentage of children. These youngsters add little to their country's economic vitality. While investing in them is wise policy, children consume resources for their education and general care that they will only begin to "repay" the system in terms of productivity and taxes when they become adults. A high percentage of senior citizens, as in Italy, is also economically suboptimal.

*Dependency ratio is a World Bank calculation of the ratio of the working-age population (ages 15–64) to the dependent population (age 14 and younger plus age 65 and older). Generally, the higher the ratio, the more economically advantaged a country is.

Data source: World Bank (2003).

also means that the cost of providing pensions and other services to retired citizens will strain a country's capacity. By 2025, for instance, an estimated 28% of Japan's population will be age 65 and older, and by 2050 fully a third of all Japanese will be of retirement age. Most European countries will also have increasingly higher percentages of retirees. Although the proportion of retired Americans will be somewhat less (13% currently, 19% in 2025, 21% in 2050) than in most other economically developed countries (EDCs), the U.S. Social Security and health care systems will still face a formidable challenge.

Education An educated population is important to national power. Although there are education variations among all countries, LDCs are especially disadvantaged compared to EDCs, as illustrated by the contrasts between Canada and Senegal in Table 8.1. It will be hard, for example, for LDCs to create educational programs that will close the gap in research and development (R&D) scientists and technicians, who number 41 per every 10,000 people in the EDCs and only 4 per 10,000 people in the LDCs. To make matters worse for LDCs, many of them suffer a substantial "brain drain," an "outflow of highly educated individuals" to EDCs, where professional opportunities are better (Carrington & Detragiache, 1999:1).

TABLE 8.1 Health and Education in Canada and Senegal

	Canada	Senegal
Health spending	$2,058	$22
Life expectancy	79	52
Children dying before age 5	0.5%	14%
Population per physician	476	10,000
Education spending	$1,715	$27
Adult literacy	99%	64%
Average years of schooling	11.6	2.6
Secondary school enrollment	97%	18%

Note: Spending for health and education is public spending per capita; life expectancy is years; average years of schooling for people age 15 and older; secondary school enrollment is the percentage of youths in that age group.
Data source: World Bank (2003).

Canada's power is enhanced by its educated and healthy population, especially relative to Senegal's disadvantaged population.

The quality of a country's education system is also important. For example, almost all Americans are literate, yet there is growing concern that the U.S. educational system is not adequately preparing students to meet the requirements of the modern world. It may be that the basic 3 Rs—reading, 'riting, and 'rithmetic—that once served to train a workforce will no longer suffice in the 21st century. Instead, the requirements will be more like the 3 Cs—computers, calculus, and communications. Another problem may be that American students during their four years of high school spend an average of only about half as much time on core subjects as do students in Japan, France, and Germany.[5] Also, a source of difficulty may be discipline in American schools. Students in U.S. classrooms are more likely than those in many, perhaps most, other countries to have their learning disrupted by the behavior problems of other students. This matter is depicted in Figure 8.2.

Whatever the cause, the achievement of American students is "middle of the pack" among EDCs, despite public funding of education that exceeds $650 billion annually. For example, of 15-year-old students in 26 EDCs evaluated in one recent study, Americans teenagers finished 15th in reading, 14th in science, and 18th in mathematics.[6] With a combined score that put it in 16th place, the U.S. achievement levels ranked well below those of the top five finishers (in order): Finland, South Korea, Japan, New Zealand, and Canada.

Yet another way to break down general educational statistics is to see how well a country trains various segments of its population. Most countries limit their power potential by underutilizing major elements of their population. For example, sexism limits the possible contribution of women in virtually all countries. In Bangladesh, for instance, 42% more male than female teenagers are enrolled in secondary school. Racial, ethnic, and other bases of discrimination add to this failure to maximize a population's potential. The fact that among adults over age 24 in the United States just 15% of African Americans and 11% of Latinos, compared to 25% of whites, have completed college means that the potential of a significant number of these disadvantaged people has been lost to the country.

Health Health problems can also sap a country's power. The health gap between Canada and Senegal shown in Table 8.1 can be supplemented by such information as

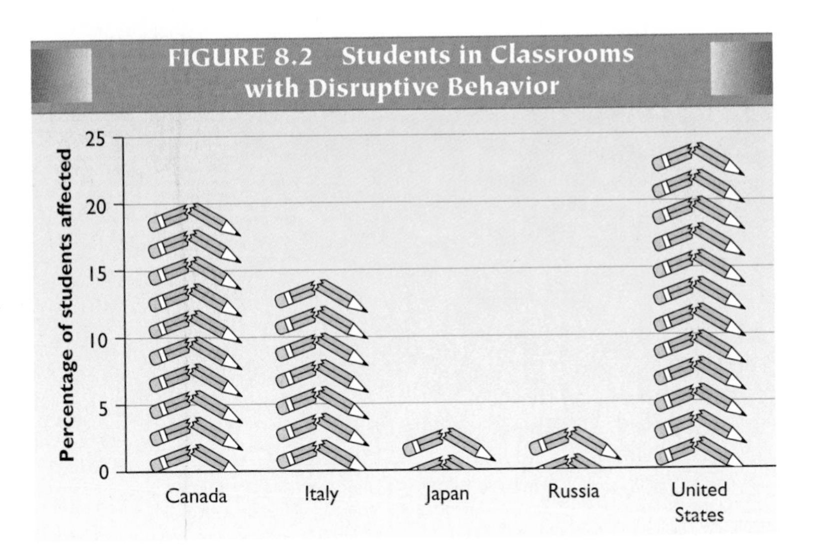

National power rests in part on a well-educated populace, and learning is difficult in a classroom that is not calm and secure. This figure shows the percentage of eighth-grade students in five countries who, according to reports by school principals, are subjected to negative behavior (such as vandalism, verbal abuse, and physical injury) that threatens a safe and orderly environment in their classroom at least weekly.

Data source: National Center for Education Statistics, *Comparative Indicators of Education in the United States and Other G-8 Countries: 2002* at http://nces.ed.gov/pubsearch/pubsinfo.asp?pubid=2003026.

the specific health problems that some countries face. AIDS is a worldwide scourge, but it is particularly devastating in Africa. About 70% of the world's 42 million HIV-infected people live in sub-Saharan Africa, where 9% of the adults are HIV-positive and there are seven countries with adult infection rates above 20%. The toll on the region is immense. The disease is killing about 2.5 million people a year there, and there are some 12 million AIDS orphans, some of whom are themselves infected and will meet an early death.

The disease is also having a profound economic impact on the continent. According to a recent UN report, "AIDS has become the biggest threat to the continent's development and its quest to bring about an African Renaissance" as several countries lose many of their "small number of highly skilled personnel in important areas of public management and core social services . . . to AIDS," and as these countries deplete their already meager resources trying to deal with the epidemic.[7]

Alcohol abuse and other attacks on health are devastating Russia and some other countries. Chain smoking, a deficient diet, and the ravages of alcohol are decimating Russia's male population. Two-thirds of all adult Russian males smoke (2.5 times the U.S. rate), and there are estimates that the average Russian adult male drinks about two quarts of vodka a week. "Sobriety is no longer the moral norm in Russia," says one health official there.[8]

The attitude of Russian men, President Boris Yeltsin once explained, is, "What kind of Russian man are you if you cannot drink?"[9] One answer is a healthy man, because a huge number of the estimated 60% of Russian men who do drink to excess die from alcohol-related diseases and accidents. Others kill themselves in despair, with Russian males having the world's highest reported annual suicide rate (73 per 100,000 males). This compares to a rate of 14 for Russian women and 28 for American men. As a result, the longevity of Russian males has actually declined substantially, and now only 48% of them (compared to 77% of Russian women) live to age 65. The threat to Russia's national strength is so palpable that one Russian government study calls it "the clearest possible threat to national security."[10]

Did You Know That:

Vodka has long undermined Russia's power. According to the *Washington Post*, in 1373 the Russians lost a battle to the Tatars because the czar's forces were too inebriated to fight. The defeated Russians were thrown into a nearby river, which was then dubbed the Reka Pianaya, the Drunk River.[1]

Morale A final factor that affects the population element of national power is the morale of a country's citizens. World War II demonstrated the power of strong civilian morale. Early in the war, Great Britain and the Soviet Union reeled under tremendous assaults by the Nazi forces. Yet the Allies hung on. Winston Churchill proclaimed in Parliament on October 9, 1940, during the darkest days of the war, that for the British people, "Death and sorrow will be the companions of our journey; hardship our garment; constancy and valor our only shield. We must be united, we must be undaunted, we must be inflexible." The British answered Sir Winston's call. They remained undaunted; they held; they prevailed.

Conversely, the collapse of national morale can lead to civil unrest and even the fall of governments. The end of the USSR in 1991 provides an example. The normally gloomy Russian outlook, which novelist Fyodor Dostoyevsky (1821–1881) described as "almost a Russian disease," has spawned dark humor, such as the joke in which one Russian meets another and asks, "How are things?" The comrade replies, "Terrible! I've hit rock bottom," to which the first Russian says, "Ah, you always were an optimist" (Javeline, 1999). Even by Russian standards, however, the populace in 1990 was disheartened, with 90% believing that the country's economic situation was dire, and 57% expressing no confidence in the future. This profound pessimism led to an almost total collapse of support for the government of Soviet President Mikhail Gorbachev and, indeed, the country's political system. On December 25, 1991, Gorbachev resigned and dissolved the Soviet Union. The "evil empire," as President Reagan called it, had been brought down by a vacuum of public support, not by the opposing superpower.

Government

The quality of a country's government is a third power element associated with the national core. The issue is not what form of government, such as a democracy or an authoritarian system, a country has. Instead the issue is *administrative competence*: whether a state has a well-organized and effective administrative structure to utilize its power potential fully. The collapse of the Soviet Union stemmed in part from its massive and inefficient bureaucratic structure, and Russia continues to struggle under poor governance. Soon after he came to power in 2000, President Vladimir Putin commented candidly that government mismanagement and corruption had so damaged the economy that they were "pushing us into the group of Third World countries."[11] Three years later, it was not clear how much, if at all, Russia had progressed toward improved governance. The arrest in late 2003 of Russia's richest capitalist, oil tycoon Mikhail Khodorkovsky, on corruption charges and the seizure of the company he headed revealed the turmoil that continues within the Russian government. The Putin government claimed it was enforcing justice, with one supporter arguing, "Russia needs law and order. Russia needs fighting against corruption."[12] But many in Russia, including top Putin advisers, saw the move as a giant step backward on the path to democracy and economic reform. Putin's chief of staff resigned and his own prime minister criticized the arrest and seizure. Whatever the rights and wrongs of the charges of corruption and the countercharges of creeping despotism being hurled back and forth, the point is that the ability of Moscow to provide honest and efficient governance, to maintain Russia's fledgling democracy, and to reform the country's economic system remains in considerable doubt.

Leadership skill also adds to a government's strength. Leadership is one of the most intangible elements of national power. Yet it can be critical, especially in times of crisis. For example, Prime Minister Winston Churchill's sturdy image and his inspiring rhetoric well served the British people during World War II. By contrast, the presidency of Boris Yeltsin, which had begun with heroics as he faced down tanks in the streets of Moscow, dissolved into incompetence as the ailing, often inebriated Yeltsin became an increasingly sad caricature of his former self.

The National Infrastructure

Another group of elements that form the foundation of state power is related to a country's infrastructure. The infrastructure of a state might be roughly equated with the skeleton

Technological capabilities are a crucial building block of national power.

of a human body. For a building, the infrastructure would be the foundation and the framing or girders. To examine the infrastructure of the state as an element of national power, the following sections will discuss technological sophistication, transportation systems, and information and communications capabilities. Each of these factors strongly affects any country's capacity in the other elements of power.

Technology

"Everything that can be invented has been invented," intoned Charles H. Duell, commissioner of the U.S. Office of Patents, in 1899.[13] Commissioner Duell was obviously both in error and in the wrong job. Most of the technology that undergirds a great deal of contemporary national power has been invented since his shortsighted assessment. Air conditioning modifies the impact of weather, computers revolutionize education, robotics speed industry, synthetic fertilizers expand agriculture, new drilling techniques allow for undersea oil exploration, microwaves speed information, and lasers bring the military to the edge of the Luke Skywalker era. Thus, technology is an overarching factor and will be discussed as part of all the tangible elements of power.

One source of U.S. strength is the considerable money that its government, corporations, and universities spend on research and development (R&D). During 2002 the United States spent $276 billion. That was more than the combined spending of $258 billion on R&D of the next five highest countries (Japan, Germany, France, Great Britain, and Italy). Another good measure of technological sophistication and capability is computing capacity. Needless to say, business, education, science, and other key elements of national power depend on computers, and, as Figure 8.3 shows, there is a vast disparity in national capabilities.

Transportation Systems

The ability to move people, raw materials, finished products, and sometimes the military throughout its territory is another part of a country's power equation. For example, one of the major hurdles that Russia must overcome to invigorate its economy is its relatively limited and decrepit transportation systems. As one standard, for every 1,000 square miles of its land territory, the United States has 14 times as many miles of paved roads and four times as many miles of railroad track than does Russia. Inadequate transportation systems are also a problem for LDCs.

Information and Communications Systems

A country's information and communications capabilities are becoming increasingly important (Rothkopf, 1998). The advent of satellites and computers has accelerated the revolution begun with radio and television. Photocopying machines, then fax machines, and now the Internet have dramatically changed communications. Enhanced communications technology increases the ability of a society to communicate within itself and remain cohesive. It also increases efficiency and effectiveness in industry, finance, and the military.

Here again, the gap between LDCs and EDCs is wide. There are, for example, approximately three times more television sets, six times more radios, three times more telephones, and 19 times more Internet users per capita in the United States than in China.

FIGURE 8.3 Comparative Computing Capacity

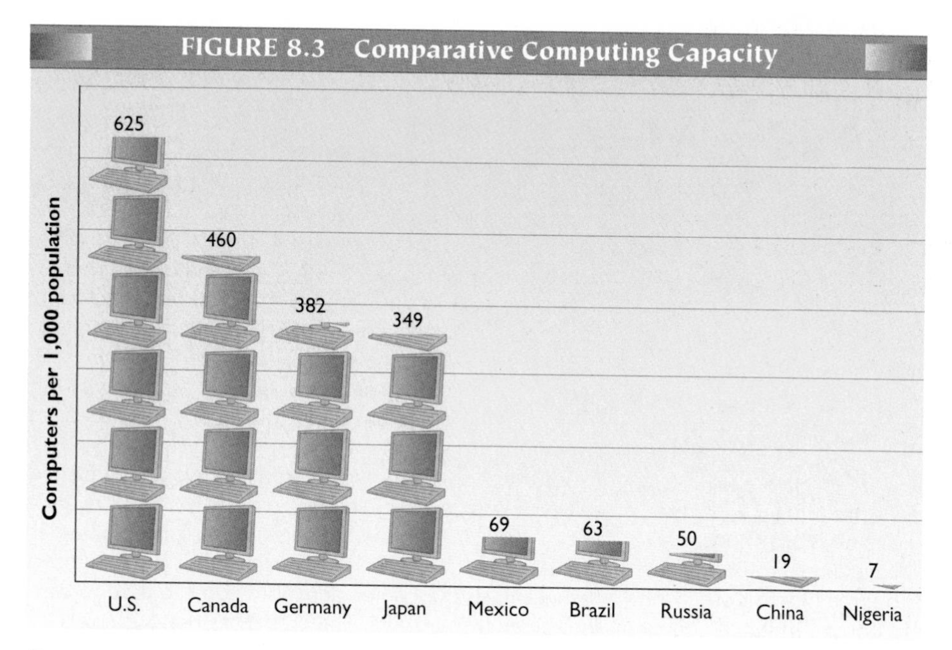

Computer capacity is a key element of a country's technological infrastructure. As this figure shows, there is a huge gap, called the "global digital divide," in global computing power.

Data source: World Bank (2003).

The Nature of Diplomacy

Now that we have explored the power foundation on which much of national diplomacy rests, we can turn to its conduct. Our discussion of diplomacy will use many diplomatic events as examples, but, in particular, it will focus on important diplomatic events that are introduced in the In the Spotlight box "Peace or War."

The Functions of Diplomacy

National diplomats serve as communication links between their countries and the rest of the world. As one scholar puts it, "Diplomats not only seek to represent their states to the world, but also seek to represent the world back to their respective states, with the objective of keeping the whole ensemble together" (Sharp, 1999:53).

Traditionally, diplomacy has focused on the national interest. Writing in the 1400s, Venetian ambassador Ermolao Barbaro asserted that "the first duty of an ambassador is . . . to do, say, advise, and think whatever may best serve the preservation and aggrandizement of his own state" (Craig & George, 1995). Whether it is conducted with honor or deceit, diplomacy is carried on by officials with a variety of titles such as president, prime minister, ambassador, or special envoy, and it is worthwhile to explore the roles that these officials and other diplomats play in promoting the national interest (Berton, Kimura, & Zartman, 1999).

Observer and reporter is one role. A primary diplomatic role has always been to gather information and impressions, to analyze them, and to report back to the home office. This information comes from activities ranging from formal meetings to the day-to-day contacts that an ambassador and other diplomats have with officials and the general public

IN THE SPOTLIGHT

Peace or War

In matters of diplomacy the stakes range from the mundane to the dramatic. For example, in 2003 U.S. diplomats negotiated the "Protocol Amending Tax Convention with Sri Lanka" treaty and also wrestled with such issues as war with Iraq. Many diplomatic events of every type are used in our exploration of diplomacy, but more than any others, you will encounter repeated references to the U.S.–North Korea nuclear crisis of 1993–1994 and its reignition in 2001; to the crises between China and Taiwan in 1996, 2000, and 2003–2004; to the U.S.-Afghanistan crisis of 2001; and to the U.S.-Iraq crisis of 2002–2003.

The U.S.-North Korea confrontation in 1993–1994 and its renewal beginning in 2002 centers on North Korea's nuclear weapons program. The confrontation began when the United States moved in 1993 to force North Korea (the Democratic People's Republic of Korea, DPRK) to give up its alleged nuclear weapons program after North Korea announced its intention to withdraw from the Nuclear Non-Proliferation Treaty (NPT) and blocked the monitoring of its nuclear plant at Yongbyon by the International Atomic Energy Agency (IAEA). Adding to the concern, the CIA reportedly believed that the DPRK probably already had one or two nuclear weapons. The image of a nuclear-armed North Korea raises grave concerns about the possibility of a nuclear nightmare occurring on the ever-tense Korean peninsula. Moreover, a nuclear-armed North Korea could force Japan and South Korea to start their own nuclear weapons programs and pressure China to expand its existing nuclear arsenal. As one South Korean analyst put it, "It would mean more nuclear weapons in Northeast Asia, more missiles and more possibilities for conflict. And when there is conflict, the damage would be increased." The impact might even spread beyond Northeast Asia: "We see a country that is designing and selling its ballistic missiles around the world," said an American diplomat. "We see a country that might export nuclear weapons."[1]

What followed was a series of diplomatic moves and countermoves that escalated to the point when in mid-1994 war seemed possible amid dire threats and military moves. Then diplomacy lowered the flame of crisis. North Korea agreed to suspend work on the nuclear reactors it was constructing, to dismantle its nuclear energy program over 10 years, and to allow IAEA inspections to resume. The United States, Japan, South Korea, and others pledged to spend some $4 billion to build two nuclear reactors in North Korea that were not capable of producing plutonium for bomb building. The West also agreed to help meet North Korea's energy needs by annually supplying it with about 138 million gallons of petroleum until new reactors are on line.

Relations between Washington and Pyongyang turned downward again after President George W. Bush took office in 2001. In June the administration signaled a harder U.S. attitude toward North Korea and indirectly criticized the incentives the Clinton administration had used to ease the earlier crisis in 1994. The president's rhetoric escalated further after 9/11 when during his 2002 State of the Union address he named North Korea a member of the "axis of evil." The picture darkened even more in October 2002 when the North Koreans told U.S. diplomats that they had recommenced making fissionable material and once again moved to block IAEA monitoring of their Yongbyon facility. The United States and others cut off their oil shipments to North Korea and demanded that it reverse its policy. Soon there was renewed talk of war, and that in turn sparked efforts to quell the danger.

The series of China-Taiwan crises featured diplomatic interplay between China, Taiwan, and the United States during the periods just before Taiwan's presidential elections in 1996, 2000, and 2004, when one or more candidates took stands that seemed to favor Taiwan declaring independence. The tensions in 2003–2004 also centered on Taiwan's adoption of a law in 2003 permitting popular referendums, a democratic technique that Beijing feared would be used to stage a public vote on independence.

Taiwan, an island located 100 miles to the east of south-central China, became politically separated from China when the Nationalist government of Chiang Kai-shek fled there in 1949 after being ousted by the communist forces of Mao Zedong. Both regimes claimed to be the legitimate

in another country. Many embassies also contain a considerable contingent of intelligence officers who are technically attached to the diplomatic service. Whatever the method, it is important for policy makers to know both the facts and the mood of foreign capitals, and the embassy is a primary source.

The value of this function is especially evident when it is absent. The intentions of North Korea, for example, are more difficult to ascertain because many countries, including the United States, do not have embassies in Pyongyang, and travel within the government of all China, including Taiwan. However, the passage of time led Taiwan to give up that fiction and to flirt with the idea of declaring its independence. China tolerates Taiwan's separate status, but Beijing has repeatedly vowed to use force to reincorporate Taiwan if the island formally declares its independence.

All three of the confrontations between Taiwan and China occurred in response to positions taken by leading candidates for the presidency of Taiwan implying they favored independence. These included President Chen Shui-bian pushing through the referendum law in Taiwan in 2003. China responded in all cases by trying to intimidate Taiwan. In 1996 this included conducting large military maneuvers in the Taiwan Strait and firing missiles into "test areas" near Taiwan's main ports. In the end, China's fear campaign failed. The United States sent two aircraft carrier–led flotillas to the area. Washington warned Beijing not to be rash and simultaneously cautioned Taipei not to be provocative. The election proceeded peacefully. The pattern was repeated in 2000. Threats and counterthreats thundered back and forth across the Pacific but fortunately remained words instead of actions. Washington deterred China by standing behind Taiwan, while also telling Taiwan that the United States would not support moves toward independence. Eventually what occurred were Beijing-Taipei-Washington negotiations in which Taipei backed down from talk of independence, Beijing stepped away from its threats, and peace was preserved.

The most recent tensions between China and Taiwan remain unresolved at this writing, but the repeat of now familiar diplomacy suggests a peaceful resolution is likely. China has made it clear that it will not tolerate an independence move by Taiwan and that it sees the referendum as a step in that direction. Speaking in New York City on the eve of a meeting with President Bush, Premier Wen Jiabao of China warned that "separatist forces" in Taiwan were trying to "use democracy only as a cover to split Taiwan away from China."[2] Lest anyone mistake the consequence, General Peng Guangqian told reporters in Beijing that "Taiwan's independence means war. This is the word of 1.3 billion people, and we will keep our word."[3] This stance brought a hopefully calming response from U.S. officials, one of whom told a reporter, "We [in the United States] don't want to see Taiwan moving toward independence. We don't want to see any unilateral moves in that direction."[4]

The crisis between Afghanistan and the United States in 2001 followed the 9/11 terrorist attacks. Washington soon became convinced that the attacks had been directed by al-Qaeda, a terrorist organization that was based in Afghanistan under the leadership of Osama bin Laden. President George W. Bush demanded that bin Laden and the rest of the leadership of al-Qaeda be turned over; the Taliban government in Kabul under the leadership of Mullah Mohammad Omar refused; war ensued.

The U.S.-Iraq crisis of 2002–2003 had been brewing since the end of the Persian Gulf War in 1991. The back and forth maneuvering over UN inspections, occasional U.S. bombing raids, and occasional mini-crises reached a full boil soon after President Bush assumed office in 2001. As was true with North Korea, the new president was determined to take a firmer stance against Iraq than had his predecessor. Even before the 9/11 terrorist attacks occurred, there were substantial sentiments in the administration to remove Saddam Hussein from power, as related in the box "Decision for War" in chapter 3. Whatever might have occurred, the events of 9/11 solidified the determination of the president to force Saddam Hussein's hand, and Iraq, like Korea, was named as part of the axis of evil. Tensions seriously mounted during the fall of 2002 as the United States sought UN resolutions supporting armed intervention in Iraq and took other measures to bring pressure on the government in Baghdad. Saddam Hussein, perhaps encouraged by the resistance in the UN to war, followed a sort of cat-and-mouse strategy of partially giving in to increased UN inspections for weapons of mass destruction (WMDs) and playing for time. The Iraqi maneuvers are even more curious in retrospect because, it seems, they did not have WMDs to hide. As is well known, the diplomats were unable to keep the peace, and the generals settled the matter on the battlefield.

country is highly restricted for the few foreigners who are there. One U.S. official noted that "compared with North Korea, the Soviet Union was a duck-soup intelligence target."[14] This lack of good information was particularly worrisome during the events of 1993 and 1994 that involved North Korea's nuclear program. "The fact of the matter is that we don't really understand what they are doing," a U.S. official commented at one point.[15] That concern persisted in 2002, with analysts unsure if North Korea was intent on developing a nuclear arsenal to increase its power, as a defensive reaction to what it

The difference between creating peace and falling into the chasm of war often rests on the skills of the diplomats representing countries that are confronting each other.

perceived as a threatening U.S. stance, or as a bargaining chip to get more aid and recognition from the United States or its allies.

Although ambassadors are still valuable as observers and reporters, the importance of these functions have declined. Countries are far less isolated from one another than they once were, and there are many new ways of using advanced technology to gather information about other countries. The result is that diplomatic reports compete with many other sources of information. This frustrates diplomats. As one U.S. official put it, "There is a diminished value in classical diplomatic reporting. If you had a choice between reading the [diplomatic] cables in your box and tuning in to CNN three times a day, you'd tune in to CNN."[16]

Negotiator is a second important role of a diplomat. Negotiation is a combination of art and technical skill that attempts to find a common ground among two or more divergent positions. For all of the public attention given to meetings between national leaders, it is ambassadors and other such personnel who conduct the vast bulk of negotiating. For example, negotiations between U.S. and North Korean diplomats in 2002–2003 resembled two boxers feeling each other out in the early rounds. At first North Korea demanded a bilateral nonaggression treaty from the United States, and Washington refused to consider any assurance on the grounds that this would be tantamount to recognizing North Korea. Later, U.S. diplomats offered verbal assurance, and even proffered the idea of some sort of written agreement that was short of a treaty and would be signed by all the region's countries. As Secretary of State Colin Powell put it, "We have made it clear we have no aggressive intent. Apparently, they want something more than a passing statement."[17] When asked whether his statement represented a shift in the U.S. position, the secretary replied, "That's what diplomacy is about."

Here again though, and especially during crises, the negotiating role of ambassadors has declined. In the immediate aftermath of the terrorist attacks on the United States in September 2001, the personal contacts among world leaders were intense. Within weeks of the attack, President Bush met in Washington with, among others, the prime ministers of France, Great Britain, Canada, Japan, and Belgium; the German chancellor, the king of Jordan; the emir of Qatar; the secretary-general of NATO; and the president of Mexico. Bush spoke by phone with the president of China and, on several occasions, with the president of Russia. President Bush also met with these two leaders, as well as many others, during the annual Asia-Pacific Economic Cooperation meeting in Shanghai, China, in mid-October.

Policy representative is a third role of a diplomat. This function includes explaining and defending the policies of the diplomat's country. Misperception is dangerous in world politics, and the role that diplomats play in explaining their countries' actions and statements to friends and foes alike is vital to accurate communications. At one point in 2003 during the shifting negotiations, a South Korean diplomat expressed the hope that "North Korea takes the message right."[18] It is the job of diplomats to try to ensure that happens.

Policy representation can also mean carrying messages from the diplomat's home government. For very powerful countries, it can also mean making demands. When, in 1972, South Vietnam resisted the U.S.-negotiated settlement, President Nixon cabled President Thieu that "all military and economic aid will be cut off . . . if an agreement is not reached" and that "I have . . . irrevocably decided to proceed . . . to sign [the agreement]. I will do so, if necessary, alone [and] explain that your government obstructs peace." As the chief diplomat of the United States, Nixon was being distinctly undiplomatic. "Brutality is nothing," he told Kissinger. "You have never seen it if this son-of-a-bitch doesn't go along, believe me" (Kissinger, 1979:1420, 1469). Thieu went along.

The Diplomatic Setting

The nature of diplomacy and how it is carried out are also affected by its setting. The setting can be roughly divided into three parts: the international system, the diplomatic environment, and the domestic connection.

The International System

One aspect of the setting is the system. As we have noted many times, the nature of the anarchical international system creates a setting in which self-interested actors pursue their diplomatic goals by using power if necessary to ensure that their goals prevail over the goals of others. That emphasis on national interest is why this chapter discusses national diplomacy and national power.

During the crisis that led to the American and British invasion of Iraq in 2003, many factors in the international system shaped the events, as discussed in detail in chapter 3. The U.S. position as the system's hegemonic power gave the United States the leeway to push forward without UN support and also arguably was part of the reason that France and other countries resisted the U.S. lead in an attempt to restore a greater balance of power. The status of the Middle East as the world's most important producer of oil was another systemic factor, as was the hostility of Arabs toward the United States for its support of Israel. The increased concern about terrorism and weapons of mass destruction in the system also entered into the mix of factors that eventually led U.S. military forces to the center of Baghdad.

The Diplomatic Environment

A second part of the diplomatic setting is determined by the relationships among the various actors who are involved in a particular matter. This part of the setting can be subdivided into four diplomatic environments: hostile, adversarial, coalition, and mediation diplomacy.

Hostile Diplomacy When one or more countries are engaged in armed clashes or when there is a substantial possibility that fighting could result, diplomacy is conducted in a hostile environment. In 2001, the maneuvering surrounding the U.S. demand on Afghanistan that it surrender those responsible for the 9/11 terrorist attacks fell distinctly within the range of **hostile diplomacy**. Almost immediately, the United States moved to deploy two aircraft carriers and numerous supporting warships to the Indian Ocean. On September 16, Bush also instructed, "The secretary of state should issue an ultimatum against the Taliban today warning them to turn over bin Laden and his al-Qaeda or they will suffer the consequences." If the Taliban do not comply, Bush instructed his advisers, "We'll attack with missiles, bombers, and boots on the ground. . . . We are going to rain holy hell on them."[19]

Adversarial Diplomacy An environment of **adversarial diplomacy** occurs at a less confrontational level when two or more countries' interests clash but when there is little or no chance of armed conflict. Even though they are allies, the diplomacy that transpired during the months before the war with Iraq in 2003 between the United States and Great Britain, on the one hand, and France and Germany, on the other, was tensely adversarial.

Adversarial diplomacy often occurs over trade disputes. When the United States increased tariffs on imported steel in 2002, many countries whose steel exports were harmed retaliated, and their citizens protested. For example, Russia suddenly decided that U.S. poultry might contain *Salmonella* and barred it. In this photograph a Muscovite holds a gallows with chicken meat dangling in front of a poster reading "No chickens' blindness!"

During a NATO conference about six weeks before the war, U.S. Secretary of Defense Rumsfeld told the assembled diplomats, including those of France and Germany, that "two or three countries" (meaning France and Germany) were guilty of "acts of irresponsibility" that were "breathtaking" and had put the UN on "a path of ridicule" and the resolve of NATO into question.[20] Reacting to the undiplomatic tone taken by Rumsfeld, German Foreign Minister Joschka Fischer told him, "I am not convinced" by the U.S. argument and prophetically added, "You're going to have to occupy Iraq for years and years. Are Americans ready for this?"[21] French Defense Minister Michèle Alliot-Marie joined the counterattack, disparaging Rumsfeld's "combative tone" and characterizing the U.S. approach as "precarious." Rumsfeld later fired back. When a reporter asked if he thought the opposition of Germany and France was an attempt to restrain U.S. unilateral power, Rumsfeld warned that "the likely effect would be that Germany and France would isolate themselves." [22]

At other times, adversarial diplomacy addresses less critical issues. President Bush in early 2002 ordered tariff increases of up to 30% on imported steel. Washington claimed the move offset unfair pricing by foreign competitors to the U.S. steel industry; critics charged the move was more about giving Republicans a political boost in big steel-producing states. Whatever the cause, countries that export steel to the United States struck back. For example, with Russia losing about $750 million a year in steel sales, Moscow moved to bar $800 million in U.S. poultry imports. With tongue in beak, the press quickly dubbed the contretemps the "cold chicken war." To the diplomats involved, however, it was serious. The American ambassador to Russia termed the dispute "the number one problem in U.S.-Russia relations in the past month," and he indicated that so many feathers had flown that diplomacy had "engaged at least five cabinet ministers on my side, and even President George W. Bush, who has spoken to President Putin directly about this."[23] Taking a different approach, the European Union filed a complaint with the World Trade Organization (WTO) that the tariffs violated international trading rules. In November 2003 the WTO ruled against the United States, and the EU threatened to put retaliatory 100% tariffs of about $2 billion on U.S. goods to equal the EU calculation of its losses to the U.S. steel tariff. Brazil, China, Japan, New Zealand, Norway, South Korea, and Switzerland also filed complaints, and the WTO ruling also allowed each of those countries to impose tariffs on their U.S. imports.

Coalition Diplomacy

When a number of countries have similar interests, often in opposition to the interest of one or more other countries, then **coalition diplomacy** becomes a significant aspect of international activity. National leaders spend a good deal of time and effort to build coalitions that will support the foreign policy initiatives of their country or of other international actors that they support. When, for instance, Iraq invaded Kuwait in August 1990, President George Bush spent much time and effort in rounding up international support for military action against Iraq. During the first four days of the crisis Bush made 23 phone calls to a dozen foreign leaders, and personally flew to Colorado to consult with British Prime Minister Margaret Thatcher, who was coincidentally speaking at a conference there.

When President George W. Bush entered the White House, he favored a more unilateralist approach to diplomacy, and was less interested in building coalitions than his father had been. The post–9/11 complexities of combating global terrorism provided the son a lesson that his father had learned earlier. The younger Bush found that he could not succeed without building a broad coalition in support of U.S. goals. In addition to a high volume of phone calls to heads of government around the world, a presidential adviser speaking in January 2002 indicated that "Since September 11, Mr. Bush has met personally with nearly 80 foreign leaders, using each session to elicit whatever backing the other nation was willing to give."[24]

Mediation Diplomacy Unlike hostile, adversarial, or coalition diplomacy, the use of **mediation diplomacy** occurs when a country that is not involved directly as one of the parties tries to help two or more other countries in a conflict resolve their differences. The United States has been involved for decades in an attempt to mediate the conflict between Israel and its Arab neighbors, especially the Palestinians, as discussed in chapter 4. The latest effort was launched in April 2002 amid intense violence between Israelis and Palestinians. Declaring "The storms of violence cannot go on. Enough is enough," President Bush proposed a "roadmap to peace" including the cessation of Palestinian attacks on Israelis and the creation of a Palestinian state.[25] Thus far the effort has come to naught in the face of continued Palestinian suicide bombings, Israeli retaliatory raids that even some Israeli see as excessive, instability in the Palestinian leadership, and a thinly veiled discussion within the Israeli government about whether it should expel Yasser Arafat from the West Bank or even assassinate him.

Nevertheless, both Israel and the Palestinian government have accepted the basic outlines, if not all the details of the roadmap. In an effort to reinvigorate the peace process, the roadmap has been supplemented by U.S. support for unofficial efforts of peace-minded Israelis and Palestinians meeting in Geneva, Switzerland, in 2003, to add details to the plan. In an unusual move, U.S. Secretary of State Colin Powell sent a letter to Israeli Yossi Beilin (a former deputy minister of foreign affairs) and Palestinian cabinet minister Yasser Abed Rabbo (a former minister of cabinet affairs), the authors of the so-called Geneva Agreement, telling them, "The United States remains committed . . . to the roadmap but we also believe that projects such as yours are important in helping to sustain an atmosphere of hope in which Israelis and Palestinians can discuss mutually acceptable resolutions to the difficult issues that confront them." In a separate statement, a U.S. State Department official portrayed Powell's initiative as "not some kind of end run around the prime minister of Israel or any other leaders in the region." But it clearly was an effort to at least expand those involved beyond the leadership of Israel and the Palestinians, both of which have frustrated the Bush administration.[26]

The Domestic Connection

Domestic politics provide yet another part of the diplomatic setting. The concept of **two-level game theory**, discussed in chapter 3, holds that to be successful a country's diplomats must find a solution that is acceptable to both the other country at the international level and, at the domestic level, to the political actors (legislators, public opinion, interest groups) in the diplomat's own country. From this perspective, the diplomatic setting exists at the domestic as well as at the international level, and is influenced by the interplay of the two levels when leaders try to pursue policies that satisfy the actors at both levels (Trumbore, 1998).

During the Taiwan crises, the leaders of China and the United States not only had to find a point of agreement between themselves, they also had to fend off domestic forces that were pushing to escalate the crisis. Prior to the 1996 crisis, China's president told the U.S. ambassador, "Any leader who lets this [Taiwan's independence] pass would be overthrown."[27] President Clinton also had to deal with strong domestic forces. In 1996, for example, House Republicans urged Clinton to commit the United States "to the defense of Taiwan."[28] To ensure that Clinton did not ignore their views, GOP legislators introduced the Taiwan Security Enhancement Act to substantially increase the U.S. commitment to Taiwan. "There is a lot of pent-up frustration about the administration's policy approach to China," a GOP aide noted.[29] The GOP did not push that bill to passage, but it served notice of the strong support of Taiwan in Congress.

The Evolution of Diplomacy

Diplomacy is an ancient art. Because of the economic and political world dominance of Europe and European-heritage countries for the past several centuries, a great deal of modern diplomatic practice can be traced through its evolution in Western practice. Still, diplomacy predates the West.

Early Diplomacy

Diplomatic records in the eastern Mediterranean region around the Tigris and Euphrates river valleys date back almost four millennia, and records from what appear to be embassies can be found from as far back as the time of the great Babylonian emperor, Hammurabi (1792–1750 B.C.). Somewhat later, many of the practices used in modern diplomacy originated in ancient Greece and Rome. Diplomatic missions are described in Homer's *Iliad* (about 850 B.C.), and the Greeks, followed by the Romans, wrote treaties, established the rudiments of international law, and used ambassadors to negotiate disputes. The Byzantine Empire, which flourished after Rome's collapse, added further to the evolution of diplomacy by specifically training negotiators and by establishing the first department of foreign affairs.

Did You Know That:

The oldest surviving diplomatic document is a cuneiform tablet written about 2,500 B.C. It is a message sent by Ibubu, chief minister to the king of Ebla (in modern Lebanon), to King Zizi of Hamazi (in modern Iran), some 1,200 miles away. In it Ibubu pledges goodwill, relates that he is sending Zizi a quantity of rare wood, and says that he wants him to "give me good mercenaries. Please send them" (Cohen, 1996:2).

Beginning in the 15th century, the Italian city-states contributed to the evolution of diplomacy through the establishment of the first permanent diplomatic missions in modern times. Italians also introduced summit meetings as a diplomatic practice and became particularly known for diplomatic artifice. Indeed, the unflattering adjective Machiavellian is an eponym after Niccolò Machiavelli of Florence, who counseled in *The Prince* (1532) that it was best to be as powerful as a lion and as sly as a fox, and who summed up his estimation of human nature with the observation that one "must start with assuming that all men are bad and ever ready to display their vicious nature whenever they may find occasion for it."

The French system is the direct predecessor of modern diplomacy. Cardinal Richelieu, who served as chief minister (1624–1642) to King Louis XIII, was the first to see diplomacy as an ongoing process rather than as an expedience, and he consolidated all foreign affairs functions under one ministry. Later, during the reign (1643–1715) of Louis XIV, the minister of foreign affairs became a member of the king's cabinet, and permanent embassies were established in all the major capitals, with lesser-ranked missions in minor capitals. It was also at the end of this era that the first diplomatic manual, *On the Manner of Negotiating with Sovereigns* (1716), was written by François de Callierres.

In general, the old diplomacy that developed mostly in Europe had several traits. *Elite domination* was one. "*L'état, c'est moi*" (I am the state), Louis XIV supposedly proclaimed with some justification, and true to that assertion, foreign policy was almost exclusively dominated by the monarch, and ministers and diplomatic corps were recruited from the nobility and gentry. *Secrecy* was a second trait of early diplomacy. Negotiations were normally conducted in secret, and even treaties were often secret. *Bilateral diplomacy* was a third trait. Although there were a few multilateral conferences, such as the Congress of Vienna (1815), **bilateral diplomacy** (direct negotiations between two countries) was the normal form of negotiation.

Modern Diplomacy

The World War I era (1914–1918) serves as a benchmark in the transition to modern diplomacy. It was the beginning of the end of European world dominance. It also marked the fall of the German, Austrian, Ottoman, and Russian emperors. Nationalistic self-determination stirred strongly in Europe and other parts of the world. New powers—the United States, Japan, and China—began to assert themselves, and they joined or replaced the declining European countries as world powers. The "old diplomacy" did not vanish, but it changed substantially. The "new diplomacy" has seven major characteristics: expanded geographic scope, multilateral diplomacy, parliamentary diplomacy, democratized diplomacy, open diplomacy, leader-to-leader diplomacy, and public diplomacy. These new practices have been greeted as "reforms," but many also have drawbacks.

Expansion of Geographic Scope

Modern diplomacy has been marked by expansion of its geographic scope. The two Hague Conferences (1899, 1907) on peace, particularly the second, with its 44 participants, included countries outside the European sphere. President Wilson's call for national self-determination foreshadowed a world of almost 200 countries. Today, the United Nations, with its nearly universal membership, reflects the truly global scope of diplomacy.

Multilateral Diplomacy

The use of conferences involving a number of nations has expanded greatly in the modern era (Best, 1999). Woodrow Wilson's call for a League of Nations symbolized the rise of **multilateral diplomacy**. There are now a number of permanent world and regional international organizations. Ad hoc conferences and treaties are also more apt to be multilateral. Before 1900, for example, the United States attended an average of one multilateral conference per year. Now, the United States is a member of scores of international organizations and American diplomats participate daily in multilateral negotiations.

Multilateral diplomacy has increased for several reasons. One is that advances in travel and communications technology allow faster and more frequent contacts among countries. Second, many global concerns, such as the environment, cannot be solved by any one country or through traditional bilateral diplomacy alone. Instead, global cooperation and solutions are required. Third, diplomacy through multilateral organizations is attractive to smaller countries as a method of influencing world politics beyond their individual power.

A fourth factor promoting multilateral diplomacy is the rise of expectations that important international actions, especially the use of military force, will be taken within the framework of a multilateral organization. President Bush said in 2001 that he would act alone if necessary against Afghanistan, but he was also careful to engage in the multilateral diplomacy necessary to win both UN and NATO support for the U.S.-led campaign. In the end, Washington and London went ahead with their invasion of Iraq in 2003 without UN or NATO support, but the efforts both capitals made to win such support made it clear that they considered it important to have although not, ultimately, absolutely necessary.

Modern diplomacy is often conducted in such parliamentary settings as the United Nations. Sometimes negotiations can involve strong exchanges of views, such as those that are evidently occurring in this photograph of UN Secretary-General Kofi Annan and U.S. Secretary of State Colin Powell. This discussion took place in February 2003 before the start of a UN Security Council session on Iraq.

Parliamentary Diplomacy

Another modern practice is **parliamentary diplomacy**. This includes debate and voting in international organizations and sometimes supplants negotiation and compromise. The maneuvering involved in parliamentary diplomacy was strongly evident in the UN during the U.S. campaign to win Security Council approval for an invasion of Iraq. That required the backing of nine of the Council's 15 members and also required a yes vote or an abstention from each of the five permanent members with veto power. As the diplomacy heated up, the United States could count on four yes votes (its own, Great Britain, Spain, and Bulgaria). Germany and Syria were definitely no votes. China, France, and Russia were opposed to war, but U.S. diplomats hoped they could get those countries to abstain. Failing that, Washington made the case that it would have a moral victory if it received nine votes, even if the resolution was vetoed. This turned the spotlight on the remaining six members: Angola, Cameroon, Chile, Guinea, Mexico, and Pakistan.

Washington's strategy, according to one U.S. diplomat, was "win backing like you would in Congress—going after votes one by one by one." And just like a campaign to influence votes in Congress, the Bush administration used a mixture of argumentation, threats, and promised rewards. Secretary of State Powell claimed there was no effort to "strong-arm" members of the Security Council: "We present our case. We don't threaten. We don't suggest that blackmail is in order."[30] But widespread reports indicated that that characterization was not true and that new or increased aid and trade opportunities (or reductions) were part of the conversations with foreign leaders. Also proffered was the ability to be involved in the postwar reconstruction of Iraq, including contracts for rebuilding and involvement in Iraqi oil development. As one U.S. diplomat conceded, "We'll put it to them [other Security Council members] simply: Do you want to be part of reconstruction and all that means—or leave it to us? They'll either want a seat at the table over the next couple of years or have to opt out now."[31]

In the end, the U.S. effort was not successful. It is not clear whether Washington would have had nine votes, but most analysts believe that would not have occurred. And it was certain that France and perhaps Russia would veto the U.S./U.K. resolution. To avoid a veto and the probability of falling short of the nine votes, the British ambassador to the UN announced, "Given the situation, the co-sponsors have agreed that we will not pursue a vote."[32]

Democratized Diplomacy

The elite and executive-dominant character of early diplomacy has changed in several ways. One change brought about by **democratized diplomacy** is that diplomats are now drawn from a wider segment of society and, thus, are somewhat more representative of their nations, rather than just the rulers of their state.

A second democratic change is the rise of the roles of legislatures, interest groups, and public opinion. Executive leaders still dominate the foreign policy–making process, but it is no longer their exclusive domain. Now, as discussed in the earlier section on the domestic setting, national executives often must conduct two-level diplomacy by negotiating with domestic actors as well as with other countries to find a mutually agreeable solution to outstanding issues.

Third, the democratization of diplomacy has promoted the conduct of public diplomacy aimed at influencing not just leaders, but also the legislatures, interest groups, and public opinion in other countries. UN Secretary-General Kofi Annan has said, "If I can't get the support of governments, then I'll get the support of the people. People move governments."[33]

Open Diplomacy

Woodrow Wilson in his Fourteen Points called for "open covenants, openly arrived at." Wilson would have approved of the fact that, much more than before, diplomacy and even international agreements are now widely reported and documented. One advantage of **open diplomacy** is that it fits with the idea of democracy because, as one scholar notes, leaders more often use secret diplomacy to "mislead the populations of their own countries" rather than to keep information from international opponents (Gibbs, 1995:213).

There are, however, advantages to secret diplomacy. Most scholars and practitioners agree that public negotiations are difficult. Early disclosure of your bargaining strategy will compromise your ability to win concessions. Public negotiations are also more likely to lead diplomats to posture for public consumption. Concessions may be difficult to make amid popular criticism. In sum, it is difficult to negotiate (or to play chess) with someone kibitzing over your shoulder. Indeed, domestic opposition to dealing with an adversary may be so intense that it may be impossible to negotiate at all.

Soon after the 9/11 terrorist attacks on the United States, the Bush administration made a series of demands on Pakistan that, in Washington's view, were crucial to the success of the U.S. response. Many of these, such as the right to use Pakistani military bases, were difficult for the government in Islamabad to accept because of the large number of militant Muslims in the country and the connection between Pakistani Pashtuns and their ethnic brethren who made up the bulk of the Taliban ranks in Afghanistan. Nevertheless, the requirements were presented strongly. "We're talking to Pakistanis in a way we've never talked to them before," one U.S. official commented.[34] The demands and the pressure were all applied in secret, however, because open diplomacy might have put Pakistan's government at risk of being overthrown if it accepted the U.S. requirements.

Leader-to-Leader Diplomacy

Modern transportation and communications have spawned an upsurge of high-level diplomacy. National leaders regularly hold bilateral or multilateral summit conferences, and foreign ministers and other ranking diplomats jet between countries, conducting

The ease of travel and the frequency with which some leaders meet has made how well they interact one factor in the success or failure of diplomacy. During the cold war, meetings between U.S. and Soviet leaders were rare. Now, President George W. Bush and President Vladimir Putin of Russia see each other several times a year and reportedly have developed a warm regard for each other that some analysts believe has helped smooth relations between Washington and Moscow. As this photograph taken in St. Petersburg, Russia, demonstrates, the normal decorous handshakes between leaders has been, for Bush and Putin, supplemented by full-scale hugging.

shuttle diplomacy. One hundred thirty years of American history passed before a president (Woodrow Wilson) traveled overseas while in office. Presidents now travel frequently. George W. Bush departed on his first state visit only 27 days after his inauguration, and during his first two years in office took nine trips abroad, visiting 18 countries. Even more common are trips of foreign leaders to Washington. Bush had 136 meetings with other leaders in his first 18 months as president. Indeed, the once-rare instances of leader-to-leader diplomacy have become nearly routine, with, for example, annual meetings of the leaders of the Group of Eight (G-8, the largest industrialized countries plus Russia).

The advent of globe-trotting, leader-to-leader diplomacy, or **summit meetings**, and the increased frequency of telecommunications diplomacy are mixed blessings. There are several *advantages*. The first is that meetings between leaders can demonstrate an important symbolic shift in relations. One of the most significant moments in the more than 50 years since the outbreak of the Korean War occurred in June 2000, when the presidents of North and South Korea met for the first time. Some agreements were reached during the meeting in Pyongyang, but their importance paled compared to the symbolic televised image of the two shaking hands, smiling, bantering, and drinking champagne. "Maybe nothing dramatic will happen right away," a clerk in Seoul noted wisely, "but most people would agree that a surprising amount of progress and understanding has been achieved already."[35]

Second, leaders can sometimes make dramatic breakthroughs. The 1978 Camp David Accords, which began the process of normalizing Egyptian-Israeli relations after decades of hostility and three wars, were produced after President Carter, Egyptian President Sadat, and Israeli Prime Minister Begin isolated themselves at the presidential retreat in Maryland. A third advantage is that rapid diplomacy can help dispel false information and stereotypes. President George H. W. Bush lauded the telephone as a helpful tool. "If [another leader] knows the heartbeat a little bit from talking [with me]," the president explained, "there's less apt to be misunderstanding."[36]

A fourth advantage of personal contact among leaders is that mutual confidence or even friendships may develop. It is probable that the adversarial diplomacy that marks much of U.S.-Russian relations will be somewhat easier in the near future than might otherwise have been the case because presidents Bush and Putin seem to get along personally. As Bush put it while meeting with Putin at Camp David in September 2003, "I like him. He's a good fellow to spend quality time with." Moreover, the president continued, "Because we've got a trustworthy relationship, we're able to move beyond any disagreement over a single issue."[37]

Clear vision and good feelings are laudable, but there are *disadvantages* to leader-to-leader diplomacy. One of these is the sheer travails of travel, as told in the Global Actors box "Presidents and Prime Ministers Come Abroad to See the World."

More substantively, leader-to-leader diplomacy may lead to misunderstandings. There are numerous instances when leaders have made and reached what each thought

GLOBAL ACTORS

Presidents and Prime Ministers Come Abroad to See the World

The thought of traveling abroad practicing world diplomacy seems pretty attractive. Your personal plane flies you to interesting places to meet important people. You stay in sumptuous guest quarters and eat royally. Not a bad deal, most people would say.

Amazingly, though, leaders often complain bitterly about the rigors of official travel. Arduous schedules and jet lag are often so exhausting that Ronald Reagan once fell asleep while listening to a speech by the pope. Similarly, the stamina of President George W. Bush, who normally goes to bed by 10:30 P.M. has often been taxed by long days and late nights. When he visited St. Petersburg, Russia, in May 2002, his host, President Putin, planned a 1 A.M. boat tour along the city's famed Neva river. "We may be friends," a White House official said, "but this was something to go to war over."[1] A bit of last-minute diplomacy got the starting time pushed back a little, but toward the end of a journey with a schedule that one reporter described as a "complete killer," the president reportedly was nearly "sleep-walking through the final stages of the trip."[2]

In addition to physical exhaustion, there are the culinary hazards of what has been waggishly labeled "mealpolitik" and "gravy-boat diplomacy." One peril is having to eat odd things to avoid injuring local sensitivities. President George H. W. Bush dined on boar's penis soup while visiting China in 1989, and Bill Clinton found moose lips on his presidential plate during a 22-course dinner hosted by President Boris Yeltsin in Russia. "This was not a chocolate dessert," joked one American official.[3] Trying to get an informal bite to eat can also be a trial for visiting leaders. When President Bush visited Great Britain in November 2003, he expressed the hope of stopping in a local pub. He was able to do that, dining with Prime Minister Tony Blair on fish and chips and mushy peas at the Dun Cow Inn in Sedgefield, England. But an uproar broke out amid reports that more than $1 million was spent on security for the lunch, making it the most expensive fish and chips meal in history. Unaccustomed food can also lead to gastric distress. Jimmy Carter was felled in Mexico City by what he undiplomatically called Montezuma's revenge, and while in Tokyo, George H. W. Bush was so indisposed that he threw up on the Japanese prime minister. It is no wonder, then, that presidents may often think of Shakespeare's *Comedy of Errors* and the lament of Dromio, "For with long travel I am stiff and weary."

Yet despite these drawbacks, presidents travel abroad frequently. Bill Clinton holds the record as most traveled, making 54 trips to 133 countries with a wanderlust that kept him abroad for 229 days, or almost 8% of his presidency. Indeed, as one critic put it, Clinton acted "like the Energizer Bunny; he . . . continued to keep on going, and going, and going."[4] Despite a reputation for not being interested in visiting other countries, President George W. Bush actually took one more trip (nine) out of the country during his first two years than did Clinton, and so could someday challenge the record.

Why do leaders travel so much? Certainly there is value in leader-to-leader diplomacy, whether it be a dramatic breakthrough or the ability to meet and evaluate other leaders. President George H. W. Bush was inclined to believe that sizing up another leader is a key element of diplomacy. As he as put it, "The best diplomacy starts with getting to know each other."[5] Foreign travel is also a way to escape domestic pressures. The time President Clinton spent overseas increased markedly during the Monica Lewinsky scandal toward the end of his presidency. Finally, visiting foreign capitals provides a relief from the difficulty of working with a cantankerous Congress and bureaucratic barons. Clinton found foreign policy more "fun" because he could make policy "with less interference and static in Congress," whereas in domestic policy even the president was but "one of a zillion decision makers."[6] Thus, like Petruchio in Shakespeare's *Taming of the Shrew,* presidents outward bound on Air Force One may muse to themselves:

> Crowns in my purse I have and goods at home,
> And so am come abroad to see the world.

was a mutual understanding, only to find to their equally mutual surprise and anger that they had misunderstood each other. Furthermore, as tricky as personal contacts may be, the telephone may present even greater difficulties. Henry Kissinger, for example, argues that "the telephone is generally made for misunderstanding. It is difficult to make a good record. You can't see the other side's expressions or body language."[38] A second substantive problem is that while leaders can disavow mistakes made by lower-ranking officials, a leader's commitments, even if not well thought out, cannot be easily retracted. "When presidents become negotiators no escape routes are left," Kissinger warns (1979:12). "Concessions are irrevocable without dishonor."

Third, specific misunderstanding and general chemistry can damage working relations between leaders instead of improving them. Kissinger (1979:142), who should know, has observed that most world leaders are characterized by a "healthy dose of ego," and when two such egos collide, "negotiations can rapidly deteriorate from intractability to confrontation." For example, relations between President Bush and German Chancellor Gerhard Schröder are difficult. They turned sour during the German parliamentary election in 2002 when the chancellor publicly castigated the president's policy toward Iraq in what the White House took to be undiplomatic language designed to improve the electoral chances of the chancellor's party. According to a U.S. diplomat, Bush felt "he was betrayed by Schröder." While leaders seldom admit to personal hard feelings, Schröder did concede at one point, "This question about Iraq has gotten personal." As for Bush, his feelings were so strong that when the two were scheduled to meet in November 2002 at a NATO summit in Prague, Czech Republic, reporters asked a U.S. spokesperson if Bush would snub the chancellor. "Is he not going to shake Schröeder's hand?" "Hell, no," the official responded. "It's not like they won't talk to each other." But they barely did. The host, Czech President Václav Havel, suggested ignoring the usual alphabetical arrangement and seating the two leaders next to each other at the conference. The White House declined, and while Bush had time for one-on-one meetings with several other leaders, he could not find time for the leader of Germany.[39] Even in the aftermath of the war, the break between the two leaders did not improve. "The personal relationship is not just damaged, it is broken, and I fear beyond repair," lamented a German official. "That is regrettable because personal trust in the negotiating parties is important for political cooperation."[40]

Public Diplomacy

The communications revolution has placed leaders and other diplomats in public view more than ever before, and their actions have an impact on world opinion that is often distinct from their negotiating positions. Among other things, this means that diplomacy is often conducted under the glare of television lights and almost everything that officials say in public is heard or read by others. Additionally, a country's overall image and the image of its leaders have become more important because of the democratization of the foreign policy process discussed above.

These changes have meant that international relations are also increasingly conducted through **public diplomacy**. The concept of public diplomacy can be defined as the process of creating an overall international image that enhances a country's ability to achieve diplomatic success. This is akin to propaganda. Public diplomacy includes traditional propaganda, but goes beyond that: it also includes what is actually said and done by political figures, practices of national self-promotion that are much the same as advertising, and other forms of public relations that are utilized by business. In practice, as we shall see, propaganda and public diplomacy overlap substantially. One scholar's concept of public diplomacy envisions a "theater of power" that is a "metaphor for the repertoire of visual and symbolic tools used by statesmen and diplomats." As players in the theater of power, leaders "must be sensitive to the impression they make on observers. . . . They surely [are] subject to the same sort of 'dramatic,' if not aesthetic, criticism of other kinds of public performances" (Cohen, 1987:i–ii).

There is also an element of public diplomacy that goes beyond presenting one's best face to involve distortions through propaganda and even outright lying. *Propaganda* is an attempt to gain influence through emotional techniques rather than logical discussion or presentation of empirical evidence. It is a process of appealing to emotions rather than minds by creating fear, doubt, sympathy, anger, or a variety of other feelings. Although the use of propaganda is as old as history, advances in communication, democratization, and the understanding of psychology have made propaganda increasingly important. In essence, if you cannot persuade another country's leaders through force or diplomacy, you can try to affect policy by persuading its people through propaganda.

By any standard, propaganda is big business. The United States, for one, operates or sponsors the Voice of America, Radio Free Europe/Radio Liberty, and Radio Martí. The U.S. Information Agency also produces Worldnet, a television service available globally, provides Web sites, and has other modern communications capabilities. Other efforts are contracted to private public relations firms. In one such effort in 2002 and 2003, the United States ran a $15 million television campaign in several Arab countries. Called "Shared Values," the media effort was meant to convince viewers that Americans were tolerant of Muslims and their beliefs and practices. In one spot, an Arab American female schoolteacher explained, "I wear a *hijab* (head covering) in the classroom where I teach. I have never had a child who thought it was weird or anything like that."[41]

Going beyond merely trying to present a good face is **disinformation**, propaganda that plants false facts. In one recent alleged example, the French ambassador wrote an open letter to the U.S. executive branch, Congress, and the media complaining of a "troubling—indeed, unacceptable—disinformation campaign aimed at sullying France's image and misleading the public." The ambassador said the stories charging France with supporting Saddam Hussein and other policies denied were false but were given to the press by "anonymous" U.S. officials. "The methods used by those propagating this disinformation," the ambassador objected, "have no place in the relationship between friends and allies. Ambassadors may disagree on important issues but should not engage in denigration and lies."[42] U.S. officials dismissed the accusation, but some analysts thought they rang true and that the stories most likely came out of the Defense Department. "It does look like the Pentagon is on its own private vendetta against France," said a respected American military analyst. "This just smacks of vengeance for pettiness' sake."[43]

The Conduct of Diplomacy

Diplomacy is a complex game of maneuvering in which the goal is to get other players to do what you want them to do. The players can number from two, in bilateral diplomacy, to many, in multilateral diplomacy. The rules of diplomacy are, at best, loose, and there is not just one mode of play. Instead, like all the most fascinating games, diplomacy is intricate and involves considerable strategy that can be employed in several ways. Thus, while diplomacy is often portrayed by an image of somber negotiations over highly polished wooden tables in ornate rooms, it is much more than that. Modern diplomacy is a far-ranging communications process.

Diplomacy as a Communications Process

In essence, diplomacy is a communications process. It involves communicating to one or more other countries or other actors what your goals, demands, requests, and other objectives are. Diplomacy also includes persuading other actors to support or comply with your objectives by communicating either the logic or morality of your point of view or by communicating the power that you can utilize to press for conformance with your goal, whether or not the other actor agrees. The diplomatic communication process is carried out through negotiation and signaling.

Negotiations occur when two or more parties communicate with one another, either directly or indirectly through an intermediary. It is very difficult to accomplish anything unless the different sides are talking. When the United States moved to quell the violence in the Middle East in early 2002, a major objective of Secretary of State Powell was to get the leadership of Israel and the leadership of the Palestinians back into negotiations with each other. Other than extremists in the Middle East, perhaps no one disagreed with Powell's assessment that "the world is in agreement that the solution will not be produced by terror or a response to terror—this is not going to get us there. What will get us there are political discussions and the sooner we can get them the better."[44]

Signaling entails saying or doing something with the intent of sending a message to another government. When leaders make bellicose or conciliatory speeches, when military forces are deployed or even used, when trade privileges are granted or sanctions invoked, or when diplomatic recognition is extended or relations are broken, these actions are, or at least should be, signals of attitude and intent to another country.

The U.S. invasion of Afghanistan in response to the 9/11 terror attacks was meant in part as a signal beyond the immediate issue. President Bush expressed worry about potential opponents doubting U.S. resolve, and it was this concern that urged Bush and his advisers to look for a response that not only dealt with the perpetrators of the terrorist attacks but also served as a signal to others. "Let's hit them hard," Bush told the chairman of the Joint Chiefs of Staff when he directed the general to send ground troops as well as warplanes and missiles against Afghanistan. "We want to signal this is a change from the past," the president explained. "We want to cause other countries like Syria and Iran to change their views [about supporting terrorism]."[45]

The Rules of Effective Diplomacy

Delineating the methods of diplomatic communications is easy. Utilizing them effectively is hard. There is no set formula that will ensure success. There are, however, several considerations that affect the chances of diplomatic success. We can examine some of these considerations by looking, in this section, at the rules of effective diplomacy, then, in the next section, by turning to the various options available for playing the great game of diplomacy. Some basic rules of effective diplomacy are:

Be realistic. It is important to have goals that match your ability to achieve them. "The test of a statesman," Kissinger has pointed out, "is his ability to recognize the real relationship of forces" (1970:47). Being realistic also means remembering that the other side, like yours, has domestic opponents. During discussions with North Korea in 1994, U.S. negotiator Robert Gallucci avoided pressing for nonvital, albeit desirable, concessions that, he said, "we recognized [as] serious [domestic] issues for [North Korea, but which] needed not to be undertaken immediately."[46] When critics charged that the Clinton administration was being too soft, a U.S. official noted pragmatically that making some concession was "better than [going to] war."[47]

Be careful about what you say. The experienced diplomat plans and weighs words carefully. Many observers feel that North Korea's antagonistic turn in 2002 may have been a defensive reaction to what it saw as threats and insults from President Bush. Associating North Korea with Nazi Germany by naming it a member of the axis of evil was inflammatory language. Another poor choice of words was President Bush's agitatedly telling a reporter, "I loathe Kim Jong Il [North Korea's leader]. I've got a visceral reaction to this guy," and "I just don't buy" objections that it would be a bad idea "if this guy were to topple."[48] It is probable that Pyongyang was alarmed by these rhetorical arrows combined with the simultaneous move toward military action against one of the other axis of evil countries, Iraq, with the announced goal of toppling its leader, Saddam Hussein.

Seek common ground. Finding common ground is a key to ending disputes peacefully. A first step to seeking common ground is to avoid seeing yourself as totally virtuous and your opponent as the epitome of evil. As a study of how peace is made and maintained puts it, "Wars are seldom a struggle between total virtue and vice. . . . But when so conceived, they become crusades that remove the possibility of finding common ground after the battles are over" (Kegley & Raymond, 1999:249).

Be flexible. While adhering to core principles may be important, being flexible on everything other than the most vital points is often wise. Discussing trying to work not only with North Korea but also with other countries in the region to resolve the nuclear confrontation, Secretary of State Powell had it right when he observed, "There are different approaches about this: Should you talk? When should you talk? Would you negotiate? What do you put on the table? Those are all issues that are worth debating."[49]

Understand the other side. Try to understand what it is your opponent really wants and to appreciate an opponent's perspective even if you do not agree with it. For example, the U.S. and international response to North Korea's resumption of its nuclear program in 2002 arguably should be tailored to what Pyongyang's real aims are. North Korea portrayed its move as defensive, with one of its diplomats accusing the United States of "hostile policies" and asserting his country's right to possess "devices to save us from a nuclear attack."[50] Another interpretation was that North Korea was playing a nuclear weapons card to try to get more aid, to force the United States to deal with it directly, and to force Washington to sign a nonaggression treaty. In the estimation of a former South Korean foreign minister, "The North Korean calculation is that [its nuclear program] increases the need to talk, from the United States' point of view, and it raises the cost of an agreement. They pile up all this leverage, or cards, and they figure each will cost something to undo to bring them back into the Non-Proliferation Treaty, to stop them from testing missiles, and to freeze their nuclear programs."[51] Still others saw North Korea as aggressively bent on becoming a nuclear weapons power. "It's still possible this is some sort of negotiating tactic," a former Clinton administration official commented, "but the weight of evidence is that they may have decided to start building up their nuclear weapons stockpile."[52]

Be patient. It is also important to bide your time. Being overly anxious can lead to concessions that are unwise and may convey weakness to an opponent. As a corollary, it is poor practice to set deadlines, for yourself or others, unless you are in a very strong position or you do not really want an agreement. Throughout the negotiations with North Korea, which were frustrating and included many setbacks, the Bush administration avoided timelines. As a former U.S. ambassador to South Korea noted, "There seems to be a recognition in the administration that what is happening in North Korea is unpleasant, and possibly destabilizing, but it is not something that is taking place at 60 miles an hour. It is going to take six to twelve months before the North Koreans can produce additional plutonium."[53]

Leave avenues of retreat open. It is axiomatic that even a rat will fight if trapped in a corner. The same is often true for countries. Call it honor, saving face, or prestige; it is important to leave yourself and your opponent an "out." Ultimatums, especially public ones, often lead to war. Whatever its other merits, President Bush's demand that Saddam Hussein leave Iraq or face war left no room for him to maneuver, and war followed 48 hours later.

Options for Conducting Diplomacy

While the above rules are solid guidelines to effective diplomacy, the practice is still more art than science. Therefore, effective diplomacy must tailor its approach to the situation and the opponent. To do this, diplomats must make choices about the channel, level, visibility, type of inducement, degree of precision, method of communication, and extent of linkage that they will use.

Conducting Direct or Indirect Negotiations

One issue that diplomats face is whether to negotiate directly with each other or indirectly through an intermediary. *Direct negotiations* have the advantage of avoiding the misinterpretations that an intermediary third party might cause. As in the old game of "Gossip," messages can become garbled. Direct negotiations are also quicker. An additional plus is that they can act as a symbol.

Indirect negotiations may also be advisable. During the confrontation with North Korea that began in 2002, the Bush administration resisted talking directly and bilaterally to Pyongyang because that would have handed a diplomatic victory to a country that the United States does not recognize. But Washington did reach out indirectly, with Secretary of State Colin Powell stressing to reporters, "We have a number of channels we're using" to communicate with Kim Jong Il's government.[54] For example, at one point North Korea dispatched two low-level diplomats to Santa Fe, New Mexico, to talk with Governor Bill Richardson, a former U.S. ambassador to the UN who had dealt with North Korea during the Clinton administration.

Direct contact symbolizes a level of legitimacy that a country may not wish to convey. Israel, for instance, long refused to negotiate openly and directly with the PLO. Indirect diplomacy can also avoid the embarrassment of a public rebuff by the other side. During the opening moves of exploring diplomatic relations in 1970, the United States and China sent oral messages through the "good offices" (friendly intermediaries) of Pakistan and Romania, and written messages were exchanged on photocopy paper with no letterheads or signatures.

Conducting High-Level or Low-Level Diplomacy

The higher the level of contact or the higher the level of the official making a statement, the more seriously will a message be taken. It implies a greater commitment, and there will be a greater reaction. Therefore, a diplomat must decide whether to communicate on a high or a low level.

High-level diplomacy has its advantages. Verbal and written statements by heads of government are noted seriously in other capitals. It was major news in diplomatic circles when in October 2003 President Bush took the occasion of a trip to Asia for an international conference to reassure North Korea and to hold out the prospect of a written commitment not to attack it. "I've said as plainly as I can say that we have no intention of invading North Korea," Bush said, adding that while signing a nonaggression treaty with North Korea was still "off the table. . . . Perhaps there are other ways to say exactly what I said publicly on paper."[55] This move, in turn, caused a shift in North Korea's position from demanding a formal treaty to being willing to meet with the United States and other countries to explore the president's intimated readiness to sign some document pledging nonaggression. The chance for a peaceful solution inched forward.

Low-level diplomacy is wiser at other times. Communications at a low level avoid overreaction and maintain flexibility. Dire threats can be issued as "trial balloons" by cabinet officers or generals and then, if later thought unwise, disavowed by higher political officers. During the Taiwan crisis of 2000, the principal leaders tended to avoid military threats, leaving that role to lesser officials. For example, an editorial in the Chinese military's newspaper, *Liberation Army Daily,* was far enough removed from official policy makers to warn provocatively that China would "spare no effort in a blood-soaked battle" if Taiwan declared independence.[56] From a position safely distant from the pinnacle of U.S. authority in the Oval Office, Undersecretary of Defense for Policy Walter Slocombe growled back that China would face "incalculable consequences" if it attacked Taiwan.[57]

Sometimes it is even prudent to use a representative who is not in the government at all. During the 2000 crisis it was diplomatically difficult for China and Taiwan officials to meet face-to-face, so, apparently, Jeremy Stone, president of the American Federation of Scientists and a close friend of Taiwan's new president, was used as an intermediary. Stone, who also has a diplomatic background in arms control, visited President-elect Chen in Taiwan. He then flew to Beijing as an "unofficial representative of Taipei," according to one Chinese official. "What we're trying to do is find ways to communicate," explained a Taiwanese source.[58]

A problem with such informal contacts is that they are sometimes suspect. In the months after the 2003 war with Iraq, reports surfaced of various last-minute peace feelers from Iraq through such intermediaries. Said one U.S. official who had been approached by a Lebanese businessman with such a purported offer, "I had doubts about whether there was a real offer, because the Iraqis had a lot of [other] ways to get in touch with the U.S."[59]

Using Coercion or Rewards to Gain Agreement

Yet another diplomatic choice is whether to brandish coercive sticks or proffer tempting carrots. To induce an opponent to react as you wish, is it better to offer rewards or to threaten punishment?

Coercive diplomacy can be effective when you have the power, will, and credibility to back it up. Just before the 1996 election in Taiwan, Beijing announced that it was going to "conduct joint ground, naval, and air exercises in and over a sea area near Taiwan."[60] This demonstration of military might included, among other things, China's firing six powerful missiles into the seas near Taiwan's two major ports, Kaohsiung and Keelung. Chinese television showed the launch of the M-9 and M-11 missiles, which can carry nuclear or conventional warheads. As breathlessly described by the Chinese narrator, "Milky-white missiles were seen deployed, nested in a mountain range. Officers and men were in full battle array. In the middle of the night, the command post issued the orders of operation. Amid the uproar of the launch came the reports: 'The first missile hits the target, the second missile hits the target.'"[61]

China regularly uses threats to deter Taiwan from declaring itself independent. Something of the intensity of Chinese feelings on the matter are captured here in this photograph of normally reserved Premier Zhu Rongji of China responding to a journalist's question about the possible use of force during the U.S.-China-Taiwan crisis in 2000.

For its part, the United States responded to the implied Chinese threat by utilizing its aircraft carriers. President Clinton ordered a major naval flotilla, centered around the carriers USS *Nimitz* and USS *Independence,* into the waters off Taiwan. The commanding admiral of the U.S. Seventh Fleet explained that "we do not want to see an escalation. China has said [it is] not going to attack Taiwan, and that's exactly what we want to see happen."[62]

There are also a number of drawbacks to coercive diplomacy. If it does not work, then those who have threatened force face an unhappy choice. On the one hand, not carrying out threats creates an image of weakness that may well embolden the opponent in the crisis at hand. Opponents in other ongoing and future confrontations may also be encouraged. On the other hand, putting one's military might and money where one's mouth is costs lives and dollars and is not necessarily successful either. Even if coercion does work, it may entail a long-term commitment that was not originally planned or desired. The Persian Gulf War with Iraq ended in February 1991, but U.S. forces have remained enmeshed in the region and fought and won another war with Iraq in 2003. Yet as of this writing a year later, the United States remains mired in the region, unable to either achieve stability or to withdraw, suffering mounting casualties on a near daily basis, and spending tens of billions of dollars on a policy that has become increasingly unpopular with the American public.

There are many times when *offers of rewards* may be a more powerful inducement than coercion. Threats may lead to war, with high costs and uncertain results. Instead, it may be possible to "buy" what you cannot "win." One song in the movie *Mary Poppins* includes the wisdom that "a spoonful of sugar helps the medicine go down," and an increase in aid, a trade concession, a state visit, or some other tangible or symbolic reward may induce agreement. Various forms of aid quelled the North Korean nuclear crisis in 1994, and in 2003 rewards again appeared to be the key to easing renewed tensions. At first the Bush administration refused to consider incentives, arguing that would be rewarding Pyongyang for reneging on the 1994 agreement. But the countries that the United States was relying on to help mediate viewed the situation differently. In the words of one Chinese diplomat, progress "depends on if the United States can have . . . more specific proposals to induce North Korea back to the negotiating table."[63] Soon the U.S. administration was taking tentative steps in that direction, with the president shifting his position from refusing to consider incentives to saying that North Korea would have to stop its nuclear program before the United States would offer incentives. "If they so choose to do so," Bush said publicly, then a "bold initiative" may be possible to halt "the suffering of the North Korean people."[64]

Often, the best diplomacy mixes carrots and sticks. Economic sanctions and other diplomatic sticks helped topple the regime of Slobodan Milosevic in October 2000. The new government refused, however, to turn him over for trial by the war crimes tribunal sitting in The Hague. What seemingly turned the trick was proffering an exceptionally attractive bunch of carrots to Belgrade. In an unspoken but obvious deal, the Yugoslav government extradited Milosevic in June 2001, and within hours the United States, the European Union, and other donor countries and organizations (such as the World Bank) meeting in Brussels pledged $1.28 billion in aid to the country.

Economic incentives are one diplomatic tool. This Dutch editorial cartoon of former Yugoslavian president Slobodan Milosevic wearing prison garb and being hanged by "donor aid" represents the widely held, and probably accurate, assumption that the decision of Yugoslavia's government to extradite him was taken in part to get international financial aid. Within hours of Milosevic's departure under guard for trial in the Netherlands in June 2001, Western donor countries offered $1.28 billion in aid to Belgrade.

Being Precise or Being Intentionally Vague

Most diplomatic experts stress the importance of being precise when communicating. There are times, however, when purposeful vagueness may be in order.

Precision is a hallmark of diplomacy. Being precise in both written and verbal communications helps avoid misunderstandings. It can also indicate true commitment, especially if it comes from the national leader.

Vagueness may at times be a better strategy. Being vague may paper over irreconcilable differences. "The Saudis have a nice way of doing things" when they do not wish to agree, says one U.S. official. "They say, 'we'll consider it.' It is not their style to say no."[65] Lack of precision also can also allow a country to retreat if necessary or permit it to avoid being too provocative. During the Taiwan elections in 1996 and 2000, the United States accomplished both goals by refusing to say exactly what it would do if China attacked Taiwan. When in 1996 a reporter asked Secretary of State Warren Christopher what would occur, he pushed aside the possibility of a Sino-American war as mere "operational details."[66]

Communicating by Word or Deed

Diplomacy utilizes both words and actions to communicate. Each method has its advantages.

Oral and written communications, either direct or through public diplomacy, are appropriate for negotiations and also can be a good signaling strategy. The possibility that North Korea's recent resumption of its nuclear weapons program could be defensive, based on fear of a U.S. attack, led to numerous public and private assurances that Pyongyang's concern was groundless. As noted, President Bush indicated that the United States has "no intention" of attacking North Korea, and Secretary of State Powell has added, "We have made it clear we have no aggressive intent."[67]

Signaling by action is often more dramatic than verbal signaling and it has its uses. There are drawbacks, though, because it is harder to retreat from dramatic deeds than from words or even subtle acts. When, in 1961, the East Germans and Soviets threatened to blockade Berlin, President John F. Kennedy took the risky step of going there and, before a throng of West Berliners, proclaiming himself a symbolic fellow citizen. "*Ich bin ein Berliner,*" Kennedy's words rang out. Both sides understood the import of the president's putting his personal honor on the line, and the crisis eased. Germans on both sides of the wall also got a good chuckle, because the president's speechwriters had made a minor grammatical error. "*Ich bin Berliner*" (I am a Berliner) is what he had wanted to say. By adding the "*ein,*" however, Kennedy had inadvertently changed the meaning of *Berliner* from citizen to jelly doughnut, locally called a *berliner.* Thus what the leader of the free world actually declared was "I am a jelly doughnut."[68]

Did You Know That:

Adding to the pastry faux pas of President Kennedy inadvertently calling himself a jelly doughnut in German, President Boris Yeltsin of Russia once fumbled in his English when he greeted a later U.S. president with "Welcome, Blin Clinton!" *Blin* means pancake in Russian.[1]

Various military actions, ranging from alerting forces, through deploying them, to limited demonstrations of force, can also be utilized. Although in the end the signal did not pressure Iraq into making concessions, the Pentagon was clearly broadcasting U.S. intent when in late 2002 it almost certainly leaked a classified report in which Secretary of Defense Donald Rumsfeld ordered U.S. forces deployed to the Persian Gulf area. Since the military usually prefers to mask its movements, many analysts concluded that the extraordinarily detailed report of aircraft carriers, Army divisions, bomber and fighter units, and other military elements being deployed was meant as a message to Iraq. An anonymous Defense Department official admitted as much, commenting, "We're going to continue to deploy forces in a steady and deliberate buildup to help the diplomatic process."[69]

By reverse logic, it is also possible to signal by not doing something. For all its frequently red-hot rhetoric, North Korea has not tested a nuclear weapon. Doing so, one analyst commented in 2003, would have proven that it did have the weapons it claimed, but, he added, "I think even they realize that would cut off all their options for a diplomatic solution."[70] In a similar way, the United States did not boost its forces in South Korea nor send the Seventh Fleet with its nuclear weapons–capable warplanes and cruise missiles near the North Korean coast.

Linking Issues or Treating Them Separately

A persistent dispute is whether a country should deal with other countries on an issue-by-issue basis or link issues together as a basis for a general orientation toward the other country. Advocates of *linking issues* argue that it is inappropriate to have normal relations on some matters with regimes that are hostile and repressive. Those who favor *treating issues separately* claim that doing so allows progress on some issues and keeps channels of communications and influence open.

During the crisis in 2000, China's stand on Taiwan became enmeshed with the fate of China's permanent normal trade relations with the United States and with China's admission to the WTO. A Chinese foreign ministry official objected that his country "firmly opposes any attempt to link these issues," and claimed that China's stand on Taiwan and "the issue of normal trade relations [are] two entirely separate issues."[71] That protest was in vain, however, and the issues remained tied together.

On a more general basis, linkage remains an ongoing and inconsistent issue in U.S. foreign policy. President Clinton argued that China's poor human rights record and authoritarian form of government should not be linked to China's trade status. One reason to delink the issues, according to Clinton, was that regular interaction would be a "force for change in China, exposing China to our ideas and ideals." The president also argued that "our engagement with China serves American interests . . . [by promoting] stability in Asia, preventing the spread of weapons of mass destruction, combating international crime and drug trafficking, [and] protecting the environment."[72] Not mentioned, but a factor, were the billions of dollars in U.S. exports and investments that go to China.

Cuba has been another matter, though, and delinkage of issues has not extended to that country. There are a number of U.S. measures, including the Helms-Burton Act (1996), that institute economic sanctions on Cuba and foreign companies doing business with Cuba in an attempt to weaken the government of President Fidel Castro. Why delinking would promote change in China and not in Cuba remains unexplained.

Maximizing or Minimizing a Dispute

Diplomats face a choice over whether to put a confrontation in a broad or narrow context. *Maximizing a dispute* by invoking national survival, world peace, or some other major principle may be advantageous because doing so increases credibility. During the 1996 Taiwan Strait crisis, China maximized the stakes by having the country's second-ranking official, Premier Li Peng, publicly depict the matter as a "core principle" involving China's "territorial integrity and the cause of reunification."[73] The drawback of maximizing a dispute is that it makes it very hard to back away from confrontation if a settlement is not reached. President Bush maximized the stakes of the crisis with Iraq. Speaking before the UN General Assembly in September 2002, he portrayed the United States, and indeed the world, as "challenged today by outlaw groups and regimes that accept no law of morality and have no limit to their violent ambitions," and he singled out Iraq's "weapons of mass murder" as the single greatest global threat.[74] That threat helped persuade Congress and the American public to back war with Iraq. Bush would have been vulnerable domestically to the charge that he did not end the threat unless the Iraqis totally capitulated to U.S. demands or were defeated in a war to remove the threat (which ironically, did not exist).

Minimizing a dispute may work positively to avoid overreactions. Once the confrontation with North Korea heated up in 2002, the Bush administration sought to cool the atmosphere by, among other things, refusing to call it a crisis. Describing it as the "C-word," one U.S. official said, "We are not thinking in those terms," and the administration labeled the North Korean decision to restart its nuclear facility as merely "regrettable," rather than using a more heated term. Some observes applauded the U.S. restraint, but others criticized it. "By feigning nonchalance, the Bush administration risks encouraging a dangerous regime to step even further forward," charged one critic, and he portrayed the use of the word "regrettable" as "the kind of word you use when the soup isn't very good before dinner."[75]

A final note is that despite the recitation of diplomatic rules and the analysis of the advantages and disadvantages of various diplomatic options in the preceding two sections, there is no substitute for skill and wisdom. Understanding how the game ought to be played does not always produce a win on the playing field of sports or a success at the negotiating table of diplomacy. Certainly you are advantaged if you know the fundamentals, but beyond that, individual capacity and field savvy provide the margin of victory.

Chapter Summary

National Power: The Foundation of National Diplomacy

1. National diplomacy is the process of trying to advance a country's national interest by applying power assets to attempt to persuade other countries to give way.
2. Power is the foundation of diplomacy in a conflictual world. National power is the sum of a country's assets that enhance its ability to get its way even when opposed by others with different interests and goals.
3. Measuring power is especially difficult. The efforts to do so have not been very successful, but they do help us see many of the complexities of analyzing the characteristics of power. These characteristics include the facts that power is dynamic, both objective and subjective, relative, situational, and multidimensional.

The Elements of Power

4. The major elements of a country's power can be roughly categorized as those that constitute (1) its national core, (2) its national infrastructure, (3) its national economy, and (4) its military. The core and infrastructure are discussed here and form the basis for economic and military power, which are analyzed in later chapters.
5. The national core consists of a country's geography, its people, and its government.
6. The national infrastructure consists of a country's technological sophistication, its transportation system, and its information and communications capabilities.

The Nature of Diplomacy

7. The functions of diplomacy include advancing the national interest through such methods as observing and reporting, negotiating, symbolically representing, intervening, and propagandizing.
8. Diplomacy does not occur in a vacuum. Instead it is set in the international system, in a specific diplomatic environment (hostile, adversarial, coalition, and mediation diplomacy), and in a domestic context.

The Evolution of Diplomacy

9. Diplomacy is an ancient art, and some of the historical functions of diplomacy are still important. Diplomacy, however, has also changed dramatically during the past century. Seven characteristics describe the new approach to diplomacy: expanded geographic scope, multilateral diplomacy, parliamentary maneuvering, democratized diplomacy, open diplomacy, leader-to-leader communications through summit meetings, and public diplomacy.
10. These changes reflect the changes in the international system and in domestic political processes. Some of the changes have been beneficial, but others have had negative consequences. At the least, diplomacy has become more complex with the proliferation of actors and options. It has also become more vital, given the possible consequences should it fail.

The Conduct of Diplomacy

11. Diplomacy is a communication process that has three main elements. The first is negotiating through direct or indirect discussions between two or more countries. The second is signaling. The third is public diplomacy.
12. Good diplomacy is an art, but it is not totally freestyle, and there are general rules that increase the chances for diplomatic success. Among the cautions are to be realistic, to be careful about what you say, to seek common ground, to try to understand the other side, to be patient, and to leave open avenues of retreat.
13. There are also a wide variety of approaches or options in diplomacy. Whether contacts should be direct or indirect, what level of contact they should involve, what rewards or coercion should be offered, how precise or vague messages should be, whether to communicate by message or deed, whether issues should be linked or dealt with separately, and the wisdom of maximizing or minimizing a dispute are all questions that require careful consideration.

For a chapter quiz, interactive activities, web links, PowerWeb articles, and much more, visit **www.mhhe.com/rourke10/** and go to chapter 8. Or, while accessing the site, click on Course-Wide Content and view recent international relations articles in the *New York Times*.

Key Terms

adversarial diplomacy
bilateral diplomacy
coalition diplomacy
coercive diplomacy
coercive power
democratized diplomacy
disinformation
hostile diplomacy
mediation diplomacy
multilateral diplomacy
objective power
open diplomacy
parliamentary diplomacy
persuasive power
power
public diplomacy
relative power
situational power
subjective power
summit meetings
two-level game theory
zero-sum game

CHAPTER

9

International Law and Morality: An Alternative Approach

FUNDAMENTALS OF INTERNATIONAL LAW AND MORALITY
- The Primitive Nature of International Law
- The Growth of International Law
- The Practice of International Law
- The Fundamentals of International Morality

THE INTERNATIONAL LEGAL SYSTEM
- The Philosophical Roots of Law
- How International Law Is Made
- Adherence to the Law
- Adjudication of the Law

APPLYING INTERNATIONAL LAW AND MORALITY
- Law and Justice in a Multicultural World
- Applying International Law and Morality to States
- Applying International Law and Morality to Individuals
- The Prudent Application of Law and Morality

THE FUTURE OF INTERNATIONAL LAW AND MORALITY

CHAPTER SUMMARY

KEY TERMS

Which is the wiser here, Justice or Iniquity?

—William Shakespeare, *Measure for Measure*

The law hath not been dead, though it hath slept.

—William Shakespeare, *Hamlet*

I establish law and justice in the land.

—Hammurabi, king of Babylon, ca. 1780 B.C.

Power not ruled by law is a menace.

—Arthur J. Goldberg, U.S. Supreme Court justice

CHAPTER OBJECTIVES

After completing this chapter, you should be able to:

- Discuss the dynamic nature of law by addressing the concept of a primitive but evolving legal system.
- Evaluate the effectiveness of international law.
- Distinguish between the different sources of international law.
- Discuss the role of morality in the international system and in international law.
- List the four essential elements of the international legal system.
- Identify and examine the roots and characteristics of international law.
- Discuss adherence to international law.
- Analyze the process of adjudication in international law.
- Enumerate problems in applying international law to different cultures.
- Identify the international legal issues that developed during the 20th century and explain how changes in the world system have affected these issues.
- Illustrate how and why international law has been applied increasingly to individuals rather than only to states.
- Analyze issues of morality in the modern international legal system and the role of morality in a future system.

This chapter focuses on international law and morality in the conduct of world politics as an alternative to the power-based diplomatic pursuit of self-interest discussed in chapter 8. It would be naive to ignore the reality that most global actors emphasize their own interests. However, this is also true in domestic systems. What is different between global and domestic systems is not so much the motives of the actors as the fact that domestic systems place greater restraints on the pursuit of self-interest than the international system does.

Legal systems are one thing that restrains the power-based pursuit of self-interest in a domestic system. Certainly, powerful individuals and groups have advantages in every domestic system. Rules are broken and the guilty, especially if they can afford a high-priced attorney, sometimes escape punishment. Still, laws in the United States cannot overtly discriminate under the "equal protection" clause of the Fourteenth Amendment to the Constitution; for example, an attorney is provided to indigent defendants in criminal cases. Thus, the law somewhat evens the playing field.

Morality is a second thing that restrains the role of power in domestic systems. We are discussing what is "right" here, not just what is legal. Whether the word is *moral, ethical, fair,* or *just,* there is a greater sense in domestic systems than there is in the international system that appropriate codes of conduct exist, that the ends do not always justify the means, and that those who violate the norms should suffer penalties. Surely, there is no domestic system in which everyone acts morally. Yet the sense of morality and justice that citizens in stable domestic systems have does influence their behavior.

What this means is that since it is possible to restrain power politics in the domestic system by the creation of legal systems and through a greater emphasis on what is moral and fair, then it is theoretically possible to use the same standards to curb the unbridled pursuit of interests in the international system. Accomplishing that will require major changes in attitudes and practices, but it can be done.

Fundamentals of International Law and Morality

What actors may and may not legitimately do is based in both international and domestic law systems on a combination of expectations, rules, and practices that help govern behavior. We will explore the fundamental nature of these legal systems and moral codes by looking first at the primitive nature, growth, and current status of international law; then by turning to issues of morality (Ku & Diehl, 1998).

The Primitive Nature of International Law

No legal system, domestic or international, emerges full blown. Each one evolves, advancing from a primitive level to more sophisticated levels. As such, any legal system can be placed on an evolutionary scale ranging from primitive to modern. Note that modern does not mean finished; people in the future may shake their heads in disbelief over how rudimentary our current legal systems are. This concept of a *primitive but evolving legal system* is important to understanding international law.

The current international legal system falls toward the primitive end of the evolutionary scale of legal systems. First, as a primitive law system, the international system does not have a formal rule-making (legislative) process. Instead, codes of behavior are derived from custom or from explicit agreements among actors. Second, there is little or no established authority to judge or punish violations of law. Primitive societies, domestic or international, have no police or courts. Instead they rely on rely on negotiation or perhaps mediation to resolve disputes and on self-help, including violence, to settle disputes that elude peaceful resolution.

Viewing international law as a primitive legal system has two benefits. One is that we can see that international law does exist, even if it is not as developed as we might wish. The second benefit is it allows us to see that international society and its law may evolve to a higher order, as have domestic systems.

The injustices of war and other aspects of international relations led the Dutch jurist and statesman Hugo Grotius (1583–1645) to look for rules to govern conflict and other interactions among states. This effort earned him the title "father of international law."

The Growth of International Law

The beginning of international law coincides with the origins of the states and their need to define and protect their status and to order their relations. Gradually, elements of ancient Jewish, Greek, and Roman practice combined with newer Christian concepts and also with custom and practice to form the beginning of an international system of law. A number of theorists were also important to the genesis of international law. The most famous was the Dutch thinker Hugo Grotius (1583–1645), whose study *De Jure Belli et Pacis* (On the Law of War and Peace) earned him the title "father of international law." Grotius and others discussed and debated the sources of international law, its role in regulating the relations of states, and its application to specific circumstances such as the justification for and conduct of war. From this base, international law expanded and changed slowly over the intervening centuries, as the interactions between the states grew and as the needs and expectations of the international community became more sophisticated.

During the last century or so, a rapid expansion of concern with international law and its practical importance has occurred. Increasing international interaction and interdependence have significantly expanded the need for rules to govern a host of functional areas such as trade, finance, travel, and communications (Armstrong, 1999). Similarly, our awareness of our ability to destroy ourselves and our environment, and of the suffering of victims of human rights abuses, has led to lawmaking treaties on such subjects as genocide, nuclear testing, use of the oceans, and human rights. Even the most political of all activities, war and other aspects of national security, have increasingly become the subject of international law. Aggressive war, for example, is outside the pale of the law. The UN's response of authorizing sanctions and then force against Iraq after that country invaded Kuwait in 1990 reflected that (Linklater, 1999). So did the refusal of most countries to support what they saw as an unjustified U.S.-led invasion of Iraq in 2003.

The Practice of International Law

One of the charges that realists make against international law is that it exists only in theory, not in practice. As evidence, critics cite ongoing, largely unpunished examples of "lawlessness" such as war and human rights abuses. The flaw in this argument is that it does not prove its point. In the first place, international law is effective in many areas. As one scholar notes, "the reality as demonstrated through their behavior is that states do accept international law as law, and, even more significant, is the vast majority of instances they . . . obey it" (Joyner, 2000:243). Furthermore, the fact that law does not cover *all* problem areas and that it is not *always* followed does not disprove its existence. There is, after all, a substantial crime rate in the United States, but does that mean there is no law?

International law is *most effective* in governing the rapidly expanding range of transnational **functional relations.** Functional interactions are those that involve "low politics," a term that designates such things as trade, diplomatic rules, and communications.

International law is *least effective* when applied to "high-politics" issues such as national security relations between sovereign states. When vital interests are involved, governments still regularly bend international law to justify their actions rather than alter their actions to conform to the law.

This does not mean, however, that the law never influences political decisions. To the contrary, there is a growing sensitivity to international legal standards, especially insofar as they reflect prevailing international norms. Both international law and world values, for instance, are strongly opposed to states unilaterally resorting to war except in immediate self-defense. Violations such as Iraq's invasion of Kuwait still occur, but they are met with mounting global condemnation and even counterforce. Now even countries as powerful as the United States regularly seek UN authorization to act in cases such as Afghanistan in 2001 and Iraq in 2003 when not long ago they would have acted on their own initiative. It is true that the United States and Great Britain ultimately went ahead in 2003 without UN support, but that does not disprove the existence of the norm against unilateral war. Indeed, the widespread condemnation of the invasion tends to show the norm does exist, and the ability of the United States to ignore the UN means only that power remains a key factor in the international system.

The Fundamentals of International Morality

Concepts of moral behavior may stem from religious beliefs, from secular ideologies or philosophies, from the standard of equity (what is fair), or from the practice of a society. We will see in our discussion of roots of international law that what a society considers moral behavior sometimes becomes law. At other times, legal standards are gradually adopted by a society as moral standards. Insofar as moral behavior remains an imperative of conscience rather than law, we can consider morality in a broad sense. Distinctions can be made between moral, ethical, and humanitarian standards and behavior, but for our purposes here, the three terms—morals, ethics, and humanitarianism—are used interchangeably.

It would be wrong—given recurring war, gnawing human deprivation, persistent human rights violations, and debilitating environmental abuse—to imagine that morality is a predominant global force. Yet it would also be erroneous to use these ills to argue that law and morality do not play a role. Instead, as one scholar describes the balance between what is ideal and real, "Contrary to what the skeptics assert, norms do indeed matter. But norms do not necessarily matter in the ways or often to the extent that their proponents have argued" (Legro, 1997:31). This state of affairs is changing, though, through a growing body of ethical norms that help determine the nature of the international system. Progress is slow and inconsistent, but it exists. American and British forces did not drop nuclear weapons on Iraq in 2003, even though it arguably could have saved time, money, and the lives of American and British troops by doing so. Many countries give foreign aid to less developed countries. National leaders, not just philosophers and clergy, regularly discuss and sometimes even make decisions based on human rights.

Consumers have rallied to the environmentalist cause to protect dolphins by purchasing only cans of tuna on which dolphin-safe logos are featured. Thus the reality is that world politics operates neither in a legal vacuum nor in a moral void.

The International Legal System

International law, like any legal system, is based on four critical considerations: the philosophical roots of law, how laws are made, when and why the law is obeyed (adherence), and how legal disputes are decided (adjudication).

The Philosophical Roots of Law

Before considering the mechanics of the legal system, it is important to inquire into the roots of law. Ideas about what is right and what should be the law do not spring from thin air. Rather, they are derived from sources both external and internal to the society they regulate.

External roots, those outside a society, provide one source of law. Some laws spring from sources external to a society. Those who look to external sources believe that some higher, metaphysical standard of conduct should govern the affairs of humankind. An important ramification of this position is that there is, or ought to be, one single system of law that governs all people.

Those who believe in the external sources can be subdivided into two schools. The **ideological/theological school of law** is one. This school of thought holds that law is derived from an overarching ideology or theology. For instance, a substantial part of international legal theory extends back to early Western proponents of international law who relied on Christian doctrine for their standards. The writings of Saint Augustine and Saint Thomas Aquinas on the law of war are examples. There are also long-standing elements of law and scholarship in Islamic, Buddhist, and other religious traditions that serve as a foundation for just international conduct.

The **naturalist school of law** relies on a second source of external principles. This view holds that humans, by nature, have certain rights and obligations. The English philosopher John Locke argued in *Two Treatises of Government* (1690) that there is "a law of nature" that "teaches all mankind, who will but consult it, that all [people] being equal and independent [in the state of nature], no one ought to harm another in his life, health, liberty, or possessions." Since countries are collectives of individuals, and the world community is a collective of states and individuals, natural law's rights and obligations also apply to the global stage and form the basis for international law.

Critics of the theory of external sources of law contend that standards based on ideology or theology can lead to oppression. The problems with natural law, critics charge, are both that it is vague and that it contains such an emphasis on individualism that it almost precludes any sense of communitarian welfare. If a person's property is protected by natural law, then, for instance, it is hard to justify taking any individual's property through taxes levied by the government without the individual's explicit agreement.

Internal roots, those from within the society, are a second basis of law. Some legal scholars reject the idea of divine or naturalist roots and, instead, focus on the customs and practices of society. This is the **positivist school of law**, which advocates that law reflects society and the way people want that society to operate. Therefore, according to positivist principles, law is and ought to be the product of the codification or formalization of a society's standards.

Critics condemn the positivist approach as amoral and sometimes immoral, in that it may legitimize immoral, albeit common, beliefs and behavior of a society as a whole or of its dominant class. These critics would say, for instance, that slavery was once widespread and widely accepted, but it was never moral or lawful, by the standards of either divine principle or natural law.

How International Law Is Made

Countries usually make domestic law through a constitution (constitutional law) or by a legislative body (statutory law). In practice, law is also established through judicial decisions (interpretation), which set guidelines (precedent) for later decisions by the courts. Less influential sources of law are custom (common law) and what is fair (equity).

Compared to its domestic equivalent, modern international lawmaking is much more decentralized. There are, according to the Statute of the International Court of Justice, four sources of law: international treaties, international custom, the general principles of law, and judicial decisions and scholarly legal writing. Some students of international law would tentatively add a fifth source: resolutions and other pronouncements of the UN General Assembly. These five rely primarily on the positivist approach but, like domestic law, include elements of both external and internal sources of law.

International treaties are the primary source of international law. A primary advantage of treaties is that they **codify**, or write down, the law. Agreements between states are binding according to the doctrine of ***pacta sunt servanda*** (treaties are to be served/carried out). All treaties are binding on those countries that are party to them (have signed and ratified or otherwise given their legal consent). Moreover, it is possible to argue that some treaties are also applicable to nonsignatories. Multilateral treaties, those signed by more than two states, are an increasingly important source of international law. When a large number of states agree to a principle, that norm begins to take on system-wide legitimacy. The 1948 Convention on the Prevention and Punishment of the Crime of Genocide, for example, has been ratified by most states. Some would argue, therefore, that genocide has been "recognized" and "codified" as a violation of international law and that this standard of conduct is binding on all states regardless of whether or not they have formally agreed to the treaty. Now people are being tried, convicted, and sentenced for genocide, as we shall discuss presently.

Did You Know That:

The word *genocide* was coined by a Jewish jurist, Raphael Lemkin, who was born in Poland and worked for the U.S. War Department during World War II. The word is derived from the Greek word *genos* (race, tribe) and the Latin suffix *cide* (to kill). Lemkin used the word in his book *Axis Rule in Occupied Europe* to include the partial, as well as complete, extermination of a people or their culture and sense of identity.

International custom is the second most important source of international law. The old, and now supplanted, rule that territorial waters extend three miles from the shore grew from the distance a cannon could fire. If you were outside the range of land-based artillery, then you were in international waters. Maritime rules of the road and diplomatic practice are two other important areas of law that grew out of custom. Sometimes, long-standing custom is eventually codified in treaties. An example is the Vienna Convention on Diplomatic Relations of 1961, which codified many existing rules of diplomatic standing and practice.

General principles of law are a third source of international law. The ancient Roman concept of *jus gentium* (the law of peoples) is the foundation of the general principles of law. By this standard, the International Court of Justice (ICJ) applies "the general principles of law recognized by civilized nations." Although such language is vague, it has its benefits. It encompasses "external" sources of law, such as the idea that freedom of religion and freedom from attack are among the inherent rights of people. More than any other standard, it is for violating these general principles that Slobodan Milosevic, the former president of Yugoslavia, was brought to trial in 2002 at the international tribunal in the Netherlands. According to the United Nations, the charges against Milosevic included nine counts of violating specific treaty law, the 1949 Geneva Conventions. But

Multilateral treaties are a prime source of international law. The four treaties (1949) and two supplementary protocols (1977) that collectively are called the Geneva Conventions form an important part of the law of war. Too often those rules have been ignored, as they allegedly were by President Charles Taylor of Liberia. But the principle expressed by the sign seen here on a wall in Liberia's capital, Monrovia, is increasingly being enforced. A month after this picture was taken in July 2003, Taylor was forced to flee to Nigeria, where he is in exile. That country's president announced that Taylor may be extradited to Sierra Leone for trial by the international tribunal that has indicted him.

the indictment was also based on *jus gentium,* including "13 counts of violations of the laws or customs of war," such as "murder; torture; cruel treatment; [and] wanton destruction of villages . . . not justified by military necessity"; and "10 counts of crimes against humanity," such as "persecutions on political, racial or religious grounds; extermination; murder; imprisonment; torture; [and] inhumane acts (forcible transfers)."[1]

Judicial decisions and scholarly writing also add to a system's body of law. In many domestic systems, legal interpretations by courts set precedent according to the doctrine of *stare decisis* (let the decision stand). This doctrine is specifically rejected in Article 59 of the Statute of the International Court of Justice, but as one scholar points out, "The fact is that all courts . . . rely upon and cite each other [as precedent] abundantly in their decisions" (Levi, 1991:50). Thus, the rulings of the ICJ, other international tribunals, and even domestic courts when they apply international law, help shape the body of law that exists. One scholar argues that this has created a "global community of courts," whose judges "are in many ways creating their own version of [an international legal] system—a bottom-up version . . . shaped by a deep respect for each other's competences and the ultimate need, in a world of law, to rely on reason rather than force" (Slaughter, 2003: 219). Judicial review is another possible role of international judicial bodies, and one that is exercised by many domestic courts. This is a court's authority to rule on whether the actions of the executive and legislative branches violate the constitution or other charter under which the court operates. The European Court of Justice has exercised that authority, and some scholars believe that the ICJ is moving cautiously toward a similar stand.

Two crucial factors in international law are how the law is enforced and what encourages compliance. These factors differ over time and for different societies.

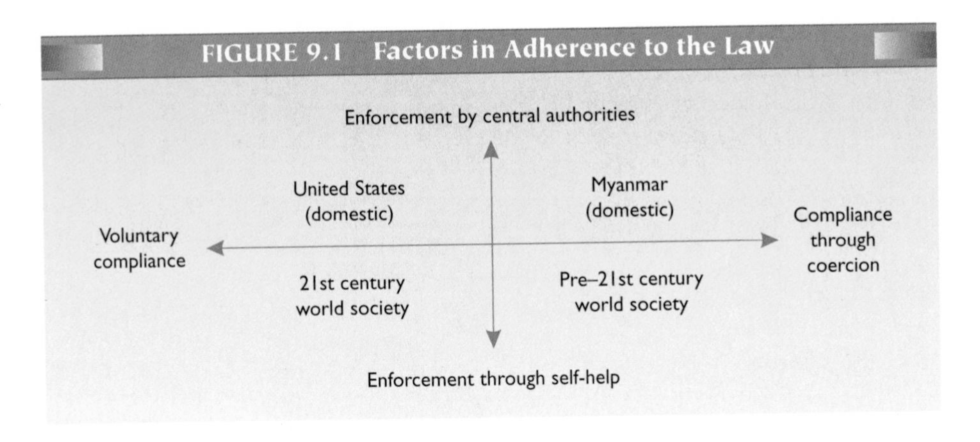

International representative assemblies are arguably a fifth source of international law. Compared to the generally recognized preceding four sources of international law, the idea that laws can come from the UN General Assembly or any other international representative assembly is much more controversial. Clearly, to date, international law is not statutory. The General Assembly cannot legislate international law the way that a national legislature does. Yet, UN members are bound by treaty to abide by some of the decisions of the General Assembly and the Security Council, which makes these bodies quasi-legislative. Some scholars contend that resolutions approved by overwhelming majorities of the General Assembly constitute international law because such votes reflect international custom and/or the general principles of law. We may, then, be seeing the beginnings of legislated international law, but, at best, it is in its genesis. Certainly, UN resolutions and mandates often are not followed, but some would argue that this means that the law is being violated rather than that the law does not exist.

Adherence to the Law

Adherence to the law is a third essential element of any legal system. What makes the law effective in any legal system is a mixture of compliance and enforcement. As Figure 9.1 represents, people obey the law because of a mixture of voluntary and coerced compliance, and they enforce the law through a mixture of enforcement by central authorities and enforcement through self-help (Hurd, 1999).

Compliance with the Law

Obedience to the law in any legal system—whether it is international or domestic, primitive or sophisticated—is based on a mix of voluntary compliance and coercion. *Voluntary compliance* occurs when the subjects obey the law because they accept its legitimacy. This means that people abide by rules because they accept the authority of the institution that made the rules (say, a legislature or a court) and/or agree that the rules are necessary for the reasonable conduct of society. *Coercion* is the process of gaining compliance through threats of violence, imprisonment, economic sanction, or other punishment.

Any society's legal system can be placed somewhere along the compliance scale between complete reliance on voluntary compliance and complete reliance on coercion. Voluntary compliance is usually more important, but the mixture of that and coercion varies widely among societies. Americans tend to obey the law voluntarily; in Myanmar (Burma) obedience to the laws of the country's military junta is primarily a function of force.

The overall degree of compliance to the law is lower in the international system than in most domestic systems, but insofar as adherence to international law has grown, it has been based more on voluntary compliance than on coercion. Legitimacy, based primarily on pragmatism, is the key to international voluntary compliance. Countries recognize the need for a system that is made predictable by adherence to laws. As we saw earlier, functional international law governing day-to-day relations between states has expanded rapidly because of their need to regulate complex international interactions such as trade, finance, communications, and diplomacy. Legitimacy based on norms is less well established, but it has also grown. Aggression, violation of human rights, and other unacceptable practices still occur, but they increasingly meet with widespread international and domestic condemnation. Unilateral military action is, for example, becoming ever more difficult for a country to launch without meeting severe criticism. Such events continue to occur, as the U.S.-led invasion of Iraq in 2003 indicates. But they occur much less often than they once did. Moreover, even countries determined to go to war will almost always make a concerted effort to gain international authorization, as the diplomacy leading up to the 2003 war again shows. It is also the case that failure to win support subjects a country, no matter how just it thinks its cause, to extensive international criticism, which, yet again, was amply evident in global reactions to the 2003 war against Iraq. A very powerful country like the United States can ignore international opposition in the short run, but there may be a price to pay later. Washington found this out when in the aftermath of the war it tried to get other countries to help shoulder the financial and military burden of occupying and rebuilding Iraq.

Enforcement of the Law

In all legal systems, enforcement relies on a combination of *enforcement through self-help* and *enforcement by central authorities*. Primitive societies rely primarily on self-help and on mediation to enforce laws and norms. As a primitive society evolves, it begins to develop enforcement authorities. Domestic systems have done this, and they rely mostly on a central authority to provide law enforcement organizations (usually the police) and sanctions (fines, prison) to compel compliance with the law. Still, even advanced legal systems recognize the legitimacy of such self-help doctrines as self-defense.

As a primitive society, the global community system continues to focus on self-help for enforcement, and neither law enforcement organizations nor sanctions are well developed at the international level. Yet there is observable movement along the evolutionary path toward a more centralized system. For example, war criminals were punished after World War II. More recently, indictments have been handed down for war crimes in Bosnia and elsewhere, and some of the accused have been tried, convicted, and imprisoned. Economic and diplomatic sanctions are becoming more frequent and are sometimes successful. Armed enforcement by central authorities is even less common and rudimentary. The UN-authorized military action against Iraq in 1991 and the NATO intervention in Kosovo in 1999 were more akin to an Old West sheriff authorizing posses to chase the outlaws than true police actions, but they did represent a step toward enforcement of international law by central authorities.

Adjudication of the Law

How a political system resolves disputes between its actors is a fourth key element in its standing along the primitive-to-modern evolutionary scale. As primitive legal systems become more sophisticated, the method of settling disputes evolves from (1) primary reliance on bargaining between adversaries, through (2) mediation/conciliation by neutral parties, to (3) **adjudication** (and the closely related process of arbitration) by neutral parties. The international system of law is in the early stages of this developmental process and is just now developing the institutions and attitudes necessary for adjudication (Roht-Arriaza, 1999).

International Courts

There are a number of international courts in the world today. The genesis of these tribunals extends back less than a century to the Permanent Court of International Arbitration established by the Hague Conference at the turn of the century. In 1922 the Permanent Court of International Justice (PCIJ) was created as part of the League of Nations, and in 1946 the current **International Court of Justice (ICJ)**, which is associated with the UN, evolved from the PCIJ. The ICJ, or so-called World Court, sits in The Hague, the Netherlands, and consists of 15 judges, who are elected to nine-year terms through a complex voting system in the UN. By tradition, each of the five permanent members of the UN Security Council has one judge on the ICJ, and the others are elected to provide regional representation, as is evident in the map on page 275.

In addition to the ICJ, there are a few regional courts of varying authority and levels of activity, including the European Court of Justice (ECJ), the European Court of Human Rights, the Inter-American Court of Human Rights, the Central American Court of Justice, and the Community Tribunal of the Economic Community of West African States. None of these has the authority of domestic courts, but like the ICJ, the regional courts are gaining more credibility.

The ECJ is particularly notable for its authority to make decisions and to have those rulings followed in areas that were once clearly within the sovereign realm of states. In 2000, for example, the court ruled that a German law barring women from holding combat positions in the military was discriminatory and that "national authorities could not . . . adopt the general position that the composition of all armed units . . . had to remain exclusively male."[2] Soon thereafter, the German army began to train women for combat. Another important decision came in 2003 when the ICJ imposed fines of up to $9 million annually on Spain for not meeting EU water quality standards for lakes and rivers in which people swim.

Additionally, people or governments sometimes change their behavior rather than face an adverse ruling by the ECJ or some other international court. One such instance involved a British law that set the age of consent at 16 for heterosexuals and 18 for homosexuals. When a 17-year-old British homosexual sued in the ECJ, arguing that the two-year differentiation was discriminatory, Prime Minister Tony Blair persuaded the House of Commons that it was wiser to lower the age of consent for homosexuals to 16 than to contest an almost certain losing case. The House of Lords blocked the measure, however, with one opponent, the Earl of Longford, reasoning, "A girl is not ruined for life by being seduced. A young fellow is." This logic escaped many. "Lord Longford is 92," wrote a columnist in the *Observer* of London, "but he acts like a man twice his age."[3] The deadlock ended when the prime minister, for only the fourth time since World War I, had Commons overrule the House of Lords by once again approving the change, thereby making it law.

Jurisdiction of International Courts

Although the creation of international tribunals during this century indicates progress, the concept of sovereignty remains a potent barrier to adjudication. The authority of the ICJ extends in theory to all international legal disputes. Cases come before the ICJ in two ways. One is when states submit legal disputes between them. The second is when one of the organs or agencies of the UN asks the ICJ for an advisory opinion.

From 1946 through late 2003, the court has averaged only about two new cases annually. Although this number has increased slightly in recent years, it remains relatively

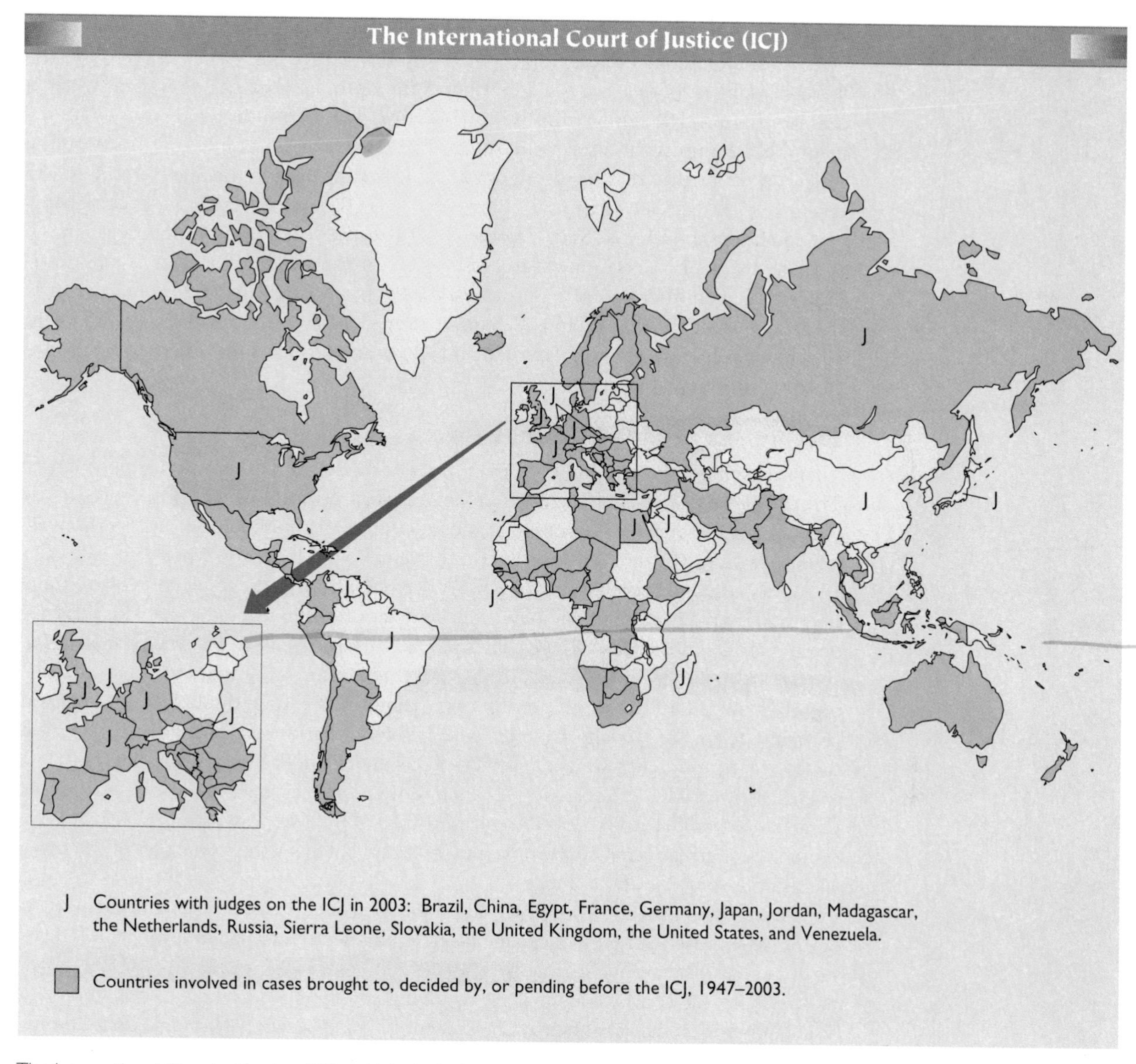

The International Court of Justice (ICJ), which sits in The Hague, the Netherlands, draws both its judges and its caseload from around the world. This map shows the home countries of the ICJ's 15 judges in 2003, and the 81 countries that have been a party in cases before the ICJ between 1947 and 2003.

few cases, given the ICJ's broad jurisdiction and the number of issues facing the world and its countries. More than any other factor, the gap between the court's jurisdiction and its actual role is a matter of the willingness of states to submit to decisions of the ICJ, to litigate cases before it, and to abide by its decisions. Although all UN member-countries are technically parties to the ICJ statute, they must also sign the so-called *optional clause* agreeing to be subject to the compulsory jurisdiction of the ICJ. About two-thirds of all countries have not done so, and others that once were adherents to the optional clause have withdrawn their consent. For example, when Nicaragua filed a case in 1984 with the ICJ charging that U.S. support of the Contra rebels and its mining of Nicaraguan harbors violated international law, the United States argued that the charges were political and, therefore, that the court had no jurisdiction. When the ICJ ruled that it did have jurisdiction in the case, the Reagan administration in 1985 withdrew U.S. consent to the optional clause.

It should be noted that not adhering to the optional clause does not mean that a country is entirely exempt from ICJ jurisdiction. It is common for treaties to have a clause that commits the signatories to submit disputes arising under the treaty to the ICJ. One such treaty that has brought two suits against the United States in the ICJ in recent years is the Vienna Convention on Consular Relations (1963). In it the signatories, including the United States, agree to settle disputes arising from the treaty in the ICJ. The treaty permits countries to assist their citizens who have been accused of serious crimes in another country. Germany in 1999 and Mexico in 2003 brought cases to the ICJ contending that various U.S. states were violating the treaty in several death penalty cases by not allowing German and Mexican consular officials access to the accused or condemned individuals.

Effectiveness of International Courts

There are some important limits on the impact of the ICJ and other international courts. The *jurisdictional limits* just discussed are one restraint. *Lack of enforcement* is a second impediment to the effectiveness of international courts. All courts rely heavily on the willingness of those within their jurisdiction to comply voluntarily or, when that fails, on a powerful executive branch to enforce court decrees. Effective domestic courts have these supports. By contrast, countries are often reluctant to follow the decisions of international courts, and the UN Secretariat, which is the ICJ executive branch, does not have the authority or power to enforce ICJ rulings. This allows countries to sometimes ignore ICJ rulings. In the death penalty cases mentioned earlier, the U.S. states involved (Arizona, Texas, and Oklahoma) rejected ICJ rulings that the executions be stayed until the convicted murderers were given their rights under the Vienna Convention on Consular Relations. The U.S. executive branch refused to intervene, and the U.S. Supreme Court in November 2003 refused to hear the case of the Mexican nationals. Arizona executed the Germans, and Oklahoma and Texas set dates for the execution of the three Mexicans involved in the ICJ cases.

Given these limitations on international courts, it is tempting to write them off as having little more than symbolic value. Such a judgment would be in error. The ICJ, for instance, does play a valuable role. Its rulings help define and advance international law. Furthermore, the court can contribute by giving countries a way, short of war, to settle a dispute once diplomacy has failed. The current ICJ case between Nicaragua and Colombia over their maritime border provides a good example. In its complaint to the ICJ, Nicaragua contested Colombia's control of a number of Caribbean islands and their surrounding territorial seas, including any possible undersea resources, such as petroleum and natural gas. Throughout history, many land and maritime border disputes have resulted in failed diplomacy, in each side seizing the other's people and property, and in war. Without an ICJ to appeal to, that might have been the outcome of the boundary dispute between Nicaragua and Honduras. With an ICJ there is an alternative option that may well lead to a peaceful settlement.

Even when countries reject ICJ jurisdiction, the court's decisions may have some effect. In the 1984 *Nicaragua v. United States* case, discussed earlier, the court heard the case anyway and ruled in Nicaragua's favor. This decision gave a black eye to the United States in the court of world opinion and strengthened the U.S. domestic opponents of the Reagan administration's policy. The United States stopped mining Nicaragua's harbors. In the long run, the capital punishment cases against the United States may have an important impact. Courts in many U.S. jurisdictions are now advising foreign defendants of their right to communicate with their country's diplomatic representatives. Moreover, the refusal of the U.S. government to try to enforce a unanimous ICJ ruling has caused a diplomatic rift with Mexico, whose president, Vicente Fox, expressed Mexico's view by canceling a trip to the United States to meet with President Bush. Perhaps most potent is the implication for Americans abroad. When they are in trouble abroad they expect to be able to communicate with U.S. diplomats, but they could be barred from doing so if other countries follow the U.S. lead. As one of the attorneys representing Mexico put it, "Americans traveling abroad are more vulnerable than ever at this point in time, and if the United States disregards the order of the world's highest court on an issue that directly affects Americans abroad [consular assistance], that sets a very dangerous precedent."[4]

The ICJ's advisory opinions also help resolve issues between IGOs and may even help establish general international law. In separate actions, the UN General Assembly and the World Health Organization each asked the ICJ to rule on the legality of using nuclear weapons. The court ruled in 1996 that "the threat or use of nuclear weapons would generally be contrary to the rules of international law applicable in armed conflict," but went on to say that it was unable to "conclude definitively whether the threat or use of nuclear weapons would be lawful or unlawful in an extreme circumstance of self-defense, in which the very survival of a state would be at stake."[5] While the ICJ's ruling was not as all-encompassing as some antinuclear advocates hoped, the decision does put any leader considering the use of nuclear weapons except in extremis on notice that he or she could wind up the defendant in some future war crimes trial.

In what may be an even higher profile instance of an advisory ruling, the General Assembly in December 2003 requested that the ICJ take up the legality of the 435-mile-long barrier wall that Israel is constructing along the Israel–West Bank border and through parts of the West Bank. The Palestinians and their supporters claim that Israel intends to use the barrier to annex part of the West Bank and the city of Jerusalem in violation of various agreements and UN resolutions dating back to the time of the Arab-Israeli armistice of 1949. Israel denies this intent, and argues that the structure is meant to make it harder for suicide bombers and other terrorists to infiltrate the country.

Finally, there is evidence that the willingness of countries to utilize the ICJ, the ECJ, and other international courts and to accept their decisions is slowly growing. The map of the ICJ's justices and cases on page 275 shows that countries around the world have justices on the court and almost half are or have been a party to its cases. Now more than 60 countries, including Canada, India, and the United Kingdom, adhere to the optional clause giving the ICJ compulsory jurisdiction over their international legal disputes. It is true that the international judicial system is still primitive, but each of the some 160 opinions issued by the PCIJ and the ICJ since 1922 is one more than the zero instances of international adjudication in previous centuries.

Applying International Law and Morality

Law and morality are easy to support in the abstract, but it is much more difficult to agree on how to apply them. To examine this, we will look at issues of cultural perspective, issues of applying international law and standards of morality equally to states and individuals, and issues of prudence.

Law and Justice in a Multicultural World

As the international legal system evolves and expands to incorporate diverse peoples, one problem it faces is the "fit" between differing culturally based concepts of law and

Many people in LDCs object that much of international law rests on Western principles. One current dispute is over patent rights. The patents on AIDS drugs keep the cost higher than many poor countries can afford. Many people, including those seen protesting here in neighboring Kenya against the U.S. pharmaceutical company Pfizer at the 13th International AIDS Conference, believe that the interests of corporations should not prevail at the expense of the tens of millions of people who are HIV-positive. Those opposed to the patents say that drug companies should be able to produce low-cost generic versions of critical patented drugs for distribution. The Western companies reply that doing so will flood the market and make the high cost of developing new generations of drugs prohibitive.

morality. Most of international law and many of the international standards of morality that currently exist and influence world politics are based on the concepts and practices of the West. This is a result of U.S. and European dominance, though, and does not mean that Western concepts are superior to those held in other parts of the world. Now, in a changing international system, Africans, Asians, Latin Americans, and other non-Westerners are questioning and sometimes rejecting law based on Western culture.

Law and Cultural Perspectives

Western and non-Western precepts of law and morality differ on numerous points (Lensu & Fritz, 1999). The *Western view* of law is based on principles designed to protect the long-dominant power of this bloc of states. Order is a primary point, as is sovereignty. Closely related is the theory of property, which holds that individuals (and states) have a "right" to accumulate and maintain property (wealth). This is a major philosophical underpinning of capitalism. Western law also relies heavily on the process and substance of law rather than on equity. Thus, there is an emphasis on courts and what the law is rather than on what is fair. One current controversy that touches on both property rights and "law versus fairness" involves HIV/AIDS and patents held by Western pharmaceutical firms. Patent drugs, which can be as much as 50 times more expensive than generic equivalents, are beyond the financial means of most less developed countries (LDCs). Even though the pharmaceutical companies have slashed prices by as much as 90% on some drugs sold in LDCs, these countries argue the drugs are still financially out of reach. They claim that their right to try to respond to the epidemic by producing the drugs themselves is more important than the Western emphasis on property rights. LDCs add that it is unfair, whatever the law may be, for the poor to suffer untreated because they cannot afford drugs that, in essence, are only available to wealthy individuals and countries.

The *non-Western view* of international law is influenced by the different cultural heritage of non-Western states, by the recent independence of those states, and by the history of exploitation their people have often suffered at the hands of the West. The newer, mostly non-Western, and mostly LDCs claim that since they had little or no role in determining the rules that govern the international system, they are not necessarily bound by preexisting agreements, principles, or practices that work to their disadvantage. These countries support sovereignty and reject aspects of international law that they claim are imperialistic abridgments of that principle. They insist on noninterference, which, for example, was one reason that many LDCs opposed the American and British intervention in Iraq in 2003. Whatever their sympathies with the plight of the Iraqis under Saddam Hussein, and whatever the LDCs' views of whether or not he posed an international danger, they are concerned that they could be the target of a future intervention. The LDCs also are keenly aware that such interventions are only launched against weaker countries and that the more powerful economically developed countries are, in effect, exempt from intervention no matter what the issue (Farer, 2003; Lang, 2003).

The LDCs also reject weighted voting schemes, such as those in the UN Security Council, the World Bank, and the International Monetary Fund, that favor the rich and powerful. The LDCs often emphasize equity over the substance and process of law. For them, the important standard is fairness, especially in terms of economic maldistribution.

Human Rights and Cultural Perspectives

Western and non-Western perspectives also differ considerably on the *rights of the individual* versus the *rights of the community.* This divergence of thought affects how human rights are defined. Imagine a scale that ranges, on one end, from a value system in which the rights of an individual are always more important than those of the community to, at the other end, a value system in which the good of the community always takes precedence over the good of the individual. Western states would generally fall toward the individualistic end of the scale; non-Western states would generally fall farther toward the communitarian end of the scale. There is, for example, a long list of rights afforded in the United States to individuals accused and even convicted of crimes. Non-Western cultures tend to think this practice gives the society too little protection; they therefore favor a more communitarian approach to ordering their society. That perspective was expressed succinctly by Singapore's foreign minister, who defended what Americans might see as draconian laws in his country, including punishment by caning for about 30 crimes ranging from attempted murder through vandalism. As the official put it, "We believe that the legal system must give maximum protection to the majority of our people. We make no apology for clearly tilting our laws and policy in favor of the majority."[6]

What constitutes a human rights abuse and what is merely a matter of clashing cultural values has been a particular sore point between the United States and China. American criticism of China on a wide range of rights issues is reflected in the annual U.S. State Department's review of global human rights. Typically, the report issued in 2003 characterized China as an "authoritarian state" whose "human rights record throughout the year remained poor" and which "continued to commit numerous and serious abuses."[7]

China rejects such criticisms. In reality, one spokesperson contends, such human rights criticisms arise largely from the fact that East and West have different conceptions of human rights. "For Asians," the official continued, "human rights do not mean the privileges of the few but of the many."[8] Using its more communitarian standards, China

Did You Know That:

Human rights groups criticize China as the country that executes the most prisoners. According to Amnesty International, there were 1,526 known executions in 31 countries during 2002. The top three countries were China (1,060), Iran (113), and the United States (71).

also accuses the United States of its own range of human rights violations. "Human rights protection provided by the U.S. Constitution is very limited," a Chinese government report asserts. It notes, for instance, that in the United States there is no right to "food, clothing, shelter, education, work, rest, and reasonable payment." The report also criticizes widespread racism as "the darkest abyss in American society" and points out that democracy is limited because "running for office requires large sums of money."[9]

Applying International Law and Morality in a Multicultural World

Given the differences in perspective between cultures, the question arises as to whether it is reasonable to try to apply the standards of law and morality at all. Those who deny that any common principles exist contend that no single standard does (or, they suspect, can) exist, at least not without global cultural homogenization, and imposing that would be **cultural imperialism**. From a Western perspective it is easy to dismiss as self-serving claims of cultural imperialism by China and other countries that are seen as human rights abusers. That would be too easy, though, and there are many analysts in the West who, without supporting the specifics of any alleged abuse, do find the fundamental argument meritorious. One American scholar writes, for instance, "We must understand and learn from other traditions while seeing them as historically conditioned—and this includes our own tradition. What we must not do . . . is elevate our own tradition to the status of 'universalism.' This is just rehashed cultural imperialism and has its roots in the dogmatic religious outlooks of the past and present." In sum, he argues, "We should realize that we create our own values, reacting to the times and climes, and rational people can disagree on what these values are."[10]

Others reject such claims of cultural imperialism as poor attempts to justify the unjustifiable. They argue that the nature of humankind is not based on culture, and, therefore, human rights are universal (Donnelly, 2003). President Chandrika Kumaratunga of Sri Lanka, for one, has expressed the opinion that "of course, every country has its own national ethos, but . . . when people talk about a conflict of values, I think it is an excuse that can be used to cover a multitude of sins" (Franck, 1997:627). Seconding this view, Secretary-General Kofi Annan told an audience in Iran, there is "talk of human rights being a Western concept, . . . [but] don't we all suffer from the lack of the rule of law and from arbitrariness? What is foreign about that? What is Western about that? And when we talk of the right [of people] . . . to live their lives to the fullest and to be able to live their dreams, it is universal."[11]

The issue of multiculturalism and human rights also raises the question of who in society gets to make decisions about what is acceptable and what is not. For example, many non-Muslims have objected to the requirement in some Muslim countries that women not be allowed to work outside the home or that they must wear veils to keep their faces from being gazed upon by men outside their immediate families. Some Muslims and others have replied that such restrictions on women are matters of culture and religion, and objections to them reflect cultural interference. A strong argument can be made for that if all or most of both men and women agree. But what if only a majority of men favor the restriction and a majority of women do not? That is the case in many Muslim countries, according to a survey conducted in 20 of them. It found that on average only a minority of men (42%) compared to a majority of women (52%) completely agreed with the unfettered right of women to work outside the home.[12] Are the restrictions, then, a matter of culture or male chauvinism?

Applying International Law and Morality to States

Traditionally, the application of international law and of standards of moral behavior in the international system has focused primarily on states. The actions of individuals have

Some people doubt whether all the world's diverse cultures can agree on one system of international law. It will be difficult, but in some areas there is growing agreement on at least fundamental principles. One such area is human rights. Most of the world's countries have agreed to the Universal Declaration of Human Rights.

not been subject to judgment. Now that is changing rapidly, as we shall see presently. This section will deal with states, and the first thing to address is whether states and individuals can be held to the same standards of law and morality. Then we can look at the specific issues of law and morality as they relate to states.

Should States Be Held to the Same Standards as Individuals?

It is common for states to act legitimately in ways that would be reprehensible for individuals. Imagine if as a private person you were having a dispute with your neighbors, and you laid siege to your neighbors' houses and somehow managed to significantly reduce their ability to feed their children and buy them medicine. As a result, some of your neighbors' children died. Would any dispute justify such actions? Most people would think not and would consider you a heinous criminal.

In a somewhat analogous situation, the United States and other countries for more than a decade continued UN-authorized economic sanctions against Iraq. Whatever the cause of the sanctions, though, one impact was that the lack of food, medicine, and other basics contributed to the deaths of several hundred thousand more Iraqi children than would have otherwise died between 1991 when the sanctions were first applied and 2003 when they ended after Saddam Hussein was driven from power. Surely those sanctions were at least partly the result of Iraq's obdurate refusal during most of the time to grant unimpeded access to UN arms inspectors. But does that settle the question? It is hard to conceive of a circumstance where we as individuals could legally or morally take action against a person that would injure that person's children. Is it moral, should it be legal, that we—the collective of states in the UN—assailed the Iraqi children to punish Iraq's regime?

Of course, we recognize differences between justifiable and inexcusable actions, but where do you draw the line? Some have argued that the state cannot be held to individual moral standards. Realist philosopher and statesman Niccolò Machiavelli wrote in *The Prince* (1513) that a ruler "cannot observe all those things which are considered good in men, being often obliged, in order to maintain the state, to act against faith and charity, against humanity, and against religion."

Proponents of state morality disagree and argue that neither national interest nor sovereignty legitimizes immoral actions. A philosopher and statesman who took this view was Thomas Jefferson. While secretary of state (1789–1793), Jefferson argued that since a society is but a collection of individuals, "the moral duties which exist between individual and individual" also form "the duties of that society toward any other; so that between society and society the same moral duties exist as between the individuals composing them" (Graebner, 1964:55).

States and Issues of Law and Morality

Traditionally, international law has concerned itself with the actions and status of states. Some of the most prominent issues are sovereignty, war, the biosphere, and human rights.

Issues of Sovereignty Sovereignty continues to be a cornerstone of the state system, but sovereignty is no longer a legal absolute. Instead, it is being chipped away by a growing number of law-creating treaties that limit action. Sovereignty is also being slowly restricted by the international community's growing intolerance of human rights abuses and other ills inflicted by governments on their people. As Secretary-General Annan puts it, sovereignty "was never meant as a license for governments to trample on human rights and human dignity. Sovereignty implies responsibility, not just power."[13] Views such as this led, for instance, to international action that ended apartheid in South Africa (1993) and forced the military junta in Haiti to flee (1994), and to the NATO bombardment of Yugoslavia until it ceased its ethnic cleansing policy in Kosovo (1999).

Issues of War Most of the early writing in international law was concerned with the law of war, and this issue continues to be a primary focus of legal development. In addition to issues of traditional state-versus-state warfare, international law now attempts to regulate revolutionary and internal warfare and terrorism.

To illustrate these diverse concerns, we can focus on the long debate on when and how war can be morally and legally fought. "Just war" theory has two parts: the cause of war and the conduct of war. Western tradition has believed that ***jus ad bellum*** (just cause of war) exists in cases where the war is (1) a last resort, (2) declared by legitimate authority, (3) waged in self-defense or to establish/restore justice, and (4) fought to bring about peace. The same line of thought maintains that ***jus in bello*** (just conduct of war) includes the standards of proportionality and discrimination. Proportionality means that the amount of force used must be proportionate to the threat. Discrimination means that force must not make noncombatants intentional targets (Rengger, 2002; Barry, 1998).

As laudable as limitations on legitimate warfare may seem, they present problems. One difficulty is that the standards of when to go to war and how to fight it are rooted in Western-Christian tradition. The parameters of *jus in bello* and *jus ad bellum* extend back to Aristotle's *Politics* (ca. 340 B.C.) and are especially associated with the writings of Christian theological philosophers Saint Augustine (Aurelius Augustinus, A.D. 354–430) and Saint Thomas Aquinas (1225–1274). As a doctrine based on Western culture and religion, not all the restrictions on war are the same as those derived from some of the other great cultural-religious traditions, including Buddhism and Islam (Silverman, 2002).

Another difficulty with the standards of just war, even if you try to abide by them, is that they are vague and controversial. To illustrate that, the Play a Part box "*Jus ad Bellum* and Iraq" asks you to assume the role of deciding whether the invasion of Iraq in 2003 by the United States and the United Kingdom was a just war or a war of aggression (Butler, 2003).

In the realm of *jus in bello,* there are some clear guidelines about what is unacceptable. The Hague Conferences (1899, 1907) and the Geneva Conventions of 1949 set down some rules regarding impermissible weapons, the treatment of prisoners, and other matters. Other treaties have banned the possession and use of biological and chemical weapons, and the ICJ has ruled that in most circumstances the use of nuclear weapons would be illegal. Most recently, the treaty establishing the International Criminal Court includes an extensive list of actions that constitute war crimes.

Still, many uncertainties exist about *jus in bello.* One recent controversy arose over the applicability of the provision of the Geneva Conventions relating to the treatment of prisoners of war with regard to the status of Taliban and al-Qaeda fighters captured by the United States in Afghanistan and held at the U.S. naval base at Guantánamo Bay, Cuba. The U.S. administration eventually took the position that Taliban prisoners were subject to the Geneva Conventions' provisions, but that al-Qaeda members were "enemy combatants," not prisoners of war, on the grounds that they were not members of a national military organization. As such, al-Qaeda prisoners can be tried by military courts, and they do not have the protection of the Geneva Conventions or of many of the rights accorded U.S. citizens and foreigners tried in U.S. civilian courts.

Another uncertainty about *jus in bello* involves how to gauge proportionality. Almost everyone would agree, for instance, that France, Great Britain, and the United States would not have been justified in using their nuclear weapons against Yugoslavia in 1999 to force it to withdraw from Kosovo or against Afghanistan in 2001 for refusing to surrender the al-Qaeda terrorists. But what if Iraq had used chemical weapons against the forces of those three countries during the Persian Gulf War in 1991 or against U.S. and British forces in 2003? Would they have been justified if they had retaliated with nuclear weapons? Some people even argue that using nuclear weapons under any conditions would violate the rule of discrimination and would thus be immoral.

The *jus in bello* standard of discrimination also involves matters of degree rather than clear lines. The U.S. preference for using aerial bombardment rather than first (or at all in some cases) risking ground combat troops has raised troublesome issues of discrimination for some observers. With respect to the U.S-led actions in Kosovo in 1999, for example, one retired U.S. Marine colonel has charged that an American "willingness-to-kill-but-not-to-die" attitude led to a bombing campaign that caused unnecessary civilian casualties. What occurred, in the colonel's view, was that "the allies' resolve was greater than the resources [troops] they were willing to commit to the action." Therefore, the colonel concludes, "Immorality resided in the mismatch" (DeCamp, 2000:43).

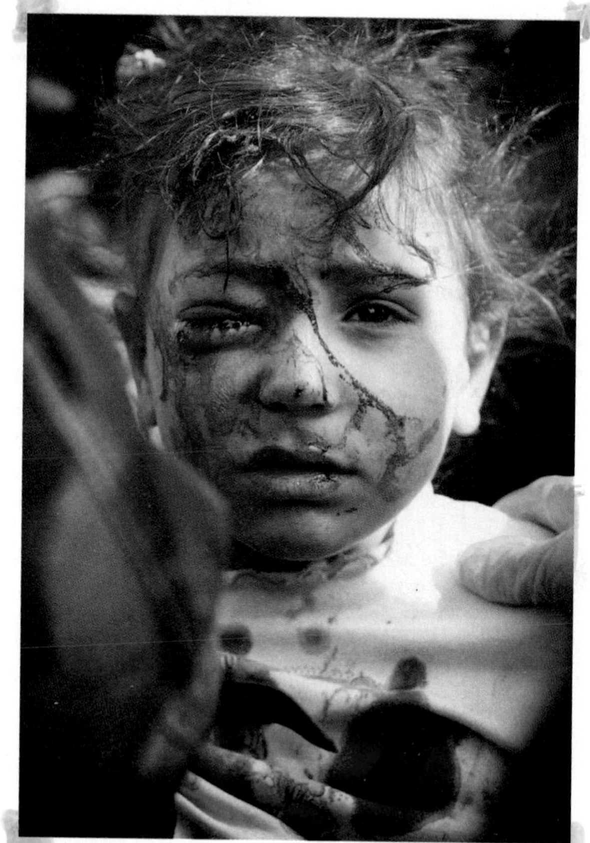

While the principles of *jus in bello,* just conduct of war, outline what is and is not permissible, the standards are not precise. One is that civilians should not be unnecessarily targeted. But civilians, like this little Iraqi girl injured in March 2003 by U.S. forces, are wounded and killed in virtually all wars. Did what happen to the girl violate *jus in bello?*

Although a few U.S. special forces were sent to Afghanistan in the early days of military operations against that

PLAY A PART

Jus ad Bellum and Iraq

The concept of *jus ad bellum,* the just cause of war, no longer exists only in theory. After World War II, the Nuremberg and Tokyo war crimes tribunals held German and Japanese leaders accountable for, among other things, waging aggressive war. More recently, UN tribunals have punished those found guilty of war crimes in the Balkans and in Rwanda. Adding to the case that aggressive war is a criminal offense under international law, the treaty that established the newly formed International Criminal Court (ICC) gives it jurisdiction "with respect to . . . the crime of aggression." Although the ICC charter does not define aggression, it does state that judging acts of war "shall be consistent with the relevant provisions of the [UN] Charter." Among these is the mandate that members "refrain in their international relations from the threat or use of force against the territorial integrity or political independence of any state." The Charter recognizes "the inherent right of individual or collective self-defense if an armed attack occurs," but apart from that contingency, the document directs that it is the Security Council that "shall determine the existence of any threat to the peace . . . or act of aggression and . . . decide what measures shall be taken." The Charter also stresses that every effort at a peaceful settlement should be made before resorting to force. These clauses closely parallel the traditional standards—that to be just, war must be the last resort, declared by legitimate authority, waged in self-defense or to establish/restore justice, and fought to bring about peace.

The issue before you is whether the United States and Great Britain had just cause for their invasion of Iraq in 2003. To find that Washington and London conducted a just war, you must be able to answer "yes" to all of the following questions:

1. *Was the war the last resort?* President George W. Bush argued it was. He told Americans, "For more than a decade, the United States and other nations have pursued patient and honorable efforts to disarm the Iraqi regime without war. . . . Every measure has been taken to avoid war."[1] President Jacques Chirac of France disagreed. He told reporters that he believed the "disarmament" of Iraq could "be done in a peaceful way," and that "War is always the worst of solutions. It's always a failure. . . . Everything should be done to avoid it."[2]
2. *Was the U.S./U.K. action taken under legitimate authority?* The United States made a legal argument that the authority to act did exist from the UN under earlier Security Council resolutions. As President Bush put it, "the Security Council did act in the early 1990s. Under Resolutions 678 and 687—both still in effect—the United States and our allies are authorized to use force in ridding Iraq of weapons of mass destruction." Taking an opposing view, Secretary-General Kofi Annan declared just before the war that if "action is taken without the authority of the Security Council, the legitimacy and support for any such action will be seriously impaired."[3]
3. *Was the war waged in self-defense or to promote justice?* Citing the threat that Iraq could give weapons of mass destruction (WMDs) to terrorists or someday use them itself, President Bush proclaimed, "The danger is clear" that the "United States has the sovereign authority to use force in assuring its own national security," and that "before it is too late to act, this danger will be removed." A statement issued in October 2002 by the heads of 60 Christian organizations disagreed. Explaining the group's position, Episcopal Bishop John B. Shane argued that just war theory differentiates between "anticipatory self-defense, which is morally justified, and preventive war, which is morally prohibited." In the case of Iraq, he continued, "I don't see the threat from Iraq to the United States as an imminent threat, so . . . military action against Iraq is inappropriate."[4]
4. *Was the war fought to bring about peace?* Here again, President Bush argued "yes," telling Americans, "The cause of peace requires all free nations . . . to work to advance liberty and peace" in the Persian Gulf region. Taking a very different view of U.S. motives, one Middle East analyst contended that the U.S. invasion of Iraq "has to do with oil and to do with

country, the overall pattern of U.S. military action once again favored heavy aerial bombardment. A much larger ground attack was launched against Iraq in 2003, but once again there was heavy bombing, some of it in urban areas. American officials went to great lengths to give assurances that all efforts were being made to avoid unnecessary civilian casualties during the campaigns against both Afghanistan and Iraq. During the Iraq war, for example, Secretary of Defense Donald H. Rumsfeld told reporters, "The empire—getting control of Iraq's enormous oil resources." The analyst then explained her belief that the motive was "not just about importing oil to the United States." Instead, "The issue is control, undermining OPEC [Organization of Petroleum Exporting States], and controlling access to oil for Germany, Japan, and the rest of Europe. This would give the United States tremendous political and economic clout in the rest of the world."[5]

It is best not to debate this issue with 20-20 hindsight. For example, whether WMDs were ultimately found and the success or failure of the postwar occupation of Iraq is not as important to determining the justice of the war as what evidence President Bush and Prime Minister Tony Blair had that a significant and imminent threat existed, what their intentions were at the onset of the war, and whether the evidence and intentions justified war. It would also be good to delve into the debate more deeply. For additional sources, begin with President Bush's televised address on March 17, 2003, justifying the U.S. position, at http://www.whitehouse.gov/news/releases/2003/03/. The U.S. argument is made in more detail in a State Department paper, "Decade of Defiance and Deception," at http://www.state.gov/p/nea/rls/01fs/14906.htm.

This box asks whether you think the U.S./U.K war against Iraq in March 2003 met the standards of jus ad bellum, *just cause of war. Just as the victors issued playing cards with the faces of Iraqi leaders they especially wanted to capture, critics of the war might argue that this ace of hearts with the picture of Prime Minister Tony Blair, perhaps accompanied by an ace of spades depicting President George Bush, would be appropriate. The Japanese protesters also believe that the two should be prosecuted in the newly formed International Criminal Court (ICC), as the sign to the right indicates.*

targeting capabilities and the care that goes into targeting, to see that the precise targets are struck and other targets are not struck is as impressive as anything anyone could see—the care that goes into it, the humanity that goes into it."[14] Others disagreed. One survey of people in 20 countries found that an average of 60% did not believe the United States tried hard enough to avoid civilian casualties, compared to 35% who believed that it did, and 5% who were unsure. As detailed in Figure 9.2, 82% of Americans thought

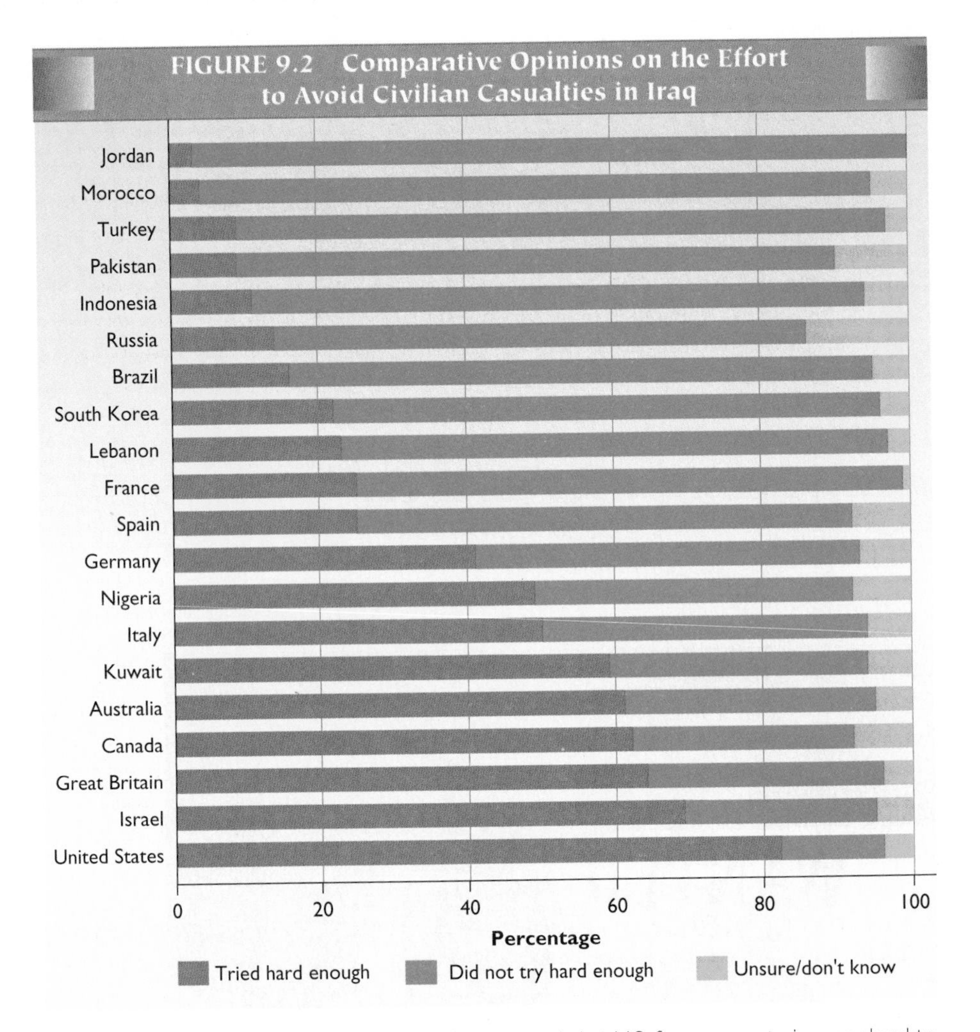

The Bush administration said, and most Americans agreed, that U.S. forces were trying very hard to avoid civilian casualties during the aerial and ground campaigns against Iraq in 2003. More often than not, respondents in Israel, Great Britain, Canada, Australia, Kuwait, Italy, and Nigeria agreed with that assessment, but a plurality or majority of the other 12 countries where the survey was taken did not think the U.S. campaign had taken sufficient care to avoid killing and wounding civilians.

Data source: The Pew Research Center for People and the Press, "Views of a Changing World," June 2003.

that their country had tried very hard to avoid killing and wounding civilians, and a majority of people in 7 other countries agreed. But in the other 12 countries, a plurality or majority of respondents disagreed.

As this discussion illustrates, the law and morality of war remain highly controversial. Most observers would support neither of the two polar views: (1) that the United States could not be held responsible no matter what the level of civilian casualties; (2) that knowingly taking actions that would kill any civilians violates the standards of *jus in bello.* It is, however, easier to question two extreme views than to clearly demarcate the dividing line between what is just and unjust.

Issues of the Biosphere Another important and growing area of international law addresses the obligation of states and individuals to use the biosphere responsibly on the theory that it belongs to no one individually and to everyone collectively. This area of law is aptly illustrated by the law of the sea.

The status of the world's oceans is a long-standing subject of international law. The international maritime rules of the road for ships have long had general acceptance. The extension of a state's territorial limits to three miles into the ocean was another widely acknowledged standard based, as noted, on international custom.

In recent years, the resource value of the seas has grown because of more sophisticated harvesting and extraction technology, and this has created uncertainty and change. Undersea oil exploration, in particular, is the source of serious dispute among a number of countries. As early as 1945, the United States claimed control of the resources on or under its continental shelf. In 1960 the Soviet Union proclaimed the extension of its territorial waters out to 12 miles, a policy that has been imitated by others, including the United States as of 1988. Several Latin American countries claimed a 200-mile territorial zone, and the United States not only established a 200-mile "conservation zone" in 1977 to control fishing but in 1983 extended that control to all economic resources within the 200-mile limit.

In an ambitious attempt to settle and regulate many of these issues, the Convention on the Law of the Sea (1982) defines coastal zones, establishes the International Seabed Authority (ISA) to regulate nonterritorial seabed mining, provides for the sharing of revenue from such efforts, and establishes the International Tribunal for the Law of the Sea to settle disputes. As of 2003, 145 countries had ratified the convention. The United States has not signed, much less ratified, the treaty amid concerns about the possible transfer of control over offshore activities (such as oil drilling) and their revenues from Washington to the ISA through decisions of the International Seabed Authority. The absence of a few countries—even a few powerful ones—should not take away from the growing body of law that protects the oceans and seas.

Issues of Human Rights International law is developing affirmatively in the area of defining human rights. International attention to the law of human rights has grown because of many factors, including the horror of the images of abuses that television reveals, the expanding efforts of individuals and organizations that promote human rights, and the growing awareness that human rights violations are a major source of international instability.

The UN Charter supports basic rights in a number of its provisions. This language was expanded in 1948 when the UN General Assembly passed the Universal Declaration of Human Rights. No country voted against the declaration, although a few did abstain. Since then, the growth of global human rights has also been enhanced by a number of important global multilateral treaties. The most important of these treaties are listed in Table 9.1. In addition to global treaties, there have been a number of regional multilateral treaties, such as the Helsinki Accords (1977), which address European human rights, and the African Charter on Human and Peoples' Rights (1990).

Much, however, remains to be done. Canada and several other countries have signed all the human rights treaties found in Table 9.1 on page 288; many other countries have not. A minority of countries have not consented to one or more of these treaties because of fears that they might be used as platforms for interfering in domestic affairs or for pressing demands for certain international policy changes, such as a redistribution of world economic resources. For instance, the United States is not a party to the conventions on the Status of Refugees (1951), on the Rights of the Child (1984), and on the Elimination of All Forms of Discrimination Against Women (1979).

The gap between existing legal standards and their application is the area of greatest concern. Gross violations of the principles set down in the multilateral treaties continue

TABLE 9.1 Adherence to Important Human Rights Treaties

Multilateral Treaty	Year	Countries* (2004)
Convention on the Prevention and the Punishment of the Crime of Genocide	1949	135
Convention Relating to the Status of Refugees	1951	142
International Convention on the Elimination of All Forms of Racial Discrimination	1965	169
International Covenant on Civil and Political Rights	1976	152
International Covenant on Economic, Social, and Cultural Rights	1976	149
Convention on the Elimination of All Forms of Discrimination Against Women	1979	177
Convention Against Torture and Other Cruel, Inhuman, or Degrading Treatment or Punishment	1984	135
Convention on the Rights of the Child	1989	192

*Indicates number of countries that have ratified or otherwise agreed to abide by the treaty.
Data source: United Nations Treaty Collection at http://untreaty.un.org/English/treaty.asp.

Most countries have signed a variety of multilateral treaties, thereby agreeing to abide by the treaties' various human rights standards. Even though not all countries have signed every treaty, and while there have also been numerous violations, many analysts argue that such treaties take on the characteristic of international law once they have been ratified by the preponderance of the world's states. As such, the standards set in these treaties may be used in a number of ways, including by international courts and tribunals, to judge the cases of states and individuals.

to occur. And the record of international reaction to violation of the standards and enforcement of them through sanctions and other means is very sporadic and often weak. Yet their existence provides a constant reminder that most of the world considers certain actions to be reprehensible. The treaties also serve, in the view of many, as a standard of international law and conduct for which states and individuals can be held accountable. Thus, the growth of human rights law has just begun. The acceptance of the concept of human rights has gained a good deal more rhetorical support than practical application, and enforcement continues to be largely in the hands of individual states with a mixed record of adherence. For all these shortcomings, though, human rights obligations are now widely discussed, world opinion is increasingly critical of violations, and real progress has been made. Exemplifying the successes and shortcomings of human rights treaties in one area, UN Assistant Secretary-General Angela E. V. King commented, "Women have made remarkable gains in health, education, and in the recognition of their human rights," yet she also had to add, "Despite this progress, much needs to be done."[15]

Applying International Law and Morality to Individuals

International law has begun recently to deal with the actions of individuals. A series of precedents in the 20th century marked this change. It is possible to divide these developments into three topics: post–World War II tribunals, current international tribunals, and the International Criminal Court (Beigbeder, 1999).

Post–World War II Tribunals

The first modern instances of individuals being charged with crimes under international law came in the aftermath of the horrors of World War II. In the Nuremberg and Tokyo war crimes trials, German and Japanese military and civilian leaders were tried for waging aggressive war, for war crimes, and for crimes against humanity. Nineteen Germans were convicted at Nuremberg; 12 were sentenced to death. Similar fates awaited convicted Japanese war criminals. Seven were hanged. Many Germans and Japanese also went to prison. Some important precedents were established. One was that those who ordered criminal acts or under whose command the acts occurred were just as liable to punishment as those who actually carried out the crimes. Another important precedent was that obeying orders was not a defense for having committed atrocities (Osiel, 1999).

There were efforts in the UN as early as 1948 to establish a permanent international tribunal to deal with genocide and other criminal affronts to humankind. Little came of the effort, however, and there were no subsequent war crimes tribunals for almost the next half-century.

Current International Tribunals

After languishing for nearly 50 years, the idea of international tribunals to deal with criminal violations of international law was resurrected by the atrocities that occurred in Bosnia and in Rwanda during the 1990s. In both places, people on all sides were abused, injured, and killed; in Bosnia it was the Muslims who were the principal victims and the Serbs who inflicted the most death and degradation between 1990 and 1995. In Rwanda the Hutus were the murderous aggressors in 1994 and the Tutsis the victims of genocide.

The atrocities in Bosnia and Rwanda shocked the conscience of the world and made it obvious, as a former UN official put it, that "a person stands a better chance of being tried and judged for killing one human being than for killing 100,000."[16] This jarring reality led to the establishment in 1994 of a tribunal for Bosnia and another for Rwanda to prosecute those who committed atrocities. The tribunal for the Balkans sits in The Hague, the Netherlands. The Rwanda tribunal is located in Arusha, Tanzania. In 1999, the authority of the Balkans tribunal was expanded to include war crimes in Kosovo.

The Hague tribunal has indicted over 110 individuals as war criminals, and more than 90 have been arrested. Of the 42 individuals whose trials had been completed by late 2003, 37 were convicted and 5 were acquitted of committing crimes such as genocide, murder, rape, and torture. Sentences have ranged up to 40 years in prison, and the convicted war criminals have been transferred from their cells in the Netherlands to other countries in Europe to serve their time.

The most important of the trials in The Hague began in 2001 against Slobodan Milosevic, the former president of Yugoslavia, who was extradited to The Hague to stand trial for crimes against Bosnian Muslims and Croats in the early 1990s and against Muslim Kosovars in the late 1990s. Milosevic declared both the court and the indictment illegal, telling the court, "The whole world knows this is a political trial."[17] Unfazed, the court entered not guilty pleas to all charges, and the prosecutors began presenting their case in February 2002 in a trial that has continued into 2004.

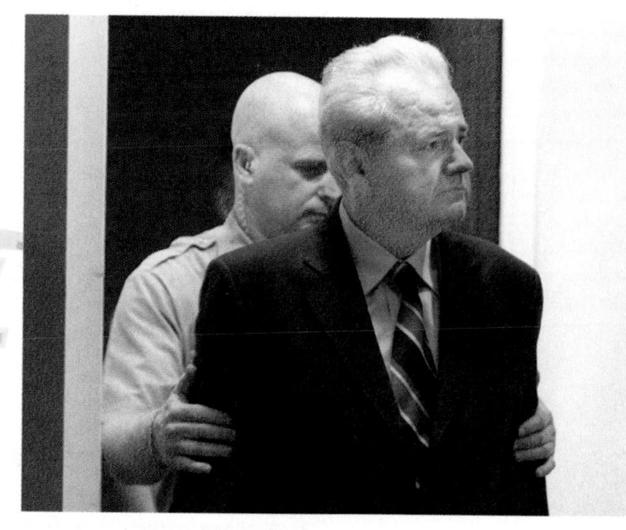

International law is increasingly being applied to individuals as well as states. Even the normal sovereign immunity of a country's leader is no longer a defense, as illustrated in the case of former Yugoslavian President Slobodan Milosevic. He is seen here in custody during his trial before a UN tribunal in the Netherlands on charges of numerous war crimes. If convicted, he could receive life imprisonment.

The Rwanda tribunal has made headway more slowly than its counterpart in The Hague, but an important step occurred in 1998 when the tribunal obtained its first conviction. Former Rwandan Prime and Minister Jean Kambanda pleaded guilty to genocide and

Did You Know That:

From his prison cell in the Netherlands, accused war criminal Slobodan Milosevic ran for Serbia's parliament during the December 2003 election. His party won enough votes to seat him but chose another individual to hold the seat "temporarily."

was sentenced to life in prison. Through late 2003, the tribunal had indicted 70 individuals and arrested 60 of them. Of these, 12 had been convicted, 1 acquitted, and 20 were on trial. Hutu civilian and military leaders have made up most, but not all, of the convicted and accused. For instance, a Belgian-born Italian citizen, Georges Henry Joseph Ruggiu, who was a radio journalist in Rwanda, was sentenced to 12 years in prison for inciting genocide. Among the many other chilling calls to mayhem he broadcast in 1994: "You [Tutsi] cockroaches must know you are made of flesh.... We will kill you."[18]

Even more recently, a UN tribunal was established in 2002 to deal with war crimes that occurred in the civil war in Sierra Leone beginning in 1996. In that afflicted country, rebels killed and mutilated many thousands of noncombatants in an attempt to terrorize the population. The rebels' favorite gruesome tactic was to hack off part of one or more of their victims' limbs so that the maimed individuals would serve as living reminders not to oppose the Revolutionary United Front (RUF). By late 2003, 13 individuals had been indicted and 9 of them were in custody. The tribunal has also indicted former Liberian President Charles Taylor on charges of aiding the RUF. He is in exile in Nigeria; its government may surrender him to the tribunal or send him back to Liberia to face trial in that country's courts.

The International Criminal Court

The advent of ad hoc international tribunals and the enforcement of international law by national courts have signaled that those who commit war crimes are at peril. But the world has also begun to recognize, as President Clinton said, that "the signal will come across even more loudly and clearly if nations all around the world . . . establish a permanent international court to prosecute . . . serious violations of humanitarian law."[19]

To that end, a UN-sponsored global conference convened in 1998 to create a permanent International Criminal Court (ICC). During the conference, a bloc of about 50 countries, with Canada as its informal leader, favored establishing a court with broad and independent jurisdiction. Secretary-General Kofi Annan supported this position, calling on the delegates in Rome to "not flinch from creating a court strong and independent enough to carry out its tasks. It must be an instrument of justice, not expediency."[20]

Other countries, including the United States, wanted a much weaker ICC. The crux of U.S. opposition to a strong ICC rested on the fear that U.S. leaders and military personnel might become targets of politically motivated prosecutions. "The reality is that the United States is a global military power and presence.... We have to be careful that it does not open up opportunities for endless frivolous complaints to be lodged against the United States as a global military power," explained the chief U.S. delegate to the talks.[21] The U.S. stand drew strong criticism. Canada's foreign minister accused the United States of wanting only a facade, "a Potemkin village," and an Italian diplomat expressed disbelief "that a major democracy . . . would want to have an image of insisting that its soldiers be given license never to be investigated."[22]

In the end, some of the reservations of the United States and some other countries were met, but over 80% of the 148 countries attending voted to create a relatively strong court. The treaty gives the ICC jurisdiction over wars of aggression, genocide, and numerous "widespread and systematic" crimes committed as part of "state, organization, or group policy" during international and internal wars. National courts will remain the first point of justice, and the ICC will be able to try cases only when they fail to do so. The UNSC can delay a prosecution for up to a year, but the vote to delay will not be subject to veto.

The ICC became a reality on April 12, 2002, when the number of countries formally agreeing to the treaty reached 60, the minimum required for the ICC treaty to take effect. That number of countries had grown to 92 by April 2004. The creation of the

The founding of the International Criminal Court, which began operation in 2003, is an important advance in the application of international law. The court and its 18 judges, headed by its president, Canada's Philippe Kirsch (center), and its two vice presidents, Akua Kuenyehia of Ghana (left) and Elizabeth Odio Benito of Costa Rica (right), will have jurisdiction over an extensive list of war crimes, including genocide, as defined in the Rome Statute of the International Criminal Court (1998), the treaty establishing the court and its authority.

court means, French President Jacques Chirac commented, that "starting now, all those who might be inclined to engage in the madness of genocide or crimes against humanity will know that nothing will be able to prevent justice."[23] The countries that have adhered to the ICC treaty met in March 2003 and elected the court's 18 judges, including Canada's Philippe Kirsch as the president of the court, and the ICC's chief prosecutor, Luis Moreno-Ocampo of Argentina. The court is expected to be fully operational by late 2004 and will begin sifting through the more than 200 complaints already filed with it.

There is little doubt that the creation of the ICC represents an important step in the advance of international law. Still, it is not clear how effective it will be. Germany, France, Great Britain, South Korea, Brazil, and a number of other notable countries have ratified the ICC treaty, but the United States, China, Russia, India, and some other important states have not. The United States remains staunchly opposed. President Clinton signed the treaty for technical reasons, but then recommended that his successor, George Bush, not submit the treaty to the Senate for ratification unless revisions were made. That was superfluous advice for Bush, who had already repeatedly expressed his opposition. Indeed in 2002, Bush directed the State Department to "unsign" the treaty through a letter to the UN declaring that the United States "does not intend to become a party to the [ICC treaty]" and that it "has no legal obligations arising from its signature (to the treaty)."[24] In another action, the president threatened to veto all UN peacekeeping operations unless U.S. troops were specifically given immunity from possible prosecution before the ICC. This issue has been resolved for now by a series of one-year exemptions from prosecution by the ICC that the Security Council has given to U.S. peacekeepers. The Bush administration has also successfully negotiated bilateral agreements with some two dozen countries, including some of those who have ratified the ICC treaty, requiring them not to surrender American nationals to the ICC.

Given its hegemonic position in the international system, the U.S. position on the court is sure to be important, perhaps critical to its success. Little change is likely while President Bush is in office. It is also the case that most Americans oppose the idea of having U.S. troops subject to trial by the ICC. This view is evident in Figure 9.3 comparing American attitudes on this question with those of people in several other countries. But some observers are optimistic about the U.S. stance in the long run. For example, the ICC's first chief judge, Philippe Kirsch, told an interviewer that he believed

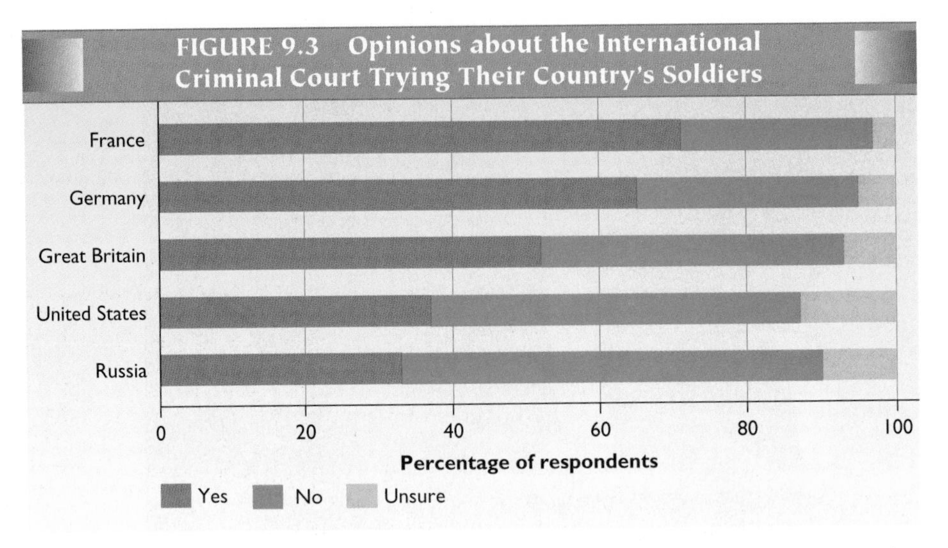

The thought of having your country's soldiers subject to trial for war crimes by the International Criminal Court is much more acceptable in some countries than others.

Note: The question asked was: In your opinion, should the International Criminal Court be allowed to try [your country's] soldiers accused of war crimes if [your country's] government refuses to try them, or not?
Data source: The Pew Research Center for People and the Press, "Views of a Changing World," June 2003.

that there will be a "progressive acceptance by those who still have doubts" as they come to see that the ICC "is in no way a political instrument but is indeed a judicial instrument with all sorts of built-in safeguards."

"In the end, this court is going to become universal," Justice Kirsch predicted. "It will not happen overnight. I think it may take a few decades to reach universality, but I believe it is only a question of time."[25]

The Prudent Application of Law and Morality

In a perfect world, everyone would act morally, obey the law, and insist that others conduct themselves in the same way. Moreover, what is legal and what is not, and what is moral and what is not, would be clear. Finally, our choices would be between good and evil, rather than between greater and lesser evils. In our imperfect world, standards and choices are often much murkier, which leads to several questions regarding the prudence of applying standards of law and morality.

Can ends justify means? One conundrum is whether an act that by itself is evil can be justified if it is done for a good cause. Some believe that ends never justify means. The philosopher Immanuel Kant took a position of **moral absolutism** in his *Groundwork on the Metaphysics of Morals* (1785) and argued that ends never justify means. He therefore urged us to "do what is right though the world should perish."

There are others who, at least in practice, maintain that what they consider to be lofty goals do justify acts that most other people would condemn as morally abhorrent. Terrorism is a case in point. For example, the Middle East terrorist group Hamas justifies suicide bombings against Israeli civilians on the grounds that the "heroic martyrdom operations . . . represent the sole weapon" available to the Palestinian people. The statement went on to argue that "denying the Palestinian people the right of self-defense and describing this as terrorism, which should have been linked with the occupation [of Palestinian lands by Israel], violates all laws and norms which granted the people's the right of

YOU BE THE PLAYWRIGHT

Would You Kill This Baby?

Here is a chance for you to rewrite the script and change the future. The setting is Braunau, Austria. The address is 219 Salzberger Vorstadt in a building once known as the Gasthof zum Pommer. There, on Easter Sunday, April 20, 1889, a child was born. It is a year later, and you have been transported back to that time and are standing in the room with the child. You are contemplating whether to kill the baby boy. If you do, you will be immediately transported back to the 21st century and will be beyond the reach of the Austrian police.

The infant is Adolf Hitler, the fourth child of Alois Schickelgruber and Klara Hitler. He is a normal, cute baby, as you can see in the accompanying picture. His parents love him, and their neighbors think he is adorable. Unlike anyone in Braunau or indeed the world in 1890, however, you know what the future holds. Baby Adolf will grow up to be the führer of Nazi Germany. His Third Reich will be responsible for the horrors of World War II and the genocidal acts against Europe's Jews, Gypsies, and others. You know that he will die by his own hand on April 29, 1945, in a bunker in Berlin. But by then it will be too late. Tens of millions of people will have died in the war in Europe and 6 million Jews and other people deemed undesirable will have perished in death camps. Should you kill the baby now?

All this may seem macabre, but the point is to struggle with what for most people would be a moral dilemma. A moral absolutist would not kill young Hitler. Someone who is amoral would have no qualms about doing it. However, most people, probably including you, are moral relativists who make moral decisions in a context. So what would you do? You can rewrite the script of history by taking a pillow and smothering baby Adolf. But would the ends justify the means? Moreover, the world drama is partly an improvisational play, so you cannot be absolutely sure of what will occur in the 1930s and the first half of the 1940s if there is a simple marker reading "Adolf Hitler, 1889–1890" at the resting place in Braunau. How do you see 1930–1945 without Hitler?

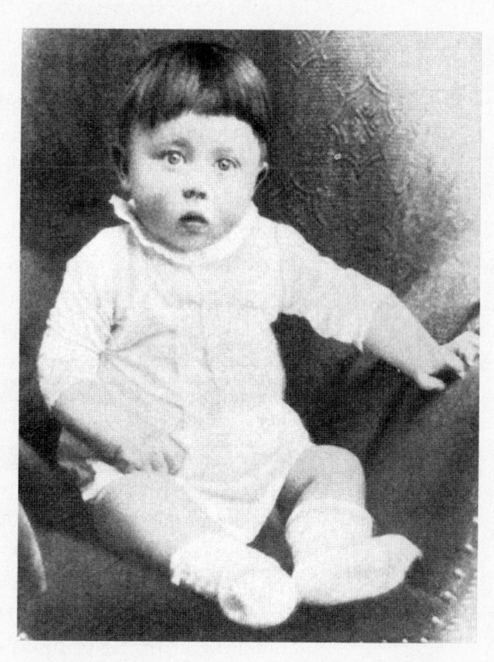

Would you kill this baby? Imagine you have been transported back to early 1890 and you are standing just out of this picture. No one but you and the child are present. The baby in this picture is Adolf Hitler, about a year after his birth on April 20, 1889, in Braunau, Austria. Given your knowledge of the horrors of World War II and the Holocaust, would you kill baby Adolf? Would the end justify the means? This and other issues are raised if one attempts to apply moral standards to the formation and conduct of foreign policy.

self-defense" and that "considering the Palestinian resistance as a terrorist act and an outlaw legitimizes occupation because it de-legitimizes its resistance."[26]

In practice, the primitive international political system can make the strict application of strong moral principles, adherence to international law, and other such altruistic acts unwise and even dangerous. Clearly, most of us do not take such an absolute position. Nor do we practice **amorality**. Instead, most people adhere to **moral relativism**. They believe that actions must be placed in context. For example, most Americans explicitly or implicitly accept capital punishment and the atomic bombings of Hiroshima and Nagasaki as somehow justified as retaliation or even as an unfortunate necessity to a better end. The problem, again, is where to draw the line. How about assassination? Explore that possibility in the You Be the Playwright box "Would You Kill This Baby?"

Should we judge others by our own standards? The issue about whether to judge others morally rests on two controversies. The first, which we have already addressed, is whether one should apply standards of international law and morality given the divergent values of a multicultural world. Some claim that doing so is cultural imperialism; others believe that at least some universal standards exist.

The second objection to any country's or even the UN's imposing sanctions or taking any other action based on another country's supposed morality or lack thereof is that it violates the sovereignty of the target country. Many Americans have few qualms about criticizing the human rights record of other countries, but they become outraged when others find American standards lacking. Capital punishment is legal and on the rise in most U.S. states, but many other countries find the practice abhorrent. Therefore they refuse to extradite accused criminals to the United States if there is a possibility of capital punishment. This has included statements by a number of countries in the aftermath of the 9/11 attacks that they would not transfer suspected terrorists to the United States if the accused faced the death penalty. Belgium was one of these countries. As its Minister of Justice Marc Verwilghen explained, "We always have said in the European Union that the execution of the death penalty is not an option."[27]

The opposition to capital punishment is intensified by the belief that there are demographic injustices in who gets executed. The UN Commission on Human Rights (UNCHR) has called for a moratorium on executions because, in part, of a UNCHR report that found that in the United States "race, ethnic origin and economic status appear to be key determinants of who will and will not receive a sentence of death."[28] Americans have regularly rejected such refusals to extradite on the grounds that executions are immoral as gross outside interference.

Is it prudent to apply moral and legal standards? Another objection to trying to apply moral principles is based on self-interest. Realists maintain that national interest sometimes precludes the application of otherwise laudable moral principles. They further contend that trying to uphold abstract standards of morality casts a leader as a perpetual Don Quixote, a pseudo knight-errant whose wish "To dream the impossible dream; to fight the unbeatable foe; . . . [and] to right the unrightable wrong," while appealing romantically, is delusional and perhaps dangerous. One danger is that you waste your reputation, your wealth, and the lives of your soldiers trying to do the impossible. A second peril springs from the reality that since not all states act morally, those who do are at a disadvantage: "Nice guys finish last."

Those who disagree with this line of reasoning contend that it fails the test of courageously standing up for what is right. They might even recall the remonstration of President John F. Kennedy, who, evoking Dante Alighieri's *The Divine Comedy* (1321), commented, "Dante once said that the hottest places in hell are reserved for those who in a period of moral crisis maintain their neutrality."[29]

More pragmatically, advocates of applying principles of law and morality contend that greater justice is necessary for world survival. This argument deals, for example, with resource distribution. It contends that it is immoral to maintain a large part of the world both impoverished and without self-development possibilities. The inevitable result, according to this view, will be a world crisis that will destroy order as countries fight for every declining resource.

One way out of the dilemma about when and to what degree law, morality, and other principles should apply to foreign policy may be to begin with the observation that it is not necessary to choose between moral absolutism and amorality. Instead, there is a middle ground of moral relativism that relies on **moral prudence** as a guiding principle. There is a secular prayer that asks for the courage to change the wrongs one can, the patience to accept the wrongs that one cannot change, and the wisdom to know the difference. From this perspective, a decision maker must ask, first, whether any tangible good is likely to result from a course of action and, second, whether the good will outweigh negative collateral consequences. By the first standard, taking high-flown principled stands when it is impossible or unlikely that you will affect the situation is quixotic. By the second standard, applying morality when the overall consequences will be vastly more negative also fails the test of prudence. But not taking action when change is possible and when the good will outweigh the bad fails the test of just behavior.

The Future of International Law and Morality

The often anarchic and inequitable world makes it easy to dismiss idealistic talk of conducting international relations according to standards of international law and morality as prattling. This view, however, was probably never valid and certainly is not true now. An irreversible trend in world affairs is the rapid acceleration of states and people interacting in almost all areas of endeavor. As these interactions have grown, so has the need for regularized behavior and for rules to prescribe that behavior. For very pragmatic reasons, then, many people have come to believe, as one analyst notes, that "most issues of transnational concern are best addressed through legal frameworks that render the behavior of global actors more predictable and induce compliance from potential or actual violators" (Ratner, 1998:78). The growth of these rules in functional international interactions has been on the leading edge of the development of international law. Advances in political and military areas have been slower, but here too there has been progress. Thus, as with the United Nations, the pessimist may decry the glass as less than half full, whereas, in reality, it is encouraging that there is more and more water in the previously almost empty glass.

All the signs point to increasing respect for international law and a greater emphasis on adhering to at least rudimentary standards of morality. Violations of international standards are now more likely to draw criticism from the world community. It is probable, therefore, that international law will continue to develop and to expand its areas of application. So too will moral discourse have an increasing impact on the actions of the international actors. There will certainly be areas where growth is painfully slow, and there will also be those who violate the principles of law and morality and who sometimes get away with their unlawful and immoral acts. But, just as surely, there will be progress.

Chapter Summary

Fundamentals of International Law and Morality

1. International law can be best understood as a primitive system of law in comparison with much more developed domestic law. There are only the most rudimentary procedures and institutions for making, adjudicating, and enforcing international law. This does not mean, however, that international law is impotent, only that it is in an earlier stage of development than domestic law.
2. As a developing phenomenon, international law is dynamic and has been growing since the earliest periods of civilization. This growth accelerated in the 20th century because the increasing level of international interaction and interdependence required many new rules to govern and regularize contacts in trade, finance, travel, communication, and other areas. The possible consequences of war have also spurred the development of international law.
3. Thus far, international law is most effective when it governs functional international relations. International law works least well in areas of "high politics," where the vital interests of the sovereign states are at

stake. Even in those areas, though, international law is gradually becoming more effective.

4. Morality is another factor in establishing the rules of the international system. It acts as a guide to action and as the basis for some international law.

The International Legal System

5. The international legal system has four essential elements: its philosophical roots, lawmaking, adherence, and adjudication.
6. The roots of law for any legal system may come from external sources, such as natural law, or from within the society, such as custom.
7. Regarding lawmaking, international law springs from a number of sources, including international treaties, international custom, general principles of law, and international representative assemblies. Some scholars argue that resolutions and other pronouncements of the UN General Assembly should be included as a significant influence.
8. Regarding adherence, international law, again like primitive law, relies mainly on voluntary compliance and self-help. Here again, though, there are early and still uncertain examples of enforcement by third parties, a feature that characterizes more advanced systems.
9. The fourth essential element of a legal system, adjudication, is also in the primitive stage in international law. Although there are a number of international courts in the world today, their jurisdiction and their use and effectiveness are limited. The International Court of Justice and other such international judicial bodies represent an increasing sophistication of international law in this area as well.

Applying International Law and Morality

10. In a still culturally diverse world, standards of international law and morality have encountered problems of fit with different cultures. Most current international law and many concepts of morality, such as the stress on individualism, are based on Western ideas and practices, and many non-Western states object to certain aspects of international law as it exists.
11. The changes in the world system in this century have created a number of important issues related to international law. Among these are the status of sovereignty, the legality of war and the conduct of war, rules for governing the biosphere, and observing and protecting human rights.
12. International law has been interpreted as applying to states. Now it is also concerned with individuals. Primarily, it applies to the treatment of individuals by states, but it also has some application to the actions of individuals. Thus people, as well as countries, are coming to have obligations, as well as rights, under international law.
13. It is not always possible to insist on strict adherence to international law and to high moral standards, yet they cannot be ignored. One middle way is to apply principles prudently.

The Future of International Law and Morality

14. With the growth of international interaction in the last century, international law has developed, and rudimentary standards of morality are being established. Although this growth has sometimes been slow, there will definitely be continued progress in the future.

For a chapter quiz, interactive activities, web links, PowerWeb articles, and much more, visit **www.mhhe.com/rourke10/** and go to chapter 9. Or, while accessing the site, click on Course-Wide Content and view recent international relations articles in the *New York Times.*

Key Terms

adjudication
amorality
codify
cultural imperialism
functional relations
ideological/theological school of law
International Court of Justice (ICJ)
jus ad bellum
jus in bello
moral absolutism
moral prudence
moral relativism
naturalist school of law
pacta sunt servanda
positivist school of law

CHAPTER

10

National Security: The Traditional Road

WAR AND WORLD POLITICS
- War: The Human Record
- The Causes of War: Three Levels of Analysis

NATIONAL MILITARY POWER
- Levels of Spending
- Weaponry: Quantity versus Quality
- Military Morale and Leadership
- Military and Political Reputation
- Military Power: The Dangers of Overemphasis

FORCE AS A POLITICAL INSTRUMENT
- Levels of Violence: From Intimidation to Attack
- The Effectiveness of Force
- The Changing Nature of War
- Classifying Warfare

UNCONVENTIONAL WARFARE
- Arms Transfers
- Special Operations
- Terrorism

CONVENTIONAL WARFARE
- Goals and Conduct
- Avoiding Unchecked Escalation

WARFARE WITH WEAPONS OF MASS DESTRUCTION
- Biological Weapons
- Chemical Weapons
- The Potential for Nuclear War
- Nuclear Weapons, Deterrence, and Strategy

CHAPTER SUMMARY

KEY TERMS

[W]hen the blast of war blows in our ears,
Then imitate the tiger:
Stiffen the sinews, conjure up the blood,
Disguise fair nature with hard-favour'd rage;
Then lend the eye a terrible aspect.

—William Shakespeare, *King Henry V*

We make war that we may live in peace.

—Aristotle, *Nicomachean Ethics,* ca. 325 B.C.

An eye for an eye only winds up making the whole world blind.

—Mohandas K. (Mahatma) Gandhi

CHAPTER OBJECTIVES

After completing this chapter, you should be able to:

- Identify reasons for studying war and summarize the human record of war, including the incidence, death toll, frequency, and severity.
- Discuss the causes of war by applying the three levels of analysis: system, state, and individual.
- Evaluate force as a political instrument and discuss its limitations.
- Discuss the escalating use of a country's military power, from intimidation to attack.
- Analyze the effectiveness of the threat and use of force in the international system.
- Discuss how the nature of war has changed as a result of nationalism and technology.
- Describe the destinations, sources, motives, and impact of international arms transfers.
- Characterize covert intervention and terrorism and distinguish between them.
- Define and describe the goals and conduct of war.
- Analyze limited nuclear-biological-chemical war as part of a battlefield strategy.
- Examine the major issues surrounding strategic nuclear war.
- Evaluate strategic nuclear weapons and strategy as ongoing factors in international politics.

War is an enigma. We bewail its existence and consequences, while we regularly wage it with exhilaration. Expressing the sentiment of many who have experienced war, General William Tecumseh Sherman cautioned in 1879, "It is only those who have neither fired a shot nor heard the shrieks and groans of the wounded who cry aloud for more blood, more vengeance, more desolation. War is hell!" General of the Army Dwight David Eisenhower agreed: "I hate war as only a soldier who has lived it can, as only one who has seen its brutality, its futility, its stupidity."

War may be hell, but it is also exhilarating for many. "I have loved war too much," King Louis XIV of France confessed in 1710. "It is well that war is so terrible—we should grow too fond of it," General Robert E. Lee wrote similarly in 1862. More than a century later, President George H. W. Bush paced the White House grounds in 1991 carrying a mini television to follow live reports of the U.S. aerial assault on Iraq. When miniature images of U.S. warplanes attacking their targets flickered on the screen, "Bush jabbed his index finger at each target on the screen as though silently declaring 'Gotcha!'"[1] Lest we think it is just the leaders who are fascinated by war, the go-with-the-troops, mini-cam images broadcast by "embedded" reporters captivated Americans in 2003. Just after war with Iraq broke out in March, 69% of Americans told one survey that they were keeping their televisions tuned to the war news, and in another poll, 41% of the respondents were willing to admit, "I just can't stop watching news about the war."[2] This was true even though so little of substance could be seen that one media expert compared the coverage to "salted peanuts . . . very tasty and almost empty of high-quality nourishment."[3]

War and World Politics

Whatever one's view of war, there is resonance to scholar Max Weber's (1864–1920) classic observation: "The decisive means for politics is violence. Anyone who fails to see this is . . . a political infant" (Porter, 1994:303). Perhaps that need not always be, but the reality for now is that countries continue to rely on themselves for protection and sometimes use threats and violence to further their interests. Thus, it is important to examine military power and to grasp the role that force plays in the conduct of international politics.

War: The Human Record

War is as ancient as humanity (Cioffi-Revilla, 2000). One reasonable number, as shown in Figure 10.1, is that there were almost 1,000 wars during the millennium that just ended. Looking even farther back, it is possible to see that the world has been totally free of significant interstate, colonial, or civil war in only about 1 out of every 12 years in all of recorded human history. The data also shows that war is not a tragic anachronism waged by our less civilized ancestors. To the contrary, political violence continues. Two ways to gauge this are by frequency and severity.

Frequency provides bad news. Over the last ten centuries, as Figure 10.1 shows, wars between countries have become more frequent, with some 30% occurring in just the last two centuries. It is true that the frequency of war in the 1900s declined somewhat from the horrific rate in the 1800s, but it is also the case that the number of civil wars increased. This means that the overall incidence of interstate and intrastate warfare remains relatively steady (Pickering & Thompson, 1998).

Severity is the truly terrible news. Again as evident in Figure 10.1, over 147 million people have died during wars since the year 1000. Of the dead, an astounding 75%

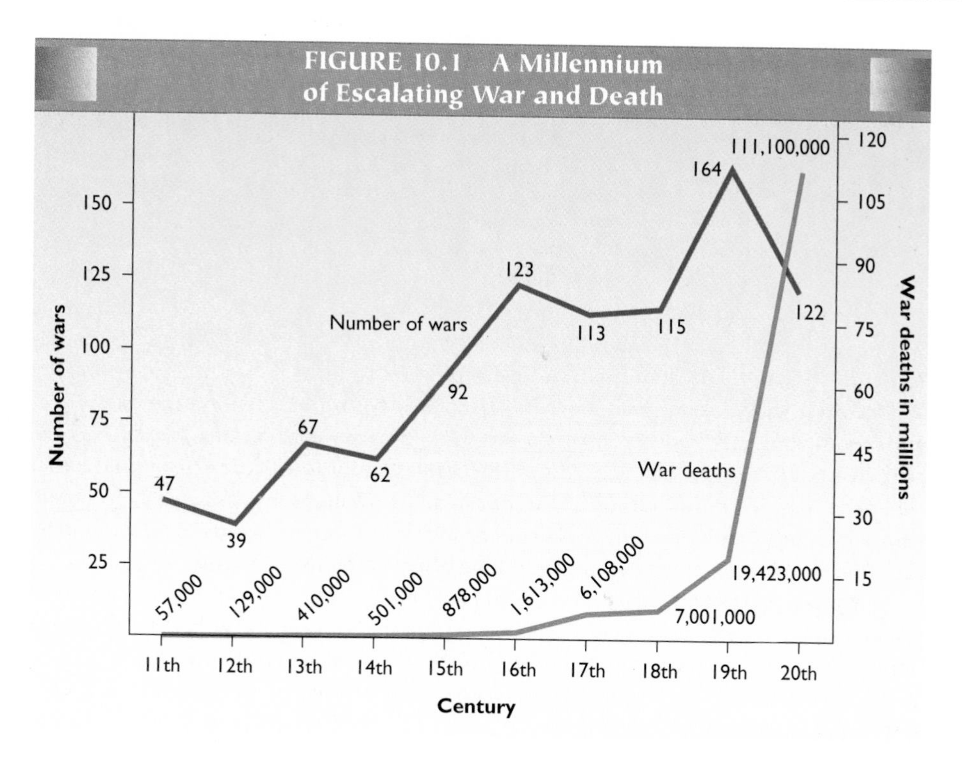

This figure shows the long-term trend in the rise of both the frequency and severity of war. Beginning in the year 1000, the number of wars in each century has usually increased. The soaring death toll of the 20th century's wars, which accounted for 75% of the millennium's total, is a truly alarming figure.

Data sources: Eckhardt (1991); author. Eckhardt defines a war as a conflict that (1) involves a government on at least one side and (2) accounts for at least 1,000 deaths per year of the conflict.

perished in the 20th century and 89% since 1800. Not only do we kill more soldiers, we also now kill larger numbers of civilians. During World War I, six soldiers died for every civilian killed (8.4 million soldiers and 1.4 million civilians). World War II killed two civilians for every soldier (16.9 million troops and 34.3 million civilians). The worst news may lie ahead. A nuclear war could literally fulfill President John F. Kennedy's warning in 1961 that "mankind must put an end to war, or war will put an end to mankind."

The Causes of War: Three Levels of Analysis

Why war? This question has challenged investigators over the centuries (Caplow & Hicks, 2002; Geller & Singer, 1998). Philosophers, world leaders, and social scientists have many theories, but there is no consensus. Further research might be able to identify a single root cause of war, but it is more likely that there is no single reason why people fight. Given this, one way to discuss the multiple causes of war is to classify them according to the three levels of analysis: system-level analysis, state-level analysis, and individual-level analysis, detailed in chapter 3.

System-Level Causes of War

Wars may be caused by a number of factors related to the general nature of the world's political system (Cashman, 1999). To illustrate that here, we can touch on four system-level variables.

The distribution of power. Recall from chapter 3 that some analysts believe that the propensity for warfare to occur within the international system is related to factors such as the system's number of poles (big powers), their relative power, and whether the poles and their power are stable or in flux. When, for example, a system is experiencing significant power transitions (that is, when some powers are rising and others are declining or even vanishing), power vacuums often occur. These can cause conflict as opposing powers move to fill the void. Postwar alliances that concentrate power by bringing victorious major countries together have also been found to be "war prone" (Gibler & Vasquez, 1998:805).

The anarchical nature of the system. Some systems analysts argue that wars occur because there is no central authority to try to prevent conflict and to protect countries. Unlike domestic societies, the international society has no effective system of law creation, enforcement, or adjudication. When the gap between U.S. demands on Iraq and what Iraq was willing to do proved unbridgeable, there was no court that could either subpoena Iraqi records or enjoin an American attack. War ensued. This self-help system causes insecurity, and, therefore, countries acquire arms in part because other countries do, creating a tension-filled cycle of escalating arms → tensions → arms → tensions.

System-level economic factors. The global pattern of production and use of natural resources is one of the system-level economic factors that can cause conflict. This was evident in 1990 when Iraq endangered the main sources of petroleum production by attacking Kuwait and threatening Saudi Arabia. A U.S-led coalition of countries dependent on petroleum rushed to defend the Saudis and to liberate the Kuwaitis (and their oil). The global gap between wealthy and poor countries is another system-level factor. Some analysts believe that the highly uneven distribution of wealth between countries and regions is one reason that a great deal of terrorism is rooted in the South.

System-level biosphere stress. Overconsumption of biosphere resources is yet another possible system-level cause of conflict. Water provides one example. This basic resource is becoming so precious in many areas that, as you will see in chapter 16, there are growing concerns that countries might soon go to war with one another over disputes about water supplies. According to one scholar, "When the empire of man over nature can no longer be easily extended, then the only way for one people to increase its standard of living is by redistributing the sources or fruits of industry from others to themselves. The surest way to do this is by extending man's empire over man" (Orme, 1998:165).

State-Level Causes of War

War may result from the very nature of states (Auerswald, 1999; Dassel, 1998). There are also several theories of war that have to do with the internal processes and conditions of countries (Morgan & Anderson, 1999; Fordham, 1998).

Militarism. Some scholars believe that states inherently tend toward militarism. One such analyst writes that "it is impossible to understand the nature of modern politics without considering its military roots" (Porter, 1994:xix). The argument is that as warfare required more soldiers and more increasingly expensive weapons, it created a need for political units with larger populations and economies. This gave rise to the state.

Externalization of internal conflict. Sometimes during domestic distress, governments try to stay in power by fomenting a foreign crisis in order to rally the populace and divert its attention. This ploy is called diversionary war or the externalization of internal conflict. Evidence indicates, for instance, that revolutionary regimes will attempt to consolidate their power by fomenting tension with other countries (Andrade, 2003). It is also the case that countries are more likely to go to war while they are experiencing times of economic distress.

Type of country. There are analysts who believe that some types of countries, because of their political structure (democratic, authoritarian) or their economic resources and wealth, are more aggressive than others. Chapter 6 discusses, for example, the democratic peace theory—the conclusion of most analysts that democratic countries are not prone to fighting with one another.

Political culture. Some scholars believe that a nation's political culture is correlated to warlike behavior. No nation has a genetic political character. Nations, however, that have had repeated experiences with violence may develop a political culture that views the world as a hostile environment. It is not necessary for the list to go on to make the point that how states are organized and how they make policy can sometimes lead to conflict and war among them.

One possible state-level cause of war occurs when a leader who is in political trouble at home tries to divert the country's attention by creating a foreign crisis. During the summer of 1998, President Bill Clinton was mired in a scandal involving sexual intimacy with White House intern Monica Lewinsky and having lied about the matter in public and in a legal deposition. In August, after terrorist bombings of U.S. embassies in Kenya and Tanzania by al-Qaeda, he ordered a cruise missile attack on a factory in Khartoum, Sudan. Clinton asserted the factory was producing chemical weapons for terrorists and for Iraq. Sudanese officials insisted it made only medicine. The Sudanese women demonstrating in this picture reflect the view of the speaker of Sudan's parliament, Hassan Turabi, who argued, "I think the president is haunted by all this campaign of Monica Lewinsky. If he lied to his own wife and betrayed his own matrimonial contract, and his own Congress and his own courts, then it is much easier to lie across the world."[1]

Individual-Level Causes of War

It may be that the causes of war are linked to the character of individual leaders or to the nature of the human species. "In the final analysis," one scholar writes, "any contemplation of war must return to . . . the nature of humanity, which yet stands as the root cause of war and the wellspring of history's inestimable tragedy" (Porter, 1994:304).

Human characteristics. Those who have this perspective believe that although it is clear that human behavior is predominantly learned, there are also behavioral links to the primal origins of humans. Territoriality, which we examined in chapter 3, is one such possible instinct, and the fact that territorial disputes are so frequently the cause of war may point to some instinctual territoriality in humans. Another possibility, some social psychologists argue, is that human aggression, individually or collectively, can stem from stress, anxiety, or frustration. The reaction of the German society to its defeat and humiliation after World War I is an example.

Individual leaders' characteristics. The individual traits of leaders may also play a role in war. One scholar has concluded after long study that "the personalities of the leaders . . . have often been decisive. . . . In all cases [studied], a fatal flaw or character weakness in a leader's personality was of critical importance. It may, in fact, have spelled the difference between the outbreak of war and the maintenance of peace" (Stoessinger, 1998:210). For example, a leader may have a personality that favors taking risks, when caution might be the better choice (Vertzberger, 1998). A leader may also have a psychological need for power. While discounting some of the more strident characterizations of Saddam Hussein as a madman, most personality analyses of Iraq's former leader characterize him as driven to seek power and to dominate, traits that made it hard for him to cooperate completely with UN arms inspectors. Individual experiences and emotions also play a role, and it is not fatuous to ask what the impact of Iraq's attempt to assassinate former President George H. W. Bush in 1993 was on his son's view of that country once he became president.

National Military Power

For good or ill, military power adds to a country's ability to prevail in international disputes. Therefore, it is appropriate to first consider the nature of military power that provides the sword for policy makers to wield. Military power is based on an array of tangible factors, such as weapons, and intangible factors, such as leadership.

Levels of Spending

Defense spending is one of the largest categories in most countries' budgets. Global military spending soared during the tense years of the cold war, peaking at nearly $1 trillion in 1987. After the end of the cold war, defense spending dropped significantly during the 1990s. By the last half of the 1990s it averaged about $730 billion, a decrease of more than 25% in current dollars and even more in real dollars (value controlled for inflation, constant dollars) from 1987. Then spending inched higher during 1999 and 2000, followed by even larger increases associated with the expansion of the U.S. defense budget in the aftermath of the 9/11 terrorist attacks, as evident in Figure 10.2. The $792 billion in current dollars (the value in the year being reported) that the world's governments spent on their militaries in 2002 equaled about 2.5% of the world gross domestic product (GDP) or about $128 for each of the world's more than 6 billion people. The United States has by far the largest defense budget. At $340 billion during 2002, it accounted for 43% of global military expenditures.

FIGURE 10.2 Trends in Global Military Spending

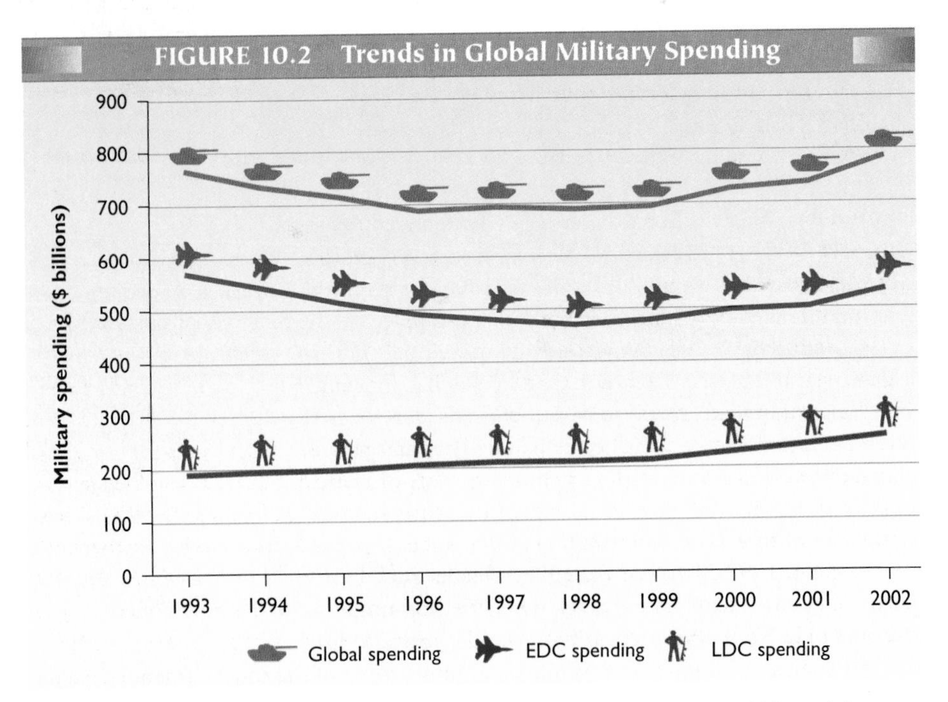

Global military spending peaked in the late 1980s, then declined into the mid-1990s, and then began to rise again, to stand in 2002 at the same level as just after the cold war, in real dollars. Notice that while LDC military spending remained much lower than EDC spending, it was on an upward trend throughout the entire period and increased 31%.

Notes: Expenditures calculated in 2000 dollars. For this chart, EDCs includes the countries of Eastern Europe, including Russia, as well as those of Western Europe, Oceania, the United States, and Canada.

Data source: Stockholm International Peace Research Institute (SIPRI), 2003.

Within Figure 10.2 it is also worth noting that military spending (in real dollars) of the world's economically less developed countries (LDCs) increased steadily during the period. The LDCs spent over $256 billion (current dollars) on their militaries in 2002. The amount was equivalent to about 4% of their collective GNPs, a percentage that the LDCs especially can ill afford because of their crying needs for spending on economic development, education, and health. A final troubling point is that the military budgets of some regions and countries have increased amid the general global decline in military spending. Military expenditures in South and East Asia increased in real dollars about 25% between 1993 and 2002, and there is an escalating arms race in the region, with China, India, and Pakistan the main contenders. China's defense spending measured in real dollars increased during the ten-year period by 219%, and India's spending for those years escalated 158%.

Weaponry: Quantity versus Quality

Very often when you see a comparison of two countries' or alliances' military might, you see a map with an overlay of small figures representing troops, tanks, planes, and other weapons. Such graphics emphasize quantity, and it always seems as if the other side's figures far outnumber your own.

> ***Did You Know That:***
> The world's smallest army is the Vatican's 100-man Swiss Guard. The original force was formed from Swiss mercenaries who had defended Pope Clement VII during the sacking of Rome in 1527 by, oddly, Charles V, the Holy Roman Emperor.

Quantity is an important military consideration, but the relative value of these figures must be modified by the cost and quality of the weapons and troops. The West, especially the United States, has tended to favor acquiring fewer but superior high-technology weapons. The wars against Iraq in 1991 and 2003, for example, were showcases for high-technology warfare as U.S. main battle tanks maneuvered at nearly highway speeds and coalition pilots used laser guidance systems to steer "smart bombs" to their targets.

The triumph of technology against Iraq must, however, be considered carefully. In the first place, high technology is very expensive. Just after the 9/11 terrorist attacks, President Bush vowed, "When I take action, I'm not going to fire a $2 million [cruise] missile at a $10 empty tent [in Afghanistan] and hit a camel in the butt."[4] Yet he did use B-2 bombers, which cost $2.1 billion each, to drop munitions on the rudimentarily armed Taliban and al-Qaeda forces. Indeed, the cost of a single B-2 is more than the yearly defense budgets of about two-thirds of the world's countries.

Second, it is difficult to calculate precisely the relative worth of a greater number of lower technology weapons versus fewer, more sophisticated, weapons. The newest U.S. fighter, the F-22, is a technological marvel that can defeat any other fighter. One has to wonder, though, whether one $150 million F-22 could defeat, say, four Russian-built SU-30 fighters (available for $37 million), which are being supplied to China, North Korea, Iran, and a variety of other countries with which U.S. relations are often strained.

It should also be remembered that the effectiveness of soldiers and military hardware is very situational. Therefore, a country's military systems need to be appropriate to the challenges they will face. American technology twice easily overwhelmed the Iraqis in the relatively open terrain near the Persian Gulf but was not able to prevail during the war in densely forested Vietnam against an even less sophisticated opponent than Iraq.

Military Morale and Leadership

Morale is a key element of military power. An army that does not fight well cannot win. Historian Stephen Ambrose, who served as a consultant for the film *Saving Private Ryan,* reflects that "in the end success or failure on D-Day [came] down to a relatively small number of junior officers, noncoms, and privates." According to Ambrose, "If the men coming in over the beaches [had] flopped down behind the seawall and refused to

The Iraqi army's lack of morale caused by poor equipment, uniforms, and supplies was one reason that it offered so little resistance during the war in 2003. The feet visible here belong to an Iraqi soldier killed in March 2003, during the initial U.S./U.K. attack. Instead of wearing combat boots, this ill-equipped soldier was wearing loafers that, themselves, were in poor repair.

advance, if the noncoms and junior officers [had] failed to lead their men up and over the seawall . . . in the face of enemy fire—why, then, the Germans would [have won] the battle and thus the war."[5]

Morale, of course, is not inherent. Russian soldiers fought with amazing valor during World War II despite conditions that, in many cases, were far worse than those that American troops faced. Yet in more recent times, the morale of Russia's soldiers has been sapped by their substandard living and working conditions; they have been poorly paid, housed, equipped, and trained. In the aftermath of the collapse of Iraq's army in 2003, some Russian military experts were worried that a similar fate might await Russia's army in a war. "Go on the street and ask who is ready to defend the motherland, and you will immediately see unpleasant parallels," fretted retired General Andrei Nikolayev, who chairs the defense affairs committee in the lower house of parliament, the State Duma. "The outcome of a war depends on the army's morale."[6]

Military leadership also plays a significant role for good or ill. There is little doubt that U.S. and British forces would have defeated the Iraqi military in 2003, but Saddam Hussein's practice of placing those most loyal to him, rather than the best officers, in command of his country's armed forces and creating many specialized units instead of a central command helped speed the rapid collapse of Iraq's army. According to one Iraqi colonel, the multiple units, some commanded by Saddam Hussein's sons, were created because "he was afraid the regular army might rise up against him." Added an Iraqi general, "There was no coordination between these armies—they hate[d] each other."[7]

Military and Political Reputation

Another power consideration is a country's reputation. Whatever real power a country may possess, its ability to influence others will depend partly on how those others perceive its capacity and will. National leaders commonly believe that weakness tempts their opponents, while a reputation for strength deters them. This has been an issue for the United States in recent decades because some observers believe, as one French general put it, that Americans want "zero-dead wars."[8] The image was formed amid the reluctance of the United States to commit ground forces in the aftermath of the frustrating Vietnam War and was heightened by the U.S. withdrawals in the face of casualties in Lebanon in 1983 and Somalia in 1993. The thinking goes that this reputation emboldened U.S. opponents, including perhaps Saddam Hussein, who argued before he invaded Kuwait, "The nature of American society makes it impossible for the United States to bear tens of thousands of casualties."[9]

The month-long air assault on Iraq before U.S. ground forces moved forward in 1991 and the exclusive use of air power to pound Yugoslavia into submission in 1999 did nothing to dispel the image that American public opinion would not tolerate significant U.S. casualties. Because President Bush believed U.S. power was being undermined by the widely held image that Americans were "flaccid" and "wouldn't fight back," he was adamant in 2001 about "putting boots on the ground" (committing ground forces) in Afghanistan.[10] Still, the actual use of U.S. troops was generally limited in favor of using anti-Taliban Afghani forces. Bush again committed ground forces in 2003, this time again in Iraq. Moreover, they launched their invasion after a much shorter aerial assault than had occurred in 1991. Still, for some the image of an American public unwilling to face casualties will probably persist in light of the deaths and wounding of American soldiers in postwar Iraq and the rapid decline in public support for a U.S. presence there.

Military Power: The Dangers of Overemphasis

Given the importance of military power as a tool of national defense and diplomacy, it is not uncommon for people to assume that the phrase "too much military power" must be an oxymoron. Exactly how much is enough is a complex question, but it is certain that there are clear dangers associated with overemphasizing military power. Three such perils deserve special mention. They are insecurity, temptation, and expense.

Military power creates insecurity. One result of power acquisition is the "spiral of insecurity." This means that our attempts to amass power to achieve security or gain other such ends are frequently perceived by others as a danger to them. They then seek to acquire offsetting power, which we see as threatening, causing us to acquire even more power . . . then them . . . then us, ad infinitum, in an escalating spiral. As evident in chapter 11's review of disarmament, the arms race is a complex phenomenon, but the interaction of one country's power and other countries' insecurity is an important factor in world politics.

Military power creates temptation. A second peril of amassing excess military power is the temptation to use it in a situation that is peripheral to the national interest. The United States went to war in Vietnam despite the fact that President Lyndon Johnson derided it as a "raggedy-ass fourth-rate country." One reason Americans intervened in Vietnam was because of a so-called arrogance of power. Had U.S. military power been more modest, the United States might have emphasized diplomacy or maybe even acquiesced to the reunification of North and South Vietnam. One can never be sure, but it is certain that it is hard to shoot someone if you do not own a gun.

Military power is expensive. A third problem with acquiring military power is that it is extremely expensive. Beyond the short-term budget decisions about choosing between domestic or defense programs and how to pay the costs, there is a longer-range concern. One scholar who studied the decline of great powers between 1500 and the 1980s concluded that "imperial overstretch" was the cause of their degeneration (Kennedy, 1988). His thesis is that superpowers of the past spent so much on military power that, ironically, they weakened the country's strength by siphoning off resources that should have been devoted to maintaining and improving the country's infrastructure. Kennedy's study did not include the Soviet Union, but it is arguable that the collapse of the USSR followed the pattern of overspending on the military, thereby enervating the country's economic core. Declinists warn that the United States is also guilty of imperial overstretch and could go the way of other great powers that rose, dominated, then fell from the pinnacle of power. Indeed, for declinists, the Bush Doctrine will hasten the U.S. downturn. "America is marching in the well-trod footsteps of virtually all of the imperial powers of the modern age," one scholar writes. "The Bush rhetoric of preventive war is a disconcerting reflection of the disastrous strategic ideas of those earlier keepers of the imperial order" (Snyder, 2002:2).

The drawing of Uncle Sam reaching beyond his grasp illustrates the view that U.S. power is declining because of "imperial overstretch," whereby the country spends too much on military power in an effort to become and remain a superpower. Other observers argue that any decline that has occurred is the result of overspending on what they see as economically unproductive programs such as care for the elderly. This might be called "social overstretch."

The **imperial overstretch thesis** has many critics (Knutsen, 1999). At the strategic level, some critics argue that far more danger is posed by a "lax Americana" than by any effort to create a "pax Americana." The reasoning is that if the United States does not exercise certain leadership as hegemon, then the international system is in danger of falling into disorder.[11] Similarly, some scholars warn that a rush to peace is only slightly less foolish than a rush to war. One study that reviewed the sharp cuts in U.S. military spending after World War II, the Korean War, and the Vietnam War concluded, "In each case the savings proved only temporary, as declining defense budgets eroded military

Many analysts agree that a country's power declines if it does not invest in its infrastructure, but they disagree about what diverts funds from that investment. Imperial overstretch theory argues that defense spending is the drain; social overstretch theory contends that appropriations for welfare, elderly care, and other such programs are sapping the economy. This figure shows the relative changes in U.S. military and social spending, but it does not answer the question of whether either or both are too high, too low, or about right.

Note: The 2004 budget is the president's budget request.
Data source: U.S. Office of Management and Budget: http://w3.access.gpo.gov/usbudget/fy2004/pdf/spec.pdf.

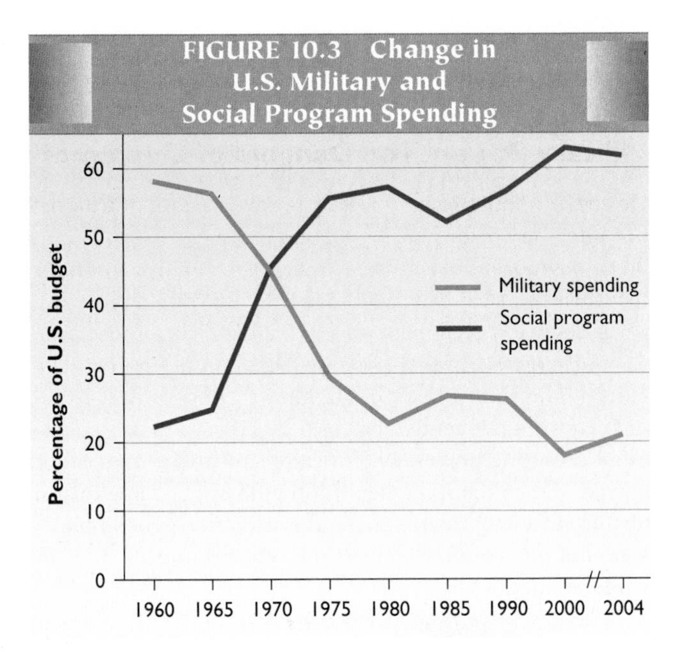

readiness and necessitated a rush to rearm in the face of new dangers abroad" (Thies, 1998:176).

Critics of Kennedy's thesis also say that it is wrong about the economic cause of decline. These critics agree with Kennedy that *overconsumption* (spending that depletes assets faster than the economy can replace them) at the expense of reinvestment (spending that creates infrastructure assets) causes decline. Whereas Kennedy argues that excessive military spending causes overconsumption, his critics say that the villain is too much social spending. This might be termed the **social overstretch thesis**. "Whether in the form of bread and circuses in the ancient world or medical care for the lower classes and social security for the aged in the modern world," the argument goes, it is social spending on the least productive elements of a society that financially drains it (Gilpin, 1981:164). It is a harsh judgment, but its advocates believe that the economic reality is that such altruistic programs may leave our spirits enriched but our coffers depleted. Consider, for example, Figure 10.3. It shows that over the long term, U.S. military spending has declined while spending on social programs has increased significantly as a percentage of the U.S. budget. It is also the case, however, that U.S. military spending accounts for more than one-third of all military spending in the world. Which, if either, category would you cut to increase spending on education, transportation, communications, and other infrastructure programs?

Force as a Political Instrument

It may be that future social scientists will be able to write of war in the past tense, but for the present we must recognize conflict as a fact of international politics. For this reason, having discussed the human record and causes of war, we should also consider levels of violence, the diplomatic and military effectiveness of force, the changing nature of warfare, and classifying warfare.

Levels of Violence: From Intimidation to Attack

A country's military power may be used in several escalating ways. These range from serving as a diplomatic backdrop that creates perceived power to direct use of military forces to defeat an opponent (Cimballa, 2002; Nathan, 2002). It also should be noted that the options provided by the five levels of violence form a multiple menu. That is, they are often exercised concurrently.

Diplomatic backdrop. Military power does not have to be used or even overtly threatened to be effective. Its very existence establishes a diplomatic backdrop that influences other countries (Freedman, 1998). "Diplomacy without force is like baseball without a bat," one U.S. diplomat has commented.[12] One obvious role of military strength is to persuade potential opponents not to risk confrontation. Military power also influences friends and neutrals. One reason why the United States has been, and remains, a leader of the West is because massive U.S. conventional and nuclear military power creates a psychological assumption by both holder and beholder that the country with dominant military power will play a strong role. This reality is what led one U.S. ambassador to China to put a photograph of a U.S. aircraft carrier on his office wall with the caption, "90,000 tons of diplomacy."[13]

Overt threats. A step up the escalation ladder is overtly threatening an opponent. That is what President Bush did in his address on March 17, 2003, when he declared, "Saddam Hussein and his sons must leave Iraq within 48 hours. Their refusal to do so will result in military conflict, commenced at a time of our choosing" and that the only way for "Iraqi military units to avoid being attacked and destroyed" was to follow the "clear instructions they would be given by U.S. forces."

Indirect intervention. A number of techniques can be used to apply military power while avoiding a commitment of your armed forces to direct combat. One approach is supplying arms and other military material or training and advisers to another government or to dissident forces. A second form of indirect intervention is sending military forces or nonuniformed operatives into another country secretly to conduct clandestine operations. Such operations can involve terrorism when the weapons supplied or the operatives sent in are involved in attacking targets beyond those that are of clear military utility.

Limited demonstration. A further escalation involves overtly wielding restrained conventional force to intimidate or harass rather than defeat an opponent. In 1996, for example, the United States attacked Iraqi military installations with about 30 cruise missiles in an effort to persuade Baghdad to end its military operations against Kurdish areas in the northern part of Iraq.

Direct action. The most violent option involves using full-scale force to attempt to defeat an opponent. Within this context, the level of violence can range from highly constrained conventional conflict, as occurred in Iraq in 2003, to unrestricted nuclear war.

Military power forms a backdrop to diplomacy and can also be used in escalating steps from threats to full-scale attacks. The F/A-18 Hornet preparing to take off is aboard the USS *Harry S. Truman*. One diplomat called aircraft carriers like the *Truman* "90,000 tons of diplomacy."

The Effectiveness of Force

Another aspect of the threat and use of force is the question of whether or not it works in a utilitarian way. It does, and one of the reasons that weapons and war persist in the international system is that they are sometimes successful. This continuing use of force is evident in the map of international conflicts between the end of WW II and 2003 on pages 310–311. The threat of violence may successfully deter an enemy from attacking you or an ally. The actual use of force also sometimes accomplishes intended goals. Given these realities, we should ask ourselves how to determine if force will be effective by utilitarian standards. Answering this question necessitates looking at measurements and conditions for success.

Measurement

Cost/benefit analysis is one of two ways of measuring the effectiveness of war. War is very expensive. There is no accurate count of the deaths in the 2003 war with Iraq but at least 20,000 and perhaps as many as 45,000 Iraqi soldiers were killed and another 2,200 or more Iraqi civilians perished. The invading U.S.-led forces had 378 soldiers killed, and that number had risen during the occupation to 830 by April 2004. As far as the financial costs, just after the war with Iraq erupted in 2003, President Bush asked Congress for $43 billion to pay for the war and another $19 billion for the occupation of Iraq. British expenses added at least another $5 billion to the total. Additionally, Iraq suffered substantial damage to roads, bridges, and other parts of its infrastructure. Were the results worth the loss of life, human anguish, and economic destruction? Although such trade-offs are made in reality, it is impossible to arrive at any objective standards that can equate the worth of a human life or political freedom with dollars spent or territory lost.

Goal attainment is the second way to judge the effectiveness of force. Generally, the decision for war is not irrational because leaders usually calculate, accurately or not, their probability of successfully achieving their goals. This calculation is called the "expected utility" of war. In the words of one study, "Initiators [of war] act as predators and are likely to attack [only] target states they know they can defeat" (Gartner & Siverson, 1996:4). By this standard, war does sometimes work. Indeed, the expected utility of force is especially apt to be positive when a major power starts the war. One study found that from 1495 to 1991, great powers that initiated wars won 60% of them (Wang & Ray, 1994). What is more, the initiators' success rate is going up. During the first three centuries (1495–1799), the initiators won 59% of the wars they fought. But during the last two centuries (1800–1991), the success rate increased, with the initiators winning 75% of the wars.

Of course, as Miguel de Cervantes noted in *Don Quixote* (ca. 1615), "There is nothing so subject to inconsistency of fortune as war." Leaders often miscalculate and, as Saddam Hussein did in 1990, start a war they ultimately lose. Also, it is sometimes hard to evaluate whether goals were attained. If the U.S. goal in 2003 was to defeat Iraq and topple Saddam Hussein, it certainly succeeded. However, since the main goal enunciated by President Bush was to destroy Iraq's nuclear program and its chemical and biological warfare capabilities, then the inability of the conquering U.S. forces to demonstrate that these had existed raises the question of whether it can be said that the United States accomplished its goals.

Conditions for Success

The next question, then, is: When does force succeed and when does it fail to accomplish its goals? There is no precise answer, but it is possible to synthesize the findings of a variety of studies and the views of military practitioners (see the Explanatory Notes section on page 553) to arrive at some rudimentary rules for the successful use of military force, especially in cases of intervention when a country has not been directly attacked. In cases of intervention, success is most likely when a country's use of military force is:

1. Taken in areas where it has a clearly defined, preferably long-standing, and previously demonstrated commitment.

2. Supported firmly and publicly by the country's leaders.
3. Supported strongly by public opinion.
4. Used to counter other military force, not to try to control political events.
5. Applied early and decisively, rather than by extended threatening and slow escalation.
6. Meant to achieve clear goals and does not change or try to exceed them.

These correlations between military action, political circumstances, and success are only preliminary and do not guarantee success. They do, however, indicate some of the factors that contribute to successful use of the military instrument.

The Changing Nature of War

Warfare has changed greatly over the centuries (Lawrence, 1998). Three factors are responsible: technology, nationalism, and strategy.

Technology has rapidly escalated the ability to kill. Successive "advances" in the ability to deliver weapons at increasing distances and in the ability to kill ever more people with a single weapon have resulted in mounting casualties, both absolutely and as a percentage of soldiers and civilians of the countries at war.

Nationalism has also changed the nature of war. Before the 19th century, wars were generally fought between the houses of nobles with limited armies. The French Revolution (1789) changed that. War began to be fought between nations, with increases in intensity and in numbers involved. France proclaimed military service to be a patriotic duty and instituted the first comprehensive military draft in 1793. The idea of patriotic military service coupled with the draft allowed France's army to be the first to number more than a million men (Avant, 2000).

As a result of technology and nationalism, the scope of war has expanded. Entire nations have become increasingly involved in wars. Before 1800, no more than 3 of 1,000 people of a country participated in a war. By World War I, the European powers called 1 of 7 people to arms. Technology increased the need to mobilize the population for industrial production and also increased the capacity for, and the rationality of, striking at civilians. Nationalism made war a movement of the masses, increasing their stake and also giving justification for attacking the enemy nation. Thus, the lines between military and civilian targets have blurred. Yet even more technology has, at other times, also reversed the connection between war effort and the nation (Coker, 2002). The high-tech forces deployed by the United States and its allies against Iraq (1991, 2003) and Yugoslavia (1995, 1999) and the quick victories that ensued largely separated the war effort from the day-to-day lives of Americans.

Strategy has also changed. Two concepts, the power to defeat and the power to hurt, are key here. The **power to defeat** is the ability to seize territory or overcome enemy military forces and is the classic goal of war. The **power to hurt**, or coercive violence, is the ability to inflict pain outside the immediate military sphere (Slantchev, 2003). It means hurting some so that the resistance of others will crumble. The power to hurt has become increasingly important to all aspects of warfare because the success of the war effort depends on a country's economic effort and, often, the morale of its citizens. Perhaps the first military leader to understand the importance of the power to hurt in modern warfare was General William Tecumseh Sherman during the U.S. Civil War. "My aim was to whip the rebels, to humble their pride, to follow them to their inmost recesses, and [to] make them fear and dread us," the general wrote in his memoirs.[14]

Traditionally wars were fought with little reference to hurting. Even when hurting was used, it depended on the ability to attack civilians by first defeating the enemy's military

International Conflicts in the Post–World War II World

War is a continuing reality in the international system. The conflicts since World War II have been less cataclysmic than that global conflagration, but the ongoing use of force means that the world cannot be sure that World War III does not lie in the future. The possibility of conflict also means that the military instrument is used in many ways, ranging from an intimidating diplomatic backdrop to a full-scale assault on an opponent.

	Conflict[1]	Start Date	Major Belligerent Countries[2] (in alphabetical order)
1	Palestine	1948	Egypt, Iraq, Israel, Jordan, Lebanon, Syria
2	Korean	1950	China, North Korea, South Korea, United Nations: United States and 11 other countries
3	Soviet-Hungarian	1956	Hungary, Soviet Union
4	Sinai	1956	Egypt, France, Israel, United Kingdom
5	Sino-Indian	1962	China, India
6	Kashmir	1965	India, Pakistan
7	Vietnam	1965	Australia, North Vietnam, South Korea, South Vietnam, United States
8	Six-Day	1967	Egypt, Israel, Jordan, Syria
9	Soviet-Czech	1968	Czechoslovakia, Soviet Union
10	Football	1969	El Salvador, Honduras
11	Indo-Pakistani	1971	India, Pakistan
12	Yom Kippur	1973	Egypt, Israel, Syria
13	Cyprus	1974	Cyprus, Turkey
14	Ogaden	1977	Ethiopia, Somalia
15	Cambodian-Vietnamese	1978	Cambodia, China, Vietnam
16	Ugandan-Tanzanian	1978	Tanzania, Uganda
17	Afghanistan	1979	Afghanistan, Soviet Union
18	Persian Gulf	1980	Iran, Iraq
19	Angola	1981	Angola, Cuba, South Africa
20	Falklands	1982	Argentina, United Kingdom
21	Saharan	1983	Chad, Libya
22	Lebanon	1987	France, Israel, Lebanon, Syria, United States
23	Panama	1989	Panama, United States
24	Persian Gulf	1990	Iraq, United Nations: United States and 7 other countries
25	Yugoslavia	1990	Bosnia-Herzegovina, Croatia, Serbia
26	Peruvian-Ecuadorian	1995	Ecuador, Peru
27	Albania	1995	Albania, Yugoslavia (Serbia-Montenegro)
28	Rwanda	1995	Burundi, Rwanda
29	East Timor	1995	Indonesia, New Guinea insurgency
30	Cameroon	1996	Cameroon, Nigeria
31	Northern Iraq	1996	Iraq, Kurdish insurgency
32	Eritrea	1997	Eritrea, Yemen
33	Iraq	1998	Great Britain, Iraq, United States
34	Kosovo	1999	Albania, NATO, Yugoslavia
35	Democratic Republic of the Congo	1998	Angola, Chad, Congo, Namibia, Sudan, Zimbabwe
36	Chechnya	1999	Chechnya, Russia
37	"War on Terrorism"	2001	Afghanistan (Taliban), al-Qaeda organization, Great Britain, United States, others
38	Iraq	2003	Great Britain, Iraq, United States

[1] "Conflict" implies at least 1,000 battle deaths.
[2] "Belligerent" implies country supplied at least 5% of the combat troops in the conflict.

International conflicts in the post–World War II world

Area of conflict

10 23 26 20

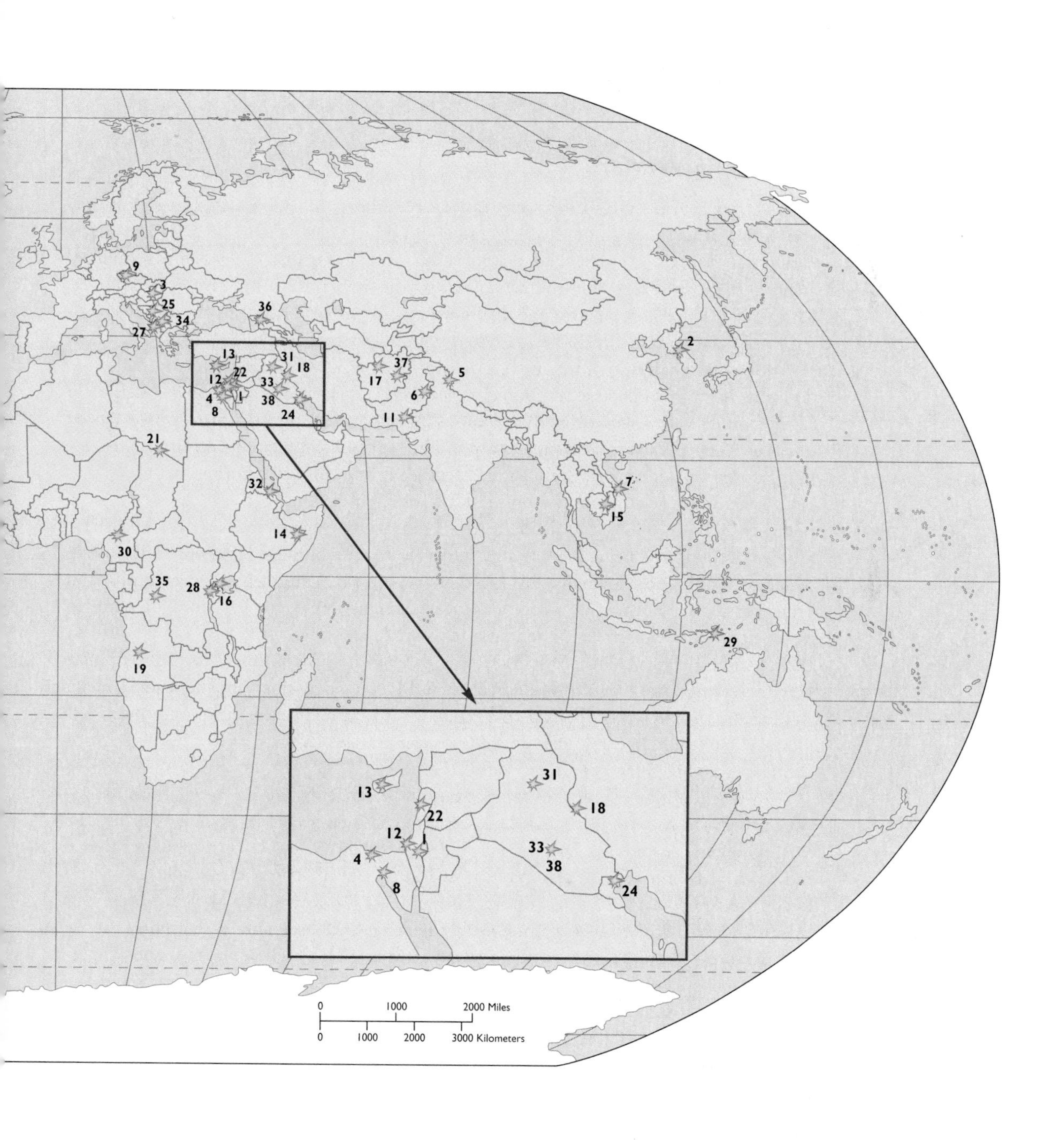
0 1000 2000 Miles
0 1000 2000 3000 Kilometers

forces. During the American Revolution, for example, the British could have utilized their power to hurt—to kill civilians in the major cities they controlled—and they might have won the war. Instead they concentrated on defeating the American army (which they could not catch, then grew too strong to overpower), and they lost.

In the modern era, the power to defeat has declined in importance relative to the power to hurt. Terrorism, guerrilla warfare, and nuclear warfare all rely extensively on the power to hurt to accomplish their ends. Even conventional warfare sometimes uses terror tactics to sap an opponent's morale. The use of strategic bombing to blast German cities during World War II is an example.

Classifying Warfare

There are numerous ways to classify warfare. One has to do with causality and intent, and distinguishes among offensive, defensive, and other types of conflict. *Offensive warfare* involves an attack launched by one country against another in the absence of a military attack or serious threat of a military attack by the targeted country. Iraq's invasion of Kuwait in 1990 is a good example. *Defensive warfare,* such as Kuwait's futile and short-lived resistance to Iraq's invasion in 1990, is the military response to aggression.

In a complicated world, however, the distinction between offensive and defensive decisions for war is not so clear. *Mutual-responsibility warfare* is one scenario. In such cases all the countries involved bear some responsibility, whether through provocative acts or missteps. World War I is a classic example. The story is complex, but in brief Austria-Hungary mobilized against Serbia after accusing it of complicity in the assassination of Archduke Franz Ferdinand, the pretender to the Austro-Hungarian throne. Russia, a friend of Serbia, mobilized to deter Austria-Hungary, but that caused Germany, Austria-Hungary's ally, to mobilize. Russia's ally, France, feared it would be defenseless if it waited, so it too mobilized. Germany, fearing that it would be caught between a mobilized France to the west and a mobilized Russia to the east, decided it had no choice but to strike first. So Germany launched an attack on France through the shortest route to Paris, neutral Belgium. Great Britain, fearing a German army on the coast of the English Channel, joined the war alongside France and Russia. Few if any of the leaders really wanted war, certainly not the war that ensued. Yet it came because, as one historian explains, "Statesmen, like soldiers, obeyed the imperatives of their offices in a system of competing and frightened national states" (Lafore, 1971:23).

Preemptive warfare is another type of conflict that defies the simple dichotomy between offensive and defensive war. This scenario has been much in the news because the Bush Doctrine, as discussed in chapter 2, declares that the speed with which violence can be launched in today's technological world dictates that "the United States can no longer solely rely on a reactive posture," and instead, "To forestall or prevent hostile acts by our adversaries, the United States will, if necessary, act preemptively." Putting theory into practice, U.S. forces moved against Iraq in March 2003. The controversy over preemptive war creates the impression that it is something new, but it is not. In a sense, the mobilization-countermobilization-war sequence of World War I involved preemptive warfare. Also, despite charges and countercharges, the line between preemption as aggression (which violates international law) and preemption as self-defense (which does not) is not precise. Even in much more constrained domestic situations, a potential victim, confronted by someone with a loaded gun, does not have to wait to be shot at before exercising his or her right of self-defense. What the law generally says is that you must be reasonably afraid that you will suffer death or injury and your response must be proportionate to the threat. Thus preemptive war in the view of many analysts is neither absolutely right nor absolutely wrong. Instead, its morality and lawfulness must be care-

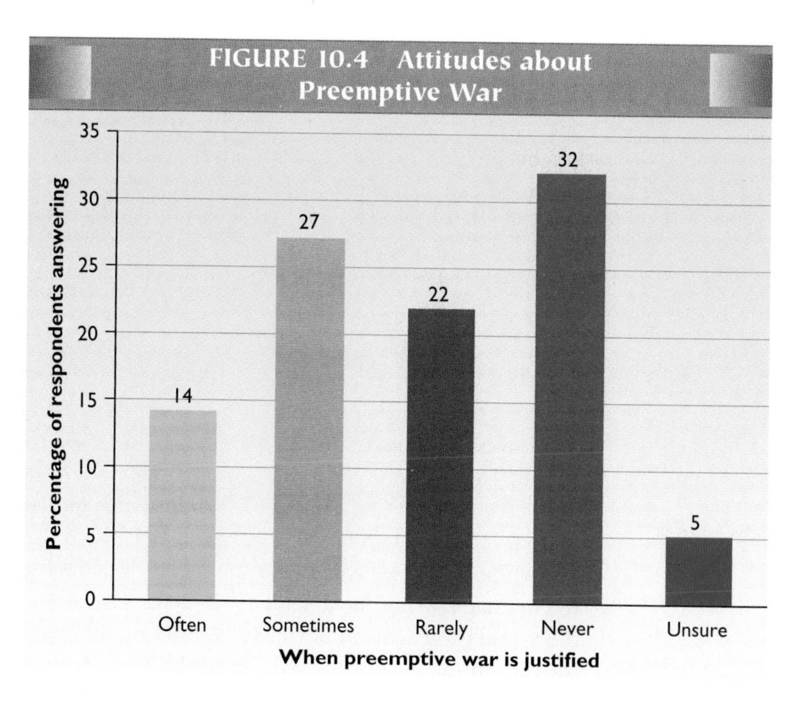

For most people, the use of preemptive war is not a matter of absolute right or wrong. From one perspective, this data indicates that a majority (54%) of the respondents in 20 countries think that preemptive war is rarely if ever justified. Another way to look at the data, though, is to see that only 32% find no circumstances that would justify preemptive warfare. Among Americans, the responses were often 22%, sometimes 44%, rarely 17%, never 13%, and unsure 4%.

Note: The question was: Do you think that using military force against countries that may seriously threaten our country, but have not attacked us, can often be justified, sometimes be justified, rarely be justified, or never be justified?
Data source: The Pew Research Center for People and the Press, "Views of a Changing World," June 2003.

fully evaluated. This view is also held by the general public. As Figure 10.4 indicates, a 2003 survey of people in 20 countries found that only 32% believe that preemptive war is never justified. More (41%) think that it is often or sometimes justified.

The changing nature of war, the increased power of weapons, and the shifts in tactics have all made classifying warfare more difficult. Studies of war and other uses of political violence divide these acts into a variety of categories. Whatever the criteria for these categories, though, the exact boundaries between various types of wars or other political phenomena are imprecise. Therefore, you should be concerned mostly with the issues involved in planning for and fighting wars. With recognition of their limits, this chapter divides international conflict into three categories: unconventional warfare, conventional warfare, and weapons of mass destruction warfare.

Unconventional Warfare

Of our three categories of force, **unconventional force** is the one that usually has the most limited geographical scope and involves the least powerful weapons. It is possible to use a variety of the instruments of violence at this level. Three ways for an outside country to apply its military power in local conflict are through (1) arms transfers, (2) special operations, and (3) terrorism.

Arms Transfers

The international supply of arms is big business, involving tens of billions of dollars annually. This global flow of arms can be properly considered as a form of intervention because, whether intended or not, arms transfers frequently either supply dissidents using unconventional warfare to battle a government or a government battling dissidents. In such scenarios, the international flow of weapons is an indirect way to intervene abroad, and it also promotes unconventional military action.

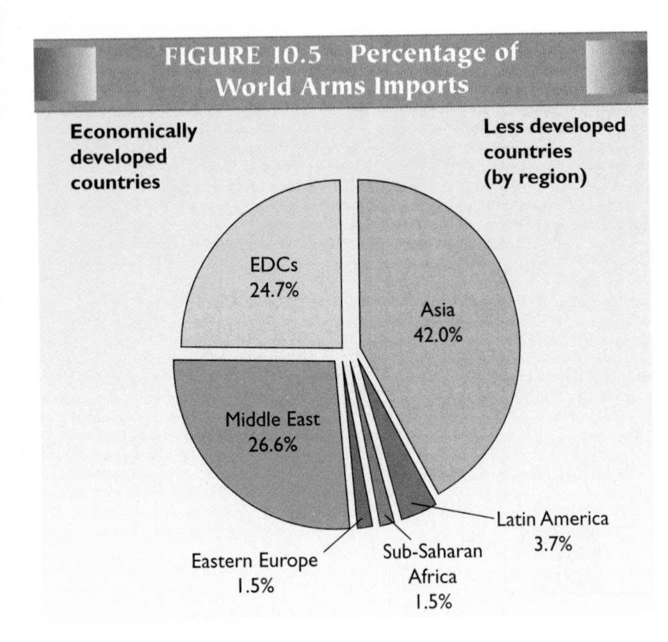

World arms exports in 2002 came to about $29 billion in current dollars. LDCs buy most of the weapons. A similar pie chart of exports would show that EDCs sell most of the weapons.

Notes: Middle East includes North Africa; Eastern Europe includes Russia and the other former Soviet republics in Europe.

Data source: Stockholm International Peace Research Institute (SIPRI), 2003, on the Web at http://projects.sipri.se/armstrade/appl3B2003.pdf.

Arms Transfers: Destinations and Sources

The export and import of arms has long been important economically and politically, but it reached new heights during the cold war, as the two hostile superpowers struggled for influence. About two-thirds of the arms that flowed in the world during the cold war were exported by the United States and the Soviet Union, while LDCs were the destination of about two-thirds of the flow of weaponry. Annual global arms transfers peaked at $36 billion (measured in constant 1990 dollars), but with the ebbing, then end of the cold war, the arms trade had declined about 45% by 2002. Still, that leaves substantial arms flow, amounting in 2002 to about $16.5 billion (1990 dollars). Figure 10.5 shows the percentage of arms imports of the various global regions. The most worrisome region is Asia, with the arms imports of East Asia increasing nearly 40% during the decade. During the period 1998–2002, China was the world's top arms importer ($8.8 billion), followed by Taiwan ($6.8 billion), India ($4.8 billion), Turkey ($4.7 billion), and Saudi Arabia ($4.4 billion). These five countries and another five (Greece, South Korea, Egypt, Great Britain, and Israel) that make up the top ten importers combined for 50% of all the major conventional military weaponry that were imported for the five-year period.

As for arms exports, the United States is by far the world's leading arms merchant. During the period 1998–2002, U.S. arms transfers accounted for 41% of the market. Russia was second (22%). These two countries and eight others (France, Germany, Great Britain, Ukraine, Italy, China, the Netherlands, and Belarus) combined for 92% of all the major conventional military weaponry transfers for the five-year period.

Arms Transfers: Motives

Several motives prompt countries to sell and give weapons to other countries or to insurgent groups. Among these motives are strengthening allies during peacetime, intervening on either side during a war or internal conflict, and striving for diplomatic influence over a recipient government or rebel group. National economic benefit is yet another, and now perhaps the predominant, motive behind arms exports. This is especially true for the world's leading arms merchant, the United States. For example, the sale of F-16 fighters is crucial to the economic well-being of Lockheed Martin Company and the approximately 12,000 workers at its Fort Worth, Texas, plant. A majority of the more than 4,200 F-16s produced or ordered since the fighter first flew in 1976 have gone to other countries, and in recent years virtually the entire production of F-16s is for export. Thus, the economic welfare of Texas is not just linked to U.S. military needs; it also depends in part on the thousands of F-16s that have been sold to over 20 countries around the world. To ensure that economic health, the administration also provides incentives. It provided Israel $2 billion in military aid in 2001, and that year Israel showed its gratitude by agreeing to purchase 52 F-16s at a cost of about $2 billion. Similarly, in late 2002, President Bush recommended that Congress give Poland a $3.8 billion loan to purchase 48 F-16s and extensive support systems.

Other countries are also eager to sell their military wares, and for some, foreign sales are a critical part of their exports. Arms exports account for over 2% of Russia's GDP, and they are even more important to essentially bankrupt North Korea. Among other "trade goods" that country has developed are such missiles as the Taepodong, with a 2,000–3,000 mile range and a price tag of $6 million, more for the international market than for Pyongyang's own use. "Our military exports are aimed at obtaining foreign money we need at present," the official Korean Central News Agency has candidly admitted.[15]

Arms Transfers: Drawbacks

It is worth belaboring the obvious to point out that selling or giving arms to other countries is not like other trade and aid transfers. There can be little doubt that countries have legitimate defense needs and that sometimes arms transfers help stabilize situations. It is also true, however, that the massive flow of arms entails drawbacks to both the importing and the exporting countries.

Cost is one danger of the weapons trade. As noted earlier, countries, especially poorer ones, face classic "guns or butter" budget decisions about whether to spend on defense or domestic programs. At least some of the billions of dollars that LDCs spend annually on arms imports could be devoted to domestic infrastructure or social programs. *Increased violence* is a second problem. Many scholars believe that the arms flow increases the level and perhaps the frequency and intensity of violence between countries and within countries. One study concludes that the consequences of the flow of weapons, especially to the LDCs, are "likely to be severe. . . . Third World countries now possess the capacity to conduct wars of greater intensity, duration, and reach." The study notes that "while no one can predict that the growing availability of modern weapons will lead to an increased frequency of armed conflict, there is a high correlation between the growing diffusion of war-making material and the increased tempo of global violence" (Klare & Lumpe, 2000:173; Parker, 1999; Sanjian, 1999; Hashim, 1998).

One of the many drawbacks of selling or otherwise transferring weapons abroad is that they often wind up in the hands of forces that commit horrific acts. Among these is the use of "boy soldiers," such as this 12-year-old brandishing his assault weapon in June 2003 in Bunia, Democratic Republic of the Congo. The boy had been impressed into the ranks of a rebel group, the Union of Congolese Patriots.

Moral corruption is a third peril of the weapons trade. According to some critics, it is immoral to supply weapons that are used to kill others. Whether or not you agree with that, it is hard not to give some credence to the view of one analyst that "one doesn't have to subscribe to the 'merchants of death' theory" to agree that "flooding the world with more efficient killing tools does not make it a safer place."[16] Another troubling moral issue is based on the fact that supplying arms to an oppressive government sometimes helps it to stay in power. Although studies show that human rights factors do play a role in determining whether or not the United States will supply another country with weapons, it is also true that "a nondemocracy still has roughly a [50%] chance of receiving U.S. arms" (Blanton, 1998:15).

Facing one's own weapons is a fourth peril that may occur. During the 1980s, the United States supplied $2 billion worth of weapons, including sophisticated, shoulder-fired Stinger surface-to-air missiles, to the Afghan rebels seeking to oust the Soviet Union from their country. Those missiles created havoc for Soviet helicopters and warplanes. More than a decade after the last Soviet soldier had departed, it was invading American troops who had to worry about the 100 or more Stinger missiles that intelligence sources indicated were in Taliban hands. Secretary of Defense Donald Rumsfeld warned publicly about a "non-trivial Stinger population" in Afghanistan, and worked to counter the threat, among other ways, by buying back the missiles for $150,000 each from various warlords.[17] There is also concern that Stingers and man-portable air-defense missiles (MANPAD) of Soviet and other origins present a terrorist threat to commercial aviation around the world.

Hypocrisy is a fifth problem associated with the arms trade. However laudable you think your goals are, it is hard to persuade others not to do what you are doing. One effort by Washington to prevent the sale of weapons to Iran by the Czech Republic left a Czech official fuming that the Americans "are preaching that we drink water while they drink wine. I consider it hypocritical."[18]

Special Operations

Not all military action involves the use of large numbers of uniformed troops against other organized military forces in classic battle scenarios. There also are approaches to violence that fall under the heading of special operations.

Special operations include overtly or covertly sending one's own special operations forces (SOFs), intelligence operatives, or paramilitary agents into another country to conduct such small-unit activities as commando operations and intelligence gathering. When these actions are aimed at an opponent's armed forces or other military targets, then the activity falls under the general heading of special operations warfare.

The use of SOFs as a form of military intervention has increased in recent decades for several reasons. First, there has been an increase in civil strife within countries. Second, attempts to topple governments or to create separatist states are now usually waged using guerrilla tactics, rather than the conventional tactics normally used in the past. More than any single reason, this change in tactics has occurred because the preponderance of high-tech weapons available to government forces makes it nearly suicidal for opposition forces to fight conventionally. Third, covert intervention avoids the avalanche of international and, often, domestic criticism that overt interventions set off. Fourth, clandestine operations allow the initiating country to disengage more easily, if it wishes, than would be possible if it overtly committed regular military forces.

Covert operations also have drawbacks. Escalating involvement can be a major problem. Interventions can begin with supplying weapons. If the arms flow does not bring victory, then the next step may be to send in advisers and special operations forces. Even if the supplier country has its doubts about wanting to commit its own armed forces, the process of intervention often causes that country's prestige to become associated with the fate of the recipient country or rebel group that is being supported. Therefore, if things continue to go badly for the recipient, then the supplier may be tempted to engage in limited combat support, and, finally, to commit to a full-scale military intervention with its own troops. This is how the United States waded ever deeper into the quagmire in Vietnam and how the Soviet Union fell into the abyss in Afghanistan.

Since the events of 9/11, SOFs have received renewed attention in the United States. President George W. Bush increased FY2004 funding for U.S. SOFs by 34% to $6.7 billion and the number of SOF active duty and reserve personnel to nearly 50,000. In addition to their use in Afghanistan and Iraq, the president has deployed SOF units to Colombia to assist in the war against leftist guerrilla armies there and to the Philippines to help that country's army in the war against Abu Sayyaf, a Muslim rebel group. The U.S. position is that these units are only meant to train and advise Colombian and Filipino forces, but some observers worry that such involvements have the potential of snaring the United States in escalating commitments, much as occurred in Vietnam. That concern was heightened in December 2003 when the head of one of the rebel groups warned, "The invasive foreign troops are a military target."[19]

Terrorism

When a survey taken in 1999 asked Americans to spontaneously name two or three top foreign policy concerns, terrorism was mentioned by only 12% of respondents. Indeed the percentage of people worried about terrorism substantially trailed the 21% of respondents who could not think of anything in the foreign policy realm that concerned them (Rielly, 1999).

In some ways the lack of concern about terrorism was not surprising. It is true that terrorism had become a persistent and nasty reality in global politics and that prior to 1999 there had been terrorist attacks in the United States. But the worst one of those, the 1995 bombing of the Federal Building in Oklahoma City, where 168 lives were lost, was perpetrated by Americans. The World Trade Center had been shaken when foreign nationals detonated a bomb in its garage in 1993, but with only 6 people killed, the incident soon faded from most people's minds. There had been other attacks on Americans, but the most sensational of these, such as the destruction of Pan Am Flight 103 over Lockerbie, Scotland, in 1988 and the bombing of the U.S. embassies in Kenya and Tanzania in 1998, had occurred overseas. However, the bubble burst on September 11, 2001, as Americans' sense of being safely remote from terrorism crashed amid the rubble of the World Trade Center and the Pentagon.

The Nature and Limits of Terrorism

One of the challenges of examining terrorism is that there is no widely accepted definition. The difficulty of coming to a common understanding of what is and is not terrorism has been underlined by the inability of the United Nations in the aftermath of the 9/11 attacks to move forward with a proposed Comprehensive Convention Against Terrorism. "The simple fact is that terrorism means different things to different people," one diplomat explained. "We couldn't find common political ground on several issues—despite the fact that the entire world is preoccupied with international terrorism."[20]

Therefore it is important to establish how the word is used here. To that end, **terrorism** is defined as (1) a form of political violence that (2) is carried out by individuals, by nongovernmental organizations, or by relatively small groups of covert government agents; that (3) specifically targets civilians; and that (4) uses clandestine attack methods, such as car bombs and hijacked airliners.

What this definition stresses is that terrorism relies exclusively on the power to hurt, that is, harming some people in order to create fear in others. Terrorists target civilians and facilities or systems (such as transportation) on which civilians rely. The objective of terrorists is not just the people they kill or physical material they destroy. Instead the true target of terrorism is the emotions of those who see or read about the act of violence and become afraid or dispirited.

It is important to note that not everyone would agree with this definition. The two main divisions involve whether noble ends can justify terrorist means and whether actions taken by uniformed military force can be classified as terrorism.

Can noble ends justify terrorist means? Some critics proffer the adage, "One man's terrorist is another man's freedom fighter," to make the point that what is terrorism to

The ultimate target of the terrorists who blew up this bus in northern Israel was not the 12 people who were killed and the 50 who were injured. Instead, the objective of the suicide bombers, who detonated explosives from their car next to the bus, was to create publicity for their cause and to instill fear among the surviving Israelis in an effort to influence policy.

some is legitimate action to others. For instance, one barrier to agreeing on language for the UN's Comprehensive Convention Against Terrorism is the insistence of many LDCs that there be wording to indicate that an armed struggle for national liberation, against occupation, or against a racist regime should not be considered terrorism. The problem with both the adage and the LDC position is that it rests on the assumption that ends can justify means, an issue discussed in chapter 9. The view here is that noble goals cannot justify reprehensible actions, and that any attack that specifically targets noncombatants is an act of terrorism.

Can actions taken by uniformed military force be classified as terrorism? Another possible criticism of the definition of terrorism used herein is that it generally excludes uniformed military personnel and government officials from being classified as terrorists. Critics of this view question why a civilian dissident who detonates a car bomb in a market, killing numerous noncombatants, is a terrorist and a military pilot who drops a bomb that kills numerous noncombatants near the target is not a terrorist.

There are two replies to this objection. The first is that intent is important. Terrorists intend to kill noncombatants. With rare exception, uniformed personnel attack military or hostile targets. Noncombatant casualties may occur, but they are not the object of the attack.

Second, it must be stressed that not all military actions are acceptable. When they are not, however, they are properly classified as war crimes under the principles of *jus in bello* (just conduct of war) discussed in chapter 9. When war crimes occur, the perpetrators should be and sometimes are brought to justice. The trial of Slobodan Milosevic, the former president of Yugoslavia, for numerous crimes committed during the 1990s in his official capacity serves as an example. It should be noted, though, that Milosevic is charged with genocide, forceful deportation, and a variety of other war crimes, not with terrorism.

A final note is that not all attacks categorized as terrorism by the United States fall within the definition of terrorism used here. For example, Washington condemned as terrorism the October 12, 2000, attack on the guided missile destroyer USS *Cole* while it was refueling in Aden. Yet despite the fact that it was suicide bombers operating a small boat laden with explosives that mangled the ship and killed 17 crew members, the fact that the target was a military vessel puts the act beyond the definition of terrorism used here. Similarly, the attacks on American, British, Italian, Polish, Spanish, and other forces in Iraq during the postwar occupation, whatever the tactics, are guerrilla warfare, not terrorism. However, the bombing of the UN's headquarters in Iraq, the murder of two Japanese diplomats, the killing of civilian contractors, and similar acts are terrorism.

Sources of Terrorism

Two sources of political terrorism concern us here. One is state terrorism, the second is transnational terrorism. As we shall see, they are closely linked.

State Terrorism To argue that most acts, even if horrific, committed by uniformed military personnel are not properly regarded as terrorism does not mean that countries cannot engage in terrorism. They can, through **state terrorism**. This is terrorism carried out directly by an established government's clandestine operatives or by others who have been specifically encouraged and funded by a country.

From the U.S. perspective, the State Department has repeatedly listed Cuba, Iran, Iraq, Libya, North Korea, Sudan, and Syria as countries guilty of state terrorism.[21] Each of these countries vehemently denies being involved in terrorism, and some of the U.S. allegations would fall outside the definition of terrorism used here. Not all acts would, though. For example, in 2003, Libya, in a letter to the UN Security Council, accepted responsibility for its agents causing the bomb destruction of Pan Am Flight 103 over Lockerbie, Scotland, in 1989 and the death of 270 people on board and on the ground. Libya agreed to pay more than $2 billion in compensation to the families of the victims, and it renounced terrorism. Additionally, Libya had earlier turned over one of the agents, Abdel Basset Ali al-Megrahi, for prosecution in Scotland's courts, and in 2002 he was convicted and sentenced to life in prison.

There have been many other accusations of state terrorism, including some against the United States. "We consider the United States and its current administration as a first-class sponsor of international terrorism, and it along with Israel form an axis of terrorism and evil in the world," a group of 126 Saudi scholars wrote in a joint statement issued in 2002.[22]

Most, but not all, such charges fall outside the definition of terrorism used here. An example of what arguably constituted terrorism involves Washington's alleged complicity in assassinations and other forms of state terrorism practiced internally by some countries in Latin America and elsewhere during the anticommunist fervor of the cold war. A secret document declassified in 1999 records the anguished views of an American diplomat in Guatemala regarding U.S. support of the Guatemalan army against Marxist guerrillas and their civilian supporters. After detailing a long list of atrocities committed by the army, the American diplomat told his superiors in the State Department, "We have condoned counter-terror . . . even . . . encouraged and blessed it. . . . Murder, torture, and mutilation are all right if our side is doing it and the victims are Communists."[23] Another example came to light in 2004 when a former Defense Department official during the Reagan administration wrote that the United States had sold technology to the Soviet Union for its natural gas pipelines that was rigged to blow up. The resulting explosion in 1982 was so powerful that it could be seen from space (Reed, 2004).

Transnational Terrorism The changes in the world that have given rise to a rapid increase in the number of international nongovernmental organizations have also expanded the number of terrorist groups that are organized and operate internationally committing **transnational terrorism**. One source, the U.S. State Department's 2003 edition of its "Report on Foreign Terrorist Organizations," lists 36 such groups, including al-Qaeda, and there are dozens of other such organizations that one source or another label as terrorist.[24]

Al-Qaeda is surely the most famous of these, and its origins and operations provide a glimpse into transnational terrorism. According to U.S. sources, al-Qaeda (the Base) was founded by Osama bin Laden, the son of a wealthy Saudi family, in the late 1980s to support Arabs fighting in Afghanistan against the Soviet Union. Once the Soviets were driven from Afghanistan in 1989, bin Laden's focus shifted to the United States. He was outraged by the presence of U.S. forces in Saudi Arabia near Mecca and Medina, the two holiest cities of Islam, and by American support of what he saw as Israel's oppression of Palestinian Muslims. Reflecting this view, he issued a *fatwa,* a religious call, in 1998 entitled "Jihad Against Jews and Crusaders," which proclaimed that "to kill the Americans and their allies—civilians and military—is an individual duty for every Muslim who can do it in any country in which it is possible to do it."[25]

American officials charge that prior to the attacks on the World Trade Center and the Pentagon, bin Laden and his followers masterminded a number of other terrorist attacks. Among these were the bombings in August 1998 of the U.S. embassies in Nairobi, Kenya, and Dar es Salaam, Tanzania, that killed more than 300 people and injured thousands of others.

Bin Laden was based in Sudan from 1991 to 1996 when he moved the headquarters of al-Qaeda to Afghanistan after international pressure forced the government of Sudan to expel him. Additionally, investigators have discovered links to al-Qaeda operatives, bank accounts, and activities in more than 50 countries. There is no accurate count of how many individuals are part of al-Qaeda, but it and other closely associated extremist groups had and probably still have several thousand members. In addition to al-Qaeda's own members, it trained many thousands of terrorists for other groups in its camps in Afghanistan and elsewhere. They derived their funding in part from bin Laden's vast personal wealth, in part from contributions from sympathizers around the world, and perhaps in part from donations from sympathetic governments. Al-Qaeda also established a sophisticated global network of bank accounts and other financial vehicles that allowed them to move money easily around the world.

The Record of Terrorism

International terrorism has become a regular occurrence (Enders & Sandler, 1999). U.S. State Department data issued in 2003 indicates that the number of attacks rose from 165 in 1968 to peak at 666 in 1987. Then terrorist attacks became less frequent. The years 1996–1998, with an average of 291 attacks annually, were the least violent three-year period in more than two decades. Violence turned sharply upward in 1999 (392 terrorist incidents) and 2000 (423 attacks). Ironically it was down in 2001 and at a relatively low level in 2002, as evident in Figure 10.6. During the period 1994 through 2002, international terrorist attacks injured almost 27,000 people worldwide, of whom approximately 5,300 died. More than half of these deaths occurred during the 9/11 attacks.

Geographically, international terrorism has been widespread, with all regions other than North America suffering frequent terrorist attacks. Thus Americans had been largely spared until the 9/11 attacks, with no fatalities in the United States due to international terrorism between the 1993 bombing of the World Trade Center in New York City that killed 6 people and the attack on it and the Pentagon eight years later. Indeed, from 1995 through 2000, only 77 Americans were killed and 751 injured by international terrorism anywhere in the world. Those relatively low numbers changed dramatically on September 11, 2001, with the attack on the World Trade Center, the worst single terrorist event in history. Including the attack on the Pentagon and the crash in

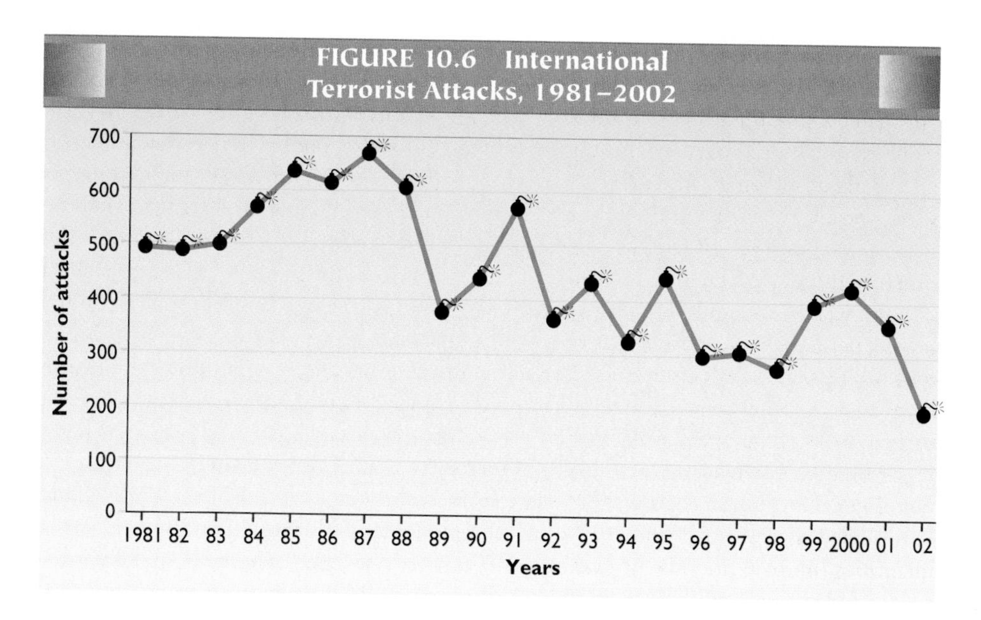

Terrorism is a constant in the world. It spiked upward in the mid-1980s, then generally declined through 1998, only to escalate anew. There were fewer terrorist attacks in 2002 than in any year in the previous two decades. Whether that reflects success for the war on terrorism or is an anomaly remains to be seen.

Data source: U.S. Department of State, *Patterns of Global Terrorism 2002*, issued April 2003.

Pennsylvania of the plane that did not reach its target, the death toll was almost 3,000 people. In 2002, 26 Americans were killed around the world, and 35 were wounded.

Terrorist Weapons and Tactics

The explosions that tore apart the World Trade Center and Pentagon and buried their victims under tons of rubble, the mangled remains of Israeli civilians in a bomb-shattered bus, the hollow stares of hostages held as pawns in the macabre game that terrorists play—these are the images of terrorism that have too often gripped us. For all the ghastly history of terrorism using conventional weapons, future possibilities are even more disturbing. Now there is a new, more terrible threat—radiological, nuclear, biological, and chemical terrorism (Gurr & Cole, 2000; Tucker, 2000). As a recent U.S. National Intelligence Estimate described the situation, for the first time "U.S. territory is more likely to be attacked" with radiological, biological, or chemical weapons using "ships, trucks, airplanes or other means" than by weapons of mass destruction from another country using its military missiles or bombers.[26]

Conventional Weapons Terrorism With relatively few exceptions, most terrorist attacks have used bombs, guns, and other conventional weapons. Data compiled by the U.S. State Department for 2002 indicates, for example, that of 30 Americans killed during international terrorist attacks, 17 died as the result of bomb blasts, 9 were killed by gunmen, and 4 died at the hands of kidnappers. Even the attacks on the World Trade Center and Pentagon in 2001, as horrific as they were, would fall under the category of a conventional weapons terrorist attack.

Radiological Terrorism There is a difference between nuclear and radiological weapons. The extraordinary difficulty of creating a nuclear chain reaction and the security surrounding existing nuclear weapons make it unlikely (but not impossible) that in the foreseeable future terrorists could acquire or construct and detonate a mini version of a military nuclear weapon. There is a much greater possibility of terrorists being able to construct a so-called dirty bomb that would use conventional explosives to disperse radioactive material over a large area. A related approach would be to destroy a nuclear power plant, spewing radioactivity into the surrounding air and water. Such scenarios would result in very few immediate or near-term deaths. Rather, the danger would be from increased levels of radiation causing future cancers, pregnancy complications, and other medical risks. There is also the potential for significant economic damage, since a radiological attack could render parts of a city or an important facility (such as a port) unsafe, perhaps for years. Thus, as one expert characterized the impact of a dirty bomb to Congress, "The effects are not instantaneous. You have long-term potential health hazards, and you also have longer-term psychological, social, and political impacts that can go on weeks, months, maybe years."[27]

The concern over the possibility of terrorists acquiring the material to fashion a radiological weapon has grown in recent years as authorities in Europe and elsewhere have seized several small (up to 12 ounces) shipments of plutonium and several larger quantities (up to 6 pounds) of uranium-235 (Cameron, 1999). There are literally hundreds of places around the world where terrorists could obtain radioactive material. Of all possible sources, however, Russia is the most likely. That country is dismantling many of its nuclear weapons, and it needs to store tons of plutonium and uranium. Russia's desperate economic condition adds to the problem. There is concern that impoverished Russian military and scientific officials might be willing to sell radioactive material to terrorist groups or states. Additionally, the partial breakdown of governmental functions throughout the former Soviet republics (FSRs) creates the possibility that the material to make a radiological bomb could be stolen.

In one of the most recent hair-raising stories, 38 warheads packed with radiological material have seemingly disappeared from a storage area in the rebellious Transdniester region of Moldova, a former Soviet republic. It is at least reasonable to assume the radiological material for the warheads was left to the ethnic Russians in Transdniester by sympathetic officers of the Russian military force that is still stationed in the region to protect it against Moldovan forces. The lethality of the radiological (not nuclear) warheads is evident in a 1994 memo obtained in 2003 by American reporters, in which a colonel in the Transdniester militia complains that uniforms of the soldiers working with the warheads became so radiologically contaminated that they had to be "destroyed by burning and burying." The fate of the warheads is unknown, but speculation centers on the possibility that they were sold to terrorists. As one Russian expert put it, "For terrorists, this [the Transdniester region] is the best market you could imagine: cheap, efficient, and forgotten by the whole world."[28]

Chemical and Biological Terrorism The existing possibility of chemical or biological attack came into sharp focus after the 9/11 attacks. There was alarm when it was learned that one of the suicide hijackers, Mohammad Atta, had made repeated trips to rural airports to learn about crop dusters. Anxiety was further heightened by the spread of anthrax through the U.S. mail to postal facilities, news organizations, and congressional offices. The resulting atmosphere spawned a spate of doomsday images of chemical and biological attacks that would leave millions dead. Most experts consider such scenarios overdrawn, and it is important to have a balanced understanding of the possibilities of chemical or biological attack and the impact of such attacks.

Causes for concern. There surely are worrisome realities. The tons of chemical weapons and agents seized from Iraq in 1991 after the Persian Gulf War bear testimony to the amount of such weapons in the world and the proliferation of the ability to produce them. Biological weapons are also a threat. A truly scary report by the U.S. Office of

Technology Assessment (OTA) worries about the possibility of terrorists spreading plague, botulism, or anthrax. The OTA anticipates that on a calm night, a light plane flying over Washington, D.C., and its surrounding area and releasing just 220 pounds of anthrax spores using a common crop sprayer could deliver a fatal dose to 3 million people.[29]

It would be comforting to think that no one would use such weapons, but that is not the case. Iraq used chemical weapons against Iran and rebellious Kurds in the 1980s. The possibilities of a terrorist chemical attack became a reality in 1995 when a Japanese cult, Aum Shinrikyo (Supreme Truth), used nerve gas in an attack on a Tokyo subway station that killed 12 people and injured 5,000. According to a confidential report that was obtained by the press in late 2003, a panel of experts convened by the UN warned, "The risk of al-Qaeda acquiring and using weapons of mass destruction . . . continues to grow," and said that the primary reason terrorists groups had not used chemical or biological weapons "is the technical complexity to operate them properly and effectively."[30]

Calls for calm. As unnerving as the possibilities of chemical and biological attack are and as unprepared as society has been to meet them, the threat also has to be kept in perspective. Providing that perspective, one scientist testifying before Congress detailed the significant difficulties of amassing enough of a chemical or biological agent to cause widespread death and injury. She told legislators, "When one retreats from the hyperbole and examines the intricacies involved in executing a mass casualty attack with [biological or chemical] agents, one is confronted with technical obstacles so high that even terrorists that have had a wealth of time, money, and technical skill, as well as a determination to acquire and use these weapons [would have difficulty doing so]."[31]

While it is impossible to rule out a biological or chemical attack that takes tens of thousands of lives, it is probably more realistic to see the likelihood of such an attack as remote. Given the problems of manufacturing and delivering substantial quantities of biological and chemical weapons, the greatest possibility of a massive attack would be the result of state terrorism, with a murderous government either launching a direct attack or supplying a transnational terrorist organization with the means to do so. The possibility of such an organization acting independently is much more limited. On balance then, the impact of a chemical or biological terrorist attack is most likely to be similar to a radiological attack. The psychological impact will far outweigh the actual casualties. This is what occurred during the anthrax incidents in the United States in late 2001. They caused only five deaths and about a dozen other infections, but that was enough to virtually close down Congress for a time and to frighten millions.

It is also the case that the United States and other countries have begun to take the threat of terrorism much more seriously, and the increased vigilance and improved security measures will make it harder for terrorists to strike. Domestically, the United States has created the Office of Homeland Security, the FBI is devoting at least 25% of its agents to counterterrorism, armed air marshals are on most flights, and numerous other actions are being taken. Internationally, there has been a massive effort to track down and destroy the international financial networks of al-Qaeda and other terrorist organizations, and the national intelligence agencies in the United States and other countries are devoting even more of their considerable technological and human intelligence assets to monitor, intervene, and disrupt terrorist groups.

Did You Know That:

Routine smallpox vaccinations in the United States ended in 1972. Prior to the 9/11 attacks, the existing U.S. stock of smallpox vaccine could have protected only 3% of Americans if a smallpox attack were to have occurred.

The Causes of Terrorism

Although the attacks of September 11, 2001, brought terrorism to the front of the international agenda, it has long existed. Understanding the causes of terrorism and its recent record are important parts of combating it.

Untangling the causes of terrorism is much like trying to understand why war occurs. As noted earlier in this chapter, there also appear to be many causes of terrorism that are rooted at each level of analysis. At the *system level of analysis,* it is possible to argue that such political violence is in part a product of the global unequal distribution of wealth. This has long existed, but globalization has brought the wealth gap into sharper focus and has also created a sense of cultural dislocation with its Westernizing impact. When the world's leaders met in Monterrey, Mexico, in 2002 to discuss globalization and economic development, many speakers made a connection between poverty and violence. Han Seung-soo, the president of the UN General Assembly, depicted poverty as "the breeding ground for violence and despair," and President Alejandro Toledo of Peru told the conference that "to speak of development is to speak also of a strong and determined fight against terrorism."[32] Not all analysts agree that poverty is related to terrorism, but if it is a factor, then eliminating terrorism might be best done through massive economic development programs (Pipes, 2002). It is important to note that despite the oil reserves in the Middle East, most people in most Muslim countries live in poor economic circumstances. This is even true in most petroleum-producing states, where the distribution of wealth is limited. These few "wealthy" states do not report poverty or income distribution statistics, but social indicators of poverty tell the tale. For example, despite their country's riches, the infant mortality rate in Saudi Arabia is more than three times that of the United States, and Saudi women are twice as likely as American women to die as a result of childbirth.

State-level analysis of the 9/11 attacks might cite the conflict between Israel and the Palestinians and the general U.S. support of Israel as causal factors. Many analysts argue that the continuing bloodshed between Israelis and Palestinians and the overwhelming view among Muslims that the United States favors Israel have evoked a fevered anger among many of them. Also cited is the presence of U.S. forces in the Middle East, especially those in Saudi Arabia near the holiest sites of Islam in Mecca and Medina. U.S. support of authoritarian regimes in Saudi Arabia and elsewhere is additionally sometimes mentioned. From this perspective, a major diplomatic effort is needed to bring peace to the Middle East and surrounding area so that Israelis and Palestinians could trade goods instead of bullets, U.S. forces could withdraw, and democracy could take root.

On the *individual level of analysis,* one looks into the psychological drives of terrorists ranging from Osama bin Laden to the numerous suicide bombers who have blown themselves to pieces attacking Israelis in cafés, shops, and meeting rooms. Like general war, there is little agreement among analysts about the causes of terrorism along these dimensions.

It is possible, however, to explain that terrorism occurs because, like war, it is effective. To begin with, there is wide agreement among serious analysts that it is misleading to treat terrorism as the irrational acts of crazed fanatics. To the contrary, terrorism occurs because many of those who use it consider it a necessary, legitimate, and effective tool to rid themselves of what they consider oppression. It is necessary, its proponents say, because it may be the only way for an oppressed group to prevail against a heavily armed government.

The effectiveness of terrorism has been further enhanced by modern conditions. First, these have increased the power of the weapons that terrorists can use. Explosives have become more deadly, huge airliners can be made into piloted missiles, and there is an increasing danger of terrorists having access to the material and means to launch a biological, chemical, or radiological attack. Second, there are an ever-greater number of tempting targets for terrorists. Urbanization brings people together so that they are more easily attacked. With eerie premonition, a U.S. senator warned in 1999 that "there is a real opportunity for a handful of zealots to wreak havoc on a scale that hitherto only armies could attain." The legislator went on to warn that targets might be "selected for their symbolic value, like the World Trade Center in the heart of Manhattan."[33] Third, modern communications have also made terrorism more efficacious because the goal of the terrorist is not to kill or injure, as such. Instead, the aim of terrorism is to gain attention for a cause and to create widespread anxiety that will, in turn, create pressure on governments to negotiate with terrorists and accede to their every demand. Without the media to transmit the news of their acts, terrorists would affect only their immediate victims, which would not accomplish the terrorists' goals.

In the end, terrorism, like most forms of violence, exists because terror tactics sometimes do accomplish their goals (Guelke, 1998; Reich, 1998). As one leading expert puts it, "Terrorism has proved a low cost, low risk, cost-effective and potentially high yield means of winning useful tactical objectives for its perpetrators, such as massive publicity, securing the release of large numbers of terrorist prisoners from jail, and the extortion of considerable sums to finance the purchase of more weapons and explosives and the launching of a wider campaign."[34]

Combating Terrorism

The most immediate concern about terrorism is how to combat it. That is made difficult by the clandestine methods used by terrorists and also by the fact that, like other forms of political violence, there is no agreement on what causes terrorism. The U.S.-led "war on terrorism" in recent years has emphasized military and economic strategies to disrupt and destroy terrorist organizations and their ability to operate. Epitomizing this approach, the U.S. State Department's 2003 report on the previous year, *Patterns of Global Terrorism 2002,* begins (p. iii) with the observation, "The evil of terrorism continued to plague the world through 2002. . . . The world is fighting terrorism on five fronts: diplomatic, intelligence, law enforcement, financial, and military." The report goes on to explain how diplomacy had created cooperation to fight terrorism, how intelligence agencies had worked to identify terrorists and uncover their plans, how law enforcement agencies in more than 100 countries had detained upwards of 3,000 suspected al-Qaeda members and associates since 9/11, how more than 160 countries had frozen over $121 million in assets of suspected terrorist groups and sympathizers, and how the military's operation Enduring Freedom had dealt heavy blows to the al-Qaeda organization and its supporting Taliban regime in Afghanistan.

What the report does not mention are any efforts to address many of the causes of terrorism discussed earlier. Critics say it is a major error not to realize that the current wave of terrorism is prompted in significant part by turmoil in the Middle East, especially between Israelis and Palestinians, and the pattern of economic and cultural threat that globalization poses to many in less developed countries. As one such critic put it, "We need to understand the root causes behind terrorism" because "military action will not prevent future terrorism, but only delay it."[35] In a debate that in some ways resembles the one on the war on drugs, some people say that too much is being spent on countering the problem and not enough on trying to cure it. What would you do? Spend heavily to attack terrorists or spend heavily to attack the roots of terrorism? Consider your answer further in the You Be the Playwright box "Prioritizing the War on Terrorism."

Conventional Warfare

The most overt form of coercive intervention is for a country to dispatch its own forces to another country. That intervention can range from such limited demonstrations of power as the numerous U.S. aerial and cruise missile attacks on Iraq between 1991 and 2003 to the global warfare seen during World War I and World War II. With the exceptions of the U.S. atomic attacks on Hiroshima and Nagasaki in 1945 and some use of chemical weapons, wars have been waged using conventional weapons.

YOU BE THE PLAYWRIGHT

Prioritizing for the War on Terrorism

As the main part of the text explains, the war on terrorism has emphasized using military and law enforcement resources to seek out and destroy terrorists, their organizations, and their financial networks. Huge sums have also been spent to defend against terrorism, with, for example, tens of billions of dollars spent on antiterrorist measures by the newly created U.S. Department of Homeland Security. Antiterrorist diplomacy has focused on encouraging most countries to pursue these tactics and warning those countries suspected of conducting or supporting terrorism to cease or face the consequences. Also as noted in the main text, much less has been done to address any of the causes of the current wave of terrorism. There is talk of increased aid for economic development, but little action has been taken. Diplomacy aimed at resolving the problems in the Middle East that analysts say contribute to terrorism has largely languished. The Israelis and Palestinians have declined to follow the Bush administration's so-called roadmap to peace. The Bush Doctrine speaks of promoting democracy, but in the Middle East that effort has been applied to conquered Iraq rather than allies such as Kuwait, Qatar, and Saudi Arabia.

Would you continue to follow the course of the war on terrorism so far, or would you rewrite the script? Below are a number of possible actions to address terrorism. Since some of them, such as diplomacy, are not exclusively monetary in nature, indicate how many of 100 priority points you would devote to each of the measures. Also put down the number of priority points that you think represent current U.S. policy. How does your allocation compare with U.S. policy and with those of other people in your class?

Your Allocation	Current Policy	Measures
_____	_____	International coercive measures, such as gathering intelligence and conducting military operations
_____	_____	International diplomacy to persuade other countries to take military and police action, including helping to fund those efforts
_____	_____	Homeland security measures, such as border and port inspections, airport and flight security, biochemical attack response preparations, increased law enforcement personnel
_____	_____	Economic development aid to ease poverty in less developed countries
_____	_____	Diplomacy to encourage Israeli-Palestinian peace, including such measures as increased aid to Israel and the Palestinians and a security guarantee to Israel
_____	_____	Diplomacy, including economic incentives, to promote democracy in all countries, including authoritarian U.S. allies
_____	_____	Diplomacy, including economic incentives, designed to stabilize the entire Middle East region sufficiently to allow the withdrawal of all land-based U.S. forces from the region

The **conventional warfare** that has been the norm throughout most of history is distinguished from other types of warfare by the tactics and weapons used. The overt use of uniformed military personnel, usually in large numbers, is what separates conventional tactics from special operations and terrorism. As for weapons, it is easier to indicate what conventional weapons are not than what they are. Generally, conventional weapons are those that rely on explosives for impact but are not nuclear/radiological, biological, or chemical weapons.

Goals and Conduct

The classic statement on the proper goal of war was made by German strategist Carl von Clausewitz in *On War* (1833). He argued that "war is not merely a political act, but also a political instrument, a continuation of political relations, a carrying out of the same by other means." Note that Clausewitz's point implies three principles that civilian and military decision makers should keep in mind.

War is a part of diplomacy, not a substitute for it. Therefore, channels of communication to the opponent should be kept open in an attempt to limit the conflict and to reestablish peace.

Wars should be governed by political, not military, considerations. Often commanders chafe under restrictions, as General Douglas MacArthur did during the Korean War (1950–1953) over his lack of authority to attack China. When generals become insubordinate, as MacArthur did, they ought to be removed from command, as he was.

War should be fought with clear political goals. When goals are not established or are later ignored, disaster looms. The stated U.S. goal at the beginning of the Korean War in 1950 was to drive North Korea's forces out of South Korea. That was soon accomplished, but instead of declaring victory, an emboldened President Truman ordered U.S. forces to move northward to "liberate" North Korea from communism. That brought China into the war. As a result, a war that arguably had already been won dragged on in stalemate for two more years and cost tens of thousands more lives. For all the later criticism of George H. W. Bush for not driving on to Baghdad and unseating Saddam Hussein, the U.S. president should get credit for not repeating Truman's mistake. The stated UN goal in 1991 was to liberate Kuwait. When that was accomplished, Bush halted hostilities. In so doing, he ended the killing and stayed within the legal confines of the UN resolution that authorized the action.

The fact that most wars are fought within limits does not mean that those boundaries are never violated. **Escalation** occurs when the rules are changed and the level of combat increases. Increasing the scope and intensity of a war, however, has always been dangerous, and it is particularly so in an era of nuclear, biological, and chemical (NBC) weapons. Not long after their entry into the war in Vietnam in the mid-1970s, Americans began to realize that continuing the war within the limits it was being fought offered little chance of victory and carried a heavy cost in lives and economics. Escalating the war by invading North Vietnam might have brought China into the war and increased the cost monumentally. Also, many Americans were sickened by the human cost to both sides; if the war had continued or escalated, there surely would have been an increase of deep divisions within the United States. Ultimately, the United States could have achieved a military victory by "nuking" North Vietnam and killing everyone there. Americans finally accepted, though, that victory was not the only thing. American troops began to withdraw from Vietnam in 1969; all U.S. troops were gone by 1973; Vietnam was reunited under Hanoi's control in 1975.

Avoiding Unchecked Escalation

The dangers of escalation and the prudence of keeping limited wars limited make it important to understand how to avoid unchecked escalation. As with most things political, there is no set formula. There are, however, a few useful standards.

Keep lines of communication open. The basic principle is that escalation (or de-escalation) should be a deliberate strategy used to signal a political message to the enemy. Accordingly, it is also important to send signals through diplomatic or public channels so that the opponent will not mistake the escalation as an angry spasm of violence or misconstrue the de-escalation as a weakening of resolve.

Limit goals. Unlimited goals by one side may evoke unlimited resistance by the other, so limiting goals is another way to avoid unchecked escalation. It is usually appropriate, for instance, that a goal should fall short of eliminating the opponent as a sovereign state! Even where unconditional victory is the aim, obliteration of the enemy population is not an appropriate goal.

Restrict geographical scope. It is often wise to limit conflict to as narrow a geographical area as possible. American forces refrained from invading China during the Korean War. Similarly, the Soviets passed up the temptation to blockade Berlin in 1962 in response to the U.S. blockade of Cuba.

Observe target restrictions. Wars can be controlled by limiting targets. Despite their close proximity, the Arabs and Israelis have never tried to bomb each other's capitals. Iraq's launch of Scud missiles against Tel Aviv and other Israeli cities in 1991 was, by contrast, a serious escalation, but it was not repeated in 2003.

Limit weapons. Yet another way to keep war limited is to adhere to the principle that the level of force used should be no greater than the minimum necessary to accomplish war aims. The stricture on weapons has become even more important in an era when there is such a great potential for the use of limited, on-the-battlefield NBC weapons. In addition to moral issues, even the limited use of NBC weapons might well set off a serious escalation that could lead to strategic nuclear war or massive biological and chemical attacks. This stricture has been followed in all international wars in recent decades, with the exception of the Iran-Iraq war in the 1980s during which Iran used mustard gas (which causes chemical burns to the lungs) and Iraq used mustard gas and tabun (a nerve agent).

Warfare with Weapons of Mass Destruction

The world's history of waging war primarily with conventional weapons does not guarantee that restraint will continue. Science and technology have rapidly increased the ability of countries to build, deploy, and potentially employ **weapons of mass destruction (WMDs)**. These nuclear, biological, and chemical weapons in the amounts and potencies that are available to national militaries can cause horrific levels of death and injury to enemy forces or civilian targets. In the pages that follow, we will deal briefly with biological and chemical weapons, then turn to a more extensive examination of nuclear weapons and strategy.

Did You Know That:

The term *weapons of mass destruction* was first used by the British press in 1937 to describe German bombers that were devastating such cities as Guernica during the Spanish Civil War (1936–1939). Germany had intervened on behalf of the eventually successful effort of the fascist nationalists to overthrow the socialist/republican government. For a sense of the destruction, find a copy of Pablo Picasso's powerful painting, *Guernica*, on the Internet.

Biological Weapons

Many historians trace the use of biological warfare to 1763 when, during an Indian uprising, the British commander in North America, Sir Jeffrey Amherst, wrote to subordinates at Fort Pitt, "Could it not be contrived to send the smallpox among those disaffected tribes of Indians?"[36] As it turns out, Sir Jeffrey's prompting was unnecessary. Soldiers at the fort had already given disease-infected blankets to members of the Shawnee and Delaware tribes.

Although the 1972 Biological Weapons Convention (BWC) bans the production, possession, and use of germ-based *biological weapons,* they continue to be a threat. For example, Russia's deputy foreign minister admitted in 1992 that the Soviet Union had until that time been violating the BWC by conducting a biological weapons research and development program since 1946 that, among other things, had amassed 20 tons of smallpox. The UN-led inspections of Iraq after the Persian Gulf War indicated that the country also had a germ warfare program that had, at minimum, produced 132,000 gallons of anthrax and botulism toxins. According to one expert, "it's far more likely than not" that, in addition to Russia, such countries as Iran, Iraq, and North Korea also have biological weapons.[37]

Chemical Weapons

Of the three components of NBC warfare, chemical weapons are the most prevalent because they are relatively easy and inexpensive to produce. Indeed, they have earned the sobriquet of "the poor man's atomic bomb." As CIA director John M. Deutch told Congress, "Chemicals used to make nerve agents are also used to make plastics and [to] process foodstuff. Any modern pharmaceutical facility can produce biological warfare agents as easily as vaccines or antibiotics."[38]

Most ominously of all, chemical weapons have been used recently. Both Iran and Iraq used them during their grueling war (1980–1988), and Iraq used them to attack rebellious Kurds in its northern provinces. The UN inspections in Iraq after the Persian Gulf War also discovered huge stores of chemical weapons, including over 105,000 gallons of mustard gas; 21,936 gallons of tabun, sarin, and other nerve gases; and over 453,000 gallons of other chemicals associated with weapons. Some of this supply was contained in munitions, such as 12,786 artillery shells filled with mustard gas and 18 warheads or bombs filled with nerve agents. There is no evidence that any chemical weapons were used during the war, but traces of mustard gas and sarin were detected on the battlefield. These may have been released inadvertently when the allied attacks destroyed Iraqi weapons depots, and some analysts suspect that exposure to these chemicals may be the cause of Gulf War syndrome, which has afflicted many veterans of the war.

The Potential for Nuclear War

The Bible's Book of Revelation speaks of an apocalyptic end to the world: A "hail of fire mixed with blood fell upon the earth; and . . . the earth was burnt up. . . . The sea became blood . . . and from the shaft rose smoke like the smoke of a great furnace and the sun and the air were darkened." Revelation laments, "Woe, woe, woe to those who dwell on earth," for many will die a fiery death, and the survivors "will seek death and will not find it; they will long to die, and death will fly from them." Whatever your religious beliefs, such a prophecy is sobering. We now have the capability to sound "the blast of the trumpets" that will kill the living and make those who remain wish to die.

Nuclear Weapons States

The world joined in a collective sigh of relief when the Soviet Union collapsed and the cold war between the two great nuclear powers ended. Almost overnight, worry about the threat of nuclear war virtually disappeared from the media and from general political discussion. Unfortunately, the perception of significantly greater safety is illusory. It is certainly true that the number of strategic nuclear weapons has declined since the end of the cold war. Nevertheless, there remains a huge number of extremely powerful nuclear weapons. Moreover, it is not at all certain that the weapons reductions that have been implemented have had the effect of reducing the chances of a nuclear war occurring.

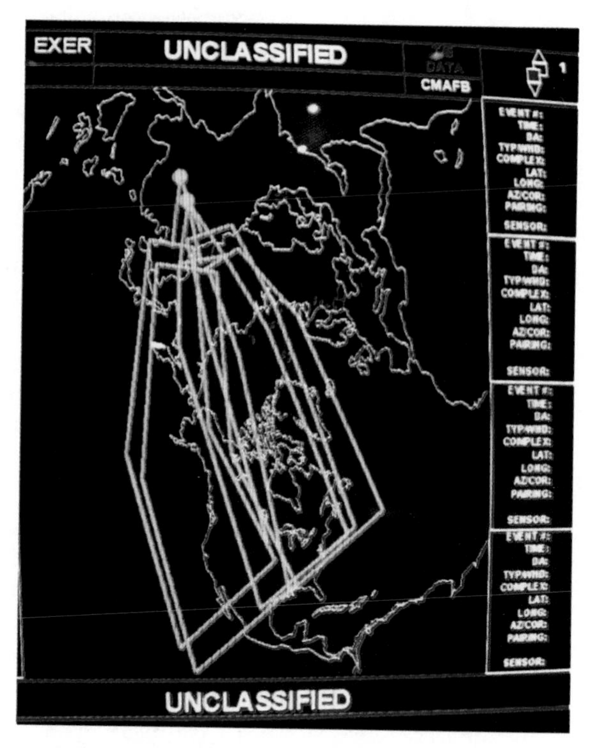

With the end of the cold war and with an increased focus on terrorism, the threat of nuclear war has faded in the minds of many. But the United States and Russia still maintain huge arsenals of nuclear weapons, and other countries, such as China, have acquired weapons or expanded their inventories. This image shows a computer screen at the North American Aerospace Defense Command Center deep inside Cheyenne Mountain in Colorado during a simulated nuclear missile attack by China on the United States. China's arsenal poses only a small threat currently, but that will change in time as it expands and modernizes its weapons systems.

The United States and Russia remain the nuclear Goliaths. In mid-2003, the U.S. deployed strategic (intercontinental-range) arsenal included 6,140 nuclear warheads and bombs and 1,040 strategic-range delivery vehicles (missiles and bombers). Russia's deployed strategic inventory was approximately 4,850 weapons and 990 delivery vehicles. Additionally, the United States has 1,120 deployed tactical (shorter-range, battlefield) nuclear weapons, and Russia has some 3,400.

China, France, Great Britain, India, and Pakistan all openly have nuclear weapons, and Israel and (perhaps) North Korea have undeclared nuclear weapons, adding another 1,300 or so nuclear devices to the volatile mix of nearly 17,000 deployed tactical and strategic nuclear devices. There are another 13,000 or so such weapons in U.S. and Russian reserve inventories or waiting for disassembly. Additionally, several countries have or are suspected of having nuclear weapons development programs, and another 30 countries have the technology base needed to build nuclear weapons.

Given this reality, it would be unwise to discount the continuing impact of nuclear weapons on world politics. One role that nuclear weapons play is to be a part of the "backdrop" of power and influence. There can be little doubt that the continuing importance of Russia, despite its tremendous travails, rests in part on its still immense nuclear arsenal. Deterrence is a second role played by nuclear weapons. Whether or not nuclear weapons will always deter conventional or nuclear attack is uncertain, but at least sometimes they have been and remain a restraining factor that deters an opponent from attacking in the first place or that limits an opponent's weapons or tactics. It is not unreasonable to conjecture, for instance, that the nuclear option that the United States, France, and Great Britain all had in the Persian Gulf War may have helped deter Saddam Hussein from using his chemical weapons in 1991. The United States again used its nuclear weapons in 2003 to threaten Iraq. Among a number of allusions by various officials to the possible use of nuclear weapons if U.S. forces faced weapons of mass destruction, Secretary of Defense Donald Rumsfeld publicly declared that the administration would "not foreclose the possible use of nuclear weapons if [so] attacked."[39]

Actual use is a third role for nuclear weapons. The atomic attacks on Hiroshima and Nagasaki demonstrate that humans have the ability and the will to use weapons of mass destruction. Therefore, it is naive to imagine that nuclear war cannot happen. To the contrary, there are several ways that a nuclear war could break out.

Did You Know That:

Eighteen Japanese survived the atomic attack on Hiroshima and also (three days later) the atomic blast in Nagasaki, where they and others had fled seeking safety after the first mushroom cloud.

How a Nuclear War Might Start

For all its potential horror, nuclear war is within the realm of possibility. Strategic analysts envision many possible scenarios.

Irrational leader. A leader who is fanatical, deranged, drunk, or otherwise out of control is one possible cause of nuclear war. What if Adolf Hitler had possessed the bomb? Were Russia's weapons safe under the control of the country's hard-drinking president, Boris Yeltsin (1990–1999)? According to reports, worried Russian generals were unsure of what could be expected of their often drunken president during a crisis.[40] It is also possible that a berserk military officer might try to use nuclear weapons, although there are numerous safety devices such as the "dual key" system and electronic "permissive action links" designed to limit such a possibility.

Calculated attack. A "bolt out of the blue" nuclear attack could also happen. This might occur if one country felt that it could deliver a first strike that would disable all or most of its opponent's strategic forces. Such an attack could come if a country believed that, combined with defensive measures, such as a national missile defense system, the strike would result in a victory with "acceptable losses." An unprovoked nuclear attack could also come as a result of a nuclear country attacking a nonnuclear country, especially if that country used chemical or biological weapons against the nuclear country.

Last gasp. Nuclear war could come as a final attempt to fend off conventional defeat. One scenario with real possibilities is to imagine a beleaguered Israel, its vaunted conventional forces finally overwhelmed by numerically superior Arab invaders, launching a last-gasp strike against Egyptian, Jordanian, and Syrian armies pounding the last Israeli defensive positions in Jerusalem near the Wailing Wall on Temple Mount, the holiest place of the Jewish people.

Inadvertent nuclear war. Of the various triggers of a nuclear war, misperception is one of the two most likely causes. The limits of rationality in decision making mean that those who command nuclear weapons can make mistakes. False intelligence that a nuclear attack is imminent or even under way, for example, might cause a leader to inadvertently strike first. In 1995, for example, Russian radar detected what appeared to be an incoming missile fired over the Norwegian Sea, and Moscow prepared to launch a retaliatory strike on the United States. Only at the last moment was it determined that the radar blip was an outgoing Norwegian scientific rocket, not an incoming U.S. missile. "For a while," said a Russian defense official, "the world was on the brink of nuclear war."[41] This was neither the first nor last such close call.

The time for American and Russian leaders to make decisions in a nuclear crisis is short, with at most 30 minutes given the flight time of a nuclear missile between the two countries. Leaders of countries close to one another, like Pakistan and India, would have much, much less time to respond. This will decrease the time to confirm reports that a nuclear attack has been launched or is about to be launched. It will also vastly increase the chances of erroneously launching what a leader sees as a counterstrike, but what, in fact, is a first strike.

This roiling red nuclear cloud captures a hint of the menace inherent in nuclear weapons. Notice the height of the mushroom cloud in this photograph, which was taken sometime in the 1950s. It is more than one mile high, as you can tell from the size of the islets surrounding Bikini Atoll below, where the blast took place. For an interactive look at the implications of a nuclear attack in your area, go to http://www.pbs.org/wgbh/amex/bomb/sfeature/blastmap.html.

Escalation. A deadly spiral is a final, not unlikely, path to nuclear war. History has demonstrated that leaders are willing to risk nuclear war even when there is no immediate and critical threat to national security. Perhaps the closest the world has ever come to nuclear war was during the 1962 Cuban missile crisis, when the Soviets risked nuclear war by placing missiles with nuclear warheads in Cuba, and the United States risked nuclear war by threatening to invade Cuba and attack the Russian forces guarding the missiles unless Moscow withdrew them.

Nuclear Weapons, Deterrence, and Strategy

There are issues of what a country's nuclear arsenal and doctrines should be that seldom enter the public debate, but that are crucial to an effective and stable arsenal. Furthermore, the post–cold war changes have brought on new challenges in strategic planning. As one expert has noted, it "is clear that there is a great debate . . . over who is the enemy and what is the target."[42] The two main issues are (1) how to minimize the chance of nuclear war and (2) how to maximize the chance of survival if a nuclear exchange does occur. It is not possible here to review all the factors that impinge on these issues, but we can illustrate the various concerns by examining deterrence and then several specific issues about weapons systems and strategy.

Weapons

The United States and the Soviet Union, now Russia, have both long relied on a triad of **strategic-range delivery vehicles**, those capable of striking more than 5,500 kilometers (3,416.8 miles) from their bases. These include (1) submarine-launched ballistic missiles (SLBMs) carried aboard ballistic missile nuclear submarines (SSBNs), (2) land-based intercontinental ballistic missiles (ICBMs), and (3) bombers. Most ICBMs are located in silos, although Russia has railroad-mobile SS-24 and road-mobile SS-25 missiles. ICBMs and SLBMs carry from one to ten warheads. Those with more than one warhead have multiple independent reentry vehicle (MIRV) capability allowing each warhead to attack a different target. All the countries with acknowledged or suspected nuclear weapons also possess shorter-range tactical delivery vehicles that are capable of delivering nuclear devices within a region or onto a battlefield.

The most powerful of these explosive devices is currently deployed on Russian SS-18 ICBMs, each of which carries 10 MIRV 750-kiloton warheads. The largest American weapons are 475-kiloton warheads, eight of which are carried on each D-5 SLBM. Nuclear weapons designed for tactical use also come in a relatively miniaturized form. Among currently deployed tactical nuclear weapons, the explosive power of U.S. B-61 bombs can be as low as 0.3 kilotons (30 tons of TNT), a yield that is approximately nine times as powerful as the ammonium nitrate bomb that destroyed the Federal Building in Oklahoma City on April 19, 1995.

Controversy over the future of such "mini-nukes" erupted in 2003 when, at the request of President Bush, Congress repealed a ten-year-old law barring the further development of nuclear weapons under 5-kiloton yields. The White House argued that it should be free to explore creating a new generation of mini-nukes to perform such tasks as penetrating deep into the ground to destroy bunkers, emitting enhanced radiation that would kill humans and other life forms but cause relatively little blast damage, and creating fireball temperatures that would destroy chemical and biological agents. Proponents argue these uses are valid and that, if nuclear weapons have to be used, it would be far better to employ a mini-nuke rather than one of the current larger nuclear devices. There are also many opponents. Speaking in 2003 on the subject of building such weapons, former Vice President Al Gore declared, "In my opinion, this would be true madness."[43] Critics charge that a false image of such weapons as relatively benign would encourage their use, taking the world beyond what, except for Hiroshima and Nagasaki, has been an absolute barrier to using nuclear weapons. Once that line is crossed, the argument goes, escalation to larger nuclear weapons will be easier. Opponents of mini-nukes also worry that if one were stolen, it could be used with devastating effect by terrorists.

Deterrence

The concept of deterrence remains at the center of the strategy of all the nuclear powers. **Deterrence** is persuading an enemy that attacking you will not be worth any potential gain. Deterrence is based on two factors: capability and credibility.

Capability. Effective deterrence requires that you be able to respond to an attack or impending attack on your forces. This capability is what India claimed it was seeking when it openly tested nuclear weapons in 1998. "Our problem is China," said an Indian official." We are not seeking [nuclear] parity with China. . . . What we are seeking is a minimum deterrent."[44] Just having weapons, however, is not enough. Since there is no way to defend against a missile attack once it is launched, deterrence requires that you have enough weapons that are relatively invulnerable to enemy destruction so that you can be assured that some will survive for a counterattack. Of all the strategic delivery systems, SLBMs are the least vulnerable; ICBMs in silos are the most vulnerable.

Credibility. It is also necessary for other states to believe that you will actually use your weapons. Perception is a key factor. The operational reality will be determined by what the other side believes rather than by what you intend. We will see, for example, that some analysts believe that relying on a second-strike capability may not always be credible.

This two-part equation for deterrence sounds simple enough on the surface, but the question is how to achieve it. The debate can be roughly divided into two schools of nuclear strategy. They are characterized by two bizarrely colorful acronyms. One is **MAD (Mutual Assured Destruction)** and **NUT (Nuclear Utilization Theory)**.

Those who favor the mutual assured destruction strategy (the MADs) believe that deterrence is best achieved if each nuclear power's capabilities include (1) a sufficient number of weapons that are (2) capable of surviving a nuclear attack by an opponent and then (3) delivering a second-strike retaliatory attack that will destroy that opponent. MADs believe, in other words, in *deterrence through punishment*. If each nuclear power has these three capabilities, then a mutual checkmate is achieved. The result, MAD theory holds, is that no power will start a nuclear war because doing so will lead to its own destruction (even if it destroys its enemy).

Those who favor nuclear utilization theory (the NUTs) contend that the MAD strategy is a mad gamble because it relies on rationality and clear-sightedness when, in reality, there are other scenarios (discussed earlier in the section "How a Nuclear War Might Start") that could lead to nuclear war. Therefore, NUTs prefer to base deterrence partly on *deterrence through damage denial* (or limitation), in contrast to the punishment strategy of MADs. This means that NUTs want to be able to destroy enemy weapons before the weapons explode on one's own territory and forces. The ways to do this are to destroy the weapons before they are launched or during flight.

Nuclear Strategy

The rapid reconfiguration of the political world and nuclear weapons inventories has muted the MAD-NUT debate, but there are still echoes in current weapons and strategy issues. To illustrate these issues, we can examine the questions of whether to ever use nuclear weapons first and whether to try to build a national missile defense system.

First Use One long-standing debate is when, if ever, to be the first to use nuclear weapons, especially to escalate from nonnuclear to nuclear warfare. The NATO alliance long held that it might launch a nuclear strike to destroy oncoming, overwhelming Soviet ground forces. More recently, Presidents Bush, the father and the son, each indirectly warned Saddam Hussein that if Iraq used biological or chemical weapons in the impending wars (1991 and 2003), Iraq faced U.S. nuclear retaliation. Similarly, President Clinton issued Presidential Decision Direction 60 (PDD-60) that anticipates the possible use of nuclear weapons in the face of biological or chemical attack. If some nation were to attack the United States with chemical weapons, the secretary of defense said, "we could make a devastating response without the use of nuclear weapons, but we would not forswear the possibility."[45]

MAD advocates are very leery of first use, warning that using nuclear weapons against a nuclear power could lead to uncontrolled escalation. Their worry is that using nuclear weapons against a nonnuclear power could undermine the norm against nuclear warfare and make it easier in the future for other nuclear powers to use their weapons against still other nonnuclear powers (Tannenwald, 1999). NUT advocates argue that, just like nuclear weapons, biological and chemical weapons are weapons of mass destruction and, therefore, deterring their use along with nuclear weapons is valid.

Missile Defense Systems Another long-standing controversy in the area of nuclear planning is whether or not to build a national missile defense system (NMDS), also called a ballistic missile defense (BMD) system. There were some thoughts of mounting

YOU BE THE PLAYWRIGHT

Thinking the Unthinkable

It is counterintuitive to think that a national missile defense system (NMDS) might be a dangerous threat to stability that could actually increase the chance of nuclear war. To help understand that position, place yourself in the Kremlin. You have a decision to make.

The year is 2015. You are president of Russia. The hopes for American-Russian friendship that flourished for a decade or so after the end of the cold war have faded. Now hostility is intense, and war is possible in the crisis you are facing.

Several events from more than a decade ago play a major role in the fearful choice you must make. One is that when the old parts of the USSR became independent countries, several contained substantial ethnic Russian minorities. The population of Latvia is 30% Russian, and your ethnic kin are 28% of Lithuania's population and 9% of Estonia's. A second factor is that each of these three Baltic republics joined the North Atlantic Treaty Organization (NATO) in 2004, making them allies of the United States and the Western European powers (Morgan & Palmer, 2003).

It was also during the presidency of George W. Bush that in 2002 the Americans withdrew from the Anti-Ballistic Missile (ABM) Treaty of 1972, which had barred both them and you from building an NMDS. The U.S. withdrawal allowed it to proceed to try to develop such a system. It took more than a decade, but your intelligence sources now tell you that within six months Washington will deploy a system capable of destroying at least 90% of incoming nuclear weapons, even if you launched all your 1,000 intercontinental and submarine-launched ballistic missiles and their approximately 4,000 warheads. You, by contrast, must continue to rely on mutual assured deterrence to counter the almost equal number of U.S. ICBMs, SLBMs, and warheads.

The immediate crisis began four months ago when, complaining of abuse, the ethnic Russians in Estonia, Latvia, and Lithuania revolted. The retaliation by these three countries against your ethnic brethren was ferocious, and outraged public opinion in your country forced you to order the Russian army into those countries to stop the slaughter. They have been occupied, but their fleeing leaders have set up governments-in-exile in Brussels and have called on their NATO allies to meet their obligation and expel your forces. NATO has begun to mass troops and air power in Poland, also a NATO ally, and to deploy naval forces in the Baltic Sea off your coast.

Your military staff is urging you to strike now. They argue that you can use 70% of your nuclear arsenal to destroy most of the American strategic delivery systems and 10% to devastate the NATO forces gathering along your borders, keeping 20% to deter a retaliatory strike. You protest that the Americans will surely retaliate, but your generals make two powerful counterarguments. One is that if you only strike U.S. strategic weapons sites and leave the population centers alone, the American president will know that if he orders a counterstrike, you will fire the remainder of your arsenal at U.S. cities, killing at least 100 million Americans. This, your military staff urges, the Americans will not

such an effort in the 1960s, but high costs and technical unfeasibility led the United States and the Soviet Union to sign the Anti-Ballistic Missile (ABM) Treaty in 1972, largely banning the testing and development of such a system. Ronald Reagan renewed the controversy when he proposed building the Strategic Defense Initiative (SDI), also labeled "Star Wars" by its critics. Reagan's vision of a comprehensive shield from missile attack was abandoned as too expensive and technically infeasible.

Advances in technology and concern about future possible nuclear attacks by "rogue states" such as North Korea once again raised the issue of building a BMD system in the late 1990s. President Clinton was ambivalent, and while he devoted funds to research, the program moved slowly. One impediment was that testing would violate the Anti-Ballistic Missile (ABM) Treaty that Washington and Moscow had signed in 1972.

That effort has been greatly speeded up by his successor, President Bush. Soon after entering office he gave Moscow the required one-year notice that the United States would withdraw from the ABM Treaty in 2002. He also directed the Pentagon to make a determined effort to build a NMDS. It will be a challenging project that may or may not ever overcome the immense technical difficulties of reliably attacking missiles early in their flight or shooting down warheads traveling through space at 18,000 miles per hour among numerous decoy warheads. The NMDS will also be expensive. Congress

The United States is determined to build a national missile defense system (NMDS), represented here by this artist's conception of a space-based laser attacking a ballistic missile during its launch phase. Proponents claim an NMDS will enhance deterrence against other nuclear weapons powers and also will provide some ability to counter a nuclear attack if one were to occur. Opponents argue an NMDS will increase the chance of nuclear war by destabilizing deterrence and by deluding leaders into thinking the unthinkable.

risk. Second, the officers point out that once the U.S. NMDS is deployed in six months, you will be at a huge disadvantage because the Americans will be able to destroy 3,600 of your 4,000 warheads before they reach their target. Even more worrisome is intelligence that the Americans might launch a first strike once their missile defense system in place. The U.S. calculation is that if they could destroy 80%, or 3,200 of your warheads in a preemptive strike, you will have to capitulate because you know that the U.S. missile defense system could destroy 720 (90%) of the remaining 800 warheads in your feeble counterstrike. Clearly, this might make what has been unthinkable, nuclear war, thinkable. Your advisers know they are asking you to make a cosmic roll of the dice, but they argue that while you may be damned if you act now, you surely will be damned if you wait. Thus you must think about the unthinkable, a preemptive nuclear strike.

The skies are heavy over Moscow this morning, and your aching brain screams for relief from the pressure. But there is none. You are the president. What is your decision?

approved over $9 billion for it in FY2004 alone. Whether spending $100 billion or more to try to build such a system is folly or a wise expenditure is a matter of opinion.

Whatever the merits of the technical and financial arguments, they are not as important as the question of whether an NMDS should be built even if it is technically and financially feasible (Cimbala, 2003). NUTs favor building an NMDS because it fits in with the damage-denial strategy by, perhaps, allowing you to destroy all or some of your opponent's weapons in flight. NUTs also argue that if your opponent believes that its weapons may not get through, the opponent is less likely to launch them and risk retaliation. MADs adamantly oppose NMDS capability as dangerously destabilizing. They argue that a defensive system detracts from assured retaliatory destruction, since second-strike missiles would be destroyed in flight. MADs also worry that a NMDS might tempt its possessor into a first strike, since the NMDS system would be most effective against a reduced retaliatory strike rather than a full-scale first strike by an opponent. This double-edged element of a NMDS, its critics say, means that it would inevitably push other nuclear powers to develop a massive number of new nuclear delivery devices capable of overwhelming any defensive system. How would you write the script about the development of such a system? To help answer that, ponder the dilemma you are presented in the You Be the Playwright box "Thinking the Unthinkable."

Chapter Summary

War and World Politics

1. War is organized killing of other human beings. Virtually everyone is against that. Yet war continues to be a part of the human condition, and its incidence has not significantly abated. Modern warfare affects more civilians than it traditionally did; the number of civilians killed during war now far exceeds that of soldiers.
2. The study of force involves several major questions: When and why does war occur? When it does happen, how effective is it? What conditions govern success or failure? What options exist in structuring the use of force?
3. Although much valuable research has been done about the causes of war, about the best we can do is to say that war is a complex phenomenon that seems to have many causes. Some of these stem from the nature of our species, some from the existence of nation-states, and some from the nature and dynamics of the world political system.

National Military Power

4. Military power is both tangible and intangible. Tangible elements of power, such as tanks, are relatively easy to visualize and measure. Intangible elements of military power, such as morale and reputation, are much more difficult to operationalize.
5. Acquiring military power also has drawbacks. It creates the temptation to use it, it makes others insecure, and it is costly. Some people argue, and others disagree, that spending too many resources on military power is a major factor in the decline of once-mighty countries. Another argument debates whether quantity or quality provides the best defense.

Force as a Political Instrument

6. Force can be used, threatened, or merely exist as an unspoken possibility. When it is used, its success requires much planning and skill. Studies have determined the ideal conditions for successful use of military force. If force is to be used, it should be employed as a means, or tool, rather than, as sometimes happens, as an end in itself.
7. Force does not have to be used to have an impact. The possession of military power creates a backdrop to diplomacy, and the overt threat of force increases the psychological pressure even more. The tools of force can be applied through arms sales and other methods of intervention. When it is used, force can range from a very limited demonstration to a full-scale nuclear attack.
8. The nature of war is changing. Technology has enhanced killing power; nationalism has made war a patriotic cause. As a result, the scope of war has expanded, which has also changed the strategy of war. The power to defeat is a traditional strategy of war, while the power to hurt has increased in significance and incidence.

Unconventional Warfare

9. Warfare can be classified into three categories: unconventional warfare (including arms transfers, special operations, and terrorism), conventional warfare, and weapons of mass destruction warfare (including nuclear, biological, and chemical weapons).
10. Arms transfers, special operations, and terrorism are unconventional methods of warfare. These have assumed more importance in recent times. The definition, sources, and history of terrorism, and their weapons and tactics have to be considered, and new strategies adopted to combat terrorism as well as to address its root causes.

Conventional Warfare

11. Conventional warfare has been the norm throughout most of history. The goals and conduct of war include avoiding unchecked escalation.

Warfare with Weapons of Mass Destruction

12. Biological, chemical, and nuclear weapons are now developed to the point where they can cause horrific levels of death and destruction. The debate (MAD versus NUT) involving how to structure nuclear weapons systems and doctrines is an example of the issues that arise as the ability to conduct war continues to change and new technology develops new weapons.

For a chapter quiz, interactive activities, web links, PowerWeb articles, and much more, visit **www.mhhe.com/rourke10/** and go to chapter 10. Or, while accessing the site, click on Course-Wide Content and view recent international relations articles in the *New York Times.*

Key Terms

conventional warfare
deterrence
escalation
imperial overstretch thesis
MAD (Mutual Assured Destruction)
NUT (Nuclear Utilization Theory)
power to defeat
power to hurt
social overstretch thesis
special operations
state terrorism
strategic-range delivery vehicles
terrorism
transnational terrorism
unconventional force
weapons of mass destruction (WMDs)

CHAPTER 11

International Security: The Alternative Road

THINKING ABOUT SECURITY
- A Tale of Insecurity
- Seeking Security: Approaches and Standards of Evaluation

LIMITED SELF-DEFENSE THROUGH ARMS CONTROL
- Methods of Achieving Arms Control
- The History of Arms Control
- The Barriers to Arms Control

INTERNATIONAL SECURITY FORCES
- International Security Forces: Theory and Practice
- International Security and the Future

ABOLITION OF WAR
- Complete Disarmament
- Pacifism

CHAPTER SUMMARY

KEY TERMS

Weapons! arms! What's the matter here?
—William Shakespeare, *King Lear*

He's mad that trusts in the tameness of a wolf.
—William Shakespeare, *King Lear*

As the bomb fell over Hiroshima and exploded, we saw an entire city disappear. I wrote in my log the words: "My God, what have we done?"
—Capt. Robert Lewis, U.S. Army Air Corps, copilot of the *Enola Gay*

A world without nuclear weapons would be less stable and more dangerous for all of us.
—British Prime Minister Margaret Thatcher

CHAPTER OBJECTIVES

After completing this chapter, you should be able to:

- Explain the issue of security by considering what insecurity means.
- Discuss limited self-defense as an approach to security.
- Characterize arms control as an approach to achieving security by limiting the numbers and types of weapons that countries possess.
- List major events and themes in the history of arms control.
- Identify the limitation and reduction of arms as important aspects of arms control.
- Discuss limits on arms transfers, focusing on the issues of proliferation and nonproliferation of weapons, including biological, chemical, and conventional weapons.
- Summarize and evaluate political, technical, and domestic barriers to arms control.
- Describe the role that international security plays in world politics.
- Discuss the abolition of war as an approach to security, focusing on disarmament and pacifism.

Security is the enduring yet elusive quest. "I would give all my fame for a pot of ale, and safety," a frightened boy cries out before a battle in Shakespeare's *King Henry V*. Alas, Melpomene, the muse of tragedy, did not favor the boy's plea. The English and French armies met on the battlefield at Agincourt. Peace—and perhaps the boy—perished. Today most of us similarly seek security. Yet our quest is tempered by the reality that while humans have sought safety throughout history, they have usually failed to achieve that goal for long.

Thinking about Security

Perhaps one reason that security from armed attack has been elusive is that we humans have sought it in the wrong way. The traditional path has emphasized national self-defense by amassing arms to deter aggression. Alternative paths have been given little attention and fewer resources. From 1948 through 2004, for example, the world states spent about 1,200 times as much on their national military budgets (about $40 trillion) as on UN peacekeeping operations (about $34 billion). It just may be, then, that the first secretary-general of the United Nations, Trygve Lie, was onto something when he suggested that "wars occur because people prepare for conflict, rather than for peace."[1]

The aim of this chapter is to think anew about security from armed aggression in light of humankind's failed effort to find it. Because the traditional path has not brought us to a consistently secure place, it is only prudent to consider alternative, less-traveled-by, paths to security. These possible approaches include limiting or abandoning our weapons altogether, creating international security forces, and even adopting the standards of pacifism.

A Tale of Insecurity

One way to think about how to increase security is to ponder the origins of insecurity. To do that, let us go back in time to the hypothetical origins of insecurity. Our vehicle is a parable. Insecurity may not have started exactly like this, but it might have.

A Drama about Insecurity

It was a sunny, yet somehow foreboding autumn day many millennia ago. Og, a caveman of the South Tribe, was searching for food. It had been a poor season for hunting and gathering, and Og fretted about the coming winter and his family. The urge to provide security from hunger for his family carried Og northward out of the South Tribe's usual territory and into the next valley.

It was the valley of Ug of the North Tribe. The same motivations that drove Og also urged Ug on, but he had been luckier. He had just killed a large antelope and Ug was feeling prosperous as he used his large knife to clean his kill. At that moment, Og, with hunting spear in hand, happened out of the forest and came upon Ug. Both the hunters were startled, and they exchanged cautious greetings. Ug was troubled by the lean and hungry look of the spear-carrying stranger, and he unconsciously grasped his knife more tightly. The tensing of his ample muscles alarmed Og, who instinctively dropped his spear point to a defensive position. Fear was the common denominator. Neither Og nor Ug wanted a confrontation, but they were trapped. Their disengagement negotiation went something like this (translated):

Ug: You are eyeing my antelope and pointing your spear at me.

Og: And your knife glints menacingly in the sunlight. But this is crazy. I mean you no harm; your antelope is yours. Still, my family is needy and it would be good if you shared your kill.

Ug: Of course I am sympathetic, and I want to be friends. But this is an antelope from the North Tribe's valley. If there is any meat left over, I'll even give you a little. But first, why don't you put down your spear so we can talk more easily?

Og: A fine idea, Ug, and I'll be glad to put down my spear, but why don't you lay down that fearful knife first? Then we can be friends.

Ug: Spears can fly through the air farther. . . . You should be first.

Og: Knives can strike more accurately. . . . You should be first.

And so the confrontation continued, with Og and Ug equally unsure of the other's intentions, with each sincerely proclaiming his peaceful purpose, but with each unable to convince the other to lay his weapon aside first.

Critiquing the Drama

Think about the web of insecurity that entangled Og and Ug. Each was insecure about providing for himself and his family in the harsh winter that was approaching. Security extends farther than just being safe from armed attacks. Ug was a "have" and Og was a "have-not." Ug had a legitimate claim to his antelope; Og had a legitimate need to find sustenance. Territoriality and tribal differences added to the building tension. Ug was in "his" valley; Og could not understand why unequal resource distribution meant that some should prosper while others were deprived. The gutting knife and the spear also played a role. But did the weapons cause tension or, perhaps, did Ug's knife protect him from a raid by Og?

We should also ask what could have provided the security to get Og and Ug out of their confrontation. If Og's valley had been full of game, he would not have been driven to the next valley. Or if the region's food had been shared by all, Og would not have needed Ug's antelope. Knowing this, Ug might have been less defensive. Assuming, for a moment, that Og was dangerous—as hunger sometimes drives people to be—then Ug might have been more secure if somehow he could have signaled the equivalent of today's 911 distress call and summoned the region's peacekeeping force, dispatched by the area's intertribal council. The council might even have been able to aid Og with some food and skins to ease his distress and to quell the anger he felt when he compared his ill fortune with the prosperity of Ug.

The analysis of our parable could go on and be made more complex. Og and Ug might have spoken different languages, worshipped different deities, or had differently colored faces. That, however, would not change the fundamental questions regarding security. Why were Og and Ug insecure? More important, once insecurity existed, what could have been done to restore harmony?

Seeking Security: Approaches and Standards of Evaluation

Now bring your minds from the past to the present, from primordial cave dwellers to yourself. Think about contemporary international security. The easiest matter is determining what our goal should be. How to do that is, of course, a much more challenging question.

Approaches to Security

There are, in essence, four possible approaches to securing peace. The basic parameters of each are shown in Table 11.1. As with many, even most matters in this book, which approach is best is part of the realist-liberal debate.

Unlimited self-defense, the first of the four approaches, is the traditional approach of each country being responsible for its own defense and amassing weapons it wishes for

TABLE 11.1 Four Approaches to Security

Security Approach	Sources of Insecurity	World Political System	Armaments Strategy	Primary Peacekeeping Mechanism	Strategy
Unlimited self-defense	Many; probably inherent in humans	State-based; national interests and rivalries; fear	Have many and all types to guard against threats	Armed states, deterrence, alliances, balance of power	Peace through strength
Limited self-defense	Many; perhaps inherent, but weapons intensify them	State-based; limited cooperation based on mutual interests	Limit amount and types to reduce capabilities, damage, tension	Armed states; defensive capabilities, lack of offensive capabilities	Peace through limited offensive ability
International security	Anarchical world system; lack of law or common security mechanisms	International political integration; regional or world government	Transfer weapons and authority to international force	International peacekeeping/peace enforcement	Peace through law and universal collective defense
Abolition of war	Weapons; personal and national greed and insecurity	Various options from pacifistic states to libertarian global village model	Eliminate weapons	Lack of ability; lack of fear; individual and collective pacifism	Peace through being peaceful

Concept source: Rapoport (1992).

The path to peace has long been debated. The four approaches outlined here provide some basic alternatives that help structure this chapter on security.

that defense. The thinking behind this approach rests on the classic realist assumption that humans have an inherent element of greed and aggressiveness that promotes individual and collective violence. This makes the international system, from the realists' perspective, a place of danger where each state must fend for itself or face the perils of domination or destruction by other states.

Beyond the traditional approach to security, there are three alternative approaches: *limited self-defense* (arms limitations), *international security* (regional and world security forces), and *abolition of war* (complete disarmament and pacifism). Each of these will be examined in the pages that follow. Realists do not oppose arms control or even international peacekeeping under the right circumstances. Realists, for instance, recognize that the huge arsenals of weapons that countries possess are dangerous and, therefore, there can be merit in carefully negotiated, truly verifiable arms accords. But because the three alternative approaches all involve some level of trust and depend on the triumph of the spirit of human cooperation over human avarice and power-seeking, they are all more attractive to liberals than to realists.

Standards of Evaluation

Now that we have identified the approaches to seeking security, the question is which one of them offers the greatest chance of safety. There is no clear answer, so it is important to consider how to evaluate the various possibilities.

To evaluate the approaches to security, begin by considering the college community in which you live. The next time you are in class, look around you. Is anyone carrying a gun? Are you? Probably not. Think about why you are not doing so. The answer is that you feel relatively secure.

Security is relative and a state of mind. Like this 19-year-old college student in Thailand who was taken hostage by a man so high on methamphetamines that he had cut himself, individuals can suddenly fall victim to violent crime. Yet most people do not carry guns because they feel safe in their domestic system. The police responded to this woman's peril and eventually subdued her assailant and freed her. By contrast, there is no one who will necessarily aid international victims of aggression. Therefore, countries in the anarchical international system rely on self-protection and create armies to defend themselves.

The word "relatively" is important here. There are, of course, dangerous people in your community who might steal your property, attack you, and perhaps even kill you. There were 16,204 homicides, 95,136 reported rapes, and 1,314,985 other violent crimes in the United States during 2002. Criminals committed another 10,450,893 burglaries, car thefts, and other property crimes. Thus, with one crime for every 24 Americans, it is clear that you are not absolutely secure. Yet most of us feel secure enough to forgo carrying firearms.

The important thing to consider is why you feel secure enough not to carry a gun despite the fact that you could be murdered, raped, beaten up, or have your property stolen. There are many reasons. *Domestic norms* against violence and stealing are one reason. Most people around you are peaceful and honest and are unlikely, even if angry or covetous, to attack you or steal your property. Established *domestic collective security forces* are a second part of feeling secure. The police are on patrol to deter criminals, and if anyone does attack you or steal your property, you can call 911; criminal courts and prisons deal with convicted felons. *Domestic disarmament* is a third contributor to your sense of security. Most domestic societies have disarmed substantially, shun the routine of carrying weapons, and have turned the legitimate use of domestic force beyond immediate self-defense over to their police. *Domestic conflict-resolution mechanisms* are a fourth contributor to security. There are ways to settle disputes without violence. Lawsuits are filed, and judges make decisions. Indeed, some crimes against persons and property are avoided because most domestic political systems provide some level of social services to meet human needs.

To return to our stress on relative security, it is important to see that for all the protections and dispute-resolution procedures provided by your domestic system, and for all the sense of security that you usually feel, you are not fully secure. Nor are countries and their citizens secure in the global system. For that matter, it is unlikely that anything near absolute global security can be achieved through any of the methods offered in this chapter or anywhere else. Therefore, the most reasonable standard by which to evaluate approaches to security is to compare them and to ask which makes you more secure.

Limited Self-Defense through Arms Control

The first alternative approach to achieving security involves limiting the numbers and types of weapons that countries possess. This approach, called **arms control**, aims at lessening military (especially offensive) capabilities and lessening the damage even if war begins. Additionally, arms control advocates believe that the decline in the number and power of weapons systems will ease political tensions, thereby making further arms agreements possible (Gallagher, 1998).

Methods of Achieving Arms Control

There are many methods to control arms in order to limit or even reduce their number and to prevent their spread. These methods include numerical restrictions; research, development, and deployment restrictions; categorical restrictions; and transfer restrictions. Several of the arms control agreements that will be used to illustrate the restrictions are detailed in the following section on the history of arms control, but to familiarize yourself with them quickly, peruse the agreements listed in Table 11.2 on page 344.

Numerical restrictions. Placing numerical limits above, at, or below the current level of existing weapons is the most common approach to arms control. This approach specifies the number or capacity of weapons and/or troops that each side may possess. In some cases the numerical limits may be at or higher than current levels. For example, both the first and second Strategic Arms Limitations Talks treaties, the two Strategic Arms Reduction Treaties (START I and II), and the Treaty of Moscow (2002) have combined to significantly reduce the number of American and Russian nuclear weapons. Although the Russian Duma refused to ratify START II unless the United States agreed to cease developing a national missile defense system, both countries later agreed to cuts in their nuclear arsenals that in many cases will exceed the reductions outlined in the treaty.

Categorical restrictions. A second approach to arms control involves limiting or eliminating certain types of weapons. The Intermediate-Range Nuclear Forces Treaty (INF) eliminated an entire class of weapons—intermediate-range nuclear missiles. The new Anti-Personnel Mine Treaty will make it safer to walk the Earth.

Development, testing, and deployment restrictions. A third method of limiting arms involves a sort of military birth control that ensures that weapons systems never begin their gestation period of development and testing or, if they do, they are never deployed. The advantage of this approach is that it stops a specific area of arms building before it starts. For instance, the countries that have ratified the Nuclear Non-Proliferation Treaty (NPT) and that do not have such weapons agree not to develop them. A related approach for weapons that have already been developed is to prohibit their deployment in certain geographic areas. The deployment of military weapons in Antarctica, the seabed, space, and elsewhere is, for example, banned.

Transfer restrictions. A fourth method of arms control is to prohibit or limit the flow of weapons and weapons technology across international borders. Under the NPT, for

TABLE 11.2 Selected Arms Control Treaties

Treaty	Provisions	Date Signed	Number of Parties
Treaties in Force			
Geneva Protocol	Bans using gas or bacteriological weapons	1925	132
Limited Test Ban	Bans nuclear tests in the atmosphere, space, or underwater	1963	124
Non-Proliferation Treaty (NPT)	Prohibits selling, giving, or receiving nuclear weapons, materials, or technology for weapons. Made permanent in 1995	1968	187
Biological Weapons	Bans the production and possession of biological weapons	1972	147
Strategic Arms Limitation Talks Treaty (SALT I)	Limits U.S. and USSR strategic weapons	1972	2
Threshold Test Ban	Limits U.S. and USSR underground tests to 150 kt	1974	2
SALT II	Limits U.S. and USSR strategic weapons	1979	2
Intermediate-Range Nuclear Forces (INF)	Eliminates U.S. and USSR missiles with ranges between 500 km and 5,500 km	1987	2
Missile Technology Control Regime (MTCR)	Limits transfer of missiles and missile technology	1987	33
Conventional Forces in Europe Treaty (CFE)	Reduces conventional forces in Europe	1990	30
Strategic Arms Reduction Treaty (START I)	Reduces U.S. and USSR/Russian strategic nuclear forces	1991	2
Chemical Weapons Convention (CWC)	Bans the possession of chemical weapons after 2005	1993	152
Anti-Personnel Mine Treaty (APM)	Bans the production, use, possession, and transfer of land mines	1997	141
Treaty of Moscow	Reduces U.S. and Russian strategic nuclear forces	2002	2
Treaties Not in Force			
Anti-Ballistic Missile (ABM) Treaty	U.S.-USSR pact limits anti-ballistic missile testing and deployment. U.S. withdrew in 2002	1972	n/a
START II	Reduces U.S. and Russian strategic nuclear forces. Not ratified by Russia	1993	1
Comprehensive Test Ban Treaty (CTBT)	Bans all nuclear weapons tests. Not ratified by U.S., China, Russia, India, and Pakistan	1996	51

Notes: The date signed indicates the first date when countries whose leadership approves of a treaty can sign it. Being a *signatory* is not legally binding; becoming a *party* to a treaty then requires fulfilling a country's ratification procedure or other legal process to legally adhere to the treaty. Treaties to which the Soviet Union was a party bind its successor state, Russia.

Data sources: Numerous news and Web sources, including the United Nations Treaty Collection at http://untreaty.un.org/.

Progress toward controlling arms has been slow and often unsteady, but each agreement listed here represents at least an attempted step down the path of restraining the world's weapons.

example, countries that have nuclear weapons or nuclear weapons technology pledge not to supply nonnuclear states with weapons or the technology to build them.

This review of the strategies and methods of arms control leads naturally to the question of whether they have been successful. And if they have not been successful, why not? To address these questions, in the next two sections we will look at the history of arms control, then at the continuing debate over arms control.

The History of Arms Control

Attempts to control arms and other military systems extend almost to the beginning of written history. The earliest recorded example occurred in 431 B.C. when Sparta and Athens negotiated over the length of the latter's defensive walls. Prior to the beginning of the 20th century, however, arms control hardly existed. Since then there has been a buildup of arms control activity. Technology, more than any single factor, spurred rising interest in arms control. The escalating lethality of weapons sparked a growing sense that an apocalypse awaited the world if humans could not restrain their ability to slaughter one another. It is possible to explore the growth of arms control activity over the last century or so in three parts. The first will cover arms control to 1990. Then the subsequent history will be divided into a discussion of attempts to control nuclear, biological, and chemical **weapons of mass destruction (WMDs)** and a discussion of controlling conventional weapons.

Arms Control through the 1980s

The modern history of arms control began with the Hague Conferences (1899, 1907). These multilateral arms negotiations did nothing about general arms levels, but some restrictions were placed on poison gas and the use of other weapons (Croft, 1997). The horror of World War I further increased world interest in arms control. The Washington Naval Conference (1921–1922) established a battleship tonnage ratio among the world's leading naval powers and, for a time, headed off a naval arms buildup. There were a number of other bilateral and multilateral arms negotiations and agreements in the 1920s and 1930s, but they all had little impact on the increasing avalanche of aggression that culminated in World War II.

Arms control efforts were spurred even more by the unparalleled destruction wrought by conventional arms during World War II and by the atomic flashes that leveled Hiroshima and Nagasaki in 1945. One early reaction was the creation in 1946 of what is now called the International Atomic Energy Agency (IAEA) to limit the use of nuclear technology to peaceful purposes.

The intensity of the cold war blocked arms control during the 1950s, but by the early 1960s worries about nuclear weapons began to overcome even that impediment. The first major step occurred in 1963, when most countries agreed to cease testing nuclear weapons in the atmosphere. Between 1945 and 1963, there were on average 25 above-ground nuclear tests each year. After the treaty was signed, such tests (all by nonsignatories) declined to about three a year, then ended in the 1980s. Thus, the alarming threat of radioactive fallout that had increasingly contaminated the atmosphere was largely eliminated. Later in the decade, the multilateral nuclear **Non-Proliferation Treaty (NPT)** of 1968 pledged its parties (countries that have completed their legal process to adhere to a treaty) to avoid taking any actions that would add to the number of countries with nuclear weapons.

During the 1970s, with cold war tensions beginning to relax substantially, and with the U.S. and Soviet nuclear weapon inventories each passing the 20,000 mark, the pace of arms control negotiations picked up. The **Anti-Ballistic Missile Treaty (ABM)** of 1972 put stringent limits on U.S. and Soviet efforts to build a ballistic missile defense (BMD) system, which many analysts believed could destabilize nuclear deterrence by undermining its cornerstone, mutual assured destruction (MAD). In 2002, President Bush withdrew the United States from the treaty in order to pursue the development and deployment of BMD systems. This controversial step is discussed in chapter 10.

The 1970s also included important negotiations to limit the number, deployment, or other aspects of weapons of mass destruction. The most important of these with regard to nuclear weapons were the **Strategic Arms Limitation Talks Treaty I (SALT I)** of 1972 and the **Strategic Arms Limitation Talks Treaty II (SALT II)** of 1979. Each put important caps on the number of Soviet and American nuclear weapons and delivery vehicles. Moscow and Washington, already confined to underground nuclear tests by the 1963 treaty, moved to limit the size of even those tests to 150 kilotons in the Threshold Test Ban Treaty (1974).

Another important advance in the realm of controlling WMDs occurred with the conclusion of the **Biological Weapons Convention** of 1972, which virtually all countries subsequently signed and ratified. Those countries with biological weapons agreed to destroy them, and all signatories agreed not to manufacture new ones.

The 1980s were a decade when arms control momentum picked up even more speed as the cold war began to wind down, reversing the trend of earlier decades when the destructive power of WMDs and the number of countries possessing them had continued to grow. The **Missile Technology Control Regime (MTCR)** was established in 1987 to restrain the proliferation of missiles. The odd designation "regime" is used for the agreement because, according to the U.S. State Department, the MTCR is an "informal political arrangement" through which signatory countries pledge not to transfer missile technology or missiles with a range greater than 300 kilometers.[2] The MTCR has not stopped the spread of missiles but has certainly slowed it down. The countries with the most sophisticated missile technology all adhere to the MTCR, and they have brought considerable pressure to bear on China and other noncompliant missile-capable countries.

A second important agreement was the U.S-Soviet **Intermediate-Range Nuclear Forces Treaty (INF)** of 1987. Because it eliminated an entire class of nuclear delivery vehicles (missiles with ranges between 500 and 5,500 kilometers), the treaty was the first pact to actually reduce the globe's nuclear arsenal. The deployment of such U.S. missiles to Europe and counter-targeting by the Soviet Union had put Europe at particular risk of nuclear war.

WMDs and Arms Control since 1990

The years since 1990 have been by far the most important in the history of the control of WMDs, especially nuclear weapons. The most significant arms control during the 1990s involved efforts to control nuclear arms. To review the changes and the controversy associated with them, we can examine three treaties to reduce strategic-range nuclear weapons: the renewal of the NPT, the efforts to ban all nuclear testing, and the treaty on chemical weapons.

Strategic Arms Reduction Treaty I After a decade of negotiations, Presidents George H. W. Bush and Mikhail Gorbachev signed the first **Strategic Arms Reduction Treaty I (START I)** in 1991. The treaty mandated significant cuts in U.S. and Soviet strategic-range (over 5,500 kilometers) nuclear forces. Each country was limited to 1,600 delivery vehicles (missiles and bombers) and 6,000 strategic explosive nuclear devices (warheads and bombs). Thus, START I began the process of reducing the U.S. and Soviet strategic arsenals, each of which contained more than 10,000 warheads and bombs.

Strategic Arms Reduction Treaty II Presidents Boris Yeltsin and George Bush took a further step toward reducing the mountain of nuclear weapons when they signed the **Strategic Arms Reduction Treaty II (START II)** in 1993. Under START II, Russia and the United States agreed that by 2007 they would reduce their nuclear warheads and bombs to 3,500 for the United States and 2,997 for Russia. The treaty also has a number of clauses relating to specific weapons, the most important of which was the elimination of all ICBMs with multiple warheads (multiple independent reentry vehicles,

MIRVs). The U.S. Senate ratified START II in 1996, but Russia's Duma delayed taking up the treaty twice, once after U.S. military action against Iraq in 1997 and a second time after the U.S.-led attack on Yugoslavia in 1999. When the Duma finally took up the treaty in 2000, it voted for a conditional ratification by including a provision specifying that the treaty would not enter into force until the U.S. Senate ratified a protocol between the two countries reaffirming the ABM Treaty. This never occurred, and START II never entered into force. As a result, the number of U.S. and Russian strategic nuclear weapons in 2004 remained about the same as what START I required, rather than the much lower level specified by START II, and the provision requiring elimination of all MIRV-capable ICBMs has not been realized.

Treaty of Moscow Even while START II was pending before Russia's Duma, Presidents Bill Clinton and Boris Yeltsin agreed in 1997 on the broad principles for a third round of START aimed at further cutting the number of nuclear devices mounted on strategic-range delivery systems to between 2,000 and 2,500. That goal took on greater substance in May 2002 when President George W. Bush met with President Vladimir Putin in Moscow and the two leaders signed the Treaty Between the United States of America and the Russian Federation on Strategic Offensive Reductions, more generally called the **Treaty of Moscow**. Under the provisions of the treaty, the two countries agree to cut their arsenals of nuclear warheads and bombs to no more than 2,200 by 2012. Unlike START I and the partially ratified START II, the Treaty of Moscow contains no provisions relating to MIRVs.

Most observers hailed the new agreement, and it was soon ratified by both countries' legislatures. There were critics, however. One characterized the treaty as "for all practical purposes meaningless," charging that it actually places no restrictions and serves only as a means for the two sides to seem to be reducing nuclear arms while being free to increase weapons if they wished.[3] This somewhat elusive quality of reductions is due to four of the treaty's clauses. For one, there is no schedule of reductions from existing levels as long as they are completed by 2012. Second, the treaty expires that year if the two sides do not renew it. Thus the two parties can have done nothing by 2012, let the treaty lapse, and never have violated it. Third, either country can withdraw with just 90 days' notice. And fourth, both countries will be able to place dismantled weapons in reserve, which would allow them to be rapidly reinstalled on missiles and deployed.

Did You Know That:

START I is about 700 pages long. The Treaty of Moscow is 3 pages long.

Such concerns, although important, should not cause one to lose track of the significant nuclear arms reductions that have taken place in the past two decades or so. The mountain of global nuclear weapons was reduced by 68% between 1986 and 2002, as Figure 11.1 illustrates. If the reductions outlined in the Moscow treaty are put into place, the United States and Russia will have accomplished a remarkable reduction of more than 80% of nuclear warheads and bombs that existed before the treaties. Moreover, if the nuclear arsenals of China and the other smaller nuclear powers remain relatively stable, the world total of nuclear weapons in 2012 will be about a third of what they are now. Even now the silos at several former U.S. ICBM sites are completely empty, some of the bases have even been sold, and part of the land has reverted to farming, bringing to fruition the words from the Book of Isaiah (2:4), "They shall beat their swords into plowshares, and their spears into pruning hooks."

The Nuclear Non-Proliferation Treaty Renewal Offsetting the good news that the number of nuclear weapons is declining is the bad news that the number of countries with nuclear weapons is growing, as indicated in the map on p. 349. Less than 60 years ago there were no countries with nuclear arms. Now there are seven countries that openly possess nuclear weapons, one country (Israel) whose nuclear arsenal is an open secret, and

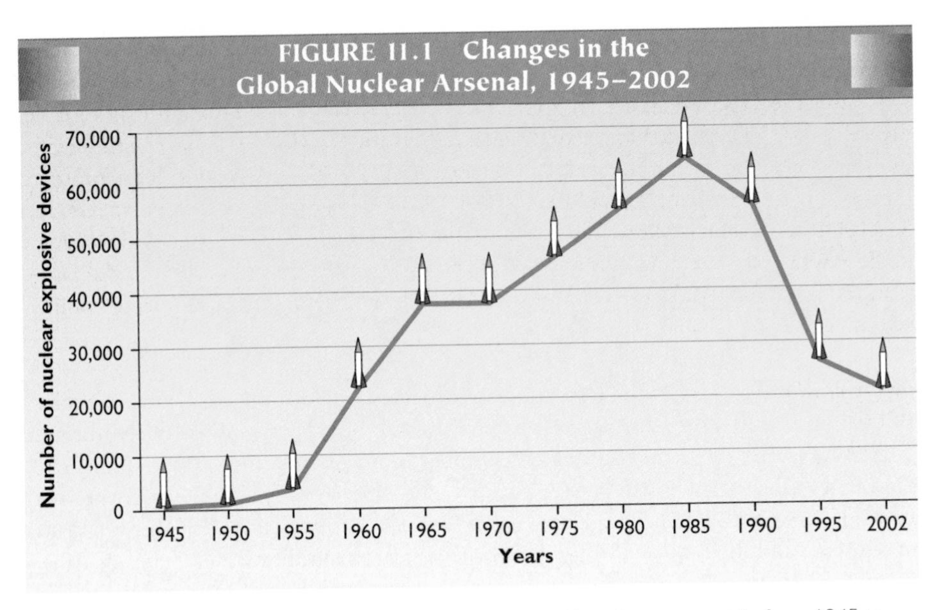

The mountain of strategic and tactical nuclear warheads and bombs grew rapidly from 1945 to 1986 when it peaked at 65,057. Then it began a steep decline and in 2002 stood at 21,022, the lowest number since 1959.

Notes: Data includes nuclear bombs and warheads in the arsenals of all acknowledged nuclear powers for the year. For 2002, estimated arsenals for India and Pakistan are included here that are not included in the *Bulletin of the Atomic Scientists* data.

Data source: Bulletin of the Atomic Scientists, 58/6 (November/December 2002):106–107.

one country (North Korea) that may well have nuclear weapons. Several other countries such as Iran have or had active programs to develop nuclear weapons.

The cornerstone of the effort to control the spread of nuclear weapons is the Nuclear Non-Proliferation Treaty (NPT). The treaty was originally signed in 1968; it was renewed and made permanent in 1995, and it has now been signed by more than 85% of the world's countries. The signatories agree not to transfer nuclear weapons or in any way to "assist, encourage, or induce any nonnuclear state to manufacture or otherwise acquire nuclear weapons." Nonnuclear signatories of the NPT also agree not to build or accept nuclear weapons and to allow the IAEA to establish safeguards to ensure that nuclear facilities are used exclusively for peaceful purposes. These efforts have been successful insofar as there are many countries with the potential to build weapons that refrain from doing so, but for all its contributions, the NPT is not an unreserved success.

At least some of the reasons that proliferation is hard to stop were evident during the negotiations preceding the NPT's renewal in 1995. Many nonnuclear countries resisted renewal unless the existing nuclear-weapons countries set a timetable for dismantling their arsenals. Malaysia's delegate to the conference charged, for instance, that without such a pledge, renewing the treaty would be "justifying nuclear states for eternity" to maintain their monopoly.[4] Gradually, however, the objections were overcome. One important factor was a pledge by the nuclear-weapons states to conclude a treaty to ban all nuclear testing. As we shall see in the next section, the United States reneged on that pledge.

Nuclear proliferation is also difficult to stem because some countries want such weapons. Neither India nor Pakistan agreed to the NPT, and the two countries acquired the dubious distinction of joining the nuclear club when they each tested nuclear weapons in 1998. Disclosures in 2004 revealed that Pakistan's chief nuclear weapons scientist,

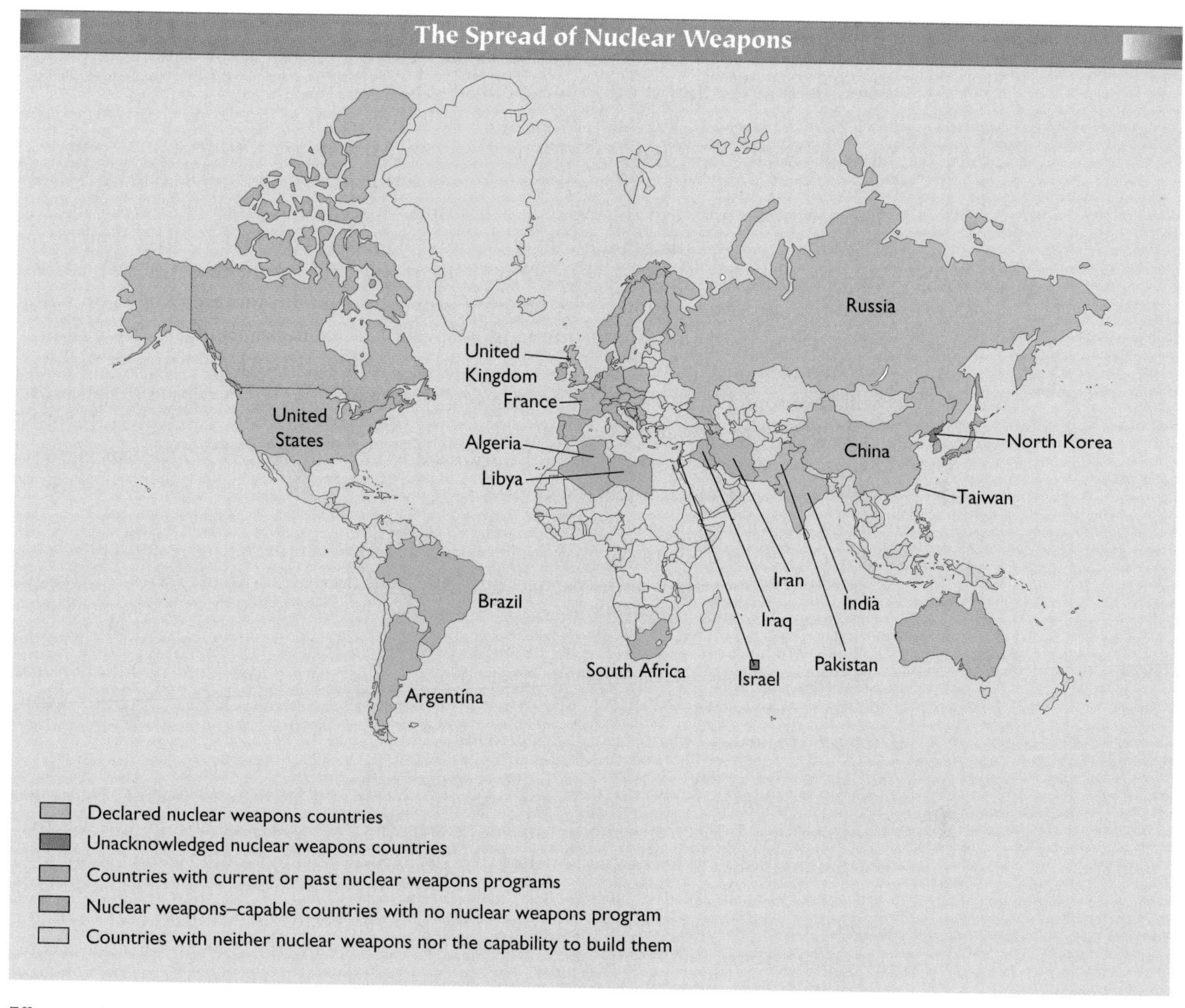

Efforts such as the Nuclear Non-Proliferation Treaty have slowed, but not stopped, the proliferation of nuclear weapons. There are now nine declared and undeclared nuclear weapons countries. Numerous other countries have the ability and, in some cases, the desire to acquire nuclear weapons.

*Israel has never acknowledged that it has nuclear weapons. North Korea claims to have them, but some outside experts do not acknowledge that as certain.

Abdul Qadeer Khan, was at the center of a multibillion dollar, multinational trafficking scheme that sent nuclear weapons technology and plans from Pakistan to Iran and Libya. This fact and the continued interest of several countries in acquiring nuclear weapons makes it easy to deride the NPT as a failure. That judgment, however, is probably too facile. For every country like India and Pakistan that can develop nuclear weapons and has, there are many other technologically advanced countries that have remained non-nuclear. These countries adhere to the NPT, which is both an expression of their animus toward proliferation and a confirmation of the treaty that supports their determination to remain without nuclear weapons.

Moreover, countries that are parties to the NPT and that do move toward developing nuclear weapons are subject to pressure from other countries for violating the treaty.

Did You Know That:

Pakistan's nuclear-warhead-capable Ghauri missile is named after Mohammad Ghauri, the 12th-century leader who began the Muslim conquest of Hindu India. India's Agni missile bears the name of the Hindu god of fire.

When concerns arose in 2003 about the nuclear energy program in Iran, the fact that the country was a party to an NPT proved an effective platform for other countries to pressure Iran to allow more complete inspections by the IAEA as required under the NPT. With the United States pressing for at least economic sanctions against Iran, the foreign ministers of France, Germany, and Great Britain traveled to Tehran and persuaded the Iranians to accept unexpected and detailed inspections of its nuclear sites by IAEA officials and also to suspend its uranium-enrichment program. Presenting the "good cop" visage, the French foreign minister told reporters, "This is a very important day. We were facing a major issue. Proliferation is a major challenge to the world, and today we found a solution to the pending issue." Taking a bit more of a bad cop stand, the British foreign minister cautioned, "The proof is not in words of the communiqué but about the implementation and compliance with the [IAEA]."[5] This view that Iran will have to deliver on its promises was furthered when the IAEA censured Iran for its earlier secrecy and warned that "further serious Iranian failures" to conform to the NPT might lead the agency to seek UN-authorized sanctions. As IAEA Director General Mohamed El Baradei noted, the censure gave Iran an "ominous message that failures in the future will not be tolerated."[6]

The issue of North Korea's nuclear program is proving even more difficult to address, but Pyongyang is also a party to the NPT, and the threat of sanctions is one factor that seems to have pushed the country to negotiate over the issue. And if it is resolved, it will be IAEA inspectors that once again begin oversight of North Korea's nuclear facilities. Adolf Hitler once described a treaty as only "a scrap of paper," and in a literal sense he was correct. But the NPT and other such scraps often prove effective, if not perfect, ways to regulate relations among countries.

The Comprehensive Test Ban Treaty Another important effort toward arms control has involved the drive to ban the testing of nuclear warheads. The first atomic test was held at Alamogordo, New Mexico, on July 16, 1945. After this first detonation, the number of tests, like the ominous cloud that symbolizes them, kept mushrooming, peaking in 1962 at 171 blasts. Then testing began to ebb in response to the negotiation of a number of treaties restricting testing (see Table 11.2), a declining need to test, and unilateral restraints. By the mid-1990s, testing nuclear weapons had declined to the point where it was unusual and was greeted with rancor. When France conducted underground tests in 1995 on uninhabited atolls in the South Pacific, there was an explosion of criticism. "An act of stupidity," thundered the prime minister of Australia in one of the milder comments.[7] The following year China exploded two bombs at its test facility under Lop Nor, bringing the global total to 2,046 tests since 1945. That figure rose to 2,051 in 1998 after India, then Pakistan conducted a series of tests that established them as the newest nuclear powers. Both countries argued they needed nuclear weapons to defend themselves, but critics charged that creating nuclear weapons was a derivative of nationalist and chauvinistic aggressive impulses. "Made with Viagra," is how one editorial cartoon in India labeled the bomb.[8] No further nuclear weapons tests have occurred after that through this writing in early 2004, as shown in Figure 11.2.

Those who share the goal of having the number of nuclear tests frozen forever at 2,051 have pinned their hopes on the **Comprehensive Test Ban Treaty (CTBT)**. The treaty was endorsed in 1996 in the UN General Assembly by the overwhelming vote of 158 to 3 (India, Libya, and Nepal; 24 other countries abstained or were absent) and opened to signature and ratification. Even though the CTBT has been signed by 155 countries and ratified by 51 of those, it has not gone into force. The reason is that it does not become operational until all 44 countries that had nuclear reactors in 1996

FIGURE 11.2 Nuclear Tests, 1945–2003

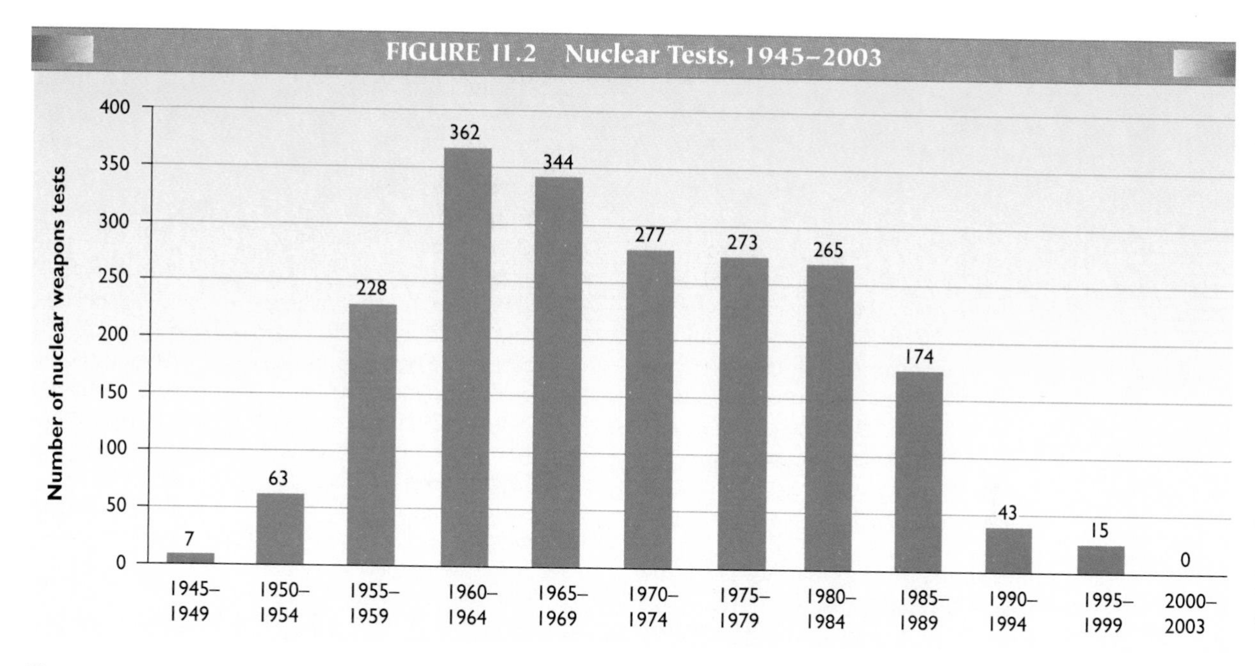

There were 2,051 known nuclear weapons tests between August 1945 and May 1998. As of this writing, no further tests have been held, raising the hope in many that the 2,051st test, conducted by Pakistan, will be the last. The goal of the Comprehensive Nuclear Test Ban Treaty is to turn that hope into a universal international commitment, but the unwillingness of several of the existing nuclear-weapons countries to ratify the treaty leaves further tests possible.

Data sources: Bulletin of the Atomic Scientists, 45/6 (November/December 1998); author's calculations.

ratify it, and several, including the United States, have not as the In the Spotlight box "Chained to the Nuclear Rock" details.

Although the Bush administration, despite its opposition to the CTBT, has maintained an informal moratorium on nuclear testing, the United States took two actions in late 2003 that indicate that it may well resume testing. In one move, President Bush signed the Energy and Water Development Appropriations Act of 2004 that included funds for the Department of Energy to create new types of nuclear weapons including low-yield mini-nukes (see chapter 10). Second, the White House authorized spending $25 million to modernize the U.S. nuclear test site in Nevada. That could set off a chain reaction of new testing. As the Russian newspaper *Pravda* editorialized, "The Moscow hawks are waiting impatiently for the USA to violate its nuclear test moratorium. . . . If the USA carries out tests in Nevada, the Kremlin will not keep its defense industries from following the bad U.S. example. They have been waiting too long since the end of the cold war."[9]

Chemical Weapons Convention Nuclear weapons were not the only WMDs to receive attention during the 1990s. Additionally, the growing threat and recent use of chemical weapons led to the **Chemical Weapons Convention (CWC)** in 1993. The signatories pledge to eliminate all chemical weapons by the year 2005; to "never under any circumstance" develop, produce, stockpile, or use chemical weapons; to not provide chemical weapons, or the means to make them, to another country; and to submit to rigorous inspection.

IN THE SPOTLIGHT

Chained to the Nuclear Rock

There are many mythological tales warning against hubris, the arrogance of seeking godlike power. In one such Greek myth, the Titan Prometheus stole fire from the gods and gave it to humankind. An angry Zeus chained Prometheus to a rock and each day sent an eagle to tear open his abdomen. To punish humans for receiving the fire, Zeus created Pandora with the capacity for curiosity. He then gave her a box containing all the travails that could plague humankind, warned her not to open it, and sent her to live in the household of Epimetheus, brother of Prometheus. There Pandora succumbed to the human trait of seeking the unknown despite its risks. She opened the box; evil escaped to bedevil the world.

There are echoes of this fable in the saga of atomic weapons. It is a tragic tale about the folly and hubris that led humans to develop the atomic fire that has given them the godlike power to destroy the Earth and all of its creatures and that has left the world unable to escape the nuclear rock that could be the site of humanity's final agony. In the modern replay of the hubris and agony of Prometheus and the folly of Pandora, the box was opened with the first atomic blast at Alamogordo, New Mexico, on July 16, 1945. Humankind now possessed the atomic fire; humankind has arguably been chained to the rock of potential nuclear destruction ever since.

As the main text indicates, blasts from 2,051 nuclear tests tore at the air and earth from the first one in 1945 until the last one in 1998. Since then the test sites have been silent.

What comes next is extremely important. One scenario includes more tests, more countries with nuclear arms and, perhaps, nuclear war. Secretary of Defense William S. Cohen was almost certainly correct when soon after India's tests he told a U.S. Senate committee that "there will be other countries that see this [testing] as an open invitation to try to acquire [nuclear weapons] technology. We have a real proliferation problem that's taking place globally."[1]

The other scenario, escaping the nuclear rock—if that is what humans wish to do—will be difficult. Some believe that one key to unlocking the chains is to forswear further testing of nuclear weapons by agreeing to the Comprehensive Test Ban Treaty (CTBT) and for eternity leaving the final total at 2,051.

To go into effect, however, the 1996 treaty requires ratification by all countries with nuclear reactors. The countries with nuclear weapons are particularly important, and of these, only France, Great Britain, and Russia have ratified the treaty. China, Israel, and the United States signed the CTBT, but have not ratified it. India and Pakistan have not even signed it.

Because of the global leadership of the United States, the absence of its ratification of the CTBT is arguably the most important barrier to the treaty becoming fully legal. When the CTBT was opened for signature, President Clinton called it "the longest-sought, hardest-fought prize in arms control history" and predicted that it would "immediately create an international norm against nuclear testing even before the treaty formally enters into force."[2] The Republican-controlled U.S. Senate did not share Clinton's enthusiasm, and it rejected the treaty in 1999. "I assure you the fight is far from over," a resolute Clinton told treaty supporters. "When all is said and done," he predicted, "the United States will ratify the treaty."[3] Perhaps, but his successor, President Bush, has expressed opposition to the treaty on the grounds that the CTBT is not verifiable and that some testing may be necessary to ensure the reliability of U.S. nuclear weapons.

There the matter stands. The Bush administration has maintained an informal moratorium on nuclear testing. "Any country that has nuclear weapons has to be respectful of the enormous lethality and power of those weapons, and has a responsibility to see that they are safe and reliable," Secretary of Defense Donald Rumsfeld explained. "To the extent that can be done without testing, clearly that is the preference. And that is why the president has concluded that, thus far, that is the case."[4]

But the Bush administration also remains unwilling to adhere to the CTBT or otherwise forswear future tests. Moreover, it continues to contemplate building new types of nuclear weapons, such as low-yield weapons that can penetrate deep underground to attack command bunkers and other hardened sites and low-yield nuclear weapons to destroy incoming warheads, as part of the national missile defense system. Such programs would almost certainly require testing to ensure they work, which could lead the United States to being the country that increases the current total of nuclear tests to 2,052 and beyond.

As with all arms control treaties, the CWC represents a step toward, not the end of, dealing with a menace. One issue is that Iraq, Libya, North Korea, Syria, and several other countries with demonstrated or suspected chemical weapons programs did not sign the treaty. Not all these refusals were necessarily sinister. Some nonnuclear states view chemical weapons as a way to balance the nuclear weapons of other countries.

Some Arab nations, for instance, are reluctant to give up chemical weapons unless Israel gives up its nuclear weapons.

A second problem with implementing a chemical weapons treaty is that many common chemicals also have weapons applications. Furthermore, some chemicals are deadly in such minute quantities that verification is extremely difficult. Perfluoroisobutene, for one, is a gas that causes pulmonary edema (the lungs fill with fluid). The chemical is clear and odorless and therefore hard to detect, has a toxic effect when dispersed in minute levels, and can be formed from the same chemical (polytetrafluoroethene) used to make nonstick frying pans.

Conventional Weapons and Arms Control since 1990

Arms control efforts in the decades following the advent of nuclear weapons in 1945 focused mostly on restraining these awesome weapons and, to a lesser degree, the other WMDs (biological and chemical weapons). In the 1990s, the world also began to pay more attention to conventional weapons inventories and to the transfer of conventional weapons.

Conventional Weapons Inventories The virtual omnipresence of conventional weapons and their multitudinous forms makes it more difficult to limit conventional weapons than nuclear weapons (Pierre, 1997). Still, progress has been made.

One major step is the **Conventional Forces in Europe Treaty (CFE)**. After 17 years of wrangling between the countries of NATO and the Soviet-led Warsaw Treaty Organization (WTO), the two sides concluded the CFE Treaty in 1990. The treaty, which has been reaffirmed by the various former Soviet republics (FSRs), cuts conventional military forces in Europe from the Atlantic to the Urals (the ATTU region). This geographic focus excludes forces in the United States and Canada and also does not affect Russian forces in Asia (east of the Ural Mountains).

The arms reductions under the CFE Treaty have been impressive. By mid-1997, forces in the ATTU region had been reduced by approximately 53,000 units of the covered weapons systems (artillery tubes, tanks, other armored vehicles, combat helicopters, and fixed-wing combat aircraft).

A supplementary step was taken in 1992 when 29 countries at the Helsinki, Finland, meeting of the Organization for Security and Cooperation in Europe (OSCE) signed a nonbinding, but still important, agreement that established the goal of reducing their troop strengths in the ATTU region. For the larger countries, the troop limits in the ATTU region now are: France (325,000), Germany (345,000), Great Britain (260,000), Russia (1,450,000), Ukraine (450,000), and the United States (250,000). The agreement, said chief U.S. negotiator Lynn Hansen, is "unprecedented in the history of Europe, [or] as far as I know, anywhere."[10]

An additional step in conventional weapons arms control came in 1997 when most of the world's nations signed the **Anti-Personnel Mine Treaty (APM)**. Details of the creation of the APM Treaty can be found in the Play a Part box "A Grassroots Treaty." The treaty prohibits making, using, possessing, or transferring land mines. The treaty became effective on March 1, 1999, six months after the 40th country had ratified it. By late 2003, 141 countries had ratified the APM Treaty, but three key countries (China, Russia, and the United States) were among those that had not, arguing that they still need to use mines. Whatever the positions of Beijing, Moscow, and Washington, the APM Treaty and the associated effort to rid the world of existing mines has had an important impact. According to the report of the 2003 meeting of the APM Treaty oversight committee, 30 million land mines had been removed by national and international efforts. Also, 46 countries had destroyed their stockpiles of mines, 10 other countries

PLAY A PART

A Grassroots Treaty

A common sight as you drive throughout the United States are roadside adopt-a-highway signs that indicate one or another civic organization or business has pledged to keep a section of the road clear of litter. Fortunately for Americans, a discarded beer can or fast-food wrapper is likely to be about the worst thing they might see or step on while walking along the country's roadways or in its field and forests. The fields of Cambodia, the paths of Angola, the hills of Afghanistan, and the countryside in dozens of other countries contain a much greater danger. In those places land mines wait with menacing silence and near invisibility. They are patient, often waiting many years to claim a victim. Land mines are also nondiscriminatory; they care not whether their deadly yield of shrapnel shreds the body of a soldier or a child. Cambodian farmer Sam Soa was trying to find his cow in a field near his village when he stepped on a mine. "It knocks you down," he remembers. "I didn't realize what had happened, and I tried to run away."[1] Sam Soa could not run away, though; the bottom of his left leg was gone.

No one knows exactly how many land mines lie in wait around the world, but a 1998 U.S. State Department report put the figure at 60 to 70 million in 60 countries.[2] Data on casualties is also imprecise, but the UN estimated in 2002 that globally land mines kill or maim between 15,000 and 20,000 annually. Among the victims, 80% are civilians and one-third are children.

The ghastly toll of mines spurred the formation of the International Campaign to Ban Land Mines (ICBL), a transnational network of more than 1,000 citizen-groups from 60 countries. Leading the ICBL was American Jody Williams, a Vermont native. She was working for a "temp agency" in Washington in 1981 when someone handed her a leaflet about protesting U.S. policy in Central America. Williams did, and that began her years of political activism. In 1991 her attention turned to land mines, and she and two others used the Internet to launch an effort that eventually became the ICBL. That organization helped build the support of countries such as Canada, necessary for the successful negotiation of the Anti-Personnel Mine (APM) Treaty (1997) banning the production, use, or sale of land mines. It was an effort that also earned Williams the Nobel Peace Prize for 1997. "When we began, we were just three people sitting in a room. It was utopia. None of us thought we would ever ban land mines. I never thought it would happen in just six years," she told a reporter.[3]

But it did happen, and the story of Jody Williams, the ICBL, and the APM Treaty is a testament to the fact that you do not have to be a president or foreign minister to play an important part in the world drama. As Williams explained her role along with many other people in the ICBL, "Together we are a superpower. It's a new definition of superpower. It's not one of us, it's everyone."[4]

For those who support the APM Treaty, much remains to be done. Tens of millions of mines remain, and mines continue to be newly deployed by countries such as India and Pakistan (along their mutual border). Certainly the ef-

were in the process of doing so, and an additional 8 countries had indicated they also would soon begin stockpile destruction programs.[11]

Conventional Weapons Transfers Another thrust of conventional arms control in the 1990s and beyond has been and will be the effort to limit the transfer of conventional weapons. To that end, 31 countries in 1995 agreed to the Wassenaar Arrangement on Export Controls for Conventional Arms and Dual-Use Goods and Technologies. Named after the Dutch town where it was organized, the "arrangement" directs its signatories to limit the export of some types of weapons technology and to create an organization to monitor the spread of conventional weapons and **dual-use technology** that has both peaceful and nonpeaceful applications.

A more recent attempt to control conventional weapons is the work of the UN Conference on the Illicit Trade in Small Arms and Light Weapons (2001). Speaking to the delegates from more than 170 countries, Secretary-General Kofi Annan called the estimated 639 million small arms and light weapons (revolvers and rifles, machine guns and mortars, hand grenades, antitank guns and portable missile launchers) that exist in

It is not necessary to be a president or prime minister to play a part on the world stage. Jody Williams was working at a "temp job" in Washington, D.C., in 1981 when she decided to get involved politically. She is pictured here outside her home in Putney, Vermont, soon after being named the recipient of the 1997 Nobel Peace Prize for her leadership of the International Campaign to Ban Land Mines and for its role in the conclusion of the Anti-Personnel Mine Treaty (1997) banning the production, use, or sale of land mines.

forts of individual countries and the UN and other IGOs will be important. But individuals can also get involved if they wish through NGOs such as the ICBL, Landmine Action, and Adopt-a-Minefield. There are no known pro–land mine groups, but you can explore the U.S. rationale for not signing the treaty in a background briefing by Department of Defense officials at http://www.defenselink.mil/news/Jul1997/x07071997_x703mine.html. If you agree, let your members of Congress and even the president know that you do.

the world, mostly (60%) in civilian hands, "deadly" and "pervasive," and he urged that they be a "focus of urgent global attention."[12] To that end, the conference called on states to curb the illicit trafficking in light weapons through such steps as ensuring that manufacturers mark weapons so that they can be traced, and tightening measures to monitor the flow of arms across borders. Most of these arms were initially supplied by the United States, Russia, and the European countries to rebel groups and to governments in less developed countries, then eventually found their way into the black market's annual multibillion-dollar flow of arms across borders. The UN program is nonbinding, but it does represent a first step toward regulating and stemming the huge volume of weapons moving through the international system. Speaking at the UN in 2003 during the biennial conference to review progress in curbing the illicit arms trade, Chairman Kuniko Inoguchi of Japan commented, "I would not claim we have achieved some heroic and ambitious outcome," but he did point to heightened awareness of the problem and to the greater willingness of countries to cooperate on the issue as evidence that the world's countries had "started to implement actions against small arms and explore what the United Nations can do."[13]

The Barriers to Arms Control

Limiting or reducing arms is an idea that most people favor. Yet arms control has proceeded slowly and sometimes not at all. The devil is in the details, as the old maxim goes, and it is important to review the continuing debate over arms control to understand its history and current status. None of the factors that we are about to discuss is the main culprit impeding arms control. Nor is any one of them insurmountable. Indeed, important advances are being made on a number of fronts. But together, these factors form a tenacious resistance to arms control.

Security Barriers

Security concerns constitute perhaps the most formidable barrier to arms control. Those who hold to the realist school of thought have strong doubts about whether countries can maintain adequate security if they disarm totally or substantially. Realists are cautious about the current political scene and about the claimed contributions of arms control.

Concern about future conflicts is one barrier to arms control. The increased possibility of countries and even terrorists using chemical, biological, and radiological weapons of mass destruction and the ability of opponents to hide their arsenals and personnel underground has led the United States to explore the creation of a new generation of very-small-yield nuclear weapons dubbed mini-nukes. Opponents argue that having such weapons would make their use more likely because they seem less terrible, and that they could even be stolen. Pictured here is a "Davy Crockett," a U.S. nuclear weapon fired from a recoilless rifle that was deployed during the 1960s and into the 1970s. The warhead weighed only 51 pounds, its egg-shaped core (nuclear material, detonator, high explosives) measured a mere 11 inches by 16 inches, and it had a blast yield of 0.01 kilotons (10 tons of TNT). Given the advances in miniaturization since the Davy Crockett was deactivated, a new generation of mini-nukes could weigh as little as 25 pounds and have a core as small as a ball 12 inches in circumference.

The Possibility of Future Conflict Worries about the future are probably the greatest barrier to arms control. For example, the anxiety during the cold war that spawned a huge arms buildup had no sooner begun to fade than fears about the threat of terrorists and "rogue" states with weapons of mass destruction escalated in the aftermath of 9/11. In the United States that spurred the Bush administration to move toward building mini-nukes. One projected use is as "bunker busters." Secretary of Defense Donald Rumsfeld told senators in 2003 that exploring the development of mini-nukes was justified on the grounds that "the world is experiencing an enormous amount of underground tunneling . . . for [weapons] production, . . . for development, [and] for storage." He argued that if "we're unwilling to even study the idea of penetrating capability [mini-nukes with the capability of burrowing into the earth and through concrete before exploding] . . . we make it advantageous for people to engage in that type of tunneling."[14] Yet another "new security" application of mini-nukes is said to be as a defense against biological or chemical attack. "Nuclear weapons can have some effect on [biological agents]. In terms of anthrax, it is said that gamma rays can destroy the anthrax spores, which is something we need to look at," General Richard Myers, the chairman of the U.S. Joint Chiefs of Staff, told reporters in 2003. "And in chemical weapons," he continued, "of course, the heat can destroy the chemical compounds and not develop that plume that conventional weapons might do that would then drift and, perhaps, bring others in harm's way."[15] A third possibility for mini-nukes is being deployed as part of a national missile defense system to guard against a ballistic missile strike by a country such as North Korea. The Department of Defense says no such plans exist, but William Schneider, Jr., chairman of the U.S. Defense Science Board, has told reporters that in

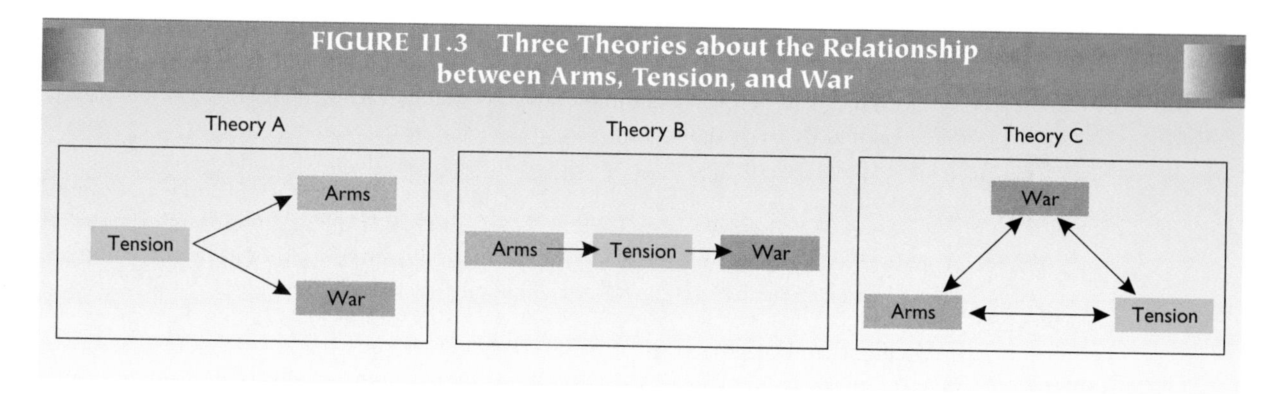

Theory A approximates the realist view, and Theory B fits the idealist view of the causal relationship between arms, tension, and use. Theory C suggests that there is a complex causal interrelationship between arms, tension, and war in which each of the three factors affects the other two.

conversations with Secretary Rumsfeld, "We've talked about it [nuclear-tipped interceptor missiles] as something that he's interested in looking at."[16]

Doubts about the Value of Arms Control Those who have doubts about arms control are also skeptical about its supposed benefits. They tend to disbelieve the often heard arguments that arms races occur and that reducing arms will increase security. The skeptics therefore reject the idea that arms control agreements necessarily represent progress (Kydd, 2000).

Arms control advocates argue that weapons create insecurity and tensions that can lead to war. Arms control skeptics doubt it. Instead, a classic tenet of realpolitik is that humans arm themselves and fight because the world is dangerous, as represented by Theory A in Figure 11.3. Given this view, realists believe that political settlements should be achieved before arms reductions are negotiated. Liberals, by contrast, agree with Homer's observation in the *Odyssey* (ca. 700 B.C.) that "the blade itself incites to violence." This is represented by Theory B in Figure 11.3.

While the logic of arms races seems obvious, empirical research has not confirmed that arms races always occur (McGinnis & Williams, 2001; Koubi, 1999). Similarly, it is not clear whether decreases in arms cause or are caused by periods of improved international relations. Instead, a host of domestic and international factors influence a country's level of armaments. What this means is that the most probable answer to the chicken-and-egg debate about which should come first, political agreements or arms control, lies in a combination of these theories. That is, arms, tension, and wars all promote one another, as represented in Theory C of Figure 11.3.

There are even arms control skeptics who argue that more weapons equal greater strength. This line of thought was evident in President Ronald Reagan's mantra, "Peace through strength." From this perspective, it is even possible that nuclear arms have increased security. Early in the atomic age, Winston Churchill observed that "it may be that we shall by a process of sublime irony" come to a point "where safety will be the sturdy child of terror and survival the twin brother of annihilation" (Nogee & Spanier, 1988:5). His point was that nuclear weapons may have made both nuclear war and large-scale conventional war between nuclear powers too dangerous to fight. There are also scholars whose work supports this view. One study suggests that "peace . . . may depend on the maintenance of credible deterrent policies. . . . Consequently, the great powers . . . should not . . . undermine the potency of their nuclear deterrent" (Huth, Gelpi, & Bennett,

1993:619). If such views are correct, then eliminating or perhaps even substantially reducing nuclear weapons levels could make war more possible and decrease security.

While these suspicions about the supposed value of arms control merit consideration, you should be chary of too easily accepting them. One caution is that such conclusions are disputed by other studies and even by some of those who commanded nuclear weapons. For example, 57 retired generals and admirals from various nuclear-weapons countries issued a manifesto in 1996, proclaiming that nuclear-weapons are now "of sharply reduced utility," and that "the ultimate objective . . . should be the complete elimination of nuclear weapons from all nations" (Schultz & Isenberg, 1997:87).

Verification Barriers

The problem is simple: Countries suspect that others will cheat. This worry was a significant factor in the rejection of the CTBT by the U.S. Senate. Majority Leader Trent Lott characterized the treaty as "ineffectual because it would not stop other nations from testing or developing nuclear weapons, but it could preclude the United States from taking appropriate steps to ensure the safety and reliability of the U.S. nuclear arsenal." Furthermore, Lott continued, "That it is not effectively verifiable is made clear by the intelligence community's inability to state unequivocally the purpose of activities under way for some number of months at the Russian nuclear test site. . . . The CTBT simply has no teeth."[17]

Possible cheating can be divided into two types: *break-out cheating* and *creep-out cheating.* A violation significant enough by itself to endanger your security would constitute a break-out. This possibility worries skeptics of arms control. Some are also hesitant about arms control because they believe there might be a reluctance to respond to creep-out cheating. In this scenario, no single violation would be serious enough by itself to create a crisis or warrant termination of the treaty. Yet the impact of successive and progressive violations might seriously upset the balance of forces.

There have been great advances in verification procedures and technologies. The most important recent procedural advance is increased **on-site inspection (OSI)**. Countries are increasingly willing to allow others to inspect their facilities, but even OSI is not foolproof, especially if the other side is not cooperative. **National technical means (NTM)** of verification using satellites, seismic measuring devices, and other equipment have also advanced rapidly. These have been substantially offset, however, by other technologies that make NTM verification more difficult. Nuclear warheads, for example, have been miniaturized to the point where 10 or more can fit on one missile and could literally be hidden in the back of a pickup truck or even in a good-sized closet. If mini-nukes are developed, they will be of backpack size. Therefore, in the last analysis, virtually no amount of OSI and NTM can ensure absolute verification.

Because absolute verification is impossible, the real issue is which course is more dangerous: (1) coming to an agreement when there is at least some chance that the other side might be able to cheat, or (2) failing to agree and living in a world of unrestrained and increasing nuclear weapons growth? Sometimes, the answer may be number 2. Taking this view while testifying before the U.S. Senate about the Chemical Weapons Convention, former secretary of state James A. Baker III counseled, "The [George H. W.] Bush administration never expected the treaty to be completely verifiable and had always expected there would be rogue states that would not participate." Nevertheless, Baker supported the treaty on the grounds that "the more countries we can get behind responsible behavior around the world . . . , the better it is for us."[18]

Domestic Barriers

As chapter 3 discusses, all countries are complex decision-making organizations. Even if they favor arms control, leaders have numerous other powerful domestic political actors

Although Pakistan and India are desperately poor countries, they both spent huge sums of money to develop nuclear weapons and the missiles to deliver them. Whatever their rational reasons might be, it is also true that emotional national pride played a role in the decisions of Islamabad and New Delhi to build nuclear weapons. That pride is evident in these Pakistanis brandishing a replica of a Shaheen (Eagle) short-range ballistic missile (SRBM) capable of delivering a nuclear warhead. The Pakistanis, who are also burning an effigy of India's prime minister, are expressing their anger during the May 2002 crisis between Pakistan and India over Kashmir.

that they must work with or, perhaps, overcome in the policy-making process. Some of the opposition that leaders face when they try to restrain or reduce arms comes from the ideological differences and policy doubts expressed above. In addition to these security and technical issues, other domestic opposition to arms control often stems from national pride and from the interrelationship among military spending, the economy, and politics.

National Pride The Book of Proverbs tells us that "pride goeth before destruction," and this statement is equally applicable to modern arms acquisitions. Whether we are dealing with conventional or nuclear arms, national pride is a primary drive behind their acquisition. For many countries, arms represent a tangible symbol of strength and sovereign equality. EXPLOSION OF SELF-ESTEEM read one newspaper headline in India after that country's nuclear tests in 1998.[19] LONG LIVE NUCLEAR PAKISTAN read a Pakistani newspaper headline soon thereafter. "Five nuclear blasts have instantly transformed an extremely demoralized nation into a self-respecting proud nation . . . having full faith in their destiny," the accompanying article explained.[20] Such emotions have also seemingly played a role in Iran's alleged nuclear weapons program. "I hope we get our atomic weapons," Shirzad Bozorgmehr, editor of *Iran News,* commented in 2003 amid international pressure on Tehran to comply with the Non-Proliferation Treaty. "If Israel has it, we should have it. If India and Pakistan do, we should, too," he explained.[21]

Military Spending, the Economy, and Politics Supplying the military is big business, and economic interest groups pressure their governments to build and to sell weapons and associated technology. Furthermore, cities that are near major military installations benefit from jobs provided on the bases and from the consumer spending of military personnel stationed on the bases. For this reason, defense-related corporations, defense plant workers, civilian employees of the military, and the cities and towns in which they reside and shop are supporters of military spending and foreign sales. Additionally, there are often bureaucratic elements, such as ministries of defense, in alliance with the defense industry and its workers. Finally, both interest groups and bureaucratic actors receive support from legislators who represent the districts and states that benefit from military spending. This alliance between interest groups, bureaucracies, and legislators forms a military-industrial-congressional complex that has been termed the **iron triangle**.

International Security Forces

The idea of forming international security forces to supplement or replace national military forces is a second approach to seeking security on the road less traveled by. This approach would enhance, not compete with, the first approach, arms control. Organizing for international security would emphasize international organizations and de-emphasize national defense forces. Thus, the creation of international security forces and the first approach, arms control, are mutually supportive.

International Security Forces: Theory and Practice

The idea of seeking security through an international organization is not new. Immanuel Kant foresaw the possibility over two centuries ago in *Idea for a Universal History from a Cosmopolitan Point of View* (1784). "Through war, through the taxing and never-ending accumulation of armament . . . after devastations, revolutions, and even complete exhaustion," Kant predicted, human nature would bring people "to that which reason could have told them in the beginning": that humankind must "step from the lawless condition of savages into a league of nations" to secure the peace. These ideas have evolved into attempts to secure the peace through such international structures as the Concert of Europe, the League of Nations, and the United Nations. An increased UN peacekeeping role has been especially evident, and other international governmental organizations (IGOs) also have occasionally been involved in international security missions (Roberts, 1996). The far-reaching language in the UN Charter related to peacekeeping can be found in the Global Actors box "The UN Charter and International Security."

An important point is that while our discussion here will focus on the UN as a global organization, much of what is said is also applicable to regional IGOs and their security forces. The **North Atlantic Treaty Organization (NATO)** is providing international security forces in Afghanistan, Bosnia-Herzegovina, and Kosovo province. Also in Europe, the European Union took on its first peacekeeping mission in 2003 when it assumed that role in Macedonia from NATO, and a second EU initiative sent its peacekeepers to the Congo later that year. Additionally on the continent, the **Organization for Security and Cooperation in Europe (OSCE)** has taken on some functions of a regional security structure. Established in 1973, the OSCE now has 55 members, including almost all the countries of Europe, Kazakhstan and several other states in Central Asia, and Canada and the United States (Flynn & Farrell, 1999). Operationally, it has begun limited field activities to, in the words of the OSCE, "work 'on the ground' to facilitate political processes, prevent or settle conflicts, and inform the OSCE community."[22] These efforts primarily involve sending monitors and other personnel to try to resolve differences, and as of late 2003, OSCE missions were operating in Albania, Bosnia, Macedonia, and more than a dozen other countries or hotspots. The largest OSCE peacekeeping effort involved the dispatch of 6,000 troops from eight countries to Albania in

GLOBAL ACTORS

The UN Charter and International Security

The fundamental idea of international security is contained in the UN Charter. Article 1 commits all members "to maintain international peace and security, and to that end, to take effective collective measures" to preserve or restore the peace. Article 24 gives to the Security Council the "primary responsibility for the maintenance of international peace and security," and by Article 25 members "agree to accept and carry out the decisions" of the council. Article 42 gives the Security Council the authority to "take such action by air, sea, or land forces as may be necessary to maintain or restore international peace and security." Key language in Article 43 requires members to "undertake to make available to the Security Council, on its call . . . armed forces . . . necessary for the purposes" of peace maintenance. The forces are subject to "special agreements" between the UN and member-countries, but the article (as written in 1945) states that the "agreements shall be negotiated as soon as possible." If you think about the implications of this language, clauses to which virtually all countries are bound legally, it is very powerful.

1997 when that country's political system collapsed into anarchy amid factional fighting (Hopmann, 1999).

Beyond Europe, the **Economic Community of West African States (ECOWAS)** has dispatched troops over the past decade or so to Guinea-Bissau, Ivory Coast, Liberia, and Sierra Leone. In July 2003, for example, ECOWAS troops from Nigeria, Ghana, Mali, and Senegal entered Liberia on a UN-authorized mission to try to bring an end to the civil war there. At the end of that year, ECOWAS peacekeepers not only remained in that country, but also in Ivory Coast and Sierra Leone. On the other side of the South Atlantic Ocean, the Organization of American States (OAS) has advanced peace on a number of fronts, including helping to settle the long and seemingly intractable border dispute between Ecuador and Peru. The potential cause of war was eliminated in 1998 when the presidents of the two countries met in Brazil to sign the Acta de Brasilia demarcating their border and establishing Argentina, Brazil, Chile, Spain, and the United States as the guarantors of the pact.

Although the UN is most often associated with peacekeeping, a number of regional organizations have also been involved. Among these is the Economic Community of West African States (ECOWAS). The Senegalese troops in this picture are part of an ECOWAS force that was deployed to Ivory Coast in 2002 to try to preserve order in the civil war–torn country.

Collective Security

One theory behind the use of international security forces through the UN and other IGOs is the concept of **collective security**. This idea was first embodied in the Covenant of the League of Nations and is also reflected in the Charter of the United Nations. Collective security is based on three basic tenets. First, all countries forswear the use of force except in self-defense. Second, all agree that the peace is indivisible. An attack on one is an attack on all. Third, all pledge to unite to halt aggression and restore the peace by supplying to the UN or other IGOs whatever material or personnel resources are necessary to deter or defeat aggressors and restore the peace.

This three-part theory is something like the idea that governs domestic law enforcement. First, self-defense is the only time an individual can use force legally. Second, acts of violence are considered transgressions against the collective. If one person assaults another, the case is not titled the victim versus the aggressor (such as *Jones v. Smith*); it is titled the society versus the aggressor *(Ohio v. Smith);* the prosecutor takes legal action and presents the case on behalf of the people. Third, domestic societies provide a collective security force, the police, and jointly support this force through taxes.

Collective security, then, is not only an appealing idea but one that works—domestically, that is. It has not, however, been a general success on the international scene. In part, applying collective security is limited by problems such as how, in some cases, to tell the aggressor from the victim. But these uncertainties also exist domestically and are resolved. The more important reason that collective security fails is the unwillingness of countries to subordinate their sovereign interests to collective action. Thus far, governments have generally maintained their right to view conflict in terms of their national interests and to support or oppose UN action based on their nationalistic points of view. Collective security, therefore, exists mostly as a goal, not as a general practice. Only the UN-authorized interventions in Korea (1950–1953) and in the Persian Gulf (1990–1991) came close to fulfilling the idea of collective security. The United States and Great Britain tried to convince the Security Council in 2003 that the situation in Iraq warranted a third such collective security action, but that effort failed.

Peacekeeping

What the United Nations has been able to do more often is implement a process commonly called **peacekeeping**. Apart from using military force, peacekeeping is quite different from collective security. The latter identifies an aggressor and employs military force to defeat the attacker. Peacekeeping takes another approach and deploys an international military force under the aegis of an international organization such as the UN to prevent fighting, usually by acting as a buffer between combatants. The international force is neutral between the combatants and must have been invited to be present by at least one of the combatants.

Some of the data regarding the use of UN peacekeeping forces and observer groups to help restore and maintain the peace are given in chapter 7 but bear repeating briefly here. During its first 58 years (1945 through 2003), the United Nations sent over 9 million soldiers, police officers, and unarmed observers from more than 130 countries to conduct 56 peacekeeping or truce observation missions. Almost 1,900 of these individuals have died in UN service. The frequency of such UN missions has risen sharply, as can be seen in Figure 7.7 on page 221. In early 2004, there were 13 UN peacekeeping forces of varying size, totaling nearly 44,000 troops, police, and military observers drawn from 91 countries in the field in Africa, Asia, Europe, and the Middle East, as shown in the accompanying map. Not shown is the 57th UN force, which in February 2004 the Security Council authorized for deployment in civil war–torn Haiti. The cost of these operations was about $2.6 billion in FY2003 and $2.2 billion in FY2004.

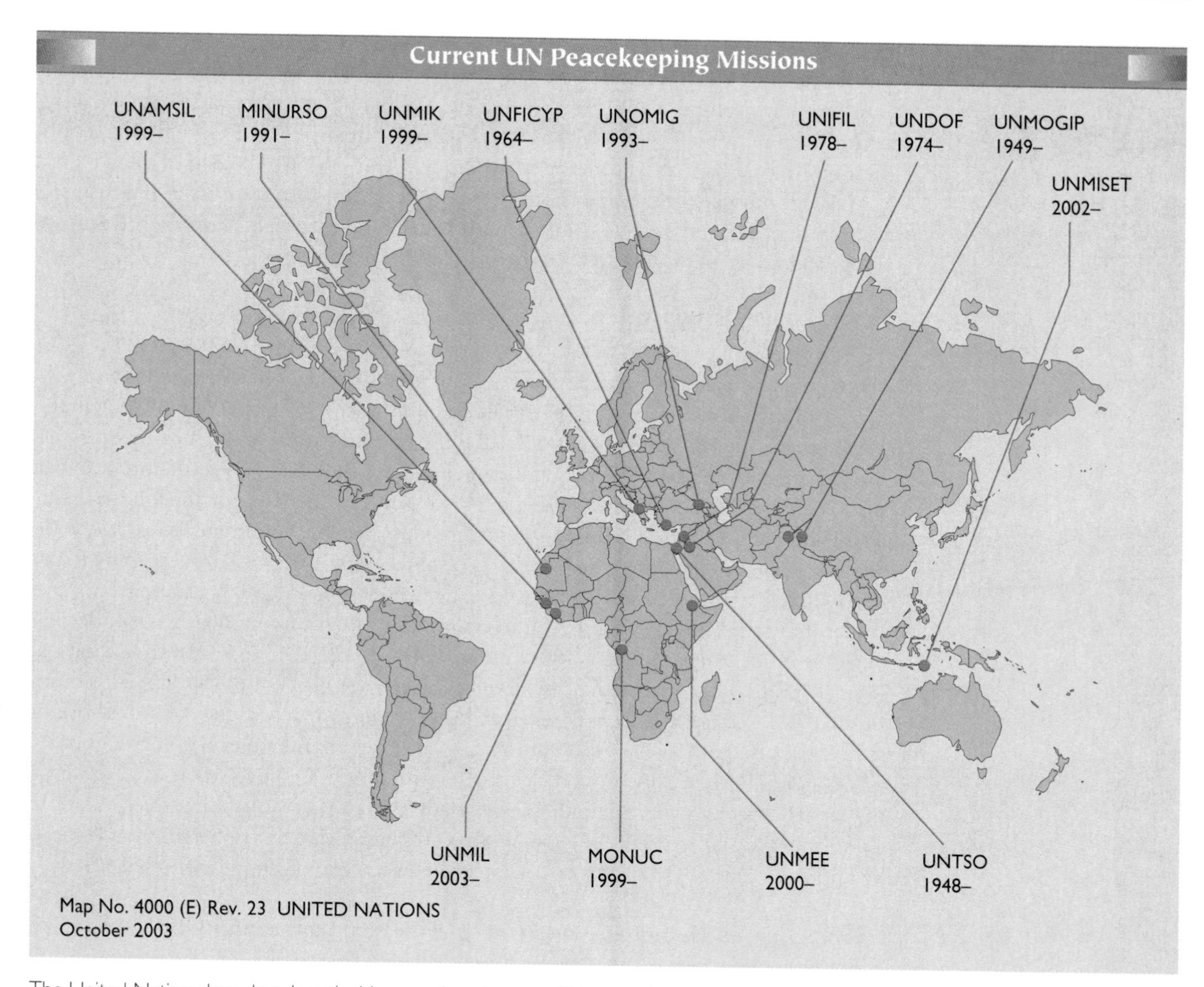

The United Nations has played a valuable peacekeeping role. This map shows the 13 peacekeeping operations active in early 2004. It is a testament to the ever-growing record of UN peacekeeping that the map would have become too confusing if it had included the other 43 peacekeeping missions that the UN had undertaken and concluded in its history. The Nobel Peace Prize for 1988 was awarded to the soldiers who have served in peacekeeping missions, thousands of whom have been killed or wounded in UN service.

Notes: UNTSO—UN Truce Supervision Organization
UNMOGIP—UN Military Observer Group in India and Pakistan
UNFICYP—UN Peacekeeping Force in Cyprus
UNDOF—UN Disengagement Observer Force
UNIFIL—UN Interim Force in Lebanon
MINURSO—UN Mission for the Referendum in Western Sahara
UNOMIG—UN Observer Mission in Georgia
UNMIK—UN Interim Administration Mission in Kosovo
UNAMSIL—UN Mission in Sierra Leone
MONUC—UN Organization Mission in the Democratic Republic of the Congo
UNMEE—UN United Nations Mission in Ethiopia and Eritrea
UNMISET—UN Mission of Support in East Timor
UNMIL—UN Mission in Liberia
Data source: http://www.un.org/Depts/dpko/dpko/home.shtml. Reprinted by permission of the United Nations Cartographic Section.

Did You Know That:

In late 2003, the five countries contributing the most UN peacekeepers were Pakistan (5,343), Bangladesh (4,274), India (2,945), Nigeria (3,342), and Ghana (2,297).

Several characteristics of UN peacekeeping actions can be noted. First, most have taken place in LDC locations, as evident on the map. Second, UN forces have generally utilized military contingents from smaller or nonaligned powers. Canada and Fiji have contributed personnel to virtually all peacekeeping efforts, and the Scandinavian countries and Ireland have also been especially frequent participants. The end of the cold war has made it possible for the troops of larger powers to take a greater part in international security missions, and in 2004, American, British, Chinese, French, German, and Russian troops and police personnel were in the field as UN peacekeepers.

Peacekeeping Issues

There are a number of important issues related to UN peacekeeping. Some of those are discussed elsewhere. For example, chapter 7 outlines the budget restraints and the unwillingness of numerous countries to pay their dues for peacekeeping to the United Nations. Yet another issue covered in chapter 7 is the use of the veto power held by the five permanent members of the UN Security Council and the growing number of countries that are voicing their discontent with a system they claim is neither fair nor any longer resembles world power realities. A third issue, addressed in chapter 9 on international law, is the demand made by the United States that its troops serving with UN peacekeeping forces be exempted by the Security Council from the jurisdiction of the International Criminal Court, and the threat of Washington to withhold its dues or veto new and continuing missions if the American stipulations are not met. As the U.S. ambassador to the UN, John Negroponte, put it while threatening to veto the renewal of the UN mission in Bosnia, "We will not ask them [American peacekeepers] to accept the additional risk of politicized prosecutions before a court whose jurisdiction over our people the government of the United States does not accept."[23] Two other issues involved with peacekeeping are whether UN forces should play a relatively passive peacemaking role or a more assertive peace enforcement function and how to ensure that humanitarian interventions by UN and other IGO military police forces are not neocolonialism by another name.

Peacekeeping and Peace Enforcement For all the contributions that UN peacekeeping efforts have made, they have sometimes been unable to halt fighting quickly (or even at all) or to keep the peace permanently. The numerous reasons for the limited effectiveness of UN forces can be boiled down to two fundamental and related problems: First, countries frequently do not support UN forces politically or financially. Second, it is often difficult to get the self-interested UN Security Council members, especially the five veto-wielding permanent members, to agree to authorize a UN mission. Even when the mission is authorized, it is often given a very narrow scope of authority to act and few troops. When the UN initially sent forces to the Balkans in 1992, the secretary-general asked for 35,000 peacekeepers. The Security Council authorized only 7,000 troops restricted to light arms and not authorized to take strong action. These limits led, at one point, to UN troops being taken hostage and chained to potential targets to deter threatened action by NATO forces.

The mounting frustrations with the reactive, passive peacekeeping approach of UN forces led to an upsurge of support for the idea of proactive **peace enforcement**. This new role would involve heavily armed UN forces with the authority to restore and maintain the peace. Such UN units would not only intervene where fighting had already broken out. They could also be deployed to imperiled countries before trouble starts, thereby putting an aggressor in the uncomfortable position of attacking UN forces as well as national defense forces.

In an effort to implement change, Secretary-General Boutros Boutros-Ghali (1992–1997) and his successor, Kofi Annan (1997–present), have called on UN members to better fund and equip UN forces and to give them sufficient personnel and a broad enough mandate (rules of engagement) that will allow them to be effective. A report issued in 2000 by a special panel appointed by Annan to study peacekeeping operations made several key points.[24] The report, which characterized its commentary as "blunt criticism" as well as recommendations, noted that "the United Nations does not wage war. Where enforcement action is required, it has consistently been entrusted to coalitions of willing states, with the authorization of the Security Council." Nevertheless, the panel urged that when peacekeepers are deployed and when they face forces that want to "spoil" the peace, "The United Nations must be prepared to deal effectively with spoilers if it expects to achieve a consistent record of success in peacekeeping." One important cause of the frequent inability of the UN to do so, the report maintained, was "the gap between verbal postures and financial and political support for prevention" by the UN's member-states. The remedy the panel recommended was not just better financing, but a change in posture for UN troops. For example, instead of maintaining impartiality toward all combatants, the UN should take the view that "where one party . . . clearly and incontrovertibly is violating [the peace], . . . continued equal treatment of all parties by the United Nations can in the best case result in ineffectiveness and in the worst may amount to complicity with evil." To implement this more assertive posture, the panel recommended bigger and better equipped forces with "robust rules of engagement," thereby making "a credible deterrent," enabling them "to mount an effective defense against violent challengers" if necessary, and empowering peacekeepers "who witness violence against civilians . . . to stop it." In yet another key recommendation, the panel called for the UN to have a "rapid and effective deployment capacity," including "the ability to fully deploy traditional peacekeeping operations within 30 days of the adoption of a Security Council resolution establishing such an operation." This could involve options ranging from national troops predesignated and trained for UN missions to a standing UN military force.

This Uruguayan solder in UN service at a checkpoint in Bunia, Democratic Republic of the Congo, in 2003, is representative of most peacekeeping forces. They are lightly armed and do not have sufficient personnel, equipment, and authority to launch proactive operations. The criticism of such forces as ineffective misses the point that political decisions establish the limits. Different decisions by the countries of the UN Security Council could lead to more potent and effective peacekeeping forces.

Reflective of the gap between the member-states' rhetoric and reality, such calls for a more effective UN peace-enforcing ability have often drawn accolades from national leaders and sometimes even pledges of support. However, change has been slow and limited. As one analyst explains the resistance of countries to further empowering the UN, "Robust peace enforcement is beyond the capacity of the United Nations. The Security Council does not have the stomach for it, contributing countries don't want to put their troops under other commanders and then have to answer questions at home when their troops get killed."[25]

Peace Enforcement: Humanitarian Intervention or Neocolonialism? Doubts about a more aggressive UN military role are not just based on nationalism and other such factors.

There is also a concern that creating a more powerful, proactive UN will undermine the sovereignty of the smaller LDCs and that the UN will become a neocolonial tool of the big powers. In the words of one UN report, "there is the understandable and legitimate concern of member states, especially the small and weak among them, about sovereignty."[26] The chaos and abuses that engulf weak countries sometimes render them mere legal fictions that have no coherent government, and they are considered so-called failed states. In such a situation, other states may have powerful emotional and political incentives to intervene, either to alleviate the suffering or to take political advantage of the turmoil. One observer notes, for example, that "the new rule whereby human rights outrank sovereignty must still prevail, because the old rule is simply dead." The problem, the analyst continues, is the "places where this new rule could be applied all too easily: weak states" (Luttwak, 2000: 61). That, arguably, allows powerful states like China to continue to abuse human rights while small countries may be "invaded" by international security forces and have their sovereignty abridged.

Other commentators worry that once the barrier of sovereignty is breached, the powerful countries will have license through the UN to impose their will on weaker countries. That suspicion is not voiced only from within LDCs, it also receives support from a recent review of UN peacekeeping activity. The analysis of the record from 1945 to 1990 led the scholar to conclude that the "interests that have been served by UN peacekeeping are those of the Western states whose interests are served by the status quo and a few non-Western states that lay claim to some prestige in international affairs through their UN activities." This use of the UN, the scholar continues, may "amount to Western interventionist foreign policy bordering on imperialism. The recent expansion of UN peacekeeping activities may indeed signal an era in which sovereignty is eroded, but only for non-Western states" (Neack, 1995:194).

International Security and the Future

What does the future hold for international security? While there are certainly many impediments on the path to international security, it would be foolish to dismiss the idea as impossible. First, it is in almost everyone's interest to prevent or contain crises, and there is a growing recognition that cooperation through the use of an international security force may often be a more effective way to maintain or restore peace than is continued reliance on unlimited national self-defense in a world capable of producing and using nuclear, biological, and chemical weapons. As such, the existence of peacekeeping has been largely a functional response to an international problem, and the increased number of missions, whether by the UN or one of the regional organizations, is evidence that the international security efforts are necessary and almost certainly have become a permanent part of world politics.

Second, it is important to see that many of the shortcomings of previous international security missions have not been due to an inherent failure of the UN (Wesley, 1997). Certainly the UN has problems, as any large political and bureaucratized organization does (Jett, 2000). But the central problem, at least in Kofi Annan's view, is that the UN has "been asked to do too much with too little."[27]

Efforts to create the nucleus of a UN ready force continue but remain controversial (Rosenblatt & Thompson, 1998). Events in the first years of the new millennium somewhat revived interest in strengthening UN forces and giving them more proactive authority. As has occurred too often, UN forces, this time in Sierra Leone in 2000, were outnumbered and outgunned by hostile forces and suffered other problems inherent in trying to deploy an army made up of various national contingents with little ability to

Does peacekeeping work? Sometimes it does, as illustrated by these "before and after" photos. The street scene in Monrovia, Liberia, pictured at the top, includes two dead people and armed rebels. It was taken on August 3, 2003, while civil war was raging in that country. Below it is a picture taken near the same spot (about where the car is in the top photo) on September 29, 2003, after the arrival of ECOWAS forces at the behest of the UN. Soon thereafter they were replaced by UN peacekeepers. For the people peacefully shopping in the lower picture, peacekeeping worked. It did not come soon enough for those lying in the street above.

work as a unified force. The worst moment came when rebels took several dozen UN peacekeepers hostage. In the aftermath of this humiliation, the Security Council more than tripled UN forces in the country to 17,500 and gave them broader authority to initiate action against the rebels. The improved UN position played an important role in creating enough stability to allow for elections in 2002. As a report more than a year later described the situation, "No one forgets . . . rebels and disenchanted government soldiers . . . hacking and burning anything that stood in their way. . . . The United Nations then arrived in force, and give or take a few hiccups, the peace has held." Now, instead of murderous troops, the capital, Freetown, has to deal with having "become one vast traffic jam," and residents have the security to complain that "a large contributor to the jam is the UN peacekeeping mission. . . . The UN's white jeeps and armored cars are everywhere."[28]

Another approach for the immediate future may be to distinguish types of international security efforts, including peacekeeping and peace enforcement missions, and to handle them differently (Mockaitis, 1999; Diehl, Druckman, & Wall, 1998). The UN's undersecretary-general for peacekeeping has contended, "Peace enforcement and serious peace restoration campaigns will . . . be the responsibility of a coalition of interested countries using their own forces but with a green light from the Council."[29] This model is much like the NATO-led interventions in Bosnia in 1995 and in Kosovo in 1999 and the International Force in East Timor in 1999. This Australian-led multinational force restored stability in East Timor before handing over responsibility for the territory to the UN in 2000. According to this model, peace enforcement would be up to heavily armed regional forces, with peacekeeping assigned to more lightly armed UN contingents. As one U.S. diplomat explains it, "There has to be a peace to keep before the blue helmets are put on the ground."[30] In the case of East Timor, at least, the model worked well. Peace was restored and protected, and the UN established a transitional administration that prepared East Timor for full independence in May 2002.

This model also resembles the intervention in Afghanistan beginning in 2001. The initial action was taken under UN authority by a U.S.-led coalition of forces that routed al-Qaeda and toppled the Taliban government. Then in 2002 the UN Security Council turned over authority to the NATO-led International Security Assistance Force to provide security in Kabul in support of the efforts of the interim government to begin the reconstruction of the country's physical and political structures.

While the exact configuration of international security forces in the future is not clear, there can be little doubt that they have become an integral part of world politics in the little more than half a century since they were first deployed. Certainly, they experience problems given their political and financial restraints. UN peacekeeping and authorized UN peace enforcement is also frequently criticized by countries that oppose a particular operation or favor commencing an operation when there is not enough support in the Security Council to authorize it. This was the case in 2003 when the UN came under a barrage of disparagement when it did not authorize an American- and British-led invasion of Iraq. But a majority of people in most countries continued to support the UN and thought that the problem was with the United States, not with the United Nations. Even a majority of Americans continued to express support. When asked in June 2003 about their basic opinion of the UN, 66% of American respondents replied "favorable," 32% replied "unfavorable," and 2% were unsure.[31] And even though most Americans were disappointed that the UN had not supported action, more of them (50%) than not (42%) were willing to concede (with 8% unsure) that the UN can still "function effectively as an international peacekeeping force."[32] Thus, in one form or another, international security forces are here to stay, and their use is likely to increase.

Abolition of War

The last of the four approaches to security that we will examine in this chapter looks toward the abolition of war. For our purposes, we will divide the discussion into two parts: complete disarmament and pacifism.

Complete Disarmament

The most sweeping approach to arms control is simply to disarm. The principal argument in favor of disarmament is, as noted, the idea that without weapons people will not fight. This rests in part on sheer inability. **General and complete disarmament (GCD)** might be accomplished either through unilateral disarmament or through multilateral negotiated disarmament.

In the case of *unilateral disarmament,* a country would dismantle its arms. Its safety, in theory, would be secured by its nonthreatening posture, which would prevent aggression, and its example would lead other countries to disarm also. Unilateral disarmament draws heavily on the idea of pacifism, or a moral and resolute refusal to fight. The unilateral approach also relies on the belief that it is arms that cause tension rather than vice versa.

Negotiated disarmament between two or more countries is a more limited approach. Advocates of this path share the unilateralists' conviction about the danger of war. They are less likely to be true pacifists, however, and they believe one-sided disarmament would expose the peace pioneer to unacceptable risk.

The GCD approach has few strong advocates among today's political leaders. Even those who do subscribe to the ideal also search for intermediate arms limitation steps. Still, the quest goes on. The UN Disarmament Committee has called for GCD, and the ideal is a valuable standard by which to judge progress as "real."

Pacifism

The second war-avoidance approach, pacifism, relies on individuals. As such, it very much fits in with the idea that people count and that you can affect world politics if you try. Unlike other approaches to security, **pacifism** is a bottom-up approach that focuses on what people do rather than a top-down approach that stresses government action.

Pacifism begins with the belief that it is wrong to kill. Leo Tolstoy, the Russian novelist and pacifist, told the Swedish Peace Conference in 1909, "The truth is so simple, so clear, so evident . . . that it is only necessary to speak it out completely for its full significance to be irresistible." That truth, Tolstoy went on, "lies in what was said thousands of years ago in four words: *Thou Shalt Not Kill.*"

Beyond this starting point, pacifists have varying approaches. There are *universal pacifists,* who oppose all violence; *private pacifists,* who oppose personal violence but who would support as a last resort the use of police or military force to counter criminals or aggressors; and *antiwar pacifists,* who oppose political violence but would use violence as a last resort for personal self-defense.

The obvious argument against pacifism is that it is likely to get one killed or conquered. Those who support pacifism make several counter-contentions. One is that there is a history of pacifism's being effective. As one scholar points out, "Nonviolence is as old as the history of religious leaders and movements." The analyst goes on to explain that "traditions embodied by Buddha and Christ have inspired successful modern political movements and leaders [such as] . . . the Indian struggle for independence under the leadership of [Mohandas K.] Gandhi and the struggle of the American blacks for greater equality under the leadership of Martin Luther King Jr." (Beer, 1990:16).

Gandhi was the great Indian spiritual leader. He began his career as a London-trained attorney earning what was then an immense sum of £5,000 annually practicing in Bombay. Soon, however, he went to South Africa, where, earning £50 a year, he defended Indian expatriates against white legal oppression. Gandhi returned to India in 1915 to work for its independence. He gave up Western ways for a life of abstinence and spirituality. Gandhi believed that the force of the soul focused on (to use the Hindi) *satyagraha* (truth seeking) and *ahimsa* (nonviolence) could accomplish what resorting to arms could not. He developed techniques such as unarmed marches, sit-downs by masses of people, work stoppages, boycotts, and what might today be called "pray-ins," whereby *satyagrahi* (truth seekers) could confront the British nonviolently. "The sword of the *satyagrahi* is love," he counseled the Indian people (Lackey, 1989:14). Gandhi became known as Mahatma (great soul) and was the single most powerful force behind Great Britain's granting of independence to India in 1947. The Mahatma then turned his soul toward ending the hatred and violence between Hindus and Muslims in independent India. For this, a Hindu fanatic, who objected to Gandhi's tolerance, assassinated him in 1948. Earlier, after the United States had dropped atomic bombs on Japan, Gandhi was moved to write that "mankind has to get out of violence only through nonviolence. Hatred can be overcome only by love. Counter-hatred only increases the surface as well as the depth of hatred." One has to suspect that had he been able to, Gandhi would have repeated this to the man who shot him.

Pacifists, especially antiwar pacifists, would also make a moral case against the massive, collective violence that is war. They would say that no gain is worth the loss. This view, they would argue, has become infinitely more compelling in the nuclear age. Consider the description of Nagasaki filed by the first reporter who flew over the city after a U.S. bomber dropped an atomic bomb, killing at least 60,000 people. "Burned, blasted, and scarred," he wrote, "Nagasaki looked like a city of death." It was a scene, he continued, of "destruction of a sort never before imagined by a man and therefore is almost indescribable. The area where the bomb hit is absolutely flat and only the markings of the building foundations provide a clue as to what may have been in the area before the energy of the universe was turned loose" (Lackey, 1989:112). Pacifists contend that even by the standards of just war conduct *(jus in bello)* adopted by nonpacifists, any nuclear attack would be unconscionable.

A final point about pacifism is that it is not an irrelevant exercise in idealist philosophy. There are some countries, such as Japan, where at least limited pacifism represents a reasonably strong political force. Moreover, in a changing world, public opinion, economic measures, and other nonviolent instruments may create what is sometimes called a "civilian-based defense." Indeed, there are efforts, such as the Program on Nonviolent Sanctions in Conflict and Defense at Harvard University's Center for International Affairs, that are working to show that those who favor nonviolence should not be considered "token pacifists" who are "tolerated as necessary to fill out the full spectrum of alternatives, with nonviolent means given serious considerations only for use in noncritical situations" (Bond, 1992:2). Instead, advocates of this approach believe that the successes of Gandhi, King, and others demonstrate that proactive techniques, including nonviolent protest and persuasion, noncooperation, and nonviolent intervention (such as sit-ins), can be successful (Bock & Young, 1999).

It is true that pacifists are unlikely to be able to reverse world conflict by themselves. They are a tiny minority everywhere. Instead, pacifism may be part of a series of so-called peace creation actions. It is an idea worth contemplating.

Chapter Summary

Thinking about Security

1. The goal of the chapter is to discuss alternative paths to security. Security is not necessarily synonymous with either massive armaments or with disarmament. There are four approaches to security: unlimited self-defense, limited self-defense, international security, and abolition of war. The first was the subject of the last chapter. This chapter investigates the other three.
2. There are four possible approaches to ensuring security. They involve restrictions on the number of arms; their development, testing, and deployment; restrictions on certain types of weapons; and the transfer of weapons. Additionally, the standards of evaluation are determined by domestic norms, domestic collective security forces, domestic disarmament, and the established domestic conflict-resolution mechanism. Despite all of the protections and dispute-resolution procedures provided by a domestic system, security is a relative term, thus making full security impossible.

Limited Self-Defense through Arms Control

3. Some people believe that, because of the nature of humans and the nature of the international system, unlimited self-defense is the prudent policy. Advocates of this approach are suspicious of arms control.
4. Limited self-defense is one means of alternative security. People who favor limited self-defense would accomplish their goals through various methods of arms control.
5. From the standpoint of pure rationality, arms control, or the lack of it, is one of the hardest aspects of international politics to understand. Virtually everyone is against arms; virtually everyone is for arms control; yet there are virtually no restraints on the explosive arms escalation in which we are all trapped. It is a story that dates back far into our history, but unless progress is made, we may not have a limitless future to look forward to.
6. There are many powerful arguments against continuation of the arms race. Arms are very costly, in direct dollars and in indirect impact on the economy. Arms are also very dangerous and add to the tensions that sometimes erupt in violence.
7. During the 1990s, efforts increased to regulate arms. Several START treaties, renewal of the Nuclear Nonproliferation Treaty (NPT), the Comprehensive Test Ban Treaty (CTBT), conventional weapons inventories, conventional weapons transfer regulation, and biological and chemical arms control are among the efforts made. There are heavy domestic pressures from the military-industrial-congressional complex and sometimes from the public against arms control.
8. There are a number of ways to implement approaches to arms control, including arms reductions, limits on the expansion of arms inventories, and prohibitions against conventional arms transfers and nuclear proliferation.

International Security Forces

9. Some people favor trying to achieve security through various international security schemes. Collective security, peacekeeping, and peace enforcement are among the most significant attempts of an international security effort. The most likely focus of this approach would be the United Nations with a greatly strengthened security mandate and with security forces sufficient to engage in peace enforcement, rather than just peacekeeping.

Abolition of War

10. Abolition of war is a fourth approach to security. One way to avoid war is through general and complete disarmament. This makes violence difficult and may also ease tensions that lead to violence. Individual and collective pacifism is another way to avoid violence. Pacifists believe that the way to start the world toward peace is to practice nonviolence individually and in ever-larger groups.

For a chapter quiz, interactive activities, web links, PowerWeb articles, and much more, visit **www.mhhe.com/rourke10/** and go to chapter 11. Or, while accessing the site, click on Course-Wide Content and view recent international relations articles in the *New York Times.*

Key Terms

- Anti-Ballistic Missile Treaty (ABM)
- Anti-Personnel Mine Treaty (APM)
- arms control
- Biological Weapons Convention
- Chemical Weapons Convention (CWC)
- collective security
- Comprehensive Test Ban Treaty (CTBT)
- Conventional Forces in Europe Treaty (CFE)
- dual-use technology
- Economic Community of West African States (ECOWAS)
- general and complete disarmament (GCD)
- Intermediate-Range Nuclear Forces Treaty (INF)
- iron triangle
- Missile Technology Control Regime (MTCR)
- national technical means (NTM)
- Non-Proliferation Treaty (NPT)
- North Atlantic Treaty Organization (NATO)
- on-site inspection (OSI)
- Organization for Security and Cooperation in Europe (OSCE)
- pacifism
- peace enforcement
- peacekeeping
- Strategic Arms Limitation Talks Treaty I (SALT I)
- Strategic Arms Limitation Talks Treaty II (SALT II)
- Strategic Arms Reduction Treaty I (START I)
- Strategic Arms Reduction Treaty II (START II)
- Treaty of Moscow
- weapons of mass destruction (WMDs)

CHAPTER

12

The International Economy: A Global Road Map

THEORIES OF INTERNATIONAL POLITICAL ECONOMY
Economic Nationalism
Economic Internationalism
Economic Structuralism
TWO ECONOMIC WORLDS: NORTH AND SOUTH
Two Economic Worlds: Analyzing the Data
Two Economic Worlds: Human Conditions
THE GROWTH AND EXTENT OF INTERNATIONAL POLITICAL ECONOMY
Trade
International Investment
Monetary Relations
Globalization and Interdependence: Debating the Future
CHAPTER SUMMARY
KEY TERMS

O, behold! The riches of the ship is come on shore.
—William Shakespeare, *Othello*

They are as sick that surfeit with too much as they that starve with nothing.
—William Shakespeare, *The Merchant of Venice*

You don't make the poor richer by making the rich poorer.
—Winston Churchill

If we make the average of mankind comfortable and secure, their prosperity will rise through the ranks.
—Franklin D. Roosevelt

CHAPTER OBJECTIVES

After completing this chapter, you should be able to:

- Explain why politics and economics are intertwined aspects of international relations.
- Analyze international political economy (IPE).
- Discuss the economic nationalist doctrine.
- Discuss the economic internationalist approaches to IPE.
- Discuss the economic structuralist approaches to IPE.
- Analyze the economic elements that form the base of the North-South axis.
- Identify the three explanations offered for the existence of the economic gap between the North and South.
- Analyze the history of IPE, focusing on the effect of changes during the last 50 years.
- Discuss how the expansion of IPE continues to be dominated by the North.
- Show the relation between the growth of trade, the rapid expansion of international financial ties, and the economic importance of monetary relations.
- Analyze the effect of increasing economic interdependence on both countries and individuals.
- Discuss the arguments for and against free international economic interchange.

Given the degree to which this text has already discussed the interplay of politics and economics, you have probably concluded correctly that, to a significant extent, economics is politics and vice versa. This chapter and the two that follow it will continue to explicate how economics and politics intertwine. The subject of this chapter is the general nature of **international political economy (IPE)**, including IPE theories, and the situation of the **economically developed countries (EDCs)** of the North and the **less developed countries (LDCs)** of the South. Chapter 13 examines the traditional political path of national economic competition (Goddard, Cronin, & Dash, 2003). Finally, chapter 14 discusses the alternative path of international economic cooperation.

It is important before delving into the subject to familiarize yourself with the distinctions between some economics terms: **gross national product (GNP**, the value of all domestic and international economic activity by a country's citizens and business) and **gross domestic product (GDP**, the value of all economic activity within a country by it its own and foreign individuals and companies); between GNP or GDP adjusted for **purchasing power parity (PPP**, as in GNP/PPP, GDP/PPP, a measure that adjusts currencies based on food, housing, and the cost of other "local" purchases); and between **current dollars** and **real dollars**. More detailed explanations of these terms, information on how to read graphs, and some commentary on the sources and reliability of economic statistics can be found in Explanatory Notes on page N-2 in the section "Economics: Technical Terms and Sources."

Theories of International Political Economy

Before getting into the details of current global economic conditions, it is appropriate to examine the broad theories about the connection between economics and politics (Burch & Denemark, 1997). As chapter 1 discusses, many political scientists believe that economic forces and conditions are the key determinants of the course of world politics. One scholar observes, "Clearly, a state perceives its international economic interests on the basis of a set of ideas or beliefs about how the world economy works and what opportunities exist within it" (Woods, 1995:161).

There are numerous schools of thought related to IPE. They can be roughly divided into economic nationalist, economic internationalist, and economic structuralist approaches. The three approaches are descriptive, in that they all purport to describe how and why conditions occur. The three approaches are also prescriptive, in that they make arguments about how policy should be conducted. These descriptions and prescriptions are summarized in Table 12.1. You should further note that economic nationalism is a realpolitik school of IPE, while economic internationalism and, especially, economic structuralism are liberal schools.

Economic Nationalism

The core of **economic nationalism** is the belief that the state should use its economic strength to further national interests. By extension, economic nationalists also advocate using a state's power to build its economic strength. Epitomizing this view, the first U.S. secretary of the treasury, Alexander Hamilton, argued that "the interference and aid of [the U.S.] government are indispensable" to protect American industry and to build U.S. economic strength (Balaam & Veseth, 1996:23).

Economic nationalists are realists who believe that conflict characterizes international economic relations and that the international economy is a zero-sum game in which

TABLE 12.1 Approaches to International Political Economy

	Economic Nationalism	Economic Internationalism	Economic Structuralism
Associated terms	Mercantilism, economic statecraft	Liberalism, free trade, free economic interchange, capitalism, laissez-faire	Marxism, dependency, neo-Marxism, neoimperialism, neocolonialism
Primary economic actors	States, alliances	Individuals, multinational corporations, IGOs	Economic classes (domestic and state)
Current economic relations	Competiton and conflict based on narrow national interest; zero-sum game	National competition but cooperation increasing; non–zero-sum game	Conflict based on classes of countries; wealthy states exploit poor ones; zero-sum game
Goal for future	Preserve/expand state power, secure national interests	Increase global prosperity	Eliminate internal and international classes
Prescription for future	Follow economic policies that build national power; use power to build national economy	Eliminate/minimize role of politics in economics; use politics	Radically reform system to end divisions in wealth and power between classes of countries
Desired relationship of politics and economics	Politics controls economic policy	Politics used only to promote domestic free markets and international free economic interchange	Politics should be eliminated by destruction of class system
View of states	Favorable; augment state power	Mixed; eliminate states as primary economic policy makers	Negative; radically reform states; perhaps eliminate states
Estimation of possibility of cooperation	Impossible; humans and states inherently seek advantage and dominance	Possible through reforms within a modified state-based system	Only possible through radical reform; revolution may be necessary
Views on development of LDCs	No responsibility to help. Also could lose national advantages by creating more competition, higher resource prices	Can be achieved through aid, loans, investment, trade, and other assistance within current system. Will ultimately benefit all countries	Exploitation of countries must be ended by fundamentally restructuring the distribution of political and economic power

Conceptual sources: Isaak (2000), Balaam & Veseth (1996), Gilpin (1996), author.

Analysts take very different approaches in describing how the international political economy works and in prescribing how it should work.

one side can gain only if another loses. As Hamilton asked rhetorically in *Federalist Paper* #6 (1787), "Have there not been as many wars founded upon commercial motives since that has become the prevailing system of nations, as were before occasioned by the cupidity of territory or dominion?" From the economic nationalist perspective, political goals should govern economic policy because the aim is to maximize state power in order to secure state interests.

To accomplish their ends, economic nationalists rely on a number of political-economic strategies. *Imperialism and neoimperialism* are one set of economic nationalist practices. Imperialism is the direct control of another land and its people for national economic gain. It was this motive that propelled Europeans outward to conquer and build the great colonial empires that dominated so much of the world until recent decades. Direct colonial control has largely died out, but many observers charge that neoimperialism (indirect control) continues to be a prime characteristic of the relationship that exists, or that EDCs try to achieve, between themselves and LDCs.

Economic incentives and disincentives provide a second set of economic nationalist practices. Countries that offer economic carrots, such as foreign aid and favorable trade policies, or that use economic sticks, such as sanctions, to promote the state's national interests are practicing economic nationalism. For example, a State Department official justified what he depicted as putting "pressure on the Cuban government through the embargo and [other economic measures]" on the grounds that "economic sanctions can be and are a valuable tool for . . . protecting our national interests."[1]

Protectionism and domestic economic support are a third set of tools that economic nationalists believe should be used to promote national power. "I use not porter [ale] or cheese in my family, but such as is made in America," George Washington once avowed.[2] From this perspective, economic nationalists are suspicious of economic interdependence on the grounds that it undermines state sovereignty and weakens the national economic strength. Economic nationalists would prefer that their respective countries use trade barriers, economic subsidies, and other policies to protect national industries, especially those with military value.

Economic Internationalism

A second theoretical and policy approach to IPE is **economic internationalism**. This approach is often also associated with such terms as capitalism, laissez-faire, economic liberalism, and free trade. Economic internationalists are liberals. They believe that international economic relations should and can be conducted cooperatively because, in their view, the international economy is a non-zero-sum game in which prosperity is available to all.

Economic internationalists contend that the best way to create prosperity is by freeing economic interchange from political restrictions. Therefore, economic internationalists (in contrast to economic nationalists) oppose tariff barriers, domestic subsidies, sanctions, and any other economic tool that distorts the free flow of trade and investment capital.

The origins of economic liberalism lie in the roots of capitalism. In one of the early expositions of capitalist theory, *The Wealth of Nations* (1776), Adam Smith wrote, "It is not from the benevolence of the butcher, the brewer, or the baker, that we expect our dinner, but from their regard to their own interest." Smith believed that this self-interest constituted an "invisible hand" of competition that created the most efficient economies. Therefore, he opposed any political interference with the operation of the invisible hand, including political meddling in trade. It was Smith's contention that "if a foreign country can supply us with a commodity cheaper than we ourselves can make it, better buy it of them with some part of the produce of our own industry, employed in a way in which we have some advantage."

Did You Know That:

The term *laissez-faire* originated with an 18th-century group of French capitalist philosophers called *les Économistes*. Reflecting their objection to government interference in the economy, their motto was *laissez-faire, laissez-passer* (let be, let pass). The views of *les Économistes* influenced the noted English capitalist philosopher Adam Smith in the writing of *The Wealth of Nations* (1776).

The pure capitalism advocated by Smith has few adherents today. Instead, most modern economic liberals favor a "mixed economy" using the state to modify the worst abuses of capitalism by preventing the formation of monopolies and by taking other steps to ensure that the competition and unequal distribution of wealth inherent in capitalism is not overly brutal. The most prominent early advocate of this approach was the British economist John Maynard Keynes, who wrote in *The End of Laissez-Faire* (1926) that while classic capitalism is "in many ways objectionable. . . . Capitalism, wisely managed, can probably be made more efficient for attaining economic ends than any alternative system" (Balaam & Veseth, 1996:49).

At the international level, Keynesian economics has influenced economic internationalists and the changes they advocate to traditional economic nationalist policies. They are moderate reforms, though, which would alter, but not radically change, either capitalism or the state-based international system. For example, the efforts in the 1940s to set up organizations such as the International Monetary Fund (IMF) and to promote trade through the General Agreement on Tariffs and Trade (GATT) reflect the Keynesian idea of using intergovernmental organizations (IGOs) and agreements to promote and, when necessary, to regulate international economic interchange. Modern liberals also favor such government interference as foreign aid and, sometimes, concessionary trade agreements or loan terms to assist LDCs to develop.

In sum, modern economic liberals generally believe in the capitalist approach of eliminating political interference in the international economy. They are modified capitalists, though, because they also favor using IGO and national government programs for two ends: (1) to ensure that countries adopt capitalism and free trade and (2) to ease the worst inequities in the system so that future competition can be fairer and current LDCs can have a chance to achieve prosperity. Thus economic liberals do not want to overturn the current political and economic international system.

Economic Structuralism

The third major approach to IPE is called **economic structuralism**. Like the other two approaches, economic structuralism has both descriptive and prescriptive elements.

Economic structuralists believe that economic structure determines politics. That is, the conduct of world politics is based on the way that the world is organized economically. Structuralists contend that the world is divided between have and have-not countries and that the "haves" (the EDCs) work to keep the "have nots" (the LDCs) weak and poor in order to exploit them. To change this, economic structuralists favor a radical restructuring of the economic system designed to end the uneven distribution of wealth and power.

Economic structuralists can be divided into two major camps. Marxist theorists are one. They see the state and capitalism as inherent sources of economic evil. The second camp is made up of dependency and world systems analysts. They do not necessarily consider capitalism evil. Instead, they advocate fundamental reforms to end economic oppression. Both types of economic structuralists believe that significant changes have to be made in the way international politics works in order to promote LDC development, but they disagree about how radical the change must be. Marxists believe that the entire capitalist-based system must be overturned and replaced with domestic and international socialist systems before economic equity can be achieved. Less radical economic structuralists stress reform of the current market system.

Marxist Theory

Marxism is perhaps the best-known strand of structuralist thought. Communist ideology, associated with Karl Marx, maintains that the economic order determines political and social relationships. Thus the distribution of wealth and the struggle between the propertied and powerful *bourgeoisie* and the poor and oppressed *proletariat* is the essence of politics. The first Soviet Communist Party chief, V. I. Lenin, applied **Marxism** to international politics. He argued in *Imperialism: The Highest Stage of Capitalism* (1916) that capitalist, bourgeois leaders had duped their proletariat workers into supporting the exploitation of other proletariat peoples through imperialism. Thus, the class struggle also included an international class struggle between bourgeois and proletariat countries and peoples.

Dependency and World Systems Theory

Two related variations of structuralist thought are dependency theory and world systems theory, which are also referred to as neo-Marxist theory and economic radical theory.

This Egyptian editorial drawing captures the view of economic structuralists, who believe that the word's wealthier countries want the world's less developed countries to remain poor in order to dominate and exploit them.

Dependency theory argues that the economically underdeveloped condition of the LDCs is caused by their exploitation by the EDCs. This is accomplished by the EDCs through indirect control of the LDCs and is driven by the EDCs' need for cheap primary resources, external markets, profitable investment opportunities, and low-wage labor. The South produces low-cost, low-profit **primary products** such as agricultural products and raw materials. These help supply the EDCs' production of high-priced, high-profit **manufactured goods**, some of which are sold to the LDCs. It is, therefore, in the interest of capitalist exploiters to keep LDCs dependent. For this reason, economic structuralists say, **neocolonialism** (neoimperialism), which operates without colonies but is nevertheless imperialistic, has created a hierarchical structure in which the rich states in the center of the world economic system dominate the LDCs on the periphery of the system. The dependency of LDCs is maintained in a number of ways, such as structuring the rules and practices of international economics to benefit the North. The economic structuralists further contend that neoimperial powers corrupt and co-opt the local elite in LDCs by allowing them personal wealth in return for governing their countries to benefit the North in such ways as keeping wages low for multinational corporations (MNCs) and ensuring low prices for the primary products needed by the EDCs.

World systems theory traces the current global economic inequality to the rise of the Western political and economic domination, especially the acceleration of that control after the onset of the Western-centered industrial revolution in the mid-1700s. Theorists who take this perspective contend that the evolution of the Western-dominated capitalist system has distorted development, leaving vast economic, social, and political disparities between the core (the EDCs) and the periphery (the LDCs) of the international system. As for countries such as South Korea, which have prospered enough to achieve standards of wealth equal to at least the least wealthy EDCs, world system theorists are apt to argue that these semiperiphery states have achieved success only by dutifully serving the interests of the EDCs. Thus, semiperiphery states are something like collaborator states that themselves exploit the periphery. Like other radical theorists, world systems theorists believe that systemwide change is possible only if there are far-reaching changes in the basic parameters of the dominant economic model of Western-dominated capitalism. Even those radical theorists who do not oppose capitalism as such are skeptical of it. They contend that it can be supported only if it is radically reformed from exploitive capitalism to cooperative capitalism, which recognizes the moral and practical advantages of ensuring at least minimally acceptable economic and social conditions for all.

Whatever their exact theoretical perspective, economic radicals would argue, for example, that the U.S. role in the Persian Gulf region dating back to World War II epitomizes neoimperialism. The devil's bargain, in the view of structuralists, is this: The United States protects or tries to protect the power of obscenely rich, profoundly undemocratic rulers of oil-rich states, such as Saudi Arabia and Kuwait, as it did in 1991. In return, the king and emir keep the price of oil down, which benefits the economies of the United States and the other oil-importing EDCs. Crude oil sold for an average of about $20 a barrel (equal to 42 gallons) in 1990. After the Persian Gulf War through 1999, oil prices dropped to an average of about $17 a barrel, a significant economic advantage to the United States and other imported-oil-dependent countries. Then, beginning in 2000, oil prices spiked up, averaging $24 a barrel during 2000–2002. Economic radical theorists are suspicious that the subsequent U.S.-led action against Iraq was motivated, at least in part, by the prospects of dominating Iraqi oil production and increasing market supply by ending the sanctions against Iraq and modernizing its production capabilities. This would lower the price in a classic supply and demand model (assuming demand does not increase proportionately or more).

Two Economic Worlds: North and South

Whether or not you subscribe to economic nationalist, internationalist, or structuralist theory, it cannot be denied that the world is generally divided into two economic spheres: a wealthy North made up of EDCs and a less wealthy South composed of LDCs. The two geographical designations result from the fact that most EDCs lie to the north in North America and Europe and most LDCs are farther to the south in Africa, Asia, and Central and South America. There are exceptions, however, and what is important is that the North and the South are distinguished from each other by economic and political factors more than by their geographical position.

Two Economic Worlds: Analyzing the Data

The economic factor is the most objective distinction between North and South. The **North** is much wealthier than the **South**, as can be ascertained by examining countries (and the 2001 per capita GNP of each). That year the two dozen wealthiest countries had an average per capita GNP of $26,510; the South's average per capita GNP was less than one-twentieth of that at $1,160. The structure of the economy is another factor that generally differentiates EDCs from LDCs. The countries of the North tend to have more diverse economic bases that rely for their income on the production of a wide variety of manufactured products and the provision of diverse and sophisticated services. The countries of the South usually depend on fewer products for their income; these are often agricultural produce or raw materials, such as minerals. In 2000, for example, agriculture accounted for 12% of the GNPs of the South and only 2% of the GNPs of the North.

It is important to note that these two classifications and the overall numbers contain some difficulties. One is that, as with most attempts to categorize the world's political and economic divisions, the classifications are imprecise and subject to change. On the sole basis of per capita GNP, for example, the World Bank divides countries into four economic groups: low income ($745 or less), lower-middle income ($746–$2,975), upper-middle income ($2,796–$9,205), and high income (more than $9,206). These groupings are illustrated in the map on page 380.

These two classifications (North-South, and the four World Bank income groups) generally coincide, but not completely. One difference is that eight countries (the oil-producing states of Bahrain, Brunei, Kuwait, Qatar, and the United Arab Emirates; and Israel, South Korea, and Singapore), which are usually classified as part of the South, fall into the high-income group. It is also important to note that some LDCs have moved a significant distance toward achieving a modern economic base. The **newly industrializing countries (NICs)** are still usually placed in the South by analysts, but countries such as South Korea ($9,460) and Argentina ($6,940) could be classified as developed market economies. The NICs are also sometimes referred to as NIEs (newly industrializing economies) to accommodate the inclusion of Taiwan ($12,228).

A second issue of classifying countries economically relates to how to treat Russia, the other former Soviet republics (FSRs), and the former communist region of Eastern

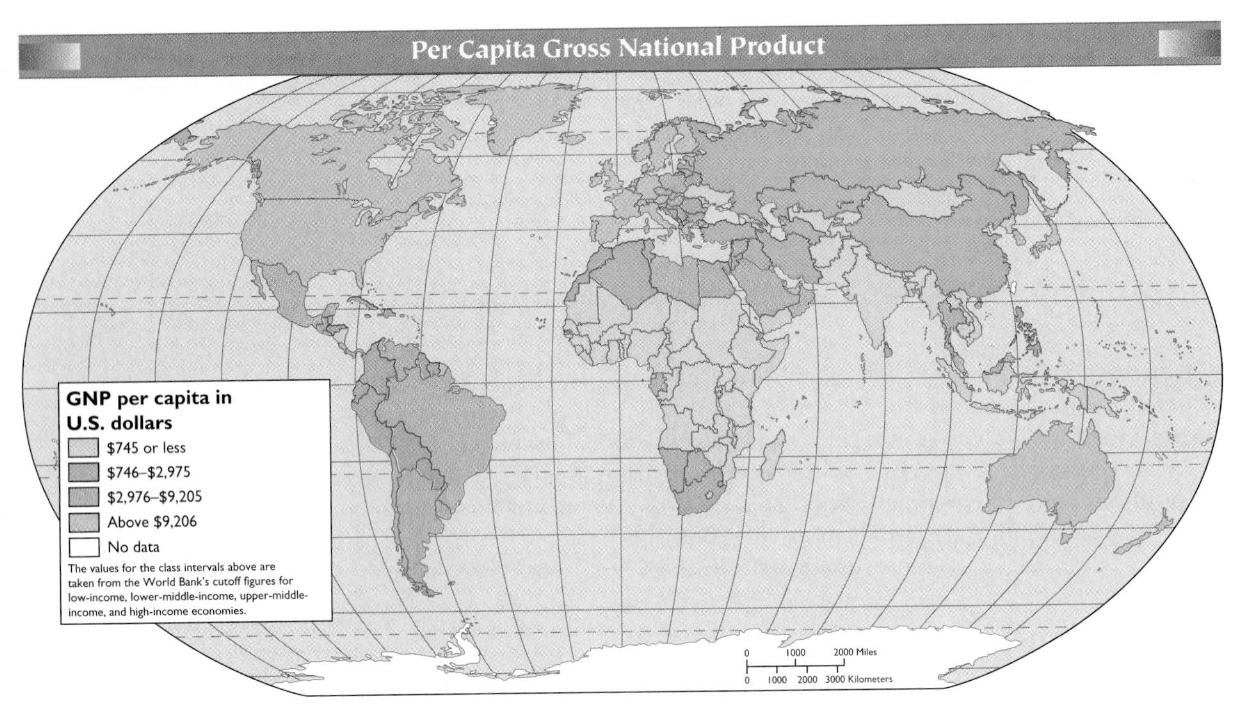

There is a great disparity in the world between a handful of countries that have a relatively small percentage of the world population but possess a huge proportion of global wealth (measured here in per capita GNP) and everyone else. The dollars that the legend uses to divide countries into economic categories do not truly convey the impact of the differences in economic circumstance. Especially if you are living in one of the poorest countries, you are much more likely to be illiterate, ill-housed, malnourished, and ill, and to die earlier than your contemporaries in the wealthy countries.

Source: From John Allen and Elizabeth Leppman, *Student Atlas of World Politics*, 6th Edition, Dushkin/McGraw-Hill, p. 60. Reprinted with permission from Dushkin/McGraw-Hill.

Europe. The World Bank designates these as transition economies (from communism to capitalism). They are also referred to as **countries in transition (CITs)**. Some of these CITs have a reasonable industrial base, although all of them have experienced significant economic difficulties during the transition. Of them, only one, Slovenia ($9,760), falls in the high-income group. Others, such as Hungary ($4,830), fall into the upper-middle-income group. Most CITs, including Russia ($1,750), are in the lower-middle-income group, but seven FSRs fall in the low-income category. Of this group of FSRs, Tajikistan ($180) is the poorest. Given the economic data, all these countries except Slovenia are treated here as LDCs.

A third concern centers on the difficulty of measuring and reporting economic data. All the statistics are only an approximation. If, for instance, you have ever had an odd job babysitting or raking leaves, have been paid for it, and have not reported your income to the government, then the GDP for your country is slightly lower than it should be. All countries, especially LDCs, have significant unrecorded economic activity. For this reason, major differences in economic circumstances, economic trends, and other macroeconomic indicators are more important than specific dollar figures.

Fourth, the cost of many items varies tremendously from country to country, undermining part of the relevance of some data, such as GNP. This issue is the focus of the In the Spotlight box "GNP-PPP: The Big Mac Standard."

For all of these difficulties, the classification of the world into a North and a South is still useful. One reason is that the classification anomalies do not disguise the fact that,

IN THE SPOTLIGHT

GNP-PPP: The Big Mac Standard

The existence of over 180 national currencies and their fluctuation in values against one another make it difficult to evaluate any country's financial status by using standard measures, such as gross national product (GNP). Using the U.S. dollar as a base to calculate exchange rates, some countries' 2001 per capita GNPs were: United States ($34,280), Argentina ($6,940), and Switzerland ($38,330). These figures might lead you to conclude that the average Swiss citizen is somewhat better off economically than the average American, who, in turn, is about five times better off than the average Argentinean.

Many economists argue, however, that these figures do not present an accurate picture because they do not reflect the prices for commonly consumed local products such as housing, public transportation, movies, and fast food. Some analysts keep track of these relative cost factors by using the ubiquitous Big Mac as a standard to compare prices. According to data on 30 countries compiled by the *Economist* (a leading British financial journal), the average 2001 Big Mac cost $2.54 in the base-price United States, and ranged from $0.78 in Argentina to $3.98 in Switzerland.[1]

To adjust GDP to reflect the actual cost of living in various countries, the World Bank and other financial institutions use GNP adjusted for purchasing power parity (PPP). This measure uses a "market basket" of items "not traded on international markets" (that is, like Big Macs, locally produced and consumed) to compare standards of living. By this standard (and again using the United States as the base), the above countries' per capita GNP-PPPs in 2001 were: United States ($34,280), Argentina ($10,980), and Switzerland ($28,769). Note that when using per capita GNP-PPP instead of just per capita GNP, the Swiss were less well off, not better off than Americans, who in turn were only three, not five, times better off than Argentineans.

It is important to see that neither the standard GNP nor the newer GNP-PPP is a fully accurate measure. GNP does not take prices of locally produced and consumed items into account. But GNP-PPP misses the fact that many items we all consume come through international trade, and the price of a barrel of imported petroleum, an imported Toyota, or an imported Mac—in this case the computer—is pretty much the same, whether you are paying for it in U.S. dollars, Argentinean pesos, or Swiss francs.

The Big Mac can also be used to analyze other kinds of data. For example, with regard to comparative wages, it takes the average worker in Kenya about three hours of labor to earn enough to buy a Big Mac. The average Lithuanian only needs to work about an hour for the wages to purchase the hamburger special, and the average American spends only ten minutes; almost less time than it takes to eat it.

as a rule, the countries of the South are poorer and less industrialized than those of the North. The data can be dry to read, but the reality behind the data is that, on average, the conditions of life for the citizens in the countries of the industrialized North are dramatically better than the living standards of the relatively deprived people who reside in the LDCs of the South.

Economic vulnerability is a second factor that unites most of the South and distinguishes it from the North. Even many upper-middle-income countries of the South have a shaky economic base that relies on one or a few products. For example, those LDCs that rely on petroleum production and export are at substantial risk when the price of oil is exceptionally low, as it was throughout most of the 1990s.

Common political experiences of the LDCs are a third reason that the North-South distinction continues to be applicable. Most LDCs share a history of being directly or indirectly dominated by the EDCs of Europe and North America or, in the case of the former communist countries, by Russia.

Two Economic Worlds: Human Conditions

Sensationalism is not the aim of this book. Still, it is hard to recount conditions of impoverishment in neutral, academic terms. Approximately 85% of the world's people live in the South, yet they produce only 21% of the global GNP. Far outpacing the fortunes of those who reside in LDCs, the 15% of the people who are fortunate enough to reside

Classifying countries economically is complex. We are used to thinking of Russia as an industrialized country, yet it is a less developed country by the World Bank's measure of per capita gross national product. The difficult economic conditions that afflict most Russians are represented by this homeless woman holding her child and begging on a snowy street in Irkutsk, Russia.

in the North produce 79% of the world's measurable GNP. Another telling calculation is that on a per capita basis, the richest 15% of the world's citizens produce $62 for every $1 produced by the 41% of the world's population who live in the poorest countries (the low-income or **least developed countries, LLDCs)**. Perhaps worse, this 62:1 ratio has doubled from a 30:1 ratio in 1960. As stark as these statistics are, their true meaning is in their social impacts. Compared with those who live in an EDC, a person who lives in an LLDC is:

- 34 times more likely to be illiterate if adult.
- 20 times more likely not to be in school if a school-age child.
- 17 times more likely to die before age 5.
- 44 times more likely not to have access to basic sanitation services.
- 48 times more likely to die during childbirth.
- 20 years earlier in the grave.

The scope of the deprivation that many in the South suffer also boggles the mind when the total number of humans affected is calculated. More than 1.1 billion people in the LDCs live in **extreme poverty**, which the World Bank defines as the condition of those trying to survive on less than $1 a day. Another 1.7 billion people struggle to sustain themselves on between $1 and $2 a day, with the two impoverished groups combining to make up about 46% of the world's population. Literacy and education are beyond the dreams of many. There are 854 million illiterate adults and 113 million children of primary-school age who are not in school in the South. The perils to health are everywhere. Governments in LDCs annually spend just $71 per capita on health care, compared to per capita expenditures of $2,376 in EDCs. Some 1.2 billion people in LDCs do not have access to safe water, and 2.5 billion are without sanitary sewer facilities. Food supplies are often inadequate, with more than 829 million people in the LDCs suffering from malnutrition. Medical facilities in the South are overwhelmed. Each physician in an LDC is responsible for about 850 people, compared to only 330 people for a physician in the North; hundreds of millions of people in the South have no access to any kind of health care. These conditions lead to disease and death on a wide scale. Infants die at a scandalously high rate, as do women during childbirth, and just 65% of the people in LDCs (compared to 85% of the people in EDCs) live to age 65.

Despite these gloomy numbers, conditions are getting better in the South in overall terms. As the 1990s ended, there were 123 million less people living in extreme poverty than when the decade began. Infant mortality rates in LDCs were down 12% during the decade; those with access to safe water and safe sanitation facilities improved 5% and 12% respectively; and life expectancy rose by three years. Also during the 1990s, illiteracy among young adults (age 15 to 24) declined 8%; and the percentage of children (age 6 to 15) in LDCs who were working rather than being in school declined 25%.

This positive overall data, while welcome, is tempered considerably by other statistics. One is that the relative economic gap between North and South is widening. This increasing disparity is evident in Figure 12.1.

Did You Know That:

The Food and Agriculture Organization (FAO) estimates that there are 829 million malnourished people in the world. At the same time, 378,000 Americans underwent liposuction surgery in 2002 to siphon excess fat from their bodies.

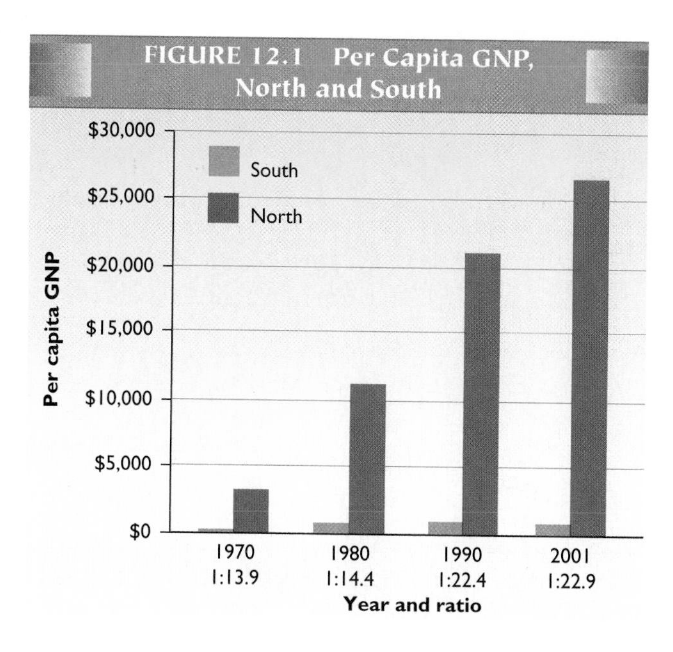

The economic gulf that divides the wealthy countries of the North and the poorer countries of the South has expanded 65%. In 1970, the average citizen in the North earned 13.9 times the average earnings of the average citizen in the South. That gap expanded to 22.9 times the average earnings in the South by 2001.

Data source: World Bank (2003).

Also troubling is that fact that conditions are declining in some countries. Sub-Saharan Africa is a particularly depressed region. Its combined per capita GNP of a scant $311 in 2001 was actually 7.5% lower in real dollars than it had been in 1965. A horrific 47% of its population lives on less than $1 a day. The region has the world's highest birthrate, and the rapidly rising population is outpacing agricultural production. A third of the population is malnourished, 17% of the region's children die before reaching age 5, and life expectancy is only 47 years. Only 60% of the people in sub-Saharan Africa have access to safe water; 29% of the children age 10 to 14 are working rather than going to school, and the adult illiteracy rate is 39%. It is unnecessary to recite more grim statistics in order to document that—relatively speaking and, in some cases, absolutely—the rich are getting richer and the poor are getting poorer.

The Growth and Extent of International Political Economy

Economic interchange between politically separate peoples predates written history. Trading records extend back to almost 3000 B.C., and archaeologists have uncovered evidence of trade in the New Stone Age, or Neolithic period (9000–8000 B.C.). Since then, economics has become an ever more important aspect of international relations. This is evident in expanding trade and the resulting increased interrelationship between international economic activity and domestic economic circumstances. We can see this by examining trade, investment, and monetary exchanges and by looking at both the general expansion of each of these factors and the uneven pattern of each.

Trade

Before beginning our discussion of the historical growth and the current extent of trade, it is necessary to note the two elements that compose trade: goods and services. **Merchandise trade** is what people most frequently associate with imports and exports.

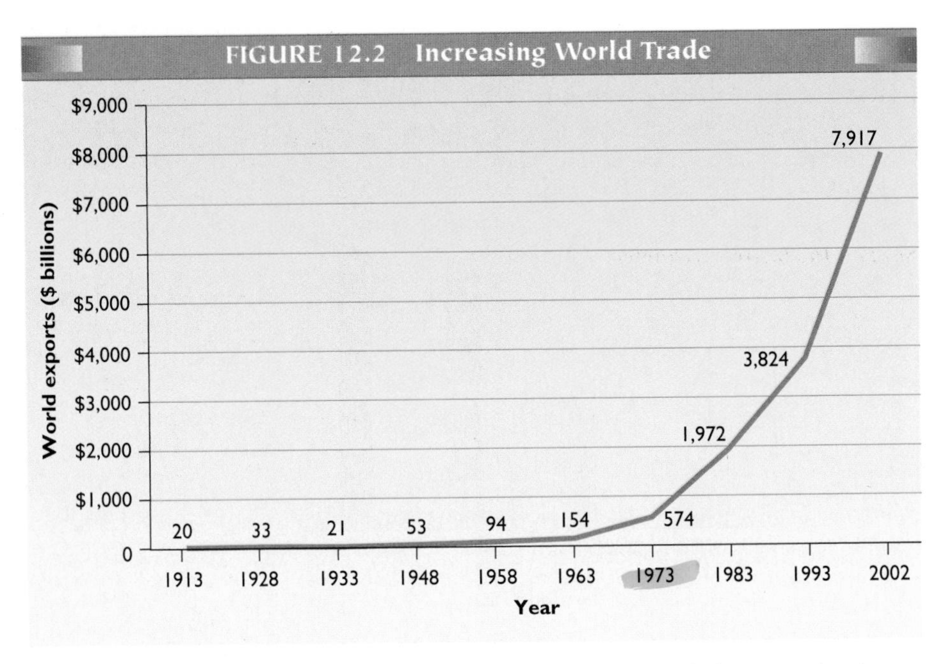

Trade, measured here in current dollar exports, has grown meteorically during recent decades. This growth is one sign of the vastly increased importance of international economic relations to individual countries and their citizens.

Data source: IMF (various years).

These goods are tangible items and are subdivided into two main categories: primary goods (raw materials) and manufactured goods. **Services trade** is less well known but also important. Services include things that you do for others. When American architects receive pay for designing foreign buildings, when U.S. insurance companies earn premiums for insuring foreign assets or people, when American movies and other intellectual properties earn royalties abroad, when U.S. trucks carry goods in Mexico or Canada, the revenue they generate is payment for the export of services. These services are a major source of income for countries, amounting to more than $1.5 trillion, or 20% of the entire flow of goods and services across international borders.

The trade in services can also have a significant impact on a country's balance of trade. In 2002 the United States had a merchandise-trade deficit of $483 billion. This was somewhat offset by a $65 billion services-trade surplus, which reduced the overall U.S. trade deficit by 13%. It is also worth pointing out that exported services do not have to be performed overseas. American colleges and universities, for example, are one of the country's largest exporters of services. More than 515,000 foreign students spent over $10 billion for tuition, room, and board at U.S. institutions of higher learning in 2002 and about another $4 billion on other aspects of college life ranging from textbooks to pepperoni pizzas.

Did You Know That:

One sign of the huge U.S. trade deficit is the literal mountain of tractor-trailer-size shipping containers building up at U.S. ports. In 2002, the Newark-Elizabeth port complex in New Jersey alone received about 1,745,000 such containers filled with imports, but shipped out only 750,000 of them carrying exports.

A General Pattern of Expanding Trade

Trade is booming, and the international flow of goods and services is a vital concern to all world states. World trade in 1913 totaled only $20 billion. In 2002 world trade stood at nearly $7.9 trillion. Even considering inflation, this represents a tremendous jump in world commerce. Figure 12.2 depicts the rise in the dollar volume of trade. Trade growth has been especially rapid during the post–World War II era of significant tariff reductions. During the 1913–1948 period of world wars, depression, and trade protectionism, trade increased at an average annual rate of only 0.8%. The postwar period has seen average annual increases at a rate of approximately 9% overall, with a somewhat slower rate (5%) since 1990. The rapid growth of trade has been caused by a number of supply and demand factors and the implementation of a free trade philosophy.

Supply: Productive Technology The industrial revolution, which began in 18th-century Europe, is one factor behind increased trade. As productivity increased, so did the supply of goods. From 1705 to 1780, prior to industrialization, world industrial production increased slowly at an annual rate of only 1.5%. Mechanization of industry boosted that average annual rate of increase to 2.6% in the four decades that followed, and to 3.3% between 1820 and 1860 (Rostow, 1978). As production rates sped up, the manufactured goods saturated local markets, and manufacturers increasingly had to seek markets for their surplus goods farther away and even across national borders. Thus, the greater volume of manufactured goods formed the supply side of trade development.

These robotic spot welders at a Ford Motors plant in Canada perform 1,270 welds per automobile on the assembly line. They are symbols of productive technology, one factor that has led to the vast expansion of trade. Using such technology, countries can produce more goods less expensively. Often the markets for this expanded supply of goods and the sources of raw material to make them are abroad.

Demand: Resource Requirements Industrialization also affected the "demand" side of international trade. During the 19th century and through World War II, importation of raw materials by the industrialized European countries was a primary force in trade, as manufacturing needs both increased demand for raw materials and outstripped domestic resource availability. During the late 1800s, for example, raw materials accounted for well over half of the goods moving across international borders. This level declined steadily during the 20th century for several reasons, one of which is that synthetic materials became an ever-larger part of the manufacturing process. Currently primary products account for only about 22% of all goods in international trade; that percentage, although it seems small, equals about $1.8 trillion dollars in primary products.

Demand: Materialism The rise in the world's standard of living, especially in the industrialized countries, has also contributed to "demand" pressure on international trade. More workers entered the wage-producing sector, and their "real" (after inflation) wages went up. The real wages of English craftspersons held relatively steady between 1300 and 1800, for instance, but beginning in 1800, after the industrial revolution, more than doubled by the 1950s.

This trend has continued into the current era. The workers of the wealthier countries have especially enjoyed increased real wages. The average real wage in the industrialized countries, for example, rose 1.8% annually between 1976 and 2002. This strengthens demand because individuals have more wealth with which to purchase domestic and imported goods and services.

Supply and Demand: Transportation Technology has also increased our ability to transport goods: to carry the supply of manufactured goods and to meet the demand for them. The development of railroads and improvements in maritime shipping were particular spurs to trade. They both increased the volume of trade that was possible and decreased per-unit transportation costs. Less than two centuries ago, all exported products were carried abroad in sailing ships or in wagons. Now foreign commerce is carried around the world by about 28,000 oceangoing merchant vessels and a vast number of trains and trucks; in just the United States, it is delivered by over 1 million large trucks and by more than 19,000 locomotives pulling almost 1.3 million freight cars.

Free Trade Philosophy The central idea of economic internationalists, that free trade will enhance overall prosperity, is rooted in the writings of capitalist economists that date back as far as the 1600s. These are reviewed later in this chapter. Whatever their validity, such theories did not come to center stage until they captured the attention of national policy makers in the wake of the global trauma occasioned by the great economic depression of the 1930s and World War II in the early 1940s. One cause for these miseries, it was said, was the high tariffs that had restricted trade and divided nations. To avoid a recurrence, the United States took the lead in reducing barriers to international trade. The General Agreement on Tariffs and Trade (GATT) came into being in 1947 when countries accounting for 80% of world commerce agreed to work to reduce international trade barriers. As a result of this and a series of related efforts, world tariff barriers dropped dramatically. American import duties, for example, dropped from an average of 60% in 1934, to 25% in 1945, to a current level of less than 4%. The tariffs of other EDCs have similarly dropped, and while the duties charged by LDCs tend to be higher, the average global tariff rate is only about 15%. Tariffs, as we will soon see, are not the only trade barrier, but their sharp reductions have greatly reduced the cost of imported goods and have strongly stimulated trade.

Uneven Patterns of Trade: North and South

The historical growth of trade, it is important to note, has not occurred evenly throughout the world. Instead, three facts about the patterns of international commerce stand out. First, as depicted in Figure 12.3, trade is overwhelmingly dominated by the EDCs in the North. These countries amass 77% of the exports in goods and services combined. The percentage of world trade shared by the LDCs is relatively small, especially in per capita figures.

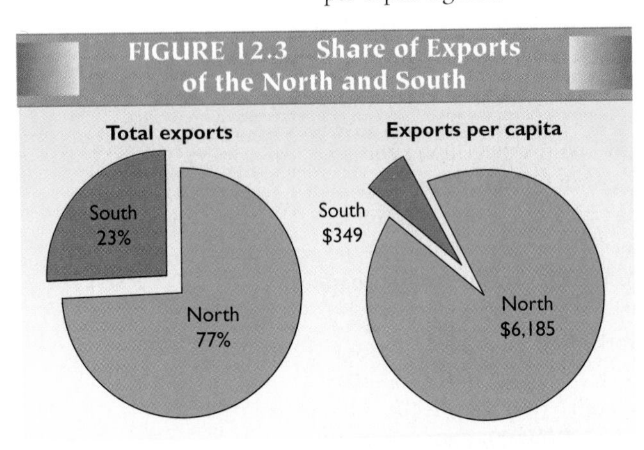

The pattern of world trade is very uneven. The North exports more than 3 times as much in good and services as does the South in overall dollars and 18 times as much on a per capita basis.

Data source: World Bank (2003).

A second, and related, pattern of world trade is that only a small percentage of global commerce occurs among LDCs. The merchandise trade among LDCs in 2002 accounted for a scant 11% of the world total. Moreover, five countries (China, Malaysia, Singapore, South Korea, and Taiwan) accounted for half of that figure measured in exports. This means that LDCs export most of their products to EDCs in a pattern of trade that leaves the LDCs heavily dependent on the EDCs for export earnings and, thus, in a vulnerable position.

A third important trade pattern involves types of exports. Merchandise exports account for 82% of what EDCs sell abroad; primary products make up only 18%. For LDCs a higher 40% of their exports are primary products, such as food, fibers, fuels, and minerals. For the poorest countries, the LLDCs, that figure is 48%. The United States and Chile provide a good comparison. Of all U.S. goods exported, manufactured products account for 82% and primary products for 18%. Chile's exports are just about the opposite, with manufactured goods at 18% and primary products at 82%. To make matters worse, just one primary product, copper, accounts for about 41% of Chile's exports. This dependence on primary products for export earnings leaves the LDCs in a disadvantaged position because the prices of primary products increase more slowly than those of manufactured goods and also because the prices for primary products are highly volatile. In this case, Chile's economy in the late 1990s was rocked by the plummeting price of copper, which was $1.33 a pound in 1995, sank to $0.66 a pound in 1999, and had risen to only $1.04 a pound in January 2004.

International Investment

Trade has not been the only form of international economic activity that has grown rapidly. There also has been a parallel expansion of international financial ties. This flow of investments can be examined by reviewing types of foreign investments and multinational corporations.

Foreign Direct and Portfolio Investment

One aspect of increased financial ties is the growth of investment in other countries. When Americans invest in British or Nigerian companies, or when Canadians invest in U.S. corporations, a web of financial interdependency is begun. Such international investment has long existed but has accelerated greatly since World War II. In 1950 U.S. direct investment abroad was $11.8 billion. By 2000 that figure had skyrocketed to $2.6 trillion. Investors in other EDCs and a few from LDCs have added to the international flow of investment capital. Currently, total world **foreign direct investment (FDI**, buying a major stake in foreign companies or real estate), is about $11 trillion. This includes $2.5 trillion in direct investments by foreign corporations and individuals in the United States and $2.4 trillion that American corporations and individuals have invested abroad. **Foreign portfolio investment (FPI)** in stocks and bonds that does not involve the control of companies or real estate is measured in the trillions. For the United States alone, foreign investors hold just over $4.1 trillion in such U.S. assets, and Americans own over $2.1 trillion in foreign portfolio investment.

Like most areas of international economics, the movement of investment in the world is not evenly distributed. Since few investors are from the South, the flow of profits from investment mostly benefits the North. Certainly, the flow of investment capital has benefits for recipient countries, but even here the distribution is mixed. About 70% of all FDI, and an even greater percentage of FPI, is made in EDCs. Furthermore, the NICs and a few other countries such as China receive most of the investment capital, and most LDCs receive little or none.

The flow of investment capital into and out of countries is an important factor in their economic well-being. FDI and, to a degree, FPI help support and expand local businesses. For example, foreigners hold about $3.6 trillion in U.S. debt instruments (mostly U.S. federal and corporate bonds), and these loans to Americans help finance the U.S. government and American businesses. Foreign investments also create earnings for investors. Americans and U.S. corporations earned $280 billion in 2002 alone from their FDI abroad.

International Investment and Multinational Corporations

To understand the flow of international investment, it is especially important to analyze the growth and practices of **multinational corporations (MNCs)**. These firms, also

This artist's image represents the reality that multinational corporations (MNCs) dominate world business in the era of globalization. Most of them are based in the United States, the European Union, or Japan. Whether, on balance, MNCs are making a contribution to global society or harming it is debatable. In the end, just as it is in domestic societies, the answer may come down to how well they are regulated.

called transnational corporations (TNCs), are at the forefront of the international movement of investment capital and private loans among countries.

An MNC is a private enterprise that includes subsidiaries operating in more than one state. This means more than merely international trading. Rather, it implies ownership of manufacturing plants and/or resource extraction and processing operations in a variety of countries. Additionally, MNCs conduct businesses abroad that supply services, such as banking, insurance, and transportation. Many observers therefore contend that MNCs are transnational organizations with operations that transcend national boundaries.

The roots of modern MNCs extend back to Europe's great trading companies, beginning with the Dutch East India Company in 1602. The level of multinational enterprise grew slowly, then expanded more quickly along with the increased European industrialization in the 19th century. By the end of that century, burgeoning American industry began to be a force, and it was not long after Henry Ford began building Model Ts that his corporation had its first subsidiary in Europe. Indeed, as early as 1902 one British author wrote a book, *The American Invaders,* warning against the takeover of the European economy by such American predators as Singer Sewing Machine, Otis Elevator, and General Electric.

Then, after World War II, the development of MNCs truly accelerated. Since 1945 direct private investment in international ventures has increased, on average, about 10% annually, and it is currently expanding at over $200 billion a year. In the process, modern MNCs became economic goliaths that account for a growing percentage of trade and other forms of international commerce.

There are now over 63,000 MNCs. They are not only numerous; they also pack enormous economic muscle. The top 100 MNCs alone have about $6 trillion in assets, employ over 13 million people, and had sales (gross corporate product, GCP) of $4.4 trillion in 2001. This GCP equaled 14% of the combined GDPs of the world's countries. It is also worth noting that of all MNCs, 77% are based in the North; all but 4 of the top 100 MNCs are based there. As a result, they contribute to the wealth and economic power of the EDCs at, some analysts would say, the expense of the South.

Did You Know That:

The MNC with the greatest number of workers is Wal-Mart, with more than 1.3 million employees. Wal-Mart has more employees in its 3,200 U.S. facilities and 1,100 foreign facilities than any of the world's 44 smallest countries have people.

Monetary Relations

The increased flow of trade and capital means that **monetary relations**, including exchange rates, interest rates, and other monetary considerations, have become an increasingly significant factor in both international and domestic economic health. This has always been true, but as trade and other economic relations have expanded, the importance of monetary interchange has increased proportionately. To begin to explore the complex area of monetary relations here and in later chapters, we can look at the evolution of the monetary system, how exchange rates work, and the calculation and impact of the balance of payments.

The Globalization of the Monetary System

The dramatic growth of world trade, international investment, and other aspects of international economic interchange already detailed in this chapter have necessarily been accompanied by a globalization of the monetary system. We can examine that by looking at the globalization of money, the globalization of financial services, North-South patterns of money and banking, and the international regulation of money.

The Globalization of Money Increased trade, investment, and other factors have set off a torrent of money moving in international channels. The volume of currency exchange has reached such a point that it is impossible to calculate very accurately, but it is not unreasonable to estimate that the currency flow is about $1.5 trillion a day, or $548 trillion a year. About two-thirds of this moves through the banking centers in just four countries: Germany, Japan, the United Kingdom, and the United States. Central banks use their monetary reserves (foreign currencies and gold) to try to control exchange rates by buying or selling currency. The problem is that these reserves amount to only about two days' worth of global currency transactions. This limits the ability of the central banks to control currency fluctuations, thereby endangering monetary exchange stability and, by extension, economic prosperity.

The Globalization of Financial Services To accommodate the globalization of money, there has been a parallel globalization of banking and other financial services. In a relatively short period of time, banks have grown from hometown to national to multinational enterprises. Another indicator of increased international financial ties is the level of international lending by private banks. Just the top 50 multinational banks controlled assets of nearly $22 trillion in 2002, giving them immense financial power in the global economy. Like MNCs, most of the biggest international banks, including the top 50, are based in the North.

These international banks play an important role in the world economy because of the influence they have over flow of loans, investment capital, and other financial transaction across borders. For example, American banks have $478 in foreign assets (such as overseas loans) and $653 million in foreign liabilities (such as foreign deposits in the banks). Moreover, many are involved in international financial services beyond traditional banking. For example, the world largest bank, Japan's Mizuho Holding, Inc. (assets: $1.3 trillion), has such nonbanking subsidiaries as Shinko Securities, a brokerage firm, and Mizuho Capital, a venture capital firm. The second largest bank, Citigroup, Inc. (assets: $1.1 trillion), owns, among other companies, Travelers Insurance, Diners Club International, and the Smith Barney brokerage house.

The International Regulation of Money As trade, transnational investing, and other forms of international economic interchange increased during the 20th century, it became clear that some mechanisms needed to be created to help regulate the rapidly expanding flow of currencies across borders. The most pressing problem was, and still is, how to stabilize the values of currencies against one another. To that end, there have been a number of regional and global efforts to keep exchange rates stable and to otherwise ensure that currency issues do not impede economic activity.

The most advanced efforts have been in the European Union, which has the European Central Bank and now a common currency, the euro. At the global level, the International Monetary Fund, which is detailed in chapter 14, has the primary responsibility for attempting to maintain monetary stability.

Exchange Rates

Of all the facets of international economic relations, one of the least understood is the importance of the ebb and flow of the world's currencies. **Exchange rates** are, very simply, the values of two currencies in relation to each other—for example, how many U.S. dollars per Japanese yen and vice versa. Exchange rates are important because they affect several aspects of the balance of payments and the health of domestic economies. Fundamentally, a decline in the exchange rate of your country's currency in relation to another country's currency means that things you buy in or from that country will be more expensive and things that the other country buys in or from you will be less expensive. If your country's currency increases in value, things you buy in or from that country will be less expensive and things that the other country buys in or from you will be more expensive. For a fuller explanation of this, see the section "How Exchange Rates Work" in the Explanatory Notes on page 554.

One example of the dramatic change in the value of a currency involves the exchange rate of the U.S. dollar versus Japan's yen (¥) since 1985, as shown in Figure 12.4. In January of that year, one dollar was worth 258 yen ($1 = ¥258). From that point, the dollar-yen exchange rate dropped to as low as $1 = ¥80 in 1995 and stood at $1 = ¥107 in January 2004. The normal way of discussing this change would be to say that the U.S. dollar in 1995 was 68% weaker versus the yen than it was in 1985 and in 2004 was 34% stronger than it was in 1995. Does weak equal bad and strong equal good, though? That depends.

If you are an American, a relatively strong dollar versus the yen is good news if you are going to buy a Japanese automobile. It will cost less. But if you are a U.S. worker producing cars, you may get laid off because relatively inexpensive foreign cars cut into the domestic market. If you are a traveler and the dollar is strong, going to Japan will be less costly because your dollar will be worth more there. If you are in the American tourist industry, however, you will be harmed by the strong dollar since fewer Japanese will visit the United States because their yen will be worth less there. The list need not go on to make the point that currency fluctuations are a two-edged sword that has both financial benefits and drawbacks no matter which way it swings.

On a more general level, if your national currency is strengthening, inflation will probably go down in your country because the foreign products you buy will be less expensive. Also, your standard of living may go up because you can buy more imported goods to improve your material well-being.

The changes in the yen/dollar exchange rate illustrate currency fluctuations.

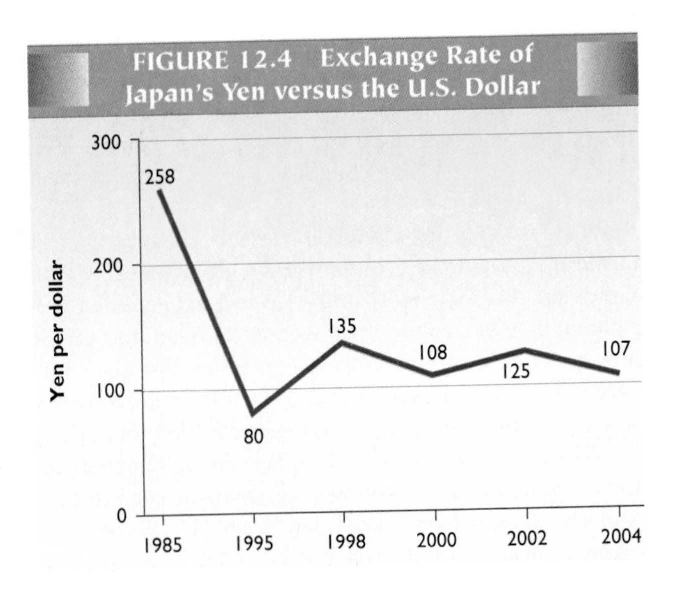

If, on the other hand, you are a U.S. manufacturer trying to sell something to the Japanese, the dollar's rise is bad news because your product's price will rise in those countries and you will probably export less. If you work for one of those companies, your standard of living could plummet if you are laid off. A declining currency, then, benefits businesses that export and may also translate into more jobs as factories expand to meet new orders.

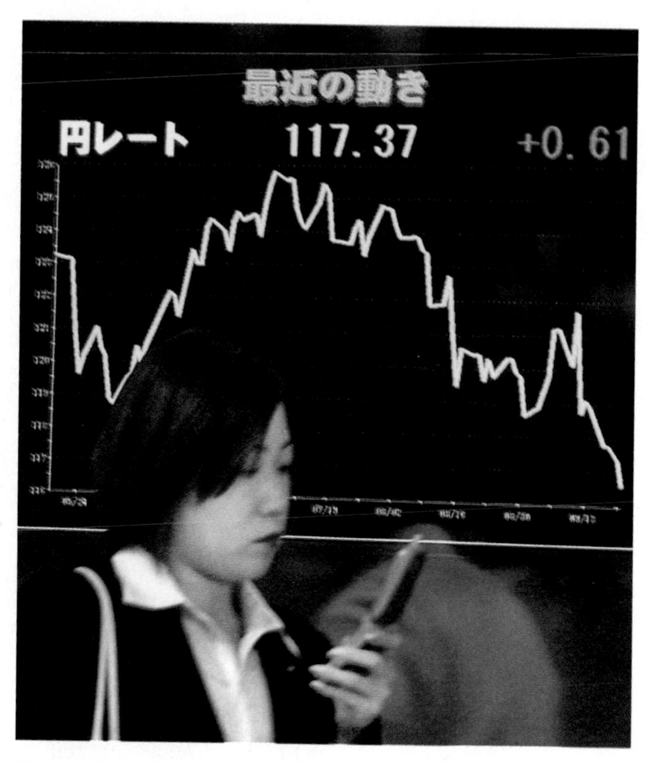

The exchange rate, the shift in values among currencies, is a major factor influencing trade, investment, and other capital flows in the global economy. The degree to which the value of currencies can fluctuate is captured in this photograph of a woman passing by a chart at Tokyo's foreign exchange market tracking the value of the yen versus the dollar. The figure "117.37" is the number of yen per dollar that day, and its current fluctuation is displayed at the end of the line to the right. The exchange rate along the vertical axis ranges from ¥126 = $1 at the top to ¥116 = $1 at the bottom. On the horizontal axis, each numbered time period is two weeks. As you can see, from its beginning point to the left, during a two-month period the number of yen per dollar fell sharply, then rose gradually, only to begin a longer term decline about mid-chart.

Balance of Payments

Along with exchange rates, another complicated aspect of international political economy that is central to understanding a country's overall health in the global economy is that country's balance of payments. Many of the matters that we have already discussed, including exports and imports, the ebb and flow of investment capital and investment returns, and international borrowing and other financial flows, combine to determine a country's **balance of payments**, a figure that represents the entire flow of money into and out of a country—that is, credits minus debits.

It is important to understand the components of the overall balance of payments to determine whether a country has a net inflow or a net outflow of financing. The United States has since 1989, when it had a balance-of-payments surplus of $15.3 billion, steadily amassed larger and larger balance-of-payments deficits, reaching $481 billion in 2002. The primary cause has been the mounting U.S. merchandise trade deficit, which grew to $483 billion that year from $101 billion in 1990. Payments on the national debt are a second factor in the growing U.S. balance-of-payments deficit. The accumulated federal debt to the private sector is over $3 trillion, and about one-third of that is to foreign bondholders to whom the U.S. government paid $72 billion in interest in 2002.

What is even more worrisome than the dollar amounts of the U.S. deficit is the rising percentage of the national economy that it represents (Krugman, 1998; Lincoln, 1998). In the 1970s and 1980s, there was a surplus. For most of the 1990s, the United States economy took in between 1% and 2% less than it spent. That shot up to 3.5% in 1999, was over 4% in 2000 and 2001, and stood at 4.7% in 2002. That worries analysts. They ask, "How much longer can the United States continue to spend more than it earns and support the resumption of global growth?" The answer is that "At some point . . . the United States' [current account deficit] . . . will become too great a burden on the U.S. economy," touching off severe financial repercussions.[3]

Globalization and Interdependence: Debating the Future

There is no doubt that the expansion of world trade, investment, and currency exchange has profoundly affected countries and their citizens. Economic **interdependence** has inexorably intertwined personal, national, and international prosperity. Domestic economics,

Not everyone sees globalization as progress. Antiglobalization protesters have tried to disrupt most recent international economic meetings, including the September 2003 ministerial meeting of the World Trade Organization held in Cancún, Mexico. Those who oppose globalization see it in terms of a predator that seems to be about to devour the Mexican farmer walking in front of the banner during the WTO meeting.

employment, inflation, and overall growth are heavily dependent on foreign markets, imports of resources, currency exchange rates, capital flows, and other international economic factors. Globalization is a reality.

What is in doubt is how much further economic interdependence will or should proceed. Indeed, there is a crucial debate being held across the world in government councils, academic circles, the media, and elsewhere about the advantages and disadvantages of economic globalization. For example, like the leaders of most EDCs, President Bush believes that "globalization is unavoidable and is positive, because it increases trade, and thus production, and thus wealth, and thus the number of jobs that there are across the world."[4] His view is no different from that of his predecessor, President Clinton, who argued, "Those who wish to roll back the forces of globalization because they fear its disruptive consequences . . . are plainly wrong. Fifty years of experience shows that greater economic integration and political cooperation are positive forces."[5] Others denounce globalization based on the capitalist "free-market" model as destructive, promoting poverty in the LDCs, damaging the environment, and causing other ills. Arguing that "our global village has caught fire," President Hosni Mubarak of Egypt has portrayed the "emerging world" as a place where "there is a bitter sentiment of injustice, a sense that there must be something wrong with a system that wipes out years of hard-won development because of changes in market sentiment."[6] Taking the same view, President Luiz Inácio Lula da Silva of Brazil objects to what he sees as the prevailing view in the EDCs that "there is now only one god—the market."[7] These views and the growing demands that the benefits of globalization be distributed more evenly mean that globalization is "fragile" according to Secretary-General Kofi Annan. "If we cannot make globalization work for all, in the end it will work for none," Annan warns. "The unequal distribution of benefits and the imbalances in global rule-making, which characterize globalization today, inevitably will produce backlash and protectionism. And that, in turn, threatens to undermine and ultimately unravel the open world economy that has been so painstakingly constructed over the course of the past half-century."[8]

The issue of the impact of globalization on the average citizen and, even more, on the poor (both countries and individuals) has caused a sharp increase in protest movements and demonstrations at meetings of the World Bank, the World Trade Organization (WTO), the IMF, and other organizations identified with promoting the agenda of free economic interchange. Some of the protests have been large and accompanied by violence. As a result, many of the international financial meetings are no longer being held in major cities and, instead, now convene in relatively isolated spots that are easier to control. For example, the resort area of Cancún, Mexico, hosted the 2003 meeting of the WTO trade talks, and the 2003 annual session of the leading EDCs, the Group of 8 (G-8), met in Évian, France, a spa resort near the Swiss border. There France deployed 15,000 police and troops in a ring that kept protesters more than 10 miles away, and Switzerland marshaled several thousand more troops on its side of the border as a bulwark against the more than 50,000 demonstrators who besieged the town.

The main points of that debate are reviewed in the following two sections that outline the case for and against free economic interchange. Think about these points as you read them and decide which view is closer to your own.

The Case for Free Economic Interchange

Advocates of free economic interchange argue from a series of economic and political propositions. Some of these involve trade or some other single aspect of international economic exchange. Other arguments are more general.

General Prosperity The most general economic argument is that trade and other forms of free economic exchange promote prosperity. Especially since the mid-20th century, trade has accounted for a rapidly growing share of the world's economic activity. Trade in 1960 equaled 12% of the collective GDPs of the world's countries. That share grew to 24% in 2001. The meaning of these numbers is that trade consumes more and more of what countries and their workers produce. Without trade, then, or with a marked decline in trade, national economies would slow, perhaps stall, or might even decline. Figure 12.5 demonstrates that trade growth helps drive economic expansion by comparing the growth of two inflation-adjusted measures: the volume of trade and real GDP.

Benefits of Specialization One economic theory supporting free trade holds that each country should efficiently do what it does best. Free trade theory dates back at least to Edward Misselden's *Free Trade or the Means to Make Trade Flourish,* published in England in 1632. Free trade theory is also associated with Adam Smith, who in *The Wealth of Nations* (1776) held that political interference in commerce created inefficiencies that harmed prosperity. This belief that free trade is economically beneficial was further propounded by the English economists David Ricardo in *On the Principles of Political Economy and Taxation* (1817) and John Stuart Mill in *Principles of Political Economy* (1848). Ricardo developed the theory of "competitive advantage," which held that everyone would benefit if each country produced and exported its most cost-efficient products. Based on this view, Mill argued that trade's "advantage consists in a more efficient employment of the productive forces of the world."

The Cost of Protectionism The reverse side of specialization is the cost of protectionism to the country erecting barriers. Tariffs and other types of trade barriers result in

FIGURE 12.5 The Growth of World Trade Volume and Real GDP

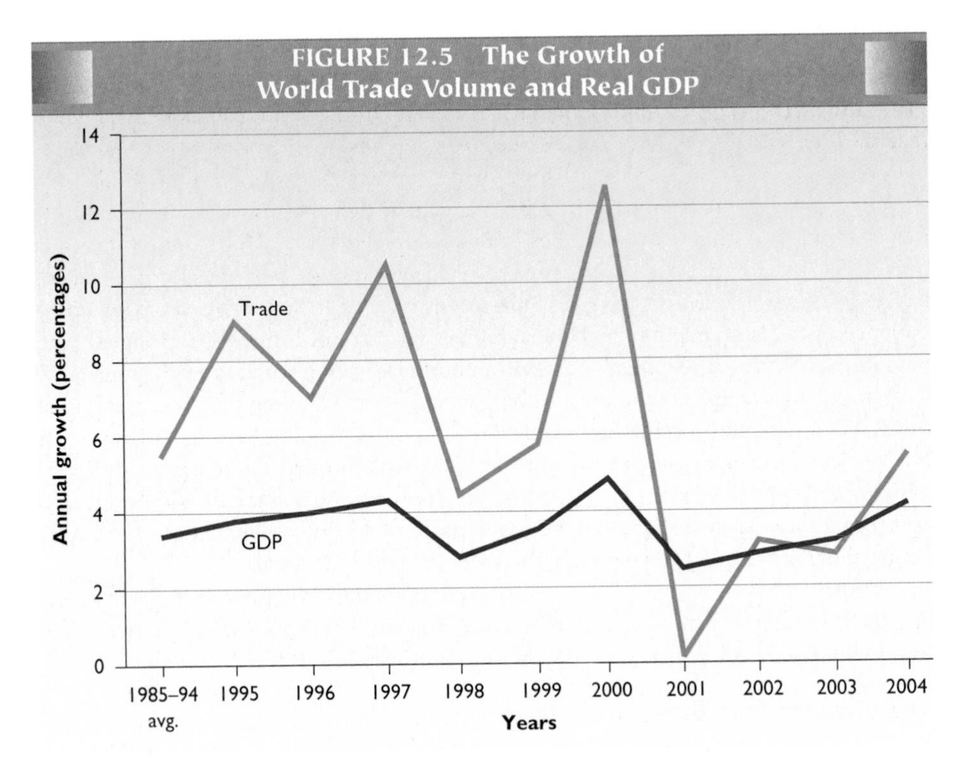

As it long has, the growth of trade has continued to outpace the growth of national economies measured in GDP since the early 1980s. This means that more and more of what countries produce is sold abroad. Therefore national economic prosperity is ever more dependent on trade.

Note: Trade volume is a measurement of trade based on adjustments for inflation, currency exchange rates, and unit prices. The percentages for 2003 and 2004 are IMF estimates.
Data source: IMF, *World Economic Outlook*, September 2003.

higher prices. This occurs because the tariff cost is passed on to consumers or because consumers are forced to buy more expensive domestically produced goods. According to the 2002 annual report of the Dallas regional U.S. Federal Reserve Bank, "In whatever guise, protectionism is pure poison for an economy." To answer the question, How much does it cost to protect a job? the report examined 20 U.S. industries that were being protected by unusually high tariffs or other restrictions. The Federal Reserve Bank's answer was that each job saved costs

> an average of $231,289. . . . Costs range from $132,870 per job saved in the costume jewelry business to $1,376,435 in the benzenoid chemical industry. Protectionism costs U.S. consumers nearly $100 billion annually. It increases not just the cost of the protected items but downstream products as well. Protecting sugar raises candy and soft drink prices; protecting lumber raises home-building costs; protecting steel makes car prices higher; and so forth. Then there are the job losses in downstream industries. Workers in steel-using industries outnumber those in steel-producing industries by 57 to 1. And the protection doesn't even work. Subsidies to steel-producing industries since 1975 have exceeded $23 billion; yet industry employment has declined by nearly two-thirds.[9]

Did You Know That:

About 75% of the $31 billion in toys sold in the United States in 2002 were imported. China accounted for two-thirds of these imports. China also shipped artificial Christmas trees and holiday ornaments to the tune of more than $2 billion to the United States.

Promotion of Competition A third economic free trade argument focuses on competition. Without foreign competition, domestic manufacturers have a captive market. However, a variety of ill effects, from price fixing to lack of innovation, may occur, especially if one corporation dominates its field or if there is monopolistic collusion among supposed

Proponents of globalization argue that one of its many benefits is the capital investment it brings into LDCs. Few Chinese are prosperous enough to own cars. Instead, most still ride bicycles like the ones seen here in front of a General Motors plant in Shanghai, China. In November 2003, GM announced that it would increase its vehicle production in China from 510,000 units annually to 760,000 units by 2006. The plant expansion will bring an infusion of capital into China, and many new workers will be hired to meet the production increase. Wages will certainly be far less than what they are for autoworkers in the EDCs, but the pay will be much greater than what the majority of Chinese who still work in agriculture make. This may, in time, lead to a picture of the workers parking their cars instead of their bikes in front of the plant.

competitors. American automakers seemingly refused to offer U.S. consumers well-built, inexpensive, fuel-efficient small cars until pressure from foreign competition forced them to reshape their product and modernize their production techniques. Competition has also spurred American manufacturers to modernize and streamline their operations to boost productivity, reduce costs, and improve competitiveness. There can be little doubt that the beating that U.S. manufacturers took at the hands of their foreign competitors, especially during the 1970s and 1980s, forced Chrysler, Ford, and General Motors to be more efficient and to offer better products.

Providing Development Capital Fourth, those who are in favor of free economic interchange contend that the flow of investment capital is an important source of development capital for LDCs. The IMF calculates that between 1991 and 2002, more than $2.1 trillion in net foreign direct investment flowed into the LDCs to bolster their economic development. It is also the case that MNC-directed investments provide EDCs with a wide variety of economic benefits. Jobs are one example. Foreign-owned MNCs employ 6 million people in the United States, or about 4% of the U.S. workforce. They pay those workers over $290 billion a year and contribute tens of billions of dollars in U.S. federal, state, and local taxes. At least some of these jobs would not have existed without foreign investment.

World Cooperation A fifth, and this time political, argument claims that free economic interchange promotes world cooperation. Functionalism argues that cooperating in certain specific functions, such as trade, can lead to cooperation in more political areas. If countries can trade together in peace, the interactions will bring greater contact and understanding. Cooperation will then become the rule rather than the exception, and this, it is thought, will lead to political cooperation and interaction. The move toward the political integration of Europe, which began with economic cooperation, is the most frequently cited example.

By a similar logic, supporters of free economic interchange also contend that the flow of investment capital around the world through MNCs promotes transnational cooperation and additionally serves the function of bringing people together through regular contact, cooperation, familiarity, and friendship.

Conflict Inhibition A sixth, and again political, argument for free economic interchange is that it restrains conflict by promoting interdependence, which makes fighting more difficult and more unlikely. In the words of one study, "Higher levels of economically important trade . . . are associated with lower incidences of militarized interstate disputes and war" (Oneal & Russett, 1997:288). One link between peace and trade is the contention that a high degree of interdependence among countries may dissuade or even prevent them from fighting. If oil and iron are necessary to fight, and if Country A supplies Country B's oil, and B supplies A's iron, then they are too enmeshed to go to war.

Much the same case is made for international investment as a restraint on conflict. Arguably, the more we own of each other, the more self-damaging it is to engage in economic or other sorts of aggression. For example, the nearly $152 billion in FDI that Japanese have in U.S. assets and the $66 billion in FDI that Americans have in Japan, not to mention the tens of billions of dollars in FPI, means that war between the two would be a financial disaster. Indeed each country has such an economic stake in the other that it has given rise to the somewhat grim joke that goes, If the Japanese were ever again to attack Pearl Harbor, they would be blowing up their own property, and if the Americans retaliated, Wall Street would suffer massive devastation.

Promoting Democracy A seventh, and once more political, argument advanced by some advocates of economic liberalization is that the openness required for free economic exchange promotes democracy. The argument, as one South Korean political scientist explains, is: "Corrupt, authoritarian governments cannot adjust to the demands of the new globalized world, where you have to have a more transparent, competitive, and rational economic structure."[10] The idea is that it is difficult to simultaneously have a free enterprise system and an authoritarian political system, and gradually the habits of independent decision making inherent in a capitalist system, the flow of ideas within the country and between it and the outside world, and the growth of powerful financial interests all work to undercut the authoritarian political regimes. For example, during the past few years, such NICs as Mexico, South Korea, and Taiwan have had their first truly democratic elections either ever, or in many decades. Particularly appealing is the thought that globalization will eventually moderate China's authoritarian government. According to one analyst, "Global markets and information technology are multiplying the channels through which outside actors can influence Chinese society and, simultaneously undermining the regime's strict control" (Moore, 2001:63; Li & Reuveny, 2003).

The Case against Free Economic Interchange

There are also several political and economic arguments for economic nationalism. Some of these involve trade or some other single aspect of international economic exchange; other arguments are more general.

Protecting the Domestic Economy The need for economic barriers to protect threatened domestic industries and workers from foreign competition is a favorite theme of domestic interest groups and politicians. "I'm not a free trader," a U.S. secretary of commerce once confessed. "The goal," he said, "is to nurture American workers and industry. It is not to adhere to some kind of strict ideology."[11] An associated argument seeks protection for new or still small, so-called infant industries. This is an especially common contention in LDCs trying to industrialize, but it is also heard worldwide. Many economists give the idea of such protection some credibility but argue that supposedly temporary protection too often becomes permanent.

Opponents of the free flow of investment capital also argue that the positive impact of creation or preservation of jobs by the inflow of investment is offset by the loss of jobs when MNCs move operations to another country or when MNCs create new jobs in another country rather than in their own home country. American MNCs, for example, employ about 500,000 more workers in other countries than foreign MNCs employ American workers in the United States. Furthermore, these opponents say, forcing well-paid workers in the United States and elsewhere to compete with poorly paid workers in LDCs depresses the wages and living conditions in EDCs. As a general statement the statistics show that this is not the case, but some types of workers, such as those in manufacturing that directly competes with foreign sources, are especially hard hit. The U.S. clothing industries, for example, have been devastated, with their combined workforce dropping from 2.1 million in 1980 to 1.2 million in 2000. During the same period, the number of American miners and primary metal workers (those in foundries) also sharply declined from 2.2 million to 1.2 million. For the regions where these industries are concentrated, the consequences are especially serious. Some types of white-collar workers in the EDCs are also increasingly at risk of having their jobs "outsourced" to workers in LDCs. For instance, in December 2003, the giant German high-technology firm Siemens announced that it would reallocate a third of its 30,000 software development jobs to China, India, Russia, and other low-wage LDCs. News reports that month indicated that IBM would follow suit, outsourcing up to 4,700 of its computer programmer and other high-tech jobs to LDCs, primarily to India, where a typical worker in the field makes $20,000 annually, compared to $75,000 to $150,000 for experienced American workers. Testifying before Congress in 2003, an official of the U.S. Department of Commerce cited statistics estimating that "over the next 15 years, 3.3 million U.S. service industry jobs—including 1 million IT [information technology] service jobs—and $136 billion in wages will 'move offshore.'" The official commented that "while other analysts offer less dramatic projections, growing number of global competitors are likely to capture increasing shares of IT and white-collar service work."[12]

Lost jobs and wages must also be measured in terms of the ripple effect that multiplies each dollar several times. A worker without a job cannot buy from the local merchant, who in turn cannot buy from the building contractor, who in turn cannot buy from the department store, and so on, rippling out through the economy. Displaced workers also collect unemployment benefits and may even wind up on public assistance programs. These costs are substantial, and although some economists find that they are less than the cost of protecting jobs, the economic costs of unemployment diminish the gains derived from free trade. Finally, there is the psychological damage from being laid off and from other forms of economic dislocation that cannot be measured in dollars and cents.

Diversification Another economic nationalist argument holds that economic diversification should be encouraged. Specialization, it is said, will make a country too dependent on a few resources or products; if demand for those products falls, then economic catastrophe will result. In reality, no modern, complex economy will become that specialized, but the argument does have simplistic appeal.

Compensating for Existing Distortions Yet another economic nationalist argument is that real-world trade distortions exist that are unaccounted for by pure economic theory. The argument goes, nice-guy free-traders will finish last when oil-producing countries set prices; authoritarian governments control exports and imports (state trading); protectionist countries erect NTBs; governments subsidize producers of export items or items that compete with imports; or governments manipulate the exchange rates of their currency by keeping them artificially low to encourage exports and discourage imports. For example, charges of currency manipulation became an increasingly prominent issue between China and the United States in 2003. Washington accused Beijing of suppressing the value of the yuan against the dollar in order to continue the tidal wave of Chinese exports heading east across the Pacific Ocean and the relative paltry flow of American exports moving in the opposite direction. With a presidential election year approaching and the White House especially worried about jobs, President Bush reportedly told visiting Chinese Premier Wen Jiabao in December 2003 that "we have to see concrete progress" toward letting the yuan rise to a realistic level against the dollar.[13] While such action may result in remedies or partial easing of existing distortions, it is unrealistic to imagine that countries will not control trade at least to some degree for economic, strategic, or domestic political reasons. Therefore, many argue that it is prudent to continue to compensate for existing distortions and that it is imprudent to take too far a lead in free trade and suffer negative consequences while others hold back.

Social, Economic, and Environmental Protection The chairman of Dow Chemical Company once confessed, "I have long dreamed of buying an island owned by no nation and establishing the world headquarters of the Dow company on . . . such an island, beholden to no nation or society" (Gruenberg, 1996:339). Critics of MNCs claim that such statements confirm their suspicions that these global enterprises use their ability to move operations around the globe to undercut protections relating to child labor, minimum wages, employment benefits, the ability of workers to organize, and many other socioeconomic standards (Rodrik, 1998). In the estimate of one analyst, "National governments have lost much of their power to direct their own economies because of the power of capital to pick up and leave." The result of the "quantum leap in the ability of transnational corporations to relocate their facilities around the world," he continues, is to make "all workers, communities and countries competitors for these corporations' favor." This competition, he worries, has set off "a 'race to the bottom' in which wages and social and environment conditions tend to fall to the level of the most desperate" (Brecher, 1993:685).

Critics of globalization also charge that, among other evils, the race to the bottom will mean gutting desirable social programs. Europe has built an extensive social welfare support system through government programs and mandates on industries (such as health insurance for workers, paid vacations, and other benefits). Such programs and benefits are costly, however, and European economies struggle to meet them while also keeping the price of their products low enough to be competitive in world markets or even at home compared to imported goods and services.

National Sovereignty One of the fastest-growing sources of sentiment against free economic interchange is the realization of many people that the process is eroding their country's national sovereignty. Many people are shocked to find that sometimes their country's laws and regulations must give way when they clash with rules of the WTO or some other international organization or agreement.

A closely related phenomenon involves the fear that foreign investors will gain control of your country's economy and will be able to influence your political processes and your culture (Bartlett & Seleny, 1998). In the 1960s U.S. investment capital seemed ready to engulf other countries' economies; Jean-Jacques Servan-Schreiber's best-seller, *The American Challenge* (1968), called on Europeans to resist foreign domination. Then, in the second half of the 1980s, when the value of the dollar plunged, the tide of foreign investment reversed. In what seemed a tidal wave of acquisition, foreign investors snapped up such quintessential American brand names as Capitol Records (Great Britain), Roy Rogers (Canada), Alka-Seltzer (Germany), and 7–Eleven (Japan). Cries rang out that the British, among others, were coming. One member of Congress fretted that "for the first time since the Revolution, Americans are being subjected to decisions and dictates from abroad."[14]

Since then, the ceaseless ebb and flow of international finance governed in large part by the rise and fall of the exchange rates of currencies has shifted the tide back and forth. Most recently, Americans have acquired more FDI assets abroad ($251 billion) than foreign interests have bought ($170 billion) in the United States.

The shifting currents of FDI flow and the fears occasioned by foreign ownership have to be put in some perspective. The U.S. economy is so huge that foreign investment is still a minor aspect of the overall economic enterprise. Total foreign investment is just .02% (two one-hundredths) of the estimated $24 quadrillion worth of privately held tangible U.S. assets. Also, foreign investment is spread broadly among many countries. In 2002, the British were the largest direct investors in the United States with $283 billion in assets, and the French were second with $171 billion in FDI. All totaled, though, there were 28 countries with $1 billion or more FDI in the United States. With such diversity, control by any outside country is impossible. It must also be remembered that Americans control more of other people's assets than others hold in U.S. assets. Maybe the British are coming, as the worry goes, with $283 billion worth of control in the United States, but the Yanks are also going, with their $255 billion FDI beachhead in the British economy.

National Security A related political economic nationalist argument involves national defense. The contention is somewhat the reverse of the "conflict inhibition," pro–free trade argument made earlier. Protectionists stress that the country must not become so dependent on foreign sources that it will be unable to defend itself. In recent years, the U.S. government has acted to protect industries ranging from specialty steels to basic textiles, partly in response to warnings that the country was losing its ability to produce weapons systems and uniforms.

Also under the rubric of national security, there is the issue of what can be called strategic trade. The question is how far a country should go in restricting trade and other economic interchanges with countries that are or may become hostile. Currently, the primary focus of the strategic trade debate is on dual-use technology that has peaceful uses but also has military applications.

Trying to maintain the U.S. lead in the multibillion-dollar global computer market, the Bush administration in 2001 raised the level above which individual licenses for computer exports to potentially hostile countries (such as China and Russia) are required from 85,000 millions of theoretical operations per second (MTOPS) to 190,000 MTOPS. While the move will help preserve the dominance of U.S. computer manufacturers in the global marketplace, it also creates concerns about how those computers will be used in countries such as China. At about the same time as the Bush administration allowed increasingly more sophisticated computers to be sold without restriction to China, the prestigious Rand Institute issued a report on the potential of a conflict with China, commenting that China was "able to take advantage of various new technologies that are commercially available. They [the Chinese] can't compete with the U.S. military across the board," the report continued, "but if they can pick niche areas, they can make life more difficult for us." From a U.S. policy-making perspective, one staff member in Congress commented that "the Rand report underscores . . . the serious undermining of U.S. national security due to relaxed restrictions on export of dual-use technologies. The Chinese threat of a 'high-tech Pearl Harbor' is well within their reach."[15]

The issue well illustrates the tug of selling billions of dollars of aircraft and other equipment abroad versus the pull of supplying a less than friendly country with the capacity to increase the sophistication of its military equipment. "The U.S. faces excruciating trade-offs," observed one former ranking U.S. trade official. "On the one hand, we have overwhelming commercial goals. On the other, we have to be careful about transferring technology, first because there could be unintended military consequences, and secondly because we could be transferring our competitiveness."[16]

Policy Tool A seventh economic nationalist argument maintains that trade is a powerful political tool that can be used to further a country's interests. The extension or withdrawal of trade and other economic benefits also has an important—albeit hard-to-measure—symbolic value. Clearly, economic tools can be used to promote a country's political goals and free economic interchange necessarily limits the availability of economic tools to pursue policy.

A current example is the U.S. embargo on most trade with and travel to Cuba, which has existed since 1960, despite the normalization over time of trade relations with the Soviet Union, China, and other countries that were or remain communist and numerous other countries, such as Saudi Arabia, that are overtly authoritarian. The debate over the wisdom of continuing the sanctions on the regime of Fidel Castro came to the fore in 2002 when former President Jimmy Carter visited Cuba and, in a televised address, expressed his hope that the Bush administration would "soon act to permit unrestricted travel between the United States and Cuba, establish open trading relationships, and repeal the embargo." Carter went on to say that "the embargo freezes the existing impasse, induces anger and resentment, restricts the freedoms of U.S. citizens, and makes it difficult for us to exchange ideas and respect."[17]

President Bush saw things very differently. As he told a convention of Cuban Americans in Florida just five days later, "Well-intentioned ideas about trade will merely prop up this dictator, enrich his cronies, and enhance the totalitarian regime. It will not help the Cuban people. With real political and economic reform, trade can benefit the Cuban people and allow them to share in the progress of our times."[18]

The Debate in Perspective

To return to the point with which we began this section, the clash between the forces that favor the advancement of free economic interchange and those that oppose it will be one of the most pivotal struggles in the years ahead. The headlong rush toward globalization that began after World War II and proceeded with growing momentum in the decades that followed has brought the world much closer to a truly global economy than seemed possible a half-century ago and has made the term "national economy" something of a misnomer. The world economy has prospered, and some countries and individuals have benefited greatly. This has been particularly true for the EDCs, but statistics make clear that even for most of the LDCs, health, education, and many other social conditions have improved. Moreover, in addition to broad support among political leaders, economists, and others, globalization is favored by most of the public, as one study found in a survey of 44 countries. Figure 12.6 shows that overall 59% of all respondents characterized globalization as good. Another 24% said they were unsure, and, significantly, only 17% characterized globalization as bad.

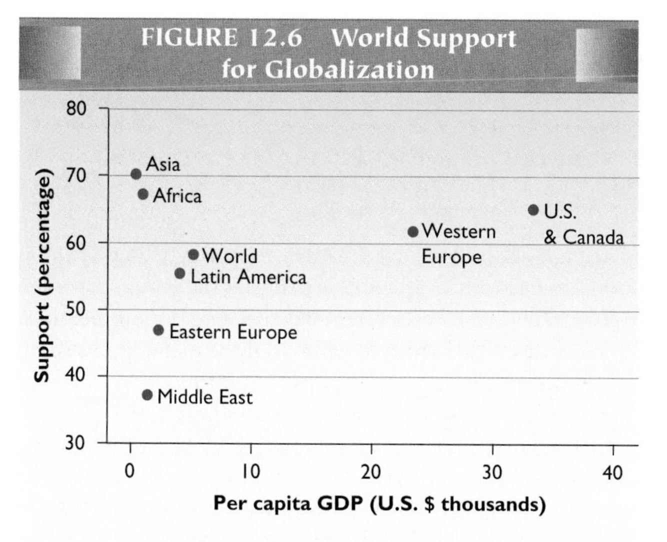

	Per capita GDP	% Good	% Bad	% Unsure
World	$5,120	59	17	24
U.S. & Canada	$33,108	66	20	12
Latin America	$4,713	57	21	22
Western Europe	$23,035	62	28	10
Eastern Europe	$2,101	47	22	31
Africa	$640	67	11	66
Asia	$480	70	9	21
Middle East	$1,187	37	22	39

This chart shows both the percentage of people in a region indicating they believe globalization is good and the average per capita GDP of the countries in that region that were included in the survey. Intuitively one might expect the greatest support for globalization to be in the more prosperous countries, and the strong support in the United States, Canada, and Western Europe meets that expectation. But defying that expectation, support is just as high or higher in Asia and Africa, the two regions with the lowest per capita GDP. Notice in the data table that the percentage of people in most regions answering "Unsure" is high, making the percentages of those responding that globalization is bad quite low in all regions. Thus support or opposition to globalization does not seem strongly linked to economic circumstance.

Notes: Japan was omitted from Asia because it is an EDC. Including Japan would have increased the region's per capita GDP but would not have significantly changed its level of support for globalization.

Data source: The Pew Research Center for People and the Press, Global Attitudes Project (2002). Calculations by author.

The advances that globalization has made and general support for it does not mean, however, that it is an unmitigated success. The changes associated with globalization have occurred in a largely unregulated international system, and, as a result, the benefits and costs that accompany most change have been unequally distributed. Other countries, their citizens, and even many people in prosperous countries have either not benefited or have been harmed. In the generally free-for-all global economic system, globalization has also been associated with such negatives as damage to the environment, the creation of sweatshops, and the utilization of child labor. In this way, economic globalization has marked parallels to the economic expansion that occurred in the aftermath of the industrial revolution in the unregulated capitalist systems in Great Britain, the rest of Western Europe, and later the United States. Their economies grew rapidly, overall data showed advancing prosperity, and some individuals accumulated huge wealth. By the mid-1800s, though, there was an increasing outcry by workers, social reformers, and others that the abuses of the system needed to be addressed. The resulting reform in the United States came during the Progressive Era around the turn of the century and the New Deal beginning in 1933, and, to a degree, continues today as Americans debate environmental policy, social welfare policy, business ethics, and other matters. This debate has now begun about economic globalization in the international system. Protesters are now common at meetings of the IMF, the World Bank, and the other institutions at the forefront of globalization. At the urging of the leaders of the LDCs and others, there is also a growing realization among the leaders of the EDCs and other supporters of globalization that, as Jordan's Queen Noor told an international conclave not long ago, "The promise of globalization is a fallacy if it is not shared," and that steps are needed to avoid "a world growing more polarized and unstable due to the widening gap between the haves and the have nots."[19]

It is also important to remember that globalization extends far beyond the growth of economic interdependence. Modern communications and travel are profoundly increasing our ability to interact. Cultures are meeting, merging, and sometimes clashing as new customs and ideas, largely exported by the dominant West, seemingly inundate the cultures of Asia, the Middle East, and elsewhere. Some matters, such as whether fast food is an advance or an abomination, are relatively minor. Others, such as the status of women and the proper relationship between church (mosque, temple) and state, are momentous. What is occurring, as Queen Noor says, is that "people whose only remaining possession is their culture are relying on ethnic and religious divisions to reinforce their sense of identity in an increasingly impersonal, homogenized world." To address that, she counsels, "Globalization . . . must shed the idea that its purpose is to mold weaker countries' cultures in the image of strong ones."

To continue the thought of Jordan's queen, what this means to the globalization debate is that globalization:

> is not an idea to be accepted or rejected, but a fact—a force to be managed with pragmatism and vision. Time and energy can be best used determining how to harness it, rather than debating its advantages or shortcomings. Whether our shared destiny is detrimental or beneficial to the world majority depends on how we approach it—with self-interest disguised as progress in the triumph of the market, or with cultural sensitivity, caution, and a true sense of participation.

Chapter Summary

Theories of International Political Economy

1. Economics and politics are closely intertwined aspects of international relations. This interrelationship has become even more important in recent history. Economics has become more important internationally because of dramatically increased trade levels, ever-tightening economic interdependence between countries, and the growing impact of international economics on domestic economics. The study of international political economy (IPE) examines the interaction between politics and economics.
2. There are many technical aspects to explaining and understanding the international political economy, and those not familiar with economic terms and methods should review the "Economics: Technical Terms and Sources" section in the Explanatory Notes on page N-2.
3. The approaches to IPE can be roughly divided into three groups: economic nationalism (mercantilism), economic internationalism (liberalism), and economic structuralism.
4. The core of the economic nationalist doctrine is the realist idea that the state should harness and use national economic strength to further national interest. Therefore, the state should shape the country's economy and its foreign economic policy to enhance state power.
5. Economic internationalists are liberals who believe that international economic relations should and can be harmonious because prosperity is available to all and is most likely to be achieved and preserved through cooperation. The main thrust of economic internationalism is to separate politics from economics, to create prosperity by freeing economic interchange from political restrictions.
6. Economic structuralists hold that world politics is based on the division of the world into have and have-not countries, with the EDCs keeping the LDCs weak and poor in order to exploit them. There are two types of economic structuralists. Marxists believe that the entire capitalist-based system must be replaced with domestic and international socialist systems

before economic equity can be achieved. Less radical economic structuralist theories include dependency and world systems theory, which stress reform of the current market system by ending the system of dependency.

Two Economic Worlds: North and South

7. Whether or not you subscribe to economic structuralist theories, it is clear that the world is generally divided into two economic spheres: a wealthy North and a much less wealthy South. There are some overlaps between the two spheres, but in general the vast majority of the people and countries of the South are much less wealthy and industrially developed than the countries of the North and their people. The South also has a history of direct and indirect colonial control by countries of the North.

The Growth and Extent of International Political Economy

8. The history of international economics is ancient, but a change that has occurred since the second half of the 20th century is that the level of economic interchange (trade, investments and other capital flows, and monetary exchange) has increased at an exponential rate.
9. Within the overall expansion of the international economy, there is, however, a pattern in which most of the trade, investment, and other aspects of international political economy are dominated by the North and work to its advantage.
10. Trade in goods and services is booming, having grown over 3,900% from $20 billion in 1913 to nearly $7.9 trillion in 2002. There has also been a rapid expansion of international financial ties. This flow of investment can be examined by reviewing types of foreign investments and multinational corporations.
11. The increased flow of trade and capital means that monetary relations, including exchange rates, interest rates, and other monetary considerations, are a significant economic factor. It is not unreasonable to estimate that the daily currency flow is $1.5 trillion, or some $548 trillion a year.
12. The expansion of world trade and investment has profoundly affected countries and their citizens. Economic interdependence has inexorably intertwined national and international economic health.
13. There are significant arguments on both sides of the question of whether or not to continue to expand free international economic interchange. Advocates of free trade contend that it results in greater efficiency and lower costs, and that international commerce promotes world cooperation and inhibits conflict. Opponents argue that economic barriers are needed to protect domestic industry, that relying on other countries is dangerous for national security reasons, and that trade can be a valuable policy tool.

For a chapter quiz, interactive activities, web links, PowerWeb articles, and much more, visit **www.mhhe.com/rourke10/** and go to chapter 12. Or, while accessing the site, click on Course-Wide Content and view recent international relations articles in the *New York Times.*

Key Terms

balance of payments
countries in transition (CITs)
current dollars
dependency theory
economically developed countries (EDCs)
economic internationalism
economic nationalism
economic structuralism
exchange rates
extreme poverty
foreign direct investment (FDI)
foreign portfolio investment (FPI)
gross domestic product (GDP)
gross national product (GNP)
interdependence
international political economy (IPE)
least developed countries (LLDCs)
less developed countries (LDCs)
manufactured goods
Marxism
merchandise trade
monetary relations
multinational corporations (MNCs)
neocolonialism
newly industrializing countries (NICs)
North
primary products
purchasing power parity (PPP)
real dollars
services trade
South
world systems theory

CHAPTER

13

National Economic Competition: The Traditional Road

NATIONAL ECONOMIC POWER: ASSETS AND UTILIZATION

National Economic Power

Methods of Manipulating Economic Interchange

Applying Economic Power

THE NORTH AND INTERNATIONAL POLITICAL ECONOMY

The National Economies of the North

National Economic Issues and Policies of the North

THE SOUTH AND INTERNATIONAL POLITICAL ECONOMY

Development in the South: Status

Development in the South: Capital Needs

Development in the South: LDC Perspectives and Policies

THE FUTURE OF NATIONAL ECONOMIC POLICY

CHAPTER SUMMARY

KEY TERMS

I greatly fear my money is not safe.

—William Shakespeare, *The Comedy of Errors*

Having nothing, nothing can he lose.

—William Shakespeare, *Henry VI, Part III*

No one can . . . love his neighbor on an empty stomach.

—Woodrow Wilson, speech, May 23, 1919

As the images of life lived anywhere on our globe become available to all, so will the contrast between the rich and the poor become a force impelling the deprived to demand a better life from the powers that be.

—Nelson Mandela, to a joint session of the U.S. Congress, October 7, 1994

CHAPTER OBJECTIVES

After completing this chapter, you should be able to:

- Analyze why politics and economics are intertwined aspects of international relations.
- Discuss how economics has taken on a more important role in international relations.
- Identify the source of economic power.
- Analyze the use of economic statecraft.
- Describe the economies of the North and their current political issues.
- Describe the economies of the South and their current political issues.
- Discuss the sources of hard currency.
- Analyze the effects of debt crisis on the global financial community and the role of loans.
- Discuss LDCs' need for investment capital and the difficulty of acquiring it.
- Evaluate the role of foreign aid in the global political community.
- Analyze the demand for a New International Economic Order.
- Identify the various impediments to free trade.
- Discuss the arguments for and against free international economic interchange.

Economic nationalism—the state-centric approach to international political economy—is the traditional road that countries have long followed. While it is true that there has been considerable movement toward liberalizing international economic relations in recent decades, economic nationalism remains the dominant practice in global economic affairs for two reasons: First, states remain the principal actors on the world stage. Second, these states most often use economic tools and formulate economic policy to benefit themselves, not the global community. This chapter will explore the economic nationalist approach, including discussions of national economic power assets and the ways that countries utilize their economic power (Milner, 1998).

National Economic Power: Assets and Utilization

The use of political power to achieve national economic goals and the reciprocal use of economic power to gain national political goals is at the core of economic nationalism. This orientation, which is also called "economic statecraft" or "mercantilism," remains in one form or another the basic approach of states to international political economy in the current state-based, quasi-anarchical system. The reason states take this self-serving approach is understandable. Each state is largely responsible for its own economic well-being. Certainly there is foreign aid, and other forms of financial assistance are available from states and from international governmental organizations (IGOs), such as the United Nations, the International Monetary Fund (IMF), and the World Bank. Such assistance, however, is neither guaranteed nor munificent. Thus, as is true for military security, economic security is based mostly on self-help.

National Economic Power

It is axiomatic that to pursue economic statecraft effectively, a country needs to possess considerable economic power. Chapter 8 has already reviewed the national infrastructure (technological sophistication, transportation systems, information and communications capabilities) that provides part of the basis for building a powerful economy. To these factors this chapter will add as determinants of national power the following: financial position, natural resources, industrial output, and agricultural output.

Financial Position

The center of any country's economic power is its basic financial position. To think about that, consider Table 13.1 and the 12 criteria of financial strength detailed there for the United States. Certainly, the U.S. economy is by far the world's largest, is prosperous, and is immensely powerful. But also, like the biblical Goliath, it has worrisome vulnerabilities. Most of the U.S. weaknesses are associated with lack of financial discipline, as detailed in the table. For example, the U.S. government during the period FY1950–FY2004 had a budget deficit for 46 of the 54 years and spent $3.8 trillion more than it raised. If accurate, the projected budgets for FY2005–FY2009 will add another $1.4 trillion to that total. One result of chronic deficit spending is that Americans are paying huge sums in interest ($156 billion in FY2004) on the $4.4 trillion in federal bonds sold to finance the debt. These figures are expected to rise in FY2009 to a $5.9 trillion debt and $299 billion in annual interest payments. Similarly, the United States had a **net trade** (exports minus imports) deficit during all but two years between 1971 and 2003, importing $3.6 trillion more in goods and services than it exported during the period.

TABLE 13.1 Measures of U.S. Financial Power

Financial Measure	Positive (+) Negative (–) Neutral (0)	United States/ Comparative
Overall GNP, 2001	+	$9.8 trillion/ 31% of world GNP
Per capita GNP, 2001	+	$34,280/ world's fifth highest
Per capita GNP/PPP, 2001	+	$34,280/ world's second highest (after Luxembourg)
Real GNP growth rate, 1995–2004	+	Good at 3.2%/ 2.7% for all EDCs
Inflation, 1995–2004	+	Low, 1.7%/ 1.5% for all EDCs
Unemployment, 1995–2004	0	Moderate, 5.1%/ 6.6% for all EDCs
Budget balance as % of GNP, 2003	–	4.3% deficit/ 3.3% deficit for all EDCs
Interest payments as % of national budget, 2000	–	13%/ 7% for all EDCs
Balance of payments as % of GNP, 2002	–	4.6% deficit/ 0.7% deficit for all EDCs
Trade balance as % of GNP, 2002	–	3.2% deficit/ 1.3% surplus for all other EDCs
Savings rate as % of disposable income, 2002	–	3.7%/ 6.5% for all other EDCs
Reserves as % of GNP, 2001	–	0.7%/ 5.5% for all other EDCs

Notes: GNP/PPP is calculated for purchasing power parity as discussed in chapter 12. Trade balance includes goods and services. Disposable income is income after taxes.

Data sources: World Bank (2003); IMF, *World Economic Outlook* (September 2003).

The United States is the largest and by far most powerful country in the world, and, except for tiny Luxembourg, Americans are the wealthiest people on Earth in terms of the purchasing power of their per capita GDP. Moreover, recent U.S. economic growth has been good, inflation has been low, and unemployment moderate. Yet there are also troubling signs for U.S. financial power including significant deficits in the federal budget, the balance of payments, and trade. Additionally, the U.S. government has high interest payments on the debt accrued from previous budget deficits. Americans also save considerably less than people in most other EDCs, making them more vulnerable to economic reverses, and the U.S. government's scant financial reserves compared to GNP limit the government's ability to intervene in the global currency exchange markets.

Deficit spending, accumulating significant foreign debts, and other such practices can weaken a country's financial position over time and even lead to collapse. This possibility is well illustrated by the recent travails of Argentina. Plagued by a variety of economic woes and unable to meet its international debts, Argentina in 2001 fell into an economic crisis that toppled several governments and set off civil unrest. The exchange rate of Argentina's currency, the peso, collapsed in early 2002, with its value versus the U.S. dollar falling 71% from US$1 = 1 peso to $1 = 3.45 pesos. The resulting higher prices for imported products and Argentineans' loss of confidence in their currency set off an inflationary spiral. For example, during six months in 2002, the price increases of cooking oil, flour, eggs, and vinegar ranged from 107% to 161%, laundry detergent was up 122%, and toothpaste crested at 111%. Other big price jumps included rice (97%), chicken (82%), and milk (67%). Also reflecting the tailspin of the peso, annual interest rates soared from 8% in 2000 to a peak of 68% in 2002. Unable to borrow money to finance operations, Argentinean businesses struggled. Construction fell 50%, and unemployment rose to 21% by midyear. The country's real GDP (controlled for inflation) declined 4.4% in 2001 and a further 10.9% in 2002. Internal reforms and assistance by the IMF and other international sources have helped Argentina begin the road to recovery. In early 2003, interest rates had fallen to 27%, inflation was down to 14%, and unemployment had declined to 16%. All these rates were still too high, but the IMF was predicting that the Argentinean economy would have a real growth rate of 5.5% for the year, and the country at least appeared to be on the road to recovery.

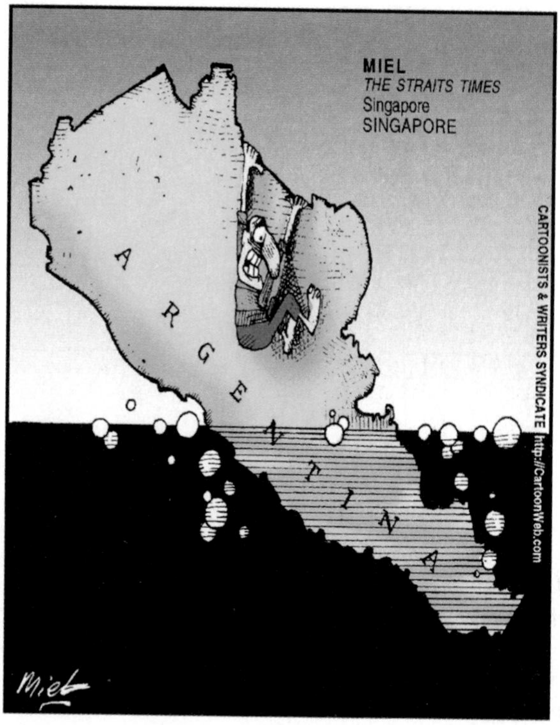

This editorial drawing from a newspaper in Singapore represents the rampant inflation, high unemployment, and other dire financial conditions that have undermined Argentina's economy and its national power since late 2001.

Natural Resources

The possession, or lack, of energy, mineral, and other natural resources has become an increasingly important power factor as industrialization and technology have advanced. Natural resources affect power in three related ways: (1) The greater a country's self-sufficiency in vital natural resources, the greater its power. (2) Conversely, the greater a country's dependency on foreign sources for vital natural resources, the less its power. (3) The greater a country's surplus (over domestic needs) of vital resources needed by other countries, the greater its power.

Each of these three related points plays a key role in determining international relationships. Lack of self-sufficiency creates a dependency on other countries. For example, the United States has a degree of vulnerability because it imports all or most of 51of the 58 minerals that the U.S. Department of the Interior lists as important to the country's economy. By contrast, some countries such as Russia and Canada are in a somewhat stronger resource position because they are more self-sufficient. Still other countries are almost totally dependent on foreign sources for their natural resource requirements. Japan, for one, imports virtually all of its primary energy supplies (oil, natural gas, and others) and 90% or more of most economically essential minerals.

The key here is not just production; it is production compared to consumption. With less than 5% of the world population, the United States produced about 11% of world's crude petroleum during 2003, putting U.S. output just behind that of the world leader, Saudi Arabia. That would seem advantageous, but it is not because the United States consumes 26% of global petroleum production. As a result, the United States in 2003 had to import approximately 11.3 million barrels (or 474.6 million gallons) of petroleum each day. One concern is that U.S. petroleum dependency makes the country vulnerable to disruptions of the flow of oil that it needs to maintain prosperity. Second, the dependency causes a huge outflow of financial resources. With imported petroleum costing Americans about $40 per barrel in mid-2004, they were spending nearly $452 million dollars a day (or $165 billion a year) importing oil.

Did You Know That:

U.S. petroleum consumption in 2002 came to 1,052 gallons per American.

Possessing a surplus of vital resources is a third important power factor. As is evident in Figure 13.1, the global imbalance of oil production has dramatically underlined this point. Oil resources have been the chief source of export revenue for many countries in the Middle East and, despite the depressed oil market during most of the 1990s, so-called black gold has allowed some of that region's countries to amass huge financial reserves. In 2003, for example, Saudi Arabia exported about $59 billion in petroleum products. Oil has also increased the global political focus on the petroleum-producing countries and on their diplomatic power, especially the countries in the Middle East, which account for about two-thirds of world petroleum reserves.

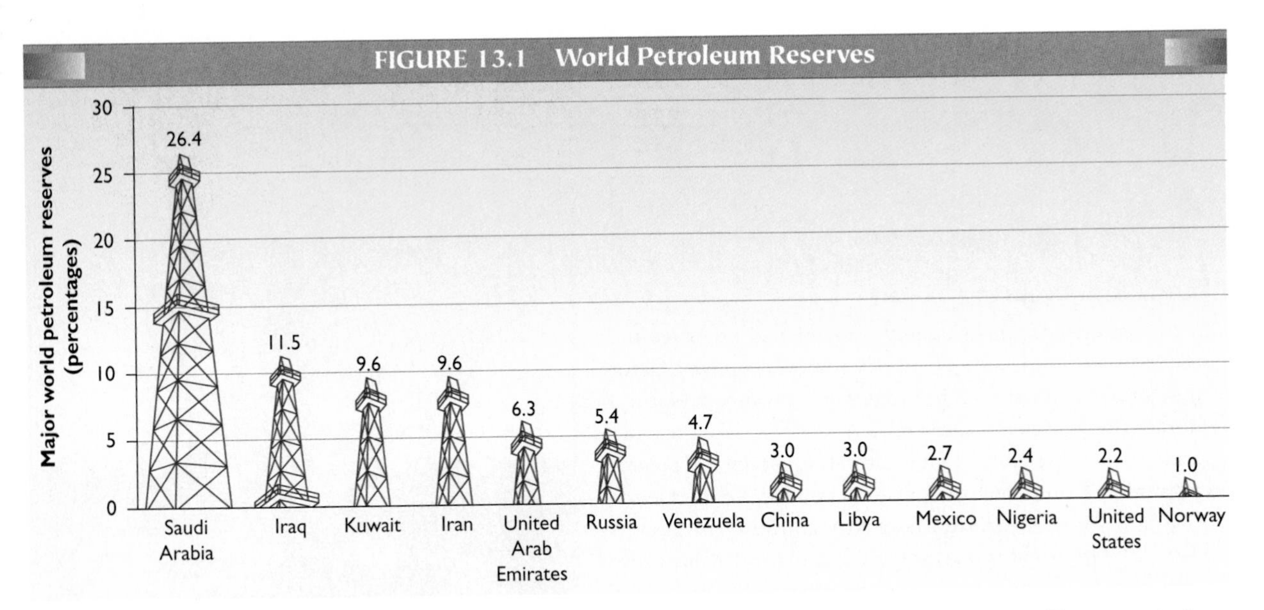

There are only 13 countries that have 1% or more of the world's oil reserves. The concentration of oil, especially in the Middle East, which has about two-thirds of the world's oil reserves, enhances the political importance and power of that region's countries.

Data source: World Almanac (2003).

Industrial Output

Even if a country is bountifully supplied with natural resources, its power is limited unless it can convert those assets into industrial goods. On a global basis, industrial production is highly concentrated. For instance, just five countries (China, Germany, Japan, Russia, and the United States) produce 55% of the world's steel. Vehicle production is another indication of industrial concentration, as indicated in Figure 13.2. It shows that in 2001 the three biggest vehicle manufacturers (Germany, Japan, and the United States) made 51% of the global total. Another 11 countries combined for 39%, with a mere 10% manufactured by 14 other countries. About 85% of the world's countries (including all those in Africa) produce no, or only a negligible number of, vehicles.

Agricultural Output

It is not common to equate food production with power. Yet a country's agricultural capacity is an important factor. Self-sufficiency varies widely in the world. The United States is basically able not only to supply its own needs but also to earn money from agricultural exports. With less than 5% of the world's population, it produces 14% of the world's cereal grains and 15% of its meat. Other countries are less fortunate. Some have to use their economic resources to import food. Others have insufficient funds to buy enough food and face widespread hunger. Many parts of Africa are in particularly desperate shape.

Another significant agricultural factor is the percentage of economic effort that a country must expend to feed its people. Countries are relatively disadvantaged if they have larger percentages of their workforce in agriculture (and thus not available for the manufacturing and service sectors), if they have to spend a great deal of their economic effort (measured as a percentage of GDP) to feed their people, and if they have to import food. Table 13.2 contrasts the agricultural efficiency of an EDC (the United States)

FIGURE 13.2 Concentration of World Vehicle Production

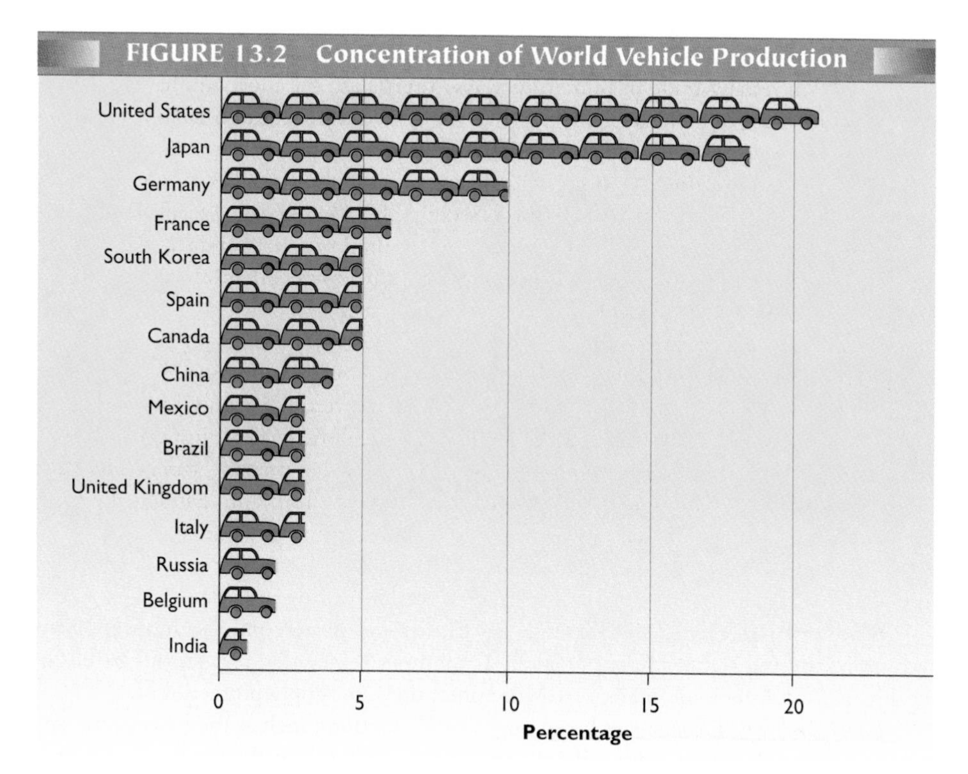

Global industry is highly concentrated. The 15 countries that produced 1% or more of the 57.5 million vehicles manufactured in 2001 accounted for 89% of world production. The biggest 3 producers manufactured just under half of all the world vehicles this year.

Data source: World Almanac (2003).

to that of an LDC (China). On each measure China is disadvantaged agriculturally. Compared to Americans, the Chinese devote much more of their economic effort and workforce to agriculture. Those workers are inefficient because they have so little farm machinery. As a result, the value of the products of each Chinese farm worker is only about 0.6% of that of an American agricultural worker. Moreover, despite its efforts, China just barely manages to feed its vast population.

TABLE 13.2 Agricultural Effort of the United States and China

Agricultural Effort	United States	China
Agriculture as % of GDP	2	15
% of workforce in agriculture	2	66
Tractors per 100 sq. miles of arable land	105	22
Value of agricultural output per worker	$50,777	$334

Data sources: World Bank (2003), Food and Agriculture Organization Web site: http://apps.fao.org/.

China and most other LDCs spend an inordinate amount of their economic effort and their workforce to feed themselves. Many EDCs spend little economic effort and few workers on agriculture, yet because of mechanization are able not only to produce enough food for domestic use but also to earn revenues by being net agricultural exporters.

Methods of Manipulating Economic Interchange

Economic nationalists, as detailed in chapter 12, believe that a state's political, military, and economic powers are inextricably linked. Therefore, economic nationalists advocate harnessing all aspects of a government's economic policy, including its foreign economic relations, to enhance the state's power. From this perspective, the movement of goods, services, investments, and other forms of economic interchange into and out of the country should be manipulated in the interest of state power by barriers and domestic support.

Barriers to Merchandise Trade

Countries can restrict trade in numerous ways. **Tariffs** are the most familiar trade barrier. Tariff rates are quite low relative to what they once were, but two qualifications are important. One is that tariff rates for EDCs are generally much lower than those for LDCs, which believe they need higher rates to protect their smaller industries from being overpowered by foreign competition. Second, the average global tariff on agricultural products is much higher than it is on manufactured products. Indeed, the protection of agriculture by tariffs and other means discussed below is perhaps the most difficult issue now facing trade negotiators.

While tariffs are generally low, especially for the EDCs, tariff hikes are still occasionally either threatened or used. Most often this occurs over economic issues. For example, during 2003 the United States brought substantial pressure to bear on China to let the exchange rate of its currency, the yuan, rise to a more realistic level against the U.S. dollar (and therefore increase U.S. exports to China). Part of that pressure was pending action in the U.S. Congress to levy a 27.5% tariff on imports from China unless the yuan was allowed to float freely against other currencies. Calling the government in Beijing a "a communist dictatorship that manipulates and cheats rather than follows the rule of law," one U.S. senator warned, "There's a perfect storm brewing in China."[1]

Nontariff barriers (NTBs) are a less-known but more common and important way of restricting trade. These NTBs are sometimes reasonable regulations based on health, safety, or other considerations. More often they are simply protectionist.

Import and export prohibitions based on political sanctions, such as the ban against importing Iraqi oil between 1990 and 2003, is one type of NTB. At the extreme, trade embargoes, such as the one that the United States has imposed on Cuban goods, may totally bar trade.

Quotas that limit the number of units that can be shipped are another form of NTB. Some quotas are imposed by importing countries; others are self-imposed by exporting countries in preference to facing imposed restrictions. One reason Japanese auto manufacturers built plants in the United States was the threat of U.S. quotas on the importation of Japanese vehicles. More recently, Washington moved in late 2003 to impose quotas on the importation of dressing gowns, knitted fabrics, and certain lingerie items from China as an opening move in an attempt to protect the U.S. textile industry and to address the yawning U.S. trade deficit with that country. Quotas are sometimes tied into tariffs. The United States sets quotas on imported raw and refined sugar by allowing only limited amounts of imports at a low or no tariff rate and setting prohibitive rates on all imports above the quota. For 2003, the U.S. import quota of 1.1 million tons was allocated among 40 countries, with the Dominican Republic receiving the largest share (185,335 tons) and ten countries limited to the lowest quota (7,258 tons).

Technical restrictions, such as health and safety regulations, are sometimes really meant to bar imports or increase their cost considerably. Even though NAFTA allows the trucks of its member-countries to carry goods across borders, many Mexican trucks are barred from the United States because they do not meet the stricter U.S. safety regulations. The European Union curtails U.S. beef imports because of the artificial hormones used in cattle feed in the United States, and the EU and many other countries imposed further restrictions in December 2003 after a single case of bovine spongiform encephalopathy (mad cow disease) was discovered in the United States. Some Americans claimed that the move was an ill-disguised attempt to further restrict U.S. exports. Still, the U.S. government had little room to complain because earlier in the year it had banned Canadian beef imports after a single case of mad cow disease had been found in the province of Alberta.

Countries sometimes use technical barriers, such as health regulations, to restrict trade. More than 60 countries banned imports of U.S. beef after a single head of cattle with mad cow disease was discovered in Washington state in December 2003. As U.S. officials traveled abroad to reassure others that U.S. beef was safe, they were often met with protests, such as the one being staged here in South Korea. Health restrictions are legitimate in trade, but in this case and others, countries sometimes use health concerns as a convenient excuse, rather than a reason, to limit imports and protect domestic economic interests.

Barriers to Trade in Services and Investment

Just as there are a wide array of merchandise trade barriers, so too there are multitudinous ways to restrict the trade in services and the flow of investment. Of the few that we can sample here, licensing requirements are one way to make it difficult for foreign professionals and companies to provide services in another country. Many countries license architects, engineers, insurance agents, stock and bond traders, and other professionals. Majority ownership requirements are a way to bar the foreign ownership of businesses within a country. India, for example, requires that all companies located in India have at least 51% Indian ownership.

Domestic Support of Trade

Countries can also attempt to gain an unfair advantage in the international marketplace. These practices all violate international trade agreements and also sometimes national law, but they are hard to eliminate completely. Conducting economic espionage, providing domestic subsidies, and encouraging dumping are just three of the many ways governments can interfere in free trade.

Economic espionage is an ongoing problem. This practice involves the theft of trade secrets from a country's companies by both friendly and hostile foreign governments (as well as private companies and individuals). The country doing the spying can then use the stolen trade secrets to build products that compete both domestically and internationally with the products of the companies that have been victimized. These activities became such a concern to U.S. economic prosperity and national power that Congress enacted the Economic Espionage Act of 1996. The protection of U.S trade secrets is assigned to the Office of the National Counterintelligence Executive (ONCE), a joint undertaking of the FBI, CIA, and other U.S. intelligence agencies. The continuing concern is illustrated in ONCE's 2001 report, which indicated, "As the world's leading industrial power and leader in technology development, the United States continues to be a prime target of foreign economic collection and industrial espionage. The United States pays a high financial price for economic espionage." The report continued, "The business community estimates that, in calendar year 2000, economic espionage cost from $100 to 250 billion in lost sales. The greatest losses to U.S. companies involve information concerning manufacturing processes and research and development."[2]

Subsidies also skew trade. These include various forms of financial support that a government gives to a company to allow it to compete unfairly in the marketplace. For example, if a country gives a company tax breaks when it produces merchandise for export, then that company can profitably sell its products both at home and abroad for less than it otherwise would be able to. In addition to tax incentives, domestic subsidies come in many forms, including direct payments to producers, providing cheap or below-cost services to producers (such as energy or transportation), and providing research and development assistance.

Many governments, for instance, heavily subsidize their agriculture industries. The EDCs provide an estimated $230 billion annually in support of agricultural business ("agribusiness") in those countries, and the LDCs' subsidies amount to at least another $100 billion. In perhaps the largest subsidy program in recent years, President George W. Bush signed legislation in 2002 that will provide an estimated $190 billion in new subsidies to U.S. agribusiness over a decade. In addition to their impact on prices, subsidies also add to the pressure on governments to use tariffs, quotas, and other means to exclude imports. As an example, in the sugar industry, the U.S. government gives loans to American producers and processors if the price goes below a set amount and takes sugar as collateral. The amount of the loans varies from year to year, but most often comes to more than $100 million in purchases. If too much foreign sugar, which sells on the international market for less than half the cost of U.S. sugar, is imported, then U.S. prices will fall and sugar price support costs will skyrocket. Therefore, in this case, through tariffs and quotas that depress the imports of sugar and keep prices high, the U.S. government protects both its budget and domestic sugar producers. The difficulty, according to critics, is that the U.S. subsidy costs taxpayers large sums. They pay for sugar itself, and the artificially high prices of sugar harm American consumers through higher prices for all the "downstream" products that use sweeteners (such as soda, candy, and jam). Additionally, the tariffs and quotas harm the many poor countries that rely heavily on sugar as an export commodity.

Did You Know That:

EDCs subsidize agriculture more than any other major economic sector. According to the UN Food and Agriculture Organization, in 2001 the average government subsidy to agribusiness per head of cattle was $436 in the EU, $1,297 in Japan, and $152 in the United States. The per capita GNP of sub-Saharan Africa was $460.

Dumping, yet another concern, occurs when a company, often with the support of its national government, sells its goods abroad at a price lower than what it sells them for at home. This violates trade laws, and complaints are regularly heard. For instance, in January 2004, the U.S. marine food industry asked the Bush administration to impose antidumping duties of up to 200% on shrimp shipments from China, Ecuador, India, Thailand, and Vietnam. Simultaneously, federal authorities in Canada opened an investigation regarding the alleged dumping of frozen pizza by U.S. firms. Such matters may seem small, but they are not for the U.S Southern Shrimp Alliance, which faces competition from imported shrimp worth $5 billion annually, or for McCain Foods of New Brunswick, Canada, which has spent $29 million expanding its frozen pizza plant there.

Applying Economic Power

States possess a variety of economic tools. It is possible to divide the economic instruments available to countries into economic incentives and economic sanctions.

Economic Incentives

States regularly offer economic incentives to induce other states to act in a desired way. Incentives include providing foreign aid, giving direct loans or credits, guaranteeing loans by commercial sources, reducing tariffs and other trade barriers, selling or licensing the sale of sensitive technology, and a variety of other techniques. Not all incentives are successful in changing another country's behavior, but they certainly do work some of the time. For example, in the aftermath of the war with Iraq in 2003, the Bush administration sought to speed the rebuilding of Iraq by dispatching former secretary of state James Baker on a global trip to press other governments to relieve Iraq of the international debt of at least $120 billion amassed under Saddam Hussein. Earlier, President Bush had barred countries that had not supported the war from participating in the lucrative reconstruction contracts, but one of the tools that Baker carried with him was Washington's willingness to reconsider that stand for countries that offered significant debt relief. While all parties denied the incentives were the reason, Baker was soon able to get positive responses from France, Germany, Russia, and other countries that had opposed the war and that were being shut out of the reconstruction process.

Economic Sanctions

Countries and alliances can use their economic power in a negative way by applying sanctions. Research indicates that countries are especially likely to do so "if there are expectations of frequent conflict with the target" (Drezner, 1998:728). Methods include raising trade barriers, cutting off aid, trying to undermine another country's currency, and even instituting blockades.

The History of Sanctions The use of **economic sanctions** dates back to at least 432 B.C. when the city-state of Athens embargoed all trade with another city-state, Megara. Then, as now, sanctions were acts of hostility, and the Megarian Decree was one of the causes of the Peloponnesian War (431–404 B.C.), in which Megara was part of the Peloponnesian League led by Sparta in its conflict with the Athenian Empire and its allies.

The point of this story is that the use of economic instruments to promote policy is ancient. In more modern times, sanctions are becoming more frequent policy tools. There were only 8 incidents of economic sanctions (0.3 per year) from 1914 through 1939. This increased to 44 incidents of sanctions (1.5 per year) between 1940 and 1969, and the number rose again to 71 incidents (3.6 per year) during the two decades of the 1970s and 1980s (Rothgeb, 1993). During the 1990s, according to another study, about 60 new sanctions were imposed by one or more countries. The United States, usually along with other countries, initiated 42 of these (Elliot & Oegg, 2002).

The increased use of sanctions has occurred, in part, because people are more aware of events in the world around them and more intent on influencing how other governments act both domestically and internationally. Sanctions are also more frequent because economic interdependence makes target countries more vulnerable to sanctions.

The increased use of sanctions also reflects the search for ways to pressure other countries without going to war. For example, in 2003, President Bush signed into law a bill authorizing him to impose sanctions on Syria if it does not, among other things, "halt [its] support for terrorism, end its occupation of Lebanon, [and] stop its development of weapons of mass destruction." Sanctions were levied in mid-2004.

Before leaving the history of sanctions, it should be noted that they are used by international organizations as well as by individual countries. The 1990s saw sanctions imposed by the UN on Libya and Sudan for supporting terrorism; on Yugoslavia for aggression in the Balkans; on Iraq for aggression against Kuwait and for failing to live up to the cease-fire agreement of 1991; on Haiti for toppling its democratic government and substituting a military regime; and, for the first time, on a rebel group, UNITA, in Angola (Cortright & Lopez, 2000; Brown, 1999).

The Effectiveness of Sanctions Economic sanctions are a blunt instrument that attempts to economically bludgeon a target country into changing some specific behavior. As such, the effectiveness of sanctions is mixed. Sometimes they can be effective. Sanctions cost South Africa tens of billions of dollars and helped push the country's white leadership to end the apartheid system. The harsh sanctions on Yugoslavia arguably helped cause the downfall of President Slobodan Milosevic in October 2000. It is also probable that the long-standing sanctions on Libya caused it to take responsibility for the bomb destruction in 1988 of Pan Am Flight 103 over Lockerbie, Scotland, and in 2003 to also agree to end its program of building weapons of mass destruction and to allow inspections by the International Atomic Inspection Agency and other international agencies. "What forced Gaddafi to act was a combination of things—U.N. sanctions . . . , his international isolation after the Soviet Union's collapse . . . and internal economic problems [caused in part by the sanctions] that led to domestic unrest," one analyst commented. An additional factor, according to a U.S. State Department official, was that "the invasion of Iraq sent a strong message to governments around the world that if the United States feels threatened by weapons of mass destruction, we are prepared to act against regimes not prepared to change their behavior."[3]

It is also the case, though, that, more often than not, sanctions fail to accomplish their goal. Some analysts place their success rate as low as 5%, but even more optimistic assessments indicate that sanctions change the behavior of a target country about one-third of the time (Elliott & Oegg, 2002; Kaempfer & Lowenberg, 1999; and Elliott, 1998). Given this limited success rate, a reasonable question is, When do they accomplish their goals? Sanctions are most likely to be effective in certain circumstances (Drezner, 2000; Shambaugh, 2000). These include instances where (1) "the goal is relatively modest," thereby minimizing the need for multilateral cooperation; (2) "the target is politically unstable, much smaller than the country imposing sanctions, and economically weak"; (3) "the sender and target are friendly toward one another and conduct substantial trade"; (4) "the sanctions are imposed quickly and decisively to maximize impact"; and (5) "the sender avoids high costs to itself," such as the loss of substantial export revenue (Elliott, 1993:34).

Whatever the evidence, sanctions remain a regularly used tool. Most are relatively limited, such as those imposed on specific products of countries accused of dumping them on another country's market. For example, the United States imposed sanctions on Vietnam in 2003 by raising the tariff on imported catfish from that country to 64% after finding that Vietnamese companies were dumping frozen fillets on the U.S. market. At a much higher level, the U.S. government in 2003 had broad economic sanctions against Burma (Myanmar), Cuba, Iran, Iraq, Liberia, Libya, North Korea, Sudan, and Zimbabwe and also had sanction policies that permit the president to penalize countries that are found to be engaged in the illicit trade in diamonds (used to finance illegal weapons purchases), narcotics production and trade, complicity in terrorism, and promotion of the proliferation of weapons of mass destruction. Some of these sanctions are in cooperation with the United Nations; others are unilateral.

Why are sanctions used so regularly as a policy tool given their limited success rate? One answer is that they can be effective, as in the role of international sanctions on Libya persuading it to abandon its WMD program in 2003. A second reason is that judging whether sanctions have worked or not is sometimes difficult. It could be argued, for example, that the UN sanctions imposed on Iraq after its defeat failed because they never did force the regime of Saddam Hussein to fully comply with the conditions imposed by the Security Council. However, a case could also be made that the sanctions did prevent Iraq from having the funds to rearm and, perhaps, to develop WMDs that could threaten the region. A third answer is that tangible success is not the only standard by which to measure sanctions. They also have a symbolic value that has nothing to do with whether they actually cause another country to change its behavior. Simply put, just as you might choose not to deal with an immoral person, so too countries can express their moral indignation by reducing or severing their interactions with an abhorrent regime (Baldwin, 2000).

The Drawbacks of Sanctions Especially given the high failure rate of sanctions, countries that apply them must be wary of the negative impact of sanctions on unintended victims. One such difficulty is that sanctions may harm economic interests other than those of the intended target. The UN sanctions imposed on Iraqi oil exports between 1991 and 2003 cost Jordan and Turkey many millions of dollars annually by way of lost revenues that they would have earned for the use of pipelines that run from Iraq through them and on to ports from which the oil is shipped.

Another drawback is that threatening or implementing sanctions can damage those who impose them. For instance, U.S. sanctions that forbade trade with other countries reduced American exports by $13 billion in 1999 alone. This accounted for only 0.9% of U.S. exported goods and services that year, but, as the study notes, "the costs of sanctions are never spread evenly" across the economy. For example, the analysis continues, "the long-standing U.S. embargo on Cuba arguably has a much larger impact on Florida than on other states" (Hufbauer & Oegg, 2003:8).

A third criticism of sanctions is that they are often the tool used by EDCs to continue their dominance of LDCs. Of the 71 incidents of sanctions applied during the 1970s and 1980s, 49 of the cases (69%) involved EDCs placing sanctions on LDCs (Rothgeb, 1993). A fourth charge against sanctions is that they may constitute a rogue action in the view of many countries that do not support them. For the 12th consecutive year and by a vote of 179 to 3, the UN General Assembly in 2003 condemned the unilateral U.S. sanctions against Cuba that have been in place since the early 1960s. Only the United States, Israel, and the Marshall Islands voted "nay," while Morocco and Micronesia abstained.

A fifth criticism is that sanctions often harm the innocent. The argument here is akin to the standard of *jus in bello* (the just conduct of war) discussed in chapter 9 that military action must not target noncombatants and must try to minimize the number of noncombatants killed and wounded as the result of even legitimate strikes. Taking the view that sanctions often do not discriminate, President Fidel Castro of Cuba has called them "noiseless atomic bombs" that "cause the death of men, women, and children."[4] Iraq provides a good example of Castro's point. There, the UN sanctions in place between 1991 and 2003 and the defiant stance of the government in Baghdad had a brutal impact. Scant supplies of food and medicine for the civilian population were among the hardships. The effects were especially devastating for children. Various studies by the UN, Harvard University's School of Public Health, and others all found that the sanctions

FIGURE 13.3 Economic Sanctions and the Death of Children

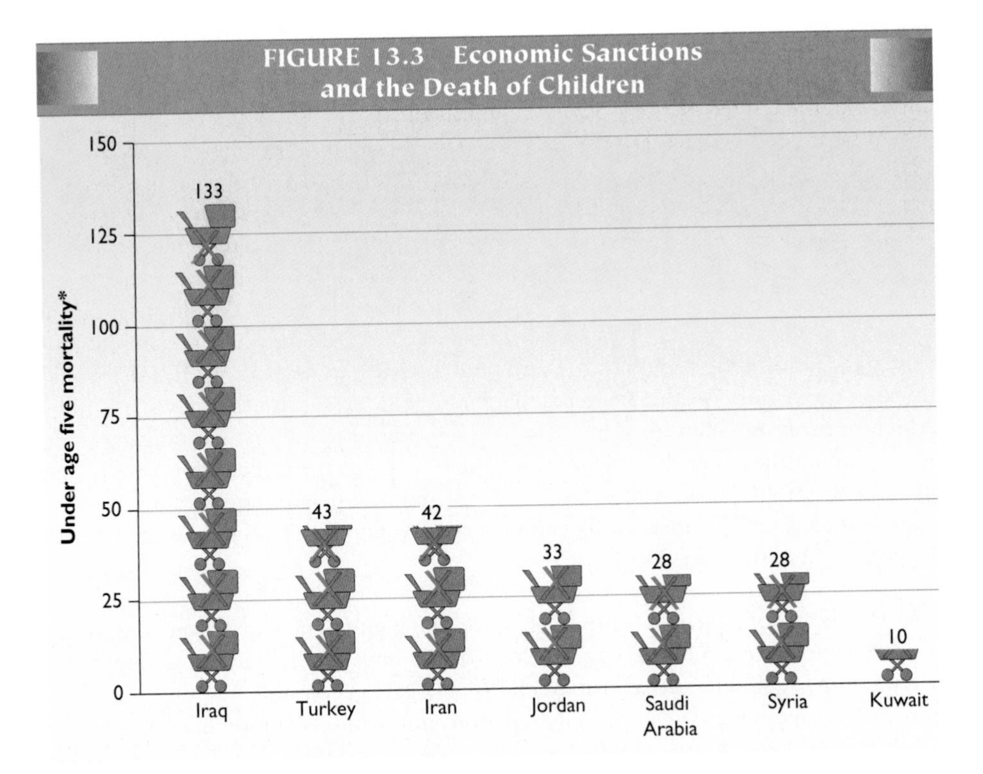

One objection to economic sanctions is that they often have the most deleterious impact on those who have the least responsibility for the actions of their government. There is little doubt that the economic sanctions that were imposed on Iraq beginning in 1990 caused many young children to die. The average death rate of small children for Iraq's six neighbors dropped markedly from 7.5% in 1990 to 3.1% in 2001, while Iraq's rate rose from 8.3% to 13.3%.

*The number of children who die before age five per 1,000 children born.

Data source: World Bank (2003).

caused (beyond normal expectations) over 1 million Iraqi children to be malnourished and upward of 500,000 to have died. This deleterious effect is evident in Figure 13.3, which compares the child mortality rate in Iraq to that of its neighbors.

The North and International Political Economy

Having reviewed national economic assets and the use of the economic instrument, we can turn to specific national economic concerns and policies. This discussion will be divided into two parts: the national economic issues and policies of the North and the national economic issues and policies of the South. By many standards, the economic position of the North is enviable. Its 2001 per capita GNP was $26,510 compared to $1,160 for the people of the South. Between 1980 and 2001, the combined GDPs of the EDCs jumped from $8 trillion to $25 trillion. That was monumental compared with a rise in the combined GDPs of the LDCs from $3 trillion to $6 trillion. Yet all is not well in the North.

The National Economies of the North

The fundamental cause of concern among EDCs is that the North's economic growth rate has slowed somewhat from its earlier high levels. The average annual real GDP growth rate of the EDCs during the 1980s was 3.4%; during the 1990s that declined to 2.3%; and between 2000 and 2003 it ebbed again to 2.1%. The number of new jobs being created in the North increased an annual average of 1.5% between 1985 and 1994; the years 1995 to 1999 saw average job growth at 1.2%; from 2000 through 2003 it was 0.9%.

There are many reasons for the deceleration of the North's economy. One is the beginning of competition from a few newly industrializing countries (NICs) of the South in the manufacturing, industrial, and service sectors. Also, the post–cold war drop in defense spending has caused some dislocation.

Yet another adjustment for the EDCs involves their entering a period that some analysts call the postindustrial economy. What this means is that through the use of robotics and other techniques, fewer and fewer workers are needed to produce more and more manufactured goods. Companies need to reduce their workforces to stay competitive internationally. Downsizing is a relatively new, and unwelcome, word in the economic vocabulary of the North. Many of the displaced workers are either unemployed or find jobs in the usually lower-paying service sector. Indeed, the shift away from manufacturing has added a whole new class of economies, service economies, to such traditional designations as primary product (agriculture, minerals) economies and industrialized economies.

Service economies are those countries that derive at least a plurality of their earnings from performing services (such as banking, education, insurance, and transportation). For most countries, domestic services (everything from flipping burgers, through almost all government activity, to acting in movies) are already the biggest part of their internal economic activity. Such services make up 73% of the U.S. GDP, compared to just 22% for industry, and 5% for primary products. Services are also becoming a more important part of exports and, therefore, the international economy. The services that Americans exported in 1980 were just 17% of all U.S. exports; in 2002 that percentage was up to 30%. Thus other countries increasingly import what Americans know and do, rather than just what they harvest, mine, and make.

For the North, the 21st century began auspiciously, with a robust 3.9% real GDP growth in 2000. However, a downturn soon followed, with growth rates of only 1% in 2001 and 1.8% each in 2002 and 2003. During the first four years the United States did relatively well with a 2.4% average growth rate. By contrast, Japan's struggling economy grew only an average of 1.4%, and the EU had an average growth rate of 1.8%. Average unemployment in the EU (8.1% during the years 2000–2003) was more than half again the rate in the United States (5.2%). As for Japan, its unemployment rate more than doubled from 2.4% in 1990 to an average of 5.2% during the years 2000–2003. Thus for the past decade or more the economy of the North has been driven by U.S. economic prosperity and expansion more than any other force. Whether that will continue is not certain. A positive view, reflected in its title, "A Second American Century," is that the United States will soon resume its strong growth. That article predicted, "If anything, American business should widen its lead over the rest of the world. France had the 17th century, Britain the 19th, and America the 20th. It will also have the 21st." It is also possible to argue that a less rosy prediction will prove more accurate. Another article, "America the Boastful," cautioned, "The current sense that the United States is on the top of the world is based on a huge exaggeration of the implications of a few good years here and a few bad years elsewhere. . . . Future historians will not record that the 21st century belonged to the United States" (Krugman, 1998:45). Whatever the future may hold, the record of the North since 1990 has accentuated the concern of each EDC with its own economy and has sometimes strained economic relations within the North. It is to these concerns and policies that we now turn our attention.

National Economic Issues and Policies of the North

Because they make up such an overwhelming percentage of the world's economic enterprise, the economic issues and policies of the North are a key determinant of the course of the global economy. For an extended period after World War II, the EDCs enjoyed good growth and were generally united politically with the United States and under its leadership. Now, with both economic and political factors changing, tensions among the EDCs are increasing.

Changes in the Economic and Political Climate in the North

The 1990s were a time of significant shifts in the international economic relations and policies of the countries of the North. There were several causes of these shifts. One, as noted, was the unsteady economic fortune of the North. During the decades of booming prosperity following World War II, the rapidly expanding international economy minimized any pressures for economic rivalry among the developed countries. Now, in a less robust economic climate, there is increased protectionist sentiment.

A second factor is the end of the cold war. The resulting changes in the international system have lessened the need for strategic cooperation among the industrialized Western allies. During the cold war with the threat of the Soviet Union looming, Western Europe, Japan, and the United States followed the advice Benjamin Franklin gave to Americans in 1776 at the signing of the Declaration of Independence: "We must all hang together, or, assuredly, we shall all hang separately." Once the USSR collapsed, the need to hang together largely dissipated. As a result, the long-standing trade disputes among the so-called trilateral countries (Japan, the United States/Canada, Western Europe) that had once been suppressed in the name of allied unity have become more acrimonious. The strains between the United States, on the one hand, and France, Germany, and other European countries, on the other, over the U.S. determination to topple the Iraqi regime of Saddam Hussein in 2003 is but one of the latest examples of the discord.

A third and related factor that has further complicated matters is that central direction has declined in the North. The United States once provided that direction. But with an upsurge in economic rivalries among the EDCs and with the American people less willing to support U.S. internationalism, Washington has lost some of its ability to lead. President George W. Bush's unilateralist approach to foreign policy has compounded this problem. Europeans were distressed by his rejection of the Kyoto Protocol on the environment, by his rejection of the International Criminal Court, by his abrogation of the Anti-Ballistic Missile Treaty, and by other actions that were taken over their objection and with little consultation. The U.S. insistence on attacking Iraq over the objection of most U.S. allies made things worse. One analyst who believes that "toppling Saddam's regime was a legitimate and necessary goal" argues that, nonetheless, "rarely in American diplomacy has the right goal been pursued so poorly. . . . The political and diplomatic effort to build a broad international coalition was a debacle. Whereas U.S. military prowess may be at an all-time high, Washington's political and moral authority has hit a new low" (Asmus, 2003:21). During its earlier weakness Western Europe might have had to tolerate being ignored by Washington, but that is much less so today. Now, increased political as well as economic integration through the European Union has created an economic bloc that rivals the size of the U.S. economy, and this has made Europeans confident enough to challenge U.S. hegemony on a range of political, economic, and social issues. "There is a rhythm of global dominance, and no country remains the first player forever," Romano Prodi, the EU's president, has observed. "Maybe [U.S. dominance] won't last. And who will be the next leading player? Maybe next will be China. But more probably, before China, it will be the united Europe," Prodi predicted. "Europe's time is almost here."[5]

There are efforts to create greater coordination in the North through such vehicles as the **Group of Seven (G-7).** This is an informal directorate of the economically most powerful Western countries (Canada, France, Germany, Great Britain, Italy, Japan, and the United States) that has met annually since 1975. In 1998 the G-7 created the **Group of Eight (G-8)** when the G-7 leaders added Russia as a member for political matters. The G-7 still exists, therefore, because the G-7 continues to meet without Russia at the finance minister level on economic issues. To avoid confusion, here the groups will be referred to as the G-8 in all their activities. The EDCs also attempt to coordinate their efforts through the World Bank and IMF, which are largely controlled by the G-8. These programs and processes are examined more fully in chapter 14.

Despite such efforts, however, the reality is that the EDCs continue to act with a sort of dual personality in the realm of international economic affairs. One set of forces within most EDCs has pressed with significant success for the continued expansion of **free economic interchange** among nations. The EU has continued to integrate; Canada, Mexico, and the United States joined together in the North American Free Trade Agreement (NAFTA); and the world extended and enhanced the General Agreement on Tariffs and Trade (GATT) and created the World Trade Organization (WTO) to administer it. All these efforts and others designed to promote economic cooperation are discussed in chapter 14.

Simultaneously, however, protectionism remains a powerful countervailing force, and there has been increased pressure within countries to follow economic nationalist policies. This pressure has been occasioned by the sagging economies of the North, by increased economic competition not only from other EDCs but also from NICs, and by a gnawing sense of economic insecurity among many people of the North. When the American public was presented with a list of policy options in 2002 and asked which they thought were important, 85% said that "protecting the jobs of American workers should be a very important U.S. foreign policy goal." Only 35% of American leaders gave job protection a high priority. It follows, then, that public attitudes have pushed national leaders to follow policies of economic nationalism (Cohen, 2000).

The result of these countervailing internationalist and nationalist economic pressures within the EDCs gives something of a schizophrenic pattern to the foreign economic policies of the North's countries. They profess support of the further internationalization of the world economy while at the same time trying to promote and protect their own national economies.

Economic Disputes among the EDCs

Trade relations among the EDCs have become more difficult in the past decade. One source of tension is that some countries have chronic trade surpluses, while others regularly run trade deficits. Japan and the United States are the two countries at the opposite ends of the scale. During the period 1985–2003, Japan accumulated a global goods and services trade surplus of $1.9 trillion, while the U.S. trade balance was a staggering $4.3 trillion deficit. Each of the 19 years, Japan had a positive balance and the United States had a negative balance. Although trade is but one aspect of a country's overall international balance of payments, it is an important one. This is reflected in Japan having a cumulative balance-of-payments surplus of $1.6 trillion during the years 1995–2003, and the United States amassing a total $3.6 trillion deficit in its balance of payments for the

IN THE SPOTLIGHT

Politics, Trade, and the U.S. Steel Tariff

The record of the administration of President George W. Bush, like that of all recent U.S. presidents, has been one of solid support for the concept of free trade. No president's policy has fully lived up to his rhetorical support of free economic interchange, but President Bush has seemed more willing than most to be persuaded by interest group pressures and domestic politics to adopt protectionist politics. For example, in March 2002 the president imposed a 30% tariff on steel imports into the United States, responding to charges by U.S. steel producers and their workers that foreign steel producers were illegally dumping their steel on the U.S. market. Critics charged that producers in other countries were simply more competitive than the inefficient U.S. producers. Some commentators also claimed that domestic politics was the real motive behind the U.S. hike in steel tariffs. One alleged that the White House goal was to improve the electoral chances of Republican candidates in Pennsylvania, Ohio, West Virginia, and other steel-producing states. Another supposed aim of the White House was to gain the support of legislators from steel-producing constituencies for a bill then pending in Congress to give the president "fast-track" authority to conclude trade treaties without congressional interference in the details.

Whatever the motives of the White House, its action set off sharp retorts from Japan, the EU, and elsewhere. The charge of dumping was rejected, with Japanese trade officials calling the U.S. tariffs a "clear-cut violation of the WTO rules."[1] Similarly, the EU's trade commissioner objected, "The U.S. decision to go down the route of protectionism is a major setback for the world trading system."[2] The EU and seven individual countries also filed an action in the WTO charging that the steel tariff increases violated U.S. treaty obligations under the General Agreement on Tariffs and Trade (GATT). Additionally, the EU, Japan, and other countries drew up a target list of products on which they would impose retaliatory tariffs if the WTO found against the United States and it still refused to roll back the tariff increase. Given their view of Bush's motive, some countries chose their targets of retaliation with politics in mind. For instance, one EU target was orange juice, an important export product in Florida, a swing state that decided the 2000 presidential election and might well also be the key to the 2004 contest.

In November 2003 Bush reversed his stand and lowered the tariffs on steel to their normal level. He was persuaded by numerous factors, some domestic. The tariffs had helped U.S. steel producers and their workers, but steel-consuming businesses (such as automobile makers) and their workers claimed that the increased cost of steel had raised the cost of their products, thereby making them less competitive with the products of other countries and costing business and jobs. Yet other industries and their employees also pressed the White House to end the extraordinary tariff on steel, claiming they were losing exports and jobs (or would do so) due to the retaliatory tariffs imposed and threatened by other countries. Domestically, then, the steel tariff did not help and arguably harmed the overall U.S. economy, and it also proved to be a political liability in such key states as automobile-producing Michigan. The administration "tried

same period. During each year Japan had a surplus; during all but one year (1991), the United States ran a deficit.

The more unilateralist foreign policy approach of President George W. Bush has extended to trade policy, creating some friction between Washington and its major trading partners. Virtually all U.S. presidents and other countries' leaders occasionally engage in protectionism, but the Bush administration has taken a number of high-profile steps that have particularly rankled its trading partners. One of these is detailed in the In the Spotlight box "Politics, Trade, and the U.S. Steel Tariff." In response to accusations that it is too protectionist, the Bush administration has replied that it has only taken action when faced with unfair trade practices. Washington also charges that the EU and others follow their own forms of protectionism. Speaking to the graduating class at West Point in May 2003, President Bush singled out the EU's virtual ban on imported genetically modified (GM) crops from the United States. The EU claims they may pose a health hazard, but Bush told his audience, "Our partners in Europe . . . have blocked all new bio-crops because of unfounded, unscientific fears."[6] Adding to the U.S. charges against the EU, the top U.S. trade official, Robert B. Zoellick, wrote in a published op-ed piece

American presidents sometimes hike tariffs or place other barriers on imports to protect one or another domestic economic interest. When President George W. Bush accused foreign steel producers of dumping their product on the U.S. market and imposed a 30% tariff on imported steel in 2002, many critics charged that the accusation was false: that he was really trying to protect an inefficient U.S. steel industry and its workers and, as a consequence, to improve Republican electoral fortunes in steel-producing states. Amid furious foreign protests and an adverse ruling by the World Trade Organization, in late 2003 Bush used this setting at a Home Depot in Lansdowne, Maryland, to announce that he was rescinding the tariff increase.

to play politics, and it looked like it was working for a while. But now it's fallen apart," commented an analyst.[3]

Bush's steel tariff increase also strengthened the view overseas that his administration was not a reliable trading partner. The suspicion that domestic politics, not the law, was behind the protectionist tariffs was confirmed in many minds when in late 2003 the WTO ruled that dumping had not occurred and that the U.S. tariff increase violated the GATT and WTO rules. Some analysts also argued that the steel tariffs harmed U.S. efforts to negotiate regional and bilateral trade agreements by creating doubts in other countries about whether the administration was willing to resist domestic pressures that always exist to protect one industry or another. The strategizing was "too clever by half," commented one such observer. "It presupposed that nobody was watching what we were doing, and it presupposed that our [U.S.] credibility was of no importance."[4]

that the EU stand was promoting world hunger. He argued that "by boosting yields, biotechnology could . . . where food is scarce, or climates harsh . . . spell the difference between life and death, between health and disease for millions." Yet, Zoellick continued, "the EU moratorium has sent a devastating signal to developing countries that stand to benefit most from innovative agricultural technologies. This dangerous effect of the EU's moratorium became evident last fall, when some famine-stricken African countries refused U.S. food aid because of fabricated fears—stoked by irresponsible rhetoric—about food safety."[7]

Such disputes are not new, but they have become more intense in recent years. How well the EDCs will be able to continue to cooperate and to avoid making conflictive economic decisions in the changed diplomatic context of the early 21st century remains to be seen. It is also well to remember that the relative prosperity of recent decades has helped smooth economic disagreements. There have been economic downturns, but none has been severe or prolonged. Whether governments could avoid the domestic pressure to resort to protectionism and other forms of economic nationalism in the midst of a sharp, extended financial recession is uncertain.

The South and International Political Economy

The economic goals of the North and South are very much alike but also very different. They are alike in that both the EDCs' and the LDCs' goals have to do with prosperity. They are different in that the North's goal is to preserve and enhance prosperity; the South's goal is to achieve it.

To further understand the economic position, goals, and policies of the LDCs, the following sections will examine economic development by looking first at the LDCs' sources of development capital and then by turning to the perspective of the LDCs on development issues. Before taking up these matters, though, it is important to look at the status of LDC development.

Development in the South: Status

There can be little doubt that on many statistical bases there has been improvement in the socioeconomic development of the South. Over the last decade, as discussed in chapter 12, the number of people living in extreme poverty is down and the infant mortality rate has been cut substantially. More people in the South have access to safe water and to adequate sanitation facilities, life expectancy has improved, and illiteracy has been reduced. Between 1985 and 2003, the real GDP of the South grew an annual average of 5.1%. Annual real per capita GDP growth was a slower but still solid 3.5%. Yet despite this progress, it would be misleading to conclude that the South is well on the road to health and prosperity. Instead, a closer examination of the South reveals many areas of concern.

Development: A Mixed Pattern

Disparity between countries is one problem with economic growth in the South. It is possible to show, for example, that for LDCs the aggregate manufacturing output, GDP, and some other factors have expanded considerably during the last 25 years, but it is also the case that these averages are misleading. This is because much of the progress was confined to a relatively few **newly industrializing countries (NICs)**, such as Argentina, Brazil, Malaysia, Mexico, Singapore, South Korea, Taiwan, and Thailand. For example, South Korea's per capita GNP in 2001 was $9,460. Much more typical is India, with a per capita GNP of just $460. Moreover, while the LDCs generally have a positive growth rate in per capita GDP, about 20% of the LDCs had a negative growth rate between 1965 and 2002. Another 20% grew during the period at less than half the average annual 2.5% growth rate of the EDCs. The point is that a few LDCs (the NICs) have made important economic progress, but most LDCs are only growing slowly, and a significant number of LDCs are actually experiencing long-term economic decline.

Disparity within countries is a second characteristic of LDC economic development. Economic class, sometimes based on race or ethnicity, is one division. Within the South there are cities with sparkling skyscrapers and luxuriant suburbs populated by well-to-do local entrepreneurs who drive Mercedes-Benzes and splash in marble pools. For each such scene, however, there are many more of open sewers, contaminated drinking water, distended bellies, and other symptoms of rural and urban human blight. In short, the scant economic benefits that have accrued in the South are not evenly distributed.

Figure 13.4 shows the percentage of income earned by the wealthiest and poorest 20% of income earners in an LDC (Brazil), an EDC (Japan), and the world's largest economy (the United States). Notice how unevenly Brazil's income is distributed, especially relative to Japan's; the wealthiest Japanese make only 3.4 times as much as the country's

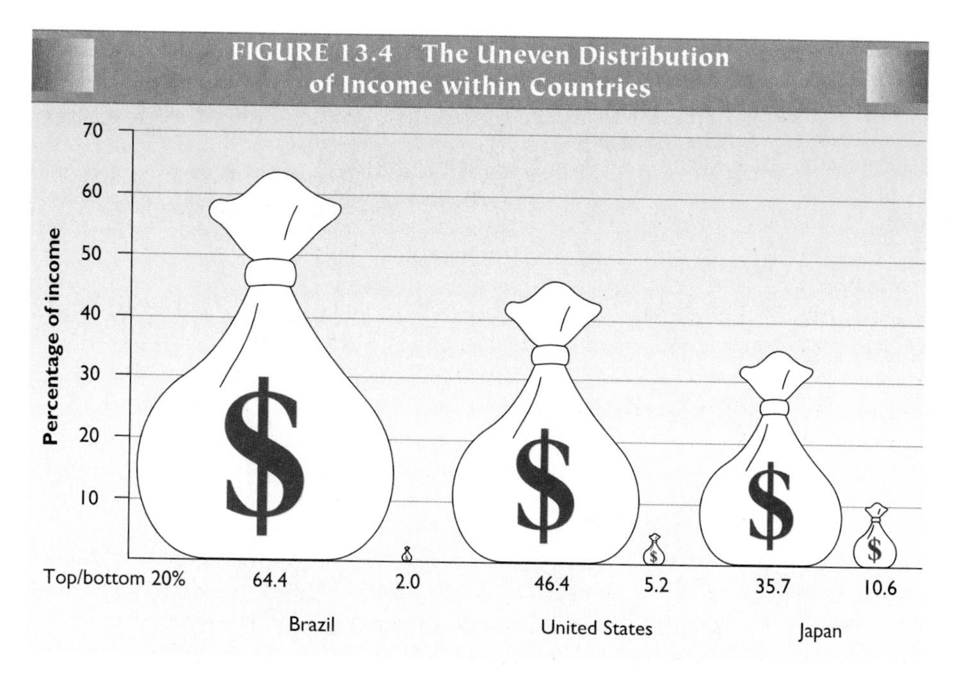

The figure shows one comparative indication of the uneven distribution of wealth within countries. The money bags represent the incomes of the wealthiest 20% of a country's income-earners and the poorest 20% in Brazil (which has one of the greatest disparities), the United States (the largest economy), and Japan (which has one of the narrowest gaps). All countries have disparities, but they tend to be much wider in the LDCs.

Data source: World Bank (2003).

poorest citizens. In Brazil the top 20% of income earners make more than 32 times what the poorest 20% of Brazilians receive. When Pope John Paul II traveled to Brazil, he spoke of "the contrasts between the two Brazils: one is highly developed, strong, and launched on the path of progress and riches; the other is seen in untold zones of poverty, suffering, illiteracy, and marginalization."[8] The data shows that this remained as true in 2001 as it was in 1991 during the pontiff's visit.

If all countries could have been crammed into Figure 13.4, you would have seen that while they all have income distribution disparities, the gaps tend to be larger in the South than in the North. It might be noted, however, that the U.S. disparity is greater than that of any other major industrialized economy and approaches the difference one would expect to find in an LDC rather than in an EDC.

Gender is another basis of economic disparity within countries. Women make up 59% of those people living in absolute poverty in the LDCs. One reason is that women comprise only 39% of the wage earners in LDCs. Adding to the disparity, data shows that women perform many more hours of unpaid household labor than do men. If this labor is included, women do 62% of the total work and (if salaries were equal, which they are not) receive only 32% of the wages.

Did You Know That:

In 2002 there were 476 billionaires in the world. Their combined assets amounted to $14.5 trillion, about the GNP of France. The wealthiest individual was Microsoft founder Bill Gates, whose $40.7 billion fortune was only slightly smaller than the GNP of Bangladesh and its 133 million people.

Modernization: A Mixed Blessing

The LDCs have benefited from advances in medicine, communications technology, and other aspects of modernization. It has been a mixed blessing, however, which has had several negative side effects for the South. *Explosive population growth* has occurred as a result of medical advances that have decreased infant mortality and increased longevity.

Modernization has proved to be a mixed blessing for many less developed countries. Rapid urbanization is a frequent but unfortunate by-product. Governments in LDCs have been unable to provide adequate services, and those flocking into cities have often found wretched conditions similar to those in this picture of the shacks, garbage-filled streets, and open sewers in the Kibera slum section of Nairobi, Kenya.

The population of sub-Saharan Africa, for instance, rose 321% from 210 million in 1960 to 674 million in 2001, and the region is expected to reach 866 million people by 2015.

Rapid urbanization has also beset the South, as the hope of finding jobs and better health, sanitation, and other social services has set off a mass migration from rural areas to cities in the South. Between 1965 and 2001 the percentage of the South's population living in urban areas grew from 22% to 42%, and it is projected to reach 53% in the year 2020. There are now approximately 175 cities in LDCs with populations over 1 million. Tokyo is the world's largest urban area (the core city and its suburbs) with 34 million people. Mexico City is the most populous LDC urban area, with about 22 million inhabitants. Sixteen of the 22 urban areas with populations above 10 million are in LDCs.

This rapid urbanization process has created a host of problems. One is the weakening of social order. Older tribal, village, and extended-family loyalties are being destroyed, with few new offsetting values and other social support systems to take their place. Second, the hope of employment is often unfulfilled, and unemployment and poverty in many cities is staggering. Third, struggling LDC governments are often unable to meet the sanitary, housing, and other needs of the flood of people moving to or being born in the cities. More than a quarter of the South's urban population is living in what the World Bank terms "absolute poverty," with nutritional, sanitary, and housing conditions below the minimum standard for health. At least a third of all urban dwellings in sub-Saharan Africa have no running water, toilets, or electricity. And despite great progress, India still has more than 112 million urban residents without access to adequate sanitation facilities.

Industrial and environmental dangers have also been undesirable by-products of development. The impact of development on the environment is detailed in chapter 16, but a brief note of the dangers is appropriate here. One problem is deforestation. This is especially critical in the South, where increased demand for wood, expanding farm and ranch acreage, and general urban growth are rapidly depleting the forests. Loss of these forests increases soil erosion, decreases oxygenation of the air, lessens rainfall, and has numerous other deleterious effects. LDC industrial development also adds to air, water, and soil pollution. This is a problem of industrialization in general, but pollution growth is especially acute in developing countries, which often cannot afford the expensive processes to cleanse emissions and dispose of waste.

Development in the South: Capital Needs

Whatever the problems and drawbacks of industrialization, the LDCs are justifiably determined to increase their development. Because of their poor economic base, most LDCs find it difficult to raise capital internally. Incomes are so low in India, for example, that less than 1% of the country's people pay income taxes. Many things can be accomplished with domestic resources and drive, but the LDCs also need massive amounts of **development capital** in order to expand and diversify their economies. "Uganda needs just two things," according to its president, Yoweri Museveni. "We need infrastructure and we need foreign investment. That is what we need. The rest we shall do ourselves."[9]

Obtaining these resources is difficult. The LDCs are constrained by limited financial reserves, especially **hard currency.** American dollars are the standard currency of international exchange. Japanese yen, European Union euros, and a handful of other currencies are also widely convertible. Guatemalan quetzals, Malaysian ringgits, and Nigerian nairas are another story. They and most LDC currencies are not readily accepted in international transactions. Since most of the world's hard-currency reserves are concentrated in the EDCs, the LDCs struggle to purchase needed imports.

A primary issue for LDCs, then, is the acquisition of hard-currency development capital. Four main sources of convertible currencies are available: loans, investment, trade, and aid. Unfortunately, there are limitations and drawbacks to each. Unless significant changes are made to increase the flow of development capital to the LDCs and to distribute it more broadly among all LDCs, the majority of them are destined to remain relatively poor for the foreseeable future.

The ability of many less developed countries to develop economically is being hindered by their heavy foreign debt. These countries use such a high percentage of what they take in from exports and other external sources of capital to pay the principal and interest on their debt that they have insufficient funds remaining to invest in the development of their economies. The debt crisis has eased somewhat in the past few years, but the debt burden remains a major problem for many LDCs.

Loans

One source of hard currency is loans extended by private or government sources. Based on a number of economic factors, in the 1970s the LDCs moved to finance their development needs by borrowing heavily from EDC banks, other private lenders, national governments, and international organizations. The upshot was that by 1982 LDC international debt had skyrocketed to $849 billion (equal to $1.6 billion in real 2000 dollars). While the rate of increase has eased, the total debt owed by the LDCs has continued to grow and stood at $2.2 trillion in 2002. Banks and other private institutional and individual bondholders are the largest creditors, followed by IGOs (such as the IMF and World Bank) and governments.

A Debt Crisis Breaks Out Most countries borrow money. During the 1800s when the United States was developing, it and its major enterprises (such as railroads) borrowed heavily from abroad to help finance expansion. More recently, the United States regularly borrows from foreigners to help pay for its persistent deficit and owes them over $1 trillion. Thus, the recent borrowing by LDCs is neither remarkable nor necessarily irresponsible.

Both borrowers and lenders must manage money carefully, however, and in the 1980s, as evident in Figure 13.5, an unwise spiral of lending and borrowing occurred. The reasons are complex, but suffice it to say that LDCs were in dire need of funds and the lenders in the EDCs had surplus capital, which they urged the LDCs to borrow. Then a global economic downturn undercut the LDCs' ability to repay their loans. At its 1987 peak, debt was nearly twice the total of the LDCs' export earnings, and the LDCs had to pay 26% of all their export earnings just to meet the annual principal and interest payments.

Argentina, Brazil, Mexico, Nigeria, and several other LDCs verged on the edge of bankruptcy and faced a seemingly lose-lose choice. They could either halt payments and thereby ruin their credit, or they could continue to try to meet their **debt service** (principal and interest payments) even though that meant an annual outflow of $100 billion that the LDCs desperately needed to provide domestic services and to develop their economies.

The North was also threatened. Banks and other creditors faced potential losses of hundreds of billions of dollars that might have driven some huge banks into insolvency. That would have cost the governments of the EDCs billions when they intervened to fend off bank failures or to repay depositors under government insurance plans.

The Debt Crisis Eases The mutual danger of the debt crisis to both the North and South led them to search for solutions. The details are complex, but a plan proposed in 1989 by U.S. secretary of the treasury Nicholas Brady began to ease the debt crisis. Under the Brady Plan during the 1990s, banks forgave over $100 billion of what the LDCs owed, lowered interest rates, and made new loans. In return, the governments of the EDCs, the IMF, and the World Bank guaranteed the loans and have increased their own lending to the LDCs. The Brady Plan has also required that the LDCs meet fiscal reform requirements negotiated with the IMF and other lenders.

The Current Debt Situation The immediate LDC debt crisis has abated, but the debt situation remains troublesome. One concern is that the LDCs still have a towering debt. Earnings from exports are one source of revenue to service debt, and the 2002 debt as a percentage of export earnings was a burdensome 135%. Among other things, this meant that the LDCs paid out $325 billion (14% of their annual export earnings) that year to meet their principal and interest obligations. While the debt service is below its 30% peak in 1985, it still represents a loss of much-needed capital for the LDCs.

The ever-present possibility that the debt issue can rapidly become a debt crisis was evident in 2001 and into 2002 when a combination of Argentina's monetary policies, its faltering economy, and its nearly $150 billion in foreign debts caused a political and financial crisis that collapsed the value of the peso, as described earlier in this chapter. One result was that throughout 2002 and well into 2003 Argentina floundered economically and failed to make payments on its debt service in the billions of dollars, as its government struggled to reach an agreement for financial support with the IMF. As a condition of making the needed loans, the IMF demanded that Argentina undertake a series of tough financial reforms, such as running a budget surplus, reforming its tax code to raise more revenue, and reducing government employment. The IMF argued that the changes were needed to correct the underlying weakness of Argentina's financial structure. The

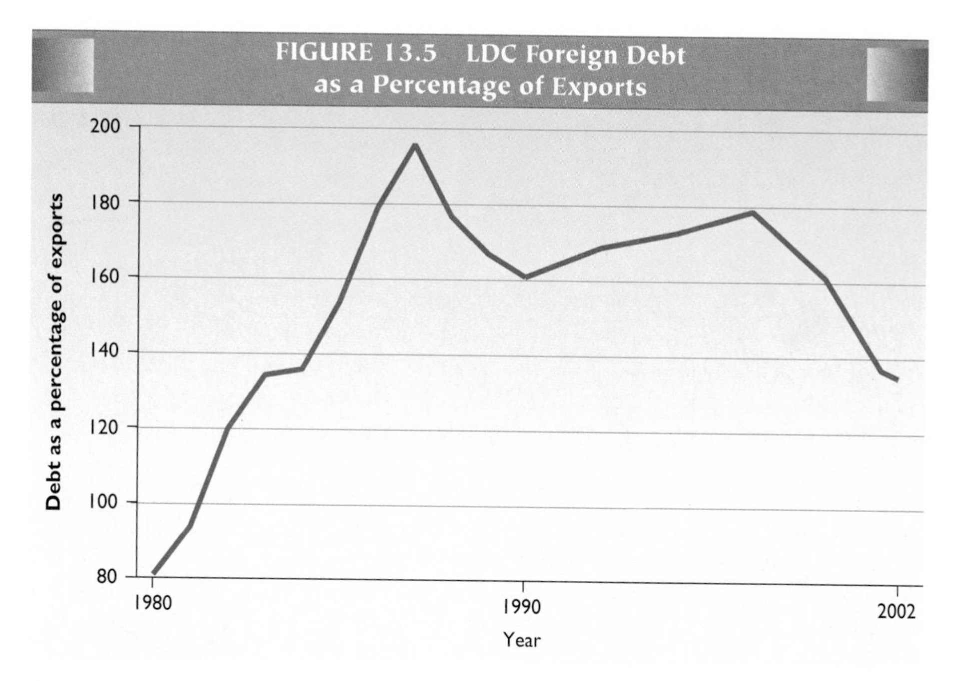

Export earnings are a key source of capital that LDCs use to pay debt. This ability was severely strained during the 1980s as the LDC's debt as a percentage of export earnings soared. Financial cooperation between the LDCs and EDCs along with an improved global economy have eased the crunch since its peak in 1987. Still, the 2002 level of debt at 135% of export earnings remains too high.

Data sources: IMF, *World Economic Outlook* (September 2003).

government in Buenos Aires responded that the IMF's conditions would make the desperate situation in Argentina even worse and might plunge it into violent political chaos. Finally in September 2003, Argentina and the IMF reached a compromise agreement for a $21 billion debt relief plan based on funds from the IMF to refinance the debt. The compromise by which the IMF eased some of its terms and Argentina agreed to a number of financial reforms was promoted with pressure from the United States and other G-7 countries that wanted to avoid either further destabilizing Argentina or risking the spread of further uncertainty about capital markets if Argentina continued to refuse to service its debts. As 2004 began, Argentina's economic difficulties were beginning to ease, and the confidence of international investors showed signs of improvement.

Private Investment

A second source of capital for LDCs is private investment through foreign direct investment (FDI) and foreign portfolio investment (FPI), as discussed in chapter 12. The flows of FDI and FPI are growing in importance as capital sources for the LDCs. Figure 13.6 shows that the combined net FDI and FPI in the LDCs skyrocketed during the 1990s. Although there is an upward trend in the proportion of global FDI that LDCs receive, with the LDCs' proportion of FDI increasing from 16% in 1990 to 27% in 1998, most funds are still being invested in EDCs.

There are several factors that temper the developmental impact of the rising flow of investment capital. First, most investment capital goes to only a handful of LDCs. China alone received 41.1% of all FDI funds that went to LDCs in 2002, and along with Brazil (10.2%) and Mexico (8.4%) received almost 60% of all LDC's FDI that year. By contrast,

FIGURE 13.6 Annual Net Private Investments in LDCs

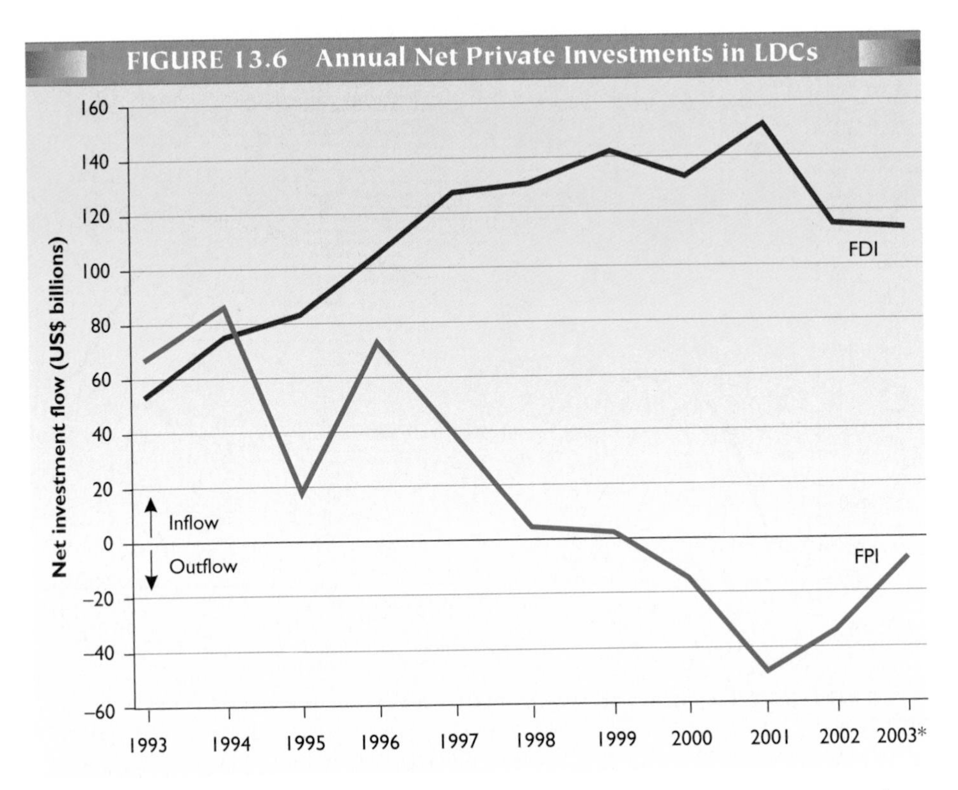

Foreign direct investment (FDI) and foreign portfolio investment (FPI) are important sources of development capital for LDCs. Notice that compared to FDI, the net flow (investments minus withdrawals) of FPI is quite unstable and beginning in 2000 became a net outflow as investors sold more assets than they bought. The sharp drop of net FPI began in 1995 and recovered briefly, but since 1997 it helped cause financial crises, among other places, in Mexico in 1995, in Asia and Russia in 1997, and in Argentina in 2001. These crises, in turn, hurt investor confidence, causing further net outflows in a destabilizing cycle that had eased but not ended by 2003. By contrast, FDI remains a strong net inflow, although the amounts have declined somewhat since 2001.

*Data estimated by the IMF.

Data source: IMF, *World Economic Outlook* (September 2003).

all of Africa received only 6.8% of the capital. Second, as evident in Figure 13.6, FPI is volatile. Third, the net flow of FPI can turn sharply negative. Mexico in 1995, much of Asia in the late 1990s, and Argentina in 2001 and 2002 suffered serious financial shocks when nervous foreign investors created net outflows of investment capital.

Trade

Export earnings are a third possible source of development capital. In light of the vast size of the world market, and because earnings from trade can be utilized by LDCs according to their own wishes, trade is theoretically the optimal source of hard currency for LDCs. Yet, in reality, the LDCs are severely disadvantaged by the pattern and terms of international trade.

There are several sources of LDC trade weakness. First, they command only 23% of the world goods and services export market. With exports equal to only $349 per person, they provide nowhere near the economic stimulus generated by the North's exports, which are over $6,000 per capita. Second, as noted earlier, just a few LDCs account for a lion's share of all the goods exported by the South. Third, most LDCs suffer a chronic trade deficit, with 74% of them needing to import more than they could export

Exports of Primary Products

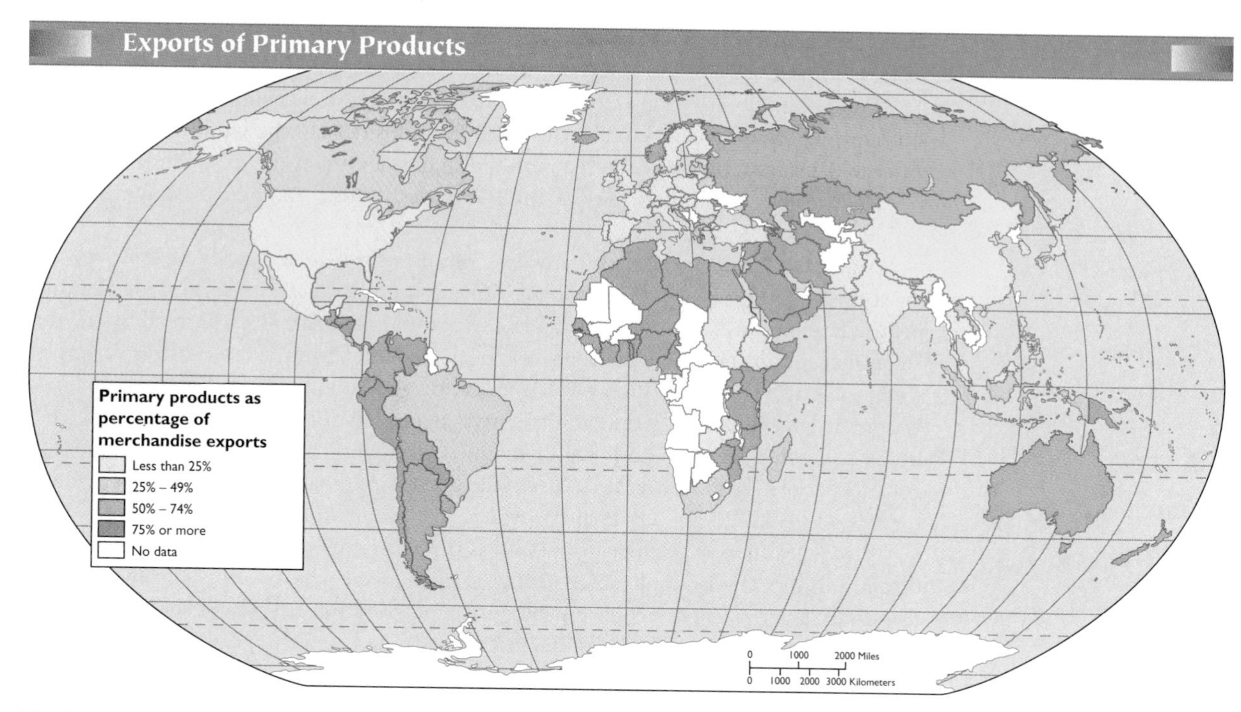

The less developed countries of the South are disadvantaged compared to the economically developed countries of the North. One reason is that the LDCs are much more reliant on primary products for export earnings. The dependency is a disadvantage because the demand for and price of primary products is unstable. Also, over the long term the value of primary products rises more slowly than manufactured products. Therefore most LDCs have increasing difficulty earning the foreign capital needed for economic development. This map shows the distribution of countries according to the percentage of their exports accounted for by primary products.

Source: John Allen and Elizabeth Leppman, *Student Atlas of World Politics*, 6th Edition, Dushkin/McGraw-Hill, p. 67. Reprinted with permission from Dushkin/McGraw-Hill.

in 2001. Many of the LDCs have staggering trade deficits that debilitate their national economies. For example, Cambodia imports were 388% of its exports in 2001, Haiti's were 265%, and Ethiopia had a 203% gap.

Fourth, LDC trade weakness stems from the heavy dependence of these countries on the export of primary products, including fibers, foodstuffs, fuels, and other minerals and raw materials, either in their unprocessed or processed forms (such as refined gasoline from petroleum or refined sugar from sugar cane). A rule of thumb is that the more dependent a country is on the export of raw or refined primary products, the poorer that country is likely to be. This rule is somewhat relaxed for a few countries, such as Kuwait, that have huge petroleum and natural gas exports combined with a small population, but even many countries, such as Angola, which export fuels remain poor because production levels are small compared to the country's population and needs. At least one indicator of the drawback of being dependent on primary products compared to manufactured ones is the fact that manufactured products constitute a majority of the exports of all but three (Australia, New Zealand, and Norway) of the EDCs, while manufactured products are a majority of the exports of only 25% of the LDCs. Trade conditions are even worse for the many LDCs that are export-dependent on one or just a few primary products. A few extreme examples (and the product and its percentage of exports) are Zambia (copper, 100%), Mauritania (iron ore, 99%), Guinea Bissau (cashew nuts, 98%), Chad (cotton, 95%) and Uganda (coffee, 91%). Dependency on a few products, especially primary products, for export earnings leaves LDCs disadvantaged because of several factors.

Product instability is one factor. Countries that rely on fish and other marine foodstuffs for export are endangered by the declining fish stocks in the world's oceans. When a freeze damages Colombia's coffee crop, a drought devastates the groundnut crops that Ghana relies on, or floods wipe out the Bangladesh jute crop, then the trade of those countries suffers greatly.

Market and price weaknesses are also common for primary products. A downturn in world demand can decimate markets. During the past decades, world trade in products such as cotton, sisal, jute, wool, and other natural fibers has been harmed by the development of synthetics. Sugar sales have been undercut by artificial substitutes and by dietary changes. Minerals such as tin and lead have also experienced market declines. Despite its recent rise, even the oil market was depressed during most of the 1990s. That leaves even what seems to be a wealthy country like Saudi Arabia vulnerable, because in 2001 its petroleum and natural gas sales made up 90% of the country's exports, accounted for 32% of the kingdom's GDP, and provided 75% of government revenue.

Price weakness for primary products is the response to the classic economic relationship of too much supply and too little demand. According to the World Bank, the real dollar price of most primary products has declined over the past several decades, while the real dollar value of manufactured goods increased sharply. Figure 13.7 shows price changes in absolute terms and also gives you some sense of the even more dramatic relative change caused by primary products going down in price while the price of manufactured goods is going up. The net result is that the primary products that LDCs export are increasingly less valuable compared to the manufactured products and the services that these countries need to import. During the period 1990–2001 alone, the real value of all LDC exports declined by 17%.

The use of trade, then, to acquire capital and to improve economic conditions has not been highly effective for most LDCs. Their pattern of merchandise trade deficits, overreliance on primary product exports, and market and price weaknesses are all disadvantages for LDCs in their trade relations with the EDCs.

Foreign Aid

A fourth possible external source of capital for LDCs is foreign aid. In some ways the flow of official development assistance (ODA) to LDCs has been impressive, amounting to over half a trillion dollars since World War II. Official ODA for 2002 was $57 billion. Currently, almost all foreign aid that is given comes from the 22 EDCs that are members of the **Development Assistance Committee (DAC)** of the Organization for Economic Cooperation and Development (OECD). Most assistance is extended through **bilateral aid** (country to country), with a smaller amount being channeled through **multilateral aid** (via the United Nations, the World Bank, and other IGOs).

Without disparaging the value or intent of past or current efforts, foreign aid has been neither a story of undisguised generosity nor one of unblemished success (Travis & Zahariadis, 2002; Koehn & Ojo, 1999; Katada & McKeown, 1998; Schraeder, Hook, & Taylor, 1998). There are a number of issues involving how aid is given and how it is spent, but the amount of aid given is the most important factor that limits its impact on the ability of LDCs to develop. Evaluating aid presents a revealing perspective about how viewing data in different ways can lead to varying conclusions. One way to analyze the data is in terms of dollars given and received by various countries. Another way to approach the data is to consider it relative to the need of recipient countries and to the wealth of donor countries. For example, measuring the aid that recipient countries get in dollars can lead to the conclusion that the amounts are impressive. Bangladesh, one of the world's poorest countries, received over $1 billion in aid in 2001, and famine-wracked

FIGURE 13.7 Commodity Price Changes, 1970–2002

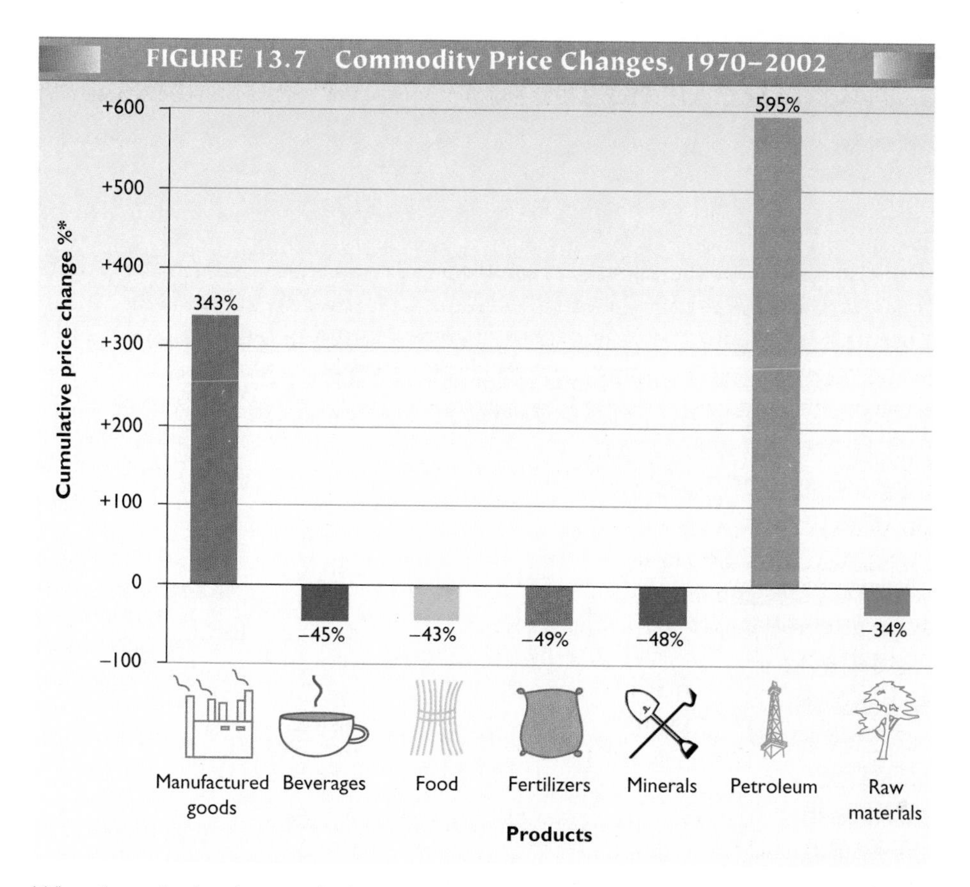

When the real price changes of primary products and manufactured goods are compared between 1970 and 2002, it is evident that the value of all primary product categories except petroleum declined, while the value of manufactured goods increased. This means that most LDCs, which substantially rely on primary products for export earnings, have an increasingly difficult time earning enough foreign capital through their exports to modernize their economies. Compounding the problem, most LDCs have to import petroleum, against which their primary produce exports have lost value.

*Measured in real dollars

Data source: World Bank (2003).

Ethiopia also received a bit over $1 billion. Yet those amounts appear less monumental when you consider the huge economic problems those countries face and the fact that the aid amounted to only $7.68 per person in Bangladesh and $16.41 per Ethiopian. Similarly, there are differing perceptual tales told by how much individual countries give in foreign aid compared to how much that is in terms of their ability to give measured by their wealth. Focusing on the United States, some people might portray the country as generously giving billions of dollars to needy countries. Others would differ, criticizing the United States for only giving a penuriously tiny fraction of its great wealth. Which perspective comes closer to reality and what future U.S. aid policy should be are matters discussed in the You Be the Playwright box "Measuring Foreign Aid."

Development in the South: LDC Perspectives and Policies

While the gap in wealth between the North and South has long existed, relations between the two economic spheres have not been static. The LDCs are now asserting with mounting intensity the proposition that they have a right to share in the world's

YOU BE THE PLAYWRIGHT

Measuring Foreign Aid

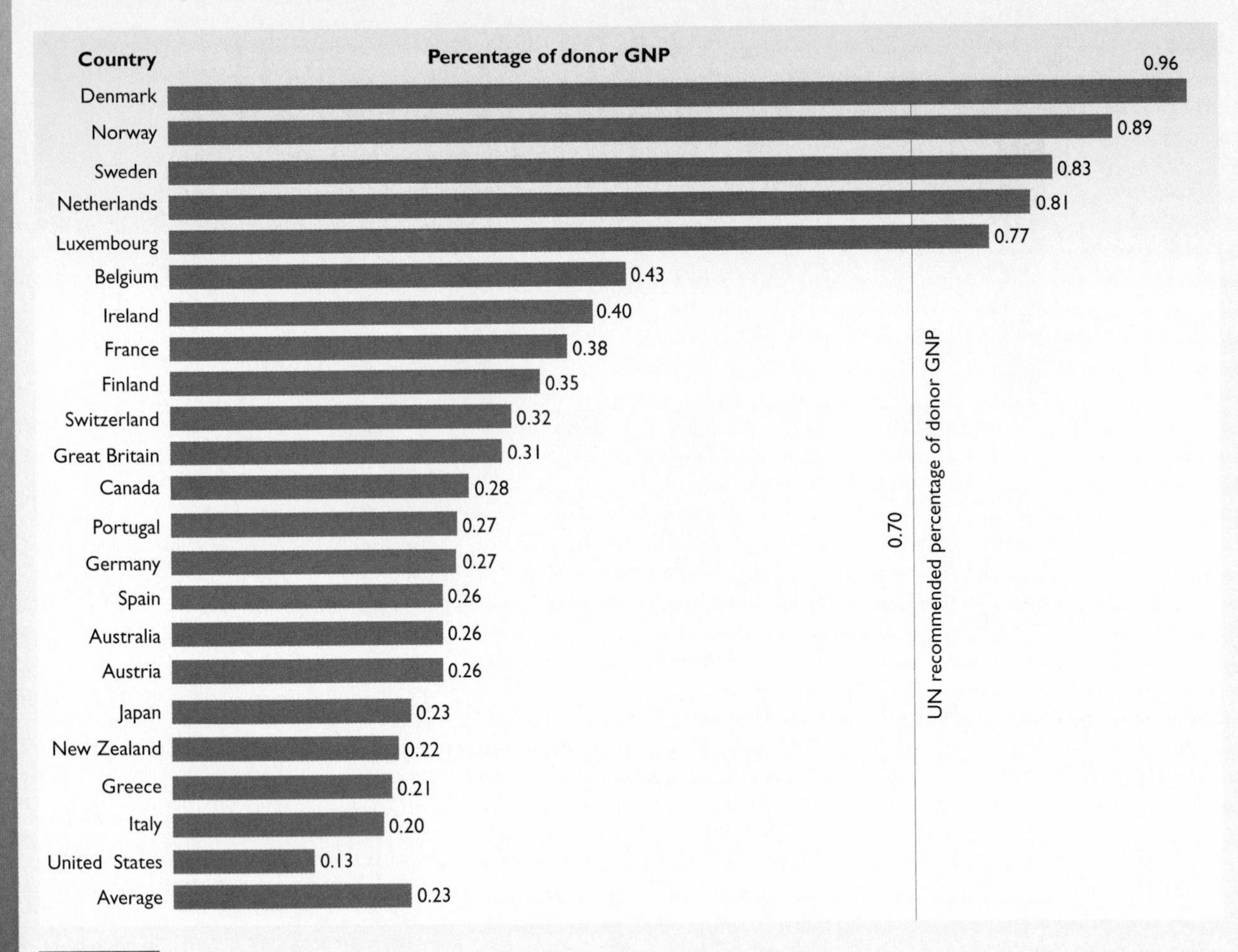

Data source: OECD statistics at http://www.oecd.org/home.

Evaluating the amount of foreign aid is a matter of perspective. Measuring it in terms of overall dollars and measuring it in terms of the donor's wealth gives very different pictures of the level of contribution. In 2002, DAC members gave $58.3 billion dollars in economic foreign aid to LDCs. Yet as impressive as that amount seems, it falls short of the amount that the UN recommends, which is that each EDC should use 0.7% of its GNP for economic assistance. This percentage was not achieved in 2002 nor has it ever been. Indeed, aid giving is moving away from, not toward that goal. In 1965 aid equaled 0.46% of the combined GNP of the DAC members. That percentage declined to 0.23 in 2002. As evident above, only 5 of the 22 countries met or exceeded that standard. If they had all given the recommended 0.7%, economic aid in 2002 would have risen to $177 billion.

More than any other DAC member, the United States provides a good test case to consider whether the aid effort of the EDCs is best described as giving a lot by distributing tens of billions of dollars or as giving only a little based on

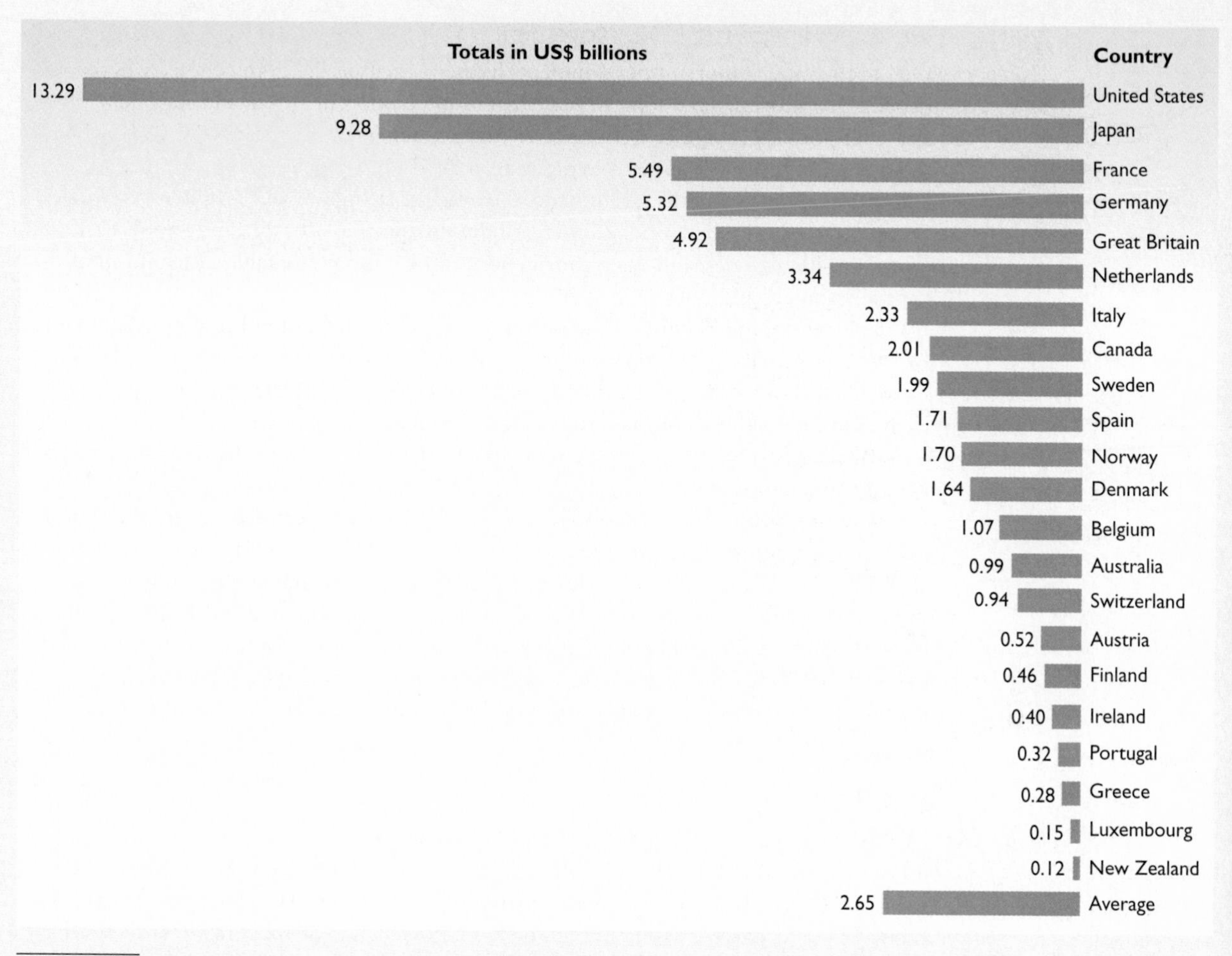

Data source: OECD statistics at http://www.oecd.org/home.

the small percentage of their wealth that goes to foreign aid. As you can see above, the United States in 2002 gave $13.29 billion in foreign aid. That considerable sum is 43% more than the next most generous country (Japan), is equal to 23% of the total aid given by the 22 DAC members, and perhaps qualifies the United States as giving a lot.

However, a less generous perspective is also presented in in the graph on page 432. It shows that when measured in terms of percentage of its GNP, the U.S. effort, 0.13%, placed it last among aid donors. In terms of their wealth, Americans gave 76% less than the Danes, only a third of the UN recommendation, and more than a third less than the next to last country, Italy.

So which perspective best describes U.S. foreign aid? More importantly, how would you write the script of future U.S. foreign aid giving? Would you increase it, keep it about the same, or decrease it? Why? And if you are going to change the amounts, how much would you write in the future budget in terms of dollars or a percentage of the U.S. per capita GNP?

As this editorial cartoon from France suggests, the people of the economically less developed countries of the South are demanding that they receive a greater share of the world's wealth, which is largely possessed by a minority of people who live in the economically developed countries of the North.

economic wealth. They have acted on a number of fronts to enhance their own economic situations and to pressure the EDCs to redistribute part of their wealth. We will examine these views and efforts in terms of the LDCs' expectations, organizational movement, demands, and actions.

Development of the LDC Movement

One of the most important developments in the last half of the 20th century was the independence movement among LDCs. Dozens of colonies in Africa and Asia demanded and won political sovereignty. Even after independence, though, many LDCs remained in an economically subservient and disadvantaged position in relation to their former colonial masters or to other dominant EDCs. Most people in LDCs are not willing to accept such marginalization, and increasingly during the last 50 years, the LDCs have joined together to demand what they believe to be a more equitable distribution of financial resources and political power.

The developing identity of the South first took the form of political nonalignment. In 1955, 29 African and Asian countries convened the Bandung Conference in Indonesia to discuss how to hasten the independence of colonial territories and how to be nonaligned in the cold war. Most of the colonies are now independent, and the cold war is over. But the Bandung Conference remains an important mark of the ongoing sense of identity among the LDCs.

Soon the South's concerns also turned to economic development. Political demands for an end to colonialism provided a role model for similar economic assertiveness. A coalition of disadvantaged countries, the Group of 77, emerged and called for creation of the first United Nations Conference on Trade and Development (UNCTAD), which met in Geneva in 1964. This conference and the Group of 77 (which has grown to 135 members) evolved into an ongoing UNCTAD organization. UNCTAD, which has 192 members, has served as a vehicle for the LDCs to discuss their needs and to press demands on the North.

LDC Demands

The development of LDC consciousness and assertiveness has led to a series of demands on the industrialized North. These came together in the Declaration on the Establishment of a **New International Economic Order (NIEO)**, which was drafted by UNCTAD and adopted as a resolution by the UN General Assembly in 1974. The NIEO declaration began by protesting the North's domination of the existing economic structure and the maldistribution of wealth. To remedy this situation, the declaration called for a number of reforms. These changes have regularly been reiterated, refined, and expanded by UNCTAD and other LDC organizations, but none of the reforms have been truly implemented. Indeed, the onward march of globalization has in many ways sharpened the demands for what UN Secretary-General Annan has termed a "Global New Deal" for the LDCs, one in which "large parts of the world are [no longer] excluded from the benefits of globalization."[10] Speaking to global business and political leaders at the World Economic Forum in early 2002, Annan bluntly told his audience, "The reality is that power and wealth in this world are very, very unequally shared, and that far too many people are condemned to lives of extreme poverty and degradation. The perception among many is that this is all the fault of globalization and that globalization is driven by a global elite, composed of, at least represented by, the people who attend this gathering."[11]

Perhaps the best recent exposition of the views of the LDCs occurred at the South's first ever general summit meeting, which occurred in 2000 at the Group of 77 conference held in Havana, Cuba. The leaders adopted a joint declaration entitled the "Havana Program of Action" that declared, "Rather than be passive witnesses of a history not of our own making, we in the South will exert every effort to shape the future through the establishment of a world order that will reflect our needs and interests."[12] That future, the document asserted, should include:

1. *Trade reforms.* The LDCs are pressing to secure improved and stabilized markets for their products. In the words of the Havana declaration, "It is necessary to adopt measures that improve access, for all products of export interest to developing countries, to the markets of developed countries by means of reducing or eliminating tariff and non-tariff barriers."
2. *Monetary reforms.* The LDCs wish to create greater stability in exchange rates and the ebb and flow of FDI and FPI. "As the recent financial crisis has illustrated," the Havana declaration noted, "financial liberalization including speculative and volatile financial flows, over which the developing countries have little controls, in the absence of adequate institutional arrangements to manage the processes, has generated significant instability in the international economies," with especially disastrous results for the developing countries.
3. *Institutional reforms.* The LDCs have long demanded greater LDC participation in the decision making of the IMF, the World Bank, and other such international financial agencies. "There is an increasing need for the reform of the international financial architecture," the Havana declaration asserted. "In this context, we should seek to ensure a more democratic and fair ordering [of decision making in financial IGOs] . . . in order to increase the effective participation of developing countries in the management of the international economy."
4. *Economic modernization.* The LDCs, from the 1974 NEIO resolution through the Havana UNCTAD summit, have called on the North to assist the South in modernizing the economies of the South through technology transfers and assistance in increasing industrial production. The LDCs gathered in Havana called on the North to assist with "measures that support capacity-building for production and export in our countries" and to "facilitate the access to, dissemination and transfer of technologies on concessional and preferential terms from developed to developing countries."
5. *Political and economic sovereignty.* The South asserts the right of each of its countries to choose its own form of government, its own economic system, and to otherwise exercise sovereign control over its internal affairs. This includes the right to control its own resources and to regulate the activities of MNCs. "We stress that every state has the inalienable right to choose political, economic, social and cultural systems of its own, without interference in any form by another state," the leaders in Havana wrote. "We also reaffirm the principle of permanent sovereignty of peoples under foreign occupation over their natural resources."
6. *Greater labor migration.* The LDCs seek greater freedom for their workers to seek employment in the more prosperous EDCs. The Havana declaration noted that "while the capital markets have been opened, including in developing countries, there has hardly been any movement in opening of the labour market in developed nations."
7. *Elimination of economic coercion.* The South tends to see sanctions as a tool used by the EDCs to punish and control LDCs. For this reason, the Havana meeting called on "developed countries to eliminate . . . unilateral economic coercive measures, inconsistent with the principles of international law" and urged "the international community to exhaust all peaceful methods before resorting to sanctions, which should only be considered as a last resort."

The less developed countries believe that their lagging economic conditions are due to unfair policies of the developed countries. To remedy these policies, the LDCs have made a series of demands for basic international economic reform. One such call was the "Havana Program of Action" formulated by the LDCs in 2000 at the Group of 77 conference held in Cuba and presided over, as seen here, by Cuba's president Fidel Castro (left) as host and Nigeria's president Olusegun Obasanjo, chairman of the G-77.

8. *Economic aid.* The meeting in Havana expressed the view that "the post–cold war period with its promise of a peace dividend has not fulfilled the hopes and expectations of the developing world. Instead, we have witnessed a weakening of the commitment of the developed countries to international cooperation in support of development." The declaration called for working toward meeting the UN's foreign aid "target of 0.7% of GNP of developed countries by the end of the first decade of the 21st century." Only five EDCs now meet that standard, as detailed in the box on pages 432–433. There are also calls for more nonpolitical multilateral aid to be given through the World Bank and other such IGOs.
9. *Debt relief.* The LDCs believe that the EDCs, the World Bank, and the IMF should "work towards outright cancellation of unsustainable debt of developing countries, and reaffirm the need of a just and lasting solution to the problem of the foreign debt of developing countries, which considers the structural causes of indebtedness and prevents the recurrence of this phenomenon in the future."

LDC Action

The LDCs have not waited passively for the EDCs to respond to their demands. They have instead taken action on a number of fronts. Not all these moves have succeeded, but they indicate the South's growing assertiveness.

Early LDC Development Policy Nationalizing MNCs, a process by which countries take over foreign corporations operating within their borders, was one early LDC approach. The oil-producing countries, for example, made Western producers surrender all or majority control of their fields and processing facilities. Many LDCs reasoned that if they controlled an industry it would operate in their interest rather than in the interest of foreign companies, investors, and governments. Perhaps, but these drastic measures caused considerable backlash and dried up the inflow of new investment money. As a result, the practice of nationalization has largely been abandoned.

Establishing cartels was a second tactic that LDCs tried initially. A **cartel** is an international trading agreement among producers who hope to control the supply and price of a primary product. The first cartel was established in 1933 to regulate tea, but the decade of the 1960s, when 18 came into existence, was the apex of cartel formation. They ranged in importance from the Organization of Petroleum Exporting Countries (OPEC) to the Asian and Pacific Coconut Community. Cartels, however, have proven generally unsuccessful. OPEC is the only important exception to that rule, but even it has had to struggle to maintain prices in the face of internal economic and political disputes (such as the Iraq-Iran war in the 1980s), the production of about 40% of the world's petroleum by non-OPEC countries, and other factors (Morse, 1999). Almost surely the efforts of the OPEC cartel to increase prices by manipulating supply has been less important to the rise of petroleum prices than the increasing demand for the product by an energy-addicted world that is evident in Figure 13.8.

Protectionism was a third, and now also rapidly declining, thrust of early LDC activity. The temptation and domestic political pressure for developing countries to use tariff and nontariff barriers to protect infant industries are strong and may in some instances even have merit. There is also an understandable common fear in the LDCs, as one Indian economist explains, "that the foreigners will exploit, dominate, and control us."[13] Protectionist policies, however, have numerous drawbacks. Most important, many economists argue that protectionism does not work for LDCs and that economic growth is positively associated with eliminating trade impediments (Bhagwati, 2002; Dollar & Kraay, 2002, 2001; Watkins 2002). Moreover, whether protectionism works or not, EDCs and the major international financial IGOs have pressed and continue to press the LDCs to open their markets. The view, as expressed in a 2003 joint statement by the heads of the IMF and the World Bank, is that "expanding trade by collectively reducing barriers is the single most powerful tool that countries, working together, can deploy to reduce poverty and raise living standards. Liberalizing trade is a core element of the strategy . . . to help developing countries achieve [greater prosperity]."[14]

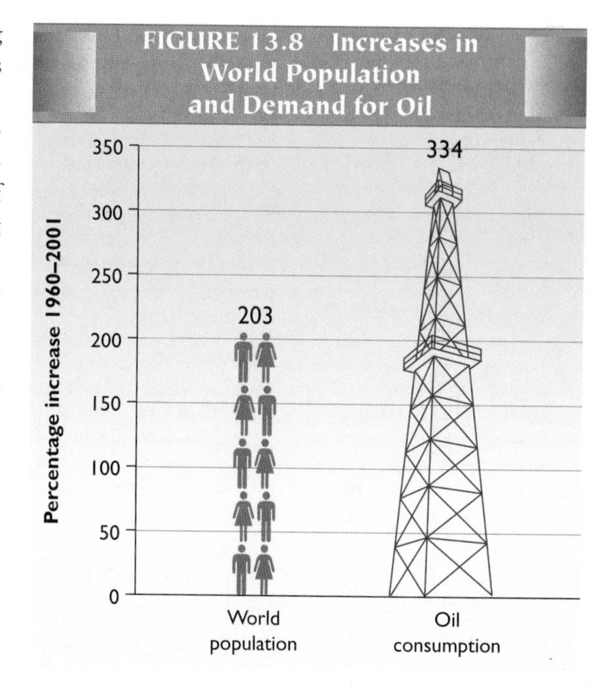

Petroleum prices have risen considerably in real dollars since 1960, but that may be more attributable to the increase in demand, which has grown 50% faster than the world population, than to OPECs efforts to manipulate prices by controlling supply.

Data sources: UN Population Fund at http://www.unfpa.org; U.S. Department of Energy at http://www.eia.doe.gov.

It must be added that eliminating trade barriers is not a panacea for reducing poverty in the LDCs. One issue is that while an LDC's overall prosperity may improve, what occurs in many such countries is that a relatively small percentage of the population benefits greatly, while little of the wealth trickles down to the poorer segments of the population (see Figure 13.4 on p. 423). Second, trade barrier reductions by the economically more fragile LDCs have to be met or even exceeded by the EDCs, especially for agriculture and other areas that are important sources of export earnings for the LDCs. The argument, as Secretary-General Annan put it in late 2003, is that many of the EDC barriers "are stifling the ability of poor countries to compete fairly in the international trading system and trade their way out of poverty."[15]

More Recent LDC Development Policy With nationalization, cartels, and protectionism proving to be mostly inefficient, even counterproductive measures, and under pressure from the United States, the IMF, and other bastions of free-market advocacy, many LDCs have turned toward trying to compete with the EDCs on their own terms. Even most of the few remaining communist countries, such as China and Vietnam, have succumbed to capitalism. Moreover, there have been some remarkable success stories, as our earlier discussion of NICs indicates. Singapore's per capita GNP is the ninth highest in the world, and South Korea's is just short of the World Bank's "high-income" category.

Yet for the LDCs, including the countries in transition (CITs, the former communist countries) that are struggling to develop their economies, the capitalist path to development has several negative by-products. One is control. To a degree, some LDCs have achieved development by suppressing democracy in favor of the political stability that outside investors favor. Second, some LDCs have also followed anti–labor union practices and other policies in order to keep wages low so that export prices can be kept down. A third drawback is that some LDCs have attracted foreign investment by having lax environmental, safety, and other regulations. Some LDCs are among the world's most polluted countries. Japan, for instance, produces 4.6 times more manufactured goods than does China; yet China's industrial emissions of carbon dioxide are 2.8 times higher than are Japan's.

Fourth, CITs and even those, such as China, that remain officially communist have found that capitalism and international economic liberalism have negative social consequences. China once stressed socioeconomic equality. Now some Chinese drive imported Mercedes, while others live in the shantytowns that have sprung up around Chinese cities. The wealthiest 20% of Chinese now take in 47% of the country's income; the poorest 20% make only 6% of the national income. That is about the same income disparity as the quintessential capitalist country, the United States.

The Future of National Economic Policy

There can be no doubt that the economic story of the last half-century has been marked by two important and related trends. The first has been the almost complete triumph of **capitalism** over competing economic models, especially Marxism and socialism. One measure of this change is the Index of Economic Freedom, which has been calculated since 1995 by the Heritage Foundation, a conservative think tank. The index measures 10 variables, including the extent or levels of government intervention in the economy, taxation, property rights, a black market, and corruption, that it believes distort a free economy.[16] By 1995 the movement toward capitalism was well under way, and that reorientation has continued since then. As evident in Figure 13.9, the percentage of countries in the economically "free" category (1–1.99) and the "mostly free" category (2–2.99) increased a combined 7% between 1995 and 2002. According to the 2003 survey, Singapore (1.50) was the most free economy, North Korea (5.00) was the least free. The U.S. rating might have been the most free, but it was reduced to 1.80 because of a 3.50 rating for high taxes.

The second important trend has been a steady movement toward ever greater economic interdependence based on an increasingly free exchange of trade, investment, and other financial activity. An array of statistics presented in this and the preceding chapter show conclusively that the movement of goods, services, investment capital, and currencies across borders has expanded exponentially. Furthermore, as we shall take up in the next chapter, the international system has created the EU, IMF, NAFTA, World Bank, WTO, and numerous global and regional organizations and arrangements to facilitate and promote free international economic interchange.

For all this evidence, it would be erroneous to conclude that the world is on a path to inevitable economic integration and that the eclipse of economic nationalism is inescapable. Indeed, there are powerful arguments against and forces opposed to globalization. "We have sunlight, but we have shadows, too," the head of the WTO commented.[17] Those shadows are cast, according to one analyst, by the fact that "today many people think that globalization is going to destroy their life as they know it. We have gotten used to the idea that globalization will inevitably succeed, but I am not so sure anymore."[18]

Other shadows have been cast by what some analysts see as a partial retreat toward protectionism even by powerful EDCs, such as the United States, that have been at the forefront of the drive toward free economic exchange and that still rhetorically espouse that goal. Warnings came from two top finance officials in separate but similar statements in November 2003. U.S. Federal Reserve Chairman Alan Greenspan cautioned, "Some clouds of emerging protectionism have become increasingly visible on today's horizon. . . .

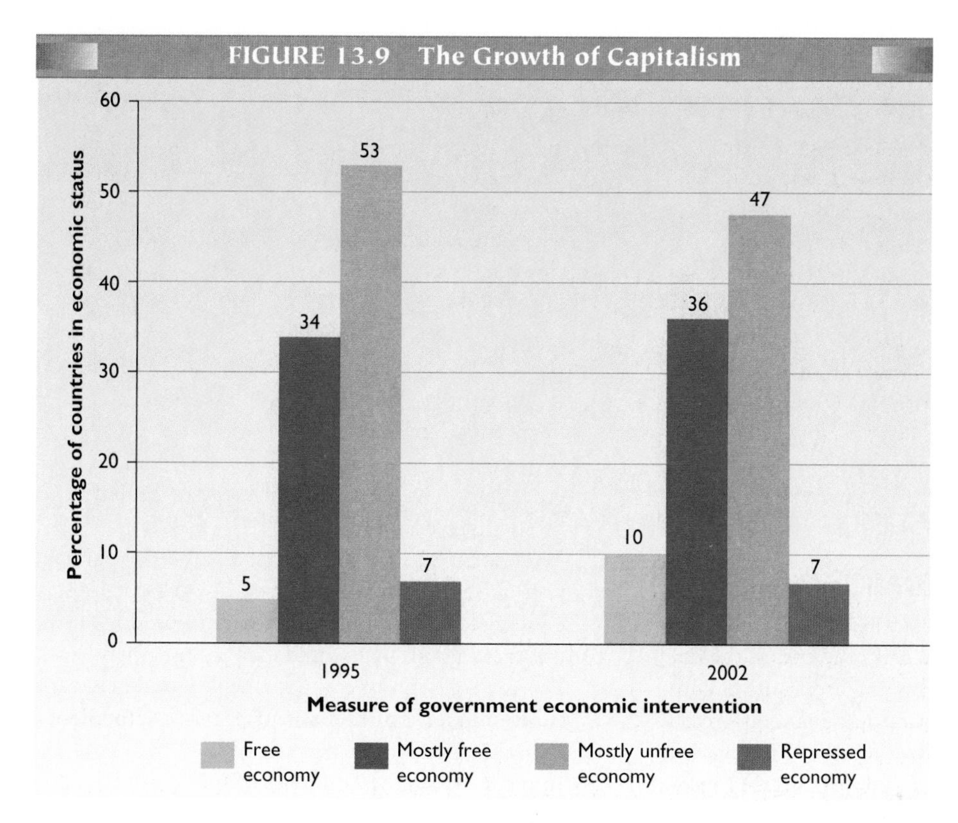

A significant change in the past few decades has been a surge in the capitalist approach to national economic management and a decline in the prevalence of other models, particularly Marxism and socialism. The shift is evident in this figure based on data from the Heritage Foundation.

Data source: Gerald P. O'Driscoll Jr., Edwin J. Feulner Jr., and Mary Anastasia O'Grady, *2003 Index of Economic Freedom*, Heritage Foundation Web site at http://index.heritage.org/.

It is imperative that creeping protectionism be thwarted and reversed." Taking the same view, the IMF's first deputy managing director Anne Krueger told an audience, "We cannot afford . . . any risk of a return to protectionism. Trade can sometimes be a controversial domestic policy issue. But governments need to resist the pressure to give in to the lobbying of narrow interest groups who cannot [be allowed to] benefit at the expense of the wider public."[19]

Whether or not globalization is to continue and to succeed without alienating the majority of LDCs, who believe they are being left behind, depends on the degree to which greater international cooperation can be achieved. The history, current status, and future of that effort are explored in chapter 14.

Chapter Summary

National Economic Power: Assets and Utilization

1. Economic nationalism still remains the dominant approach in global economic affairs even though the trend toward international economic liberalization has grown in importance.
2. The stronger role being played by international economics means that political relations between countries have been increasingly influenced by economic relations. Domestically also, politics significantly affect economic policy. Domestic political pressures are important

determinants of tariff policies and other trade regulations. Trade can also be used as a diplomatic tool.

3. Economic strength is a key element of every country's overall power. Economic power is based on financial position, natural resources, industrial output, agricultural output, and international competitiveness.
4. Countries use their economic power through a mixture of positive incentives and negative sanctions. While each approach is sometimes successful, both incentives and, particularly, sanctions are difficult to apply successfully and have numerous drawbacks.
5. There are a variety of barriers to the unimpeded international movement of trade and capital that countries use to pursue economic nationalism. These include such barriers as tariffs, nontariff barriers, and licensing requirements.

The North and International Political Economy

6. The economies of the North are prosperous compared to those of the South. With the end of the cold war and with a variety of changing economic circumstances, however, the situation has changed greatly. The EDCs are experiencing a number of economic difficulties, including the pressure of entering into a period of postindustrial economy, and economic tensions among them have increased.

The South and International Political Economy

7. The economies of the South are relatively weak compared to those of the North. Also, in the South there is great disparity in wealth among and within countries. A few NICs have expanding and modernizing economies. There is also, in most LDCs, a small wealthy class of people and a much larger class of impoverished people.
8. The LDCs need hard currency capital to buy the goods and services that will allow them to develop their economies. The four basic sources of hard currency are loans, foreign investment, trade, and foreign aid. There are, however, problems with each of these sources.
9. Loans are unsatisfactory because of high repayment costs. The debt crisis has eased, but LDC debt is growing once again and could threaten the global financial community.
10. Investment capital has grown in amount and importance in recent years. Still, investment capital flows mostly into just a few LDCs.
11. The catch-22 of trade is that the LDCs' primary products, their main exports, do not earn them enough capital to found industries to produce manufactured goods that would earn more money.
12. Foreign aid is minor compared with world needs and is often given on the basis of political expediency rather than economic necessity.
13. In recent years, the countries of the South have begun to make greater demands for economic equity to press the North to join in establishing a New International Economic Order.

The Future of National Economic Policy

14. In order for globalization to succeed, the economic interests of LDCs and EDCs have to be mutually accommodated by international economic cooperation.

For a chapter quiz, interactive activities, web links, PowerWeb articles, and much more, visit **www.mhhe.com/rourke10/** and go to chapter 13. Or, while accessing the site, click on Course-Wide Content and view recent international relations articles in the *New York Times*.

Key Terms

bilateral aid
capitalism
cartel
debt service
Development Assistance Committee (DAC)
development capital
economic sanctions
free economic interchange
Group of 7 (G-7)
Group of Eight (G-8)
hard currency
multilateral aid
net trade
New International Economic Order (NIEO)
newly industrializing countries (NICs)
nontariff barriers (NTBs)
protectionism
tariff

CHAPTER

14

International Economic Cooperation: The Alternative Road

GLOBAL ECONOMIC COOPERATION: BACKGROUND
- The Origins of Economic Cooperation
- Global Economic Cooperation: EDC Prosperity
- Global Economic Cooperation: LDC Development

GLOBAL ECONOMIC COOPERATION: THE INSTITUTIONS
- The United Nations and Economic Cooperation
- Trade Cooperation: The GATT and the WTO
- Monetary Cooperation: The IMF
- Development Cooperation: The World Bank Group

REGIONAL ECONOMIC COOPERATION
- Europe
- The Western Hemisphere
- Asia, the Pacific, and Elsewhere
- The Future of Regionalism

CHAPTER SUMMARY

KEY TERMS

The gods sent not
Corn for the rich men only.
—William Shakespeare, *Coriolanus*

Happy are they that can hear their detractions, and can put them to mending.
—William Shakespeare, *Much Ado about Nothing*

If a house be divided against itself, that house cannot stand.
—Mark 3:25

The Lord so constituted everybody that no matter what color you are you require the same amount of nourishment.
—Will Rogers, *The Autobiography of Will Rogers*

CHAPTER OBJECTIVES

After completing this chapter, you should be able to:

- Discuss why economic cooperation and integration will prove to be pivotal determinants of future international relations.
- Analyze the specialized cooperative efforts currently at work on the world stage.
- List the most significant development agencies involved in granting loans and aid to less developed countries.
- Discuss the reasons leading to growing international monetary cooperation, giving special attention to the International Monetary Fund.
- Evaluate how the European Union exemplifies efforts at international or regional economic integration.
- Trace the evolution of the North American Free Trade Agreement and assess its effects on the region and the world.
- Describe efforts at regionalism that have emerged at least partly in response to the economic integration occurring in Europe and North America.

This chapter is the last of three that examine international political economy. Chapter 12 laid out the global economic road map. Chapter 13 took up economic nationalism, which is characterized by self-interested economic competition among and between the states of the North and of the South. Economic nationalism persists and, in some aspects, is on the rise. It may even eventually provide prosperity to all states and peoples.

There are, however, economic internationalists and structuralists who condemn the harvest that we reap from this nationalist economic strategy. They believe that the global economic future will be better if countries cooperate economically, or even integrate their economies. Whereas chapter 13 explores the economic nationalist path, this chapter assesses the alternative route of greater international cooperation. This assessment will first examine global cooperation, then turn its attention to regional efforts. As you will see, one aspect of cooperation among the economically developed countries (EDCs) of the North is an effort to ensure that their relative prosperity continues. An even more important goal of economic cooperation, arguably, is to improve the circumstances of the less developed countries (LDCs) of the South, and we will pay particular attention to economic development programs. Within these broader topics, this chapter will also deal with a variety of more specific issues, such as child labor and the puzzle of how to continue to grow economically while simultaneously protecting the environment from the negative by-products of economic expansion.

Global Economic Cooperation: Background

The thought of moving toward a very different way of dealing with the international economy is more than theory. It is a process that has made substantial progress and one that many scholars, practitioners, and other analysts think can and should become the dominant paradigm in the future. At the global level, it is appropriate to first look at the background of economic cooperation. Then we will turn to detailing the most important international economic institutions.

The Origins of Economic Cooperation

Economic nationalism has long been the prevailing reality, but it is also true that economic cooperation and regulation have become increasingly commonplace, albeit still limited, elements of national and international economics. The liberal idea of creating a global economy based on free economic interchange and interdependence dates back several hundred years, as elaborated in chapter 12. This view was slow to take hold, though, and did not begin to shape international economic relations to any great extent until the 1930s and 1940s. A combination of the strife that had marked the 20th century to that point and the Great Depression that was gripping the world in the 1930s led an increasing number of leaders to agree with the view of the longest-serving U.S. secretary of state (1933–1944), Cordell Hull, that "international commerce is not only calculated to aid materially in the restoration of prosperity everywhere, but it is the greatest civilizer and peacemaker in the experience of the human race" (Paterson, Clifford, & Hagan, 2000:121).

While the tensions that led to World War II kept international economic reform on the political back burner for a decade, the war added to the impetus to change the structure and course of world politics. With the United States leading the anti-Axis alliance and then the anticommunist West, the capitalist EDCs moved during the years 1943–1948 to create the foundation for a new international economic order. The EDCs created a number of global and regional intergovernmental organizations (IGOs) to reduce national economic barriers and to otherwise handle a range of economic interactions across national boundaries. The most prominent of these IGOs are the World Bank, the International Monetary Fund (IMF), the General Agreement on Tariffs and Trade (GATT, both a treaty and an organization; the organization was renamed the World Trade Organization, WTO), and the United Nations, with its numerous economic agencies and responsibilities, which was brought into existence by the U.S.-led victors at the end of World War II. Although the UN was created to address a broad range of global issues, it had and continues to have an important economic role.

Thus began the current era of enhanced global and regional economic cooperation. Trade and the flow of international capital grew rapidly. These successes and the need to further regulate the increased economic interchanges led to yet more agreements and IGOs dedicated to still further reductions of national economic barriers. The European Union (EU) and the North American Free Trade Agreement (NAFTA) are just two of the more recent IGOs or treaties that facilitate the free flow of goods, services, and capital. We will examine them by first taking up global efforts, then by turning to regional ones.

Global Economic Cooperation: EDC Prosperity

The United States and other countries that in the 1940s initiated the movement toward greater economic cooperation were all EDCs, and their goal was to renew and maintain their prosperity. Initially, little attention was paid to the South, much of which still had colonial status. Economic cooperation has come to include efforts to develop the South, but there remains an important dimension of cooperation among countries of the North to maintain their prosperity.

In addition to creating the IMF, World Bank, and WTO to help ensure their post–World War II economic health, the EDCs also later founded other institutions for the same purpose. The first of these, the **Organization for Economic Cooperation and Development (OECD)**, was established in 1961 by the United States, Canada, 15 Western European countries, and Turkey (an LDC admitted because it was a member of the North Atlantic Treaty Organization [NATO]) to coordinate economic policy among the Western EDCs. Several other EDCs subsequently became members. A second LDC, Mexico, was admitted in 1994 after it became linked to the United States and Canada under the North American Free Trade Agreement (NAFTA). Since then, South Korea, the Czech Republic, Hungary, Poland, and Slovakia (all LDCs, albeit relatively prosperous ones) have also joined. Still, the bulk of the OECD's 30 member-states are EDCs, making the organization something of a "rich man's club." The OECD serves as forum for member-countries to discuss economic issues, it generates copious statistics and numerous studies, and it offers economic advice and technical assistance. Like almost all major economic IGOs, the OECD in recent years has also become increasingly involved with the LDCs and such issues as globalization and sustainable development, and it has established links with some 70 LDCs, ranging from Brazil, China, and Russia to the least developed countries (LLDCs) in sub-Saharan Africa and elsewhere.

If the OECD is a reasonably exclusive club of prosperous member-countries, the **Group of Eight (G-8)** is equivalent to the executive board. The G-8 does not have a formal connection to the OECD, but it does represent the pinnacle of economic power. The G-8 began in 1975 as the **Group of Seven (G-7)**, which included the seven most economically powerful Western countries (Canada, France, Germany, Great Britain, Italy, Japan, and the United States). The group's annual meeting in 1997 expanded membership for political matters to include Russia. The group officially became the Group of Eight (G-8) the following year. In some sense, however, the G-7 continues to exist because the original seven agreed they would meet as the G-7 without Russia on financial

The annual Group of Eight (G-8) meeting among the world's seven leading economic powers and Russia serves as a platform for the leaders of these countries to discuss a range of political and economic issues of mutual concern, and to coordinate policy. The meetings also provide a way for the leaders to get to know one another in both formal and informal settings, as evident in this photograph of (from left to right in the foreground) Prime Minister Tony Blair of Great Britain, President Jacques Chirac of France, President Vladimir Putin of Russia, and Chancellor Gerhard Schröder of Germany enjoying a lighter moment during the 2003 meeting of the G-8 in Evian, France.

issues and as the G-8 with the Russian president on political issues. To avoid confusion, the group will be referred to as the G-8 in all its activities.

Whatever the G-number, the most important issue is the impact of the process. There are numerous G-8 meetings at the ministerial level, but the apex is the annual summit meeting. The G-8 has become one focus of the ire of antiglobalization forces, and its meetings, like those of other Western economic IGOs, increasingly drew large, often violent protests beginning in the mid-1990s. After being besieged by antiglobalism protesters during their 2001 meeting in Genoa, Italy, the leaders of the G-8 decided to move their meetings to more remote sites where security would be easier. Locations of the most recent meetings have been Kananaskis, Canada, a resort area 55 miles west of Calgary, Alberta (2002), Evian, France, a resort town along the Swiss border (2003), and Sea Island, Georgia, in the United States (2004). While the G-8 remains primarily devoted to economic coordination among the leading EDCs, it has also expanded the scope of its meetings. This shift was reflected by the summary of the chair (host President Jacques Chirac) of the 2003 meeting. His summary of the meeting indicated that it addressed three major subjects: global (not just EDC) economic growth, enhancing environmentally sustainable development, and improving security in the areas of terrorism, nonproliferation, and illicit international small arms sales. Reflecting their broadening focus, the G-8 leaders also took up issues concerning Iraq, Israel and Palestine, North Korea, Afghanistan, and Iran. Additionally, the G-8 leaders met with the leaders of Algeria, Brazil, China, Egypt, India, Malaysia, Mexico, Nigeria, Saudi Arabia, Senegal, and South Africa, as well as representatives from the UN, the World Bank, the IMF, and the WTO.

Many analysts conclude that the annual summits play a positive, if not always clear-cut role. As one scholar writes, the member-countries "do comply modestly with the decisions and consensus generated [at the annual economic summit meetings]. Compliance is particularly high in regard to agreements on international trade and energy." The analyst also points out that the meetings provide "an important occasion for busy leaders to discuss major, often complex international issues, and to develop the personal relations that help them" both to "respond in an effective fashion to sudden crises or shocks" and "shape the international [economic] order more generally."[1] Also, the group takes up political and social issues. There are other analysts who fault the G-8 for not achieving more concrete results and cite this as a reason why the meetings of the G-8, which were once major news stories, have more recently been far from front-page news. As one analyst put it after reviewing the 2003 G-8 summit, it had been important as a meeting to begin the reconciliation of the leaders after the divisions that had occurred over the war with Iraq, but beyond that, "the substantive results from Evian were copious in quantity but weak in quality."[2]

Global Economic Cooperation: LDC Development

Commentary in other parts of this book has explored the economic gap between the EDCs and LDCs and its associated political and social consequences (chapters 2 and 12) and the historical roles that the industrial revolution, military technology, colonialism, and other factors have played in the creation and persistence of that gap (chapter 2). The concern here is what can and should be done. More specifically, what can and should the countries of the North do to assist the countries of the South?

Approaches to Economic Development

As noted in chapter 12, there are three fundamental approaches to international political economy (IPE). Each of these gives very different answers to the questions of why great economic disparity exists in the world and what, if anything, to do about it.

The Economic Nationalist Approach Economic nationalists operate from a realpolitik orientation and believe that each country should look out for itself first and foremost. Therefore, economic nationalists argue that an EDC should be governed by its own national interest when formulating trade, investment, and aid policies toward the South. Furthermore, economic nationalists suspect that the South's calls for greater equity are, in essence, attempts to change the rules so that the LDCs can acquire political power for themselves.

Economic nationalists view the political economy as a zero-sum game in which gains made by some players inevitably mean losses for other players. It is a perspective that leads economic nationalists to worry that extensive aid to LDCs may be counterproductive for both the donor and the recipient. The reasoning often uses a **lifeboat analogy**. This image depicts the world as a lifeboat that can support only so many passengers. The people of the EDCs are in the boat. The billions of poor are in the sea, in peril of drowning, and clamoring to get aboard. The dilemma is that the lifeboat is incapable of supporting everyone because there are not enough resources. Therefore, if everyone gets in, the lifeboat will sink and all will perish. The answer, then, is to sail off with a sad but resolute sigh, saving the few at the expense of the many in the interest of common sense. An extension of this logic, economic nationalists suggest, is that providing food and medicine to the already overpopulated LDCs only encourages more childbearing, decreases infant mortality, and increases longevity, and thereby worsens the situation by creating more people to flounder and drown in the impoverished sea.

The Economic Internationalist Approach Economic internationalist theorists believe that development can be achieved within the existing international economic structure. This belief is related to the idealist approach to general world politics. Economic internationalists believe that the major impediments to the South's development are its weakness in acquiring capital, its shortage of skilled labor, and some of its domestic economic policies, such as centralized planning and protectionism. These difficulties can be overcome through free trade and foreign investment supplemented by loans and foreign aid and through reduced government interference in the economy. Such policies, economic internationalists believe, will allow unimpeded international economic exchange among states, which will

Some people use a lifeboat analogy to argue against extending massive aid to the less developed countries. The logic is that a lifeboat can support only so many passengers, and that the economic boat will be swamped and its current passengers (those in the wealthy countries) figuratively drowned (impoverished) with little or no benefit to the poor countries struggling in poverty. Others argue that everyone is in the same boat, and that whether it becomes a luxury liner or like the *Titanic* goes down at sea depends on how well all the passengers are doing.

eventually create prosperity for all. Thus, for economic internationalists, the global economy is not a zero-sum game. They believe it is possible to integrate LDCs into the world economic system by eliminating imperfections in the current system while maintaining the system's basic structure and stability.

As for the lifeboat analogy, economic internationalists contend that we are not in (or out of) a lifeboat at all. Instead, they say, we are all inescapably sailing on the same vessel, perhaps the SS *World,* to a common destiny. From this perspective, we can all reach the home port of prosperity, or we can all suffer the fate of the *Titanic,* which struck an iceberg and sank in the North Atlantic in 1912. The 1,513 passengers who drowned came from both luxurious first-class and steerage accommodations, but they found in death the equality inherent in all humans. Commenting in this vein, UN Secretary-General Kofi Annan told the economic elite attending the World Economic Forum in 2002, "None of us, I suggest, can afford to ignore the condition of our fellow passengers on this little boat. If they are sick, all of us risk infection. And if they are angry, all of us can easily get hurt."[3]

The Economic Structuralist Approach Scholars of the structuralist school of thought believe that the political-economic organization of the world's patterns of production and trade must be radically altered for the LDCs to develop. In terms of the lifeboat analogy, economic structuralists believe that not only should the poor be allowed into the boat, but that they should also at least share command with, and perhaps supplant, the wealthy captains who have been sailing the vessel in their own interests and at the expense of others. Marxists would not shun a peaceful change of command if that were possible, but they are not averse to a mutiny if necessary.

Incentives and Resistance to Development

It is obvious that the three different IPE approaches to the general conduct of global economic affairs and to North-South relations present markedly different descriptions of, and even more dramatically different prescriptions for, the conduct of political–economic relations. To help decide which of the three contains the greatest element of truth, it is appropriate to turn to an examination of the current status of global incentives to get more LDCs in the lifeboat and the resistance to that goal.

Incentives to Assist the Development of the South There are several incentives for the North to try to assist the South. One of these is moral; the others are pragmatic.

Humanitarian compassion is one reason to assist the South. The concept that each domestic society has an obligation to provide at least a minimally acceptable level of existence for its people has taken firm hold throughout most of the world. This has led all countries, especially the wealthy ones, to adopt a wide range of economic and social programs to help those in need. National borders have created a sense of boundaries relating to whom a country does or does not have a moral responsibility to help, but as chapters 4 and 6 relate, those borders are artificial creations that are increasingly less relevant in today's interconnected world.

Decreased international violence is one of the pragmatic ways that the North will benefit from increased prosperity in the South, according to aid advocates. This view contends that the poor are becoming increasingly hostile toward the wealthy. Modern communications have heightened the South's sense of relative deprivation—the awareness of a deprived person (group, country) of the gap between his or her circumstances and the relatively better position of others. Research shows that seeing another's prosperity and knowing that there are alternatives to your own impoverished condition causes frustration and a sense of being cheated that often leads to resentment and sometimes to violence.

Perhaps it was the 9/11 attacks that provided the wake-up call, but when world leaders met in Monterrey, Mexico, in 2002 to discuss LDC development, a constant theme was the connection between poverty and violence. "Poverty in all its forms is the greatest single threat to peace [and] security," the head of the WTO told delegates.[4] Echoing that theme, Secretary-General Annan warned another group of economic leaders, "Left alone in their poverty, these countries are all too likely to collapse or relapse into conflict and anarchy, a menace to their neighbors and potentially, as the events of the 11th of September so brutally reminded us, a threat to global security."[5]

Increased economic prosperity for the EDCs is another benefit that many analysts believe will result from the betterment of the LDCs. This view maintains that it is in the North's long-term economic interest to aid the South's development. After World War II, the United States launched the Marshall Plan, which gave billions of dollars to Europe. One motivation was the U.S. realization that it needed an economically revitalized Europe with which to trade and in which to invest. Europe recovered, and its growth helped drive the strong growth of the American economy. In the same way, according to many analysts, helping the South toward prosperity would require an immense investment by the North. In the long run, though, that investment would create a world in which many of the 1.3 billion Chinese could purchase Fords, more of India's 1 billion people could afford to travel in Boeing airplanes, and a majority of the 124 million Nigerians and 168 Brazilians could buy Dell personal computers. It is true that a developed South will compete economically with the North, but economic history demonstrates that increased production and competition bring more, better, and cheaper products that improve the standard of living for all.

One argument for extending massive economic aid to less developed countries is that if they grow prosperous they can buy the products of the United States and other developed countries. This 2003 photograph in Beijing, China, of commuters and even a worker delivering goods, shows that bicycles are still the most common form of transportation in that country. Currently there are 7 cars per 1,000 people in China, compared to 475 cars per 1,000 Americans. That means a huge potential market for auto manufacturers, almost all of which are headquartered in the EDCs.

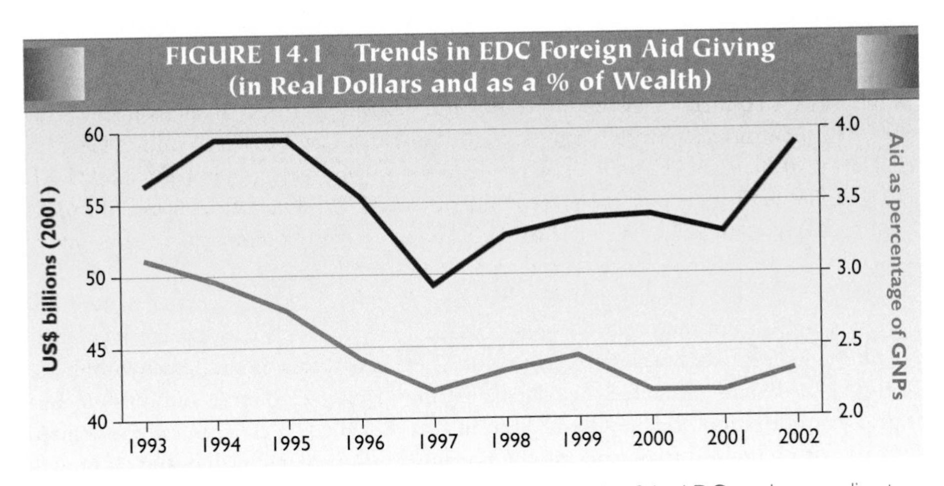

Despite a great deal of rhetoric from the EDCs about the needs of the LDCs and responding to them, there has been no movement to substantially increase foreign aid. Measured in real dollars, aid giving has been static. As for their aid effort compared to wealth, the EDCs gave 26% less of their collective GNPs in 2002 than they did in 1993.

Data source: OECD at http://www.oecd.org.

Resistance to Development Whatever the moral and pragmatic arguments for promoting LDC prosperity may be, the North has been slow to respond to the development needs of the South. Among the reasons are a continuing strong sense of economic nationalism, internal pressure from interest groups to preserve advantages such as agricultural subsidies, domestic opposition to foreign aid, and the sense based on political nationalism that the EDCs are not responsible for causing, continuing, or correcting the wealth gap with the LDCs. One indication of this stance by the EDCs, as we have noted, is that foreign economic aid-giving by the EDCs has been relatively static when measured in real dollars (controlled for inflation), and aid has dropped off substantially when measured as a percentage of GNP, as indicated in Figure 14.1.

Efforts to bring the North and South together directly to marshal resources and coordinate programs have also shown very limited results. The initial UN-sponsored meeting that brought the leaders of the North and South together was held in 1981. This meeting and a number of others on development that have followed have helped increase international awareness among the policy makers of the North about the need for development, have elicited expressions of concern, and have even brought some financial support. Still, the outcome has been that the North has been unwilling to take the actions needed to rapidly advance the South's development.

An example of the continuing gap between rhetoric and reality, between what is needed to address development and what is offered, was provided by the most recent of the North-South meetings, the **International Conference on Financing for Development (ICFD)**, which was held in March 2002 in Monterrey, Mexico. The conference was attended by 50 heads of government, ranging from George Bush to Fidel Castro, the leaders of the World Bank, IMF, and other top financial IGOs, representatives of numerous NGOs (such as Focus on the Global South, headquartered in Thailand), and representatives of the Institute of Canadian Bankers and other business entities.

The challenge to the conference was put forth by Kofi Annan. "All serious studies concur that we cannot achieve [our development goals] without at least $50 billion a year of additional official aid," he told the delegates. "The clearest and most immediate test of the Monterrey spirit," Annan continued, "is whether the donor countries will provide that aid." He went on to recognize that "some donors may still be skeptical, because they are not convinced that aid works," but added, "To them, I say, 'look at the record.' There is abundant evidence that aid does work."[6]

To some degree, the leaders of the EDCs were responsive. France's President Jacques Chirac proposed meeting the long-standing UN goal of "allocating 0.7% of the wealth of the industrialized countries to development of the poor countries." The European Union pledged to add $7 billion a year by 2006 to the aid that its members collectively contribute, and President Bush announced that he would ask Congress to increase U.S. economic aid by 50% to about $15 billion by 2005. Whatever the intentions of these and other leaders, however, such promises are unlikely to be fulfilled and, even if progress is made, it will almost surely fall short of the 0.7% standard. As leaders of democratic countries, Chirac, Bush, and others must convince their respective national legislatures to appropriate the funds they indicated as a goal. The fact, as Figure 14.1 indicates, that foreign aid measured in real dollars has been static and as a percentage of donor countries' respective GNPs has been going down creates skepticism that the leaders of the EDCs literally mean what they say, or, even if they do, that they will be able to win large aid increases. To meet the 0.7% goal, France would have to increase its aid 184% from its 2002 level (0.38% of GNP) and U.S. aid would have to jump 538% from its 2002 level (0.13%). In sum, one does not want to be unduly pessimistic, but meeting the goals of the Monterrey conference and adequately funding development in the South will require a substantial change in the recent historical trends among the recalcitrant rich.

Global Economic Cooperation: The Institutions

The most obvious manifestation of the move toward economic cooperation and globalization that began in earnest in the 1940s is the array of global and regional IGOs that have been created to try to regulate and enhance the world economy. Of the global IGOs, the most important are the UN, the WTO, the IMF, and the World Bank.

The United Nations and Economic Cooperation

The UN serves as a global umbrella organization for numerous agencies and programs that deal with economic issues through the UN General Assembly (UNGA), the United Nations Economic and Social Council (UNESCO), and other UN divisions and associated agencies. The economic focus of the UN can be roughly divided into two categories: global economic regulation and the economic development of the South.

The UN and Global Economic Regulation

The UN is involved in a number of areas related to global economic cooperation. The regulation of transnational (or multinational) corporations (TNCs/MNCs) is one such area. The need to regulate business first became apparent at the national level. As a result, the sometimes predatory practices of capitalist corporations have been partially restrained by domestic laws enacted over the past century or so. In the United States, for instance, the Progressive Era of the late 1800s and early 1900s led to efforts to rein in the so-called robber barons of big business through the passage of such legislation as the Sherman Antitrust Act (1890) and the establishment of such agencies as the Federal Trade Commission (1914).

Now, some people worry that globalization has allowed business to escape regulation. These critics, therefore, favor creating global regulations and oversight ("watchdog") agencies similar to those in most EDCs. "Are we really going to let the world become a global market without any laws except those of the jungle?" President François Mitterrand of France once asked at a UN-sponsored economic conference. "Should we leave the world's destiny in the hands of those speculators who in a few hours can bring to nothing the work of millions of men and women?"[7] In response to such concerns, the UN's Center for Transnational Corporations was established as part of the effort to create global standards and regulations to limit the inherently self-serving practices of capitalist corporations.

Creating global labor standards is a related area of economic regulation. At the national level, for example, it was during the American Progressive Era that workers began to organize widely into unions. The American Federation of Labor, for one, was established in 1886. The U.S. government also began to regulate labor through such statutes as the Federal Child Labor Law (1916) and to create agencies such as the Department of Labor (1913) to promote the welfare of workers. Similarly, the UN is trying to make progress on labor conditions at the international level through such affiliated specialized agencies as the United Nations Children's Fund (UNICEF) and the International Labor Organization (ILO).

Child labor is one of the principal current concerns of the ILO. It estimates that there are over 186 million children aged 5 to 14 who are performing more than light or casual "economic activity." About 88% of these children are engaged in what the ILO classifies as hazardous work. A further subset of child workers are the 8.4 million who are enmeshed in slavery, prostitution and pornography, or who are boy soldiers, all of which the ILO terms "unconditional worst forms of child labor."

Such abuses have long existed, but it is only in the past few years that the world community has turned more seriously to addressing the issue. For example, an ILO-sponsored international conference led to an agreement known as the Worst Forms of Child Labour Convention (1999). The convention bars countries from inflicting on children any form of compulsory labor similar to slavery (including being forced to become a child soldier), using children for illicit activities (prostitution, pornography, drug trafficking), and having children do work that is inherently dangerous. As of early 2004, the treaty had been ratified by 132 countries and was well on its way to becoming part of international law. Protocols outlawing the sale of children, their being forced into armed conflict, or into prostitution and pornography also have been attached to the Convention on the Rights of the Child (1989).

The UN and the Economic Development of the South

The second focus of UN economic activity has been on the economic development of the LDCs. One role that the UN plays is providing a forum where world leaders from North and South occasionally come together. During the Millennium Summit sponsored by the UN in September 2000, one lunch table included Nigeria's president, Olusegun Obasanjo, U.S. president Bill Clinton, UN secretary-general Kofi Annan, China's president Jiang Zemin, British prime minister Tony Blair, and several other leaders. "The wishes of the developing world are simple," President Obasanjo told President Clinton and Prime Minister Blair. "We are all living in the same house, whether you are developed or not developed. . . . [But some of us] are living in superluxurious rooms; others are living in something not better than an unkempt kitchen where pipes are leaking and where there is no toilet. We [in the South] are saying," Obasanjo continued, "Look . . . let [those] living in the superluxurious rooms pay a bit of attention to those who are living where the pipes are leaking, or we'll all be badly affected. That's the message."[8] The

Millennium Summit also agreed that in two years the leaders of North and South should meet again, and that gathering came to pass in the form of the UN-sponsored International Conference on Financing for Development held in Monterrey, Mexico.

The UN also has numerous programs to promote development. Many of the UN's programs began during the mid-1960s in response to the decolonization of much of the South and the needs and demands of the new countries. The General Assembly, for example, created the **UN Development Programme (UNDP)** in 1965 to provide both technical assistance (such as planning) and development funds to LDCs. The UNDP's budget of just over $2.5 billion is obtained through voluntary contributions from the member-countries of the UN and its affiliated agencies. With offices in 166 LDCs, the UNDP especially focuses on grassroots economic development, such as promoting entrepreneurship, supporting the Development Fund for Women, and transferring technology and management skills from EDCs to LDCs.

Another important UN organization, the **UN Conference on Trade and Development (UNCTAD)**, was founded in 1964 to address the economic concerns of the LDCs. With 192 members, UNCTAD has virtually universal membership. There is an UNCTAD summit conference every four years, with the eleventh and most recent conference held in São Paulo, Brazil, in June 2004. The organization has a small budget of about $70 million. Its primary functions are to gather information and, even more importantly, to serve as a vehicle for the formation and expression of LDC demands for reforms in the structure and conduct of the international political economy, as discussed in chapter 13. For example, the UNCTAD gathering in Brazil concentrated on development in an era of globalization with an emphasis on "ways to make trade work for development, bearing in mind the outcomes [pledges of support by EDCs] of the recent summits on Financing for Development [Monterrey, Mexico, 2002] and Sustainable Development [Johannesburg, South Africa, 2002]."[9] UNCTAD's basic view, as expressed by its secretary-general, Rubens Ricupero, is that "it is not the amount and pace of international integration that counts, but its quality. A world economic system that fails to offer poorer countries, and the poorer parts of the populations within them, adequate and realistic opportunities to raise their living standards will inevitably lose its legitimacy in much of the developing world. And without this legitimacy," Ricupero warned, "no world economic system can long endure."[10]

While UNCTAD itself includes virtually universal membership and addresses general issues of trade and LDC development, the organization spun off a closely associated bloc called the **Group of 77 (G-77)**, named after the LDCs that issued the Joint Declaration of the Seventy-Seven Countries at the end of the first UNCTAD conference. Since then the G-77 has expanded to include 135 members. In 2000, as detailed in chapter 13, the leaders of the G-77 countries gathered in Havana, Cuba, for the organization's first summit meeting since the initial one that founded it in 1964. Much like the recent UNCTAD meetings, the Havana summit stressed the need to narrow the economic gap between the few EDCs and the many LDCs. In particular, the meeting called for debt relief.

Trade Cooperation: The GATT and the WTO

While the UN addresses the broad range of global economic issues, there are a number of IGOs that focus on one or another specific area of economic interchange. One of the most prominent of these specialized economic IGOs on the global level is the **General Agreement on Tariffs and Trade (GATT)**. It was founded in 1947 to promote free trade. For most of its existence, the name GATT was the source of considerable confusion because it was both the name of a treaty and the name of the organization headquartered in Geneva, Switzerland. That confusion has now ended. The GATT treaty was amended to create the **World Trade Organization (WTO)**, which superseded the GATT organization as of January 1, 1995. Therefore, references to the organization (even before 1995) will use WTO; the treaty will be referred to as the GATT. Whatever its name, the organization's initial membership of 23 countries has expanded to 146 members. Russia and Saudi Arabia are the only countries of significant economic note that are not WTO members, but they and 21 other countries have applied for membership. The trade of the full members accounts for approximately 90% of all world trade. The GATT and the WTO have played an important role in promoting the meteoric expansion of international trade. The organization has sponsored a series of trade negotiations that have greatly reduced tariffs and nontariff barriers (NTBs), such as import quotas.

The Latest Revisions of the GATT: The Uruguay Round

The eighth and most recent completed round of negotiations to revise the GATT in order to further reduce trade barriers was convened in Punta del Este, Uruguay, in 1986. The **Uruguay Round** proved to be the most difficult in GATT history, and it was not concluded until 1994.

Did You Know That:

Indicative of the complexity of modern trade negotiations, the 1994 GATT revision is some 26,000 pages long and weighs about 385 pounds.

The GATT revisions related to reducing economic barriers are complex. They address the nature and trade details of some 10,000 products and myriad businesses and other commercial interchanges. There are, for example, four paragraphs on the importation of "soft-ripened cow's milk cheese" and how to distinguish that kind of cheese from other kinds of cheese.

What is important, though, is that, overall, the countries that signed the Uruguay Round document agreed to reduce their tariffs $744 billion over a 10-year period by cutting them one-third on average. Agricultural tariffs were included in the GATT for the first time, and the agreement also further reduced or barred many NTBs. The signatories also agreed to institute within five years effective protection of intellectual property, such as patents, copyrights, trade secrets, and trademarks.

The Structure and Role of the WTO

To deal with the complexities of the GATT and to handle the disputes that will inevitably arise, the Uruguay Round also created the WTO. It is headquartered in Geneva, Switzerland, and currently headed by Director-General Supachai Panitchpakdi, a former deputy prime minister of Thailand, who took office in 2002.

Countries can file complaints against one another for violation of the GATT. The WTO has the power to enforce the provisions of the GATT and to assess trade penalties against countries that violate the accord. While any country can withdraw from the WTO by giving six months' notice, that country would suffer significant economic perils because its products would no longer be subject to the reciprocal low tariffs and other advantages WTO members accord one another. When one country charges another with a trade violation, a three-judge panel under the WTO hears the complaints. If the panel finds a violation, the WTO may impose sanctions on the offending country. Each country has one vote in the WTO, and sanctions may be imposed by a two-thirds vote. This means, among other things, that domestic laws may be disallowed by the WTO if they are found to be de facto trade barriers.

Despite grumbling by critics about the loss of sovereignty, the WTO judicial process has been busy. From 1995 through January 2004, the WTO handled 305 cases. The first case in 1995 involved a complaint by Singapore against Malaysia related to its prohibition of imports of polyethylene and polypropylene. Case number 305 filed in early 2004 by the United States charged Egypt with maintaining illegally high tariffs on textiles and apparel products. The pattern of complaints and whom they are made against shows that all types of countries are both complainants and respondents. This pattern is illustrated in Figure 14.2, which is based on the 50 most recent cases (extending from May 2002 to January 2004) as of this writing. The United States was involved in 42% of those cases, 6 times as a complainant and 15 times as a respondent. It is reasonable to conclude that the frequency of the U.S. status of respondent is almost surely a function of the size of the U.S. economy, rather than any tendency to target the United States, given the fact that the European Union was involved in 36% of all cases, filing 5 complaints and responding to 13 others.

The operation and value of the WTO hearing process was evident in the global dispute that flared up in 2002, after the United States dramatically hiked steel tariffs to protect the U.S. steel industry from what the Bush administration claimed was the below-cost dumping of foreign steel into U.S. markets. Dumping is illegal under the GATT. This set off a flurry of cases at the WTO, with Washington filing complaints about the alleged dumping, and the countries whose steel industries would be harmed by the increased U.S. tariffs also seeking relief from the WTO.

As related in the chapter 13 box, "Politics, Trade, and the U.S. Steel Tariff," what might have turned into a nasty trade war was averted because the WTO provided a way to resolve the dispute and to avoid the bilateral retaliation, counter-retaliations, and occasional wars that have marked trade disputes in the past. Some countries took quick retaliation against the United States by restricting their purchase of U.S. goods, but the EU, Japan, and most other countries were satisfied to sue the United States in the WTO and to threaten retaliation if Washington lost the dispute and still refused to give way. In the end that was not necessary. The initial WTO decision was against the U.S. tariff, and before the U.S. appeal could be heard, the United States withdrew it in late 2003. President Bush claimed that the U.S. steel producers had recovered from the unfair competition, and that, therefore, the tariff hike was no longer necessary. Most observers concluded, however, that the president had wisely chosen not to risk major damage to the relatively free trade system and to the WTO, which the United States had been instrumental in creating.

FIGURE 14.2 The Distribution of Complainants in the WTO

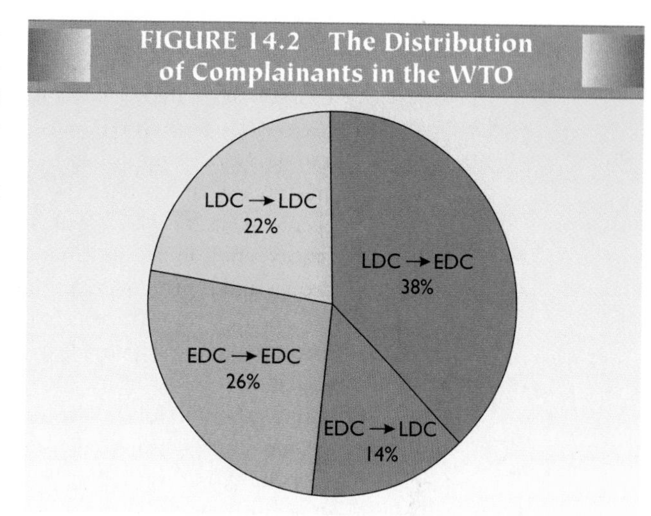

An average of 33 complaints have been filed with the WTO every year since it heard its first trade dispute in 1995. This sample of 50 cases from May 2002 through January 2004 indicates that there is no overwhelming pattern of complaints and respondents that differentiate LDCs and EDCs. Most commonly, LDCs file complaints against EDCs, but that is not surprising given the sensitivity of trade-dependent LDCs to EDC policies. The fact that the least frequent pattern is EDCs filing complaints against LDCs is also unexceptional, given the limited impact that the trade policies of most individual LDCs can have on the immensely larger economies of the EDCs.

Note: The country type (EDC or LDC) to the left of the symbol → is the complainant; the country type to the right of the arrow is the respondent: complainant → respondent.

Data source: WTO at http://www.wto.org/english/tratop_e/dispu_e/dispu_status_e.htm. Calculations by author.

The Future of the GATT and the WTO

Although the WTO has gotten off to a promising start, its future is not clear. There are a number of potential problem areas. *The tension between sovereignty and global governance* is one issue. The WTO's authority to rule on trade cases is a step toward supranationalism that contravenes traditional state sovereignty. The question is what will happen if one or more member-countries, especially powerful ones, refuse to abide by the WTO rules and reject the findings of the judicial process. So far, when Washington and the EU have lost a case, they have quietly given way, as the United States did in 2003 in the face of an adverse WTO ruling on the steel tariffs. What remains to be seen, however, is the reaction when a highly sensitive case is brought before the WTO.

Criticism of the WTO as an agent of globalization is a second and related issue. The WTO epitomizes globalization, which makes the WTO a lightning rod for the antiglobalization campaign. Like most other meetings of the major economic IGOs in recent years, WTO meetings have drawn throngs of protesters. They were at the recent WTO ministerial meeting in Cancún, Mexico, despite the now common tactic of holding such meetings in rural or resort settings and away from urban centers. The range of complaints against the WTO parallel those against other aspects of globalization: The organization is not democratic, it is dominated by capitalist EDCs, it works against common people, and it promotes environmentally unsound policies. Expressing that point of view at Cancún, a representative of Friends of the Earth Europe argued, "If the talks collapse that is good news: it could open the door to more sustainable trade."[11] Other WTO opponents at Cancún were even more fervent. Indeed, one of them, Lee Kyung-hae, a 55-year-old South Korean farmer, stabbed himself to death as a protest. A group of Korean farmers in Cancún issued a statement claiming, "Mr. Lee committed suicide after seeing how the WTO was killing peasants around the world." According to witnesses, Lee told other protesters, "Don't worry about me, just struggle your hardest," as he plunged a knife into his heart.[12]

Disagreement over how to further revise the GATT to reduce barriers to global economic interchange is a third and perhaps the key issue facing the WTO. The WTO agreed to attempt that at its periodic ministerial meeting, which gathered in Doha, Qatar, in November 2001. The meeting, perhaps influenced by a sense of shocked unity in the aftermath of 9/11, set the ambitious goal of reaching a new set of agreements in just three years, less than half the time it took to complete the Uruguay Round.

The next major steps forward in the **Doha Round** was to be marked when the top economic representatives of the WTO members convened at another ministerial meeting, this time in Cancún, Mexico, in September 2003. Speaking to the delegates, WTO director-general Panitchpakdi contended, "We face a choice here in Cancún. Either we continue to strengthen the multilateral trading system and the world economy or we flounder. . . . The eyes of the world are on this conference and people will judge us by the choice we make. There is only one possible answer. We have to deliver on the first choice."[13]

Perhaps, but the delegates took the second choice. At least temporarily, the timetable set by the Doha meeting was derailed amid acrimony, especially between the EDCs and the LDCs. The issues are complex, but, in short, the two sides disagree about what the priorities should be, and that dispute came to a head in the 2003 meeting, as told in the In the Spotlight box "Collapse in Cancún."

What the collapse of the Cancún ministerial talks will mean for the future of the Doha Round, and indeed the WTO, GATT, and the future of economic globalization remains to be seen. In the immediate aftermath, there were gloomy predictions from almost every quarter. Singapore's trade minister saw "serious implications" for trade.[14] In the same vein, the EU's trade commission fretted that the collapse of the talks was "not only a severe blow for the WTO but also a lost opportunity for developed and developing countries alike."[15] About the only bright spot was, in the view of some delegates from LDCs, that the G-21 had stood its ground. For one, Malaysia's trade minister exulted, "The developing countries have come into their own. This [meeting] has made it clear that developing countries cannot be dictated to by anybody."[16] But WTO Director-General Panitchpakdi warned that the LDCs would have to pay a price. "While some non-governmental organizations—and even some delegations—briefly celebrated the collapse in Cancún," he said later, "I can assure you no one is celebrating now. There is a sharp realization that the $1 billion a day spent on farm subsidies [by EDCs] will continue unabated."[17]

IN THE SPOTLIGHT

Collapse in Cancún

The sunny skies and calm seas at the Mexican resort of Cancún were a stark contrast to the turbulence that beset the September 2003 ministerial meeting of the World Trade Organization (WTO). It had convened to advance the Doha Round, the latest series of negotiations to further reduce economic barriers under the General Agreement on Tariffs and Trade.

The economically developed countries (EDCs) wanted to focus on the so-called Singapore issues, named for the location of the 1996 ministerial meeting at which they were introduced. The issues include such matters as competition (the EDCs want to restrict cartels and price fixing), transparency (ensuring corruption does not hinder trade), intellectual property rights (protecting the patents of EDC companies), government procurement (ensuring foreign companies can compete), and investment restrictions (such as limits of foreign ownership of business and real estate). By contrast, the less developed countries (LDCs) wanted to downplay these issues and instead focus on reducing EDCs barriers to agricultural imports. A particular target is the approximately $300 billion in annual subsidies that the EDCs give to their farmers and agribusinesses, thereby truncating the ability of the LDCs to send their raw and processed agricultural products to the United States, the European Union (EU), Japan, and other EDCs. For the first time at GATT talks, Brazil, China, India, and other leading LDCs formed at least a temporary coalition, styled the G-21 (G-20 or G-22 by some accounts), to press their demands. A representative of Brazil speaking for the G-21 said the only path to progress was one that would "pave the way to fundamental reform of agricultural trade," and the commerce minister of India proclaimed that "subsidies on all [agricultural] products have to eventually go."[1]

From the perspective of many LDC delegates, the talks failed because of the recalcitrance of the EDCs. "They were not generous enough; there was just not enough on the table for developing countries," argued the delegate from Jamaica. "If the developed countries had offered more to the developing countries, it would have created an atmosphere more conducive to a settlement." Agreeing, a representative of Oxfam, a British-based development advocacy group, contended, "In the past, rich countries made deals behind closed doors without listening to the rest of the world. They tried it again in Cancún. But developing countries refused to sign a deal that would fail the world's poorest people." The U.S. delegate saw the cause of the collapse quite differently. The problem, according to U.S. Trade Representative Robert Zoellick, was that some countries emphasized "rhetoric as opposed to negotiation" and that "a number of countries just thought it [the conference] was a freebie; they could just make whatever points they suggested, argue, and not offer and give. Whether developed or developing, there were 'can-do' and 'won't-do' countries here," Zeollick added. "The rhetoric of the 'won't-dos' overwhelmed the concerted efforts of the 'can-dos.'" As result, he concluded, "now they are going to face the cold reality of that strategy: coming home with nothing. That's not a good result for any of us."[2]

The passage of time soon also saw a movement to revive negotiations by those who believed that they were too important to the future to be allowed to founder. For example, a month later at the meeting of the 21-country Asia-Pacific Economic Cooperation (APEC) forum in Bangkok, Thailand, the final joint communiqué of the APEC leaders "reaffirmed the primacy of the multilateral trading system, and agreed that the Doha [Round] offers the potential for real gains for all economies, particularly developing economies." The leaders went on to express their "strong support for continuing . . . to advance the [Doha Round]," and they agreed to "re-energize the negotiation process" and to "press for an ambitious and balanced outcome."[18] By late in 2003, trade ministers were meeting again to try to revive the Doha Round, but there were no signs of progress. Belaboring the obvious, a top WTO official told reporters, "Personally I have my doubts that it can all be done by 2004 to be very honest."[19] That was an understatement of the difficulties ahead.

Many of the issues facing the negotiators pit the EDCs against the LDCs, as indicated. The LDCs are disinclined to move very far on the Singapore issues that concern the EDCs, and the EDCs are loath to seriously reduce the agricultural subsidies that are at the top of the LDCs' agenda. Other concerns, such as social and environmental issues,

Less developed countries are pressing hard on the economically developed countries to end the subsidies, high tariffs, and other methods of protecting the EDCs' agricultural interests. But the EDCs are also under heavy pressure from their domestic sector to preserve the barriers against agricultural imports. In this 2003 photograph, a Japanese farmer dressed as a rice ball is among those protesting in Tokyo against efforts in the World Trade Organization to open Japan to more rice imports, thereby threatening the livelihoods of Japan's rice farmers.

are also present and more crosscutting. The EU, for one, wants the Doha Round of talks to include negotiations about how to structure trade policy to enhance the protection of the environment, consumer and worker rights, and public health. In a curious alliance, the LDCs and United States are among the countries that maintain that such matters are adequately dealt with by the current GATT and that social and environmental regulations could in some cases be used as an excuse to practice protectionism. Labor standards are yet another point of controversy. The EU is among those advocating the inclusion on standards for the protection of workers in any new revision of the GATT. The United States seems ambivalent on this matter, and the LDCs worry that the EDCs could evoke labor standards to weaken the competitiveness of goods from the South by driving up its labor costs.

Monetary Cooperation: The IMF

As trade and the level of other international financial transactions have increased, the need to cooperate internationally to facilitate and stabilize the flow of dollars, marks, yen, pounds, and other currencies has become vital. To meet this need, a number of organizations have been founded. The **International Monetary Fund (IMF)** is the most important of these.

Early Monetary Regulation

The formation of the IMF stemmed in part from the belief of many analysts that the Great Depression of the 1930s and World War II were both partly caused by the near-chaotic international monetary scene that characterized the years between 1919 and 1939. Wild inflation struck some countries. Many countries suspended the convertibility of their currencies, and the North broke up into rival American, British, and French monetary blocs. Other countries, such as Germany, abandoned convertibility altogether and adopted protectionist monetary and trade policies. It was a period of open economic warfare—a prelude to the military hostilities that followed.

As part of postwar planning, the Allies met in 1944 at Bretton Woods, New Hampshire, to establish a new monetary order. The **Bretton Woods system** operated on the basis of "fixed convertibility into gold." The system relied on the strength of the U.S. dollar, which was set at a rate of $35 per ounce of gold.

The delegates at Bretton Woods also established the IMF and several other institutions to help promote and regulate the world economy. Thus, like the GATT, the IMF was created by the West, with the United States in the lead, as part of the liberalization of international economic interchange. The specific role of the IMF in attempting to provide exchange rate stability will be discussed in the next section.

The Bretton Woods system worked reasonably well as long as the American economy was strong, international confidence in it remained high, and countries accepted and held dollars on a basis of their being "as good as gold." During the 1960s and the early 1970s, however, the Bretton Woods system weakened, then collapsed. The basic cause was the declining U.S. balance-of-payments position and the resulting oversupply of dollars held by foreign banks and businesses. Countries were less willing to hold surplus dollars and increasingly redeemed their dollars for gold. U.S. gold reserves fell precipitously, and in 1971 this forced the United States to abandon the gold standard. In place of fixed convertibility, a new system, one of "free-floating" currency relations, was established. The conversion from a fixed standard to floating exchange rates in the international monetary system increased the IMF's importance even more because of the potential for greater and more rapid fluctuations in the relative values of the world's currencies.

In the initial period after the end of the Bretton Woods system, international money managers assumed that exchange rates among the EDCs would fluctuate slowly and within narrow boundaries. This has not been true. Instead, the exchange rates of most currencies have fluctuated greatly. Figure 12.4 on page 390 and the associated discussion of the fluctuation of the Japanese yen (¥) versus the U.S. dollar illustrate this volatility. In January 1985, one dollar equaled 258 yen ($1 = ¥258). A decade later the yen value had changed 68% and stood at $1 = ¥80 in 1995. Then it moved in the opposite direction by 56% and in January 2004 was $1 = ¥107.

Such large fluctuations occur because governments have frequently had difficulty managing international monetary exchange rates. To do so, a country's central bank, for example, may choose to create demand by buying its own currency if it wishes to keep its price up. The price goes up because of increased demand for a limited supply of currency. Conversely, a central bank that wishes to lower the value of its currency may create a greater supply by selling its currency. Governments sometimes even cooperate to control any given currency by agreeing to buy or sell it if it fluctuates beyond certain boundaries. Given the more than $1.5 trillion in currency exchanges each day, however, even the wealthiest countries with the largest foreign reserves often find themselves unable to adequately regulate the rise and fall of their currencies.

The Role of the IMF

The IMF began operations in 1947 with 44 member-countries. Since then the IMF has grown steadily, and in 2004 membership stood at 184. Indeed, about the only countries not in the IMF are those few (such as Nauru, which uses the Australian dollar) that do not have their own currency and have adopted the currency of a larger neighbor. The IMF's headquarters are in Washington, D.C. The managing director of the IMF since 2000 is Horst Köhler, a German and former president of the European Bank for Reconstruction and Development.

The IMF's primary function is to help maintain exchange-rate stability by making short-term loans to countries with international balance-of-payments problems because of trade deficits, heavy loan payments, or other factors. In such times, the IMF extends a line of credit to the country, which can be used to draw upon IMF funds in order to help meet debt payments, to buy back its own currency (thus maintaining exchange-rate stability by balancing supply and demand), or take other financial steps.

The IMF receives its usable funds from hard currency reserves ($296 billion in 2003) placed at its disposal by wealthier member-countries and from earnings that it derives from interest on loans made to countries that draw on those reserves. The IMF also holds more than $100 billion in reserves in LDC currencies, but they do not trade readily in the foreign exchange markets and, therefore, are of little practical use.

To help stabilize national currencies, the IMF has **Special drawing rights (SDRs)** that serve as reserves on which central banks of needy countries can draw. SDR value is based on an average, or market basket, value of several currencies, and SDRs are acceptable as payment at central banks. In January 2004, one SDR equaled about 1.505 U.S. dollars (SDR = $1.505). A country facing an unacceptable decline in its currency can borrow SDRs from the IMF and use them in addition to its own reserves to counter the

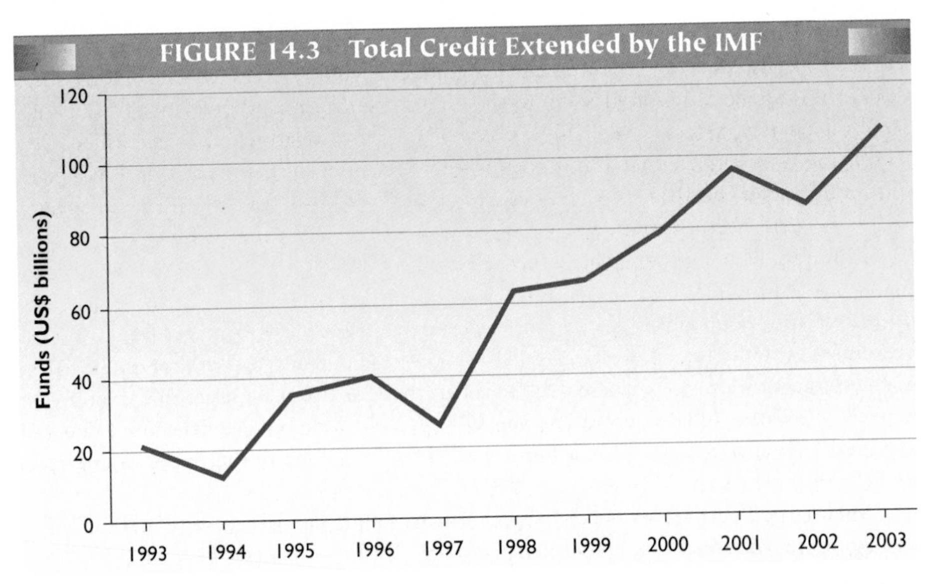

The rapid growth of the world economy and the need to keep currencies stable in a free-floating exchange rate environment have led to increasing importance for the IMF. Almost all of the IMF's funds go to developing and transitional economies to support the value of their currencies.

Note: Sources express data in SDRs; conversion to dollars by author using average SDR rate for each year.

Data source: IMF Web site at http://www.imf.org/external/index.htm.

price change. At the end of 2003, the IMF had SDR 71.9 billion ($107.9 billion) in credit lines extended to 88 countries. Of that amount, 57 countries had actually drawn SDR 55.0 billion ($82.4 billion). The three countries that had drawn the largest amounts were Brazil ($19 billion), Turkey ($16 billion) and Argentina ($10 billion). The growth of total IMF credit lines extended by the IMF from 1994 through 2003 is shown in Figure 14.3.

While SDRs have helped, they have not always been sufficient to halt instability. One problem is that the funds at the IMF's command are paltry compared to the immense daily flow of about $1.5 trillion in currency trading. Also, monetary regulation is difficult because countries often work at odds with one another.

Controversy about the IMF

Although the IMF has played a valuable role and has many supporters, it has not been above criticism (Feldstein, 1998). Indeed, in recent years the IMF has been one focus of the struggle over globalization. The controversies regarding the IMF may be divided into two categories: voting and conditionality.

Voting The first issue centers on the formula that determines voting on the IMF board of directors. Voting is based on the level of each member's contribution to the fund's resources. On this basis, the United States (17%), Japan (6%), Germany (6%), France (5%), and Great Britain (5%), which combine to make up less than 3% of the IMF membership, cast 39% of the votes on the board. Adding in the rest of the EDCs gives them well over half the IMF votes. By contrast, the 39 countries of sub-Saharan Africa that constitute 21% of the IMF's membership control less than 5% of its votes. This wealth-weighted system has two ramifications. One is that the formula gives the small percentage of the world's people who live in EDCs a solid majority of the votes. This apportionment has led to LDC charges that the fund is controlled by the North and is being used as a tool to dominate the LDCs.

Conditionality The second criticism of the IMF is that it imposes unfair and unwise conditions on countries that use its financial resources. Most loans granted by the IMF to LDCs are subject to **conditionality**. This refers to requirements that the borrowing country take steps to remedy the situations that, according to the IMF, have caused the recipient's financial problems.

Foreign banks and other sources of external funding also base their decisions on the degree to which an applicant country has met the IMF's terms. The IMF's conditions press the LDCs to move toward a capitalist economy by such steps as privatizing state-run enterprises, reducing barriers to trade and to the flow of capital (thus promoting foreign ownership of domestic businesses), reducing domestic programs in order to cut government budget deficits, ending domestic subsidies or laws that artificially suppress prices, and devaluing currencies (which increases exports and makes imports more expensive).

For example, Argentina's economy fell into turmoil that reached a crisis stage in December 2001. During the following 18 months, the government in Buenos Aires sought a $10 billion credit line from the IMF to support the exchange rate of the Argentine peso, to help it meet the debt service on its immense foreign debt, and to otherwise stem the economy's free fall. The IMF, which had long been extending credit to Argentina, offered to help, but only if the country took a number of steps, such as drastically reducing the spending of both the national and provincial governments, to correct the problems that the IMF saw as the cause of the economic difficulty. On the surface such conditions sound prudent, but in reality they have their drawbacks.

First, LDCs charge that the *IMF conditions violate sovereignty* by interfering in the recipients' policy-making processes. In Argentina, most provincial governors resisted the demand by the IMF that they slash their budget deficits. The IMF "should go to hell," growled the governor of one of the country's provinces. "The only thing lacking is for us to pull down the Argentine flag and replace it with the IMF's," he continued. Taking a similar view, one Argentinean senator characterized the deference to the IMF director as "paying homage to a viceroy." It must be added that not everyone, Argentineans and outsiders included, agreed with such complaints. Economist Marcelo Lascano of the University of Buenos Aires rejoined that the IMF director acted "as a viceroy" because Argentina needed outside direction. "The problem doesn't lie with [the IMF], but with the Argentine leadership," Lascano said.[20] Second, some critics have contended that *conditionality intentionally or unintentionally maintains the dependency relationship.* Reacting to the conditions laid down by the IMF in 1997 and 1998 to assist Asia's faltering economies, *Matichon,* a daily newspaper in Thailand, editorialized that the conditions amounted to "economic colonialism."[21] Taking a similar view, President Eduardo Duhalde of Argentina (2002–2003) blamed part of his country's crisis on "domination" by the industrialized world.[22]

Third, critics charge that *IMF conditions often harm economies in LDCs* by requiring "cookbook" plans of fiscal austerity and other stringent conditions and by not sufficiently tailoring plans to the circumstances of individual countries. During the IMF-Argentina negotiations, Harvard economist Jeffrey Sachs argued that the IMF was overemphasizing "one theme alone: that Argentina's economic crisis is the result of fiscal profligacy, the result of a government living beyond its means. So it emphasizes the need for Argentina to cut budget expenditures." The problem with this remedy, according to Sachs, is that the cuts in government spending increase unemployment and otherwise depress Argentina's economy, an approach he compared to "the 18th-century medical

The International Monetary Fund demands that countries in financial trouble meet IMF conditions for economic reform before they can receive funds to stabilize the country's currency and restructure its debt. This demand has met with strong criticism from many national leaders and economists. The view of many Argentineans to the IMF conditions is evident in this photograph. Protesters in Buenos Aires wear robes with the Spanish acronym of the IMF and carry a coffin with a top resembling the country's flag, symbolizing what they said was the death of Argentina's social welfare system.

practice in which doctors 'treated' feverish patients by drawing blood from them, weakening the patients further and frequently hastening their deaths."[23]

Fourth, critics charge that *IMF conditions often destabilize governments.* While a stable government is a key factor during times of financial trouble, critics claim that the reforms the IMF demands are often so politically difficult to institute that they undermine the very government that the IMF needs to work with and that needs to remain viable in order to deal with the crisis. Reflecting that concern in Argentina, one observer commented, "The IMF has the wrong idea if they think Duhalde or any president can immediately make the kinds of reforms they are demanding and still be left standing in the morning."[24] Giving some credence to that view, some of the efforts of the government to meet such IMF demands as raising taxes and reducing government spending sparked riots in the country. A fifth line of criticism contends that *the IMF undermines social welfare* by pushing countries to cut their budget, thereby reducing social services, laying off government workers, and taking other steps that harm the quality of life of their citizens. Taking that view, Argentina's new president, Nestor Kirchner, said he would not meet the IMF's requirements "at the cost of delaying education and the good health of Argentina's children."[25]

The Defense of the IMF Accusations are not equivalent to a guilty verdict, and it is important to understand the justifications for the ways in which the IMF operates. With respect to the voting formula, the reply to inequality is that since it is the EDCs that provide the funds, they should have a proportionate share of the say in how they are invested. Defenders say that a formula based, for example, on one vote for every member-country would mean that it would be the countries in financial difficulty, the borrowers, and not the countries supplying the loan money to the IMF, that would make decisions on the IMF's policies. That, IMF defenders say, would not work with domestic bank loans, and it would be an ill-advised policy for the IMF or any other financial institution.

As for conditionality, the IMF acknowledges that its demands often cause hardship. But it argues that the required reforms are necessary to correct the problems that led the borrower country into financial difficulty in the first place. Without reform, IMF defenders contend, there would be an unsupportable continuing cycle of crisis and loans, crisis and loans that would constitute "throwing good money after bad," as the phrase goes. Reflecting this view during Argentina's economic meltdown, Horst Köhler, the head of the IMF, argued, "What Argentina needs now is growth and growth requires savings, investment, and a working banking system." As for the bitter side-effects of following the IMF's prescribed regimen, Köhler stated, "One also must recognize that without pain, it won't get out of this crisis, and the crisis—at its root—is homemade." Others, including U.S. national security adviser Condoleezza Rice, agreed. "We [in the Bush administration] truly believe that if they [the Argentines] can just do the things that the IMF is requesting that they do, we believe that they can find a way back to sustainable growth," Rice said. She indicated that the U.S. position "is not an unwillingness to have international assistance go to Argentina. It is an understanding that the conditions have to be right so that those resources actually make a difference."[26]

It is also the case that the IMF may be easing its stern stance somewhat. The agreement between Argentina and the IMF to refinance the country's debt reflected a compromise in which the IMF considerably reduced its requirements. Like many compromises it left many on both sides dissatisfied. Some talked of an IMF "cave in," while others protested that "if the national government . . . with the IMF . . . [causes] utility rate increases, there will be more hunger and there will be more unemployment."[27] The organization has also conceded that in the past it may have pushed countries to open their economies too quickly to globalization. In a 2003 report that the IMF chief economist called "sobering," an IMF study group found, "If financial integration has a positive effect on growth, there is as yet no clear and robust empirical proof that the effect is quantitatively significant." Therefore, the report concluded, "the evidence . . . suggests that financial integration should be approached cautiously."[28]

Still, at the beginning of 2004, Argentina remained at odds with its creditors and the IMF. The country was threatening to repay as little as 25% of the $88 billion in loans it had defaulted on in 2002 and arguing that paying more would harm the country's economic recovery. For their part, the IMF, commercial banks, and other sources of capital were warning that further lines of credit and other capital flows into Argentina were in peril. A representative of Argentina's creditors warned the country had "crossed the line (in terms) of their strategy being economically rational," and another observer cautioned that unless reasonable debt payments were made, "there won't be any significant foreign investment [in Argentina], and without investment in the power sector, for example, the economy is going to start having problems."[29] Thus it remains unclear whether the IMF-Argentina agreement in 2003 and the upturn in the country's economy was the beginning of a long-term recovery aided by outside help or a lull in the storm that could leave Argentina even more financially distressed and isolated than it already is.

Before concluding our discussion of the IMF, it is important to note that there are several other monetary IGOs that make contributions. On a global scale, the oldest and largest (founded in 1930) is the Bank for International Settlements (BIS). The BIS has

55 members, including all the major EDCs and a number of economically important LDCs such as China and Saudi Arabia. The BIS serves several functions. One is as a meeting ground where its members' central banks discuss global monetary issues. Second, the BIS provides expertise to assist the central banks of those LDCs and other countries that are struggling with fiscal stability. Third, the BIS has assets ($205 billion in 2003) deposited by the central banks of its members, and it uses these funds for purposes such as maintaining currency exchange stability. Finally, there are a number of regional monetary policies and institutions, such as the European Central Bank and the Arab Monetary Fund, that are affiliated with larger regional organizations.

Development Cooperation: The World Bank Group

A third type of multilateral economic cooperation involves granting loans and aid for the economic development of LDCs. The most significant development agency today is the **World Bank Group**, which is commonly referred to simply as the World Bank. The word "group" relates to the fact that it has four agencies, which are detailed below.

World Bank Operations

Like the IMF and GATT/WTO, the World Bank was established in the World War II era to promote the postwar economic prosperity of the United States and its allies, especially those in Western Europe. In line with that purpose, the World Bank's first loan ($250 million) went to France in 1947 for postwar reconstruction. Since then through 2003, total loans by the World Bank have amounted to about $561 billion.

Over time, the World Bank's priorities have shifted more and more to assisting the development of the South. Illustrating this, the World Bank's *Annual Report 2003* noted the "the importance of pledges made at the International Conference on Financing for Development at Monterrey in March 2002 underscored the importance of the collective effort needed to attain the Millennium Development goals (MDGs), including the goal of reducing poverty by half by the year 2015." "For the World Bank," the report continued, "this has translated into a special focus on implementation in four priority sectors that are key to meeting some of the MDGs—education for all, HIV/AIDS, water and sanitation, and health."

Of the four main parts of the World Bank, the *International Bank for Reconstruction and Development (IBRD)* was the first established (1946). It has lending policies that most closely resemble those of a commercial bank, applying standards of creditworthiness to recipients and the projects they wish to fund and charging some interest. In 2003, the IBRD drew on the funds donated by its 184 members to make loans of $11.2 billion to fund 99 projects in 37 countries.

A second agency, the *International Development Association (IDA),* was created in 1960 and has a separate pool of funds drawn from member contributions. It has 164 members, and it focuses on making loans at no interest to the very poorest countries to help them provide better basic human services (such as education, health care, safe water, and sanitation), to improve economic productivity, and to create employment. During 2003, the IDA extended $7.3 billion in loans to fund 141 projects in 55 countries. Given its focus on the LDCs, about a third of all IDA money went to sub-Saharan Africa, whereas very few loans of the slightly more commercial IRBD went to countries in that region.

The *International Finance Corporation (IFC),* a third agency, was established in 1956 and has 175 members. It makes loans to companies in LDCs and guarantees private foreign or domestic investment aimed at establishing or improving companies and business opportunities in LDCs. This contrasts with the IBRD and the IDA, which mostly make loans to governments for public projects. Because of its goal of enhancing capitalism, the IFC, more than any of the other multilateral banks, has been favorably received in the

United States. The IFC's loans for 2003 came to $3.9 billion to 204 private enterprises in 64 countries. Because of the unstable business climates in many countries, many of the IFC's loans are risky.

The *Multilateral Investment Guarantee Agency (MIGA)* is the fourth and newest of the World Bank Group agencies, having been established in 1988. It specializes in promoting the flow of private development capital to LDCs by providing guarantees to investors against part of any losses they might suffer due to noncommercial risks (such as political instability). The agency in 2003 issued $1.4 billion in guarantees on approximately five times the amount of private capital invested in LDCs. Like the IFC, the MIGA, with 162 members, is autonomous from the World Bank, but draws on the bank's administrative, analytical, and other services.

Controversy about the World Bank Group

Like the IMF, the agencies that make up the World Bank Group do a great deal of good, but they have also been the subject of considerable controversy. One point of criticism involves the North's domination of the South. Individuals from EDCs have headed the three most important economic IGOs (the IMF, World Bank, and GATT/WTO) throughout most of their history. All IMF managing directors have been Europeans. The GATT/WTO was also headed by Europeans or in one case a New Zealander, until Supachai Panitchpakdi of Thailand became its director-general in 2002. And the president of the World Bank has always been American. Exemplifying the Western leaders is the ninth and current (since June 1995) head of the World Bank, James D. Wolfensohn. He holds MBA and JD degrees and has been an attorney, a Wall Street investment officer, and a consultant on international investing to more than 30 multinational corporations. As further evidence of the North's domination, critics also point out that the World Bank Group, like the IMF, has a board of directors with a voting formula that gives the majority of the votes to the handful of EDCs. Therefore, as is the case for the IMF, the United States, the countries of the European Union, and Japan control a majority of the votes. What all this means, from the perspective of the LDCs, is that the origins and experiences of these Western executives and their EDC-dominated boards of directors limit their ability to understand, much less sympathize with the perspectives and problems of the LDCs. A harsher interpretation of the dominance of the financial IGOs by the North is that they are vehicles for neoimperialist control of the LDCs by the EDCs. For example, Martin Kohr, a Malaysian economist who heads an NGO called Third World Network, charges, "Economically speaking, we are more dependent on the ex-colonial powers than we ever were. The World Bank and the IMF are playing the role that our ex-colonial masters used to play."[30]

A second complaint about the World Bank is simply that it provides too little funding. Figures such as $23.8 billion in total World Bank commitments to or guarantees of projects in 2003 sound less impressive in light of the fact that they have declined in terms of real dollars. For example, World

Supporters of the World Bank believe that it has made an important contribution to the economic development of the countries of the South. Detractors argue that the World Bank is part of the structure by which the North dominates the international economy, and, among other things, point to the fact that the World Bank president has always been an American. The ninth and latest American to head the bank, James Wolfensohn, is seen here addressing a recent press conference.

Bank commitments and guarantees in 1995 were $21.5 billion. Adjusted for inflation, this comes to $26.0 billion in 2003 current dollars, making the $23.8 billion actually spent a real decline of 21% since 1995. It should be noted though, that the bank relies on contributions from the EDCs to fund its operations, and as noted earlier in this chapter and in chapter 13, the official development aid that includes the funding for the World Bank has been static during the last decade.

The terms of the loans are a third sore spot. The World Bank is caught between the North's concentration on "businesslike," interest-bearing loans and the South's demands that more loans be unconditionally granted to the poorest countries at low rates or with no interest at all. While the IDA made 50% of its loans in 2003 to sub-Saharan Africa, the more "commercial" IBRD extended 49% of its commitments to just five countries (Argentina, Brazil, China, Colombia, and Mexico). By contrast, sub-Saharan Africa receive only 10% of the IBRD's loans, with two-thirds of that going to just one country, Nigeria. Adding to what critics say is too conservative an orientation by the World Bank, the IFC and MIGA only finance projects that meet with the Western, capitalist model.

Such criticisms and the more general uneasiness about globalization have made the World Bank, like the WTO and IMF, the target of massive street protests. Although the 2003 meeting in Washington, D.C., actually found more police than demonstrators at the barricades, other recent meetings have been less tranquil. Demonstrations in Prague, the Czech Republic, at the 2001 meeting were so intense that the World Bank scrapped a development conference scheduled to be held in Barcelona, Spain, the following year and held it by telecommunications in cyberspace. Such protests take their toll. After one recent meeting, the bank's president confessed, "It was impossible not to be affected."[31] Certainly, it would be too strong to say that such protests have an immediate dramatic effect, but they do add to the pressure that affects policy. That is evident in shifts over the last decade of the World Bank and other global financial IGOs toward a greater willingness to support social programs and to address the needs of the world's least developed countries.

Regional Economic Cooperation

For all the far-reaching economic cooperative efforts at the global level, the degree of activity and economic cooperation and integration at the regional level is even more advanced (El-Agraa, 1999). One area of cooperation is finance through the nine regional development banks. In terms of loan commitments, the largest of these (and their loans in 2002) were the 46-member Inter-American Development Bank ($6.8 billion), the Asian Development Bank ($5.7 billion), and the European Bank for Reconstruction and Development ($3.0 billion), which focuses on projects in the European CITs. Many other regional banks are much more limited in their funding. The 2002 loans of the poorly funded African Development Bank, for example, amounted to just over $1 billion, despite its region's pressing needs, and that year the Caribbean Development Bank managed a mere $115 million in loans to the distressed countries in its region.

Multilateral **regional trade organizations (RTOs)** provide an even more numerous and rapidly expanding example of the growth of regional economic cooperation. Notice two things in the map on page 465 that details the membership of 29 regional trade organizations. First, there are relatively few countries that are not in some trade group. Second, numerous countries are in more than one. Some RTOs, in truth, are little more than shell organizations that keep their goals barely alive. Yet the very existence of each organization represents the conviction of its members that, compared to standing alone, they can achieve greater economic prosperity by working together through economic cooperation or even economic integration.

Regional Trade Organizations and Agreements

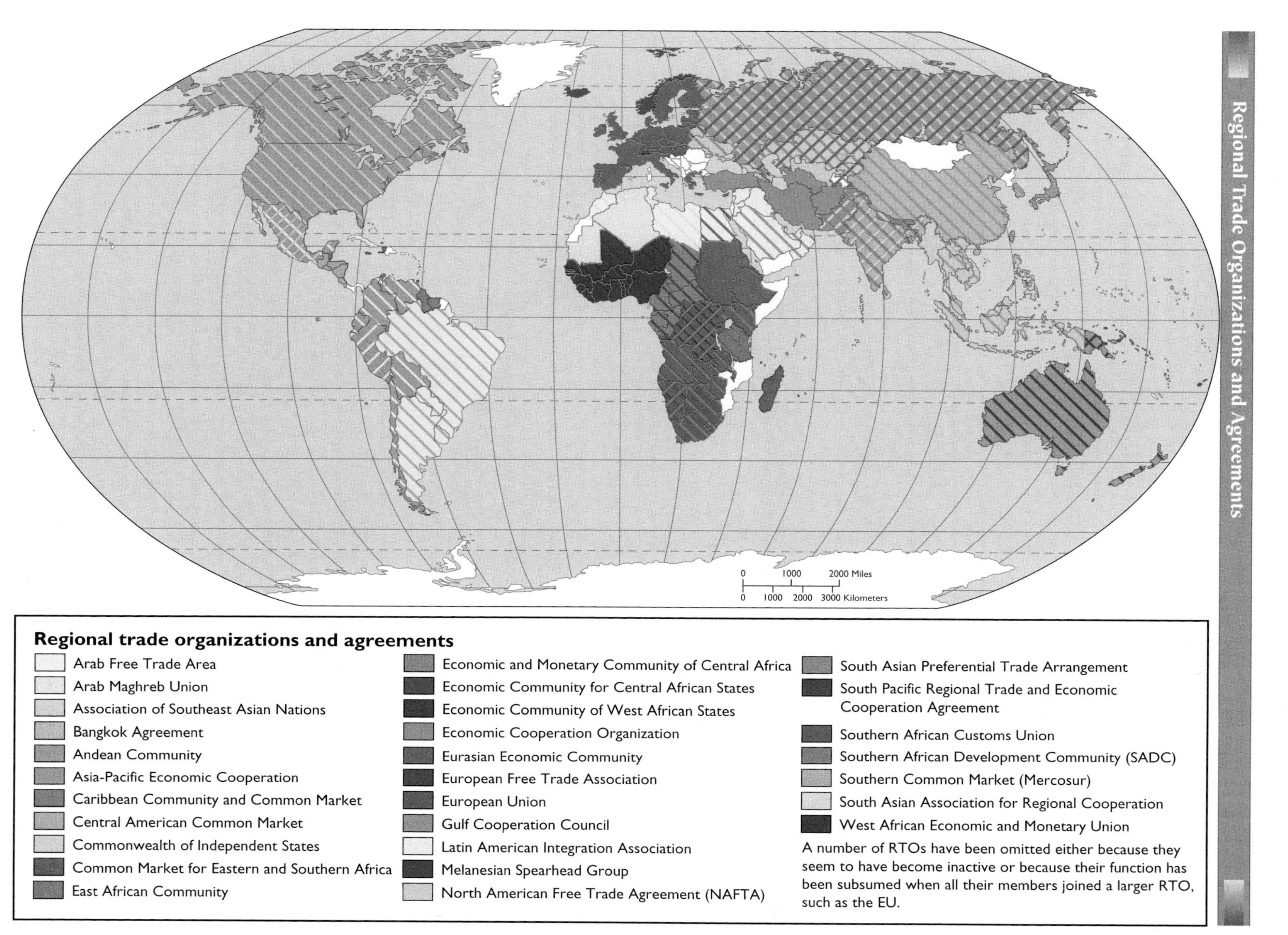

Global trade is characterized by an increasingly expansive and complex pattern of regional trade organizations.

Economic cooperation is a process whereby sovereign states cooperate with one another bilaterally or multilaterally through IGOs (such as the IMF) or processes (such as the G-8 meetings). *Economic integration* means such a close degree of economic intertwining that, by formal agreement or informal circumstance, the countries involved begin to surrender some degree of sovereignty and act as an economic unit. There is no precise point when economic cooperation becomes economic integration. It is more a matter of moving along a continuum ranging from economic isolation, through mercantile policy, then to economic cooperation, and finally to economic integration. Even this stage has its steps, as countries move progressively from creating a relatively *free trade area* (eliminating many or most trade barriers) through a *customs union* (adding common tariff and nontariff barriers against external countries), a *common market* (eliminating barriers to the free flow of labor, capital, and other aspects of economic interchange among members), an *economic union* (harmonizing economic policies such as tax and social welfare), to achieving *monetary union* (Feld, 1979).

Among the RTOs, the EU has moved farthest along this continuum, and, except for three hold-out members, has established a monetary union. Other RTOs are much less integrated, and, indeed some may never develop beyond loose agreements of preferential trade policies among the members. It is also worth noting that the process of economic integration is not the result of a single strand of activity. Rather, integration is a complex phenomenon that results from the interaction and mutual strengthening of transnational trade and finance, of IGOs and NGOs, and of transnational values and international law.

To expand our discussion of economic integration, we now turn our attention to the progress that has been made along the continuum toward integration. This will entail an examination of regional integration in Europe, North America, and the Pacific region.

Europe

The European Union is by far the most extensive regional effort. This European organization of 25 member-countries has moved substantially toward full economic integration. It has also traveled in the direction of considerable political cooperation. The evolution of the EU's economic integration since the early 1950s and its organizational structure and political development are discussed in chapter 7. Given this background, it is possible to make a few summary points about the current status and future of the EU's progress toward economic and political integration that reflect the earlier discussion.

One such point is that the EU took a huge stride forward when its new common currency, the euro, went into general circulation on January 1, 2002, and began to replace the German mark, French franc, Italian lira, and the other national currencies of most of the other EU members. In addition to the monetary union that a common currency will bring to the EU, there is a great deal of political symbolism in the willingness of the French, Germans, Italians, and others to give up their respective national currencies, which are visible representations of the state and sovereignty.

A second observation is that the expansion of the EU's membership to 25 in 2004 has created an even larger economic unit than the already imposing 15-member EU. With 455 million residents, the EU's population is 60% larger than that of the United States. The combined GNPs of the 25 EU countries in the expanded EU, at about \$10.5 trillion (2002), is equivalent to that of the United States (\$10.4 trillion), and the 25 EU countries' exports of \$3.9 trillion (2002) in goods and services are nearly three times U.S. exports of \$1.4 trillion. In sum, the EU has come to rival and by some measures surpass the United States economically, and that will strengthen the EU economically and politically.

The Western Hemisphere

Economic cooperation in the Western Hemisphere does not yet rival the level found in Europe, but the process is under way. The origins of hemispheric distinctiveness and a U.S. consciousness of its connection to the hemisphere date back many years. The first hemispheric conference met in 1889. A U.S. proposal to establish a customs union was thwarted by the other 17 countries that attended, but they did create the first regional organization, the International Bureau of American Republics. That later became the Pan-American Union, then, by the Rio Treaty of 1948, the Organization of American States (OAS). The first summit of most of the hemisphere's heads of government occurred in Punta del Este, Uruguay, in 1967. These events and trends have recently led to several important trade efforts discussed in the following sections.

The North American Free Trade Agreement (NAFTA)

Canada, Mexico, and the United States took the first major step toward multilateral economic integration in the Western Hemisphere when they concluded the **North American Free Trade Agreement (NAFTA)**, which took effect in 1994. The more than 2,000-page agreement established schedules for reducing tariff and nontariff barriers to trade by 2004 in all but a few hundred of some 20,000 product categories and by 2009 for all products. Also under NAFTA, many previous restrictions on foreign investments and other financial transactions among the NAFTA countries will end, and investments in financial services operations (such as advertising, banking, insurance, and telecommunications) flow much more freely across borders. Intra-NAFTA transportation has also become much easier. Truck and bus companies now have largely unimpeded access across borders. There is a standing commission with representatives from all three countries to deal with disputes that arise under the NAFTA agreement.

There can be little doubt that NAFTA has had an important impact on the three trading partners. Since 1994, trade, investment, and other forms of economic interchange among the three countries have grown extensively and faster than otherwise might have been expected. For example, trade among them, which was extensive even before NAFTA, has grown even more since 1994, and intra-NAFTA trade is a key component of the exports of all three partners, as can be seen in the data on merchandise trade in Figure 14.4. Canada is the most dependent on intra-NAFTA trade, with 90% of its exports going to the United States and Mexico. Mexico's level of intra-NAFTA trade is not much less, with 84% of exports going to its NAFTA partners. Another index of the importance of NAFTA is that total U.S.-Canada trade of $380 billion is the world's largest two-way commercial relationship. The United States is least dependent, albeit still heavily so, on NAFTA trade, with 39% of U.S. exports going to Canada and Mexico.

There is little doubt that NAFTA has increased trade, investment, and other aspects of financial interchange among the three partners, but beyond that it is difficult to be precise about specific impacts. The most important reason is that in a rapidly changing global economic environment, it is difficult to precisely separate out changes caused by NAFTA from the many other forces at work.

There was and, to a degree, still is a vigorous debate going on in each of the three countries about the pros and cons of NAFTA. The economic impact of NAFTA on the consumers, workers, and business of the three partners engenders both praise and criticism in each of the three countries. Canada is the least affected because it has relatively little interchange with Mexico and because a preexisting U.S.-Canada free trade agreement (1988) means that NAFTA has not dramatically affected trading relations between the two. For Americans, there certainly have been losses. Many American businesses have relocated facilities to Mexico, establishing *maquiladoras,* manufacturing plants just

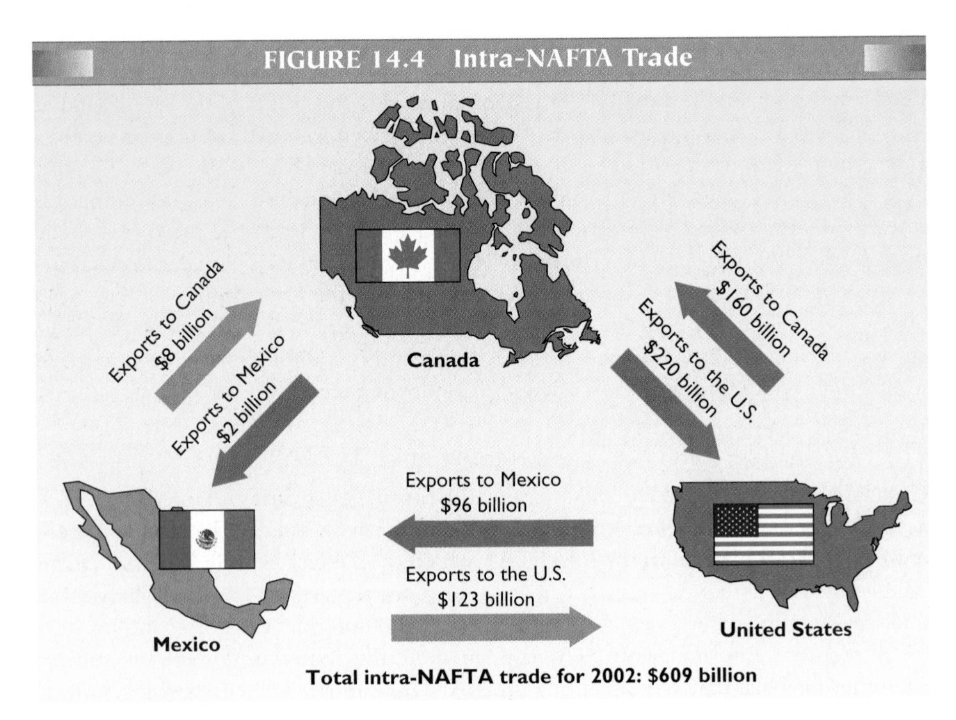

The North American Free Trade Agreement has accounted for a rapid rise in trade among Canada, Mexico, and the United States since the treaty went into effect in 1994. There are now plans for a Western Hemisphere free trade zone, the Free Trade Area of the Americas.

Data source: IMF (2002).

south of the border, which produce goods for export to the United States. According to a U.S. Department of Labor study, U.S. jobs lost because of this shift of production and other job losses due to imports from Mexico totaled 507,000 between late 1993 and late 2002. "NAFTA was extremely destructive to the manufacturing base in this country, particularly the apparel and textile industries," claims a union representative.[32] Yet it can also be said that the strong U.S. economy created many new jobs and that unemployment during the period was relatively low. Furthermore, other Americans gained from NAFTA. Consumers, for instance, benefited from lower prices for goods imported from Mexico. Such gains often are less noticed, however, than are losses. As one economist explains, "The gains are so thinly spread across the country that people don't thank NAFTA when they buy a mango or inexpensive auto parts."[33]

Of all the NAFTA partners, the pact has had the greatest effect on Mexico, in large part because both the size and the strength of its economy are so much less than those of the United States and Canada. Mexico's maquiladora program was initiated by Mexico to promote industrialization by giving special tax and other advantages to industries in a zone near the United States and, thus, had existed for almost 30 years before NAFTA was concluded. But during the remainder of the 1990s, the number of plants increased 67% to almost 3,700, production doubled, and the number of employees tripled to approximately 1.4 million. Wages are low, with an assembly-line worker making about $1.50 an hour, but that is more than twice Mexico's minimum wage and higher than many industrial wages elsewhere in the country. "NAFTA gave us a big push," Mexican President Vicente Fox contended recently, "It gave us jobs. It gave us knowledge, experience, technological transfer."[34]

Did You Know That:

Maquiladora is derived from the Spanish word *maquila*, the charge levied by millers to process grain, and was used since most of the maquiladora plants processed parts produced in the United States into finished products. The verb *maquilar* means to assemble.

Most Mexicans disagree. Whereas 68% of all Mexicans favored NAFTA in 1993 just before it went into operation, a later survey in 2003 found that support had dropped to

One impact of the North American Free Trade Agreement was to spur the growth of industrialization in Mexico's maquiladora plants. They assemble merchandise for sale primarily in the United States, including items such as this 2004 Chrysler PT Cruiser being built by Mexican workers at the Daimler Chrysler plant in Toluca, Mexico.

45%. Giving voice to that view, Mexico's ambassador to the United States told an audience that NAFTA was the equivalent of Mexico having "a weekend fling" with a United States that "isn't interested in a relationship of equals with Mexico, but rather in a relationship of convenience and subordination."[35] Whatever the accuracy of that characterization, it put the diplomat at odds with his president, and he was soon replaced.

On balance, the data reveals a much less optimistic picture than presented by President Fox, although perhaps not as distressing as portrayed by the ambassador. On the plus side Mexico's economy has become more diversified and its exports have risen sharply. Its per capita GNP at about $6,200 (2002) is higher than that of any country in Central or South American except Argentina. Yet in real terms Mexico's economy has only grown slowly, increasing an average of 0.9% between 1995 and 2002, compared to 3.3% for Canada's economy and 2.4% for the U.S. economy. Some segments of Mexico's economy have been particularly hard hit. For example, corn farmers in central and southern Mexico have suffered greatly from the incoming tidal wave of subsidized U.S. corn. For all the problems, it is not clear that all or most of Mexico's very mixed economic fortunes can be attributed to NAFTA. One reason for the slowdown in the country's economy in the past few years has been that its role as a provider of low-cost exports to the United States has been substantially undercut by China, where an average factory worker's wages are less than half of his or her Mexican counterpart. As a result, production dropped 30% between 2000 and 2002 in the maquiladora zone, with some 850 maquiladoras shutting down and employment declining by 20%.

The Free Trade Area of the Americas

It is possible that NAFTA may also be another step toward integration of all or most of the Western Hemisphere. Trade cooperation in the hemisphere moved toward a new, higher level in 1994 with the beginning of an effort to create what has been tentatively named the **Free Trade Area of the Americas (FTAA)**. The idea is a natural extension of the proliferation of regional trade organizations in the era of globalization and the existence of several RTOs in the Western Hemisphere, as shown in the map on p. 471. Partly in response to the increasing size and power of the EU and in the same atmosphere that led to the creation of NAFTA, the United States began to push in the early 1990s to establish an RTO that would include all or most of the countries in North, Central, and South America, and in the Caribbean.

Preliminary negotiations culminated in 1994 when the heads of 34 countries met at the Summit of the Americas in Miami, Florida. Only Cuba was excluded. The conference agreed to aim at the creation of a free trade zone in the hemisphere by 2005. The leaders also agreed to a series of more than 100 specific political, environmental, and economic programs and reforms, and the conference ended in near-euphoria. "When our work is done, the free trade area of the Americas will stretch from Alaska to Argentina," predicted President Bill Clinton. "In less than a decade, if current trends continue, this hemisphere will be the world's largest market."[36]

If it proceeds as planned, the FTAA will link the Western Hemisphere in a single market that in 2005 will have an estimated 875 million people producing $13.6 trillion worth of goods and services. However, it is very much in question whether that will come to pass. The prospects for the FTAA to be completed by 2005 are especially dubious. The bargaining over the details has been difficult. As excited as they are about access to the U.S. markets, the hemisphere's LDCs are equally as nervous about dropping their protections and being drowned in a tidal wave of American imports and services, and about having American investors snap up local businesses and other property. The idea will be an equally hard sell in the United States, where many Americans will fear that their jobs will wind up in the hands of an underpaid Bolivian, Honduran, or perhaps Uruguayan worker. President Clinton was fond of borrowing an image that John Kennedy often used: "As they say on my own Cape Cod, a rising tide lifts all boats. And a partnership, by definition, serves both partners." Another possibility, Prime Minister Owen Arthur of Barbados told President Clinton in Miami, is that "a rising tide can . . . overturn small boats."[37]

Meetings of the leaders of the Western Hemisphere, the first in Quebec City, Canada, in 2001 and the second in Monterrey, Mexico, in January 2004 have not yielded significant visible progress. Each meeting reaffirmed the 2005 goal, yet wide disagreements continue to exist that will make it extraordinarily difficult to meet that target date. The issues are very much akin to those that caused the breakdown of the WTO's Cancún ministerial meeting in 2003. In his opening remarks at the 2004 conference, President George Bush propounded a strong free market approach. "We must also chart a clear course toward a vibrant free market," he told the assembled heads of state. "Over the long term, trade is the most certain path to lasting prosperity."[38] But several other heads of state saw the road to development differently. Reacting to such instances of protectionism as the U.S. steel tariff and to the multibillion-dollar subsidization of U.S. agriculture, they expressed doubt about the willingness of the United States to open its markets and keep them open. In more general terms, they argued that the U.S. stance would produce more of the type of globalization that, in their view, makes the rich richer and, at best, leaves the poor somewhere between poor and no better off. Brazil's President Luiz Inácio Lula da Silva depicted the 1990s as "a decade of despair" caused by "a perverse [globalization] model that wrongly separated the economic from the social, put stability against growth and separated responsibility from justice."[39] And Venezuelan President Hugo Chavez predicted that if it worked like other aspects of globalization, the FTAA would be "an infernal machinery that, minute by minute, produces an impressive number of poor."[40] As noted, the Monterrey conference ended with a reaffirmation of the goal of concluding the FTAA by the end of 2005, but most observers considered that little more than a diplomatic way to adjourn a divisive meeting with a patina of harmony.

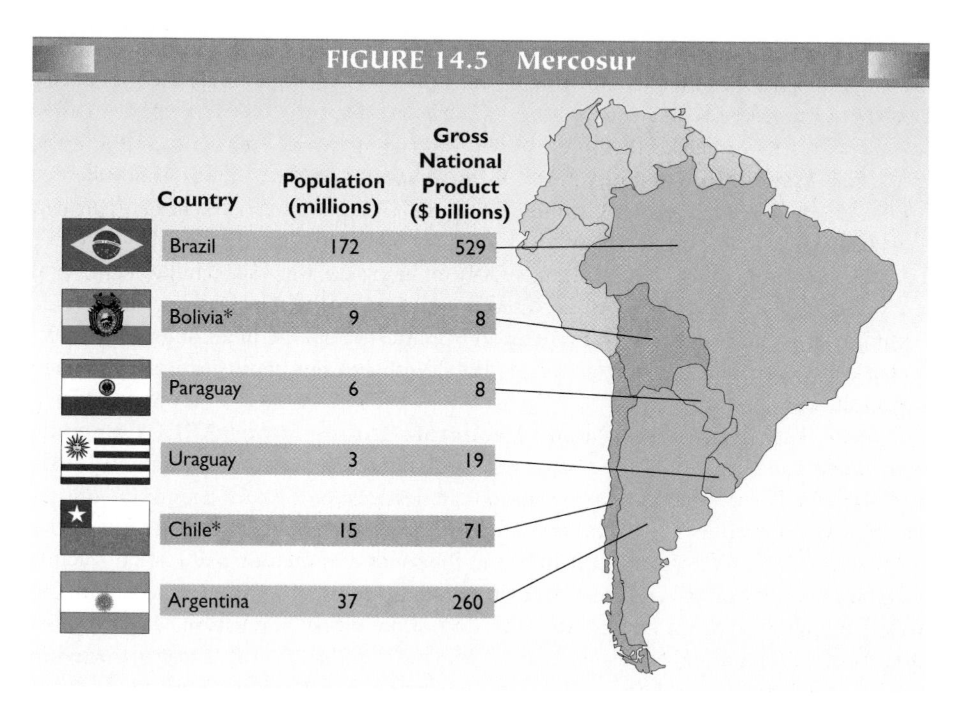

The Southern Common Market (Mercosur) is an example of one of the several important and growing regional free trade organizations, A key issue for the future of the Western Hemisphere is whether it will unite into a single free trade organization, the Free Trade Area of the Americas (FTAA), or whether the hemisphere will be divided into two rival trade blocs, Mercosur and the North American Free Trade Agreement (NAFTA).

*associate members

Data source: World Bank (2003).

Mercosur

Whatever the future of the FTAA, a number of countries have undertaken or continued efforts to establish or expand their own trade treaties. The **Southern Common Market (Mercosur)** is of particular note. Mercosur was established in 1995 by Argentina, Brazil, Paraguay, and Uruguay. Chile and Bolivia became associate members in 1996 and 1997, respectively. They are negotiating full membership, and Colombia, Ecuador, Peru, and Venezuela have evinced interest in joining Mercosur. Including just its four full and two associate members, Mercosur is a market of 242 million people with a combined GDP of $895 billion, as shown in Figure 14.5.

A number of issues, including Argentina's economic crisis, have slowed the negotiations to expand Mercosur, but that effort has recently been reinvigorated by Brazil. President Lula da Silva is trying to strengthen the organization as a counterweight to the United States in the hemisphere. "We have to unite," he told an audience in Peru. "We need to create a South American nation. The more policies we have in common, the better we will be able to succeed in big negotiations, above all in trying to break down WTO's protectionist barriers and prevent the FTAA becoming an instrument that suffocates our chances of growth."[41]

Asia, the Pacific, and Elsewhere

The impulse for regional ties has not been confined to Europe and the Americas. Other regions have also begun to form their own groups. There are four Arab and seven sub-Saharan African trade groups. The three Slavic FSRs (Belarus, Russia, and Ukraine) agreed in 1993 to negotiate cooperation agreements with an eye to a future economic union. Adding to that, Belarus and Russia agreed in 1994 to move to unify their monetary systems based on the Russian ruble.

Even more portentous than these efforts is the trend toward regionalism in the Pacific. The **Association of Southeast Asian Nations (ASEAN)** was established in 1967 and now includes Brunei, Cambodia, Indonesia, Laos, Malaysia, Myanmar (Burma), the Philippines, Singapore, Thailand, and Vietnam. The ASEAN countries have a combined population of over 520 million, a GNP of approximately $610 billion, and total exports of about $405 billion. As discussed in chapter 7, ASEAN, like some other trade organizations, is also working to forge greater political cooperation among its members and to try to bargain as a group (as the EU does) with external countries and other trade organizations.

More recently, the **Asia-Pacific Economic Cooperation (APEC)**, an oddly named structure, began in 1989 and may be evolving toward becoming a regional trade organization. The 21-member organization includes most of the countries of the greater Pacific Ocean region. The members range in the eastern Pacific from Russia in the north, through Southeast Asia, to Australia in the south. On the other side of the Pacific, members extend from Canada in the north, through Mexico, to Chile in the south. The APEC members account for slightly over 40% of the world population, about 60% of the global GDP, and half of all merchandise trade. APEC has a small secretariat based in Singapore, but it is symbolic of APEC's still-tentative status that it has not added a word such as "organization" or "community" to the end of its name.

The first of what have become annual summit meetings of the APEC leaders took place in Seattle, Washington, in 1993. The United States hoped for an agreement in principle to move toward a free trade zone, an Asia-Pacific Economic Community. Among other reasons, that effort was forestalled by strains between LDCs and EDCs about the course of globalization. As one Japanese diplomat put it, "there are a variety of concerns, especially among the developing nations, that we proceed with some caution."[42] As a result, classifying APEC as a regional trade organization is using the term liberally, although that is done here because of the importance the annual meetings have assumed as a forum for discussions among the United States, Japan, China, and other leading members. Still, progress toward APEC integration has been slow. There have been agreements in principle, for example, to achieve "free and open trade and investment" in the Asia-Pacific region. Japan and the United States are to remove all their barriers by the year 2010, with the rest of the APEC members achieving a zero-barrier level by 2020. It remains unclear whether this will occur, given such factors as China's already rising trade surplus with the United States and Japan's uncertain economy. Beyond this, few specific agreements have resulted from these summits, but they are part of a process of dialogue that helps keep lines of communication open.

Beyond Asia, regional trade pacts are even less developed. The various efforts to give life to them in the Middle East have fallen prey to the region's political problems, to the fact that many of the oil production–dependent economies have little to trade with one another, and to other problems. Similarly, Africa's regional trade groups have languished in the face of the continent's poverty and frequent political turmoil.

The Future of Regionalism

The precise role that regional trading blocs will play on the world stage is unclear. Some observers believe that such groupings will help integrate regions, improve and strengthen the economic circumstances of the regions' countries and people, and provide a stepping-stone to world economic integration, just as the EEC was part of the genesis of the EU and just as NAFTA led to the FTAA agreement. Other analysts are worried that while regional blocs (no matter what their level of integration) must still adhere to the GATT/WTO rules and decisions with respect to trade with other blocs and countries, the RTOs will become increasingly closed trading areas and that competition among the blocs will cause a breakdown of the GATT and the construction of higher trade barriers among the blocs. This would lead regionalism away from the integrative model economic internationalists (liberals) favor and toward a competitive model closer to that pictured by economic nationalists (realists). Furthering the concern about the growth in the number of RTOs and their membership is the rise of additional free trade areas and customs unions through bilateral agreements between two countries (the United States and Singapore, 2001), between two RTOs (the Commonwealth of Independent States and the Latin American Integration Association, 2003), and between an RTO and a nonmember country (the EU and Chile, 2002). The WTO refers collectively to the RTOs and the bilateral free trade agreements by the confusing name "regional trade agreements," but they might better be termed **preferential trade agreements (PTAs)** because each establishes preferential treatment–related tariffs and nontariff barriers and because an increasing number have no relationship to a specific region. Figure 14.6 shows the dramatic recent increase in the number of PTAs. The WTO estimates that 70 more have not yet been reported to it and an additional 70 are being negotiated.

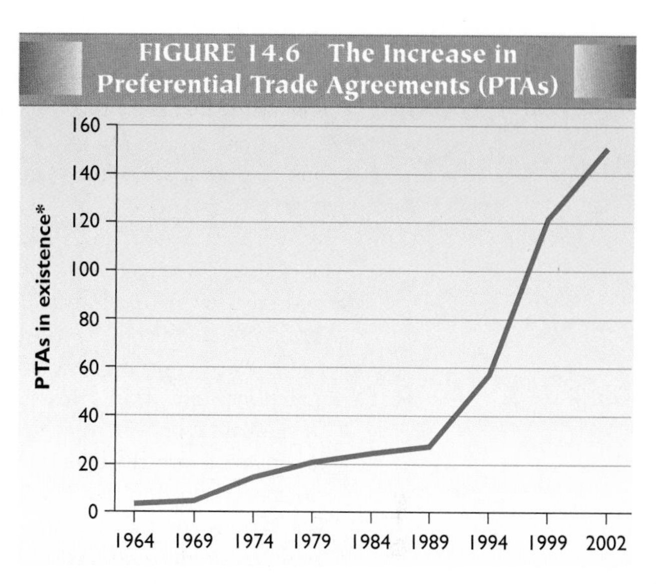

The WTO believes, and some analysts agree, that the marked increase in preferential trade agreements is a sign of stress in global and regional trade integration and, in particular, is an indication that the most powerful EDCs, individually and collectively, are seeking to continue to dominate trade by dealing bilaterally with individual LDCs.

*Only those PTAs still in force as of 2003 are indicated.

Data source: WTO, *World Trade Report* (2003).

The WTO argues in its 2003 *World Trade Report* (p. 46) that "the seeds" for the growth in the number of PTA in the 1990s "were arguably sown in the 1980s" and were "driven then by the seemingly bleak prospects for progress on the multilateral agenda." The report (p. 51) points out that "the proliferation of [PTAs] . . . has meant overlapping membership for many countries" and suggests diplomatically that "this patchwork of agreements and diverse treatments of issues . . . carries the risk that some provisions are mutually inconsistent and may hamper trade by creating complexity and uncertainty." In other words, the WTO worries that the effort to create ever-larger trade units is being undermined by a hodgepodge of PTAs.

The WTO also argues that the RTOs do not work, especially for the LDCs. According to the head of the WTO, bilateral and regional pacts are an unsatisfactory substitute for global trade liberalization because "they are by their very nature discriminatory. None has really succeeded in opening markets in sensitive areas like agriculture. They add to the complexities of doing business by creating a multiplicity of rules. And the poorest countries tend to get left out in the cold." That view is seconded by trade analyst Robert Scollay at Auckland University, New Zealand, who finds the growth of bilateral country-country and RTO-country PTAs particularly troublesome. A generic problem is that PTAs create trade distortions by advantaging "in" countries and disadvantaging "out" countries. The other problem is the bargaining power of the hub country or RTO. What can result is something of a wagon-wheel arrangement, where a powerful hub has bilateral agreements (the spokes) with countries on the rim. These are unlikely to be equal because of the power of the hub compared to the individual countries on the rim. This arrangement is particularly being used to protect agricultural markets, he believes. "The U.S. is clearly pursuing that kind of agenda," Scollay contends, and he also sees evidence of the same in the agenda of the EU and Japan. "If Japan finds it can make progress on bilaterals on a fairly wide front without including agriculture, it is a huge disincentive for them to go anywhere near the WTO," he reasons.[43]

In sum, it is possible to view the future of regionalism in two ways. The optimistic view is that regional organizations will provide a path to greater regional integration, not just economically, but also socially and politically, as the European Union has. This positive view of the future also sees regional trade blocs within regions merging and serving as increasingly broad-based building blocks to global free economic interchange and increased world cooperation along other political, social, and environmental fronts. The pessimistic view is that the rise of RTOs and other forms of PTAs are undermining the globalization of free economic interchange represented by the WTO. Adding to the negative image is the concern that some PTAs are serving to reinforce dependency relations between hub EDC and LDCs on the rim. Those critical of the proliferation of RTOs also worry that in the future they will not lead to greater global integration and cooperation but rather serve as new bases of competition and conflict, substituting regional rivalries for national rivalries. The most likely path lies somewhere between the two extremes, yet either of them is possible.

Chapter Summary

Global Economic Cooperation: Background

1. This chapter discusses the global and regional attempts of countries to cooperate to address the economic issues that face them and to find common interests and solutions.

Global Economic Cooperation: The Institutions

2. A wide variety of general intergovernmental organizations (IGOs) and efforts are devoted to economic cooperation. The UN maintains a number of efforts aimed at general economic development, with an emphasis on the less developed countries (LDCs).
3. Many specialized intergovernmental organizations (IGOs) are also involved in economic cooperation; some examples are the Organization for Economic Cooperation and Development and the Group of Eight.
4. Economic nationalists, economic internationalists, and economic structuralists all offer different explanations of why the relative deprivation of the South exists. The three schools of thought also have varying prescriptions about what, if anything, to do to remedy the North-South gap in economic development.
5. Trade cooperation has grown through the new General Agreement on Tariffs and Trade (GATT) and its administrative structure, the World Trade Organization (WTO), and great strides have been taken toward promoting free trade.
6. Among monetary institutions, the International Monetary Fund is the primary organization dedicated to stabilizing the world's monetary system. The IMF's primary role in recent years has been to assist LDCs and CITs to prosper by reducing their foreign debt.
7. The IMF, however, attaches conditions to its assistance, and this practice has occasioned considerable criticism, especially regarding the voting formula, conditionality, capitalism, and social justice.
8. A number of international organizations provide developmental loans and grants to countries in need. The best known of these is the World Bank Group, which consists of several interrelated subsidiaries. These organizations also primarily extend aid to EDCs, but, like the IMF, some analysts criticize the conditions they attach.

Regional Economic Cooperation

9. There are also several regional efforts aimed at economic integration. The European Union and the North American Free Trade Agreement are the most important of these.

10. By far the most developed is the European Union. The EU has been experiencing some sharp difficulties but has also showed great resilience. It has made great strides in reaching the highest point of integration: converting to a single European currency, the euro.

11. There is disagreement whether the growth in the number and membership of regional trade organizations and the establishment of other forms of preferential trade agreements is a positive or negative development for global economic cooperation, and, by extension, cooperation in other areas.

For a chapter quiz, interactive activities, web links, PowerWeb articles, and much more, visit **www.mhhe.com/rourke10/** and go to chapter 14. Or, while accessing the site, click on Course-Wide Content and view recent international relations articles in the *New York Times.*

Key Terms

Asia-Pacific Economic Cooperation (APEC)
Association of Southeast Asian Nations (ASEAN)
Bretton Woods system
conditionality
Doha Round
Free Trade Area of the Americas (FTAA)
General Agreement on Tariffs and Trade (GATT)
Group of 77 (G-77)
Group of Eight (G-8)
Group of Seven (G-7)
International Conference on Financing for Development (IFCD)
International Monetary Fund (IMF)
lifeboat analogy
North American Free Trade Agreement (NAFTA)
Organization for Economic Cooperation and Development (OECD)
preferential trade agreement (PTA)
regional trade organizations (RTOs)
Southern Common Market (Mercosur)
special drawing rights (SDRs)
UN Conference on Trade and Development (UNCTAD)
UN Development Programme (UNDP)
Uruguay Round
World Bank Group
World Trade Organization (WTO)

CHAPTER

15

Preserving and Enhancing Human Rights and Dignity

THE NATURE OF HUMAN RIGHTS

NEGATIVE HUMAN RIGHTS: FREEDOM FROM ABUSES

- Abuse of Individual Rights
- Abuse of Group Rights
- The International Response to Individual and Group Human Rights Issues

POSITIVE HUMAN RIGHTS

- Food
- Health
- Education

CHAPTER SUMMARY

KEY TERMS

The sun with one eye vieweth all the world.

—William Shakespeare, *Henry VI, Part I*

And your true rights be term'd a poet's rage.

—William Shakespeare, "Sonnet XVII"

Recognition of the inherent dignity and of the equal and inalienable rights of all members of the human family is the foundation of freedom, justice, and peace in the world.

—preamble to the Universal Declaration of Human Rights, 1948

CHAPTER OBJECTIVES

After completing this chapter, you should be able to:

- Discuss the two types of human rights.
- Examine the two types of individual rights.
- Discuss the prevalence of human rights abuses and the ideological justification for those abuses.
- Identify the focus of modern international efforts to ease human rights abuses.
- Analyze the political barriers to human rights efforts and the progress that has been made.
- Evaluate the global problems related to population growth and food shortages, and assess international efforts to address them.
- Evaluate the global problems related to health and assess international efforts to address them.
- Analyze the role of education in achieving human rights and the organizations developed to improve levels of education.

As we near the end of this introduction to world politics, it is appropriate to pause momentarily to remember that, amid all the sound and fury, politics ought to be about maintaining or improving people's quality of life. We have been exploring whether the traditional state-based international system that operates on self-interested competition can best accomplish that or whether the goals of politics can be better attained by transforming the international system into one that emphasizes cooperation and the rule of law, an enhanced authoritative role for international organizations, and diminished state sovereignty. This and the next chapter continue that inquiry by addressing, in this chapter, the human rights and social dignity of the world's people and, in the next, the condition of the biosphere that they inhabit. These two topics are closely linked because the future rests in considerable part on how well the political system nurtures its two most valuable assets: people and the biosphere.

It is important to stress that while the discussions of the human condition and the environment are divided into two chapters, the two subjects are intrinsically intertwined. The size of the globe's population and the need to feed people and supply their material needs is putting tremendous pressure on the capacity of the biosphere to provide resources and to absorb waste. This can be addressed in part by improving the social, educational, and economic status of people, thereby eventually leading to slower population growth, wiser land use, better control of pollution, and other steps that will ease the pressure on the environment. Reciprocally, protecting the biosphere now will ensure that the land, seas, and atmosphere that the human condition depends upon can yield the fresh water, foodstuffs, minerals, and other natural resources necessary for prosperity.

Indeed, the intersection of people and their environment and the combined impact of the two on the social and economic future are so strong that the World Bank in the mid-1990s devised an approach called *green accounting* to measure the *comprehensive wealth* of countries. **Green accounting** includes overall and per capita gross national product (GNP) and other traditional measures of national wealth and then adds two other factors: One is "human capital," which calculates the productive capacity of a country's population by its education, health, and how well all segments are able to participate equally; the second factor is "natural capital," which includes the quality and quantity, as appropriate, of land, air, water, and natural resources. Estimating natural and human capital is even more difficult than arriving at GNP figures, but the results are valuable. Nobel Prize–winning economist Robert M. Solow contends that green accounting is an advance over the traditional approach to measuring assets because "what we normally measure as capital is a small part of what it takes to sustain human welfare." Therefore, adds another economist, green accounting "is a valuable thing to do even if it can only be done relatively crudely."[1]

Turning the emphasis away from mere production helps us to focus on the economic reality that any economic unit needs to add to its national core and infrastructure in order to remain prosperous. If, for example, the owner of a farm devotes all of the farm's financial and human resources to producing crops and neither takes care to avoid depleting the soil and water supplies nor devotes resources to keeping the workers healthy and to training them in the latest farm methods, then, even though production may soar in the short term, the farm's long-term prospects are not good. Similarly, countries face an increasingly bleak future if they do not preserve and, when possible, replenish their natural and human capital. As one observer put it, such "countries are [inflating] income by selling off the family jewels."[2]

The Nature of Human Rights

Before moving to a detailed discussion of human rights, it is important to explain the broad concept of human rights used here. We are used to thinking about human rights in terms of *individual human rights,* that is, freedom from specific abuses or restrictions, especially by governments. The U.S. Bill of Rights, for example, prohibits (except in extreme cases) the government from abridging individual Americans' right to exercise their religion or free speech and from committing a variety of other abuses. These are called **negative rights**, those things that the government and perhaps others cannot do to individuals or groups (such as discriminate based on race, ethnicity, gender, or other inherent demographic characteristics).

Beyond negative rights, there is another range of rights that are more collective in nature. These are called **positive rights**. They include those basic necessities that a society and its government are arguably obligated to provide as best they can in order to assure certain qualitative standards of life for everyone in the community. By the standard of positive rights, every person has the right to exist in at least tolerable conditions. Among these are receiving adequate education, nutrition, housing, sanitation, health care, and the other basics necessary to live with dignity and security and to be a productive individual. Whether society is defined in narrow national terms or broader global terms is a matter of controversy.

Whatever the focus, though, one scholar suggests that the most fruitful way to think about human rights is to begin with the idea that "ultimately they are supposed to serve basic human needs." These basic human needs, which generate corresponding rights, include, among others (Galtung, 1994:3, 72):

- "Survival needs—to avoid violence": The requisite to avoid and the right to be free from individual and collective violence.
- "Well-being needs—to avoid misery": The right to adequate nutrition and water; to movement, sleep, sex, and other biological wants; to protection from diseases and from adverse climatological and environmental impacts.
- "Identity needs—to avoid alienation": The right to self-expression; to realize your potential, to establish and maintain emotional bonds with others; to preserve cultural heritage and association; to contribute through work and other activity; and to receive information about and maintain contact with nature, global humanity, and other aspects of the biosphere.
- "Freedom needs—to avoid repression": The right to receive and express opinions, to assemble with others, to have a say in common policy; and to choose in such wide-ranging matters as jobs, spouses, where to live, and lifestyle.

There is broad agreement among scholars that a right is a justified claim to something. To say, for instance, that you have a right to freedom of religion means you have a legitimate claim to believe whatever you wish. However, a key question is what justifies claiming a right. Where does it come from? As noted in chapter 9, there are two schools of thought, the universalist and the relativist, about the basis of human rights. **Universalists** believe that human rights are derived from sources external to society. Depending on the universalist, the source may be one or another theological or ideological doctrine or it may be natural rights. This last concept holds that the fact of being human carries with it certain rights that cannot be violated or can only be violated in extremis. Universalists therefore believe that there is a single, prevailing set of standards of moral behavior on which human rights are based and that these rights are immutable.

Relativists (from cultural relativism) argue from a positivist point of view and claim that rights are the product of a society's contemporary values. Relativists therefore contend that in a world of diverse cultures, no single standard of human rights exists or is likely to exist short of the world becoming completely homogenized culturally. Those who believe in the cultural relativism of rights also tend to view attempts to impose standards of rights by one culture on another as cultural imperialism. The cultural relativist point of view also means that rights are not timeless; they can change with changing social norms.

The universalist approach to human rights contends that they are the same for all people everywhere and that they cannot be revoked or abridged by any government. It is a view of human rights that is captured in this photograph of a woman in India protesting alleged police brutality.

To see the difference between the two views of rights, consider slavery. Legal slavery existed throughout history until Saudi Arabia and Yemen officially abolished it in 1962 and, by some standards, until Mauritania decreed its end, not for the first time, in 1980. Numerous international treaties now enunciate a right not to be held in slavery. The questions here are two: First, was there always a right not to be a slave, one that existed through all of history, even when slavery was common? Or did the right come into being by sometime in the early-to-mid-19th century, by which time most countries had abolished slavery and the international slave trade, thereby reflecting a new social norm? Second, at the point in the 1800s when it could be said that prevailing international standards had concluded that slavery was a human rights violation, did that right not to be enslaved extend to everyone everywhere, or did it only apply to those countries that had abolished it? Universalists would argue that the right not to be a slave always existed, that the change in attitudes two centuries ago merely recognized that right, and that, therefore, the right applied to all people. A cultural relativist would argue that the right was granted, that it did not exist until it was widely recognized, and that at least for an extended time it only existed where it was the norm.

As chapter 9 discusses, it is not uncommon to hear those in the non-Western world argue that many of the rights asserted in such international documents as the Universal Declaration of Human Rights, which was adopted in 1948 by an overwhelming vote of the UN General Assembly, are based on the values of the politically dominant West. Positivists contend that many of these Western values, such as individualism and democracy, are not held as strongly in other cultures. Therefore, the argument goes, attempts by the West to impose its concept of rights, even if well intended, constitute cultural imperialism. There are, however, leaders in non-Western cultures who reject these assertions of cultural relativism. Burmese political activist and 1991 Nobel Peace Prize winner Aung San Suu Kyi (1995:14) writes that claims about "the national culture" are often distorted in an effort "to justify the policies and actions of those in power." She goes on to argue, "It is precisely because of the cultural diversity of the world that it is necessary for different nations and peoples to agree on those basic human values which will act as a unifying factor."

It must be said that differences over what constitutes a human right are not only matters of Western and non-Western philosophies. There are also vigorous disputes between countries of similar cultural heritage and even within countries. One source of different views about positive and negative rights can be traced to how much a society

FIGURE 15.1 Views About Success in Life

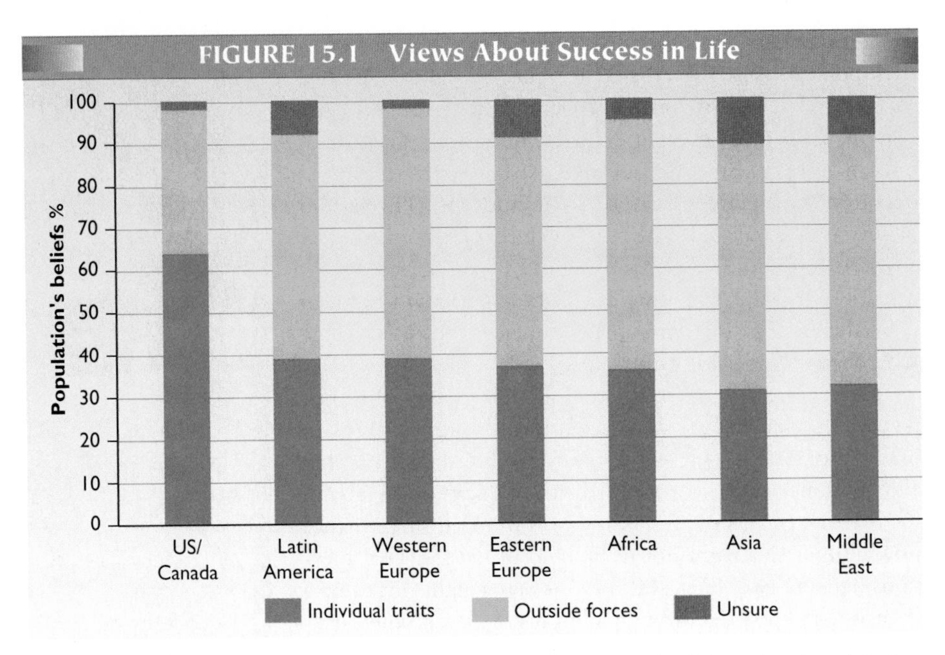

One determinant of how a society perceives positive and negative rights is based on how it feels about success. People in some countries emphasize the importance of individual talent and effort in achieving success rather than the influence of outside forces, such as what country a person is born in, or whether a person is a member of a privileged or disadvantaged demographic group in their country. Americans and Canadians are much more likely than people elsewhere to attribute success to individual characteristics. Indeed, it is interesting to note in this chart that the percentage of people believing that outside forces pretty much control success is fairly consistent across geographic areas, except for the United States and Canada, which on average have percentages almost exactly opposite of everyone else.

Note: The question was whether or not people agreed that "Success in life is pretty much determined by forces outside our control." For clarity, the "agree" answer is labeled "outside forces" and the "disagree" answer is labeled "individual traits."

Data source: The Pew Research Center for People and the Press, "Views of a Changing World, 2003"

believes that individual success or failure is based on each person's effort or outside forces such as that person's place in society. Americans and Canadians have a much stronger individualist attitude about personal success than do people elsewhere in the world. For example, asked if they agreed that "success in life is pretty much determined by forces outside our control," 65% of Americans disagreed, with only 32% agreeing and 3% unsure. The percentages for Canadians were almost identical. By contrast, in 44 other countries across all continents the combined percentages came close to being reversed. On average, only 35% of the respondents in those countries disagreed, with 58% agreeing and 7% unsure. The percentages broken down for different geographical groups are presented in Figure 15.1. Given the differences, it is hardly surprising that there are different views of positive and negative liberty. This became apparent in a survey that asked people in the United States, four Western European countries, and five Eastern European countries which they thought more important for a government to do: (1) follow the negative liberty standard of not interfering in people's freedom to pursue their goals or (2) adhere to the positive liberty standard of acting to ensure that no one in the society is in need. Among Americans, 58% favored the negative liberty approach. Only 33% of Western Europeans and 29% of Eastern Europeans took this view. Instead, 59% of Western Europeans and 60% of Eastern Europeans (compared to 33% of Americans) favored the positive liberty approach (with the remainder of each group unsure).[3]

Negative Human Rights: Freedom from Abuses

Most rights that societies and their states extend (the relativist view) or recognize as valid (the universalist view) are negative rights that prohibit the government and often others (such as organizations and companies) from doing certain things. Although they overlap, these rights can be subdivided into individual rights to such things as freedom of speech and assembly, and group rights, which involve prohibitions against discriminating against categories of people based on ethnicity, gender, race, and other such "in-born" factors. These are often thought of as civil rights.

Abuse of Individual Rights

Oppression is the tool of dictators, who violate individual rights by arbitrarily arresting and punishing people; by depriving them of their property without the due process of law; and by abridging their freedom to freely speak, organize, travel, and associate with other individuals and groups. That such abuses are all too common is evident in data from one survey that ranked countries' respect for political and civil rights on two separate scales, 1 (free) to 7 (oppressive), that resulted in country scores ranging from 2 (best) to 14 (worst). Figure 15.2 illustrates that individual rights are still moderately to severely restricted in most of the world's countries. Indeed, 59 countries fall at or below the seriously oppressive score of 10.

It is likely that you, like most of the people who read this book, live in the United States, Canada, or some other country that has attained a ranking of 2 on the Freedom House scale and where individual rights, while far from ideal, have progressed over time. Indeed, it is hard for those of us fortunate enough to live in such countries to imagine how widespread and how harsh oppression can be. Whether or not you agreed with the U.S.-led invasion of Iraq in 2003, there can be no doubt that President George Bush was correct in his 2004 State of the Union message when he asserted, "Had we failed to act . . . Iraq's torture chambers would still be filled with victims—terrified and innocent. The killing fields of Iraq—where hundreds of thousands of men and women and children vanished into the sands—would still be known only to the killers."[4] Nor do the abuses of some Iraqi prisoners by American guards negate that. Detailing lurid tales of repression would be easy, for there are many. It will suffice here, however, to note that the abuse of human rights is generally associated with authoritarian governance of the state, a topic extensively reviewed in chapter 6. The abuse of individual rights is also often linked to the abuse of groups. For example, the Sunni Muslim–dominated government of Saddam Hussein not only committed atrocities against individual political opponents, it also carried out horrific attacks against Shiite Muslims and on the Kurds, a non-Arab Muslim

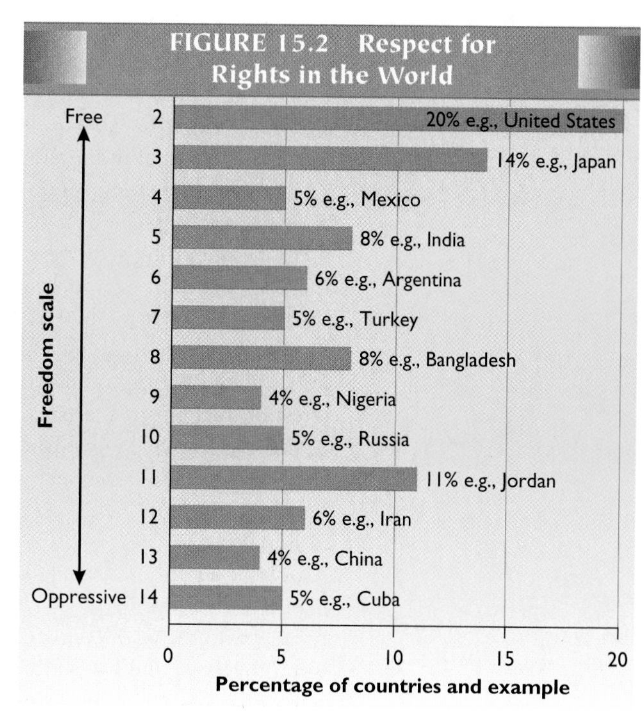

Oppression of individual and group rights remains common. Although about a third of all countries fall into the laudable 2 and 3 categories, about as many fall into categories 10–14, which includes those countries where rights are tenuous at best and brutally abused at worst.

Notes: Percentages do not equal 100 because of rounding. Scores are based on a rating system of 1 to 7 used by Freedom House to evaluate political rights and civil liberties. An example of a country in each category is included.

Data source: Freedom House, *Freedom House Survey 2003* at http://www.freedomhouse.org/research/index.htm. Calculations by author.

group in Iraq's north. It must be noted, though, that democracies also commit abuses. The United States has counted itself a democracy from its founding, yet it permitted slavery from that time until the adoption of the Thirteenth Amendment to the Constitution in 1865. Moreover, abuses of African Americans and other groups by domestic state and local governments continued under so-called Jim Crow laws, and the authorities too often turned a blind eye to such individual abuses as the lynching of nearly 3,500 blacks between 1882 and 1968. One of the many advantages of democracy in today's world is that such abuses are much less common than they are in authoritarian states, but issues continue to exist globally related to the treatment of many groups, including women, children, ethnic and racial groups, religious groups, indigenous people, and refugees and immigrants. It is to these problems that we can now turn our attention.

Abuse of Group Rights

Whether the focus is race, ethnicity, gender, sexual orientation, religious choice, or some other trait, there are few human characteristics or beliefs that have not been the target of discrimination and abuse somewhere in the world. One important cause is the "we-they" sense of group identification often associated with nationalism (as discussed in chapter 4) that leads people to value the group they identify with and to see those in other ("they") groups as different. Too frequently, different does not mean "I'm OK, you're OK," but instead means that you are inferior and someone to be feared or oppressed. Evidence of such attitudes extends as far back into history as we can see. Genocide is a modern term, but the practice is ancient. The Roman philosopher and statesman Seneca (ca. 8 B.C.–A.D. 65) wrote in *Epistles* that Romans were "mad, not only individually, but nationally" because they punished "manslaughter and isolated murders" but accepted "the much vaunted crime of slaughtering whole peoples."

In the intervening centuries, attitudes on racial or other forms of demographic superiority and oppression have often played a destructive role in history. Many of today's divisions and problems are, for example, a legacy of the racism that combined with political and economic nationalism to rationalize oppression. The ideas of biologist Charles Darwin in *The Origin of Species* (1859) were bastardized through **social Darwinism** to justify colonial domination of the "unfit" (nonwhites) by the "fit" (whites). Racism also joined with religion to build a case in the Western mind that subjugation was in the interest of uncivilized and pagan—that is, nonwhite, non-Christian—societies. Symbolic of this racist self-justification is Rudyard Kipling's "White Man's Burden," penned in 1899 to persuade Americans to seize the Philippines: "Take up the White Man's burden," the verse urged, "To serve your captives' need." Kipling argued it was a noble undertaking to try to civilize those whom he described as "Your new-caught, sullen peoples, / Half devil and half child," even though doing so would earn whites "The blame of those ye better / The hate of those ye guard." Such ideas continued to exist broadly into the 20th century, as evidenced by the continuation of widespread colonialism into the second half of that century. It was also the basis of fascism, expressed among other places by Adolf Hitler's view that war and conquest were "all in the natural order of things—for [they make] for the survival of the fittest" and that, as he asserted in *Mein Kampf* (1925), "all occurrences in world history are only expressions of the races' instinct of self-preservation."

Other sources of discrimination and abuse of groups within a society come from any one or combination of feelings of superiority, lack of tolerance, or lack of concern. For example, the status of women has always been determined in significant part by the assumption long held by most men and even by many women that male dominance was natural because, as Plato put it in *The Republic,* men were the "watch dogs of the flock" and should bear the burden of conducting war and "the other duties of guardianship," whereas "in these duties the light part must fall to the women because of the weakness of their sex." The work of Charles Darwin also lent a patina of scientific theory to the practice of male dominance, based on his argument in *The Descent of Man* (1871) that "man is more courageous, pugnacious and energetic than woman, and has a more inventive genius." Darwin went on to assert that "the chief distinction in the intellectual powers of the two sexes is [shown] by man's attaining to a higher eminence, in whatever he takes up, than can woman—whether requiring deep thought, reason, or imagination, or merely the use of the senses and hands." Such attitudes are less pervasive than they once were, but they continue to exist widely, overtly or covertly, and are especially strong in some societies. This was documented in a survey's finding that approval of gender equality ranged from a high of 82% in Western countries, through 60%–65% in Asia and sub-Saharan Africa, to 55% in Muslim countries (Inglehart & Norris, 2002, 2003a).

Women

In our discussion of the plight of a diversity of demographic groups, it is appropriate that we begin with the largest of all minority groups, women. Females constitute about half the world's population, but they are a distinct economic-political-social minority because of the wide gap in societal power and resources between women and men. Compared to men, women are much less likely to have a salaried job, are much less likely to hold a professional position, are much more likely to be illiterate, and are much more likely to be living below the poverty line (Rhein, 1998).

Women, Armed Conflict, and Abuse Economic and educational deprivations seem to pale when compared to the violence inflicted on women. A recent UN Development Fund for Women (UNIFEM) report, *War, Women, and Peace* (2002), begins with the observation of the study panel members that while they had read the distressing statistics about the extensive violence suffered by women noncombatants in conflict, nevertheless,

> We were completely unprepared for the searing magnitude of what we saw and heard in the conflict and post-conflict areas we visited . . . [and] for the horrors women described. Wombs punctured with guns. Women raped and tortured in front of their husbands and children. Rifles forced into vaginas. Pregnant women beaten to induce miscarriages. Fetuses ripped from wombs. Women kidnapped, blindfolded, and beaten on their way to work or school. We heard accounts of gang rapes, rape camps, and mutilation. Of murder and sexual slavery. We saw scars of brutality so extreme that survival seemed for some a worse fate than death. (p. 9)

It is important to stress that the attacks on women often are not just individual acts of sexual aggression. Instead, according to the report, women's "bodies become a battleground over which opposing forces struggle. Women are raped as a way to humiliate the men they are related to. . . . In societies where ethnicity is inherited through the male, 'enemy' women are raped and forced to bear children." Additionally, "Women are kidnapped and used as sexual slaves to service troops, as well as to cook for them and carry their loads from camp to camp. They are purposely infected with HIV/AIDS, a slow, painful murder" (p. 10). Adding to the toll on women, many flee the fighting and become refugees. In fact of all refugees, women and their children make up a substantial majority—up to 80% of those who are forced from their homes and become refugees in another country or internally displaced persons. Without adequate food, shelter, or health care, many women fall victim to disease. Other women who are trapped in these desperate conditions, the report relates, "are forced or left with little choice but to become sex workers . . . ; their bodies become part of a barter system, a form of exchange that buys the necessities of life" (p. 11). To compound the problem, desperation often continues after women return home—if that is what razed dwellings, dead husbands and other family members, and no means of economic support can be termed. Such graphic language is not meant to be sensationalistic, but to convey the reality of what women suffer because they are women and to help overcome the fact that, as the UNIFEM report puts it, "Violence against women in conflict is one of history's great silences" (p. 9).

Women, Society, and Abuse All the abuses noncombatant women suffer are, grimly, a small proportion of the violence and other forms of abuse that women endure globally. These abuses occur in significant part because of the same attitudes and lack of recourse that make women so vulnerable during conflict. Some of the deprivations involve overt violence. According to the UN, at least one-third of all women have been beaten, coerced into sex, or otherwise abused at least once in their life, and, depending on the country, 40% to 70% of all female murder victims are killed during domestic violence.

Domestic violence against women is a global human rights crisis that the transnational network of IGOs, such as the UN Fund for Women, and NGOs, such as Women Against Violence, are working to ease. This shocking photo shows one victim of domestic violence. The husband of Nayyar Shahzaidi, a Pakistani woman, sliced off her nose because he feared she would cheat on him. He then sent her back to her parents' home where, ashamed of her disfigurement, she is likely to remain secluded for the rest of her life. Whether or not this woman's husband was punished was not reported, but it is not uncommon for officials to ignore such horrors. Other women in South Asia suffer what are arguably even worse fates, such as so-called bride burning, but abuse is found in every region.

Another form of assault on women comes through sex-selective abortions or the neglect of infant girls. Globally, there are about 60 million fewer girls (age 0 to 15) than normal population figures would expect. For example, although it is normal for about 5% more girls than boys to be born and survive to age six, India's recent census found that nationally there were 7.3% more boys than girls in that age group. The gap reached 21% in some localities. This means that annually in India alone, about 157,000 more girls than normal either die or are aborted as female fetuses because of gender bias. India bans the use of ultrasound to determine sex, but the procedure is reportedly readily available. "Society needs to recognize this discrimination," a 2003 UN Population Fund (UNFPA) study counsels. "Girls have a right to live just as boys do. Moreover, a missing number of either sex, and the resulting imbalance, can destroy the social and human fabric as we know it."[5]

Other girls are subjected to female genital mutilation (FGM), sometimes euphemistically called female circumcision. This procedure ranges in severity from, at minimum, a clitoridectomy (the excision of the clitoris), which deprives a female of all sexual sensation, to infibulation, the cutting away of all of a female's external genitalia and labial tissue. It is widely performed on adolescent and pre-adolescent girls in central and North Africa, and the UN estimates that as many as 130 million women and girls alive currently have undergone the procedure and that each year another 2 million are subjected to it. Beyond the psychological trauma, FGM, which is usually performed by individuals without medical training operating in unsanitary settings, is extraordinarily painful and dangerous, carrying a significant rate of infection.

Another unhappy fate awaits over 2 million impoverished women in many countries who annually are sold or forced to go into de facto slavery in their own countries or abroad. Some become domestic servants, who are often mistreated. The sale of young women and even girls (and young men and boys) into heterosexual or homosexual slavery is also relatively common in some places, and the U.S. State Department has estimated that there are 2.3 million people who have been forced into prostitution and transported across international borders. Those impressed in their own country add millions more to this number. Most of the women in sexual servitude are located in the LDCs, but many are also in the EDCs. Indeed, so many women from Russia, Ukraine, and other former Soviet republics have been forced physically or by poverty into prostitution in other countries, especially in Europe, Canada, and the United States, that this sad trafficking in women has become known as the "Natasha trade" (Hughes, 2000). These women can be purchased for as little as $1,500, and as one pimp in Canada recently assured a reporter, "I can get 10 to 15 to 20 girls shipped to me in a week."[6]

Economic, educational, and political discrimination, although less immediately disabling than violence, also takes its toll on women. As related in chapter 5, the UN Development Programme's (UNDP) gender development index, which rates the level of equality of women compared to men using a range of economic and social political criteria, finds that equality is nonexistent. According to the 2003 calculation, Norway was least unequal, with a rating of 0.941 out of 1.000, and Niger finished last of the 74 countries, with an abysmal rating of 0.279. A separate gender empowerment measure based on the status of women in politics and business similarly found no country that could boast of treating its women equally. Because of data gaps, only 69 countries were rated, but among these Norway again did best at 0.837, with Yemen in a distant last place with a 0.127 rating. What these statistics translate into economically is less opportunity and wages and more poverty for women. Studies of market (for pay) and nonmarket (such as homemaking) work activities indicate that women work more than men in virtually all countries, yet they receive substantially less money than men do, especially in LDCs. From the beginning, women are disadvantaged because they receive less education, with girls 50% more likely not to be in school than boys. Even when they do work as adults, they receive lower wages. One review of wage rates in 47 EDCs and LDCs found that on average women made 28% less than men for full-time work. The bottom line of all these elements of economic deprivation is that women are much more vulnerable economically. There is no more single telling statistic than the fact that women constitute approximately 70% of all those living below the poverty line in their respective countries.

Gender Abuse and the Law Sometimes the abuses are sanctioned by law, but more often the rights of women are simply ignored by male-dominated governments. In some cases, there are also economic incentives for governments to ignore abuses. Prostitution is a huge business in Southeast Asia, as elsewhere, and the females—often poor girls and women who are forced or duped into sexual slavery—bring in billions of dollars. The UN has estimated, for example, that the revenue generated by sex tourism and other aspects of the illicit sexual trade ranges between 2% and 14% of the GNPs of Indonesia, Malaysia, Thailand, and the Philippines. According to the UN report, the "revenues [the sex trade] generates are crucial to the livelihoods and earning potential of millions of workers beyond the prostitutes themselves."[7]

Did You Know That:

Only about 25% of the world's countries have laws against domestic abuse.

Most often, civil law and social strictures reinforce one another. This is so in Saudi Arabia, where women are treated as second-class citizens. Women cannot live independently; they are not permitted to drive, and there is widespread gender segregation in schools, universities, and workplaces. Saudi women are disadvantaged compared to men in matters of marriage, divorce, and child custody. All women are required to wear a black scarf to cover their head and an *abaya* (robe) that completely covers them except for their eyes, hands, and feet. If they fail to do so, they are subject to harassment, or even physical

YOU BE THE PLAYWRIGHT

Sovereignty, Democracy, the *Shari'ah,* and Women's Rights in Iraq

Speaking to the nation in his 2004 State of the Union address, President George Bush expressed his determination to bring democracy to Iraq. "Today our coalition is working with the Iraqi Governing Council to draft a basic law, with a bill of rights," he assured his listeners. The president also looked forward to soon restoring the governance of Iraq to Iraqis, telling his audience, "We're working with Iraqis and the United Nations to prepare for a transition to full Iraqi sovereignty by the end of June [2004]." Fine words! But accomplishing them would not be easy. One pitfall involved the status of Iraqi women.

It is reasonable to assume that both democracy and a bill of rights would include equal political and civil rights for women. Within very wide boundaries, sovereignty means Iraq being its own master, deciding its laws and policies without outside interference. The problem is that the rights of Iraqi women and sovereignty for Iraq collided, and that threatened U.S. disengagement.

Soon after a leftist, pan-Arab revolution overthrew the country's last monarch, King Faisal II, in 1958, Iraq established a relatively progressive civil code that gave women more legal status and rights than possessed by women in most other Arab countries. For example, the code prohibited marriage below age 18, arbitrary divorce, and favoring males in child custody and property inheritance disputes. The Baathist regime headed by Saddam Hussein that took power in 1968 left the basic laws in place and continued a largely secular, if despotic, legal and judicial system.

Then, of course, the United States toppled Saddam Hussein and the Baath Party from power in April 2003 and set up the Iraqi Governing Council to create a democratic Iraq and to oversee the country's transition toward control of its own affairs. Among its earlier actions, in December 2003 the council voted to repeal the parts of the civil code dealing with women. Under a new government, the council decreed, such matters as marriage, divorce, child custody, and property rights would be under the jurisdiction of religious courts presided over by clerics making decisions based on *shari'ah* (the law of the Koran). Reportedly the 25-member council took the action after only 15 minutes' discussion and did so when two of its three female members had temporarily left the chamber to attend to other business.

Many Iraqi women voiced outrage. Amira Hassan Abdullah, a Kurdish lawyer, protested, "This will send us home and shut the door, just like what happened to women in Afghanistan. The old law wasn't perfect, but this one would make Iraq a jungle. Iraqi women will accept it over their dead bodies." Agreeing, jurist Zakia Ismael Hakki praised the 1959 code as giving women a "half-share in society," and predicted, "This new law will send Iraqi families back to the Middle Ages. It will allow men to have four or five or six wives. It will take away children from their mothers. It will allow anyone who calls himself a cleric to open an Islamic court in his house and decide about who can marry and divorce and have rights. We have to stop it."[1]

Speaking for the council, spokesman Hamid al-Khifaey argued that transferring jurisdiction over family matters from civil courts to religious ones was what Iraqis wanted. "It is only right that people use the doctrine they believe in to sort out their family affairs and family problems," he claimed.[2] Indicating what that might mean for the status of women from the council's view, one of its members, Ibrahim al-Jafaari, told reporters, "Islam makes a woman the responsibility of her father until she marries, and then she is the responsibility of her husband." He added that "a man is worth two women," according to the Koran, but

punishment, by the so-called religious police, the government-funded Committee for the Propagation of Virtue and the Prevention of Vice. Women's rights organizations do not exist in the country, nor does any woman have a role of importance in the government.

The struggle to advance women's status under the law and to ensure enforcement of women's rights continues in many countries, with many of the socially conservative Middle Eastern countries being a particular legal desert for women. In some cases, there is even the possibility that the laws will regress and women will lose the rights they have, as explained in the You Be the Playwright box "Sovereignty, Democracy, the *Shari'ah,* and Women's Rights in Iraq."

Children

Children are not commonly considered a minority group. But insofar as they are dominated and sometimes abused by others, children fall well within the range of the groups

In late 2003, the Governing Council of Iraq, which the United States set up, repealed what was a progressive (for the Middle East) civil code governing family relations and other matters pertaining to women. President George Bush promised to bring democracy to Iraq, but a new Iraqi government might well favor traditional Muslim law. This could lead to actions, such as barring women from wearing nontraditional clothes like those on the student in the foreground at Al-Mustansiriyah University in Baghdad, or, indeed, forbidding women from going to the university at all. Would democracy be better served by letting the Iraqis make their own decisions about how to treat women or by insisting that women receive equal rights?

cautioned, "We have to be careful about taking verses in isolation."[3]

If you were president of the United States, how would you proceed? You could tell your administrator in Iraq to insist that the council reverse its repeal and also include a full and explicit set of rights for women in Iraq's new constitution. That would make Iraq more democratic in one way. But would it be democratic to impose your say over the vote of the governing council? Moreover, the council might refuse. That could disrupt your timetable for returning Iraq to sovereignty during the summer of 2004, a result that would anger Iraqis and perhaps also mightily dismay Americans and endanger your reelection in November.

So what would you do? Would you hold firm for defending the rights of women in post-occupation Iraq even if it meant that the United States had to continue to exercise control for an extended time beyond your goal? Or would you let the governing council's majority-vote action stand, thereby allowing Iraq to proceed to self-governance and enabling you to tell voters that the end of U.S. involvement in Iraq was in sight?

that suffer because of their lack of economic and political power and because they are often denied rights accorded to the dominant segments of society.

Besides conditions such as lack of adequate nutrition that deny to a vast number of children any opportunity for a fulfilling life, children endure a variety of abuses. Being forced to work is one of them. According to the 2002 data of the International Programme for the Elimination of Child Labour (IPEC), a division of the International Labor Organization (ILO), there are 186 million children aged 5 to 14 that are performing more than light or casual economic work. About 88% of these children are engaged in what the ILO classifies as hazardous work. One of eight children between the ages of 5 and 9 works, and that rises to nearly one in four between 10 and 14. To make matters worse, nearly 60% of these children are doing what the IPEC classifies as hazardous work. Adding further to the problem, 5.4 % of the children between ages 5 and 9 and 13.1% of those aged 10 to 14—or over 110 million children in total—work instead of

The UN and associated agencies are slowly moving to institute economic regulations to end corruption, labor abuses, and other problems. Child labor is one such concern, with the International Labor Organization a leader in the effort to create a world where scenes such as the one pictured here cease to exist. This young girl is at work carrying bricks at a construction site in Myanmar rather than going to school and playing as she should be. Bricks such as the eight she is carrying weigh between 3 and 4 kilos each, meaning that the total weight pressing down her neck and spine is somewhere between 53 and 71 pounds.

going to school. The percentage of child laborers ranges from about 2% in the EDCs to as high as 29% in sub-Saharan Africa.

The most disturbing statistics of all related to the 8.4 million children involved in what IPEC terms "unconditional worst forms of child labor." This includes children in five categories (and the number of children in each): internationally trafficked children (1.2 million), forced and bonded labor (5.7 million), armed conflict (so-called boy soldiers, 0.3 million), prostitution and pornography (1.8 million), and illicit activities (such as drug sales, 0.6 million).[8] Child prostitution is especially prevalent in Southern Asia and Latin America. "Brazil may be the worst in the world, but nobody really knows," says a UN representative in Brazil.[9] There are many reasons— ranging from abuse at home to economic desperation—why children turn to prostitution; it is also the case that many children are sold by their families. A recent UN report related the example of Lam, a 15-year-old Vietnamese girl who was sold by her grandmother to purveyors for a brothel in Cambodia. According to the report, the price for girls like Lam ranges between $50 and $200. Other individuals are kidnapped by sex-slavers to supply the multibillion-dollar sex trade. An astronomical rate of AIDS and other sexually transmitted diseases are among the myriad dangers these children face.

The treatment of children is certainly the proper concern of national governments, but it is also an international issue. It is estimated that each year 10 to 12 million men travel internationally as "sex tourists" to exploit children. Clothes, shoes, and other products manufactured by children are sold in international trade; you may be wearing one of these products even as you read these words. The wars and civil strife that ruin the lives of boy soldiers and other children are often rooted in world affairs.

Ethnic and Racial Groups

Strife and oppression based on ethnicity and race are still unsettlingly common. Until international pressure through economic sanctions and other actions finally compelled South African whites to surrender political power in 1994, racism persisted officially through the apartheid system that permitted 6.5 million whites to dominate the other 29 million black, Asian, and "colored" (mixed-race) people. Also in 1994 the slaughter of Tutsis by Hutus in Rwanda and the recurring violence between these two groups in Burundi and Rwanda provided a terrible example of racial/ethnic hate politics. To cite just a few of the many more recent examples, ethnic-based rivalries tore at the lives of the people of Afghanistan, the Iraqi government assailed its Kurdish minority, Tamils and Sinhalese continued killing one another in Sri Lanka, Tibetans unwillingly continued to be governed by China, and Cyprus remains split between Greeks and Turks. The previous discussions of these ethnic and racial tensions, especially in chapter 4, make further comments redundant here; it is only necessary to reiterate that ethnic and racial identification are a key component of the tensions and conflict that make nationalism one of, if not the most, divisive elements of human politics.

Religious Groups

Strife and oppression based entirely or in part on religion is also common on the world stage, as the conflict in Northern Ireland, the conflict in Sudan between the Muslim government and non-Muslim rebels, the slaughter of Bosnian Muslims and Kosovars by Orthodox Bosnian Serbs, and other conflicts attest. There are also, as detailed in chapter 5, numerous efforts by religious fundamentalists in India, Israel, Northern Ireland, several Muslim countries, and elsewhere to align the legal codes and religious laws of their respective countries and to force everyone, regardless of their personal beliefs, to follow those theocratic laws. Even in countries where there is no move to supplant civil with theocratic law, religious intimidation is not uncommon.

Racism, anti-Semitism, and other disturbing forms of hatred are also on the rise in Europe. Russia and Eastern Europe have witnessed the reemergence of overt and not infrequent verbal and physical assaults on Jews. Public opinion surveys in some countries reveal that many negative images of Jews persist. One poll found 59% of Russians agreeing with the statement, "Jews have too much power in the world of business." Other former communist countries in Europe are also seeing more overt anti-Semitism. A survey in Poland found that one-third of all respondents thought Jewish influence "too great" in the country, and 31% admitted to being somewhere between "extremely" and "slightly" anti-Semitic. Even more recently, Tel Aviv University's annual review on global anti-Semitism reported that 57% of 311 anti-Semitic incidents that occurred in 2002 happened in Western Europe.

Indigenous Peoples

The history of the world is a story of mass migrations and conquests that have often left the indigenous people of a region as a minority in national political systems imposed on their traditional tribal or other political structures. The most familiar of these groups to many readers probably are the numerous native peoples of North and South America commonly lumped together as "Indians," or more contemporarily referred to by such designations as Native Americans and Mezo-Americans. The Eskimos or Inuits of Canada and Alaska (as well as Greenland and eastern Siberia), and native Hawaiians in that U.S. state are also indigenous peoples. All together, there are approximately 5,000 indigenous groups with a total of 300 million people residing in more than 70 countries on five continents.

The efforts of various indigenous groups in Central and South America have also become increasingly well known. The unrest in the southern area of Chiapas in Mexico is associated in part with the alienation of the impoverished Mayan and other indigenous peoples of that region from the Mexican government. This feeling of oppression is supported by UN data that finds that on the UNDP's Human Development Index, the level of development of the Mexican people is 27% higher than that of the country's indigenous peoples. This relative poverty, even in what used to be called **Third World** countries, has led to the term **Fourth World** to designate indigenous peoples collectively.

One of the particular efforts of indigenous peoples in recent years has been their effort to protect their traditional home areas politically and environmentally from the incursion of the surrounding cultures. The spread of people and commercial activities such as logging and mining into the vast interior areas of the Amazon River system has increasingly degraded the health, environment, and other aspects of the life of the indigenous peoples of that region. The Yanomami people of Brazil and Venezuela provide an example. The Yanomami (the word means "human being") had little contact with outsiders before the mid-1980s when the lure of gold brought prospectors and miners far up Brazil's rivers and into the Yanomami's forest retreats. The invasion has left the

Yanomami devastated by the diseases, mercury, and other toxins brought by the miners, and, on occasion, by violence aimed at forcing the tribe off its lands. Their numbers have shrunk since the mid-1980s by about 10%, to 19,000.

Beyond the Amazon basin, similar stories are common. Representatives of the Khwe people of Botswana traveled to the annual UN Commission on Human Rights convention in Geneva, Switzerland, to seek help in fending off their threatened expulsion from the Kalahari Desert to make way for tourism facilities. "We came without any promise of getting anything done," said John Hardbattle, leader of the First People of the Kalahari organization. "We felt that if we can't get help at the UN, then we won't get it anywhere else."[10] As Hardbattle recognized, the ability of aboriginal groups to resist the hunger of powerful outside forces for resources and land is limited. They depend in part on gaining world attention and help. That has just begun, as we will see later.

Refugees and Immigrants

Many commentators have accurately noted the rise of ethnic and racial strife, religious fundamentalism, and other xenophobic movements in recent years. One clear indication of that nativist tendency is evident in the upsurge in negative feeling in many quarters of the world toward immigrants and refugees. The post–cold war spasm of civil wars and other internal violence, added to the economic desperation of many people, has set off a flood of refugees. "Migration is the visible face of social change," as a report by UNFPA puts it.[11] According to the United Nations High Commissioner for Refugees, 10.4 million refugees were living outside their native countries at the beginning of 2003. While still distressingly high, this figure was well below its peak over the past quarter century of 17.9 million and the lowest total since 1982. Also in 2003, there were 1 million people in other countries seeking asylum and an additional 5.8 million internally displaced persons who, while still living in their own country, had been forced to flee their homes, villages, and cities.

Beyond those classes of people, millions of people have legally or illegally entered other countries to find work. The tide of refugees and immigrants, legal and illegal, has been met with increasing resistance. When asked whether immigrants have a good or bad effect on their country, a plurality of people in 28 countries replied bad, with a plurality in 13 countries answering good, and 3 countries evenly divided on the issue. When people were queried about increasing restrictions on people coming to their country, the reactions to immigrants, refugees, foreign workers, and other outsiders were even starker. On average, a resounding 72% of the respondents favored stricter controls. Only 22% opposed stricter controls, with 6% unsure. Opposition was very high in the EDCs, especially the United States, Canada, and Western Europe, where, on average, 76% wanted tougher restrictions. But opposition was even slightly higher in Latin America (77%) and sub-Saharan Africa (79%). East Europeans (67%), Asians (61%), and Middle Easterners (66%) were also solidly for raising barriers to entry.[12] This survey was taken in 2002, and some of the strong feelings may have been a post-9/11 reaction to worries about terrorism. Still, there can be little doubt that increased immigration is broadly unpopular throughout the world.

To a degree, the feelings against immigrants, refugees, and others entering a country may result from racial, ethnic, religious, and other biases. But there are other causes. As discussed in chapter 5, people in most countries see their national cultures being diluted by the cross-acculturation associated with globalization. It is also the case that coping with refugees and economically driven illegal immigrants is costly. Countries donate billions of dollars to assist refugees overseas, and many countries also spend vast sums on their border patrols and on other domestic programs to stem the influx of refugees and undocumented immigrants, to assist those who are admitted or who slip in, and to return some of those who do arrive to their country of origin. Such costs can be a severe strain for LDCs that suffer a large influx of refugees, and the funds available through the UN and other IGOs and private NGOs are almost never adequate to fully house, feed, and otherwise care for the refugees. There are also other potential problems. For one, when refugees have fled from fighting, the conflict may sometimes spread to the new area to which they have gone.

Whatever attitudes may be about the inflow of refugees and immigrants, it is certain that the tide will be unending as long as people in some countries are subject to endemic violence and poverty. The Kevin Costner movie *Field of Dreams* revolved around the line, "If you build it, they will come." To those who daily face death, disease, and hunger, any safe haven and especially the EDCs' societies of relative peace and material wealth represent a field of dreams. And people in danger and destitution will come. Barriers can lower the stream, but arguably a better way that would address the cause and also avoid the perpetual spending of vast sums on aid, immigration control, and other programs is to help the South develop quickly and achieve political stability so that it can build a field that at least meets minimum needs of sustenance and safety. It is conceivable that if Mexico's standard of living were to increase substantially, for example, many of its citizens would no longer undergo the dislocation and risk the physical danger that leaving home and slipping into the United States entails. "We have a good argument now, a very concrete one," for helping the LDCs, the prime minister of Denmark told a UN conference, "which is, if you don't help the Third World . . . , then you will have these poor people in your society."[13]

The International Response to Individual and Group Human Rights Issues

It would be naive to argue that the world has even begun to come close to resolving its numerous individual and group human rights issues; it would be equally wrong to deny that a start has been made and that one aspect of globalization is the increased concern for and application of human rights principles (Tomuschat, 2004; Moravcsik, 2000). The way to evaluate the worth of the efforts that we are about to discuss is to judge their goals and to see them as the beginnings of a process that only a few decades ago did not exist at all. Whatever country you live in, the protection of human rights has evolved over an extended period and is still far from complete. The global community has now embarked on an effort similar to your country's effort. It will take time, however, and it will be controversial (Monshipouri, Englehart, Nathan, & Philip, 2003; Brysk, 2002).

The United Nations is at the center of global human rights activity (Pace, 1998). The basis for concern is the UN's charter, which touches on human rights in several places (Eide, 1998; Korey, 1998). More specific is the **Universal Declaration of Human Rights,** which was adopted by the UN General Assembly in 1948 by a vote of 48 in favor, 8 countries abstaining, and 2 countries absent. The United States and all the Western allies were among those voting in favor; the abstaining countries were such notably undemocratic states as the Soviet Union and its allies, Saudi Arabia, and then–white-controlled South Africa. The Universal Declaration clearly supports the universalist approach, rather than the relativist approach to human rights by declaring in Article 1, "All human beings are born free and equal in dignity and rights," and by further proclaiming in Article 2, "Everyone is entitled to all the rights and freedoms set forth in this Declaration, without distinction of any kind."

Because it is not a treaty, the Universal Declaration does not directly bind countries, but its overwhelming passage makes it arguably part of the global norms that are one of the bases of international law. Many of the rights enunciated in the Universal Declaration

The Universal Declaration of Human Rights, which was adopted overwhelmingly by the UN General Assembly in 1948, is the foundation of the many human rights treaties that have been subsequently concluded. This photograph shows college students in Hong Kong at what was one of many gatherings in 1998 to celebrate the 50th anniversary of the Universal Declaration of Human Rights.

are also included in two other multilateral treaties: the International Covenant on Civil and Political Rights (1966) and the International Covenant on Economic, Social and Cultural Rights (1966). About 75% of all countries have agreed to these pacts. Like the other major countries, China and the United States have signed both treaties, but the United States has not ratified the latter treaty, and China has not ratified either of them. In addition to these two basic treaties and the Universal Declaration, there are nearly two dozen other UN-sponsored covenants that address children's rights, genocide, racial discrimination, refugees, slavery, stateless persons, women's rights, and other human rights issues (Kent, 1999). These agreements and human rights in general are monitored by the United Nations Commission on Human Rights (UNCHR).

There are also a number of regional conventions and IGOs that supplement the principles and efforts of the UN. The best developed of these are in Western Europe and include two human rights covenants. These are adjudicated by the European Court of Human Rights and by the UN Commission on Human Rights, as discussed in chapters 7 and 9. Domestic courts also increasingly apply human rights law (Jayawickrama, 2003). Additionally, there are a substantial number of NGOs, such as Amnesty International and Human Rights Watch, that are concerned with a broad range of human rights. These groups work independently and in cooperation with the UN and regional organizations to further human rights. They add to the swell of information about, and criticisms of, abuses and help promote the adoption of international norms that support human rights.

It would be foolish to imagine that being a party to one, some, or even all of these treaties by itself prevents a country from abusing human rights. Iraq is a party to both the International Covenant on Civil and Political Rights and the International Covenant on Economic, Social and Cultural Rights in 1971, yet throughout its 33 years, Saddam Hussein's regime egregiously abused many, even most, of the rights set forth in both covenants. Indeed, the impact of such treaties, the efforts of IGOs and NGOs, and the general progress of human rights have, as noted, been mixed. One problem is political selectivity, which disposes all countries to be shocked when opponents transgress against human rights and to ignore abuses by themselves, by their allies, and by countries that they hope to influence. The United States regularly proclaims its commitment to the global spread of democracy, yet continues to support the governments of Saudi Arabia and several other unabashedly authoritarian regimes. Another impediment is the claim that cultural standards are different, and, therefore, what is a human rights violation in one country is culturally acceptable in another. A third issue is the standard of sovereignty, which continues to be used by some countries to reject outside interference in domestic abuses, and by other countries as a reason for ignoring those abuses. There are repeated signs, however, that the sovereignty defense is wearing thin. For example, when Americans were asked in late 2002 whether the record of Saddam Hussein's "human rights violations are enough to require the United Nations to support U.S. military action against Iraq," 50% replied yes, only 34% said no, and 16% were unsure.[14]

While it would be wrong to overestimate the advance of human rights, it would equally be an error not to recognize that progress has been achieved in the advancement of human rights by declarations of principle, by numerous treaties, and by the work of the UN, Amnesty International, and other IGOs and NGOs. The frequency and horror of the abuses that they highlight increasingly are penetrating the international consciousness and disconcerting the global conscience. The 1993 UN-sponsored World Conference on Human Rights (WCHR) held in Vienna, Austria, provides an example. As is true for international forums on most issues, the WCHR witnessed political fissures along several lines. Some Asian, Muslim, and other countries resisted broad declarations of human rights based on what they see as Western-oriented values. This charge of cultural imperialism also led them to oppose the appointment of a high commissioner for human rights to head the UNCHR and give it more impact. In the end, though, some advances were made in both defining global human rights and creating and empowering a high commissioner. To clarify human rights, the WCHR declared that "all human rights are universal and indivisible and interdependent and interrelated," while adding that "the significance of national and regional particularities and various historical, cultural, and religious backgrounds must be kept in mind" when defining rights and identifying and condemning abuses (Burk, 1994:201). Those who advocated appointing a high commissioner were able to overcome the roadblocks erected at the WCHR by subsequently bringing the issue before the UN General Assembly, which created the post. To give a bit more detail on the efforts of the UN, other IGOs, and NGOs in the area of human rights, we can turn to their activities with respect to women, children, ethnic and racial groups, religious groups, indigenous people, and refugees and immigrants.

Women

A great deal of the human rights attention and some of the most vigorous international human rights efforts in recent years have focused on women. The most significant progress has been made in the realm of identifying the maltreatment of women as a global problem, identifying some of the causes and worst abuses, and defining women's rights. This has placed the issue of women solidly on the international agenda. For example, the UN General Assembly's Third Committee, which specializes in social, cultural, and humanitarian issues, spent less than 2% of its time discussing women's rights from 1955 to 1965. That percentage had risen almost sevenfold by the mid-1980s, and, indeed, has become the second most extensively discussed issue (after racial discrimination) in the Third Committee.

A major symbolic step occurred with the UN declaration of 1975 as International Women's Year and the kickoff of a Decade for Women. Numerous conferences brought women together to document their status. Funding for projects to benefit women was begun through the establishment of such structures as the UN Fund for Women (UNIFEM). The adoption of the **Convention on the Elimination of All Forms of Discrimination Against Women (CEDAW**, the treaty) in 1979 was a path-breaking step in defining women's rights on an international level. As of December 2003, 175 countries had agreed to the treaty, with the United States one of the few that had not.

This rise in the level of consciousness also led to a number of other institutional changes at the UN. The organization created the Division for the Advancement of Women, which is responsible for addressing women's issues and promoting their rights. In this role, the division administratively supports both the Commission on the Status of Women (CSW), which is the main UN policy-making body for women, and the Committee on the Elimination of Discrimination Against Women (CEDAW, the committee), which monitors the implementation of the 1979 convention on women's rights. The division has also organized four UN world conferences on women.

Of these, the most important was the fourth **World Conference on Women (WCW)**, which convened in Beijing in 1995. During the planning for the conference, its chairwoman urged that "the road to Beijing must be paved with vision and commitment" (Burk, 1994:239). Some 3,000 delegates from 180 countries, including the U.S. delegation headed by Hillary Rodham Clinton and Secretary of State Madeleine Albright, attended the official convention, and about 30,000 delegates representing some 2,000 NGOs gathered at the parallel NGO convention in nearby Huairou. The meetings constituted the largest conclave of women in history. Not only did women meet and strengthen their already formidable network of women's groups, but their message was carried outward by the 2,500 reporters who covered the conferences.

The final report of the WCW demanded an end to discrimination against and the abuse of women, called for their economic empowerment, and urged public and private organizations to lend their moral and economic support to the cause of advancing the status of women worldwide. While the Beijing conference's platform was not binding on states, it set a standard that has had an impact. The following year, for example, the Hague tribunal for war crimes in the Balkans for the first time held that sexual abuse was a war crime and indicted eight Bosnian Serb soldiers for the rape of Bosnian Muslim women.

Five years later a special UN General Assembly session and a parallel NGO conference, collectively called the Beijing + 5 Conference, brought 10,000 delegates together in New York City to review the progress of the goals adopted by the WCW. In addition to continuing the important networking of women and the pressure on governments to address women's issues, Beijing + 5 adopted additional goals such as increasing the availability and affordability of treatment for women and girls afflicted with HIV and AIDS.

Finally, there have been advances in other contexts to further the rights of women. One notable stride occurred through the treaty that created the **International Criminal**

Court (ICC). It specifies in Article 7 (Crimes Against Humanity) that such crimes "when committed as part of a widespread or systematic attack directed against any civilian population, with knowledge of the attack," include, among others, acts of "rape, sexual slavery, enforced prostitution, forced pregnancy, enforced sterilization, or any other form of sexual violence of comparable gravity." Currently accused war criminals are being prosecuted at the existing tribunals in The Hague (for the Balkans) and in Tanzania (for Rwanda) for such depravities, and the world has now served notice that rape and related abuses are war crimes. The ICC has now been formed at its seat in The Hague, the Netherlands, and is, in the view of MADRE, a U.S.-based women's rights NGO, "a critical new tool in the defense of human rights for women and their families around the world."[15]

There is also evidence that the rising international condemnation of the abuse of women is having some impact on norms and practices within countries. A number of countries where FGM has been practiced have passed laws against it, and there are indications that the procedure is on the decline. In Burkina Faso, for example, performing FGM now carries penalties of up to three years in prison and a $1,500 fine (a monumental sum in that poor country), and a 2004 report estimates that the number of girls undergoing FGM has dropped from 70% to a relatively small minority. Surely reforms have come slowly in many countries, but it is important to realize that repeated, even if grudging rhetorical recognition that reforms are needed is part of the process of eventual substantive change. It is noteworthy, for example, that Yemen, the country that finished in 148th place on the UNDP's 2003 gender development index and dead last on its gender empowerment index, felt constrained to ratify CEDAW. Moreover, in 2003 Yemen not only created a Ministry of Human Rights, but appointed a woman, Amat Alaleem Ali Alsoswa, as its first head. Yemen is unlikely to become a feminist mecca in the near term, but change it has.

Children

Serious international efforts to protect the rights of children have only recently begun, but there have already been worthwhile steps. UNICEF is the most important single agency, but it is supported by numerous other IGOs. The efforts of UNICEF are also supported and supplemented by a wide range of NGOs, such as End Child Prostitution in Asian Tourism, which was established in 1991 by child welfare groups in several Asian countries. Their common goal, in the words of UNICEF's executive director, is to "ensure that exploitive and hazardous child labor becomes as unacceptable in the next century as slavery has become in this. Children should be students in school, not slaves in factories, fields, or brothels."[16]

One noteworthy advance is the **Convention on the Rights of the Child**. Work on it began in 1979, which was designated by the UN as the International Year of the Child. A treaty was adopted unanimously by the UN General Assembly in 1989 and made available for signature and ratification by the world's countries. The convention outlines a wide range of collective and individual rights for all persons under the age of 18. If all countries and people abided by the convention, the sexual exploitation of children, the use of boy soldiers, the diversion of children from their education to work, and many other abuses would end.

It is a mark of hope that the convention garnered enough ratifications to go into force in less than a year and also quickly became the most widely ratified human rights treaty in history. Indeed, as of early 2004, every country in the world save the United States and the failed state of Somalia was a party to the treaty. Among other concerns in the United States was whether the convention would abridge the possibility in some U.S. states that minors convicted of capital crimes can be executed once they reach age 18.

A second important effort on behalf of children was the World Congress Against Commercial Sexual Exploitation of Children, which met in Stockholm, Sweden. Representatives of 122 national governments, the UN and other IGOs, and 471 NGOs attended the 1996 conference. The authority of such international meetings is severely limited, but they do serve a valuable function by focusing attention on issues. As the congress's general rapporteur, Vitit Muntarbhorn of Thailand, noted, "There can be no more delusions—no one can deny that the problem of children being sold for sex exists, here and now, in almost every country in the world."[17]

Despite the near impossibility of opposing children's rights in theory, the effort to protect them in practice, like most international human rights programs, runs into the problems of nationalism and parochialism. Countries resist being told what to do, and they are better able to see what others should do than what they themselves should do. India's representative to the UNCHR in Geneva reacted to criticism of the number of children being exploited in her country by lashing out at "finger pointing" by other countries and recounting that when India had tried to garner support for a global ban on sex tourism, the effort had met resistance from Germany, Japan, Korea, and the Netherlands. Displaying ads in German magazines offering "boys of any color, size, or age," the delegate from India related that other countries had told her, "We are not willing to ban promotion of sex tours."[18]

Ethnic, Racial, and Religious Groups

The global effort to combat intolerance has also been furthered by a series of international conferences to highlight the problem and seek solutions. The first two met in Geneva, Switzerland, in 1978 and 1983. The third, the World Conference against Racism, Racial Discrimination, Xenophobia and Related Intolerance (WCAR) convened in Durban, South Africa, in 2001. The meeting brought together official delegations from 160 countries. Like most UN conferences, there was also an unofficial parallel conference that brought together representatives of hundreds of NGOs ranging alphabetically from ABC Ulwazi (South Africa) to the Zoroastrian Women's Organization (Iran).

Unfortunately for the future of a united struggle against intolerance, the Durban conference fell into acrimonious debate over what some saw as an undiplomatic truculence (and others viewed as justified candor) on the part of delegations from the South. This was captured in the comments of the host, South African president Thabo Mbeki. Opening the conference, he told the assembly, "It became necessary that we convene in Durban because together we recognized the fact there are many in our common world who suffer indignity and humiliation because they are not white." Therefore, he continued, "Their cultures and traditions are despised as savage and primitive and their identities denied. . . . To those who have to bear the pain of this real world, it seems the blues singers were right when they decried the world in which it was said, 'If you're white you're alright; if you are brown, stick around; if you are black, oh brother! Get back, get back, get back!' "[19]

Wrangling between North and South particularly focused on two issues raised in preliminary resolutions. One was the demand by African countries that the countries of Western Europe and the United States that long ago were involved in the slave trade apologize and perhaps pay reparations. The other sore point centered on Israel and the Palestinians. Draft language favored by Muslim countries labeled Israel a "racist apartheid state" and demanded an end to the "ongoing Israeli systematic perpetration of racist crimes, including war crimes, genocide, and ethnic cleansing."[20]

Even before the meeting, this strident stand caused Canada, Great Britain, the United States, and a number of other Western countries to downgrade their delegation. Then when the attack on Israel persisted, the U.S. delegation withdrew altogether. "I have taken this decision with regret," Secretary of State Colin Powell said. "[But] I know that you do not combat racism by conferences that produce declarations containing hateful language," he concluded.[21]

While the conference expanded and strengthened the **transnational advocacy network (TAN)** against intolerance, the image that it projected abroad was one of "all the wrong news," as one delegate put it.[22] As the conference drew to a close, UN Human Rights Commissioner Mary Robinson optimistically told the delegates, "We have not been deterred from making a breakthrough here in Durban." Probably more accurate was the evaluation of an Australian representative, who lamented, "Far too much of the time at the conference was consumed by bitter divisive exchanges on issues which have done nothing to advance the cause of combating racism."[23]

More positively, efforts to define the rights of ethnic, racial, and religious groups have been part of the major human rights documents such as the International Covenant on Economic, Social, and Cultural Rights and the Convention on the Prevention and Punishment of the Crime of Genocide. There have also been some specific agreements, such as the **International Convention on the Elimination of All Forms of Racial Discrimination** (1969). It is a step forward that 169 countries have been willing to agree to this document, which, among other things, proclaims that its signatories are "convinced that any doctrine of superiority based on racial differentiation is scientifically false, morally condemnable, socially unjust and dangerous, and that there is no justification for racial discrimination, in theory or in practice, anywhere."[24]

These efforts have been supplemented by some levels of enforcement. The earlier international pressure on South Africa to end legal racism was an important step. The international tribunals investigating and trying war crimes committed in the Balkans and in Rwanda are further evidence that persecution based on ethnicity, race, or religion are increasingly considered an affront to the global conscience.

Indigenous Peoples

The UN General Assembly proclaimed 1993 to be the International Year of the Indigenous Peoples (Pritchard, 1998). The following year, representatives of some of the more than 5,000 indigenous peoples agreed to an International Covenant on the Rights of Indigenous Nations that prescribed relations among the groups and between each of them and the country in which it is located. The efforts of indigenous people have also been furthered by numerous NGOs, including the International Indian Treaty Council, the World Council of Indigenous Peoples, the Inuit Circumpolar Conference, and the Unrepresented Nations and Peoples' Organization. The causes of indigenous peoples were also furthered when the Nobel Peace Prize Committee made its 1992 award to Rigoberta Menchú of Guatemala in recognition of her efforts to advance the rights of her Mayan people in her country and to further the welfare of indigenous people globally.

Refugees and Immigrants

International efforts on behalf of refugees have provided very mixed results. There have been a number of efforts to define the status and the rights of both international and internal refugees. An early effort was the 1951 Convention Relating to the Status of Refugees (1951). This document charged the UN with providing assistance to people who were being persecuted in their countries or who feared persecution if returned to their home countries. The convention also defined the basic rights of refugees and minimum standards for their treatment and has served, among other things, as a foundation for subsequent efforts on behalf of refugees. It is also true, though, that it is one of the least widely ratified of the UN's major human rights treaties. Because of concerns that they might be required to open their borders to refugees or extend rights to those who

The UN High Commissioner for Refugees is the lead organization for providing housing, food, and other types of support for the millions of refugees worldwide. Representative of that effort, this August 2003 picture shows Chechen women at a refugee camp in Russia telling UNHCR Goodwill Ambassador Angelina Jolie about their plight.

managed to arrive unbidden, only 140 countries have signed and ratified it, with the United States among those missing countries.

Aid to refugees, while scant compared to their actual need, presents a somewhat brighter picture. The effort on behalf of displaced persons in the early 1950s led to the creation of the UN High Commissioner for Refugees in 1951 with wide responsibility for refugee rights and needs. Also formed that year was the International Organization for Migration (IOM), a body specifically concerned with the movement of refugees either to new homes or back to their former homes, as appropriate. Additionally, there are a number of IGOs, such as the International Red Cross (and its Muslim counterpart, the International Red Crescent), Oxfam, and others, which are involved in providing food, clothes, shelter, and other necessities.

Positive Human Rights

Compared to the negative rights that we have been discussing, positive human rights are much less often recognized or enumerated in the legal structure of countries or in international law. Yet they exist. For example, the U.S. Constitution mostly includes negative rights, but it does positively specify in Article IV, Section 4, "The United States shall guarantee to every state in the union a republican form of government, and shall protect each of them against invasion and . . . domestic violence." In other words, the U.S. federal government is obligated to ensure that all states maintain a democratic form of government, to repel invaders, and if needed to preserve domestic order. Many U.S. state constitutions are more expansive in codifying positive rights. For instance, the Connecticut state constitution declares in Article VIII, Section 1, "There shall always be free public elementary and secondary schools in the state. The general assembly shall implement this principle." Note that the article does not say children cannot be denied the right to seek education (a negative right); it obligates the state to provide free elementary and secondary schooling. Moreover, the article does not simply provide the legislature with the power to establish and fund schools. It mandates the General Assembly to act ("shall"). Less clearly, there has been an effort at both the U.S. federal and state levels to establish the notion that providing many basic services (such as housing, food, and health care for the needy) are obligations on the government, not merely options. This move is evident in the vast array of federal programs, such as food stamps and Medicare, which provide funding according to a formula (rather than by specific legislative appropriation) and which are commonly referred to as "entitlement programs." This phrase has a political point. It is meant to imply a positive obligation. These programs have not been held to be a right by the federal courts, but the important thing to see is that at least some Americans are thinking of them in terms of positive rights, and it is not unthinkable that in time they could become widely recognized as such, including by the courts.

Although the Universal Declaration of Human Rights that the United States, among others, voted for and, indeed, helped draft, mostly contains negative rights, it does also enumerate positive rights. Article 22 specifies that:

> Everyone, as a member of society, has the right to social security and is entitled to realization, through national effort and international co-operation and in accordance with the organization and resources of each State, of the economic, social and cultural rights indispensable for his dignity and the free development of his personality.

Being more specific about some of these positive rights, Article 25 states in part:

> Everyone has the right to a standard of living adequate for the health and well-being of himself and of his family, including food, clothing, housing and medical care and necessary social services, and the right to security in the event of unemployment, sickness, disability, widowhood, old age or other lack of livelihood in circumstances beyond his control.

Certainly one set of pressing problems for the world community involves preserving and enhancing human dignity by protecting and improving the physical condition of humans (Lauren, 1998). These issues are partly economic in nature and are being addressed by the international economic cooperation efforts discussed in chapter 14. It is also the case, in the view of many, that food, health, and the other quality of life matters that we will take up in this section fall under the rubric of human rights (Speth, 1998). For example, the UN-sponsored World Food Summit that met in 1996 reasserted the principle found in the Universal Declaration by asserting that there is a "right to adequate food and the fundamental right of everyone to be free from hunger."[25] If, indeed, there is such a right, then an obligation exists. As one scholar explains it, "Since adequate food is a human right, the obligations apply internationally. The rights and the corresponding obligations do not end at national borders. Under human rights law, the international community is obligated to create conditions that will end hunger in the world" (Kent, 2002). A right to adequate nutrition, to a reasonable standard of health, and to a basic education are not the only ones that some people lay claim to as positive rights, but they will serve to illustrate the need and the response.

Food

Just over two centuries ago, Thomas Malthus predicted in his *Essay on the Principle of Population* (1798) that the world's population would eventually outpace the world's agricultural carrying capacity. For the two centuries since Malthus's essay, human ingenuity has defied his predictions. The question is whether it can continue to do so, given the rapidly increasing global population.

The Index of Human Development

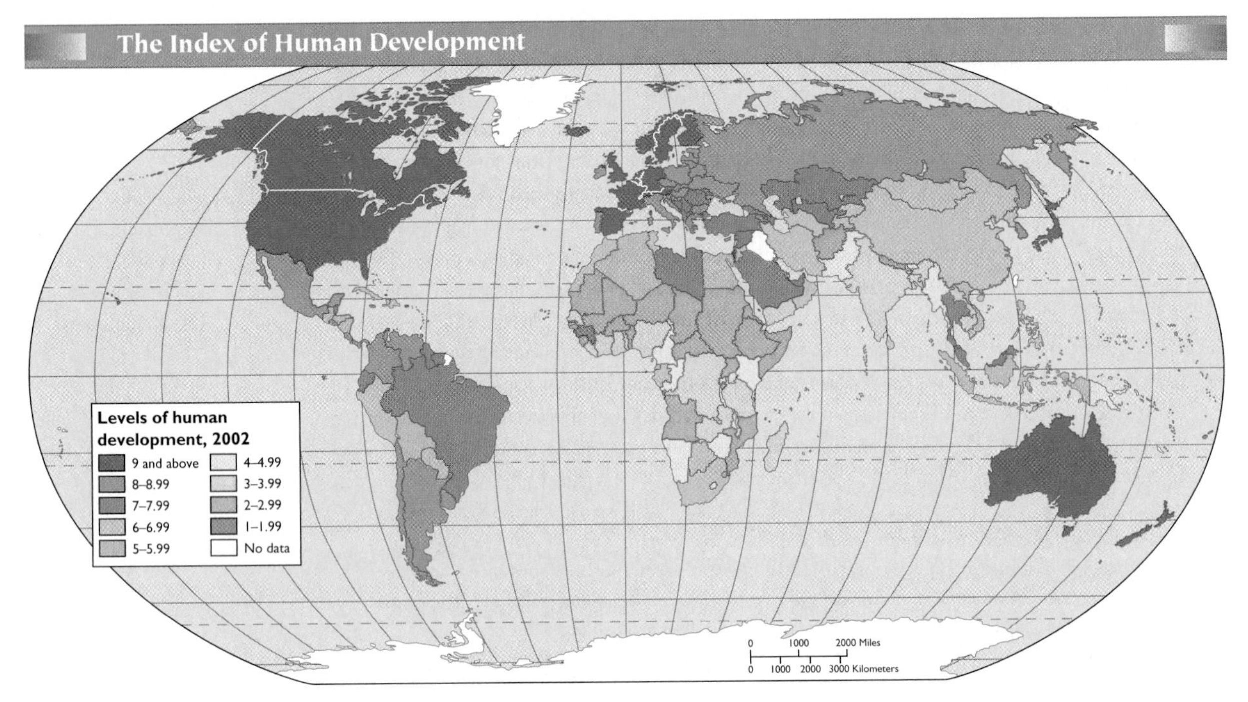

The level of human rights and dignity around the world is measured in part by the Index of Human Development. The index, which was developed by the United Nations Development Programme, includes such gauges as health, literacy, income, and education. As you can see, the level of development that people enjoy or endure, as the case may be, varies greatly.

Source: John Allen and Elizabeth Leppman, *Student Atlas of World Politics*, 6th Edition, Dushkin/McGraw-Hill, p. 509. Reprinted with permission from Dushkin/McGraw-Hill.

There are two basic food problems. One is the *short-term food supply.* Regional shortages inflict real human suffering. Hunger—indeed, starvation—is most common in Africa, where many countries face a severe shortage of food. In addition to the multitudes that have died from starvation or diseases stemming from malnutrition, agricultural insufficiency has a host of negative economic impacts that range from sapping the vigor of the population to consuming development funds for food relief. The UN's Food and Agriculture Organization (FAO) estimates that around the globe over 800 million people are undernourished; some 15 million a year die from outright starvation or from diseases brought on by malnutrition.

The *long-term adequacy* of the food supply is also a significant issue. There have been important strides in the LDCs over the past few decades toward agricultural self-sufficiency. The food supply and crop yields (amount produced per acre) have grown over 50% since 1970 due to the "green revolution" (the development and widespread introduction of high-yielding rice, wheat, and other grains), the increased use of fertilizers and pesticides, better irrigation, more mechanization, and other agricultural advances. Among the poorest countries (the LLDCs) where the problem has been most acute, the food production index increased 81% between 1981 and 2001, while the population rose 55%. One result was that undernourishment in the LDCs fell from 28% of their collective total population in 1981 to 17% in 2001. Still, 17% remains unacceptably high, and there are causes for long-term concern.

Causes of the Food Problem

Population growth is one. At current fertility levels (average number of babies born per woman), the world population will grow more than 50% to 9.9 billion by 2050. If the population growth rate slows as much as the UN Population Fund (UNFPA) projects, the population will be 8.9 billion. That is better, but it is still a 48% increase during the first half of the 21st century. Because the highest population growth rate is in the LLDCs, the number of people they have to feed will grow 20% during just the first 15 years of the century. As a result, agriculture will be hard pressed to keep up. The ability to increase yields per unit of farmland is not infinite, which means that new acreage will have to be devoted to agriculture. This clearing of land is causing deforestation, aggravating a range of problems such as greenhouse warming, wildlife habitat destruction, and water pollution from pesticide and fertilizer runoff. Accelerating the problem is the fact that a great deal of current agricultural land is being lost to urbanization, degradation due to ill-use, and other causes. The FAO calculates that 38% of the world's original cropland (some 2.1 million square miles, almost two-thirds the area of the United States) has been lost to agriculture, and that a combination of increasing population and loss of arable land has cut the world's cultivated land to six-tenths of an acre per mouth to feed.

It is also important to note that some countries are already not keeping up. Whether the problem is inability to afford modern methods and technology, lack of adequate water and arable land, or political strife, many countries are in serious trouble. There are 38 LDC countries whose per capita food production declined during the 1990s. Cuba had the worst record, with an average annual drop of 6.5% in its per capita production.

Maldistribution of food is a second problem. In 2000 the world produced enough food to allow for 2,757 calories per person in the world. Thus, for now at least, the world has the agricultural capacity to feed everyone adequately. Resources and consumption, however, are concentrated in relatively few countries. In the EDCs, daily food consumption averages a waist-expanding 3,240 calories a day. In significant segments of the South calorie intakes were at belt-tightening low levels. The sub-Saharan countries of Africa, for example, averaged only 2,183 calories per capita daily.

Nutritional content represents a third, and even greater gap between the ability of the North and South to meet dietary needs. Protein deficiency is particularly common in the LLDCs. Most people in Africa, for instance, consume less than 60 grams of protein per day per capita and in some countries they average as little as 30 grams. The recommended daily intake is about 55 grams for sedentary individuals, which means that in the LLDCs, where manual labor is the norm, protein deficiency is also the norm. The lack of protein is especially detrimental to children because of the role it plays in developing both healthy bodies and brain tissue, and there are over 300 million children in LDCs who suffer from stunted growth, poor cognitive development, and other ills due to protein malnutrition. Vitamin A deficiency, also common in LLDCs, is the cause of visual impairment in over 100 million children a year. Adding to the nutritional woes of the South, 740 million people suffer from disorders such as mental retardation, delayed motor skill development, and stunting caused by iodine deficiency, even though this can be cheaply remedied by the use of iodized salt.

Political strife is a fourth problem. In many countries with severe food shortages, farms have been destroyed, farmers displaced, and food transportation disrupted by internal warfare. Sierra Leone, one of the recent tragic examples, now produces 19% less food than the already meager supply it managed to provide in 1991 before it was overtaken by strife.

The International Response to the Food Problem

A number of international efforts are under way. Some deal with food aid to meet immediate needs, while others are dedicated to increasing future agricultural productivity.

Emergency Food Aid Supplying food aid to areas with food shortages is a short-term necessity to alleviate malnutrition and even starvation. Grains constitute about 95% of food

Although it is not widely reported, the staff of relief agencies often work in dangerous conditions, as this photograph of a World Food Programme facility in Iraq illustrates. The WFP office was located in the UN headquarters in Baghdad, which was destroyed in August 2003 when a bomb hidden in a cement truck detonated. Twenty-two people died; more than 100 others were injured.

aid. About 10 million tons of grains and more limited amounts of other foodstuffs are donated each year, of which about 65% comes from the United States. Some of the aid is given bilaterally, but a good deal of the assistance goes through a number of multilateral food aid efforts. The UN's World Food Programme (WFP) is the largest. It distributes food in crisis situations, delivering 3.7 million tons of food in 2002 to feed 72 million during 130 relief operations in 75 countries. About 88% of WFP aid goes to countries that have experienced food emergencies because of natural causes or political strife; the other 12% to development projects. In 2002, the WFP received $1.6 billion in grains and other foodstuffs. While these contributions are laudable, they meet only about two-thirds of the emergency food needs identified by the WFP and amounted in 2001 to only about $22 per individual whom the WFP tried to sustain. There are also a variety of NGOs, such as Food for the Hungry International, that are active in food aid.

Agricultural Development The development of agricultural techniques and capabilities is crucial if there is to be any hope of future self-sufficiency. This is particularly important to the 8 countries that suffer what the FAO labels critical food security (all sources of supply are less than 65% of need) and to another 20 countries that have low food security (supply is 65% to 75% of need).

On a bilateral basis, many countries' programs include agricultural development aid. There is also a multilateral effort. The oldest agricultural IGO is the FAO. Founded in 1945, it has 188 members and an annual budget of approximately $750 million. The FAO supplies food aid and technical assistance to LDCs. The agency has been criticized for a variety of its policies, including putting too much emphasis on short-term food aid and not enough effort into long-range agricultural growth. This, in addition to the growing recognition of the food problem, has led to the establishment of several other global food efforts.

One of these is the International Fund for Agricultural Development (IFAD), a specialized UN agency. IFAD began operations in 1977 and is specifically dedicated to environmentally sustainable agricultural development projects in rural areas of the poorest LDCs. The agency raises its funds through the voluntary contributions of its 163 member-countries, and disburses about $450 million annually in loans and grants to support projects in agriculturally struggling countries. These efforts are supplemented by several UN-associated organizations involved in various donor, investment, and research efforts in agriculture. Finally, there are a variety of regional and specialized organizations that address agricultural issues.

World Food Conferences A key event in both the area of short-term aid and especially the agricultural development effort was the 1974 World Food Conference held in Rome. Among its other actions, the conference sponsored the creation of IFAD and various structures associated with the UN Economic and Social Council to monitor the global food supply and its delivery to needy countries and people.

A second global conference, the 1996 **World Food Summit**, met at FAO headquarters in Rome and was attended by the heads of more than 80 governments and representatives from more than 100 other governments. Reflecting the declining commitment of the EDCs to foreign aid, though, the leaders of most of the industrialized countries were not present. The United States, for example, sent its secretary of agriculture. The tone of the meeting was set by the first plenary speaker, Pope John Paul II, who called on the world's countries to "eliminate the specter of hunger from the planet" and to "jointly seek solutions so that never again will there be hungry people living side by side with people in opulence. . . . Such contrasts between poverty and wealth cannot be tolerated."[26]

Without the strong support of the EDCs, though, there was little of immediate substance that the summit could accomplish. It did, however, establish the goal of reducing the number of undernourished people from 800 million to 400 million by 2015. It also reaffirmed the UN's traditional standard that the EDCs should devote 0.7% of their respective GDPs to development aid, including food and agricultural assistance. Third, in a move that rankled Washington and some other capitals, the conference resolved that "food should not be used as an instrument for political and economic pressure."[27] This swipe at economic sanctions came just days after the UN General Assembly voted overwhelmingly to urge the United States to end its embargo against Cuba.

The continuing problems with supplying adequate calories and nutrition to a large number of LDCs occasioned a review of the efforts since the 1996 conference. The World Food Summit—Five Years Later conference, organized by the FAO, was held in Rome during June 2002. The fifth year review was necessary, in the estimation of Jacques Diouf, the FAO's director-general, because little progress was being made toward achieving the goal to cut the number of malnourished people in half, set by the 1996 conference. "There is very little evidence," according to Diouf, "of the large-scale purposive action needed to get to grips with the underlying causes of hunger."[28]

Health

The state of medical care, sanitation, and other conditions related to health in some areas of the world is below a level imaginable by most readers of this book. While health care is well below EDC standards in nearly all LDCs, it is in the LLDCs that the greatest need exists. As one measure, the EDCs annually spend $130 per capita on health care for every $1 spent by the LLDCs. By another measure, there are 8 times as many physicians per person and 5 times as many hospital beds per capita in the EDCs as there are in the LLDCs. The health of people within these countries is an international concern for reasons beyond personal well-being. A healthy population is vital to economic growth because healthy people are economically productive and because unhealthy people often consume more of a society's resources than they produce.

The fate of children is one way to think about health care. In LLDCs, 27% of all children born have low birth weights (less than 5.5 pounds), which is one reason why in these countries children under age five die at a rate that is 17 times higher than for children in the North. Compared to children in the EDCs, those in the LLDCs are more frequently exposed to disease because of poor sanitation and other factors, they are more vulnerable to disease because of malnutrition, and they more often succumb to disease because basic medical care is not available. Overall, an estimated 70% of the children under age five in the LDCs who die each year perish from infectious and parasitic diseases that are easily preventable and claim only 1% of the children in the EDCs. "No famine, no flood, no earthquake, no war has ever claimed the lives of this many children a year," the director of the UN Children's Fund (UNICEF) once lamented."[29]

As grim as these figures are, they were once much worse. A few decades ago as few as 1 in 20 children in LLDCs received any vaccinations; now 61% receive protection against diphtheria, whooping cough, and polio. For this and other reasons, child mortality in the LLDCs is down 29% since 1980. The advance in the health of children has been paralleled in adults. Their health prospects in LLDCs are far below those in EDCs, but also like the children in the LLDCs, the adults are in better health and live longer than in previous decades.

Did You Know That:

Plague in its various forms (bubonic, septicemic, and pneumonic) remains a threat. The disease is transmitted by fleas from infected rodents to humans. There were 2,603 reported cases in 14 countries during 2000. Untreated, the mortality rate is about 60%. Medical care reduces that to about 15%.

Much of the credit for these advances goes to the **World Health Organization (WHO)**, headquartered in Geneva, Switzerland. The UN-affiliated WHO was created in 1946. It has 192 members and an annual budget of about $2.2 billion from the UN and from other sources. The crusade against smallpox provides a heartening example of WHO's contributions. Smallpox was a scourge throughout human history. There were over 131,000 cases worldwide in 1967 when WHO began a 10-year campaign to eradicate the disease. By 1977 smallpox was confined to a single case in Somalia; no case has been reported since 1978. Polio is another disease whose death may be imminent. The annual global incidence has been cut 99% from 350,000 reported cases in 125 countries during 1988 to 1,919 cases in 7 countries during 2002. "We are on the verge of eradicating this debilitating disease," a WHO official proudly and accurately proclaimed.[30]

Optimism based on progress is offset by continuing problems and new threats. For all the progress made, far too many people in the South suffer and die from diseases, nutritional deficiencies, and even starvation. Also, diseases once thought to be on the decline can reassert themselves catastrophically. Tuberculosis is one such disease. WHO declared in 1993 that TB had resurged after a period of declining new cases. Now over 40 million people have TB, and 8 million new cases are reported each year. Indeed, TB has become the leading cause of death from a single infectious agent and, in WHO's estimate, over 150 million people will get sick and 36 million will die of TB between 2002 and 2020 if prevention and treatment programs are not improved.

New problems add to these old worries. The worldwide AIDS epidemic, for one, is a global killer. At the beginning of 2004, one of every 155 people, about 40 million people, worldwide were HIV-positive. That was a net annual increase of 2 million cases, a grim statistic derived from subtracting the 3 million people who died from AIDS-related causes from the 5 million new HIV-positive people. Some countries are truly devastated. More than 20% of the populations of seven sub-Saharan countries are HIV-positive, with Botswana having an especially disturbing 39% infection rate. Perhaps the most tragic victims are the 2.5 million children under age 15 who are HIV-positive. A half million of them died in 2001, and were sadly replaced by 700,000 new cases. Other children will fall victim to AIDS in a different way. In Botswana, about 40% of pregnant women were HIV-positive. The UN estimates that by the end of the decade well over 10 million children will lose their mothers to AIDS. These millions of orphans are a human tragedy,

The dark reality of this loving photograph of Ingrid Kealotswe and her son Onilegape in Gaborone, Botswana, in 2003 is that both are HIV positive. Perhaps they are able to smile because some hope has been kindled by the AIDS drugs that are being provided free of charge to them by their government with the assistance and through the efforts of the World Health Organization and other international agencies.

and they will also be an added economic burden on countries that are already struggling economically.

Yet other horrific emerging diseases lurk in the shadows and threaten to spread, as AIDS has, to a world with few or no natural or manufactured immunological defenses. SARS (severe acute respiratory syndrome) spread from China to other parts of the world in 2003, and an outbreak of cases in China in 2004 carried the portent that the disease was far from contained. A few years earlier in 1999, the mosquito-transmitted West Nile virus began to infect Americans, and in 2003, a total of 9,100 of them fell ill with the disease, and 223 died. The beginning of 2004 brought news that a strain of avian influenza had spread from domestic fowl to humans in Asia, killing 18 of the 23 people with confirmed cases (as of February 2004) and creating alarm that it could spread globally. Also in the extraordinarily lethal category is the Ebola virus. It was discovered in 1976 and is named for the river in Zaire where it was first detected. The most recent outbreak of the disease was in the Republic of the Congo in January 2004. Although most outbreaks have been contained, with, for example, only 29 Congolese succumbing most recently, what makes the disease alarming is its 90% fatality rate. Thought to be transmitted by monkeys (as HIV/AIDS may have been, evolving from simian immunodeficiency virus, SIV), the Ebola virus causes a hemorrhagic fever, beginning with fever and chills, and then usually progressing to vomiting, diarrhea, and other acute symptoms. Finally, the victim's blood fails to clot, and he or she dies from internal bleeding from the gastrointestinal tract and other internal organs. The ability of local medical personnel aided by WHO and other international agencies to contain outbreaks of new and recurring horrors such as Ebola are applaudable. Nevertheless, one WHO physician cautions, "There are almost certainly diseases out there waiting to get us. What is happening is that human beings are invading territories where no human beings have been before. We're cutting down forests; we're going to areas to develop agriculture where there wasn't any before. Human beings are coming into contact with animals and insects they never met before."[31]

What makes these diseases even more of a world problem than they once were is the flow of humans and their products around the globe, which means that diseases can be spread very quickly from continent to continent. A person who contracts an exotic disease in one place can board an airplane and, 12 hours later, be stifling a sneeze while sitting next to you in a restaurant. Therefore, the work of WHO has become increasingly pivotal to combating new and persistent diseases worldwide.

Education

Education, like health, affects more than just the quality of life. Education is also a key to increased national and international productivity, population control, and other positive social goals. Promotion of education remains primarily a national function, but there are a number of international efforts. For one, the United Nations Educational, Scientific, and Cultural Organization (UNESCO) sponsors several programs. These national and international efforts are slowly paying off. In the 1950s less than 30% of all children in LDCs ever attended any school; now almost all children begin the first grade and more than half go on to begin secondary school. Overall, the level of adults with at least rudimentary literacy has increased to about 77% in the LDCs. The data is even more encouraging if younger people (aged 15–24) are considered. Of this group in LDCs, 85% are literate.

The increasing percentages should not disguise the crying needs that still exist. More than 1 billion adults are still illiterate, and their personal and societal productivity is limited. There is also a gender gap in education, especially in LDCs, where males are 13% more likely to be literate than females. An optimistic note is that the gap is only 8%

Girls in many countries are still less likely to go to school or to remain in school than are boys. This gender disparity has decreased considerably, however, through the efforts of the United Nations Educational, Scientific, and Cultural Organization and other international agencies. This change has improved the chances that these girls in Hargeisa, Somalia, and other girls around the world will be able to play a fuller, more equal role in their societies than has been the case.

among people aged 15 to 24. The averages also tend to disguise regional areas of profound educational deprivation. In sub-Saharan Africa, adult illiteracy is 38%. The statistics showing an increase of literacy in LDCs also tend to cloud the fact that most people have received just a few years of primary education. For LDCs, the average years of schooling is only 5.5 years, with that figure dropping to 4.4 years in the LLDCs. In some sub-Saharan Africa countries as few as 20% of the people have finished primary school. Here again, the data is more encouraging for current youngsters. Except in places where civil war and other forms of violence prevent it, most children in LDCs are receiving at least some primary schooling, even though many do not complete that phase, and there are about 38 million primary-age children who are not in school. At the next level, 58% of the appropriate age group is attending secondary school, although, again, the completion rate is far below that in EDCs. Whereas about 59% of the relevant age groups of children in LDCs are in secondary school, that figure drops off to 46% in the LLDCs.

The postsecondary school level is attained by only 10% of LDC students, compared with 62% of students in EDCs. Expenditures on education also vary widely between LDCs and EDCs, which annually spend 27 times as much per student than the LDCs can manage. In our technological age, the lack of advanced training is a major impediment to development. In the North there are nearly 10 times as many scientists and technicians per capita as there are in the South. That imbalance is 80 times as many per capita for the LLDCs.

At the end of this section on positive rights and the lengthier discussion of negative rights, it is worthwhile to ask yourself how you feel about them. If a right is a justifiable claim, are these claims justified by whatever standard you believe should apply? Also, to the extent that you believe various rights exist, do the restraints of negative rights and the obligations of positive rights apply only in your own country or are they universal? To begin to answer these questions, consider the You Be the Playwright box "A Global Bill of Rights." Think about and debate them, as the box suggests. While doing that, particularly note which rights you believe are or should be positive rights. Items 23, 24, and 25 fall into that category; others may if you believe that they carry with them a positive obligation for societies and their governments to fulfill them. If you believe that an obligation exists, does it end at national borders, or does it extend to humankind?

YOU BE THE PLAYWRIGHT

A Global Bill of Rights

It is easy to assert that people have, or ought to have, rights, especially when we think ours are being violated. It is much harder to agree on what rights all people (regardless of place, status, or demographic trait) should have and which, therefore, we and our governments should respect and protect.

The following list of rights is drawn in close paraphrase from almost all of the clauses of the Universal Declaration of Human Rights. This declaration was adopted in 1948 by the UN General Assembly with no dissenting votes (albeit with abstentions by the Soviet bloc countries, Saudi Arabia, and South Africa). The rights that the UN membership recognized with near-unanimity illustrate two of the important controversies about rights. One is the matter of cultural relativism. The Universal Declaration of Human Rights (UNDHR) in its preamble implicitly rejects the positivist concept that rights are culture-based by recognizing the existence of "inalienable rights of all members of the human family." The second controversy is whether rights involve only prohibitions on governments, and perhaps people, against specific abuses (such as abridging free speech), or whether rights extend to quality of life criteria (such as health and economic condition). You will note that beginning with number 20, the rights enumerated by the Universal Declaration include several quality of life standards.

One thing that you can do with this list, in your class or with your friends, is to constitute yourselves as the World Constitutional Convention, debate the various clauses of the UNDHR, and decide whether to ratify or reject each one of them. You might also decide to open them up for amendment. Finally, note clause 27 and ponder whether it provides too much of an escape clause that potentially allows governments to violate rights and to assert that doing so is necessitated by "the just requirements of morality, public order, and the general welfare in a democratic society."

How say you to the propositions that:

1. Everyone has the right to life, liberty, and security of person. Ratify___ Reject___
2. No one shall be held in slavery or servitude; slavery and the slave trade shall be prohibited in all their forms. Ratify___ Reject___
3. No one shall be subjected to torture or to cruel, inhuman, or degrading treatment or punishment. Ratify___ Reject___
4. All are equal before the law and are entitled without any discrimination to equal protection of the law. Ratify___ Reject___
5. No one shall be subjected to arbitrary arrest, detention, or exile. Ratify___ Reject___
6. Everyone charged with a penal offense has the right to be presumed innocent until proved guilty according to law in a public trial [and to have] all the guarantees necessary for his [or her] defense. Ratify___ Reject___
7. Everyone has the right to freedom of movement and residence within the borders of each state. Ratify___ Reject___
8. Everyone has the right to leave any country, including his own, and to return to his country. Ratify___ Reject___
9. Everyone has the right to seek and to enjoy in other countries asylum from persecution. Ratify___ Reject___
10. No one shall be arbitrarily deprived of his nationality nor denied the right to change his nationality. Ratify___ Reject___
11. Adults, without any limitation due to race, nationality, or religion, have the right to marry or not to marry and to found a family. They are entitled to equal rights both during marriage and at its dissolution. Ratify___ Reject___

(continued)

YOU BE THE PLAYWRIGHT

A Global Bill of Rights *(continued)*

12. Everyone has the right to own property alone. No one shall be arbitrarily deprived of his property. Ratify___ Reject___

13. Everyone has the right to freedom of thought, conscience, and religion; to change religion or belief; and in public or private to manifest that religion or belief in teaching, practice, worship, and observance. Ratify___ Reject___

14. Everyone has the right to freedom of opinion and expression; this includes freedom to hold opinions without interference and to seek, receive, and impart information and ideas through any media and regardless of frontiers. Ratify___ Reject___

15. Everyone has the right to freedom of peaceful assembly and association. Ratify___ Reject___

16. No one may be compelled to belong to an association Ratify___ Reject___

17. Everyone has the right to take part in the government of his country, directly or through freely chosen representatives. Ratify___ Reject___

18. Everyone has the right to equal access to public service in his country. Ratify___ Reject___

19. The will of the people shall be the basis of the authority of government; this will shall be expressed in periodic and genuine elections which shall be by universal and equal suffrage and shall be held by secret vote or by equivalent free voting procedures. Ratify___ Reject___

20. Everyone has the right to work, to free choice of employment, to just and favorable conditions of work, and to protection against unemployment. Ratify___ Reject___

21. Everyone, without any discrimination, has the right to equal pay for equal work. Ratify___ Reject___

22. Everyone has the right to form and to join trade unions for the protection of his interests. Ratify___ Reject___

23. Everyone has the right to a standard of living adequate for the health and well-being of himself and of his family, including food, clothing, housing and medical care, and necessary social services, and the right to security in the event of unemployment, sickness, disability, widowhood, old age, or other lack of livelihood in circumstances beyond his control. Ratify___ Reject___

24. Motherhood and childhood are entitled to special care and assistance. All children, whether born in or out of wedlock, shall enjoy the same social protection. Ratify___ Reject___

25. Everyone has the right to education. Education shall be free, at least in the elementary and fundamental stages. Elementary education shall be compulsory. Technical and professional education shall be equally accessible to all on the basis of merit. Ratify___ Reject___

26. Parents have a prior right to choose the kind of education that shall be given to their children. Ratify___ Reject___

27. In the exercise of his rights and freedoms, everyone shall be subject only to such limitations as are determined by law solely for the purpose of securing due recognition and respect for the rights and freedoms of others and of meeting the just requirements of morality, public order, and the general welfare in a democratic society. Ratify___ Reject___

Chapter Summary

The Nature of Human Rights

1. Rights can be divided between negative rights, those that others cannot violate, and positive rights, those that others are obligated to ensure everyone attains.
2. This chapter discusses the universalist and relativist schools of thought about the origin of rights.
3. Human rights abuses are widespread. They spring from intolerance, authoritarianism, societal biases, and other causes, and they are often rationalized by pseudoscientific theories, such as social Darwinism, and by repressive ideologies, such as fascism.

Negative Human Rights: Freedom from Abuses

4. The discussion of negative human rights, the abuses of them, and the efforts to ease them focuses on women, children, ethnic and racial groups, religious groups, indigenous peoples, and refugees and immigrants.
5. The area of human rights is one of the most difficult to work in because violations are usually politically based. Therefore, efforts to redress them are often resented and rejected by target countries. The greatest progress has been made in adopting a number of UN declarations, such as the Universal Declaration of Human Rights, and multilateral treaties that define basic human rights. The enforcement of human rights is much less well developed, but the rising level of awareness and of disapproval of violations on a global scale are having a positive impact. There are also many IGOs, such as the UN Human Rights Commission, and NGOs, such as Amnesty International, that work to improve human rights.

Positive Human Rights

6. The discussion of positive human rights focuses on what some people claim are the rights to adequate nutrition, health prevention and care, and education.
7. Population growth, the underproduction of food, and the maldistribution of the food that is produced are factors contributing to food shortages and inadequate nutrition for many people in LDCs. International organizations, such as the Food and Agriculture Organization, attempt to provide short-term food relief and long-term agricultural assistance to countries facing nutritional shortages.
8. Many people in LDCs face disease and lack of medical care to degrees that boggle the minds of most people in EDCs. Some of the diseases, such as AIDS, can become a world health threat. The World Health Organization, other IGOs, and many NGOs are attempting to bring better health care to people globally.
9. The ability of individuals to achieve a higher quality of life and the ability of countries to develop economically depend in substantial part on education. More than 1 billion adults are still illiterate, many more have only the most rudimentary education, and the personal and societal productivity of these people is limited. The United Nations Educational, Scientific, and Cultural Organization is one of many international organizations working to improve education in the LDCs.

For a chapter quiz, interactive activities, web links, PowerWeb articles, and much more, visit **www.mhhe.com/rourke10/** and go to chapter 15. Or, while accessing the site, click on Course-Wide Content and view recent international relations articles in the *New York Times.*

Key Terms

Convention on the Elimination of All Forms of Discrimination Against Women (CEDAW)
Fourth World
green accounting
International Convention on the Elimination of All Forms of Racial Discrimination
International Criminal Court (ICC)
negative rights
positive rights
relativists
social Darwinism
Third World
transnational advocacy network (TAN)
Universal Declaration of Human Rights
universalists
World Conference on Women (WCW)
Convention on the Rights of the Child
World Food Summit
World Health Organization (WHO)

CHAPTER

16

Preserving and Enhancing the Global Commons

TOWARD SUSTAINABLE DEVELOPMENT

The Ecological State of the World

Sustainable Development

SUSTAINABLE DEVELOPMENT: POPULATION AND RESOURCES

Population Issues and Cooperation

Resource Issues and Cooperation

Resource Conservation: The Global Response

SUSTAINABLE DEVELOPMENT: THE ENVIRONMENT

Environmental Issues

Environmental Protection: The International Response

CHAPTER SUMMARY

KEY TERMS

Comfort's in heaven, and we are on the earth.

—William Shakespeare, *Richard II*

Dear earth, I do salute thee with my hand.

—William Shakespeare, *Richard II*

Over the long haul of life on this planet, it is the ecologists, and not the bookkeepers of business, who are the ultimate accountants.

—Stewart L. Udall, U.S. secretary of the interior

Only in the last moment of human history has the delusion arisen that people can flourish apart from the rest of the living world.

—Edward O. Wilson

CHAPTER OBJECTIVES

After completing this chapter, you should be able to:

- Explain the concept of sustainable development and consider whether it is possible or desirable.
- Summarize the debate regarding environmental degradation and possible solutions.
- Discuss the issues of the world's growing population and efforts to control population growth.
- Analyze the global problems related to population and industrialization, including their causes.
- Discuss current efforts toward international environmental cooperation and speculate about their future role.

This chapter deals with ecological concerns and cooperation, but in many ways it is an extension of the human rights issues in chapter 15. One connection between the two chapters is the normative question, Should we care? Clearly, the view in this text is that we all should care. Self-interest compels us to attend to issues of the world's expanding population, the depletion of natural resources, the increase of chemical discharges into the environment, and the impact of these trends on the global biosphere. You will see that new approaches are needed because solutions attempted by single countries will be insufficient to solve the problems we humans face collectively. The issues discussed in this chapter are transnational problems. Therefore, their solution requires transnational programs achieved through international cooperation (Zurn, 1998).

Toward Sustainable Development

Before taking up specific issues, it is helpful to understand how they are related. To do this, we will discuss two overarching controversies. One debate concerns the *ecological state of the world*. You will see presently that some analysts are truly alarmed about the future. Other observers believe that worries about the ecosphere are frequently overwrought. The second overarching controversy focuses on **sustainable development**. The issue is whether (or perhaps, *how*) the world can continue simultaneously to sustain development *and* to protect its environment. Another important term is **carrying capacity**, which is the largest number of humans that the Earth can sustain indefinitely at current rates of per capita consumption of natural resources.

The Ecological State of the World

Just as the U.S. president delivers an annual State of the Union address to Congress, each year the Worldwatch Institute assesses the ecological state of the world in a book, *The State of the World*.[1] We should follow its lead and regularly take stock of the Earth we all live on.

A good place to start is the "green accounting" approach discussed in chapter 15 that adds "natural capital," as well as "human capital," to the standard economic measurements (such as gross national product, GNP) to measure the wealth of a country, region, or the world. From this perspective, one group of 13 scientists set out to place a value on Earth's ecological systems by assigning a dollar value to 17 different natural functions (such as water supply, soil formation, oxygen generation by plants) based on either the economic value they supply or what it would cost to replicate them artificially.[2] The estimates of the scientists ranged from $16 trillion to $54 trillion, with $33 trillion as a median figure. Even without increasing the value of the natural capital since the estimates were made in 1997, $33 trillion is about the size of the world's GNP in 2003. More importantly, whatever the exact value may be, it is clear that in sheer dollars and cents, the globe's ecological systems are extraordinarily valuable.

A second preliminary question about the state of the world's ecological systems is to ask how important they are to us, irrespective of monetary value. The answer is that we cannot get along unless they are in reasonably good working order. Using medical analogies, one scientist refers to the biosphere as "the planet's life-support system," and another scientist called it humankind's "umbilical cord." He added, "Common sense and what little we have left of the wisdom of our ancestors tells us that if we ruin the Earth, we will suffer grievously."[3]

There is no controversy over the immense financial value of the biosphere and our dependence on it. Consensus ends, however, when we turn to the question of the current and future ecological state of the world. Here the range of opinions can be roughly divided into two camps: the environmental pessimists and the environmental optimists.

Environmental pessimists are those analysts who assess the state of the world and believe that human activity is causing serious, in some cases irreversible, damage to the environment. They further worry that the environmental damage will increasingly cause human suffering: severe and devastating storms due to global warming, skin cancer due to ozone layer depletion, warfare over scarce natural resources, and other problems. This school of thought charges that those who ignore the environmental degradation that is already occurring and hope that new energy supplies and other scientific and technological innovations will make strong conservation unnecessary are akin to the proverbial ostrich that keeps its head planted firmly in the sand so that it can avoid seeing trouble.

Environmental optimists charge that environmental pessimists are like Chicken Little, running about in a panic because of the false belief that the sky is falling. Environmental pessimists reply that the optimists are like the proverbial ostrich that sticks its head in the sand to avoid seeing danger. Until you are fully informed, perhaps the best approach is to be a wise environmental owl who carefully considers all the arguments and evidence. These particular owls were gathered in Banff, Alberta, Canada, in April 2002 to urge a meeting of the G-8 environment ministers (who were preparing for the G-8 summit meeting in June) to take steps to protect spotted owls.

Those who contribute to the annual *State of the World* volume are among the environmental pessimists group. The 2003 edition of the book warns that, "depending on the degree of misery and biological impoverishment that we [humans] are prepared to accept, we have only one or perhaps two generations [20 to 40 years] in which to reinvent ourselves" (p. 5). It is imperative to do so, the study warns, because, "by virtually every broad measure, our world is in a state of pervasive ecological decline." The analysis concedes that such "damage assessments have an air of unreality about them," but argues this is so because "few of us ever encounter the toxic waste, soil degradation, or unsustainable mining and logging to support our collective consumption," activities that are occurring yet constitute largely "invisible threats." Some pessimistic analysts even foresee "environmental scarcities" as the cause of future warfare among states desperate to sustain their economies and quality of life. According to one study, scarcities of renewable resources are already causing some conflict in the world, and there may be "an upsurge of violence in the coming decades . . . that is caused or aggravated by environmental change" (Homer-Dixon, 1998:342).

Environmental optimists reject this gloomy view of the world and its future. Indeed, some optimists believe that the pessimists resemble Chicken Little, the protagonist in a children's story who was hit on the head by a shingle that had fallen off the barn roof. Convinced that he had been struck by a piece of the sky, Chicken Little panicked and raced around the barnyard crying, "The sky is falling, the sky is falling," thereby creating unfounded pandemonium. Optimists tend to chastise the ecology movement for promoting "green guilt" by alarming people. "On average we overworry about the environmental areas," one such critic notes. That is not necessary, he continues, because "things are actually getting better and better, and they're likely to do so in the future." He concedes, "This does not mean that there are no problems," but reassuringly argues they "are getting smaller" (Lomborg, 2003:312).

Optimists say that the sky remains safely in its traditional location and that with reasonable prudence there is no need to fear for the future. They argue that we will be able to meet our needs and continue to grow economically through conservation, population restraints, and, most importantly, through technological innovation. They believe that new technology can find and develop additional oil fields. Synthetics can replace natural resources. Fertilizers, hybrid seeds, and mechanization can increase crop yields. Desalinization and weather control can meet water demands. Energy can be drawn from nuclear, solar, thermal, wind, and hydroelectric sources. In sum, according to one of the best-known optimists, economist Julian Simon (1994:297), not only do the scientific facts indicate that "the current gloom-and-doom about a 'crisis' of our environment is all wrong," but "almost every economic and social change or trend points in a positive direction." In fact Simon was so sure of his view that in 1980 he made a $1,000 bet with an equally convinced pessimist, biologist Paul Ehrlich, author of *The Population Bomb,* about the prices of five basic metal ores in 1990. Ehrlich wagered that population demands would drive the prices up; Simon bet they would not. A decade and nearly a billion people later, the prices were all down. Ehrlich sent Simon a check.

It is important to note that most optimists do not dismiss the problems that the world faces. "Progress does not come automatically," Simon wrote, "and my message is not complacency. In this I agree with the doomsayers—that our world needs the best efforts of all humanity to improve our lot." That effort will be provided, he continued, expressing his profound optimism, by our "ultimate resource . . . people—especially skilled, spirited, and hopeful young people . . . who will exert their wills and imaginations for their own benefit, and so inevitably they will benefit not only themselves but the rest of us as well" (p. 306).

Sustainable Development

Industrialization and science have been two-edged swords in their relationship to the environment and the quality of human life. On the positive side, industrialization has vastly expanded global wealth, especially for the economically developed countries (EDCs). Science has created synthetic substances that enhance our lives; medicine has dramatically increased our chances of surviving infancy and has extended adult longevity. Yet, on the negative side, industry consumes natural resources and discharges pollutants into the air, ground, and water. Synthetic substances enter the food chain as carcinogens, refuse to degrade, and have other baleful effects. Similarly, decreased infant mortality rates and increased longevity are positive, yet they have also been major factors promoting the world's rapid population growth.

All these phenomena and trends, however, are part of modernization and are unlikely to be reversed. The dilemma is how to protect the biosphere and, at the same time, advance human socioeconomic development. This conundrum overarches specific issues such as population, habitat destruction, and pollution.

Pessimists would certainly see this concern as immediate and critical, but even most optimists would concede that the challenge would be vastly compounded if you were to increase the industrial production and standard-of-living levels of the 5.2 billion people who live in less developed countries (LDCs) in the South up to the levels enjoyed by the less than 1 billion people who reside in the North.

The Conundrum of Sustainable Development

Here is the problem you should ponder as you read the rest of this chapter: If the minority of the world's population who live in EDCs use most of the resources and create most of the pollution, how can the South develop economically without accelerating

World Ecological Regions

The world has many ecological areas. There is one issue that all these diverse areas share: the environmental health of each of them has been degraded and continues to be further threatened by human activity. Without international cooperation, it is improbable that the conundrum of sustainable development can be successfully resolved.

Source: John Allen and Elizabeth Leppman, *Student Atlas of World Politics,* 6th Edition, Dushkin/McGraw-Hill, pp. 532–533. Reprinted with permission from Dushkin/McGraw-Hill.

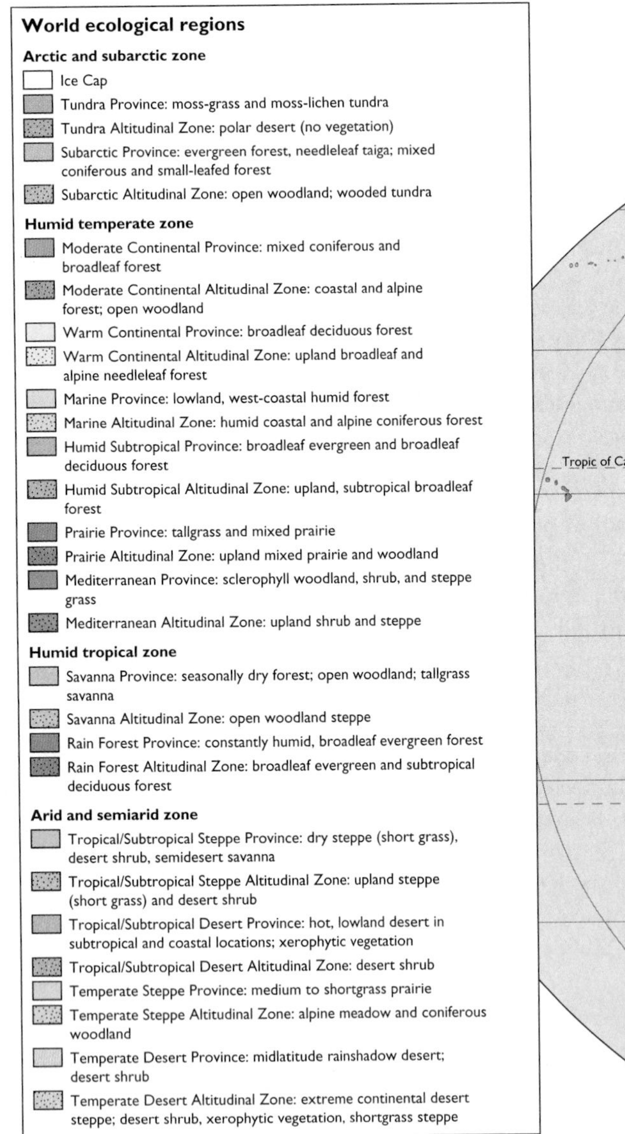

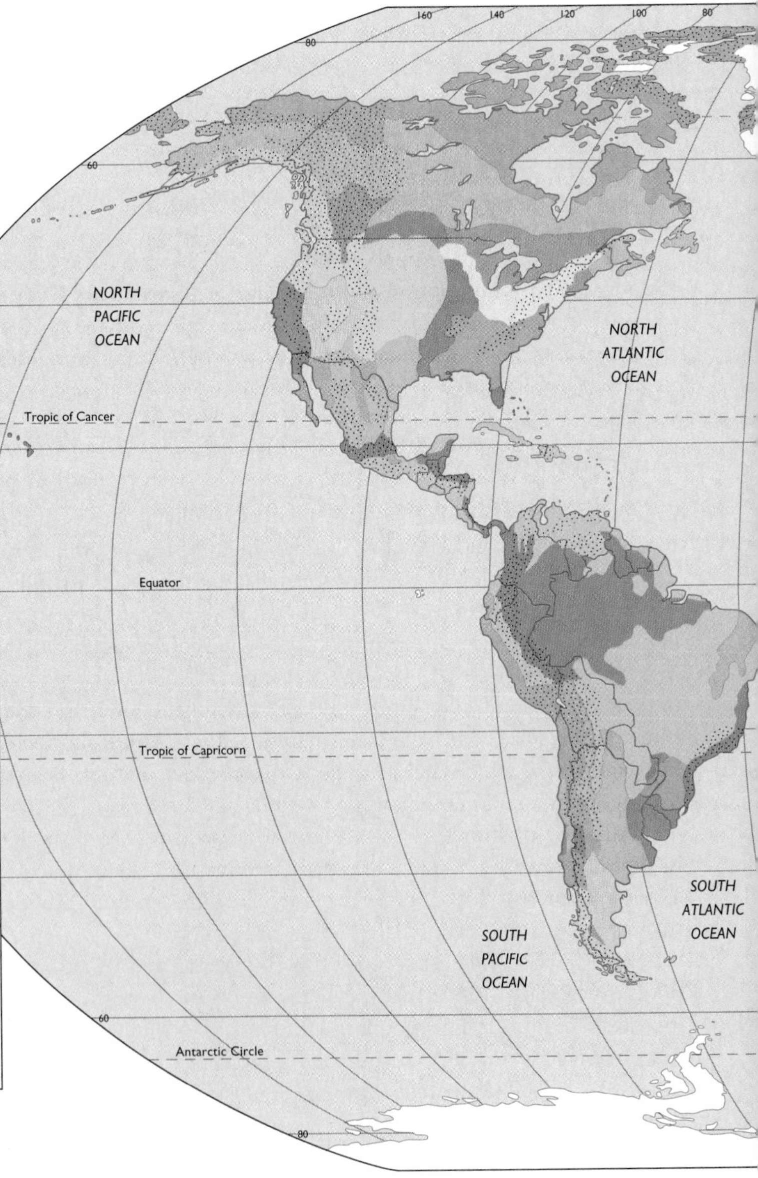

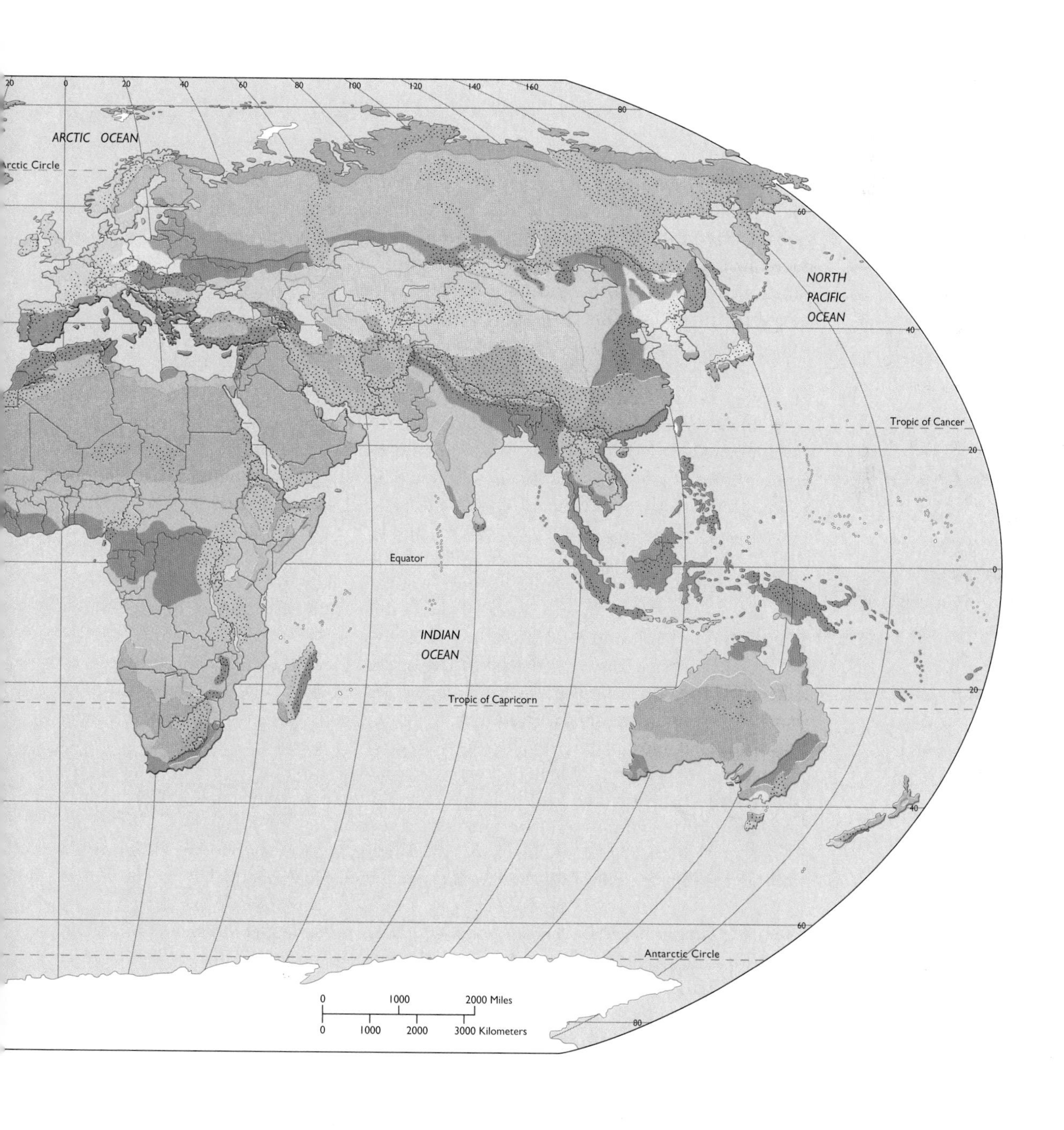
ARCTIC OCEAN
Arctic Circle
NORTH
PACIFIC
OCEAN
Tropic of Cancer
Equator
INDIAN
OCEAN
Tropic of Capricorn
Antarctic Circle
0 1000 2000 Miles
0 1000 2000 3000 Kilometers

the ecological deterioration that already exists? Think about what consumption would be like if China were economically developed and the Chinese per capita consumption of petroleum and minerals and per capita CO_2 emissions were equal to that of Americans. Figure 2.4 on page 54 illustrates this. Given the fact that China's population is about four times that of the United States, a fully developed China with a per capita consumption equal to the current U.S. level would more than triple the two countries' combined CO_2 emissions. By the same standard, the two countries' petroleum consumption would increase more than 300% and their consumption of minerals would jump more than 400%. Furthermore, if you were to bring the rest of the LDCs up to the U.S. level of resource use and emissions discharge, then you would hyperaccelerate the depletion of natural resources and the creation of pollution. Clearly, this is not acceptable. Less clear is what to do. Other than doing nothing, the options fall into two broad categories: restricting development and paying the price for environmentally sustainable development.

Option 1: Restricting Development Preserving the environment by consuming less is one possibility. What is necessary, according to one analyst, is to institute "an integrated global program to set permissible levels" for consumption and emission, to mobilize huge financial resources for resource conservation and pollution control, and to create "effective international institutions with legally binding powers . . . to enforce [the] agreed-upon standards and financial obligations" (Johansen, 1994:381). Those who advocate stringent programs believe that even if they seem unpalatable to many people now, eventually we will be better off if we make the sacrifices necessary to restrain development and preserve the environment.

Objections to such solutions leap to mind. Are we, for instance, to suppress LDC development? If the Chinese do not acquire more cars, if Indians are kept in the fields instead of in factories, and if Africans continue to swelter in the summer's heat without air conditioners, then accelerated resource use and pollution discharges can be partly avoided. As we saw in chapter 13, however, the LDCs are demanding a global "New Deal," as Secretary-General Annan has called it, that will allow them to develop industrially and technologically.[4] The EDCs cannot "try to tell the people of Beijing that they can't buy a car or an air-conditioner" because they pollute, said one Chinese energy official. "It is just as hot in Beijing as it is in Washington."[5]

Another possible answer is for the people of the North to use dramatically fewer resources and to take the steps needed to reduce pollution drastically. Polls show that most people favor the theory of conservation and environmental protection. Yet practice indicates that, so far, most people are also unwilling to suffer a major reduction in their own conveniences or standards of living. Efforts to get more Americans to use mass transit, for example, have had very little success. Proposals to raise U.S. gasoline taxes (thereby reducing consumption and raising environmental protection revenue) have met with strong political opposition. Laws could be passed mandating compact cars, but Americans would probably vote anyone out of office who threatened their SUVs and pickup trucks.

Option 2: Paying the Price for Environmentally Sustainable Development A second possibility is to pay the price to create and distribute technologies that will allow for a maximum balance between economic development and environmental protection. Without modern technology and the money to pay for it, China, for example, poses a serious environmental threat. China now stands second behind the United States in terms of national CO_2 emissions. A primary reason is that China generates most of its commercial power by burning coal, which is very polluting. In 2001, China consumed almost 1.4 billion tons of coal, about 26% of the world total. That, combined with the country's economic development, is a major reason why China's per capita CO_2 emissions rose 91% between 1980 and 2000, while the rest of the world's emissions went up 59%. Even on a per capita basis, China's emissions increased 53% during the period, compared to a 12% global per capita increase.

There are choices, but each has trade-offs. One option is to install pollution control equipment such as "stack scrubbers" to clean the emissions from burning coal. That would aid the environment, but it would be hugely expensive. For example, an announcement in 2003 stated that the cost to retrofit a huge coal-fired generating plant in Bulgaria with stack scrubbers and other equipment, which would clean up its sulfur dioxide emissions by 95%, came to $650 million. Bulgaria had EU backing for the project, and China and other LDCs would need similar support to meet the costs of reducing the discharge of pollutants. Another approach China could take is to consume more oil to decrease the use of coal. Oil imports would be vastly expensive, however, which could affect the country's socioeconomic development. Increased oil consumption at the level China would need would also accelerate the depletion of the world's finite petroleum reserves. Moreover, the new oil fields that are being found often lie offshore, and drilling endangers the oceans.

A third possibility is using hydroelectricity to provide relatively nonpolluting energy. This requires the construction of dams that flood the surrounding countryside, displace its residents, and spoil the pristine beauty of the river valley downstream. China, for example, is trying to ease its energy crunch and simultaneously develop clean hydroelectric power by building the massive, $25 billion Three Gorges Dam and hydroelectric project on the Yangtze River. The project, which rivals the Great Wall of China in scope, will vastly increase the availability of clean power to rural provinces by generating 18,200 megawatts of electricity without burning highly polluting coal. The dam will also help stem floods that have often caused catastrophic damage and death downstream. To accomplish these benefits, however, the dam will create a 370-mile-long reservoir, inundating over 200 cities, towns, and villages, forcing 1.3 million people from their homes. The rising water will submerge numerous archeological sites and what many consider one of the most scenic natural areas in the world. Moreover, a collapse of the dam from structural failure, earthquake or other natural disaster, or military attack could cause a flood of unimaginable proportions. Critics also charge that as the reservoir covers some 1,500 factories, hospitals, dumps, and other sites containing human and industrial waste, the water will become contaminated as the pollutants seep into it. Thus, the Three Gorges project is an almost perfect illustration of the difficulty of sustainable development. Even though the project will ease some environmental problems (in this case, coal burning) it will also have an adverse impact on people and on the environment.

Even if you can cut such Gordian knots, you will encounter other problems: the short-term costs of environmental protection in terms of taxes to pay for government programs; the high costs of products that are produced in an environmentally acceptable way and that are themselves environmentally safe; and the expense of disposing of waste in an ecologically responsible manner.

Moreover, since the LDCs are determined to develop economically, yet must struggle to pay the costs of environmentally sound progress, the North will have to extend significant aid to the South to help it develop in a relatively safe way. Money is needed to create nonpolluting energy resources, to install pollution control devices in factories, and to provide many other technologies. The costs will be huge, with some estimates exceeding $120 billion a year. Billions more are needed each year to help the LDCs stem their—and the world's—spiraling population.

One way that China is trying to achieve sustainable development is by building the immense Three Gorges Dam to generate electricity and cut down on the need to burn coal. Yet the project had major drawbacks, one of which is illustrated by this 2003 photograph of the last few residents leaving the nearly deserted city of Fengjie, once home to 100,000 people. The new 370-mile-long reservoir behind the dam will submerge numerous cities and towns, displacing 1.3 million people and creating concern that waste from abandoned factories, hospitals, dumps, and other sites will leak into the lake and eventually also pollute the Yangtze River downstream.

Is the North willing to pay this price? Polls show that people in many countries are concerned about global warming, ozone layer destruction, deforestation, wildlife destruction, and acid rain. Cross-national polls also regularly find that a majority of respondents say that their governments should do more to protect their country's environment and also to be involved in the global environmental effort. Yet surveys additionally find that a majority of citizens think that their tax burdens are already too heavy and are reluctant to support large expenditures on environmental programs. One illustrative poll asked Americans if they would be willing or unwilling "to pay much higher taxes in order to protect the environment?" In response, 30% replied they were willing, but 40% said they were unwilling, and the remaining 30% declared themselves neutral or unsure.[6] This resistance will work against any attempt to amass the funds that need to be spent internationally to help the LDCs simultaneously develop and protect the environment.[7]

The Politics of Sustainable Development

There is not a great deal of debate over the fact that future development has to occur in a way that does not lay further waste to the biosphere. But what to do and who is responsible for doing it is a much more difficult question, and the lack of resolution of that issue has hampered efforts to fashion an overall global approach to achieving the goal of sustainable development. There are sections later in this chapter that address problems and programs associated with the atmosphere, water, land, and other elements of the biosphere, but before taking those up, it is appropriate to review the global approach to sustainable development and its politics at its broadest level.

The first step to dealing with any problem is recognizing that there is an issue. That this has been accomplished regarding sustainable development is demonstrated by the convening of two UN-sponsored "Earth Summits," one in 1992 and the other in 2002. However, both illustrate the limits to progress and the political disagreements that stand in the way.

Earth Summit I The convening in 1992 of the **United Nations Conference on Environment and Development (UNCED)** meeting in Rio de Janeiro symbolized the growing concern with the environment and how to achieve sustainable development. Popularly dubbed Earth Summit I, the conference was attended by 178 countries and 115 heads of state. Some 8,000 journalists covered the proceedings, and 15,000 representatives of NGOs attended a nearby parallel conference. The official conference produced Agenda 21 (an 800-page document covering 112 topics that constitute a nonbinding blueprint for sustainable development in the 21st century) and two treaties (the Biodiversity Convention and the Global Warming Convention).

Beyond this simple recounting of the facts, Earth Summit I illustrated the often-divisive politics of environmental protection. In particular, the North and the South were at odds on many issues. The LDCs argued that the burden of sustainable development should fall substantially on the EDCs for several reasons. First, the already industrialized EDCs had caused most of the problems through their consumption of natural resources and their discharges of pollutants onto the land and into the air and water. Second, the LDCs contended that restrictions on development should either not apply to them for an extended time or should be much less stringent than those restricting the EDCs. This was justified, in the LDCs' view, because the EDCs had already achieved their development and it was unfair to ask the LDCs not to achieve what the EDCs already had. Indeed, some in the LDCs suspect that EDC efforts to restrict their development may be part of a neocolonial effort to keep the LDCs poor, weak, and dependent.

Third, the LDCs reasoned, they were too poor to develop their considerable resources in an environmentally sustainable way and, therefore, the EDCs should significantly increase aid to help the LDCs do so. For their part, most of the EDCs, especially the United States, believed that the LDCs had to join in taking significant steps, such as protecting their forests from commercial logging and from clearing for agricultural and industrial use. The EDCs also rejected the notion that they should bear a disproportionate share of the burden by restricting their economies without the LDCs doing so too, and by paying a significant part of the costs associated with whatever programs the LDCs did adopt.

These divisions created what amounted to a stand-off. The EDCs averted efforts by the LDCs to force them to set binding timetables for reducing the use of fossil fuels and the emissions of CO_2 and other gases that contribute to global warming. The North also resisted making major financial commitments. "We do not have an open pocketbook," President George H. W. Bush observed.[8] Similarly, the South avoided restrictions, including those pertaining to forest resources. "Forests are clearly a sovereign resource—not like atmosphere and oceans, which are a global commons," said Malaysia's chief negotiator. "We cannot allow forests to be taken up in global forums."[9] Given the various divisions, it was not surprising that neither the Biodiversity nor Global Warming Convention created legally binding mandates (Swanson, 1999).

Was the Earth Summit a failure? Not really. At the time, Norway's prime minister observed, "We owe the world to be frank about what we have achieved in Rio: Progress in many fields, too little progress in most fields, and no progress at all in some fields."[10] One of the conference's successes was that it symbolized the recognition that sustainable development was a problem significant enough to bring virtually all of the world's countries together. Second, Agenda 21 and the two conventions served to enunciate goals and actions to address the problem. Thus, Earth Summit I helped set the stage.

Earth Summit II Defining problems, propounding principles, and establishing goals are, however, only preliminaries to solving problems, and the lack of sufficient progress persuaded the UN to convene the **World Summit on Sustainable Development (WSSD)** in 2002. Secretary-General Kofi Annan explained the need for a second Earth Summit: "The . . . conceptual breakthrough achieved at Rio has not . . . proved decisive enough to break with business as usual. . . . There is a gap between the goals and the promises set out in Rio and the daily reality [of what has been accomplished]." To address that gap, representatives (including 104 heads of state or government) of almost all of the world's countries and some 8,000 NGOs gathered in Johannesburg, South Africa. Including the 4,000 reporters who covered the event, attendance at the conference exceeded 21,000.

The political disputes during the conference, dubbed Earth Summit II, were similar to those that bedeviled Earth Summit I. For their part the United States and some other EDCs were neither willing to commit to what they saw as lofty rhetoric and attempts to obligate them to vast amounts of aid nor to focus on their policies and not those of the LDCs. As one U.S. official put it before the convention, "The world community does not need to negotiate new goals or create new global bureaucracies." Instead, she continued, the best approach is through "effective domestic policies" so that "sustainable development can be achieved in a way that benefits both developing and developed nations"[11] Others disagreed with this approach. During his opening address to the conference, Secretary-General Annan urged the delegates to "stop being economically defensive, and start being politically courageous. . . . The richest countries must lead the way. They have the wealth. They have the technology. And they contribute disproportionately to global environmental problems."[12]

Given the political divides, the advances made by the WSSD were modest but were an advance over those of UNCED a decade earlier. The EDCs announced new funding commitments. Speaking to the delegates, U.S. Secretary of State Powell said the Bush administration would seek to increase U.S. aid for economic development from $10 billion to $15 billion within three years, and the FY2004 budget submitted by Bush projected this increase, even if not until year four (FY2007). The conference also adopted some important new targets, such as cutting by 50% the number of people without access to basic sanitation by 2015; using and producing chemicals in ways that do not adversely affect human health and the environment by 2020; maintaining or restoring the world's fisheries to sustainable levels by 2015; and achieving by 2010 a significant reduction in the rate that biological diversity is being lost through the extinction of species of flora and fauna.

Still, many were disappointed in the results. As the *State of the World* 2003 put it, "The lack of detail in these commitments and the acrimony that preceded them" at the conference left many participants "pessimistic about the world's ability to move forward." Moreover, the report continued, "The severe North-South splits . . . seemed deeper than ever" (p. xvi). "It's a battle, a conflict of interest between developed and developing countries," observed Emil Salim, a former Indonesian environment minister who helped organize the conference.[13]

Again, as in 1992, the question must be raised about whether the conference was a success or a failure. Perhaps Kofi Annan provided a good perspective when he was asked that question at the end of the conference. "I think we have to be careful not to expect conferences like this to produce miracles," he advised a press conference. "It is not one isolated conference that is going to do this whole thing. What happens is the energy that we create here, the commitments that have been made, and what we do on the ground as individuals, as civil society, as community groups and as governments and private sector."[14]

During Earth Summit I, its secretary-general, Canadian diplomat Maurice Strong, characterized achieving sustainable development as a "Herculean task."[15] This remains as true today as it was in 1992. We can gain further perspective on the problem by examining some of the key issues regarding the biosphere and its inhabitants, and the possibility of achieving international cooperation toward sustainable development. We will first consider population. Then we will turn to concerns over such resources as minerals, forests, wildlife, and water. Last, the chapter will take up environmental issues, including pollution of the ground, water, air, and upper atmosphere.

Sustainable Development: Population and Resources

Throughout history, humans have taken their world for granted. We have assumed that it will always be here, that it will yield the necessities of life, and that it will absorb what is discarded. For several millennia this assumption proved justifiable. The Earth was generally able to sustain its population and replenish itself.

Now, the exploding human population and technology have changed this. Not only are there five times as many people as there were just a little more than 150 years ago, but our technological progress has multiplied our per capita resource consumption and our per capita waste and pollutant production. Technological wizardry may bring solutions, as the optimists predict, but such solutions are uncertain; for now the reality is that the world faces a crisis of carrying capacity—the potential of no longer being able to sustain its population in an adequate manner or being able to absorb its waste. To put this as an equation:

Exploding population × Spiraling per capita resource consumption × Mounting waste and pollutant production = Potential catastrophe

Population Issues and Cooperation

On Tuesday, October 12, 1999, the world population passed the 6 billion mark. That is a stunning number. It took all of human history to the year 1804 for the population to reach 1 billion. Adding the next billion people took just 123 years. Getting to 7 billion is expected to take just 13 years. China alone, with its 1.3 billion inhabitants, has more people than there were humans in the entire world less than 200 years ago. According to the United Nations Population Fund (UNFPA), the world population in 2050 will be 8.9 billion, and will not stabilize until it reaches about 10.5 billion around the year 2200. Given a reasonably finite amount of resources and ability to absorb waste, this growing population presents a challenge to the Earth's carrying capacity. A sense of both the number of people, now and in the future, in each region and of the varying rates of population growth among the regions can be gained from Figure 16.1 and the accompanying map.

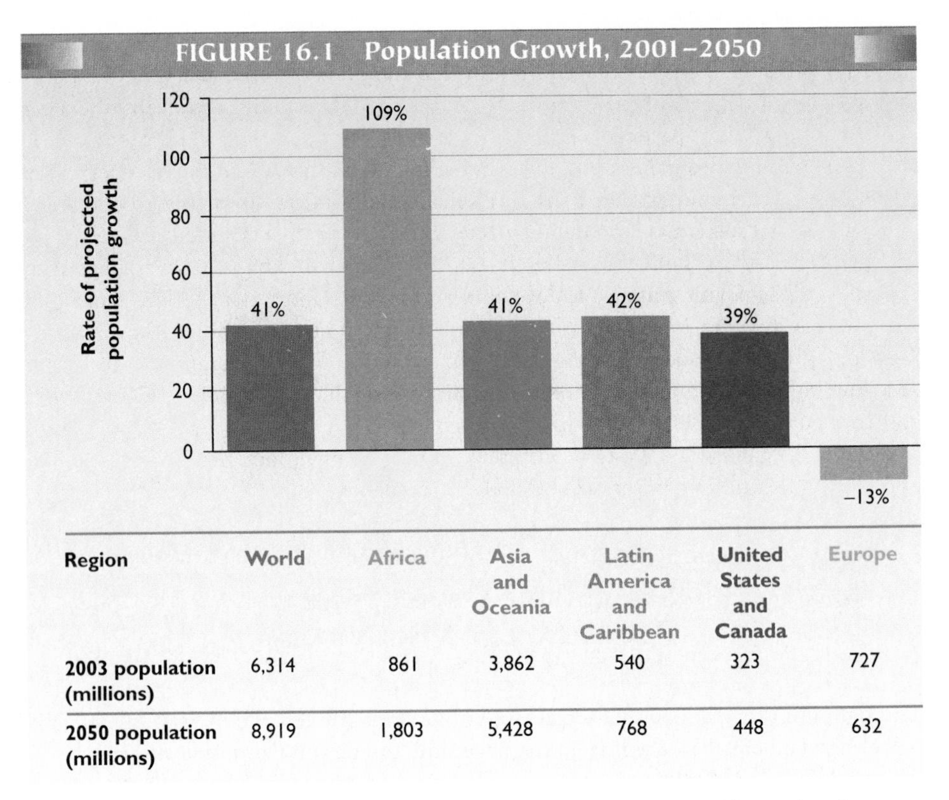

Region	World	Africa	Asia and Oceania	Latin America and Caribbean	United States and Canada	Europe
2003 population (millions)	6,314	861	3,862	540	323	727
2050 population (millions)	8,919	1,803	5,428	768	448	632

World population growth is not even. The burden of additional people will fall most heavily on the regions with a predominance of less developed countries, which have scant resources to support their burgeoning populations.

Note: The numbers do not add precisely across because of rounding.

Data source: United Nations Population Division at http://esa.un.org/unpp/p2k0data.asp.

To a significant degree, the expanding population is the result of improving human health. *Fewer deaths* is one factor. Infant mortality has decreased; adult longevity has increased. These two factors combine to mean that even in areas where the birthrate declines, the population growth rate sometimes continues to accelerate. For example, the birthrate in the LLDCs declined from 45 births per 1,000 population in 1960 to 29 in 2001. But during the same period, advances in health and other conditions decreased the crude death rate (annual deaths of people per thousand) from 22 to 11 as life expectancy rose from 44 years to 58 years. The net result is that the rapidly declining death rates have more than offset the more slowly declining birthrates and resulted in an annual population growth of 2.7% during the 41-year period.

The huge population base of 6.3 billion is another factor in population growth. This problem is one of mathematics. Although the average woman has 45% fewer babies now than in 1970, there are so many more women in their childbearing years that the number of babies born continues to go up. During the next decade, some 3 billion women will enter their childbearing years. At the current fertility rate (average number of children born per woman in her childbearing years), these women will have 8.1 billion children, of which 7.5 billion will live to at least age 5. Happily, most of this tidal wave of children will grow up. When they do, most of them will also become parents. That will be a joyous event for them, but it will not be a blessed event for the embattled ecosphere.

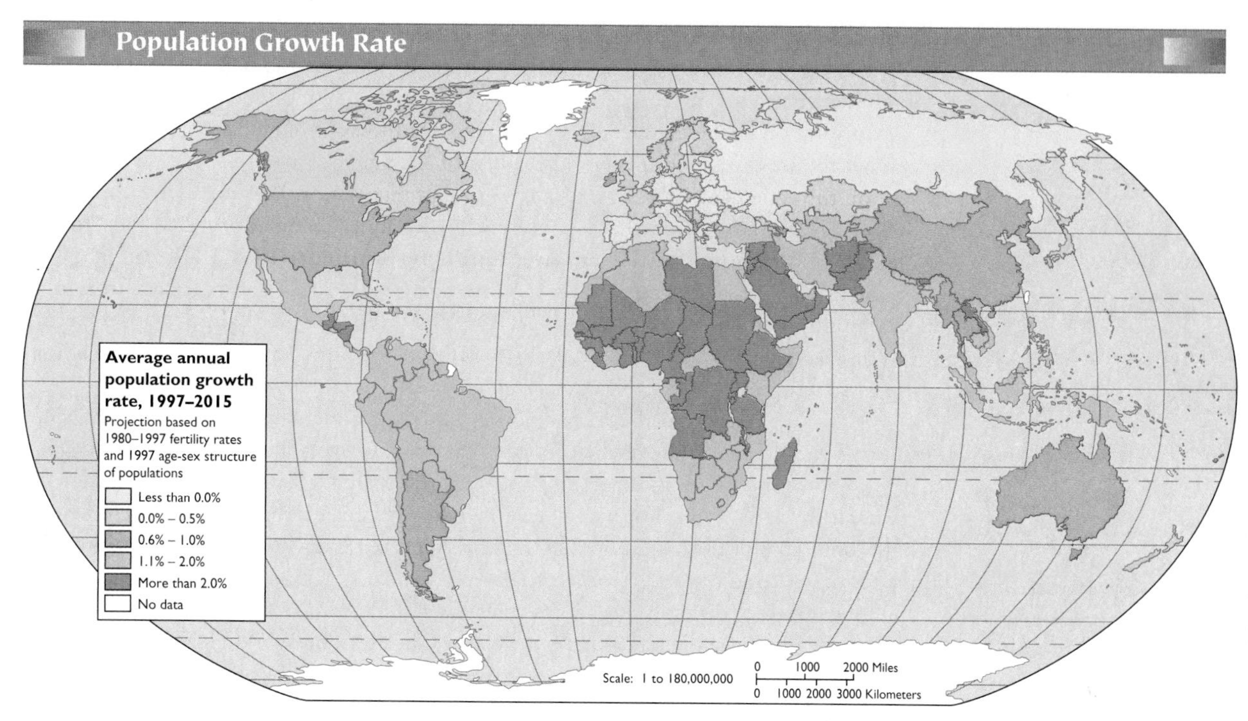

The world's population approximately quadrupled during the 20th century. We continue to strain the Earth's resources by adding about 1 billion people every 13 years. Although Figure 16.1 and this map use slightly different data parameters, they are complementary. What you can see in this map is a graphic representation that the growth of population is not evenly spread around the globe. The most rapid growth is in less developed countries of the South, which will struggle to house, educate, feed, and otherwise care for their burgeoning populations. At the same time, many of the economically developed countries of the North are near or even below the zero population growth rate. For these countries, an aging population will present a different set of challenges than face the LDCs with their massive number of children.

Source: John Allen and Elizabeth Leppman, *Student Atlas of World Politics*, 6th Edition, Dushkin/McGraw-Hill, p. 542. Reprinted with permission from Dushkin/McGraw-Hill.

IGO and NGO Responses to the Population Problem

The effort to control global population growth is led appropriately by the United Nations. There are a number of associated organizations and programs within the UN's purview. Of these, UNFPA, a subsidiary organ of the UN General Assembly, is the largest. The agency began operations in 1969 and focuses on promoting family planning services and improving reproductive health in LDCs. During its history, UNFPA has provided nearly $6 billion to support population programs in the vast majority of the world's countries. The organization is funded through voluntary contributions, and in 2001 had a budget of $378 million donated by about 120 countries. In addition to its own programs, the agency helps coordinate the programs of other related IGOs, NGOs, and national governments. Within the UN and its associated agencies, these include the United Nations Children's Fund (UNICEF) and the World Health Organization (WHO). UNFPA's efforts are further supplemented by and often coordinated with NGOs such as the International Planned Parenthood Federation (IPPF). This British-based organization, which was founded in 1952, operates its own international family planning programs and also links the individual planned parenthood organizations of about 150 countries. The IPPF is funded by these national organizations, by private contributions, and by donations from approximately 20 countries. Like a number of other IGOs in the population control and reproductive health area, the IPPF has consultative status with the UN.

In addition to these general responses, the need to control global population growth also led the UN to begin the World Population Conference series to focus world attention on the issue, seek solutions, and galvanize an international cooperative effort to address it. There have been three conferences, the most recent of which, the **United Nations Conference on Population and Development (UNCPD)**, met in Cairo, Egypt, in 1994. It was organized by UNFPA and brought together delegates from over 170 countries and a large number of NGOs. The session focused on population control and on reproductive health. Each year, for example, over 400,000 women (99% of whom live in LDCs) die from complications of pregnancy and childbirth.

Abortion presents a particularly emotional issue for both its supporters and opponents. Only about 2% of all countries ban abortion even if a woman's life is in danger, but beyond that, whether and under what circumstances abortions are legal varies greatly. Abortions to protect a woman's physical or mental heath are legally available in 90% of the EDCs but in only about 50% of LDCs. Among the LDCs, China and India both permit abortions, giving about 75% of the world's women access to abortion. Abortions that are unsafe, either in countries where abortion is illegal or severely restricted or in countries with an inadequate health care system, are a major threat to women's health. The World Health Organization estimates that about 20 million women a year undergo unsafe abortions and about 80,000 of these women die, accounting for about 20% of the maternal mortality rate. There are estimates that in some countries, which both restrict abortions and are exceptionally poor, over half of all maternal mortality is the result of illegal abortions.

While the related goals of restraining population growth, improving reproductive health, and empowering women were hardly debatable, how to achieve these ends sparked considerable controversy at the conference. The dispute centered on the charge that the conference was moving toward supporting social and even legal pressure on people to limit the number of children they had, advocating abortion, and promoting other practices to which the critics objected. Several predominantly Muslim countries refused to attend the conference, and the Sudanese government charged that it would result in "the spread of immoral and irreligious ideas."[16] The Roman Catholic Church was also critical. Following the conference, Pope John Paul II wrote to the head of the UNFPA asserting that the conference had "ignore[d] the rights of the unborn," emphasizing his opposition to methods of "finality," such as sterilization and abortion, and calling them a "violation of human rights, especially [those] of women." As an alternate approach, the pontiff contended that the world would be better off if societies promoted development that improved the lot of families, rather than denying the right to be born.[17] The Vatican's view drew furious criticism. For one, Prime Minister Gro Harlem Brundtland of Norway, who was head of WHO (1998–2003), charged that "morality becomes hypocrisy if it means accepting mothers' suffering or dying in connection with unwanted pregnancies and illegal abortions and unwanted children."[18]

The result of all this was a series of compromises. The document's language on promoting safe abortion was qualified by adding the phrase, "in circumstances in which abortion is legal," and it specified, "In no case should abortion be promoted as a method of family planning." The 1994 Cairo conference unanimously approved a "Program of Action" calling for spending $5.7 billion annually by the year 2000 on international programs to foster family planning. Funding never reached that goal, but the heightened awareness of the population problem and the closely associated issue of women's reproductive health and the postconference activity of the delegates and others did help to increase funding from $1.3 billion in 1993 to $2.2 billion in 2000.

Approaches to Reducing the Birthrate

Whether the programs being developed are engendered by IGOs and NGOs or by global conferences such as the UNCPD, there are two basic approaches to reducing the birthrate. *Social approaches* are one. These provide information about birth control and encouragement to practice it. The social approach also involves making birth control devices and pills, sterilization, and, in some cases, abortion programs available. At the national level, many LDCs have made strong efforts, given their limited financial resources. In Thailand, for instance, 72% of all couples practice contraception (the contraceptive prevalence rate), a rate that is higher than in most EDCs.

These national efforts are supported by the UNFPA, other IGOs, and NGOs, and their combined efforts have had an impact. During the early 1960s, the contraceptive prevalence rate in the LDCs was only 9%. Now about 49% of couples in LDCs practice birth control. This contraceptive prevalence rate falls off drastically in the least developed countries (LLDCs), where it is only 23%. There are at least 15 countries in which the rate is a mere 10% or less.

Economic approaches to population growth can also be successful. There is a clear relationship between poverty and birthrates. In 2001, the birthrate per 1,000 population in the EDCs was 12. In the LLDCs it was 29, with sub-Saharan Africa at 39, more than triple the EDC rate. How does one explain the link between population and poverty? One commonly held view is that overpopulation causes poverty. This view reasons that with too many people, especially in already poor countries, there are too few resources, jobs, and other forms of wealth to go around. Perhaps, but that is only part of the problem, because it is also true that poverty *causes* overpopulation (Catley-Carlson & Outlaw, 1998). The LLDCs tend to have the most labor-intensive economies, which means that

Perhaps the best way to decrease population growth is to provide women with increased educational and occupational opportunities. The international effort to promote these is symbolized by this picture of a Palestinian woman in Gaza reading *We Mean Business*, by Susan Norman (Boston: Longman Publishing, 1993). The woman is in a facility run by the White Ribbon Alliance, a UN-affiliated NGO that works to make pregnancy and childbirth safe for all women and infants.

children are economically valuable because they help their parents with farming or, when they are somewhat older, provide cheap labor in mining and manufacturing processes. As a result, cultural attitudes in many countries have come to reflect economic utility. Having a large family is also an asset in terms of social standing in many societies with limited economic opportunities.

Furthermore, women in LDCs have fewer opportunities to limit the number of children they bear. Artificial birth control methods and counseling services are less readily available in these countries. Another fact is that women in LDCs are less educated than are women in EDCs. It is therefore harder to convey birth control information, especially written information, to women in LDCs. Additionally, women in LDCs have fewer opportunities than do women in EDCs to gain paid employment and to develop status roles beyond that of motherhood. The inadequacies in financial, educational, and contraceptive opportunities for women are strongly correlated to high fertility rates. One way to see relationships is to consider Figure 16.2, which compares Malawi and the United States. Even within LDCs, the relationship between economics and the number of children a woman is likely to have is clear. Among one group of LLDCs, women in the top economic 20% had a fertility rate of 3.3; for women in the bottom 20% the rate was 6.2.

The evidence that poverty causes population increases has spurred efforts to advance the economic and educational opportunities available to women as an integral part of population control. This realization was one of the factors that led the UN to designate 1975 as International Women's Year and to kick off the Decade for Women. That year the UN also convened the first World Conference on Women (WCW). These initiatives were followed in 1976 by the establishment of the UN Development Fund for Women (UNIFEM, after its French acronym). The Fund works through 10 regional offices to improve the living standards of women in LDCs by providing technical and financial support to advance the entry of women into business, scientific and technical careers, and other key areas. UNIFEM also strives to incorporate women into the international and national planning and administration of development programs and to ensure that the issues of particular concern to women such as food, security, human rights, and reproductive health are kept on the global agenda. The UN also established the International Research and Training Institute for the Advancement of Women with the task of carrying out research, training, and information activities related to women and the development process. Headquartered in the Dominican Republic, the institute conducts research on the barriers that impede the progress of women in social, economic, and political development.

The Impact of International Population Control Efforts

The effort to reduce global population growth is a success story. Part of this is due to the work of IGOs, NGOs, and national government. Improved economic conditions in many LDCs and the slowly improving economic and educational status of women in many countries has also played a role. As a result, the average global fertility rate has declined from 4.9 in 1970 to 2.6 in 2001. The goal is 2.1, which is considered the stable replacement rate, although as infant mortality and crude death rates continue to drop, it may even be necessary to reach 2.0 or slightly lower to stabilize the population. Even better news is that the UNFPA estimates the population growth has slowed somewhat and is expected to continue to decelerate. As recently as 1994, the population was expanding at 94 million a year, and the UN was estimating that it would reach 11.6 billion by 2150. Now the population is projected to level off almost 2 billion people short of that. Even this positive change has mixed components, however, because the fastest population increases are occurring in the very poorest countries (the least developed countries, LLDCs). Between

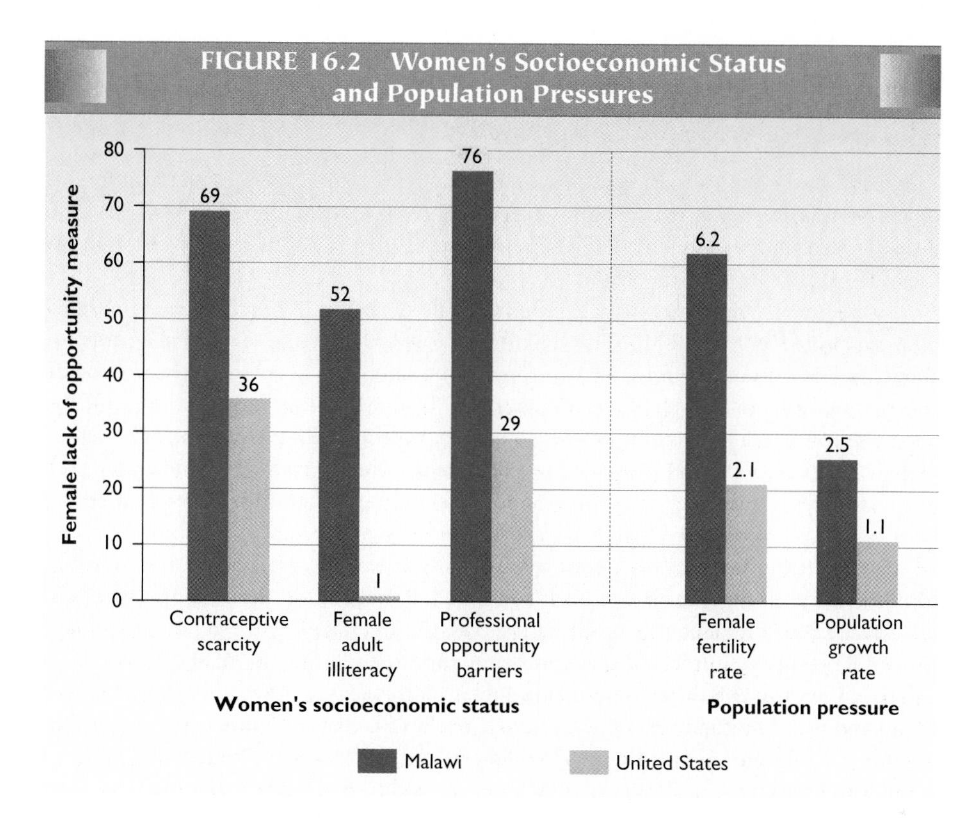

There is a strong relationship between the lack of availability to women of contraceptive programs, education, and professional and other economic opportunities (represented by the three categories to the left) and upward population pressures (represented by the two categories to the right). Notice that compared to the United States, the measures for Malawi related to the lack of opportunities for women in the three left categories are reflected by greater upward population pressures in the two categories on the right. The evidence indicates that the best way to control population growth is to enhance women's opportunities.

Notes: Contraceptive scarcity: percentage of females age 15–49 who (or whose partners) are not using some form of contraception; Female illiteracy: percentage of age 15 or more; Professional opportunity barriers: degree of lack of equality in political, professional, and economic opportunities that make up the gender empowerment measure (GEM) of the UNDP; Female fertility rate: number of children the average woman will have during her childbearing years; Population growth rate: annual growth population data on scale and converted to a 100 base for comparison.

Data sources: World Bank (2003); UNDP (2001, 2003).

2000 and 2050, the population of these countries will increase about 250%, six times faster than the world as a whole. Moreover, as one demographer commented about the easing of the population growth rate, "The difference is comparable to a tidal wave surging toward one of our coastal cities. Whether the tidal wave is 80 feet or 100 feet high, the impact will be similar."[19] Therefore, good news does not mean the problem is solved or that the efforts of the UN and other organizations are complete.

Resource Issues and Cooperation

Recent decades have witnessed increased warnings that we are using our resources too quickly. Most studies by individual analysts, governmental commissions, and private organizations have concluded that the rates at which humans are depleting energy, mineral, forest, land, wildlife, fishery, and water resources are matters calling for a level of concern ranging from caution to serious alarm.

Petroleum, Natural Gas, and Minerals

The supply of oil, gas, and mineral resources is one area of concern. At the forefront of these worries are the cost and supply of energy resources. The energy issue has such immense economic and environmental ramifications that it set off a war when Iraq invaded Kuwait in 1990.

World energy needs are skyrocketing. Global energy production increased roughly 33% between 1980 and 2000. The burning of fossil fuels (coal, oil, gas) accounts for about 79% of output. Burning wood, crop residue, and other forms of biomass provide another 11% of the energy. Nuclear energy, at 7%, was the third largest source. Of the most environmentally friendly sources of energy, hydroelectric power generated 2% of global energy, and 1% was produced by solar, geothermal, wind, wave, and other such power sources. Of the various sources, nuclear energy production by far increased the most rapidly, growing more than tenfold over the last two decades.

At one time the world had perhaps 2.3 trillion barrels of oil beneath its surface. More than half of that has already been consumed. Projections of future use are tricky, as are estimates for the discovery of future reserves. On one hand, there can be little doubt that oil is a finite resource and that it is being consumed at the rate of about 25 billion barrels a year. On the other, new techniques are discovering previously unknown reserves and bringing them into production. The result is that the known reserves of petroleum actually increased from 1.007 trillion barrels in 1996 to 1.213 trillion barrels in 2003. The U.S. Geological Survey, which performs the even more difficult task of estimating how much undiscovered oil exists, raised its estimates from 539 billion barrels in 1994 to 649 barrels in 2000. This means that it is not accurate to take the known reserves (1.213 trillion barrels) in 2003, divide it by current annual consumption (25 billion barrels), and conclude that the oil fields will run dry in 48.5 years, or sometime in 2051. Nevertheless, petroleum reserves are a concern because the supply is exhaustible and because new finds are smaller and less attractive to utilize (deeper, under the ocean, in environmentally sensitive land areas).

> ***Did You Know That:***
>
> The world's first oil well was drilled in 1859 in Titusville, Pennsylvania. Sold as a lubricant, oil initially averaged $25 a barrel, compared to about $40 a barrel in mid-2004. Adjusted for inflation, the 1859 price is equal to about $550 a barrel today.

The story for natural gas is nearly the same. New discoveries, enhanced extraction methods, and other factors may have an impact on the timing, but the bottom line is that the supply is finite and at some point, perhaps within the lifetime of people being born today, it will be exhausted.

Coal is an abundant energy source that will last almost 500 years at current consumption rates, but it is a major pollutant if not controlled by expensive technology. The development of hydroelectric power is attractive in some ways, but it is expensive (albeit increasingly less so) to develop. Moreover, as noted earlier, damming rivers creates environmental and social problems. Nuclear power is yet another alternative, and some countries have become reliant on it. For example, France generates 40% of all its commercial energy by nuclear power. These countries are exceptions, however. Only 28 countries generate nuclear power, and on average it amounts to only about 20% of their total commercial energy production. Additionally, there are high costs and obvious hazards to nuclear power. Some people advocate developing wind, solar, geothermal, and other such sources of power. So far, though, cost, production capacity, and other factors have limited the application of these energy sources and will continue to do so unless there are major technological breakthroughs.

Dealing with the supply and demand for energy also requires understanding use patterns. The vast majority of all energy is used by the EDCs. Most of the growing demand for energy, by contrast, is a result of increased needs by the countries of the South.

During the period 1980–2000, the energy consumption of EDCs increased 36%, while the LDCs' energy use increased 51%. Most of the LDC increase was because of population growth rather than modernization. This is evident in the modest 7% per capita energy use increase by the LDCs during the two-decade period compared to the 17% increase in per capita energy consumption in the EDCs. What these patterns reveal is that the most immediate way to deal with energy consumption is to restrain per capita increases in the North and to reduce population growth in the South.

Pressure on the supply of fossil fuel resources has the highest political profile, but there are also many other minerals being rapidly depleted. Based on world reserves and world use, some minerals that are in particularly short supply (and estimates of the year that the Earth's supply will be exhausted given known reserves) include copper (2056), lead (2041), mercury (2077), tin (2053), and zinc (2042). Certainly, discoveries of new sources or the decline of consumption based on conservation or the use of substitutes could extend those dates. But it is also possible that the time interval to depletion could narrow if, for instance, extraction rates accelerate as LDCs develop.

The resource puzzle, as mentioned, is how to simultaneously (1) maintain the industrialized countries' economies and standards of living, (2) promote economic development in the South (which will consume increased energy and minerals), and (3) manage the problems of resource depletion and environmental damage involved in energy and mineral production and use. If, for instance, the South were to develop to the same economic level as the North, if the LDCs' energy-use patterns were the same as the North's currently are, and if the same energy resource patterns that exist now persisted, then petroleum reserves would almost certainly soon be dry. Natural gas and many other minerals probably would also quickly follow oil into the museum of geological history.

Forests and Land

For many who will read this book, the trees that surround them and the very land on which they stand will hardly seem like natural resources and will certainly not seem to be endangered. That is not the case. There are serious concerns about the depletion of the world's forests and the degradation of its land.

Forest Depletion The depletion of forests and their resources concerns many analysts. Data compiled by the UN Food and Agriculture Organization (FAO) and other sources indicates that the increase in world population and, to a lesser degree, economic development are destroying the world's forests. Some 1 billion people depend on wood as an energy source, and many forests have disappeared because of such domestic needs as cooking and heating. Forests are also being cleared to make room for farms and grazing lands. Forests and woodland still cover about 30% of the Earth's land area. Once, however, they occupied 48% of the land area, and tree cover is declining by about 1% every five years. Logging is a major factor, but forests are also being drowned by hydroelectric projects and being strip-mined for minerals. Acid rain and other environmental attacks increase the toll on trees. Whatever the cause, the result is that some 35,000 square miles of forest are being lost every year. This is a loss roughly equivalent to clear-cutting Portugal.

Forest loss is not spread evenly across the world. Through conservation, reforestation, and (less positively) importing forest products from the LDCs, the EDC forests are actually growing by 0.1% a year. By contrast 0.3% of the LDCs' forests are disappearing annually, and for the LLDCs the loss rate is 0.8%. Significant stretches of Brazil, China, East Africa, and Malaysia have been nearly denuded of their forests. The tropical forests, which account for over 80% of all forest losses, are of particular concern. Fifty years ago, 12% of the Earth's land surface was covered by tropical forest; now just 6% is. The Amazon River Basin's tropical forest in Brazil and the surrounding countries is an especially

Each year the world's forest shrink as trees are cut and land is cleared. It is easy to decry this and to advocate a halt to forest destruction, but what does one say to the poor Indonesian farmer seen here using fire and a machete to clear land so that he can plant crops and feed his family?

critical issue. This ecosystem is by far the largest of its kind in the world, covering 2.7 million square miles, about the size of the 48 contiguous U.S. states. The expanding populations and economic needs of the region's countries have exerted great pressure on the forest. For example, the Amazon Basin has recently been losing 9,000 square miles (an area about the size of Massachusetts) of forest every year.

LDCs recognize the problem, but there are powerful economic incentives for them to continue clearing forest land. Domestically, it helps open farmland and economic development. Internationally, the annual global trade in wood and wood products (such as paper, pulp, and resins) is over $200 billion, and poor countries are cutting their trees and exporting the wood to earn capital to pay off their international debt and to finance economic development. It is easy to blame the LDCs for allowing their forests to be overcut, but many in those countries ask what alternative they have. "Anyone, American, Dutch or whatever, who comes in and tells us not to cut the forest has to give us another way to live," says an official of Suriname (a former Dutch colony). "And so far they haven't done that." Instead, what occurs, charges the country's president, is "eco-colonialism" by international environmental organizations trying to prevent Suriname from using its resources.[20]

Deforestation has numerous negative consequences. One is global warming, which we will discuss in a later section. Another ill effect of forest depletion is that with a shrinking supply of wood and an increased demand for cooking and heating, the cost of wood goes up and may swallow a third of a poor family's income in some African cities. In some rural areas, wood is so scarce that each family must have at least one member working nearly full-time to gather a supply for home use. The devastation of the forests is also driving many forms of life into extinction. A typical 4-square-mile section of the Amazon Basin rain forest contains some 750 species of trees, 125 kinds of mammals, 400 types of birds, 160 different kinds of reptiles and amphibians, and perhaps 300,000 insect species. The loss of biodiversity has an obvious aesthetic impact, and there are also pragmatic implications. Some 25% of all modern pharmaceutical products contain ingredients originally found in plants. Extracts from Madagascar's rosy periwinkle, for example, are used in drugs to treat children's leukemia and Hodgkin's disease. A drug called Taxol, derived from the Pacific yew, is a promising treatment for breast and ovarian cancer. Many plants also contain natural pesticides that could provide the basis for the development of ecologically safe commercial pesticides to replace the environmental horrors (such as DDT) of the past.

Did You Know That:

Eating less meat has many environmental benefits. The production of one pound of beef requires 7 pounds of grain, which use 7,000 gallons of water to grow. For each resulting pound of meat, cattle discharge 12 pounds of feces and other organic pollutants and copious amounts of ozone layer–depleting methane. Of all U.S. grain produced, 70% goes to feed livestock.

Land Degradation Not only are the forests in trouble, so too is the land. Deforestation is one of the many causes of soil erosion and other forms of damage to the land. Tropical forests rest on thin topsoil. This land is especially unsuited for agriculture, and it becomes exhausted quickly once the forest is cut down and crops are planted or grazing takes place. With no trees to hold soil in place, runoff occurs, and silt clogs rivers and bedevils hydroelectric projects. Unchecked runoff can also significantly increase the chances of down-river floods, resulting in loss of life and economic damage.

Honduras is one of the many countries that environmental scientists had identified as endangered by deforestation. As one study relates, "They [the scientists] were right. In October 1998, Hurricane Mitch slammed into the Gulf [of Mexico] coast of Central America and stalled there for four days. Nightmarish mudslides obliterated entire villages," the study continues; "half the population of Honduras was displaced, and the country lost 95% of its agricultural production. And in the chaos and filth of Mitch's wake, there followed tens of thousands of additional cases of malaria, cholera, and dengue fever" (Bright, 2000:23).

According to the United Nations Environmental Programme (UNEP), 3.5 million square miles (about the size of China or the United States) of land is moderately degraded, 1.4 million square miles (about equal to Argentina) is strongly degraded, and 347,000 square miles (about the same as Egypt) is extremely degraded (beyond repair). At its worst, *desertification* occurs. More of the world's surface is becoming desertlike because of water scarcity, timber cutting, overgrazing, and overplanting. The desertification of land is increasing at an estimated rate of 30,600 square miles a year, turning an area the size of Austria into barren desert. Moreover, that rate of degradation could worsen, based on UNEP's estimate that 8 billion acres are in jeopardy.

Wildlife

The march of humankind has driven almost all the other creatures of the Earth into retreat and, in some cases, into extinction. Beyond the impact of deforestation, there are many other by-products of human civilization, ranging from urbanization to pollution, that destroy wildlife habitat. Whatever its cause, a decrease in the planet's wildlife will be an immeasurable loss to humans. The drug Capoten, which is used to control high blood pressure, is derived from the venom of the Brazilian pit viper. And the American Heart Association has identified an anti–blood-clotting drug based on substances found in bat saliva that is effective in preventing heart attacks in humans. Many endangered species have no known immediate pragmatic value. Nevertheless, a world without giant pandas, hooded cranes, Plymouth red-bellied turtles, and Chinese river dolphins will be a less diverse, less appealing place.

Unfortunately, some species do have economic value. The estimated $20 billion annual illegal trade in feathers, pelts, ivory, and other wildlife products is leading to the capture and sale or slaughter of numerous species, including many that are endangered. A snow leopard pelt fetches $1,000 in Afghanistan, Komodo dragons and orangutans bring $30,000 on the black market in Indonesia, and the price of a radiated tortoise from Madagascar is $5,000. Often the species are less exotic and the illegal hunting is closer to home. The U.S. National Park Service reported in early 2004 that poachers annually kill more than 40,000 bears per year in the United States alone. Bear paws can bring $1,000 or more in Asia, where they are eaten. The supposed medicinal value for a range of ailments (including convulsions, fever, and hemorrhoids) places a price tag of up to $3,000 on a bear's gall bladder. During the last

The Convention on the International Trade in Endangered Species has provided some relief to many endangered species by banning the international sale of live wildlife or wildlife products, such as skins. This picture shows the confiscated pelts of a tiger and leopard being burned by customs officials at Mumbai's (Bombay) international airport. The blaze was meant to send out a signal to those engaged in the illegal wildlife trade that India's government is serious about protecting endangered wildlife. Still, saving the tiger and other species is difficult because of their monetary value to poachers. A tiger skin can fetch $900, a canine tooth goes for $125, and each claw brings $10. Other parts of the big cat are used in traditional medicines. Men hoping to improve their virility pay $800 for a potion made from a tiger penis, and tiger bones, which are said to relieve rheumatism, sell for $180 a pound.

half of the 1990s, U.S. officials intercepted more than 70 shipments of bear parts to Asia and concede that many more were smuggled out.

Humans further add to the destruction of wildlife through pollution. In recent memory, there have been several disastrous discharges from oil tankers in Alaska, off the Galápagos Islands, and elsewhere that have spilled up to 11 million gallons per incident, devastating the fish, birds, animals, and other creatures in the water and along the nearby shores. Probably the most damaging of all is human encroachment for settlement, farming, and other uses in a process that has felled forests, filled in swamps, and otherwise destroyed plants and the habitat of wildlife.

It should be noted that on the issue of wildlife, like many other matters discussed in this chapter, there are optimists who believe that the problem is being grossly overstated. According to Julian Simon, "a fair reading of the available data suggests a rate of extinction not even one one-thousandth as great as the one the doomsayers scare us with." Simon was careful to say that he was not suggesting "that we should ignore possible dangers to species." He contended, though, "we should strive for a clear and unbiased view of species' assets so as to make sound judgments about how much time and money to spend on guarding them."[21] Other analysts have agreed with that assessment (Lomborg, 2001).

Human food requirements put increasing pressure on the ocean's fish, mollusks, and crustaceans. The importance of marine life as a source of food plus the demands of a growing world population increased the marine (saltwater) catch from 19 million tons in 1950 to over 90 million tons by the early 1990s. Given the FAO's estimate that the sustainable annual yield of Earth's oceans is between 69 and 96 million tons, it became clear that a crisis point had been reached. Since then, a combination of conservation and the scarcity of fish has kept the catch stable, with a total of 92 million tons taken in 2001. Still, the pressure on many marine species remains severe. Among other implications, the damage to the world's fisheries, which supply 16% of the animal protein humans consume, poses a health threat to countries that rely on fish for vital protein supplies. Especially imperiled would be Asia and Africa, where fish contribute over 25% of the often already inadequate animal protein in the diet of the regions' inhabitants.

Water

The final resource that we will examine here is perhaps the most basic of all. Along with oxygen, water is an immediate need for almost all life forms. Seventy-one percent of the Earth's surface may be covered by water, but 96.5% is salt water, and 2.4% is in the form of ice or snow. This leaves just 1.1% readily available for human consumption. A significant part of this is polluted, and drinking it poses serious health risks. Moreover, this scarce drinkable water supply is threatened, and the cry "Water, water, everywhere, / Nor any drop to drink" of Samuel Taylor Coleridge's ancient Mariner may foreshadow the shortages of the future. Increased agricultural and industrial use, pollution, and other factors are depleting or tainting water supplies. Freshwater use, after tripling between 1940 and 1975, has slowed its growth rate to about 2% to 3% a year. Much of this is due to population stabilization and conservation measures in the developed countries. Still, because the population is growing and rainfall is a constant, the world needs to use an additional 7.1 trillion gallons each year just to grow the extra grain needed to feed the expanding population.

Complicating matters even more, many countries, especially LDCs, have low per capita supplies of water, as you can see in the accompanying map. The world per capita average availability is 7,044 cubic meters. There are currently 25 countries with an annual availability of less than 1,000 cubic meters of water per person. Given the fact that Americans annually use 1,677 cubic meters of water per capita, the inadequacy of less than 1,000 cubic meters is readily apparent.

Per Capita Water Availability

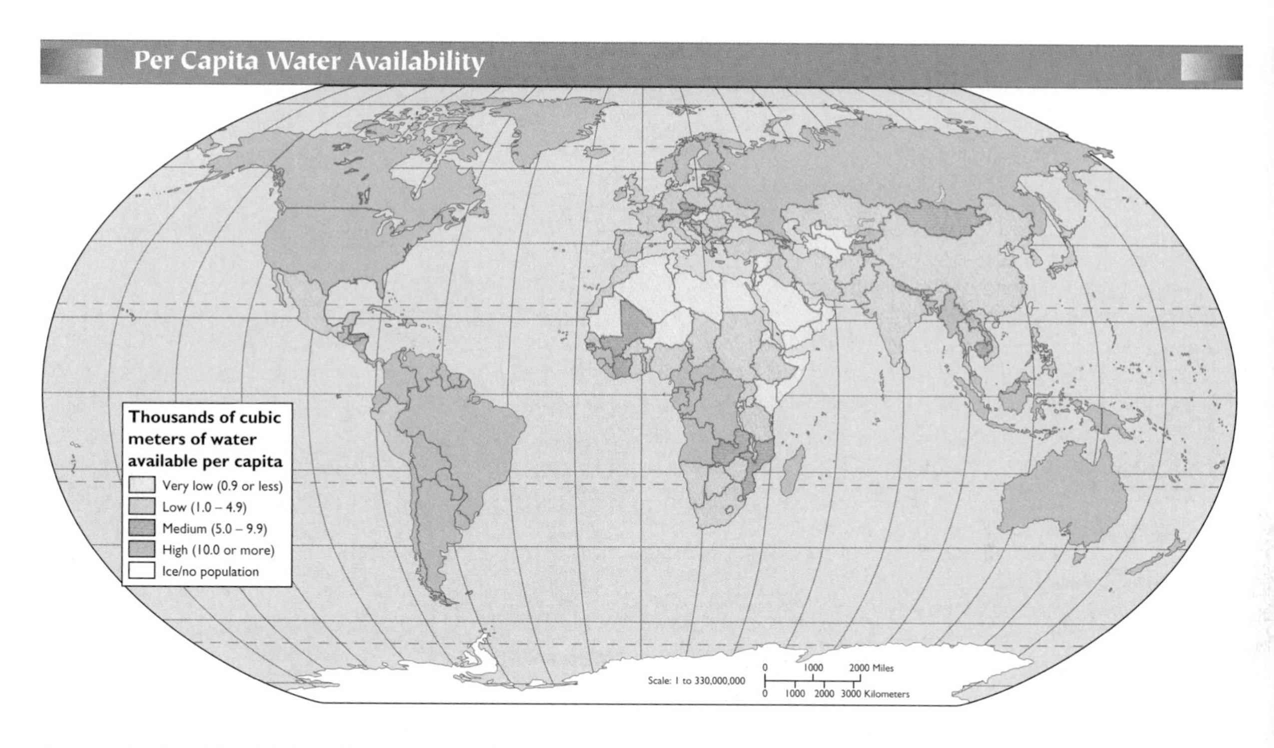

A report by the United Nations Commission on Sustainable Development warns that 1.2 billion people live in countries facing "medium-high to high water stress."

Data source: World Resources Institute (2003).

To make matters worse, the water usage in the LDCs will increase as they develop their economies. These increases will either create greater pressure on the water supply or will limit a country's growth possibilities. Globally, most freshwater is used for either agriculture (70%) or industry (21%), with only 9% for domestic (personal) use. Industrialized countries, however, use greater percentages for industry and more water per capita overall than LDCs. It follows then, that as the LDCs industrialize, their water needs will rise rapidly. China provides an example: Water use for industry, which amounted in 1980 to 46 billion cubic meters, increased 107% to 95 billion cubic meters in 1999. Adding to the problem in many countries, a great deal of the water needed for drinking is being contaminated by fertilizer leaching, industrial pollution, human and animal wastes, and other discharges.

Overall, according to a grim UN report in 2003, the average per capita water supply worldwide by 2050 will decline by one-third, leaving 7 billion people in 60 countries facing a water shortage. "Of all the social and natural crises we humans face, the water crisis is the one that lies at the heart of our survival and that of our planet Earth," commented the director general of the United Nations Educational, Scientific, and Cultural Organization (UNESCO) when the report was issued.[22] Such a projection coming to pass could lead to a competition for water and to international tensions. There are, for example, 19 countries that get 20% or more of their freshwater from rivers that originate outside their borders. The security of these countries would be threatened if upstream countries diverted that water for their own purposes or threatened to limit it as a political sanction. Such possibilities have led some analysts to suggest that in the not-too-distant future the access to water supplies could send "thirsty" countries over the brink of war.

IN THE SPOTLIGHT

The Death of a Sea

There are few stories better than that of the sad fate of the Aral Sea to illustrate humankind's abuse of the environment and its devastating consequences. The inland sea is located between Kazakhstan to the north and Uzbekistan to the south. In 1960, when those countries were still part of the Soviet Union, the sea was the world's fourth-largest inland body of water, covering 26,300 square miles, an area about the size of Belgium and the Netherlands combined.

Then, beginning in the 1960s, Soviet agriculture demands and horrendous planning began to drain water from the sea and from the two great rivers (the Amu Darya from the north and the Syr Darya from the south) that feed it faster than the water could be replenished.

This man and his fishing boat have been left high and dry by the environmental mismanagement that has drained the Aral Sea of 75% of its water. Exactly where it lies now, the boat was once tied to a pier in the Aral Sea port of Munak, Uzbekistan. Now the shore is 50 miles away.

The sea started to shrink rapidly. As it did, the level of its salinity rose, and by 1977 the catch from the once-important fishery had declined by over 75%. Still the water level continued to fall, as the sea provided irrigation for cotton fields and for other agricultural production. The same Soviet planning that brought the world the Chernobyl nuclear plant disaster in Ukraine stood by paralyzed as the Aral Sea began to disappear before the world's eyes.

Now, in reality, the geographical name Aral Sea is a fiction, because it has shrunk in size and depth so much that a land bridge separates the so-called Greater Sea to the north from the Lesser Sea to the south. What was a single sea has lost 75% of its water and 50% of its surface area in the past 40 years. That is roughly equivalent to draining Lake Erie and Lake Ontario. The Uzbek town of Munak was once the Aral Sea's leading port, with its fishermen harvesting the sea's abundant catch. Now there are few fish, but even if there were many, it would not help the people of Munak. The town is now in the middle of a desert; the shoreline of the Lesser Sea is 50 miles away.

Before leaving this unhappy catalog of types of environmental abuse and turning to the happier topic of resource conservation, it is worth noting that damage to one aspect of the environment can also adversely affect others. This is readily obvious in the In the Spotlight box "The Death of a Sea" which details the impact of poor water conservation. Fishery stock depletion, desertification, and salinization are among other disasters that have befallen the Aral Sea and the countries and people on its shrinking shores.

Resource Conservation: The Global Response

While pessimists and optimists disagree about how serious the problems are and how immediate and drastic remedies need to be, it is certain that mineral, forest, wildlife, and water resources must be more carefully managed and conserved. After several millennia of unchecked resource use, people are now beginning to act with some restraint and to cooperate in conservation causes. All the various individual and organized efforts cannot be mentioned here, but a few illustrative examples will serve to demonstrate the thrust of these activities.

Land and Wildlife

Desertification is one area in which the international community has begun to act. Some 100 countries signed the Convention on Desertification in 1994 to coordinate efforts for land preservation and reclamation projects. More recently, 122 countries agreed in 2000 to a treaty that will eventually ban 12 so-called dirty dozen pollutants, such as PCBs and dioxins, which have been linked to birth defects and other genetic abnormalities.

Progress is also being made in the preservation of forest and wildlife resources. Membership in environmental groups has grown dramatically. In several European countries and in the European Union, "green parties" have become viable political forces. For example, they have 34 (5%) of the seats in the European Parliament and Germany's Green Party has 55 seats (9%) in the Bundestag. The growing interest in flora and fauna is also increasing the so-called ecotourism trade, which some sources estimate makes up as much as a third of the nearly $500 billion annual tourism industry. For this reason, many countries are beginning to realize that they can derive more economic benefit from tourists shooting pictures than from hunters shooting guns or loggers wielding chain saws.

Although the world's list of endangered species is still growing, these threatened species are also now gaining some relief through the Convention on the International Trade in Endangered Species (CITES). Elephants were added in 1989 to the CITES list of endangered species, and the legal ivory trade has dropped from 473 tons in 1985 to zero. About 500 elephants a year are still being killed for their ivory by poachers, but that is far better than the annual toll of 70,000 elephants during the last decade before they were protected under CITES. Wild cats, reptiles, and other types of wildlife have also found greater refuge, and the international sale of their skins has declined drastically. The global trade in live primates, birds, and reptiles has seen similar decreases. Individual countries have also acted to suppress poaching and punish those engaged in the illegal sales of wildlife. In late 2003, for example, Chinese officials impounded 1,276 illegal pelts from 32 tigers, 579 leopards, and 665 otters that had been smuggled into the country. It was the largest seizure in China's history, and a particularly helpful sign from a region that is the destination of a great deal of the illegal trade in wildlife, especially in parts used in traditional medicine. Penalties, it should be noted, are especially stringent for such activity in China, which has executed 28 wildlife smugglers since 1990.

The Seas and Fisheries

One major step at the international level came in 1994 when the UN's convention on the Law of the Sea went into effect. Agreed to by 145 countries, not including the United States, the treaty gives countries full sovereignty over the seas within 12 miles of their shores and control over fishing rights and oil- and gas-exploration rights within 200 miles of their shores. That should help improve conservation in these coastal zones. Additionally, an International Seabed Authority, headquartered in Jamaica, has been established. It will help regulate mining of the seabed in international waters and will receive royalties from those mining operations to help finance ocean-protection programs.

National and international efforts are also being made in other areas. A 64% decline between the mid-1980s and the mid-1990s in the catch of demersal fish (such as cod, flounder, and haddock) in the northwest Atlantic prompted both Canada and the United States to severely limit or temporarily ban catches in rich fishing grounds such as the Grand Banks and the Georges Bank off their North Atlantic coasts. On an even broader scale, 99 countries, including all the major fishing countries, agreed in 1995 to

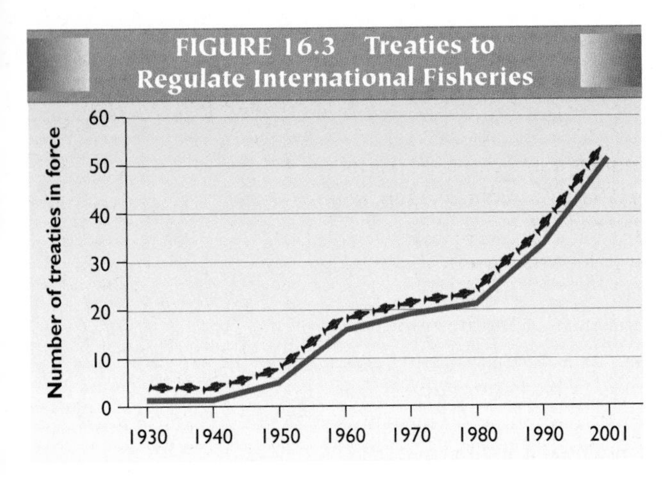

The rapid growth, especially in recent decades, of the number of treaties regulating fishing in international waters demonstrates that countries recognize the danger posed by seriously depleted stock of fish, crustaceans, and other marine wildlife and are cooperating to address the problem. Although the rapidly ascending line is for marine fisheries treaties, it also underscores the upsurge in the number of international agreements in nearly every area of biosphere regulation and conservation.

Data source: Internet Guide to Fisheries Law at http://www.oceanlaw.net/texts/index.htm.

an international treaty that will regulate the catch of all the species of fish (such as cod, pollock, tuna, and swordfish) that migrate between national and international waters. As evident in Figure 16.3, the treaty was part of the rapidly growing number of international pacts to regulate the marine catch that have made fishing, as one diplomat put it, "no longer a free-for-all situation."[23]

Despite its relatively minor economic impact, there is no issue of marine regulation that sparks more emotion than the control of whaling. At the center of the controversy is the International Whaling Commission (IWC), which was established in 1946. Amid outcries against whaling that had often exceeded 30,000 whales a year and decimated their population, the IWC reduced the limits and finally banned commercial whaling in 1986. That did not end the killing of whales, but it did reduce the number of whales killed annually, with Japan and Norway each taking about 650 whales and Iceland taking 36 in 2003. The whaling is done under the guise of IWC rules that allow it for scientific study, but the meat is sold commercially to supposedly pay for the research.

The contentiousness of the whaling issue was evident at the IWC's 2003 conference, as it frequently had been before. Japan requested a significant increase in its "scientific quota," which the IWC rejected resoundingly. Taking a stronger conservationist position than it had in the past, the IWC also established a committee to study and give advice on threats to marine mammals from pollution, sonar gear, ships, global warming, and even whale watching. The IWC's moves delighted some and angered others. A pleased Humane Society International official portrayed the IWC as "moving out of the old mindset—that everything has to be killed—into the more embracing notion that the earth is getting smaller and smaller and we have to treat all our resources with more care."[24] Taking a very different stand, Iceland's delegate to the IWC complained, "It's very clear that conservation is part of it, but conservation is there to ensure the continuation of whaling. It's a means to an end."[25] The representative noted that according to IWC figures, there are about 1 million minke whales, the species that makes up over 90% of the whales taken each year. Some conservationist groups disagree, but even the lowest estimates exceed 300,000. Opponents of the committee charged that the IWC was exceeding its charter by concerning itself with other cetaceans (dolphins and porpoises).

Did You Know That:

In 2003, whale meat was selling for about $11 a pound in Japan and about $7.40 a pound in Iceland.

Whatever one's view of whaling, it is important to note that the overall numbers of most whale species and other marine wildlife are recovering. For one, the Pacific gray whale population has doubled since conservation began, and it is no longer on the U.S. endangered species list. However, whales reproduce very slowly, and it is also true that other species, such as the right whale, with only 400 surviving animals, remain at the edge of extinction. And while Galápagos fur seals, once at the edge of extinction, now have a viable population, a marine oil spill off the Galápagos Islands in 2000 wiped out 60% of the marine iguanas that live there and nowhere else. Thus, what has been accomplished is the beginning, rather than the culmination, of conservation efforts.

One of the themes of this book is the role that you as an individual can play on the world stage, and the protection of marine mammals provides one more example of that. For example, public pressure, which the industry refers to as the "Flipper" factor (after the 1960s TV series), forced U.S. tuna canners to demand that suppliers use dolphin-safe methods of netting to save dolphins. That was followed in 1990 by a U.S. law banning the importation of tuna caught without dolphin-safe methods. Other governments have followed suit. Concern over an increase in the number of dolphins dying as a result of fishing by European fleets led the European Union in 2002 to station observers on suspect fishing boats that may be using methods that do not minimize the chances of dolphins being killed. Other IGOs and NGOs are also involved. The Inter-American Tropical Tuna Commission sponsors a program that stations a monitor onboard all large tuna vessels. The result is that the number of dolphins killed annually has dropped from over 200,000 before 1990 to an estimated 3,000 in 2002.

StarKist DOLPHIN SAFE

Faced with adverse public opinion and economic boycotts, known in the tuna canning industry as the "Flipper factor," Starkist and all other major U.S. tuna canners now display logos, such as this one, to assure their consumers that the tuna are not taken using nets that kill dolphins.

Sustainable Development: The Environment

In the environmental equation on p. 521, the ever-growing world population and its increasing consumption of resources are only part of the problem. The third part of that equation is the mounting waste and pollutant production that comes from the excretions of over 6 billion people and the untold billions of domestic animals they keep for food or companionship and from the discharges of polluting gases, chemicals, and other types of waste into the water, air, and ground by industry, governments, and individuals.

Environmental Issues

The state of the biosphere is related to many of the economic and resource issues we have been examining. Like the concerns over those issues, international awareness and activity are relatively recent and are still in their early stages. Several concerns that have an environmental impact, such as desertification, deforestation, and biodiversity loss, have already been discussed. The next sections will look at ground pollution, water pollution, air pollution, global warming, and ozone layer depletion.

Ground Pollution

The pollution of the land is a significant problem, but the territorial dominance of states renders this issue primarily domestic and, therefore, outside the realm of international action. Exporting solid waste for disposal does, however, have an international impact. With their disposal sites brimming and frequently dangerous, EDCs annually ship millions of tons of hazardous wastes to LDCs. Financial considerations have persuaded some countries to accept these toxic deliveries. Sending old tires, batteries, and other refuse to the LDCs has now been joined by so-called e-dumping, which involves sending millions of the computers that have broken or been discarded overseas for disposal. One news story about such dumping in China described one site there with a "huge mound of computer circuit boards, broken cathode ray tubes and burning plastic components that leak toxic acids and heavy metals into stagnant water systems." Often, to avoid bans on exporting waste, the computers are supposedly exported for recycling. What occurs, though, is that small amounts of valuable minerals (gold, platinum, silver, copper, and palladium) found on some motherboards are sometimes extracted, and the rest of the unit is dumped, where it threatens ground and water pollution and also poses a health threat to the throngs of poor who scavenge in the dumps for anything they might sell. In the view of one NGO report, "The export of e-waste remains a dirty little secret of the high-tech revolution."[26]

Although the practice of, in essence, using LDCs as disposal sites is widely condemned and illegal in some shipping and receiving countries, the UN reports that "the volume of transboundary movements of toxic wastes has not diminished." Even more alarmingly, the report went on to warn, "The wastes are sent to poor countries lacking the infrastructure for appropriate treatment. They are usually dumped in overpopulated areas in poor regions or near towns, posing great risks to the environment and to the life and health of the poorest populations and those least able to protect themselves."[27] A closely associated international aspect of ground pollution is that it is often caused by waste disposal by multinational corporations (MNCs), which may set up operations in LDCs because they have fewer environmental regulations.

Water Pollution

There are two water environments: the marine (saltwater) environment and the freshwater environment. Water pollution is damaging both.

Marine pollution has multiple sources. Spillage from shipping, ocean waste dumping, offshore mining, and oil and gas drilling activity taken together account for a significant part of the pollutants that are introduced into the oceans, seas, and other international waterways. Petroleum is a particular danger. Spills from tankers, pipelines, and other parts of the transportation system during the 1990s dumped an annual average of 110,000 tons of oil into the water, and discharges from offshore drilling account for another 20,000 tons. The flow of oil from seepage and dumpsites on land or oil discharge into inland waters making their way to the ocean is yet another large man-made source, with these sources annually adding about 41,000 tons of oil to the marine environment. Some spills are spectacular, such as the August 2003 grounding on Pakistan's coast of the Greek oil tanker *Tasman Spirit,* which spilled 28,000 tons (7.5 million gallons), but less noticed are the many smaller spills that add to the damage.

Many of the world's lakes, rivers, and oceans have been befouled by the dumping of trash, garbage, and untreated sewage. As this almost darkly humorous photograph taken at the bottom of the Red Sea in 2003 illustrates, people have even discarded their toilet bowls into the Earth's waters.

Another major part of the marine pollution is carried by the rivers, which serve as highways that carry human sewage, industrial waste, pesticide and fertilizer runoff, petroleum spillage, and other pollutants into the seas. One of the worst sources is fertilizers, and their global use has grown from about 40 million metric tons a year in 1960 to some 156 million metric tons annually in the late 1990s. Another major source is the exploding world population, which creates ever more intestinal waste. Many coastal cities are not served by sewage treatment facilities. Sewage is the major polluter of the Mediterranean and Caribbean seas and the ocean regions off East Africa and Southeast Asia. Industrial waste is also common. Adding to the problem, ships, coastal cities, business, and others with trash to dispose have long found the marine waters a cheap and seemingly out-of-sight place to dump garbage and all sorts of debris.

Of these pollutants, the influx of excess nitrogen into the marine system is especially damaging. Human activities, such as using fertilizers and burning fossil fuels, add about 210 million metric tons to the

140 million metric tons generated by natural processes. Excess nitrogen stimulates eutrophication, the rapid growth of algae and other aquatic plants. When these plants die in their natural cycle, the decay process strips the water of its dissolved oxygen, thereby making it less and less inhabitable for aquatic plants, fish, and other marine life. To make matters worse, some algae blooms are toxic and take a heavy toll on fish, birds, and marine mammals. The Baltic Sea, Black Sea, the Caribbean, Mediterranean Sea, and other partly enclosed seas have been heavily afflicted with eutrophication, and even ocean areas such as the northeast and northwest coasts of the United States have seen a significant increase in the number of algae blooms in the last quarter century. Inasmuch as 99% of all commercial fishing is done within 200 miles of continental coasts, such pollution is especially damaging to fishing grounds.

Freshwater pollution of lakes and rivers is an international as well as a domestic issue. The discharge of pollutants into lakes and rivers that form international boundaries (the Great Lakes, the Rio Grande) or that flow between countries (the Rhine River) is a source of discord. Additionally, millions of tons of organic material and other pollutants that are dumped into the inland rivers around the world eventually find their way to the ocean. Freshwater pollution is also caused by acid rain and other contaminants that drift across borders.

Air Pollution

The world's air currents ignore national boundaries, making air pollution a major international concern. To illustrate the many sources of air pollution and problems associated with it, we will explore the acid rain issue.

Acid rain is caused by air pollutants that contaminate water resources and attack forests through rainfall. Sulfur dioxide (SO_2) and nitric acids from the burning of fossil fuels and from smelting and other industrial processes are the major deleterious components of acid rain. The damage done by acid rain has followed industrialization. The United States, Canada, and Europe were the first to suffer. Especially in the northern part of the United States and in Canada there has been extensive damage to trees, and many lakes have become so acidified that most of the fish have been killed.

Europe has also suffered extensive damage. About a quarter of the continent's trees have sustained moderate to severe defoliation. The annual value of the lost lumber harvest to Europe alone is an estimated $23 billion. The ecotourism industry in once verdant forests around the world is also in danger, imperiling jobs. The death of trees and their stabilizing root systems increases soil erosion, resulting in the silting-up of lakes and rivers. The list of negative consequences could go on, but that is not necessary to make the point that acid rain is environmentally and economically devastating.

The good news is that pollution control in the EDCs has substantially reduced new air pollution. Annual EDC emissions of SO_2, for instance, have declined dramatically. As one example, U.S. emissions dropped almost 50% between 1970 and 2002. The bad news is that the improvement in the EDCs is being more than offset by spiraling levels of air pollution in the LDCs. This is particularly true in Asia. There, rapid industrialization combined with the financial inability to spend the tens of billions of dollars needed to control SO_2 emissions is expected to more than triple annual SO_2 emissions from 34 million tons in 1990 to about 115 million tons in 2020.

Air pollution from sulfur dioxide, nitrogen dioxide, and suspended particles (such as dust and soot) cause about 500,000 deaths a year, according to the World Health Organization. The majority of those are in Asia, where most of the major cities exceed WHO guidelines for suspended particles. For example, compared to Paris, Beijing's SO_2 concentration is 6 times higher, its nitrogen oxides (NO_x) level is twice as high, and its suspended particles measure is 7 times as high. Beijing's pollution exceeds the WHO safety standard for SO_2 by 80% and for NO_x by 205%. There are no accepted standards for the safe level of suspended particulates, but few who have ever traveled to Beijing would claim that its air is healthy.

Global Warming

Many scientists believe—and some disagree—that the Earth is experiencing a gradual pattern of global warming. The cause is said to be the accumulation of carbon dioxide (CO_2) and other gases, especially methane and chlorofluorocarbons (CFCs), in the upper atmosphere. This creates a blanket effect, trapping heat and preventing the nightly cooling of the Earth. Reduced cooling means warmer days, producing what is known as the **greenhouse effect** based on the way an agricultural greenhouse builds up heat by permitting incoming solar radiation but hindering the outward flow of heat.

Global Warming: What We Know Three things are beyond dispute. First, the global emissions of greenhouse gases has risen signficantly. The primary cause has been a significant increase in the emission of CO_2 from burning fossil fuels as a result of the industrial revolution and the rapid growth in the world population. For one or both of these reasons, methane, CFC, and other greenhouse gas discharges have also increased by large amounts. For example, annual global CO_2 emissions more than quadrupled between 1950 and 2000. This connection between industrialization and CO_2 emissions is evident in Figure 16.4.

Deforestation also contributes to increased levels of CO_2 in the atmosphere, since trees convert CO_2 into oxygen by the process of photosynthesis. Thus a sort of double negative is created by burning fossil fuels and cutting down trees. Just one way to calculate this is to compare the CO_2 impacts of an SUV and a big tree. With gasoline putting about 20 pounds of CO_2 into the atmosphere per gallon burned, an SUV driven 12,000 miles a year and getting 15 miles per gallon annually emits 16,000 pounds of CO_2. A large tree can absorb about 48 pounds of CO_2 each year. Therefore, to someday offset their vehicle use, each SUV owner should consider planting 333 trees a year.

> ***Did You Know That:***
>
> The first warning about global warming was issued in 1896 by Swedish chemist Svante Ahrrenius, who wrote that "we are evaporating our coal mines into the air."

A second certainty is that atmospheric CO_2 concentrations have risen. The greenhouse gases emitted into the atmosphere linger there for up to 200 years before dissipating. As a result, CO_2 concentrations have increased 34% since the beginning of the industrial revolution in the mid-1700s. The increase was slow at first, then rapid in the second half of the 20th century. Of the overall increase in the 250 years between 1750 and 2000, 60% of the buildup occurred after 1949.

Third, the global temperature is rising. Scientists estimate that over the last century the Earth's average temperature has risen 0.6°C/1.1°F. In fact, 1998 was the warmest year in recorded history, 2003 and 2002 tied for the second hottest years, and 2001 was the next warmest on record. The five hottest years on record have all occurred since 1997, and the 10 hottest since 1990.

Global Warming: What Is in Dispute Two things about global warming are controversial. One is whether global warming is caused by humans or is a natural phenomenon. As one atmospheric scientist accurately notes, "I don't think we're arguing over whether there's any global warming. The question is, What is the cause of it?"[28] The second issue is whether global warming will have dire consequences or is an impact that will in some cases be beneficial and in other cases can be addressed using modern technology.

Environmental pessimists contend that humans are causing global warming. The third and most recent report (2001) of the UN-sponsored Intergovernmental Panel on Climatic Change (IPCC) notes that "the present CO_2 concentration has not been exceeded during the past 420,000 years and likely not during the past 20 million years." Based on such evidence, the panel reasoned, "Human activities have increased the atmospheric

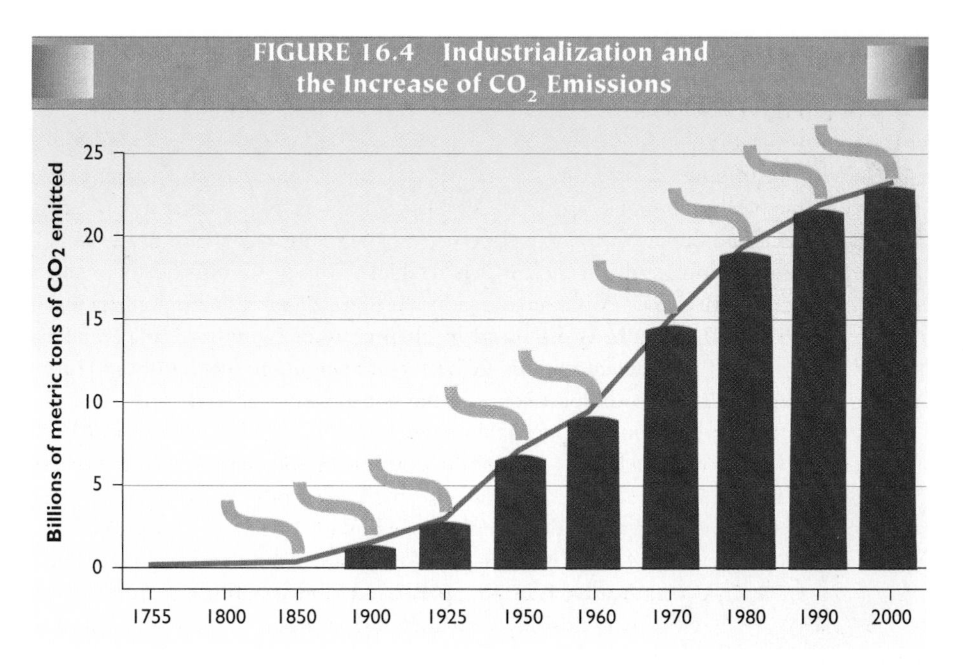

Since the industrial revolution began in the mid-1700s, the discharge of CO_2 into the air by the industrial burning of coal, gas, oil, and other fossil fuels has rapidly increased. The majority of scientists who study this believe that these emissions are creating a global warming effect that is significantly altering the Earth's climate.

Note: The measure used here follows the World Bank reporting of mass of carbon weight, which is calculated by multiplying the carbon element weight used by the CDIAC by 3.664.

Data source: U.S. Department of Energy, Carbon Dioxide Information Analysis Center at http://cdiac.esd.ornl.gov/.

concentrations of greenhouse gases . . . since the pre-industrial era." Given the unprecedented levels of greenhouse gases, the rise in global temperatures, and the role of humans in discharging those into the atmosphere, the IPCC report concluded that "emissions of greenhouse gases . . . due to human activities continue to alter the atmosphere in ways that are expected to affect the climate." The report also rejected natural climate change as the cause of global warming, arguing, "The observed warming is inconsistent with model estimates of natural internal climate variability."[29]

Environmental pessimists are also alarmed about the impact of global warming. The IPCC report concluded that, given current trends, the world's average temperature could increase another 0.8°C/1.4°F to 3.2°C/5.8°F by the year 2100. For comparison, the temperature increase since the last ice age is estimated to be between 2.8°C/5°F and 5°C/9°F. The pessimists believe this change has already altered rainfall, wind currents, and other climatic patterns, and that the deleterious effects, such as the melting of the polar ice caps and the rise of sea levels, will escalate during the coming century as temperatures continue to rise. For example, a report issued in 1999 by the Goddard Space Science Institute estimated that the Arctic ice cover had thinned by 45% over the previous 40-year period, with the size of the ice cover shrinking by about 14,000 square miles, an area larger than Delaware and Maryland combined. According to IPCC, such melting could cause sea levels in different regions to rise between 3.5 inches and 37 inches, with the floods displacing well over 100 million people over the next century. Particularly at risk are island countries, 42 of which have formed the Alliance of Small Island States. The question, as the president of the Maldives, an Indian Ocean island country, put it in an address to the UN Millennium Summit in 2000, is, "When the UN

Did You Know That:

La Niña is marked by unusually cold water in the mid-Pacific; El Niño is marked by unusually warm water in the same region. The term *El Niño* originated with South American fishermen who noticed that unusually warm water would appear some years near Christmas. This led to the name, which means "little boy" and refers to the Christ child. Since La Niña is something of the opposite of El Niño, that name soon came into use.

meets [in 2100] to usher in yet another century, will the Maldives and other low-lying nations be represented here?" Noticing that his five-minute time limit had elapsed, the Maldives' president finished with the thought, "My time at the podium is up. But I pray that that of my country is not."[30]

Important, sometimes dramatic, weather changes are yet another possible peril from global warming. Warming affects ocean temperatures and currents and upper atmosphere wind patterns, which control patterns of rainfall, temperature, and other climatic variables. Droughts could occur in some places; other areas could see much heavier precipitation including periods of torrential rainfall. As discussed in chapter 1, El Niño/La Niña (unusual warming/cooling) conditions are both occurring more commonly and more strongly than in the past. These have been cited as at least one cause of, among other things, deluges that have devastated Central America in 1999 and 2001, drought conditions in Southeast Asia and the U.S. southeast, and the alternating periods of very wet and very dry weather along the U.S. West Coast. In May 2003, Rick Ochoa, head of the U.S. Bureau of Land Management's weather program, predicted a busy wildfire season for the year and added, "We see increasing fire problems because of global warming, we know that drier conditions will exist over the next 10 to 20 years, and we have to figure out what actions to take."[31] He turned out to be unsettlingly correct. Five months later, Southern California was assailed by 13 simultaneous wildfires that charred 750,000 acres, incinerated at least 3,600 houses and other buildings, and killed 22 people. Estimated costs to fight the fires, assist the displaced, and rebuild were about $2 billion.

Global warming is not an abstract concept; it is a reality that affects most people in one way or another. Many scientists blame the El Niño/La Niña phenomena associated with global warming for the alternating very wet and very dry conditions along the U.S. West Coast. In late 2003, such dry conditions in southern California contributed to the numerous and massive wildfires that incinerated vast tracts of land and thousands of houses, caused $2 billion in damage, and killed 22 people. Representing the losses and disruption of people's lives caused by the fires is this photograph of the flames consuming a school zone sign near World High School in Lake Arrowhead, California.

The list of negative impacts of global warming cited by the IPCC is longer, but detailing all of it is not necessary to make the point that the panel projects unfortunate consequences for many. The panel concedes that there have been and will be some benefits, with, for example, areas that were once very dry or extremely cold becoming more agriculturally productive. Overall, though, it concludes that the positive results "are expected to diminish as the magnitude of climate change increases. In contrast many identified adverse effects are expected to increase in both extent and severity with the degree of climate change. When considered by region, adverse effects are projected to predominate for much of the world, particularly in the tropics and subtropics."

Environmental optimists treat the pessimists as alarmists. First, the optimists point out that Earth has natural warming and cooling trends and attribute a good part of the current global warming to this natural cycle, rather than human activity. They note that the Earth cooled somewhat in the 1950s and 1960s, and some predict that the cooling trend will resume over the next few decades. Other environmental optimists do not believe that increases will be huge, either because they will not occur in any significant way or because offsetting factors, such as increased cloudiness, will ease the effect. According to one such scientist, "The prospects for having a modest climate impact instead of a disastrous one are quite good."[32]

Optimists also downplay the damage from global warming. "It should be pretty clear," says one, "that warming to date didn't demonstrably dent health and welfare very much." There is no reason, he added, "to expect a sudden [greater danger] in the next 50 years."[33] Moreover, the optimists predict that some areas could benefit and most could adapt to the changes brought on by global warming (Moore, 1998). Drought in the lower and middle latitudes would ruin some present agricultural areas, the logic goes, but new ones would be created and would prosper at higher latitudes. Farmers in colder regions might have their growing seasons and bounty increased. Moreover, optimists argue that the world can use its technological and financial resources to deal with whatever climate change does occur. Danish scientist Bjørn Lomborg argues, for example, that while global warming is important, it "is not a problem that in any way will damage our future dramatically." According to his calculations, the damage from global warming will come to between $5 trillion and $8 trillion dollars. He concedes that this is "not a trivial amount," but points out that it is not overwhelming. Taking the 2000 world GNP of $31.4 trillion, and projecting it out over 50 years ($1.57 quadrillion), $8 trillion would come to 0.05% of that total.

Global Warming: What to Do? The key issue in the global warming debate is what to do. Keep in mind that stabilizing emissions at current levels or even cutting them back marginally will not solve the problem. Doing that would only keep the growth of global warming steady or slightly slow it. Stopping it requires significant reductions in the emission of global gases. Economic cost cuts both ways. In the long run, addressing global warming may have great financial benefits such as reduced energy costs and significant savings from dealing with the damage done by fires, storms, and other perils associated with global warming. In the short term, however, the costs will be substantial, requiring spending to clean emissions, develop alternative energy sources, enhance mass transportation, offset losses to companies and workers harmed by energy consumption and emission targets, and otherwise pay for all that needs to be done. Spending the money to reduce emissions in the EDCs without financially helping the LDCs to achieve similar cuts would be like shutting one window in a two-window room to keep out the cold. Citizens would bear these costs through higher taxes and higher costs for the products they consume. Lifestyle is another factor. To reverse global warming, people will not have to revert to living in unheated caves, eating raw meat, and walking everywhere. But the day of the SUV could surely be over. Vehicles will have to be much more fuel efficient, mass transit into and within cities might be mandatory, and, in general people would have to turn down the heat, wear warmer sweaters in winter, and make many other adjustments large and small in how they live throughout the year. Safety is yet another factor. Greater reliance on nuclear energy might be needed as coal-fired and oil-fired generators are shut down. Environmentalists claim that with enough investment solar power and other clean energy sources can meet needs. But that would take time and the theory has not been clearly demonstrated on a large scale.

Not making a concerted effort to reverse global warming also gives one pause. There are growing immediate costs. As noted just the fires in Southern California in October 2003 cost $2 billion, and the blazes there consumed only about 10% of the 7 million acres that burned in the United States during 2003. The budget that President Bush submitted to Congress in early 2004 called for spending $2.2 billion for wildfire prevention and firefighting, a 10% increase over the year before. Other costs are less obvious, including the increased cost of food due to crop losses from adverse weather and increased insurance costs to help offset the payouts for fire and storm damage. Even if you do not live in one of the houses that burned, not addressing global warming can affect your lifestyle. It is hyperbole to say that skiers could become an endangered species, but they already have to search harder for snow. A 2003 UNEP report that focused on

YOU BE THE PLAYWRIGHT

Considering Kyoto

Concern about global warming grew to a point that in 1992 most of the countries of the world concluded the United Nations Framework Convention on Climate Change (UNFCCC). In it they agreed to take steps domestically to ease pressure on the climate and engage in negotiations to establish an international approach to address the problem. At the third round of discussions, which were held in Kyoto, Japan, in 1997, the conferees drafted a protocol (supplement) to the UNFCCC called the Kyoto Protocol.

The negotiations at Kyoto were intense. Often the divisions were along North-South lines. Some proposals wanted the EDCs to cut emissions by 12% to 15% by 2012, a standard many EDCs found unacceptable. The LDCs wanted promises of massive aid to help them stem pollution; the EDCs were reluctant to make specific commitments. The EDCs did not expect the LDCs to meet the same stringent targets, they did want some upper limits on future emissions. As President Bill Clinton put the U.S. position, there had to be "meaningful participation by key developing nations."[1] To this, Mark Mwandosya of Tanzania, who headed the LDC caucus in Kyoto, rejoined, "Very many of us are struggling to attain a decent standard of living for our people. And yet we are constantly told that we must share in the effort to reduce emissions so that industrialized countries can continue to enjoy the benefits of their wasteful lifestyle."[2]

The final agreement requires the EDCs to reduce greenhouse gas emissions by about 7% below their 1990 levels by 2012. The protocol also allows the EDCs to trade emissions quotas among themselves. If, say, the United States fails to meet its goal, it can buy emissions quota units from another EDC that has exceeded its goal. The pact relies on good conscience; there are no sanctions for failure to meet the standards. EDCs can also earn credits for excess omissions by funding projects in LDCs that reduce the emission of greenhouse gases or otherwise promote sustainable development. As for the LDCs, they were encouraged to do what they can but exempted from specific targets for reducing emissions. The negotiators decided that the agreement would go into effect when ratified by at least 55 countries representing at least 55% of the world's emissions of greenhouse gases at that point. At the end of 2003 the protocol had still not gone into force. It had 120 ratifications, but those countries represented only 40.2% of the global CO_2 emissions, leaving ratification 14.8% short.

Most of the EDCs including Canada, France, Germany, Great Britain, Italy, and Japan have ratified the Kyoto Protocol. The easiest way to put the treaty into force would be to have it ratified by the United States, whose emissions were calculated at 36.2% under the protocol. Russia is the other major emitter (17.4%) that has not ratified, and it also could single-handedly meet the ratification standard. The question here is whether the United States should join with the other EDCs and ratify the Kyoto Protocol or continue to reject it.

ski resorts in Europe's Alps, the United States, and Canada concluded that in the foreseeable future, "many resorts, particularly the traditional, lower altitude resorts of Europe, will be either unable to operate as a result of lack of snow or will face additional costs, including artificial snowmaking, that may render them uneconomic."[34] The study concluded that any ski resort lower than about 4,300 feet was imperiled by a future of unreliable snow.

Amid all these economic and social costs, it is certain that neither alternative—doing something significant or not doing so—is risk free or cost free. Yet policy decisions have to be made, and if the choice is to do little or nothing, then it is better to take that option consciously than by inert default. Given the stakes, it is hardly a surprise that the choice is intricately entwined in politics, and that interaction and the policy issue are considered in the You Be the Playwright box "Considering Kyoto."

Ozone Layer Depletion

In contrast to the debate over global warming, there is little doubt about the depletion of the ozone layer and the damage that it causes. Atmospheric ozone (O_3) absorbs ultraviolet (UV) rays from the sun, and, without the ozone layer 10 to 30 miles above the

The protocol was greeted in the United States by caustic condemnation in many quarters. A representative of a U.S. business denounced the protocol as "unilateral economic disarmament [by the EDCs]." Republican leaders in Congress also criticized it. The Senate GOP leader declared that Congress "will not ratify a flawed treaty," and the Speaker of the House called it an "outrage" that would cripple the U.S. economy.[3] Some in the United States applauded the agreement, and Senator John Kerry (D-MA) chastised opponents of the protocol for using "Chicken Little" scare tactics. These are "the very same people who spent millions of dollars opposing the Clean Air Act, the very same people who told America that that would be the end of our economy, that [the U.S. automobile industry] would shut down."[4] Although the United States finally signed the protocol, the level of criticism and the approaching presidential election persuaded Clinton not to submit the pact to the Senate for ratification.

Vice President Al Gore had been the chief U.S. negotiator in Kyoto, and what might have occurred had he been elected president in 2000 cannot be known. But the U.S. position under President George W. Bush was clear during the campaign. "I oppose the Kyoto [treaty]," he told reporters. "It is ineffective, inadequate, and unfair to America because it exempts 80% of the world, including major population centers such as China and India, from compliance."[5] It was no surprise, then, that not long after becoming president, Bush directed that the United States withdraw as a signatory of the Kyoto Protocol.

In the intervening years, the president has both been attacked and defended for this position. The EU's Environment Commissioner described Bush's position as "irresponsible," and in 2002 the EU formally approved the protocol.[6] Environmentalists and other Americans also joined in criticizing the president. Others supported the president. Writing in early 2004, a former U.S. secretary of energy rejected the "political alarmism over global warming" and argued the "cold, hard facts take the heat out of global warming."[7] For his part, Bush held firm. "The Kyoto treaty would severely damage the United States' economy, and I don't accept that," Bush told reporters. Placing himself squarely in the camp of environmental optimists, he expressed his belief that "we can grow our economy and, at the same time, through technologies, improve our environment."[8]

There the matter rested in early 2004. Going into the presidential election, the incumbent Bush remained steadfast. All the Democratic candidates favored the direction the Kyoto Protocol was taking, although some wanted to renegotiate parts of it. Assume for now that one of those Democrats has won the 2004 election or perhaps that a re-elected George Bush has a change of heart and presents the protocol to the Senate for ratification after the new Congress convenes. You are the U.S. senator from your state. It is your chance to change the script of international environmental policy. How would you vote on the ratification of the Kyoto Protocol: Yea or Nay?

planet, human life could not exist. The ozone layer is being attacked by emissions of chlorofluorocarbons (CFCs), a chemical group used in refrigerators, air-conditioners, products such as Styrofoam, many spray can propellants, fire extinguishers, and industrial solvents. The chemical effect of the CFCs is to deplete the ozone by turning it into atmospheric oxygen (O_2), which does not block ultraviolet rays. This thinning of the ozone layer increases the penetration through the atmosphere of ultraviolet-B (UV-B) rays, which cause cancers and other mutations in life forms below. Scientists estimate that each 1% decrease in the ozone layer will increase UV-B penetration 1.3%. This can increase the rate of various types of skin cancer from 1 to 3%. The impact of this on Americans was noted in chapter 1. Australia and New Zealand have measured temporary increases of as much as 20% in UV-B radiation, and light-skinned Australians have the world's highest skin cancer rate. Another possible deleterious effect of increased UV-B bombardment came to light when a study of the water surrounding Antarctica, over which a 3.86-million-square-mile hole—about the size of Europe and with as much as a 70% depletion of atmospheric O_3—occurs annually. There scientists found evidence of a 6% to 12% decline in plankton organisms during the period of the annual ozone hole. Such losses at the bottom of the food chain could restrict the nutrition and health of fish and eventually of

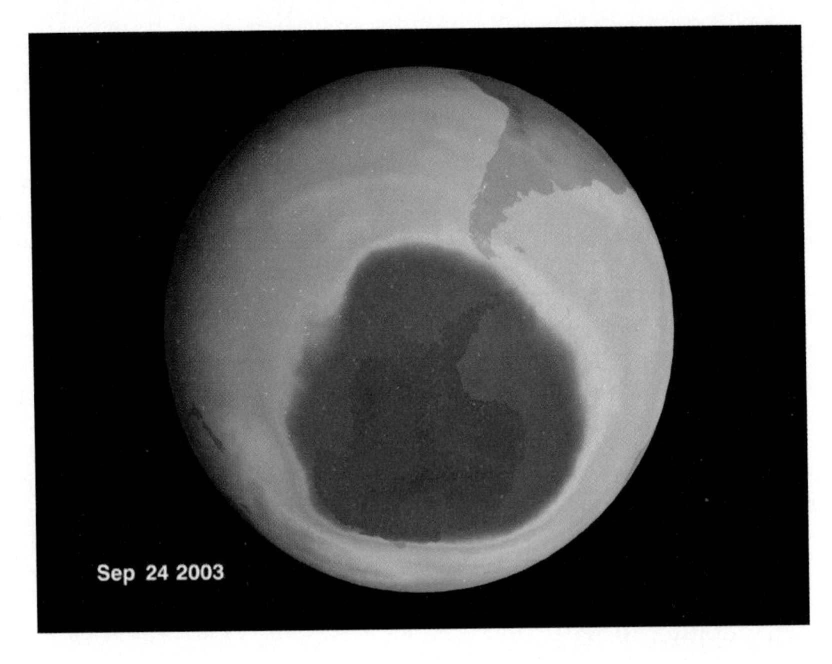

The attack on the ozone layer by chemicals that humans discharge is quite obvious in this 2003 NASA image. The landmass toward the bottom of the photograph is Antarctica. It is clearly visible through the nearly depleted ozone hole in the atmosphere that appears over the continent each year. South America to the north is less visible because it is still partly shielded.

humans farther up the food chain. Ozone levels over the rest of the world have declined less than over the South Pole, but they are still down about 10% since the 1950s.

Environmental Protection: The International Response

Like many of the other issues discussed in this chapter, environmental problems have been slowly growing for centuries. They accelerated rapidly in the 20th century, however, and in some cases they have now reached hypervelocity growth rates. Only recently has widespread public and governmental concern been sparked. The result is that programs are just beginning. Most of the work that has been done has had a national focus, and there have been many advances. In a great part of the developed world, where the problems were most acute and where the resources to fund programs were available, water is cleaner, acid rain is being curbed, trees are being planted, toxic wastes are being dealt with better, recycling is under way, and a host of other positive programs have stemmed and sometimes even reversed the flood tide of pollution.

There has also been progress at the international level. There are many IGOs and NGOs that focus on one or more environmental programs. The UN has become involved in a number of environmental efforts. These began with the 1972 Conference on the Human Environment in Stockholm, which led to the establishment of the United Nations Environmental Programme (UNEP). The work of the many IGOs that are concerned with preserving and enhancing the biosphere is supplemented by a vast host of NGOs dedicated to the same purpose. It is also increasingly common for trade treaties, such as the North American Free Trade Agreement, and other international pacts to include environmental protection clauses. Additionally, countless local organizations and even individuals are involved in international environmental activism.

Protecting the Ozone Layer

Among its other accomplishments, the UNEP sponsored a 1987 conference in Montreal to discuss protection of the ozone layer. There, 46 countries agreed to reduce their CFC production and consumption by 50% before the end of the century. Subsequent amendments to the Montreal Convention at quadrennial conferences, the last of which was held in Nairobi, Kenya, in 2003. The major issue was a U.S. move to increase its permitted use of methyl bromide, a pest control. The effort was rejected.

Overall, there is relatively good news on ozone depletion. The annual buildup of CFC concentrations reversed itself from 5% in the 1980s to a slight decline beginning in 1994, only seven years after the Montreal Convention. Somewhat modifying this good news is the fact that the CFC buildup had increased so rapidly in the years before 1987 that, in the estimate of one scientist, "We might be back to 1979 [CFC concentration] levels sometime around 2050 or so."[35]

The scientist might have added "If we are lucky" to that prediction because there are uncertainties. The most important of these has to do with sustainable development and the economic advancement of the LDCs. The substitutes for CFCs in refrigerants and other products are expensive, and the estimates of phasing out CFCs worldwide range up to $40 billion. Therefore LDCs will be hard-pressed to industrialize and provide their citizens with a better standard of living while simultaneously abandoning the production and use of CFCs. For example, refrigerators, which not long ago were rare in China, are becoming more and more commonplace. China has pledged to end CFC production by 2010, but it still has 27 CFC plants operating, and ending production with outside help now would be better than ending it (hopefully) alone later.

Easing Global Warming

Progress on dealing with global warming has been more limited. The reduction of CFCs will have a positive impact because of their role in global warming. The significant reduction of CO_2 discharges will be more difficult. There is increased recognition of the need to act, however, and a UNEP-sponsored World Climate Conference convened in Geneva in 1990 with the CO_2 problem as a major focus. At that meeting of 130 countries, most EDCs pledged to stabilize or reduce greenhouse gas emissions by the year 2000. The United States, however, declined to join in because of concern about the cost and the negative domestic economic impact. The global effort to reduce greenhouse gas emissions was reconfirmed in the Global Warming Convention signed at the 1992 Earth Summit. Further progress occurred when President Clinton agreed to drop the U.S. reservation to that treaty's suggested timetables for reducing emissions.

Progress on that treaty will, however, be difficult to put into effect. The next major effort to give practical application to the goal of easing the threat of global warming came in Kyoto, Japan, in 1997. The events leading up to the conference, its outcome, and the implications are related in the You Be the Playwright box "Considering Kyoto" on pages 544–545.

Addressing Other Environmental Concerns

There has also been progress on a range of other environmental concerns, such as international dumping. The 1989 Convention on the Control of Transboundary Movements of Hazardous Wastes and Their Disposal (the Basel Convention), signed by 105 countries in Switzerland, limits such activity. In 1991 almost all African states signed the Bamako Convention in Mali banning the transboundary trade in hazardous wastes on their continent. The limits in the Basel Convention were stiffened further in reaction to the continued export of hazardous wastes under the guise of declaring that the materials were meant for recycling or as foreign aid in the form of recoverable materials. Great Britain alone exported 105,000 tons of such toxic foreign aid in 1993 to 65 LDCs, a practice that one British opposition leader called the "immoral . . . dumping of our environmental problems in someone else's backyard."[36] As of January 1, 1998, all such shipments for recycling and recovery purposes were banned.

Less developed countries are becoming more adamant about not accepting toxic wastes from industrialized countries. At the same time, these latter countries are closing their own dumps. The question is, Where will the oil-soaked rags, the soiled Pampers, and the rest of humanity's waste products go?

While the control of some areas of environmental concern, such as greenhouse gases, has been frustratingly slow, other areas have shown much better progress. Preventing oil spills in the oceans and seas is one such bright spot, with overall incidents in the early 2000s down 77% from the 1970s and large spills down 89% during the period.

Note: All spills are those reported over 7 tons. Large spills are those over 700 tons. 2000s is through 2002.

Data source: International Tanker Owners Pollution Federation, "Oil Tanker Spill Statistics," at www.itopf.com/stats03.pdf.

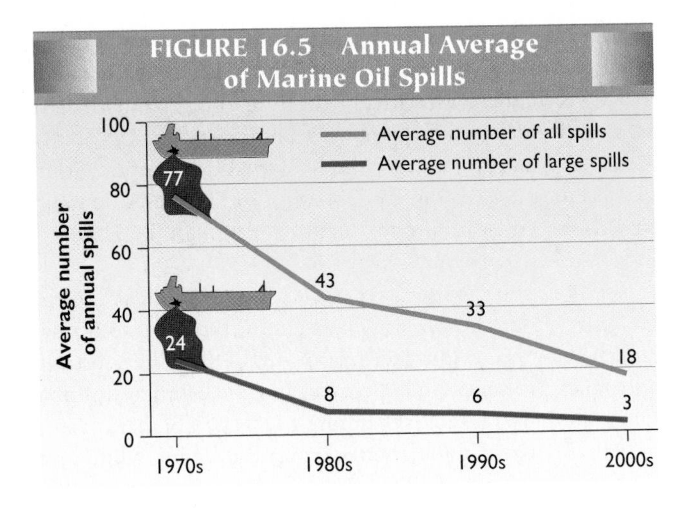

Marine pollution has also been on the international agenda for some time, and progress has been made. One of the first multilateral efforts was the International Convention for the Prevention of Pollution from Ships. More recently, 43 countries, including the world's largest industrial countries, agreed in 1990 to a global ban on dumping industrial wastes in the oceans. It went into effect in 1995. The countries also agreed not to dispose of nuclear waste in the oceans. These efforts have made a dramatic difference for marine oil spills as Figure 16.5 demonstrates. During the 1970s, the average year saw 312,000 tons of oil spew into the oceans and seas; that spillage was down to 33 tons a year during 2000–2002. National governments are also taking valuable enforcement steps, with, for instance, the U.S. Justice Department fining 10 cruise lines a total of $48.5 million between 1993 and 2002.

After reading this chapter and the chapters on international law, international organization, arms control, and economic cooperation, it is easy to be discouraged. The problems are immense and complex; barriers to cooperation are formidable; failure to find solutions carries potentially dire consequences. And sometimes when you begin to think that you are making progress, as the world has in recent years, a setback occurs. Still, the world must and does continue to try to preserve and improve the condition of the Earth and its people. It is true that the current level of cooperation, when compared with the problems, seems woefully inadequate, but that does not mean that we should despair.

The message here is to avoid the extremes of either unguarded optimism or hopeless pessimism. It is equally unwise to take the rosy "It's darkest before the dawn" approach or the gloom-and-doom approach represented by comedian Eddie Murphy's observation, "Sometimes it's darkest before the light goes out completely."

Don't sell the early efforts that we have discussed in this chapter and elsewhere too short. It is only during the last century, and really since World War II, that the need to cooperate has penetrated our consciousness and our conscience. The intervening years have been a microsecond in human history. In that sense, much has been done. Yet much remains to be done to secure the future, and the microseconds keep ticking by.

This book began its discussion of the alternative nationalist and internationalist approaches to world politics by using Robert Frost's poem about two roads diverging in a wood. The choice of which road to take is yours to make individually, as well as a group choice for all of humankind. Your present and, more important, your future will be determined by the road you follow. It will be hard to turn back. So, as Shakespeare tells us in *Richard III*, "Go, tread the path that thou shalt ne'er return."

Chapter Summary

Toward Sustainable Development

1. This chapter deals with international ecological concerns and cooperation. Self-interest—some people would say self-survival—compels us to attend to issues concerning the world's expanding population, the depletion of natural resources, the increase of chemical discharges into the environment, and the impact of these trends on the global biosphere.
2. A key concept and goal is sustainable development. The question is how to continue to develop industrially and otherwise while simultaneously protecting the environment. Given the justifiable determination of the LDCs to develop economically, the potential for accelerated resource depletion and pollution production is very high.
3. There is a wide range of views about how great the environmental threats are and what can and should be done to address them.

Sustainable Development: Population and Resources

4. Population is a significant problem facing the world, with the global population surpassing the 6 billion mark. The 1994 UN Conference on Population and Development in Cairo marked the latest step in the effort to control population and the associated attempts to improve women's reproductive and other rights. There are also numerous international organizations, such as the United Nations Population Fund, working in the area. The most effective way to control population is to improve the educational and economic status of women and to make contraceptive services widely available.
5. Increasing population and industrialization have rapidly increased the use of a wide range of natural resources. It is possible, using known resources and current use rates, to project that petroleum, natural gas, and a variety of minerals will be totally depleted within the present century. The world's forests, its supply of freshwater, and its wildlife are also under population and industrialization pressure. There are many international governmental and nongovernmental organizations and efforts, symbolized by the 1992 Earth Summit, to address these problems.

Sustainable Development: The Environment

6. Population growth and industrialization are also responsible for mounting ground pollution, water pollution, air pollution, global warming, and ozone layer depletion due to atmospheric pollution. Work in other areas, such as reducing CO_2 emissions, has only just begun and is difficult because of the high costs.
7. The efforts at international cooperation in the areas discussed in this chapter return us to the question of standards of judgment. It is easy to view the vast extent of the problems facing the globe, to measure the limited effort being made to resolve them, and to dismiss the entire subject of international cooperation as superficial. It is true that not nearly enough is being done. But it is also true that only a very few decades ago nothing was being done. From that zero base, the progress made since World War II is encouraging. The only question is whether or not we will continue to expand our efforts and whether or not we will do enough, soon enough.

For a chapter quiz, interactive activities, web links, PowerWeb articles, and much more, visit **www.mhhe.com/rourke10/** and go to chapter 16. Or, while accessing the site, click on Course-Wide Content and view recent international relations articles in the *New York Times.*

Key Terms

carrying capacity
environmental optimists
environmental pessimists
greenhouse effect
sustainable development
UN Conference on Environment and Development (UNCED)
United Nations Conference on Population and Development (UNCPD)
World Summit on Sustainable Development (WSSD)

An Epilogue to the Text/ A Prologue to the Future

Where I did begin, there shall I end.
—William Shakespeare, *Julius Caesar*

So here it is some months later, and we are at the end of this book and this course. Finals await, and then, praise be, vacation. That well-deserved break from your academic labors brings you to an implicit point of decision about what to do with this text, the other course readings, and the knowledge you have gained from your instructor. One option is to sell what books you can back to the bookstore and forget the rest. I can remember from my undergraduate days how attractive an idea that sometimes seemed.

But then, is that really the best option? Probably not. We began our semester's journey with the idea that we are all inescapably part of the world drama. There may be times when we want to shout, "Stop the world, I want to get off," but we cannot. We have also seen that we are both audience and actors in the global play's progress. At the very least, we are all touched by the action in ways that range from the foreign designer jeans that we wear to, potentially, our atomized end.

We can leave it at that, shrug our shoulders, and complain and mumble at the forces that buffet us. But we also can do more than that. We do not have to be just passive victims. We can, if we want and if we try, help write the script. The plot is ongoing and improvisational. The final scene is yet unwritten. We are not even sure when it will occur. It could be well into the far distant future—or it could be tomorrow. This, more than any particular point of information, is the most important message. You are not helpless, and you owe it to yourself and your fellow humans to take an active role in your life and in the world's tomorrows.

The world is beset by great problems. War continues to kill without cessation. The specter of terrorism increasingly haunts many people as they go about their daily lives. A billion-dollar diet industry prospers in many countries of the North due to the fact that many of its citizens are overweight, while in the South, infants and the elderly starve to death in the dry dust. As if localized malnutrition were too slow and selective, we globally attack our environment with the waste products of our progress, and the human population tide threatens to overwhelm the Earth's ability to sustain the people who live on it. Of even more immediate peril, an expanse of nuclear mushroom clouds could instantly terminate our biosphere's more evolutionary decay.

To face these problems, we have, at best, a primitive political system. Sovereignty strengthens nationalities but divides the world. Frontier justice is the rule. As in a grade-B western, most of the actors carry guns on their hips and sometimes shoot it out. The law is weak, and the marshals have more authority in theory than in practice.

There are few anymore who really try to defend the system of assertive sovereignty as adequate for the future. Clearly, it is not. What is less certain is what to do next and how to do it. Cooperation, humanitarianism, enlightenment, and other such words provide easy answers, but they are vague goals. Real answers are difficult to come by. They may involve tough choices; we may be asked to give up some things now so that they will not be taken later, to curb our lifestyle, to risk arms control in the hope of avoiding nuclear war, and to think of the world in terms of "we."

At every step there will be those who urge caution, who counsel self-preservation first, who see the world as a lifeboat. Maybe they will be right—but probably not. We *have* begun to move toward a more rational order. Many chapters clearly show this. But they also show how limited and fragile this progress has been. This is where you come in. Your job is to work to make the world the place you want it to be. It is your job to consider the problems, to ponder possible solutions, to reach informed opinions, and to act on your convictions. Think? Yes, of course. But also DO!! That is what is really important.

We began this study with the thought from Shakespeare's *Henry V* that "the world [is] familiar to us and [yet] unknown." My hope is that this text and the course you have just about completed have made the world more familiar, less unknown to you. What you do with what you have learned is now the issue. Will you treat this moment as an end? Or is it a beginning? Heed, if you will, the counsel of Shakespeare's King Lear:

Be governed by your knowledge and proceed.

Explanatory Notes

PAGE 49. **Some Matters of Terminology: EDC/LDC.** The use of the acronym EDC for economically developed country is not common in the literature. I am using "economically developed" here instead of simply "developed" in order to stress the economic factor and to avoid the all-too-common stereotype of the countries of the South as culturally or otherwise inferior. Indeed, the designation LDC, or less developed country, is misleading in the same way. Less economically developed country (LEDC) would be preferable, and politically and economically disadvantaged country (PEDC) would be better still, because these terms would recognize that the countries are in a relatively weak international political and economic position. The acronym LDC, however, is so common that I will continue to use it. The South is also referred to frequently as the Third World, although this term is rapidly becoming outmoded. It has been used somewhat inconsistently, but it generally has meant LDCs, especially those not aligned with either of the two superpowers during the cold war era. It may seem odd to refer to Third World countries when we do not refer to Second World ones, but the term has been useful to designate those countries that are not only politically and economically disadvantaged but that have invariably suffered through or are still undergoing a direct or an indirect colonial experience. It would be reasonable, therefore, to classify many of the former Soviet republics as Third World countries. Poor, mostly Muslim Uzbekistan, for example, was until recently something of a colony of the Russian-dominated Soviet state. The point is that such countries, many of which have had unfortunate experiences with politically and militarily powerful EDCs, share similar views of EDCs and their alleged role in causing and maintaining the LDCs' unjust economic and politically disadvantaged status. Finally, some analysts have used the words "core" and "periphery" to designate, respectively, those countries with power as being at the center of the political system and those without much power on the margins. These nuances need not concern us here. Therefore, the terms North, EDC, developed country, and core country all mean about the same thing; as do South, LDC, Third World, and periphery country.

PAGE 72. **Names in Non-Western Cultures.** Names in many parts of the world do not follow the format familiar to Americans, Canadians, and others whose names are most likely to follow the European tradition of a first (given) name followed by a family name (surname). In China, the Koreas, Vietnam, and many other countries in Asia, the custom is to place the surname first, followed by the given name. Thus, Zhu Rongji would be addressed formally as Premier Zhu. Given the greater formality followed in China (and most of the rest of the world) compared to the United States, only Zhu's family and very close friends would call him Rongji. Japan presents something of a twist on this practice. Like most other North and East Asian people, the Japanese in their own usage place the surname first. But the very externally oriented Japanese have long practiced putting the given name first in all communications with the outside world. Thus internally in Japanese characters, the Japanese would refer to their prime minister as Koizumi (surname) Junichiro (given name). Externally in English or other languages, he would be designated Junichiro Koizumi. There are also countries in which only one name is used. Najibullah is the entire name of the Soviet-backed president of Afghanistan overthrown by U.S.–backed rebels in 1992. In somewhat the same way, the familiar name of Saddam Hussein of Iraq creates some confusion. Originally, he was given his father's name (Hussein) coupled with what could be construed as a surname, al-Takrit, after the Takrit region of his home in Iraq. The designation "Saddam" is not a name as such. Rather it is an adopted political appellation meaning "one who confronts." In this way, he was President Hussein, but his familiar name is also Hussein. Finally, Spanish-heritage surnames often have longer and shorter versions that relate to family and origin. The full name of the Mexican president elected in 2000 is Vicente Fox Quesada. After the first long form he would be referred to as President Fox. In the same way, former Costa Rican president and 1987 Nobel Peace Prize winner Oscar Arias Sanchez is President Arias.

PAGE 308. **The Conditions for Military Success.** Elements for success are those of George, Hall, and Simons (1971), which include (1) strong U.S. determination, (2) a less determined opponent, (3) clear U.S. goals, (4) a sense of urgency to accomplish these goals, (5) adequate domestic political support, (6) usable military options, (7) fear of U.S. escalation by the opponent, and (8) clarity concerning terms of the peaceful settlement. Other elements of success have been provided by Blechman and Kaplan (1978) and include (1) the opponent finds the threat credible, (2) the opponent is not yet fully committed to a course of action, (3) the goal is maintaining the authority of a particular regime abroad, (4) force is used to offset force by an opponent, (5) the goal is to have an opponent continue current behavior, that is, to deter a change in behavior, (6) the action is consistent with prior policy, (7) there has been previous U.S. action in the area, (8) U.S. involvement begins early in the crisis, (9) military action is taken rather than threatened, and (10) strategic forces become involved, thus signaling seriousness of purpose. Caspar Weinberger's six criteria included (1) vital U.S. interests must be at stake, (2) there must be a clear intention of winning, (3) political and military objectives must be clearly defined, (4) sufficient military force must be employed to gain the objective, (5) there must be reasonable congressional and public support, and (6) combat should be a last resort. General Colin Powell's comments, made during a press interview, were not as easily enumerated as Weinberger's, but they generally agreed with the criteria of the then–secretary of defense. Powell's views can be found in the *New York Times,* September 29, 1992.

PAGE 374. **Economics: Technical Terms and Sources.** The terms *gross national product* (GNP) and *gross domestic product* (GDP) are similar but not interchangeable. GNP measures the sum of all goods and services produced by a country's nationals whether they are in the country or abroad. Thus GNP includes data such as the profits of a country's MNCs. Some sources, such as the World Bank, use the term "gross national income" (GNI) to refer to GNP. By the same logic, GNP does not include profits from production in one's country by foreign MNCs. GDP includes only income within a country (by both nationals and foreigners) and excludes foreign earnings of a country's nationals. The fact that some countries report only GNP and others report only GDP creates slight statistical comparison anomalies.

The most recent change in calculating a country's production of wealth is the addition of "purchasing power parity" (PPP) to the calculation. Because GDP or GNP is expressed in a single currency, usually the U.S. dollar, it does not fully account for the difference in prices for similar goods and services in different countries. Some countries are more expensive than the United States. Refer to the box "GNP-PPP" on page 381 for a complete explanation of GNP-PPP. There is certainly value to PPP adjustments, but this book uses unadjusted figures. Using both adjusted and unadjusted figures would created more confusion than clarity, and the reason for using the unadjusted GDP/GNP is that since many of the industrial and technological products that LDCs wish to acquire come from abroad, the cost to the LDC is not affected by PPP. A U.S. tractor that costs $50,000, costs $50,000 whether you buy it in the United States or Kenya. Therefore, PPP masks the gap in international purchasing power between LDCs and EDCs and inflates the economic position of LDCs compared to EDCs in the world economy.

All monetary values in this book are in current U.S. dollars (US$), unless otherwise noted. There are two ways to express monetary values. One is in current dollars, which means the value of the dollar in the year reported. Because of inflation, using current dollars means that, for example, the percentage increase in *value* of exports will rise faster than the percentage increase in the *volume* of exports over any period. The second way to express monetary value is in *real dollars,* or uninflated dollars. This means that the currency is reported in terms of what it would have been worth in a stated year. In this book, monetary value is in current U.S. dollars except where noted. Therefore, you could say either that a car in 2004 cost $15,395 or that (assuming a 4% inflation rate) it cost $10,000 in real 1993 dollars. Note that you figure inflation by compounding the rate, that is, multiplying $10,000 by 1.04 × 1.04 × 1.04. . . . The number 100 is used as a baseline in many of the figures in this and other chapters. It is used to show relative change. This number is an abstraction and has no value as such. It simply allows comparisons of later growth or decline. It is used instead of zero to avoid pluses and minuses before subsequent data. For example, if you earned $5,000 in 1993 and a friend earned $7,000, and you wished to compare later earning growth, you would make 1993 earnings for both of you equal to 100. Then, if in 2004 you earned $8,000, but your friend earned only $4,000 (using increments of 10 to equal each $1,000), your earnings would be expressed as 130 and your friend's earnings would be 70. You may find that the data, such as trade expressed in dollars, used in this book for any given year or period varies somewhat from what is cited by another source. Most of the data is based on extensive compilations and complex calculations completed by the sources cited or by the author. But the reporting organizations, such as the U.S. government, the United Nations, the IMF, the World Bank, and GATT all use slightly different assumptions and inputs in calculating their final figures. Most of the major sources used herein include careful discussion of exactly how they arrive at their conclusions. You may refer to these if you wish a detailed explanation of their methodologies. The key, then, usually is not to focus too much on specific numbers, especially if they come from different sources. Rather it is best to concentrate on patterns, such as the rate of growth or decline of trade over a period of years. Unless specifically noted, this chapter relies on the latest editions at the time of writing of the following sources for financial, trade, and other economic data: International Monetary Fund, *Direction of Trade Statistics,* Washington, D.C.; IMF, *International Financial Statistics*; IMF, *World Economic Outlook*; IMF, *IMF Survey*; U.S. Central Intelligence Agency (CIA), *The World Factbook,* (U.S.) Bureau of the Census and U.S. Economics and Statistics Administration, *Statistical Abstract* of the United States, *World Almanac,* World Bank, *World Development Report,* World Resources Institute, *World Resources.* Several further comments on these sources are appropriate. One is that many are periodic publications. The most current year used is shown, but historical data may also be drawn from various issues in the current or earlier years. Second, some sources of historical data are not shown because of the sheer mounting volume of citation that would be necessary through multiple editions of this study. Where it is not cited herein, historical data sources are cited in earlier editions of *International Politics on the World Stage.* Third, full bibliographic citations for most of the sources listed here can be found in this volume's bibliography.

PAGE 390. **How Exchange Rates Work.** To begin to understand the mysteries of how exchange rates work and the impact of their fluctuation, consider the following two scenarios: the first with the dollar ($) equal to the post–World War II high of 258 yen (¥), which was the case in early 1985; and the second with the dollar equal to the 2004 value of ¥107. For illustration, assume that one automobile costs ¥3,096,000 to manufacture in Japan and another costs $18,000 to build in Detroit. Let us further suppose that an average Japanese worker makes ¥1,806 an hour; an American makes $10 an hour. Manufacturing costs and wages are not directly affected by exchange rates and, therefore, remain constant.

Automobile Imports at a ¥258 = $1 Exchange Rate

- At ¥258 to the dollar, the equivalent cost is $12,000 for the Japanese car (¥3,096,000 ÷ ¥258) and ¥4,644,000 for the U.S. car ($18,000 × ¥258).
- It will take the Japanese worker earning ¥1,806 ($7) an hour a total of 1,714 work hours (¥3,096,00 ÷ ¥1,806) to buy the Japanese car and 2,571 work hours (¥4,644,000 ÷ ¥1,806) to buy the U.S. car. The Japanese worker will probably buy the Japanese car.
- It will take the American worker earning $10 (¥2,580) an hour a total of 1,200 work hours (¥3,096,000 ÷ ¥2,580) to buy the Japanese car and 1,800 work hours ($18,000 ÷ $10) to buy the U.S. car. The American worker will probably buy the Japanese car.

- With both the Japanese and the American worker buying Japanese cars, Japanese automobile exports to the United States will rise and U.S. exports to Japan will decline.

Automobile Imports at a ¥107 = $1 Exchange Rate

- At ¥107 per dollar, the equivalent cost is $28,935 for the Japanese car (¥3,096,000 ÷ ¥107) and ¥1,926,000 for the U.S. car ($18,000 × ¥107).
- It will take the Japanese worker earning ¥1,806 ($16.88) an hour a total of 1,714 work hours (¥3,096,000 ÷ ¥1,806) to buy the Japanese car and 1,066 work hours (¥1,926,000 ÷ ¥1,806) to buy the U.S. car. The Japanese worker will probably buy the U.S. car.
- It will take the American worker earning $10 (¥1,070) an hour a total of 2,893 work hours (¥3,096,000 ÷ ¥1,070) to buy the Japanese car and 1,800 work hours ($18,000 ÷ $10) to buy the U.S. car. The American worker will probably buy the U.S. car.
- With both the Japanese and the American worker buying U.S. cars, exports from Japan will decline and U.S. exports will rise.

Endnotes

CHAPTER 1

1. Robert J. Samuelson, "End of Illusion," *Washington Post National Weekly Edition,* September 17–23, 2001.
2. *New York Times,* December 28, 1997.
3. National Geographic Society, "National Geographic—Roper 2002 Global Geographic Literacy Survey," November 2002.
4. *New York Times,* January 22, 1996.
5. International Federation of Red Cross and Red Crescent Societies, *World Disasters Report, 2002,* available on the Web at http://www.ifrc.org/PUBLICAT/index.asp.
6. *New York Times,* August 28, 2002.
7. *Hartford Courant,* May 4, 2003. The physician was Paul Epstein, associate director of the Center for Health and Global Environment at Harvard University's medical school.
8. Gallup Poll, January 4, 2002, found on the Web at http://www.gallup.com.
9. *New York Times,* November 28, 1995.
10. *New York Times,* August 14, 1992.
11. *New York Times,* July 29, 1996.
12. John J. Mearsheimer and Stephen M. Walt, "Keeping Saddam Hussein in a Box," *New York Times,* February 2, 2003.
13. *New York Times,* October 6, 1995.

BOX, For and Against the War in Iraq, p. 14

1. Quoted in Mina Hamilton, "In Memory of Abbie Hoffman," *Dissident Voice,* May 16, 2003, on the Web at http://www.dissidentvoice.org/Articles4/Hamilton_Hoffman.htm.
2. ABC News/*Washington Post* on March 17, 2003. Data supplied by the Roper Center for Public Opinion Research, University of Connecticut. The question was straightforward: "Would you support or oppose the United States going to war with Iraq?"
3. Dan Reiter and Erik R. Tillman, "Public, Legislative, and Executive Constraints on the Democratic Initiation of Conflict," *The Journal of Politics* 64 (2002): 810–827.
4. Quoted in Alfred M. Lilienthal, "J. William Fulbright: A Giant Passes," *Washington Report on Middle East Affairs,* April/May 1995, p. 50.

CHAPTER 2

1. French foreign minister Hubert Védrine, quoted by Joseph Nye from *The Economist,* October 23, 1999.
2. *Moscow Times,* May 28, 2003.
3. *Hartford Courant,* May 29, 2003.
4. *New York Times,* June 1, 2003.
5. For example, see *Public Perspective,* March/April, 2003, p. 20 for a chart of public responses to that question between 1945 and 2002.
6. *Hartford Courant,* September 5, 1995.
7. U.S. Government, White House, "A National Security Strategy for a New Century," released January 5, 2000, and found on the Web at http://usinfo.state.gov/regional/ar/natsec2k.htm#4.
8. *Time,* June 1, 1992.
9. U.S. Government, White House, "A New Security Strategy for a New Century," released January 5, 2000, and found on the Web at http://usinfo.state.gov/regional/ar/natsec2k.htm#4.
10. *Time,* June 1, 1992.

BOX, The Bush Doctrine, p. 49

1. George W. Bush, "The National Security Strategy of the United States of America, a Report to the Nation," September 17, 2002, available on the Web at http://www.whitehouse.gov/nsc/nss.html.

CHAPTER 3

1. *The Sunday Herald* (Scotland), May 13, 2001.
2. BBC News, December 12, 1999, on the Web at http://news.bbc.co.uk/1/hi/world/europe/557700.stm.
3. Richard Hooker, *Western Civilizations: An Internet Classroom and Anthology,* Washington State University, on the Web at http://www.wsu.edu:8080/~dee/WORLD.HTM.
4. *Washington Post,* April 30, 2003.
5. *New York Times,* May 5, 1994.
6. CBS News, November 15, 2002, on the Web at http://www.cbsnews.com/stories/2002/11/15/world/.
7. Robert Dreyfuss, "The Thirty-Year Itch," *Mother Jones,* March/April 2003, Internet edition at http://www.motherjones.com/news/feature/2003/10/ma_273_01.html.
8. Michael Klare, professor of peace and world security studies at Hampshire College, quoted in Dreyfuss, "The Thirty-Year Itch."
9. Michael Lynch, managing director, Strategic Energy and Economic Resources, quoted in Faye Bowers, "Driving Forces in War-Weary Nations," *The Nation,* February 25, 2003, Internet edition at http://www.csmonitor.com/2003/0225/p03s01-woiq.html.
10. *Investor's Business Daily, Christian Science Monitor* poll, April 1–6, 2003. Data provided by The Roper Center for Public Opinion Research, University of Connecticut.
11. *Guardian Unlimited,* April 15, 2003.
12. Steven Kull, *Americans on Expanding NATO: A Study of U.S. Public Attitudes* (College Park, MD: Center for the Study of Policy Attitudes and Center for International and Security Studies, February 13, 1997).
13. *Investor's Business Daily, Christian Science Monitor* poll, 2002. Data provided by The Roper Center for Public Opinion Research, University of Connecticut.

14. "Letter from the President to the Speaker of the House of Representatives and the President Pro Tempore of the Senate," October 9, 2001, State Department Web site at http://usinfo.state.gov/topical/pol/terror/01100909.htm.
15. Transcript of joint press conference, October 21, 2001, on the White House Web site at http://www.whitehouse.gov/news/releases/2001/10/20011021-3.html.
16. *New York Times,* September 17, 1995.
17. *Washington Post,* July 23, 2003.
18. *Washington Post,* July 25, 2003.
19. *Washington Post,* July 25, 2003.
20. *New York Times,* October 12, 2003.
21. Representative James Leach, quoted in the *New York Times,* September 26, 1993.
22. *Washington Post,* January 28, 2002.
23. *Washington Post,* February 1, 2002.
24. Chicago Council on Foreign Relations and the German Marshall Fund of the United States, *Worldviews 2002,* report issued September 4, 2002, found on the Web at: http://www.worldviews.org/.
25. *Washington Post,* March 4, 2003.
26. *Washington Post,* February 12, 2002.
27. *Washington Post,* October 30, 2002.
28. *Washington Post,* January 27, 2002.
29. *New York Times,* September 21, 2001.
30. Fareed Zakaria in *Newsweek,* October 15, 2001, on the Web at http://www.msnbc.com/news/639057.asp.
31. Gallup Poll Web site at http://www.gallup.com/poll/summits/islam.asp.
32. *Hartford Courant,* June 18, 1998.
33. *New York Times,* June 1, 1998.
34. *Hartford Courant,* June 18, 1998.
35. The adviser was Arthur Goldberg. The quote is from Robert Dallek, *Flawed Giant: Lyndon Johnson and His Times, 1961–1973* (New York: Oxford University Press, 1998) as reproduced in a review of the book. Sean Wilentz, "Lone Starr Setting," *New York Times Book Review,* April 12, 1998, p. 6.
36. *Washington Post,* January 27, 2002.
37. Quotes from *Washington Post,* August 10, 2003.
38. Lloyd Etheredge, "Will the Bush Administration Unravel?" June 2001, on the Web at http://www.policyscience.net/.
39. Quotes from *Washington Post,* February 3, 2002.
40. *New York Times,* June 17, 1991.
41. Bush's remarks were made during an interview with Linda Douglas of KNBC, Jim Lampley of KCBS, and Paul Moyer of KABC in Los Angeles, California, June 15, 1991.
42. The quote is from Robert Woodward, *Bush at War* (New York: Simon & Schuster, 2002), which appeared in David Frum, "The Disloyal Powell Should Be Sacked," *National Post* (Canada), November 26, 2002.
43. Colin Powell, PBS Frontline series, "The Gulf War: An Oral History," on the Web at http://www.pbs.org/wgbh/pages/frontline/gulf/oral/powell/5.html.
44. Doug Wead, "Bush Completes Father's Unfinished Business," op-ed piece, *USA Today,* June 15, 2003. Wead was an aide to George H. W. Bush.
45. *Albany Times-Union,* November 10, 2002.
46. Pew Research Center, "Views of a Changing World 2003: War with Iraq Further Divides Global Publics," June 3, 2003, on the Web at http://people-press.org/reports/display.php3?ReportID=185.
47. Press conference, October 11, 2001, on the Web at http://www.whitehouse.gov.
48. Pew Research Center, "Views of a Changing World 2003: War with Iraq Further Divides Global Publics," June 3, 2003, on the Web at http://people-press.org/reports/display.php3?ReportID=185.
49. *USA Today* poll, September 2002. Data provided by The Roper Center for Public Opinion Research, University of Connecticut.
50. Pew Research Center, "Views of a Changing World 2003: War with Iraq Further Divides Global Publics," June 3, 2003, on the Web at http://people-press.org/reports/display.php3?ReportID=185.
51. Richard Brookhiser, "The Mind of George W. Bush," *Atlantic Monthly,* April 2003, pp. 55–69.

BOX, The Decision for War, p. 74

1. Elizabeth Drew, "The Neocons in Power," *New York Review of Books,* June 12, 2003.
2. The letter can be found on the Web site of the Project for a New American Century at http://newamericancentury.org/iraqclintonletter.htm.
3. *Washington Post,* January 12, 2003.
4. *Washington Post,* January 12, 2003.
5. *Washington Post,* January 12, 2003.

CHAPTER 4

1. Gallup/CNN/*USA Today* poll, June 2003. Data provided by The Roper Center for Public Opinion Research, University of Connecticut.
2. *Toronto Star,* August 31, 2001.
3. *Hartford Courant,* April 8, 1994.
4. *New York Times,* May 11, 1998.
5. *Hartford Courant,* September 7, 2003. The remark was made some months earlier.
6. Martha Brill Olcott of the Carnegie Endowment for International Peace, quoted in *The Kansas City Star,* November 26, 2001, found on the National Geographic Society Web site at http://news.nationalgeographic.com/news/2001/11/1126_wireafghan.html.
7. Quoted on the Web site of Consortiumnews.com, February 7, 2000, at http://www.consortiumnews.com.
8. *New York Times,* October 6, 1995.
9. *New York Times,* June 8, 1994.
10. Henry J. Kaiser Family Foundation, Harvard School of Public Health survey, February 2002. Data provided by The Roper Center for Public Opinion Research, University of Connecticut.
11. Chicago Council on Foreign Relations, German Marshall Fund. Methodology survey, June 2002. Data provided by The Roper Center for Public Opinion Research, University of Connecticut.
12. From "Patrie" in *Dictionaire Philosophique,* 1764.
13. *New York Times,* August 2, 1994. The anthropologist was Eugene Hammel.
14. *New York Times,* April 10, 1994.
15. Statement in "Report of the Secretary-General on the Work of the Organization," quoted in the *Hartford Courant,* September 9, 1999.
16. *Time,* March 12, 1990.

17. James's comment was in a letter, "The Philippine Tangle," to the editor of the *Boston Evening Transcript,* March 1, 1899, in reference to the desire for independence of the Filipinos.
18. Wilson's speech to Congress was on February 11, 1918.
19. Harvard's Rupert Emerson quoted in Wiebe (2001), p. 2.

BOX, The Elusive Quest for Kurdistan, p. 110

1. *USA Today,* April 10, 2003.

BOX, J'Accuse! Nationalism on Trial, p. 125

1. The scholars were Karl Popper and Tom Narirn, quoted in Wiebe (2000), p. 3.
2. This widely quoted view is from Einstein's *The World as I See It* (1934).
3. Michael Lind, "Nationalism and Its Discontents," *Washington Monthly,* January 2001, on the Web at http://www.washingtonmonthly.com/features/2001/0112.lind.html.

CHAPTER 5

1. *Time,* June 15, 1996.
2. *Washington Post,* January 29, 2000.
3. The Pew Research Center for People and the Press, "Views of a Changing World," June 2003.
4. *Hartford Courant,* September 19, 1999.
5. *Hartford Courant,* March 7, 1996.
6. Pauline Maier, "No Sunshine Patriot," a review of *Tom Paine: A Political Life* (Boston: Little Brown, 1995) in the *New York Times Book Review,* March 12, 1995, 1–et. seq.
7. All data on attitudes toward European and national political identification in this section are drawn from Eurobarometer 59, Spring 2003.
8. Richard M. Nixon, *Beyond Peace* (New York: Random House, 1994), excerpted in *Time,* May 2, 1994.
9. The Pew Research Center for People and the Press, "Views of a Changing World," June 2003.
10. *New York Times,* August 24, 1994.
11. *New York Times,* June 9, 1996.
12. The Pew Research Center for People and the Press, "What the World Thinks in 2002."
13. Former Syrian prime minister Maaruf al-Dawalibi, quoted in the *New York Times,* June 2, 1993.
14. *New York Times,* February 27, 1998.
15. Gallup Poll Web site at http://www.gallup.com/poll/releases/pr020308.asp.
16. *Washington Post,* October 7, 2002. The poll was conducted in 2002.
17. *USA Today*-CNN-Gallup poll, reported in the *Arizona Republic,* March 5, 2001.
18. Sheik Abdalah bin Biyah, a member of the Supreme Council of Mosques and a professor of theology at King Abdelziz University in Jidda, Saudi Arabia, quoted in the *New York Times,* June 2, 1993.
19. *New York Times,* April 14, 1996.
20. The Pew Research Center for People and the Press, "Views of a Changing World," June 2003.
21. *Hartford Courant,* July 10, 1992.
22. Survey in the *New York Times,* June 7, 2000.
23. *New York Times,* September 16, 1995.
24. *New York Times,* April 10, 1995.
25. *New York Times,* April 10, 1995.
26. David Shenk of the Columbia University Freedom Forum Media Studies Center, quoted in the *New York Times,* April 14, 1996.

BOX, And Never the Twain Shall Meet: Until Now, p. 135

1. *New York Times,* April 24, 1992.
2. Tom McCarthy, chief executive officer of the Asian Basketball Confederation, on the Web at http://www.gluckman.com/NBA.html.

BOX, India, Pakistan, Religion, and the Bomb, p. 153

1. *New York Times,* February 16, 1998.
2. *New York Times,* May 16, 1998.
3. *Newsweek,* June 8, 1998.
4. *Washington Post,* February 15, 2002.

CHAPTER 6

1. Kenneth Roth, executive director of Human Rights Watch, in the *New York Times,* July 1, 2001.
2. Senator Larry E. Craig of Idaho, in the *Washington Post,* August 22, 2001.
3. Representative Ron Paul, *Congressional Record,* July 17, 2001, p. H4022.
4. *New York Times,* February 26, 1992.
5. *New York Times,* June 25, 2002.
6. *The Internet Encyclopedia of Philosophy* at http://www.utm.edu/research/iep/d/donoso.htm.
7. Maurice Glele-Ahanhanzo, UN Special Rapporteur of the Commission on Human Rights. InterPress Service World News, September 20, 1998, on the Web at http://www.oneworld.org/ips2/sept98/ 12_34_035.html.
8. *Le Monde,* May 8, 1998.
9. *Chicago Tribune,* September 28, 2001.
10. *Deutsche Welle,* September 12, 2003.
11. *New York Times,* January 28, 1998.
12. CNN.com, April 20, 2000.
13. The Pew Research Center for People and the Press, "Views of a Changing World," June 2003.
14. All data in this paragraph is from The Pew Research Center for People and the Press, "Views of a Changing World," June 2003.
15. The Pew Research Center for People and the Press, "Views of a Changing World," June 2003. That report and its updates contain data from surveys taken in both 2002 and 2003.
16. *Hartford Courant,* February 25, 1994.
17. All data in this paragraph is from Chicago Council on Foreign Relations and the German Marshall Fund of the United States, *Worldviews 2002,* September 4, 2002, at http://www.worldviews.org/.
18. CNN.com, January 24, 2003.
19. Opening statement by Han Seung-soo, president of the General Assembly of the UN, at the International Conference on Financing for Development, Monterrey, Mexico, March 21, 2002, at http://www.un.org/ga/president/56/speech/020321.htm.
20. The report, issued in 2000, is available at http://www.cia.gov/cia/reports/nie/report/nie99-17d.html.
21. CNN.com, April 30, 2000.
22. *Flash Eurobarometer* 133, September/October 2002.

BOX, The Future of Tibet, p. 169

1. CNN.com, May 23, 2001.
2. The White House, Office of the Press Secretary, Statement by the Press Secretary on the Meeting with the Dalai Lama, May 23, 2001, at http://usembassy.state.gov/tokyo/wwwhse0181.html.

Did You Know That, p. 174

1. *New York Times,* July 23, 1996.

CHAPTER 7

1. Declaration of the Twenty-Seventh Annual Ministerial Conference, United Nations headquarters, New York City, September 25, 2003, at http://www.g77.org/Docs/Decl2003.htm.
2. BBC News, February 11, 2003.
3. Valery Fyodorov, director of the Center for Political Trends in Moscow, quoted in the *Christian Science Monitor,* February 11, 2003.
4. BBC News, August 22, 2003.
5. Churchill made the widely quoted statement on June 26, 1954, while visiting the United States. Various papers printed it the next day.
6. Address to the General Assembly, July 16, 1997, UN Document SG/SM/6284/Rev.2.
7. World Federalist Association at http://www.wfa.org/about/.
8. *Manchester Guardian Weekly,* July 27, 1997.
9. *Washington Post,* October 5, 2003.
10. BBC News, July 18, 2003.
11. BBC News, October 28, 2003.
12. *New York Times,* June 28, 2000.
13. Speech by Joschka Fischer at Humboldt University in Berlin, May 12, 2000.
14. BBC News, May 22, 2000.
15. Address to the Council on Foreign Relations, New York, April 22, 1997, UN document SG/SM/6218.
16. Permanent Mission of Germany to the United Nations at http://www.germany-info.org/UN/ un_reform.htm.
17. President Frederick J. T. Chiluba of Zambia, quoted in the *New York Times,* October 23, 1995.
18. Fifty-Sixth General Assembly, November 1, 2001.
19. UN press release GA/9692, December 20, 1999.
20. UN press release SG/SM/8965, October 27, 2003.
21. *New York Times,* March 6, 1995.
22. Address at commencement at the Massachusetts Institute of Technology, Cambridge, June 5, 1997, UN Document SG/SM/6247.
23. CNN.com, March 11, 2003.
24. CNN.com, September 23, 2003.
25. Associated Press wire, October 3, 2003.
26. Associated Press wire, October 4, 2003.
27. Address to the Council on Foreign Relations, New York, January 19, 1999, UN Document SG/SM/6865.
28. James Traub, "Kofi Annan's Next Test," *New York Times Magazine,* March 29, 1998.
29. *New York Times,* September 12, 1995.
30. *New York Times,* December 26, 1996.
31. Address to "Empower America," Washington, D.C., October 16, 1998, UN Document SG/SM/6754.
32. *New York Times,* November 6, 1994.
33. *Time,* October 30, 1995.
34. *New York Times,* July 17, 1997.
35. *New York Times,* October 4, 2002.
36. Address at Princeton University, November 24, 1997, UN Document SG/SM/6404.
37. *New York Times,* January 8, 1997.
38. *New York Times,* September 18, 1994.
39. Kofi Annan, "The Unpaid Bill That's Crippling the UN," an op-ed piece, *New York Times,* March 9, 1998.
40. Hammarskjöld's widely quoted statement is attributed to the *New York Times,* June 27, 1955.

BOX, When Is a Banana a Banana? p. 207

1. Reuters press dispatch, January 12, 2002.
2. *New York Times,* October 6, 1994.

BOX, Much Ado about Something, p. 214

1. *Time,* December 2, 1991.

BOX, Santa Claus or Scrooge? The United States and the UN Budget, p. 218

1. *Time,* October 30, 1995.
2. Worldview 2002 survey, June 2002. Data provided by The Roper Center for Public Opinion Research, University of Connecticut.
3. Fox News survey, February 2003. Data provided by The Roper Center for Public Opinion Research, University of Connecticut.
4. Gallup/CNN/*USA Today* poll, August, 2003. Data provided by The Roper Center for Public Opinion Research, University of Connecticut.

CHAPTER 8

1. Churchill told this story in a speech on October 24, 1928, and it can be found, among other places, in Robert Rhodes James, ed., *Winston S. Churchill: His Complete Speeches 1897–1963, Vol. 5* (London: Chelsea House/Bowker, 1974), p. 5421.
2. *New York Times,* March 7, 1996.
3. *USA Today,* March 18, 2003.
4. *New York Times,* February 24, 1998.
5. The Report of the National Education Commission on Time and Learning, 1994, at http://www.ed.gov/pubs/PrisonersOfTime/index.html.
6. National Center for Education Statistics, *Comparative Indicators of Education in the United States and Other G-8 Countries: 2002* at http://nces.ed.gov/pubsearch/pubsinfo.asp?pubid=2003026.
7. Joint United Nations Programme on HIV/AIDS (UNAIDS) and World Health Organization (WHO), *AIDS Epidemic Update December 2001,* p. 16.
8. Andrei Memin, president of the Public Health Association, quoted in the *Hartford Courant,* November 24, 1995.
9. *New York Times,* May 10, 1996.
10. *New York Times,* June 8, 1997.
11. *Washington Post,* July 2, 2001.
12. *Washington Post,* November 1, 2003.
13. *Time,* July 15, 1996.
14. *Time,* June 13, 1994.
15. *New York Times,* May 29, 1994.

16. *Washington Post,* April 13, 1990.
17. *Washington Post,* January 9, 2003.
18. *Washington Post,* January 9, 2003.
19. *Washington Post,* February 1, 2002.
20. DoD News, February 28, 2003, at http://www.defenselink.mil/news/.
21. *Washington Post,* February 9, 2003.
22. *Washington Post,* February 9, 2003.
23. BBC News, March 31, 2002.
24. CBS News, January 20, 2002.
25. *Washington Post,* April 5, 2002.
26. ABC News online, November 8, 2003.
27. Ambassador J. Stapleton Roy's recollection of what Jiang said. *New York Times,* July 3, 1995.
28. *New York Times,* March 7, 1996.
29. *New York Times,* February 27, 2000.
30. BBC News, February 24, 2003.
31. *Los Angeles Times,* February 25, 2003.
32. Associated Press, March 17, 2003.
33. *New York Times,* March 3, 1998.
34. *Washington Post,* January 28, 2002.
35. *New York Times,* June 15, 2000.
36. *Time,* April 9, 1990.
37. CBS News, September 29, 2003.
38. *New York Times,* February 3, 1996, p. A11.
39. All quotes from the *Prague Post,* November 22, 2002.
40. Hans-Ulrich Klose, head of the foreign affairs committee in the German parliament, quoted by the Associated Press, May 18, 2003.
41. CBS News, January 16, 2003.
42. The letter can be found at http://www.info-france-usa.org/news/statmnts/2003/levitte_us051503.asp.
43. Michael O'Hanlon of the Brookings Institution in Washington, quoted in the *Washington Post,* May 22, 2003.
44. *Washington Post,* February 1, 2002.
45. *Washington Post,* February 2, 2002.
46. *Hartford Courant,* September 18, 1994.
47. *Hartford Courant,* October 14, 1994.
48. CBS News, November 19, 2002. The reporter was Bob Woodward, as reported in his book *Bush at War* (New York: Simon & Schuster, 2002).
49. *Washington Post,* January 9, 2003.
50. *Washington Post,* January 12, 2003.
51. Statement by Han Sung Joo in the *Washington Post,* January 12, 2003.
52. Joel Wit of the Center for Strategic and International Studies, quoted in the *Washington Post,* January 10, 2003.
53. *Washington Post,* December 29, 2002.
54. *Washington Post,* January 9, 2003.
55. KnightRidder News Service, October 19, 2003.
56. *New York Times,* February 27, 2000.
57. *New York Times,* March 6, 2000.
58. *Washington Post,* April 1, 2000.
59. *Washington Post,* November 6, 2003.
60. *New York Times,* March 16, 1996.
61. *New York Times,* March 16, 1996.
62. Vice Admiral Archie Ray Clemins, quoted in the *New York Times,* March 17, 1996.
63. *Washington Post,* September 4, 2002.
64. *Washington Post,* January 14, 2003.
65. Assistant Secretary of Defense Joseph Nye, quoted in the *New York Times,* October 4, 1994.
66. *USA Today,* March 11, 1996.
67. *Washington Post,* January 9, 2003.
68. *New York Times,* April 30, 1988.
69. *Washington Post,* December 28, 2002.
70. *Washington Post,* October 3, 2003.
71. *New York Times,* March 1, 2000.
72. *New York Times,* June 18, 1998.
73. *New York Times,* March 18, 1996.
74. *New York Times,* September 13, 2002.
75. Kurt Campbell of the Center for Strategic and International Studies, quoted in the *Washington Post,* December 29, 2002.

Did You Know That, p. 238

1. *Washington Post,* July 2, 2001.

Did You Know That, p. 261

1. BBC News, June 15, 2001.

BOX, Peace or War, p. 242

1. All quotes from the *Washington Post,* January 12, 2003.
2. CNN.com, December 9, 2003.
3. PBS.org, *Newshour* extra, December 9, 2003.
4. CNN.com, December 9, 2003.

BOX, Presidents and Prime Ministers Come Abroad to See the World, p. 253

1. *Time,* May 28, 2002.
2. BBC, May 28, 2002. The reporter was BBC's Nick Bryant.
3. *New York Times,* August 4, 1998.
4. Representative Larry Craig, October 5, 1998, *Congressional Record,* p. S11405.
5. *New York Times,* February 19, 2001.
6. *Time,* October 31, 1994.

CHAPTER 9

1. UN Web site at http://www.un.org/icty/glance/milosevic.htm.
2. European Court of Justice Case C-285/98, January 11, 2000, paragraph 29.
3. *New York Times,* August 4, 1998.
4. Associated Press, February 5, 2003.
5. *New York Times,* July 9, 1996.
6. *New York Times,* May 5, 1994.
7. U.S. State Department, Bureau of Democracy, Human Rights, and Labor, Country Reports on Human Rights Practices, 2002, released March 31, 2003.
8. *Newsweek,* November 29, 1993.
9. *New York Times,* March 5, 1997.
10. Thomas Riggins, "Why Humanists Should Reject the Social Contract," March 20, 2001, Corliss Lamont Chapter of the American Humanist Association Web site at http:// www.corliss-lamont.org/hsmny/contract.htm. Professor Riggins teaches the history of philosophy at the New School for Social Research and at New York University.
11. Address at the University of Tehran on Human Rights Day, December 10, 1997, UN Document SG/SM/6419.
12. The Pew Research Center for People and the Press, "Views of a Changing World," June 2003.

13. Address at Ditchley Park, United Kingdom, June 26, 1998, UN Document SG/SM/6313.
14. Radio Free Europe release, April 9, 2003. http://www.rferl.org/nca/features/2003/04/09042003175158.asp.
15. Statement to the Sixth African Regional Conference on Women, November 26, 1999 at http://www.uneca.org/eca_resources/Major_ECA_Websites/6thregionalconference/html/conference/speech_angela_ev_king.htm.
16. Taken from the Web at http://worldnews.miningo.com/msub.12.htm.
17. BBC.com, July 4, 2001.
18. CNN.com, June 1, 2000.
19. Remarks by President Bill Clinton, University of Connecticut, October 15, 1995.
20. *New York Times,* June 16, 1998.
21. *New York Times,* August 13, 1997.
22. *New York Times,* June 10, 1998, and June 15, 1998, respectively.
23. *Washington Post,* April 12, 2002.
24. Letter from Undersecretary of State for Arms Control and International Security John Bolton to Secretary-General Kofi Annan. *Hartford Courant,* May 6, 2002.
25. Interview of April 29, 2002, in Judicial Diplomacy on the Web at http://www.diplomatiejudiciaire.com/UK/ICCUK7.htm.
26. Statement of the Islamic Resistance Movement, Hamas-Palestine, issued December 17, 2001, in reaction to the speech of President Arafat, on the Web at http://www.jmcc.org/new/01/dec/hamasstate.htm.
27. Associated Press, October 8, 2001.
28. *New York Times,* April 7, 1998.
29. Kennedy's remark on June 24, 1963, can be found in the *Public Papers of the President of the United States: John F. Kennedy, 1963.*

BOX, *Jus ad Bellum* and Iraq, p. 284

1. All quotes from President George W. Bush are from his address to the nation, March 17, 2003.
2. CNN.com, February 24, 2003.
3. *New York Times,* March 11, 2003.
4. Quoted on the Web at http://www.why-war.com/news/2002/10/12/iraqwarn.html.
5. Phyllis Bennis of the Institute for Policy Studies, quoted in Margot Patterson, "Beyond Baghdad: Iraq Seen as First Step to Extend U.S. Hegemony," *National Catholic Reporter,* December 12, 2002.

CHAPTER 10

1. *Time,* January 28, 1991.
2. The polls were taken by the Pew Research Center, March 2003 and April 2003, respectively. Data provided by The Roper Center for Public Opinion Research, University of Connecticut.
3. Joan Shorenstein of Harvard University's Center on the Press, Politics, and Public Policy, quoted in Sherry Ricchiardi, "Close to the Action," *American Journalism Review,* May/June 2003, p. 30.
4. *Newsweek,* September 24, 2001.
5. *Newsweek,* July 13, 1998.
6. *Boston Globe,* May 9, 2003.
7. *Washington Post,* July 20, 2003.
8. *Newsweek,* November 26, 1994.
9. *Time,* October 1, 1990.
10. *Washington Post,* January 11, 2002.
11. Jacob Heilbrunn and Michael Lind, "The Third American Empire," an op-ed piece in the *New York Times,* January 2, 1996.
12. Charles H. Thomas II, former U.S. envoy to Bosnia, quoted in the *New York Times,* November 29, 1995.
13. *Washington Post,* April 13, 2001.
14. Gary W. Gallagher, "At War with Himself," a review of Michael Fellman, *Citizen Sherman: A Life of William Tecumseh Sherman* (New York: Random House, 1995) in the *New York Times Review of Books,* October 22, 1995, p. 24.
15. *New York Times,* June 17, 1998.
16. Nicholas Berry, senior analyst, Center for Defense Information, on the CDI Web site at www.cdi.org.
17. Agence France Presse, December 4, 2001.
18. Vladimir Diouhy, Czech minister of industry and trade, quoted in the *New York Times,* February 13, 1994.
19. *Washington Post,* November 30, 2003.
20. Interpress Service World News, November 29, 2001.
21. 2001 Report on Foreign Terrorist Organizations at http://www.state.gov/s/ct/rls/rpt/fto/2001/5258.htm.
22. *Washington Post,* April 24, 2002.
23. *Washington Post,* April 24, 2002.
24. The list is available at http://www.state.gov/s/ct/rls/fs/2003/17065.htm/.
25. World Islamic Front Statement, "Jihad Against Jews and Crusaders," February 23, 1998, on the Web site of the Federation of American Scientists at http://www.fas.org/irp/world/para/docs/980223-fatwa.htm.
26. *Washington Post,* January 11, 2002.
27. John Pike, director of the Global Security Organization, testifying before the U.S. Senate Committee on Foreign Relations, quoted in an ABC News report, March 6, 2002.
28. Vladimir Orlov, founding director of the Center for Policy Studies in Moscow, a group that studies proliferation issues, quoted in the *Washington Post,* December 7, 2003.
29. *World Press Review,* September 1996.
30. Associated Press, November 15, 2003.
31. Amy Smithson on the Web site of the Henry L. Stimson Center at http://www.stimson.org/cbw/?SN=CB2001121259; and testifying before the U.S. House Committee on Energy and Commerce, on the congressional Web site at http://energycommerce.house.gov/107/hearings/10102001Hearing390/Smithson622.htm.
32. BBC News, March 22, 2002.
33. Senator Pat Robert of Kansas, quoted in the *Washington Post National Weekly Edition,* October 1–7, 2001.
34. Paul Wilkenson, "The Strategic Implications of Terrorism," on the Web site of the Center for the Study of Terrorism and Political Violence at http://www.st-and.ac.uk/academic/intrel/research/cstpv/publications1d.htm.
35. Bill Christison, a retired CIA official, writing "Why the War on Terror Won't Work," *Counterpunch,* March 4, 2002. On the Web at http://www.counterpunch.org/christison1.html.
36. Elizabeth A. Fenn, "Biological Warfare, Circa 1750," an op-ed piece in the *New York Times,* April 11, 1998.
37. Alan Zellicoff of Sandia National Laboratories, quoted in the *Hartford Courant,* April 2, 2000.

38. *New York Times,* February 25, 1996.
39. *New York Times,* February 14, 2003.
40. Colonel General Lev Rokhlin, quoted in *Time,* June 3, 1996.
41. *Time,* May 19, 1997.
42. *New York Times,* October 26, 1994.
43. BBC.com, August 8, 2003.
44. *New York Times,* July 7, 1998.
45. *Washington Post,* March 12, 2002, quoting Defense Secretary William Perry's 1996 statement.

CHAPTER 11

1. *Labor,* September 6, 1947.
2. U.S. Department of State Web site at http://www.state.gov/www/global/arms/np/mtcr/mtcr96.html.
3. Arms expert Christopher E. Paine, testifying before the U.S. Senate, Committee on Foreign Relations, during hearings, "Treaty on Strategic Offensive Reductions: The Moscow Treaty," July 23, 2002.
4. *New York Times,* May 12, 1996.
5. *Washington Post,* October 21, 2003.
6. Associated Press, November 27, 2003.
7. *Time,* September 18, 1995.
8. *Newsweek,* May 25, 1998.
9. *Pravda,* December 16, 2003.
10. *Hartford Courant,* July 7, 1992.
11. United Nations Mine Action Service, Fifth Meeting of All State Parties, September 2003.
12. United Nations Department of Disarmament Affairs Web site at http://www.un.org/Depts/dda/CAB/smallarms/sg.htm.
13. United Nations Foundation, UN Wire, July 14, 2003, at http://www.unwire.org/News/328_426_6550.asp.
14. U.S. Senate, Committee on Armed Services, hearing, "On the Defense Department Budget for Fiscal Year 2004 and Posture of the U.S. Armed Forces," February 13, 2003.
15. Radio Free Europe, May 21, 2003.
16. *Washington Post,* April 11, 2002.
17. *Congressional Record,* October 13, 1999, p. S12549.
18. *New York Times,* September 12, 1996.
19. *Newsweek,* May 25, 1998.
20. *New York Times,* May 31, 1998.
21. *Washington Post,* March 11, 2003.
22. Organization for Security and Cooperation in Europe Web site at http://www.osce.org/field_activities/field_activities.htm.
23. Radio Free Europe, July 1, 2002.
24. Report of the Panel on United Nations Peace Operations, 2002, at http://www.un.org/peace/reports/peace_operations/.
25. J. Stephen Morrison, the director of Africa programs at the Center for Strategic and International Studies in Washington, quoted in the *New York Times,* May 10, 2000.
26. Report of the Panel on United Nations Peace Operations, 2002, at http://www.un.org/peace/reports/peace_operations/.
27. *New York Times,* January 6, 1995.
28. BBC News, December 17, 2003.
29. *New York Times,* May 4, 1997.
30. *New York Times,* October 3, 1999.
31. German Marshall Fund of the United States poll, June 2003. Data provided by The Roper Center for Public Opinion Research, University of Connecticut.
32. NBC News/*Wall Street Journal* poll, April 2003. Data provided by The Roper Center for Public Opinion Research, University of Connecticut.

BOX, Chained to the Nuclear Rock, p. 352

1. *New York Times,* May 17, 1998.
2. *New York Times,* September 25, 1996.
3. *New York Times,* October 14, 1999.
4. *Washington Post,* January 7, 2002.

BOX, A Grassroots Treaty, p. 354

1. *New York Times,* May 1, 1996.
2. U.S. Department of State report, "Hidden Killers: The Global Landmine Crisis," 1998, on the Web at http://www.state.gov/www/global/arms/rpt_9809_demine_toc.html.
3. CNN, June 18, 1997.
4. *New York Times,* September 4, 1997.

CHAPTER 12

1. Michael Ranneberger, testifying at U.S. Congress, House of Representatives, Hearings Before the Subcommittee on Trade of the Committee on Ways and Means, May 7, 1998.
2. Quoted in Michael Lind, "Why Buy American?" a review of Alfred E. Eckes, Jr., *U.S. Foreign Trade Policy Since 1776* (Chapel Hill: University of North Carolina Press, 1995), in the *New York Times Book Review,* October 29, 1995.
3. Catherine L. Mann, "Is the U.S. Current Account Deficit Sustainable?" *Finance & Development* (a quarterly magazine of the IMF), March 2000, 37/1, on the IMF Web site at http://www.imf.org/external/pubs/ft/fandd/2000/03/ mann.htm.
4. White House press release, May 26, 2002, at http://www.whitehouse.gov.
5. Clinton's remarks were made on January 29, 2000, and can be found on the Web at http://www.usembassy-mexico.gov/et000131WEF.html.
6. *New York Times,* February 1, 1999.
7. Address to the World Economic Forum, January 26, 2003, at http://www.weforum.org/.
8. Address to the World Economic Forum, January 28, 2001, at http://www.weforum.org/.
9. U.S. Federal Reserve Bank of Dallas, *2002 Annual Report* at http://www.dallasfed.org/fed/annual/2002.
10. *New York Times,* May 28, 1998.
11. *New York Times,* November 2, 1996.
12. Testimony of Assistant Secretary of Commerce for Technology Policy Bruce P. Mehlman before the Committee on Small Business, U.S. House of Representatives, June 18, 2003, on the Web at http://www.technology.gov/Testimony/BPM_030618.pdf.
13. *Hartford Courant,* December 12, 2003.
14. Representative Joseph Gaydos in the *Congressional Record,* April 13, 1988.
15. All quotes are from Charles R. Smith, "Rand Report Warns of Conflict with China," June 20, 2001, on the NewsMax Web site at http://www.newsmax.com/.
16. *New York Times,* October 30, 1996.
17. *Washington Post,* May 15, 2002.
18. White House press release, May 20, 2002, at http://www.whitehouse.gov.

19. These and subsequent comments by Queen Noor are from her address to the Aspen Institute, August 22, 2000, at http://yaleglobal.yale.edu/about/pdfs/global_culture.pdf.

BOX, GDP-PPP: The Big Mac Standard, p. 381

1. The Big Mac Standard can be found at http://www.economist.com/markets/Bigmac/Index.cfm.

CHAPTER 13

1. *Boston Globe,* December 10, 2003.
2. Office of the National Counterintelligence Executive. Annual Report to Congress on Foreign Economic Collection and Industrial Espionage, 2001, on the Web at http://www.ncix.gov/pubs/reports/fy01.htm#a.
3. *Washington Post,* December 20, 2003. The analyst was Ray Takeyh, a Libya expert at the National Defense University. The State Department official spoke anonymously.
4. *New York Times,* October 23, 1995.
5. *Washington Post,* May 22, 2002.
6. *New York Times,* May 22, 2003.
7. Robert B. Zoellick, "United States v. European Union," *Wall Street Journal,* May 21, 2003.
8. *New York Times,* April 4, 1991.
9. *New York Times,* March 2, 1997.
10. BBC News, February 12, 2000.
11. *New York Times,* February 5, 2002.
12. This and the following quotes related to the G-77 summit are from the "Havana Program of Action," April 14, 2000, found on the UNCTAD Web site at http://www.g77.org/.
13. *Time,* September 19, 1995.
14. United Nation Foundation, UN Wire, November 21, 2003.
15. United Nation Foundation, UN Wire, November 21, 2003.
16. The annual Index to Economic Freedom is available at the Heritage Foundation Web site at http://index.heritage.org/.
17. *New York Times,* February 5, 2002.
18. Klaus Schwab, director of the Davos Forum, quoted in Thomas L. Friedman, "The Revolt of the Wannabes," a column in the *New York Times,* February 7, 1996.
19. Both quotes are from United Nation Foundation, UN Wire, November 21, 2003.

BOX, Politics, Trade, and the U.S. Steel Tariff, p. 420

1. *Washington Post,* May 18, 2002.
2. Press release, March 5, 2002, on the European Union Web site at http://www.eurunion.org.
3. Economist Bruce Bartlett, senior fellow at the National Center for Policy Analysis, quoted in the *Washington Post,* September 19, 2003.
4. Bartlett, quoted in the *Washington Post,* September 19, 2003.

CHAPTER 14

1. John Kirton, University of Toronto G-7 Research Group, "What Is the G-7," November 10, 1996, on the Web at http:un/1.library.utoronto.ca/.
2. Nicholas Bayne, "Impressions of the Evian Summit, 1–3 June 2003," 2003 Evian Summit: Analytical Studies, G-8 Information Center, University of Toronto, http://www.g7.utoronto.ca/evaluations/.
3. Associated Press, February 5, 2002.
4. BBC News, March 22, 2002.
5. Associated Press, February 5, 2002.
6. Address on March 22, 2002, International Conference on Financing for Development Web site at http:// www.un.org/esa/ffd/.
7. *Hartford Courant,* March 12, 1995.
8. *New York Times,* September 7, 2000.
9. UNCTAD XI section of the UNCTAD Web site at http://www.unctad.org/Templates/StartPage.asp?intItemID=2068.
10. Web site for UNCTAD's tenth meeting at http://www.unctad-10.org/index_en.htm.
11. BBC News, September 13, 2003.
12. BBC News, September 11, 2003.
13. BBC News, September 10, 2003.
14. CNN, September 15, 2003.
15. BBC News, September 15, 2003.
16. CNN, September 15, 2003.
17. *New Zealand Herald,* January 14, 2004.
18. 2003 Leaders' Declaration, Bangkok, Thailand, October 23, 2003, APEC Web site at http://www.apecsec.org.sg/apec/leaders__declarations.html.
19. BBC News, December 16, 2003.
20. All quotes in this paragraph from Inter Press Service News Agency, April 17, 2002.
21. *New York Times,* February 17, 1998.
22. *Washington Post,* January 15, 2002.
23. Jeffrey D. Sachs, "IMF 'Cure' Is Adding to Crisis in Argentina," op-ed piece in the *Irish Times,* May 4, 2002.
24. Artemio Lopez, chief economist for EquisResearch, quoted in the *Washington Post,* May 3, 2002.
25. BBC News, May 26, 2003.
26. *Washington Post,* April 30, 2002.
27. BBC News, September 11, 2003.
28. BBC News, March 19, 2003.
29. Both quotes from Reuters, January 30, 2004.
30. Comments in a speech, January 22, 1999, on the Web at http://www.oneworld.net/guides/imf_wb/front.shtml.
31. *New York Times,* April 18, 2000.
32. Mark Levinson, chief economist for the Union of Needletrades, Industrial and Textile Employees, quoted in the *Virginian-Pilot,* January 14, 2004.
33. Gary Hufbauer of the Institute for International Economics, quoted in the *Virginian-Pilot,* January 14, 2004.
34. *BusinessWeek,* December 22, 2003.
35. *BusinessWeek,* December 22, 2003.
36. *New York Times,* December 11, 1994.
37. Both quotes are from the *New York Times,* December 12, 1994.
38. Address on January 13, 2004, on the White House Web site at http://www.whitehouse.gov/.
39. *Guardian Unlimited,* January 14, 2004.
40. *Washington Post,* January 14, 2004.
41. *Miami Herald,* September 13, 2003.
42. *New York Times,* November 19, 1993.
43. The statements by the head of the WTO and Robert Scollay are both from the *New Zealand Herald,* January 14, 2004.

BOX, Collapse in Cancún, p. 455

1. BBC News, September 13, 2003.
2. Both quotes from the *Washington Post,* September 15, 2003.

CHAPTER 15

1. Both quotes, the second by Robert Repetto of the World Resources Institute, are from the *New York Times,* September 19, 1995.
2. Paul Portney of Resources for the Future, quoted in the *New York Times,* September 19, 1995.
3. The Pew Research Center for People and the Press, "Views of a Changing World," June 2003.
4. *New York Times,* January 21, 2004.
5. UN Population Fund (UNFPA), *Missing: Mapping the Inverse Child Sex Ratio in India,* June 2003, p. 1.
6. *Toronto Star,* January 18, 2004.
7. International Labor Organization, *The Sex Sector: The Economic and Social Bases of Prostitution in Southeast Asia,* 1998, quoted in the *New York Times,* August 20, 1998.
8. International Programme for the Elimination of Child Labour, "Every Child Counts," 2002, on the International Labour Organization Web site at http://www.ilo.org/public/english/standards/ipec/simpoc/others/globalest.pdf.
9. Toronto *Globe and Mail,* August 26, 1996, reproduced in the *World Press Review,* November 1996.
10. *New York Times,* March 31, 1996.
11. *Hartford Courant,* July 7, 1993.
12. The Pew Research Center for People and the Press, "Views of a Changing World," June 2003.
13. *New York Times,* March 11, 1995.
14. Survey by Fox News, December 2003. Data provided by The Roper Center for Public Opinion Research, University of Connecticut.
15. MADRE press release, April 12, 2002, on the Web at http://www.madre.org/criminalcourt.html.
16. *Hartford Courant,* December 12, 1996.
17. Report on the World Congress Against Commercial Sexual Exploitation of Children, taken in December 1996 from the UNICEF Web site at http://www.childhub.ch/webpub/csechome/.
18. Quoted in Barbara Crossette, "Snubbing Human Rights," *New York Times,* April 28, 1996.
19. *Guardian Unlimited,* September 1, 2001.
20. *Guardian Unlimited,* September 3, 2001.
21. Secretary of State Powell on the State Department Web site at http://www.state.gov/p/io/uncnf/wcar/.
22. *Hartford Courant,* September 8, 2001.
23. *Hartford Courant,* September 8, 2001.
24. BBC, September 8, 2001, on the Web at http://news.bbc.co.uk/hi/english/world/africa/newsid_1530000/1530976.stm.
25. Final document of the World Food Summit, November 17, 1996, taken from the Web at http://www.fao.org/wfs/final/rd-e.htm.
26. CNN.com, November 13, 1996.
27. Final document of the World Food Summit, November 17, 1996, taken from the Web at http://www.fao.org/wfs/final/rd-e.htm.
28. United Nations *Chronicle,* 2001, Issue 3, at http://www.un.org/Pubs/chronicle/2001/issue3/0103p12.html.
29. *Hartford Courant,* December 17, 1992.
30. World Health Organization press release, October 19, 2001.
31. CNN.com, October 18, 1995.

BOX, Sovereignty, Democracy, the Shari'ah, and Women's Rights in Iraq, p. 486

1. Both quotes from the *Washington Post,* January 16, 2004.
2. *Hartford Courant,* January 14, 2004.
3. *Hartford Courant,* January 26, 2004.

CHAPTER 16

1. The *State of the World* series is an annually published project of the Worldwatch Institute, with articles by a group of analysts on a variable agenda of issues related to the environment. The 2003 project director was Gary Gardner. The series is published by W. W. Norton, New York.
2. *New York Times,* May 20, 1997.
3. *New York Times,* May 20, 1997.
4. *Washington Post,* February 12, 2000.
5. *New York Times,* November 29, 1995.
6. National Opinion Research Center poll, 2000. Data provided by The Roper Center for Public Opinion Research, University of Connecticut.
7. *Time,* December 12, 1990.
8. *Hartford Courant,* June 8, 1992.
9. *New York Times,* June 12, 1992.
10. *Hartford Courant,* June 15, 1992.
11. Under Secretary of State for Global Affairs Paula Dobriansky, on the Web site of the U.S. Embassy in Indonesia at http://www.usembassyjakarta.org/press_rel/wssd_bali4.html.
12. September 2, 2003, on the WSSD site at http://www.un.org/events/wssd/statements/.
13. Reuters wire story, June 7, 2002.
14. September 4, 2003, on the WSSD site at http://www.un.org/events/wssd/pressconf/.
15. *Time,* June 1, 1992.
16. *New York Times,* August 31, 1994.
17. *L'Observatore Romano,* n.d.
18. *New York Times,* September 6, 1994.
19. *New York Times,* December 31, 1997.
20. *New York Times,* September 4, 1995.
21. Julian Simon, "Environmentalists May Cause the Truth to Become Extinct," an op-ed piece in the *Hartford Courant,* June 15, 1992.
22. *Washington Post,* March 5, 2003.
23. Satya Nandan of Fiji, chairman of the conference that in 1995 concluded the Agreement for the Implementation of the Law of the Sea Convention Relating to the Conservation and Management of Straddling Fish Stocks and Highly Migratory Fish Stocks; quoted in the *Hartford Courant,* August 4, 1995.
24. Executive Vice President Patricia Forkan, quoted in *Time,* June 30, 2003.
25. *Time,* June 30, 2003.
26. Both quotes are from the *Asia Times,* August 8, 2003. The NGOs that issued the report were the Basel Action Network and the Silicon Valley Toxics Coalition.
27. UN Human Rights Commission, UN Document E/CN.4/1998/10, "Adverse Effects of the Illicit Movement and Dumping of Toxic and Dangerous Products and Wastes on the Enjoyment of Human Rights," January 20, 1998.
28. *New York Times,* February 29, 2000.

29. International Panel on Climate Change, *Climate Change 2001,* at http://www.ipcc.ch/.
30. *New York Times,* September 6, 2000.
31. CNN.com, May 31, 2003.
32. *New York Times,* August 19, 2000.
33. *New York Times,* February 29, 2000.
34. BBC.com, December 2, 2003.
35. NASA's Marshall Space Flight Center, *Science@NASA* article, September 17, 2001, at http://www.southpole.com/headlines/y2001/ast17sep_1.htm. The scientist was Paul Newman of the Goddard Space Flight Center.
36. *Manchester Guardian Weekly,* March 20, 1994.

BOX, Considering Kyoto, p. 544

1. *New York Times,* December 12, 1997.
2. *New York Times,* November 20, 1997.
3. The quotes are from the *New York Times,* December 12 and 13, 1997.
4. CNN.com, December 14, 1997.
5. *Hartford Courant,* October 19, 2000.
6. Radio Free Europe release, March 29, 2001.
7. James Schlesinger, an op-ed piece in the *Hartford Courant,* January 27, 2004.
8. *Washington Post,* June 5, 2002.

Glossary

Adjudication The legal process of deciding an issue through the courts. 273

Adversarial diplomacy A negotiation situation where two or more countries' interests clash, but when there is little or no chance of armed conflict. 245

Amorality The philosophy that altruistic acts are unwise and even dangerous, or that morality should never be the absolute guide of human actions, particularly in regard to international law. 293

Anarchical political system An anarchical system is one in which there is no central authority to make rules, to enforce rules, or to resolve disputes about the actors in the political system. Many people believe that a system without central authority is inevitably one either of chaos or one in which the powerful prey on the weak. There is, however, an anarchist political philosophy that contends that the natural tendency of people to cooperate has been corrupted by artificial political, economic, or social institutions. Therefore, anarchists believe that the end of these institutions will lead to a cooperative society. Marxism, insofar as it foresees the collapse of the state once capitalism is destroyed and workers live in proletariat harmony, has elements of anarchism. 32

Anti-Ballistic Missile Treaty (ABM) A treaty signed by the United States and the Soviet Union (now Russia) in 1972 that barred the two countries from developing and deploying a system to shoot down ballistic missiles. The United States withdrew from the treaty in 2001 in order to pursue the development and deployment of a national missile defense system. 345

Anti-Personnel Mine Treaty (APM) A treaty signed in 1997 and effective in 1999 that commits its adherents not to produce, stockpile, or transfer antipersonnel land mines, to destroy any current inventory of mines, and to remove all mines they have planted. The United States is among the handful of countries that has not agreed to the treaty. 353

Appeasement policy A policy advocated by the British and French toward the Germans following World War I. The hope was to maintain peace by allowing Hitler to annex the Sudentenland part of Czechoslovakia. 39

Arms control A variety of approaches to the limitation of weapons. Arms control ranges from restricting the future growth in the number, types, or deployment of weapons; through the reduction of weapons; to the elimination of some types of (or even all) weapons on a global or regional basis. 343

Asia-Pacific Economic Cooperation (APEC) A regional trade organization founded in 1989 that now includes 18 countries. 472

Association of Southeast Asian Nations (ASEAN) A regional organization that emphasizes trade relations, established in 1967; now includes Brunei, Cambodia, Indonesia, Laos, Malaysia, Myanmar (Burma), the Philippines, Singapore, Thailand, and Vietnam. 472

Asymmetrical warfare A strategy by which a national military or other armed force, including a terrorist organization, that is relatively small and lightly equipped attacks a militarily stronger opponent by using unconventional means, such as terrorism, or with limited unconventional weapons, such as nuclear explosives and material, biological agents, or chemical agents. 47

Authoritarian government A political system that allows little or no participation in decision making by individuals and groups outside the upper reaches of the government. 70, 172

Authoritarianism A type of restrictive governmental system where people are under the rule of an individual, such as a dictator or king, or a group, such as a party or military junta. 173

Balance of payments A figure that represents the net flow of money into and out of a country due to trade, tourist expenditures, sale of services (such as consulting), foreign aid, profits, and so forth. 391

Balance of power A concept that describes the degree of equilibrium (balance) or disequilibrium (imbalance) of power in the global or regional system. 36

Beijing + 5 Conference A meeting held at the UN in New York City in 2000 to review the progress made since the fourth World Conference on Women held in 1995. 159

Bilateral diplomacy Negotiations between two countries. 249

Bilateral (foreign) aid Foreign aid given by one country directly to another. 430

Biological Weapons Convention A multilateral treaty concluded in 1972. The parties to the treaty agree not to develop, produce, stockpile, or acquire biological agents or toxins "of types and in quantities that have no justification for prophylactic, protective, and other peaceful purposes" and to destroy any such material that they might have. 346

Biopolitics This theory examines the relationship between the physical nature and political behavior of humans. 84

Bipolar system A type of international system with two roughly equal actors or coalitions of actors that divide the international system into two poles. 39, 65

Bretton Woods system The international monetary system that existed from the end of World War II until the early 1970s; named for an international economic conference held in Bretton Woods, New Hampshire, in 1944. 456

Bureaucracy The bulk of the state's administrative structure that continues even when leaders change. 75

Bush Doctrine The belief of President George W. Bush that the United States has a responsibility to promote democracy, capitalism, and other American values throughout the world and that it is permissible for the United States to take preemptive military action to prevent military or terrorist attacks. 48

Capitalism An economic system based on the private ownership of the means of production and distribution of goods, competition, and profit incentives. 438

Carrying capacity The number of people that an environment, such as Earth, can feed, provide water for, and otherwise sustain. 511

Cartel An international agreement among producers of a commodity that attempts to control the production and pricing of that commodity. 436

Chemical Weapons Convention (CWC) A treaty that was signed and became effective in 1995 under which signatories pledge to eliminate all chemical weapons by the year 2005; to submit to rigorous inspection; to never develop, produce, stockpile, or use chemical weapons; and to never transfer chemical weapons to another country or assist another country to acquire such weapons. 351

Civil society The voluntary and private (not controlled by the government) economic, cultural, and other interactions and associations of individuals. 132

Clash of civilizations Samuel P. Huntington's thesis (1996, 1993) that the source of future conflict will be cultural. 148

Coalition diplomacy A negotiation situation where a number of countries have similar interests, which are often in opposition to the interests of one or more other countries. 246

Codify To write down a law in formal language. 270

Coercive diplomacy The use of threats or force as a diplomatic tactic. 259

Coercive power "Hard power" such as military force or economic sanctions. 231

Cognitive decision making Making choices within the limits of what you consciously know. 81

Cold war The confrontation that emerged following World War II between the bipolar superpowers, the Soviet Union and the United States. Although no direct conflict took place between these countries, it was an era of great tensions and global division. 40

Collective security The original theory behind UN peacekeeping. It holds that aggression against one state is aggression against every member and should be defeated by the collective action of all. 362

Communism An ideology that originated in the works of Friedrich Engels and Karl Marx that is essentially an economic theory. As such, it is the idea that an oppressed proletariat class of workers would eventually organize and revolt against those who owned the means of production, the bourgeoisie; a political system of government applied in China, and elsewhere, wherein the state owns the means of production as a system to expedite Engels and Marx's economic theory. 174

Communitarianism The concept that the welfare of the collective must be valued over any individual rights or liberties. 176

Comprehensive Test Ban Treaty (CTBT) A treaty that bans all testing of nuclear weapons. The treaty was signed in 1996 but will not go into force until ratified by the major nuclear weapons powers. The United States Senate rejected ratification in 2001. 350

Conditionality A term that refers to the policy of the International Monetary Fund, the World Bank, and some other international financial agencies to attach conditions to their loans and grants. These conditions may require recipient countries to devalue their currencies, to lift controls on prices, to cut their budgets, and to reduce barriers to trade and capital flows. Such conditions are often politically unpopular, may cause at least short-term economic pain, and are construed by critics as interference in recipient countries' sovereignty. 459

Confederation A group of states that willingly enter into an alliance to form a political unit for a common purpose, such as economic security or defense; it is highly interdependent, but has a weak directorate organization, thus allowing the individual states to maintain a fairly high degree of sovereignty. 200

Constructivism An approach to analysis based on the notion that our understanding of the world and our relationship to it is based on our individual norms, experiences, and other factors that shape our perceptions. 141

Containment doctrine U.S. policy that sought to contain communism, during the cold war. 40

Convention on the Elimination of All Forms of Discrimination Against Women (CEDAW) Adopted by the UN General Assembly in 1979 and subsequently adhered to by over 90% of all countries, the treaty defines what constitutes discrimination against women and sets forth an agenda for national action to end it. 494

Convention on the Rights of the Child Adopted unanimously by the UN General Assembly in 1989, with sufficient ratifications to go into effect in 1990, the convention outlines a wide range of collective and individual rights for all persons under the age of 18. 495

Conventional Forces in Europe Treaty (CFE) A treaty negotiated between the countries in NATO and the (now defunct) Soviet-led Warsaw Pact that placed numerical limits on a range of conventional "heavy" weapons, including tanks and other armored combat vehicles, artillery, and fixed-wing and rotary combat aircraft permitted in the so-called Atlantic-to-the-Urals Zone (ATTU) region. 353

Conventional warfare The application of force by uniformed military units usually against other uniformed military units or other clearly military targets using weapons other than biological, chemical, or nuclear weapons. 326

Council of the European Union The most important decision-making body on the EU. The Council represents the member-states through each member's representatives, which can range from the head of state to specialized ministers (such as agriculture). Also known as the Council of Ministers. 202

Countries in transition (CITs) Former communist countries such as Russia whose economies are in transition from socialism to capitalism. 380

Court of Justice The most important court in the European Union. 204

Crisis situation A circumstance or event that is a surprise to decision makers, that evokes a sense of threat (particularly physical peril), and that must be responded to within a limited amount of time. 71

Cultural imperialism The attempt to impose your own value system on others, including judging others by how closely they conform to your norms. 280

Current dollars The value of the dollar in the year for which it is being reported. Sometimes called inflated dollars. Any currency can be expressed in current value. *See also* Real dollars. 374

Debt service The total amount of money due on principal and interest payments for loan repayment. 426

Decision-making process The manner by which humans choose which policy to pursue and which actions to take in support of policy goals. The study of decision making seeks to identify patterns in the way that humans make decisions. This includes gathering information, analyzing information, and making choices. Decision making is a complex process that relates to personality and other human traits, to the sociopolitical setting in which decision makers function, and to the organizational structures involved. 81

Democracy/democratic government The most basic concept describes the ideology of a body governed by and for the people; also the type of governmental system a country has, in terms of free and fair elections and levels of participation. 70, 172

Democratic peace theory The assertion that as more countries become democratic, the likelihood that they will enter into conflict with one another decreases. 181

Democratized diplomacy The current trend in diplomacy where diplomats are drawn from a wider segment of society, making them more representative of their nations. 251

Dependency theory The belief that the industrialized North has created a neocolonial relationship with the South in which the less developed countries are dependent on and disadvantaged by their economic relations with the capitalist industrial countries. 378

Détente A cold war policy involving the United States, the Soviet Union, and China, which sought to open relations among the countries and ease tensions. 40

Deterrence Persuading an opponent not to attack by having enough forces to disable the attack and/or launch a punishing counterattack. 332

Development Assistance Committee (DAC) The 22 member-countries of the Organization for Economic Cooperation and Development that give official development aid. 430

Development capital Monies and resources needed by less developed countries to increase their economic growth and diversify their economies. 425

Disinformation False stories that are given to the media, placed on the Internet, or otherwise broadcast as part of a propaganda effort to undermine a country, leader, or organization. 255

Doha Round The ninth and latest round of GATT negotiations to reduce barriers to international free economic interchange. The round is named after the 2001 WTO ministerial meeting in Doha, Qatar, where agreement to try to negotiate a new round of reductions in barriers by 2005 was reached. 454

Dual-use technology Technology that has peaceful uses but also has military applications. 354

Economic Community of West African States (ECOWAS) A regional group of 15 countries founded in 1975. Its mission is to promote economic integration, and it has also taken on some peacekeeping activities through its nonpermanent function called Economic Community's African States Monitoring Group (ECOMOG). 361

Economic interdependence See *Interdependence.* 48

Economic internationalism The belief that international economic relations should and can be conducted cooperatively because the international economy is a non–zero-sum game in which prosperity is available to all. 376

Economic nationalism The belief that the state should use its economic strength to further national interests, and that a state should use its power to build its economic strength. 374

Economic sanctions Economic measures imposed by a country or international governmental organization on one or more countries to change their behavior. These sanctions include such tools as refusing to purchase another country's product, refusing to sell it something that it needs, freezing its accounts in your country, or imposing punitive tariffs and quotas on its products. 413

Economic structuralism The belief that economic structure determines politics, as the conduct of world politics is based on the way that the world is organized economically.

A radical restructuring of the economic system is required to end the uneven distribution of wealth and power. 377

Economically developed country (EDC) An industrialized country mainly found in the Northern Hemisphere. 49, 374

Environmental optimists Those analysts who predict that the world population will meet its needs while continuing to grow economically through conservation, population restraints, and technological innovation. 512

Environmental pessimists Those analysts who predict environmental and ecological problems, based on current trends in ecology and population pressure. 512

Escalation Increasing the level of fighting. 327

Ethnonational group An ethnic group in which a significant percentage of its members favor national self-determination and the establishment of a nation-state dominated by the group. 47, 101

Ethology The comparison of animal and human behavior. 84

European Commission A 20-member commission that serves as the bureaucratic organ of the European Union. 203

European Communities (EC) Established in 1967, the EC was a single unit whose plural name (Communities) reflects the fact that it united the European Coal and Steel Community, the European Economic Community, and the European Atomic Energy Community under one organizational structure. The EC evolved into the European Union beginning in 1993. 201

European Economic Community (EEC) The regional trade and economic organization established in Western Europe by the Treaty of Rome in 1958; also known as the Common Market. 200

European Parliament The 626-member legislative branch of the European Union. Representation is determined by population of member-countries, and is based on five-year terms. 203

European Union (EU) The Western European regional organization established in 1983 when the Maastricht Treaty went into effect. The EU encompasses the still legally existing European Community (EC). When the EC was formed in 1967, it in turn encompassed three still legally existing regional organizations formed in the 1950s: the European Coal and Steel Community (ECSC), the European Economic Community (EEC), and the European Atomic Energy Community (EURATOM). 200

Eurowhites A term to distinguish the whites of Europe and of Australia, Canada, New Zealand, the United States, and other countries whose cultures were founded on or converted to European culture from other races and ethnic groups, including Caucasian peoples in Latin America, the Middle East, South Asia, and elsewhere. 36

Exceptionalism The belief by some that their nation or other group is better than others. 116

Exchange rate The values of two currencies relative to each other—for example, how many yen equal a dollar or how many lira equal a pound. 390

Extreme poverty A World Bank term for the condition of those living on less than $1 per day. 382

Failed states Countries in which all or most of the citizens give their primary political loyalty to an ethnic group, a religious group, or some other source of political identity. Such states are so fragmented that no one political group can govern effectively and, thus, are more legal entities than functioning governments. 111

Fascism An ideology that advocates extreme nationalism, with a heightened sense of national belonging or ethnic identity. 174

Feminism The theory of, and the struggle for, equality for women. 142

Feudal system Medieval political system of smaller units, such as principalities, dukedoms, and baronies, ruled by minor royalty. 30

Fiscal year (FY) A budget year, which may or may not be the same as the calendar year. The U.S. fiscal year runs from October 1 through September 30 and is referred to by its ending date. Thus, FY2002 ran from October 1, 2001, through September 30, 2002. 61

Foreign direct investment (FDI) Buying stock, real estate, and other assets in another country with the aim of gaining a controlling interest in foreign economic enterprises. Different from portfolio investment, which involves investment solely to gain capital appreciation through market fluctuations. 387

Foreign policy–making actors The political actors within a state—including political executives, bureaucracies, legislatures, political opponents, interest groups, and the people—who influence the foreign policy process. 73

Foreign policy process A concept that includes the influences and activities within a country that cause its government to decide to adopt one or another foreign policy. 71

Foreign portfolio investment (FPI) Investment in the stocks and the public and private debt instruments (such as bonds) of another country below the level where the stock- or bondholder can exercise control over the policies of the stock-issuing company or the bond-issuing debtor. 387

Formal powers Authority to act or to exert influence that is granted by statutory law or by the constitution to a political executive or to another element of government. 73

Fourth World A term used to designate collectively the indigenous (aboriginal, native) people of the countries of the world. 489

Fourth World Conference on Women (WCW) The largest and most widely noted in a series of UN conferences on the status of women. This international meeting took place in Beijing, China, in 1995. 159

Free economic interchange The absence of tariffs and nontariff barriers in trade between countries. 419

Free Trade Area of the Americas (FTAA) The tentative name given by the 34 countries that met in December 1994 at the Summit of the Americas to the proposed Western Hemisphere free trade zone that is projected to come into existence by the year 2005. 470

Frustration-aggression theory A psychologically based theory that frustrated societies sometimes become collectively aggressive. 83

Functional relations Relations that include interaction in such usually nonpolitical areas as communication, travel, trade, and finances. 268

Functionalism International cooperation in specific areas such as communications, trade, travel, health, or environmental protection activity. Often symbolized by the specialized agencies, such as the World Health Organization, associated with the United Nations. 193

Fundamentalism Religious traditionalism and values incorporated into secular political activities. 151

Gender opinion gap The difference between males and females along any one of a number of dimensions, including foreign policy preferences. 80

General Agreement on Tariffs and Trade (GATT) The world's primary organization promoting the expansion of free trade. Established in 1947, it has grown to a membership of over 100. 451

General and complete disarmament (GCD) The total absence of armaments. 369

Globalization A multifaceted concept that represents the increasing integration of economics, communications, and culture across national boundaries. 127

Green accounting An approach to measure the comprehensive wealth of countries by calculating "human capital" (such as education, health, and equality) and "natural capital" (the quality and quantity of air, land, water, and natural resources), as well as such traditional economic measures as gross national product. 477

Greenhouse effect The process by which the accumulation of carbon dioxide and other gases in the Earth's upper atmosphere arguably cause an increase in temperature by creating a thermal blanket effect that prevents some of the cooling that occurs at night as the Earth radiates heat. 540

Gross domestic product (GDP) A measure of income within a country that excludes foreign earnings. 7, 374

Gross national product (GNP) A measure of the sum of all goods and services produced by a country's nationals, whether they are in the country or abroad. 50, 374

Group of Eight (G-8) The seven economically largest free market countries plus Russia (a member on political issues since 1998). 419, 443

Group of Seven (G-7) The seven economically largest free market countries: Canada, France, Germany, Great Britain, Italy, Japan, and the United States. 419, 443

Group of 77 (G-77) The group of 77 countries of the South that cosponsored the Joint Declaration of Developing Countries in 1963 calling for greater equity in North-South trade. This group has come to include more than 120 members and represents the interests of the less developed countries of the South. 451

Groupthink How an individual's membership in an organization/decision-making group influences his or her thinking and actions. In particular there are tendencies within a group to think alike, to avoid discordancy, and to ignore ideas or information that threaten to disrupt the consensus. 86

Hague system Name given to the peace conferences held in the Netherlands in 1899 and 1907. This serves as the first example of an international attempt to improve the condition of humanity. 191

Hard currency Currencies, such as dollars, marks, francs, and yen, that are acceptable in private channels of international economics. 425

Head of government The ranking official in the executive branch who is politically and constitutionally invested with the preponderance of authority to administer the government and execute its laws and policies. 73

Hegemonic power A single country or alliance that is so dominant in the international system that it plays the key role in determining the rules and norms by which the system operates. It dominates the system and has a central position in both making and enforcing the norms and modes of behavior. Hegemon is a synonym for a hegemonic power. 65

Hegemony Exercising dominant power in the international system. See *hegemonic power.* 43

Heuristic devices A range of psychological strategies that allow individuals to simplify complex decisions. Such devices include evaluating people and events in terms of how well they coincide with your own belief system ("I am anticommunist; therefore all communists are dangerous"), stereotypes ("all Muslims are fanatics"), or analogies ("appeasing Hitler was wrong; therefore all compromise with aggressors is wrong"). 82

Holy Roman Empire The domination and unification of a political territory in Western and Central Europe that lasted from its inception with Charlemagne in 800 to the renunciation of the imperial title by Francis II in 1806. 29

Horizontal authority structure A system in which authority is fragmented. The international system has a mostly horizontal authority structure. 59

Hostile diplomacy A situation where negotiation takes place in an environment where one or more countries are engaged in armed clashes or when there is a substantial possibility that fighting could result. 245

Ideological/theological school of law A set of related ideas in secular or religious thought, usually founded on identifiable thinkers and their works, that offers a more or less comprehensive picture of reality. 269

Ideology Interconnected theological or secular ideas that establish values about what is good and what is not, and that indicate a course of action, create perceptual links among adherents, and perceptually distinguish those who adhere to a given ideology from those who do not. 101

Idiosyncratic analysis An individual-level analysis approach to decision making that assumes that individuals make foreign policy decisions and that different individuals are likely to make different decisions. 88

Imperial overstrech thesis The idea that attempting to maintain global order through leadership as a hegemon, especially through military power, is detrimental to the hegemon's existence. 305

Imperialism A term synonymous with colonization, meaning domination by Northern Eurowhites over Southern nonwhites as a means to tap resources to further their own development. 36

Individualism The concept that rights and liberties of the individual are paramount within a society. 176

Individual-level analysis An analytical approach that emphasizes the role of individuals as either distinct personalities or biological/psychological beings. 81

Industrial revolution The development of mechanical and industrial production of goods that began in Great Britain in the mid-1700s and then spread through Europe and North America. 36

Informal powers Authority to act or to exert influence that is derived from custom or from the prestige within a political system of either an individual leader or an institution. 73

Instrumental theory of government The notion that the purpose of political units and their governments is to benefit the people who established them and that the continued legitimate existence of these organizations rests on whether and how well they perform their tasks. 171

Interdependence The close interrelationship and mutual dependence of two or more domestic economies on each other. 391

Interest group A private (nongovernmental) association of people who have similar policy views and who pressure the government to adopt those views as policy. 77

Intergovernmental organizations (IGOs) International/transnational actors that are composed of member countries. 60, 191

Intermediate-Range Nuclear Forces Treaty (INF) A treaty between the United States and Soviet Union signed in 1987 that pledged the two countries to destroy all their ground-launched ballistic and cruise missiles with ranges of between 500 and 5,500 kilometers. 346

Intermestic The merger of *inter*national and do*mestic* concerns and decisions. 5

International Conference on Financing for Development (ICFD) A UN-sponsored conference on development programs for the South that met in Monterrey, Mexico during March 2002. Fifty heads of state or government, as well as by over 200 government cabinet ministers, leaders from NGOs, and leaders from the major IGOs attended the conference. 448

International Convention on the Elimination of All Forms of Racial Discrimination Adopted in 1965 and in effect in 1969, the treaty defines and condemns racial discrimination and commits the states that are party to it to "pursue by all appropriate means and without delay a policy of eliminating racial discrimination in all its forms and promoting understanding among all races." 497

International Court of Justice (ICJ) The world court, which sits in The Hague with 15 judges and is associated with the United Nations. 274

International Criminal Court (ICC) The permanent criminal court with jurisdiction over genocide and other crimes against humanity. The court, seated in The Hague, the Netherlands, began its operations in 2003. 494

International Monetary Fund (IMF) The world's primary organization devoted to maintaining monetary stability by helping countries to fund balance-of-payment deficits. Established in 1947, it now has 170 members. 456

International political economy (IPE) An approach to the study of international relations that is concerned with the political determinants of international economic relations and also with the economic determinants of international political relations. 374

International organizations Organizations that conduct business across national boundaries and have members from or units operating in more than one country. International organizations whose members are countries are called intergovernmental organizations. International organizations whose membership consists of individuals or private groups are called nongovernmental organizations. 191

International system An abstract concept that encompasses global actors, the interactions (especially patterns of interaction) among those actors, and the factors that cause those interactions. The international system is largest of a vast number of overlapping political systems that extend downward in size to micropolitical systems at the local level. *See also* System-level analysis. 28

Iron triangle An alliance between interest groups, bureaucracies, and legislators that forms a military-industrial-congressional complex. 360

Irredentism A minority population's demand to join its motherland (often an adjoining state), or when the motherland claims the area in which the minority lives. 109

Issue areas Substantive categories of policy that must be considered when evaluating national interest. 71

Jus ad bellum The Western concept meaning "just cause of war," which provides a moral and legal basis governing causes for war. 282

Jus in bello The Western concept meaning "just conduct of war," which provides a moral and legal basis governing conduct of war. 282

Leader-citizen opinion gap Differences of opinion between leaders and public, which may have an impact on foreign policy in a democratic country. 79

League of Nations The first, true general international organization. It existed between the end of World War I and the beginning of World War II and was the immediate predecessor of the United Nations. 192

Least developed countries (LLDCs) Those countries in the poorest of economic circumstances. In this book, this includes those countries with a per capita GNP of less than $400 in 1985 dollars. 382

Less developed countries (LDCs) Countries, located mainly in Africa, Asia, and Latin America, with economies that rely heavily on the production of agriculture and raw materials and whose per capita GDP and standard of living are substantially below Western standards. 50, 374

Levels of analysis Different perspectives (system, state, individual) from which international politics can be analyzed. 50

Liberals Analysts who reject power politics and argue that people are capable of finding mutual interests and cooperating to achieve them. 18

Lifeboat analogy An image that compares global economic circumstances to that of a lifeboat which can safely accomodate only so many people. Therefore those fortunate enough to be in the boat will be endangered if they try to rescue too many of those still in the water, whatever their peril. This analogy represents the view that the world has only so much "carrying capacity" (such as natural resources) and that economic competition creates a zero-sum game, one in which the betterment of one player or groups of players can only come at the expense of others. 445

Limited membership council A representative organization body of the UN that grants special status to members who have a greater stake, responsibility, or capacity in a particular area of concern. The UN Security Council is an example. 210

Limited unipolar system A configuration of the international system in which there is one power center that plays something less than a fully dominant role because of a range of external and/or internal restraints on its power. 43

Maastricht Treaty The most significant agreement in the recent history of the European Union (EU). The Maastricht Treaty was signed by leaders of the EU's 12 member-countries in December 1991 and outlines steps toward further political-economic integration. 202

MAD (mutual assured destruction) A situation in which each nuclear superpower has the capability of launching a devastating nuclear second strike even after an enemy has attacked it. The belief that a MAD capacity prevents nuclear war is the basis of deterrence by punishment theory. 333

Majority voting A system used to determine how votes should count. The theory of majoritarianism springs from the concept of sovereign equality and the democratic notion that the will of the majority should prevail. This system has two main components: (1) each member casts one equal vote, and (2) the issue is carried by either a simple majority (50 percent plus one vote) or, in some cases, an extraordinary majority (commonly two-thirds). 211

Manufactured goods Items that required substantial processing or assembly to become usable. Distinct from primary products, such as agricultural and forestry products, that need little or no processing. 378

Marxism The philosophy of Karl Marx that the economic (material) order determines political and social relationships. Thus, history, the current situation, and the future are determined by the economic struggle, termed dialectical materialism. 377

McWorld This concept describes the merging of states into an integrated world. Benjamin Barber coined this term to describe how states are becoming more globalized, especially with the growth of economic interdependence. 46

Mediation diplomacy A negotiation situation where a country that is not involved directly as one of the parties tries to help two or more conflicting sides to resolve their differences. 247

Merchandise trade The import and export of tangible manufactured goods and raw materials. 383

Microstate A country with a small population that cannot survive economically without outside aid or that is inherently so militarily weak that it is an inviting target for foreign intervention. 120

Mirror image perception The tendency of two countries or individuals to see each other in similar ways, whether positive or negative. 93

Missile Technology Control Regime (MTCR) A series of understandings that commits most of the countries capable of producing extended-range missiles to a ban on the export of ballistic missiles and related technology and that also pledges MTCR adherents to bring economic and diplomatic pressure to bear on countries that export missile-applicable technology. 346

Monarchism A political system that is organized, governed, and defined by the idea of the divine right of kings, or the notion that because a person is born into royalty, he or she is meant to rule. 174

Monetary relations The entire scope of international money issues, such as exchange rates, interest rates, loan policies, balance of payments, and regulating institutions (for example, the International Monetary Fund). 388

Moral absolutism A philosophy based on the notion that the ends never justify the means, or that morality should be the absolute guide of human actions, particularly in regard to international law. 292

Moral prudence The idea that there is a middle ground between amorality and moral absolutism that acts as a guide to human actions, particularly in regard to international law. 294

Moral relativism A philosophy that human actions must be placed in context as a means to inform international law. 293

Multilateral diplomacy Negotiations among three or more countries. 249

Multilateral (foreign) aid Foreign aid distributed by international organizations such as the United Nations. 430

Multinational corporations (MNCs) Private enterprises that have production subsidiaries or branches in more than one country. 62, 387

Multinational states Countries in which there are two or more significant nationalities. 106

Multipolar system A world political system in which power is primarily held by four or more international actors. 36

Multistate nation A nation that has substantial numbers of its people living in more than one state. 108

Munich analogy A belief among post–World War II leaders, particularly Americans, that aggression must always be met firmly and that appeasement will only encourage an aggressor. Named for the concessions made to Hitler by Great Britain and France at Munich during the 1938 Czechoslovakian crisis. 82

Munich Conference A meeting between France, Germany, Great Britain, and Italy in 1938, during which France and Great Britain, unwilling to confront Hitler, acquiesced with Germany's decision to annex the Sudetenland (part of Czechoslovakia). This appeasement of Germany became synonymous with a lack of political will. 39

Nation A group of culturally and historically similar people who feel a communal bond and who feel they should govern themselves to at least some degree. 99

National technical means (NTM) An arms control verification technique that involves using satellites, seismic measuring devices, and other equipment to identify, locate, and monitor the manufacturing, testing, or deployment of weapons or delivery vehicles, or other aspects of treaty compliance. 358

Nationalism The belief that the nation is the ultimate basis of political loyalty and that nations should have self-governing states. *See also* Nation-state. 38, 99

Nation-state A politically organized territory that recognizes no higher law, and whose population politically identifies with that entity. *See also* State. 101

Naturalist school of law Those who believe that law springs from the rights and obligations that humans have by nature. 269

Negative rights Prohibitions to having something done to an individual or a group. These rights are usually expressed in such terms as, "the government may not . . ." 478

Neocolonialism The notion that EDCs continue to control and exploit LDCs through indirect means, such as economic dominance and co-opting the local elite. 378

Neofunctionalism The top-down approach to solving world problems. 194

Neoliberals Analysts who believe the conflict and other ills that result from the anarchical international system can be eased by building global and regional organizations and processes that will allow people, groups, countries, and other international actors to cooperate for their mutual benefit. 18

Neorealists Analysts who believe that the distribution across and shifting of power among states in the anarchical international system is a causal factor that determines the actions of states and, thus, the dynamics of world politics. 17

Net trade The difference between exports and imports, either overall or for specific commodities. For example, if a state exports $10 billion in agricultural products and imports $8 billion dollars in agricultural products, that country has a net agricultural trade surplus of $2 billion. 405

New International Economic Order (NIEO) A term that refers to the goals and demands of the South for basic reforms in the international economic system. 434

Newly industrializing countries (NICs) Less developed countries whose economies and whose trade now include significant amounts of manufactured products. As a result, these countries have a per capita GDP significantly higher than the average per capita GDP for less developed countries. 50, 379

Nongovernmental organizations (NGOs) International (transnational) organizations with private memberships. 60,145

Non-Proliferation Treaty (NPT) A multilateral treaty concluded in 1968, then renewed and made permanent in 1995. The parties to the treaty agree not to transfer nuclear weapons or in any way to "assist, encourage, or induce any nonnuclear state to manufacture or otherwise acquire nuclear weapons." Nonnuclear signatories of the NPT also agree not to build or accept nuclear weapons. 345

Nontariff barrier (NTB) A nonmonetary restriction on trade, such as quotas, technical specifications, or unnecessarily lengthy quarantine and inspection procedures. 410

Norms A principle of right action that is binding on members of a group and serves to regulate the behavior of the members of that group. The word is based on the Latin *norma*, which means a carpenter's square or an accurate measure. Norms are based on custom and usage and may also become part of formal law. Norms are recognized in international law under the principle of *jus cogens* (just thought), which states that a standard of behavior accepted by the world community should not be violated by the actions of a state or group of states. In domestic systems, "common law" is equivalent to norms in the international system. 58

North The economically developed countries (EDCs) including those of Western Europe, the United States and Canada in North America, Japan in Asia, and Australia and New Zealand in Oceania. 49, 379

North American Free Trade Agreement (NAFTA) An economic agreement among Canada, Mexico, and the United States that went into effect on January 1, 1994. It will eliminate most trade barriers by 2009 and will also eliminate or reduce restrictions on foreign investments and other financial transactions among the NAFTA countries. 467

North Atlantic Treaty Organization (NATO) An alliance of 19 member-countries, established in 1949 by Canada, the United States, and most of the countries of Western Europe to defend its members from outside, presumably Soviet-led, attack. In the era after the cold war, NATO has begun to admit members from Eastern Europe and has also expanded its mission to include peacekeeping. 46, 360

NUT (Nuclear Utilization Theory) The belief that because nuclear war might occur, countries must be ready to fight, survive, and win a nuclear war. NUT advocates believe this posture will limit the damage if nuclear war occurs and also make nuclear war less likely by creating retaliatory options that are more credible than massive retaliation. 333

Objective power Assets a country objectively possesses and has the will and capacity to use. 232

On-site inspection (OSI) An arms control verification technique that involves stationing your or a neutral country's personnel in another country to monitor weapons or delivery vehicle manufacturing, testing, deployment, or other aspects of treaty compliance. 358

Open diplomacy The public conduct of negotiations and the publication of agreements. 251

Operational code A perceptual phenomenon that describes how an individual acts and responds when faced with specific types of situations. 93

Operational reality The process by which what is perceived, whether that perception is accurate or not, assumes a level of reality in the mind of the beholder and becomes the basis for making an operational decision (a decision about what to do). 93

Organization for Economic Cooperation and Development (OECD) An organization that has existed since 1948 (and since 1960 under its present name) to facilitate the exchange of information and otherwise to promote cooperation among the economically developed countries. In recent years, the OECD has started accepting a few newly industrializing and former communist countries in transition as members. 443

Organization for Security and Cooperation in Europe (OSCE) Series of conferences among 34 NATO, former Soviet bloc, and neutral European countries that led to permanent organization. Established by the 1976 Helsinki Accords. 360

Pacificism A bottom-up approach to avoidance of war based on the belief that it is wrong to kill. 369

Pacta sunt servanda Translates as "treaties are to be served/carried out" and means that agreements between states are binding. 270

Parliamentary diplomacy Debate and voting in international organizations to settle diplomatic issues. 250

Peace enforcement The restoration of peace or the prevention of a breach of the peace by, if necessary, the assertive use of military force to compel one or more of the sides involved in a conflict to cease their violent actions. 364

Peacekeeping The use of military means by an international organization such as the United Nations to prevent fighting, usually by acting as a buffer between combatants. The international force is neutral between the combatants and must have been invited to be present by at least one of the combatants. *See also* Collective security. 362

Perceptions The factors that create a decision maker's images of reality. 90

Persuasive power "Soft power" such as moral authority or technological excellence. 232

Plenary representative body An assembly, such as the UN's General Assembly, that consists of all members of the main organization. 209

Political culture A concept that refers to a society's general, long-held, and fundamental practices and attitudes. These are based on a country's historical experience and on the values (norms) of its citizens. These attitudes are often an important part of the internal setting in which national leaders make foreign policy. 72

Political executives Those officials, usually but not always in the executive branch of a government, who are at the center of foreign policy making and whose tenures are variable and dependent on the political contest for power. 73

Political identity The perceived connection between an individual and a political community (a group that has political interest and goals) and among individuals of a political community. Nationalism is the dominant political identity of most people, but others, such as religion, do exist as a primary political identity and are becoming more common. 99, 140

Popular sovereignty A political doctrine that holds that sovereign political authority resides with the citizens of a state. According to this doctrine, the citizenry grant a certain amount of authority to the state, its government, and, especially, its specific political leaders (such as monarchs, presidents, and prime ministers), but do not surrender ultimate sovereignty. 33, 103

Positive rights Obligations on a society and its government to try to provide a certain qualitative standard of life that, at a minimum, meets basic needs and perhaps does not differ radically from the quality of life enjoyed by others in the society. These rights are usually expressed in such terms as "the government shall . . ." 478

Positivist school of law Those who believe that law reflects society and the way that people want the society to operate. 269

Postmodernism This theory holds that reality does not exist as such. Rather, reality is created by how we think and our discourse (writing, talking). As applied to world politics, postmodernism is the belief that we have become trapped by stale ways of conceiving of how we organize and conduct ourselves. Postmodernists wish, therefore, to "deconstruct" discourse. 140

Power The totality of a country's international capabilities. Power is based on multiple resources, which alone or in concert allow one country to have its interests prevail in the international system. Power is especially important in enabling one state to achieve its goals when it clashes with the goals and wills of other international actors. 230

Power pole An actor in the international system that has enough military, economic, and/or diplomatic strength to often have an important role in determining the rules and operation of the system. Power poles, or simply poles, have generally been either (1) a single country or empire or (2) a group of countries that constitute an alliance or bloc. 36, 63

Power to defeat The ability to overcome in a traditional military sense—that is, to overcome enemy armies and capture and hold territory. 309

Power to hurt The ability to inflict pain outside the immediate battle area; sometimes called coercive violence. It is often used against civilians and is a particular hallmark of terrorism and nuclear warfare. 309

Preferential trade agreement (PTA) A bilateral or multilateral agreement within a region or across regions to cooperate to reduce trade barriers and also often to advance other areas of economic cooperation and integration. PTAs are called regional trade agreements by the World Trade Organization, and neither term is synonymous with a regional trade organization, a narrower term used by the World Trade Organization to define multilateral, regional economic pacts. 473

President of the Commission Comparable to being president of the European Union (EU), this person is the director of the 20-member European Commission, the policy-making bureaucratic organ of the EU. 203

Primary products Agricultural products and raw materials, such as minerals. 378

Procedural democracy A form of democracy that is defined by whether or not particular procedures are followed, such as free and fair elections or following a set of laws or a constitution. 177

Protectionism Using tariffs or nontariff barriers such as quotas or subsidies to protect a domestic economic sector from competition from imported goods or services. 437

Protestant Reformation The religious movement initiated by Martin Luther in Germany in 1517 that rejected the Catholic Church as the necessary intermediary between people and God. 31

Public diplomacy A process of creating an overall international image that enhances your ability to achieve diplomatic success. 254

Purchasing Power Parity (PPP) A measure of the relative purchasing power of different currencies. It is measured by the price of the same goods in different countries, translated by the exchange rate of that country's currency against a "base currency," usually the U.S. dollar. 374

Rally effect The tendency during a crisis of political and other leaders, legislators, and the public to give strong support to a chief executive and the policy that leader has adopted in response to the crisis. 71

Real dollars The value of dollars expressed in terms of a base year. This is determined by taking current value and subtracting the amount of inflation between the base year and the year being reported. Sometimes called uninflated dollars. Any currency can be valued in real terms. *See also* Current dollars. 374

Realists Analysts who believe that countries operate in their own self-interests and that politics is a struggle for power. 16

Realpolitik Operating according to the belief that politics is based on the pursuit, possession, and application of power. 38

Regime A complex of norms, treaties, international organizations, and transnational activity that orders an area of activity such as the environment or oceans. 197

Regional government A possible middle level of governance between the prevalent national governments of today and the world government that some people favor. The regional structure that comes closest to (but still well short of) a regional government is the European Union. 199

Regional trade organization (RTO) An agreement and the organization to administer it between three or more countries in a geographical region to cooperate to reduce trade barriers and often to advance other areas of economic cooperation and integration. RTO is not synonymous with regional trade agreement, a broader term used by the World Trade Organization to define bilateral and cross-regional agreements as well as multilateral regional ones. 464

Relative power Power measured in comparison with the power of other international actors. 232

Relativists A group of people who subscribe to the belief that human rights are the product of cultures. 479

Renaissance A period of cultural and intellectual rebirth and reform following the Dark Ages from approximately 1350 to 1650. 31

Role How an individual's position influences his or her thinking and actions. 86

SALT I The Strategic Arms Limitation Talks Treaty signed in 1972. 346

SALT II The Strategic Arms Limitation Talks Treaty signed in 1979 but withdrawn by President Carter from the U.S. Senate before ratification in response to the Soviet invasion of Afghanistan. 346

Secretariat The administrative organ of the United Nations, headed by the secretary-general. In general, the administrative element of any IGO, headed by a secretary-general. 213

Self-determination The concept that a people should have the opportunity to map their own destiny. 119

Services trade Trade based on the purchase (import) from or sale (export) to another country of intangibles such as architectural fees; insurance premiums; royalties on movies, books, patents, and other intellectual properties; shipping services; advertising fees; and educational programs. 384

Situational power The power that can be applied, and is reasonable, in a given situation. Not all elements of power can be applied to every situation. 233

Social contract The implicit understanding agreed to by those who merged into a society and created a government. The social contract details the proper functions of and prohibitions on government. 171

Social Darwinism A social theory that argues it is proper that stronger peoples will prosper and will dominate lesser peoples. 482

Social overstretch thesis The idea that spending money on altruistic social welfare programs to support the least productive people in society financially drains that economy. 306

South The economically less developed countries (LDCs), primarily located in Africa, Asia, and Latin America. 50, 379

Southern Common Market (Mercosur) A regional organization that emphasizes trade relations, established in 1995 among Argentina, Brazil, Paraguay, and Uruguay, with Chile (1996) and Bolivia (1997) as associate members. 471

Sovereignty The most essential characteristic of an international state. The term strongly implies political independence from any higher authority and also suggests at least theoretical equality. 165

Special drawing rights (SDRs) Reserves held by the International Monetary Fund that the central banks of member-countries can draw on to help manage the values of their currencies. SDR value is based on a "market-basket" of currencies, and SDRs are acceptable in transactions between central banks. 457

Special operations The overt or covert use of relatively small units of troops or paramilitary forces, which conduct commando/guerrilla operations, gather intelligence, and perform other specialized roles. Special operations forces in the U.S. military include such units as the U.S. Green Berets, Seals, and Delta Force; Great Britain's Special Air Services (SAS), and Russia's Special Purpose Force (SPETSNAZ). 316

State A political actor that has sovereignty and a number of characteristics, including territory, population, organization, and recognition. 32, 59

State building The process of creating both a government and other legal structures of a country and the political identification of the inhabitants of the country with the state and their sense of loyalty to it. 104

State of nature A theoretical time in human history when people lived independently or in family groups and there were no societies of nonrelated individuals or governments. 171

State terrorism Terrorism carried out directly by, or encouraged and funded by, an established government of a state (country). 319

State-centric system A system describing the current world system wherein states are the principal actors. 59

State-level analysis An analytical approach that emphasizes the actions of states and the internal (domestic) causes of their policies. 70

Stateless nation A nation that does not exercise political control over any state. 109

Strategic Arms Reduction Talks Treaty I (START I) A nuclear weapons treaty signed by the Soviet Union and the United States in 1991 and later re-signed with Belarus, Kazakhstan, Russia, and Ukraine that will limit Russia and the United States to 1,600 delivery vehicles and 6,000 strategic explosive nuclear devices each, with the other three countries destroying their nuclear weapons or transferring them to Russia. 346

Strategic Arms Reduction Talks Treaty II (START II) A nuclear weapons treaty signed by the Soviet Union and the United States in 1993, which established nuclear warhead and bomb ceilings of 3,500 for the United States and 2,997 for Russia by the year 2003 and that also eliminated some types of weapons systems. As of February 1997 the treaty had not been ratified by the Russian parliament and, therefore, the treaty is not legally in effect. 346

Strategic-range delivery vehicle A missile or bomber capable of delivering weapons at a distance of more than 5,500 kilometers (3,416.8 miles). 331

Subjective power A country's power based on other countries' perception of its current or potential power. 232

Substantive democracy A form of democracy that is defined by whether qualities of democracy, such as equality, justice, or self-rule, are evident. 177

Summit meetings High-level meetings for diplomatic negotiations between national political leaders. 252

Superpower A term used to describe the leader of a system pole in a bipolar system. During the cold war, the Soviet Union and the United States were each leaders of a bipolar system pole. 39

Supranational organization An organization that is founded and operates, at least in part, on the idea that international organizations can or should have authority higher than individual states and that those states should be subordinate to the supranational organization. 199

Sustainable development The ability to continue to improve the quality of life of those in the industrialized countries and, particularly, those in the less developed countries while simultaneously protecting the Earth's biosphere. 53, 511

System-level analysis An analytical approach that emphasizes the importance of the impact of world conditions (economics, technology, power relationships, and so forth) on the actions of states and other international actors. 58

Tariff A tax, usually based on percentage of value, that importers must pay on items purchased abroad; also known as an import tax or import duty. 410

Terrorism A form of political violence conducted by individuals, groups, or clandestine government agents that attempts to manipulate politics by attacking noncombatants and nonmilitary targets in order to create a climate of fear. 317

Terrorist groups Groups of individuals that are not officially part of a government but attack nonmilitary targets using bombs and other methods to inflict pain on an opponent rather than defeat that opponent in a traditional military sense. Many terrorist groups draw individuals from more than one country and operate across national boundaries. 62

Theocracy A political system that is organized, governed, and defined by spiritual leaders and their religious beliefs. 173

Third World A term once commonly used to designate the countries of Asia, Africa, Latin America, and elsewhere that were economically less developed. The phrase is attributed to French analyst Alfred Sauvy, who in 1952 used *tiers monde* to describe neutral countries in the cold war. By inference, the U.S.-led Western bloc and the Soviet-led Eastern bloc were the other two worlds. But since most of the neutral countries were also relatively poor, the phrase had a double meaning. Sauvy used the older *tiers*, instead of the more modern *troisième*, to allude to the pre-Revolutionary (1789) third estate (*tiers état*), that is, the underprivileged class, the commoners. The nobility and the clergy were the first and second estates. Based on this second meaning, Third World came most commonly to designate the less developed countries of the world, whatever their political orientation. The phrase is less often used since the end of the cold war, although some analysts continue to employ it to designate the less developed countries. 40, 489

Transnational actors Organizations that operate internationally, but whose membership, unlike IGOs, is private. 60

Transnational advocacy networks (TANs) IGOs, NGOs, and national organizations that are based on shared values or common interests and exchange information and services. 146, 497

Transnational corporations (TNCs) Transnational corporations are business enterprises that conduct business beyond just selling a product in more than one country. Companies with factories in several countries are TNCs, as are banks with branches in more than one country. The businesses are also referred to as multinational corporations (MNCs). The two terms are synonymous; TNC is used herein based on UN usage. 62

Transnational terrorism Terrorism carried out either across national borders or by groups that operate in more than one country. 320

Transnationalism Extension beyond the borders of a single country; applies to a political movement, issue, organization, or other phenomena. 127

Treaty of Amsterdam (1997) The most recent agreement in a series of treaties that has further integrated the economic and political sectors of the European Union. 202

Treaty of Moscow A treaty signed in 2002 by President George W. Bush and President Vladimir Putin. Under the treaty's provisions, the United States and Russia agree to reduce their nuclear arsenals of nuclear warheads and bombs to no more than 2,200 by 2012. When presidents Bill Clinton and Boris Yeltsin had earlier committed to the general levels established in the treaty, they had referred to the potential accord as the third Strategic Arms Reduction Treaty (START III), but that name was abandoned by Bush and Putin. 347

Treaty of Westphalia The treaty that ended the Thirty Years' War (1618–1648). The treaty signals the birth of the modern state system and the end of the theoretical subordination of the monarchies of Europe, especially those that had adopted Protestantism, to the Roman Catholic Church and the Holy Roman Empire. While the date of 1648 marked an important change, the state as a sovereign entity had begun to emerge earlier and continues to evolve. 31

Tribalism A term used by scholar Benjamin Barber to decribe the internal pressure on countries that can lead to their fragmentation and even to their collapse. 46

Two-level game theory The concept that in order to arrive at satisfactory international agreements, a country's diplomats actually have to deal with (at one level) the other country's negotiators and (at the second level) legislators, interest groups, and other domestic forces at home. 74, 247

UN Conference on Environment and Development (UNCED) Often called Earth Summit I or the Rio Conference, this gathering in 1992 was the first to bring together most of the world's countries, a majority of which were represented by their head of state or government, to address the range of issues associated with sustainable development. 519

UN Conference on Population and Development (UNCPD) A UN-sponsored conference that met in Cairo, Egypt, in September 1994 and was attended by delegates from more than 170 countries. The conference called for a program of action to include spending $17 billion annually by the year 2000 on international, national, and local programs to foster family planning and to improve the access of women in such areas as education. 524

UN Conference on Trade and Development (UNCTAD) A UN organization established in 1964 and currently consisting of all UN members plus the Holy See, Switzerland, and Tonga, which holds quadrennial meetings aimed at promoting international trade and economic development. 451

UN Development Programme (UNDP) An agency of the UN established in 1965 to provide technical assistance to stimulate economic and social development in the economically less developed countries. The UNDP has 48 members selected on a rotating basis from the world's regions. 451

UN General Assembly (UNGA) The main representative body of the United Nations, composed of all 191 member-states. 209

UN Security Council The main peacekeeping organ of the United Nations. The Security Council has 15 members, including 5 permanent members. 210

Unanimity voting A system used to determine how votes should count. In this system, in order for a vote to be valid, all members must agree to the proposed measure. Abstention from a vote may or may not block an agreement. 212

Unconventional force The application of force using the techniques of guerrilla warfare, covert operations, and terrorism conducted by military special forces or by paramilitary groups. Such groups frequently rely on external sources for funds and weapons. Unconventional warfare is sometimes waged against nonmilitary targets and may use conventional weapons or weapons of mass destruction. 313

Unipolar system A type of international system that describes a single country with complete global hegemony. 65

United Nations (UN) An international body created with the intention to maintain peace through the cooperation of its member-states. As part of its mission, it addresses human welfare issues such as the environment, human rights, population, and health. Its headquarters are located in New York City, and it was established following World War II to supersede the League of Nations. 192

Universal Declaration of Human Rights Adopted by the UN General Assembly, it is the most fundamental internationally proclaimed statement of human rights in existence. 491

Universalists A group of people who subscribe to the belief that human rights are derived from sources external to society, such as from a theological, ideological, or natural rights basis. 478

Uruguay Round The eighth round of GATT negotiations to reduce tariffs and nontariff barriers to trade. The eighth round was convened in Punta del Este, Uruguay, in 1986 and its resulting agreements were signed in Marrakesh, Morocco, in April 1994. 452

Vertical authority structure A system in which subordinate units answer to higher levels of authority. 59

Veto A negative vote cast in the UN Security Council by one of the five permanent members; has the effect of defeating the issue being voted on. 212

Weapons of mass destruction (WMDs) Generally deemed to be nuclear weapons with a tremendous capability to destroy a population and the planet, but also include some exceptionally devastating conventional arms, such as fuel-air explosives, as well as biological, and chemical weapons. Weapons of mass destruction warfare refers to the application of force between countries using biological, chemical, and nuclear weapons. 47, 328

Weighted voting A system used to determine how votes should count. In this system, particular votes count more or less depending on what criterion is deemed to be most significant. For instance, population or wealth might be the important defining criterion for a particular vote. In the case of population, a country would receive a particular number of votes based on its population, thus a country with a large population would have more votes than a less-populated country. 211

West Historically, Europe and those countries and regions whose cultures were founded on or converted to European culture. Such countries would include Australia, Canada, New Zealand, and the United States. The majority of the populations in these countries are also "white," in the European, not the larger Caucasian, sense. After World War II, the term West took on two somewhat different but related meanings. One referred to the countries allied with the United States and opposed to the Soviet Union and its allies, called the East. The West also came to mean the industrial democracies, including Japan. *See also* Eurowhites. 33

Westernization of the international system A number of factors, including scientific and technological advances, contributed to the domination of the West over the international system that was essentially created by the Treaty of Westphalia (1648). 33

World Bank Group Four associated agencies that grant loans to LDCs for economic development and other financial needs. Two of the agencies, the International Bank for Reconstruction and Development (IBRD) and the International Development Association (IDA), are collectively referred to as the World Bank. The other two agencies are the International Finance Corporation (IFC) and the Multilateral Investment Guarantee Agency (MIGA). 462

World Conference(s) on Women (WCW) A series of UN-sponsored global conferences on the status of women. Of these, the most recent was the fourth WCW held in Beijing in 1995. 494

World Food Summit Specifically, a 1996 meeting in Rome attended by almost all the world's countries and dedicated to addressing both the short-term and long-term food needs of less developed countries. More generically, world food summit refers to any of a number of global meetings held on the topic. 503

World government The concept of a supranational world authority to which current countries would surrender some or all of their sovereign authority. 199

World Health Organization (WHO) A UN-affiliated organization created in 1946 to address world health issues. 504

World Summit on Sustainable Development (WSSD) Often called Earth Summit II, this conference was held in Johannesburg in 2002. It was attended by almost all countries and by some 8,000 NGOs, and it established a series of calls for action and timetables for ameliorating various problems. 520

World systems theory Based on Marxist constructs, this perspective emphasizes the interrelationships among all actors and forces within the capitalist world economic system and demonstrates how the structure of that system conditions outcomes. 378

World Trade Organization (WTO) The organization that replaced the General Agreement on Tariffs and Trade (GATT) organization as the body that implements GATT, the treaty. 452

Xenophobia Fear of others, "they-groups." 117

Zero-sum game A contest in which gains by one player can only be achieved by equal losses for other players. A non–zero-sum game is a situation in which one or more players, even all players, can gain without offsetting losses for any other player or players. 232

Zionism The belief that Jews are a nation and that they should have an independent homeland. 109

Abbreviations

The following abbreviations are used in the text:

ABM	Anti-Ballistic Missile (treaty)
APEC	Asia-Pacific Economic Cooperation
APM	Anti-Personnel Mine (treaty)
ASEAN	Association of Southeast Asian Nations
ATTU	Atlantic to the Urals Zone (region)
BIS	Bank for International Settlement
BMD	Ballistic Missile Defense
BWT	Biological Weapons Treaty
CEDAW	Convention on the Elimination of All Forms of Discrimination Against Women
CFE	Conventional Forces in Europe (treaty)
CIS	Commonwealth of Independent States
CIT	Country in Transition
CITES	Convention on the International Trade in Endangered Species
CSW	Commission on the Status of Women
CTBT	Comprehensive Test Ban Treaty
CWC	Chemical Weapons Convention
DAC	Development Assistance Committee
EC	European Communities
ECB	European Central Bank
ECJ	European Court of Justice
ECOSOC	Economic and Social Council
ECOWAS	Economic Community of West African States
ECSC	European Coal and Steel Community
EDC	Economically Developed Country
EEC	European Economic Community
EMS	European Monetary System
EMU	European Monetary Union
EP	European Parliament
EPA	Environmental Protection Agency
EPP	European People's Party
EU	European Union
EURATOM	European Atomic Energy Community
FAO	Food and Agriculture Organization (United Nations)
FDI	Foreign Direct Investment
FIS	Front for Islamic Salvation
FPI	Foreign Portfolio Investment
FSR	Former Soviet Republic
FTAA	Free Trade Area of the Americas
G-7	Group of Seven
G-8	Group of Eight
G-77	Group of 77
GATT	General Agreement on Tariffs and Trade
GCD	General and Complete Disarmament
GCP	Gross Corporate Product
GDP	Gross Domestic Product
GEF	Global Environmental Facility
GNP	Gross National Product
GPS	Global Positioning System
HDI	Human Development Index
IAEA	International Atomic Energy Agency
IBRD	International Bank for Reconstruction and Development
ICBM	Intercontinental Ballistic Missile
ICC	International Criminal Court
ICFD	International Conference on Financing for Development
ICJ	International Court of Justice
IDA	International Development Association
IFAD	International Fund for Agricultural Development
IFC	International Finance Corporation
IFOR	International Force
IGO	Intergovernmental Organization
ILO	International Labor Organization
IMF	International Monetary Fund
INF	Intermediate-Range Nuclear Forces (treaty)
IOM	International Organization for Migration
IPCC	International Panel on Climatic Change
IPE	International Political Economy
IPPF	International Planned Parenthood Federation
IWC	International Whaling Commission

JCS	Joint Chiefs of Staff
LDC	Less Developed Country
LLDC	Least Developed Country
MAD	Mutual Assured Destruction
MAI	Multilateral Agreement on Investment
MFN	Most-Favored-Nation
MIGA	Multilateral Investment Guarantee Agency
MIRV	Multiple-Independent-Reentry-Vehicle
MNC	Multinational Corporation
MTCR	Missile Technology Control Regime
NAFTA	North American Free Trade Association; North American Free Trade Agreement
NAM	Non-Aligned Movement
NATO	North Atlantic Treaty Organization
NBC	Nuclear-Biological-Chemical
NGO	Nongovernmental Organization
NIC	Newly Industrializing Country
NIEO	New International Economic Order
NPT	Non-Proliferation Treaty
NSC	National Security Council
NTB	Nontariff Barrier
NTM	National Technical Means
NUT	Nuclear Utilization Theory
OAS	Organization of American States
OAU	Organization of African Unity
ODA	Official Development Aid
OECD	Organization for Economic Cooperation and Development
OPEC	Organization of Petroleum Exporting Countries
OSCE	Organization for Security and Cooperation in Europe
OSI	On-Site Inspection
P5	Permanent 5
PCIJ	Permanent Court of International Justice
PLA	People's Liberation Army (China)
PLO	Palestine Liberation Organization
PNA	Palestine National Authority
PNTR	Permanent Normal Trade Relations
PPP	Purchasing Power Parity
RTA	Regional Trade Agreement
RTO	Regional Trade Organization
SALT	Strategic Arms Limitation Talks
SDF	Self-Defense Force (Japan)
SDI	Strategic Defense Initiative
SDR	Special Drawing Right
SEA	Single European Act
SLBM	Sea-Launched Ballistic Missile
SPE	Socialist Party of Europe
START	Strategic Arms Reduction Talks
TAN	Transnational Advocacy Network
THAAD	Theater High Altitude Area Defense
TI	Transparency International
TNC	Transnational Corporation
UN	United Nations
UNCED	United Nations Conference on Environment and Development
UNCHR	United Nations Commission on Human Rights
UNCPD	United Nations Conference on Population and Development
UNCTAD	United Nations Conference on Trade and Development
UNDHR	Universal Declaration of Human Rights
UNDP	United Nations Development Programme
UNEP	United Nations Environmental Programme
UNESCO	United Nations Educational, Scientific, and Cultural Organization
UNFPA	United Nations Population Fund
UNGA	United Nations General Assembly
UNICEF	United Nations Children's Fund
UNIDO	United Nations Industrial Development Organization
UNIFEM	UN Development Fund for Women
UNSC	United Nations Security Council
VAT	Value-Added Tax
WCHR	World Conference on Human Rights
WCW	World Conference on Women
WEDO	Women's Environment and Development Organization
WEU	Western European Union
WFC	World Food Council
WHO	World Health Organization
WTO	World Trade Organization

References

Abbott, Kenneth W., and Duncan Snidal. 1998. "Why States Act Through Formal International Organizations." *Journal of Conflict Organization,* 42:3–32.

ADL (Anti-Defamation League). 1999. *Highlights from a September 1999 Anti-Defamation League Survey on Anti-Semitism and Societal Attitudes in Russia.* New York: Martilla Communications Group. Also available at the ADL Web site at http://www.adl.org/frames/front_israel.html.

Ahmad, Zakaria Haji, and Baladas Ghoshal. 1999. "The Political Future of ASEAN After the Asian Crisis." *International Affairs,* 75:759–778.

Alter, Karen J. 1998. "Who Are the 'Masters of the Treaty'? European Governments and the European Court of Justice." *International Organization,* 52:121–148.

Alulis, Joseph, and Vickie Sullivan, eds. 1996. *Shakespeare's Political Pageant: Essays in Politics and Literature.* Boulder, CO: Rowman & Littlefield.

Amadife, Emmanuel N. 1999. *Pre-Theories and Theories of Foreign Policy–Making.* Lanham, MD: University Press of America.

Anderson, Benedict. 1991. *Imagined Communities: Reflections on the Origin and Spread of Nationalism,* rev ed. New York: Verso Books.

Andrade, Lydia M. 2003. "Presidential Diversionary Attempts: A Peaceful Perspective." *Congress & the Presidency,* 30:55–79.

Annan, Kofi. 2002. "Foreword." In *State of the World 2002.* Christopher Flavin, Hilary French, Gary Gardner et al. New York: W. W. Norton.

Apodaca, Clair, and Michael Stohl. 1999. "United States Human Rights Policy and Foreign Assistance." *International Studies Quarterly,* 43:185–198.

Armstrong, David. 1999. "Law, Justice and the Idea of a World Society." *International Affairs,* 75:563–598.

Art, Robert J., and Kenneth W. Waltz. 2003. *The Use of Force: Military Power and International Politics,* 6th ed. Lanham, MD: Rowman & Littlefield.

Ashley, Richard K. 1989. "Living on Border Lines: Man, Poststructuralism, and War." In *International/Intertextual Relations,* eds. James Der Derian and Michael J. Shapiro. New York: Lexington Books.

Asmus, Ronald D. 2003. "Rebuilding the Atlantic Alliance." *Foreign Affairs,* 82/5:20–31.

Astorino-Courtois, Allison. 1998. "Clarifying Decisions: Assessing the Impact of Decision Structures on Foreign Policy Choices During the 1970 Jordanian Civil War." *International Studies Quarterly,* 42:733–754.

Auerswald, David. P. 1999. "Inward Bound: Domestic Institutions and Military Conflicts." *International Organization,* 53:469–504.

Avant, Deborah. 2000. "From Mercenaries to Citizen Armies: Explaining Change in the Practice of War." *International Organization,* 54:41–73.

Baker William D., and John R. O'Neal. 2001. "Patriotism or Opinion Leadership? The Nature and Origins of the 'Rally 'Round the Flag' Effect." *Journal of Conflict Resolution,* 45: 661–688.

Balaam, David N., and Michael Veseth. 1996. *Introduction to International Political Economy.* Upper Saddle River, NJ: Prentice Hall.

Baldwin, David A. 2000. "The Sanctions Debate and the Logic of Choice." *International Security,* 24/3:80–107.

Baradat, Leon P. 2003. *Political Ideologies.* 8th ed. Englewood Cliffs, NJ: Prentice-Hall.

Barber, Benjamin R. 1995. *Jihad vs. McWorld.* New York: Times Books/Random House.

Barber, Benjamin R. 1996. *Jihad vs. McWorld: How Globalism and Tribalism Are Reshaping the World.* New York: Ballantine Books, Inc.

Barber, James David. 1985. *Presidential Character,* 3rd ed. Englewood Cliffs, NJ: Prentice Hall.

Barnett, Michael N., and Martha Finnemore. 1999. "The Politics, Power, and Pathologies of International Organizations." *International Organization,* 53:699–732.

Barry, James A. 1998. *The Sword of Justice: Ethics and Coercion in International Politics.* Westport, CT: Praeger.

Bartlett, David, and Anna Seleny. 1998. "The Political Enforcement of Liberalism: Bargaining, Institutions, and Auto Multinationals in Hungary." *International Studies Quarterly,* 42:319–338.

Beer, Francis A. 1990. "The Reduction of War and the Creation of Peace." In *A Reader in Peace Studies,* ed. Paul Smoker, Ruth Davies, and Barbara Munske. New York: Pergamon.

Beigbeder, Yves. 1999. *Judging War Criminals: The Politics of International Justice.* New York: St. Martin's.

Beiner, Ronald, ed. 1999. *Theorizing Nationalism.* Albany: State University of New York Press.

Beitz, Charles R. 1999. *Political Theory and International Relations.* Princeton: Princeton University Press.

Belgrad, Eric A., and Nitza Nachmias. 1997. *The Politics of International Humanitarian Aid Operations.* Westport, CT: Praeger.

Bender, Peter. 2003. "America: The New Roman Empire?" *Orbis,* 47:145–159.

Berton, Peter, Hiroshi Kimura, and I. William Zartman. 1999. *International Negotiation: Actors Structure/Process, Values.* New York: St. Martin's.

Best, Geoffrey. 1999. "Peace Conferences and the Century of Total War: The 1899 Hague Conference and What Came After." *International Affairs,* 75:619–634.

Betts, Richard K. 1998. "The New Threat of Mass Destruction." *Foreign Affairs,* 77/1:26–45.

Bhagwati, Jagdish. 2002. "Trading for Development: The Poor's Best Hope." *The Economist,* June 22, 25–28.

Blanton, Shannon Lindsey. 1998. "U.S. Arms Transfers and the Promotion of Global Order." Paper presented at the International Studies Association convention, Minneapolis.

Blanton, Shannon Lindsey. 2000. "Promoting Human Rights and Democracy in the Developing World: U.S. Rhetoric versus U.S. Arms Exports." *American Journal of Political Science,* 44:123–133.

Bloomfield, Lincoln P., and Allen Moulton. 1997. *Managing International Conflict: From Theory to Policy.* New York: St. Martin's Press.

Bock, Peter, and Nigel Young. 1999. *Pacifism in the Twentieth Century.* Syracuse, NY: Syracuse University Press.

Boesche, Roger. 2002. *The First Great Realist: Kautilya and His Arthashastra.* Lanham, MD: Lexington Books.

Bohman, James. 1999. "International Regimes and Democratic Governance: Political Equality and Influence in Global Institutions." *International Affairs,* 75:499–514.

Bond, Doug. 1992. "Introduction." In *Transforming Struggle: Strategy and the Global Experience of Nonviolent Direct Action.* Cambridge, MA: Program on Nonviolent Sanction in Conflict and Defense, Center for International Affairs, Harvard University.

Brandes, Lisa C. O. 1994. "The Liberal Feminist State and War." Presented at the annual meeting of the American Political Science Association, New York.

Brecher, Jeremy. 1993. "Global Village or Global Pillage." *The Nation,* December 6.

Brecher, Michael, and Jonathan Wilkenfeld. 1997. *A Study of Crisis.* Ann Arbor: University of Michigan Press.

Breuning, Marijke. 2003. "The Role of Analogies and Abstract Reasoning in Decision-Making: Evidence from the Debate over Truman's Proposal for Development Assistance." *International Studies Quarterly,* 47:229–245.

Bright, Chris. 2000. "Anticipating Environmental 'Surprise,'" In *State of the World 2000,* ed. Lester R. Brown, et al. New York: W. W. Norton.

Brooks, Stephen G. 1997. "Dueling Realisms." *International Organization,* 51:445–478.

Brown, Michael E., ed. 2003. *Grave New World: Security Challenges in the 21st Century.* Washington, DC: Georgetown University Press.

Brown, Sarah Graham. 1999. *Sanctioning Saddam: The Politics of Intervention in Iraq.* New York: St. Martin's.

Brown, Seyom. 1992. *International Relations in a Changing Global System.* Boulder, CO: Westview.

Brown, Seyom. 1998. "World Interests and the Changing Dimension of Security." In *World Security: Challenges for a New Century,* 3rd ed., ed. Michael T. Klare and Yogesh Chandran. New York: St. Martin's.

Brysk, Alison, ed. 2002. *Globalization and Human Rights.* Berkeley, CA: University of California Press.

Bueno de Mesquita, Bruce. 2002. "Domestic Politics and International Relations." *International Studies Quarterly,* 46:1–10.

Bueno de Mesquita, Bruce J., and James D. Morrow. 1999. "Sorting Through the Wealth of Nations." *International Security,* 24/2:56–73.

Bueno de Mesquita, Bruce J., and Randolph M. Siverson. 1993. "War and the Survival of Political Leaders: A Comparative Analysis." Presented at the annual meeting of the American Political Science Association, Washington, DC.

Bull, Hedley, and Adam Watson. 1982. *The Expansion of International Society.* London: Oxford University Press.

Bunch, Charlotte, and Roxana Carillo. 1998. "Global Violence against Women: The Challenge to Human Rights and Development." In *World Security: Challenges for a New Century,* 3rd ed., ed. Michael T. Klare and Yogesh Chandran. New York: St. Martin's.

Burch, Kurt, and Robert A. Denemark, eds. 1997. *Constituting International Political Economy: International Political Economy Yearbook, vol. 10.* Boulder, CO: Lynne Rienner.

Bureau of the Census. *See* (U.S.) Bureau of the Census.

Burgess, Stephen F. 1998. "The Limits of Westphalia Sovereignty and Genocide in Africa." Paper presented at the International Studies Association convention, Minneapolis.

Burk, Erika. 1994. "Human Rights and Social Issues." In *A Global Agenda: Issues Before the 49th General Assembly,* ed. John Tessitore and Susan Woolfson. Lanham, MD: University Press of America.

Burrowes, Robert J. 1996. *The Strategy of Nonviolent Defense.* Albany: State University of New York Press.

Butler, Michael J. 2003. "U.S. Military Intervention in Crisis, 1945–1994." *Journal of Conflict Resolution,* 47:226–248.

Byman, Daniel L., and Kenneth M. Pollack. 2001. "Let Us Now Praise Great Men." *International Security,* 25/4:107–146.

Calleo, David P. 2003. *Rethinking Europe's Future.* Princeton, NJ: Princeton University Press.

Cameron, Gavin. 1999. *Nuclear Terrorism: A Threat Assessment for the Twenty-First Century.* New York: St. Martin's.

Campbell, Tom, Jeffrey Goldsworthy, and Adrienne Stone, eds. 2003. *Protecting Human Rights: Instruments and Institutions.* Oxford, U.K.: Oxford University Press.

Caplow, Theodore, and Louis Hicks. 2002. *Systems of War and Peace.* Lanham, MD: University Press of America.

Caprioli, Mary. 1998. "Why Democracy?" In *Taking Sides: Clashing Views on Controversial Issues in World Politics,* 8th ed., ed. John T. Rourke. Guilford, CT: Dushkin/McGraw-Hill.

Caprioli, Mary. 2000. "The Myth of Women's Pacifism." In *Taking Sides: Clashing Views on Controversial Issues in World Politics,* 9th ed., ed. John T. Rourke. Guilford, CT: McGraw-Hill/Dushkin.

Caprioli, Mary, and Mark Boyer. 2001. "Gender, Violence and International Crisis." *Journal of Conflict Resolution,* 45:503–518.

Carrington, William J., and Enrica Detragiache. 1999. "How Extensive Is the Brain Drain?" *Finance & Development,* 36/2:108.

Carruthers, Susan L. 1998. "Not like the US? Europeans and the Spread of American Culture." *International Affairs,* 74:883–892.

Carter, Ralph G. 2003. "Leadership at Risk: The Perils of Unilateralism." *PS: Political Science & Politics,* 36/1:17–22.

Cashman, Greg. 1999. *What Causes War? An Introduction to Theories of International Conflict.* Lanham, MD: Lexington Books.

Catley-Carlson, Margaret, and Judith A.M. Outlaw. 1998. Poverty and Population Issues: Clarifying the Connections." *Journal of International Affairs,* 52:233–252.

Chafetz, Glenn, Michael Spirtas, and Benjamin Frankel, eds. 1999. *Origins of National Interests.* Essex, U.K.: Frank Cass.

Chan, Stephen, Peter G. Mandaville, and Roland Bleiker, eds. 2001. *The Zen of International Relations: IR Theory from East to West.* New York: Palgrave Macmillan.

Chan, Stephen, and Jarrod Weiner, eds. 1998. *Twentieth Century International History.* New York: St. Martin's.

Chittick, William O., and Lee Ann Pingel. 2002. *American Foreign Policy: History, Substance and Process.* New York: Seven Bridges Press.

Chrystal, Jonathan. 1998. "A New Kind of Competition: How American Producers Respond to Incoming Foreign Direct Investment." *International Studies Quarterly,* 42:513–543.

CIA. *See* U.S. (CIA).

Cimballa, Stephen J. 2002. *Military Persuasion in War and Policy: The Power of Soft.* Westport, CT: Praeger.

Cimballa, Stephen J. 2003. *Shield of Dreams: Missile Defenses and Nuclear Strategy.* Westport, CT: Praeger.

Cioffi-Revilla, Claudio. 2000. "Ancient Warfare: Origins and Systems." In *Handbook of War Studies II,* ed. Manus I. Midlarsky. Ann Arbor, MI: University of Michigan Press.

Cioffi-Revilla, Claudio. 2000. *Origins of the International System: Mesopotamian and West Asian Politics, 6000 B.C. to 1500 B.C.* Denver: Long-Range Analysis of War Project, University of Colorado.

Clapham, Christopher. 1999. "Sovereignty and the Third World State." *Political Studies,* 47:522–537.

Cockburn, Cynthia. 1999. "Gender, Armed Conflict and Political Violence: A Background Paper." Washington, DC: World Bank.

Cohen, Raymond. 1987. *Theater of Power: The Art of Diplomatic Signaling.* Essex, U.K.: Longman.

Cohen, Stephen D. 2000. *The Making of United States International Economic Policy,* 5th ed. Westport, CT: Praeger.

Coker, Christopher. 2002. *Waging War Without Warriors? The Changing Culture of Military Conflict.* Boulder, CO: Lynne Rienner.

Colaresi, Michael. 2001. "Great Power Rivalry and the Leadership Long Cycle." *Journal of Conflict Resolution,* 45:569–584.

Conversi, Daniel. 2002. *Ethnonationalism in the Contemporary World: Walker Connor and the Study of Nationalism.* London: Routledge.

Cortright, David, and George A. Lopez, eds. 1996. *Economic Sanctions: Panacea or Peacebuilding in a Post–Cold War World?* Boulder, CO: Westview.

Cortright, David, and George A. Lopez. 2000. *The Sanctions Decade: Assessing UN Strategies in the 1990s.* Boulder, CO: Lynne Rienner.

Cortright, David, and Geroge A. Lopez, eds. 2002. *Smart Sanctions: Targeting Economic Statecraft.* Lanham, MD: Rowman & Littlefield.

Cox, Dan G. 2002. "Making Sense of Poll Results: Ambiguity in the Interpretation of Foreign Policy Questions Regarding the United Nations." *International Journal of Public Opinion Research,* 14:218–219.

Cox, Robert W., ed. 1997. *The New Realism: Perspectives on Multilateralism and World Order.* New York: St. Martin's.

Craig, Gordon A., and Alexander L. George. 1995. *Force and Statecraft: Diplomatic Problems of Our Time,* 3rd ed. New York: Oxford University Press.

Croft, Stuart. 1997. *Strategies of Arms Control: A History and Typology.* New York: St. Martin's.

Croucher, Sheila, L. 2003. "Perpetual Imagining: Nationhood in a Global Era." *International Studies Review,* 5:1–24.

Croucher, Sheila, L. 2003a. *Globalization and Belonging: The Politics of Identity in a Changing World.* Lanham, MD: Rowman & Littlefield.

Culter, A. Claire, Virginia Haufler, and Tony Porter, eds. 1999. *Private Authority and International Affairs.* Albany: State University of New York Press.

Cusimano, Maryann, ed. 1998. *Beyond Sovereignty: Issues for a Global Agenda.* New York: St. Martin's.

Daalder, Ivo H., and James M. Lindsay. 2003. "The Bush Revolution: The Remaking of America's Foreign Policy." Paper presented at the conference on The Bush Presidency: An Early Assessment, Woodrow Wilson School, Princeton University, Princeton, NJ, May 27, 2003.

Dahbour, Omar. 2003. *The Illusion of the Peoples: A Critique of National Self-Determination.* Lanham, MD: Lexington Books.

Dalton, Russell J., Wilhelm Burklin, and Andrew Drummond. 2001. "Public Opinion and Direct Democracy." *Data Journal of Democracy,* 12/4:141–154.

Danspeckgruber, Wolfgang. 2002. *The Self-Determination of Peoples: Community, Nation, and State in an Interdependent World.* Boulder, CO: Lynne Rienner.

Dassel, Kurt. 1998. "Civilians, Soldiers, and Strife: Domestic Sources of International Aggression." *International Security,* 23:107–140.

Dassel, Kurt, and Eric Reinhardt. 1999. "Domestic Strife and the Initiation of Violence at Home and Abroad." *American Journal of Political Science,* 43:56–85.

de la Garza, Rodolfo, and Harry Pachon, eds. 2000. *Latinos and U.S. Foreign Policy: Representing the "Homeland"?* Landover, MD: Rowman & Littlefield.

DeCamp, William T. 2000. "The Big Picture: A Moral Analysis of Allied Force in Kosovo." *Marine Corps Gazette,* 84/2: 42– 44.

Der Derian, James. 1988. "Introducing Philosophical Traditions in International Relations." *Millennium,* 17:189–193.

Destler, I. M., Leslie H. Gelb, and Anthony Lake. 1984. *Our Own Worst Enemy: The Unmaking of American Foreign Policy.* New York: Simon & Schuster.

Diamond, Larry. 2003. "Universal Democracy?" *Policy Review,* 119:3–26.

Diehl, Paul F. 2001. *The Politics of Global Governance: International Organizations in an Interdependent World.* Boulder, CO: Lynne Rienner.

Diehl, Paul F., Daniel Druckman, and James Wall. 1998. "International Peacekeeping and Conflict Resolution: A Taxonomic Analysis with Implications." *Journal of Conflict Resolution,* 42:33–55.

DiIulio, John J. 2003. "Inside the Bush Presidency: Reflections of an Academic Interloper." Paper presented at the conference on The Bush Presidency: An Early Assessment, Woodrow Wilson School, Princeton University, Princeton, NJ, May 27, 2003.

Dollar, David, and Aart Kraay. 2001. "Trade, Growth and Poverty." *Finance & Development,* 38/3. Web edition at: http://www.imf.org/external/pubind.htm.

Dollar, David, and Aart Kraay. 2002. "Spreading the Wealth." *Foreign Affairs,* 81/1:1–18.

Donnelly, Jack. 2003. *Universal Human Rights in Theory and Practice.* Ithaca, NY: Cornell University Press.

Drezner, Daniel W. 1998. "Conflict Expectations and the Paradox of Economic Coercion." *International Studies Quarterly,* 42:709–732.

Drezner, Daniel W. 2000. "Bargaining, Enforcement, and Multilateral Sanctions: When Is Cooperation Counterproductive?" *International Organization,* 54:73–102.

Dror, Yehezkel. 1971. *Crazy States: A Counterconventional Strategic Issue.* Lexington, MA: D. C. Heath.

Druckman, Daniel. 1994. "Nationalism, Patriotism and Group Loyalty: A Social Psychological Perspective." *Mershon International Studies Review,* supplement to *International Studies Quarterly,* 38:43–68.

Dunn, John. 1995. "Introduction: Crisis of the Nation State." In *Contemporary Crisis of the Nation State,* ed. John Dunn. Oxford, U.K.: Blackwell.

Ehrenreich, Barbara, and Katha Pollitt, 1999. "Fukuyama's Follies." *Foreign Affairs,* 78/1:118–129.

Eichengreen, Barry. 1998. "Geography as Destiny." *Foreign Affairs,* 77/2:128–139.

Eide, Asbjorn. 1998. "The Historical Significance of the Universal Declaration." *International Social Science Journal,* 50: 475–498.

Eland, Ivan. 2002. "The Empire Strikes Out: The 'New Imperialism': and Its Fatal Flaws." *Policy Analysis,* #469. Washington, DC: Cato Institute.

Elliott, Kimberly Ann. 1993. "A Look at the Record." *Bulletin of the Atomic Scientists,* November.

Elliott, Kimberly Ann. 1998. "The Sanctions Glass: Half Full or Completely Empty?" *International Security,* 23:50–65.

Elliott, Kimberly Ann, and Barbara L. Oegg. 2002. "Economic Sanctions Reconsidered—Again." Paper presented at International Studies Association Convention, New Orleans, LA, March 23–26, 2002.

Elman, Colin. 1996. "Why Not Neorealist Theories of Foreign Policy?" *Security Studies,* 6:7–53.

Enders, Walter, and Todd Sandler. 1999. "Transnational Terrorism in the Post–Cold War Era." *International Studies Quarterly,* 43:145–167.

Esposito, John. 2002. *Unholy War: Terror in the Name of Islam.* New York: Oxford University Press.

Etzioni, Amitai. 1993. "The Evils of Self-Determination." *Foreign Policy,* 89:21–35.

Everts, Philip, and Pierangelo, Isernia, eds. 2001. *Public Opinion and the Use of Force.* London: Routledge.

Falk, Richard. 1999. "World Prisms: The Future of Sovereign States and International Order." *Harvard International Review,* 21/3:30–35.

(FAO) Food and Agricultural Organization. 1995. "Forest Resources Assessment 1990: Global Synthesis." *FAO Forestry Paper 124.* Rome: FAO.

Farer, Tom J. 2003. "The Ethics of Interventions in Self-Determination Struggles." *Human Rights Quarterly,* 25: 382–406.

Farrell, Robert H. 1998. *The Dying President: Franklin D. Roosevelt, 1944–1945.* Columbia: University of Missouri Press.

Fearon, James D., and David D. Laitin. 2003. "Ethnicity, Insurgency, and Civil War." *American Political Science Review,* 97:75–90.

Feld, Werner J. 1979. *International Relations: A Transnational Approach.* New York: Alfred Publishing.

Feldstein, Martin. 1998. "Refocusing the IMF." *Foreign Affairs,* 77/2:46–71.

Fitzsimons, David M. 1995. "Thomas Paine's New World Order: Idealistic Internationalism in the Ideology of Early American Foreign Relations." *Diplomatic History,* 19:569– 582.

Florea, Natalie, Mark A. Boyer, Michael J. Butler, Magnolia Hernandez, Kimberly Weir, Scott W. Brown, Paula R. Johnson, Ling Meng, Haley J. Mayall, and Clarisse Lima. 2003. "Negotiating from Mars to Venus: Some Findings on Gender's Impact in Simulated International Negotiations." Paper presented at the International Studies Association, Northeast Convention, November 2003, Providence, RI.

Flynn, Gregory, and Henry Farrell. 1999. "Piecing Together the Democratic Peace: The CSCE and the 'Construction' of Security in Post–Cold War Europe." *International Organization,* 53:505–535.

Foot, Rosemary, S. Neil MacFarlane, and Michael Mastanudo, eds. 2003. *U.S. Hegemony and International Organizations.* New York: Oxford University Press.

Fordham, Benjamin. 1998. "The Politics of Threat Perception and the Use of Force: A Political Economy Model of U.S. Uses of Force, 1949–1994." *International Studies Quarterly,* 42:567–590.

Fordham, Benjamin O. 2002. "Domestic Politics, International Pressure, and the Allocation of American Cold War Military Spending." *Journal of Politics,* 64:63–89.

Fowler, Michael Ross, and Julie Marie Bunck. 1995. *Law, Power, and the Sovereign States: The Evolution and Application of the*

Concept of Sovereignty. University Park: University of Pennsylvania Press.

Foyle, Douglas C. 1997. "Public Opinion and Foreign Policy: Elite Beliefs as a Mediating Variable." *International Studies Quarterly,* 41:141–170.

Franck, Thomas M. 1997. "Is Personal Freedom a Western Value?" *American Journal of International Law,* 91:593– 627.

Fraser, Arvonne S. 1999. "Becoming Human: The Origins and Development of Women's Human Rights." *Human Rights Quarterly* 21:853–906.

Freedman, Lawrence. 1998. "Military Power and Political Influence." *International Affairs,* 74:36–49.

Freedom House. 1997. *Freedom in the World: The Annual Survey of Political Rights & Civil Liberties, 1996–1997.* New Brunswick, NJ: Transaction.

Fukuyama, Francis. 1989. "The End of History?" *National Interest,* 16:3–18.

Fukuyama, Francis. 1998. "Women and the Evolution of Politics." *Foreign Affairs,* 77/5:24–40.

Fuller, Graham E., and Rend Rahim Francke. 2000. *The Arab Shi'a: The Forgotten Muslims.* New York: St. Martin's.

Gabel, Matthew. 1998. "Public Support for European Integration: An Empirical Test of Five Theories." *Journal of Politics,* 60:333–355.

Gaenslen, Fritz. 1997. "Advancing Cultural Explanations." In *Culture and Foreign Policy,* ed. Valerie M. Hudson. Boulder, CO: Lynne Rienner.

Gallagher, Nancy W., ed. 1998. *Arms Control: New Approaches to Theory and Policy.* Newbury Park, U.K.: Frank Cass.

Galtung, Johan. 1994. *Human Rights in Another Key.* Cambridge, U.K.: Polity Press.

Garrett, Geoffrey, R., Daniel Kelemen, and Heiner Schulz. 1998. "The European Court of Justice, National Governments, and Legal Integration in the European Union." *International Organization,* 52:149–176.

Gartner, Scott Sigmund, and Randolph M. Siverson. 1996. "War Expansion and War Outcome." *Journal of Conflict Resolution,* 40:4–15.

Gartzke, Erik. 1998. "Kant We All Just Get Along? Opportunity, Willingness, and the Origins of the Democratic Peace." *American Journal of Political Science,* 42:1–27.

Gartzke, Erik, Quan Li, and Charles Boehmer. 2001. "Investing in the Peace: Economic Interdependence and International Conflict." *International Organization,* 55:391–438.

Gaus, Gerald F. 2000. *Political Concepts and Political Theories.* Boulder, CO: Westview.

Geller, Daniel S. 1993. "Power Differentials and War in Rival Dyads." *International Studies Quarterly,* 37:173–193.

Geller, Daniel S., and J. David Singer. 1998. *Nations at War: A Scientific Study of International Conflict.* Cambridge, U.K.: Cambridge University Press.

Gellner, Ernest. 1995. "Introduction." In *Nations of Nationalism,* ed. Sukumar Periwal. Budapest: Central European University Press.

Gelpi, Christopher, and Peter D. Feaver. 2002. "Speak Softly and Carry a Big Stick? Veterans in the Political Elite and the American Use of Force." *American Political Science Review,* 96:779–793.

George, Alexander L. 1994. "Some Guides to Bridging the Gap." *Mershon International Studies Review,* 39:171–172.

Gibbs, David N. 1995. "Secrecy and International Relations." *Journal of Peace Research,* 32:213–238.

Gibler, Douglas M., and John A. Vasquez. 1998. "Uncovering the Dangerous Alliances, 1495–1980." *International Studies Quarterly,* 42:785–810.

Gilbert, Alan. 1999. *Must Global Politics Constrain Democracy? Great-Power Realism, Democratic Peace, and Democratic Internationalism.* Princeton, NJ:Princeton University Press, 1999.

Gilbert, Mark F. 2003. *Surpassing Realism: The Politics of European Integration Since 1945.* Lanham, MD: Rowman & Littlefield.

Gilpin, Robert. 1981. *War and Change in World Politics.* Cambridge, U.K.: Cambridge University Press.

Goddard, C., Patrick Cronin Roe, and Kishore C. Dash, eds. 2003. *International Political Economy,* 2nd ed. Boulder, CO: Lynne Rienner.

Goff, Patricia M. 2000. "Invisible Borders: Economic Liberalization and National Identity." *International Studies Quarterly,* 44:533–62.

Goldsmith, Jack, and Stephen D. Krasner. 2003. "The Limits of Idealism." *Daedalus,*132:47–63.

Goldstein, Melvyn C. 1997. *The Snow Lion and the Dragon: China, Tibet and the Dalai Lama.* Berkeley: University of California Press.

Graebner, Norman, ed. 1964. *Ideas and Diplomacy.* New York: Oxford University Press.

Grant, Rebecca, and Kathleen Newland, eds. 1991. *Gender and International Relations.* Bloomington: Indiana University Press.

Grantham, Bill. 1998. "America the Menace: France's Feud with Hollywood." *World Policy Journal,* 15/2:58–66.

Gray, Colin S. 1994. "Force, Order, and Justice: The Ethics of Realism in Statecraft." *Global Affairs,* 14:1–17.

Green, Michael. 1996. *Arming Japan: Defense Production, Alliance Politics, and the Post-War Search for Autonomy.* Baltimore: Johns Hopkins University Press.

Greenfeld, Liah. 1992. *Nationalism: Five Roads to Modernity.* Cambridge, MA: Harvard University Press.

Greenstein, Fred I. 2003. "The Leadership Style of George W. Bush." Paper presented at the conference on The Bush Presidency: An Early Assessment, Woodrow Wilson School, Princeton University, Princeton, NJ, May 27, 2003.

Greider, William. 1997. *The Manic Logic of Global Capitalism.* New York: Simon & Schuster.

Gruenberg, Leon. 1996. "The IPE of Multinational Corporations." In *Introduction to International Political Economy,* ed. David N. Balaam and Michael Veseth. Upper Saddle River, NJ: Prentice Hall.

Guelke, Adrian. 1998. *The Age of Terrorism and the International Political System.* New York: St Martin's.

Guibernau, Montserrat. 1996. *Nationalisms: The Nation-State and Nationalism in the Twentieth Century.* Cambridge, U.K.: Polity Press.

Gurr, Nadine, and Benjamin Cole. 2000. *The New Face of Terrorism: Threats from Weapons of Mass Destruction.* New York: St. Martin's.

Gurr, Ted Robert, Monty G. Marshall, and Deepa Khosla. 2001. *Peace and Conflict 2001: Armed Conflicts, Self- Determination Movements, and Democracy.* College Park Maryland: Integrated Network for Societal Conflict Research at the University of Maryland. Available on the Web at http://www.bsos.umd.edu/cidcm/peace.htm.

Haass, Richard N. 1997. *The Reluctant Sheriff: The United States After the Cold War.* New York: Council on Foreign Relations.

Hagen, Joe D. 2001. "Does Decision Making Matter: Systemic Assumptions vs. Historical Reality in International Theory." *International Studies Review,* 3:2 (summer): 5– 46.

Hall, John. 1995. "Nationalism, Classified and Explained." In *Notions of Nationalism,* ed. Sukumar Periwal. Budapest: Central European University Press.

Hall, Rodney Bruce. 1999. *National Collective Identity: Social Constructs and International Systems.* New York: Columbia University Press.

Hannum, Hurst. 1999. "The Specter of Secession." *Foreign Affairs,* 77/2:13–19.

Harbour, Frances V. 1998. *Thinking About International Ethics: Moral Theory and Cases from American Foreign Policy.* Boulder, CO: Westview.

Harnisch, Sebastian. 2001. "The Hegemon and the Demon": U.S. Nuclear Learning vis-à-vis North Korea." Unpublished paper on the Web at http://www.uni-trier.de/uni/fb3/politik/liba/harnisch/Pubs/Hegemon-Demon-Final.pdf.

Hashim, Ahmed S. 1998. "The Revolution in Military Affairs Outside the West." *Journal of International Affairs,* 51:431– 446.

Hawkins, Darren. 1999. "Transnational Activists as Motors for Change." *International Studies Review,* I/1:119–122.

Hayden, Deborah. 2003. *Pox: Genius, Madness, and the Mysteries of Syphilis.* New York: Perseus.

Heasley, James E., III. 2003. *Organization Global Governance: International Regimes and the Process of Collective Hegemony.* Lanham, MD: Lexington Books.

Hechter, Michael. 2000. *Containing Nationalism.* Oxford, U.K.: York: Oxford University Press.

Helco, Hugh. 2003. "The Bush Political Ethos." Paper presented at the conference on The Bush Presidency: An Early Assessment, Woodrow Wilson School, Princeton University, Princeton, NJ, May 27, 2003.

Held, David. 1987. *Models of Democracy.* Stanford, CA: Stanford University Press.

Henderson, Earl Anthony. 1999. "The Democratic Peace through the Lens of Culture, 1820–1989." *International Studies Quarterly,* 42/3:461–484.

Henderson, Errol A. 2002. *Democracy and War: The End of an Illusion?* Boulder, CO: Lynne Rienner.

Henry, Charles P., ed. 2000. *Foreign Policy and the Black (Inter) National Interest.* Albany: State University of New York Press.

Hensel, Paul R., Gary Goertz, and Paul F. Diehl. 2000. "The Democratic Peace and Rivalries." *Journal of Politics,* 62:1173–1189.

Heo, Uk, Eban J.Christensen, and Tatyana Karaman. 2003. "Power Parity, Alliance, Differential Growth, and Great Power War." *Armed Forces & Society,* 29:449–459.

Herek, Gregory M., Irving L. Janis, and Paul Huth. 1987. "Decision-Making During International Crises: Is the Quality of Progress Related to the Outcome?" *Journal of Conflict Resolution,* 31:203–236.

Hermann, Margaret G. 1998. "One Field, Many Perspectives: Building the Foundations for Dialogue." *International Studies Quarterly,* 42/4:605–620.

Hermann, Margaret G. 2001. "How Decision Units Shape Foreign Policy: A Theoretical Framework." *International Studies Review,* Special Issue, "Leaders, Groups, and Coalitions: Understanding the People and Processes in Foreign Policy Making," 47–82.

Hermann, Margaret G., and Joe D. Hagan. 1998. "International Decision Making: Leadership Matters." *Foreign Policy,* No. 110 (Spring):124–137.

Hermann, Margaret B., Thomas Preston, Baghat Korany, and Timothy M. Shaw. 2001. "Who Leads Matters; The Effects of Powerful Individuals." *International Studies Review,* Special Issue, "Leaders, Groups, and Coalitions: Understanding the People and Processes in Foreign Policy Making," 83–132.

Hetherington, Marc J., and Michael Nelson. 2003. "Anatomy of a Rally Effect: George W. Bush and the War on Terrorism." *Political Science and Politics,* 36:37–42.

Heymann, Philip B. 2002. "Dealing with Terrorism: An Overview." *International Security,* 26/3:24–38.

Higgins, Rosalyn. 1994. *Problems and Process: International Law and How We Use It.* New York: Oxford University Press.

Hirst, Paul, and Grahame Thompson. 1996. *Globalization in Question: The International Economy and the Possibilities of Governance.* Cambridge, U.K.: Polity Press.

Hix, Simon. 1999. *The Political System of the European Union.* New York: St. Martin's.

Hobbes, Heidi H., ed. 2000. *Pondering Postinternationalism: A Paradigm for the Twenty-First Century.* Albany, NY: State University of New York Press.

Hobsbawm, Eric. 2001. "Democracy Can Be Bad for You." *New Statesman* 14/626 (March 5, 2001): 25–28.

Hoffmann, Stanley. 1995. "The Crisis of Liberal Internationalism." *Foreign Policy,* 98:159–179.

Hoffman, Stanley. 2003. "World Governance: Beyond Utopia." *Daedalus,* 132:27–35.

Holsti, Ole R. 1997. *Public Opinion and American Foreign Policy.* Ann Arbor: University of Michigan Press.

Homer-Dixon, Thomas. 1998. "Environmental Scarcity and Intergroup Conflict." In *World Security: Challenges for a New Century,* 3rd ed., ed. Michael T. Klare and Yogesh Chandran. New York: St. Martin's.

Hopmann, P. Terrence. 1999. *Building Security in Post–Cold War Eurasia: The OSCE and U.S. Foreign Policy.* Washington, DC: United States Institute of Peace.

Horne, John. 2002. "Civilian Populations and Wartime Violence: Toward an Historical Analysis. *International Social Science Journal,* 26:426–435.

Hossay, Patrick. 2002. *Contentions of Nationhood: Nationalist Movements, Political Conflict and Social Change in Flanders, Scotland, and French Canada.* Lanham, MD: Lexington Books.

Hout, Will. 1997. "Globalization and the Quest for Governance." *Mershon International Studies Review,* 41:99–106.

Hufbauer, Cary Clyde, and Barbara Oegg. 2003. "The Impact of Economic Sanctions on U.S. Trade: Andrew Rose's Gravity Model." *International Economics Policy Briefs,* Number PB03-4, April 2003. Washington DC: Institute for International Economics.

Hughes, Donna M. 2000. "The 'Natasha' Trade: The Transnational Shadow Market of Trafficking in Women." *Journal of International Affairs,* 53:625–652.

Huntington, Samuel. 1993. "The Clash of Civilizations." *Foreign Affairs,* 72(3):56–73.

Huntington, Samuel P. 1996. *The Clash of Civilizations and the Remaking of World Order.* New York: Simon & Schuster.

Huntington, Samuel P. 1999. "The Lonely Superpower." *Foreign Affairs,* 78/2 (March/April 1999):35–49.

Huntley, James Robert. 1998. *Pax Democratics: A Strategy for the Twenty-First Century.* New York: St. Martin's.

Hurd, Ian. 1999. "Legitimacy and Authority in International Politics." *International Organization,* 53:379–408.

Huth, Paul K. 1996. *Standing Your Ground: Territorial Disputes and International Conflict.* Ann Arbor: University of Michigan Press.

Huth, Paul K., Christopher Gelpi, and D. Scott Bennett. 1993. "The Escalation of Great Power Militarized Disputes: Testing Rational Deterrence Theory and Structural Realism." *American Political Science Review,* 87:609–623.

Ikenberry, G. John. 2001. "Getting Hegemony Right." *The National Interest,* (Spring) 63:17–24.

Ikenberry, G. John, ed. 2002. *America Unrivaled: The Future of the Balance of Power.* Ithaca, NY: Cornell University Press.

Inglehart, Ronald. 2003. "How Solid Is Mass Support for Democracy—And How Can We Measure It?" *PS, Political Science and Politics,* 36/1:51–57.

Inglehart, Ronald, and Pippa Norris. 2002. "Islam and the West: Testing the Clash of Civilizations Thesis." Faculty Research Working Paper Series. John F. Kennedy School of Government. Harvard University.

Inglehart, Ronald, and Pippa Norris. 2003. "The True Clash of Civilizations." *Foreign Policy,* 136:63–70.

Inglehart, Ronald, and Pippa Norris. 2003a. *Rising Tide: Gender Equality and Cultural Change Around the World.* New York: Cambridge University Press.

Isaak, Robert A. 2000. *Managing World Economic Change: International Political Economy,* 3rd ed. Upper Saddle River, NJ: Prentice-Hall.

Isernia, Pierangelo, Zoltan Juhasz, and Hans Rattinger. 2002. "Foreign Policy and the Rational Public in Comparative Perspective." *Journal of Conflict Resolution,* 46:201–225.

Ishiyama, John T., and Marijke Breuning. 1998. *Ethnopolitics in the "New" Europe.* Boulder, CO: Lynne Rienner.

Iyer, Pico. 1996. "The Global Village Finally Arrives." In *Annual Editions: Global Issues 96/97.* Guilford, CT: Dushkin/McGraw-Hill.

Jackson, Robert. 1999. "TI Sovereignty in World Politics: A Glance at the Conceptual and Historical Landscape." *Political Studies,* 47:431–56.

Jackson, Robert, and Georg Sørenson. 2003. *Introduction to International Relations: Theories and Approaches,* 2nd ed. Oxford, U.K.: Oxford University Press.

Jacobsen, John Kurt. 2003. "Dueling Constructivisms: A Post-Mortem on the Ideas Debated in Mainstream IR/IPE." *Review of International Studies,* 29:39–60.

James, Alan. 1999. "The Practice of Sovereign Statehood in Contemporary International Society." *Political Studies,* 47:457–573.

James, Patrick. 2002. *International Relations and Scientific Progress: Structural Realism Reconsidered.* Columbus: Ohio State University Press.

Jaquette, Jane S. 1997. "Women in Power: From Tokenism to Critical Mass." *Foreign Policy,* 108:23–97.

Javeline, Debra. 1999. "Protest and Passivity: How Russians Respond to Not Getting Paid." Davis Center for Russian Studies, Harvard University. Published on the Web at http://data.fas.harvard.edu/~javeline/draft1.htm.

Jayawickrama, Nihal. 2003. *The Judicial Application of Human Rights Law: National, Regional and International Jurisprudence.* Cambridge, U.K.: Cambridge University Press.

Jervis, Robert. 1999. "Realism, Neoliberalism, and Cooperation: Understanding the Debate." *International Security,* 24:42–63.

Jett, Dennis C. 2000. *Why Peacekeeping Fails.* New York: St. Martin's.

Jewett, Aubrey W., and Marc D. Turetzky. 1998. "Stability and Change in President Clinton's Foreign Policy Beliefs, 1993–96," *Presidential Studies Quarterly,* 28:638–676.

Johansen, Robert C. 1994. "Building World Security: The Need for Strengthened International Institutions." In *World Security: Challenges for a New Century,* ed. Michael T. Klare and Daniel C. Thomas. New York: St. Martin's.

Jones, Howard. 1988. *The Course of American Diplomacy,* 2nd ed. Chicago: Dorsey.

Jones, R. J. Barry. 1999. "Globalization and Change in the International Political Economy." *International Affairs,* 75/2: 357–369.

Jowitt, Ken. 2003. "Why the Bush Doctrine Makes Sense." *Hoover Digest,* 2003/2 (Spring). On the Web at http://www-hoover.stanford.edu/publications/digest/.

Joyner, Christopher C. 2000. "The Reality and Relevance of International Law in the Twenty-First Century." In *The Global Agenda: Issues and Perspectives,* ed. Charles W. Kegley, Jr., and Eugene R. Wittkopf. Boston: McGraw-Hill.

Jung, Hwa Yol. 2002. *Comparative Political Culture in the Age of Globalization.* Lanham, MD: Lexington Books.

Jutta, Joachim. 2003. "Framing Issues and Seizing Opportunities: The UN, NGOs, and Women's Rights." *International Studies Quarterly,* 47:247–274.

Kaempfer, Willliam H., and Anton D. Lowenberg. 1999. "Unilateral Versus Multilateral International Sanctions: A Public Choice Perspective." *International Studies Quarterly,* 43:37–58.

Kaplan, Robert D. 1999. "Was Democracy Just a Moment?" In *Stand: Contending Issue and Opinion, World Politics,* ed., Marc Genest. Boulder, CO: Coursewise Publishing.

Kapstein, Ethan B., and Michael Mastanduno, eds. 1999. *Realism and State Strategies After the Cold War.* New York: Columbia University Press.

Karl, Terry Lynn. 1999. "The Perils of the Petro-State: Reflections on the Paradox of Plenty." *Journal of International Affairs,* 53:31–51.

Katada, Saori N., and Timothy J. McKeown. 1998. "Aid Politics and Electoral Politics: Japan, 1970–1992." *International Studies Quarterly,* 42:591–600.

Kateb, George. 2000. "Is Patriotism a Mistake?" *Social Research,* 67:901–923.

Keane, John. 1994. "Nations, Nationalism, and Citizens in Europe." *International Social Science Journal,* 140:169– 184.

Kegley, Charles W., Jr., and Gregory A. Raymond. 1999. *How Nations Make Peace.* New York: St. Martin's.

Kelman, Herbert C. 2000. "The Role of the Scholar-Practitioner in International Conflict Resolution." *International Studies Perspective,* 1:273–288.

Kennedy, Paul. 1988. *The Rise and Fall of the Great Powers.* New York: Random House.

Kent, Ann. 1999. *China, the United Nations, and Human Rights: The Limits of Compliance.* Philadelphia: University of Pennsylvania Press.

Kent, George. 2002. "Food Trade and Food Rights." *United Nations Chronicle,* 39/1. Online edition at http://www.un.org/Pubs/chronicle/2002/issue1/0102p27.html.

Keohane, Robert O. 1998. "International Institutions: Can Interdependence Work?" *Foreign Policy,* 110:82–96.

Keohane, Robert O., and Lisa L. Martin. 1995. "The Promise of Institutionalist Theory." *International Security,* 20/1:39–51.

Keohane, Robert O., and Joseph S. Nye, Jr. 1999. "Globalization: What's New? What's Not? (And So What?)." *Foreign Policy,* 114:104–119.

Keylor, William. 1996. *The Twentieth Century World.* New York: Oxford University Press.

Kille, Kent J., and Roger M. Scully. 2003. "Executive Heads and the Role of Intergovernmental Organizations: Expansionist Leadership in the United Nations and the European Union." *Political Psychology,* 24:175–190.

Kim, Samuel S. 1997. "China as a Great Power." *Current History,* 96:246–251.

Kimura, Masato, and David A. Welch. 1998. "Specifying 'Interests': Japan's Claim to the Northern Territories and Its Implications for International Relations Theory." *International Studies Quarterly,* 42:213–244.

Kinsella, David, and Bruce Russett. 2002. "Conflict Emergence and Escalation in Interactive International Dyads." *Journal of Politics,* 64:1045–1069.

Kissinger, Henry A. 1970. "The Just and the Possible." In *Negotiation and Statecraft: A Selection of Readings,* U.S. Congress, Senate Committee on Government Operations, 91st Cong., 2nd sess.

Kissinger, Henry A. 1979. *The White House Years.* Boston: Little, Brown.

Kissinger, Henry A. 1982. *Years of Upheaval.* Boston: Little, Brown.

Kissinger, Henry A. 1994. *Diplomacy.* New York: Simon & Schuster.

Klare, Michael T., and Yogesh Chandrani, eds. 1998. *World Security: Challenges for a New Century,* 3rd ed. New York: St. Martin's.

Klare, Michael T., and Lora Lumpe. 2000. "Fanning the Flames of War: Conventional Arms Transfers in the 1990s." In *World Security: Challenges for a New Century,* 3rd ed., eds. Michael T. Klare and Yogesh Chandrani. New York: St. Martin's.

Knutsen, Torbjorn L. 1999. *The Rise and Fall of World Orders.* New York: St. Martin's.

Koehn, Peter H., and Olatunde J. B. Ojo. 1999. *Making Aid Work: Innovative Approaches for Africa at the Turn of the Century.* Lanham, MD: University Press of America.

Korbin, Stephen. 1996. "The Architecture of Globalization: State Sovereignty in a Networked Global Economy." In *Globalization, Governments and Competition.* Oxford, U.K.: Oxford University Press.

Korey, William. 1998. *NGOs and the Universal Declaration of Human Rights: The Curious Grapevine.* New York: St. Martin's.

Koubi, Vally. 1999. "Military Technology Races." *International Organization,* 53:537–565.

Krasner, Stephen D. 1999. *Sovereignty: Organized Hypocrisy.* Princeton, NJ: Princeton University Press.

Krasno, Jean, Bradd C. Hayes, and Donald C. F. Daniel, eds. 2003. *Leveraging for Success in United Nations Peacekeeping Operations.* Westport, CT: Praeger.

Krause, Keith, and W. Andy Knight, eds. 1995. *State, Society, and the UN System: Perspectives on Multilateralism.* Tokyo: United Nations University Press.

Krauthammer Charles. 1991. "The Unipolar Moment." *Foreign Affairs, America and the World, 1990/91,* 23–33.

Kriesberg, Louis. 1992. *International Conflict Resolution.* New Haven, CT: Yale University Press.

Krosnick, Jon, and Shibley Telhami. 1995. "Public Attitudes Toward Israel: A Study of the Attentive and Issue Publics." *International Studies Quarterly,* 39:535–554.

Krugman, Paul. 1998. "America the Boastful." *Foreign Affairs,* 77/3:32–45.

Ku, Charlotte, and Paul F. Diehl. 1998. *International Law: Classic and Contemporary Readings.* Boulder, CO: Lynne Rienner.

Kuttner, Robert. 1998. "Globalism Bites Back." *American Prospect,* 37 (March-April, 1998):6–8.

Kydd, Andrew. 2000. "Arms Races and Arms Control: Modeling the Hawk Perspective." *American Journal of Political Science,* 44:228–244.

Lackey, Douglas. 1989. *The Ethics of War and Peace.* Englewood Cliffs, NJ: Prentice Hall.

Lafore, Laurence. 1971. *The Long Fuse. An Interpretation of the Origins of World War I,* 2nd ed. Philadelphia: J. B. Lippincott.

Lang, Anthony F., Jr., ed. 2003. *Just Intervention.* Washington, DC: Georgetown University Press.

Lauren, Paul Gordon. 1998. *The Evolution of International Human Rights.* Philadelphia: University of Pennsylvania Press.

Lawrence, Philip K. 1998. *Modernity and War: The Creed of Absolute Violence.* New York: St. Martin's.

Legro, Jeffrey W. 1996. "Culture and Preferences in the International Cooperation Two-Step." *American Political Science Review,* 90:118–137.

Legro, Jeffrey W. 1997. "Which Norms Matter: Revisiting the 'Failure' of Internationalism." *International Organization*, 51:31–63.

Legro, Jeffrey W., and Andrew Moravcsik. 1999. "Is Anybody Still a Realist?" *International Security*, 24/2:5–55.

Legro, Jeffrey W. and Andrew Moravcsik. 2001. "Faux Realism: Spin Versus Substance in the Bush Foreign-Policy Doctrine." *Foreign Policy* 125:80–82.

Lemke, Douglas, and William Reed. 2001. "War and Rivalry Among Great Powers." *American Journal of Political Science*, 45:457–469.

Lensu, Maria, and Jan-Sefan Fritz, eds. 1999. *Value Pluralism, Normative Theory, and International Relations.* New York:St. Martin's.

Leogrande, William M. 2002. "Tug of War: How Real Is the Rivalry Between Congress and the President over Foreign Policy?" *Congress & the Presidency*, 29:113–118.

Lepgold, Joseph. 1998. "Is Anyone Listening? International Relations Theory and the Problem of Policy Relevance." *Political Science Quarterly*, 113:43–63.

L'Etang, Hugh. 1970. *The Pathology of Leadership.* New York: Hawthorne Books.

Levi, Werner. 1991. *Contemporary International Law*, 2nd ed. Boulder, CO: Westview.

Levinson, David. 1998. *Ethnic Groups Worldwide.* Phoenix, AZ: Oryx Press

Li, Quan, and Rafael Reuveny. 2003. "Economic Globalization and Democracy: An Empirical Analysis." *British Journal of Political Science*, 33:29–54.

Lincoln, Edward J. 1998. "Japan's Financial Mess." *Foreign Affairs*, 77/3:57–66.

Lind, Michael. 1994. "In Defense of Liberal Nationalism." *Foreign Affairs*, 73(3):87–99.

Lindsay, James M. 1994. "Congress, Foreign Policy, and the New Institutionalism." *International Studies Quarterly*, 38:281–304.

Linklater, Andrew. 1999. "The Evolving Spheres of International Justice." *International Affairs*, 75:473–482.

Litfin, Karen T. 1994. *Ozone Discourses: Science and Politics in Global Environmental Cooperation.* New York: Columbia University Press.

Locher, Birgit and Elizabeth Prügl. 2001. "Feminism and Constructivism: World Apart or Sharing the Middle Ground?" *International Studies Quarterly*, 45:111–129.

Lomborg, Bjørn, 2001. *The Skeptical Environmentalist: Measuring the Real State of the World.* New York: Cambridge University Press.

Lomborg, Bjørn. 2003. "Debating the Skeptical Environmentalist." In *Taking Sides: Clashing View on Controversial Issues in World Politics*, 11th ed., ed. John T. Rourke. Guilford, CT: McGraw-Hill/Dushkin.

Lopez, George A., Jackie G. Smith, and Ron Pagnucco. 1995. "The Global Tide." *Bulletin of the Atomic Scientists*, 51/6 (July/August):33–39.

Lugo, Luis E. 1996. *Sovereignty at the Crossroads? Morality and International Politics in the Post–Cold War Era.* Lanham, MD: Rowman & Littlefield.

Luttwak, Edward. 2000. "Kofi's Rule: Humanitarian Intervention and Neocolonialism." *The National Interest* 58 (Winter): 57–62.

MacIver, Don. 1999. *The Politics of Multinational States.* New York: St. Martin's.

Macridis, Roy C., and Mark L. Hulliung. 1996. *Contemporary Political Ideologies.* New York: Harper-Collins.

Malone, David M., and Yuen Foong Khong, eds. 2003. *Unilateralism and U.S. Foreign Policy: International Perspectives.* Boulder, CO: Lynne Rienner.

Mandaville, Peter G. 2000. "Territory and Translocality: Discrepant Idioms of Political Identity." Paper presented at the International Studies Association Convention, Los Angeles, CA, March 2000.

Mandaville, Peter. 2002. "Reading the State from Elsewhere: Toward an Anthropology of the Postnational." *Review of International Studies*, 28:199–207.

Mansbach, Richard W. 1996. "Neo-This and Neo-That: Or, 'Play It Sam' (Again and Again)." *Mershon International Studies Review*, 40:90–95.

Mansfield, Edward D., and Helen V. Milner. 1999. "The New Wave of Regionalism." *International Organization*, 53: 589–628.

Mansfield, Edward D., and. Brian M. Pollins. 2001. "The Study of Interdependence and Conflict: Recent Advances, Open Questions, and Directions for Future Research." *Journal of Conflict Resolution*, 45:834–860.

Marshall, Bryan W., and Brandon C. Prins. 2002. "The Pendulum of Congressional Power: Agenda Change, Partisanship, and the Demise of the Post–World War II Foreign Policy Consensus." *Congress & the Presidency*, 29:195–212.

Marshall, Monty G., and Ted Robert Gurr. 2002. *Peace and Conflict, 2003: A Global Survey of Armed Conflicts, Self-Determination Movements, and Democracy.* College Park, MD: Center for International Development and Conflict Management.

Marx, Anthony W. 2003. *Faith in Nation: Exclusionary Origins of Nationalism.* New York: Oxford University Press.

Mattli, Walter, and Anne-Marie Slaughter. 1998. "Revisiting the European Court of Justice." *International Organization*, 52:177–210.

Maurer, Andreas. 2003. "The Legislative Powers and Impact of the European Parliament." *Journal of Common Market Studies*, 41:227–248.

Mayall, James. 1999. "Sovereignty, Nationalism, and Self- Determination." *Political Studies*, 47/3:474–502.

Maynes, Charles William. 1998. "The Perils of (and for) an Imperial America." *Foreign Policy*, 111:503–521.

McCormick, John. 1999. *Understanding the European Union.* Boulder, CO: Westview Press.

McGinnis, Michael Dean, and John T. Williams. 2001. *Compound Dilemmas: Democracy, Collective Action, and Superpower Rivalry.* Ann Arbor: University of Michigan Press.

McKay, David. 1999. "The Political Sustainability of European Monetary Union." *British Journal of Political Science*, 29: 463–486.

McKeown, Timothy J. 2001. "Plans and Routines, Bureaucratic Bargaining, and the Cuban Missile Crisis." *Journal of Politics,* 63:1163–1191.

Mearsheimer, John J. 2001. *The Tragedy of Great Power Politics.* New York: W. W. Norton.

Mearsheimer, John J., and Stephen Walt. 2003. "An Unnecessary War." *Foreign Policy,* 134:50–59.

Mercer, Jonathan C. 1996. *Reputation and International Politics.* Ithaca, NY: Cornell University Press.

Meunier, Sophie. 2000. "What Single Voice? European Institutions and EU-US Trade Negotiations." *International Organization,* 54/2:103–135.

Meyer, Mary K., and Elisabeth Prügel, eds. 1999. *Gender Politics in Global Governance.* Lanham, MD: Rowman & Littlefield.

Midlarsky, Manus. 1999. "Democracy and Islam: Implications for Civilizational Conflict and the Democratic Peace." *International Studies Quarterly,* 42:485–512.

Milner, Helen V. 1998. "International Political Economy: Beyond Hegemonic Stability." *Foreign Policy,* 110:112–123.

Mockaitis, Thomas R. 1999. *Peace Operations and Interstate Conflict: The Sword or the Olive Branch.* Westport, CT: Praeger.

Monshipouri, Mahmood, Neil Englehart, Andrew J. Nathan, and Kavita Philip, eds. 2003. *Constructing Human Rights in the Age of Globalization.* Armonk, NY: M. E.Sharpe.

Moore, Gale. 1998. *Climate of Fear: Why We Shouldn't Worry About Global Warming.* Washington, DC: Cato Institute.

Moore, Rebecca R. 2001. "China's Fledgling Civil Society." *World Policy Journal,* 18/1:56–66.

Moore, Will H., and David J. Lanoue. 2003. "Domestic Politics and U.S. Foreign Policy: A Study of Cold War Conflict Behavior." *Journal of Politics,* 65:376–397.

Moravcsik, Andrew. 1997. "Taking Preferences Seriously: A Liberal Theory of International Politics." *International Organization,* 51:513–554.

Moravcsik, Andrew. 2000. "The Origin of Human Rights Regimes: Democratic Delegation in Postwar Europe." *International Organization,* 54:217–252.

Morgan, T. Clifton, and Christopher J. Anderson. 1999. "Domestic Support and Diversionary External Conflict in Great Britain, 1950–1992." *Journal of Politics,* 61:799–814.

Morgan, T. Clifton, and Glenn Palmer. 2003. "To Protect and Serve: Alliances and Foreign Policy Portfolios." *Journal of Conflict Resolution,* 47:180–203.

Morgenthau, Hans W. 1973, 1986. *Politics among Nations.* New York: Knopf. Morgenthau's text was first published in 1948 and periodically thereafter. Two sources are used herein. One is the fifth edition, published in 1973. The second is an edited abstract drawn from pp. 3–4, 10–12, 14, 27–29, and 31–35 of the third edition, published in 1960. The abstract appears in Vasquez 1986:37–41. Pages cited for Morgenthau 1986 refer to Vasquez's, not Morgenthau's, book.

Morse, Edward L. 1999. "A New Political Economy of Oil?" *Journal of International Affairs,* 53:1–30.

Mortimer, Edward, and Robert Fine. 1999. *People, Nation, and State: The Meaning of Ethnicity and Nationalism.* New York: St. Martin's.

Mower, A. Glenn, Jr. 1997. *The Convention of the Rights of the Child: International Law Support for Children.* Westport, CT: Greenwood.

Muldoon, James P., Jr. 2003. *The Architecture of Global Governance.* Boulder, CO: Westview.

Murray, A. J. H. 1996. "The Moral Politics of Hans Morgenthau." *The Review of Politics,* 58:81–109.

Namkung, Gon. 1998. *Japanese Images of the United States and Other Nations: A Comparative Study of Public Opinion and Foreign Policy.* Doctoral dissertation. Storrs, CT: University of Connecticut.

Nathan, James A. 2002. *Soldiers, Statecraft, and History: Coercive Diplomacy and the International Order.* Westport, CT: Praeger.

Neack, Laura. 1995. "UN Peace-Keeping: In the Interest of Community or Self?" *Journal of Peace Research,* 32:181– 196.

Neuman, Stephanie. 1998. *International Relations Theory and the Third World.* New York: St. Martin's.

Nogee, Joseph L., and John Spanier. 1988. *Peace Impossible—War Unlikely: The Cold War Between the United States and the Soviet Union.* Glenville, IL: Scott, Foresman.

Nye, Joseph. 2000. *Understanding International Conflicts,* 3rd ed. New York: Longman.

Nye, Joseph S., Jr. 2002. "Limits of American Power." *Political Science Quarterly,* 117:545–559.

O'Leary, Brendan. 1997. "On the Nature of Nationalism: An Appraisal of Ernest Gellner's Writings on Nationalism." *British Journal of Political Science,* 27:191–222.

Oneal, John R., and Bruce M. Russett. 1997. "The Classical Liberals Were Right: Democracy, Interdependence, and Conflict, 1950–1985." *International Studies Quarterly,* 41:267– 294.

Oneal, John R., and Bruce Russett. 1999. "The Kantian Peace: The Pacific Benefits of Democracy, Interdependence, and International Organizations, 1885–1992." *World Politics,* 52: 1–37.

O'Neill, Barry O. 1997. "Power and Satisfaction in the Security Council." In *The Once and Future Security Council,* ed. Bruce Russett. New York: St. Martin's.

Opello, Walter C., Jr., and Stephen Rosow. 1999. *The Nation-State and Global Order: A Historical Introduction to Contemporary Politics.* Boulder, CO: Lynne Rienner.

Oren, Ido. 2003. *Our Enemies and the U.S.: America's Rivalries and the Making of Political Science.* Ithaca, NY: Cornell University Press.

Orme, John. 1998. "The Utility of Force in a World of Scarcity." *International Security,* 22/3:138–167.

Osiander, Andreas. 1998. "Rereading Early Twentieth-Century IR Theory: Idealism Revisited." *International Studies Quarterly,* 42:409–432.

Osiel, Mark. 1999. *Obeying Orders: Atrocity, Military Discipline, and the Law of War.* New Brunswick, NJ: Transaction.

Owen, John M., IV, 2001. "Transnational Liberalism and U.S. Primacy." *International Security,* 26:117–153.

Pace, John P. 1998. "The Development of Human Rights Law in the United Nations, Its Control and Monitoring Machine." *International Social Science Journal,* 50:499–512.

Pagden, Anthony. 1998. "The Genesis of 'Governance' and Enlightenment Conceptions of the Cosmopolitan World Order." *International Social Science Journal,* 50:7–16.

Paquette, Laura. 2003. *Analyzing National and International Policy: Theory, Method, and Case Studies.* Lanham, MD: Lexington Books.

Park, Bert Edward. 1994. *Ailing, Aging, Addicted: Studies of Compromised Leadership.* Lexington, KY: University Press of Kentucky.

Parker, Christopher S. 1999. "New Weapons for Old Problems: Conventional Proliferation and Military Effectiveness in Developing States." *International Security,* 23/4:119–147.

Paterson, Thomas G. J., Garry Clifford, and Kenneth J. Hagen. 2000. *American Foreign Relations: A History, Vol. II: Since 1945,* 5th ed. Boston: Houghton Mifflin.

Patrick, Stewart, and Shepard Forman, eds. 2002. *Multilateralism and U.S. Foreign Policy: Ambivalent Engagement.* Boulder, CO: Lynne Rienner.

Paul, T. V., G. John Ikenberry, and John A. Hall. 2004. *The Nation-State in Question.* Princeton, NJ: Princeton University Press.

Peterson, John, and Elizabeth Bomberg. 1999. *Decision-Making in the European Union.* New York: St. Martin's.

Pew Research Center for the People and the Press. 2003. *Views of a Changing World, 2003.* Washington, DC: Pew Research Center for the People and the Press.

Phan, Chau T. 1996. "International Nongovernmental Organizations, Global Negotiations, and Global Activist Networks: The Emergence of INGOs as Partners in the Global Governance Process." *International Organization,* 51:591– 622.

Philpott, Daniel. 1999. "Westphalia, Authority, and International Society." *Political Studies,* 47/3:566–589.

Pickering, Jeffrey, and William R. Thompson. 1998. "Stability in a Fragmenting World: Interstate Military Force, 1946–1988." *Political Research Quarterly,* 51:241–264.

Pierre, Andrew J., ed. 1997. *Cascade of Arms: Managing Conventional Weapons Proliferation.* Washington, DC: Brookings Institution.

Pipes, Daniel. 2002. "God and Mammon: Does Poverty Cause Militant Islam?" *National Interest,* 66:14–21.

Porter, Bruce D. 1994. *War and the Rise of the State.* New York: Free Press.

Powell, Robert. 1996. "Stability and the Distribution of Power." *World Politics,* 48:239–267.

Powlick, Philip J., and Andrew Z. Katz. 1998. "Defining the American Public Opinion/Foreign Policy Nexus." *Mershon International Studies Review,* 42/1:29–62.

Pritchard, Sarah, ed. 1998. *Indigenous Peoples, the United Nations, and Human Rights.* New York: St. Martin's.

Qvortrup, Mads. 2002. *A Comparative Study of Referendums: Government by the People.* Manchester, U.K.: Manchester University Press.

Rabkin, Jeremy. 1994. "Threats to U.S. Sovereignty." *Commentary,* 97(3):41–47.

Ramet, Sabrina P. 2000. "The So-Called Right of National Self-Determination and Other Myths." *Human Rights Review,* 2:84–103.

Ratner, Steven R. 1998. "International Law: The Trials of Global Norms." *Foreign Policy,* 110:65–81.

Razavi, Shahra. 1999. "Seeing Poverty Through a Gender Lens." *International Social Science Journal,* 51:473–483.

Reardon, Betty A. 1990. "Feminist Concepts of Peace and Security." In *A Reader in Peace Studies,* ed. Paul Smoker, Ruth Davies, and Barbara Munske. Oxford, U.K.: Pergamon Press.

Reed, Thomas C. 2004. *At the Abyss: An Insider's History of the Cold War.* New York: Ballantine.

Reich, Walter, ed. 1998. *Origins of Terrorism: Psychologies, Ideologies, Theologies, States of Mind.* Princeton, N.J.: Woodrow Wilson Center Press.

Reiter, Dan, and Erik R. Tillman. 2002. "Public, Legislative, and Executive Constraints on the Democratic Initiation of Conflict." *Journal of Politics,* 64:810–837.

Reiter, Dan, and Allan C. Stam. 2002. *Democracies at War.* Princeton, NJ: Princeton University Press.

Renan, Ernest. 1995. "Qu'est-ce Qu'une Nation?" In *Nationalism,* ed. John Hutchinson and Anthony D. Smith. New York: Oxford University Press.

Rengger, Nicholas. 2002. "On the Just War Tradition in the Twenty-First Century." *International Affairs,* 78:353–363.

Renshon, Stanley A. 1995. "Character, Judgment, and Political Leadership: Promise, Problems, and Prospects of the Clinton Presidency." In *The Clinton Presidency: Campaigning, Governing, and the Psychology of Leadership,* ed. Stanley Renshon. Boulder, CO: Westview.

Renshon, Stanley A., and Deborah Welch Larson, eds. 2002. *Good Judgment in Foreign Policy: Theory and Application.* Lanham, MD: Rowman & Littlefield.

Reynolds, Andrew. 1999. "Women in the Legislatures and Executives of the World: Knocking at the Highest Glass Ceiling." *World Politics,* 514: 547–569.

Rhein, Wendy. 1998. "The Feminization of Poverty: Unemployment in Russia." *Journal of International Affairs,* 52:351–367.

Rhodes, Edward. 2003. "The Imperial Logic of Bush's Liberal Agenda." *Survival,* 45:131–154.

Richards, Diana. 1993. "A Chaotic Model of Power Concentration in the International System." *International Studies Quarterly,* 37:55–72.

Rielly, John E. 1999. "Americans and the World: A Survey at Century's End." *Foreign Policy,* 114:97–113.

Roberts, Adam. 1996. "From San Francisco to Sarajevo: The UN and the Use of Force." *Survival,* 37/4 (Winter):7–28.

Rodrik, Dani. 1998. *Has Globalization Gone Too Far?* Washington, DC: Institute for International Economics.

Roht-Arriaza, Naomi. 1999. "Establishing a Framework." *Journal of International Affairs,* 52:473–492.

Rose, Gideon. 1998. "Neoclassical Realism and Theories of Foreign Policy." *World Politics,* 51:144–169.

Rosenau, James N. 1998. "The Dynamism of a Turbulent World." In *World Security: Challenges for a New Century,* 3rd ed., ed. Michael T. Klare and Yogesh Chandran. New York: St. Martin's.

Rosenblatt, Lionel, and Larry Thompson. 1998. "The Door of Opportunity: Creating a Permanent Peacekeeping Force." *World Policy Journal,* 15:36–47.

Rossiter, Clinton. 1960. *The American Presidency,* 2nd ed. New York: Harcourt Brace Jovanovich.

Rostow, Walt W. 1978. *The World Economy.* Austin: University of Texas Press.

Rothgeb, John M., Jr. 1993. *Defining Power: Influence and Force in the Contemporary International System.* New York: St. Martin's.

Rothkopf, David J. 1998. "Cyberpolitik: The Changing Nature of Power in the Information Age." *Journal of International Affairs.* 51:325–360.

Rourke, John T. 1983. *Congress and the Presidency in U.S. Foreign Policy Making: A Study of Interaction and Influence, 1945–1982.* Boulder, CO: Westview.

Rourke, John T. 1993. *Presidential Wars and American Democracy: Rally 'Round the Chief.* New York: Paragon.

Rourke, John T., Richard P. Hiskes, and Cyrus Ernesto Zirakzadeh. 1992. *Direct Democracy and International Politics.* Boulder, CO: Lynne Rienner.

Ruggie, John Gerard. 1998. "What Makes the World Hang Together? Neo-Utilitarianism and the Social Constructivist Challenge." *International Organization,* 52:855–885.

Rummel, R. J. 1995 "Democracy, Power, Genocide, and Mass Murder." *Journal of Conflict Resolution,* 39:3–26.

Rusk, Dean, as told to Richard Rusk. 1990. *As I Saw It.* New York: W. W. Norton.

Russett, Bruce. 2000. "How Democracy, Interdependence, and International Organizations Create a System for Peace." In *The Global Agenda: Issues and Perspectives,* ed. Charles W. Kegley, Jr., and Eugene R. Wittkopf. Boston: McGraw-Hill.

Ryan, Stephen. 2000. *The United Nations and International Politics.* New York: St. Martin's.

Saideman, Stephen M. 2001. *The Ties That Divide: Ethnic Politics, Foreign Policy, and International Conflict.* New York: Columbia University Press.

Sanjian, Gregory. 1999. "Promoting Stability or Instability? Arms Transfers and Regional Rivalries, 1950–1991." *International Studies Quarterly,* 43:641–670.

Saunders, Robert M. 1994. "History, Health and Herons: The Historiography of Woodrow Wilson's Personality and Decision-Making." *Presidential Studies Quarterly,* 24:57–77.

Schafer, Mark, and Scott Crichlow. 2002. "The Process-Outcome Connection in Foreign Policy Decision Making: A Quantitative Study Building on Groupthink." *International Studies Quarterly,* 46:45–68.

Schmidt, Brian C. 1997. *The Political Discourse of Anarchy.* Albany: State University of New York Press.

Schmidt, Brian C. 1998. "Lessons from the Past: Reassessing the Interwar Disciplinary History of International Relations." *International Studies Quarterly,* 42:433–460.

Schneider, Gerald, Katherine Barbieri, and Nils Petter Gleditsch, eds. 2003. *Globalization and Armed Conflict.* Lanham, MD: Rowman & Littlefield.

Schraeder, Peter J., Steven W. Hook, and Bruce Taylor. 1998. "Clarifying the Foreign Aid Puzzle: A Comparison of American, Japanese, French, and Swedish Aid Flows." *World Politics,* 50:294–324.

Schultz, Kathryn R., and David Isenberg. 1997. "Arms Control and Disarmament." In *A Global Agenda: Issues Before the 52nd General Assembly of the United Nations,* ed. John Tessitore and Susan Woolfson. Lanham, MD: Rowman & Littlefield.

Schultz, Kenneth A. 1999. "Do Democratic Institutions Constrain or Inform? Contrasting Two Institutional Perspectives on Democracy and War." *International Organization,* 53: 233–266.

Schulzinger, Robert D. 1989. *Henry Kissinger: Doctor of Diplomacy.* New York: Columbia University Press.

Schweller, Randall L. 1997. "New Realist Research on Alliances: Refining, Not Refuting, Waltz's Balancing Proposition." *American Political Science Review,* 4:927–930.

Schweller, Randall L. 1998. *Deadly Imbalances: Tripolarity and Hitler's Strategy of World Conquest.* New York: Columbia University Press.

Schweller, Randall L., and David Priess. 1997. "A Tale of Two Realisms: Expanding the Institutions Debate." *Mershon International Studies Review,* 41:1–32.

Scott, James M., and Ralph G. Carter. 2002. "Acting on the Hill: Congressional Assertiveness in U.S. Foreign Policy." *Congress & the Presidency,* 29:151–170.

Scully, Roger, and David M. Farrell. 2003. "MEPs as Representatives: Individual and Institutional Roles." *Journal of Common Market Studies,* 41:269-288.

Sen, Amartya. 1999. *Development as Freedom.* New York: Alfred A. Knopf.

Setala, Maija. 1999. *Referendums and Democratic Government.* New York: St. Martin's.

Seymour, Michel. 2000 "Quebec and Canada at the Crossroads: A Nation Within a Nation." *Nations and Nationalism,* 6:227–256.

Shaheed, Farida. 1999. "Constructing Identities: Culture, Women's Agency and the Muslim World." *International Social Science Journal,* 51:61–75.

Shambaugh, George E., IV. 1996. "Dominance, Dependence, and Political Power: Tethering Technology in the 1980s and Today." *International Studies Quarterly,* 40:559–588.

Shambaugh, George E. 2000. *States, Firms, and Power: Successful Sanctions in United States Foreign Policy.* Albany, NY: State University of New York Press.

Sharp, Paul. 1999. "For Diplomacy: Representation and the Study of International Relations." *International Studies Review,* 1:33–58.

Sharp, Paul. 2001. "Making Sense of Citizen Diplomats: The People of Duluth, Minnesota, as International Actors." *International Studies Perspective,* 2:131–150.

Sherman, Dennis, and Joyce Salisbury. 2004. *The West in the World,* 2nd ed. Boston: McGraw-Hill.

Shlaim, Avi. 1999. *The Iron Wall: Israel and the Arab World.* New York: W. W. Norton.

Shinko, Rosemary. 2004 (forthcoming). "Postmodernism: A Genealogy of Humanitarian Intervention." In *Making Sense of IR Theory,* ed. Jennifer Sterling-Folker. Boulder, CO: Lynne Rienner.

Silverman, Adam L. 2002. "Just War, Jihad, and Terrorism: A Comparison of Western and Islamic Norms for the Use of Political Violence." *Journal of Church and State,* 44:73–92.

Simon, Craig. 1998. "Internet Governance Goes Global." In *International Relations in a Constructed World,* eds. Vendulka Kubalkova, Nicholas Onuf, and Paul Kowert. Armonk, NY: M. E. Sharpe.

Simon, Julian L. 1994. "More People, Greater Wealth, More Resources, Healthier Environment." In *Taking Sides: Clashing Views on Controversial Issues in World Politics,* 6th ed., ed. John T. Rourke. Guilford, CT: Dushkin.

(SIPRI) Stockholm International Peace Research Institute. Annual Editions. *SIPRI Yearbook.* Oxford, U.K.: Oxford University Press.

Slantchev, Branislav. L. 2003. "The Power to Hurt: Costly Conflict with Completely Informed States." *American Political Science Review,* 97:123–133.

Slaughter, Anne-Marie. 2003. "The Global Community of Courts." *Harvard International Law Journal,* 44:217–219.

Slaughter, Anne-Marie. 2003a. "Everyday Global Governance." *Daedalus,* 132:83–89.

Snyder, Jack. 2002. "Myths of Empire, Then and Now." Morton-Kenney Public Affairs Lecture Series. Department of Political Science, Southern Illinois University, Carbondale, IL.

Snyder, Robert S. 1999. "The U.S. and Third World Revolutionary States: Understanding the Breakdown in Relations." *International Studies Quarterly,* 43:265–290.

Sobel, Richard. 2001. *The Impact of Public Opinion on U.S. Foreign Policy Since Vietnam—Constraining the Colossus.* Oxford, U.K.: Oxford University Press.

Sørensen, Georg. 1999. "Sovereignty: Change and Continuity in a Fundamental Institution." *Political Studies,* 47:590–609.

Sørensen Georg. 2001. *Changes in Statehood: The Transformation of International Relations.* London: Palgrave.

Soroos, Marvin S. 1997. *The Endangered Atmosphere: Preserving a Global Commons.* Norman: University of Oklahoma Press.

Spegele, Roger D. 1996. *Political Realism in International Theory.* Cambridge, U.K.: Cambridge University Press.

Speth, James Gustave. 1998. "Poverty: A Denial of Human Rights." *Journal of International Affairs,* 52:277–292.

Spruyt, Hendrik. 1994. *The Sovereign State and Its Competitors: An Analysis of Systems Change.* Princeton, NJ: Princeton University Press.

Steinbruner, John. 2003. "Confusing Ends and Means: The Doctrine of Coercive Pre-emption." *Arms Control Today,* 33/1 (January/February). On the Web at http://www.armscontrol.org/.

Sterling-Folker, Jennifer. 1997. "Realist Environment, Liberal Process, and Domestic-Level Variables." *International Studies Quarterly,* 41:1–26.

Sterling-Folker, Jennifer. 2002. *Theories of International Cooperation and the Primacy of Anarchy: Explaining U.S. International Monetary Policy-Making After Bretton Woods.* Albany: State University of New York Press.

Stoessinger, John G. 1998. *Why Nations Go to War,* 7th ed. New York: St. Martin's.

Strange, Susan. 1997. *The Retreat of the State: The Diffusion of Power in the World Economy.* New York: Cambridge University Press.

Sutterlin, James. 2003. *The United Nations and the Maintenance of International Security,* 2nd ed. Westport, CT: Praeger.

Swanson, Timothy. 1999. "Why Is There a Biodiversity Convention? The International Interest in Centralized Development Planning." *International Affairs,* 75:307–331.

Sylvester, Caroline. 1994. "A Review of J. Ann Tickner's *Gender in International Relations.*" *American Political Science Review,* 87:823–824.

Taber, Charles S. 1989. "Power Capability Indexes in the Third World." In *Power in World Politics,* ed. Richard J. Stoll and Michael D. Ward. Boulder, CO: Lynne Rienner.

Talbott, Strobe. 2000. "Self-Determination in an Interdependent World." *Foreign Policy,* 118 (Spring 2000):152– 163.

Tamir, Yael. 1995. "The Enigma of Nationalism." *World Politics,* 47:418–440.

Tammen, Ronald L., et al. 2002. *Power Transitions: Strategies for the Twenty-First Century.* New York: Chatham House/Seven Bridges Press.

Tannenwald, Nina. 1999. "The Nuclear Taboo: The United States and the Normative Basis of Nuclear Non-Use." *International Organization,* 53:433–468.

Taras, Ray, and Rajat Ganguly. 1998. *Understanding Ethnic Conflict: The International Dimension.* New York: Longman.

Tarrow, Sidney. 2001. *Rethinking Europe's Future.* Princeton, NJ: Princeton University Press.

Taylor, Paul. 1999. "The United Nations in the 1990s: Proactive Cosmopolitanism and the Issue of Sovereignty." *Political Studies,* 47: 538–565.

Tehranian, Majid. 1999. *Global Communication and World Politics: Domination, Development, and Discourse.* Boulder, CO: Lynne Rienner.

Thies, Wallace J. 1998. "Deliberate and Inadvertent War in the Post–Cold War World." In *Annual Editions, American Foreign Policy 98/99,* ed. Glenn P. Hastedt. Guilford, CT: Dushkin/McGraw-Hill.

Thompson, Kenneth W. 1995. *Fathers of International Thought: The Legacy of Political Theory.* Baton Rouge: Louisiana State University Press.

Thompson, William R., and Richard Tucker. 1997. "A Tale of Two Democratic Peace Critiques." *Journal of Conflict Resolution,* 41:428–454.

Tomuschat, Christian. 2004. *Human Rights: Between Idealism and Realism.* Oxford, U.K.: Oxford University Press.

Travis, Rick, and Nikolaos Zahariadis. 2002. "A Multiple Stream Model of U.S. Foreign Aid Policy." *Policy Studies Journal,* 30:495–514.

Trumbore, Peter F. 1998. "Public Opinion as a Domestic Constraint in International Negotiations: Two-Level Games in the Anglo-Irish Peace Process." *International Studies Quarterly,* 42:545–565.

Trumbore, Peter F. 2003. "Victims or Aggressors? Ethno-Political Rebellion and Use of Force in Militarized Interstate Disputes." *International Studies Quarterly,* 47:183–201.

Tsygankov, Andrei P. 2003. "The Irony of Western Ideas in a Multicultural World: Russia's Intellectual Engagement with the 'End of History' and 'Clash of Civilizations.'" *International Studies Review,* 5:53–76.

Tucker, Jonathan B. 2000. *Toxic Terror: Assessing Terrorist Use of Chemical and Biological Weapons.* Cambridge, MA: MIT Press.

Turner, Frederick C., and Alejandro L. Corbacho. 2000. "New Roles for the State." *International Social Science Journal,* 163:109–120.

UN, Department of Economic and Social Affairs, Population Division. 2004. At http://www.undp.org/.

(UN, UNICEF) United Nations Children's Fund. Annual editions. *State of the World's Children.* New York: Oxford University Press.

(UNDP) United Nations Development Programme. Annual editions. *Human Development Report.* New York: Oxford University Press.

United Nations. *See* (UN).

(U.S.) Bureau of the Census. Annual editions. *Statistical Abstract of the United States.* Washington, DC.

U.S. (CIA) Central Intelligence Agency. Annual editions. *World Fact Book.* Washington, DC: GPO.

Vandenbroucke, Lucien. 1991. *Perilous Options: Special Operations in U.S. Foreign Policy.* Unpublished dissertation, University of Connecticut. A manuscript based on Vandenbroucke's revised dissertation was published in 1993 under the same title by Oxford University Press.

Vasquez, John A., ed. 1986. *Classics of International Relations.* Englewood Cliffs, NJ: Prentice Hall.

Vasquez, John, and Marie T. Henehan. 2001. "Territorial Disputes and the Probability of War, 1816–1992." *Journal of Peace Research* 38/2:123–138.

Vertzberger, Yaakov Y. I. 1994. "Collective Risk Taking: The Decisionmaking Group and Organization." Presented at the annual meeting of the International Studies Association, Washington, DC.

Vertzberger. Yaakov Y. I. 1998. *Risk Taking and Decision Making: Foreign Military Intervention Decisions.* Stanford, CA: Stanford University Press.

Vlahos, Michael. 1998. "Entering the Infosphere." *Journal of International Affairs,* 51:497–526.

Voeten, Erik. 2000. "Clashes in the Assembly." *International Organization,* 54:185–216.

Walker, Stephen G., Mark Schafer, and Michael D. Young. 1998. "Systematic Procedures for Operational Code Analysis: Measuring and Modeling Jimmy Carter's Operational Code." *International Studies Quarterly,* 42:175–189.

Wallace, William. 1999. "The Sharing of Sovereignty: The European Paradox." *Political Studies,* 47:503–521.

Walt, Stephen M. 1996. "Alliances: Balancing and Bandwagoning." In *International Politics,* 4th ed., ed. Robert J. Art and Robert Jervis. New York: HarperCollins.

Wang, Kevin H., and James Lee Ray. 1994. "Beginnings and Winners: The Fate of Initiators of Interstate Wars Involving Great Powers Since 1495." *International Studies Quarterly,* 38:139–154.

Watkins, Kevin. 2002. "Making Globalization Work for the Poor." *Finance & Development,* 39/1. Web edition at http://www.imf.org/external/pubind.htm.

Wead, Douglas. 2003. *All the President's Children: Triumph and Tragedy in the Lives of America's First Families.* New York: Atria.

Wear, Spencer R. 1998. *Never at War: Why Democracies Will Not Fight One Another.* New Haven, CT: Yale University Press.

Weisband, Edward. 2000. "Discursive Multilateralism: Global Benchmarks, Shame, and Learning in the ILO Labor Standards Monitoring Regime." *International Studies Quarterly,* 44:643–666.

Weiss, Linda. 1998. *The Myth of the Powerless State.* Ithaca, NY: Cornell University Press.

Wendt, Alexander. 1992. "Anarchy Is What States Make of It: The Social Construction of Power Politics." *International Organization,* 46:335–370.

Wesley, Michael. 1997. *Casualties of the New World Order: The Causes of Failure of UN Missions to Civil Wars.* New York: St. Martin's.

Wiebe, Robert H. *Who We Are: A History of Popular Nationalism.* Princeton, NJ: Princeton University Press.

Wohlforth, William C. 1999. "The Stability of a Unipolar World." *International Security,* 24/1:5–41.

Woods, Ngaire. 1995. "Economic Ideas and International Relations: Beyond Rational Neglect." *International Studies,* 39: 161–180.

World Almanac and Book of Facts. Annual editions. New York: Funk & Wagnalls.

World Bank. 2003. *World Development Indicators 2003.* Washington, DC: World Bank.

World Bank. Annual editions. *World Development Report.* New York: Oxford University Press.

World Resources Institute. Annual editions. *World Resources.* New York: Oxford University Press.

Zakaria, Fareed. 1993. "Is Realism Finished?" *National Interest,* 32:21–32.

Zakaria, Fareed. 1996. "Speak Softly, Carry a Veiled Threat." *New York Times Magazine,* February 18.

Zehfuss, Maja. 2002. *Constructivism in International Relations: The Politics of Reality.* New York: Cambridge University Press.

Zhang, Ming, and Ronald N. Montaperto. 1999. *A Triad of Another Kind.* New York: St. Martin's.

Zielonka, Jan. 1998. *Explaining Euro-Paralysis: Why Europe Is Unable to Act in International Politics.* New York: St. Martin's.

Zuckerman, Mortimer B. 1998. "A Second American Century." Foreign Affairs, 77-3:13–31.

Zurn, Michael. 1998. "The Rise of International Environmental Politics: A Review of Current Research." *World Politics,* 50:617–649.

Index

Page numbers in *italics* indicate boxes, tables, photos, charts, etc. Page numbers in **bold** indicate definitions.

A

Abdullah, Amir Hassan, *486*
abortion, population control and, 523
Abrams, Elliott, *74*
absolute poverty, 424
Abu Sayyaf (Philippines), 317
Acheson, Dean, 74
acid rain, 539
actors, in foreign policy, 73
  bureaucracies, 75–76
  heads of government, 73–75
  interest groups, 77–78
  legislatures, 76–77
  political opposition, 77
  the public, 78–80
Adams, John, 144
adjudication, **273**–274
adversarial diplomacy, **245**–246
Afghanistan
  al-Qaeda in, 320, 325
  as failed state, 111
  Muslim sectarianism in, 156
  Soviet Union in, 316
  Taliban regime in, 111, 245, 316, 325, 368
  theocracy in, 173
  topography of, 234–235
  UN in, 166, 368
  U.S. military aid to, 315–316
  U.S. retaliation against, 3, 73, *243,* 245, 249, 256, 283, 304, 316
Africa
  colonization and decolonization of, *37*
  deforestation in, 529
  demands for slavery reparations, 496
  FDI in, 428
  sub-Sahara, 116, 383, 424, 471, 506
  trade groups in, 471
  African Charter on Human and Peoples' Rights (1990), 287
  African Union, 200
  age distribution, 235–236, *236*
  aggression
  as cause of war, 301
  external, 117–118
agricultural development, 502
agricultural output, as economic force, *309,* 408–409
AIDS, 185–186, 238, 278–279, *278,* 504–505
air pollution, 539–540
airplane, invention of, 128, *129*
Akhand Bharat, 153
al-Jafaari, Ibrahim, *486–487*
Al-Jazeera, 129–130, *130*
al-Khifaey, Hamid, *486*
al-Megrahi, Abdel Basset Ali, 319
al-Qaeda, 3, *63,* 76, 166, *243,* 245, 283, 320, 323, 325, 368
Albania, 108
Albright, Madeleine, 24–25, 178, 224, 494
Alliot-Marie, Michèle, 183, 246
Amazon River Basin, 529–530
ambition, decision making and, 89–90
Ambrose, Stephen, 303–304
"America the Boastful," 417
American Challenge, The (Servan-Schreiber), 399
American exceptionalism, 72–73
American Federation of Labor, 450
American Federation of Scientists, 259
American Invaders, The, 388
American Revolution, 33, 103, 176
Amherst, Sir Jeffrey, 328
Amnesty International, *279,* 492–493
amorality, **293**
Amsterdam, Treaty of, **202**
Anglican Church, 102–103
Angola, 414, 429
animus dominandi, 17
Annan, Kofi, 197, 208, 211, *214, 215,* 223, 224, 225, *250,* 280, 290, 354–355, 392–393, 446, 450, 516, 520, 521
anthrax, as weapon, 323, 356
Anti-Ballistic Missile (ABM) Treaty (1972), 334, *334, 344,* **345**, 418
Anti-Personnel Mine (APM) Treaty, 343, *344,* **353**–354, *354–355*
anti-Semitism, 489
antiwar pacifists, 369
apartheid, 166, 282, 414, 497
appeasement policy, **39**
Arab Cooperation Council, 200
Arafat, Yasser, 167, 212–213
Aral Sea, *534*
Argentina, 174, 428, 471
  economy of, 406–407, *407,* 459–460, *460,* 461
Aristotle, 25, 28, 282
Armitage, Richard, *74*
arms control, 48, **343**–344, *344*
  barriers to, 356, *357,* 358–360
  Chemical Weapons Convention (CWC), *344,* 351–353
  Comprehensive Test Ban Treaty (CTBT), *344,* 350–351
  conventional weapons, 353–355
  Nuclear Non-Proliferation Treaty renewal, 347–350
  START I and II, 346–347
  through 1980s, 345–346
  Treaty of Moscow, *344,* 347
  UN and, 220
  WMDs and arms control since 1990, *344,* 346–351
  See also security; war
arms transfers, 313–316, *314*
  See also military power; war
Ashcroft, John, 82
Asia, arms transfers to, 314
Asia-Pacific Economic Cooperation (APEC), 455, **472**
Asian and Pacific Coconut Community, 436
Asian Development Bank, 464
Association of Southeast Asian Nations (ASEAN), 48, 200, **472**
asymmetrical warfare, **47**
Atta, Mohammad, 322
ATTU region, CFE in, 353
Augustine, Saint, 269, 282
Aung San Suu Kyi, 479
Australia, 177, *432–433*
Austria, 175, *432–433*
Austro-Hungarian empire, 103, 312
authoritarian government, **70**–71, **172**
authoritarianism, **173**

authority, organization of, 59
automobiles, world production of, *409*
avian influenza, 505
axis of evil, 82, 91–92, 94, *243,* 256
Axis Rule in Occupied Europe, 270

B

B–2 stealth bomber, *230,* 303
Bahrain, 379
Baker, James A., III, 68, 358, 413
balance of payments, *391,* **391**
balance of power, **36**
balance-of-power politics, 66
Balkans, 117, 166, 364
See also individual countries
ballistic missile defense (BMD) system. *See* national missile defense system (NMDS)
Bamako Convention, 547
Bandarnaike, Sirimavo Ratwatte Dias, 177
Bandung Conference, 434
Bangladesh, *364, 423*
Bank for International Settlement (BIS), 461–462
Baradei, Mohamed El, 350
Barbaro, Ermolao, 241
Barber, Benjamin, 45–46
Basel Convention, 547
basketball, in China, *135*
Bateer, Mengke, 135
Begin, Menachem, 252
behavior norms, in international system, 68–70
Beijing + 5 conference, 159
Beilin, Yossi, 247
Belarus, 314
Belgium, *432–433*
Benito, Elizabeth Odio, *291*
Benker, Charlotte, *129*
Berlusconi, Silvio, 175
Bharatiya Janata Party (BJP), *153*
"Big Mac standard," *381*
Bikini Atoll, *331*
bilateral aid, **430**
bilateral diplomacy, **249**
bin Laden, Osama, 3, 130, *243,* 245, 320
biological factors, in decision making, 84–86
biological weapons, 283, 322–323, 328, 356
Biological Weapons Convention (1972), 328, *344,* **346**
biopolitics, **84**–86
biosphere
law and morality issues, 286–287
system-level stresses on, 300
bipolar system, **39**–42, *64,* **65**
Black Death, 10–11, 185–186, *186,* 323
Blair, Tony, *45,* 71, 81, 93, *253,* 274, *285, 444,* 450
BMD system. *See* national missile defense system (NMDS)
Bolivia, 471
Bolshevism, 39, *39*
Bolton, John, *74*
Bosnia, 289, 364
Botswana, 490
botulism, as weapon, 323
Boutros-Ghali, Boutros, 214–215, *214,* 217, 364–365
boycotts, by consumers, 12–13
Bozorgmehr, Shirzad, 359
Brady Plan, 426
Brazil
child prostitution in, 488
computing capacity, *241*
deforestation in, 529
FDI in, 427
income earned, 422–423, *423*
in Mercosur, 471
Yanomami of, 489–490
break-out cheating, in arms control, 358
Bretton Woods system, **456**–457
Brezhnev, Leonid I., 40
Brundtland, Gro Harlem, 177
Brunei, 379
bubonic plague, 10–11
Buddha, 138
bureaucracy, 75, **75**
bureaucratic survival, 86–87
Burundi, 104
Bush Doctrine, **48**, *49,* 215, 305, *326*
Bush, George H. W., *91*
assassination attempt, 301
CTBT and, 358
diplomacy of, 252, *253*
Persian Gulf War, 82, 246–247, 298, 327, 333
realpolitik approach of, 20
"Wimp Factor," 90
Bush, George W., 13–14, *22, 45,* 83, *91*
Afghanistan military action, 73, 249, 304
agricultural subsidies legislation signed by, 412
Anti-Ballistic Missile Treaty, *334, 344,* 345, 418
China and, 398
computer sales to China, 399–400
Dalai Lama meeting, *169*
diplomatic travel of, 252, *253*
"fast track" authority issue, 72
foreign policy, 72, 79
free market approach, 470
on globalization, 392
ICC and, 291
informal moratorium on nuclear testing, *352*
Iraq war leadership, 69, 73, *74,* 81, 85–86, 93, 229, *243, 284–285,* 301, 333, 413, 481, *486*
Kyoto treaty opposition, *545*
legal versus real authority of, 75
military technology statement, 303
neoconservatives in administration of, 182
North Korean diplomacy, 258
operational code of, 94
personality, 89, 92, 301
public support of, 71
as realist, 21
"roadmap to peace" in Middle East, 247
sense of duty, 94
September 11, 2001 behavior, 86
special operations budget increased by, 316–317
steel tariff, 246, *420–421*
Syria sanctions, 414
Treaty of Moscow, 347
unilateralist approach, 182, 247, 418, 420
world leaders and, 252, 254
Bush, Laura, 85

C

California, wildfires in, 541, *542,* 543
Callierres, François de, 248
Camp David Accords (1977), 252
Canada
computing capacity, *241*
education in, *238*
foreign aid from, *432–433*
in G–7, 443
health in, *237,* 238
individualism in, 480, *480*
military expenditures, 7
as multinational state, 106–107
in OECD, 443
as trilateral country, 418
in World War I, 312
Cancún meeting (WTO), 454, *455*
capital punishment, in international law, 276–277, 294
capitalism, 437, **438**, *439*
carbon dioxide emissions, *54,* 516, 540, *541*
See also global warming
Card, Andrew H., Jr., 87
carrying capacity, **511**
Carter, Jimmy, 83, 252, *253,* 400
Carthage, 65
Castro, Fidel, 400, 415, *436*
Catholic Church. *See* Roman Catholic Church
Cato the Elder, 65
CEDAW. *See* Convention on the Elimination of All Forms of Discrimination Against Women (CEDAW)
Central American Court of Justice, 274

Central Commission for the Navigation of the Rhine, 193
Cervantes, Miguel de, 308
Ceylon. *See* Sri Lanka
CFCs. *See* chlorofluorocarbons (CFCs)
Chad, 429
Chamberlain, Neville, 39
change, pace of, 36, 38
chaos theory, 66
Charlemagne, 102
Charles V (Holy Roman Emperor), *303*
Chavez, Hugo, 470
Chechnya, 47, 112–113, *112*
chemical and biological terrorism, 322–323
chemical weapons, 283, 328–329
Chemical Weapons Convention (CWC), *344,* 350–351
Cheney, Richard, *74*
child labor. *See* labor
children
  Convention on the Rights of the Child, 495
  economic value of, 526
  health, 503–504
  human rights of, 486–488, 495–496
  UNICEF, 495
  World Congress Against Commercial Sexual Exploitation of Children, 496
Chile, 386–387, 471
China, 166–167, *167*
  abortions in, 524
  agricultural efficiency, 408–409, *409*
  armed forces in, 234
  arms imports and exports, 314
  capital investment in, *395*
  capitalism in, 437, 438
  communitarianism in, 114
  computer sales to by U.S., 399–400
  computing capacity, *241*
  currency manipulation accusations, 398
  democracy in, 396
  diplomatic recognition of, 168
  e-dumping in, 537
  economic development in, *447*
  environmental issues, 516–517
  exports, *394*
  FDI in, 427
  global role of, 45
  globalization and, 396
  human rights in, 279–280, *279,* 492
  Internet usage in, 130
  in Korean War, 327
  military expenditures, 7
  nonmissionary attitude, 73
  nuclear weapons in, 232, *242,* 330, 332, 347, 350
  role of in North Korea crisis, 44
  SARS in, 505
  as signatory to CTBT, *352*
  Sinocentrism in, 72
  Taiwan and, *242–243,* 248, 258–259, *259,* 261–262
  Three Gorges Dam, 517, *518*
  Tibet and, *169*
  in UN, 209
  U.S. and, 279–280, 399–400, 410
  Western pop culture in, *135*
  WTO admission, 261–262
  See also Taiwan
Chirac, Jacques, 43, 66, 133, 175, 196, *284,* 444, *444*
chlorofluorocarbons (CFCs), 10, 545, 547
Christianity, conflict with Islam, 153, *156*
Christopher, Warren, 261
Churchill, Winston, 36, 89, 197, 225, 228, 357
CIA, in Iraq decision making, 75, 76, 323
Citigroup, 389
CITs. *See* countries in transition (CITs)
city-states, 28, 29, 32
civil society, **132**
clash of civilizations, **148**
Clausewitz, Carl von, 326–327
Clement VII (Pope), *303*
climate, as element of power equation, 235
Clinton, Bill
  BMD system, 334
  China trade status, 262
  on CTBT, *352*
  diplomatic travel, *253*
  education, 24–25
  "fast track" authority issue, 72
  foreign policy, 71, 72
  on FTAA, 470
  Global Warming Convention, 547
  on globalization, 392
  ICC, 291
  Kyoto Protocol, *544*
  letter from neoconservatives on Iraq, *74*
  as liberal, 20–21
  at Millennium Summit, 450
  on nationalism, 115
  personality, 89
  Presidential Decision Directive 60 (PDD–60), 333
  scandal involving, *301*
  Taiwan crises, 248
  worldview, 93–94
Clinton, Hillary Rodham, 494
CNN, 129, *130*
coal, as fuel, 517, 528
coalition diplomacy, **246**–247
codification, **270**
coercive diplomacy, **259**–260
coercive power, **231**–232
cognitive consistency, 81–82
cognitive decision making, **81**–82
Cohen, William S., *352*
cold war, 39–**40**, 418
collective security, **362**
Colombia, 276, 316
colonialism, 33, 36, *37,* 45, 114, 153–154, 434, 459
Columbus, Christopher, 30
Committee for the Propagation of Virtue and the Prevention of Vice, 486
common market, 466
Common Sense (Paine), 139
communications, 129–131, 261
communism, **174**
Communist Manifesto, The (Engels, Marx), 139
communitarianism, **176**–177
community, rights of, 279
Community Tribunal of the Economic Community of West African States, 274
competition, 21–22, 394–395
compliance, with international law, 272–273
Comprehensive Convention Against Terrorism (proposed), 317, 318
Comprehensive Test Ban Treaty (CTBT), 71, *344,* **350**–351, *352,* 358
Concert of Europe, 360
Conference on Environment and Development (UNCED), 146
Conference on Population and Development (UNCPD), 159
Conference on the Illicit Trade in Small Arms and Light Weapons (2001), 354–355
Congress of Vienna, 249
constructivism, 139, *141,* **141**–142
consumer boycotts, 12–13
consumer products, as part of common culture, 133–134
containment doctrine, **40**
contraception, 525
Convention Against Torture and Other Cruel, Inhumane, or Degrading Treatment or Punishment, *288*
Convention on the Control of Transboundary Movement of Hazardous Wastes and Their Disposal, 547
Convention on the Elimination of All Forms of Discrimination Against Women (CEDAW), *288,* **494**
Convention on the International Trade in Endangered Species, *531*
Convention on the Law of the Sea, 197, *198,* 287
Convention on the Preservation and Protection of Fur Seals, 197, *198*

Convention on the Prevention and Punishment of Genocide (1948), 270, *288,* 497
Convention on the Rights of the Child (1989), *288,* 450
Convention Relating to the Status of Refugees, *288,* 497–498
Conventional Forces in Europe Treaty (CFE), *344,* **353**
conventional warfare, 325–3**26**, 353–355
See also war
conventional weapons, 320, 354–355
cooperation, 22–23
Cortés, Juan Donoso, 172
cost/benefit analysis, of war, 308
Council of the Baltic Sea States, 197
Council of the European Union, **202**–203
countries in transition (CITs), **380**
Court of Justice (European Union), 204
covert operations, 316–317
creep-out cheating, in arms control, 358
crisis situation, **71**
CTBT. *See* Comprehensive Test Ban Treaty (CTBT)
Cuba, 319, 262, 400, 414, 415, 501
Cuban missile crisis, 40, 87, 331
cultural globalization, 131–132
global reaction to cultural homogenization, 136–137, *137*
spread of common culture, 133–134, *133*
See also multiculturalism
cultural groups, 77
cultural homogenization, 136–137, *137*
cultural imperialism, **280**, 479
cultural relativism, 479
cultural transnationalism, 148–150
culture, Western. *See* Western culture
current dollars, **374**
custom, as source of law, 270
customs union, 466
cycle theories, concerning power changes, 66
Czechoslovakia, 123

D

da Silva, Luiz Inácio, *45,* 392, 470, 471Dalai Lama, *169*
Dante Alighieri, 294
dar al-harb, 151, 155
Darwin, Charles, 482
"Davy Crockett" mini-nuke, *356*
de Tocqueville, Alexis, 181
death penalty, international law and, 276–277, 294
debt service, **426**
decision-making process, **81**
biological factors, 84–86
cognitive factors, 81–82
emotional factors, 83
groupthink, 86–87
leaders and their individual traits, 87–94
policy quality and, *88*
psychological factors, 83
Declaration of Independence, 103, 171, 172, 417
Declaration on the Establishment of a New International Economic Order (NIEO), **434**
defense spending, 7–8, 7
defensive warfare, 312
deforestation, 501, 529–530, 540
Delian League, 191
democide, 180
democratic peace theory, **181**
democracy
early development, 29
globalization and, 396
nationalism and, 113
procedural, 177
spread of, *176*
substantive, 177
world politics and, 176
attitudes about democracy, 179–180
economic development, 179, *180*
exclusiveness-inclusiveness, 177–178
individualism-communitarianism, 176–177
process-outcome, 177
security, 180–181
Democracy in America (de Tocqueville), 181
democratic government, **70**–71, **172**
democratic nationalism, 33
Democratic Republic of the Congo, *315, 365*
democratic theory, 175–176
democratized diplomacy, **251**
Denmark, *432–433*
dependency theory, 377–379, **378**
Descartes, René, 137–138
Descent of Man, The (Darwin), 483
description, as goal of political science, 24
desertification, 531
détente, **40**
deterrence, **332**–333
Deutch, John M., 329
Development Assistance Committee (DAC), **430**, *432–433*
development capital, 395, **425**
diamond trade, for illegal weapons purchases, 414–415
diplomacy
adversarial, 245–246
bilateral, **249**
coalition diplomacy, 246–247
as communications process, 255–256
effective, 256–257
functions of, 241–245
historical, 248–249, *248*
hostile, 245
mediation diplomacy, 247
modern, 249
democratized diplomacy, 251
expansion of geographical scope, 249
leader-to-leader diplomacy, 251–254
multilateral diplomacy, 249
open diplomacy, 251
parliamentary diplomacy, 250–251
public diplomacy, 254–255
multilateral view of, 94
options, 257
coercion, 259–260
direct or indirect negotiations, 258
high-level or low-level diplomacy, 258–259
linking or separating issues, 261–262
maximizing or minimizing disputes, 262
precision or vagueness, 260–261
words or actions, 261
setting of, 245
coalition diplomacy, 246–247
diplomatic environment, 245–246
domestic connection, 247–248
international system, 245
by UN, 219
war as part of, 327
diplomatic recognition, as measure of statehood, 168
direct action, in global relations, 12–13
direct voting, 14
disarmament
domestic, 342
general and complete, **369**
negotiated, 369
UN and, 220
unilateral, 369
Discourse on Method (Descartes), 137–138
disease control, 10–11
disinformation, **255**
diversification, 396
diversity, 114
Divine Comedy, The (Dante), 294
divine right of kings, 33
Dobriansky, Paula, *74*
Doha Round, 454, 455
dollars, current and real, 374
domestic abuse, 484–485
domestic disarmament, 342
domestic economic support, 376
domestic economy, globalization and, 396–397
domestic security, 180
Don Quixote (Cervantes), 308
Dostoyevsky, Fyodor, 239
Dow Chemical Corporation, 398

downsizing, 417
Dreyfus, Alfred, *125*
dual-use technology, **354**, 399–400
Dubois, Pierre, 191
Duhalde, Eduardo, 459
dumping, of goods, 412–413

E

e-dumping, 537
Earth Summit I, 222, 519–520
Earth Summit II, 520–521
East Timor, 21, 47, 114, *121,* 123, 220, 368
Ebadi, Shirin, *52*
Ebola virus, 505
ecology, world, 511–513, *514–515*
See also environmental issues; sustainable development
economic colonialism, 459
Economic Community of West African States (ECOWAS), 200, *361,* **361**, *367*
economic cooperation, 442–443, 466
in Asia and Pacific, 471–472
EDC prosperity, 443–444
in Europe, 466
future of regionalism, 472–474
LDC development, 444–448
regional, 464, *465,* 466
trade (GATT and WTO), 451–456
in Western Hemisphere, 467–470, *471*
economic development
democracy and, 179, *180*
economic internationalist approach, 445–446
economic nationalist approach, 445
economic structuralist approach, 446
incentives for, 446–447
nationalism and, 114
resistance to, 448–449, *448*
See also less developed countries (LDCs)
economic espionage, 412
economic groups, 78
economic incentives and disincentives, 376
economic integration, 466
economic interdependence, **48**–49, 63, 67–68, **391**–393, 438
economic internationalism, *375,* **376**–377, 445–446
economic nationalism, **374**–376, *375,* 405, 409, 445
economic power, 413
incentives, 412
sanctions, 413–416
methods of manipulating economic interchange, 409
domestic trade support, 411–413
merchandise trade barriers, 510
services and investment trade barriers, 411
national economic power, 405, *406*
agricultural output, 408–409, *409*
financial position, 405–407
industrial output, 408, *409*
natural resources, 407, *408*
See also international political economy (IPE)
economic sanctions, **413**, 414–416, *416*
economic statecraft, 405
economic structuralism, *375,* 377, **377**, 446
economic union, 466
economically developed countries (EDCs), **49**–50, *51, 54,* 68, 157, 183, **374**, 375, *375*
economic cooperation and prosperity, 442–444
economic issues and policies, 418–420, *420–421*
economic sanctions used by, 415
education in, 236–237, *237*
energy consumption in, 529
environmental issues and sustainable development, 513, 516–521, *544–545*
GDPs of, 417
globalization and, 396–397
information and communication systems in, 240
international trade, 386–387
military spending, *302,* 303
national economies, 417–418
nontariff barriers, 410
population and age distribution, 236, *236*
tariffs, 410
war among, 232
WTO and, 454–456, *455*
See also economic cooperation; economic development
economy
postindustrial, 417
service, 417
ECOWAS. *See* Economic Community of West African States (ECOWAS)
Ecuador, 361
education, 505–506
EEC. *See* European Economic Community (EEC)
ego, decision making and, 89–90
Egypt, 314
Ehrlich, Paul, 513
Einstein, Albert, *125*
Eisenhower, Dwight David, 298
El Niño/La Niña, 9
empire, 29
employment, international trade and, 6
"End of History, The?," 176
End of Laissez-Faire, The (Keynes), 376
endangered species, 531–532, *531*
Energy and Water Development Appropriations Act (2004), 351
enforcement, of international law, 273
Engels, Friedrich, 139, 140, 174
English, as common language, 133, *134*
entertainment media, cultural homogenization and, 136
environmental issues, 8–10, 52–54, 537, 547–548
air pollution, 539–540
Conference on Environment and Development (Earth Summit), 146, 222
global warming, 540–544, 547
ground pollution, 537–538
Kyoto Protocol, 418, *544–545*
ozone layer depletion, 544–547, *546*
United Nations Environmental Programme (UNEP), 9–10, 217, 221
water pollution, 538–539
See also ecology; sustainable development
environmental optimists, **512**–513, 542–543
environmental pessimists, **512**, 540–541
Epistles (Seneca), 482
equal voting, *212*
Eritrea, 85, 123
escalation, of war, **327**–328
Eskimos. *See* indigenous peoples
Essay on the Principle of Population (Malthus), 499
ethical principles, in international politics, 19–21
Ethiopia, 85
ethnonational groups, **47**, *101,* **101**, 105, 107–108, *115,* 123
ethology, **84**–85
EU. *See* European Union (EU)
euro, 206
Eurobarometer, 205
Eurocorps, 65
Europe, 38–39, 200
European Atomic Energy Community (EURATOM), 200
European Bank for Reconstruction and Development, 464
European Central Bank, 389
European Commission, **203**
European Communities (EC), 201
European Court of Human Rights, 274
European Court of Justice, 271, 274
European Economic Community (EEC), 200
European Parliament (EP), 202, **203**–204, *204*
European People's Party, 203
European Union (EU), 45, 48, 59, **200**, 438
anthem of, *201*
ban on imports of genetically modified crops, 420–421
citizenship in, 167, 188

as confederation, 200
Council of the European Union, **202**–203
economic development funds donated by, 449
economic integration of, 419
euro as official currency, 206
Eurocorps and, 65
as example of regional transnationalism, 147, 161
food and agriculture issues, *207*
future of, 104–105, 205–208
GATT revisions, 456
government of, 202–204
Kyoto treaty, *545*
membership and organizational structure, *201*
membership in, 14–15
monetary regulation, 389
origins and evolution, 200–202
protectionism by, 420–421
as RTO, 466
trade barriers against U.S., 410
Treaty of Nice, 15
unemployment, 417
U.S. steel tariff and, 246, *420*
See also intergovernmental organizations (IGOs)
exceptionalism, *116,* **116**–117
exchange rates, *390,* **390**–391
exclusiveness, in democracy, 177–178
external expectations, 86
extreme poverty, **382**

F

F–16 fighter, 314
F–22 fighter, 303
failed states, **111**, 170
FAO. *See* Food and Agriculture Organization (FAO)
fascism, **174**–175
"fast track" authority of president, 72
FBI. *See* Federal Bureau of Investigation (FBI)
FDI. *See* foreign direct investment (FDI)
Federal Bureau of Investigation (FBI), 76
Federal Child Labor Law (1916), 450
Federal Trade Commission, 449
Federalist Paper #6 (Hamilton), 375
female genital mutilation, 484, 495
feminism, 139, 140, *141,* **142**–144
See also women
feudal system, **30**–31
films, as part of common culture, 133–134
financial markets, international, 6–7
financial services, globalization of, 389
Finland, 177, *432–433*
fiscal year (FY), **6**
Fischer, Joschka, 246
Flying Cloud, 128
Food shortages, 499–503
Food and Agriculture Organization (FAO), *382, 412,* 500, 501, 502
force, as political instrument, 306–309
See also war
foreign aid, 430–431, *432–433, 448*
foreign direct investment (FDI), **387**, 399, 427–428, *428*
foreign policy, 70
actors, 73–80
decision process and quality of, *88*
government type, 70–71
national voice in, 77
policy type, 71–72
political culture, 72–73
pure, 71–72
situation, 71
foreign portfolio investment (FPI), **387**, 427–428, *428*
forests, sustainable development and, 529–530
former Soviet republics (FSRs), 111–113, 114, 353, 379–380, 471–472
"Fourteen Points" (Wilson), 19, *20,* 251
Fourth World, **489**
Fox, Vicente, 277, 468, 469
FPI. *See* foreign portfolio investment (FPI)
France
ambivalence toward American culture in, 136–137
arms transfers by, 314
diplomatic system in, 248
draft in, 33
foreign aid from, *432–433*
in G–7, 443
Napoleonic, 33, 235
nuclear power in, 528
nuclear weapons in, 330, 350
ratification of CTBT, *352*
Revolution, 33, *33,* 103, 139, 176
troops in ATTU region, 353
U.S. invasion of Iraq and, 183, 196, 245–246, 251, 418
view of U.S., *93*
in World War I, 312
Franco, Francisco, 174
Franklin, Benjamin, 418
Franks, Tommy, *74*
free economic interchange, **419**
free trade, 49, 386, 466
Free Trade Area of the Americas (FTAA), 469–4**70**
Free Trade or the Means to Make Trade Flourish (Misselden), 393
Freedom Party (Austria), 175
French Revolution, 33, *33,* 103, 139, 176
freshwater pollution, 539
Friends of the Earth, 145, 454
Frost, Robert, 15–16
frustration-aggression theory, **83**
FTAA. *See* Free Trade Area of the Americas (FTAA)
Fukuyama, Francis, 85, 176
Fulbright, J. William, *14*
functionalism, **193**–194
fundamentalism, **151**

G

game theory. *See* two-level game theory
Gandhi, Indira, 178
Gandhi, Mohandas K., 370
Gates, Bill, *423*
GATT. *See* General Agreement on Tariffs and Trade (GATT)
Gaza, 167, 168
GDP. *See* gross domestic product (GDP)
gender
abuse and the law, 485–486
as basis of economic disparity, 423
in decision making, 85–86, *85*
in democracy, 177–178
See also women
gender development index, 485
gender gap, worldwide, 157–158, *158*
gender opinion gap, **80**
General Agreement on Tariffs and Trade (GATT), 199, 377, 386, 419, *420,* 443, **451**–452, 454
general and complete disarmament, **369**
genetically modified (GM) crops, 420–421
Geneva Conventions, 166, 270, *271,* 283
genital mutilation, 144
genocide, *270*
geography
comparative knowledge of, *4*
as element of power, 234
Germany
arms transfers by, 314
Berlin blockade, 261
computing capacity, *241*
foreign aid from, *432–433*
in G–7, 443
Hitler in, 39
ICJ and, 276
invasion of Iraq and, 183
Nazi period, 117
as perceived by members of the EU, 207–208
reunification of, 41–42, 123
troops in ATTU region, 353
U.S. invasion of Iraq and, 196, 245–246, 418
view of U.S., *93*
in World War I, 38, 39, 312
Ghana, *364*
Gibraltar, 14–15
global warming, 8–9, *10,* 540
deforestation and, 530
disputed issues, 540–543
known issues, 540
solutions, 543–544, 547
Global Warming Convention, 547
globalism, 122

globalization, 46, **127**–128, *395*
business regulation and, 450
of communications and transportation, 128–131, *132*
cultural, 131–137, *137*
debate on, 393–402, *401*
economic, 131, *132,* 442
economic interdependence, 391–393
national interest and, 182
sovereignty and, 398–399, 453
transnationalism and, 137
WTO as agent of, 454
GNP. *See* gross national product (GNP)
Gorbachev, Mikhail S., 41–42, 239
Gore, Al, 14, 24–25, 332, *545*
governance
as element in power equation, 239
leadership skill, 239
theories of, 172, *173*
authoritarian, 172–173
communism, 174
fascism, 174–175
monarchism, 174
theocracy, 173–174
government
administrative competence, 239
types of, 199–200
Great Britain
age of consent in, 274
arms imports and exports, 314
exportation of hazardous waste, 547
foreign aid from, *432–433*
in G–7, 443
geographical isolation of, 234
house of Stuart in, 103
in Iraq War, 219, 233, 245–246, 268, *284–285,* 304
nuclear weapons in, 330
ratification of CTBT, *352*
troops in ATTU region, 353
VAT exemptions, 204
in World War I, 312
Great Depression, 442
Greece, 108–109, 314, *432–433*
ancient, city-states in, 28–29, 175, 191, 248, 413
green accounting, **477**, 511
"green peril," 157
greenhouse effect, **540**
Greenpeace International, 146, 197
Greenspan, Alan, 438–439
gross domestic product (GDP), *5,* **7**, *394,* 417
gross national product (GNP), *5,* **62**, **374**, *380, 381, 383*
Grotius, Hugo, 192, 267, *267*
ground pollution, 537–538
Groundwork on the Metaphysics of Morals (Kant), 292
Group of 7 (G–7), **419**, 427, **443**–444
Group of 8 (G–8), 393, **419**, **443**–444, *444*
Group of 77, 195, 434–435, *436,* **451**
groupthink, **86**–87
Guatama, Siddhartha, 138
Guatemala, 319
Guinea Bissau, 429
gunpowder, introduction of, 30, *32*

H

Hadley, Stephen, 75
Hague Conferences, 274, 283, 345
Hague system, **191**–192
Haider, Jörge, 175
Haiti, 166, 282, 414
Hakki, Zakia Ismael, *486*
Hale, Nathan, *125*
Hamilton, Alexander, 374, 375
Hammarskjöld, Dag, 213–214, 225
Hammurabi, 248
Han Seung-soo, 183, 324
Hanseatic League, 32
Hardbattle, John, 490
Havana Program of Action, 434–436, *437,* 451
Havel, Václav, 254
Hawaiian independence movement, 120, *120*
hazardous waste, 547
head of government, **73**
health, as element in power equation, *237,* 238
health care, in LDCs, 382
health issues, 503–505
hegemonic power, **65**
hegemony, **43**
Helms-Burton Act (1996), 262
Helsinki Accords (1977), 287
Henry VIII (England), 31, 102–103
Heritage Foundation, 438
heuristic devices, used in decision-making process, **82**–83
Hindu nationalist party, *153*
Hindutva, 153
Hitler, Adolf, 39, 83, 89, 117, 174, *293,* 330, 350, 482
Ho Chi Minh, 40
Hobbes, Thomas, 17, 171
Hoffman, Abbie, *14*
Hollywood, as part of common culture, 133–134
Holy Roman Empire (HRE), **29**, 102, 165
Homeland Security Department, *326*
Homer, 357
Honduras, 531
Hong Kong, *492*
horizontal authority structure, **59**
hostile diplomacy, **245**
Hu Jintao, 43
human development index, *500*
human rights, 50–52, 478–481
adherence to treaties, *288*
cultural perspectives on, 279–280
food, 499–503
group rights abuses, 482–483
children, 486–488
ethnic and racial groups, 488
indigenous peoples, 489–490
refugees and immigrants, 490–491
religious groups, 489
women, 483–486, *486–487*
human development index, *500*
IGOs and, 221–222
individual rights abuses, 481–482, *481*
international response to, 491–493
children, 495–496
ethnic, racial, and religious groups, 496–497
indigenous peoples, 497
refugees and immigrants, 497–498
women, 493–495
law and morality issues, 287–288, *288*
positive, 498–499
Human Rights Watch, 493
humanitarian intervention, 365–366
Hungary, 14
Huntington, Samuel P., 148
Hussein, Saddam, 21–22, *43,* 69, *74,* 81, *82,* 86, 87, 90, 91, 93, *100, 110,* 130, 155, 156, 229, 233, *243,* 281, 415, *486*
human rights abuses by, 481, 493
invasion of Kuwait, 304
military leadership, 304
in Persian Gulf War, 327, 330
personality of as cause for war, 301
hydroelectricity, 517

I

IBRD. *See* International Bank for Reconstruction and Development (IBRD)
ICC. *See* International Criminal Court (ICC)
ICJ. *See* International Court of Justice (ICJ)
IDA. *See* International Development Association (IDA)
Idea for a Universal History from a Cosmopolitan Point of View (Kant), 139, 360
ideological/theological school of law, **269**
ideology, **101**
idiosyncratic analysis, 87–89, **88**
IFAD. *See* International Fund for Agricultural Development (IFAD)
IFC. *See* International Finance Corporation (IFC)

IGOs. *See* international governmental organizations (IGOs)
ILO. *See* International Labor Organization (ILO)
IMF. *See* International Monetary Fund (IMF)
IMMARSAT, 194
immigrants, 490–491, 497–498
imperial overstretch thesis, *305,* **305**–306
imperialism, 36, 113–114, 375
Imperialism; The Highest Stage of Capitalism (Lenin), 377
implementation, of foreign policy initiatives, 76
import and export prohibitions, 410
inclusiveness, in democracy, 177–178
income distribution, 422–423, *423*
independence, *164,* 165
Index of Economic Freedom, 438
India
  abortions in, 524
  CTBT and, *352*
  independence, 370
  military expenditures, 7
  nuclear weapons in, *153,* 232–233, 330, 332, 348–349, 359, *359*
  Pakistan and, *152–153*
  religious fundamentalism in, *153*
  UN peacekeepers contributed by, *364*
indigenous peoples, 489–490, 497–498
individual interests, as alternative to national interests, 183
individual-level analysis, **81**
  humans as a species, 81–86
  leaders and individual traits, 87–94
  organizational behavior, 86–87
  of terrorism, 324
individualism, **176**–177
individuals
  applying international law and morality to, 288–292
  rights of, 279
industrial output, as economic force, 408
industrial revolution, **36**, *37,* 385
industrialization, global warming and, *541*
infant mortality, 382, 522
infectious diseases, as global health threat, 186, *186*
information and communication systems, as part of power equation, 240
information filtering, 75
Inoguchi, Kuniko, 355
instrumental theory of government, **171**
international security forces, 48
Inter-American Court of Human Rights, 274
Inter-American Development Bank, 464
interest groups, role of in foreign policy, 77–78
intergovernmental organizations (IGOs), **191**, *192*
  activities, 217–222
  economic issues, 443
  European Union as, 200–208
  financial, 463
  future of, 223–225
  growth of, 193–195
  leadership, administration, and finance, 213–217
  organization and membership issues, 208–213
  origins, 191–193
  roles, 195
    center of cooperation, 197
    as independent international actor, *60,* **60**, 187, 198
    interactive arena, 195–197
    as supranatural organization, 198–200, **199**
  UN as, 208–225
Intergovernmental Panel on Climatic Change (IPCC), 540–541
Intermediate-Range Nuclear Forces Treaty (INF), 343, *344,* **346**
intermestic, **5**
intermestic policy, **72**
International AIDS conference, *278*
International Atomic Energy Agency (IAEA), 194, *242,* 345, 350
International Bank for Reconstruction and Development (IBRD), 462, 464
International Campaign to Ban Land Mines (ICBL), *354–355*
International Civil Aviation Organization, 197
International Conference on Financing for Development (ICFD), **448**–449
International Convention for the Prevention of Pollution from Ships, 548
International Convention on the Elimination of All Forms of Racial Discrimination, *288,* **497**
International Court of Justice (ICJ), 270, 271, **274**–277, *275, 284*
  optional clause, 275–276
International Covenant on Civil and Political Rights (1966), *288,* 492
International Covenant on Economic, Social, and Cultural Rights, *288,* 497
International Covenant on the Rights of Indigenous Nations, 497
International Criminal Court (ICC), 51, 290–292, *291,* 364, 418, **494–495**
International Development Association (IDA), 462, 464
International Finance Corporation (IFC), 462–463
International Fund for Agricultural Development (IFAD), 502
international governmental organizations (IGOs), 2, 187, 523–524
International Indian Treaty Council, 497
International Labor Organization (ILO), 487
international law
  adherence to, 272–273, *272*
  adjudication, 273–277
  application of law and morality, 292–295
  applied to individuals, 288–292
  applied to states, 280–288
    standards, 281–282
  growth of, 267
  International Criminal Court, 290–292
  law and morality issues, 282–288
  multiculturalism and, 277–280
  philosophical roots, 269–270
  practice of, 267–268
  primitive nature of, 266–267
  UN and, 222
International Maritime Organization, 197, *198*
International Monetary Fund (IMF), 194, 211–212, 377, 389, 393, 427, 438, 443, 457–458, 458–462, *458*
International Organization for Migration (IOM), 498
International Planned Parenthood Federation (IPPF), 523–524
international political economy (IPE), 16, **374**, *375*
  economic internationalism, 376–377
  economic nationalism, 374–376
  economic structuralism, 377–379
  EDCs and LDS, 379–383, *382*
  foreign direct and portfolio investment, 387
  globalization and interdependence, 391–402
  monetary relations, 388–391, *391*
  multinational corporations, 387–388
  North, 379–383, 416, 417–421
  perspectives and policy, 431, 434–438
  South, 379–383, 422–425, 425–431
  trade, 383–387, *384*
  See also economic nationalism
International Programme for the Elimination of Child Labour (IPEC), 487–488
International Red Cross/Red Crescent, 9
international representative assemblies, as source of law, 272
International Research and Training Institute for the Advancement of Women, 526

International Seabed Authority (ISA), 197, *198,* 287
international security, democracy and, 180–181
International Security Assistance Force (NATO), 368
international system, **28**
- actors in, 59–63
- anarchical nature of, 300
- ancient Greece and Rome, 28–29
- behavior norms, 68–70
- economic patterns, 67–68, 300
- eighteenth and nineteenth centuries, 32, 33, 36
- Middle Ages, 29–32
- power in, 63–67
- twentieth century, 36, 38–42
- twenty-first century, 42–54
- war causes and, 300
- Westernization of, 33, 36, 45
- *See also* levels of analysis

International Telegraphic (Telecommunications) Union, 193, 194
international trade, 383–384
- domestic support of, 411–413
- effect of on personal finances, 5–6
- employment and, 6
- expansion of, 63
- exports as percentage of GNP/GDP, *5*
- LDCs in, 428–430, *431*
- merchandise trade, 383–384
- in Middle Ages, 31
- North and South, 386–387, *386*
- pattern of expansion, 384–386, *384*
- services trade, 384
- strategic, 399–400
- world dependence on, *5*

international treaties and customs, as source of law, 270
International War Crimes Tribunal for the Balkans, 166
International Whaling Commission, 197, *198*
International Women's Year, 526
Internet, the, 46, 130, 133
Inuit Circumpolar Conference, 497
Inuits. *See* indigenous peoples
investment capital, international, 6
"invisible hand," 376
IOM. *See* International Organization for Migration (IOM)
IPCC. *See* Intergovernmental Panel on Climatic Change (IPCC)
IPE. *See* international political economy (IPE)
IPEC. *See* International Programme for the Elimination of Child Labour (IPEC)
IPPF *See* International Planned Parenthood Federation (IPPF)
Iran
- chemical weapons used by, 329
- nuclear weapons technology in, 349, 350, 359
- as part of axis of evil, 82, 91–92, *92*
- state terrorism by, 319
- theocratic elements in, 173
- U.S. sanctions against, 414
- war with Iraq, 154, 155

Iraq
- Baath party in, *486*
- chemical weapons in, 322–323, 329, 330, 333
- debt relief for, 413
- human rights abuses in, 481, 493
- invasion of Kuwait, 218, 246–247, 267, 300
- Muslim sectarianism in, 156
- as part of axis of evil, 82, 91–92, *92, 243*
- state terrorism by, 319
- topography of, 235
- UN inspections, 328, 329
- UN sanctions against, 267, 281, 414, 415–416
- U.S. sanctions against, 414
- war with Iran, 154, 155
- women's rights in, *486–487*
- *See also* Iraq War (2003); Persian Gulf War

Iraq War (1990) . *See* Persian Gulf War
Iraq War (2003), *13, 14,* 21, 44, *49, 69,* 73, 82, 85–86, 260, 333
- adversarial diplomacy, 245–246
- armaments, *230*
- casualties, 285–286, *285,* 308
- conventional war aspects of, 233
- decision-making process, 74, 81
- diplomatic communications, 261
- foreign support for, 68, 418
- as guerrilla war, 233
- information filtering, 75
- Iraq military morale, 304, *304*
- *jus ad bellum* and, 284–285, *284–285*
- Kurds in, *110*
- national interests and, 186
- oil as basis for, *68*
- rally effect and, 71
- rebuilding, 413
- U.S. ultimatum, 229, 300
- victory declaration, *233*
- White House Iraq Group, 87

ireedentism, **109**
ireedentist nationalism, 104
Ireland, 108, *432–433*
iron triangle, **360**
ISA. *See* International Seabed Authority (ISA)
Islam, 151–152
- culture, 148–150
- nationalism and, 154–155
- and non-Islamic world, 155
- political heritage, 152–154
- sectarianism, 155–156
- traditionalism and secularism, 156–157
- *See also* Muslims

Israel
- arms imports by, 314
- barrier on West Bank border, 277
- declaration of independence, 168
- diplomatic recognition of, 170
- economic classification of, 379
- foreign policy, 79
- geography of, 234
- military expenditures, 7
- Muslim beliefs about, 496–497
- relations with Palestinians, 109–111, 151
- as signatory to CTBT, *352*
- terrorism in, *318*
- undeclared nuclear weapons in, 330, 348
- U.S. military aid to, 314

issue-oriented groups, 78
Italian Social Movement (MSI), 175
Italy, 104, 175, *236, 238,* 248, 314, *432–433,* 443
Ivory Coast, 361, *361*

J

J'Accuse, 125
Jahre Viking, 128
James, William, 119
Japan
- banking, 389
- computing capacity, *241*
- education in, *238*
- exchange rate, *390, 391*
- foreign aid from, *432–433*
- foreign direct investments in U.S., 396
- foreign trade, 131
- in G–7, 443
- global goods and services surplus, 419–420, *420–421*
- income earned, 422–423, *423*
- military expenditures, 7
- North Korea and, *242*
- nuclear attacks on, 330, 345, 370
- population of, 236
- role of in international system, 39
- theocracy in, 173
- as trilateral country, 418
- unification of, 104
- U.S. nontariff barriers, 410
- U.S. steel tariff against, *420–421*
- women in, *160*
- WTO and, *456*

Jefferson, Thomas, 282
Jiang Zemin, 450
jihad, 151–152
Jihad vs. McWorld: How Globalism and Tribalism Are Reshaping the World, 45–46

jobs, outsourcing of, 397
John Paul II, Pope, 22, 113, 524
Johnson, Lyndon, 85, 89, 99, 304
Johnson, Shoshana, *13*
Jolie, Angelina, *498*
judicial review, 271
jus ad bellum, **282**–283, *284–285*
jus gentium concept, 270–271
jus in bello, **282**–283, 370, 415

K

Kambanda, Jean, 289–290
Kant, Immanuel, 139, 181, 292, 360
Karzai, Hamid, 133
Kashmir, Indian and Pakistan in, *153, 359*
Kelvin, Lord (William Thomson), 128
Kennedy, John F., 40, 87, 261, 294
Kenya, *7,* 317, 320
Keynes, John Maynard, 376–377
KFOR. *See* Kosovo Force (KFOR)
Khan, Abdul Qadeer, 349
Khastgir, Parma, 159–160
Khomeini, Ayatollah Ruholla, 155
Khwe people, 490
Kim Jong Il, 256, 258
King, Angela E., 288
King, Martin Luther, Jr., 370
Kipling, Rudyard, *135,* 482
Kirchner, Nestor, 460
Kiribato, 120, *120*
Kirsch, Philippe, 291–292, *291*
Kissinger, Henry, 73, 89, 92, 182, 245, 253, 254, 256
Köhler, Horst, 457, 461
Koizumi, Junichiro, *45*
Koran (Qur'an), 151, 156, *486*
Korea, as multistate nation, 108
Korean War, 327
Kosovo, 47, 166, 283
  battle of, (1389), 117
Kosovo Force (KFOR), 108, 166
Krauthammer, Charles, 42–43, 44
Krueger, Anne, 439
Kuenyeha, Akua, *291*
Kumaratunga, Chandrika, *179,* 280
Kurdish Security Zone, *110*
Kurds, as stateless nation, 109, *110*
Kuwait, 47, 68, 82, 154, 218, 246–247, 267, 300, 379, 429
Kyoto Protocol, 418, *544–545*

L

labor
  child, 450, 488
  EU protection of, 456
  global standards for, 450
Lake, Anthony, 87
land degradation, 530–531
language, as part of common culture, 133, *133*
Lascano, Marcelo, 459
law. *See* international law
Law of the Sea Treaty, 197, *198,* 287
Le Pen, Jean-Marie, 175, *175*
leader-citizen opinion gap, **79**–80
leader-to-leader diplomacy, 251–254
leaders
  ego and ambition, 89–90
  individual traits of, 87–88
  perceptions, 90–94
  personal experiences, 90
  personality, 88–89
  physical and mental health, 89
leadership, as part of power equation, 239
League of Nations, **192**, 274, 360
least developed countries (LLDCs), **382**, 386–387, 500, 503–504, 506, 522, 525
Lee, Robert E., 105, 298
legal systems. *See* international law
legislatures, effect of on foreign policy initiatives, 76–77
Lemkin, Raphael, *270*
Lenin, Vladimir, 39, 174, 377
Leningrad, siege of, 236
Leo III, Pope, 102
less developed countries (LDCs), 40–50, **50**, *51,* 53–54, *54,* 68, 157, 183, **374**, 375, *375*
  arms transfers to, 314–315
  capital investment in, *395*
  capital needs, 425–431, *427, 431, 432–433*
  capitalism in, 437
  Comprehensive Convention Against Terrorism and, 318
  Declaration on the Establishment of a New International Economic Order, 434–436, *437*
  deforestation in, 530
  development status, 422–425
  economic sanctions used against, 415
  education in, 236–237, *237,* 505–506
  energy consumption in, 529
  environmental issues and sustainable development, 513, 516–521, *544–545*
  fears about UN peacekeeping in, 366
  foreign debt, *425, 427*
  globalization and, 396–397
  Group of 77, 195, 434–435, *436*
  health issues, 503–504
  information and communication systems in, 240
  international law and, 278–279, *278*
  in international political economy, 375, *375,* 377, 378, 379–381
  international trade, 386–387
  military spending, *302,* 303
  nontariff barriers, 410
  perspectives and policies, 431, 434
  population issues, 521–526
  tariffs, 410
  water use, 533
  WTO and, 454–456, *455*
  See also economic development
L'État, c'est moi, 248–249
levels of analysis, **58**
  individual level, 81–94
  state level, 70–80
  system level, 58–70
Leviathan (Hobbes), 17
Lewinsky, Monica, *301*
Li Peng, 262
liberalism, 16, *17,* 18–21, 22–23, *49,* 139
liberals, **18**
Liberia, *220, 271, 367,* 414
Libya, 319, 349, 414, 415
Lie, Trygve, 213
lifeboat analogy, *445,* **445**
limited membership council, **210**
Limited Test Ban Treaty (1963), *344,* 345
limited unipolar system, **43**–44
Lind, Michael, *125*
Lindbergh, Charles A., *129*
Lithuania, membership in EU, 14
LLDCs. *See* least developed countries (LLDCs)
loans, to LDCs, 425–427, *427*
local authority, in Middle Ages, 30
Locke, John, 171, 269
Lockheed Martin Company, 314
Lomborg, Bjorn, 543
Lott, Trent, 358
Louis XIII (France), 248
Louis XIV (France), 248–249, 298
Lula da Silva, Liz Inacio, 392, 470, 471
Luther, Martin, 31
Luxembourg, *432–433*
Lynch, Jessica, *13*

M

Maastricht Treaty, **202**
Macarthur, Gen. Douglas, 327
Macedonians, 108–109
Machiavelli, Niccolò, 248, 282
MAD. *See* mutual assured destruction (MAD)
mad cow disease, 410, *411*
MADRE, 495
majority voting, **211**
Malaysia, 529
Maldives, 541–542
Malta, 14
Malthus, Thomas, 499
manufactured goods, **378**
Mao Zedong, 130, 168, 174, *242*
maquiladora program, 468–469, *468, 469*
Marcus Aurelius, 138
marine pollution, 538–539, 548, *548*
Marshall Plan, 447
Marx, Karl, 139, 140, 174

Marxism, **377**
mass production, 31
materialism, international trade and, 385
Mauritania, 429
Mazzini, Guiseppe, *125*
Mbeki, Thabo, 496
McWorld, 45–4**6**, 188
mechanization, 385
mediation diplomacy, **247**
Meditations (Marcus Aurelius), 138
Megarian Decree, 413
Mein Kampf (Hitler), 83, 117, 482
Meir, Golda, 178
Menchú, Rigoberta, 497
mercantilism, 405
merchandise trade, **383**–384
Mercosur. *See* Southern Common Market (Mercosur)
Mexico
  citizenship in, 168
  computing capacity, *241*
  emigration from, 491
  FDI in, 427
  ICJ and, 276–277
  maquiladora program, 468–469, *468, 469*
  military expenditures, 7
  in OECD, 443
microstates, *120,* **120**–121
Middle Ages, 29–32, 191
Middle East conflict
  mediation of, 247, 255–256, *326*
  See also Israel; Palestinians
MIGA. *See* Multinational Investment Guarantee Agency (MIGA)
militarism, 300
military draft, 12
military power, 302
  danger of overemphasis., 305–306
  force as political instrument, 306–309
  military and political reputation, 304–305
  morale and leadership, 303–304
  spending level, 7–8, *7, 47,* 302–303, *302*
  weaponry, 303
  See also war
military security. *See* security
military technology, in Middle Ages, 30
Mill, John Stuart, 393
Millennium Summit, 450–451, 541–542
Milosevic, Slobodan, 50–51, 166, 260, 270–271, 289–290, *290,* 318, 414
mini-nukes, 356, *356,* 357
minorities, global distribution of, *106–107*
mirror-image perception, *93,* **93**
MIRVs. *See* multiple independent reentry vehicles (MIRVs)
Misselden, Edward, 393
missile defense systems, 333–335, *334–335*
Missile Technology Control Regime (MTCR), *344,* **346**
Mitterrand, François, 450
Mizuho Holding, Inc., 389
modernization, in LDCs, 423–425
modified multipolar system, 44–45
Moldova, 322
monarchism, **174**
monetary regulation, 456–457
  See also International Monetary Fund (IMF)
monetary relations, **388**–389
monetary union, 466
Montreal Guidelines on Land-Based Pollution, 197
Montreal Protocol, 10
moral absolutism, **292**–293
moral prudence, **294**–295
moral relativism, **293**
morale, military, 238–239, 303–304
morality, 266
  applied to states, 280–281
  international fundamentals of, 268–269, 292–295
  See also international law
Moreno-Ocampo, Luis, 291
Morgenthau, Hans, 17, 19, 21
Mubarak, Hosni, *45*
Muhammad, 151
multiculturalism, law and justice and, 277–278, 278–280
multilateral aid, **430**
multilateral diplomacy, **249**
multilateral regional trade organizations (RTOs), 464, *465,* 466
multinational corporations (MNCs), 48, **387**
  domestic economy and, 396–397
  as international actors, *2, 62,* **62**, 398
  international investments by, 387–388, *388*
  North and South economic issues, 378
  UN regulation of, 449–450
Multinational Investment Guarantee Agency (MIGA), 463
multinational states, **106**–108
multiple independent reentry vehicles (MIRVs), 347
multipolar power structure, 43, 44–45
multipolar world system, **36**, 38–39, *64*
multistate nation, **108**–109
Munich analogy, **82**–83
Munich Conference, **39**
Muslims
  anti-American sentiment of, 155, 324
  countries with majority Muslim population, *154*
  in FSRs, 114
  multiculturalism and, 280
  opinions of U.S. actions, 83
  in Persian Gulf War, 195–196
  sense of threat and solidarity among, *149*
  in U.S., *78*
  See also Islam
Mussolini, Benito, 174, 175
mutual assured destruction (MAD), **333**–335, 345
mutual-responsibility warfare, 312
Myanmar (Burma), 414
Myers, Richard, 356

N

NAFTA. *See* North American Free Trade Agreement (NAFTA)
Nakamura, Kuniwo, 222
Namibia, 123
Napoleon Bonaparte, 36, 192, 235
nation, **99**–101
  infrastructure, 239–240
  information and communication systems, 240
  technology, 240
  transportation systems, 240
  national core, 234
  age distribution, 235–236, *236*
  education, 236–237, *237*
  geography, 234–235
  government, 239
  health, *237,* 238
  morale, 238–239
  population, 235, *236*
  See also nationalism
nation-states, **101**–102
  See also nationalism
National Alliance (Italy), 175
national economic power, 405–409, 438–439
national interest, as standard of conduct, 181–183
national missile defense system (NMDS), 333–335, *334–335,* 345
National Security Council, in Iraq decision making, 75
National Socialism, 174
national technical means (NTM), 358
nationalism, 28–29, **38**, **99**, **100**, 101, *125*
  beneficent face of, 113–114
  clash of cultures and, 148
  democratic, 33
  future, 123–124
  human rights abuses and, 482
  Islam and, 154–155
  "populist-romantic," 103–104
  in practice
    multinational states, 106–108
    multiple nations, multiple states, 111–113
    multistate nation, 108–109
    one state, one nation, 105
    stateless nation, 109–111
  problems with, 115–118

recent past and present, 122–123, *123*
rise and ascendancy of, 102–104, 249
self-determination as goal, 119–121
war and, 309
world government and, 199–200
Native Americans. *See* indigenous peoples
nativism, 490
NATO. *See* North Atlantic Treaty Organization (NATO)
natural gas, sustainable development and, 528–529
natural resources, 68, 407, *408*
See also environmental issues; sustainable development
naturalist school of law, **369**
Naval Conference (1921–22), 345
negative rights, **478**
negotiated disarmament, 369
negotiation, 244, 255–256
Negroponte, John, 364
neo-fascism, 175
neo-nazism, 175
neocolonialism, 154, 365–366, **378**
neoconservative ideology, *22, 74,* 182
neofunctionalism, **194**
neoimperialism, *49,* 375
neoliberals, **18**, 22
neorealists, **17**–18
net trade deficit, **405**
Netherlands, *432–433*
Netherlands, the, 314
New Deal, 401
New Zealand, 177, *432–433*
newly industrializing countries (NICs), **50**, *51,* **379**, 396, 417, **422**
NGOs. *See* nongovernmental organizations (NGOs)
Nicaragua, 275–276
Nice, Treaty of, 15, 202
Nigeria, *241, 364*
9/11. *See* September 11, 2001 attacks
Nixon, Richard M., 40, 89, 244–245
Nonaligned Movement (NAM), 194–195
nongovernmental organizations (NGOs), *2,* **60**–61, *61,* **145**–147, *146,* 147, **191**, 523–524
nonmissionary attitude, 73
nontariff barriers (NTBs), **410**
Noor, Queen (Jordan), 401–402
Noriega, Manuel, 219
North American Free Trade Agreement (NAFTA), 419, 438, 443, **467**–469, *468,* 473
North Atlantic Treaty Organization (NATO), **40**, **360**
Bosnia mission, 368
CFE and, 353
expansion of, 65, 72
International Security Assistance Force, 368
Kosovo intervention, 273, 368
possibility of nuclear strike against Soviet forces, 333
North (economically developed countries), **49**–50, *51,* **379**
See also economically developed countries (EDCs)
North Korea, 44
arms exports by, 315
diplomacy with South Korea, 252
diplomatic relations with, 242–244, 256, 258
nuclear weapons, *242,* 244, 260, 261, 262, 330, 348, 350
as part of axis of evil, 82, 91–92, *92, 243,* 256
state terrorism by, 319
U.S. sanctions against, 414
Norway, 177, *432–433*
NTM. *See* national technical means (NTM)
nuclear, biological, and chemical (NBC) weapons, 327, 328
See also arms control; weapons of mass destruction (WMDs); *individual types of weapons*
Nuclear Non-Proliferation Treaty (NPT), *242,* 343–344, *344,* **345**, 347–350
nuclear power, 528
nuclear utilization theory (NUT), **333**–335
nuclear weapons
biological agents and, 356
compared to radiological weapons, 321–322
Comprehensive Test Ban Treaty (CTBT), 71, *344,* **350**–351
deterrence and strategy, 331–335
how nuclear war might start, 330–331
legality of use, 277, 283
mini-nukes, 356, *356,* 357
states having, *153,* 329–330, *348, 349*
testing, *351*
See also arms control; weapons of mass destruction (WMDs)
Nuremberg war crimes trials, 288–289
NUT. *See* nuclear utilization theory (NUT)
Nye, Joseph, 229–230

O

OAS. *See* Organization of American States (OAS)
Obasanjo, Olusegun, *45, 436,* 450
objective power, **232**
observation and reporting, as function of diplomacy, 241–244
oceans
law and morality issues, 287
marine pollution, 538–539, 548, *548*
protection of, 532
Odyssey, The (Homer), 357
offensive warfare, 312
Office of Technology Assessment (OTA), 322–323
oil. *See* petroleum
on-site inspections (OSI), **358**
On the Law of War and Peace (Grotius), 192, 267
On the Manner of Negotiating with Sovereigns (de Callieres), 248
On the Principles of Political Economy and Taxation (Ricardo), 393
On War (Clausewitz), 326–327
OPEC. *See* Organization of Petroleum Exporting States (OPEC)
open diplomacy, **251**
operational code, **93**
operational reality, **93**
Oppenheimer, J. Robert, 65
oppression, internal, 117
optional clause, for ICJ, 275–276
order, as Western cultural value, 278
Organization for Economic Cooperation and Development (OECD), 430, **443**
Organization for Security and Cooperation in Europe (OSCE), 353, **360**–361
Organization of American States (OAS), 219, 361, 467
Organization of Petroleum Exporting States (OPEC), 436–437, *437*
organizational behavior, 86–87
Origin of Species, The (Darwin), 482
Ottoman empire, 103
outsourcing, 397
ozone layer, 10, 544–547, *546*

P

pacifism, **369**–370
pacta sunt servanda, **270**
Paine, Thomas, 104, 139, 144
Pakistan
CTBT and, *352*
India and, *152–153*
Iraq war and, 251
nuclear weapons in, *153,* 232–233, 330, 348–349, *349,* 359, *359*
religious fundamentalism in, *153*
UN peacekeepers contributed by, *364*
Palau, 123, 222
Palestine Liberation Organization (PLO), 154, 258
Palestine National Authority (PNA), 168
Palestinians
diplomatic recognition of, 168, 170
Israel and, 109–111, 151
as stateless nation, 109–111, 167
UN and, 208–209
U.S. support of Israel and, 157
West bank barrier, 277

Pan Am Flight 103 (Lockerbie), 317, 319
Pan-American Union, 467
Pan-Arab sentiment, 154
Panitchpakdi, Supachai, 452, 454, 463
Paraguay, 471
parliamentary diplomacy, **250**–251
Partnership for Principle 10, 146
patent rights, 278, *278*
Patterns of Global Terrorism, 2002, 325
Peace Corps, 50
peace enforcement, **364**–365
peacekeeping, 219–220, *221,* **360**, *363,* 364–365
Peloponnesian War, 413
Peloponnesian War, The (Thucydides), 25
perceptions, in decision-making process, **90**–94
perfluoroisobutene, 353
Perle, Richard, *74*
Permanent Court of International Arbitration, 274
Permanent Court of International Justice (PCJI), 274
Perón, Juan, 164
Perpetual Peace (Kant), 181
Persian Gulf War, 68, *80,* 82, 90, 259–260, 283, 300, 301, 304, 330
persuasive power, **232**
Peru, 361
petroleum
  in international relations, 47, *68*
  oil spills, 532, *548*
  as source of export revenue, 407
  sustainable development and, 528–529
  U.S. production of, 407
  world reserves, *408*
Philippines, 316–317
Piestewa, Lori, *13*
plague. *See* Black Death
Plato, 173, 194, 482–483
plenary representative body, **209**
Poland, 234, 314
polarity, 42–45
policy representation, as diplomatic role, 244–245
polio, 504
political culture, **72**–73
political executives, **73**
political identity, **99**, **140**
political opposition, role of in foreign policy, 77
political science, description as goal, 23–25
political systems, *173*
political violence, 11–12
politics, women in, 160
Politics (Aristotle), 28, 282
Polo, Marco, 30
popular sovereignty, **33**, **103**
population
  abortion issues, 524
  birthrate reduction, 525–526
  as cause of food shortages, 500–501
  as element in power equation, *6,* 235
  IGO and NGO response to overpopulation, 523–524
  in LDCs, 423–424, 523–526
  as measure of statehood, 167–168
  poverty and, 525–526
  sustainable development and, 521–523, *522, 523*
  world, 8, *8, 9*
population-based voting, *212*
Population Bomb, The (Ehrlich), 513
"populist-romantic" nationalism, 103–104
Portugal, foreign aid from, *432–433*
positive rights, **478**
positivist school of law, **269**–270, 479
postindustrial economy, 417
postmodernism, 139, **140**, *141*
poverty
  absolute, 424
  extreme, 382
  overpopulation and, 525–526
  violence and, 446–447
Powell, Colin, *74,* 75, 90, 244, 247, 250, *250,* 256, 258
power, **230**
  balance of, 36
  coercive, 231–232
  distribution of and war, 300
  distribution of in international system, 63–67
  hegemonic, 65
  national core as element of, 234–239
  nature of, 229–234
  objective, 232
  persuasive, 232
  polar structure of, 42–45, 63, *64,* 65
  relative, 232
  situational, **233**
  subjective, 232
power poles, in world system, **36**, **63**, *64,* 65
power politics, 22–23
  See also realism
power to defeat, **309**
power to hurt, **309**, 312
PPP. *See* purchasing power parity (PPP)
precision, in diplomacy, 260–261
prediction, as goal of political science, 24
preemptive warfare, 312–313, *313*
preferential trade agreements (PTAs), *473,* **473**
prescription, as goal of political science, 24–25
President of the Commission (European Commission), **203**
Presidential Decision Directive 60 (PDD–60), 333
price weakness, 430
primary products, **378**, 429, *429*
Prince, The (Machiavelli), 248, 282
Principles of Political Economy (Mill), 393
private pacifists, 369
procedural democracy, **177**
Prodi, Romano, 203
product instability, 430
Program on Nonviolent Sanctions in Conflict and Defense (Harvard), 370
Progressive Era, 401, 449, 450
Project for the New American Century, *74*
propaganda, 255
property, Western theory of, 278
prostitution
  child, 488
  forced, 143–144, 485
protectionism, 376, 393–394, 419, 420–421, **437**, 438–439
Protestant Reformation, **31**
psychological factors in decision making, 83
PTAs. *See* preferential trade agreements (PTAs)
public diplomacy, **254**–255
public opinion, *71,* 78–80, *80*
Punic Wars, 65
purchasing power parity (PPP), 374, *381*
pure foreign policy, **71**–72
Putin, Vladimir, 43, 75, 239, 246, 252, *253,* 347, *444*

Q

Qatar, 379
quotas, as nontrade barrier, 410

R

Rabbo, Yasser Abed, 247
racism, 489, 496–497
Radio Free Europe/Radio Liberty, 253
Radio Martí, 255
radiological terrorism, 321–322
rally effect, *71,* **71**
Rankin, Jeannette, 77
rationality, internal boundaries on, 81
Reagan, Ronald
  diplomacy, *253*
  "peace through strength," 357
  as realist, 21
  Soviet Union as "evil empire," 239
  Strategic Defense Initiative (SDI), 334
  technology sales to Soviet Union, 319
  withdrawal of consent to optional clause for ICJ, 276
real dollars, **374**
realism, 16–19, *17,* 21–23, 25, *49,* 139, 182
realists, **16**–17
realpolitik, **38**–39
  See also realism

recommendations, from bureaucracies, 76
Recovery of the Holy Land, The, 191
Reformation, Protestant, **31**
refugees, 490–491, 497–498
regime, **197**
Regime for Oceans and Seas, 197, *198*
regime theory, 197
regional government, **199**
relative power, **232**
relativists, **479**
religion, transnational, world politics and, 150–151
religious authority, 29
religious fundamentalism, 151, 490
Renaissance, **31**
Republic, The, 194, 482–483
research, in political science, 25
research and development (R&D), 240
Revolutionary United Front (Sierra Leone), 290
Ricardo, David, 393
Rice, Condoleezza, *24, 130*
Richard I (England), *110*
Ricupero, Rubens, 451
Rights of Man, The (Paine), 104, 139
Rio Declaration, 146
Rio Treaty (1948), 467
Rodman, Peter W., *74*
roles, in decision making, **86**
Roman Catholic Church, 29, 31, 102, 165, 524
Rome
  ancient, 65, 104, 138, 248
  sacking of, *303*
Rome Statute (ICC), *291*
Roosevelt, Franklin Delano, 89, 225
Rousseau, Jean-Jacques, 18
RTOs. *See* multilateral regional trade organizations (RTOs)
Ruggiu, Georges Henry Joseph, 290
Rumsfeld, Donald, 68, *74,* 83, 183, 246, 261, 284–285, 316, *352*
Rusk, Dean, 86
Russia
  arms transfers by, 314, 315
  Bolshevism in, 39, *39*
  climate in, 235
  computing capacity, *241*
  Czarist, 111–112
  economy, *382*
  education in, *238*
  in G-8, 443
  German invasion of (WWII), 235
  governance in, 239
  health and alcohol abuse in, 238
  military expenditures, 7
  nationalism in, 118, *118*
  nuclear weapons in, 329–330, *329,* 331
  radiological weapons in, 322
  ratification of CTBT, *352*
  reaction to U.S. steel tariff increases, 246
  relative size of, 235
  strategic-range delivery vehicles in, 331–332
  as successor state to Soviet Union, 209, 231
  troops in ATTU region, 353
  in UN, 209
  U.S. invasion of Iraq and, 196, 251
  U.S. relations, 252
  in World War I, 312
  See also Soviet Union
Rwanda, 47, 104, 107–108, 289–290

S

Sachs, Jeffrey, 459
Sadat, Anwar, 252
Sadik, Nafis, 160
Saladin, *110*
SALT I, SALT II. *See* Strategic Arms Limitation Talks (SALT I and II)
San Marino, 166–167, *167*
sanctions, UN, 219
Santer, Jacques, 203
SARS. *See* severe acute respiratory syndrome (SARS)
Saudi Arabia, 154, 314, 407, 485–486
Sbaataryn, Yanjamaa Nemendeyen, 177
Schneider, William, Jr., 356–357
Schroeder, Gerhard, *444*
scientific innovation, 38, *38*
"Second American Century, A," 417
Secretariat (UN), **213**
secular authority, 29–30
security, 47–48, 339–340
  approaches to, 340–341, *341*
  democracy and, 180–181
  future issues, 366, 368
  globalization and, 399–400
  international security forces, 360–362
  standards of evaluation, 341–343
  See also arms control; war
self-determination, **119**–121, 249
self-expectations, 86
self-reliance, in security issues, 47
Seneca, 482
Senegal, *237,* 238
separatists, 101
September 11, 2001 attacks, 3, 11, 86, 294, 320–321
  Afghanistan and, 3, 73, *243,* 245
  change in attitude toward North Korea and, *242*
  diplomatic actions, 244, 251
  due to terrorist groups, 63, 94
  economic effect, 5
  increased special operations due to, 316–317
  intelligence information about, 76, 320
  rally effect and, 71
  self-reliance and, 47
  state-level analysis of, 324
  See also terrorism
Serbia, in World War I, 312
Servan-Schreiber, Jean-Jacques, 399
service economy, 417
services trade, **384**
severe acute respiratory syndrome (SARS), 11, 505
sex tourism, 488, 496
Shane, John B., *284*
shari'ah, 156, *486–487*
Sherman Antitrust Act (1890), 449
Sherman, William Tecumseh, 309
Shiite Muslims, 155–156
Shinko Securities, 389
Siemens, 397
Sierra Leone, civil war in, 290, 366, 368
signaling, as diplomatic tool, 256, 261
Simon, Julian, 513
Singapore, 379, 437
Sinocentrism, 72–73, *72*
situational power, **233**
slavery, 482, 484, 496
Slovenia, 14
smallpox, *323,* 328, 504
Smith, Adam, 376, 393
social contract, **171**
Social Contract, The (Rousseau), 18
social Darwinism, **482**
social overstretch thesis, **306**
Socialist Party of Europe (SPE), 203
socialization, in decision making, *85*
SOFs. *See* special operations forces (SOFs)
Solow, Robert M., 477
Somalia, 495
South Africa, 166, 282, 414, 497
South Korea
  arms imports by, 314
  economics, 378, 379, 437
  North Korea and, *242,* 252
  population of, *236*
South (less developed countries), **50**, *51,* **379**
  See also less developed countries (LDCs)
South Pacific Forum, 197
Southern Common Market (Mercosur), 48, *471,* **471**
sovereignty, *2,* 22, **28**, 32, **165**, 187
  as defense of government mistreatment of citizens, 165–166
  development of, 165
  globalization and, 398–399, 453
  IMF and, 459
  independence and, 165
  law and morality issues, 282
  popular, 33, 103
  used as repression against internal rebellion, 166
  as Western cultural value, 278

Soviet Union
  in Afghanistan, 316
  Anti-Ballistic Missile (ABM) Treaty, 334, *334*
  arms transfers from, 314
  biological weapons in, 328
  in cold war, 39–40
  collapse of, 41–42, 46–47, 123, 239, 305, 418
  creation of, 39
  ethnonational populations in, 111–113, 118
  as "evil empire," 239
  rise of in international system, 39–40
  as superpower, 231
  territorial waters of, 287
  U.S. technology sales to, 319
  See also Russia
Spain, fascism in, 174, 234, *432–433*
Spanish-American War, 36
Special Drawing Rights (SDRs), **457**–458
special operations, **316**–317
special operations forces (SOFs), 316–317
specialization, benefits of, 393
"Speech on Dictatorship" (Cortés), 173
spoilers, 365
Sri Lanka, women officeholders in, 177, 280
Stalin, Josef, 89, 174
Stalingrad, siege of, 235
"Star Wars". *See* Strategic Defense Initiative (SDI)
stare decisis, 271
state-building nationalism, 104
state-centric system, **59**
state-level analysis, **70**
  actors, 73–80
  political culture, 72–73
  of terrorism, 324
  type of government, situation, policy, 70–72
state of nature, **171**
state terrorism, **319**
stateless nation, **109**–111
states, **59**, **165**
  as actors, 59
  challenges to authority of, 45–46
  as core political organization, 172
    democracy and world politics, 176–181
    national and other interests, 181–183
    theories of governance, 172–176
  defined, 165
    domestic support, 170
    internal organization, 170
    population, 167–168
    sovereignty, 165–168
    territory, 167
  as dominant political actors, 32
  duration of independence, *164*
  economic prosperity as key role, 185
  externalization of internal conflicts, 300
  failed, 111
  future of, 184–188
  general welfare as key role, 185
  as international actors, *2*
  international law applied to, 280–281
  multinational, 106–108
  number of, *123*
  physical safety as key role, 185
  purposes of, 170–172
  sovereignty, 165–168, 170
  territorial, 28
  wars created by, 300–301
  world map of, *34–35*
  See also nationalism
stereotypes, 82
Stoicism, 138, 191
Stone, Jeremy, 259
Strategic Arms Limitation Talks (SALT I and II), 343, *344*, **346**
Strategic Arms Reduction Treaties (START I and II), 343, *344*, 346–347
Strategic Defense Initiative (SDI), 334
strategic-range delivery vehicles, **331**–332
strategic trade, 399–400
subjective power, **232**
subsidies, economic, 412, *412*
substantive democracy, **177**
success, views about, *480*
successor states, 209
Sudan
  sanctions against, 414
  state terrorism by, 319
summit meetings, **252**
Sunni Muslims, 155–156
superpowers, **39**–40, *67*
supranational organizations, 198–200, **199**
sustainable development, **53**, *54*, **511**
  attainment of, 513, 516–518
  politics of, 518–519
    Earth Summit I, 519–520
    Earth Summit II, 520–521
  population issues, 521–527
  resource conservation, 534–537
  resource issues and cooperation, 527–533, *533*, *534*
  See also ecology; environmental issues
sweatshops, *131*
Sweden, 7, *432–433*
Switzerland, 15, 177, 234, *432–433*
Syria, 319, 414
system-level analysis, **58**–59
  behavior norms, 68–70
  economic patterns, 67–68
  power relationships, 63–65, *64*
  structural characteristics, 59
    actors, 59–63
    interactions, 63
    organization of authority, 59
  of terrorism, 323–324

T

Taiwan, 170
  arms imports by, 314
  China crises, *242–243*, 248, 258–259, *259*, 261–262
  diplomatic recognition of, 168
  effective ejection from UN, 209
  See also China
Taliban regime, 111, 245, 316
Tanzania, U.S. embassy attack, 317, 320
tariffs, **410**
Taylor, Charles, 51, *271*, 290
technology, 38, *38*
  expanding trade and, 385
  as part of power equation, 240
  in war, 309
television, as part of common culture, 134
Telfah, Sajida Khairallah, 86
Tenet, George, *153*
territorial state, 28
territoriality, 84–85
  as cause of war, 301
territory, as measure of statehood, 167
terrorism, 50, 94, **317**
  arms control and, 356
  causes, 323–325
  combating, 325
  nature and limits of, 317–319
  record of, 320–321, *321*
  sources of, 319–320
  weapons and tactics, 321–323
  See also September 11, 2001 attacks; unconventional force; war
terrorist groups, as actors, **62**–63
Thailand, theocracy in, 173
Thatcher, Margaret, 65, 178
The Republic (Plato), 173
theocracy, **173**–174
Third Crusade, *110*
Third World, **40**, **489**
Thomas Aquinas, Saint, 269, 282
Three Gorges Dam, 517, *518*
Threshold Test Ban Treaty (1974), *344*, 346
Thucydides, 25
Tibet, 168, *169*, 170, 173
Tilger, Mary, *186*
TNCs. *See* transnational corporations (TNCs)
Tokyo war crimes trials, 288–289
Toledo, Alejandro, 324

topography, as element of power, 234–235
trade. *See* international trade
transnational actors, **60**
transnational advocacy networks (TANs), **146, 497**
transnational communications, 130–131, *131*
transnational corporations (TNCs), 388, 449–450
See also multinational corporations (MNCs)
transnational interest groups, 78
transnational terrorism, 319–**320**
transnationalism, **127**, 137–138
as alternative to nationalism, 138
contemporary, 139–140, *141*
constructivism, 141–142
feminism, 142–144
postmodernism, 140
reactions to, 144
cultural, 148–150
early, 138–139
future, 161
movements, 157–160
organizations, 145–147
regional, 147–148
religion, 150–157
sources of, 137–138
transportation
globalization of, 128–129
international trade and, 385–386
as part of power equation, 240
Treaty of Moscow, 343, *344,* **347**
Treaty of Versailles, 89
tribalism, 45–46, **46**–47, 188
trilateral countries, 418
tripolar system, *64*
Truman, Harry S., 73, 327
tuberculosis, 504
Turabi, Hassan, *301*
Turkey, *110,* 314, 443
two-level game theory, **74**–75, **247**–248
Two Treatises of Government (Locke), 269

U

überfremdung, 175
Uganda, *236,* 429
Ukraine, 314, 353
ummah, 151, 154
UN. *See* United Nations (UN)
unanimity voting, **212**–213
UNCED. *See* United Nations Conference on Environment and Development (UNCED)
unconventional force, **313**
arms transfers, 313–316, *314*
special operations, 316–317
terrorism, 317–325
See also war
UNCPD. *See* United Nations Conference on Population and Development (UNCPD)
UNCTAD. *See* United Nations Conference on Trade and Development (UNCTAD)
UNDP. *See* United Nations Development Programme (UNDP)
UNESCO. *See* United Nations Educational, Scientific, and Cultural Organization (UNESCO)
UNFCCC. *See* United Nations Framework Convention on Climate Change (UNFCCC)
UNFPA. *See* United Nations Population Fund (UNFPA)
UNGA. *See* United Nations, General Assembly
UNICEF. *See* United Nations Children's Fund (UNICEF)
UNIFEM. *See* United Nations, Development Fund for Women; United Nations Development Fund for Women (UNIFEM)
unification nationalism, 104
unilateral disarmament, 369
Union of Congolese Patriots, *315*
"Unipolar Moment, The" (Krauthammer), 42–43, 44
unipolar power structure, 42–43, *64,* **65**
unipolar system, limited, 43–44
UNITA, UN sanctions against, 414
United Arab Emirates, 379
United Nations
Center for Transnational Corporations, 450
Convention Relating to the Status of Refugees, *288,* 497
United Nations Children's Fund (UNICEF), 217, 222, 495, 523
United Nations Commission on Human Rights (UNCHR), 221–222, 294, 492
United Nations Conference on Environment and Development (UNCED), 222, **519**–520, 520–521
United Nations Conference on Population and Development (UNCPD), **524**
United Nations Conference on Trade and Development (UNCTAD), 343, **451**
United Nations Development Fund for Women (UNIFEM), 221, 483, 494, 526
United Nations Development Programme (UNDP), **451**, 485
United Nations Educational, Scientific, and Cultural Organization (UNESCO), 449, 505, 533
United Nations Environmental Programme (UNEP), 9–10, 217, 221, 531, 543–544
United Nations Framework Convention on Climate Change (UNFCCC), *544*
United Nations Population Fund (UNFPA), 501, 521, 523, 524, 526
United Nations (UN), 45, *60,* **191**, 360
activities, 217, 218–220, 220–222
arms control by, 220
Charter, 104, 160, 211, 218, *284,* 287, *361*
Development Fund for Women, 221
Disarmament Committee, 369
economic development goals, 449–451
evaluation and future of, 223–225, *224*
General Assembly, **209**–210
Declaration on the Establishment of a New International Economic Order, 434
Israeli barrier along West Bank border, 277
legality of nuclear weapons, 277
sources of conflict in, 196
Universal Declaration of Human Rights, *281,* 287, 479, 491, *492,* 499, *507–508*
geographic and demographic imbalance in, 210–211
High Commissioner for Refugees, 490, 498, *498*
human rights issues, 491–493
inequitable veto in, 211
as international security protector, *361,* 362
Iraq and
1991 military action against, 273
inspections, 328, 329
Iraq War (2003), 213, 216, 224, *243,* 250–251, 268, *284–285*
sanctions, 267, 281
leadership, administration, and finance, 213, *218,* 316–317
multinational conferences convened by, 146, 159
organization, 208, *209*
basis of representation issues, 209–211
membership issues, 208–209, *210*
voting issues, 211–213, *212*
peacekeeping by, 187, 219–220, *221,* 362, *363,* 364–366, *365,* 366
sanctions by, 414
Secretariat, **213**, 276
Security Council, 192–193, **210**–213, 224
as source of international law, 272

United Nations (UN) *(continued)*
as symbol of cooperative globalism, 122
women in, 160
Women Watch, 1
United States
Afghanistan retaliation, 3, 73, *243,* 245, 256
agricultural efficiency, 408–409, *409*
anti-Muslim sentiment in, 155
children's rights, 495
China and, 279–280
Civil War, 309
in cold war, 40
colonialism, 36
computing capacity, *241*
Constitution, 171, 498
crime in, 342
Cuba sanctions, 262
Cuban missile crisis, 40
currency manipulation by China, 398
Declaration of Independence, 103, 171, 172, 417
democracy in, 180, 181
Department of Labor, 450
dependence on imports, 6
economic development aid from, 449
economic sanctions imposed by, 414–415
economy, *380, 381,* 399
balance of payments, 391
budget deficit, 405–406, *406*
direct investment abroad, 387
effects of globalization, 396–397
exchange rate, 390–391, *390, 391*
exports, 386–387
foreign direct investments in Japan, 396
GDP, 417
national debt, 6–7
national economic power, 405–406, *406*
subsidies, 412, *412*
trade barriers, 420
trade deficit, *384,* 405, 419–420, *420–421*
unemployment, 417
education in, *238*
ethnonational groups in, 105
exceptionalist attitude in, 72–73
"fast track" authority of president, 72
Federal Child Labor Law (1916), 450
Federal Reserve Bank, 394
Federal Trade Commission, 449
foreign aid, 431, *432–433*
foreign opinions of, 83
in G-7, 443
gasoline taxes, 516
global role of, 44, *44*
Hawaiian independence movement, 120, *120*
hegemony of, 43
human rights issues in, 482, 492
illegal immigration, 491
individualism in, 114, 480, *480*
in International Criminal Court, 291–292, 364, 418
in international system, 39
internationalism of, 418
Iraq War (2003), *13, 14,* 21, 44, *49,* 68, *69,* 71, *74,* 196, 216, 219, 229, *233,* 268
jobs exported from, 6
Kyoto Protocol, *544–545*
Marshall Plan, 447
mass transit, 516
membership in ICJ, 275–276
in Middle East, 247, 255–256
military
Anti-Ballistic Missile (ABM) Treaty, 334, *334*
arms transfers, 314
Comprehensive Test Ban Treaty, 351
desire for "zero-dead" wars, 304
imperial overstretch thesis, 305–306, *305*
military aid offered, 314, 315–316
mini-nukes, 356, *356,* 357
national missile defense system (NMDS), 333–335, *334–335*
nuclear weapons, 329–330, *329,* 351
spending, *7,* 302, 303, 305–306
Strategic Defense Initiative (SDI), 334
strategic-range delivery vehicles, 331–332
technology, 303
troops in ATTU region, 353
withdrawal from Anti-Ballistic Missile Treaty, 334, *334, 344,* 345, 418
mineral imports, 407
Muslims in, *78*
as nation-state, 105
NATO and, 65
neoimperialism in Persian Gulf, 378–379
North Korea and, *242,* 244, 256, 257, 258, 260, 261, 262
in OECD, 443
Office of Homeland Security, 323
offshore rights, 287
Persian Gulf War, 68, 196
petroleum production and consumption, 407, *407, 408*
political and moral authority of, 418–419
population and age distribution, 236
propaganda of, 255
protectionism by, 419, 420–421, *420–421,* 453
rejection of CTBT, 358
Revolution, 33, 103, 176, 312
Russia and, 246, 252
Sherman Antitrust Act (1890), 449
slavery in, 482
social programs spending in, 306, *306*
steel tariff, *420–421,* 453
Sudan factory attack, *301*
Taiwan crises, 242–243, 248, 258–259, *259,* 261–262
terrorist attacks on, 320–321
embassy bombings (Kenya and Tanzania), *301,* 317, 320
Homeland Security, *326*
Oklahoma Federal Building, 317
World Trade Center (1993), 317, 320
See also September 11, 2001 attacks
as trilateral country, 418
United Nations and, *218,* 364, 368
Vietnam War, 11–12, 21, 40, 244–245, 305
views on other countries, *93*
voter turnout, *4*
women in, 159, *160*
universal authority, in Middle Ages, 29–30, 31–32
Universal Declaration of Human Rights, *281,* 287, 479, **491**–492, *492,* 499, *507–508*
Universal Postal Union, 193
universalists, **478**
UNSC. *See* United Nations, Security Council
Uruguay, 471
Uruguay Round, **452**
U.S. Geological Survey, 528
U.S. Information Agency, 255
USS *Cole* attack, 319
USS *Harry S. Truman, 307*
USSR. *See* Soviet Union
Uwilingiyamana, Agathe, 108

vagueness, in diplomacy, 260–261
Vajpayee, Atal Behari, 43, *153*
VAT (value-added tax), 201, 204
Vatican, defense force, *303*
Venezuela, Yanomami of, 489–490
vertical authority structure, **59**
veto, **212**–213
Vienna Convention on Consular Relations (1963), 276
Vietnam, 437
Vietnam War, 11–12, 21, 40, 244–245, 304, 305, 327
violence
domestic norms against, 342
economic issues and, 446–447

Voice of America, 255
voting
direct, 14
equal, population-based, and wealth-based, *212*
global effect of, 13–14
majority, 211
unanimity, 212–213
weighted, 211–212

W

Wal-Mart, *388*
Wang Zhi-zhi, *135*
war
abolition of, 369
complete disarmament, 369
pacifism, 369–370
causes, 299
individual-level, 301
state-level, 300–301
system-level, 299–300
changing nature of, 309, 312
classification of, 312–313, *313*
conventional, 325–326
escalation avoidance, 327–328
goals and conduct, 326–327
as fading phenomenon, 232
human record, 298–299, *299*
international conflicts in post-World War II era, *310–311*
law and morality issues, 282–286
measuring effectiveness of, 308
strategy, 309, 312
unconventional, **313**
arms transfers, 313–316, *314*
special operations, 316–317
terrorism, 317–325
with weapons of mass destruction, 328
chemical weapons, 328–329
deterrence and strategy, 331–335
potential for nuclear war, 329–331
See also arms control; military power; security
war criminals, 273
war on terrorism. *See* terrorism
Warsaw Pact, **40**
Warsaw Treaty Organization (WTO), 353
water
per capita availability of, *533*
pollution of, 538–539, 548, *548*
sustainable development and, 531–533, *533, 534*
WCAR. *See* World Conference Against Racism, Racial Discrimination, Xenophobia and Related Intolerances (WCAR)
WCHR. *See* World Conference on Human Rights (WCHR)
wealth, distribution of, 68, 477
wealth-based voting, *212*
Wealth of Nations, The (Smith), 376, 393
weapons of mass destruction (WMDs), **47**–48, *49*, **66**, 93, 224, *243*, 283, **328**, **345**
biological weapons, 328
chemical weapons, 328–329
deterrence and strategy, 329–331, 335
nuclear war potential, 329–330, *329*
See also arms control; nuclear weapons; security
weather, global warming and, 542
Weber, Max, 298
weighted voting, **211**–212
Wen Jiabao, 398
West Bank, 167, 168, 212
West Nile virus, *186*, 505
Western culture, 133, 134, *135*, 148–150, 278–279
Westernization, of international system, **33**, 36
Westphalia, Treaty of, **31**, 32, 36
WFP. *See* World Food Programme (WFP)
White House Iraq Group, 87
"White Man's Burden, The" (Kipling), 482
WHO. *See* World Health Organization (WHO)
Wickremesinghe, Ranil, *179*
wildlife
Convention on the International Trade in Endangered Species, 531
sustainable development and, 531–532
Williams, Jody, *2, 354–355*
Wilson, Woodrow, 19, *20*, 89, 119, 171, 252
"Fourteen Points," 19, *20*, 251
League of Nations, 192, 249
WMDs. *See* weapons of mass destruction (WMDs)
Wolfensohn, James D., 463, *463*
Wolfowitz, Paul, *74*
women
Convention on the Elimination of All Forms of Discrimination Against Women (CEDAW), 494
domestic abuse of, 484–485
economic and educational advancement of, 526
economic, political, and educational discrimination against, 485
education, *506*
female infanticide, 484
forced labor of, 484–485
forced prostitution, 485
genital mutilation of, 484, 495
International Women's Year, 526
MADRE, 495
military service by, 12, *13*
in politics, 160, 177–178, *178*
rights of, 51–52
socioeconomic status and population pressures, *527*
transnational women's movement, 158–160
UN Development Fund for Women (UNIFEM), 221, 483, 494
violence against, 143–144, 483–484
World Conference on Women (WCW), 146, 159–160, 494, 526
worldwide gender gap, 157–158, *158*
See also feminism; gender
Women Watch, 159
Woods, Tiger, *135*
world affairs, comparative knowledge of, *4*
World Bank, 48, 194, 211–212, 221, 393, 424, 438, 443, 462–464, **462**
World Conference Against Racism, Racial Discrimination, Xenophobia and Related Intolerances (WCAR), 496–497
World Conference on Human Rights (WCHR), 493
World Conference on Sustainable Development, 146, *146*
World Conference on Women (WCW), 146, 159–160, 494
World Congress Against Commercial Sexual Exploitation of Children, 496
World Council of Indigenous Peoples, 497
world court. *See* International Court of Justice (ICJ)
World Disasters Report 2002, 9
World Federalist Association, 199
World Food Conference (1974), 502
World Food Programme (WFP), 502, *502*
World Food Summit (1996), **503**
World Food Summit-Five Years Later, 503
world government, **199**–200
World Health Organization (WHO), 11, 222, 277, **504**
world politics
democracy and, 176–181
disease control, 10–11
environmental issues, 8–10
making a difference, 12–15
personal finances and, 5–6
political violence, 11–12
realism versus liberalism in, 15–16, *17*
assessing reality, 23
competition and cooperation, 21–23
nature of politics, 16–21
religion and, 150–151

world politics *(continued)*
studying, 3–5, 23–25
war and, 298–301
world population. *See* population
world states, *34–35*
World Summit on Sustainable Development (WSSD), **520**–521
world system. *See* international system
world systems theory, **378**
World Trade Center attack (1993), 317, 320
See also September 11, 2001 attacks
World Trade Organization (WTO), 48, 59, 187, 199, 246, 261–262, 393, 419, *420–421,* 438, 443, **452**
as agent of globalization, 454
Cancún meeting, 454, *455*
distribution of complainants, 452–453, *453*
Doha Round, 454, 455
future of, 453–456
structure and role of, 452–453
World War I, 38–39, 192, 249, 299, 312, 345, 447
World War II, 39–40, 122, 299, 345, 442
World Wide Web. *See* Internet, the
Worldnet, 255
Worst Forms of Child Labour Convention (1999), 450
Wright, Orville, 128
Wright, Wilbur, 128
WSSD. *See* World Summit on Sustainable Development (WSSD)

X

xenophobia, **117**

Y

Yalta Conference, 89
Yanomami people, 489–490
Yao Ming, *135*
Yeltsin, Boris, 89, 238, *253, 261,* 330
Yemen, 495
Yippies, *14*
Youth International Party ("Yippies"), *14*
Yugoslavia, *69, 101,* 260
breakup of, 123
ethnonational groups in, 108, *117*
Kosovo and, 47, 166, 283
NATO bombing of, 282, 283, 304
UN sanctions against, 414

Z

Zambia, 429
zero-sum game, **232**
Zhu Rongji, *259*
Zimbabwe, 414
Zionism, **109**
Zoellick, Robert B., 420–421
Zola, Émile, *125*

Credits

Chapter 1. 10 Associated Press/AP; 11 Associated Press/AP; 13 Associated Press/AP; 14 (left & right) Associated Press/AP; 22 Associated Press/AP; 24 Reuters NewMedia Inc./Corbis.

Chapter 2. 31 Corbis; 33 Associated Press/AP; 41 Farrell Grehan/Corbis; 43 Reuters NewMedia Inc./Corbis; 45 Reuters NewMedia Inc./Corbis; 48 Rick Friedman/Corbis; 52 European Press Photo Agency/EPA; 53 Rickey Rogers/Reuters NewMedia Inc./Corbis.

Chapter 3. 60 UN photo by M. Grant; 68 James Leynse/Corbis; 69 AFP/Corbis; 76 Images.com/Corbis; 78 AFP/Corbis; 82 Olivier Coret/In Visu/Corbis; 84 Associated Press/AP; 85 Steve Raymer/Corbis; 91 Brooks Craft/Corbis; 92 Associated Press/AP

Chapter 4. 98 Images.com/Corbis; 100 AFP/Corbis; 101 Images.com/Corbis; Nayef Hashlamoun/Reuters; 112 AFP/Corbis; 121 Reuters NewMedia Inc./Corbis.

Chapter 5. 129 Lester Lefkowitz/Corbis; 130 AFP/Corbis; 131 Associated Press/AP; 135 Associated Press/AP; 143 Associated Press/AP; 146 Associated Press/AP; 148 Associated Press/AP; 152 Associated Press/AP; 156 Associated Press/AP; 161 NASA.

Chapter 6. 165 W. Cody/Corbis; 169 Touhig Sion/Corbis Sygma; 175 Associated Press/AP; 179 Reuters NewMedia Inc./Corbis; 184 Don Hammond/Corbis; 185 Associated Press/AP; 186 Associated Press/AP.

Chapter 7. 193 Howard Davies/Corbis; 195 Lester Lefkowitz/Corbis; 196 Reuters NewMedia Inc./Corbis; 204 Reuters NewMedia/Corbis; 206 AFP/Corbis; 215 Associated Press/AP; 220 European Press Photo Agency, EPA; 223 Reuters NewMedia Inc./Corbis.

Chapter 8. 230 Reuters NewMedia Inc./Corbis; 233 Arko Datta/ Reuters NewMedia Inc./Corbis; 240 Mendola/Doug Chezem/Corbis; 244 Images.com/Corbis; 246 AFP/Corbis; 250 AFP Photo/Don Emmert/Corbis; 252 Putin hugs Bush; 259 AFP/Corbis; 260 Schot/CWS.

Chapter 9. 267 Corbis/Bettmann; 271 Reuters NewMedia Inc./Corbis; 278 Corbis; 281 UN; 283 Reuters NewMedia Inc./Corbis; 285 Associated Press/AP; 289 AFP/Corbis; 291 Reuters NewMedia Inc./Corbis; 293 Bettmann/Corbis.

Chapter 10. 301 Associated Press/AP; 304 David Leeson/Dallas Morning News/Corbis; 307 Associated Press/AP; 315 EPA/DPA; 318 Reuters NewMedia Inc./Corbis; 329 Reuters NewMedia Inc./Corbis; 331 Corbis; 335 Reuters NewMedia Inc./Corbis.

Chapter 11. 342 Reuters NewMedia Inc./Corbis; 355 Associated Press/AP; 356 Bettmann/Corbis; 359 AFP/Corbis; 361 AFP/Corbis; 365 EPA/DPA; 367 (top & bot.) EPA/Associated Press/AP.

Chapter 12. 378 Gamaa/*Al Ahram Weekly*/Cairo/CWS; 382 Gideon Mendel/Corbis; 385 Paul A. Souders/Corbis; 388 Sanford/Agliolo/Corbis; 391 AFP/Corbis; 392 Juan Carlos Ulate/ Reuters NewMedia Inc./Corbis; 395 Qilai Shen/European Press Agency/AP .

Chapter 13. 407 Miel, *Straits Times,* Singapore, CWS; 411 Stringer/Reuters NewMedia Inc./Corbis; 421 William Philpott/Reuters NewMedia Inc./Corbis; 424 Reuters NewMedia Inc./Corbis; 434 Plantu/CWS; 436 AFP/Corbis.

Chapter 14. 444 Associated Press/AP; 445 Images.com/Corbis; 447 Guang Niu/Reuters NewMedia Inc./Corbis; 456 AFP/Corbis; 460 Reuters NewMedia Inc./Corbis; 463 Reuters NewMedia Inc./Corbis; 469 Keith Danemiller/Corbis/Saba.

Chapter 15. 479 AFP/Corbis; 484 Lynsey Addario/Corbis; 487 Shepard Sherbell/Corbis/Saba; 488 Associated Press/AP; 492 AFP/Corbis; 498 UNHCR/Corbis; 502 Stephanie Sinclair/Corbis; 504 Associated Press/AP; 506 Associated Press/AP.

Chapter 16. 512 Associated Press/AP; 518 EPA, Feature China Files; 525 Associated Press/AP; 530 Charles O'Rear/Corbis; 531 Timepix; 534 David Turnley/Corbis; 538 The Cover Story/Corbis; 542 Bruce Chambers/Orange County Register/Corbis; 546 NASA; 547 De Angelis, *Il Popolo,* Rome, CWS.

U.S.
CANADA
UNITED STATES
NORTH
PACIFIC
OCEAN
NORTH
ATLANTIC
OCEAN
MEXICO
Tropic of Cancer
U.S.
Equator
GUYANA
SURINAME
FRENCH
GUIANA
(FR)
COLOMBIA
VENEZUELA
ECUADOR
PERU
BRAZIL
BOLIVIA
PARAGUAY
CHILE
ARGENTINA
URUGUAY
WESTERN
SAMOA
TONGA
Tropic of Capricorn
SOUTH
PACIFIC
OCEAN
SOUTH
ATLANTIC
OCEAN
Antarctic Circle
U.S.
THE
BAHAMAS
300 Miles
300 Kilometers
CUBA
MEXICO
DOMINICAN
REPUBLIC
PUERTO RICO
JAMAICA
HAITI
BELIZE
ST. KITTS AND NEVIS
ANTIGUA AND BARBUDA
GUATEMALA
HONDURAS
CARIBBEAN
SEA
DOMINICA
MARTINIQUE
ST. LUCIA
EL
SALVADOR
NICARAGUA
ST. VINCENT AND THE GRENADINES
BARBADOS
GRENADA
COSTA RICA
TRINIDAD AND TOBAGO
PANAMA
COLOMBIA
VENEZUELA
Scale: 1 to 125,000,000
1000
2000 Miles
1000
2000
3000 Kilometers